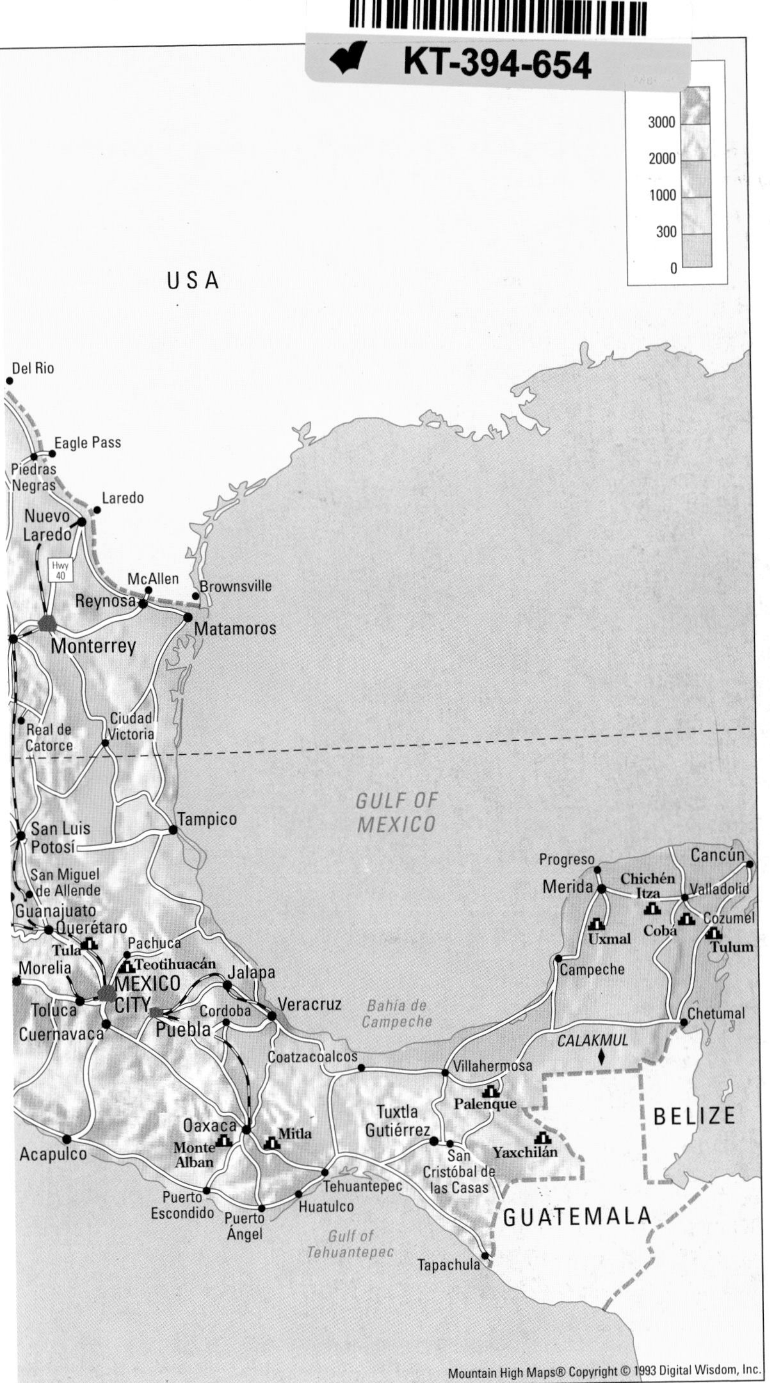
3000
2000
1000
300
0
USA
Del Rio
Eagle Pass
Piedras Negras
Laredo
Nuevo Laredo
Hwy 40
McAllen
Brownsville
Reynosa
Matamoros
Monterrey
Real de Catorce
Ciudad Victoria
GULF OF MEXICO
Tampico
San Luis Potosí
San Miguel de Allende
Guanajuato
Querétaro
Tula
Pachuca
Teotihuacán
Morelia
MEXICO CITY
Jalapa
Toluca
Cuernavaca
Puebla
Cordoba
Veracruz
Bahía de Campeche
Coatzacoalcos
Oaxaca
Monte Alban
Mitla
Acapulco
Puerto Escondido
Puerto Ángel
Huatulco
Tehuantepec
Gulf of Tehuantepec
Tuxtla Gutiérrez
San Cristóbal de las Casas
Villahermosa
Palenque
Yaxchilán
Tapachula
GUATEMALA
BELIZE
CALAKMUL
Campeche
Chetumal
Progreso
Merida
Uxmal
Chichén Itza
Cobá
Cancún
Valladolid
Cozumel
Tulum
Mountain High Maps® Copyright © 1993 Digital Wisdom, Inc.

△ Playa del Carmen

The **Rough Guide** to

Mexico

written and researched by

John Fisher

with additional contributions by

Adrien Glover, Daniel Jacobs,
Sheelah Kolhatkar, Roger Norum, Zora O'Neill,
Paul D. Smith, Ross Velton

NEW YORK • LONDON • DELHI

www.roughguides.com

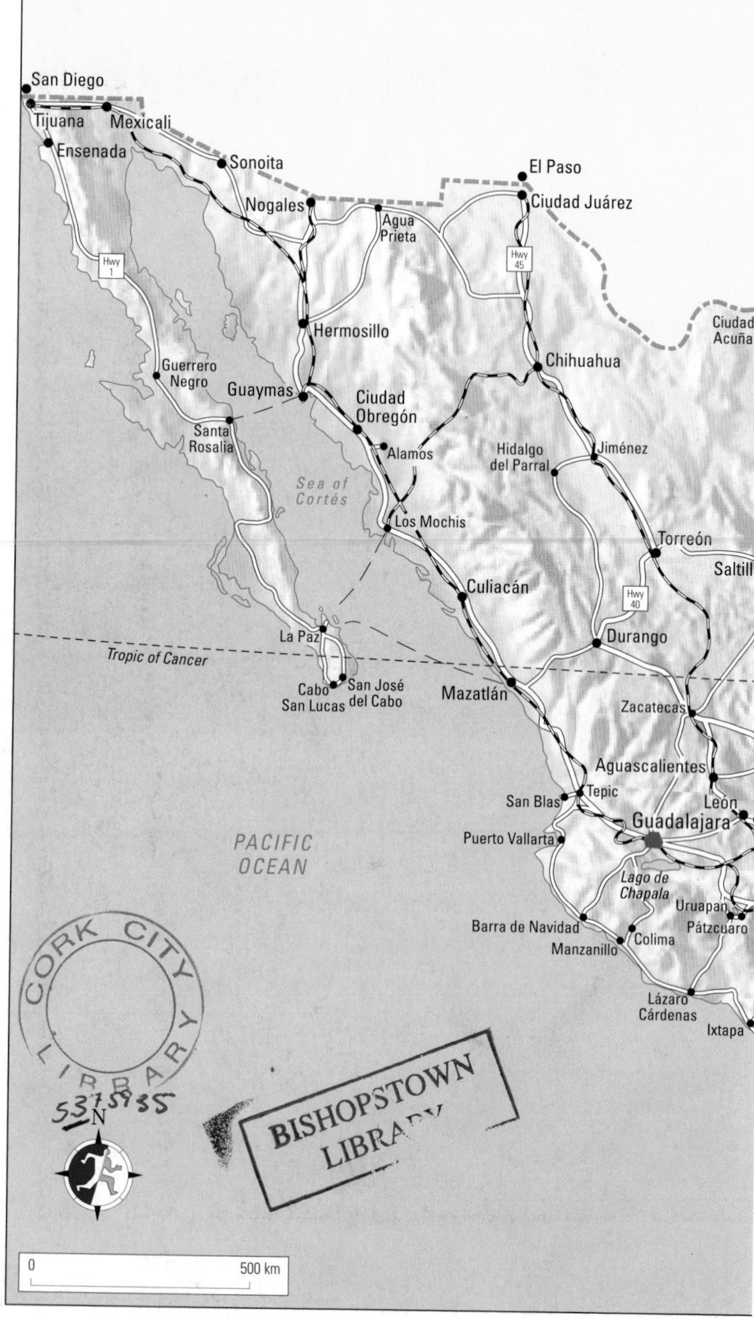
San Diego
Tijuana
Mexicali
Ensenada
Sonoita
El Paso
Ciudad Juárez
Nogales
Agua Prieta
Hwy 1
Hwy 45
Ciudad Acuña
Hermosillo
Chihuahua
Guerrero Negro
Guaymas
Ciudad Obregón
Santa Rosalia
Alamos
Hidalgo del Parral
Jiménez
Sea of Cortés
Los Mochis
Torreón
Saltillo
Culiacán
Hwy 40
La Paz
Durango
Tropic of Cancer
Cabo San Lucas
San José del Cabo
Mazatlán
Zacatecas
Aguascalientes
Tepic
San Blas
León
Guadalajara
Puerto Vallarta
PACIFIC OCEAN
Lago de Chapala
Uruapan
Pátzcuaro
Barra de Navidad
Colima
Manzanillo
Lázaro Cárdenas
Ixtapa
N
0
500 km

Introduction to

Mexico

Mexico enjoys a cultural blend that is wholly unique: it's among the fastest-growing industrial powers on the planet with sprawling cities full of modern architecture, yet it still appears, in places, like a half-forgotten Spanish colony, while the influence of native American culture, five hundred years after the Conquest, remains extraordinarily strong.

Each aspect can be found in isolation, but far more often, throughout the republic, the three co-exist – indigenous markets, little changed in form since the arrival of the Spanish, thrive alongside elaborate colonial churches in the shadow of the skyscrapers of the Mexican miracle. Occasionally, the marriage is an uneasy one, but for the most part it works surprisingly well. The people of Mexico reflect it, too: there are communities of full-blooded **indígenas**, and there are a few – a very few – Mexicans of pure **Spanish** descent. The great majority of the population, though, is **mestizo**, combining both traditions and, to a greater or lesser extent, a veneer of urban sophistication.

Despite encroaching US influence, a tide accelerated by the North American Free Trade Agreement (NAFTA), and close links with the rest of the Spanish-speaking world (an avid audience for Mexican soap operas), the country remains resolutely individual. Its music, its look, its sound, its smell rarely leave you in any doubt about where you are, and the thought "only in Mexico" – sometimes in awe, sometimes in exasperation, most often in simple bemusement – is rarely far from a traveller's mind. The strength of Mexican identity perhaps hits most clearly

Fact file

- Bordering the US, Guatemala and Belize, Mexico is technically part of **North America**. The country covers an **area** of virtually two million square kilometres and has a **population** of more than 100 million. Well over 20 million of them live in the capital and its immediate vicinity in the Valley of México.
- Physically, Mexico is a country of tremendous variety. The north is largely arid **semi-desert**, the south **tropical** and forested. The **volcanic mountains** of the centre rise to 5700m.
- The **economy** is growing rapidly, especially since the signing of **NAFTA**. Chief **exports** are oil and related products, silver and other metals and minerals, along with manufactured goods produced using Mexican labour in the border zone.
- Mexico is a **federal republic**, with a presidential system loosely based on that of the US. In practice, a single party, the PRI, governed from the establishment of the modern constitution in 1917 until President Vicente Fox Quesada, from the PAN opposition party, was elected in 2000.

▽ Cactus

if you travel overland across the border with the United States: this is the only place on earth where a single step will take you from the "First" world to the "Third". It's a small step that really is a giant leap.

You have to be prepared to adapt to travel in any country that is still "developing" and where change has been so dramatically rapid. Although the **mañana** mentality is largely an outsiders' myth, Mexico is still a country where timetables are not always to be entirely trusted, where anything that can break down will break down (when it's most needed), and where any attempt to do things in a hurry is liable to be frustrated. You simply have to accept the local temperament – that work may be necessary to live but it's not life's central focus, that minor annoyances really are minor, and that there's always something else to do in the meantime. At times it can seem that there's incessant, inescapable noise and dirt. More deeply disturbing are the extremes of ostentatious wealth and absolute poverty, most poignant in the big cities where unemployment and austerity measures imposed by the massive foreign debt have bitten hardest. But for the most part this is a friendly, fabulously varied and enormously enjoyable place in which to travel.

> **Any attempt to do things in a hurry is liable to be frustrated**

Physically, Mexico resembles a vast horn, curving away south and east from the US border with its final tip bent right back round to the north. It is an extremely mountainous country: two great ranges, the Sierra Madre Occidental in the west and the Sierra Madre Oriental in the east, run down parallel to the coasts, enclosing a high, semi-desert plateau. About halfway down they are crossed by the volcanic highland area in which stand Mexico City (or México; see the box overleaf) and the major centres of population. Beyond, the mountains run together as a single range through the southern states of Oaxaca and Chiapas. Only the eastern tip – the Yucatán peninsula – is consistently low-lying and flat.

Where to go

The north of Mexico, relatively speaking, is dull, arid and sparsely populated outside of a few industrial cities – like **Monterrey** – which are heavily American-influenced. The **Baja California** wilderness has its devotees, the border cities can be exciting in a rather sleazy way, and there are beach resorts on the Pacific, but most of the excitement lies in central and southeastern Mexico.

△ Mountain road, Sierra Tarahumara

México versus Mexico City

For clarity, we've referred to Mexico's capital as Mexico City throughout this guide, though its literal translation "Ciudad de México" is rarely used. To Mexicans it is known simply as México, La Ciudad, or El DF (El "day effay") – the Distrito Federal being the administrative zone that contains most of the urban areas. It's a source of infinite confusion to visitors, but the fact is that the country took its name from the city, and "México" in conversation almost always means the latter. The nation is La República, or occasionally in speeches La Patria – very rarely is it referred to as Mexico.

It's in the highlands north of and around the capital that the first really worthwhile stops come, with the bulk of the historic colonial towns and an enticingly spring-like climate year-round. Coming through the heart of the country, you'll pass the silver-mining towns of **Zacatecas** and **Guanajuato**, the historic centres of **San Miguel de Allende** and **Querétaro**, and many smaller places with a legacy of superb colonial architecture. **Mexico City** itself is a nightmare of urban sprawl, but totally fascinating, and in every way – artistic, political, cultural – the capital of the nation. Around the city lie the chief relics of the pre-Hispanic cultures of central Mexico – the massive pyramids of **Teotihuacán**; the main Toltec site at **Tula**; and **Tenochtitlán**, heart of the Aztec empire, in the capital itself. **Guadalajara**, to the west, is a city on a more human scale, capital of the state of **Jalisco** and in easy reach of **Michoacán**: between them, these states share some of the most gently scenic country in Mexico – thickly forested hills, studded with lakes and

▽ Copper Canyon train

△ Azulejos domes, Puerto Vallarta

ancient villages – and a reputation for producing some of the finest crafts in a country renowned for them.

South of the capital, the states of Oaxaca and Chiapas are mountainous and beautiful, too, but in a far wilder way. The city of **Oaxaca**, especially, is one of the most enticing destinations in the country, with an extraordinary mix of colonial and indigenous life, superb markets and fascinating archeological sites. **Chiapas** was the centre of the Zapatista uprising, though visitors are little affected these days, and the strength of indigenous traditions in and around the market town of **San Cristóbal de las Casas**, together with the opening-up of a number of lesser-known Maya cities, continue to make it a big travellers' centre. East into the **Yucatán** there is also traditional indigenous life, side by side with a tourist industry based around the magnificent Maya cities – **Palenque**, **Chichén Itzá** and **Uxmal** above all, but also scores of others – and the burgeoning new Caribbean resorts that surround **Cancún**. The capital, **Mérida**, continues its provincial life remarkably unaffected by the crowds all around.

On the Pacific coast, **Acapulco** is just the best-known of the destinations. Northwards, big resorts like **Mazatlán** and **Puerto Vallarta** are interspersed with hundreds of miles of empty beaches; to the south there is still less development, and in the state of Oaxaca there are some equally enticing shores. Few tourists venture over to the Gulf coast, despite the attractions of **Veracruz** and its mysterious ruins. The scene is largely dominated by oil, the weather too humid most of the time, and the beaches can be a disappointment.

The border cities can be exciting in a rather sleazy way

Before the Spanish

When the Spanish arrived in what is now Mexico in 1519, they were astonished to find a thriving, previously unknown civilization, in many ways as sophisticated as the one they had left behind. In fact, the Aztec empire was still evolving and expanding its domain. But where had they come from? These are some of the main names you'll come across on your travels:

- **Olmec** The earliest known civilization flourished in the low-lying jungles of southern Veracruz and Tabasco from around 1150 BC. We know little of the Olmecs, but their legacy speaks of a complex, highly organized society, and their religious and artistic legacy can be seen in everything that followed.
- **Teotihuacán** A vast, imposing city and the first of the powerful, centralizing cultures to dominate the high, central plain that has been the heart of Mexico ever since. At the height of its power from about 250 to 750 AD.
- **Maya** While Teotihuacán dominated the centre, an even more impressive society ruled over much of southeastern Mexico, Guatemala and beyond. At their height, the Maya population may have been around two million, based around at least forty substantial cities.
- **Zapotec** Based in the area around Oaxaca in the southwest, the Zapotecs developed the first known writing and calendar in the region – they too reached the height of their power in the Classic Period.
- **Toltec** After the fall of Teotihuacán, many groups vied for power in central Mexico. The Toltecs held sway over the region from their capital at Tula from around 900 to 1200 AD.
- **Aztec** The Aztecs (or Mexica or Tenochca) were the last and most successful of a series of invaders from the north. When its development was interrupted by the Spanish invasion, their empire had existed for less than a hundred years, yet had already grown to dominate an area equal to that of any of its predecessors.

△ Oxcutzcab market

When to go

To a great extent, the physical terrain in Mexico determines the **climate** – certainly far more than the expected indicators of latitude and longitude. You can drive down the coast all day without conditions changing noticeably, but turn inland to the mountains and the contrast is immediate: in temperature, scenery, vegetation, even the mood and mould of the people around you. Generalizations, therefore, are difficult.

Summer, from June to October, is in theory the rainy season, but just how wet it is varies wildly from place to place. In the heart of the country you can expect a heavy but short-lived downpour virtually every afternoon; in the north hardly any rain falls, ever. Chiapas is the wettest state, with many minor roads washed out in the autumn, and in the south and low-lying coastal areas summer is stickily humid too, with occasional spectacular tropical storms. Winter is the traditional tourist season, and in the big beach resorts like Acapulco and Cancún, December is the busiest month of the year. Mountain areas, though, can get very cold then: indeed nights in the mountains can be extremely cold at any time of year, so carry a sweater.

In effect there are now tourists all year round – sticking on the whole to the highlands in summer and the coasts in winter. Given a totally free choice, November is probably the ideal time to visit, with the rains over, the land still fresh, and the peak season not yet begun. Overall, though, the climate is so benign that any time of year will do, so long as you're prepared for some rain in the summer, some cold in winter, and for sudden changes which go with the altitude at any time.

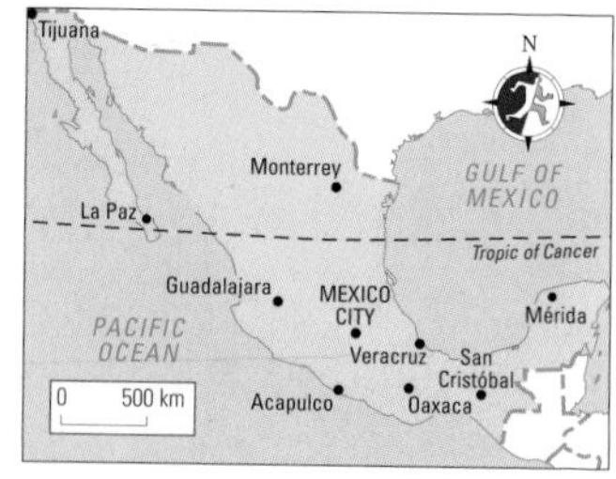

Average temperatures and rainfall

	Jan		Mar		May		Jul		Sep		Nov	
	Max	Min	Max	Min	Max	Min	Max	Min	Max	Min	Max	Min
Acapulco (˚F)	88	72	88	72	90	77	91	77	90	77	90	75
Rainfall (inch)	0.5		0.2		0		8		11		0.6	
Guadalajara (˚F)	73	45	82	48	88	57	79	59	79	59	77	50
Rainfall (inch)	0.5		0.3		1		7		7		0.5	
La Paz (˚F)	73	55	79	55	91	63	97	73	95	73	84	63
Rainfall (inch)	0.3		0		0		1		1		0.5	
Mérida (˚F)	82	64	90	68	93	70	91	73	90	73	84	66
Rainfall (inch)	1		0.5		3		5		7		1	
Mexico City (˚F)	72	43	81	50	81	55	75	55	73	55	73	48
Rainfall (inch)	0.5		0.5		3		6		5		0.5	
Monterrey (˚F)	68	48	79	55	88	68	93	72	93	72	73	54
Rainfall (inch)	1		1		2		3		4		1	
Oaxaca (˚F)	82	46	90	54	90	59	82	59	81	59	82	50
Rainfall (inch)	2		1		5		8		11		2	
San Cristóbal (˚F)	68	41	72	45	72	48	72	50	70	50	68	45
Rainfall (inch)	2		2		7		7		14		3	
Tijuana (˚F)	68	43	70	46	73	54	81	61	81	61	73	50
Rainfall (inch)	2		1		0.2		0		0.5		1	
Veracruz (˚F)	77	64	79	70	86	77	88	75	88	77	82	70
Rainfall (inch)	1		1		4		9		12		2	

To convert Fahrenheit to Centigrade, subtract 32, multiply by 5 and divide by 9.

To convert inches to millimeters, multiply by 25.4.

38

things not to miss

It's not possible to see everything that Mexico has to offer in one trip – and we don't suggest you try. What follows is a selective taste of the country's highlights: traditional markets, Maya ruins, relaxing beaches and spectacular landscapes. They're arranged in five colour-coded categories, which you can browse through to find the very best things to see and experience. All highlights have a page reference to take you straight into the guide, where you can find out more.

01 **Diving** Page **780** • From its northern Pacific to its southern Caribbean coasts, Mexico has some fantastic diving opportunities. Some of the best are to be found in the coral reefs off Isla Cozumel.

02 Great pyramid of Cholula Page **469** • The remains of the largest pyramid ever built may not be overly impressive now, but the fascinating tunnels that honeycomb it reveal elements of earlier temples and steep ceremonial stairways.

03 The Voladores de Papantla Page **569** • This ancient religious rite is now put on as much for tourists in the larger towns and cities as it is for locals in their villages, but it's no less breathtaking for that.

04 Cenotes, Valladolid Page **759** • Swim in the pools here, one of which has the roots of a huge alamo tree stretching down into it.

05 Sian Ka'an Biosphere Reserve Page **790** • One of the largest protected areas in Mexico, this stunning coastline comprises tropical forest, fresh- and salt-water marshes, mangroves and a section of the longest barrier reef in the western hemisphere.

06 Silver jewellery from Taxco Page **480** • No matter that this town is an interesting place in itself, Taxco offers the most exquisitely produced silverware in the country.

07 Football Page **440** • If you're a footy fan then you can't afford to miss out on the spectacular buzz generated by matches at Mexico City's Estadio Azteca, site of the 1970 and 1986 World Cups.

08 Tulum Page **785** • An important Maya spiritual and cultural centre and one of the most picturesque of all the sites, looking out across the Caribbean from its clifftop setting.

09 Whale-watching Page **94** • Ecotourism is ever more popular in Baja California, and with good reason. From December to April, for example, you can see some of the thousands of Alaskan grey whales which have come to mate in the lagoons of Guerrero Negro, San Ignacio, and Bahía Magdalena.

10 Tortillas Page **49** • The tortilla is the basis of many traditional Mexican dishes, from tacos to enchiladas. Fresh, cheap and available almost everywhere you go, it's the ultimate fast food.

11 Museo Frida Kahlo Page **416** • Politics, art and national identity combine at the home of Frida Kahlo, where she and her husband Diego Rivera – two of Mexico's most iconic artists – played host to Leon Trotsky.

12 Tequila in Tequila Page **247** • The blue agave is the basis for the archetypal Mexican drink, which is the main reason for being in Tequila. Over 100 million litres of tequila are manufactured every year, a process you can see at the distilleries here.

13 Coffee Page **51** • Veracruz is something of a garden state, growing some of the best produce in Mexico, and the coffee from Veracruz is no exception.

14 Chichén Itzá Page **750** • The most famous of the Maya sites, although its history remains uncertain. The impact of the ruins and carvings is undeniable, however, and it's well worth staying nearby so you can see them over a couple of days.

15 Monarch Butterfly Sanctuary Page **272** • Between November and mid-April, witness the amazing sight of millions of Monarch butterflies settling on the landscape, turning it a vibrant orange with their distinctive colouring.

16 Guanajuato Page **310** • This gorgeous colonial town, sandwiched into a narrow ravine, is home to one of the country's finest Baroque churches, a thriving student life, and a relaxed café and bar culture.

17 Chiles Page **48** • It's hard to escape from chiles in Mexican cooking, but this can only be a good thing – with at least a hundred varieties, their taste and degrees of intensity vary greatly, forming the basis of many a national dish. The jalapeño pepper is the one you'll encounter most.

18 Rodeo Page **438** • If you don't like the idea of seeing a bullfight, rodeos are almost as good a traditional spectator sport – the ultimate *charrería* (cowboy) event.

19 The Zócalo, Mexico City Page **376** • The heart of the modern city, of ancient Tenochtitlán and of Cortés' city, surrounded by the oldest streets, the cathedral, Aztec ruins, and the Palacio Nacional.

20 Day of the Dead Pages **57 & 261** • Celebrated on November 1 (and right through to the next day) with fervour across all of Mexico, nowhere are the festivities as vibrant – and moving – as on Lago de Pátzcuaro, when locals converge on the island of Janitzio in their canoes, a single candle alight in each one.

21 **Hammock** Page **727** • String a hammock from tree to tree and relax as locals do. Mérida, in the Yucatán, is the best place in the country to pick one up.

22 **Yaxchilán** Page **690** • Visit the remote ruins of this Classic Period Maya site and stay in the nearby Lacandón Maya community of Lacanhá Chansayab.

23 **El Tajín** Page **569** • Once the most important ancient city on the Gulf coast, by the time of the Conquest it had been forgotten and was only rediscovered by accident in 1785. Even now it remains one of the most mysterious archeological sites in Mexico – no one even knows who built it.

24 Oaxaca market Page **597** • Any market in Mexico is a feast for the senses, and in Oaxaca you'll find some of the best shopping in the entire country.

25 Tula Page **454** • The fantastic pre-Hispanic pyramid site of Tula, with its striking large statues atop the main pyramid, succeeded Teotihuacán as the Valley of México's great power.

26 Mariachis Page **432** • Probably the best-known of all Mexican music styles, you'll find *mariachi* played the length and breadth of the country. During the evenings hundreds of *mariachis* compete in Mexico City's Plaza Garibaldi for the crowds' attention and money in a blur of silver-spangled *charro* finery and grand sombreros.

27 Museo Nacional de Antropología Page **401** • Mexico's best and most important museum, with an enormous collection of artefacts from all the major pre-Columbian cultures.

28 Xochimilco Page **421** • Get punted around the canals here, taking in the carnival atmosphere and dazzling colours while being serendaded by *mariachi* bands, then wander the streets of Xochimilco town and visit the flower and fruit market.

29 The Bonampak murals Page **688** • Hidden deep in the forest until 1946, the ancient temples at Bonampak are home to the renowned murals depicting vivid scenes of Maya life – and sacrifice.

30 Lago de Pátzcuaro Page **261** • Beyond its famous Day of the Dead celebrations, the enchanting lake is a worthy destination in itself.

31 Palenque Page **680** • This Maya site is remarkable not only for its distinct architectural style but also for its setting – surrounded by hills covered in jungle, right at the edge of the great Yucatán plain.

32 Turquoise waters and white-sand beaches Page **101** • The Pacific coast around Bahía Concepción is classic picture-postcard material and a must for all beach lovers.

33 Calakmul Page **726** • Partially restored and in the heart of the jungle, this is considered the biggest archeological area in Mesoamerica, with a stunning seven thousand buildings in its central area alone.

34 The zócalo in Veracruz Page **557** • One of the most enjoyable places in the republic in which to chill out. In the evening, the tables under the *portales* of the plaza fill up, and the drinking and the marimba music begin.

35 The Rivera murals Page **380** • Diego Rivera's work is inextricably linked with the Mexicans' sense of national identity, a particularly powerful theme in his classic murals at the Palacio Nacional.

36 Oaxacan textiles Pages **607 & 612** • Some of the country's best-made and most imaginative textiles are to be found in the city of Oaxaca – though you can go one better and buy them direct from the villages where they are made.

37 The Copper Canyon Page **169** • Whether on the breathtaking train ride here from the west coast or hiking along the canyon and visiting the beautiful towns along its floor, a visit to the canyon is a definite highlight of any trip to northern Mexico.

38 Santo Domingo church, Oaxaca Page **595** • A sixteenth-century architectural feast, carved and decorated inside and out, rated by Aldous Huxley as "one of the most extravagantly gorgeous churches in the world".

Contents

Using this Rough Guide

We've tried to make this Rough Guide a good read and easy to use. The book is divided into six main sections, and you should be able to find whatever you want in one of them.

Colour section

The front colour section offers a quick tour of Mexico. The **introduction** aims to give you a feel for the place, with suggestions on where to go. We also tell you what the weather is like and include a basic country fact file. Next, our authors round up their favourite aspects of Mexico in the **things not to miss** section – whether it's a local festival, amazing sight or a special hotel. Right after this comes the Rough Guide's full **contents** list.

Basics

The Basics section covers all the **pre-departure** nitty-gritty to help you plan your trip. This is where to find out which airlines fly to your destination, what paperwork you'll need, what to do about money and insurance, about Internet access, food, security, public transport, car rental – in fact just about every piece of **general practical information** you might need.

Guide

This is the heart of the Rough Guide, divided into user-friendly chapters, each of which covers a specific region. Every chapter starts with a list of **highlights** and an **introduction** that helps you to decide where to go, depending on your time and budget. Likewise, introductions to the various towns and smaller regions within each chapter should help you plan your itinerary. We start most town accounts with information on arrival and accommodation, followed by a tour of the sights, and finally reviews of places to eat and drink, and details of nightlife. Longer accounts also have a directory of practical listings. Each chapter concludes with **public transport** details for that region.

Contexts

Read Contexts to get a deeper understanding of how Mexico ticks. We include a brief **history**, articles about **ancient belief systems**, the **environment**, **wildlife** and **music**, together with a detailed further reading section that reviews dozens of **books** relating to the country.

Language

Our language section gives you all the **Mexican Spanish** you'll need to get by, with **everyday phrases** and an extensive **menu reader**, followed by **glossaries** of terms used throughout the guide.

Index + small print

Apart from a **full index**, which includes maps as well as places, this section covers publishing information, credits and acknowledgements, and also has our contact details in case you want to send in updates and corrections to the book – or suggestions as to how we might improve it.

Chapter list and map

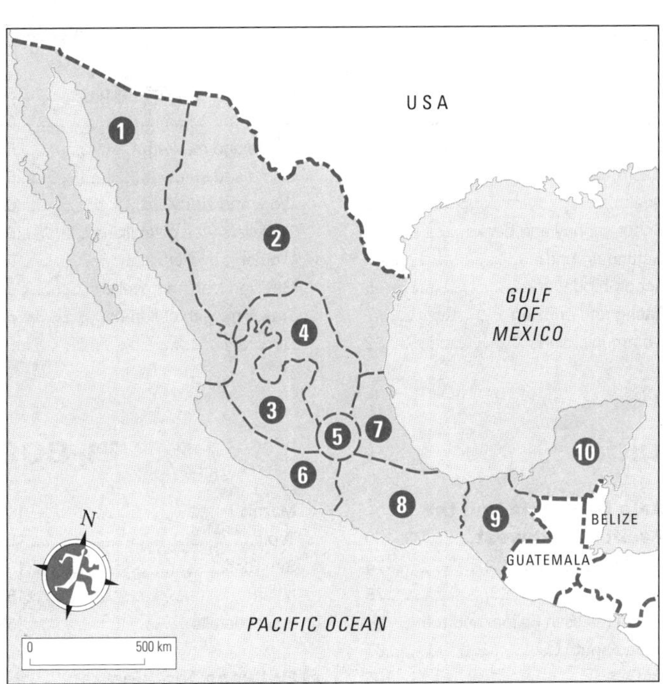

Contents

Colour section i–xxiv

Basics 9–70

Guide 71–802

Contexts 803–870

Language 871–881

small print and Index 897–912

Basics

Basics

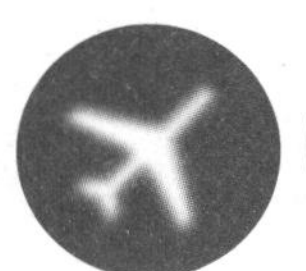

Getting there

The quickest and easiest way to get to Mexico is to fly. Going overland from the US won't save you much money, if any, but becomes rather more convenient the nearer you live to the border. Unless you've got your own boat, getting there by water is only normally possible on a cruise ship.

Barring special offers and airpasses, the best fares will carry certain restrictions, such as advance booking (an **Apex** ticket, for example, which must be booked at least fourteen days before departure) and fixed dates, with a penalty charge if you change your schedule. They may also limit your stay – typically to between 7 and 21 days. Many airlines offer **youth** or **student fares** to those 25 and younger, though requirements vary; a passport or driving licence is sufficient proof of age, though these tickets are subject to availability and can have eccentric booking conditions – If you qualify, you'll save perhaps eight to ten percent, but you'll need to book as far in advance as possible, as seat availability at these prices is limited. It's worth remembering that most cheap round-trip fares involve spending at least one Saturday night away and that many will only give a percentage refund if you need to cancel or alter your journey.

You can often cut costs by going through a **specialist flight agent** – either a consolidator (in North America), who buys up blocks of tickets from the airlines and sells them at a discount, or a discount agent, who in addition to dealing with discounted flights may also offer special **student and youth fares** and a range of other travel-related services such as travel insurance, rail passes, car rentals, tours and the like. Some agents specialize in charter flights, which may be cheaper than any available scheduled flight, but again departure dates are fixed and withdrawal penalties are high. Don't automatically assume that tickets purchased through a travel specialist will be cheapest, however – once you get a quote, check with the airlines and you may turn up an even better deal. A further possibility is to see if you can arrange a **courier flight**, although you'll need a flexible schedule, and preferably be travelling alone with very little luggage. In return for shepherding a parcel through customs, you can expect to get a deeply discounted ticket. You'll probably also be restricted in the duration of your stay.

To some extent, the fare will depend on the **season**. Though prices to Mexico City (or México, also referred to as "El DF") and non-resort destinations show little if any fluctuation, fares to Mexico are otherwise highest around Easter, from early June to mid-September and at Christmas and New Year, when prices – especially to the resort areas – will run higher than in low season. Prices drop during the "shoulder" seasons – mid-September to early November and mid-April to early June – and you'll get the best deals during the low season, November to April (excluding Christmas and the New Year, of course). Note also that flying at weekends adds to the round-trip fare; the typical lowest round-trip Apex prices quoted below assume midweek travel in high season.

If Mexico is only one stop on a longer journey, you might want to consider buying a **Round-the-World (RTW) ticket**. Some travel agents can sell you an "off-the-shelf" RTW ticket that will have you touching down in about half a dozen cities; others will have to assemble one for you, which can be tailored to your needs but is apt to be more expensive.

Online travel agents

Many airlines and discount travel websites offer you the opportunity to book your tickets **online**, cutting out the costs of agents and middlemen. Good deals can often be found through discount or auction sites, as well as through the airlines' own websites.

Online booking agents and general travel sites

www.cheapflights.com (in US, UK and Ireland); **www.cheapflights.ca** (in Canada); **www.cheapflights.com.au** (in Australia). Flight deals, travel agents, plus links to other travel sites.
www.cheaptickets.com Discount flight specialists (US only).
www.deckchair.com Bob Geldof's online venture, drawing on a wide range of airlines.
www.etn.nl/discount.htm A hub of consolidator and discount agent web links, maintained by the nonprofit European Travel Network.
www.expedia.com (in US); **www.expedia.ca** (in Canada); **www.expedia.co.uk** (in UK). Discount airfares, all-airline search engine and daily deals.
www.flyaow.com Online air travel info and reservations site.
www.geocities.com/thavery2000 Has an extensive list of airline toll-free numbers (from the US) and websites.
www.hotwire.com Bookings from the US only. Last-minute savings of up to forty percent on regular published fares. Travellers must be at least 18 and there are no refunds, transfers or changes allowed. Log-in required.
www.lastminute.com (in UK); **www.lastminute.com.au** (in Australia). Offers good last-minute holiday package and flight-only deals.
www.priceline.com (in US); **www.priceline.co.uk** (in UK). You make an offer of what you will pay for a flight on a certain date and if they find a ticket at an equivalent value, a non-refundable, non-transferable and non-changeable ticket will be purchased. Savings run as high as forty percent off standard fares, but you cannot specify flight times and you need to be sure about dates as you are locked into the ticket. Bid low at the beginning.
www.skyauction.com Bookings from the US only. Auctions tickets and travel packages using a "second bid" scheme. The best strategy is to bid the maximum you're willing to pay, since if you win you'll pay just enough to beat the runner-up regardless of your maximum bid.
www.smilinjack.com/airlines.htm Lists an up-to-date compilation of airline website addresses.
www.travelocity.com Destination guides, hot web fares and best deals for car rental, accommodation and lodging as well as fares. Provides access to the travel agent system SABRE, the most comprehensive central reservations system in the US.
www.travelshop.com.au Australian website offering discounted flights, packages, insurance, and online bookings.

Flights from the US and Canada

There are flights to Mexico from just about every major **US** city, but the cheapest and most frequent depart from "gateway" cities in the south and west, most commonly LA, Dallas, Houston and Miami.

If you live close to the border, it's usually cheaper to cross into Mexico and take an **internal flight** (which you can arrange through your local travel agent). If it's a resort that you want, you'll probably find that at least one of the airlines offers an attractive deal including a few nights' lodging (see "Packages and organized tours", p.14).

Aeroméxico and Mexicana fly direct to dozens of destinations in Mexico, and can make connections to many others; the bigger US airlines have connections to Mexico City and the more popular resorts. **Fares** are most competitive from Dallas and Houston, where round-trip flights to Mexico City start around US$275, rising to US$400–450 to Acapulco and Cancún (sometimes less if you don't mind an indirect flight, changing planes en route), and US$450 to Mérida. From LA, figure on US$300 to Mexico City, US$400 to Acapulco and US$450 to Mérida or Cancún. Flights from Miami to Mérida or Cancún are also good value, hovering between US$300 and US$400 round-trip. From New York, a round-trip flight to Mexico City or Cancún should cost around US$350, rising to US$450 for Mérida, or US$475 for Acapulco. There are direct flights to many parts of Mexico from numerous US airports, but in any case adding a feeder flight from any city to one of the main gateways should be straightforward.

Charter, promotional, student/youth and other **discounted** fares routinely run US$100–200 lower than those listed above.

There are few direct scheduled flights **from Canada** to Mexico, although Air Canada flies from Toronto, Vancouver and Montreal to Mexico City, and from Toronto and Montreal to Cancún, and charter flights are plentiful in the winter. There's even currently a Japan Airlines flight from Vancouver to

Mexico City en route from Tokyo. Your options expand greatly if you fly via the US. Typical lowest round-trip fares are: Montreal to Mexico City Can$850, to Cancún Can$875, and to Acapulco Can$1250; Toronto to Mexico City Can$850, to Cancún Can$850, and to Acapulco Can$1150; and from Vancouver to Mexico City Can$900, to Cancún Can$900, and to Acapulco Can$1000.

Airlines in the US and Canada

Aero California ⓣ1-800/237-6225, ⓦwww.abstravel.com/aerocalifornia. LA to Durango, Hermosillo, Manzanillo, Mazatlán, Monterrey, Mexico City and Puerto Vallarta.

Aeroméxico ⓣ1-800/237-6639 or 713/939-0077, ⓦwww.aeromexico.com. Atlanta, Chicago, Dallas, Houston, Las Vegas, LA, Miami, New York, Oakland, Phoenix, Salt Lake City, San Diego and Vancouver to Mexico City; Atlanta, LA, Las Vegas, Miami, New York, Ontario, Phoenix and Tucson to Guadalajara; Atlanta, Cincinnati, LA, Miami and New York to Cancún; LA to Acapulco, Aguascalientes, Hermosillo, Ixtapa, León/Bajío, Los Cabos and Mérida; New York to Acapulco, Monterrey and Puerto Vallarta; San Antonio to Aguascalientes and Monterrey; Ontario, California to Los Cabos; El Paso to Chihuahua and Durango; Houston to Ixtapa; San Diego to Los Cabos; Las Vegas, Phoenix, Salt Lake City and Tucson to Hermosillo; Atlanta and Las Vegas to Monterrey; Salt Lake City and Tucson to Mazatlán; Miami to Mérida.

Air Canada ⓣ1-888/247-2262, ⓦwww.aircanada.ca. Montreal, Toronto and Vancouver to Mexico City; Montreal and Toronto to Cancún.

Alaska Airlines ⓣ1-800/252-7522, ⓦwww.alaska-air.com. LA to Cancún, Guadalajara, Ixtapa, Los Cabos, Manzanillo, Mazatlán and Puerto Vallarta; Seattle to Cancún, Guadalajara, Ixtapa, Los Cabos and Puerto Vallarta; Portland to Ixtapa, Los Cabos, Manzanillo, Mazatlán and Puerto Vallarta; San Francisco to Ixtapa, Los Cabos and Puerto Vallarta; Anchorage to Cancún and Los Cabos; Fairbanks and Spokane to Puerto Vallarta; Reno to Ixtapa and Manzanillo; San Diego and Spokane to Los Cabos.

America West Airlines ⓣ1-800/235-9292, ⓦwww.americawest.com. Phoenix to Acapulco, Cancún, Guadalajara, Hermosillo, Ixtapa, Los Cabos, Mazatlán, Mexico City and Puerto Vallarta; Las Vegas and Spokane to Mexico City; Burbank, Las Vegas, San José and Spokane to Puerto Vallarta; St Louis to Ixtapa; Dallas to Mazatlán; Las Vegas, New York and Sacramento to Los Cabos; Bakersfield and Medford to Guadalajara.

American Airlines ⓣ1-800/433-7300, ⓦwww.aa.com. Boston, Burbank, Chicago, Dallas, LA, Miami, Philadelphia and Seattle to Mexico City; Chicago, Dallas, LA, Miami, New York, Phoenix, St Louis, San Francisco, Seattle and Tampa to Cancún; Dallas to Aguascalientes, Guadalajara, León/Bajío, Los Cabos, Monterrey and Puerto Vallarta; LA, Phoenix and Raleigh to Los Cabos; New York and Indianapolis to León/Bajío; Oakland and Richmond to Puerto Vallarta; New Orleans, New York and Philadelphia to Guadalajara.

Aviacsa ⓣ1-888/528-4227, ⓦwww.aviacsa.com.mx. Chicago, Houston, Las Vegas and LA to Monterrey; Houston and Oakland to Mexico City; LA to León/Bajío; Las Vegas to Guadalajara.

Continental Airlines ⓣ1-800/231-0856, ⓦwww.continental.com. Houston to Acapulco, Aguascalientes, Cancún, Chihuahua, Cozumel, Guadalajara, Ixtapa, León/Bajío, Los Cabos, Mazatlán, Mérida, Mexico City, Monterrey and Puerto Vallarta; Newark to Cancún, Cozumel, León/Bajío, Mexico City, Monterrey and Puerto Vallarta; Atlanta, Chicago, Cleveland, Salt Lake City and San Francisco to Mexico City; Albuquerque, Chicago, Cleveland, Columbus, Oakland, Orlando, Philadelphia, Raleigh, Sacramento, San Antonio and West Palm Beach to Cancún; Boston, Las Vegas and San Antonio to Acapulco; Birmingham to Aguascalientes; Cleveland to Los Cabos; Jacksonville, LA and Miami to León/Bajío; Tampa to Cozumel; Charleston to Mazatlán; Indianapolis and Greeensboro to Chihuahua; St Louis to Ixtapa; Charlotte, Columbia SC, Dallas and Toronto to Monterrey; Austin, Birmingham, Cincinnati, Dallas and Philadelphia to Guadalajara; Fort Lauderdale and Phoenix to Puerto Vallarta; Columbus and San Antonio to Mérida.

Delta Air Lines ⓣ1-800/241-4141, ⓦwww.delta.com. Atlanta, Chicago, Dallas, Houston, Las Vegas, LA, Miami, New York, Phoenix, Salt Lake City and San Diego to Mexico City; Atlanta, LA, Las Vegas, Ontario, Phoenix and Tucson to Guadalajara; LA to Acapulco, Aguascalientes, Hermosillo, León/Bajío and Puerto Vallarta; Atlanta, New York and San Antonio to Monterrey; San Antonio to Aguascalientes; El Paso to Chihuahua; San Diego to Los Cabos; Salt Lake City and Tucson to Hermosillo and Mazatlán; Phoenix and Las Vegas to Hermosillo; Miami to Mérida.

Japan Airlines ⓣ1-800/525-3663, ⓦwww.japanair.com. Vancouver to Mexico City.

Mexicana ⓣ1-800/531-7921, ⓦwww.mexicana.com. Austin, Chicago, Dallas, LA, Miami, Montreal, Oakland, Portland,

Sacramento, San Antonio, San Francisco, San José, Toronto, Vancouver and Washington to Mexico City; Austin, Dallas, Miami, San Francisco and Toronto to Cancún; Las Vegas, LA, Oakland, Portland, Sacramento, San Francisco and Vancouver to Guadalajara; Chicago to Durango, Guadalajara, León/Bajío, Monterrey, Puerto Vallarta and Zacatecas; LA to Cancún, León/Bajío, Los Cabos and Mazatlán; El Paso to Chihuahua; Oakland to Zacatecas; Vancouver to Monterrey.

Northwest ⓣ1-800/447-4747, ⓦwww.nwa.com. Detroit and Washington to Mexico City; Memphis to Cancún.

Taca US ⓣ1-800/535-8780, Canada ⓣ1-888/261-3269, ⓦwww.taca.com. VICA, Mayan and Latino airpasses.

United Airlines ⓣ1-800/538-2929, ⓦwww.ual.com. Boston, Chicago, LA, Miami, New York, San Antonio, San Francisco, Seattle and Washington to Mexico City; LA to Cancún, Guadalajara, León/Bajío, Los Cabos, Mazatlán and Zacatecas; Chicago to Guadalajara, Monterrey and Puerto Vallarta; Oakland and San Francisco to Guadalajara; Miami to Cancún.

US Airways ⓣ1-800/622-1015, ⓦwww.usairways.com. Charlotte, Pittsburgh and Washington to Cancún; Charlotte to Cozumel.

Discount travel companies in the US and Canada

Air Courier Association ⓣ1-800/282-1202, ⓦwww.aircourier.org. Courier flight broker. Membership (3 months/$19, 1yr/$29, 3yr/$58, 5yr/$87) also entitles you to twenty percent discount on travel insurance and name-your-own-price non-courier flights.

Council Travel ⓣ1-800/2COUNCIL, ⓦwww.counciltravel.com. Student/budget travel agency with branches in many US cities (flights from US only).

eXito ⓣ1-800/655-4053 or 970/482-3019, ⓦwww.exitotravel.com. Latin America independent travel specialists. Their webpage has a particularly useful airfare finder and much other invaluable information.

International Association of Air Travel Couriers ⓣ308/632-3273, ⓦwww.courier.org. Courier flight broker with membership fee of US$45 per year or US$80 for two years.

Last Minute Club ⓣ1-877/970-3500, ⓦwww.lastminuteclub.com. Canada-based travel club specializing in stand-by flights and packages.

Now Voyager ⓣ212/459-1616, ⓦwww.nowvoyagertravel.com. New York-based courier flight broker and consolidator.

STA Travel US ⓣ1-800/781-4040, Canada 1-888/427-5639, ⓦwww.sta-travel.com. Worldwide discount travel firm specializing in student/youth fares, with branches in the New York, Los Angeles, San Francisco and Boston areas; also student IDs, travel insurance, car rental and other travel needs.

Travel Avenue ⓣ1-800/333-3335, ⓦwww.travelavenue.com. Full-service travel agent that offers discounts in the form of rebates.

Travel CUTS Canada ⓣ1-800/667-2887, US ⓣ1-866/246-9762, ⓦwww.travelcuts.com. Canada's main student travel firm, specializing in student fares, IDs and other travel services.

Packages and organized tours

Hundreds of independent companies offer good-value **package tours** to Mexican resorts, as do the tour arms of most major North American airlines. Packages are generally only available for the more commercialized destinations, such as Cabo San Lucas, Mazatlán, Puerto Vallarta, Acapulco, Ixtapa or Cancún, and travel agents usually only give you one or two weeks. If, however, what you want is a week on a Mexican beach, your best bet is to comb the Sunday newspaper travel sections for the latest bargains and then see if your local travel agent can turn up anything better. Prices vary tremendously by resort, season and style of accommodation, but one week in a good hotel in any of the resorts above will generally start at US$500 per person. Prices may be less than that on last-minute deals, available a week or two before the departure date. The busiest times for North Americans travelling to Mexican resorts are during Christmas and college spring break, when you'll be less likely to get the flight or the fare you want.

In addition, literally hundreds of **specialist companies** offer tours of Mexico based around hiking, biking, diving, bird-watching and the like. See p.16 for just a few of the possibilities; a travel agent should be able to point out others. Remember that bookings made through a travel agent cost no more than going through the tour operator – indeed, many tour companies sell only through agents. Unless stated, the prices we've quoted do not include the cost of actually getting to Mexico. For operators that run trips exclusively for travellers with disabilities see p.64.

Airpasses in Mexico

If you want to visit several destinations in a fairly short time (and even travel onwards to Central or South America), then there are a few **airpasses** worth considering – these can be especially useful if combined with the flexibility of an open-ended ticket.

The **MexiPass** consists of prebooked and prepaid coupons for internal flights on Mexicana and Aeroméxico (including subsidiaries Aerocaribe and Aerocozumel, serving Yucatán) at discount prices for travellers from outside Mexico. Travel into Mexico can be on any airline (but some fares are lower if you use Mexicana or Aeroméxico), the pass is valid for ninety days, costs the same from every supplier and you'll need to purchase a minimum of two coupons and book routes and dates in advance. Date (but not route) changes can be made without paying a penalty, provided space is available on the flight you want. Prices are for one-way flights, based on zones, increasing the further you fly, and do not include domestic departure taxes (currently US$16 per flight): Mexico City to Acapulco, for example, is US$80; Mexico City to Cancún US$150; Oaxaca to Mérida US$120. The **MexiPass Inter** is similar, but also includes international flights on the Mexican carriers between the USA, Canada and South America, and you need to buy at least three coupons. It offers real advantages on the longer flights: for example, Miami–Mexico City–Oaxaca–Cancún–Miami will cost US$490; and Toronto–Mexico City–Oaxaca–Cancún–Havana (Cuba)–Mexico City–Toronto costs US$890.

If you're travelling to Mexico and also want to fly to Central or South America, then Taca's **Latin Air Flexi Pass** (valid on Taca, Aviateca and Lacsa) is worth thinking about. The pass links North American gateways and cities in Mexico with all the capitals and some other cities in Central America, as well as with some destinations in South America and the Caribbean. For example, a routing Mexico City–Guatemala City–Flores–Belize–San José will be around US$485, saving almost one-third on flying the same route without the pass.

The potential permutations are mind-boggling, but the savings can be considerable; you need to think seriously about what you want to see, and in what order, before you go. The best way to find out how (or if) an airpass will benefit you is to call either the airlines concerned or a specialist flight agent.

More countercultural, and arguably better value, are **overland routes** covered by **Green Tortoise Adventure Travel**. Converted school buses provide reasonably comfortable transport and sleeping space for up to 35 people; the clientele comes from all over the world, and communal cookouts are the rule. Most of their tours depart from the San Francisco headquarters, but add-on journeys from Boston, New York and many points along the Pacific Coast are easily arranged on one of Green Tortoise's cross-country services. The routes that currently include Mexico are the nine- and fifteen-day overland adventures through Baja from November to April (US$490–700), or a seventeen-day Baja trip in February including two days' whale-watching (US$750), a 28-day San Francisco–Cancún "Winter Migration" (US$1090–1200), and a fifteen-day Yucatán trip (US$700 plus airfare to Cancún). For more information, contact their main office at 494 Broadway, San Francisco, CA 94133 (ⓣ415/956-7500 or 1-800/TORTOISE, ⓦwww.greentortoise.com).

Package tour operators in the US and Canada

Future Vacations ⓣ1-888/788-2545, ⓦwww.futurevacations.com. Vacation packages in Acapulco, Cancún, Cozumel, Los Cabos and Puerto Vallarta.

Globus ⓣ1-800/755-8581, ⓦwww.globusjourneys.com. Nine-day Copper Canyon tour from US$1499.

International Student Tours Canada ⓣ1-888/472-3933, ⓦwww.istours.com. Student group-travel company offering resort packages to Mazatlán (a week from Can$989 including airfare) and Puerto Vallarta (a week from Can$979 including airfare).

Majestic Mexico Tours ⓣ1-877/MEX-MEX2, ⓦwww.mexico-tours.com. First-class sightseeing tours celebrating colonial Mexico. seven-day Colonial Cities tour from US$879 plus airfare, fourteen-day Grand Tour from US$2029 plus airfare.

Pleasant Holidays – Mexico ⓣ1-800/742 9244, ⓦwww.2mexico.com. Getaways to various beach resorts including Acapulco, Cancún, Cozumel, Ixtapa, Los Cabos, Mazatlán and Puerto Vallarta.

Suntrips ⓣ1-800/SUNTRIPS, ⓦwww.suntrips.com. Wholesale travel company offering resort packages to Cabo San Lucas, Puerto Vallarta, Cancún and Cozumel from Denver and Oakland.

Specialist tour operators in the US and Canada

Adventure Center ⓣ1-800/228-8747, ⓦwww.adventure-center.com. Specializes in ecologically sound adventure travel. A fifteen-day "Ancient Civilizations" trip through Oaxaca, Chiapas and the Yucatán, for example, starts at US$995.

Adventures Abroad ⓣ1-800/665-3998, ⓦwww.adventures-abroad.com. Canada-based travel planners providing small-group tours. A seven-day tour of the Yucatán's ancient sites costs US$1246; a nine-day tour of central Mexico (Toluca, Morelia, Pátzcuaro, Guadalajara, Guanajuato, San Miguel de Allende) starts at US$944.

Backroads ⓣ1-800/GO-ACTIVE, ⓦwww.backroads.com. Hiking, biking and kayaking tours to Baja California and other destinations, starting at US$2298 per person for a six-day trip.

Baja Expeditions ⓣ1-800/843-6967, ⓦwww.bajaex.com. Sea kayaking, whale-watching, snorkelling and scuba diving, among other tours. Five days' whale-watching in February or March costs US$1925 including flight from San Diego; diving packages start at US$365 per person for two days' diving and three nights' accommodation.

Ecosummer Expeditions ⓣ1-800/465-8884, ⓦwww.ecosummer.com. Sea kayaking and whale-watching in Baja from US$1195.

G.A.P. Adventures ⓣ1-800/465-5600, ⓦwww.gap.ca. Guided adventure trips (some camping); US$1395 for three weeks on the Ruta Maya through the Yucatán, Chiapas, Guatemala and Belize, or US$995 for a two-week "Ancient Civilizations" trip from Mexico City to Cancún.

Global Exchange ⓣ1-800/497-1994 or 415/255-7296, ⓦwww.globalexchange.org. Organization campaigning on international issues which offers "Reality Tours" to increase American travellers' awareness of real life in other countries, costing US$750 on average.

Mountain Travel Sobek ⓣ1-888/MTSOBEK, ⓦwww.mtsobek.com. Outdoor active adventure trips including sea kayaking or whale-watching in Baja (7 days for US$1390), or a Copper Canyon hike (8 days for US$1790).

Questers Worldwide Nature Tours ⓣ1-800/468-8668, ⓦwww.questers.com. Offer small-group, eleven-day overland tours exploring the natural history of the Copper Canyon for US$2430.

S&S Tours ⓣ1-800/499-5685 or 520/458-6365, ⓦwww.ss-tours.com. Adventure tours in the Copper Canyon, whale-watching in Baja California, or colonial cities and monarch butterflies in Michoacán. Six- to nine-day tours range from US$1495 to US$2190.

Smithsonian Journeys ⓣ1-877/EDU-TOUR, ⓦwww.si.edu/tsa/sst/start.htm. Educational tours including nine days in the Copper Canyon for US$2995, or a thirteen-day Maya tour in Chiapas, the Yucatán, Guatemala and Honduras for US$4990.

Suntrek ⓣ1-800/SUNTREK, ⓦwww.suntrek.com. Overland adventure tours, including two weeks on the Ruta Maya from US$799, three weeks in Mexico City, Oaxaca, Chiapas and the Yucatán from US$1077, or a six-week "Gran Traversa" from LA to Cancún from US$2039.

Wilderness Travel ⓣ1-800/368-2794, ⓦwww.wildernesstravel.com. Twelve days on the Ruta Maya in Chiapas, Guatemala and Honduras from US$2895 (depending on how many people take the tour), and eight days' sea kayaking in Baja from US$1495.

Overland from the US

There are more than forty **frontier posts** along the US–Mexican border. Many of them, however, are only open during the day, and more or less inaccessible without your own transport (for a full list and map, see ⓦwww.ibwc.state.gov/LANDBOUN/BRIDGES/body_bridges_crossings.htm). The main ones, open 24 hours a day, seven days a week, are, from west to east:

San Diego, California – Tijuana, Baja California Norte.
Calexico, California – Mexicali, Baja California Norte.
Nogales, Arizona – Nogales, Sonora.
Douglas, Arizona – Agua Prieta, Sonora.
El Paso, Texas – Ciudad Juárez, Chihuahua.
Laredo, Texas – Nuevo Laredo, Tamaulipas.
Brownsville, Texas – Matamoros, Tamaulipas.

By bus

North American **bus travel** is pretty grim compared to the relative comfort of Amtrak, but you have a wider range of US border posts to choose from. Count on at least 45 hours' journey time from New York to a Texas frontier post (US$99–159), or at least eleven and a half hours from San Francisco to Tijuana (US$53–57) – and a further day's travel from either point to Mexico City.

Since the North American Free Trade Agreement (NAFTA), many Mexican bus companies now also cross the border into the US, so that you can pick up a bus back into Mexico as far north as Houston or LA.

Greyhound (Ⓣ1-800/229-9424, Ⓦwww.greyhound.com) runs regularly to all the major border crossings, and some of their buses will take you over the frontier and to a Mexican bus station, which saves a lot of hassle. Greyhound agents abroad should also be able to reserve your through tickets with their Mexican counterparts, which is even more convenient but involves a lot of pre-planning.

A cheap and cheerful alternative to the rigours of Greyhound travel is an overland tour in one of Green Tortoise's summer-of-love style buses (see "Packages and organized tours" on p.15).

By rail

US passenger **train** services reach the border at El Paso, on the LA–Dallas line. El Paso is served by Amtrak's *Texas Eagle* (three times weekly from Chicago, St Louis, Little Rock, Dallas, Tucson and LA) and *Sunset Limited* (three times weekly from Orlando, Jacksonville, New Orleans, Houston, Tucson and LA). The journey takes 19 hours from Houston, 26 from Dallas, 37.5 from Orlando, 16 from LA, and 49 from Chicago.

Afternoon arrivals on these services give you plenty of time to get across the frontier, have supper in Ciudad Juárez, and get an evening bus departure down to Mexico City.

Check current **timetables** with Amtrak (Ⓣ1-800/USA-RAIL, Ⓦwww.amtrak.com).

By car

Taking your own **car** into Mexico will obviously give you a great deal more freedom, but it's an option fraught with complications. Aside from the border formalities, you'll have to contend with the state of the roads, the style of driving and the quality of the fuel – these considerations are dealt with in more detail on p.42.

US, Canadian, British, Irish, Australian, New Zealand and most European **driving licences** are valid in Mexico, but it's a good idea to arm yourself with an International Driving Licence – available to US citizens for a nominal fee from the American Automobile Association (Ⓣ1-800/AAA-HELP, Ⓦwww.aaa.com), and to Canadian drivers from the Canadian Automobile Association (Ⓣ613/247-0117, Ⓦwww.caa.ca). If you run afoul of a Mexican traffic cop for any reason, show that first, and if they abscond with it you at least still have your own (more difficult to replace) licence.

As a rule, you can drive in Baja and the Zona Libre (the border area extending roughly 20km into Mexico) without any special **formalities**. To drive elsewhere in Mexico, however, you must obtain a temporary importation permit (around US$25) from the Departamento de Migración at the border. This must be paid for using a major credit card, otherwise you'll be asked for a refundable bond – the amount depends on the make and age of your vehicle, but it will be at least US$400 for a car less than four years old, and can reach well over US$1000 – plus nonrefundable tax and commission. You'll need to show registration and title for the car, plus your driver's licence and passport, and you'll probably be asked to supply photocopies of these and of your tourist card. The permits are good for 180 days. To make sure you don't sell the car in Mexico or a neighbouring country, you'll also be required either to post a cash bond equal to the vehicle's book value, deposited at a branch of Banejército (which has offices at border posts for the purposes), or to give an imprint of a major credit card (Visa, MasterCard, Diners Club or Amex). Plastic is obviously preferable, although it carries a US$24.20 fee, especially as you can only get a refund of a cash deposit at the same border post where you paid the bond – paying by plastic you can return via any border crossing you like. Note that your importation permit is subject to a six-month time limit, during which you can drive your car out of Mexico and return, but there are penalties in force if you exceed the limit, including forfeiture of your vehicle.

Similar conditions apply if you want to sail to Mexico in **your own boat**. For further details, see Ⓦwww.tijuana.com/boatcrossing.

With few exceptions, US auto **insurance** policies don't cover mishaps in Mexico. Take out a Mexican policy, available from numerous agencies on either side of every border post. Rates depend on the value of the vehicle and what kind of coverage you want, but figure on US$11 or so a day for basic liability. Fourteen days' coverage is US$94.25 with Mexico Insurance Services and full coverage for a US$10,000 vehicle is US$154.80. To arrange a policy before leaving the US, call Instant Mexico Insurance Services (Ⓣ1-800/345-4701, Ⓦwww.mexonline.com/instant1.htm); International Gateways (Ⓣ1-800/423-2646); Oscar Padilla Mexican Insurance (Ⓣ1-800/258-8600, Ⓦwww.mexicaninsurance.com); or Sanborn's Insurance (Ⓣ1-800/222-0158, Ⓦwww.sanbornsinsurance.com). The last is the acknowledged leader in the field.

To get **discounts on insurance**, it might be worthwhile joining a travel club, such as Discover Baja Travel Club (Ⓣ1 800/727-BAJA) or Sanborn's Sombrero Club (Ⓣ1-800/222-0158). These clubs typically also offer discounts on accommodation and free travel advice. Annual dues are US$25–40. For more on general insurance policies, see p.29.

The American Automobile Association and Canadian Automobile Association produce **road maps** and route planners for travel to Mexico, and members may qualify for discounted insurance at affiliated border agencies. However, emergency/breakdown services apply only in the US and Canada.

Cruises

Several lines offer **cruises** on the Pacific coast, most popularly between LA and Acapulco, stopping at Los Cabos, Mazatlán, Puerto Vallarta and Zihuatanejo. Others ply the Caribbean side out of Miami, taking in Cozumel, Playa del Carmen and other Mexican destinations. **Prices** start at US$600 per person (plus airfare to the starting point), and go (way) up from there.

Agencies specializing in cruises include Cruise Adventures (Ⓣ1-800/248-7447, Ⓦwww.cruiseadventures.com) and Cruise World (Ⓣ1-800/228-1153, Ⓦwww.cruiseworldtours.com).

North American cruise lines

Carnival Cruise Lines Ⓣ1-888/CARNIVAL, Ⓦwww.carnival.com.
Clipper Cruise Lines Ⓣ1-800/325-0010, Ⓦwww.clippercruise.com.
Norwegian Cruise Line Ⓣ1-800/327-7030, Ⓦwww.ncl.com.
Royal Caribbean Cruises US & Canada Ⓣ1-800/398-9819, UK Ⓣ0800/018 2917, Ⓦwww.royalcaribbean.com.

Flights from Britain

The only direct scheduled flights **from Britain** are with British Airways, three times weekly from London Heathrow to Mexico City. Flying from anywhere else in the British Isles, or to any other destination in Mexico,

Border formalities

Crossing the border, especially on foot, it's easy to go straight past the immigration and customs checks. There's a free zone south of the frontier, and you can cross at will and stay for up to three days. Make sure you do get your **tourist card** stamped and your bags checked, though, or when you try to continue south you'll be stopped after some 20km and sent back to complete the formalities.

means you have to change planes somewhere.

Good deals can be found with a number of European carriers, which fly to Mexico **via European hubs**. Another possibility is to fly **via the US** and either continue overland or buy an onward flight once in the country. New York is usually the cheapest place to get to from London, but it's only halfway to Mexico City. LA or Houston are logical points from which to set off overland. Both of these cities, and Miami, also have reasonably priced onward flights to a number of Mexican destinations. For more on getting to Mexico from North America, see p.12.

Ticket prices to Mexico are usually lower than to other Latin American destinations, and competition is such that there are often bargains available, especially if you can be flexible with dates. Tickets are usually valid for between three and six months, sometimes up to one year, but some tickets work out cheaper if you're away less than thirty days, and budget tickets may have fixed dates that you cannot change. If you want to fly into one city and out of another, travel to different destinations in Mexico, or even other countries in the region, then it's worth considering an open-return ticket, perhaps in conjunction with an airpass (see box on p.15).

Official fares, quoted by the airlines, are generally more expensive than those booked through a flight or travel agent. To find discount agents, check the travel pages of the broadsheet papers or listings magazines, Teletext or the Internet, though websites in the UK are not so directly geared to finding Mexican destinations as their US counterparts (for online booking agents, see p.12). STA Travel's website (see p.21) has a reasonable farefinder too. Deciding which flight option is best for you can be a little complex; as always, a good flight specialist – such as North South, Journey Latin America or Trailfinders (see p.21) – is the best first call to weed through the possibilities.

Prices for scheduled return flights (excluding taxes – about £50, or more if you're routed through the US) from London to Mexico City range from £450 low season to £650 or more in high season. Charter flights to Mexico are fairly common now, usually flying out of Gatwick or Manchester to Cancún, Acapulco or Puerto Vallarta. Charter fares, sometimes under £350 in the low season, can also be very good value any time outside school holidays, though they can go as high as £870 in August, and your stay will probably be limited to two or four weeks. The best way to find out about charters is to call Sky Deals (ⓣ0800/000747, ⓦwww.skydeals.com), who sell tickets for all the main operators. Otherwise, try My Travel (ⓣ0870/241 2567, ⓦwww.mytravel.co.uk), whose charters offer the largest choice of Mexican destinations.

British Airways' **direct flights from London** often work out to be very good value, especially in the high season, when you might be able to get one for around £520 (plus tax) if you book early. Several European airlines offer connecting flights from Britain to Mexico, and often work out surprisingly good value. Iberia flies daily via Madrid from London Heathrow to Mexico City and Cancún; they also fly from Manchester to Mexico City via Barcelona, though you may have to take an additional flight from Barcelona to Madrid. Air France via Paris, and Lufthansa via Frankfurt also offer daily connecting flights to Mexico City from several British airports.

It's simple enough to **fly to the US** on one of the main European or US carriers and continue from there – most of the airlines we've listed will get you to Mexico City (and often other destinations in the Republic) the same day. New York is usually the cheapest destination in the US, but it's a long way from Mexico; for speediest connections, it's usually best to fly to Miami (on BA, American or Virgin), Houston (Continental) or Atlanta (Delta). The cheapest high-season fares are usually on Continental or Virgin (connection at Miami with Aeroméxico), but these probably won't beat flights via Europe. If you want a stopover on a budget flight, you'll generally pay upwards of £100 more, though it may be worthwhile if you also want to spend some time in the US.

It's worth checking if your transatlantic carrier has an **airpass** deal for non-US residents – most major US airlines do – by which you purchase coupons in Britain at a flat rate for a certain number of flights (with a usual minimum of three) in North America. Depending on the airline, the pass will usually also include one or more destinations in Mexico and Canada. To fly NYC–Mexico City–San Francisco–NYC on American, for example, because you'd need to change planes at Dallas between Mexico City and New York or San Francisco, you'd need a five-flight pass (valid for sixty days), which would cost £685. A similar itinerary on Continental would require a four-flight pass (also valid on Northwest Airlines), costing £439 in low season, £369 in high season. For more on getting to Mexico from North America (including overland routes) see pp.12–18.

For Mexican destinations other than the capital, Continental have the widest choice, serving Acapulco, Aguascalientes, Cancún, Chihuahua, Cozumel, Ixtapa, Guadalajara, León/Bajío, Los Cabos, Mazatlán, Mérida, Monterrey and Puerto Vallarta. American are not far behind, serving Aguascalientes, Cancún, Guadalajara, León/Bajío, Los Cabos, Monterrey and Puerto Vallarta, and Delta are third, with most of their routes bar Mexico City and Guadalajara requiring a change of plane at LA.

Flights from Ireland

There are currently no **direct scheduled flights** from Ireland to Mexico. Your cheapest way to get there will almost certainly be to take one of the numerous daily flights **to London** from Dublin, Cork, Shannon or Belfast and then connect with one of the transatlantic flights detailed above or, from Dublin, to fly **via Europe** with Air France or Iberia. Lufthansa doesn't currently connect the same day, but it is possible to connect with its daily flight from Frankfurt by taking the early morning Aer Lingus flight there from Dublin. British Airways, in conjunction with Aer Lingus, can fly you to London from Dublin, Cork or Shannon in time to meet your connection, but from Belfast, you will need to change at Glasgow or Manchester to get to London for your onward flight. You can also fly from Ireland **via the US**, with Delta from Dublin via Atlanta, or with Continental from Dublin or Shannon via New York (Newark). The cheapest place to buy your ticket will almost certainly be a discount travel agent such as usitNow rather than from the airlines themselves. Expect to pay around €700 low season, €1200 high season, plus tax (around €100, depending on where you change planes) for the cheapest return tickets from Dublin to Mexico, €50–100 more from Cork or Shannon. From Belfast or Derry, expect to pay around £800 low season, £1300 high season, plus tax (around £100).

Airlines in Britain and Ireland

Aer Lingus Republic of Ireland ⓣ0818/365000, Northern Ireland ⓣ0845/084 4444, ⓦwww.aerlingus.ie.
Aeroméxico ⓣ020/7801 6234, ⓦwww.aeromexico.com.
Air France UK ⓣ0845/0845 111, ⓦwww.airfrance.com/uk, Ireland ⓣ01/605 0383, ⓦwww.airfrance.com/ie.
American Airlines UK ⓣ0845/778 9789 or 020/8572 5555, Ireland ⓣ01/602 0550, ⓦwww.aa.com.
British Airways UK ⓣ0845/773 3377, Ireland ⓣ1800/626 747, ⓦwww.ba.com.
Continental UK ⓣ0800/776464, ⓦwww.continental.com/uk, Ireland ⓣ1890/925 252, ⓦwww.continental.com/ie.
Delta UK ⓣ0800/414767, Ireland ⓣ01/407 3165, ⓦwww.delta.com.
Iberia UK ⓣ0845/601 2854, Ireland ⓣ01/407 3017, ⓦwww.iberiaairlines.co.uk.
KLM UK ⓣ0870/507 4074, ⓦwww.klmuk.com. London, Aberdeen, Birmingham, Bristol, Cardiff, Edinburgh, Humberside, Leeds, Manchester, Newcastle, Norwich and Teesside to Mexico City via Amsterdam.
Lufthansa UK ⓣ0845/773 7747, Ireland ⓣ01/844 5544, ⓦwww.lufthansa.co.uk. London, Dublin, Edinburgh, Birmingham, Manchester and Newcastle to Mexico City via Frankfurt.
Méxicana ⓣ020/8492 0000, ⓦwww.mexicana.com.mx.
Ryanair Ireland ⓣ0818/303 030, UK ⓣ0871/246 0000, ⓦwww.ryanair.com.
Taca UK ⓣ0870/241 0340, ⓦwww.grupotaca.com. Central America airpasses.
United UK ⓣ0845/844 4777, ⓦwww.unitedairlines.co.uk.
Virgin Atlantic UK ⓣ01293/747747 ⓦwww.virgin-atlantic.com.

Travel agents in Britain and Ireland

Aran Travel International Ireland ⓣ091/562 595, ⓦwww.homepages.iol.ie/~arantvl/aranmain.htm. Good-value flights.
Bridge the World UK ⓣ0870/444 7474, ⓦwww.bridgetheworld.com. Round-the-world tickets, and good deals aimed at the backpacker market.
Joe Walsh Tours Ireland ⓣ01/676 0991, ⓦwww.joewalshtours.ie. General budget fares agent.
Journey Latin America UK ⓣ020/8747 3108 or 8747 8315, ⓦwww.journeylatinamerica.co.uk. Leaders in the field on airfares and tours to Latin America; some of the best prices on high-season flights.
Lee Travel Ireland ⓣ021/427 7111, ⓦwww.leetravel.ie. Flights and holidays.
Maxwell's Travel Ireland ⓣ01/677 9479. Latin America specialists; representatives for many of the UK tour operators listed below, including Exodus and Explore.
North South Travel UK ⓣ&ⓕ01245/608 291, ⓦwww.northsouthtravel.co.uk. Friendly, competitive travel agency, offering discounted fares worldwide – profits are used to support projects in the developing world, especially the promotion of sustainable tourism.
Premier Travel Northern Ireland ⓣ028/7126 3333, ⓦwww.premiertravel.uk.com. Discount flight specialists.
South American Experience UK ⓣ020/7976 5511, ⓦwww.southamericanexperience.co.uk. Flight and tailor-made itinerary specialists; very good airfare prices.
STA Travel UK ⓣ0870/1600 599, ⓦwww.statravel.co.uk. Specialists in low-cost flights and tours for students and those 25 and younger, though other customers welcome.
Top Deck UK ⓣ020/7244 8000, ⓦwww.topdecktravel.co.uk. Long-established agent dealing in discount flights.
Trailfinders UK ⓣ020/7628 7628, ⓦwww.trailfinders.co.uk, Ireland ⓣ01/677 7888, ⓦwww.trailfinders.ie. One of the best-informed and most efficient agents for independent travellers; produce a very useful quarterly magazine worth scrutinizing for round-the-world routes.
Travel Cuts UK ⓣ020/7255 2082 or 7255 1944, ⓦwww.travelcuts.co.uk. Canadian company specializing in budget, student and youth travel and round-the-world tickets.
usitNOW Republic of Ireland ⓣ01/602 1600, Northern Ireland ⓣ028/9032 7111, ⓦwww.usitnow.ie. Ireland's main student and youth travel specialists.

Packages and tours

Many companies offer **package tours** to Mexico, and there's an enormous choice to suit all budgets. Trips range from two weeks in a luxury beach hotel to trekking in the Sierra Madre; visits to native markets in Oaxaca or a camping tour of Maya sites in Yucatán. Wildlife trips are popular too – you can watch whales off the Baja coast or seek rare birds in the cloudforests of Chiapas. Group tours save the hassle of making your own arrangements and can be good value. The tours are generally relaxed and friendly, usually led by someone from the UK who knows the area, and in many cases there's also a local guide. Several firms offer **tailor-made itineraries**, whereby you decide what you'd like and they arrange it for you. The list below covers the best and most experienced UK operators; all can provide detailed information on each trip. Prices quoted do not include the airfare unless stated, and are of course subject to change, as well as to supplements for things like single room occupancy. Many tours operate in winter only, though several run year-round.

Specialist tour operators in Britain and Ireland

Bales Worldwide UK ⓣ0870/241 3208, ⓦwww.balesworldwide.com. Family-owned company offering a high-quality two-week escorted cultural tour taking in all of Mexico's most famous sights, from £2820 including airfare.
Cathy Matos Mexican Tours UK ⓣ020/8492 0000, ⓦwww.cathymatosmexico.com. Wide variety of tailor-made tours, including colonial cities, beaches, sightseeing and archeology tours, whale-watching and weddings. Located in the UK office for Mexicana.
Discover the World – Wildlife Encounters UK ⓣ01737/218800, ⓦwww.wildlife-encounters.co.uk. Eight days' whale-watching in Baja from £1885 including airfare.
Dragoman UK ⓣ01728/861133, ⓦwww.dragoman.com. Well-established overland firm offering an eight-week "Central American Explorer" from Mexico to Panama from £1740 plus US$750 for food, or a four-week tour of Mexico, Belize and Guatemala from £895 plus US$400, partly camping, partly in hotels. Also available online from Ireland, the US, Canada, Australia, New Zealand and Europe.

Exodus UK ⓣ020/8675 5500, Ireland ⓣ01/677 1029, ⓦwww.exodus.co.uk. Seventeen-day Ruta Maya tour in Mexico, Guatemala and Belize from £970 plus US$150.
Explore Worldwide UK ⓣ01252/344161, ⓦwww.exploreworldwide.com. Fifteen-day "Indian Mexico" tour (including visits to Guatemala and Belize – Yucatán extension also possible) from £799 plus US$240, or a fifteen-day Sierra Madre trek, partly camping, from £725 plus US$245.
Mountain Travel Sobek UK ⓣ01494/448901, ⓦwww.mtsobek.com. Outdoor active adventure trips including sea kayaking or whale-watching in Baja (7 days for US$1390), or a Copper Canyon hike (8 days for US$1790).
Travelbag Adventures UK ⓣ01420/541007, ⓦwww.travelbag-adventures.com. Small-group hotel-based tours including a fifteen-day "Lost Empires" tour of central Mexico from £929, and a fifteen-day "Realm of the Maya" tour in the Yucatán, Chiapas, Guatemala and Belize from £899. A good outfit that will tailor itineraries to meet your needs.
Trek America UK ⓣ01295/256777, ⓦwww.trekamerica.com. Small-group adventure trips, camping or staying at budget hotels across Mexico, including a fourteen-day "Mexican Adventure" for £506, sixteen days on the Ruta Maya for £819, or a ten-day "Mexican Highlights" trek for £607 – flights, food and hotels (where used) are extra.
Trips Worldwide UK ⓣ0117/311 440, ⓦwww.tripsworldwide.co.uk. Friendly, experienced company with an inspired range of tailor-made itineraries to Mexico. Also agents for many other recommended tour operators.
Wild Oceans UK ⓣ0117/965 8333, ⓦwww.wildwings.co.uk. Naturalist-led tours to observe whales (including blue whale research project), sealions and other wildlife in the Sea of Cortés; accommodation on board a comfortable 28-metre boat. From £2499 for fourteen days, including airfare.

Flights from Australia and New Zealand

The **high season** for flights to Mexico from Australia and New Zealand comprises mid-June to mid-July, and mid-December to mid-January. You can count on paying A$200–400 more at peak season than the fares quoted below.

From Australia the cheapest flights – **fares** quoted are from major cities, including Brisbane, Cairns, Sydney and Melbourne – are with Japan Airlines (JAL) to Mexico City via Tokyo or Osaka (A$1879). Alternatives are with Air New Zealand via Auckland (A$1989), and United Airlines via Los Angeles (A$2499). **From New Zealand**, your cheapest choices are Air Tahiti Nui in combination with either Delta or Continental (from NZ$2199), American Airlines (NZ$2879), or JAL (NZ$2989).

One of the best deals, mile for mile, on **RTW fares from Australia** is offered by the Star Alliance airline group (including Air New Zealand, Lufthansa, Thai, Singapore, Varig and Mexicana). Prices and deals vary, but the best deal is A$2590/NZ$3099 for 26,000 miles and up to five stops. A similar deal is offered by the Global Alliance (including Qantas, British Airways, Cathay Pacific, American and LanChile), for A$2869 /NZ$3099, and higher mileage with up to fifteen stops is available from both groups for not a great deal more.

Airlines

Aerolineas Argentinas Australia ⓣ02/9252 5150, New Zealand ⓣ09/379 3675, ⓦwww.aerolineas.com.au.
Aeroméxico Australia ⓣ02/9959 3922, ⓦwww.aeromexico.com.
Air New Zealand New Zealand ⓣ0800/737 000, ⓦwww.airnz.co.nz, Australia ⓣ13/2476, ⓦwww.airnz.com.au.
Air Tahiti Nui New Zealand ⓣ09/308 3360, ⓦwww.airtahitinui.fr.
Delta Australia ⓣ02/9251 3211, New Zealand ⓣ09/379 3370, ⓦwww.delta.com.
Japan Airlines (JAL) Australia ⓣ02/9272 1111, New Zealand ⓣ09/379 9906, ⓦwww.japanair.com.
Mexicana Australia ⓣ03/9699 9355, New Zealand ⓣ09/914 2573, ⓦwww.mexicana.com.mx.
Qantas Australia ⓣ13/1313, ⓦwww.qantas.com.au, New Zealand ⓣ0800/808 767, ⓦwww.qantas.co.nz.
United Australia ⓣ13/1777, ⓦwww.unitedairlines.com.au, New Zealand ⓣ09/379 3800 or 0800/508 648, ⓦwww.unitedairlines.co.nz.

Discount travel agents

Flight Centre Australia ⓣ13/3133 or 02/9235 3522, ⓦwww.flightcentre.com.au, New Zealand ⓣ0800/243 544 or 09/358 4310, ⓦwww.flightcentre.co.nz.

Holiday Shoppe New Zealand ⓣ0800/808 480, ⓦwww.holidayshoppe.co.nz.
Northern Gateway Australia ⓣ1800/174 800, ⓦwww.northerngateway.com.au.
STA Travel Australia ⓣ1300/360 960, ⓦwww.statravel.com.au, New Zealand ⓣ0508/782 872, ⓦwww.statravel.co.nz.
Student Uni Travel Australia ⓣ02/9232 8444, ⓦwww.sut.com.au, New Zealand ⓣ09/379 4224, ⓦwww.sut.co.nz.
Trailfinders Australia ⓣ02/9247 7666, ⓦwww.trailfinders.com.au.

Tour operators

Adventure World Australia ⓣ02/8913 0755, ⓦwww.adventureworld.com.au, New Zealand ⓣ09/524 5118, ⓦwww.adventureworld.co.nz. eight days in Mexico City, Taxco and Acapulco from A$782/NZ$805 plus airfare, or 21 days in Mexico, Guatemala and Cuba from A$8183/NZ$8635 including airfare, or resort holidays in Cancún, Cozumel, Playa del Carmen, Puerto Vallarta, Mazatlán, San José del Cabo or Ixtapa. Agents for UK operators Dragoman and Explore Worldwide.
Latin Link Adventure New Zealand ⓣ03/525 9945. Offer a 28-day multi-city tour including Mexico City, Oaxaca, Chiapas, the Yucatán and Guatemala in October for around NZ$8590 including airfare from Auckland.
Mexico.com.au Australia ⓣ1800/200 700, ⓦwww.mexico.com.au. Booking agency for accommodation throughout Mexico.
South America Destinations Australia ⓣ1800/337050 or 03/9725 4655, ⓦwww.south-america.com.au. Offer a seven-day Colonial Cities tour, a six-day Copper Canyon Railway tour, or a four-day city break in Mexico City.
South America Travel Centre Australia ⓣ1800/655 051 or 03/9642 5353, ⓦwww.satc.com.au. Tours on offer include twelve days in Mexico City, Oaxaca and Acapulco from A$1750, seven days in the colonial cities of central Mexico from A$1580, or 22 days on the Ruta Maya in Mexico, Guatemala and Belize from A$2275.
World Expeditions Australia ⓣ1300/720 000, ⓦwww.worldexpeditions.com.au, New Zealand ⓣ0800/350 354, ⓦwww.worldexpeditions.co.nz. Offer a fourteen-day "Mayan World" tour in Chiapas and Guatemala from A$3990, or a 22-day trip including Oaxaca and Mexico City too from A$5450 (not including airfare). They also have offices in the US (ⓣ1-888/464-8735, ⓦwww.weadventures.com) and UK (ⓣ020/8870 2600, ⓦwww.worldexpeditions.co.uk) .

Visas and red tape

Citizens of the US, Canada, the UK, Ireland, Australia, New Zealand and much of Western Europe need no visa to enter Mexico as tourists for less than 180 days. Other Western Europeans can stay for 90 days. Non-US citizens travelling via the US, however, may need a US visa. Visitors entering by land are subject to a US$18.50 entry fee, which will be includeed in your ticket if arriving by air.

What every visitor does need is a valid **passport** and a **tourist card** (or FMT – *folleto de migración turística*). Tourist cards are free, and if you're flying direct, you should get one on the plane, or from the airline before leaving. A good travel agent should be able to arrange one for you, too. Otherwise they're issued by Mexican consulates, in person or by post. Every major US city and most border towns have a Mexican consulate; tourist cards and vehicle import forms are also available from all AAA offices in California, Arizona, New Mexico and Texas. Finally, failing all these, you should be able to get tourist cards at airports or border crossings on arrival. However, if they've run out, you'll have to twiddle your thumbs until the next batch comes in, and if your passport is not issued by a rich Western country, you may encounter difficulty in persuading border officials to give you a card at all; it's therefore preferable to get one in advance. Entering from Belize or Guatemala, it's not at all uncommon for border posts to run out of tourist cards, or for officials to (illegally) demand a fee for issuing them.

Most people officially need a passport to pick up their tourist card, but for US and Canadian citizens all that's required is proof of citizenship (an original birth certificate or notarized copy, for instance, or naturalization papers), along with some form of photo ID (such as a driver's licence). US and Canadian citizens can even enter Mexico without a passport if they carry such documents plus their tourist card with them, but it's not advisable, since officials checking your ID may not be aware of this right.

A tourist card is valid for a single entry only, so if you intend to enter and leave Mexico more than once you should pick up two or three. On the card, you are asked how long you intend to stay. You should always apply for longer than you need, since getting an extension is a frustrating and time-consuming business. You don't always get the time you've asked for in any case: in particular, at Mexico's borders with Belize and Guatemala to the south, you will probably only get thirty days (though they may give you more if you specifically ask), and entering via Chiapas state means you're likely only to get fifteen days (extensions unlikely). Especially if you are not from a rich country, you may also be asked to show bank statements or other proof of sufficient funds for your stay.

A tourist card isn't strictly necessary for anyone who only intends to visit the northern border towns and stay less than three days (though you still need a passport or photo ID). In fact, the twenty-kilometre strip adjoining the US border is a duty-free area into which you can come and go more or less as you please; heading further south beyond this zone, however, there are checkpoints on every road, and you'll be sent back if you haven't brought the necessary documents and been through customs and immigration.

Don't lose the tourist card stub that is given back to you after immigration inspection. You are legally required to carry it at all times, and if you have to show your papers, it's more important than your passport. It also has to be handed in on leaving the country – without it, you may encounter hassle and delay.

Should you lose your tourist card, or need to have it renewed, head for the nearest immigration department office (Departamento de Migración); there are downtown branches in the biggest cities. In the case of renewal, it's far simpler to cross the border for a day and get a new one on re-entry than to apply for an extension; if you do apply to the immigration department, it's wise to do so a couple of weeks in advance, though you may be told to come back nearer the actual expiry date. Whatever else you may be told, branches of SECTUR (the tourist office) cannot renew expired tourist cards or replace lost ones – they will only make sympathetic noises and direct you to the nearest immigration office.

Visas, obtainable only through a consulate (in person or by mail), are required by nationals of South Africa and most non-industrialized countries, as well as by anyone entering Mexico to work, or to study or for more than six months. Business visitors need a Business Authorization Card available from consulates, and usually a visa too. Anyone under 18 needs written consent from their parents if not accompanied by both of them (if accompanied by one, they need written consent from the other).

US visas

Non-US citizens travelling through the US on the way to or from Mexico, or stopping over there, may need a **US visa**. If there's even a possibility you might stop in the US, unless you are Canadian or from a country on the US visa waiver scheme, obtaining a visa in advance is a sensible precaution. You can expect to wait in line wherever you apply in person, but you can always apply by mail instead, provided you allow enough time (usually four weeks). A number of countries, including Britain, Ireland, Australia, New Zealand, Singapore, the Netherlands, Denmark, Sweden, Norway and Germany, but not South Africa, are on a visa waiver scheme, designed to speed up lengthy immigration procedures. Visa waiver forms are available from travel agencies, the airline during check-in, or on the plane, and must be presented to immigration on arrival. Be sure to return the part stapled into your passport when you leave the US: if it isn't returned within the visa expiry time, computer records automatically log you as an illegal alien. If re-entering the US by land from Mexico, you will need to have a form with you in order to be exempt from visa requirements, so make sure you get one in advance. Getting a US visa in Mexico will be a nightmare of waiting in line and frustration.

Many US airports do not have transit lounges, so even if you are on a through flight you may have to go through US immigration and customs. This can easily take two hours, so bear the delay in mind if you have an onward flight to catch.

Mexican consulates and embassies abroad

The following all issue visas and tourist cards. To find the address of an embassy or consulate not listed here, see Ⓦwww.sre.gob.mx/delegaciones/dire.htm.

Australia

14 Perth Ave, Yarralumla, Canberra, ACT 2600 Ⓣ02/6273 3963, Ⓦwww.embassyofmexicoinaustralia.org.

Belize

20 N Park St, Belize City Ⓣ02/230193 or 230194, Ⓦwww.embamexbelize.gob.mx.

Canada

45 O'Connor St, Suite 1500, Ottawa, ON K1P 1A4 Ⓣ613/233-8988, Ⓦwww.embamexcan.com; 2055 Peel, Suite 1000, Montreal, PQ H3A 1V4 Ⓣ514/288-2502, Ⓦwww.consulmex.qc.ca; 199 Bay St, Suite 4440, Commerce Court W, Toronto, ON M5L 1E9 Ⓣ416/368-2875, Ⓦwww.consulmex.com; 710–1117 W Hastings St, Vancouver, BC V6E 2K3 Ⓣ604/684-3547, Ⓦwww.consulmexvan.com.

Cuba

C 12, #518, Miramar, Playa, Havana 6 Ⓣ7/204 7722 to 7725, Ⓔembamexc@enet.cu.

Guatemala

The embassy is at Nivel 7, Edificio Centro Ejecutivo, 15 C 3–20, Zona 10, Guatemala City Ⓣ02/333 7254 to 7258, Ⓦwww.sre.gob.mx/guatemala. There are also consulates at Offices J-2 and J-300, 3rd floor, Edificio Plaza Corporativa Reforma, Torre Jardín, Av Reforma 6–64, Zona 9, Guatemala City Ⓣ02/339 1007 to 1009 and 21 Av 8–64, Zona 3, Quetzaltenango Ⓣ09/767 5542, Ⓔmexicoq@xela.net.gt.

Ireland

43 Ailesbury Rd, Ballsbridge, Dublin 4 Ⓣ01/260 0699, Ⓔembasmex@indigo.ie.

New Zealand

111–115 Customhouse Quay, 8th floor, Wellington Ⓣ04/472 0555, Ⓦwww.mexico.org.nz.

UK

8 Halkin St, London SW1X 7DW Ⓣ020/7235 6393, Ⓦwww.mexicanconsulate.org.uk.

US

2827 16th St, NW, Washington, DC 20009–4260 Ⓣ202/736-1000, Ⓦwww.sre.gob.mx/eua; and in nearly fifty other US towns and cities, among them those in the border states listed below:
Arizona 1201 F Ave, Douglas, AZ 85607 Ⓣ520/364-3107, Ⓦwww.consulmexdouglas.com; 51 N Grand Ave, Nogales, AZ 85621 Ⓣ602/287-3381 or 3386, Ⓔconsulmex2@mchsi.com.
California 408 Heber Ave, Calexico, CA 92231 Ⓣ619/357-3863, Ⓔconsulmexcal@earthlink.net; 1549 India St, San Diego, CA 92101 Ⓣ619/231-8414, Ⓦwww.sre.gob.mx/sandiego.
Texas 724 E Elizabeth St, Brownsville, TX 78520 Ⓣ956/542-2051, Ⓦwww.sre.gob.mx/brownsville; 2398 Spur 239, Del Rio, TX 78840 Ⓣ830/775-2352, Ⓔconsulmexdel.titular@wcsonline.net; 140 N Adams St, Eagle Pass, TX 78852 Ⓣ830/773-9255 or 9256, Ⓔconsulmx@wcsonline.net; 910 E San Antonio Ave, El Paso, TX 79901 Ⓣ915/533-8555, Ⓦwww.sre.gob.mx/elpaso; 1219 Matamoros St, Laredo, TX 78040 Ⓣ956/723-6369, Ⓦwww.sre.gob.mx/laredo; 600 S Broadway St, McAllen, TX 78501 Ⓣ956/686-0243, econsumexmc@aol.com; 127 Navarro St, San Antonio, TX 78205 Ⓣ210/227-1085 or 1086.

Embassies and consulates in Mexico

Contact details for embassies and consulates not listed here can be found at Ⓦwww.sre.gob.mx/delegaciones/acreditadas. Further details of embassy and consulate locations can be found in the "Listings" sections for the relevant cities in this book.

Australia Rubén Darío 55, Colonia Polanco, 11580 Mexico City ⓣ55/5531-5225, ⓦwww.mexico.embassy.gov.au; and in Guadalajara and Monterrey.
Canada Schiller 529, Colonia Rincón del Bosque, Polanco, 11560 Mexico City ⓣ55/5724-7900, ⓦwww.canada.org.mx; and in Acapulco, Cancún, Guadalajara, Mazatlán, Monterrey, Oaxaca, Puerto Vallarta, San José del Cabo and Tijuana.
Ireland Blv Manuel Avila Camacho 76, 3rd floor, Colonia Lomas de Chapultepec, 11000 Mexico City ⓣ55/5520-5803, ⓔembajada@irlanda.org.mx.
New Zealand José Luis Lagrange 103, 10th floor, Colonia Los Morales, Polanco, 11510 Mexico City ⓣ55/5283-9460, ⓔkiwimexico@compuserve.com.mx.
UK Río Lerma 71, Colonia Cuauhtémoc, 06500 Mexico City ⓣ55/5207-2089, ⓦwww.embajadabritanica.com.mx; and in Acapulco, Cancún, Ciudad Juárez, Guadalajara, Monterrey, Tijuana and Veracruz.
USA Paseo de la Reforma 305, Colonia Cuauhtémoc, 06500 Mexico City ⓣ55/5080-2000, ⓦwww.usembassy-mexico.gov; and in Ciudad Juárez, Guadalajara, Hermosillo, Matamoros, Mérida, Monterrey, Nogales, Nuevo Laredo and Tijuana; addresses for these and for consular agents in other Mexican cities are listed on ⓦwww.usembassy-mexico.gov/edirector.html.

Customs

Duty-free allowances into Mexico are three bottles of liquor (including wine), plus four hundred cigarettes or fifty cigars or 250g of tobacco, plus twelve rolls of camera film or camcorder tape. The monetary limit for duty-free goods is US$300. Returning home, note that it is illegal to take antiquities out of the country, and penalties are serious.

Information, websites and maps

The first place to head for information, and for free maps of the country and many towns, is the Mexican Government Ministry of Tourism (Secretaría de Turismo, abbreviated to SECTUR), which has offices throughout Mexico and abroad. It's always worth stocking up in advance with as many relevant brochures and plans as they'll let you have, since offices in Mexico are frequently closed or have run out.

Once you're in Mexico, you'll find tourist offices (sometimes called *turismos*) run by SECTUR, in addition to some run by state and municipal authorities; quite often there'll be two or three rival ones in the same town. It's quite impossible to generalize about the services offered: some are extremely friendly and helpful, with free information and leaflets by the cart-load; others are barely capable of answering the simplest enquiry. We have listed these in the relevant city and regional sections throughout the guide. You can also call SECTUR toll-free round the clock in Mexico at ⓣ1-800/903-9200, or from the US or Canada on ⓣ1-800/482-9832.

Mexican tourist offices overseas

US

300 N Michigan Ave, 4th floor, Chicago, IL 60601 (ⓣ312/606-9252, ⓕ312/606-9012, ⓔMgtochi@cis.compuserve.com); 10103 Fondern St, 5th floor, Houston, TX 77096 (ⓣ713/772-3819, ⓕ713/772-6058, ⓔMgtotx@ix.netcom.com); 2401 W 6th St, Los Angeles, CA 90067 (ⓣ310/351-2075, ⓕ310/351-2074, ⓔ104045,3647@compuserve.com); 21 E 63rd St, 3rd floor, New York, NY 10021 (ⓣ212/821-0304, ⓕ212/821-0367, ⓔMilmgto@interport.net); 1200 NW 78th Ave, Suite 203, Miami, FL 33126–1817 (ⓣ305/718-4095 or 4096, ⓔMgtomia@gate.net).

Canada

1 Place Ville Marie, Suite 1931, Montreal, PQ H3B 2C3 (Ⓣ450/871-1052, Ⓔturimex@cam.org); 2 Bloor St W, Suite 1502, Toronto, ON M4W 3E2 (Ⓣ416/925-2753, Ⓔmexto3@inforamp.net); 999 W Hastings St, Suite 1110, Vancouver, BC V6C 2W2 (Ⓣ604/669-2845, Ⓕ604/669-3498).

UK

Wakefield House, 41 Trinity Square, London EC3N 4DT Ⓣ020/7488 9392, Ⓦwww.mexicotravel.co.uk.

Websites

Mexico is fairly well advertised on the **Internet**, which can be an excellent source of information for trip planning, as well as learning about the country, although there is a surprising dearth of official online tourist information, and few sites with any kind of decent listings.

Government advisories

The latest information and advice on travel in Mexico is put out by Western governments for their citizens, sometimes over-cautious, but well informed, regularly updated, and always worth reading before making travel plans, and again before departure.

US State Department
Ⓦtravel.state.gov/mexico.html
Canadian Foreign Affairs Department
Ⓦwww.dfait-maeci.gc.ca/latinamerica/mexico-en.asp
UK Foreign Office
Ⓦwww.fco.gov.uk/travel/countryadvice
Australian Foreign Affairs Department
Ⓦwww.dfat.gov.au/geo/mexico/index.html

Other useful websites

Amnesty International Ⓦweb.amnesty.org/library/eng-mex/index. Amnesty's latest information on the human rights situation in Chiapas and nationwide.

Exploring Colonial Mexico Ⓦwww.colonialmexico.com. A site run by Espadaña Press concentrating on art and architecture from the colonial era, with an excellent archive of photos and information on sites throughout Mexico.

INEGI Ⓦwww.inegi.gob.mx. Website of the Mexican government's National Institute for Statistics, Geography and IT, with tables of statistical and geographical information, and maps of things like climate and vegetation. Some, but not all, is posted in English.

Latin American Information Centre (LANIC) Ⓦwww.lanic.utexas.edu/la/mexico. An excellent source of background information, logically laid out with extensive links covering topics such as history, politics, culture, religion and food; the premier Latin American academic website.

Mesoweb Ⓦwww.mesoweb.com. A huge collection of articles and resources on pre-Columbian Mexico and Central America, including the latest archeological news, maps, timelines, features on archeological sites, and articles about all aspects of life in ancient Mexico.

Mexican Channel Ⓦwww.trace-sc.com. Links to Mexican newpapers, magazines and business news sites.

Mexico Connect Ⓦwww.mexconnect.com. Features and articles on Mexican culture, mostly by Americans residing in Mexico. You have to log in to read the articles in full.

Mexican Wave Ⓦwww.mexicanwave.com. Billed as "Europe's Gateway to Mexico", this site has news, features, stories, hotel reviews and travel tips for visitors to Mexico.

Mexico Travel Ⓦwww.mexico-travel.com. Run by the Mexican Tourism Ministry, and formerly quite a comprehensive site, this has now been pared down to a brief review of the country's eight most popular beach resorts (Acapulco, Cabo San Lucas, Cancún, Cozumel, Ixtapa, Manzanillo, Mazatlán and Puerto Vallarta).

Mexico Travel Guide Ⓦwww.go2mexico.com. Online travel guide with features and articles on culture, the environment and living in Mexico, as well as a phrasebook-style "Spanish helper".

Ruins of Mexico Ⓦwww.geocities.com/atlantis01mx/index.html. An online guide to Mexico's archeological sites, with photos, plans and explanations, which aims eventually to cover all sites, both major and minor. To date it is still largely under construction, but what's on it so far is excellent.

SECTUR UK Ⓦwww.mexicotravel.co.uk. General tourist information on Mexico and tips for visitors, put out by the Mexican Tourism Ministry's London office, but not updated too often.

US National Weather Service Ⓦweather.noaa.gov/weather/MX_cc.html. Highly detailed reports on weather conditions at locations across Mexico.

Weather Underground Ⓦwww.wunderground.com/global/MX.html. User-friendly reports on weather conditions at locations across Mexico.

Maps

You should be able to find a reasonable **map** of Mexico in any of the outlets listed below, and in many large bookshops besides. A number of country maps, such as those published by Collins (1:3,300,000), Geocenter (1:2,500,000) and Map Productions (1:3,300,000), make some attempt to show relief, but this tends to make other details harder to read. On the Collins map, ridiculously, all detail ends at the US and Guatemalan borders, which is a nuisance if you need to navigate across them. Rough Guides, in conjunction with the World Mapping Project, have produced our own map, with roads, contours and physical features all clearly shown, and printed on rip-proof, waterproof plastic. Obviously we recommend it, and if you compare it for price and clarity with the competition, we are confident that you will prefer it too.

In Mexico itself, the best maps are those published by Patria, which cover each state individually, and by Guía Roji, who also publish a Mexican road atlas and a Mexico City street guide. Both makes of map are widely available – try branches of Sanborn's or large Pemex stations.

More detailed, large-scale maps – for hiking or climbing – are harder to come by. The most detailed, easily available area maps are produced by International Travel Map Productions, whose 1:1,000,000 Travellers' Reference Map series includes the peninsulas of Baja California and the Yucatán. INEGI, the Mexican government map-makers, also produce very good topographic maps on various scales. They have an office in every state capital and an outlet at Mexico City's airport. Unfortunately, stocks can run rather low, so don't count on being able to buy the ones that you want.

Map outlets

In the US and Canada

Adventurous Traveler US ⓣ1-800/282-3963, ⓦwww.AdventurousTraveler.com.
Book Passage 51 Tamal Vista Blvd, Corte Madera, CA 94925 ⓣ1-800/999-7909, ⓦwww.bookpassage.com.
Distant Lands 56 S Raymond Ave, Pasadena, CA 91105 ⓣ1-800/310-3220, ⓦwww.distantlands.com.
Elliot Bay Book Company 101 S Main St, Seattle, WA 98104 ⓣ1-800/962-5311, ⓦwww.elliotbaybook.com.
Globe Corner Bookstore 28 Church St, Cambridge, MA 02138 ⓣ1-800/358-6013, ⓦwww.globecorner.com.
Map Link 30 S La Patera Lane, Unit 5, Santa Barbara, CA 93117 ⓣ1-800/962-1394, ⓦwww.maplink.com.
Rand McNally US ⓣ1-800/333-0136, ⓦwww.randmcnally.com. Around thirty stores across the US; dial ext 2111 or check the website for the nearest location.
The Travel Bug Bookstore 2667 W Broadway, Vancouver, BC V6K 2G2 ⓣ604/737-1122, ⓦwww.swifty.com/tbug.
World of Maps 1235 Wellington St, Ottawa, ON K1Y 3A3 ⓣ1-800/214-8524, ⓦwww.worldofmaps.com.

In the UK and Ireland

Blackwell's Map and Travel Shop 53 Broad St, Oxford OX1 3BQ ⓣ01865/793550, ⓦmaps.blackwell.co.uk.
Easons Bookshop 40 O'Connell St, Dublin 1 ⓣ01/858 3881, ⓦwww.eason.ie.
Heffers Map and Travel 20 Trinity St, Cambridge CB2 1TJ ⓣ01865/333 536, ⓦwww.heffers.co.uk.
Hodges Figgis Bookshop 56–58 Dawson St, Dublin 2 ⓣ01/677 4754.
The Map Shop 30a Belvoir St, Leicester LE1 6QH ⓣ0116/247 1400, ⓦwww.mapshopleicester.co.uk.
National Map Centre 22–24 Caxton St, London SW1H 0QU ⓣ020/7222 2466, ⓦwww.mapsnmc.co.uk.
Newcastle Map Centre 55 Grey St, Newcastle-upon-Tyne NE1 6EF ⓣ0191/261 5622.
Scotland's Map Centre 50 Couper St, Glasgow G4 0DL ⓣ0141/552 4394, ⓦwww.johnsmith.co.uk/smc/index.htm.
Stanfords 12–14 Long Acre, London WC2E 9LP ⓣ020/7836 1321; 29 Corn St, Bristol BS1 1HT ⓣ0117/929 9966; 39 Spring Gardens, Manchester M2 2BG ⓣ0161/831 0250; ⓦwww.stanfords.co.uk; maps by mail or phone order are available on this number and via ⓔsales@stanfords.co.uk.

In Australia and New Zealand

The Map Shop 6–10 Peel St, Adelaide, SA 5000 ⓣ08/8231 2033, ⓦwww.mapshop.net.au.

Mapland 372 Little Bourke St, Melbourne, Vic 3000 ⓣ03/9670 4383, ⓦwww.mapland.com.au.
Mapworld 173 Gloucester St, Christchurch ⓣ0800/627 967 or 03/374 5399, ⓦwww.mapworld.co.nz.
Perth Map Centre 900 Hay St, Perth, WA 6000 ⓣ08/9322 5733, ⓦwww.perthmap.com.au.
Specialty Maps 46 Albert St, Auckland 1001 ⓣ09/307 2217, ⓦwww.specialtymaps.co.nz.

Insurance

There are no reciprocal health arrangements between Mexico and any other country, so travel insurance is essential.

Credit and charge cards (particularly American Express) often have certain levels of medical or other insurance included, and travel insurance may also be included if you use a major credit or charge card to pay for your trip. Some package tours, too, may include insurance.

Before paying for a new policy, however, it's worth checking whether you are already covered: some all-risks home insurance policies may cover your possessions when overseas, and many private medical schemes include cover when abroad. In Canada, provincial health plans usually provide partial cover for medical mishaps overseas, while holders of official student/teacher/youth cards in Canada and the US are entitled to meagre accident coverage and hospital inpatient benefits. Students will often find that their student health coverage extends during the vacations and for one term beyond the date of last enrolment.

After exhausting the possibilities above, you might want to contact a specialist travel insurance company, or consider the travel insurance deal we offer (see box below). A typical travel insurance policy usually provides cover for the loss of baggage, tickets and – up to a certain limit – cash or cheques, as well as cancellation or curtailment of your journey. Most of them exclude so-called dangerous sports unless an extra premium is paid: in Mexico this can mean scuba diving, whitewater rafting, windsurfing and trekking, though probably not kayaking or jeep safaris. Many policies can be chopped and changed to exclude coverage

Rough Guide travel insurance

Rough Guides Ltd offers a low-cost travel insurance policy, especially customized for our statistically low-risk readers by a leading British broker, provided by the American International Group (AIG) and registered with the British regulatory body, GISC (the General Insurance Standards Council). There are five main Rough Guides insurance plans: No Frills for the bare minimum for secure travel; Essential, which provides decent all-round cover; Premier for comprehensive cover with a wide range of benefits; Extended Stay for cover lasting four months to a year; and Annual Multi-Trip, a cost-effective way of getting Premier cover if you travel more than once a year. Premier, Annual Multi-Trip and Extended Stay policies can be supplemented by a "Hazardous Pursuits Extension" if you plan to indulge in sports considered dangerous, such as scuba diving or trekking. For a policy quote, call the Rough Guide Insurance Line: toll-free in the UK ⓣ0800/015 09 06 or ⓣ+44 1392 314 665 from elsewhere. Alternatively, get an online quote at www.roughguides.com/insurance.

you don't need – for example, sickness and accident benefits can often be excluded or included at will. If you do take medical coverage, ascertain whether benefits will be paid as treatment proceeds or only after return home, and whether there is a 24-hour medical emergency number. When securing baggage cover, make sure that the per-article limit – typically under US$800/£500 – will cover your most valuable possession. If you need to make a claim, you should keep receipts for medicines and medical treatment, and in the event you have anything stolen, you must make an **official statement** to the police and obtain a copy of the declaration (*copia de la declaración*) for your insurance company.

Health

It's always easier to become ill in a foreign country with a different climate, different food and different germs, still more so in a country with lower standards of sanitation than you might be acccustomed to. Most travellers, however, get through Mexico without catching anything more serious than a dose of Montezuma's Revenge. You will still want the security of health insurance (see "Insurance" on p.29), but the important thing is to keep your resistance high and to be aware of the health risks linked to poor hygiene, untreated water, mosquito bites, undressed open cuts and unprotected sex.

What you eat and drink is crucial: a poor **diet** lowers your resistance. Be sure to eat enough of the right things, including a good balance of protein (meat, fish, eggs or beans, for example), carbohydrates, vitamins and minerals. Eating plenty of fibre helps to avoid constipation – black beans can be a good source of fibre in Mexican food. Peeled fresh fruit will keep up your vitamin and mineral intake; it might be worth taking daily multivitamin and mineral tablets with you, but they're really no substitute for fresh fruit and vegetables. It's also important to eat enough – an unfamiliar diet may reduce the amount you eat, drink plenty of fluids (bottled water is widely available) and get enough sleep and rest, as it's easy to become run-down if you're on the move a lot, especially in a hot climate.

The lack of **sanitation** in Mexico is often exaggerated, and it's not worth being obsessive about it or you'll never enjoy yourself. Even so, a degree of caution is wise – don't try anything too exotic in the first few days, before your body has had a chance to adjust to local microbes, and avoid food that looks like it has been on display for a while or not freshly cooked. You should also steer clear of salads, and peel fruit before eating it. Avoid raw shellfish, and don't eat anywhere that is obviously dirty (easily spotted, since most Mexican restaurants are scrupulously clean) – street stalls in particular are suspect. For advice on water, see box opposite.

For comprehensive coverage of the health problems encountered by travellers worldwide, consult the *Rough Guide to Travel Health* by Dr Nick Jones.

Vaccinations

There are no required inoculations for Mexico, but it's worth visiting your doctor at least four weeks before you leave to check that you are up to date with **tetanus**, **typhoid** and **hepatitis A** shots. Those travelling from the US or Canada will have to pay for inoculations, available at any immunization centre or at most local clinics. Most

GPs in the UK have their own travel clinics where you can get advice and certain vaccines on prescription, though they may not administer some of the less common immunizations. Normal travel clinics can be more expensive, but you won't need to make an appointment. In Australia and New Zealand, vaccination centres are less expensive than doctors' clinics. Most will also sell travel-associated accessories, including mosquito nets and first-aid kits.

Intestinal troubles

Despite all the dire warnings below, a bout of **diarrhoea** ("Montezuma's Revenge", or simply *turista* as it's also known in Mexico) is the only medical problem you're likely to encounter. No one, however cautious they are, seems to avoid it altogether, largely because there are no reliable preventive measures. It's caused by the bacteria in Mexican food, which are different from (as well as more numerous than) those found in other Western diets, and is compounded by the change in food intake and routine.

If you go down with a mild dose of the runs unaccompanied by other symptoms, this will probably be the cause. If your diarrhoea is accompanied by cramps and vomiting, it could be **food poisoning** of some sort. Either way, it will probably pass of its own accord in 24–48 hours without treatment. In the meantime, it's essential to replace the fluid and salts you're losing, so

What about the water?

In a hot climate and at high altitudes, it's essential to increase **water** intake to prevent dehydration. Most travellers, and most Mexicans if they can, stay off the tap water, although a lot of the time it is in fact drinkable, and in practice impossible to avoid completely: ice made with it, unasked for, may appear in drinks, utensils are washed in it, and so on.

Most restaurants and *licuaderías* use **purified water** (*agua purificada*), but always check; most hotels have a supply and will often provide bottles of water in your room. Bottled water (generally purified with ozone or ultraviolet) is widely available, but stick with known brands, and always check that the seal on the bottle is intact since refilling empties with tap water for resale is common (carbonated water is generally a safer bet in that respect).

There are various methods of **treating water** while you are travelling, whether your source is from a tap or a river or stream. Boiling it for a minimum of five minutes is the time-honoured method, but it is not always practical, will not remove unpleasant tastes, and is a lot less effective at higher altitudes – including much of central Mexico, where you have to boil it for much longer.

Chemical sterilization, using either chlorine or iodine tablets or a tincture of iodine liquid, is more convenient, but leaves a nasty aftertaste (which can to some extent be masked with lemon or lime juice). Chlorine kills bacteria but, unlike iodine, is not effective against amoebic dysentery and giardiasis. Pregnant women or people with thyroid problems should consult their doctor before using iodine sterilizing tablets or iodine-based purifiers. Too many iodine tablets can cause gastrointestinal discomfort themselves. Inexpensive iodine removal filters are available and are recommended if treated water is being used continuously for more than a month or is being given to babies.

Purification, involving both filtration and sterilization, gives the most complete treatment. Portable water purifiers range in size from units weighing as little as 60g, which can be slipped into a pocket, up to 800g for carrying in a backpack. For those planning to spend time in remote areas where clean water is not available, some of the best water purifiers on the market are made in Britain by Pre-Mac. For suppliers worldwide contact Pre-Mac International Ltd, Unit 5, Morewood Close, Sevenoaks, Kent TN13 2HU ⓣ01732/460333, ⓦwww.pre-mac.com.

drink lots of water. If you have severe diarrhoea, and whenever young children have it, add oral **rehydration salts** – *suero oral* (brand names: Dioralyte, Electrosol, Rehidrat). If you can't get these, dissolve half a teaspoon of salt and three of sugar in a litre of water. Avoid greasy food, heavy spices, caffeine and most fruit and dairy products; some say bananas, papayas, guavas and prickly pears (*tunas*) are a help, while plain yogurt or a broth made from yeast extract (such as Marmite or Vegemite, if you happen to have some with you) can be easily absorbed by your body when you have diarrhoea. Drugs like Lomotil or Imodium plug you up – and thus undermine the body's efforts to rid itself of infection – but they can be a temporary stop-gap if you have to travel. If symptoms persist for more than three days, or if you have a fever or blood in your stool, seek medical advice (see "Getting medical help" on p.36).

Medical resources for travellers

Websites

ⓦ health.yahoo.com Information on specific diseases and conditions, drugs and herbal remedies, plus advice from health experts.

ⓦ www.fitfortravel.scot.nhs.uk Scottish NHS website carrying information about travel-related diseases and how to avoid them.

ⓦ www.istm.org International Society for Travel Medicine site, with a full list of clinics specializing in international travel health.

ⓦ www.tmvc.com.au Lists Travellers Medical and Vaccination Centres in Australia and New Zealand, plus general travel health information.

ⓦ www.tripprep.com Destination information such as necessary vaccinations for most countries, including Mexico, but you have to register to access it.

In the US and Canada

Canadian Society for International Health 1 Nicholas St, Suite 1105, Ottawa, ON K1N 7B7 ⓣ613/241-5785, ⓦwww.csih.org. Distributes a free pamphlet, "Health Information for Canadian Travellers", containing an extensive list of travel health centres in Canada.

Centers for Disease Control 1600 Clifton Rd NE, Atlanta, GA 30333 ⓣ1-800/311-3435 or 404/639-3534, ⓦwww.cdc.gov. Publishes outbreak warnings, suggested inoculations, precautions and other background information for travellers. Useful website plus International Travelers Hotline on ⓣ1-877/FYI-TRIP.

International Association for Medical Assistance to Travellers (IAMAT) 417 Center St, Lewiston, NY 14092 ⓣ716/754-4883, ⓦwww.sentex.net/~iamat, and 40 Regal Rd, Guelph, ON N1K 1B5 ⓣ519/836-0102. A non-profit organization supported by donations, it can provide a list of English-speaking doctors in Mexico, climate charts and leaflets on various diseases and inoculations.

International SOS Assistance Eight Neshaminy Interplex Suite 207,Trevose, PA 19053-6956 ⓣ1-800/523-8930, ⓦwww.intsos.com. Members receive pre-trip medical referral info, as well as overseas emergency services designed to complement travel insurance coverage.

MEDJET Assistance ⓣ1-800/9MEDJET, ⓦwww.medjetassistance.com. Annual membership programme for travellers (US$175 for individuals, US$275 for families) that, in the event of illness or injury, will fly members home or to the hospital of their choice in a medically equipped and staffed jet.

Travel Medicine ⓣ1-800/TRAVMED, ⓦwww.travmed.com. Sells first-aid kits, mosquito netting, water filters, reference books and other health-related travel products.

Travelers Medical Center 31 Washington Square W, New York, NY 10011 ⓣ212/982-1600. Consultation service on immunizations and treatment of diseases for people travelling to developing countries.

In the UK and Ireland

British Airways Travel Clinics 213 Piccadilly, London W1J 9HQ ⓣ0845/600 2236 (Mon–Fri 9.30am–6pm, Sat 10am–5pm, no appointment necessary) and 101 Cheapside, London EC2V 6DT (Mon–Fri 9am–5pm, appointment required), ⓦwww.britishairways.com/travel/healthclinintro. Vaccinations, tailored advice from an online database and a complete range of travel healthcare products.

Communicable Diseases Unit Brownlee Centre, Glasgow G12 0YN ⓣ0141/211 1062. Vaccination centre.

Dun Laoghaire Medical Centre 5 Northumberland Ave, Dun Laoghaire, Co Dublin ⓣ01/280 4996, ⓕ280 5603. Advice on medical matters abroad.

Hospital for Tropical Diseases Travel Clinic 2nd floor, Mortimer Market Centre, off Capper St, London WC1E 6AU ⓣ020/7388 9600 (Mon–Fri 9am–5pm by appointment only). A consultation costs £15 which is waived if you have injections or buy malaria pills. A recorded Health Line (ⓣ0906/133 7733; 50p per min) gives hints on hygiene and illness prevention as well as listing appropriate immunizations.

Liverpool School of Tropical Medicine Pembroke Place, Liverpool L3 5QA ⓣ0151/708 9393. Walk-in vaccination clinic, Mon–Fri 1–4pm.

MASTA (Medical Advisory Service for Travellers Abroad) 40 regional clinics (call ⓣ0870/606 2782 for the nearest). Also operates a pre-recorded 24-hour Travellers' Health Line (UK ⓣ0906/822 4100; 60p per min), giving written information tailored to your journey by return of post, or you can get a personalized health brief for £4.99 on line at ⓦwww.masta.org.

Nomad Pharmacy surgeries 40 Bernard St, London WC1N 1LE, and 3–4 Wellington Terrace, Turnpike Lane, London N8 0PX ⓣ020/7833 4114 (Mon–Fri 9.30am–6pm, call to book vaccination appointment). They give advice free if you go in person, or their telephone helpline is ⓣ0906/863 3414 (60p per min).

Trailfinders immunization clinics (no appointments necessary) at 194 Kensington High St, London W8 7RG ⓣ020/7938 3999 (Mon–Fri 9am–5pm except Thurs to 6pm, Sat 9.30am–4pm).

Travel Health Centre Dept of International Health and Tropical Medicine, Royal College of Surgeons in Ireland, Mercers Medical Centre, Stephen's St Lower, Dublin 2 ⓣ01/402 2337. Pre-trip advice and inoculations.

Travel Medicine Services PO Box 254, 16 College St, Belfast BT1 6BT ⓣ028/9031 5220. Offers medical advice before a trip and help afterwards in the event of a tropical disease.

Tropical Medical Bureau Grafton Buildings, 34 Grafton St, Dublin 2 ⓣ01/671 9200, ⓦtmb.exodus.ie. Medical articles, trip advice and innoculations.

In Australia and New Zealand

Travellers' Medical and Vaccination Centres
27–29 Gilbert Place, Adelaide, SA 5000 ⓣ08/8212 7522, ⓔadelaide@traveldoctor.com.au.
1/170 Queen St, Auckland ⓣ09/373 3531, ⓔauckland@traveldoctor.co.nz.
5/247 Adelaide St, Brisbane, Qld 4000 ⓣ07/3221 9066, ⓔbrisbane@traveldoctor.com.au.
5/8–10 Hobart Place, Canberra, ACT 2600 ⓣ02/6257 7156, ⓔcanberra@traveldoctor.com.au.
Moorhouse Medical Centre, 9 Washington Way, Christchurch ⓣ03/379 4000, ⓔchristchurch@traveldoctor.co.nz.
270 Sandy Bay Rd, Sandy Bay, Hobart, Tas 7005 ⓣ03/6223 7577, ⓔhobart@traveldoctor.com.au.
2/393 Little Bourke St, Melbourne, Vic 3000 ⓣ03/9602 5788, ⓔmelbourne@traveldoctor.com.au.
Level 7, Dymocks Bldg, 428 George St, Sydney, NSW 2000 ⓣ02/9221 7133, ⓔsydney@traveldoctor.com.au.
Shop 15, Grand Arcade, 14–16 Willis St, Wellington ⓣ04/473 0991, ⓔwellington@traveldoctor.co.nz.

Malaria and dengue fever

Malaria, caused by a parasite that lives in the saliva of Anopheles mosquitoes, is endemic in some parts of Mexico. Areas above 1000m (such as the capital) are malaria-free, as are Cancún, Cozumel, Isla Mujeres, and all the beach resorts of the Baja and the Pacific coasts. Daytime visits to archeological sites are risk-free, too, but low-lying inland areas can be risky, especially at night. It's a good idea to take chloroquine (brand names: Nivaquin, Resochin, Avloclor, Aralen), starting one week before you arrive and continuing for a month afterwards. Chloroquine is unsuitable for sufferers of various complaints such as epilepsy and psoriasis but daily proguanil (brand name Paludrine) can be used in its place.

If you go down with malaria, you'll probably know. The fever, shivering and headaches are like severe flu and come in waves, usually beginning in the early evening. Malaria is not infectious, but can be dangerous and sometimes even fatal if not treated quickly. If no doctor is available, take 600mg of quinine sulphate three times daily for at least three days, followed by three Fansidar (available from a local pharmacy) taken together.

The most important thing, obviously, is to avoid **mosquito** bites. Though active from dusk till dawn, female Anopheles mosquitoes prefer to bite in the evening. Wear long sleeves, skirts or trousers, avoid dark colours, which attract mosquitoes, and put repellent on all exposed skin, especially feet and ankles, which are their favourite targets. Plenty of good brands are sold locally, though health departments recommend carrying high-DEET brands available from travel clinics at home. An alternative is to burn coils of pyrethrum incense such as Raidolitos (these are readily available and burn all night if whole, but break easily). Sleep under a net if you can – one that hangs from a single point is best (you can usually find a way to tie a string across your room to hang it from). Special mosquito nets for hammocks are available in Mexico.

Another illness spread by mosquito bites is **dengue fever**, whose symptoms are similar to those of malaria, plus a headache and aching bones. Dengue-carrying mosquitoes are particularly prevalent during the rainy season and fly during the day, so wear insect repellent in the daytime if mosquitoes are around. The only treatment is complete rest, with drugs to assuage the fever – unfortunately, a second infection can be fatal.

Other bites and stings

Other **biting insects** can be a nuisance. These include bed bugs, sometimes found in cheap hotels – look for squashed ones around the bed. Sandflies, often present on beaches, are quite small, but their bites, usually on feet and ankles, itch like hell and last for days. Head or body lice can be picked up from people or bedding, and are best treated with medicated soap or shampoo.

Scorpions are mostly nocturnal and hide during the heat of the day under rocks and in crevices, so poking around in such places when in the countryside is generally ill-advised. If sleeping in a place where they might enter (such as a beach cabaña), shake your shoes out before putting them on in the morning, and try not to wander round barefoot. The sting of some scorpions is dangerous and medical treatment should always be sought – cold-pack the sting in the meantime. **Snakes** are unlikely to bite unless accidentally disturbed, and most are harmless in any case. To see one at all, you need to search stealthily – walk heavily and they will usually slither away. If you do get bitten or stung, remember what the snake or scorpion looked like (kill it if you can do so without receiving more bites), try not to move the affected part (tourniquets are not recommended – if you do use one, it is *vital* to relieve it for at least ninety seconds every fifteen minutes), and seek medical help: antivenins are available in most hospitals.

Heat and altitude problems

Two other common causes of health problems are **altitude** and **the sun**. The solution in both cases is to take it easy. Especially if you arrive in Mexico City, you may find any activity strenuous, and the thin air is made worse by the high concentration of pollutants. Allow yourself time to acclimatize. If going to higher altitudes (climbing Popocatépetl, for example), you may develop symptoms of Acute Mountain Sickness (AMS), such as breathlessness, headaches, dizziness, nausea and appetite loss. More extreme cases may cause vomiting, disorientation, loss of balance and coughing up of pink frothy phlegm. The simple cure – a slow descent – almost always brings immediate recovery.

Tolerance to the sun, too, takes a while to build up: use a strong **sun screen** and, if you're walking during the day, wear a hat or keep to the shade. Be sure to avoid dehydration by drinking enough (water or fruit juice rather than beer or coffee and you should aim to drink at least three litres a day), and don't exert yourself for long periods in the hot sun. Be aware that overheating can cause **heatstroke**, which is potentially fatal. Signs are a very high body temperature without a feeling of fever, accompanied by headaches, disorientation and even irrational behaviour. Lowering body temperature (a tepid shower, for example) is the first step in treatment.

Less serious is **prickly heat**, an itchy rash that is in fact an infection of the sweat ducts caused by excessive perspiration that doesn't dry off. A cool shower, zinc oxide powder and loose cotton clothes should help.

HIV and AIDS

Over 47,000 cases of **AIDS** (**SIDA**) have been reported in Mexico, mostly in the centre of the country, and especially in the capital. It is estimated that a further 150,000 people or more are **HIV**-positive. While the problem in Mexico is no worse than in many other countries, it is still a risk and you should take all the usual precautions to avoid contracting it. In particular, to contemplate casual sex without a condom, whether with a Mexican or a fellow traveller, would be madness – carry some with you (preferably from home; if buying them in Mexico, check the date and remember that heat affects their durability). They will also protect you from numerous other sexually transmitted diseases.

Should you need an injection or any invasive procedure, make sure that the equipment is sterile (it might be worth bringing a sterile kit from home); any blood you receive should be screened, and from voluntary rather than commercial donor banks. If you have a shave from a barber, make sure a clean blade is used, and don't submit to processes such as ear-piercing, acupuncture or tattooing unless you can be sure that the equipment is sterile.

Hepatitis and other diseases

Hepatitis A is transmitted through contaminated food and water, or through saliva, and thrives in conditions of poor hygiene. It can lay a victim low for several months with exhaustion, fever and diarrhoea, and can even cause liver damage. The Havrix vaccines have been shown to be extremely effective; though expensive (around US$150/£95 for a course of two shots), protection lasts for ten years. Gamma globulin vaccines are no longer used as they are blood products and there are concerns with regard to the transmission of new variant CJD.

Hepatitis symptoms include a yellowing of the whites of the eyes, general malaise, orange urine (though dehydration can also cause this) and light-coloured stools. If you think you have it and are unable immediately to see a doctor, it is important to get lots of rest, avoid alcohol and do your best not to spread the disease. If medical insurance coverage is an issue, you can go to a pathology lab (most towns have them) to get blood tests before paying a greater amount to see a doctor. More serious is **hepatitis B**, which is extremely contagious and passed through blood or sexual contact. Vaccinations are recommended if you will be in contact with those with weaker immunity systems, for example, working around medical patients or with children. Ideally three doses are given over six months but if time is short, there are other options which take one to two months with a booster given after a year.

Typhoid and cholera are spread in the same way as hepatitis A. **Typhoid** produces a persistent high fever with malaise, headaches and abdominal pains, followed by diarrhoea. Vaccination can be by injection or orally, but the oral alternative is less effective, more expensive and only lasts a year, as opposed to three for a shot in the arm. **Cholera** appears in epidemics rather than isolated cases – if it's about, you will probably hear about it. Cholera is characterized by sudden attacks of watery diarrhoea with severe cramps and debilitation. The vaccination is no longer given as it is ineffective.

Immunizations against **mumps**, **measles**, **TB** and **rubella** are a good idea for anyone who wasn't vaccinated as a child and hasn't had the diseases, and it's worth making sure you are covered for **tetanus**. You don't need a shot for yellow fever unless you're coming from a country where it's endemic (in which case you need to carry your vaccination certificate), and the polio vaccine is no longer necessary as the disease has been eradicated from the Americas.

Rabies exists in Mexico and the rabies vaccine is advised for anyone who will be more than 24 hours away from medical help. The best advice is simply to give dogs a wide berth, and not to play with animals at all, no matter how cuddly they may look. A bite, a scratch or even a lick from an infected animal could spread the disease – rabies is potentially fatal so if you are bitten, assume the worst and get medical help as quickly as possible. While waiting, wash any such wound immediately but gently with soap or detergent and apply alcohol or iodine if possible. If you decide to get the vaccination, you'll need three shots spread over a four-week period prior to travel.

Travellers' first-aid kit

The items you might want to carry with you, especially if you're planning to go trekking or spend time in the more remote areas of Mexico, are:

Antiseptic cream

Insect repellent

Hydrocortisone/calamine lotion or any of the creams specifically designed to take the itch out of insect bites

Plasters/band aids

Water sterilization tablets or **water purifier**

Lint/gauze and sealed bandages

Knee supports

A course of **flagyl antibiotics**

Imodium (Lomotil) for emergency diarrhoea treatment

Paracetamol/aspirin (useful for combating the effects of altitude)

Multivitamin and mineral tablets

Rehydration sachets

Getting medical help

For minor medical problems, head for a **farmacia** – look for a green cross and the Farmacia sign. Pharmacists are knowledgeable and helpful, and many speak some English. They can also sell drugs over the counter (if necessary) that are only available by prescription at home. One word of warning however: in many Mexican pharmacies you can still buy drugs such as Entero-Vioform and Mexaform, which can cause optic nerve damage and have been banned elsewhere; it is not a good idea, therefore, to use local brands unless you know what they are.

For more serious complaints you can get a list of English-speaking **doctors** from your government's nearest consulate (see p.25) or from MedToGo health and safety travel service (Ⓦ www.medtogo.com), which has a directory of English-speaking physicians and hospitals. Big hotels and tourist offices may also be able to recommend medical services. Every Mexican border town has hundreds of doctors experienced in treating gringos (**dentists**, too), since they charge less than their colleagues across the border. Every reasonably sized town should also have a state- or Red Cross-run **health centre** (*centro de salud*), where treatment is free.

Costs, money and banks

Mexico is not as cheap as it once was, despite the instability of its currency. Although, in general, costs are lower than you'll find at home, compared with the rest of Central or South America, prices here can come as something of a shock.

In the long term, the trade agreement with the US and Canada (NAFTA) can probably be expected to keep costs (and, one hopes, wages) rising, though prices will fluctuate somewhat as the peso goes down against the dollar, and inflation moves in to fill the gap. As the peso is so unstable, all prices in the text of the guide section of this book are quoted in US dollars (US$); be aware, however, that these will be affected by unpredictable factors such as inflation and exchange rates. The latest developments and your own common sense will determine how you apply them. When appropriate in the Basics section of this book, prices are quoted in both US dollars and British pounds. We've averaged the rate at US$1.6 to £1, but check The Universal Currency Converter (www.xe.com) for up-to-date conversions.

Costs

The developed tourist resorts and big cities are invariably more expensive than more remote towns, and certain other areas also have noticeably higher prices – among them the industrialized north, especially along the border, Baja, and all the newly wealthy oil regions. Prices can also be affected by **season** and many hotels raise their prices during busy times of the year. Summer, Christmas and Easter are the peak times for Mexican tourists and areas like Acapulco and Cancún, which attract large numbers of overseas visitors, put their prices up during the high season. **Special events** are also likely to be marked by price hikes. Nonetheless, wherever you go you can probably get by on US$300/£190 a week (you could reduce that if you hardly travel around or hitchhike, stay only on campsites or in hostels, live on basic food and don't buy any souvenirs, but that requires a lot of discipline), while on US$600/£375 you'd be living well.

Accommodation prices range from just a few dollars for a beach cabaña to upwards of US$100/£63 for five-star luxury. A room in a cheap hotel costs US$10–15/£6–10 per person and a room in the mid-range US$25–50/£15–30. **Food prices** can also vary wildly, but you should always be able to get a substantial meal in a basic Mexican restaurant for around US$4/£3. Most restaurant bills come with fifteen percent IVA (Impuesto de Valor Añadido, or Valued Added Sales Tax) added; this may not always be included in prices quoted on the menu. If you intend to travel around a lot, **transport** could be another major expense because distances are so huge. On a per-kilometre basis, however, prices are still quite reasonable: Mexico City to Acapulco, for example, a journey of over 400km, costs less than US$40/£25 by first-class bus, while a 24-hour journey such as Mexico City to Cancún (1800km) works out at around US$90/£55.

As always, if you're **travelling alone** you'll end up spending more – sharing rooms and food saves a substantial amount. In the larger resorts, you can get apartments for up to six people for even greater savings. If you have an **international Student or Youth Card**, you might find the occasional reduction on a museum admission price, but don't go out of your way to obtain one, since most concessions are, at least in theory, only for Mexican students. Cards available include the ISIC card for full-time students and the Go-25 youth card for under-26s, both of which carry health and emergency insurance benefits for Americans, and are available from youth travel firms such as STA Travel. Even a college photo ID card might work in some places.

Service is hardly ever added to bills, and the amount you tip is entirely up to you – in cheap places, it's just the loose change, while expensive venues tend to expect a full fifteen percent. It's not standard practice to tip **taxi drivers**.

Currency

The "new Mexican Peso", or **Nuevo Peso**, usually written $, was introduced in 1993 and is made up of 100 centavos (¢, like a US cent) – it's the equivalent of 1000 old pesos. Bills come in denominations of $20, $50, $100, $200 and $500, with coins of 10¢, 20¢, 50¢, $1, $2, $5, $10 and $20. The use of the dollar symbol for the peso is occasionally confusing; the initials MN (*moneda nacional* or national coin) are occasionally used to indicate that it's Mexican, not American money that is being referred to.

Currency exchange

The easiest kind of **foreign currency** to change in Mexico is cash US dollars. US dollar travellers' cheques come second; Canadian dollars and other major international currencies such as pounds sterling, yen and euros are a poor third, and you'll find it hard to change travellers' cheques in those currencies. Quetzales and Belize dollars are best got rid of before entering Mexico (otherwise, your best bet for changing them is with tourists heading the other way).

Correspondingly, you'll get the best rates for cash dollars, slightly lower rates for dollar travellers' cheques, and rates lower still for other currencies: indeed, it is a good idea to change other currencies into US dollars at home before coming to Mexico, since the difference in the exchange rate more than outweighs the amount you lose in changing your money twice.

Although the **banks** have all been nationalized, each is run differently. The Banco Nacional de Mexico (known as Banamex) is probably the most efficient; Bancomer, almost as widespread, is also good, as is the smaller Banco del Atlántico. Banks are generally open Monday to Friday from 9.30am until 5pm, though often with shorter hours for exchange. The commission charged varies from bank to bank, while the exchange rate, in theory, is the same – fixed daily by the government. Generally, only larger branches of the big banks, plus some in tourist resorts, are prepared to change currencies other than dollars – and even then at worse rates than you would get for the dollar equivalent. **Automatic Teller Machines (ATMs)**, or cash dispenser machines, are now widespread in Mexico and make a useful alternative (see opposite).

Casas de cambio (exchange offices) are open longer hours and at weekends, and have varying exchange rates and commission charges; they also tend to have shorter queues and less bureaucratic procedures. They usually give better rates than banks, but it's always worth checking, especially if you're changing travellers' cheques. Occasionally, casas de cambio give rates for Canadian dollars, sterling and other currencies that are as good as those they give for US dollars, so again it's worth shopping around, especially if you intend to change a large sum.

If you're desperate, many **hotels**, **shops** and **restaurants** that are used to tourists are prepared to change dollars or accept them as payment, but rates will be very low. There isn't much of a **black market** in Mexico since exchange regulations are relatively loose, and it's not really worth bothering with unless it comes about through trustworthy personal contacts or you want to do someone a favour.

Cash and travellers' cheques

In touristy places, such as Acapulco and Tijuana, US dollar bills are almost as easy to spend as pesos. Of course the big disadvantage with cash is that once stolen or lost, it's obviously gone forever. For that reason, most travellers prefer to bring plastic and/or travellers' cheques (personal cheques are virtually worthless in Mexico). But do bring some **dollars cash** – sometimes you won't be able to change anything else. It's also a good idea to have a mixture of denominations, including a wad of single dollar bills, and to try to bring some pesos (US$50/£30-worth, say), just in case you're unable to change money on arrival, or would rather not wait in a long line to do so. Although few US banks keep foreign currency on hand, and banks in Britain, Australia and New Zealand are unlikely to stock Mexican pesos, you should be able to order them from your bank's foreign desk if you give them a few days' notice; or you may find them at specialist exchange desks at the airport.

Travellers' cheques have the obvious advantage over cash that if they are lost or stolen, the issuing company will refund them on production of the purchase receipt. For that reason, keep the receipt safe and separate from the cheques themselves, along with a record of the serial numbers and a note of those ones you have already cashed. If your cheques do get lost or stolen, the issuing company will expect you to report the loss to their local office immediately. You pay one to two percent commission to buy the cheques, and usually get a lower rate of exchange for them, but it's worth it for the peace of mind.

When buying travellers' cheques, get a sensible mix of denominations, and stick to the established names – Thomas Cook, American Express, Visa or one of the major American banks – not only because these will be more recognized, but also because there will be better customer service should they be lost or stolen.

Credit and cash cards

Major **credit cards** are widely accepted and handy for emergencies. Visa and

MasterCard are the best; American Express and other charge cards are usually only accepted by expensive places, but an Amex card is worth it for the other services it offers, such as mail pick-up points and dollar travellers' cheque purchase. Credit cards are not accepted in the cheapest hotels or restaurants, nor for most bus tickets, but you can use them to get cash advances from banks. Usually there's a minimum withdrawal of around US$75–100.

In addition, you can get cash 24 hours a day from **ATMs** in most sizeable towns in Mexico, using credit cards or ATM cash cards from home. Banamex and Bancomer machines accept Visa and MasterCard plus debit cards from the Cirrus and PLUS systems, which allow account holders to withdraw money directly from their current/checking accounts back home. In some border towns you can find cash machines pay out in US dollars.

Make sure before you leave home that your personal identification number (**PIN**) will work abroad. Remember that cash withdrawals on credit cards are treated as loans, with interest accruing daily from the date of withdrawal; there may be a transaction fee on top of this, but this does not usually apply to debit cards, which often give a better exchange rate than a bank. Be aware that technical hitches are not uncommon – though rare, it has been known for machines not to dispense cash but to debit your account anyway. Finally, take extra care when you're withdrawing money from ATMs, especially at night; it's best done with a friend beside you.

A compromise between travellers' cheques and plastic is **Visa TravelMoney**, a disposable pre-paid debit card with a PIN which works in all ATMs that take Visa cards. You load up your account with funds before leaving home, and when they run out, you simply throw the card away. You can buy up to nine cards to access the same funds – useful for couples or families travelling together – and it's a good idea to buy at least one extra as a back-up in case of loss or theft. There is also a 24-hour toll-free customer assistance number at ⓣ1-800/847-2911. The card is available in most countries from branches of Thomas Cook and Citicorp. For more information, check the Visa TravelMoney website at ⓦusa.visa.com/personal/cards/visa_travel_money.html.

Phone numbers for lost cards or cheques

American Express ⓣ1-866/247-6878
Diners Club ⓣ55/5258-3220
MasterCard ⓣ1-800/307-7309
Thomas Cook/MasterCard (for travellers'cheques) ⓣ1-800/223-7373
Visa ⓣ1-800/847-2911

Wiring money

Wiring money is a fast but expensive way to send funds abroad and should be considered only as a last resort. Money can be sent via MoneyGram or Western Union (see below) and should be available for collection, from the company's local agent, within a few minutes of being sent. Fees depend on the amount being transferred and both companies charge on a sliding scale, so sending larger amounts of cash is better value. For example, wiring US$100/£63 to Mexico will cost US$23/£14 whilst US$1000/£625 will cost around US$80/£50.

It's also possible to have money wired directly from a bank in your home country to a bank in Mexico, although this is somewhat less reliable because it involves two separate institutions. If you take this route, the person wiring the funds to you will need to know the telex number of the receiving bank.

Money-wiring companies

Moneygram US ⓣ1-800/955-7777, Canada ⓣ1-800/933-3278, UK ⓣ0800/018 0104, Ireland ⓣ1850/205 800, Australia ⓣ1800/230 100, New Zealand ⓣ0800/262 263, ⓦwww.moneygram.com.
Western Union US & Canada ⓣ1-800/325-6000, UK ⓣ0800/833 833, Ireland ⓣ1800/395 395, ⓦwww.westernunion.com. Australia ⓣ1800/501 500, New Zealand ⓣ0800/270 000.

Getting around

Distances in Mexico can be huge, and if you're intending to travel on public transport, you should quickly get used to the idea of long, long journeys. Getting from Tijuana to Mexico City, for example, could take nearly two days nonstop. Although public transport at ground level is frequent and reasonably efficient everywhere, taking an internal flight at least once may be worthwhile for the time it saves.

Buses

Within Mexico, **buses** (long-distance buses are called *camiones*, rather than *autobuses*, in Mexican Spanish) are by far the most common and efficient form of public transport. There are an unbelievable number of them, run by a multitude of companies and connecting even the smallest of villages. Long-distance services generally rely on very comfortable and dependable vehicles; remote villages are more commonly connected by what look like (and often are) recycled school buses from north of the border.

There are basically two **classes** of bus, first (*primera*) and second (*segunda*), though on major long-distance routes there's often little to differentiate them. First-class vehicles have reserved seats, videos and air-conditioning, though an increasing number of second-class lines have the same comforts. The main differences will be in the number of stops – second-class buses call at more places, and consequently take longer to get where they're going – and the fare, which is about ten percent higher on first-class services, and sometimes a lot more. You may be able to get a discount with a student card, though it's unlikely. Most people choose first-class for any appreciably long distance, and second for short trips or (obviously) for destinations only served by a second-class local bus, but you should certainly not be put off second class if it seems more convenient – and it may even prove less crowded. **Air-conditioning** is not necessarily a boon – there's nothing more uncomfortable than a bus with sealed windows and a broken air-conditioner. The **videos**, mostly Hollywood action movies, in English with subtitles, aren't necessarily tasteful family viewing, and may contain scenes of violence that are not suitable for children.

On important routes there are also **deluxe** or **pullman** buses, with names like Primera Plus or Turistar Plus and fares around thirty percent higher than those of first-class buses. They have few if any stops, and waitress service and free snacks and drinks over longer distances, comfortable airline-style seating, and air conditioning that works – be sure to keep a sweater handy, as it can get very cold. They may also be emptier, which could mean more space to stretch out and sleep. Almost all pullman services have computerized reservations and may accept credit cards in payment: these facilities are increasingly common with the larger regular bus lines too.

Most towns of any size have a modern bus station, known as the **Central Camionera** or **Central de Autobuses**. Don't let the word "central" fool you, as they are usually located a long way from the town centre. Where there is no unified terminus you may find separate first- and second-class terminals, or individual ones for each company, sometimes little more than bus stops at the side of the road. In almost every bus station, there is some form of baggage deposit (left luggage) office – usually known as a **guardería**, **consigna** or simply **equipaje**, and costing about US$0.30/£0.20 per item per hour. Before leaving anything, make sure that the place will be open when you come to collect. If there's no formal facility, staff at the bus companies' baggage dispatching offices can often be persuaded to look after things for a short while.

Always check your **route** and **arrival time**, and whenever possible buy **tickets** from the bus station in advance to get the best (or any) seats; count on paying about US$4–6/£3–4 for every 100km covered. There is very rarely any problem getting a place on a bus from its point of origin or from really big towns. In smaller, mid-route places, however, you may have to wait for the bus to arrive (or at least to leave its last stop) before discovering if there are any seats – the increased prevalence of computerized ticketing is easing the problem. Often there are too few **seats**, and without fluent and loud Spanish you may lose out in the fight for the ticket clerk's attention. Alternatively, there's almost always a bus described as *local*, which means it originates from where you are (as opposed to a *de paso* bus, which started somewhere else), and tickets for these can be bought well in advance.

Weekends, holiday season, school holidays and fiestas can also overload services to certain destinations: again the only real answer is to buy tickets in advance. However, you could also try the cheaper second-class lines, where they'll pack you in standing, or take whatever's going to the next town along the way and try for a *local* from there. A word with the driver and a small tip can sometimes work wonders.

Terms to look out for on the timetable, besides *local* and *de paso*, include *vía corta* (by the short route) and *directo* or *expreso* (direct/nonstop – in theory at least). *Salida* is departure, *llegada* arrival. A decent road map will be extremely helpful in working out which buses are going to pass through your destination.

The legendary craziness of Mexican bus drivers is largely a thing of the past, and many bus companies have installed warning lights and buzzers to indicate when the driver is exceeding the speed limit (though these are often ignored by the driver). In recent years the government has been trying to improve the safety record through regular mechanical checks and also by keeping tabs on the drivers.

Trains

Mexico's **railways** were privatized in 1995, and since then, though more freight is carried by rail, all passenger services have been withdrawn bar two services run especially for tourists. The first of these is the **Copper Canyon Railway** in Chihuahua, an amazing scenic journey that rates as one of the country's top tourist attractions (see p.169). The other is the *Tequila Express* from Guadalajara to Amatitan, carrying tourists to the home of Mexico's most famous liquor (see p.241).

Flights

There are more than fifty airports in Mexico with regular passenger **flights** run by local airlines, plus several smaller airports with feeder services. The two big companies, both formerly state-owned and with international as well as domestic flights, are Aeroméxico and Mexicana, which between them connect most places to Mexico City, usually several times a day. Their monopoly is being challenged by a handful of smaller airlines that are growing rapidly and offering greater numbers of destinations all the time. Of these, Aviacsa serves the Yucatán, Chiapas, Oaxaca, Guadalajara, Acapulco, Cancún, Tijuana and Monterrey. Aerolineas Internacionales and Aero California also cover most major destinations, while Aeromar operates mainly in the north. The stiff competition between these airlines serves to keep prices steady and relatively low. Information about them is not usually available in cities not served by them, nor from Aeroméxico and Mexicana offices, though a good travel agent should be able to help track down details.

Internal **airfares** reflect the popularity of the route: the more popular the trip, the lower the price. Thus the flight from Tijuana to Mexico City costs little more than the first-class bus, while the much shorter, but less popular flight from Tijuana to Chihuahua costs no less. Obviously, fares like the first are a real bargain, but even on more expensive routes they can be well worth it for the time they save. While the smaller airlines might be cheaper, the price of a ticket on a particular flight doesn't normally vary from agent to agent. There are few discounts, and it's usually twice as much for a round-trip as a one-way ticket.

Mexicana and Aeroméxico offer multi-flight **airpasses**, available only outside Mexico (see the box on p.15 for details).

Domestic airlines

Aero California US ⓣ1-800/237-6225, Mexico ⓣ55/5207-1392, ⓦwww.abstravel.com/aerocalifornia.
Aerolineas Internacionales US ⓣ949/752-0058, Mexico ⓣ&ⓕ7/311-5114 or 5115, ⓦwww.aerolineas.cc.
Aerolitoral Mexico ⓣ1-800/800 AERO, ⓦwww.aerolitoral.com.mx.
Aeromar US ⓣ1-800/950 0747, Mexico ⓣ1-800/AEROMAR or 5133-1111, ⓦwww.aeromar.com.mx.
Aeroméxico US ⓣ1-800/237-6639, Mexico ⓣ1-800/021-2622, ⓦwww.aeromexico.com.
Aviacsa US ⓣ1-888/528-4227, Mexico ⓣ1-800/711-6733, ⓦwww.aviacsa.com.mx.
Mexicana US ⓣ1-800/531-7921, Mexico ⓣ1-800/501-9900, ⓦwww.mexicana.com.mx.

Ferries

Ferries connect Baja California with a trio of ports on the Pacific mainland: Santa Rosalía to Guaymas, and La Paz to Mazatlán and Topolobampo (for Los Mochis). For detailed information on **schedules** see ⓦwww.mexconnect.com/mex_/mexicoferryw.html. For fares, see ⓦwww.sematur.com.mx/tarifas.asp. There are also smaller boats to islands off the Caribbean coast: from Chetumal to Xcalak, from Cancún to Isla Mujeres and from Playa del Carmen and Puerto Morelos to Cozumel (the ferry from Puerto Morelos is for cars only and doesn't carry foot passengers). Though not as cheap as they once were, all these services are still pretty reasonable: see the relevant chapters for current fares.

Driving

Getting your **car** into Mexico properly documented (see "Getting there" on p.17) is just the beginning of your problems. Although most people who venture in by car enjoy it and get out again with no more than minor incidents, driving in Mexico does require a good deal of care and concentration, and almost inevitably involves at least one brush with bureaucracy or the law. In general, police have eased up of late in response to pressure from above to stop putting the bite on tourists.

Renting a car in Mexico – especially if done with a specific itinerary in mind, just for a day or two – avoids many problems and is often an extremely good way of seeing quickly a small area that would take days to explore using public transport. In all the tourist resorts and major cities there are any number of competing agencies, with local operations usually charging less than the well-known chains. You should check **rates** carefully, though, to make sure they include insurance, tax and the mileage that you'll need. Daily rates with unlimited mileage start at around US$50/£30; weekly rates usually cost the same as six days. For shorter distances, mopeds and motorbikes are also available in some resorts but most of the large, international companies don't deal with them because of the high frequency of accidents.

Drivers from the US, Canada, Britain, Ireland, Australia and New Zealand will find that their **licences** are valid in Mexico, though an international can be useful, especially if your domestic one has no photo on it. It's important to remember you are required to have all your documents with you when driving. Insurance is not compulsory, but you'd be foolhardy not to get some sort of policy.

The government oil company, Pemex, has a monopoly and sells two types of **fuel**: Premio (leaded) and Magna Sin (unleaded), both of which cost slightly more than regular unleaded north of the border, at about US$2 per US gallon. Magna Sin is increasingly available, in response to howls of outrage from US motorists who have ruined their engines using Premio.

Mexican **roads and traffic**, however, are your chief worry. Traffic circulates on the right, and the normal speed limit is 40kph (25mph) in built-up areas, 70kph (43mph) in open country, and 110kph (68mph) on the freeway. Some of the new highways are excellent, and the toll (*cuota*) superhighways are better still, though extremely expensive to drive on. Away from the major population centres, however, roads are often narrow, winding and potholed, with livestock wandering across at unexpected moments. Get out of the way of Mexican bus and truck drivers (and remember that if you signal left to them on a stretch of open road, it means it's clear to overtake). Every town and village on the road, however tiny, limits the speed of through traffic with a series of *topes* (concrete or metal speed bumps) across the road. Look out for the warning signs and take them seriously; the bumps are often huge. Most people suggest, too, that you should never drive at night (and not just for road safety reasons: see the box on p.44) – sound advice, even if not always practical. Any good road map should provide details of the more common symbols used on Mexican **road signs**, and SECTUR have a pamphlet on driving in Mexico in which they're also featured. One convention to be aware of is that the first driver to flash their lights at a junction, or where only one vehicle can pass, has the right of way: they're not inviting you to go first.

In most large towns you'll find extensive **one-way systems**. Traffic direction is often poorly marked (look for small arrows affixed to lampposts), though this is less of a problem than it sounds: simply note the directions in which the parked cars, if not the moving cars, are facing.

Parking in cities is another hassle – the restrictions are complicated and foreigners are easy pickings for traffic police, who usually remove one or both plates in lieu of a ticket (retrieving them can be an expensive and time-consuming business). Since **theft** is also a real threat, you'll usually have to pay extra for a hotel with secure parking. You may well also have to fork out over on-the-spot "fines" for traffic offences (real or concocted). In the capital, residents' cars are banned from driving on one day of every week, determined by their licence number (see box on p.358): the ban applies to foreign cars, but rented vehicles are exempt.

Unless your car is a basic-model VW, Ford or Dodge (all of which are manufactured in Mexico), **spare parts** are expensive and hard to come by – bring a basic spares kit. Tyres suffer particularly badly on burning-hot Mexican roads, and you should carry at least one good spare. Roadside *vulcanizadoras* and *llanteros* can do temporary repairs; new tyres are expensive, but remoulds aren't a good idea on hot roads at high speed. If you have a breakdown, there is a free highway mechanic service known as the **Ángeles Verdes** (Green Angels). As well as patrolling all major routes looking for beleaguered motorists, they can be reached by phone on ⓣ55/5250-8221 (although they don't actually operate inside the capital, where you can try calling the Mexican Automobile Association on ⓣ55/5242-0262). The Ángeles Verdes speak English.

Should you have a minor **accident**, try to come to some arrangement with the other party – involving the police will only make matters worse, and Mexican drivers will be just as anxious to avoid doing so. If you witness an accident, you may want to consider the gravity of the situation before getting involved. Witnesses can be locked up along with those directly implicated to prevent them from leaving before the case comes up – so consider if your involvement is necessary to serve justice. In a serious incident, contact your consulate and your Mexican insurance company as soon as possible.

For further sound advice on driving in Mexico, see the ASIRT report, on line at ⓦwww.asirt.org/RoadTravelReports/Mexico.pdf.

Car rental agencies

In North America

Avis US ⓣ1-800/331-1084, Canada ⓣ1-800/272-5871, ⓦwww.avis.com.
Budget ⓣ1-800/527-0700, ⓦwww.budgetrentacar.com.
Dollar ⓣ1-800/800-4000, ⓦwww.dollar.com.
Hertz US ⓣ1-800/654-3001, Canada ⓣ1-800/263-0600, ⓦwww.hertz.com.
Holiday Autos ⓣ1-800/422-7737, ⓦwww.holidayautos.com.
National ⓣ1-800/227-7368, ⓦwww.nationalcar.com.
Thrifty ⓣ1-800/367-2277, ⓦwww.thrifty.com.

In the UK

Avis ⓣ0870/606 0100, ⓦwww.avis.co.uk.
Budget ⓣ0800/181181, ⓦwww.budget.co.uk.
Hertz ⓣ0870/844 8844, ⓦwww.hertz.co.uk.
Holiday Autos ⓣ0870/400 0099, ⓦwww.holidayautos.co.uk.
National ⓣ0870/536 5365, ⓦwww.nationalcar.co.uk.
Thrifty ⓣ01494/751600, ⓦwww.thrifty.co.uk.

In the Republic of Ireland

Avis ⓣ01/605 7500, ⓦwww.avis.ie.
Budget ⓣ0903/27711, ⓦwww.budget.ie.

Hertz ⓣ01/676 7476, ⓦwww.hertz.ie.
Holiday Autos ⓣ01/872 9366, ⓦwww.holidayautos.ie.
Thrifty ⓣ1800/515 800, ⓦwww.thrifty.ie.

In Australia

Avis ⓣ13/6333 or 02/9353 9000, ⓦwww.avis.com.au.
Budget ⓣ1300/362 848, ⓦwww.budget.com.au.
Dollar ⓣ02/9223 1444, ⓦwww.dollarcar.com.au.
Hertz ⓣ13/3039, ⓦwww.hertz.com.au.
Holiday Autos ⓣ1300/554432, ⓦwww.holidayautos.com.au.
National ⓣ13/1045, ⓦwww.nationalcar.com.au.
Thrifty ⓣ1300/367 227, ⓦwww.thrifty.com.au.

In New Zealand

Avis ⓣ09/526 5231 or 0800/655 111, ⓦwww.avis.co.nz.
Budget ⓣ09/976 2222, ⓦwww.budget.co.nz.
Hertz ⓣ0800/654321, ⓦwww.hertz.co.nz.
National ⓣ0800/800115, ⓦwww.nationalcar.co.nz.
Thrifty ⓣ09/309 0111, ⓦwww.thrifty.co.nz.

Hitching

It's possible to **hitch** your way around Mexico, but it can't be recommended – certainly not in the north. Lifts are relatively scarce, distances vast, risks high, and the roadside often a harsh environment if you get dropped at some obscure turn-off. You may also be harassed by the police. Many drivers – especially truck drivers – expect you to contribute to their expenses, which you may think rather defeats the object of hitching. Quite apart from all this, hitching is not safe: robbery is common, and women in particular (but also men) are advised not to hitch alone. You should wait to know where the driver is going before getting in, rather than stating your own destination first, sit by a door and keep your baggage to hand in case you need to leave in a hurry (feigned carsickness is one way to get a driver to stop). Particularly avoid areas frequented by *bandidos*, such as those listed in the box below.

That said, to get to villages where there's no bus or simply to while away the time spent waiting for one, you may find yourself hitching and you'll probably come across genuine friendliness and certainly meet people you wouldn't otherwise enocunter. It does help if your Spanish will stretch to a conversation.

Local transport

Public transport within Mexican towns and cities is always plentiful and inexpensive, though crowded and not particularly user-friendly. Mexico City has an extensive, excellent **Metro** system, and there are smaller metros in Guadalajara and Monterrey, but elsewhere you'll be reliant on **buses**, which pour out clouds of choking diesel fumes; often there's a flat-fare system, but this varies from place to place. Wherever possible we've indicated which bus to take and where to catch it, but often only a local will fully understand the

Banditry: a warning

You should be aware when driving in Mexico, especially in a foreign vehicle, of the danger of **bandits**. Robberies and even more serious assaults of motorists do occur, above all in the northwest and especially in the state of Sinaloa. Sometimes robbers pose as police, sometimes as hitchhikers or motorists in distress, so think twice about offering a lift or a helping hand. They may also try to make you stop by indicating there's something wrong with your vehicle. On the other hand, remember that there are plenty of legitimate police checkpoints along the main roads, where you must stop. Roads where there have been regular reports of problems, and where you should certainly try to avoid driving at night, include Hwy-15 (Los Mochis–Mazatlán) and express Hwy-1 in Sinaloa, Hwy-5 (Mexico City–Acapulco) in Guerrero, Hwy-75 (Oaxaca–Tuxtepec), Hwy-57 (San Luis Potosí–Matahuela), and near the border, in particular on Hwy-2 (Mexicali–Agua Prieta) and Hwy-40 (Matamoros–Monterrey). The US embassy in Mexico advises never driving after dark.

intricacies of the system and you may well have to ask: the main destinations of the bus are usually marked on the windscreen, which helps.

In bigger places *combis* or **colectivos** offer a faster and perhaps less crowded alternative for only a little more money. These are minibuses, vans or large suburbans (sport utility vehicles) that run along a fixed route to set destinations; they'll pick you up and drop you off wherever you like along the way, and you simply pay the driver for the distance travelled. In Mexico City, *combis* are known as **peseros**.

Regular **taxis** can also be good value, but be aware of rip-offs – unless you're confident that the meter is working, fix a price before you get in. In the big cities, there are often tables of fixed prices posted at prominent spots. At almost every airport and at some of the biggest bus stations you'll find a booth selling vouchers for taxis into town at a fixed price depending on the part of town you want to go to – sometimes there's a choice of paying more for a private car or less to share. This will invariably cost less than just hailing a cab outside the terminal, and will certainly offer extra security. In every case you should know the name of a hotel to head for, or they'll take you to the one that pays the biggest commission (they may try to do this anyway, saying that yours is full). Never accept a ride in any kind of unofficial or unmarked taxi.

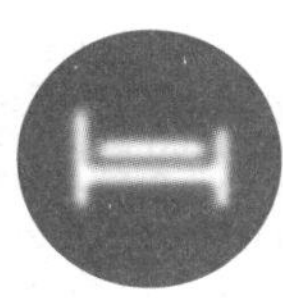

Accommodation

Mexican hotels may describe themselves as anything from *paradores*, *posadas* and *casas de huéspedes* to plain *hoteles*, all terms that are used more or less interchangeably. A *parador* is totally unrelated to its upmarket Spanish namesake, for example, and although in theory a *casa de huéspedes* means a small cheap place like a guesthouse, you won't find this necessarily to be the case.

Finding a room is rarely difficult – in most old and not overly touristy places the cheap hotels are concentrated around the main plaza (the zócalo), with others near the market, train station or bus station (or where the bus station used to be, before it moved to the outskirts of town). In bigger cities, there's usually a relatively small area in which you'll find the bulk of the less expensive possibilities. The more modern and expensive places often lie on the outskirts of towns, accessible only by car or taxi. The only times you're likely to have big problems finding somewhere to stay are in coastal resorts over the peak Christmas season, at Easter, on Mexican holidays, and almost anywhere during a local fiesta, when it's well worth trying to reserve ahead.

All rooms should have an official **price** displayed, though this is not always a guide to quality – a filthy fleapit and a beautifully run converted mansion may charge exactly the same, even if they're right next door to each other. To guarantee quality, the only recourse is seeing your room first – you soon learn to spot which establishments have promise. You should never pay more than the official rate (though just occasionally the sign may not have kept up with inflation) and in the low season you can often pay less. The charging system varies: sometimes it's per person, but usually the price quoted will be for the room regardless of how many people occupy it, so sharing can mean big savings. A room with one double bed (*cama matrimonial*) is almost always cheaper than a room with two singles (*doble* or *con dos camas*), and most hotels have large "family" rooms with several beds, which are tremendous value for groups. In the big resorts, there are lots of apartments that sleep six or more and include cooking facilities, for yet more savings. A little gentle haggling rarely goes amiss, and many places will have some rooms that cost less, so just ask (*¿Tiene un cuarto mas barato?*).

Air-conditioning (*aire acondicionado*) is a feature that inflates prices – it is frequently optional. Unless it's quite unbearably hot and humid, a room with a simple **ceiling fan** (*ventilador*) is generally better; except in the most expensive places, the air-conditioning units are almost always noisy and inefficient, whereas a fan can be left running silently all night and the draught helps to keep insects away. It might seem too obvious to mention, but be careful of the ceiling fans, which are often quite low. Don't stand on the bed, and keep well clear of them when removing any clothes from the upper body. In winter, especially at altitude or in the desert, it will of course be heating rather than cooling that you want – if there isn't any, make sure there's enough bedding and ask for extra blankets if necessary.

When looking at a room, you should always check its **insect proofing**. Cockroaches and ants are common, and there's not much anyone can do about them, but decent netting will keep mosquitoes and worse out and allow you to sleep. If the mosquitoes are really bad you'll probably see where previous occupants have splattered them on the walls – it is the same story for bedbugs around the bed.

Campsites, hammocks and cabañas

There is not usually much alternative to staying in hotels. **Camping** is easy enough if you are hiking in the backcountry, or happy simply to crash on a beach, but robberies are common, especially in places with a lot of tourists. There are very few organized campsites, and those that do exist are first and foremost trailer parks, not particularly pleasant to pitch tents in. Of course, if you have a van or **RV** you can use these or park just about anywhere else – there are a good number of facilities in the well-travelled areas, especially down the Pacific coast and Baja.

If you're planning to do a lot of camping, an **international camping card** is a good investment, serving as useful ID and getting you discounts at member sites. It is available from home motoring organizations.

In a lot of less official campsites, you will be able to rent a **hammock** and a place to sling it for the same price as pitching a tent (around US$4/£2.50), maybe less, and certainly less if you're packing your own hammock (Mexico is a good place to buy these, especially in and around Mérida, Yucatán).

Beach huts, or **cabañas**, are found at the more rustic, backpacker-oriented beach resorts, and sometimes inland. Usually just a wooden or palm-frond shack with a hammock slung up inside (or a place to sling your own), they are frequently without electricity, though as a resort gets more popular, they tend to transform into sturdier beach bungalows with modern conveniences and higher prices. At backwaters and beaches too untouristed for even cabañas, you should still be able to sling a hammock somewhere (probably the local bar or restaurant, where the *palapa* serves as shelter and shade).

Youth hostels

There are over thirty official **youth hostels** in Mexico, charging around US$10 per person for basic, single-sex dorm facilities. A YH

Accommodation price codes

All the accommodation listed in this book has been categorized into one of nine **price codes**, as set out below. The prices quoted are in US dollars and normally refer to the cheapest available room for two people sharing in high season.

- ❶ less than US$5
- ❷ US$5–10
- ❸ US$10–15
- ❹ US$15–25
- ❺ US$25–40
- ❻ US$40–60
- ❼ US$60–80
- ❽ US$80–100
- ❾ more than US$100

card is not usually necessary, but you may pay more without one. **Rules** are strict in some places (no booze, 11pm curfew, up and out by 9am) but others are open 24 hours and provide kitchen facilities, laundry, travel advice, Internet and other services. At **holiday** periods they're often taken over completely by Mexican groups. The International Youth Hostels website is at Ⓦwww.iyhf.org; or by visiting the websites of the two Mexican youth hostel associations listed below, you'll be able to view a fairly comprehensive list of Mexican youth hostels complete with addresses and phone numbers. Those with email usually provide an electronic reservation service.

Youth hostel associations

In Mexico

Red Mexicana de Alojamiento para Jóvenes (REMAJ) República de Guatemala, Col Centro, México DF 06020 Ⓣ55/5518-1726, Ⓦwww.hostellingmexico.com. This is Mexico's official branch of Hostelling International, and has seven hostels nationwide.

Asociación Mexicana de Albergues Juveniles Insurgentes Sur 421, Edificio "A", Despacho 1401-B, Col Hipodromo Condesa, México DF 06170 Ⓣ55/5574-9729, Ⓦwww.hostels.com.mx. This organization is not affiliated to HI, but in fact runs a larger number of hostels (28 nationwide).

North America and overseas

US Ⓣ202/783-6161, Ⓦwww.hiayh.org.
Canada Ⓣ1-800/663-5777 or 613/237-7884, Ⓦwww.hostellingintl.ca.
England and Wales Ⓣ0870/770 8868, Ⓦwww.yha.org.uk.
Scotland Ⓣ0870/155 3255, Ⓦwww.syha.org.uk.
Ireland Ⓣ01/830 4555, Ⓦwww.irelandyha.org.
Northern Ireland Ⓣ028/9032 4733, Ⓦwww.hini.org.uk.
Australia Ⓣ02/9261 1111, Ⓦwww.yha.com.au.
New Zealand Ⓣ0800/278 299 or 03/379 9970, Ⓦwww.yha.co.nz.

Eating and drinking

Whatever your preconceptions about Mexican food, if you've never eaten in Mexico, they will almost certainly be wrong. It bears very little resemblance to the concoctions served in "Mexican" restaurants or fast-food joints in other parts of the world – certainly you won't find chile con carne outside the tourist spots. Nor, as a rule, is it especially spicy; indeed, a more common complaint from visitors is that after a while it all seems rather bland.

Where to eat

Basic meals are served at **restaurantes**, but you can get breakfast, snacks and often full meals at cafés too; there are **take-out** and **fast-food** places serving sandwiches, tortas (filled rolls) and tacos (tortillas folded over with a filling), as well as more international-style food; there are establishments called **jugerías** (look for signs saying "Jugos y Licuados") serving nothing but wonderful juices (*jugos*), *licuados* (fruit blended with water or milk) and fruit salads; and there are **street stalls** dishing out everything from tacos to orange juice to ready-made crisp vegetable salads sprinkled with chile-salt and lime. Just about every **market** in the country has a cooked-food section, too, and these are invariably the cheapest places to eat, if not always in the most enticing surroundings. In the big cities and resorts, of course, there are international restaurants too – **pizza** and **Chinese** food are ubiquitous. **Argentinian** restaurants are the places to go for well-cooked, quality steaks.

Salsa

Since so much Mexican food is simple, and endlessly repeated in restaurant after restaurant, one way to tell the places apart – and a vital guide to the quality of the establishment – is by their **salsa**. A restaurant with a quality salsa on the table will probably serve up some decent food, whereas a place which takes no pride in its salsa often treats its food in the same manner. To a certain extent you can tell from the presentation: a place that has grubby salsa dishes on the table and rarely changes them, probably just refilling them from a supermarket-bought can, will not take the same pride in its food as a *casero* (home-cooking) restaurant that proudly puts its own salsa on the table in a nice bowl.

Frequently you will be served a variety of salsa and sauces, including bottles of commercial hot sauce (Tapatío, Tabasco, Yucateco), but there should always be at least one home-made salsa concoction. Increasingly this is **raw**, California-style salsa: tomato, onion, chile and cilantro (coriander leaves) finely chopped together. More common, though, are the traditional **cooked** salsas: either green or red, and relatively mild (start eating with caution, just in case). The recipes are – of course – closely guarded secrets, but again the basic ingredients are tomato (the verdant Mexican tomatillo in green versions), onion and one or more of the hundreds of varieties of chile.

When you're travelling, as often as not the food will come to you; at every stop people clamber onto buses and trains (especially second-class ones) with baskets of home-made foods, local specialities, cold drinks or jugs of coffee. You'll find wonderful things this way that you won't come across in restaurants, but they should be treated with caution, and with an eye to hygiene.

What to eat

The basic Mexican diet is essentially one of **corn** (*maíz*) and its products, supplemented by **beans** and **chiles**. These three things appear in an almost infinite variety of guises. Some dishes are spicy (*picante*), but on the whole you add your own seasoning from the bowls of home-made chile sauce on the table – these are often surprisingly mild, but they can be fiery and should always be approached with caution.

There are at least a hundred different types of **chile**, fresh or dried, in colours ranging from pale green to almost black, and all sorts of different sizes (large, mild ones are often stuffed with meat or cheese and rice to make **chiles rellenos**). Each has a distinct flavour and by no means all are hot (which is why we don't use the English term "chilli" for them), although the most common, chiles jalapeños, small and either green or red, certainly are. You'll always find a chile sauce (**salsa**; see box above) on the table when you eat, and in any decent restaurant it will be home-made; no two are quite alike. Chile is also the basic ingredient of more complex cooked sauces, notably **mole**, which is Mexico's version of a curry, traditionally served with turkey or chicken, but also sometimes with enchiladas (rolled, filled tortillas). There are several types of mole, the two most common being the rather bland *mole verde*, and the far richer and more exciting **mole poblano**, a speciality of Puebla. Half of the fifty or so ingredients in this extraordinary mixture are different types of chile, but the most notable ingredient is chocolate, and unless you hate chocolate, you should definitely try *mole poblano* at least once while you are in Mexico. Another speciality to look out for is **chiles en nogada**, a bizarre combination of stuffed green peppers covered in a white sauce made of walnuts and cream cheese or sour cream, topped with red pomegranate: the colours reflect the national flag and it's served especially in September around Independence Day, which is also when the walnuts are fresh.

Beans (*frijoles*), an invariable accompaniment to egg dishes – and with almost everything else too – are of the pinto or kidney variety and are almost always served **refritos**, ie boiled up, mashed, and "refried" (though actually it is the first time they're fried). They're even better if you can get them whole in some kind of country-style soup or stew, often with pork or bacon, as in **frijoles charros**.

Corn, in some form or another, features in virtually everything. In its natural state it is known as *elote* and you can find it roasted on the cob at street stalls or in soups and stews such as **pozole** (with meat). Far more often, though, it is ground into flour for **tortillas**, flat maize pancakes of which you will get a stack to accompany your meal in any cheap Mexican restaurant (in more expensive or touristy places you'll get bread rolls known as *bolillos*). Tortillas can also be made of wheatflour (*de harina*), which may be preferable to outsiders' tastes, but these are rare except in the north.

Tortillas form the basis of many specifically Mexican dishes, often described as **antojitos** (appetizers, light courses) on menus. Simplest of these are **tacos**, tortillas filled with almost anything, from beef and chicken to green vegetables, and then fried (they're usually still soft, not at all like the baked taco shells you may have had at home). With cheese, either alone or in addition to other fillings, they are called **quesadillas**. **Enchiladas** are rolled, filled tortillas covered in chile sauce and baked; **enchiladas suizas** are filled with chicken and have sour cream over them. **Tostadas** are flat tortillas toasted crisp and piled with ingredients – usually meat, salad vegetables and cheese (smaller bite-size versions are known as *sopes*). Tortillas torn up and cooked together with meat and (usually hot) sauce are called **chilaquiles**: this is a traditional way of using up leftovers. Especially in the north, you'll also come across **burritos** (large wheatflour tortillas, stuffed with anything, but usually beef and potatoes or beans) and **gorditas** (delicious fat corn tortillas, sliced open, stuffed and baked or fried). Also short and fat are **tlacoyos**, tortillas made with a stuffing of mashed beans, often using blue cornflour, which gives them a rather bizarre colour.

Cornflour, too, is the basis of **tamales** – found predominantly in central and southern Mexico – which are a sort of cornmeal pudding, stuffed, flavoured, and steamed in corn or banana leaves. They can be either savoury, with additions like shrimp or corn kernels, or sweet when made with something like coconut.

Except in the north, **meat** is not especially good – beef in particular is usually thin and tough; pork, goat and occasionally lamb are better. If the menu doesn't specify what kind of meat it is, it's usually pork – even steak (*bistec*) can be pork unless it specifies **bistec de res**. For thick American-style steaks, look for a sign saying "Carnes Hereford" or for a "New York Cut" description (only in expensive places or in the north or at fancier resorts). **Seafood** is almost always fresh and delicious, especially the spicy shrimp or octopus cocktails which you find in most coastal areas (**coctél/campechana de camarón** or **pulpo**), but beware of eating uncooked shellfish, even *ceviche* (though the lime juice it is marinaded in does kill off most of the nasties). **Eggs** in country areas are genuinely free-range and flavoursome. They feature on every menu as the most basic of meals, and at some time you must try the classic Mexican combinations of **huevos rancheros** (fried eggs on a tortilla with red salsa) or **huevos a la mexicana** (scrambled with onion, tomato and chile).

Vegetarian food in Mexico

Vegetarians can eat well in Mexico, although it does take caution to avoid meat altogether. Many Mexican dishes are naturally meat-free and there are always fabulous fruits and vegetables available. Most restaurants serve vegetable soups and rice, and items like quesadillas, chiles rellenos, and even tacos and enchiladas often come with non-meat fillings. Another possibility is **queso fundido**, simply (and literally) melted cheese, served with tortillas and salsa. Eggs, too, are served anywhere at any time, and many *jugerías* serve huge mixed **salads** to which grains and nuts can be added.

However, do bear in mind that vegetarianism, though growing, is not particularly common, and a simple cheese and chile dish may have some meat added to "improve" it. Worse, most of the fat used for frying is animal fat (usually lard), so that even something as unadorned as refried beans may not be strictly vegetarian (especially as a bone or some stock may have been added to the water the beans were originally boiled in). Even so-called vegetarian restaurants, which can be found in all the big cities, often include chicken on the menu. You may well have better luck in pizza places and Chinese or other ethnic restaurants.

Meals

Traditionally, Mexicans eat a light breakfast very early, a snack of tacos or eggs in mid-morning, lunch (the main meal of the day) around two o'clock or later – in theory followed by a siesta, but decreasingly so, it seems – and a late, light supper. Eating a large meal at lunchtime can be a great way to save money – almost every restaurant serves a cut-price **comida corrida**.

Breakfast (*desayuno*) in Mexico can consist simply of coffee (see "Drinking", below) and *pan dulce* – sweet rolls and pastries that usually come in a basket; you pay for as many as you eat. More substantial breakfasts consist of eggs in any number of forms (many set breakfasts include *huevos al gusto*: eggs any way you like them), and at fruit juice places you can have a simple *licuado* (see "Drinking", below) fortified with raw egg (*blanquillo*). Freshly squeezed orange juice (*jugo de naranja*) is always available from street stalls in the early morning.

Snack meals mostly consist of some variation on the taco/enchilada theme (stalls selling them are called *taquerías*), but tortas – rolls heavily filled with meat or cheese or both, garnished with avocado and chile and toasted on request – are also wonderful, and you'll see take-out torta stands everywhere. Failing that, you can of course always make your own snacks with bread or tortillas, along with fillings such as avocado or cheese, from shops or markets.

You can of course eat a full meal in a restaurant at any time of day, but you'd do well to adopt the local habit of taking your main meal at **lunchtime**, since this is when comidas corridas (set meals, varied daily) are served, from around 1pm to 5pm: in more expensive places the same thing may be known as the *menu del día* or *menu turístico*. Price is one good reason: you'll usually get three or four courses for US$5/£3 or less (sometimes half that price in fact), which can't be bad. More importantly the comida is an affordable alternative to the budget traveller's staples of eggs, tacos and beans. They include food that doesn't normally appear on menus such as home-made soups, stews, local specialities, puddings and elusive vegetables.

A typical comida will consist of "wet" soup, probably vegetable, followed by "dry" soup – most commonly *sopa de arroz* (simply rice seasoned with tomato or chile), or perhaps a plate of vegetables, pasta, beans or guacamole (avocado mashed with onion, and maybe tomato, lime juice and chile). Then comes the main course, followed by pudding, usually fruit, *flan* or *pudin* (crème caramel-like concoctions) or rice pudding. The courses are brought quickly, sometimes all at once, and in the cheaper places you may have no idea what you're going to get until it arrives, since there'll simply be a sign saying "comida corrida" and the price.

Some restaurants also offer set meals in the evening, but this is rare, and on the whole going out to **eat at night** is much more expensive.

Drinking

The basic drinks to accompany food are water or beer. If you're drinking **water**, stick to bottled stuff (*agua mineral* or *agua de Tehuacán*) – it comes either plain (*sin gas*) or carbonated (*con gas*).

Jugos, licuados and refrescos

Soft drinks (*refrescos*) – including Coke, Pepsi, Squirt (fun to pronounce in Spanish), and Mexican brands such as apple-flavoured Sidral (which are usually extremely sweet) – are on sale everywhere. Far more tempting are the real **fruit juices** and licuados sold at shops and stalls displaying the "Jugos y Licuados" sign and known as *jugerías* or *licuaderías*. Juices (**jugos**) can be squeezed from anything that will go through the extractor. Orange (**naranja**) and carrot (**zanahoria**) are the staples, but you should also experiment with some of the more obscure **tropical fruits**, most of which are much better than they sound. **Licuados** are made of fruit mixed with water (**licuado de agua** or simply **agua de . . .**) or milk (**licuado de leche**) in a blender, usually with sugar added, and are always fantastic. **Limonada** (fresh lemonade) is also sold in many of these places, as are **aguas frescas** – flavoured cold drinks, of which the most common are **horchata** (rice milk flavoured with cinnamon) and **agua de arroz** (like an iced rice pudding drink – delicious), **agua de jamaica** (hibiscus) or **de tamarindo** (tamarind). These are also often served in restaurants or sold in the streets from great glass jars. Make sure that any water and ice used is purified – street stalls are especially suspect in this regard. Juices and licuados are also sold at many **ice-cream** parlours – *neverías* or *paleterías*. The ice cream, more like Italian *gelato* than the heavy-cream US varieties, can also be fabulous and comes in a huge range of flavours.

Coffee and tea

A great deal of **coffee** is produced in Mexico, and in the growing areas, especially the state of Veracruz, as well as in the traditional coffee-houses in the capital, you will be served superb coffee. In its basic form, **café solo** or **negro**, it is strong, black, often sweet (ask for it *sin azúcar* for no sugar), and comes in small cups. For weaker black coffee ask for **café americano**, though this may mean instant (if you do want instant, ask for "Nescafé"). White is **café cortado** or **con un pocito de leche**; **café con leche** can be delicious, made with all milk and no water (ask if it's "hecho de leche"). **Espresso** and **cappuccino** are often available too, or you may be offered **café de olla** – stewed in the pot for hours with cinnamon and sugar, it's thick, sweet and tasty. Outside traditional coffee areas, however, the coffee is often terrible, with only instant available (if you look like a tourist they may automatically assume you want instant anyway).

Tea (**té**) is often available too, and you may well be offered a cup at the end of a comida. Usually it's some kind of herb tea like **manzanillo** (camomile) or **yerbabuena** (mint). If you get the chance to try traditional **hot chocolate** ("the drink of the Aztecs"), then do so – it's an extraordinary, spicy, semi-bitter concoction, quite unlike the milky bedtime drink of your childhood.

Alcohol

Mexican beer, or *cerveza*, is excellent. Most is light, lager-style *cerveza clara*, the best-known (but least flavoursome) examples of which are Sol and Corona. Other examples are Bohémia, Superior, Dos Equis and Tecate, but you can also get dark (*oscura*) beers, of which the best are Negra Modelo, Indio and Tres Equis. Pacífico, originally from the west coast, is gaining popularity among the national brands. Try a *michelada,* a beer cocktail made by adding ice, lime, Worcestershire and tabasco sauce to dark beer and rimming the glass with salt. The milder *chelada* is a light beer mixed with plenty of lime and salt, and both are refreshing on a sunny day.

You'll normally be drinking in bars, but if you don't feel comfortable – this applies to women, in particular (for more on which, see overleaf) – you can also get takeout from most shops, supermarkets and, cheapest of all, *agencias*, which are normally agents for just one brand. When buying from any of these places, it is normal to pay a **deposit** of about 30–40 percent of the purchase price: keep your receipt and return your bottles to the same store. Instead of buying 330ml bottles, you go for the 940ml vessels known as *caguamas* (turtles), or in the case of Pacífico, *ballenas* (whales).

Wine (*vino* – *tinto* is red, *blanco* is white) is not seen a great deal, although Mexico does produce a fair number of perfectly good ones. You're safest sticking to the brand names like Hidalgo or Domecq, although it may also be worth experimenting with some of the new labels, especially those from Baja California, which are attempting to emulate the success of their neighbours across the border and in many cases have borrowed American techniques and wine-makers.

Tequila, distilled from the agave cactus-like plant and produced mainly in the state of Jalisco, is of course the most famous of Mexican spirits, usually served straight with lime and salt on the side. Lick the salt and bite into the lime, then take a swig of tequila (or the other way round – there's no correct etiquette). The best stuff is aged (*añejo* or *reposado*) for smoothness; try Sauza Hornitos, which is powerful, or Commemorativo, which is unexpectedly gentle on the throat. Mexico is currently experiencing a minor tequila crisis as a result of a boom in its popularity, both at home and abroad. The plants take around seven years to mature so the surge in demand has left reserves of the agave plant depleted and triggered a significant rise in prices.

Mescal (often spelled *mezcal*) is basically the same drink, but made from a slightly different type of plant, the maguey, and younger and less refined. In fact, tequila was originally just a variety of mescal. The spurious belief that the worm in the mescal bottle is hallucinogenic is based on confusion between the drink and the peyote cactus, which is also called mescal; by the time you've got down as far as the worm, you wouldn't notice hallucinations anyway.

Pulque, a mildly alcoholic milky beer made from the same cactus, is the traditional drink of the poor and sold in special bars called *pulquerías*. The best comes from the state of Mexico City, and is thick and viscous – it's a little like palm wine, and definitely an acquired taste. Unfermented *pulque*, called *aguamiel*, is sweet and non-alcoholic.

Drinking other spirits, you should always ask for **nacional**, as anything imported is fabulously expensive. **Rum** (*ron*), gin (*ginebra*) and **vodka** are made in Mexico, as are some very palatable **brandies** (brandy or coñac – try San Marcos or Presidente). Most of the **cocktails** for which Mexico is known – margaritas, piñas coladas and so on – are available only in tourist areas or hotel bars, and are generally pretty strong. **Sangrita** is a mixture of tomato and fruit juices with chile, often drunk as a mixer with tequila.

For drinking any of these, the least heavy atmosphere is in **hotel bars**, tourist areas or anything that describes itself as a "ladies' bar". Traditional **cantinas** are for serious and excessive drinking, have a thoroughly threatening, macho atmosphere, and usually bar women; more often than not, there's a sign above the door prohibiting entry to "women, members of the armed forces, and anyone in uniform". Big-city cantinas are to some extent more liberal, but in small and traditional places they remain exclusively male preserves, full of drunken bonhomie that can suddenly sour into threats and fighting.

Communications

Although on the face of it Mexico has reasonably efficient postal and telephone systems, phoning home can be a tricky business, while packages have a tendency to go astray in both directions. One thing to watch is the outrageous cost of international phone calls, faxes and telegrams – call collect or use a calling card wherever possible. Better still, see if you can make your international calls over the Internet.

Mail

Mexican postal services (*correos*) are reasonably efficient. Airmail to the capital should arrive within a few days, but it may take a couple of weeks to get anywhere at all remote. **Post offices** (generally Mon–Fri 9am–3pm, Sat 9am–1pm) usually offer a poste restante/general delivery service: letters should be addressed to Lista de Correos at the Correo Central (main post office) of any town; all mail that arrives for the Lista is put on a list updated daily and displayed in the post office, but is held for only two weeks. You may get around that by sending it to "Poste Restante" instead of "Lista de Correos" and having letter-writers put "Favor de retener hasta la llegada" (please hold until arrival) on the envelope; letters addressed thus will not appear on the Lista. Letters are often filed incorrectly, so you should have staff check under all your initials, preferably use only two names on the envelope (in Hispanic countries, the second of people's three names, or the third if they've four names, is the paternal surname and the most important, so if three names are used, your mail will probably be filed under the middle one) and capitalize and underline your surname. To collect, you need your passport or some other official ID with a photograph. There is no fee.

American Express also operates an efficient mail collection service, and has a number of offices all over Mexico – most useful in Mexico City, where the address for the most central branch is: c/o American Express, Paseo de la Reforma 350, Planta Baja, Col Juárez, 06600 México DF. They keep letters for a month and also hold faxes (Ⓕ 55/5208-5903). If you don't carry their card or cheques, you have to pay a fee to collect your mail, although they don't always ask.

Sending letters and cards is also easy enough, if slow. Anything sent abroad by air should have an **airmail** (*por avión*) stamp on it or it is liable to go surface. Letters should take around a week to North America, two to Europe or Australasia, but can take much longer (postcards in particular are likely to be slow). Anything at all important should be taken to the post office and preferably **registered** rather than dropped in a mail box, although the dedicated airmail boxes in resorts and big cities are supposed to be more reliable than ordinary ones.

Sending **packages** out of the country is drowned in bureaucracy. Regulations about the thickness of brown paper wrapping and the amount of string used vary from state to state, but most importantly, any package must be checked by customs and have its paperwork stamped by at least three other departments, which may take a while. Take your package (unsealed) to any post office and they'll set you on your way. Many stores will send your purchases home for you, which is a great deal easier. Within the country, you can send a package by bus if there is someone to collect it at the other end.

Telegram offices (*telégrafos*) are frequently in the same building as the post office. The service is super-efficient, but international ones are very expensive, even if you use the cheaper overnight service. In most cases, you can get across a short message for less by phone or fax.

Mobile phones

If you want to use your mobile phone in Mexico, you'll need to check with your phone provider whether it will work there, and how the calls are charged. Foreign mobile phones are unlikely to work in most of Mexico, even though there are two GSM providers, Radiomovil (Telcel) and Pegaso Comunicaciones (Movistar). Radiomovil has roaming agreements with AT&T, Cingular and T-mobile in the US, Microcell in Canada, Hutchison, O_2, T-Mobile and Vodafone in the UK, Optus and Telestra in Australia, and MTN in South Africa, among other operators worldwide, but both GSM providers are new, and their coverage of the country is so far confined largely to urban areas around Mexico City. It is also possible to obtain a tri-band phone, which will cover local frequencies, but these can be pricey and generally, until GSM coverage is wider, it is better to rent a mobile while you are in the country. This is easy enough, costing around US$4.50–6 per day for a pay-as-you-go phone, with cards widely available nationwide.

For further information on using your mobile in Mexico, including a coverage map and list of overseas mobile phone companies with roaming agreements for Mexico, see Ⓦ www.gsmworld.com/roaming/gsminfo/cou_mx.shtml. More general information about using your mobile abroad can be found at Ⓦ www.telecomsadvice.org.uk/features/using_your_mobile_abroad.htm.

Phones

Local phone calls in Mexico are cheap, and some hotels will let you call locally for free. Coin-operated public phones, rapidly disappearing, also charge very little for local calls. Internal **long-distance calls** are best made with a phonecard. These are available from telephone offices and stores near phones that use them (especially in bus and train stations, airports and major resorts). Many newer public phones say they accept credit cards; in practice, however, they often don't.

Slightly more expensive are **casetas de teléfono**, phone offices where someone will make the connection for you. There are lots of them, as many Mexicans don't have phones of their own: they can be simply shops or bars with public phones, indicated by a phone sign outside, in which case you may only be allowed to make local calls. However, many are specialist phone and fax places displaying a blue-and-white **Larga Distancia** (long-distance) sign. You're connected by an operator who presents you with a bill afterwards – once connected, the cost can usually be seen clicking up on a meter. There are scores of competing companies, and the new ones, like Computel, tend to be better; many take credit cards. Prices vary, so if you're making lots of calls it may be worth checking a few out. There are *casetas* at just about every bus station and airport.

Wherever you make them from, **international calls** are fabulously expensive – using a phonecard is the easiest option, though even the highest denomination ones won't last long. From a cardphone, you pay US$1 per minute to the US or Canada, US$2 to the British Isles or Europe, US$2.50 to Australia or New Zealand. You pay similar or slightly higher rates from a *caseta* (though costs vary more than you'd expect, so shop around); calling from a hotel is very extravagant indeed. One of the cheapest ways to make an international call is via the Internet, a service available from a limited but growing number of Internet offices. This can cost as little as US$0.40 a minute to anywhere in the world. Another alternative is to arm yourself in advance with a charge card or calling card that can be used in Mexico; you'll be connected to an English-speaking operator and will be billed at home at a rate that is predictable (if still high). You should be able to get through to the toll-free numbers from any working public phone.

It is also possible to **call collect** (*por cobrar*). In theory you should be able to make an international collect call from any public phone, by dialling the international operator (☎090) or getting in touch with the person-to-person direct-dial numbers listed below, though it can be hard to get through. At a *caseta* there may be a charge for making the connection, even if you don't get through, and a hotel is liable to make an even bigger charge.

Faxes can be sent from (and received at) many long-distance telephone *casetas*: again the cost is likely to be astronomical.

Dialling codes

To call **collect** or **person-to-person**, dial ☎92 for interstate calls within Mexico, ☎96 for the US and Canada, ☎99 for the rest of the world.

Calling from long-distance public phones

Mexico interstate ☎01 + area code + number
US and Canada ☎00 + area code + number
UK ☎00 44 + area code (minus initial zero) + number
Ireland ☎00 353 + area code (minus initial zero) + number
Australia ☎00 61 + area code (minus initial zero) + number
New Zealand ☎00 64 + area code (minus initial zero) + number

Calling Mexico from abroad

From US and Canada ☎011 52 + area code + number
From UK, Ireland and New Zealand ☎00 52 + area code + number
From Australia ☎0011 52 + area code + number

Calling card numbers

US and UK **calling card** numbers for English-speaking operator and home billing are as follows:
AT&T ☎01-800/288-2872
BT ☎01-800/123-0244
Canada Direct ☎01-800/123-0200 or 1-800/021-1994
ekit ☎1-888/206-5546 or 1-877/237-6347
Sprint ☎01-800/210-2273

Email and the Internet

The **Internet** is booming in Mexico – most urban school children are computer-literate and public access facilities are springing up all over the place. **Internet cafés** are easy to find in all the larger cities and resort destinations, and the level of service is usually excellent, although servers tend to crash with greater frequency than they do at home. In smaller towns and villages, such facilities are still rare. Depending on where you are, Internet access can cost anything from US$0.50 to US$2.50 an hour. Major tourist resorts can be the most expensive places, and it's best there to look for cheaper Internet cafés around the town centre that are frequented by Mexicans and avoid those in the luxury hotel zones. Internet facilities in large cities are usually open from early morning until late at night, but in smaller towns they have shorter opening hours and may close altogether at weekends. Most home email accounts can be accessed from other computers, such as those in Mexican cybercafés: if you don't already know how to do this, ask your service provider, or alternatively set up a free web-based account with Hotmail (Ⓦwww.hotmail.com) or Yahoo! (Ⓦwww.yahoo.com), which you can access from anywhere with an Internet connection.

The media

Few domestic newspapers carry much foreign news, and the majority of international coverage does not extend beyond Latin America. Papers are lurid scandal sheets, brimming with violent crime depicted in full colour. Each state has its own press, however, and they do vary: while most are little more than government mouthpieces, others can be surprisingly independent.

Probably the best national paper, if you read Spanish, is the new *Reforma*, which, although in its infancy, has already established an excellent reputation for its independence and political objectivity. Also worth a read is *La Jornada*, which with its unashamedly left-wing agenda is quite daringly critical of government policy, especially in Chiapas, and whose journalists regularly face death threats as a result. As the press has gradually been asserting its independence since 1995, subjects such as human rights, corruption and drug trafficking are increasingly being tackled, but journalists face great danger if they speak out, not only from shady government groups but also from the drug traffickers. In 2002 for example, two journalists were murdered, probably by agents of drug cartels, and nine were detained by the authorities, mostly under Mexico's punitive defamation laws. Eight journalists on the paper *Norte de Ciudad Juárez*, including the editor, were also threatened with imprisonment by a Chihuahua judge for reporting on corruption involving a powerful local politician and businessman.

On Mexican **TV** you can watch any number of US shows dubbed into Spanish – it's most bizarre to be walking through some shantytown as the strains of some highly familiar theme tune come floating across the air. Far and away the most popular programmes are the *telenovelas* – soap operas that dominate the screens from 6pm to 10pm and pull in audiences of millions. Each episode seems to take melodrama to new heights, with nonstop action and emotions hammed-up to the maximum for the riveted fans. Plot lines are like national news, while *telenovela* stars become major celebrities, despite their ludicrously over-the-top acting styles. **Cable and satellite** are now widespread, and even quite downmarket hotels offer numerous channels, many of them American.

Radio stations in the capital and Guadalajara (among others) have programmes in English for a couple of hours each day, and in many places US broadcasts can also be picked up. If you have a short-wave radio, you can pick up the BBC World Service, which is broadcast on various frequencies depending on the time of day. The main ones are 5975KHz, 6195KHz, 11,675KHz, 11,835KHz and 15,390KHz. Full details of programmes and frequencies can be found on the BBC website at Ⓦwww.bbc.co.uk/worldservice. The Voice of America broadcasts 24 hours on a number of frequencies including 5995KHz, 6130KHz, 7405KHz, 9455KHz, 9775KHz, 11,695KHz and 13,790KHz (full details of schedules and frequencies at Ⓦwww.voa.gov).

Opening hours and holidays

It's almost impossible to generalize about opening hours in Mexico; even when times are posted at museums, tourist offices and shops, they're not always adhered to.

The **siesta**, though, is still around, and many places will close for a couple of hours in the early afternoon, usually from 1pm to 3pm. The strictness of this is very much dependent on the climate; where it's hot – especially on the Gulf Coast and in the Yucatán – everything may close for up to four hours in the middle of the day, and then reopen until 8pm or 9pm. In central Mexico, the industrial north and highland areas, hours are more like the standard nine-to-five, and shops do not close for lunch.

More specifically, **shops** tend to keep fairly long hours, say from 9am to 8pm, though many will close for a couple of hours in the middle of the day. Post offices are open Monday to Friday 9am–3pm, Saturday 9am–1pm, and the central post office in a large town will usually be open until 6pm weekdays. Banks are generally open Monday to Friday 9.30am–5pm.

Museums and galleries tend to open from about 9am or 10am to 5pm or 6pm. Many have reduced entry fees – or are free – on Sunday, and most are closed on Monday. Some museums may close for lunch, but archeological sites are open right through the day.

Public holidays

The main **public holidays**, when virtually everything will be closed, are listed below. In addition, many places close on January 6 (Twelfth Night/Reyes).

Jan 1	New Year's Day
Feb 5	Anniversary of the Constitution
March 21	Benito Juárez Day
Good Friday and Easter Saturday	
May 1	Labor Day
May 5	Battle of Puebla
Sept 1	Presidential address to the nation
Sept 16	Independence Day
Oct 12	Día de la Raza/Columbus Day
Nov 1/2	All Saints/Day of the Dead
Nov 20	Anniversary of the Revolution
Dec 12	Virgin of Guadalupe
Dec 24–26	Christmas

Fiestas and entertainment

Stumbling, perhaps accidentally, onto some Mexican village **fiesta** may prove to be the highlight of your travels. Everywhere, from the remotest Indian village to the most sophisticated city suburb, will take at least one day off annually to devote to partying. Usually it's the local saint's day, but many fiestas have pre-Christian origins and any excuse – from harvest celebrations to the coming of the rains – will do.

Traditional dances and music form an essential part of almost every fiesta, and most include a procession behind some revered holy image or a more celebratory secular parade with fireworks. The only rule is that no two will be quite the same. The most famous, spectacular or curious **fiestas are listed at the end of each chapter** of this guide, but there are many others, and certain times of year are party time almost everywhere.

Carnaval, the week before Lent, is celebrated throughout the Roman Catholic world, and is at its most exuberant in Latin America. It is the last week of taking one's pleasures before the forty-day abstinence of Lent, which lasts until Easter. Like Easter, its date is not fixed, but it generally falls in February or early March. Carnaval is celebrated with costumes, parades, eating and dancing, most spectacularly in Veracruz and Mazatlán, and works its way up to a climax on the last day, Mardi Gras or Fat Tuesday.

The country's biggest holiday, however, is **Semana Santa** – Holy Week – beginning on Palm Sunday and continuing until the following Sunday, Easter Day. Still a deeply religious festival in Mexico, it celebrates the resurrection of Christ, and has also become an occasion to venerate the Virgin Mary, with processions bearing her image a hallmark of the celebrations. During Semana Santa, expect transport to be totally disrupted as virtually the whole country is on the move, visiting family and returning from the big city to their village of origin: you will definitely need to plan ahead if travelling then. Many places close for the whole of Holy Week, and certainly from Thursday to Sunday.

Secular **Independence Day** (Sept 16) is in some ways more solemn than the religious festivals with their exuberant fervour. While Easter and Carnaval are popular festivals, this one is more official, marking the historic day in 1810 when Manuel Hidalgo y Costilla issued the Grito (Cry of Independence) from his parish church in Dolores, now Dolores Hidalgo, Guanajuato, which is still the centre of commemoration. You'll also find the day marked in the capital with mass recitation of the Grito in the zócalo, followed by fireworks, music and dancing.

The **Day of the Dead** is All Saints' or All Souls' Day and its eve (Nov 1–2), when offerings are made to ancestors' souls, frequently with picnics and all-night vigils at their graves. People build shrines in their homes to honour their departed relatives, but it's the cemeteries to head for if you want to see the really spectacular stuff. Sweetmeats and papier-mâché statues of dressed-up skeletons give the whole proceedings a rather gothic air.

Christmas is a major holiday, and again a time when people are on the move and transport booked solid for weeks ahead. Gringo influence is heavy nowadays, with Santa Claus and Christmas trees, but the Mexican festival remains distinct in many ways, with a much stronger religious element (virtually every home has a nativity crib). **New Year** is still largely an occasion to spend with family, the actual hour being celebrated with the eating of grapes. Presents are traditionally given on Twelfth Night or Epiphany (Jan 6), which is when the three Magi of the Bible arrived bearing gifts – though things are shifting into line with Yankee custom, and more and more people are exchanging gifts on December 25. One of the more bizarre Christmas events takes place at Oaxaca, where there is a public display of nativity cribs and other sculptures made of radishes.

Dance

Traditional **dances**, complicated and full of ancient symbolism, are often a fiesta's most extraordinary feature. Many of the most famous – including the **Yaqui stag** dance and the dance of **Los Viejitos** (the little old men) – can be seen in sanitized form at **Ballet Folklórico** performances in Mexico City or on tour in the provinces. Many states, too, have regular shows put on by regional *folklórico* companies, and many *indígenas* help make ends meet by putting on their people's traditional dances for tourists. The spectacular **Voladores** flying dance of the Totonacs of Veracruz state, for example, is performed regularly at Papantla and the nearby archeological sites.

You should try at least once to see dance in its authentic state, performed by enthusiastic amateurs at a village celebration. Some of the most impressive are the plant and animal **Las Varitas** and **Zacamson** dances of the Huastecs in the southeastern corner of San Luis Potosí state, performed for the festivals of San Miguel Arcángel (Sept 28–29) and Virgen de Guadalupe (Dec 12). Information is available from tourist offices. Less indigenous are the **Moros y Cristianos** dances celebrating the victories of the Christian *Reconquista* over the Muslim Moors in eighth- to fifteenth-century Spain, and widely performed in Mexico to this day. Of more recent origin, the **masked dance** held on Mardi Gras in Huejotzingo, northwest of Puebla, re-enacts nineteenth-century battles between Mexicans and the French troops of Emperor Maximilian.

Sport

You'll find facilities for golf, tennis, sailing, surfing, scuba diving and deep-sea fishing – even horseback riding and hunting – provided at all the big resorts.

Sport fishing is enormously popular in Baja California and the big Pacific coast resorts, while freshwater bass fishing is growing in popularity too, especially behind the large dams in the north of the country. The gentler arts of **diving** and **snorkelling** are big on the Caribbean coast, with world-famous dive sites at Cozumel and on the reefs further south. The Pacific coast is becoming something of a centre for **surfing**, with few facilities as yet (though you can rent surfboards in major tourist centres such as Acapulco and Mazatlán) but plenty of Californian surfers who follow the weather south over the winter. The most popular places are in Baja California and on the Oaxaca coast, but the biggest waves are to be found around Lázaro Cárdenas in Michoacán. A more minority-interest activity for which Mexico has become a major centre is **caving**. With a third of the country built on limestone, there are caverns in most states that can be explored by experienced potholers or spelunkers.

The Ministry of Tourism publishes a leaflet on participatory sport in Mexico, and can also advise on such things as licences and seasons.

Spectator sports

Mexico's chief spectator sport is **soccer** (*fútbol*). Mexican teams have not been notably successful on the international stage, but going to a game can still be a thrilling experience, with vast crowds for the big ones. The capital and Guadalajara are the best places to see a match and the biggest game in the domestic league, "El Clásico", between Chivas from Guadalajara and América from Mexico City, fills the city's 150,000-seater Aztec stadium to capacity. **Baseball** (*béisbol*) is also popular, as is **American football** (especially on TV). **Jai alai** (also known as **frontón**, or **pelota vasca**) is Basque handball, common in big cities and played at a very high speed with a small hard ball and curved scoop attached to the hand; it's a big gambling game.

Mexican **rodeos** (*charreadas*), mainly seen in the north of the country, are as spectacular for their style and costume as they are for the events, while **bullfights** remain an obsession: every city has a bullring – Mexico City's Plaza México is the world's largest – and the country's *toreros* are said to be the world's most reckless, much in demand in Spain. Another popular bloodsport, usually at village level, is **cockfighting**, still legal in Mexico and mainly attended for the opportunity to bet on the outcome.

Masked **wrestling** (*lucha libre*) is very popular in Mexico, too, with the participants, Batman-like, out of the game for good should their mask be removed and their secret identity revealed. Nor does the resemblance to comic-book superheroes end in the ring: certain masked wrestlers have become popular social campaigners out of the ring, always ready to turn up just in the nick of time to rescue the beleaguered poor from eviction by avaricious landlords, or persecution by corrupt politicians. For more on wrestling, see p.439.

Crafts and markets

The craft tradition of Mexico, much of it descended directly from arts practised long before the Spanish arrived, is still extremely strong. Regional and highly localized specialities survive, with villages throughout the republic jealously guarding their reputations – especially in the states of Michoacán, Oaxaca, Chiapas and the Yucatán. There's a considerable amount of Guatemalan stuff about too.

Crafts

To buy crafts, there is no need these days to visit the place of origin – **craft shops** in Mexico City and all the big resorts gather the best and most popular items from around the country. On the other hand, it's a great deal more enjoyable to see where the articles come from, and certainly the only way to get any real bargains. The good stuff is rarely cheap wherever you buy it, however, and there is an enormous amount of dross produced specifically for tourists.

FONART shops, which you'll come across in major centres throughout Mexico, are run by a government agency devoted to the promotion and preservation of crafts – their wares are always excellent, if expensive, and the shops should be visited to get an idea of what is potentially available. Where no such store exists, you can get a similar idea by looking at the best of the tourist shops.

Among the most popular items are: **silver**, the best of which is wrought in Taxco, although rarely mined there; **pottery**, almost everywhere, with different techniques, designs and patterns in each region; **woollen goods**, especially blankets and *sarapes* from Oaxaca, which are again made everywhere – always check the fibres and go for more expensive natural dyes; **leather**, especially tyre-tread-soled *huaraches* (sandals), sold cheaply wherever you go; glass from Jalisco; **lacquerware**, particularly from Uruapán; and **hammocks**, the best of which are sold in Mérida.

It is illegal to buy or sell **antiquities**, and even more criminal to try taking them out of the country (moreover, many items sold as valuable antiquities are little more than worthless fakes) – best to just look.

Markets

For bargain hunters, the **mercado** (market) is the place to head. There's one in every Mexican town, which on one day of the week, the traditional market day, will be at its busiest with villagers from the surrounding area bringing their produce for sale or barter. By and large, of course, *mercados* are mainly dedicated to food and everyday necessities, but most have a section devoted to crafts, and in larger towns you may find a separate crafts bazaar.

Unless you're completely hopeless at bargaining, **prices** will always be lower in the market than in shops, but shops do have a couple of advantages. First, they exercise a degree of quality control, whereas any old junk can be sold in the market; and second, many established shops will be able to ship purchases home for you, which saves an enormous amount of the frustrating bureaucracy you'll encounter if you attempt to do it yourself.

Bargaining and **haggling** are very much a matter of personal style, highly dependent on your command of Spanish, aggressiveness and to some extent on experience. The old tricks (never show the least sign of interest, let alone enthusiasm; walking away will always cut the price dramatically) do still hold true; but most important is to know what you want, its approximate value, and how much you are prepared to pay. Never start to haggle for something you definitely don't intend to buy – it'll end in bad feelings on both sides. In shops there's little chance of significantly altering the official price unless you're buying in bulk, and even in markets most food and simple household goods have a set price (though it may be doubled at the sight of an approaching gringo).

Crime and safety

Despite soaring crime rates and dismal-sounding statistics, you are unlikely to run into trouble in Mexico as long as you stick to the well-travelled paths. Even in Mexico City, which has an appalling reputation, the threat is not that much greater than in many large North American and European cities.

Obviously there are areas of the cities where you wander alone, or at night, at your peril; but the precautions to be taken are mostly common sense and would be second nature at home. Travelling in the Zapatista-controlled areas of the state of Chiapas you will undoubtedly come across guerrillas and the army, but tourists are a target of neither and you shouldn't encounter any trouble.

Avoiding theft

Petty theft and **pickpockets** are your biggest worry, so don't wave money around, try not to look too obviously affluent, don't leave cash or cameras in hotel rooms, and do deposit your valuables in your hotel's safe if it has one (make a note of what you've deposited and ask the hotelier to sign it if you're worried). **Crowds**, especially on public city transport, are obvious hot spots: thieves tend to work in groups and target tourists. Distracting your attention, especially by pretending to look for something (always be suspicious of anyone who appears to be searching for something near you), or having one or two people pin you while another goes through your pockets, are common ploys, and can be done faster and more easily than you might imagine. Razoring of bags and pockets is another gambit, as is the more brutish grabbing of handbags, or anything left unattended even for a split second. When carrying your valuables, keep them out of sight under your clothes. If you are held up, however, don't try any heroics: hand over your money and rely on travellers' cheque refund schemes and credit card hotlines if appropriate. One trick is to carry a cheap wallet with US$20 and an old identification card, while hiding the bulk of your cash in a money belt. If you end up in the wrong situation, you can hand over the wallet and cut your losses. **Mugging** is less common, but you should steer clear of obvious danger spots, such as deserted pedestrian underpasses in big cities – indeed, avoid all deserted areas in big cities. When using ATM machines, use those in shopping malls or enclosed premises, and only in daylight when there are plenty of people around. **Robbery and sexual assault** on tourists by cab drivers are not unknown, and the US State Department advises its citizens against hailing a cab in the street in the capital,

Mexico City (see p.370). Instead, phone for a radio cab or, failing that, take the next best option and get a cab from an official *sitio*. At night the beaches in tourist areas are also potentially dangerous.

When travelling, keep an eye on your bags (which are safe enough in the luggage compartments underneath most buses). Hold-ups of buses happen from time to time, and you may well be frisked on boarding to check for arms, since the bandits are most often passengers on the bus.

Drivers are likely to encounter problems if they leave anything in their car. The **vehicle** itself is less likely to be stolen than broken into for the valuables inside. To avoid the worst, always park legally (and preferably off the street) and never leave anything visible inside the car. Driving itself can be hazardous, too, especially at night (see box, p.44).

Police

Mexican **police** are, in the ordinary run of events, no better or worse than any other; but they are very badly paid, and **graft** is an accepted part of the job. This is often difficult for foreign visitors to accept, but it is a system, and in its own way it works well enough. If a policeman accuses you of some violation (and this is almost bound to happen to drivers at some stage), explain that you're a tourist, not used to the ways of the country – you may get off scot-free, but more likely the subject of a "**fine**" will come up. Such on-the-spot fines are open to negotiation, but only if you're confident you've done nothing seriously wrong and have a reasonable command of Spanish. Otherwise pay up and get out.

These small bribes are known as *mordidas* (bites), and they may also be extracted by border officials or bureaucrats (in which case, you could get out of paying by asking for a receipt, but it won't make life easier). In general, it is always wise to back off from any sort of confrontation with the police and to be extremely polite to them at all times.

Emergencies

In the event of trouble, dial ⑦06 for the police **emergency operator**. Most phone booths give the number for the local Red Cross (Cruz Roja) – but don't expect the phone to be answered promptly.

Far more common than the *mordida* is the **propina**, or tip, a payment that is made entirely on your initiative. There's no need to do this, but it's remarkable how often a few pesos complete paperwork that would otherwise take weeks, open doors that were firmly locked before, or even find a seat on a previously full bus. All such transactions are quite open, and it's up to you to literally put your money on the table.

Should a crime be committed against you – in particular if you're robbed – your relationship with the police will obviously be different, although even in this eventuality it's worth considering whether the lengthy hassles you'll go through make it worth reporting. Some insurance companies will insist on a police report if you're to get any refund – in which case you may practically have to dictate it to the officer and can expect little action – but others will be understanding of the situation. American Express in Mexico City, for example, may accept without a murmur the fact that your cheques have been stolen but the theft was not reported to the police. The department you need in order to *presentar una denuncia* (report the theft officially) is the Procuradoría General de Justicia.

The Mexican **legal system** is based on the Napoleonic code, which assumes your guilt until you can prove otherwise. Your one phone call should you be jailed should be to your **consulate** – if nothing else, they'll arrange an English-speaking lawyer. You can be held for up to 72 hours on suspicion before charges have to be brought. Mexican jails are grim, although lots of money and friends on the outside can ameliorate matters slightly.

Drugs

Drug offences are the most common cause of serious trouble between tourists and the authorities. Under heavy pressure from the US to stamp out the trade, local authorities are particularly happy to throw the book at foreign offenders.

A good deal of **marijuana** (known as *mota*) – grown primarily in Guerrero ("Acapulco Gold"), the Yucatán, Sinaloa, Oaxaca, and Michoacán (redder in colour, and generally considered the best) – continues to be cultivated in Mexico, despite US-backed government attempts to stamp it out (at one time, imports of Mexican marijuana were so high that the DEA had crops sprayed with paraquat). Although cannabis is widely used, it remains strictly illegal, and foreigners caught in **possession** are dealt with harshly; for quantities reckoned to be for distribution you can wave goodbye to daylight for a long time. For possession of small quantities, you can expect a hefty fine, no sympathy and little help from your consulate.

Other naturally occurring drugs – Mexico has more species of psychoactive plants than anywhere else in the world – still form an important part of many indigenous rituals. **Hallucinogenic mushrooms** can be found in many parts of the country, especially in the states of Oaxaca, Chiapas and México, while the **peyote cactus** from the northern deserts is used primarily by the Huichols, but also by other indigenous peoples. The authorities turn a blind eye to traditional use, but use by non-indigenous Mexicans and tourists is as strongly prohibited as that of any other illegal drug, and heavily penalized. Expect searches and hotel raids by police if staying in areas known for peyote.

Cocaine trafficking is a national problem, as Mexico is a major staging post on the smuggling route from Colombian supply to American demand. Well-connected gangs involved in the trade – especially in Guadalajara, Ciudad Juárez and Tijuana – are often more powerful than the police and local government. Use of cocaine is also widespread and growing; **crack** is a blight in parts of the capital and in certain northern cities, approaching levels once seen in American cities. The best advice as far as this unpleasant trade goes is to steer as clear as possible.

Work and study

There's virtually no chance of finding temporary work in Mexico unless you have some very specialized skill and have arranged the position beforehand. Work permits are almost impossible to get hold of. The few foreigners who manage to find work do so mostly in language schools. It may be possible, though not legal, to earn money as a private English tutor by simply advertising in a local newspaper or on notice boards at a university.

The best way to extend your time in Mexico is on a **study programme** or **volunteer project**. A US organization called **AmeriSpan** selects language schools throughout Latin America, including Mexico, to match the needs and requirements of students, and provides advice and support. For further information, call (from the US or Canada) ⓣ1-800/879-6640 or 215/751-1100, ⓕ215/751-1986, ⓦwww.amerispan.com.

Study and work programmes

From the US

AFS Intercultural Programs ⓣ1-800/876-2377 or 212/299-9000, ⓦwww.usa.afs.org. Runs summer experiential programmes aimed at fostering international understanding for teenagers and adults.

American Friends Service Committee ⓣ215/241-7295, ⓦwww.afsc.org. Summer volunteer work camps in Mexican villages for 18–26-year-olds. Spanish language skills required.

American Institute for Foreign Study ⓣ1-800/727-2437, ⓦwww.aifs.com. Language study and cultural immersion for the summer or school year, as well as au pair and Camp America programmes.

Association for International Practical Training ⓣ1-800/994-2443 or 410/997-2200, ⓦwww.aipt.org. Summer internships for students who have completed at least two years of college in science, agriculture, engineering or architecture.

Bernan Associates ⓣ1-800/274-4888, ⓦwww.bernan.com. Distributes UNESCO's encyclopedic *Study Abroad* book.

Council on International Educational Exchange (CIEE) ⓣ1-800/2COUNCIL, ⓦwww.ciee.org. The nonprofit parent organization of Council Travel, CIEE runs summer, semester and academic-year programmes, and publishes *Work, Study, Travel Abroad and Volunteer! The Comprehensive Guide to Voluntary Service in the US and Abroad.*

Experiment in International Living ⓣ1-800/345-2929 or 802/257-7751, ⓦwww.usexperiment.org. Summer programme for high-school students, focusing on community service, language study, ecology, the arts, and outdoor adventure, staying with a host family as part of the local community.

Global Exchange ⓣ415/255-7296, ⓦwww.globalexchange.org. A not-for-profit organization that leads "reality tours", giving participants the chance to learn about the country while seeing it. Check out their detailed website for information on "travel seminars" looking at issues such as culture, music, health, religion or agriculture.

School for Field Studies ⓣ1-800/989-4418, ⓦwww.fieldstudies.org. Study abroad programme focused on environmental problem solving.

Studyabroad.com ⓣ610/499-9200, ⓦwww.studyabroad.com. Language programmes, semester-long and year-long courses, internships, and a page on their website devoted specifically to Mexico.

Volunteers for Peace ⓣ802/259-2759, ⓦwww.vfp.org. Nonprofit organization with links to a huge international network of "workcamps", two- to four-week programmes that bring volunteers together from many countries to carry out needed community projects. Most workcamps are in summer, with registration in April–May. Annual directory costs US$20.

World Learning ⓣ1-800/257-7751 or 802/257-7751, ⓦwww.worldlearning.org. Its School for International Training (ⓣ1-800/336-1616, ⓦwww.sit.edu) runs accredited college semesters in Oaxaca, comprising language and cultural studies, homestay and other academic work.

From the UK and Ireland

British Council ⓣ020/7930 8466. Produce a free leaflet which details study opportunities abroad. The Council's Central Management Direct Teaching (ⓣ020/7389 4931) recruits TEFL teachers for posts worldwide (check ⓦwww.britishcouncil.org/work/jobs.htm for a current list of vacancies), and its Central Bureau for International Education and Training (ⓣ020/7389 4004, ⓦwww.centralbureau.org.uk) enables those who already work as educators to find out about teacher development programmes abroad. It also publishes a book, *Year Between*, aimed principally at gap-year

Earthwatch

Earthwatch matches volunteers with scientists working on a particular project. Recent expeditions in Mexico have included excavations of ancient megafauna in San Miguel de Allende, investigations into pre- and post-Conquest religious architecture in the Yucatán, and a survey of carnivores in the tropical dry forests of Jalisco. Fascinating though this work is, it's not a cheap way to see the country: volunteers must raise US$700–4000 (average about US$2000) for each one- to two-week stint as a contribution to the cost of research. For more information, access their website (ⓦwww.earthwatch.org), or contact one of the following:

Earthwatch HQ 3 Clock Tower Place, Suite 100, PO Box 75, Maynard, MA 01754 ⓣ1-800/776-0188 or 978/461-0081.

Earthwatch Europe 267 Banbury Rd, Oxford OX2 7HT, UK ⓣ01865/318838, ⓦwww.earthwatch.org/europe.

Earthwatch Australia 126 Bank St, South Melbourne, Vic 3205 ⓣ03/9682 6828, ⓦwww.earthwatch.org/australia.

students, detailing volunteer programmes, and schemes abroad.

BTCV ⓣ01491/821600, ⓦwww.btcv.org.uk. One of the largest environmental charities in Britain, with branches across the country, also has a programme of international working holidays (as a paying volunteer), with a comprehensive brochure available.

Council Exchange (CIEE) ⓣ020/7478 2000. International study and volunteer work programmes for students and recent graduates.

International House ⓣ020/7518 6999, ⓦwww.ihlondon.com. Head office of a reputable English-teaching organization which offers TEFL training leading to the award of a Certificate in English Language Teaching to Adults (CELTA), and recruits for teaching positions in Britain and abroad.

VSO (Voluntary Service Overseas) ⓣ020/8780 7200, ⓦwww.vso.org.uk. Highly respected charity that sends qualified professionals (in the fields of education, health, community and social work, engineering, information technology, law and media) to spend two years or more working for local wages on projects beneficial to developing countries.

From Australia and New Zealand

Australian Volunteers International ⓣ03/9279 1788, ⓦwww.ozvol.org.au. Postings for up to two years in developing countries.

Council Exchange (CIEE) ⓣ02/8235 7000, ⓦwww.councilexchanges.org.au. International study and volunteer work programmes for students and recent graduates.

Travellers with disabilities

Mexico is not well equipped for people with disabilities, but it is improving all the time and, especially at the top end of the market, it shouldn't be too difficult to find accommodation and tour operators who can cater for your particular needs. The important thing is to check beforehand with tour companies, hotels and airlines that they can accommodate you specifically. The list below details organizations that can advise you as to which tour operators and airlines are the most reliable.

If you stick to beach resorts – Cancún and Acapulco in particular – and upmarket tourist hotels, you should certainly be able to find places that are wheelchair-friendly and used to having disabled guests. US chains are very good for this, with Choice, Days Inn, Holiday Inn, Leading Hotels of the World, Marriott, Radisson, Ramada, Sheraton and Westin claiming to have the necessary facilities for at least some disabilities in some of their hotels. Always check in advance, however, that the hotel of your choice can cater for your particular needs.

You'll find that, unless you have your own transport, the best way to travel inside the country may prove to be by air, since trains and buses rarely cater for disabled people, and certainly not for wheelchairs. Travelling on a lower budget, or getting off the beaten track, you'll find few facilities. Ramps are few and far between, streets and pavements not in a very good state, and people no more likely to volunteer help than at home. Depending on your disability, you may want to find an able-bodied helper to accompany you. If you cannot find anyone suitable among your own friends or family, the organizations listed below may be able to help you get in touch with someone.

Contacts for travellers with disabilities

In the US and Canada

Access-Able ⓦwww.access-able.com. Online resource for travellers with disabilities.

Directions Unlimited 123 Green Lane, Bedford Hills, NY 10507 ⓣ1-800/533-5343 or 914/241-1700. Travel agency specializing in bookings for people with disabilities.

Mobility International USA 451 Broadway, Eugene, OR 97401 ⓣ541/343-1284, ⓦwww.miusa.org. Information and referral services, access guides, tours and exchange programmes. Annual membership US$35 (includes quarterly newsletter).

Society for the Advancement of Travelers with Handicaps (SATH) 347 5th Ave, New York, NY 10016 ⓣ212/447-7284, ⓦwww.sath.org. Nonprofit educational organization that has actively represented travellers with disabilities since 1976.

Wheels Up! ⓣ1-888/38-WHEELS, ⓦwww.wheelsup.com. Provides discounted airfare, tour and cruise prices for disabled travellers; also publishes a free monthly newsletter and has a comprehensive website.

In the UK and Ireland

Disability Action Portside Business Park, 189 Airport Rd W, Belfast BT3 9ED ⓣ028/9029 7800. Provides information about access for disabled travellers abroad.

Holiday Care 2nd floor, Imperial Building, Victoria Rd, Horley, Surrey RH6 7PZ ⓣ0845/124 9971, minicom ⓣ0845/124 9976, ⓦwww.holidaycare.org.uk. Provides free lists of accessible accommodation abroad. Information on financial help for holidays available.

Tripscope Alexandra House, Albany Rd, Brentford, Middlesex TW8 0NE ⓣ0845/758 5641, ⓦwww.tripscope.org.uk. This registered charity provides a national telephone information service offering free advice on international transport for those with a mobility problem.

In Australia and New Zealand

ACROD (Australian Council for Rehabilitation of the Disabled) PO Box 60, Curtin, ACT 2605 ⓣ02/6282 4333; Suite 103, 1st floor, 1–5 Commercial Rd, Kings Grove, NSW 2208 ⓦwww.acrod.org.au. Provides lists of travel agencies and tour operators for people with disabilities.

Disabled Persons Assembly 4/173–175 Victoria St, Wellington ⓣ04/801 9100 (also TTY), ⓦwww.dpa.org.nz. Resource centre with lists of travel agencies and tour operators for people with disabilities.

Women travellers

So many oppressive limitations are imposed on women's freedom to travel that any advice or warning seems merely to reinforce the situation. That said, machismo is engrained in the Mexican mentality and, although it's softened to some extent by the gentler mores of indigenous culture, a degree of harassment is inevitable.

On the whole, most hassles will be limited to comments (*piropos*, supposedly compliments) in the street, but even situations that might be quite routine at home can seem threatening without a clear understanding of the nuances of Mexican Spanish. It's a good idea to **avoid eye contact** – wearing sunglasses helps. To avoid matters escalating, any provocation is best ignored totally. Mexican women are rarely slow with a stream of retaliatory abuse, but it's a dangerous strategy unless you're very sure of your ground – coming from a foreigner, it may also be taken as racism.

Public transport can be one of the worst places for harassment, especially groping in crowded situations. On the Mexico City Metro, there are separate women's carriages and passages during rush hours. Otherwise, if you get a seat, you can hide behind a newspaper.

Any problems are aggravated in the big tourist spots, where legendarily "easy" tourists attract droves of would-be gigolos.

Mexico City can feel overwhelming, though if you're from a big city yourself, it may not seem that different, and requires the same common sense. Away from the cities, though, and especially in indigenous areas, there is rarely any problem – you may as an outsider be treated as an object of curiosity (or even resentment), but not necessarily with any implied or intended sexual threat. And wherever you come across it, such curiosity can also extend to great friendliness and hospitality. On the whole, the further from the US border you get, the easier things will become – though some women find other Latin American countries further south, which are less used to tourists, infinitely worse.

The restrictions imposed on **drinking** are without a doubt irksome: women are simply and absolutely barred from the vast majority of cantinas, and even in so-called Ladies' Bars "unescorted" women may be looked at with suspicion or even refused service. Carrying a bottle is the only answer, since in small towns the cantina may be the only place that sells alcoholic drinks.

Gay and lesbian travellers

There are no federal laws governing homosexuality in Mexico, and hence it's legal. There are, however, laws enforcing "public morality", which although they are supposed only to apply to prostitution, are often used against gays. While 1997 saw the election of Mexico's first "out" congresswoman, the left-wing PRD's Patria Jiménez, President Fox's right-wing party, PAN, has been running anti-gay campaigns in towns and states that it controls, closing gay bars in Monterrey and passing an ordinance against "abnormal sexual behaviour" in Guadalajara.

There are in fact a large number of gay **groups** and **publications** in Mexico – we've supplied two contact addresses below. The lesbian scene is not as visible or as large as the gay scene for men, but it's there and growing. There are gay bars and clubs in the major resorts and US border towns, and in large cities such as the capital, and also Monterrey, Guadalajara, Veracruz and Oaxaca; elsewhere, private parties are where it all happens, and you'll need a contact to find them.

As far as popular **attitudes** are concerned, religion and machismo are the order of the day, and prejudice is rife, but attitudes are changing. Soft-porn magazines for gay men are sold openly on street stalls and, while you should be careful to avoid upsetting macho sensibilities, you should have few problems if you are discreet. Many Mexicans of both sexes are bisexual, though they do not see themselves as such. In Juchitán, Oaxaca, on the other hand, gay male transvestites, known as *muxes*, are accepted as a kind of third sex, and the town even has a transvestite basketball team.

HIV and **AIDS** (SIDA) are as much a threat in Mexico as anywhere else in the world, and the usual precautions are in order. You can check the latest gay rights situation in Mexico on the International Gay and Lesbian Human Rights Commission website at Ⓦwww.iglhrc.org, and information on the male gay scene in Mexico (gay bars, meeting places and cruising spots) can be found in the annual *Spartacus Gay Guide*, available in bookshops at home. As for contacts within Mexico: lesbians can get in touch with Grupo Lesbico Patlatonalli, Apartado Postal 1-623, CP 44100, Guadalajara, Jalisco (Ⓣ&Ⓕ33/3632-0507); while for gay men, CIDHOM (Centro de Información y

Documentación de las Homosexualidades en México), Cerrada Cuaunochtli 11, Col. Pueblo Quieto, Tlalpan, México DF 14040 (ⓣ55/5666-5436, ⓔcidhom@laneta.apc.org), can offer information.

International gay and lesbian travel contacts

Damron US ⓣ1-800/462-6654 or 415/255-0404, ⓦwww.damron.com. Publisher of the *Men's Travel Guide*, a pocket-sized yearbook full of listings of hotels, bars, clubs and resources for gay men; the *Women's Traveler*, which provides similar listings for lesbians; and *Damron Accommodations*, which provides detailed listings of over 1000 accommodations for gays and lesbians worldwide. All are offered at a discount on the website.

Dreamwaves Holidays UK ⓣ0870/042 2475, ⓦwww.gayholidaysdirect.com. Online gay and lesbian travel agent, offering good deals on all types of holiday. Also lists gay- and lesbian-friendly hotels around the world.

Gay and Lesbian Tourism Australia ⓦwww.galta.com.au. Directory and links for gay and lesbian travel in Australia and worldwide.

Gay Travel dot.com US ⓣ1-800/GAY-TRAVEL, ⓦwww.gaytravel.com. Gay online travel agent, offering accommodation, cruises, tours and more.

Gay Travel UK ⓦwww.gaytravel.co.uk. Online gay and lesbian travel agent, offering good deals on all types of holiday. Also lists gay- and lesbian-friendly hotels around the world.

International Gay & Lesbian Travel Association US ⓣ1-800/448-8550 or 954/776-2626, ⓦwww.iglta.org. Trade group that can provide a list of gay- and lesbian-owned or -friendly travel agents, accommodation and other travel businesses.

Madison Travel UK ⓣ01273/202 532, ⓦwww.madisontravel.co.uk. Established travel agents specializing in packages to gay- and lesbian-friendly mainstream destinations, and also to gay/lesbian destinations.

Parkside Travel Australia ⓣ08/8274 1222, ⓔparkside@herveyworld.com.au. Gay travel agent associated with local branch of Hervey World Travel; all aspects of gay and lesbian travel worldwide.

Silke's Travel Australia ⓣ1800/807 860 or 02/8347 2000, ⓦwww.silkes.com.au. Long-established gay and lesbian specialist, with the emphasis on women's travel.

Tearaway Travel Australia ⓣ1800/664 440 or 03/9510 6644, ⓦwww.tearaway.com. Gay-specific business dealing with international and domestic travel.

Travelling with children

A minor under the age of 18 can enter the country with either their own passport or on the passport of a parent with whom they are travelling.

Travelling with younger kids is not uncommon – you will find that most Mexicans dote on children and they can often help to break the ice with strangers. The main problem, especially with small children, is their extra vulnerability. Even more than their parents, they need protecting from the **sun**, unsafe **drinking water**, **heat** and unfamiliar **food**. Chile in particular may be a problem for kids who are not used to it. Remember too that **diarrhoea** can be dangerous for younger children: rehydration salts (see p.32) are vital if your child goes down with it. Make sure too, if possible, that your child is aware of the dangers of rabies and other animal-borne illnesses; keep children away from all animals and consider a **rabies** shot.

For touring, hiking or walking, **child-carrier backpacks** are ideal: they can weigh less than 2kg and start at around US$75/£50. If the child is small enough, a fold-up buggy is also well worth packing – especially if they will sleep in it, while you have a meal or a drink.

One thing to be aware of, if you try to keep your children away from such things, is the level of on-screen violence typical of the movies shown on buses. You may wish to find seats away from the screen when travelling on long-distance bus journeys to avoid the level of gore that is likely to be shown.

US contacts for travellers with children

Rascals in Paradise ⓣ415/921-7000, ⓦwww.rascalsinparadise.com. Can arrange scheduled and customized itineraries built around activities for kids.

Travel With Your Children ⓣ212/477-5524 or 1-888/822-4388. Publish a regular newsletter, *Family Travel Times* (ⓦwww.familytraveltimes.com), as well as a series of books on travel with children including *Great Adventure Vacations With Your Kids*.

Senior travellers

Mexico is not a country that offers any special difficulties – or any special advantages – to older travellers, but the same considerations apply here as to anywhere else in the world. If choosing a package tour, consider one run by an organization such as Saga, Vantage or Elderhostel, which is specifically designed for over-50s.

If travelling independently, don't choose too punishing a schedule. Remember that in many parts of Mexico, high altitude, desert heat and tropical humidity can tire you out a lot faster than you might otherwise expect, and especially in such conditions it is wise to take it easy. If you plan on doing a lot of sightseeing, consider setting aside a few days when you have absolutely nothing specific to do. As far as comfort is concerned, first-class buses are generally pretty pleasant, with plenty of legroom, though the videos they show may not be entirely to your liking (time was, they used to show classics from the golden age of Mexican cinema, the 1940s, but nowadays it's shoot-em-up Hollywood action films). Second-class buses can be rather more boneshaking, and you won't want to take them for too long a journey if you can avoid it. Rail was always a more tranquil way to travel, but apart from the Copper Canyon Railway (see p.169), train travel is alas now a thing of the past.

Most of the hotels we recommend in this book should more than meet your needs, and in general even relatively low-budget hotels are clean and comfortable. Remember that senior citizens are often entitled to **discounts**, especially when visiting tourist sights, but also on occasion for accommodation and transport, something which it's always worth asking about.

Contacts for senior travellers

Elderhostel US & Canada ⓣ1-877/426-8056, ⓦwww.elderhostel.org. Runs an extensive worldwide network of educational and activity programmes, cruises and homestays for people over 60 (companions may be younger). Programmes generally last a week or more and costs are in line with those of commercial tours.

Saga Holidays US & Canada ⓣ1-800/343-0273, ⓦwww.sagaholidays.com; UK ⓣ0130/377 1111, ⓦwww.holidays.saga.co.uk. The biggest and most established specialist in tours and holidays aimed at older people.

Vantage Deluxe World Travel ⓣ1-800/322-6677, ⓦwww.vantagetravel.com. Specializes in worldwide group travel for seniors.

Directory

Addresses In Mexico addresses are frequently written with just the street name and number (thus: Madero 125), which can lead to confusion as many streets are known only as numbers (C 17). Calle (C) means Street; Avenida (Av), Bulevar (Blv), Calzada and Paseo are other common terms – most are named after historical figures or dates. An address such as Hidalgo 39 8° 120, means Hidalgo no. 39, 8th floor, room 120 (a ground-floor address would be denoted PB for Planta Baja). Many towns have all their streets laid out in a numbered grid fanning out from a central point – often with odd-numbered streets running east–west, even ones north–south. In such places a suffix – Ote (for Oriente, East), Pte (for Poniente, West), Nte (for Norte, North), or Sur (South) – may be added to the street number to tell you which side of the two central dividing streets it is.

Airport tax A departure tax is payable when flying out of Mexico (the equivalent of US$40). This is included in the price of most air tickets, but be sure to check when buying.

Alphabetical order Remember when looking things up in directories that "CH", "LL" and "Ñ" are considered separate letters in Spanish, so CH comes after C, LL after L and Ñ after N.

Electricity Theoretically 110 volts AC, with simple two-flat-pin rectangular plugs, so most North American appliances can be used as they are. Travellers from the UK, Ireland, Australasia and Europe should bring along a converter and a plug adapter. Cuts in service and fluctuations in the current do occur, and in cheap hotels any sort of appliance that draws a lot of current may blow all the fuses as soon as it's turned on.

Emergency General emergency number ⓣ080; Police ⓣ060; Fire ⓣ068; Ambulance ⓣ065; Green Angels (emergency highway breakdown) ⓣ55/5250-8221; toll-free tourist advice ⓣ01-800/903-9200.

Film and camera equipment Film is manufactured in Mexico and, if you buy it from a chain store like Woolworth's or Sanborn's rather than at a tourist store, costs no more than at home (if you buy it elsewhere, be sure to check the date on the box, and be suspicious if you can't see it). Up to twelve rolls of film can be brought into Mexico, and spare batteries are also a wise precaution. Any sort of camera hardware, though, will be prohibitively expensive. Slide film is hard to come by, too.

Laundry *Lavanderías* are ubiquitous in Mexico as the majority of households don't own a washing machine. Most charge by the kilo and for a few dollars you'll get your clothes back clean, pressed and perfectly folded, in less than 24 hours. Many hotels also offer laundry services that, although convenient, tend to charge by the item, adding up to a considerably greater cost.

Time zones Four time zones exist in Mexico. Most of the country is on GMT–6 in winter, GMT–5 in summer (first Sunday in April till last Sunday in October), the same as US Central Time. Baja California Sur, Sinaloa Nayarit and Chihuahua are on GMT–7 in winter, GMT–6 in summer, the same as Mountain Time. Baja California Norte is on GMT–8 in winter, GMT–7 in summer, the same as the US West Coast (Pacific Time); and finally, Sonora is also on GMT–7 all year round, and does not observe daylight saving time.

Toilets Public toilets in Mexico can be quite filthy, and sometimes there's no paper, although there will often be someone selling it outside for a couple of pesos. Toilets are usually known as *baños* (literally bathrooms) or as *excusados* or *sanitarios.* The most common signs are Damas (Ladies) and Caballeros (Gentlemen), though you may find the more confusing Señoras (Women) and Señores (Men) or even the symbols of Moon (Women) and Sun (Men). Always carry some toilet paper with you: it's easy enough to buy in Mexico, but it's never there when you need it.

Guide

Guide

Baja California and the Pacific Northwest

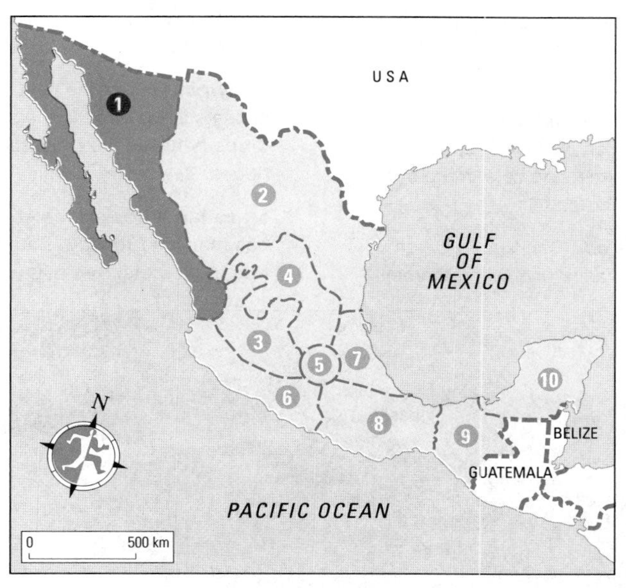

CHAPTER 1 Highlights

* **The Baja Peninsula** If you have the opportunity to travel the length of it, do so. There is no other drive so consistently beautiful and adventurous. See p.92

* **San Ignacio** Watching the grey whales is one of the most moving experiences to be had in Baja. See p.97

* **Bahía Concepcíon** Kayak alongside dolphins in these serene aquamarine waters. See p.103

* **La Paz** During carnival time, relax on the beach by day, then watch the action from a streetside café in the evening. See p.106

* **Cabo San Lucas** Catch marlin, dive with hammer-heads and whale sharks, and see a 2000-metre underwater "sandfall". See p.111

* **Todos Santos** Stay at the fabled *Hotel California*, the reported inspiration of the eponymous Eagles' song. See p.120

* **Puerto Peñasco** Visit the massive Pinacate Biosphere Reserve, a fifty-kilometre-wide volcanic field of giant craters home to all manner of wildlife. See p.125

* **Guaymas** One of the best sunsets in Mexico, as the sun drops between the mountain ridges. See p.131

* **Mazatlán** A tropical resort that has managed to stay relatively true to its roots. See p.142

△ Playa de Balandra, La Paz

1

Baja California and the Pacific Northwest

Mexico's northwest is something of a bizarre – and initially uninviting – introduction to the country. Certain aspects of what you see here resonate as you travel further south, yet in many ways it's atypical: at once desert and the country's most fertile agricultural region, wealthy and heavily Americanized, yet in parts strikingly impoverished, drab and barren. Nor is the climate exactly welcoming – although the ocean and local conditions help produce one or two milder spots, summer temperatures can hit 50°C, while winter nights in the desert drop to freezing levels.

Travelling overland from the US west coast you're clearly going to come this way, but on the whole the best advice is to push on through the northern part at least, perhaps stopping at the shrimping town of **Puerto Peñasco** or checking out the many beaches near **Guaymas**, or visiting **Alamos**, the colonial silver-mining town at the foot of the sierras. Once you've crossed the Tropic of Cancer there's a tangible change – the country is softer and greener, the climate less harsh. Here you begin to find places that could be regarded as destinations in their own right, such as the enormous all-out resort of **Mazatlán**, or the quieter Pacific beaches around **San Blas**, where you might be tempted to stay more than just a night or two.

There's a straightforward choice of **routes**: down from Tijuana through the Baja Peninsula and onwards by ferry from La Paz; or around by the mainland road, sticking to the coast all the way or possibly cutting up into central Mexico, either by railway from Los Mochis to Chihuahua, or by road from Mazatlán to Durango. However, while the mainland route is quicker if your only aim is to get to Mexico City, drivers should note that there have been numerous reports of assaults on motorists, especially between Los Mochis and Culiacán in Sinaloa. Not only is Baja's Hwy-1 safer, the narrow strip of land that it traverses, passing through rugged mountains and long stretches of empty shoreline, must rank as one of Mexico's most beautiful drives. The route is also cheaper – the ferries are good value if you travel as a deck passenger.

That said, **Baja California**'s plentiful devotees mostly arrive in light planes or in vehicles capable of heading off across the punishing desert tracks, laden down with fishing and scuba gear. Without such means of transport, it's difficult to get to most of the peninsula's undeniable attractions – completely

isolated beaches, prehistoric cave paintings in the hilly interior, excellent fishing and snorkelling, and some great surfing and windsurfing spots. On the bus all you do is pound down Hwy-1, still a relatively new road and low on facilities. However, there are beautiful beaches that you can get to in the south by public transport, more crowded ones around Tijuana in the north, and if you're heading straight for the big Pacific resorts – Mazatlán, Puerto Vallarta and on towards Acapulco – it makes a lot of sense to come this way. Early in the year you can witness extraordinary scenes at **Scammon's Lagoon**, near Guerrero Negro, when hordes of **whales** – participating in the longest known mammal migration – congregate just offshore to calve. Further south you'll find turquoise waters and white-sand beaches around **Mulegé**, in Bahía Concepción. Most coastal towns in Baja Sur offer fantastic opportunities for diving, fishing and kayaking, but **Loreto**, **La Paz** and **Los Cabos** are the standouts among them.

Border checks

Crossing the border, do not forget to go through **immigration and customs** checks. As everywhere, there's a free zone south of the frontier, and you can cross at will. Try to continue south, though, and you'll be stopped after some 20km and sent back to get your **tourist card** (US$22) stamped. You can drive throughout Baja without special papers, but if you're planning to continue on the ferries across to the mainland you need to do the necessary paperwork at the border: attempting to rectify your error in La Paz or Santa Rosalía is fraught with difficulties.

On the **mainland route**, too, most people stick rigidly to the highway – over 2000km of it from Tijuana to Tepic, where the main road finally leaves the coast to cut through the mountains to Guadalajara. Here at least there's the option to stray from the highway; it's a relatively populous area, and from towns all along the route local buses run to villages in the foothills of the Sierra Madre or down to beaches along the Sea of Cortés and, later, the Pacific. Then again you can leave the coast entirely, heading inland by road or rail over the mountains. On the whole, though, the equation is simple: the further south you travel, the more enticing the land becomes. For the first stages it's a question of getting as far in one go as you can stand – try to make it as far as Guaymas, or even Alamos. By the time you reach Mazatlán the pace becomes more relaxed, and you'll increasingly come across things to detain you such as village fiestas, tropical beaches and mountain excursions. **Beyond Tepic** you're faced with the choice of following the mainstream and heading inland towards the central highlands, or sticking to the coast, where there's a good road all the way to Acapulco and beyond.

As everywhere, **buses** are the most efficient and fastest form of transport, though if you intend to visit out-of-the-way places, you're best off renting a car, as bus routes generally stick to the main highways. Buses run the entire length of the coast road, and from Nogales or Tijuana to Mexico City, frequently down through Baja. Unfortunately the Mexicali–Nogales–Guadalajara railway is no longer open for service to the public, although there is still the possibility of a private company restarting the service. There are also a number of **flights** taking advantage of deregulated airspace to link the major towns all the way down the coast. Flights to and from Mexico City can be especially competitive. Even on less used and therefore more expensive routes, an hour-long flight can be a tempting alternative to a ride of ten hours or more.

If you're **driving**, it's very much quicker to arrive via Nogales, as Baja highways are busier and have more police checkpoints. Even if you're coming from Mexico's west coast, you'll save a considerable time by taking US highways via Tucson. You will, however, encounter numerous tolls, and over a long distance the costs can add up, but you always have the option of taking the free – *libre* – roads, which often parallel the toll roads. Heading down through Baja you could be delayed for a day or two trying to get your car onto a ferry (see p.10) – book ahead if at all possible. **Hitching** should be regarded here only as a last resort: beyond the normal dangers, the long-distance traffic moves fast and is reluctant to stop, and it's exceedingly hot and therefore dangerous if you get stranded by the roadside.

Tijuana and the Baja Peninsula

The early Spanish colonists believed Baja California to be an island and, after failing to find any great riches or to make much impact in converting the inhabitants to Christianity, they left it pretty much alone. Aside from the many ancient cave paintings, there's little of historic interest beyond a few old mission centres, and almost all you see dates from the latter half of the twentieth century, in particular since Hwy-1 was opened in 1973. Development has continued apace and in the south new resorts are springing up all the time, while what in the early nineteenth century was simply Aunt Juana's ranch (Rancho Tía Juana) became a border crossing in 1848 and has not looked back since. The westernmost point of the country, **Tijuana** now ranks as one of Mexico's most populous cities. Prohibition in the US was the biggest individual spur to development, but the city has never been slow to exploit its neighbour's desires, whether they be for sex, gambling or cheap labour. As if it didn't already have enough of a notorious reputation, the area along Tijuana's border now sees the world's highest rate of human trafficking, including the illegal immigrant and sex-slave trade.

Tijuana

TIJUANA is the quintessential Mexican border town – with every virtue and vice that this implies. More than 36 million people cross the border every year – the vast majority of them staying only a few hours – so it can boast with some justification of being the "World's Most Visited City". This is not to say it's somewhere you should plan to hang around; but if you want to stop off before starting a long trek down the peninsula, Tijuana is certainly your most practical choice. There's no shortage of reasonable hotels, although as you'd expect, most things are far more expensive than they are further south.

Above all, the town is geared towards dealing with hordes of day-trippers, which means hundreds of tacky souvenir stands, cheap medical care, dentists and auto-repair shops, and countless bars and restaurants, pricey by Mexican standards but cheaper than anything you'll find in San Diego. One thing you won't find much of any more – at least not anywhere near the centre of town – is the prostitution and the sex shows for which the border towns used to be notorious. This is to some extent the result of a conscious attempt to clean the city up, due in part to US efforts to discourage sex tourism. The trade does still exist in pockets, but it's not nearly as overt as a decade ago. Tijuana does still thrive on **gambling**, though, with greyhound racing every evening; jai alai from 8pm every night except Wednesday in the huge downtown Frontón Palacio; and **bullfights** throughout the summer (May–Sept) at two rings, one right on the coast, the other a couple of kilometres southeast of the centre. At the off-track betting lounges all around Tijuana, you can place money on just about anything that moves and monitor progress on the banks of closed-circuit TVs.

△ Playa Norte, Mazatlán

The parts of the city most tourists don't see fit less easily into expectations. **Modern Tijuana** is among the wealthiest cities in the Mexican republic, buoyed by the region's duty-free status and by *maquiladora* assembly plants (raw or semi-assembled materials are brought across the border duty-free, assembled by cheap Mexican labour, and re-exported with duty levied only on the added value). Downtown, beyond the areas where most tourists venture, the modern concrete and glass wouldn't look amiss in southern California. The flip side of the boom lies along the border, where shantytowns sprawl for miles: housing for the labourers and also, more traditionally, the final staging post for the bid to disappear north. Starting from the coast, the city now stretches out for around 19km along the US border.

Arrival and information

As in so many places in Mexico, Tijuana's Central Camionera, or **long-distance bus station** (Ⓣ664/626-1701 for information), is miles from the centre – almost thirty minutes on the blue-and-white local bus marked "Centro" which runs through town on Calle 2-A (Juárez) and passes the border on the way to the terminal. For the trip from the bus station, the city bus is preferable to a taxi, which can legally charge an extortionate fare of around US$15, though you can always haggle if you have the patience. Taxis to other points in Tijuana are not so bad, provided the meter is working, but you'll still save a lot by using the local busline. Some buses from Rosarito and Ensenada run by Elite and Norte de Sonora drop you either right at the border or at the Central Vieja bus station where, at the corner of 1st and Madero, you're in the middle of Tijuana. ABC, a relatively small bus company running routes between cities in Baja, has a terminal a few blocks away.

The **airport** (Ⓣ664/683-2418 or 2118) is slightly closer to town than the bus station, and frequent buses run from there into town; cabs, found on the street in front of the airport, are costly at around US$10 after bargaining.

Information

Of Tijuana's three very helpful **tourist offices**, two are right at the border – one for pedestrians, another for drivers (insurance available) – either of which is well worth a visit to pick up a free map and some leaflets. The **main tourist office** is right in the centre of downtown at Revolución and 1st (weekdays 9am–7pm; Ⓣ664/684-0537 or 0538, Ⓦwww.seetijuana.com), while on the opposite corner you'll find the often even more helpful **Tourism Protection Office** (Mon–Fri 8am–8pm, Sun 10am–3pm; Ⓣ664/688-0555). This is the office to head for if you become the victim of crime, a rip-off or simply want to make a complaint (with so many tourists Tijuana may feel safe enough, but there's plenty of petty crime and occasionally drug-related violence. They also have some maps and general information. There is also an informal, general information **booth** at Revolución and Calle 3.

Accommodation

In comparison to the rest of Mexico, you pay more for **accommodation** in Tijuana and get less for your money – at least there's plenty of choice. Watch out for noise and security if you're staying in the centre. None of the budget places along Calle 1 heading west from Revolución is recommended – parti-cularly not for lone women – as most of your fellow guests will only be staying for an hour or less. The more expensive hotels, mostly further out, are better value, but there's little point staying at these unless you're here on business.

Crossing the border at Tijuana

If you have the right documentation, crossing the border (known as *la linea*, or The Line) is normally a breeze, though you may have to wait – especially during commuter hours (Mon–Fri 8–10am & 4–6pm) – and US immigration can be pretty intimidating if you're entering the States. Heading into Mexico, the main worry is making sure that you have your tourist card stamped at *migración* – people only visiting Tijuana, Ensenada and San Felipe don't need to do this. The border is open 24 hours a day.

On the **US side**, San Ysidro, there's excellent local transport into downtown San Diego – buses (US$1.50) and trams ("San Diego Trolley"; 5am–1am & hourly through Sat night; US$2.50) run every few minutes – and there are plenty of alternatives if you're heading further north. Vans and minibuses, as well as Greyhound and other services, run almost constantly to Los Angeles; the Greyhound terminal is right by the border. **San Ysidro** itself, at least around the border, has little to offer: you'll find American fast-food places, a few secondhand clothes stores, money exchanges, motor insurance offices, and a number of car parks charging US$5–12 a day. There are also a few **motels** – closest to the border are the *Gateway Inn* (Ⓣ619/428-2251; ⑥) and *Holiday Lodge* (Ⓣ619/428-1105; ⑤).

On the **Mexican side** it's only a short walk downtown – through the Viva Tijuana shopping mall, over the footbridge, and along Calle 1 to Revolución. Alternatively you can catch a bus headed downtown (look for those marked "Centro" or "Revolución") or to the bus station (blue-and-white buses marked "Buena Vista/Central Camionera") from the public bus and taxi terminal right by the entrance to Viva Tijuana. There are also fixed-fare yellow taxis that stop between calles 2 and 3 on Madero and can take you to the Central Camionera for about US$2.

It's also possible to **cross the border by shuttle bus**, though it usually costs more and sometimes takes longer than walking over and picking up transport the other side; taking a bus can, however, help avoid the painfully long queues during commuter hours. For example, Mexicoach (Revolución and 7th) and Transportes Diamante (Revolución, a block and a half below 1st) both run shuttles to San Ysidro (US$1.50); Mexicoach also operates a shuttle service between the border and Revolución. Another option for avoiding queues is to **cross the border by short-term rented bicycle**; a few enterprising Mexicans have capitalized on the busy border traffic by renting bikes to travellers wishing to avoid the often long wait, so they can cross in the bicycles-only lane. Usually around rush hour just outside either side of the border, you'll see a few men peddling bicycles of all shapes and sizes. You hop on one, ride through customs and immigration, then deliver it to his associate waiting just on the other side – this racket currently costs about US$5.

Caesar Revolución 1079 at C 5 Ⓣ664/688-0550. Time-worn place whose restaurant claims to have invented the Caesar salad. Has seen better days, but surprisingly good value given its classy setting. ⑤

Catalina C 5 2059 at Madero Ⓣ664/685-9748. Modernized hotel in older building with clean, spacious rooms with en-suite bathrooms. ④

Geni Revolución 417, below C 1 (no phone). Basic, but acceptable and inexpensive, the rooms here are quite literally all bed, with little space for much else. Note that if you're taller than 5ft, you'll have a tough time standing in the bathrooms. ③

Grand Hotel Tijuana Agua Caliente 4500 Ⓣ664/681-7000, Ⓦwww.grandhoteltijuana.com. Twin 23-storey towers mark Tijuana's fanciest hotel, where deluxe, plush rooms have every amenity you'd expect from a high-class business hotel, including access to tennis courts, a pool and a disco. ⑨

Hotel Arreola Revolución 1080 Ⓣ664/685-9081. A basic motel, clean with hot showers, a bit pricey for what you get. ⑤

Hotel Lafayette Revolución 325 Ⓣ664/685-3940. A spare yet pleasant hotel with a family touch, though it can be noisy. Good prices for singles, better rates for groups. ③

Motel Díaz Revolución 650, below C 1 Ⓣ664/685-7148. Acceptable rooms set around a courtyard, worth the money if you need parking. ⑤

Nelson Revolución 721 at C 1 ☎664/685-4302, Ⓦwww.bajavisual.com/hotelnelson. Pleasant, old-fashioned, respectable hotel in a convenient, but noisy location. Rooms have cable TV. ❻

Plaza de Oro Revolución 588, below 1st ☎664/638-4112. Comfortable, modern place with cable TV but little character. ❺

St Francis C 2 between Revolución and Madero ☎664/685-4903. This clean, old-fashioned hotel has been around since the 1920s. They have decent rooms and a breezy, wood-trimmed lobby in which to pass the time. ❹

Villa de Zaragoza Madero 1480 at C 7 ☎664/685-1832. Modern, upmarket US-style motel offering TVs and phones in its rooms. Also has suites with kitchenettes. Laundry available. ❻

Downtown Tijuana

If you're here to shop, drink and party, you need not wander far from the uninterrupted stream of bars, dance clubs, malls, markets and souvenir stalls, and more or less permanent crowds on Avenida Revolución between 1st and 8th streets. If you're after anything else, you're in the wrong town, though there are a few purpose-built attractions to occupy some time. Buses between

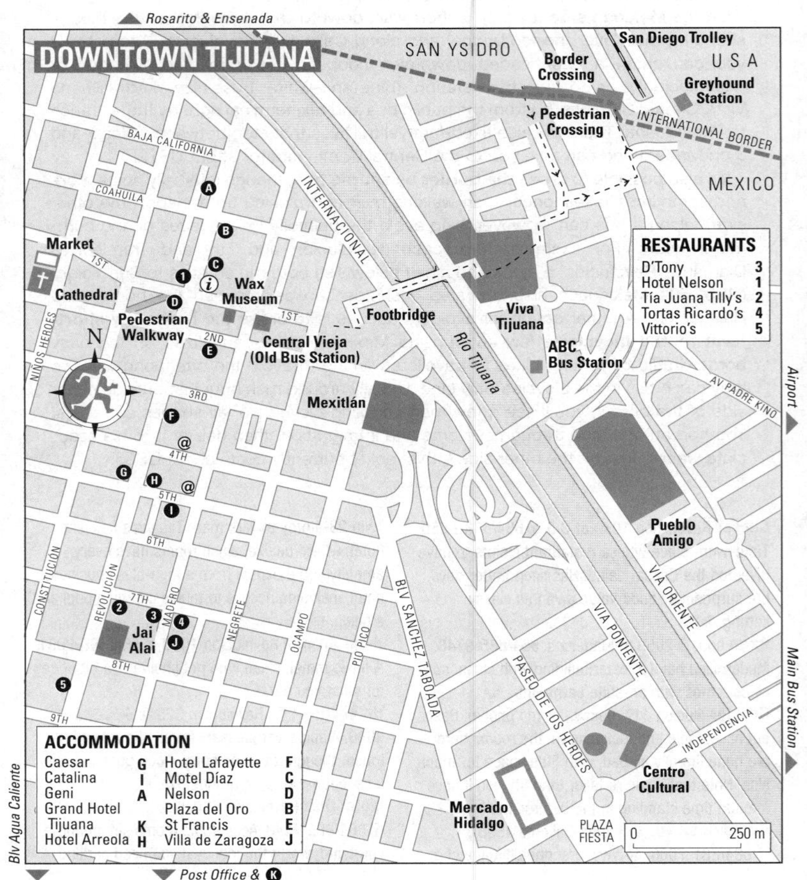

the centre and the border pass the **Centro Cultural** (ⓣ664/687-9600 ext 301), the modernist, out-of-place structure resembling Disney's Epcot Center globe. Designed by Pedro Ramírez Vázquez – the architect responsible for Mexico City's Aztec stadium and Anthropological Museum – it's said to represent the earth breaking out of its shell. Inside, the **Cine Planetario** (Mon–Fri 3–9pm, Sat & Sun 11am–9pm; US$5) hosts a multimedia spectacular on its giant Cinemax screen; the programme changes every four months or so, sometimes featuring English-language films. There are also regular exhibitions and shows, a restaurant and the inevitable shopping arcade, along with a **museum** (Tues–Sun 10am–8pm; US$2), which is not at all bad as an introduction to Mexican culture and art, despite the fact that almost everything you see is a reproduction. **El Lugar del Nopal**, Calle 6 and Avenida G, is a cultural centre that hosts a variety of artistic events, including exhibitions and live music.

Lesser attractions include the now run-down **Mexitlán** (mid-May to mid-Sept daily 10am–10pm, except Mon; mid-Sept to mid-May Wed–Fri 10am–5pm, Sat & Sun 9am–9pm; US$1.25), a miniature national theme park with models of famous Mexican buildings, folklore performances and more restaurants and shops, which is hard to miss as you approach town from the border. There is also a new and very tacky **wax museum** at Madero and 1st (don't waste the US$1.50), and various modern **shopping malls**. Most of these are given over to a mix of duty-free goods and stalls selling souvenirs, fake designer clothing and jewellery – two of the biggest are Viva Tijuana, which you'll walk through on the way to the centre if you cross the border on foot, and Pueblo Amigo.

Eating

If you expect great restaurants to satisfy the high number of visitors, you'll be disappointed. On the main drag everything is aimed at foreign tastes: US-style Mexican restaurants, almost all of them with loud music and a contrived party atmosphere. **Plaza Fiesta**, diagonally opposite the Centro Cultural, has a wide variety of restaurants and fast-food places; you'll find a similar, though smaller, range in any of the shopping plazas.

More authentic Mexican food can be found in the surrounding streets, especially on Madero and Constitución, but despite the fact that migrants from all over Mexico bring their cuisine with them – naming their *lonchería* or *taquería* after their home state – there's nothing particularly exciting, even here.

Antojitos Bíbi's in the Mercado Hidalgo. Clean and inexpensive place for simple meals all day. Close to the Centro Cultural.

D'Tony corner of Madero and C 7. If you accidentally ended up in Tijuana for your honeymoon, this is the spot to go. Romantic, upscale Argentine restaurant with the best steak in town and a great selection of South American wines. Tango is piped in round-the-clock.

Hotel Nelson Revolución and C 1. Decent-value and very popular Mexican place, serving good food in large portions.

Punto Café Plaza Fiesta. Trendy, low-key place with outside seating, magazines to flick through and an incredible range of coffees.

Tapiro Constitución between C 2 and C 3. Bargain sit-down taco joint, with US$0.50 bite-sized tacos.

Tía Juana Tilly's Revolución 1420 at C 7. Slick, predictable Tex-Mex restaurant with terrace, linked to the jai alai hall. Bow-tied waiters serve up main courses (steak, chicken, seafood) for around US$7–12.

Tortas Ricardo's Madero at C 7. A massive range of excellent Mexican dishes served in American diner surroundings. Delicious tortas and enchiladas. Open late.

Vittorio's Revolución 1687 at C 9. Full range of well-prepared Italian dishes as well as Mexican staples. Good pizza and great espresso.

Drinking and nightlife

Nearly all the action in Tijuana happens close to Revolución, where numerous **nightclubs** pump out soft rock, commercial r&b and hip-hop. English is the lingua franca, dollars are the currency of choice, and the playlist is solidly North American. With competition fierce, cover charges are rare and drinks are often offered two for the price of one: walk along Revolución and pick the most appealing joint on the night. More traditional **Mexican bars**, as well as those featuring "exotic dancers" cluster around 1st and Constitución and on Revolución at 6th – most places are open until at least 2am.

The pedestrianized Plaza Fiesta (see "Eating" p.83) offers the most obvious alternative to the hard-sell party atmosphere of the main drag. Though smaller and slightly calmer, this area, crammed with bars and clubs, offers more variety and certainly feels less Americanized.

The Cave Revolución 1137 between 5th and 6th. Much the same as all the other tourist-oriented places, but at ground level so you can see what you are getting yourself into.

Diamante Disco Revolución and 1st. The least intimidating of the seedy Latin music bars but still not recommended for unaccompanied women.

People's Sports and Rock Revolución 786 at C 2. Consistently one of the better bars, with a slightly harder edge to the music, frequented by both tourists and locals. Be prepared for the roving bar staff to pour tequila down your throat in an effort to loosen the purse strings.

Las Pulgas Revolución 1127 opposite jai alai. Modern *norteña* disco with a huge dance floor plays to crowds of 20-something locals and tourists. Open until 6am.

Salón de Baile 6th between Revolución and Madero. Don't be put off by the lurid wall paintings: this is the real thing – a traditional dance hall with an almost Caribbean feel, playing salsa, *cumbia* and *norteño*. Look for the sign with the big red star.

El Torito Revolución between C 2 and C 3. Loads of American day and evening trippers cross the border in search of cheap beer and spring-break behaviour; many of them end up here. Also see *Caribbean*, next door with a slightly more mod interior, but the same deal.

Listings

Airlines Aero California, Paseo de los Héroes 95, Plaza Río Local C-20 ☎664/684-2100; Aeroméxico, Revolución 1236 ☎664/688-3465; and Mexicana at the airport ☎664/682-4184.

American Express Office is in Viajes Carrousel travel agency (Mon–Fri 9am–6pm, Sat 9am–noon) way out on Sanchez Taboada at Clemente Orozco, and their exchange rates are poor.

Banks and exchange US dollars are accepted almost everywhere – rates are usually fair, but always check beforehand. Changing money is not a problem, with casas de cambio on virtually every corner. Most offer good rates – almost identical to those north of the border – though few of them accept travellers' cheques, and if they do, they charge a heavy commission. For cheques you're better off with a bank, most of which are on Constitución, a block over from Revolución.

Books Sanborn's, at Revolución and C 8, has books and magazines, some from the US, though it primarily functions as a food chain.

Buses The Central Camionera is reached on local blue-and-white buses marked "Buena Vista" or "Central Camionera", which run through the centre on C 2-A and pass the border on the way to the terminal; or by metered or fixed-fare yellow taxis. From the station there are departures to almost all Mexican destinations, with numerous departures at all hours to the west coast and hourly buses down Baja. Tijuana to Cabo San Lucas (24hr trip) will cost you US$90, and a ticket to Mexico City (36–48hr) will cost you at least US$100. Some operators offer large discounts for students – though primarily only during Mexican university vacations (July–Aug, Dec) – so bring ID. The Central Vieja bus station, at Madero and 1st, handles buses to Rosarito (hourly 8am–8pm). For US destinations you can pick up Greyhound buses (roughly hourly 6am–6pm) from the Central Camionera; they go on to pick up from the Central Vieja station, then cross the border, stopping at San Ysidro. Slightly more expensive, Transportes Intercalifornias run nine times daily from the airport, Camionera

Central, the centre of town and both sides of the border to Los Angeles.

Car rental Alamo ⓣ664/686-4040 or 2400; Budget ⓣ664/634-3303 or 3304; Hertz ⓣ664/607-3949; and National ⓣ664/683-5500 or 4745.

Consulates Australia/Canada, German Gedovius 5-202, Zona Río ⓣ664/684-0461; UK, Salónas 1500 ⓣ664/681-7323; US, Tapachula 96 ⓣ664/681-7400.

Flights The airport is reached on buses marked "Aeropuerto" from Madero and 2nd. Though they vary greatly depending on demand, flights to the rest of Mexico, and particularly to the capital (16 daily; 3hr), can be surprisingly cheap from Tijuana, sometimes the same price as a first-class bus. Flights to other destinations are less competitive, such as Guadalajara, Acapulco, La Paz, as there are fewer flights and they can charge more. Viajes La Mesa, at Madero and 1st (ⓣ664/688-1511), can help with bookings, but it pays to shop around for the best prices.

Internet access You'll find inexpensive Internet joints off Revolución; the best is Space, at C 5 and Madero, with a very fast connection (open 24hr; US$1.50/hr). Also try Intercom Site, C 4 between Madero and Revolución, assuming you can stand the teeming youngsters playing video games alongside you (daily 8am to midnight; US$1.50/hr).

Left luggage Bags can be left at the Central Camionera (daily 6am–10.30pm), in lockers at the Greyhound station on the US side of the border (24hr), or next door at Pro-Pack (Mon–Sat 9am–6pm).

Post office Negrete and C 11 (Mon–Fri 8am–4pm, Sat & Sun 9.30am–1pm), though to send international mail you're better off crossing the border and using the American postal system.

Telephones The post office (see above) has *larga distancia* phones, as does the Central Camionera, but again you're better off making long-distance calls from the US side of the border.

Rosarito

If you want to escape the hectic pace and noise of Tijuana, head for **ROSARITO**, about 45 minutes' bus ride on the old road to Ensenada. **Beaches** in Tijuana are invariably crowded and dirty, so Rosarito – with its longer and sandier, yet scarcely less crowded or littered beach – is a good alternative and provides a more restful atmosphere. The hotels and condo developments that abut the beach are better value than those in the centre, making it worthwhile to stay out near the water. If at all possible, avoid visiting during March and April, when spring-breakers make the town difficult to bear for all who insist on remaining sober.

Rosarito was until recently part of the city of Tijuana, but became a municipality when local politicians realized that it was capable of generating its own tourism dollars. Since 1997, it has also become an attraction for movie aficionados who have come to see **Fox Studios Baja**, just south of town at km 32.8 on the free highway to Ensenada. This bit of Hollywood-in-Mexico, originally created for the filming of *Titanic*, is now a massive full-time production facility that utilizes its seventeen-million-gallon oceanfront tank for water-based films (including *Pearl Harbor* and *Tomorrow Never Dies*). Tours are available on Sundays (US$8) and some Saturdays (provided they are not filming). The *Titanic* model, created at 95 per cent scale, has been disassembled, but much of the set is viewable in storage. While you're there, you can also visit **Foxploration**, a new cinema-based theme park located in the same complex (Mon–Fri 9am–7pm, Sat & Sun 10am–6.30pm; ⓣ661/614-9444, ⓦwww.foxploration.com).

To **get to Rosarito** from Tijuana, take one of the colectivo taxis that leave from Madero between calles 4 and 5, or head for the old bus station at Madero and 1st, from where buses leave every hour or so; to **get back**, just flag down a bus or colectivo on Juárez, Rosarito's main street. Rosarito's **tourist office** (Mon–Fri 9am–5pm & Sat & Sun 11am–4pm; ⓣ661/612-0200) is inconveniently situated a twenty-minute walk to the north on the road to Tijuana, and is not really worth the effort. You could try the more central Rosarito Beach Convention and Visitors Bureau (Mon–Fri 9am–6pm; ⓣ661/662-0396), Ciprés 101 at Juárez. There aren't really any budget **hotels** left here; your best bet is probably the *Hotel California* (ⓣ661/612-2550; ④). Slightly more expensive is the *Motel Sonia* (ⓣ661/612-1260; ⑤) at Juárez and Plama. Right on the beach with ocean views is the *Hotel Los Pelicanos* (ⓣ661/612-0445; ⑦). The style and charm that made the upscale *Rosarito Beach Hotel* (ⓣ661/612-0144; ⑦) a hotbed for scandalous affairs among the Hollywood glitterati during the Prohibition years has largely been obliterated by modern refurbishment, but the older rooms still have some character. Along the single street behind the beach is a row of restaurants, cafés and bars, some of them pretty good, in particular the **fish restaurants** and a couple of cafés that serve decent cappuccino and cakes. The focus of party-goers is *Papas and Beer*, where beach volleyball and knocking back as much Corona as possible is the order of the day.

If you're **continuing south** to Ensenada and beyond, you can pick up long-distance buses (at least hourly) at the autopista toll-booth 1km south of the tourist office, past the *Rosarito Beach Hotel*. The coast road down through Rosarito – now supplanted by the motorway to Ensenada – is an attractive drive, lined with seaside villas and condos.

Surfing

Though it has gained mythical status as the lifestyle of blond-haired, hedonism-seeking men from southern California, surfing is an age-old sport. Reliefs discovered in coastal Peru, some over 5000 years old, depict native peoples navigating the waves on boards made from reeds. Hawaii has evidence of surfing in scenes carved into rock that date back 1500 years.

The practice was brought from Polynesia to Hawaii during a period of migration in the fourth century AD. It wasn't until the early twentieth century that Hawaiian Duke Kahanamoku, an Olympic swimmer, actor and the greatest surfer of his time, popularized the sport internationally. Surfing took off in California and continued to evolve in board design and riding techniques. Californians crossed the border into Baja to seek out some of its legendary waves, and the sport became established in Mexico.

There are different types of surfboads, which influence surfing style and performance. The **longboard** is over 2.5m long, has a single fin and rounded features. This traditional type of board is superior for cruising and is the easiest to stand on, but is difficult to manoeuvre out past the breaking waves. The **shortboard** is under 2.5m, has three fins and a pointy front tip. These boards are easier to steer, but require more skill to gain your initial balance. Hybrid, mid-size boards, also referred to as **funboards** are ideal for learning to surf. The following words are a few basic necessary terms:

Close-out (n./v.) A wave that does not crest and gradually break to the left or to the right, but folds over at once and is almost impossible to ride.

Goofy foot (n.) Style of surfing with the left foot at the back end (tail) of the board. The back foot steers and, therefore, people typically favour the right foot.

Hang ten (v.) To stand on the front end (nose) of a longboard, thereby dangling all ten toes off the tip.

Kook (n.) An inexperienced surfer unfamiliar with surfing etiquette.

Leash (n.) The cord that attaches the surfboard to a Velcro strap around the ankle of the surfer.

Point break (n.) A wave that breaks at the tip of a promonotory of land and continues down its side for a longer distance than a normal wave.

Ensenada, San Felipe and the road south

ENSENADA, just ninety minutes on from Tijuana by the toll road and sitting on Bahía de Todos Santos, is packed at weekends with both partying groups of southern Californians and crowds of cruise-ship passengers. Nevertheless, it remains far calmer, cheaper and smaller than Tijuana and is a good jumping-off spot for ecotourism destinations further south. As a major port and fish-processing centre it is also home to some industry, including one of the nation's largest wineries, although the wine is of distinctly average quality.

When the European explorers first sailed into Ensenada's waters almost four hundred years ago, the lack of fresh water made permanent settlement difficult, but over the next two hundred years Bahía de Todos Santos became a popular port of call for whaling ships, fur traders, Spanish treasure fleets and the pirate ships which sought them, and by around 1870 it had developed into a supply point for missionaries working along the northern Mexican frontier. When gold reserves were discovered that year nearby in Real de Castillo, miners rushed in, but at the beginning of the twentieth century the mines closed and the population dwindled, leaving Ensenada to revert to little more than a small fishing village. A renaissance came in the late 1930s with the rise of agriculture in the Mexicali Valley, and the port became a point of export for the produce. When the paved highway from Tijuana was opened some forty years later American tourist dollars began to pour in.

Almost all the action is squeezed into a few streets around the **harbour**: seafront **Bulevar Costero** (aka Lázaro Cárdenas), **Avenida Mateos** (or Calle 1), which runs parallel to and as far inland as **Avenida Juárez** (Calle 5). Here you'll find scores of souvenir shops and outfits offering sport-fishing trips, as well as the bulk of the bars, hotels and restaurants – the majority of visitors come here to eat, drink, shop and little else. If you do want to explore further, you could check out the **view** from the Chapultepec Hills, overlooking town from the west, or visit the Bodegas de Santo Tomás **winery**, one of Baja's largest, which offers tours and regular tastings at Miramar 666 between calles 6-A and 7-A (tours Mon–Sat every hour between 10am and 3pm; US$5-10; ⓣ646/178-3333). Most of the wines are only passable; if it isn't offered, ask to try the white sherry, a local favourite. The Museo Histórico Regional, at Gastélum off Mateos (Mon–Fri 9am–5pm, Sat & Sun 11am–5pm; US$2.50; ⓣ646/178-3692), has rotating exhibitions on the peoples and cultures of Ensenada and Northern Baja. From December through to March, the California grey whale migration from the Arctic to the Baja's Pacific coast can be seen on daily **whale-watching tours** from Ensenada, which go to Bahía de Todos Santos, although what you'll see is as nothing compared to what's further south: Caracol Museo de Ciencias, Obregón 1463 and also on one of the piers (ⓣ646/178-7192), can arrange trips for you.

Ensenada is close to a number of beaches and attracts its share of surfers. Baja Surf Shop on Costero and Miramar rents equipment for US$20 a day. As in other parts of Baja it can be difficult to get to many of the best beaches without your own transport; however, you can catch a local propane-powered "Brisa" bus from Macheros and Mateos (every 30min; US$0.60) to **Surzal** and **San Miguel**, the closest surfing **beaches** (rocky and not for beginners). The best **beaches** for swimming and sunbathing are at **Estero**, some 10km to the south, 2km off the main road; occasional local buses run past these to perhaps the most startling attraction in the area, **La Bufadora** geyser. The combined action of wind, waves and an incoming tide periodically forces a huge jet of

ENSENADA

Bus Station

La Bufadora & San Quentin

Bodegas Santo Tomás Winery

Federal Highway Patrol

Riviera del Pacífico Cultural Center

Museum of History

Arts & Crafts Center

Arroyo de Lusenada

Marina

Puerto de Ensenada

Equinoxio

Cursos

Regional History Museum

Open Air Fish Market

AVENIDA LOPEZ MATEOS

AVENIDA RIVIERA

LAS ROCAS

LAS BRISAS

BLV COSTERO (LÁZARO CÁRDENAS)

BLV LÓPEZ MATEOS

CASTILLO

BLANCARTE

ALVARADO

SEGUNDA

TERCERA

CUARTA

RIVEROLL

JUÁREZ

SEXTA

GASTÉLUM

MACHEROS

MIRAMAR

RUIZ

OBREGÓN

PASEO CALLE PRIMERA

VIRGILIO URIBE

RYERSON

N

0 200 m

ACCOMMODATION

Bahía	F
Hotel Río	G
Misión Santa Isabel	D
Motel América	A
Motel Caribe	E
Motel Pancho	B
Perla del Pacífico	H
Posada El Rey Sol	C

RESTAURANTS, CAFÉS & BARS

Angelo's Ristorante	1
Las Brasas	4
Café Café	5
Café Tomas	6
El Charro	4
Hussong's Cantina	2
Papas and Beer	3
Pueblo Café-Deli	7

sea water up through a small vent in the roof of an undersea cavern, in ideal conditions reaching 25–30m. Even though it's more than 20km off the main road and encircled by an annoying number of souvenir stands that rather spoil the atmosphere, it's worth a visit. To get there take a micro from the Tres Cabezas park on Costero at the bottom of Riveroll to Maneadero and another from there, or a US$10 taxi from town.

Ensenada itself hosts numerous events aimed squarely at the large US encampment in town, from sporting contests to food and wine festivals. The **Newport to Ensenada Yacht Race**, in April, is one of the largest international regattas in the world, with yachts leaving Newport, California, on a Friday afternoon and finishing in Ensenada a day later, when the partying commences and the town gets packed. April is also when the **Rosarito–Ensenada Bike Ride** draws thousands of cyclists here for the scenic eighty-kilometre "fun ride" from Playa de Rosarito to Ensenada, while off-road racing is the theme *du jour* during the Baja 100 (June) and the Baja 2000 (Nov). Culinary events kick off in August, when some of Baja's better wineries and vineyards host the ten-day **Fiestas de la Vendimia**, where wine-tastings and wine-themed competitions and parties are held at the wineries and in town; for information about tickets for the ten-day festival ask at the tourist office. The town celebrates **Independence Day** with a week of festivities.

Arrival, information and getting around

The **bus station** (with guardería) is at Calle 11 and Avenida Riveroll: turn right and head down Riveroll to reach the bay – head left when you reach Mateos for the centre of town. There's a second, smaller station a couple of blocks down Riveroll between calles 8 and 9, which handles frequent services to Tijuana. The very helpful COTUCO **tourist office** (Mon & Tues 9am–5pm, Wed–Fri 9am–7pm, Sat & Sun 9am–5pm; ⓣ646/178-2411, ⓦwww.ensenada-tourism.com) is on Costero at the corner of Gastélum, where the main road enters town; the SECTUR **tourism protection office** is at Costero 1477 and Rocas (same hours). The **post office** (Mon–Fri 8am–7pm, Sat 9am–1pm) is at Club Rotario 93 and Mateos. **Rental cars** are available at Hertz on Riveroll and 2a (ⓣ646/178-2982). Browse the **Internet** at *Equinoxio*, 267 Costero and Miramar (Mon 9am–10pm, Tues–Sat 8am–10pm, Sun 10am–9pm; US$2/hr), where there's a fast connection, many terminals and a full café, or at Compunet next to Hertz (Mon–Fri 9am–10pm, Sat & Sun 10am–9pm; US$1.50/hr). You'll find a great collection of used **books** and magazines at The Bookseller, no. 240 on Calle 4 at Obregón (Tues–Sat 10am–6pm). The Baja California Language College (ⓣ646/174-1741, ⓦwww.bajacal.com), 1287 Avenida Riveroll, offers excellent **Spanish courses**, which last a weekend or several months. Try to find a copy of either the *Gringo Gazette* or *Ensenada Tour* for information on goings-on about town; both are free and available from most establishments on Mateos.

Accommodation

If you're hoping for somewhere to **stay** at the weekend – the best time to be here for the nightlife – you'd be well advised to book ahead, or arrive early; during the week there should be no problem. Most of the hotels are on Mateos and Costero between Riveroll and Espinoza; though **rates** in general are high (and hiked at weekends), you'll find cheaper places on Mateos. Just one block east of the tourist strip lies a grubbier zone where the best deals are to be had, but the area is not as safe as Mateos.

Bahía Mateos 850 between Riveroll and Alvarado ⓣ646/178-2101, ⓦwww.hotelBahia.com.mx. Huge, popular place with wide range of rooms, some with ocean views. Prices go down US$20 during the week, and they've got a large pool. ❻

Hotel Río Miramar 231 at C 2a ⓣ646/178-3733. A good deal, but off the strip in the dodgy zone. Though it sees its share of hourly clientele, the family-run hotel has clean rooms, friendly staff and a secure car park. Choose one of the newly renovated rooms in the centre of the hotel. ❸

Misión Santa Isabel Castillo 1100 at Costero ⓣ646/178-3345, ⓦwww.baja4fun.com/misionsantaisabel. Modern colonial-style motel, with good rooms, a pool, and their restaurant *El Campanario*, which overlooks the bay. ❻

Motel América Mateos 1309 at Espinoza ⓣ646/176-1333. Well off the strip, this clean, no-frills roadside inn has decent-priced rooms, some with kitchenettes. ❹

Motel Caribe Mateos 628 at Blancarte ⓣ646/178-3481. Without a doubt the best budget deal in town: clean, if simple, rooms right in the centre of the action, though it can be a little noisy when the cruise-ship passengers are let loose on the street below. ❹

Motel Pancho Alvarado 211 at C 2a ⓣ646/178-2344. Newly renovated, this very clean place has "luxury" rooms for a few dollars more, though the only difference here seems to be stucco walls and a huge mirror. ❹

Perla del Pacífico Miramar 229 across from *Río* ⓣ646/178-3051. Similar clientele to the *Río*, and the atmosphere isn't nearly as inviting: shabby, dark, small rooms line dingy hallways with peeling paint. You can save a few dollars if you're willing to share a bathroom with other guests. ❸

Posada El Rey Sol Blancarte 130 at Mateos ⓣ646/178-1601, ⓦwww.elreysol.com. Good hotel in central location offering clean rooms in a motel-style layout, a pool and jacuzzi. After check-in, you get an hour of complimentary margarita-drinking at the bar. ❼

Eating and drinking

There's plenty of choice of places to **eat and drink** near the hotels, including a few inexpensive taco stands on and off Mateos. For good, reasonably priced food, particularly breakfasts, try the *Plaza Café*, at Mateos between Gastélum and Miramar. *El Charro*, Mateos 454, is a well-established colonial-style restaurant serving roast chicken and Mexican food at good prices until late, while their next-door neighbour, *Las Brasas*, is smaller and less formal, offering a similar menu at similar prices. The bohemian *Café Café*, Mateos and Gastélum, is low-key, with backgammon, couches, and walls plastered with surrealist and indigenous art, much of which is for sale; the congenial owner Memo also has the low-down on cultural happenings around town. *Pueblo Café-Deli*, Mateos and Ruíz, is a stylish and popular bar also serving a wide variety of food, including pastries and traditional Mexican dishes. *Café Tomas*, at Mateos 335, although it seems to have not-so-subtly appropriated both the Starbuck's aesthetic and its prices, has some very good international coffee and a nice patio in the back; they open at 6am. For a romantic Italian dinner with decent prices, head to *Angelo's Ristorante* (ⓣ646/178-1970) a few storefronts down from *Hussong's* (see below).

The stalls at the fish market, by the harbour, sell fish tacos and other **seafood** at a fraction of the price of the fancy restaurants that line Costero. If you do want to sit down and don't mind missing out on the views, for excellent, plain seafood, try *Mariscos Playa Azul*, Riveroll 113, or *El Palmar* at Mateos and Obregón. Among the numerous **Chinese restaurants** is the upmarket *China Land*, at Riveroll 1149, by the bus station.

For **places to drink**, *Hussong's Cantina* at Ruíz 113, opened in 1892, is a sawdusted watering hole that has become a landmark and survives largely unchanged, much appreciated by the regulars who come here day and night; you can catch some great local *norteña* music here. *Papas and Beer* is probably the best-known Ensenada chain bar, where lively crowds pack the downstairs restaurant by day and imbibe round-the-clock upstairs in a relentless party atmosphere. For a slightly less tourist-filled night, try the increasingly popular discotheque *Octopus*, Riveroll 225 at Segunda, or *VIP*, just around the corner from *Papas and Beer*, which caters to the local student crowd. *MangoMango*, Mateos 335, and the restaurant at *El Cid*, Mateos 993, both have salsa bands on Saturdays and sometimes offer free dance classes in the evening.

San Felipe

With so few places in northern Baja boasting a decent beach and reasonable public transport, the prospect of **SAN FELIPE**, a growing Sea of Cortés resort on a dead-end road 200km south of Mexicali, might seem attractive. In truth, its appeal is limited: the entire bay is strung with RV parks, and the dunes between here and the encircling folded ridges of the San Pedro Martír mountains reverberate to the screaming engines of dune buggies and balloon-tyred ATVs. If you're planning to continue south down Baja, then do just that. But San Felipe does have good swimming – at least at high tide – and if you are confined to the north, it's a good place to rent a catamaran or just relax for a day or so.

San Felipe first came to the attention of fishermen who, in the early 1950s, took advantage of the new tarmac road – built to serve the American radar station to the south on what is now called Punta Radar – to exploit the vast schools of tortuava, a species now fished onto the endangered list. Since the 1980s, the fishing village has grown to accommodate the November-to-April influx of holiday-makers from north of the border and college students on spring break. Apart from lying on the beach, you can rent **dirt bikes** and ATVs from a couple of places along the malecón (around US$20 an hour), **catamarans** (similar price; just ask along the beach wherever you see one), or indulge in a little **sport fishing**. Tours are arranged through a couple of places at the northern end of the malecón.

If the road through the cactus desert south of here to Hwy-1 ever gets improved to the point that it can be negotiated by low-clearance vehicles, this could become an interesting alternative route to southern Baja, but for the moment the hamlet of **Puertecitos**, 85km south (no public transport), is as far as ordinary cars can get – and even then with difficulty.

Practicalities

Buses from Mexicali (4 daily; 3hr) and Ensenada (2 daily; 3hr 30min) arrive 1km inland: turn left out of the bus station and right down Manzanillo to get to Avenida Mar de Cortés, which runs parallel to the sea. At the junction, the **tourist office** (Mon–Fri 8am–7pm, Sat 9am–3pm, Sun 10am–1pm; ⓣ646/577-1155) gives out a map of the town but little else. North from here along Cortés there's a *farmacia* where you can **change money** (Mon–Fri 9am–6pm) and, beyond, a Bancomer but no ATM. The **post office** is on Mar Blanco just off Chetumal, five blocks inland. **Hotels** in San Felipe are not particularly cheap, though there are a couple of decent mid-range choices: *La Hacienda*, Chetumal 125 (ⓣ646/577-1608; ❻), is marginally better than *Chapala Motel*, Mar de Cortés 142 (ⓣ646/577-1240; ❻), but the best of all is *El Capitán Motel*, Mar de Cortés 298 (ⓣ646/577-1303; ❻), closer to the water with pool, TVs and a/c; note that their prices go down during the week by around US$20. **Camping** is best at the RV parks to the north of town, notably *Ruben's RV Trailer Park*, Golfo de California (ⓣ646/577-2021; ❸), or you can just camp on the beach around the bottom of Chetumal, where there are showers and toilets.

Not surprisingly, **seafood** is the staple diet here, with several restaurants and numerous stands selling shellfish cocktails along the front. Head for *The Bearded*

Clam, the ill-named hole-in-the-wall at the northern end of the beachfront malecón, or *The Red Lobster* at *La Hacienda* hotel.

On to the 28th parallel

Beyond Ensenada you head into Baja California proper – barren and god-forsaken. At times the road runs along the coast, but for the most part the scenery is dry brown desert, with the peninsula's low mountain spine to the left and nothing but sand and the occasional scrubby cactus around the road. The towns are generally drab, dusty and windswept collections of single-storey shacks that belie the area's supposed wealth. At **SANTO TOMÁS**, 45km from Ensenada, the *El Palomar* motel (☎646/153-8002; ❻), with pool (a whopping US$7 even if you're a guest), trailer park and restaurant, makes a good place to break the journey; the town itself is known for its wine and a deserted Dominican mission. If you can get off the highway, the attractions of the desert and its extraordinary vegetation become clearer.

Sixty-five kilometres past Santo Tomás, just beyond Colonet, a road turns inland towards the **Parque Nacional San Pedro Martír**. The side road, unsurfaced but in good condition, winds almost 100km up into the sierra, which includes Baja's highest peaks at over 3000m – where it snows in winter. As you climb, the land becomes increasingly green and wooded, and at the end of the road astronomical observatories take advantage of the piercingly clear air. There are breathtaking views in every direction. Numerous poorly defined trails wind through the park, but again, there's no public transport and you need to be fully equipped for wilderness camping if you want to linger.

San Quintín

SAN QUINTÍN is the first town of any size south of Ensenada, and even here, though there are a couple of big hotels, most of the buildings look temporary. There's no reason to stop here unless you intend to head to **Bahía San Quintín**, which is undeniably attractive, with five cinder-cone volcanoes as a backdrop to a series of small sandy beaches, and endless fishing (though not without a permit) and superb clam digging that draw campers and RV tourists. The closest of the beaches are some 20km from town, 5km from the highway, and there's no public transport to reach them.

Buses from Ensenada stop at **Lázaro Cárdenas**, 5km south of town. If you want a **place to stay**, the *Hotel La Pinta* (☎616/165-9008; ❼) is the luxury option, right on the beach 3km off the highway, some 8km south of Lázaro Cárdenas. More realistic alternatives include *Cielito Lindo* (no phone; ❻), close to *La Pinta*, and *Molino Viejo* (☎616/171-3353; ❺) – from where fishing trips can be organized – on the bay; or one of the motels in town: *Romo* (☎616/165-2396; ❹), which also has a decent **restaurant**; the spartan *Real del Cora* at km 193 (☎616/166-8576; ❺); and at km 191 the decent *Chavez* (☎616/165-2005; ❹). There are also plenty of **camping** spots around the bay if you come equipped, and RV sites at the *Molino Viejo*. Should you need **Internet** access while in San Quintín, Internet Milenio has several computers (US$2) and is right on the transpeninsular highway at km 195.

El Rosario and Cataviña

Some 60km beyond San Quintín, the highway passes through **EL ROSARIO**, the original site of a Dominican mission. Founded in 1774, the mission was forced by a shortage of water in 1802 to move 3km downstream to **El Rosario de Abajo**, where you can see the ruins: nowadays, however, it's little more than a BMX track for local kids, and definitely not worth getting off the bus for. El Rosario is just another staging point, and modern El Rosario de Arriba consists of just a couple of petrol stations, a few restaurants and two **motels**. *El Rosario* (Ⓣ616/165-8850; ④), as you come into town, is good value, if noisy, with trucks roaring down the hill throughout the night, while the *Motel Sinai* (Ⓣ616/165-8818; ④), at the town's southern edge, is quieter and may work out cheaper. There's a rather rocky beach 12km south at Punta Baja.

Beyond El Rosario, the road turns sharply inland, to run down the centre of the peninsula for some 350km to Guerrero Negro. It's a bizarre landscape of cactus – particularly yucca, *cirios*, unique to this area, and *cardones*, which can grow over 16m tall – and rock, with plenty of strange giant formations; much of it is protected within the **Parque Natural del Desierto Central de Baja California**. In the heart of this area is **CATAVIÑA**, comprising a dozen or so buildings strung along the highway, complete with luxury **hotel**, *La Pinta* (Ⓣ646/176-2601, Ⓦwww.lapintahotels.com; ⑧), restaurants and trailer park. There's cheaper accommodation at *Rancho Santa Inés*, a couple of kilometres south (no phone; ④), whose rooms double as dorms when necessary – you can also eat here, but the *Café La Enramada* opposite *La Pinta* is cheaper. *Cabañas Lindas*, a nearly abandoned motel just north of *La Pinta* on the east side of the highway, rents out a dozen or so rustic rooms. If you have to stop, and you need shoestring accommodation, this could be an option, but seems as dependable as the wind. If you do stop, take time to look at some of the giant boulders; not far off the highway at Km 171, just before Cataviña, is **La Cueva Pintada**, a tiny cave beneath a huge rock decorated with ancient paintings that include circles, dots, sunbursts and stick figures. Incidentally, if you're driving through Cataviña, fill your tank at the informal roadside **fuel** station here – the petrol may be pricey, but there's no other station for quite some distance.

Bahía de los Ángeles

The turn-off for **BAHÍA DE LOS ÁNGELES**, a growing resort on the Sea of Cortés, is about 100km further on from Cataviña. Still a small place, some 70km off Hwy-1, the town sits on the eponymous bay, which teems with sea life and is hemmed in by contorted mountains. There's little more than a few hotels, cafés and fishing boats. Most visitors are an older generation of North Americans who arrive by light plane or in RVs. If you're passing through here, visit the small bilingual **museum** (daily 9am–noon & 2–4pm; free) marked by a narrow-gauge locomotive, a relic of the gold and copper mines that first attracted Europeans to the area. Mining history and that of the local ranchero life is well covered, along with details of sea life in the bay. The **Isla Ángel de la Guarda**, out in the bay, is the biggest island in the Sea of Cortés and the focus of numerous diving and fishing trips. There are no official rental agencies for **scuba**, **snorkelling** or **fishing gear**, but the hotels can organize equipment rental and you should be able to strike a deal by asking around.

There's an underdeveloped, frontier feeling in Bahía. The town has no bus service at all: hitching from the main highway is a possibility, but be prepared for a long wait. Like everything else here, **hotels** are expensive. The best are the very pleasant *Costa del Sol* (Ⓣ646/178-8167, Ⓔcostadelsolhotel@hotmail.com; ⑤) and the aging *Villa Vitta* (Ⓣ615/650-3208, ⑤), both of which have pools, restaurants and all the creature comforts. *Casa Díaz* (Ⓣ617/650-3206; ④) and *Las Hamacas* (Ⓣ665/650-3208; ④) are slightly less luxurious (though the latter is often more popular than the former). *Guillermo's Trailer Park* (Ⓣ615/650-3209; ⑥

Ecotourism and Baja Sur

The meeting of the **Colorado River** with the huge underwater canyons of the **Sea of Cortés** and the strong currents of the **Pacific Ocean** creates a plankton-wealthy environment in the waters around Baja that supports an extensive food chain and, in turn, an amazingly diverse aquatic culture. Inland, the combination of five mountain ranges, most notably the **Sierra de Juárez** in the north and the **Sierra de la Giganta** in the south, constitute the backbone of the peninsula and contain the petroglyphs of some of Baja's first inhabitants, dating back an estimated 1500 years. Inhospitable desert stretches away from these mountains to marshland, mangrove-lined rivers, coastal dunes and miles of untouched beaches.

With so many natural sights, **ecotourism** has become big business in Baja, particularly in the less developed southern portion of the peninsula, **Baja Sur** – running from Guerrero Negro nearly 1000km south to Cabo San Lucas at the bottom tip. Perhaps the most enticing excursion of all here is to see the annual grey whale migration, when thousands of Alaskan **grey whales** travel some 10,000km to mate and breed in the warm-water lagoons of Guerrero Negro, San Ignacio, and Bahía Magdalena, from December to April. San Ignacio is also the base for jumping off into the Sierra de San Francisco to view the mountains and their giant **cave paintings**. Further south, the tranquil aquamarine bays and islands of the Sea of Cortés near Mulegé, Loreto and La Paz, offer the best **sea kayaking** in Mexico. Off the southern edge of the peninsula lives Cabo Pulmo, the only living **coral reef** on the western shore of the North American continent which, not surprisingly, is home to hundreds of open-sea species and is treasured among divers.

It would be quite easy to spend weeks exploring the local environment, and as the tourist population expands each year, new tour companies crop up and it can be hard to sift through the marketing and understand exactly where to go. Listed below are the favourite activities and the best areas from which to embark.

Whale-watching

There are three main "sanctuaries" where you can see grey whales mating and breeding. Most whales congregate in **Ojo de Liebre** (see p.96), just off Guerrero Negro, where **tours** are plentiful and charge about US$40–45 for transportation to the lagoon, four hours of boat travel and lunch. Many people, though, prefer the lagoon 150km south near **San Ignacio** (see p.97), where the town itself is also an attraction, as are the local birds, caves and mission church. The least-visited of the three sanctuaries is **Bahía Magdalena**, located near Ciudad Constitución, 140km south of Loreto and 216km north of La Paz – if you've bypassed Guerrero Negro and San Ignacio, then Bahía Magdalena is your last opportunity to view the whales within a sanctuary.

Most southern towns offer whale-watching tours as well, but keep in mind that you will be paying exorbitant prices for transportation to the west coast, where they will likely take you to one of the sanctuaries – a four-hour/US$40 whale tour could easily become a fourteen-hour/US$130 affair from Loreto, La Paz or anywhere else further south. That said, many whales speed past the three

for rooms) and the frequently deserted *La Playa RV Park* both have **camping**; for free camping, walk to the beaches to the south. All of the hotels have **restaurants**, but *Guillermo's* has the best location, with palapas right on the beach. For **fishing**, Joel Moreno at the *Costa del Sol* is a good guide and offers trips (5–7hr) in the waters around the Isla Ángel de la Guarda, for up to six for a total of US$100–140, a good price considering the high cost of fuel. The folks at *Costa del Sol* will also set you up with a tour guide for the hour-long hike to the **gold mine** and rent kayaks for US$25 a day.

sanctuaries and head further south along the coast; some even make the turn around the tip of the peninsula and into the Sea of Cortés. If you can't make it to one of the sanctuaries, you at least have the option of watching them from the shore, where you can see them pop up some 50m out: Todos Santos (see p.120) and the western side of Cabo San Lucas (see p.111) are particularly good. Tour operators running out of Guerrero Negro and San Ignacio are listed overleaf and on p.98 respectively.

Cave painting tours

Between Bahía de los Angeles and Loreto sits the **Sierra de San Francisco**, recently declared a World Heritage Site by UNESCO because of five hundred historic rock-art sites contained within it. Many of the famed sites are 45km north of San Ignacio, so most people choose **San Ignacio** (see p.97) as their base for excursion. Tours are also a good option from **Guerrero Negro** (see below) in the north, and **Mulegé** in the south (see p.101); see the relevant entries for operators. Towns further south will have tours, but again, you will be paying exorbitant prices for the transportation costs north. The land is now protected by the Instituto Nacional de Antropología e Historia (INAH), and they require you to be accompanied by a guide and to seek permission before setting out (tour companies/guides will help you with this). **Tours** generally last anywhere from five hours to several days; a five-hour tour will cost US$30–45 per person, depending on the length of your hike and transportation required from the tour. Having your own transportation will usually cut these costs in half.

Sea kayaking

The waters around Baja are so picturesque and rich in marine life that nearly everyone will be drawn to try their hand at sea kayaking. It's as good a way as any to explore the bays, snorkel the ledges around the many islands and, for the more ambitious, to make your way down the coast. On the road south, the first real spot for even a novice to put in would be **Mulegé** (see p.101). There's no abundance of kayak-rental agencies in this area, but the few that exist have cornered the market and can offer you any related gear you could ever need. The standard open-top kayaks go for about US$30 per day, wet suit and fins another US$6 or so. Week-long packages bring the per day price down to US$20, including the necessary VHF radio, optional wet suit and snorkel gear. **Loreto** (see p.105) and **La Paz** (see p.106) are also phenomenal options for sea kayaking. Trips to Isla del Carmen off Loreto and to Isla Espíritu Santo off La Paz pose more extended challenges and seem to attract their share of experienced kayakers. Dozens of companies compete for business in each of these towns – see the relevant entries for details – so gear rental will always be reasonable, with half-day tours starting at around US$40 and full-day tours at about US$65. Some companies offer week-long all-inclusive kayak "safaris" that can creep up towards US$1000. **Los Cabos** (see p.111) also has its share of kayak adventures, but none particularly rewarding as in the north.

Guerrero Negro

Continuing on the main highway, there's little between Cataviña and the 28th parallel, where an enormous metal monument, and a hotel, mark the border of Baja California Norte and **Baja California Sur**; you'll have to set your watch forward an hour when you cross, unless Baja California Norte is on **Daylight Saving Time** (April–Oct), in which case there's no change. **GUERRERO NEGRO**, just across the border, offers little in the way of respite from the heat and aridity that has gone before (winters, however, can find the town quite chilly). Flat and fly-blown, it's an important centre for salt production, surrounded by vast saltpans and stark storage warehouses. At most times of year you'll want to do little more than grab a drink and carry straight on. In January and February (and, peripherally, Dec & March–May), however, Guerrero Negro is home to one of Mexico's most extraordinary natural phenomena, when scores of **grey whales** congregate to calve just off the coast.

The whales, which spend most of their lives in the icy Bering Sea around Alaska, can be watched (at remarkably close quarters; the young are sometimes left stranded on the beaches) from an area within the **Parque Natural de la Ballena Gris**, which surrounds the Laguna Ojo de Liebre. The laguna is also known as **Scammon's Lagoon** after the whaling captain Charles Melville Scammon, who first brought the huge potential of the bay to the attention of rapacious whalers in 1857 – the town gets its name from the *Black Warrior*, an overladen whaling ship that sank here a year later.

During the season there are organized **whale-watching trips**, and an observation tower that guarantees at least a distant sighting. Although talk turns every year to restricting numbers or banning boats altogether, there are currently more tours and **boat trips** than ever. If you can take one, then do so – it's an exceptional experience, and many visitors actually get to touch the whales, which sometimes come right up to bobbing vessels, engines switched off. Whale-watching trips are run from *Don Miguelito*'s and *Mario's* (see below): both charge around US$40 per person for a four-hour trip, including a complimentary drink or two. Laguna Whale Watching Tours (Ⓣ615/157-0050, Ⓔlaguna@intecnet.com.mx), a rather professional outfit on Emiliano Zapata next to the *Motel San Ignacio*, also offer the standard trip for about the same price; they generally run two trips a day. Malarrimo Eco-Tours (Ⓣ615/157-0100, Ⓦwww.malarrimo.com) also run whale tours, plus they offer eight-hour tours to the Sierra de San Francisco to see cave paintings from October until December. If you are heading south, keep in mind that you will have two more opportunities to go whale-watching, at San Ignacio and Ciudad Insurgentes.

To **watch the whales from the shore**, you'll need your own vehicle (preferably 4WD): head south from town until you see the park sign, from where a poor sand track leads 24km down to the lagoon. Midway there's a **checkpoint** where you must register your vehicle and its occupants, and at the park entrance a fee of around US$3 is charged. To see the whales you'll need to get up early or stay late, as they move out to the deeper water in the middle of the day.

Practicalities

If you want to stay in Guerrero Negro, you can choose from numerous **hotels and motels** strung out along the main drag, Zapata. Perhaps the best is the *Motel Cabañas Don Miguelito* (Ⓣ615/857-0250; ❺), to the right as you enter town, with clean rooms with TV, RV spaces and a good seafood restaurant. Further into town, the *Motel Las Dunas* (Ⓣ615/157-0650; ❹), on Zapata and División del Norte, is simple, clean and friendly, though sometimes a little noisy. You'll find much the same at *Las Ballenas* (Ⓣ615/157-0116; ❹) on Victoria, which offers a dozen or so basic rooms with TV; or, on the north side of Zapata, there's the good but overpriced and almost antiseptic *Hotel El Morro* (Ⓣ615/157-0414; ❺), whose rooms have fans and cable TV. Equally satisfactory and cheaper alternatives are the *Motel San Ignacio* (Ⓣ615/857-0270; ❹), offering older, stuffy, sink-in-the-bedroom lodging as well as a modern, pricier section which has more comfortable rooms with full bath, or the *Motel Brisa*

Salina (no phone; ④), also on the main strip, which offers rustic rooms with some local colour, a/c, TV and private parking. On the budget front, there are several to choose from: try *Motel Salparaíso*, on Noyola (no phone; ③), which has pleasant rooms just off the main drag (follow the signs). You can also **camp** on nearby beaches for free – it's usually allowed even inside the park, though you need your own transport to get there.

There are plenty of **restaurants** along the main street, though only a few ever seem to be open at any one time. *Malarrimo*, next to *Don Miguelito's*, has good seafood and is another place to check about whale-watching trips; *El Asadero Norteño* serves meaty northern specialities; *Mario's* (Ⓣ615/157-0788), on the entrance to the highway, is good for breakfast and the basics; also try *Don Gus*, an agreeable place by the bus station where you can eat huge US$15 shrimp platters and gaze at one of the region's salt flats. Fresh produce can also be purchased from Supermercado La Ballena, on Zapata.

Buses from Guerrero Negro's bus station, near the hotels, are irregular. The six services (one local) which head **north** to Tijuana (US$37), and the one to Mexicali, leave at night or early morning; the eight **southbound** services – two local, running all the way to La Paz (US$40) – depart either early in the morning or in the late afternoon and evening. You'll find **Internet** at the aptly titled Café Internet (US$2.50/hr) on Zapata 100m from *Brisa Salina*.

San Ignacio

Leaving Guerrero Negro, the highway heads inland again for the hottest, driest stage of the journey, across the Desierto Vizcaíno. In the midst of this landscape, **SAN IGNACIO** comes as an extraordinary relief. At the very centre of the peninsula, this is an oasis in every sense of the word: not only green and shaded but, with some of the few colonial buildings in Baja, a genuinely attractive little town that just may entice you to stay longer than a night's stopover.

The settlement was founded by the Jesuits in 1728, but the area had long been populated by the indigenous **Guaicura**, attracted by the tiny stream, the only fresh water for hundreds of miles. Underneath the surfaced road between the highway and town is the small dam that the settlers built to form the lagoon that still sustains the town's agricultural economy, mostly based on the Mediterranean staples of dates, figs, grapes, olives, limes and oranges. San Ignacio's **church**, built by the first arrivals and probably the best example of colonial architecture in the whole of Baja California, dominates the attractive, shaded plaza. Early missionaries were responsible, too, for the attractive palm trees that give the town its character.

In the bleak sierras to the north and south are numerous **caves**, many decorated with **ancient paintings**. Not much is known about the provenance of these designs, beyond the fact that they were painted at different periods and bear little resemblance to any other known art in this region of the world. Some archeological studies estimate them to be several thousand years old, though opinions still vary considerably: native legend, as related to the earliest colonists, has it that they are the product of a race of giants from the north. Certainly many of the human figures – most paintings depict hunters and their prey – are well over 2m tall. The cave paintings are, however, extremely hard to visit, reached only by tracks or mule paths and almost impossible to find without a guide (which is also a legal requirement for visits). If you're determined, join one of the **tours** arranged from the hotels in town or through any of the operators listed in the box (both overleaf), though all can be pricey.

At the beginning of the year, the same places also organize **whale-watching trips** (again, see box below) to the nearby Laguna San Ignacio, considered by some as a better place to spot the animals than Guerrero Negro. The waters of the town's lagoon attract hundreds of species of birds to San Ignacio, which nest in its environs; in fact, if you stay overnight, you can't help but notice that the birds and frogs between them produce a rainforest-like soundtrack, a rather surreal feeling in the middle of a desert. For a nominal fee, informal **bird-watching tours** can be arranged at *Rice & Beans* (see below).

Practicalities

The centre of San Ignacio lies almost 3km off the main highway where all the **buses** stop. Upon arrival you may be lucky enough to pick up a taxi, otherwise it's a thirty-minute walk down the road through the palms. There are two newer budget **hotels**, both of which are near the main highway. The *Baja Oasis*, just southeast of town, offers clean and comfortable rooms (no phone, Ⓔbajaoasis@yahoo.com; ❹). A good deal is *Rice & Beans* (Ⓣ615/154-0283; ❺); from the bus stop, walk west to where a small road parallels the highway,

Tours and trips from San Ignacio

Although whales are most in evidence throughout January and February (recent censuses have counted between 300 and 600 at one time), **whale-watching** tours are offered from December to April. Ecoturismo Kuyima (Ⓣ615/154-0070, Ⓦwww.kuyima.com), opposite the mission in town, is the best **tour operator** of all, but you could also try El Padrino and Antonio Aguilar Eco Tours (Ⓣ615/154-0089 or 0059, Ⓔelpadrino@prodigy.net.mx), opposite the *La Pinta* hotel. Kuyima charge about US$40 all-inclusive, while El Padrino charge a flat rate of US$120 for up to six people, lodging not included. Most tours provide transportation, but if you have your own you can cut your expenses considerably – although the dirt road to Laguna San Ignacio from San Ignacio can be tough on a small car – and you can hire a guided *panga* when you arrive from any number of local guides, which should run to about US$30 per person for about three hours. Ecoturismo Kuyima (see above) has a **camp** at the lagoon, with tents and clean palapas with solar power, plus they serve food. It's possible to visit and return in one day, but it's better to stay the night (❹ all-inclusive) as the whales are best seen in the early morning when they venture into the shallow waters.

Cave painting tours from San Ignacio focus on the area of Sierra de San Francisco, about 45km north of San Ignacio, where nearly five hundred sites exist across around 11,000 square kilometres; tour operators also run cave painting tours that begin in San Ignacio and usually pass through the little town of San Francisco de la Sierra and head for the easily accessible Cueva del Ratón, or remoter ones such as the Cueva Pintada and Cueva de las Flechas in Canón San Pablo, which requires a minimum of two days. Tours are fairly expensive, so if you want to save some cash you can arrange a mule trip at Sierra de San Francisco. However, you will need your own transport to get there: at Km 118, 45km north of San Ignacio, you'll find a road heading east to San Francisco de la Sierra, and the first site is just over 2km further on. Note that you must always be accompanied by a guide and that you are required to get **INAH permission**, gained in San Ignacio from Cuco Arce, the INAH rep in San Ignacio (Ⓣ615/154-0215 or 0222; Mon–Sat 8am–3pm); an easier alternative, though, is to stop at Ecoturismo Kuyima (see above) on the square and ask. Once you've got permission, sort out a guide and a mule and you'll be able to camp in the area – an excellent way to see a variety of paintings. Note that **flash photography** is not allowed in the caves.

and the hotel is a few blocks on. There are refreshingly clean rooms here, with hot showers, and plenty of space to **camp** (US$5 per car and all passengers, US$10 for electricity and showers). The hospitable owner is a long-time resident and can organize any activity you want in San Ignacio. The restaurant, too, serves an ample menu of excellent seafood and traditional Mexican dishes, from morning until night. Try the house specialty, *caldo de pescado*, a fish soup made from fresh local catch. On the road into town you pass a number of other places where you could pitch a tent: *La Posada Motel*, at Carranza 22 (Ⓣ615/154-0313; ❹), southeast of the zócalo, is also inexpensive, though there's no a/c, while *La Pinta* (Ⓣ615/154-0300, Ⓦwww.lapintahotels.com; ❻) is the luxury alternative. Some of the other **trailer parks** along the highway and on the road into town have camping space; the most useful, *El Padrino* (Ⓣ615/154-0089), almost opposite *La Pinta*, charges US$5 per person.

Of the many **places to eat** around the central plaza, *Restaurant Chalita* is a traditional Mexican choice (and has a few rooms, if poor value at US$15 per person); *Tota's* is better but somewhat more Americanized, and they are quite often closed in the off-season, while *Rice & Beans'* restaurant is another good choice. The town is short on most other facilities.

Santa Rosalía

The highway emerges on the east coast at **SANTA ROSALÍA**, which is also the terminal for the ferry to Guaymas. An odd little town, wedged in the narrow river valley of the Arroyo de Santa Rosalía, it was built as a port to ship copper from the nearby French-run mines of the El Boleo company (see box, overleaf). Nowadays, the mines are virtually exhausted and the smelters stand idle, though much of the equipment still lies around town, including parts of a rusting narrow-gauge railway. The government still claims to be developing a plan to employ modern techniques to extract the last of the ore from the five million tonnes of tailings, a move that would provide a much needed financial boost to a community that struggles by on revenue from fishing and the plaster mines on the Isla de San Marcos to the south. To date, however, little real progress has been made on this front.

The town itself feels like no other town in Baja. Built by French miners, it has somewhat of a transient feel, and many of its buildings look strikingly un-Mexican. Santa Rosalía does possess a certain charm that continually attracts tourists to break their trip along the peninsula. The streets are narrow and crowded, while the workers' houses in the valley resemble those in the Caribbean, with low angled roofs over hibiscus-flanked porches, and grander colonial residences for the managers rim the hill to the north. Look out especially for the **church** on Obregón, a prefabricated iron structure designed by Eiffel and exhibited in Paris before it was shipped here.

Practicalities

Hwy-1 runs along the coast, passing between Santa Rosalía's harbour and Parque Morelos. Five avenues – Obregón, Constitución, Carranza, Sarabia and Montoya – run perpendicular to the coast, crossing the numbered calles.

Santa Rosalía's new **bus station** (and ferry terminal) lies just two minutes' walk south of Parque Morelos. Only the 5pm to Tijuana originates here. All others are *de paso* and may at times be full, though if you arrive early enough the friendly staff can generally call ahead to locate a seat for you. Northbound buses call in the evening or very early in the morning, while those heading south stop mostly in the late morning and late evening. **Ferries** leave twice a week (Wed & Sun at 8am) for the seven-hour trip to Guaymas. Tickets (which cost US$51 for a reclining seat, twice that for a four-berth cabin, US$141 for a two-person *cabina*, nothing for a bike and US$240 for a small car) go on sale at the terminal from 6am, but check times and reserve in advance (Ⓣ615/152-0013), or buy your ticket from a travel agent, as the timetable may change. Car drivers should ensure that their papers are in order for the mainland (see "Border checks" on p.77).

The best-value hotels will be just as you walk into the centre from the bus/ferry terminal. The eclectically furnished *Olvera* (Ⓣ615/152-2550; ❹) and the somewhat bland *Hotel del Real* (Ⓣ615/152-0068; ❹) are both on Parque Morelos, and have rooms with TV and a/c; those with just a fan run about US$5 less. *Hotel 6* (Ⓣ615/152-0595; ❸), at Calle 6 and Constitución, has tiny no-frills rooms, and the longtime backpacker's favourite *Blanco y Negro* (Ⓣ615/152-0080; ❹), whose cheapest rooms share a bath, is just off the south-west corner of Plaza Juárez, four blocks in from the waterfront. The more modern *Minas de Santa Rosalía* (Ⓣ615/152-1060; ❹) on Obregón at Calle 10, is good value. They offer large rooms with tiled bath, hot water, a/c and TV; several even have small balconies. The *Hotel Francés* (Ⓣ615/152-2052; ❺) is a beautiful colonial building on the hill to the north of town, and worth the little bit more for its relative luxury. The *El Morro* (Ⓣ615/152-0414; ❺), on the highway a short way south of town, offers even more comfort, with sea views, pool and restaurant, and a good beach nearby.

Santa Rosalía's copper mines

While walking in the hills in 1868, one José Villavicencio chanced upon a **boleo**, a blue-green globule of rock that proved to be just a taster of a mineral vein containing more than twenty percent copper. By 1880 the wealth of the small-scale mining concessions came to the notice of the **Rothschilds**, who provided finance for the French El Boleo company to buy the rights and found a massive extraction and smelting operation. Six hundred kilometres of tunnels were dug, a foundry was shipped out from Europe, and a new wharf built to transport the smelted ore north to Washington State for refining. Ships returned with lumber for the construction of a new town, laid out with houses built to a standard commensurate with their occupier's status within the company. Water was piped from the Santa Agueda oasis 15km away, and labour was brought in: Yaqui from Sonora as well as two thousand Chinese and Japanese who supposedly found that Baja was too arid to grow rice and soon headed off to the Mexican mainland. By 1954, falling profits from the nearly spent mines forced the French to sell the pits and smelter to the Mexican government who, though the mines were left idle, continued to smelt ore from the mainland until the early 1990s.

If you fancy a short desert walk, pick a cool part of the day and make a circuit of what remains of the mining equipment and the tunnels that riddle the hills to the north. None of the mines is fenced, so take a torch and explore cautiously. Following Calle Altamirano from Eiffel's Iglesia Santa Bárbara, you reach the massive kilometre-long above-ground duct, built of furnace slag, which once conveyed fumes from the smelter to the hilltop stack. You can walk along the top of it to the chimney for a superb view of the town and surrounding desert. From here, choose one of the numerous paths that head away inland to a series of gaping maws in the hillside. You can return the same way or pick your way straight down to the town or, with enough time, continue among the low cacti on the mesa, working your way down to the top end of Santa Rosalía.

Sadly, no French **restaurants** remain as a reminder of the town's beginnings, but the *Panadería El Boleo* produces some of the best baked goods in these parts, even if the baguettes aren't as crisp as the real thing. Restaurants in general aren't up to much, though you can eat well enough at *Terco's Pollito*, Obregón at Calle Playa. Next to the *Hotel del Real* there's a wonderful morning place, which has a good coffee and breakfast selection; they will prepare *huevos* any way you like them. Several inexpensive places are scattered along Obregón, many selling great fish and seafood tacos. Try *Hot Dogs Exquisitos* on Calle 6 just down from the *Hotel 6*, where you can enjoy a filling evening meal as you watch TV outside with the family who runs the joint. *Restaurant Regio*, on the highway just as you come into town, plays the role of local truck stop; they have tacos and quesadillas for US$1 apiece, as well as more expensive meals.

Both **banks** are on Constitución, and have ATMs: Bancomer changes cheques until noon, Banamex accepts only bills until 1pm. If you are heading south, note that Mulegé does not have a bank and this will be your last chance for money until Loreto. The **post office** is on Constitución at Calle 2, and there's a **phone** outside the *Hotel del Real*. There are a few places with **Internet** access: *Internet Café*, on Calle 6 just off Obregón (Mon–Sat 8am–2pm & 4–10pm; US$2/hr), and its sibling *Café Internet*, on Obregón and Playa (Mon–Sat 9am–10pm; US$2/hr).

Mulegé and around

Some 60km to the south of Santa Rosalía lies **MULEGÉ**, a small village on the site of an ancient mission. Like San Ignacio, it's a real oasis. Tucked into a lush valley, the village sits underneath a myriad of palms on the north bank of the Río Santa Rosalía. Roughly 960km south of the US border, Mulegé has a definite feel of the tropics, a fruit-growing centre that's also popular with kayakers. The town is also one of the most peaceful and laid-back in Baja, helped in part by some superb beaches strung out along the coast to the south. Yet again you'll miss out on the best of them without some means of getting about, but here hitching is at least a realistic possibility – many visitors commute to the beaches daily, particularly during the high season (mid-Oct to April).

There's not a great deal to see in Mulegé, though you could check out the the unkempt **Museo Mulegé** (Mon–Sat 8.30am–3pm; US$1 suggested donation), set on a hillside above town; head a couple blocks away from the centre towards the ocean, then follow the trail leading up the hill to the museum. Built nearly a hundred years ago, it is housed in a former prison known as the "prison without doors", as it allowed its inmates to work in town in the mornings and afternoons; some were even married in town. Visitors can enter the prison cells and view a number of local artefacts. The **Misión Santa Rosalía**, founded in 1705 and completed sixty years later, sits atop a hill overlooking Mulegé. The church only opens for the occasional mass, but it's still well worth the hike up for the spectacular view from above the palms. Follow Zaragoza south underneath the highway bridge until you see the dirt road that climbs to the mission.

Mulegé practicalities

From the **bus stop** it's a ten-minute walk into Mulegé: follow the side road, take the right fork onto Martínez, then a second right onto Zaragoza and the plaza. A schedule of *de paso* services (the only way out of town) is posted at the

Activities and trips around Mulegé

Other than as a springboard for the beaches to the south, the main reason to stop at Mulegé is to go diving or take one of the **cave painting tours** out to the Sierra de Guadalupe. This range boasts the densest collection of rock art in Baja (at least 700 paintings), as well as some of the most accessible, requiring as little as five hours for the round-trip. Getting a group together to cut costs shouldn't prove a problem in high season, but you still need to shop around as the tours differ considerably. Expect to pay US$40 per person or half that with your own transportation. Overnight excursions are possible too, including a night at a 260-year-old ranch, and two different cave locations. Otherwise, Ciro Romero can take you to the cave paintings (Ⓣ615/153-0481, Ⓔcirocuesta@yahoo.com.mx) for similar prices. Lastly, head to *Las Casitas* (see below), which also acts as an informal tourist office for information on other local attractions and tours.

For **snorkelling and diving trips**, head to Cortez Explorers (Ⓣ615/153-0500, Ⓦwww.cortez-explorer.com; open 4–7pm) at Moctezuma 75-A; prices begin at US$60 per person. They also rent **mountain bikes** (US$15 per day) and all-terrain vehicles (US$20 per hr). A beginner's resort course costs US$90, a snorkelling trip US$35 (including equipment). You can also rent snorkel gear from them and go about it yourself: Punta Prieta – north of the lighthouse, a short walk from town – is still an unknown gem, even though it's really the only place you can dive or snorkel that can be reached by the shore (other spots must be accessed by boat). Follow Madero as it hugs the river, and before you reach the lighthouse you'll meet a dirt road; take a left and it will take you past an old hotel and a school before you reach Punta Prieta.

small café with the "ABC" sign near the bus stop. Heading south, all services currently pass through during late morning or late evening; northbound buses mostly pass in the afternoon.

If you want to **stay** in Mulegé, you have a choice of either cheap and very basic *casas de huéspedes* or relatively upmarket hotels. The *Hacienda* (Ⓣ615/153-0021; ❺), on Madero just off the plaza, is the pick of the latter, with its small pool, pleasant courtyard and parking, though *Las Casitas*, Madero 50 (Ⓣ615/153-0019, Ⓔlascasitas1962@hotmail.com; ❺), the former home of Mexican poet José Gorosave, has its charm, with an orchard-like yard and dribbling fountains. Budget alternatives include the small, shaded *Casa de Huéspedes Nachita* (Ⓣ615/153-0140; ❷), a family-run place with the most laid-back staff you'll find in Baja, and the slightly more comfortable *Manuelita* (Ⓣ615/153-0175; ❹), both on Moctezuma, the left fork as you head into Mulegé from the highway, and, with slightly larger rooms, the somewhat musty *Canett* (Ⓣ615/153-0272; ❸), on Madero beyond the church. The newer *La Noria* (Ⓣ615/153-0195; ❸), on the highway just north of town, has simple rooms but you'll probably suffer from the noise of the highway. For an altogether more peaceful stay, try the rapidly expanding *Hotel Mulegé* (Ⓣ615/153-0090; ❺) on the left as you head into town at Moctezuma 15; the hotel plans to add a pool, roof bar, and ATM in the near future. Just south of town on the east side of the Transpeninsular at Km 139, the luxurious *Serenidad* (Ⓣ615/153-0530, Ⓦwww.serenidad.com; ❼, closed Sept) has some great summer three-night-stay specials, and many of its guests fly into the private airstrip. **Campers** should head 1km south of the bus stop (or along the dirt road on the south side of the river from Mulegé) to *Huerta Saucedo RV Park* – also called *The Orchard* (Ⓣ615/153-0300) – where two can pitch a tent for US$8 and guests can rent canoes on the Río Mulegé.

Mulegé doesn't offer a huge amount of **eating and drinking** options, but what's there is quite good. The majority of the North American long-stayers and a good many Mexicans gravitate towards the decent and reasonably priced restaurant and bar at *Las Casitas* (see opposite). You could also try *Los Equipales*, Moctezuma and Zaragoza, a mid-range steak and seafood place serving large portions – a steak complete with soup, salad and potatoes costs US$10; alternatively there's the less formal and cheaper *El Candil* on the plaza, another gringo rendezvous spot that does excellent breakfasts of fruit, eggs, ham, bacon, toast and potatoes for US$3. *La Palapa*, on the highway south and past the Pemex petrol station, also does great breakfasts. If you happen to be around on Sunday night, head to *Eduardo's* for some of the best Chinese food on the peninsula; it's inexpensive, but be prepared to wait some time for service. To eat on the cheap, try *Pollos del Castillo*, which serves great chicken tortas.

Mulegé has no banks, although *Rosario's Patio* serves as a **casa de cambio** with mediocre rates (Mon–Sat 9am–1pm & 4–8pm), on Moctezuma two blocks off the plaza; note that travellers' cheques are not widely accepted in town. If you're strapped for cash, try La Tienda, on Martínez, which primarily sells books, camera film plus diving and fishing accessories but also accepts payment by ATM cards. The owners are also a great source of local **information**. The small **post office** is on Martínez, and outside it you'll find long-distance **phones**; there are also some at Padilla grocery store at Zaragoza and Martínez. If you find yourself staying for a few days and need a **laundry**, Lavamática Claudia, at Zaragoza and Moctezuma, washes, dries and folds your clothes for about US$4 per load. You can find a few **Internet** terminals with dial-up on Moctezuma, three blocks from the bus stop (Mon–Sat 9.30am–8pm & Sun 10am–2pm; US$2/hr).

Bahía Concepción

There is good diving and fishing immediately around Mulegé, but the best beaches are between 10km and 50km south of town along the shore of **Bahía Concepción**. The bay ranges from 3km to 6.5km wide, is 48km long and is enclosed on three sides and dotted with islands. The blue-green waters, peaceful bays and white-sand beaches are beautiful and relatively undeveloped – though you will at times find teams of RVs lining the waters – and it's a good place to break your journey for a day or so before travelling south. As far as **kayaking** goes, there are few places better than Bahía Concepción.

The best stretches of sand include **Playa Punta Arena**, some 16km down the highway followed by 2km along a dirt road, where there are some basic palapa shelters to rent. **Playa Santispac**, some 5km further on, is right on the highway – despite the early stages of development and occasional crowds of RVs, it still has plenty of room to camp (for a fee) and enough life to make staying here longer-term a realistic option, though there are free open palapas to hang out under during the day if you just want to stop for a swim. **Posada Concepción**, just south of Santispac, shows the beginnings of Cabo-style development and has permanent residents; *EcoMundo* here, at Km 111 (no phone, ⓔecomundo@aol.com), is an environmentally minded place offering standard palapa (US$12) and tent (US$8) accommodation, plus they rent out kayaks for a day or longer (from US$25 per day, reservations a must); they've also added more luxurious honeymoon palapas (US$20), for those seeking a little more privacy. Facilities include a natural hot spring for guests, a barbecue pit, an excellent little bookstore, a restaurant and a bar. To get there, hire a taxi in Mulegé for US$12, or hitch a ride (a widely accepted practice around Mulegé); if you are coming from Loreto by bus, some drivers will let you off

Diving and fishing around Baja California

Nowhere in Baja California is more than 90km from either the Pacific Ocean or the Sea of Cortés, and both bodies of water support an abundance of **sea life**. The unmatched variety of marine environments makes the Sea of Cortés one of the richest seas in the world, with over eight hundred species of fish and more than twice as many shellfish. Throughout the peninsula you'll see RVs and off-road vehicles laden with fishing tackle, dinghies and scuba gear, headed for remote fish camps or sheltered bays to launch the dive boat.

Diving

The most popular **diving** areas in the north are **Islas Los Coronados**, off Tijuana, but only served by organized trips from San Diego north of the border; and **Punta Banda** and **Islas de Todos Santos**, off Ensenada. In the south, where the waters are a good deal warmer and the fish dramatically colourful, the best dives are off the coast of **Mulegé** and **Bahía de Concepción** just south of Mulegé, **Loreto**, **La Paz** and **Los Cabos**. In the waters off San José del Cabo, the giant reef known as **Cabo Pulmo** offers the chance to dive amidst schools of hammerheads, whale sharks, tunas and sea lions; many proclaim it to be Baja's best diving spot. From August to November you'll find the ideal combination of water clarity and warmth.

Recent years have seen a dramatic increase in Baja's tourist numbers, especially in the south, and **dive shops** are plentiful once you cross the Baja Sur line. Diving is not cheap, though, and having your own gear will cut costs in half. The average two-tank all-inclusive outing will cost you US$70–100, and the prices generally increase the closer to Los Cabos you choose to dive. Many dive shops will offer something called a "resort" course for US$100 – a basic introduction to scuba diving and guided shallow underwater dives, perfect for someone with zero experience. The more extensive Open Water Diver certification takes four or five days and will cost you at least US$350, but this certifies you to dive in most waters of the world. Recommended **dive operators** for various locations are listed in the guide text.

Fishing

Fishing in Baja can be spectacular, especially so in the south. The favourite holes have always been near **La Paz** and around **Cabo San Lucas**, the small fishing village of **La Playita** just east of **San José del Cabo**, and the rest of the **East Cape**, where the nearby Gordo Banks seamount produces more marlin, tuna, wahoo, sailfish, and dorado for anglers each year than anywhere else in Mexico. Most large towns have established charters, while towns like Bahía de los Angeles offer cheaper, more rustic adventures. **Fishing charters** offer one of two services: either less formal fishing from a *panga* that can carry up to three anglers, or the giant marina-based fleets with boats that can accommodate up to six. *Pangas* charge anywhere from US$150 to US$200 for six hours, the larger boats upwards of US$450, including food, drinks and gratuity. These trips generally begin at about 6am and last from five to eight hours. **Shore-fishing** is an option almost anywhere in Baja, though as with fishing charters, a **fishing licence** is required. While fishing charters provide this, if you're on your own you will need to ask about them at the local tourist office. Tour operators are listed in the relevant town entries.

at Km 111. Further south there are few facilities for anything other than camping: **Playa El Coyote**, where there's also a hot spring, and **Playa El Requesón**, another couple of popular, beautiful beaches, are the last and the best opportunities for this (US$5 for each). Note that there's no fresh water available at either, but locals drop by in the early morning and afternoon selling everything from water to fresh shrimp. Your other best bet is renting kayak, snorkelling or scuba equipment from the reputable Las Parras Tours in Loreto (see below).

Loreto

LORETO, the next town down the coast, is a far bigger place than Mulegé, and is on the site of the earliest permanent settlement in the Californias. Founded in 1697 as the head of the Jesuit missions to California, and later taken over by the Franciscans, it was in practice the administrative capital of the entire territory for some 130 years until a devastating hurricane struck in 1829. More recently it has been a popular escape for fishing and diving enthusiasts, and nowadays it's enjoying something of a renaissance, boosted by the development of southern Baja California as a whole. A super-resort along the lines of Cancún was planned some 10km south of town in **Nopoló** – an airport laid out, roads and electricity put in – but the momentum slowed and priorities were shifted elsewhere. As of now there's just the *Stouffer Presidente* hotel, a tennis centre and the beginnings of further construction, along with talk of development picking up again. The main upshot appears to be that downtown Loreto itself has been spruced up in expectation, but prices have risen accordingly. There is also the tidy, if impersonal, malecón along Bulevar López Mateos, backing the tolerable **town beach**, and, with transport, you can reach some more great stretches of sand a few miles to the south – and good camping territory, too.

The original **mission church**, the Misión Nuestra Señora de Loreto, is still standing and, though heavily restored after centuries of earthquake damage, its basic structure – solid, squat and simple – is little changed. The inscription over the door, which translates as "The head and mother church of the missions of upper and lower California", attests to its former importance, as does the Baroque altarpiece originally transported here from Mexico City. Next door a small **museum** (Mon & Wed–Sun 9am–1pm; US$1.25) chronicles the early conversion and colonization of Baja California, and houses a declaration of Loreto as the historical capital of the Californias.

Loreto is yet another superb place for **diving** and **kayaking**. Las Parras (Ⓣ613/135-1010, Ⓦwww.lasparrastours.com), at Madero 16 next to the *Café Olé*, is an established if sometimes pricey **tour** operator and can set you up with gear for diving, kayaking and snorkelling. A two-tank dive will run you US$75, a full eight-hour day of kayaking US$25. They also do tours to see cave paintings and whales, though these are far pricier than those from San Ignacio. *Baja Outpost*, which is also a bed-and-breakfast (see overleaf), can also set you up with diving equipment and tours at comparable prices.

Practicalities

From Loreto's **bus station** (Ⓣ613/135-0767) it's a fifteen-minute walk east along Salvatierra to the mission church and central plaza, and a further five minutes in the same direction to the beach. From Loreto five buses head north daily (from the afternoon to late evening) and another handful run south (8am–midnight) to La Paz, five long hours away (US$18). If you're confined to the main road there's really nothing to detain you. El Juncalito, about 15km south of Loreto, is a nice spot with an RV park. Ciudad Constitución, about halfway to La Paz, is a large, modern town with plenty of facilities and is the gateway to Puerto San Carlos and Bahía Magdalena, the southernmost of the whale sanctuaries. Puerto San Carlos, 40km west, has hotels, a trailer park, a petrol station and bus service to Ciudad Constitución. Loreto's **airport**

(ⓣ613/135-0454) is a US$6 taxi ride from town and has daily flights to La Paz and numerous cities in mainland Mexico, as well as international flights to Los Angeles.

Between the bus station and the beach are the best of the town's budget **hotels**, including the *Motel Salvatierra* (ⓣ613/135-0021; ❹), Salvatierra 123, near Allende, which is better value than the *Posada San Martín* (ⓣ613/135-0442; ❸) at Juárez 14, two blocks north of the plaza. *Hotel Palmas Altas* (ⓣ613/135-1429; ❹), on Adolfo, offers a decent trailer-home environment, a small pool and tiny though acceptable rooms, while the *Motel Brenda* (ⓣ613/135-0707; ❹), on Juárez between Marquez de León and Ayuntamiento, is a step up from these and somewhat cleaner, offering slightly larger rooms with TV, a/c and hot water. Other hotels are relatively expensive, catering mainly to wealthier diving buffs and people who know the area well; of these, the best are the beachfront *Oasis* (ⓣ613/135-0112, ⓦwww.hoteloasis.com; ❼, three blocks south of the plaza, which has a pool and all the trappings; and the *Posada de las Flores* (ⓣ613/135-1162, ⓦwww.posadadelasflores.com; ❽), near the mission at Salvatierra and Madero, a hacienda-style luxury option with a rooftop garden and an Italian restaurant. Otherwise, the B&B *Baja Outpost* (ⓣ613/125-1134, ⓦwww.bajaoutpost.com; ❻), on the malecón, has comfortable palapas and rooms with slightly arty decor, and the owner also offers dive, snorkel and kayak trips. **Campers** should head towards the beaches north of town for a free spot, or walk 1km south along Madero to *Loreto Shores RV Park*. On the way is *Villas de Loreto* (ⓣ613/135-0586, ⓦwww.villasdeloreto.com; ❼ including breakfast and bike rental), which has a pool, a restaurant and a dive shop, and rents out kayaks.

Finding simple Mexican **food** is no problem at taco stands along Hidalgo or at fancier places around the plaza, notably the popular *Café Olé*, which does good-value breakfasts and antojitos; and try the cinnamon rolls. *Tiffany's Pisa Parlour* on Hidalgo south of the plaza serves excellent, if pricey, pizza, though they are not always open in the off-season. *Tío Lupe's*, a short walk down from *Tiffany's* on Salvatierra, offers a standard Mexican menu, but also has local seafood and a few continental dishes. *La Terraza*, also on Hidalgo but closer to the malecón, cooks similar food, though it is somewhat cheaper and, as you may have guessed, has a terrace.

The English-speaking **tourist office** (Mon–Fri 8am–3pm; ⓣ613/135-0411) is located in the Palacio de Gobierno at Madero and Salvatierra. **Car rental** is currently available only from Budget (ⓣ613/135-1149) just off the malecón. **Bancomer** on the plaza, has a 24-hour ATM; the staff change travellers' cheques until 2.30pm. The **post office** is on Deportiva, just off Salvatierra on the way into town, behind the Cruz Roja building. Salvatierra offers a number of **Internet** joints, though Café Internet (Mon–Sat 8am–9pm & Sun 9am–1pm; US$2/hr) is the cheapest of them all, located a few minutes from the bus station on Salvatierra just as it meets Hidalgo.

La Paz

Everyone ends up in **LA PAZ** eventually, if only to get the ferry out, and it seems that most of the population of Baja California Sur is gravitating here, too. The outskirts are an ugly sprawl, their development outpacing the spread of paved roads and facilities. But the town centre, modernized as it is, has managed to preserve something of its quiet colonial atmosphere. You can stroll along the waterfront malecón, and, for a change, the beach in town looks inviting enough for a swim – though there are no guarantees on the cleanliness of the water.

The Bay of La Paz was explored by **Cortés** himself in the first years after the Conquest – drawn, as always, by tales of great wealth – but he found little to interest him and, despite successive military and missionary expeditions, La Paz wasn't permanently settled until the end of the eighteenth century. It then grew rapidly, however, thanks to the riches of the surrounding sea, and above all as a pearl-fishing centre. American troops occupied the town during the Texan war, and six years later it was again invaded, by William Walker in one of his many attempts to carve himself out a Central American kingdom; by this time it was already capital of the territory of California. The pearl trade has pretty much dried up – a mystery disease wiped out most of the oysters – but since the 1960s La Paz has continued to boom. It was buoyed by tourists who were at first flown in, then boosted by the growing ferry service and is now primarily fed by the hordes pouring down Hwy-1.

The best time to visit is from November to May, as summers can be unbearably hot. During the last week in February La Paz holds its **carnival**, with colourful parades and cultural events transforming the town; book ahead if you plan to come during this time. The event, which is less Río de Janeiro bacchanalia and more county fair, begins on Saturday at dusk with scores of themed floats parading down the malecón. You'll find a huge variety of live music played all over town till the wee hours, though the most interesting venues are found in the small bandstands at the end of the parade strip. If you do decide

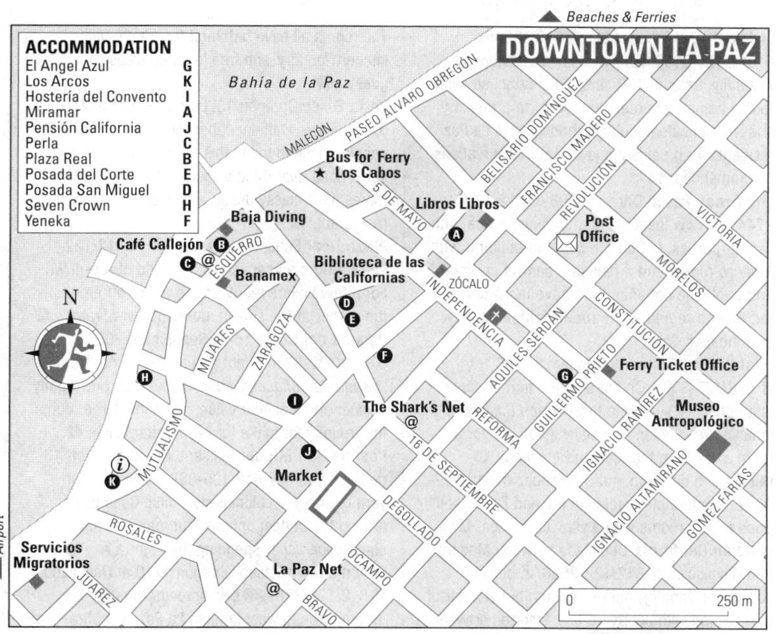

BAJA CALIFORNIA AND THE PACIFIC NORTHWEST | La Paz

to stay in La Paz during the carnival, you will need to make reservations as the town overflows with visitors.

Arrival and information

If you arrive in La Paz by bus you'll be stuck at the **bus station** about 5km out in the suburbs at Jalisco and Independencia. Long-distance services often arrive in the middle of the night and you may have no choice but to walk into town, though this is not recommended: you're best off trying to arrive in the daytime. During the day you might be lucky enough to pick up one of the irregular buses ("Centro/Camionera"); a taxi should cost around US$4. **Ferry** passengers arriving at Pichilingue (see box, p.110) are better off – there should be buses to town, and also colectivo taxis. From the airport, 12km south, there's a fixed-rate taxi service (US$15).

The most useful **tourist office** (daily 8am–10pm; ⓣ612/122-5939) is in the centre, on the waterfront at Obregón and Bravo, though there is another with the same hours and information on the highway 5.5km north of town.

Accommodation

Most of the inexpensive **hotels**, where rooms are good value by Baja standards, are within a few blocks of the zócalo; some of the older fancier places are downtown too, but the newer ones tend to be out along the coast. The **youth hostel**, on Forjadores (ⓣ612/122-4615; ❷), has reasonably priced, impersonal dorms, inconvenient for town but fairly close to the bus station; turn right up Jalisco, left along Isabel la Católica, following the one-way traffic to the right, then take the next right and right again, around 1km in all. The nearest **campsite** is *El Cardón Trailer Park* (ⓣ612/124-0078, ⓔelcardon@latinmail.com), about 2km out on the road north.

El Ángel Azul Independencia 518 at Prieto ⓣ612/125-5130, ⓦwww.elangelazul.com. A tastefully restored 150-year-old courthouse, with rooms around a garden courtyard, an art gallery and a small café popular with long-term La Paz residents for breakfast and coffees. Reservations recommended. ❼

Los Arcos Paseo Obregón 498 ⓣ612/122-2744, ⓦwww.losarcos.com. Popular place with fishing parties, set on the bay. Old building with modern rooms and a pleasant central courtyard and pool. The cabañas here have more character, though regular-style rooms without a view are cheaper. ❽

Hostería del Convento Madero Sur 85 ⓣ612/122-3508. On the site of a former convent and uncannily similar to the *Pensión California*, but smaller and quieter, especially if you ask for a room away from the road and the lobby. ❸

Miramar 5 de Mayo and Domínguez ⓣ612/122-0672. Comfortable hotel with a/c and TV; a good price for the rooms with a view of the sea. ❻

Pensión California Degollado between Madero and Revolución ⓣ612/122-2896, ⓔpension-california@prodigy.net.mx. A worn but wonderful old building with courtyard and assorted artwork. The rooms all have bath and fan. Communal kitchen, laundry, and free Internet access for guests. ❸

Perla Paseo Obregón 1570 at La Paz ⓣ612/122-0777, ⓦwww.hotelperlabaja.com. Once the most popular place in town, this Spanish colonial gem is still a good deal. Tiled throughout, western-style rooms have classy decor; a/c, pool and restaurant. ❼

Plaza Real Esquerro and Callejón ⓣ612/122-9333. Bright and spacious, but kind of run-down. For a few dollars more, you're better off around the corner at the similar, but superior, *Miramar*. ❺

Posada del Corte 16 de Septiembre 202 ⓣ612/122-8240. Right around the corner from *Posada San Miguel*, with less character but slightly cleaner and a similar value; has some large rooms for groups that make for even better value. ❹

Posada San Miguel Belisario Domínguez, off 16 de Septiembre ⓣ612/125-8888. Simple, courtyard rooms in a colonial-style villa. Good value among the budget options, but may also have some *cucarachas* spending the night. ❸

Seven Crown Paseo Obregón 1710 at Degollado ⓣ612/128-7787, ⓔsevencrown@prodigy.net.mx. The newest hotel in La Paz, this ultramodern waterfront spot is decked out in glass, steel, aluminium and tile. Rooms are sleek and many have direct views of the bay. Indoor pool, jacuzzi, business centre and all the expected amenities of a high-class city hotel. ❽–❾

Yeneka Madero, near the zócalo ☎612/125-4688. Eccentric decor and comfortable, clean rooms; also has a café. The helpful staff actually encourage you to negotiate your room rate. ❹

The Town and around

There's not a great deal to see in La Paz itself and if you're staying for any length of time you should head for the beaches. If you're just hanging around waiting for a ferry, however, you can happily fill a day window-shopping in the centre – dozens of stores selling everything from clothes, cosmetics and varied bric-a-brac take advantage of the duty-free zone – and browsing around the market. The small **Museo Antropológico** (Mon–Fri 8am–6pm, Sat 9am–2pm; free), at 5 de Mayo and Altamirano, is also worth a passing look: exhibits include photos of cave paintings and an ethnological history of the peninsula. This is as good as Baja museums get, but has no English labelling. More information on all aspects of Baja, some of it in English, is available in the Biblioteca de las Californias, opposite the cathedral on the zócalo, or at Libros Libros at Constitución 195.

Beaches ring the bay all around La Paz, but the easiest to get to are undoubtedly those to the south, served by the local bus that runs along Obregón to the ferry terminal at Pichilingue. Decent ones are **Playa del Tesoro**, shortly before Pichilingue, and **Playa Pichilingue**, just beyond the ferry station. Both have simple facilities, including a restaurant. The best, however, is **Playa de Balandra**, actually several beaches around a saltwater lagoon with eight shallow bays, most of which are no more than waist-deep: three buses leave the malecón from 10am daily and traverse the beach route, taking you here for US$3; the last bus back is 5pm.

There are plenty of opportunities for fishing and diving, and for **boat trips** into the bay; just stroll along the malecón to find people offering the latter – **Isla Espíritu Santo** is a popular destination, as is **Los Islotes**, a small group of islands that hosts a colony of **sea lions** – or check the "Listings" (see overleaf) for details of specific operators.

Eating and drinking

Wandering round La Paz you'll find dozens of places to **eat** – the seafood, above all, is excellent. There are numerous inexpensive local restaurants near the market, especially on Serdán and 16 de Septiembre, and around the zócalo.

Bismark II Altamirano and Degollado ☎612/122-4854. Excellent seafood without having to pay inflated seafront prices. Also runs a *taquería* towards the southern half of Obregón, with some of the best tacos in town.

Las Brisas del Mar Obregón at Colegio Militar ☎612/123-5055. Nearly all-Mexican clientele who come for the seafood, despite the prices.

El Carrito Obregón at Morelos ☎612/125-6658. Unpretentious and popular with locals who come for the *ceviche* and other great seafood, all reasonably priced.

Kiwi Obregón at 5 de Mayo. Great local and regional cuisine for decent prices, with tables set right in the sand on the beach. Try the scrumptious stuffed fish fillet, a house specialty.

La Media Luna Obregón 755. Slightly upscale restaurant and bar, with great seafood; also a good spot for sunset drinks.

Seven Crown Obregón 1710 at Degollado ☎612/128-7787. This newly built minimalist hotel may have pricey rooms, but its stylish roof bar and restaurant, open to non-guests, have wonderful views of the water, with several small terraces for those seeking private sunset inebriation.

Super Tacos de California Esquerro, near Serfin bank. Seafood tacos and help-yourself salad stand. A lobster taco is US$2.50.

Taquería Muello Hacienda near Serfin bank, and a half-block from the malecón. Hugely popular taco stand; try the potato special.
Tequilas Bar and Grill Mutualismo and Ocampo. Equally enjoyed by tourists and locals, a bar whose friendly atmosphere centres around the pool table.
La Terraza Obregón 1570 at La Paz. Café-restaurant under the *Hotel Perla*. Popular spot to watch the world go by, though food can be lacklustre and pricey for what you get.

Listings

Airlines and flights Aerocalifornia ⓣ612/125-1023, ⓦwww.aerocalifornia.com.mx; and Aeroméxico ⓣ612/122-0091 or 0092, ⓦwww.aeromexico.com; for comprehensive flight details, contact the Viajes Perla travel agency, on the corner of 5 de Mayo and Dominguéz (Mon–Sat 8.30am–7.30pm & Sun 9am–2pm; ⓣ612/122-8666). The airport is 8km southwest from town, reached by an expensive taxi ride.
American Express Esquerro 1679, behind the *Hotel Perla* (Mon–Fri 9am–2pm & 4–6pm, Sat 9am–2pm; ⓣ612/122-8300).
Banks Most banks lie between the zócalo and the waterfront.

The ferry from La Paz

If you're planning to take the **ferry** across the Sea of Cortés to **Mazatlán** or **Topolobampo** (the port for Los Mochis), you should buy tickets as far ahead of time as possible: cabins – *turista* (four bunks), *cabina* (two bunks) or *especial* (suite) – and space for cars are often overbooked. There's rarely any problem going *salón* class (entitling you to a reclining seat), for which tickets are only available a day in advance. On balance, for most people, *salón* is the best option, as the cabins can be freezing if the a/c works and stiflingly hot if not. Sleeping out on deck can be a pleasant experience. **Departures** for the eighteen-hour run to Mazatlán on SEMATUR leave daily at 3pm and with TMC (a smaller, cargo-focused line) every other day at 5pm; those for the five-hour sail to Topolobampo (Bajaferries) leave Wednesday to Monday at 3pm.

You can make **reservations** at the downtown ticket offices of the **ferry operators**: SEMATUR, 5 de Mayo and Prieto (ⓣ612/125-2366, ⓦwww.ferrysematur.com.mx), where you'll need to arrive early and be prepared to wait in line; direct at the terminal (ⓣ612/122-5005); Baja Ferries, Morelos 720 (ⓣ612/125-7443, ⓦwww.bajaferries.com); or through local travel agents. Ferry schedules change frequently and it's always best to call ahead to check the schedule. The cost of **tickets** to Topolobampo with Bajaferries, running a newly built, 300-cabin ship, ranges from US$23 for a reclining seat to US$69 for a cabin and US$180 for a small car, and tickets can be paid for with major credit cards. For the trip to Mazatlán with SEMATUR, a *salón* class ticket costs US$66, a *turista* ticket is US$170, a cabin is US$208, and a small car will cost US$202. **Bicycles** go free.

Before buying tickets, car drivers should ensure they have a **permit to drive** on the mainland. This should have been obtained when crossing the border into Mexico, but if not you may have some joy by taking your vehicle and all relevant papers along to the customs office at the ferry terminal a couple of days before you sail. If for some reason you've managed to get this far without having your **tourist card** stamped, you should also attend to that before sailing – there's an immigration office at Obregón 2140, between Juárez and Allende.

To **get to the ferry** itself, which sails from the terminal at Pichilingue, some 14km away, go to the old bus station on the malecón – straight down Independencia from the zócalo – and, again, get there early. There is only one bus an hour, on the hour (8am–5pm; US$1), or take a taxi from town (US$15). Arrive at the ferry by 1.30pm. According to signs at the terminal, it is illegal to take your own **food** on board, but since the catering is so poor, everyone does and nobody seems to mind. Try one of the *loncheros* by the docks for quesadillas, burritos, and drinks to take along.

Bookstore Libros Libros, Constitución 195, sells many English-language newspapers and books.
Buses La Paz bus station (Ⓣ612/122-6476) is also the southern terminus for the peninsula buses. Ten regular daily services head north, three going as far as Tijuana, 22 hours away (at 8am, 10am, and 10pm), another to Mexicali (1pm). Buses leave roughly hourly (6.30am–6.30pm) for Cabo San Lucas and San José del Cabo; some are routed via Todos Santos, others take the eastern route direct to San José. The western route is quicker and more scenic as it follows the coast for quite a way below Todos Santos.
Car rental Most car rental agents have offices at the airport or on the malecón, including: Alamo Ⓣ612/122-6262; Avis Ⓣ612/122-2651; Budget Ⓣ612/122-7655 or 123-1919); Dollar (Ⓣ612/122-6060; Hertz Ⓣ612/122-5300; National Ⓣ612/125-6585; and Thrifty Ⓣ612/125-9696.
Internet access Several Internet joints line the malecón. *Café Callejón*, just in from the water on Callejón, has a restaurant and outdoor café (daily 8.30am–10pm, US$1/hr); The Shark's Net, 16 de Septiembre and Aquiles Serdán, claims to be open 24 hours (US$1.50/hr); La Paz Net, as you head away from the malecón on Ocampo, on the right just past Revolución (closed Sun, US$2/hr).
Laundry La Paz Lava, Mutualismo 260 Ⓣ612/122-3112 (daily 8am–midnight; US$2/load).
Post office Corner of Revolución and Constitución.
Spanish courses Se Habla La Paz, Madero 540 Ⓣ612/122-7763, Ⓦwww.sehablalapaz.com.
Tours and activities Baja Diving and Service, 1665 Obregón (Ⓣ612/122-1826), offer good diving and snorkelling tours and courses. For decent kayak rental and snorkelling outings to nearby volcanic islands, or to the sea-lion colony at Los Islotes, try Baja Outdoor Activities (BOA), Madero and Campeche y Tamaulipas (Ⓣ612/125-5636, Ⓦwww.kayactivities.com), a half-hour walk from downtown La Paz on the road to Pichilingue next to the *Hotel El Moro*; full- and half-day packages from US$30. Otherwise, operators include: Katun (Ⓣ612/348-5609; Ⓦwww.katun-tours.com), Juárez 1445 at Callejón, who run mountain-biking and sea-kayaking trips; Scuba Baja Joe (Ⓣ612/122-4006, Ⓦwww.scubabajajoe.com) on Obregón and Ocampo, who offer competitively priced dive packages; Funbaja (Ⓣ612/121-5884, Ⓦwww.funbaja.com), Km 2.5 on the road to Pichilingue, who run all kinds of aquatic outings; and The Cortés Club (Ⓣ612/121-6120, Ⓦwww.Cortésclub.com), at Km 5 on the road to Pichilingue, who run beginner's through to dive-master courses for PADI dive certification.

Los Cabos and the East Cape

Beyond La Paz, the coastline becomes increasingly developed: modern, commercialized and resort-weary. **Los Cabos**, the series of capes and beaches around the southern tip of the Baja Peninsula, is one of the fastest-developing tourist areas in Mexico – heavily promoted by the authorities and a boom area for the big hotel chains and resort builders. Undeniably beautiful, and home to most of the luxury resorts, golf courses and beaches you see on the postcards, it's not a place for the budget traveller to venture unprepared. Not far south of La Paz the highway splits: the fast new road cuts across to the Pacific to run straight down the west coast to **Cabo San Lucas**; the old route trails through the mountains, emerging only briefly above the Sea of Cortés on its long journey to **San José del Cabo**. At the moment, the coastal towns between La Paz and San José are mostly inaccessible without a 4WD, but the state still hopes to extend Cabo development to the **East Cape**, and the construction of two new highways, though currently still in the planning stages, will open up over a hundred kilometres of untouched beaches and small fishing villages, for better or for worse.

Cabo San Lucas

The bay of **Cabo San Lucas**, at the southernmost tip of Baja, was once a base for pirate vessels waiting to pounce on Spanish treasure ships. Even fifteen years

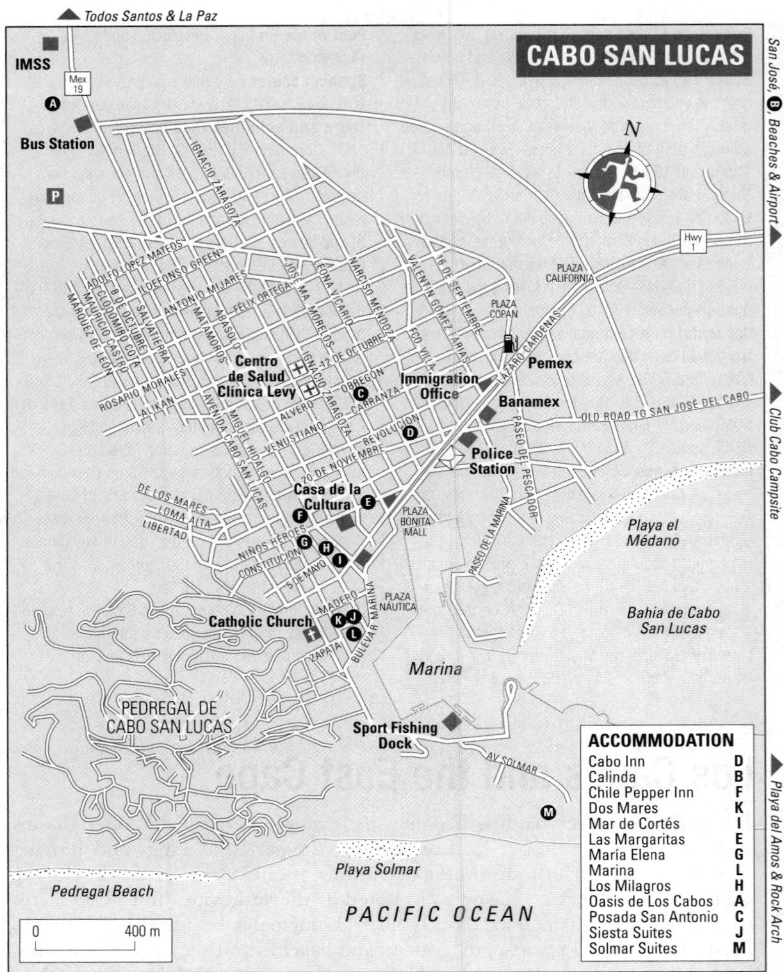

ago, it was little more than a fishing and canning village occasionally visited by adventurous sports fishermen with the means to sail or fly to town. It quickly earned a reputation for the marlin that could be caught here, and the bay is now full of sleek, radar-equipped fishing yachts.

In recent years, the once quiet town has rapidly become the focal point of Los Cabos: million-dollar condos have sprung up, palms have been transplanted, golf courses have been laid, water has been piped in from San José and everywhere is kept pristine. More like an enclave of the US than part of Mexico, preserving almost nothing that is not geared to tourism, it can be fun for a day or two, unless, of course, you want to fish or dive. Though prices are higher than in neighbouring San José (see p.116), there's much more of a party atmosphere, with a younger crowd. Currently there are over 3500 rooms for rent and the local feeling is that 10,000 is the next feasible "goal", which would equate the town with the long-established resorts such as Mazatlán or Acapulco. Even a mammoth Wal-Mart has opened here, alongside Puerto Paraíso, an enormous mall on the marina comprising a convention centre, a theatre complex, a bowling alley a huge parking outlet and condos. Other plans include an artificial island to sit in the bay, complete with restaurants and bars.

Arrival and information

Buses from La Paz (roughly hourly 6am–7pm; 2–3hr) and San José del Cabo (roughly hourly 7am–10pm; 30min) stop on the highway about 2km outside the city, and from there it's a twenty-minute walk or a US$3 taxi ride. From the **airport** (see p.118), catch a taxi to San José and a bus from there. Another option is the direct shuttle to town; returning to the airport, the shuttle leaves from the *Plaza Las Glorias* hotel at the marina. Surprisingly, Cabo has no official tourist office, just dozens of places dishing out maps and **information**, and usually throwing in some timeshare patter while they're at it; you can, however, visit the campy but informative Ⓦwww.allaboutcabo.com.

Accommodation

The most affordable way to enjoy the sand and water around Cabo San Lucas is to stay in San José (see p.118) and visit for the day on one of the frequent buses. If you do decide to stay here for any reason, however, you have the choice of a few good-value places (though none is cheap); if you're here out of season (May–Oct) you may find dramatically reduced rates at one of the swanky beachfront hotels.

Camping on the local Playa Médano is not encouraged by the beachfront restaurateurs, nor is it particularly safe – with all the tourists, Cabo does have its share of petty crime – but you could toss down a sleeping bag on one of the relatively secluded beaches nearby. Local **RV parks** include *Vagabondos del Mar* (Ⓣ624/143-0290), 3km east; *Club Cabo* (Ⓣ624/143-3348, Ⓦwww.mexonline.com/clubcabo.htm), 4km east down a dirt road, which also has a hotel (❹) and a pool; and *Faro Viejo* at Abasolo and Mijares in town. All camping costs US$10–12.

Cabo Inn 20 de Noviembre at Leona Vicario Ⓣ624/143-0819, Ⓦwww.allaboutcabo.com/caboinn.htm. Small, quiet rooms with a proper local feel just two blocks from the marina – a former brothel, it has now gained a slightly bohemian travellers' atmosphere. All rooms have a/c, plus there's a small pool, a sun deck and free coffee for guests. ❻

Calinda Km 4.5 on the highway towards San José Ⓣ624/145-8044, Ⓦwww.hotelescalinda.com.mx. If you are looking to stay on the water without the extreme expense of most other places, this Cabo old-timer has had a face-lift and is the best value oceanfront hotel, set away from the party. ❽

Dos Mares north side of Zapata, east of Hidalgo Ⓣ624/143-0330. A good location right by the marina and close to the action, rooms here have TV, plus there's a tiny pool, as well as some studios with kitchens. ❺

Mar de Cortés Lázaro Cárdenas between Guerrero and Matamoros Ⓣ624/143-0032, Ⓦwww.mardecortez.com. Colonial-style decor in a lovely planted setting with a mix of older and modern, larger rooms around a pool; some have terraces and all have a/c. Also has a good restaurant. ❻

María Elena Matamoros near Cárdenas and Niños Héroes Ⓣ624/143-3296. A basic place in the less touristy area between the bus station and town. Nothing special, but fairly clean rooms and just next to a laundromat. ❺

Las Margaritas Plaza Aramburo 7 Ⓣ624/143-6770 Ⓔmargaritas@real-turismo.com. Smack in the middle of Cabo, with spacious and likeable rooms, all with a/c, TV and kitchens. ❼

Marina Marina at Guerrero Ⓣ624/143-0030; Ⓔostmc@prodigy.net.mx. Right across from the marina, with small rooms and a pool. Can be noisy, but perfectly acceptable. ❻

Los Milagros Matamoros 116 ⓣ624/143-4566, ⓦwww.losmilagros.com.mx. Tasteful, studio-like rooms, a small pool and a sun deck make this a real find, just a few blocks from the action. Reservations recommended. ❻

Oasis de los Cabos on the road to Todos Santos, next to the bus station ⓣ624/143-2098. Brand-new place with a pool and clean rooms, handy if you arrive late at the bus station. ❺

Posada San Antonio Morelos by Obregón ⓣ624/143-7353. An old budget hotel a few blocks from the strip, with dark and simple rooms. ❸

Siesta Suites on Zapata between Hidalgo and Guerrero, two blocks in from the *Plaza Las Glorias* ⓣ624/143-2773, ⓦwww.loscabosguide.com/siestasui.htm. This expat-run establishment has been around for ten years and offers clean, studio rooms with TV, a/c, free local calls, and close proximity to the marina. ❺

Solmar Suites Playa Solmar, 1km west towards Finisterra ⓣ624/143-3535, in US ⓣ1-800/344-3349, ⓦwww.solmar.com. Deluxe oceanfront resort offering the whole enchilada: two heated swimming pools with swim-up bars, lap pool, 15-person jacuzzi, fitness centre, lighted tennis courts and nightly *mariachi* entertainment. Rooms themselves are predictable, but many have stunning ocean views. Check out their three-nights-plus-meals deal, which can be as little as US$160 off-season. ❼

The Town

With its great sands and fascinating marine life, Cabo San Lucas is one of the most attractive spots in Baja. Above all there's the huge **rock arch** at Finisterra – Land's End, where the Sea of Cortés meets the Pacific – an extraordinary place, with a clear division between the shallow turquoise sea water on the left and the profound blue of the ocean on the right. A colony of sea lions lives on the rocks roundabout. Only the adventurous can walk over the rocks (from *Solmar Suites* or Playa Solmar) to the arch, but there are plenty of trips out here from the **marina**, most of which take in one of the small surrounding beaches, more often than not **Playa del Amor**, which boasts strands on both seas. A round-trip to Playa del Amor by water taxi will cost a negotiable US$7.

Around the marina, down the nearby streets and along the **Playa Médano**, the town's closest safe-swimming beach, hawkers constantly tout trips in glass-bottomed boats, fishing, water-skiing, paragliding or bungee jumping, and will rent anything from horses to off-road quad bikes to jet skis and underwater gear. Competition is fierce, prices change and places come and go, so shop around. **Scuba diving** and **snorkelling** are perhaps the most rewarding of these activities, though the best sites (out towards Finisterra) can only be reached by boat. For gear rental, snorkelling trips and scuba courses, check out the many companies along Bulevar Marina, especially in the plazas. Or simply rent a snorkel and fins at the marina (US$7), take a water taxi to Playa del Amor, and swim back to **Pelican Rock**, where the underwater shelf is home to schools of tropical fish. Experienced divers shouldn't miss the rim of a marine canyon also off Playa del Amor, where unusual conditions at 30m create a "**sandfall**" with streams of sand starting their 2000-metre fall to the canyon bottom. The marine life in such a habitat is unique to beachfront areas. One of the most popular dives is to **Cabo Pulmo**, the giant coral reef (though this is more easily reached from San José) where some of the larger members of the underwater food chain make their home.

Eating, drinking and nightlife

For reasonably inexpensive **food**, head for Morelos and the streets away from the waterfront. The more touristy places – some of them the most expensive in Baja – cluster around the marina and along Hidalgo. At night, such places compete for partying patrons by offering **happy hours** (often 6–8pm) and novel cocktails. There's little difference between them; stroll along and take your pick.

Billygan's Island Playa Médano. One of the three beach bar-restaurants that caters to beach party-goers, from 9am till 11pm. Breakfast, lunch and dinner right on the sand, and tropical drinks poured and consumed fairly nonstop.

Cabo Wabo Guerrero between Lázaro Cárdenas and Madero. Rocker Sammy Hagar owns this boisterous club (and they make a popular tequila of the same name). Loud and lively, often with a heavy charge, but still a good place to hear live music – and if you're going here around a holiday, perhaps you can catch Sammy himself on stage.

Francisco's Café del Mundo marina waterfront. The best coffee in town. Delicious cakes, US newspapers, magazines and a harbour view.

Giggling Marlin Blv Marina at Matamoros. A Cabo institution, drawing an older set than other places on the strip. Mostly a place to drink and dance to Latin standards: chances of getting out without hearing *La Bamba* are slim.

Mariscos Mocambo Morelos at Revolución. Unpretentious seafood restaurant popular with Mexicans and the fisherman crowd. Has a number of tasty regional specialties, the Grilled Red Snapper, for example. New location under an enormous palapa.

The Office Playa Médano. Restaurant and bar which, along with its neighbours, *Billygan's Island* and *Pirata Cavendish*, pumps out rock classics and offers happy hours. Expensive food and not to everyone's taste, though they do offer a large seafood menu. Out of the three, is known best for its rowdy parties.

Oye Como Va Guerrero at Zapata. New curbside Mexican joint with exceptional and cheap tortas, tacos, and breakfasts, as well as comida corrida.

La Perla Lázaro Cárdenas between Matamoros and Abasolo. Very inexpensive and suprisingly untouristy place right in the tourist zone. Good Mexican staples and *licuados*.

Restaurant Orale Zaragoza and 16 de Septiembre. A down-to-earth, inexpensive Mexican place. Great food and a friendly staff.

El Squid Roe directly across from the marina. If you're here for spring break, this Cabo classic should be your first stop; a wild party atmosphere with table dancing allowed, if not encouraged. Open late.

Listings

Airlines For airport enquiries, call ☎624/142-0341. Airlines include: Aeroméxico ☎624/142-0397; Alaska ☎624/149-5800; Continental ☎624/142-3890; Mexicana ☎624/143-5352; and United ☎624/142-2880.

Banks and exchange There's an ATM, and the best exchange rates, at Bancomer (cheques cashed 8.30am–noon) on Lázaro Cárdenas at Hidalgo; after hours, several casas de cambio (one by *Giggling Marlin*; see above) offer decent rates until 11pm.

Bookstore Libros Libros, Blv Marina 20.

Buses Aquila ☎624/143-7878 or 7880. Buses leave hourly for Tijuana and the border (24hr; US$90) via La Paz (2hr 30min; US$10).

Car rental Avis ☎624/143-4606 or 146-0201; Budget ☎624/143-4190 or 1522; Hertz ☎624/146-5088 or 142-0375; National ☎624/143-1414; and Thrifty ☎624/146-5030 or 143-1666.

Consulates US ☎624/143-3566; Canada ☎624/142-4333.

Emergencies Police ☎624/143-3997 or 142-0361; Hospital ☎624/143-1594.

Internet access and phones Cabomix, on Matamoros at Niños Héroes, has the best rates in town and also has phones (including Internet phone services); there are also several small Internet places near the old bus station at Zaragoza and 16 de Septiembre, as well as a number of good but expensive Internet providers along the strip, including Internet Services on Plaza Náutica.

Post office On Lázaro Cárdenas, east of the marina (Mon–Fri 9am–6pm).

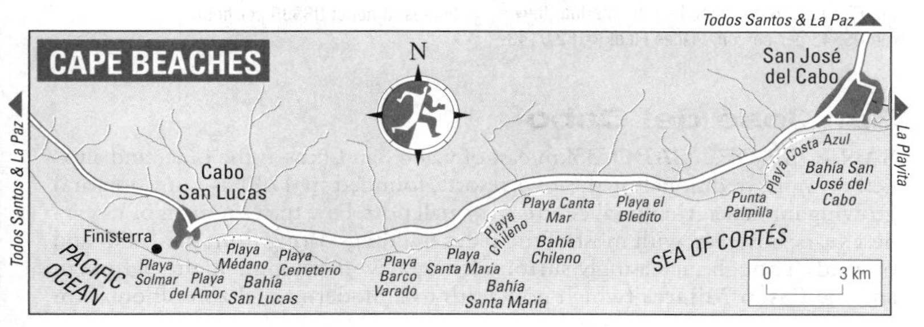

The cape beaches

The highway between Cabo San Lucas and San José del Cabo gives access to a wealth of superb **beaches**, many of them visible from the road. Unfortunately, as condo and hotel development continues, access, especially for those on foot, is becoming increasingly difficult. You could just ride along until you see one you fancy, but if you have a preference and are using the bus between the two towns, make sure the driver is prepared to let you off at your desired stop. Be aware that swimming may not be safe at all beaches due to very strong currents.

Apart from Solmar Del Amor and La Playita, all **distances** are measured east from Cabo San Lucas towards San José del Cabo, 33km away.

Solmar, 1km west. Pacific-side beach with strong undertow. Whale-watching Jan–April.

Del Amor, in centre. Boat-access beach spanning the two seas out by El Arco. Great snorkelling on the marina side.

Médano, 1km. Cabo's beach. Sand, restaurants, bars and abundant aquatic paraphernalia to rent. Can be uncomfortably crowded.

Cementerio, 4km. Beautiful swimming beach. Access on foot from Médano.

Barco Varado, 9km. Shipwreck beach. The remains of a Japanese trawler that sank in 1966 is the main diving focus. Surfing and rock reefs, too. Access very difficult: take the marked access road off the highway, but watch the rocks on your way down.

Santa María, 12km. Scuba and snorkelling on rock reefs at both ends. Excellent swimming. Easy access, not far from road.

Punta Chileno, 14km. Excellent swimming and snorkelling and you can usually find water-sports equipment rental right on the beach. Easiest access of all.

Canta Mar, 16km. Appropriately dubbed "surfing beach". Occasional point breaks.

Punta Palmilla, 27km. Good safe beach used by San José hotel residents needing escape from the strong riptide closer to home. Point and reef breaks when surf's up.

Costa Azul, 29km. Consistently the region's best surfing beach. Shore break but rocks at low tide.

La Playita, 2.5km east of San José via a dirt road. Secluded and excellent for fishing; swimming is also possible, but look out for the plentiful surfers.

Tours and activities Land's End Divers (ⓣ624/143-2200, ⓦwww.mexonline.com/landsend.htm), at A-5 in the marina, has good rates for their dive packages. Ecological snorkelling adventures are offered by Cabo Expeditions (ⓣ624/143-2700, ⓦwww.allaboutcabo.com/caboexpeditions.htm), in the *Plaza Las Glorias* hotel on the marina; they run US$45 per person. Pisces Fleet (ⓣ624/143-1288, ⓦwww.piscessportfishing.com), in the marina, run marlin-fishing trips (US$60–100 per person). Solmar Fleet (ⓣ624/143-3535), in the *Solmar Suites* hotel, is an equally established fishing fleet and has similar rates. Rancho Collins (ⓣ624/143-3652), near Playa Médano, east of *Billygan's Island*, hires out horses at about US$35 per hour.

San José del Cabo

SAN JOSÉ DEL CABO, 33km east of Cabo San Lucas, is the older and altogether more traditional of the two resorts, founded in 1730 as a mission and growing into an agricultural centre and small port. Few traces remain of its earliest years, however, with most of the older buildings dating from the 1880s and onwards. Though increasingly surrounded by new development, the old **plaza** and the **Paseo Mijares** (which now leads to a modern hotel zone about 1km seaward) are still more or less intact, and there's a small local **museum** in the Casa de la Cultura. The numerous shops and restaurants that line the streets and shady courtyards are interesting enough, the latter offering a good variety of cuisine, but prices are high. Visitors, however, tend to come for the aquatic flora and fauna, and most of the hotels can help arrange tours, guides and equipment, but you'd be wise to shop around.

To get to the **beaches** it's a considerable walk down Mijares to the hotel zone, and on from there to find empty sand: the beaches stretch for miles so keep walking until you find a quiet spot. Some 2km east is the lesser-known alternative **Pueblo La Playa (La Playita)**, a hundred-year-old fishing village that offers numerous options for sport fishing; try Gordo Banks Pangas (ⓣ624/142-1147, ⓦwww.gordobanks.com). The waters at the seamount of Gordo Banks here house the highest concentrations of gamefish in the waters of Los Cabos. The **estuary** just northeast of town is home to hundreds of birds and makes for an interesting hour or two; it can be reached by kayak or on foot. The town celebrates its annual **festival** the third week in March – as good a time as any to visit.

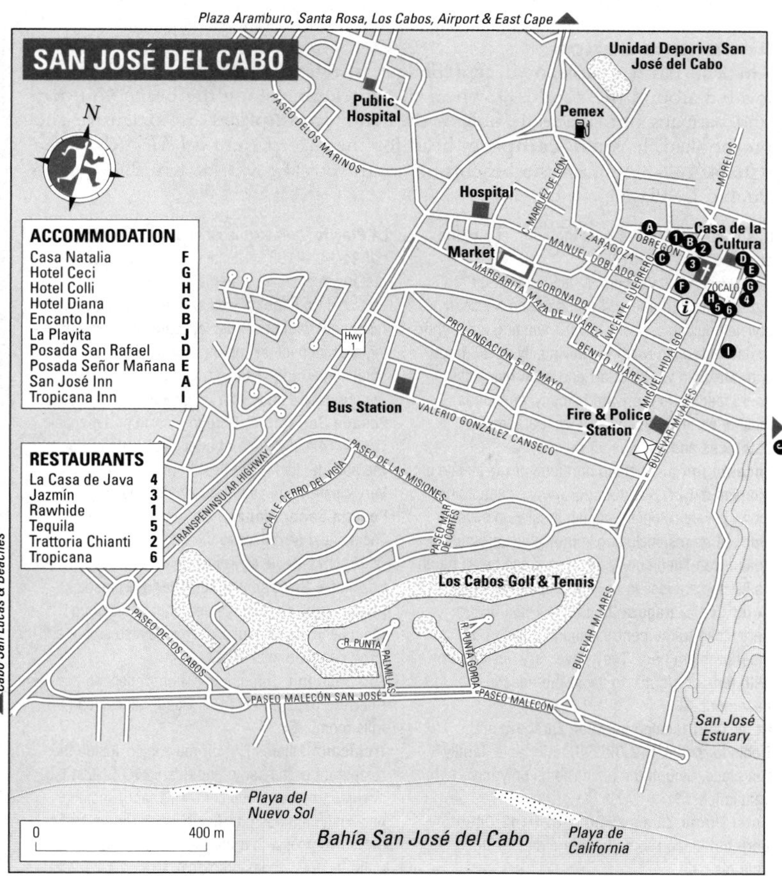

Arrival and information

Alaska, American, Mexicana, Aero California and Aeroméxico all fly to **San José airport**, which serves both resorts. It's located 11km north of town, and runs services from several Mexican and US West Coast cities, and a few East Coast cities. Shuttle vans run into town (US$10, though you may be able to bargain directly with the drivers down to US$5). Taxis are the most expensive option (US$14–16). The third, least recommended option is to walk the 2.5km to the highway and jump on one of the frequent local buses that stop on the highway near town. Do not change money at the airport, as the rates given here are among the worst in Mexico; you're much better off at the banks or ATMs in town. The **bus station** (Águila: ⓣ624/142-1100) is about fifteen minutes' walk from the centre: turn left out of the station along Gonzales and then, after 1km, left onto Mijares and to the zócalo – easily spotted by the church towers. Zaragoza crosses Mijares at this point; Obregón and Doblado run parallel to and either side of Zaragoza. The tourist office, Mauricio Castro at Plaza San José, is quite far out on the highway, but they do offer helpful **information** on the Cabos area (ⓣ624/142-3310, ⓦwww.loscabos.gob.mx).

Accommodation

San José has a couple of decent budget **hotels**, the cheapest of which are located around the zócalo. Down in the hotel zone along the beach you may find bargains out of season, but on the whole most places are expensive and pre-booked. If you're **camping**, head for the pricey *Brisa del Mar RV Resort* (ⓣ624/142-3999), on the beachfront southwest of town (at Km 29.5), or to Pueblo La Playa.

Casa Natalia Mijares 4, at the north end of the zócalo ⓣ624/142-5100, ⓦwww.casanatalia.com. A new and rather striking architectural mix of European and Mexican styles, housing a classy, award-winning hotel and restaurant; each room is individually decked out with Mexican works of art and each has glass doors leading to a private balcony. Amenities include an in-room spa service, personal bathrobes and daily paper delivery. ❾

Encanto Inn just behind northend of the zócalo on Morelos ⓣ624/142-0388, ⓦwww.elencantoinn.com. Lovely colonial Spanish hotel with several types of rooms, including some suites, around a quaint tree-lined courtyard . Rates can be as much as 50 percent less in the low season. ❼

Hotel Ceci Zaragoza 22 ⓣ624/142-0051. Very close to the centre, though noise is the chief problem here. They have very basic rooms with fans or a/c; try to avoid the ones in the basement. ❸

Hotel Colli Hidalgo between Zaragoza and Doblado ⓣ624/142-0725. Comfortable, family-run place, though the plain rooms only have fan ventilation. ❹

Hotel Diana Zaragoza 30 ⓣ624/142-0490. Bare but clean rooms have a/c and TV but little else. ❹

La Playita 2km southeast of central San José ⓣ624/142-4166, ⓔlaplayitahotel@prodigy.net.mx. A pleasant waterside alternative that's removed from the crowds, a three-storey hotel and restaurant with comfortable, spare rooms overlooking a small pool and an outdoor dining area. The hotel can arrange fishing trips for you and the restaurant will cook your catch. ❼

Posada San Rafael Obregón, north of the zócalo ⓣ624/142-3878. A lot better than it looks from the outside, this is the best bet in its price class. Very clean rooms and friendly staff. ❸

Posada Señor Mañana northeast corner of the zócalo (just next door to the Casa de la Cultura) ⓣ624/142-0462, ⓦwww.srmanana.net. Run by a hospitable Swedish woman, offering spacious, palm-lined surroundings and charming, clean rooms with or without a/c. There's also a pool and large common kitchen. ❺

San José Inn Obregón between Degollado and Guerrero ⓣ624/142-2464. Good-value, clean no-frills rooms. ❸

Tropicana Mijares just off the zócalo, inside the restaurant of the same name ⓣ624/142-2311, ⓦwww.tropicanacabo.com. This fancy-looking establishment has tidy, luxury-style rooms and an attractive pool with a bar around a large stone patio; price includes breakfast. ❽

Eating, drinking and nightlife

There's a huge variety of upmarket **restaurants** downtown along Mijares, but it's more difficult to find places with local prices – look around Zaragoza and Obregón.

La Baguette on the eastern side of the square. Decent pastries and bread for US$1, open daily 8am–8pm.

Cactus Jack's three blocks south of the zócalo. Serves inexpensive Mexican breakfasts and seafood dishes off a large international menu, but the karaoke and big-screen TV here are the main draw for the locals.

La Casa de Java Mijares 8. Cosy, with breakfast all day. The relaxed atmosphere also makes it a perfect place to have a coffee and take time out to read the papers.

La Cenaduría del Poncho on the zócalo. Good local food and pleasant atmosphere; has a great terrace overlooking the square. Ask for a free *cerveza* or *sopa tortilla* with any meal.

La Dolce... on the zócalo. Standard Italian cuisine, including tasty pizzas and wines for relatively good prices. Popular among tourists.

Don Emiliano Mijares 27. Traditional Mexican cuisine accompanied by live music every night.

French Riviera Doblado and Hidalgo. Somewhat impersonal, but still a good coffee and snack spot, just off the square. Crepes for US$5.

Jazmín Morelos one block west of the zócalo. The best-value traditional Mexican food in town. Also has excellent breakfasts.

Mi Cocina Mijares 4, inside *Casa Natalia*. Mostly about presentation – meaning smaller portions and exquisite wines – but the torch-lit atmosphere is captivating.

La Picazón Gonzalez s/n, just a short walk west from the main highway and buses. All sorts of great inexpensive Mexican seafood specialties and antojitos served outside in a colourful, tropical atmosphere. Try the *tacos del pulpo al mojo de ajo* – soft tacos with octopus cooked in garlic.

La Playita at the beach in Pueblo La Playa. Serves wonderful seafood (including your own day's catch if you like) in a breezy palapa.

Rawhide Obregón and Guerrero. An expat-run Southwest American cantina serving ribs and burgers, with a menu that includes such dishes as Buckshot Macaroni and Cheese.

Tequila Doblado 1011 between Mijares and Hidalgo. The top choice in town, with a quaint garden atmosphere and attentive (overly attentive) waiting staff; overpriced wines and cigars.

Trattoria Chianti Obregón at Morelos. Serves excellent Italian food in a romantic courtyard setting; the pasta dishes and wood-fired pizza oven here make it a local gringo favourite.

Tropicana just off the zócalo on Mijares. Another favourite, this colonial-style restaurant has a very nice tiled, palapa sitting area, and serves excellent seafood, often with Cuban dancers providing entertainment.

Listings

Airlines For airport enquiries, call ⓣ624/142-0341. Airlines include: Aeroméxico ⓣ624/142-0397; Alaska ⓣ624/149-5800; Continental ⓣ624/142-3890; Mexicana ⓣ624/143-5352; and United ⓣ624/142-2880.

Banks and exchange You'll find both ATMs and the town's best rates at Bancomer, on Zaragoza and Morelos (Mon–Fri 8.30am–4pm, Sat 10am–4pm), and Banamex, Mijares and Coronado (Mon–Fri 9am–4pm, Sat 10am–2pm).

Bookstore Libros Libros, Mijares 41. Also sells English-language newspapers.

Buses Águila ⓣ624/142-1100. Buses to Loreto (6hr; US$33) via Cabo San Lucas (30min; US$2) and La Paz (3hr; US$12) leave hourly. Also serve Tijuana (24hr; US$105).

Car rental Avis ⓣ624/142-1180 or 146-0201; Hertz ⓣ624/142-0375. National ⓣ624/142-2424; Quick ⓣ624/142-4600, ⓦwww.quickrentacar.com; Thrifty ⓣ624/142-1671.

Consulates Canada ⓣ624/142-4333.

Emergencies Police ⓣ624/143-3997 or 142-0361; hospital ⓣ624/143-1594.

Internet access and phones Espacio Internet, on Doblado five blocks west of the zócalo, across from the Coppola department store, has cheap rates (daily 10am–9pm, US$3/hr). Trazzo Digial Internet, off the zócalo, is more expensive, but has a much faster connection and reasonably priced international phone service (Mon–Fri 8am–9pm, Sat 9am–7pm, US$4/hr).

Post office On Mijares, on the way to the hotel zone from the beach (Mon–Fri 9am–6pm).

Tours and activities Lienzo Charro offers relatively inexpensive horseback tours to the surrounding mountains, while next door at Motosol shop (ⓣ624/143-9310, ⓦwww.atvsmotosol.com)

you can book ATV tours to the beach and mountains for around US$50; head to the corner of Mijares and Cansesco. EcoTours de Baja also runs trips to nearby Santiago and Miraflores (Ⓣ624/143-0775, Ⓔcapeland@prodigy.net.mx). Aztec Surf shop (Ⓣ624/146-9898, Ⓦwww.aztecsurf.com), 10min walk from the bus station down the Transpeninsular, rents boards for US$20/day, including rash guard, wax, and a roof rack; they also offer lessons for US$45. Bajawild, on Obregón and Guerrero, has kayaks and snorkeling rental (Ⓣ624/148-2222, Ⓦwww.bajawild.com). The botanical garden/museum Cacti Mundo is now open on Mijares just north of the golf course, exhibiting 11,000 examples of the plant from all over Mexico (Ⓣ624/146-9191; US$6, though students and seniors get a 50 per cent discount).

Los Barriles

On the eastern side of the peninsula, the land is rapidly being bought up and converted into residential property. Roughly 120km south of La Paz and 40km north of Cabo San Lucas, the East Cape encompasses Punta Pescadero, Los Barriles, Buena Vista, La Rivera, Cabo Pulmo and Los Frailes. The largest and most accessible resort is **LOS BARRILES**, a major **fishing** and **windsurfing** centre that takes advantage of the near-constant strong breeze in the bay. The wind, best in winter, is brilliant for experienced windsurfers (less so for beginners) and makes this a regular venue for international competitions. Hotels are expensive, and you almost certainly need to have booked in advance during high season in January and February; but you should be able to camp, either at one of the nearby trailer parks, or on the beach. Oddly, neither fishing nor windsurfing is easily arranged on the spot, and there's almost nowhere you can turn up and find an inexpensive room; *Hotel Palmas de Cortés* (Ⓣ624/141-0050, Ⓦwww.bajaresorts.com/palmas.htm; ❽) is the landmark **resort** here, well established and able to arrange activities and outings for you. Their room prices always include three meals, and they have good deals for groups. A block away, you can stop for a bite at *Tío Pablo's*, a US expat-run restaurant with a mammoth menu of delicious burgers, fish and salads.

Todos Santos

On the new road along the west coast, just north of the Tropic of Cancer, the farming town of **TODOS SANTOS** marks the halfway point between Cabo San Lucas and La Paz. It's also the closest thing to an exception to all the rules about the cape region, with great beaches in easy reach, affordable hotels and a bus service.

Founded in 1723 as a Jesuit mission, the fortunes of Todos Santos have risen and fallen ever since, at one time a successful farming community, then destroyed by an eighteenth-century indigenous uprising and introduced European diseases, before gaining then losing status as a major place for sugar-cane growing. In the 1970s, with the creation of the Transpeninsular highway, throngs of surfers came in search of giant waves, followed in the 1980s by an artistic crowd, many of whom settled here. When Hwy-19 was subsequently completed, the town became more easily accessed from La Paz and Los Cabos and now many drive here to experience some of the best **surfing** in Baja. There's also some great **whale-watching** to be had from the shore: sit on any of the beaches in the winter months and you are bound to see several of the creatures.

Today, the pleasant, leisurely paced town is home to a thriving community of artists, with a popular week-long **art festival** each February. There are plenty of galleries for you to check out, and if you feel like turning your own hand to being creative, you can join any of the **workshops**, teaching everything from writing to watercolours, pottery, and even improvisational theatre. Check the local monthly publication *El Calendario* for details, or look in the bookstore, Juárez at Hidalgo, for *El Tecolote Libros* magazine. Take the historic house **tours**, offered occasionally, and learn about the people and events that have woven themselves into town lore; again, details are posted around town. The most notorious bit of lore may well be that the local *Hotel California*, recently reopened, was the inspiration for the Eagles' signature song.

As for **beaches**, **Punta Lobos** and **San Pedrito** are among several strung out between here and Cabo San Lucas, the first few within a half-hour's walk: several blocks west from the centre is a dirt road marked with a sign that reads "Aviso oficial" (if you can't find it, ask around), which brings you to the south edge of Punta Lobos. From here, the rest of the beaches line the coast for 10km south: **San Pedro** (also known as **Las Palmas**) is beyond **Punta Lobos** and is excellent for swimming; **Los Cerritos**, 12km south (50m beyond Km 64), is also a good option for swimming. Note that due to riptides, steeply shelving beaches and rogue waves, only these last two beaches are safe for **swimming**.

Arrival and information

The highway runs through the middle of Todos Santos at Calle Colegio Militar. Here, and on parallel Juárez, are the **bank**, shops, **post office** and telephones. *El Tecolote* on Hidalgo at Juárez has a great selection of new and used **books**. The **bus** will drop you at the corner of Colegio Militar and Zaragoza.

Accommodation

Cabañas Quiñones 3km from the zócalo; follow signs from Juárez and Topete T 612/126-5113. Handful of small cottages with tiny kitchens, large bedrooms, private bath and ocean-view patios. Also has limited laundry facilties. 4

Hacienda Inn Todos Santos signposted along a dirt road north of town T 612/145-0073, W www.haciendainntodossantos.com. The lavish gardens, pool and Moorish domes are impressive, if out of place, at this near-luxury hotel with TV, a/c, fireplaces and a few rooms with kitchens; some rooms have ocean views. There's also a restaurant and laundry services – without your own transport, however, it's a bit far from town. 6

Hotel California Morelos, three blocks west of the main highway T 612/145-0525, E hotelcaliforniareservations@hotmail.com. Even if you're not on the trail of Eagles lore, an evening's stay at this gem might make it worth parting with some of those pesos you've been setting aside for a rainy day. The new owners have completed a beautiful restoration of the building, and the rooms are multicultural *mestizos* of Mexican and Moorish decor. Pool, sea views. 9

Hotel Miramar Verduzco and Pedrajo, three blocks west of the main highway T 612/825-0321. Basic rooms, some with sea views, a short walk from the beach but a little longer to the centre of town. The hotel has a laundry and pool. 4

Motel Guluarte Juárez at Morelos T 612/825-0006. Still one of the cheapest places in town. Fifteen rooms with fridge and fan (some have a/c and TV). Also has a small pool and car park, and sits next to a nice little market. 3

Todos Santos Inn Legaspi between Topete and Obregón T 612/145-0040, W www.mexonline.com/todossantosinn.htm. Four elegantly decorated rooms in a historic house, run by a US expat and right in the heart of the town, surrounded by excellent art galleries; the best luxury option in town. Has a wonderful garden patio too. Reservations recommended. 7

Way of Nature follow the signs from the Farmacia Guadalupe on Juárez T 612/126-6060, W www.wayofnature.com. Quiet B&B and meditation centre amid palms and farmland just west of town, a 5min walk from the beach. Accommodation is in palapa-like huts or hotel-style rooms, and breakfast is included. Camping is also possible. T'ai chi, yoga and massages are on offer, plus you can rent surf and boogie boards. No smoking or alcohol allowed in the rooms. 4

Eating

Places to eat are mainly on Colegio Militar: you'll find street stalls around the bus-stop area and a couple of decent restaurants at the traffic lights a block away.

Caffé Todos Santos Centenario 33 and Topete, three blocks north and two west from the bus stop ⓣ612/145-0340. Decorated by local artists, this expat-run café does fine breakfasts, coffees, teas, muffins and bagels. Their lunch and dinner menus are great as well, though the service can be a bit slow.

La Coronela inside the *Hotel California*. Good, slightly highbrow Mexican cuisine with a country slant, and tapas on a separate menu. The store next door sells everything from local handicrafts to Afghan carpets.

Lonchería Carla Hidalgo just off the road into town. An open-air café with flavourful quesadillas and burritos for US$1 apiece.

Mariscos Mi Costa on Colegio Militar at Ocampo. Excellent seafood place with a relaxed atmosphere, also serving decent tacos. Try the *sopa de mariscos* or shrimp *ceviche*.

Santa Fe on the zócalo at Centenario. A Todos Santos landmark, with excellent but pricey Italian food, best known for its homemade pasta. Set in a former hacienda with a lovely garden. Closed Tues.

Shut-up Frank's south of Pemex on the highway towards Cabo. The town's only sports bar, replete with great burgers and some traditional Mexican food.

Tacos Chilakos corner of Juárez and Hidalgo. Regarded as one of the best places for tacos in Baja.

The mainland route

The extraordinary desert scenery first grabs your attention on the **mainland route through the northwest** of the country. Between Tijuana and Mexicali, especially, stretches a region of awesome barrenness. As you continue south through the states of Sonora and Sinaloa, the desert becomes rockier, which, along with the huge cacti, makes for some archetypal Mexican landscapes. Only as you approach Mazatlán does the harshness finally start to relent, and some colour creep back into the land.

Historically, this part of Mexico was little more favoured than Baja California. The first Spanish explorers met fierce resistance from a number of indigenous tribes – the Pima, Seri and Yaqui are still among the least-integrated of Mexico's peoples – and it wasn't until the late seventeenth century that the Jesuit missionary **Padre Kino** established a significant number of permanent settlements. During the dictatorship of Porfirio Díaz, new roads and railways were established, and after the **Revolution** these links were used to open the region to irrigation and development programmes, leading to considerable agricultural wealth. Today the big **ranches** of Sonora and Sinaloa are among the richest in Mexico.

El Gran Desierto

If the peninsula of Baja California is desolate, the northern part of the state – to Mexicali and beyond into northern Sonora – is infinitely, yet spectacularly, more so. The **drive from Tijuana to Mexicali** is worthwhile for the views alone, as the mountains suddenly drop away to reveal a huge salt lake and hundreds of miles of desert below. This is **El Gran Desierto**, and it's a startlingly sudden change from the landscape that precedes it: the western escarpment up from Tijuana through **Tecate** (the small border town where the famous beer comes from) and beyond is relatively fertile and climbs deceptively gently, but the rains from the Pacific never get as far as the eastern edge, where the land falls away dizzily to the burnt plain and the road teeters between crags seemingly scraped bare by the ferocity of the sun. The heat at the bottom is incredible, the road down terrifying – the danger of its constant precipices proven by the piles of twisted metal at the bottom of so many of them. The more recent addition of the fast toll road has tamed the route somewhat, but it's still a fantastic trip.

Mexicali

MEXICALI, too, is hot – unbearably so in summer, though winter nights can drop below freezing – but despite its natural disadvantages it's a large, wealthy city, the capital of Baja California Norte and an important road and rail junction for the crossing into the States. It's also an increasingly important destination for Mexican migrants looking for work in the *maquiladoras* and, as in Tijuana 160km to the west, the city's hinterland is rapidly being covered by shantytown sprawl. While there may be an exotic ring to the name, there's nothing exotic about the place, and if you come looking for a movieland border town, swing-door saloons and dusty dirt streets, you'll be disappointed. There's more chance of choking on exhaust fumes or getting run over trying to cross the street. The name of the town is a sweet-sounding hybrid of Mexico and California, with an appalling sibling across the border, **CALEXICO**.

Though less touristed and industrialized than many of the larger border towns, it's not a place where you'd choose to spend time. Mexicali is really only valuable as a stop-off on the journey south, a daunting trip of at least nine hours on the bus to Hermosillo, the first place you might remotely choose to take a break, and a further hour and a half to the relatively more appealing Guaymas.

If you happen to be around during October you'll find a few cultural activities in town – live music, dance, cockfights and the like – taking place as part of the **Fiesta del Sol**; at any other time of year you can fill an hour browsing the local history exhibits at the free **Museo Regional de la Universidad de Baja California**, on Reforma.

Arrival and information

The Mexicali **border crossing** is open 24 hours and, except at morning and evening rush hours, is usually relatively quiet, with straightforward procedures. Remember to visit *migración* if you're travelling further on into Mexico. In **Calexico**, Imperial Avenue leads straight to the border, lined with handily placed automobile insurance offices, banks and exchange places that offer almost identical rates to those in Mexicali; the **Greyhound** bus station is one block from the frontier on 1st Street.

It's possible to get a Golden State bus from LA to the **Central Camionera** in Mexicali: the bus only comes as far as the border, where they bundle you into a taxi for the rest of the journey (included in bus fare). The **airport** lies some 20km to the east; supposedly fixed-price **taxis** (US$18, but you can bargain the price down by half) and minibuses shuttle passengers into town. You'll find a host of **car rental** booths at the airport.

Broad avenues lead away from the frontier: straight ahead is López Mateos, which will eventually take you directly out of town, passing close by the **bus terminal** on the way. To the left, off López Mateos and following the covered walkway from the border, stretches Madero, which, along with parallel Reforma, is the main commercial street downtown. The **local bus stand** is at the back of the small market just up from the border – a couple of blocks up López Mateos to the right. **Taxis** wait at ranks around the junction of López Mateos and Madero.

The **tourist information** booth (nominally daily 8am–7pm), well hidden opposite the vehicle entrance at the border, seldom seems to be open; the **main office** (Mon–Fri 9am–4pm; ☎686/556-1072) is a very long way down López Mateos at Calafia in the Centro Cívico, a journey not worth making unless you have a special reason. There are several **banks** and casas de cambio very close to the border – Bancomer, on Madero, is closest, and Banamex a couple of blocks up Madero near the **post office**. You can find **Internet access** at the *Mexicali Café*, López Mateos 485, at Morelos (Mon–Sat 9am–10pm; US$1/hr).

Accommodation

Most of Mexicali's cheaper hotels can be found in the older streets around the border, although as with most border towns, the cheapest places are a bit suspicious and are frequently of the hourly-rate type. If you're looking for somewhere more predictable, **Calexico** is a safer bet, with several motels charging under US$40 per night. Try for example the *Don Juan Motel*, 344 4th St East, between Hefferman and Heber (☎760/357-3231; ❺), or the newly renovated *El Rancho* (☎760/357-2458; ❺) opposite, both a short walk from the border.

In **Mexicali**, probably the cheapest acceptable hotel in the centre is *16 de Septiembre*, Altamirano 353 (☎686/552-6070; ❸), just south of Mateos; try to ignore the scantily clad women who line the stairway around dinner time. The *Hotel del Norte*, Madero 205 just off López Mateos (☎686/552-8101 ext 03, ⓔhoteldelnorte@hotmail.com; ❺), is one of the first things you see as you cross the border; it has a better interior than you might expect at first glance. The clean *Imperial*, Madero 222 (☎686/553-6333; ❺), and *Plaza*, Madero 366 (☎686/552-9757; ❺), in the next block, are simpler places and slightly less expensive. For less than the *Del Norte*, the *Hotel San Juan Capistrano*, Reforma 646 (☎686/554-6831; ❺), a few blocks further from the border, is a far better deal – a rather bland business hotel with a decent restaurant. Though it's a hike from the centre, *Hotel Burbujas*, Cansada and Independencia in Pueblo Nuevo (no phone; ❸), is one of the city's better – and safer – bargains. To get there, take a US$3 cab or a bus marked either "Calle 3" or "Wisteria" from the border and get off at Independencia, then walk one block. The *Motel Azteca de Oro*, Calle de la Industria 600 (☎686/557-1433; ❹), right by the train station, is comfortable and handy for transport: the *camionera* is only about ten minutes' walk away up López Mateos. More expensive hotels are mainly on the outskirts, particularly along Juárez – the modern, international-style *Lucerna*, for example, at Juárez 2151 (☎686/566-4700; ❼). One exception is the newer *Crowne Plaza*, near the Centro Cívico on López Mateos at Avenida de los Héroes (☎686/557-3600; ❾).

Eating

There are plenty of places to **eat** in the border area, too, with lots of stalls and small restaurants around the market and on Madero and Reforma. The restaurant in the *Del Norte* is convenient, and better than the hotel itself, while on Reforma at Calle D, about six blocks down, *La Parroquia*, though a bit touristy, serves good Mexican food. Entirely off the tourist track are the many restaurants and cafés in and around the Centro Cívico, on Independencia a couple

Moving on from Mexicali

Mexicali's **Central Camionera** (☎686/557-2410; with guardería) is 4km from the border on Independencia at Anahuac, close to the new **Centro Cívico** development and not far off López Mateos. To get there, take a "Calle 6" bus from the local bus stand off Mateos. Altogether well over fifty buses a day head **south** (twenty to Mexico City), and there's at least one local service an hour to **Tijuana**. Golden State has an office at the station: three buses leave daily for Los Angeles via Palm Springs. On the other hand, you'll have far more choice, and save a few dollars, if you walk across the border to Calexico's Greyhound station. **Flights** to Mexico City and Acapulco leave daily from the airport 20km east of town. Unfortunately, the **train** to Nogales and Guadalajara is no longer a commercial service.

of blocks from the Central Camionera. The Centro itself has a branch of *Sanborn's*, reliable as ever. *Café Petunias*, at Plaza Cholula 1091 off Calafia, is one of many in this area serving sandwiches, juices and lunch to office workers and shoppers.

Beyond Mexicali

Beyond Mexicali the road towards central Mexico trails the border eastwards, while the rail line cuts south around the northern edge of the Sea of Cortés – between them rises the Sierra del Pinacate, an area so desolate that it was used by American astronauts to simulate lunar conditions. Not far out of Mexicali you cross the border from Baja California into the state of **Sonora**; you'll have to put your watch forward an hour when you cross, unless Baja California Norte is on Daylight Saving Time (April–Oct), in which case there's no change.

There's little to stop for on the road. You'll pass through **San Luis Río Colorado**, something of an oasis with a large cultivated valley watered by the Colorado River, and **Sonoita** (or Sonoyta), a minor border crossing on the river of the same name. Both are pretty dull, though they have plenty of facilities for travellers passing through. Past Sonoita the road cuts inland and turns to the south, hitting the first foothills of the Sierra Madre Occidental, whose western slopes it follows, hugging the coast, all the way to Tepic. At **Santa Ana** it meets the Nogales road, and near the tiny village of **Benjamin Hill** rejoins the rail tracks. If you're travelling north you may well have to change buses at Santa Ana (especially en route to Nogales – there are far more buses to Mexicali), though there's little reason to venture outside the bus terminal.

Puerto Peñasco

On the former rail route there's just one place of any size, **PUERTO PEÑASCO**, a shrimping port that, while not particularly attractive, does have good beaches that attract large weekend crowds from across the border (Tucson is only about three hours away). The town has exploded over the past few years, and it's in danger of joining other Mexican resort towns that have grown too fast for their own good. Some colour is added to the place by local claims that during Prohibition, Puerto Peñasco was favoured by Al Capone as a base from which to smuggle *mescal* into the States.

Arrival and information

There's a good road down here from Sonoita, and a new one east to Caborca, not far from Santa Ana. Incidentally, if you're taking the bus from Nogales (there's only one per day) or arriving in the evening by car, you should be able to catch a spectacular sunset on the way; the road itself is fairly flat, but is flanked on all sides by the picturesque sierras and makes for some unforgettable vistas. If you have your own vehicle you may fancy the new detour, especially as it's quite easy to cut east to Caborca and rejoin the main road there. **Buses** are infrequent, with a couple of daily services each to Hermosillo, Mexicali and Nogales. The bus stations are located a few kilometres outside of town. One of the omnipresent white taxis (US$1.50 for a ride anywhere inside town) should get you to wherever you need to be.

The brochure-happy **tourist office** (Mon–Fri 9am–4pm; ⓣ638/383-6122) borders the outskirts of town on the road (Juárez) to Sonoita, and can set you up with a tour of the town and environs, including El Pinacate. Be sure to grab a copy of either the *Rocky Point Times* or *Join Us Here in Rocky Point*, both of which have a detailed town map as well as information on tours and activities, available for free at many local establishments. If you need to log on to the **Internet**, your best bet is Café Internet CiberChat, Calle 13 at Encinas (daily 10am–10pm, US$1/hr).

Accommodation

The cheap accommodation which seemed so commonplace here just a few years ago may now well be a thing of the past. **Rooms** tend to fill up and be more expensive when the weekend crowd shows up, but even mid-week and off-season you'll have a tough time if you are looking for budget accommodation.

Arizona Motel Pino Suárez and Calle 17, near Plaza Las Glorias ⓣ638/383-6502. Friendly staff at this fairly new motel in a quiet neighbourhood, offering clean, though somewhat cramped rooms with a/c and cable TV. ❺

La Casa del Puerto one block from the church in the old port ⓣ638/383-6209. Tasteful studios and one-bedroom suites with jacuzzi, sun deck, palapas and bar. A good deal for groups, the rooms here have luxurious touches, and prices drop slightly out of season. They also rent out kayaks and boogie boards at reasonable rates. ❼

Hotel Plaza Peñasco Av Sinaloa near the road to Caborca ⓣ638/383-5910. Best of the "budget" hotels, this clean outfit offers basic rooms, a pool with a bar, cable TV, and a secure car park. ❹

July Pino Suárez and Calle 15 (no phone). Much larger rooms than the *Arizona* a few blocks away, though this place is often full. 3min walk from the beach. ❹

Posada La Roca Primero de Junio 2, in the old port ⓣ638/383-3199. One of the oldest buildings in town, the rooms in this great stone building are cooled by the rock they're set in, though they all have a/c in case you need it. Ostensibly hosted Al Capone while he was surveying business options in Mexico. ❺

The Town and around

Though the **old port** used to be the centre of town, tourist dollars are pushing development along the coast in both directions, and now the action is divided between the malecón and Calle 13 across the harbour. From the old port, the main Bulevar Juárez runs nearly parallel to the water before heading off towards Sonoita. Many of the town's more reasonable hotels can be found around Calle 13, between Juárez and the colossal *Hotel Plaza Las Glorias* on the water.

There are plenty of opportunities for **fishing**, **diving** and **sailing** here; head to Sun 'n Fun Dive Shop (ⓣ638/383-5450, ⓦwww.sun-n-fun-divers.com) at the edge of the old port, where you can sort out diving excursions, rent gear as well as sign up for a fishing trip, a sunset cruise and even a clam-digging outing. Just up the street you'll find Pompano's Landing (ⓣ638/385-6036), which offers low-cost fishing trips, tours and paragliding. Most trips will bring you to **San Jorge Island** where you can swim with sea lions and dolphins and perhaps spot the rare and protected species of seahorse that lives here. The greatly changing tide brings hordes of crabs, oysters and starfish into the tide pools. You can also rent ATVs (US$20/hr) and jet skis (US$45/hr) at a host of places on Calle 13 towards the beach.

Another nearby attraction is the **El Pinacate Biosphere Reserve** (Mon–Sat 9am–5pm), 52km north of Puerto Peñasco on the road to Sonoita; buses don't stop here, but if you have your own transport it's worth the twenty-minute drive to the edge of the park and this phenomenal expanse of red cinder cones and craters. The latter are so massive – such as El Elegante, 1km wide and 120m deep – they can be seen from space, and the terrain is so other-worldly that NASA used it to help train the astronauts for the lunar-lander *Apollo 11*. You only need cover the first 25km to see El Elegante. Camping is allowed by arrangement with the visitor centre at the edge of the park; permits are given on a first-come, first-served basis. For more information, check with the tourist office in town.

Eating

Seafood stalls are gathered at the end of Eusebio Kino, while for more substantial Mexican food you can head for *Los Arcos* on Eusebio Kino at Tamarindos.

Café Plaza Las Glorias Inside the *Plaza Las Glorias*. One of Rocky Point's more upscale restaurants, they offer high-priced but very good seafood and international cuisine. Little atmosphere but stunning views. Bring your credit card or a wad of cash.

La Casa del Capitán follow Juárez to Antonio's liquor store; from there you'll see the entrance to the path leading to the top of the mountain – a 15min walk to the top. One of the nicest restaurants in town, and great for romantic dinners, with its postcard views of the town and the sea. They offer a full international menu, with a number of house seafood specialties, and live music at sunset.

Flavio's Malecón and Primero de Junio in the old port. Unpretentious place right on the boardwalk, favoured by residents for its excellent seafood and local prices.

The Friendly Dolphin Alcantan 44 in the old port. Local favourite with a full seafood menu and decent prices. Adorned with antique pictures of Mexico, the restaurant also serves on an outdoor patio upstairs. Occasionally one of the owners will play guitar and sing to the tables.

Gamma's Calle 13 right on the water, across from *Plaza las Glorias*. No-frills stand-by serves the best seafood in Puerto Peñasco, though not the place for a romantic dinner. Try the *ceviche*.

JJ's Cantina Cholla Bay. A beach-party seafood joint that does great fish. An excellent place to watch the sunset over the bay if you don't mind the American feel – monthly events, for example, include "Whiplash Racing" and "Bathtub Races".

Lily's Kino and Zaragoza. Standard Mexican fare at US prices, popular with Americans and always buzzing; the patio seating is great for people-watching.

La Ramada at Calle 13 and Francisco Villa. Inexpensive open-air taco and burrito stand with simple, cheap, and tasty food; try the meat-stuffed potatoes.

Sushi Sun Calle 13 and Elias Callas. Though it appears to be similar to many other Mexican restaurants, this mid-range place serves sushi that locals swear by. Specialties include tempura and Matsuri rolls, both made with local *camarones*. They also deliver.

Nogales to Hermosillo

Relative to most of the frontier, **NOGALES** (its name means "walnut trees", though few are in evidence) is a reasonably pleasant town. Although there is also a Nogales on the American side of the boundary, the closest US city of any size is the somewhat distant university town of Tucson, meaning that

Nogales is not part of a cross-border metropolis like Ciudad Juárez or Tijuana. It is a smaller, less frenetic place and therefore has a lower level of street hustling, vice and general nightlife options – but that is not to say those things do not exist.

The **Nogales pass** has been a significant staging post since explorers first travelled this way, and there is evidence of settlements in the area dating back to several thousand years BC. After the Conquest, it was used by Spanish explorers and surveyors, followed in rapid succession by evangelizing Jesuits (especially the celebrated Padre Kino) and Franciscans on their way to establish missions in California. Nogales itself remained no more than a large ranch, often existing in a state of virtual siege under harassment from the Apaches, until the war with the US and the ceding of Arizona, New Mexico, Texas and Alta California to the Americans in 1848. Thereafter, with the border passing straight through, the town was deliberately developed by both sides to prevent the periodic raids of the other. Yankee troops marched through a few years later, protecting Union supplies shipped in through Guaymas during the Civil War, and there was a constant traffic of rustling and raids from both sides – culminating in the activities of Pancho Villa in the years leading up to the Mexican Revolution. The railway to the coast brought the final economic spur, and the town's chief business remains that of shipping Sonora's rich agricultural produce to the States. Just over the border on the US side an excellent little **museum** of local history (Thurs–Sun 10am–4pm; free), run by the Pimeria Alta Historical Society, records all this, and some of the traditions of the Pima, whom this land originally belonged to.

There's little to see between Nogales and Santa Ana, and still less on the long stretch of desert highway from Santa Ana to Hermosillo. Shortly before Santa Ana, however, you pass through the small town of **Magdalena**, where most buses briefly stop. Here there's a mausoleum containing, under glass, the recently discovered remains of **Padre Kino**. Kino, "Conquistador of the Desert", was a Spanish Jesuit priest who came to Mexico in 1687 and is credited with having founded 25 missions and converted at least seven local indigenous tribes – among them the Apaches of Arizona and the Pima, Yuma and Seri of Sonora.

Nogales practicalities

Mexican Nogales is a provincial town, not a bad place in which to rest up and acclimatize for a day or two, though accommodation is pricier than in towns further from the US. Crossing the border (24hr) is straightforward; remember to have your tourist card stamped by *migración* if you're heading further south – there's also an office at the bus station where they can do this. Immediately by the border, the small **tourist office** (daily 9am–5pm; ☎631/312-0666) has a limited amount of local information and maps, while just beyond this you're in an area teeming with blanket stalls and cafés, and a few hotels. These last are concentrated on two streets leading away from the border: Obregón, which eventually becomes the highway south, and Juárez. There are several **banks**, most with ATMs (some giving US dollars), and casas de cambio along López Mateos and Obregón, but if you want to phone or send mail you're better off doing so across the border. You can find a good **Internet** café, Cyberflash, fifty steps from the border crossing on Internacional (Thurs–Tues 10am–10pm; US$1.50/hr).

If you're looking for an affordable **place to stay**, there's no need to go any further: possibilities include the *Imperial*, Internacional 79 (☎631/312-1458; ❹), right by the border fence west of the checkpoint and probably as basic as you'd want on your first night in Mexico; the *San Carlos*, Juárez 22 (☎631/312-1346; ❺), with more frills, including TV, a/c and free Internet access for guests; and the *Olivia*, Obregón 125 (☎631/312-4695; ❹), another step up in class. There are plenty of cafés and **restaurants** in the same area; *Café Olga*, on Juárez just across the border, is a Nogales institution. Many of the alternatives are far more touristy, some with live *mariachi* in the evenings: *Coco Loco*, Obregón 64, and *El Greco*, Pierson and Obregón, are good examples.

The main **bus station**, which is bordered by several smaller terminals, is on the highway about 5km south of town – local buses (signed "Central Camionera") run from the border, or you can take a taxi, which will cost around US$10. Southbound departures from the *camionera* – which has all the usual facilities including long-distance phones and guardería – are frequent, going as far south as Guadalajara (26hr) and Mexico City (34hr), though currently only TBC runs a direct route to Puerto Peñasco (3pm; 6hr; US$16), which leaves from the TBC station, several blocks north of the main terminal. On the other side of the border, the **Greyhound** station is right by the customs office; buses leave every one or two hours (6.45am–6.45pm) for Tucson and Phoenix. The **Nogales–Guadalajara train** is no longer operating as a commercial service, and there is little chance it will restart as such in the near future.

Agua Prieta

To the east lies another border crossing, **AGUA PRIETA**, just across from Douglas, Arizona. Still a quiet town that sees few tourists, it's gradually growing thanks to the *maquiladora* assembly plants on both sides of the border, and to new roads linking the town to **Janos** (for Ciudad Juárez and Nuevo Casas Grandes) and Hermosillo. Despite the fact that these roads are barely marked on many maps, they're paved highways, and Agua Prieta is thus on the only route from central Mexico to the Pacific between the border and Mazatlán; several buses a day run in each direction. If you're **staying** over, try the *Hotel Plaza* (no phone; ❺) on the central plaza, or the *Hotel La Hacienda* (☎633/338-0621; ❻), Calle 1 at Avenida 6, though you may find better value in Douglas, where there's a *Motel 6* (☎602/364-2457; ❺) among other inexpensive motels.

Hermosillo

From a distance **HERMOSILLO**, the state capital of Sonora, is an odd-looking place, surrounded by strange rock formations and presided over, right in the centre, by a tall outcrop crowned by radio masts, lit up at night like a helter-skelter. Close up, though, it's less interesting – the boom of the last half-century has wiped out almost everything that might have survived of the old town. Some of the earliest organized **revolutionaries**, including General Alvaro Obregón, were locals, as were many of the early presidents of revolutionary Mexico: Obregón himself, Huerta, whom he overthrew, Plutarco Elías Calles and Abelardo Rodríguez. Their many monuments and the streets named after them reflect the pride in local history. Today this is a thriving city and big ranching supply centre, with overflowing meat markets and shops full of tack gear, cowboy hats and boots.

While it's interesting enough to experience such a stereotypically Mexican town, there's no reason to stay here long; in any case, Hermosillo, spread out and car-oriented, is not geared to welcoming visitors, especially those without their own vehicle. If you do have to, or want to, spend time here, head down to the **beaches** at Bahía de Kino. Short stays can be enlivened by strolling down Serdán past the market, and taking a look at the attractive plaza around the cathedral, across Rosales from the bottom of Serdán. Or check out the **Centro Ecológico de Sonora**, about 5km south on Bulevar Rosales (closed Mon & Tues); take the "Luis Orcí" bus.

Arrival and information

Although the city sprawls, **downtown** Hermosillo is relatively compact. The highway comes into town as Bulevar Eusebio Kino, known as Bulevar Rosales as it runs north–south through the centre of town; crossing it, Bulevar Luis Encinas passes the **bus station** (ⓣ658/213-4455), 3km east of the centre, leaving town to the west, past the airport towards Bahía de Kino (see opposite). Virtually everything you might want to see lies in an area bounded by these two, as well as Juárez and Serdán, the main commercial street downtown, which runs past the bottom of the distinctive hill known as the Cerro de la Campaña.

From the rather isolated **Central Camionera** (with guardería), take a "Ruta 1" microbus, a van (marked "Ranchito") or a "Multirutas" town bus across the main road to get downtown. Taxis are rather expensive (US$4) and the drivers unwilling to bargain. Almost all the buses passing through Hermosillo are *de paso*, and at times it can be very hard to get on. However, TBC (depot outside the Central Camionera and left a few paces) run a local service to Guaymas, Navojoa and, four times daily, to Alamos. From the **airport**, a short way out on the road towards Bahía de Kino, you can pick up one of the usual fixed-fare taxis.

The **tourist office** (Mon–Fri 8am–3pm & 5–7pm, Sat 10am–1pm; ⓣ658/217-0060) is in the Edificio Sonora Norte, at Comonfort and Paseo Canal; they generally prove helpful, though they have little printed information and seem to come across few visitors.

Other facilities and shops are mostly on Serdán, including numerous **banks** and casas de cambio (there's also a handy Bancomer, with ATM, at Matamoros and Sonora, on the plaza a block from the *Monte Carlo* hotel). The **post office** is at the corner of Serdán and Rosales. Should you want to book a flight out, there is a **travel agency** inside the *Hotel San Alberto* (ⓣ658/212-2670). For surfing the **Internet**, try Contacto X at Niños Héroes and Guerrero (Mon–Sat 11am–11pm, Sun 1–8pm; US$1.50/hr) or visit Biblioteca (no relation to the real library) right by the post office.

Accommodation

Nearly all the cheaper **hotels** in Hermosillo are strikingly poor value, but some very pleasant mid-range places cater to business people and the wealthy rancheros who come here for the markets. One budget favourite with very helpful staff is the *Hotel Washington*, at Noriega 68 near Guerrero (ⓣ658/213-1183; ❹), with good-value rooms, excellent hot showers and free coffee in the lobby. Otherwise, the *Hotel Niza*, Plutarco Elías Calles 66, just off Serdán near the market (ⓣ658/217-2028; ❹), has a good location, but not great atmosphere. Much nicer, if you can afford them, are a couple of businesslike places down on Rosales: the solidly comfortable *Hotel San Alberto*, Serdán and Rosales (ⓣ658/213-1840; ❺), and the colonial-style *Hotel Kino*, Pino Suarez 151, just off Rosales near the cathedral plaza (ⓣ658/213-3131; ❻), which is really a motel but has all facilities including a pool. The more expensive hotels, and a number of motels, are almost all in the hotel zone, a long way from the centre on Kino.

Eating

Downtown Hermosillo is surprisingly short of decent **places to eat**: Serdán and the surrounding streets are lined with plenty of juice bars and places selling tortas and other snacks, but locals in search of fancier food tend to get in their cars and head for the restaurants situated on the main boulevards or in the hotel zone. All the hotels mentioned above have restaurants that are at least passable, and there are several places on and around the plaza by the *Hotel Monte Carlo*: try *Napy's*, Matamoros 109 between Noriega and Morelia; the vegetarian restaurant and wholefood shop *Jung*, Niños Héroes 75 between Matamoros and Guerrero; or *La Fabula Pizza*, a branch of a chain at Morelia 34 between Matamoros and Juárez. *Rin-Rin Pizza*, just west of the *Hotel Washington* (see opposite), is an option for cheaper but greasier pizza.

Bahía de Kino

Offering the nearest beaches to Hermosillo, **BAHÍA DE KINO**, 117km west, is a popular weekend escape for locals and increasingly a winter resort for Americans, many of whom have second or retirement homes here. There are two settlements around the bay: the old fishing village of **Kino Viejo**, a dusty collection of corrugated-iron huts, passed over by the fruits of development, and the younger **Kino Nuevo** – basically a single road strung with one-storey seafront houses, trailer parks, and a couple of hotels and restaurants. There's really not a lot to it, but the beach is good, with miles of sand – and the offshore islets and strange rock formations make the sunsets even more spectacular.

This whole area used to be inhabited by the **Seri** peoples, and there are still a few communities living round about: one such, on the offshore **Isla del Tiburón** (Shark Island), was relocated when the island was made into a wildlife refuge. You may come across Seri hawking traditional and not-so-traditional ironwood carvings along the beach in Kino Nuevo. The tiny **Museo de los Seris** (Tues–Fri 8am–6pm; US$0.50), on the "plaza" in the middle of Kino Nuevo, gives a little more information on Seri history.

Buses leave Hermosillo from a small bus station on Sonora, a block and a half east of the *Monte Carlo*. There are about nine a day – hourly from 5.30am to 9.30am, then every two hours up to 5.30pm – with more at busy weekends; they take around two hours. There are few hotels in town, and none caters to anyone on a budget; one of the last places on the road is the *Trailer Park Bahía Kino* (Ⓣ662/242-0216), where during off-season you should be able to pitch a tent for US$15. If you are reasonably discreet and careful with your stuff, **camping** on the Kino Nuevo beach is also a possibility. Opposite the trailer park, the restaurant *Jorges* is a good place to make enquiries about the local area, to sample the local **seafood**, or simply to enjoy a beer and watch the sun go down. The *Hotel Saro* (Ⓣ662/242-0007; ❺), soon after you enter Kino Nuevo, has a/c and TV, and another decent restaurant; otherwise, try the nicer *Posada del Mar Hotel* (Ⓣ662/242-0155; ❻), which has a pool, also at the southern end of town. The *Posada Las Aves*, Veracruz near Nautla (Ⓣ662/242-0242; ❻), is perhaps your best option, as it's quite clean and only two blocks from the water.

Guaymas and around

Back on the route south the next major stop is **GUAYMAS**, an important port with a magnificent, almost enclosed natural harbour, where the mountains come right down to the sea. Although Guaymas claims a proud history – seemingly every adventurer whose eyes ever turned greedily to Mexico sent a gunship into the bay – there's really nothing to see beyond a couple of grandiose Porfiriano bank buildings on the main street. Nonetheless, if you have to choose somewhere to stop, this is definitely a more attractive option than Hermosillo, ninety minutes away, or Los Mochis, six hours on.

The Americans, the French and the British have all at one time or another attempted to take Guaymas (only the Americans had any real success, occupying the town in 1847–48). At one point, a French count, **Gaston Raousset de Bourbon,** attempted to carve out an empire in Sonora with the tacit support of the then president General Santa Ana. Raousset invaded twice, holding Guaymas for several months in 1852, but his second attempt in 1854 was less successful and ended with most of the pirates, the count included, captured and shot. There are monuments to the hero of that battle – one General Yañez – all over town.

Today, Guaymas is still a thriving fishing and naval centre and makes few concessions to tourism. At the waterfront there's an attractive plaza where you can sit and look out over the deep bay, alive with the comings and goings of ships, and the scores of fishing boats at anchor. It would be a fantastic site for outdoor waterfront cafés, but unfortunately the dockside is still rough and looks more like a building site. Still, it's a pleasant spot, and there are also some good beaches a short bus ride away.

Arrival

Virtually everything that happens in Guaymas happens on Serdán, the main drag, which brings southbound traffic from the highway into town from the west, and leaves to the east for Ciudad Obregón via the docks, passing the now defunct train station.

The **airport**, off the highway west of town, is closer, though here you'll have to rely on taxis for transport. Most people arrive by **bus**, however: the three terminals serving Tres Estrellas, Norte de Sonora, Baldamero Corral (TBC) (☎622/224-2949) and Pacífico are right opposite each other on Calle 14 at Rodríguez, a couple of blocks off Serdán and within walking distance of all the action. **Ferries** from Santa Rosalía arrive at the docks 2km east of the centre, easily reached on local buses along Serdán.

Accommodation

From the bus stations, Rodríguez leads towards the centre, the street numbers rising as you go. In the first block you pass what looks like a Venetian castle, but is in fact the town jail. The best of the budget **places to stay** in Guaymas is the *Casa de Huéspedes Lupita*, Calle 15 no. 125 (☎622/224-1945; ❷), by the prison

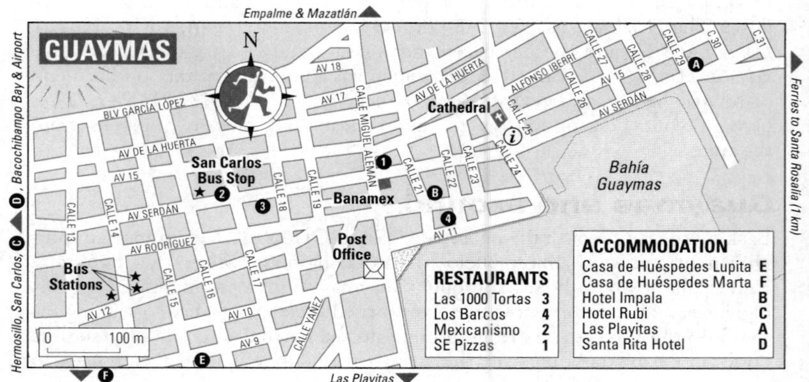

and just a block from the bus stations. You'll pay a few dollars more for a/c and private bath. Nearby is their smaller sister hotel *Casa de Huéspedes Marta*, at Calle 13 and Avenida 9 (☎622/222-8332; ❷), with similar rooms and slightly higher prices. For a little more comfort, carry on into town and try the *Hotel Impala*, Calle 21 at Avenida 12, one block off Serdán (☎622/224-0922; ❹), an older place whose prices are inflated because it has had a face-lift, or the *Hotel Rubi*, Serdán and Calle 29 at the far end of the waterfront (☎622/224-0169; ❹), better value for simple, quiet courtyard rooms with private bath, TV and a/c. In the other direction, at Serdán and Mesa (aka Calle 9), the *Santa Rita Hotel* (☎622/222-8100; ❹) is also worth a try (not to be confused with the more expensive motel of the same name). Perhaps the best place to stay is the comfortable motel–trailer park complex, *Las Playitas* (☎622/221-5196; ❸), which offers furnished cottages in a quiet spot overlooking the bay. It's out of town on the coast at nearby Las Playitas (see below; take a taxi, or the local bus).

Eating

Mercado Municipal, a block off Serdán on Calle 20, sells fresh food good for picnics, but Guaymas has plenty of inexpensive, no-nonsense **places to eat**. On Calle 17 and Serdán you'll find a well-priced buffet at *Mexicanismo*, open until midnight every day. Further up, between calles 17 and 18, and also at Calle 10, *Las 1000 Tortas* dishes out tasty tortas, tacos, quesadillas and comidas. Off to the right you'll find *Restaurant Mandarin*, a Mex-Chinese place in the *Hotel Impala*. Opposite Banamex, *SE Pizzas* also offer a great buffet deal, all you can eat and a soft drink for US$3. To sample some of the town's best **seafood** head for *Los Barcos* on the seafront, Avenida 11 at Calle 20, with its huge palapa dining area.

Listings

Banks Mostly on Serdán, including Bancomer at C 18, and Banamex at C 20. Both have 24hr ATMs.
Buses Many first-class buses on the Mazatlán–Hermosillo run stick to the main highway, skipping Guaymas. There are, however, second-class buses in both directions. TBC runs buses to Mazatlán, Alamos, Tucson and Phoenix.
Ferries Boats to Santa Rosalía in Baja California leave from the docks about 2km beyond Guaymas centre – just about any bus heading east on Serdán will take you there. There are currently three sailings a week (Mon, Thurs and Sat, 10pm) and you buy tickets from the terminal (sales and reservations Mon–Sat 8am–3pm; ☎622/222-2324) or at the TNS bus station; check the timetable and reserve in advance if possible, which you'll need to do if you plan to take a car across. Single fares for the 7hr crossing are US$41 for a reclining seat, US$115 sharing a simple four-berth cabin and US$200 for a small car. Ferries may not sail if the wind is too strong.
Internet access Available near Banamex on Calle 20, just north of Serdán, or at Joakin's Internet Café, Calle 28 off Serdán.
Post office Avenida 10 just off Calle 20 (Calle Miguel Alemán), which runs south from Serdán and round the side of the bay.
Telephones Farmacia Bell, Serdán at C 22, as well as in the bus terminal.
Tourist information A tiny booth is at Serdán and Calle 25, right across from the waterfront.
Tours and activities Be sure to pick up the "What is There to do in San Carlos" brochure at the tourist information booth, which lists several dozen outfitters who offer everything from fishing, diving, golf, to the newest rage down here, kite-surfing.

Beaches around Guaymas

You may be told that there are beaches at **LAS PLAYITAS**, on the other side of Guaymas' bay. Don't believe it: the *Las Playitas* motel–trailer park has a pool and a good restaurant, but the beach is entirely wishful thinking. If you've a couple of hours to kill, though, it is interesting to take the bus out this way for the ride – you can stay on all the way and eventually it will turn round and head back home. You get to see the shipbuilding industry, the fish-freezing and processing centres, and some fine views of the outer stretches of the wreck-strewn bay.

The best beach, and the one the locals use, is at **MIRAMAR**, an upmarket suburb on Bacochibampo Bay, a few kilometres north of Guaymas. On balance, this is your best bet for swimming, though there is more happening 16km further north at **SAN CARLOS** (also sometimes known as "Nuevo Guaymas" in an attempt to foster increased tourism), a town in the infant stages of becoming a larger resort geared towards a mainly retired clientele, with a marina, a golf course and scores of villas and half-completed developments linked to the highway north by a long avenue of transplanted palms. There are some lovely-looking bays here, but access to the shore is difficult, and most of the beaches you can reach are stony. As compensation you can rent all manner of **diving and fishing** gear or go on sightseeing **cruises** at Gary's (ⓣ622/226-0049, ⓦwww.garysdiveshop.com), about 1km south of the marina; they also have a fast broadband Internet connection available every day except Sunday. If you want to **stay**, the *Totonaka RV Park* (ⓣ622/226-0481, ⓦwww.mexonline.com/totonaka.htm; ❺) is as good a deal as any, on the right-hand side as you enter town; they also offer free Internet usage from their office. *Posada del Desierto Apartments* (ⓣ622/226-0467, ⓔpasadadesierto@yahoo.com; ❺) has inexpensive apartments, though the deals are much better if you have a group of three or more. There are some decent **eating** options; *Rosa's Cantina* on the main strip serves fine tortas and other Mexican dishes, and next door there's an unnamed taco joint attached to the equally anonymous farmacia, another good option for cheap eats. If you want some excellent seafood, try *Charly's Rock* across from the *Totonaka RV Park*; the restaurant serves enormous lobsters and is also a good spot to have a drink and watch the sun go down. If you happen to be in town at the weekend, head to the Santa Rosa Market where you can buy an excellent sirloin steak for US$2, which they'll cook for free.

Head over the hill beyond San Carlos and you'll come to **ALGODONES**, where *Catch-22* was filmed – the beaches here are private. If you have your

The Yaqui

Between Guaymas and Ciudad Obregón lies the valley of the Río Yaqui, traditional home of the **Yaqui** people. The Yaqui were perhaps the fiercest and most independent of the Mexican peoples, maintaining virtual autonomy until the beginning of the twentieth century. Rebellions and, at times, outright war against the government of the day were frequent – the most significant coming in 1710 and again, after Independence, in 1852. The last major uprising was in 1928 during the brief presidency of General Alvaro Obregón. The president, himself a Sonoran, was assassinated in Mexico City but his plans for the development of the northwest laid the basis for peace with the Yaqui; this was aided, no doubt, by the fact that earlier regimes had shipped rebels out wholesale to work on the tobacco plantations of Oaxaca. Today the Yaqui enjoy a degree of self-rule, with eight governors, one for each of their chief towns, but their cultural and political assimilation has been rapid. One surviving element of Yaqui culture is the celebrated **Danza del Venado**, or "Stag Dance", not only performed frequently at local festivals in the villages of this area but also at folklore festivals throughout the republic – and it forms one of the centrepieces of the Ballet Folklórico in Mexico City. The chief dancer wears a deer's head, a symbol of good (the stag being the sacred animal of the Yaqui), and is hounded by one or more coyote dancers, falling eventually, after a gallant struggle, to these forces of evil.

own transport, head past the *Plaza San Carlos* and turn left towards the water onto any dirt road, which will bring you to an uncrowded, public beach.

Buses for Miramar and San Carlos leave Guaymas every thirty minutes or so from Calle 19 by the post office, but it's easier to catch them as they head up Serdán, for example at the corner of Calle 18. It can take up to an hour to reach San Carlos. To get to Las Playitas, hop on the bus marked "Parajes" from Calle Miguel Alemán; to get to Algodones from San Carlos, follow the strip that leads to the marina and its restaurants, or take a taxi.

Ciudad Obregón to Alamos

On the main highway, there's little to tempt you to stop between Guaymas and the Sonora state border. **CIUDAD OBREGÓN**, founded in 1928 and named after the president, has thrived on the agricultural development that accompanied the plans to utilize the Río Yaqui. Thanks to the irrigation schemes and huge dams upriver it's now a very large and uncompromisingly ugly town. About the only draw is for fans of cowboy clothing: locally produced **straw stetsons** are among the best and least expensive you'll find anywhere.

NAVOJOA, too, is a rather dull farming town. Where it scores over Ciudad Obregón is in having a reasonably priced hotel, a good market, and above all in being the jumping-off point for Alamos (see below). If you have some time to pass here, it's well worth checking out the **Museo Yaqui** on Calle Allende and 5 de Febrero. Most **buses** (usually *de paso*) pull into either the TBC or Transportes de Pacífico stations, near each other around the junction of Guerrero and Calle No Reelección a couple of hundred metres away from the train station. Local buses to Alamos (hourly 6.30am–6.30pm) generally leave from either station. The Transportes de Pacífico bus station is handy for one of the town's cheaper **hotels**, the *Aduana* (❷) on Ignacio Allende, which has a/c rooms and a restaurant-bar inside. Unless it's necessary, you're better off heading straight through to Alamos.

Alamos

The existence of **ALAMOS**, a Spanish colonial town and national historical monument just five hours' drive from the US border and 50km southeast of Navojoa, hasn't escaped the notice of scores of Americans – predominantly artists and retirees – who have chosen to settle here over the last forty years or so, often renovating the otherwise doomed-to-decay colonial architecture. The expat community lives in near-complete social isolation from the local Mexicans, but the necessary economic interaction at least stops Alamos going the way of so many other ex-mining villages in the region. A ride out here to this patch of green makes a very pleasant respite from the monotony of the coastal road. And it's a great place to do nothing for a while: a tour of the town takes no longer than a couple of hours, and there's little else to do but walk in the mountains (an exceedingly hot exercise in summer). The meeting here of the Sonoran and Sinaloan deserts at the foot of the Sierra Madre Occidental has created a fairly distinct ecosystem, home to a broad range of flora and fauna. In particular, this is a **bird-watching** mecca, boasting several hundred different species. Thousands of people descend upon Alamos at the end of January for the annual week-long Ortiz Tirado **music festival**, in honor of the late Dr Alfonso Ortiz Tirado, sometimes referred to as the "Mexican Pavarotti". Accommodation is usually booked solid at this time, so reservations are a must.

Coronado was the first European to pass through this area in 1540, spending most of his time trying to subjugate the Mayo and Yaqui, unaware that below his feet lay some of the richest **silver ore** in Mexico. Silver was discovered late in the seventeenth century and Alamos became Mexico's northernmost silver-mining town, within a century a substantial city with its own mint, on the coastal branch of the Camino Real, and the most prosperous town north of Guadalajara. With Mexican Independence, control fell into the hands of the Alamada family who, despite having initially productive mines, spent the rest of the nineteenth century protecting their property from political wranglings and petty feuds, and watching over the region's decline. The mint closed in 1896, and even the brief existence of a railway only served to help depopulate a dying town. Alamos languished until the 1940s, when an American, **William Levant Alcorn**, bought numerous houses here and set about selling the property to his countryfolk. A bank was built in 1958, an airstrip opened, and a paved road from Navojoa was finished two years later. Today the population hovers around the 10,000 mark.

The Town and around

The town's focal point is the beautiful old arcaded **plaza** and the elegant eighteenth-century **cathedral**. Opposite the arcade on the Plaza de Armas, the mildly diverting **Museo Costumbrista de Sonora** (Mon–Fri 9am–1pm & 3–6pm; US$1) illustrates the town's zenith through a mock-up of the mine, and grainy photos of moustachioed workers (note that it's all done in Spanish, however). More interesting are the town's magnificent old Andalucian-style **mansions**, brooding and shuttered from the outside, but enclosing beautiful flower-filled patios. If poking your head through gaping doorways and visiting the restaurants or bars of houses converted into swanky hotels doesn't satisfy your curiosity, you can take an hour-long **house tour** (Sat 10am; US$8), which leaves from by the bank on the Alameda and visits some of the finest, predominantly American-owned, homes. You could also hire one of the informative, English-speaking **guides**

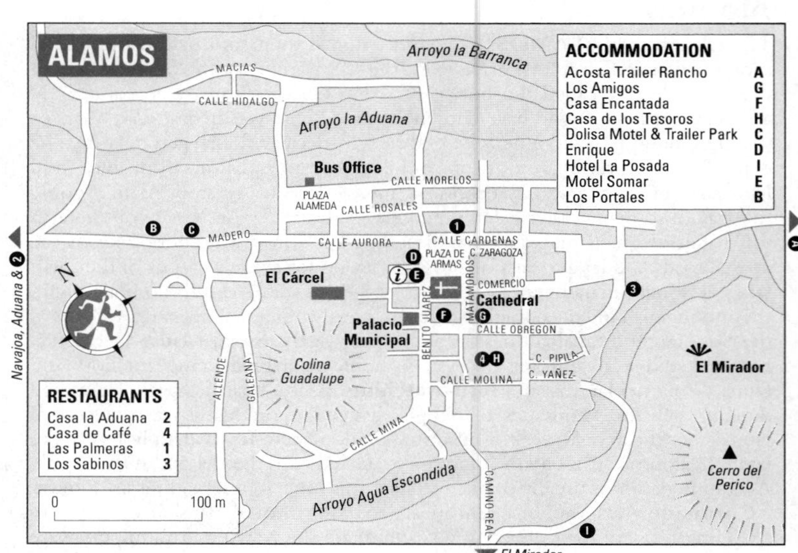

who hang out in front of the tourist office (see below) and can walk you around the town and up to **El Cárcel**, a weathered stone jail that overlooks the town from Colina Guadalupe – the views alone are worth the trip – where you can buy crafts woven by the tiny prison's handful of detainees. Guides may also take you to **El Mirador**, the best vantage point in town, from where you can see the whole of Alamos and take in the beautiful vistas of the surrounding Sierra Madre.

Arrival and information

From Navojoa hourly **buses** run to Alamos (6.30am–6.30pm; 1hr), arriving at the bus station on Morelos by the Alameda. There is a **Bancomer**, with an ATM, across the park on Rosales. Follow Rosales east, then Juárez south to reach the Plaza de Armas, the cathedral and the enthusiastic **tourist office** (Mon–Fri 9am–1pm & 3–6pm, Sat & Sun 9am–1pm; ⓣ647/428-0450), in the same location as the *Los Portales* hotel – walk up to the hotel, and underneath the veranda is the tourist office. For reliable information talk to Celsa in *Las Palmeras*, or *Los Amigos* (see below) produces a good pamphlet on the history of Alamos. The **post office** is on the approach into town, opposite the *Dolisa Motel and Trailer Park*. There are a few places with **Internet** access in town; try Compuimagen, Morelos 37 (7.30am–11pm), or head to *Los Amigos* (see below).

For **moving on from Alamos**, there are six daily TBC buses (ⓣ647/428-0175) leaving for Navojoa, Guaymas and Hermosillo in the morning, returning in the late afternoon and evening.

Accommodation

Low-cost accommodation in Alamos is hard to come by, but there are some beautiful, moderately priced hacienda-style places, with cool rooms ranged around orchid-draped courtyards. You'll pay ten to twenty percent less outside the high season of November to April. The town also boasts two **trailer parks**, both offering some rooms: *Dolisa Motel and Trailer Park* (ⓣ647/428-0131; ❸–❹), a convenient though often crowded site at the entrance to town (open all year); and *Acosta Trailer Rancho,* about 1km east of town (Oct–April; ⓣ647/428-0246; ❷–❸), a secluded park with camping spots and a pool. To get there, follow Morelos east across the usually dry Arroyo La Aduana, then turn left at the cemetery.

Los Amigos Obregón 3 ⓣ647/428-1014, ⓔjmtoevs@hotmail.com. Charming B&B with a café, Internet access, a newsstand, burgeoning art gallery and book swap; is also the source of the Alamos newsletter. The rooms are spacious and good value and their palapa is a great place from which to watch the activity in the square at dusk. ❻
Casa de los Tesoros Obregón 10 ⓣ647/428-0400. Just along from the *Casa Encantada*, up behind the cathedral, this eighteenth-century former convent now has a pool and beautifully decorated rooms. A/c for summer, fireplace for winter. Add US$4 if you'd like breakfast. ❼
Casa Encantada Obregón 2 ⓣ647/428-5760. Beautiful 300-year-old mansion with fully refitted rooms, some with a/c. The same people also run *Hotel La Mansión* across the road, which has a pool. Breakfast included. Closed Jun–Sept. ❻
Enríque Juárez on the Plaza de Armas ⓣ647/428-0280. Comfortable and cheap rooms around a planted courtyard. The best budget option in town, though only one room has a private bath. ❸
Hotel La Posada Follow signs from *Casa de los Tesoros* ⓣ647/428-0045. Luxuriously furnished apartments with kitchen and all modern conveniences; large group rooms available. ❻
Motel Somar On the approach into town, near the *Dolisa Motel and Trailer Park* ⓣ647/428-0195. Big and soulless but cheap and clean. Rooms have bath and fan. ❹
Los Portales Juárez on the Plaza de Armas ⓣ647/428-0211. Beautiful restored hacienda, formerly owned by the Alamada family and currently owned by the Alcorns, with pleasant rooms around a broad stone courtyard, but no a/c or pool. ❺

Eating and drinking

The best **restaurants** in Alamos are at the fancier hotels, in particular the *Casa Encantada*, *La Posada* and *Casa de los Tesoros*. Opposite *Hotel La Mansión* is *La Casa de Café*, a great breakfast place for scrumptious coffee and cake in the courtyard. Right on the plaza, *Las Palmeras* serves excellent Mexican food at very reasonable prices, and *Los Sabinos* (follow signs from *Los Tesoros*) is also highly recommended for steak. There are a number of run-of-the-mill cheaper places around the **market** that fronts onto the Alameda, and locals make for the roaming taco stand *Fortino's* when it lands in front of the cathedral at weekends. If you have your own transport, try *Casa La Aduana*, about 4km outside of town on the road to Navojoa; at the signpost for Aduana, take the dirt road for about 2km into the hills. They serve Spanish and French dishes with a Mexican twist.

Into Sinaloa: Los Mochis

As you continue down the coast and cross into the state of Sinaloa, the next place of any size is **LOS MOCHIS**, another modern agricultural centre, broad-streeted and rather dull, but a major crossing point for road, rail and ferry, and above all the western terminus of the incomparable **rail trip** between here and Chihuahua through the Barranca del Cobre (see box, p.141).

The various modes of **transport** into and out of this area are infuriating in their inability to connect – even the bus stations are on opposite sides of town – and the Chihuahua–Los Mochis route is now the only rail option. The ferry, meanwhile, leaves from the port at Topolobampo, 24km away, and although the Chihuahua line goes there, the train doesn't carry passengers beyond Los Mochis. Again, see the box on p.141.

No matter how you arrange things, if you're taking the ferry or train you'll have little choice but to **stay** at least one night here – and don't expect much excitement. The sweltering grid of streets that makes up Los Mochis has no real focus, but what there is of a **town centre** is on Hidalgo, between Prieto and Leyva. From the Tres Estrellas station, head right along Juárez and then, after four blocks, left onto Leyva; from Pacífico turn left along Morelos and take the next left onto Leyva.

To kill an afternoon you could pop out to **TOPOLOBAMPO**, a strange place on an almost Scandinavian coastline of green, deeply inset bays – there's water all around but the ocean itself is invisible and the ferry steams in through a narrow channel, appearing suddenly from behind a hill into what seems a

Driving in Sinaloa

If you have your own vehicle, you should take particular care in Sinaloa. The usual hazards of Mexican **driving** seem amplified (for more on which see p.42), especially around Culiacán, where there are some particularly hazardous stretches of Hwy-15 and there have been reports of robberies and attacks; the smooth new toll road that avoids this is extremely expensive and is also said to be prey to bandits. More importantly, remote areas of the state are notorious **drug-growing** centres, and inquisitive strangers are not welcome, so stick to the main roads and don't even think about hitching here. For the same reason, there's an especially high concentration of checkpoints along the highways.

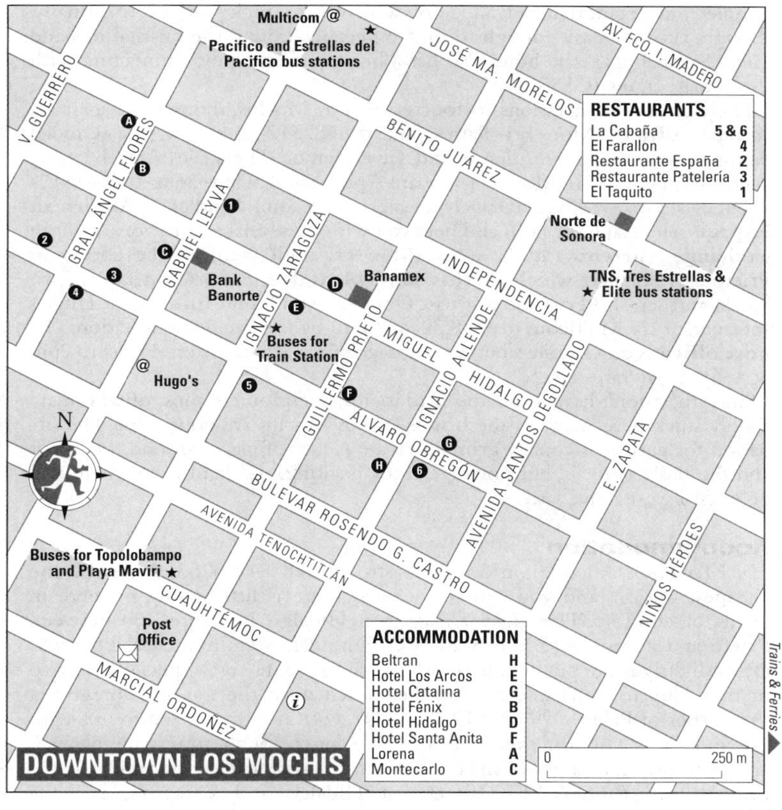

landlocked lake. There are no beaches, unfortunately, but you might persuade a local fisherman to take you out for a ride round the bay and a swim off the boat. The Sociedad Cooperativa de Servicios Turísticos runs trips out to the offshore islands, some of which host colonies of sea lions. The beach favoured by locals is **Playa Maviri**, ten minutes by bus from Cuauhtémoc, between Zaragoza and Prieta.

Practicalities

The Pacífico and Estrella del Pacífico **bus stations** are next to each other on Morelos between Zaragoza and Leyva. Norte de Sonora, Tres Estrellas and Elite are based on Santos Degollado, between Juárez and Morelos, within easy walking distance of most downtown hotels and restaurants. The **train station** is 3km from the centre and, although there are frequent buses (marked "Colonia Ferrocarril") from Zaragoza, between Hidalgo and Obregón, you can't rely on them to get you there in time for the 6am departure or to meet the late-evening arrival of trains from Chihuahua. **Taxi** fares in Los Mochis are a long-established rip-off, so grin and bear it: if you're aiming to catch an early morning train, try to gather a group of people and arrange in advance for a driver to pick you up. Normally, though, taxis are easy enough to find, especially around the bus stations and *Hotel Santa Anita* – the hotel also has a bus for guests only, connecting with the tourist trains (US$5).

There are few concessions to tourism in Los Mochis, though you'll find a **tourist office** (Mon–Fri 9am–3pm; ⓣ668/812-6640) in the Unidad Administrativa building, Allende and Cuauhtémoc. The Viajes Aracely travel agent, Obregón 471 (Mon–Fri 8.30am–7pm, Sat 8.30am–2pm; ⓣ668/812-2084, ⓕ815-8787, ⓔventasaracely@viajesaracely.com), handles all **American Express** needs, and they can also help you with train-related questions. You can **exchange currency** at Banamex (Mon–Fri until 2pm), at the corner of Prieto and Hidalgo, which also has an ATM, as does Banorte on Leyva. Two blocks further on Leyva and just past Obregón, you'll find **Internet** at Hugo's Internet, or try Multicom (daily 8.30am–9pm) by the Pacífico bus station. The **post office** is on Ordoñez, between Zaragoza and Prieto (Mon–Fri 9am–2pm & 4–6pm, Sat 9am–1pm).

Since they don't have to try too hard to attract customers, most of whom are simply stuck here, many of the **hotels** in Los Mochis are poor value. The situation for **eating** is equally grim: there are plenty of places around the hotels and the bus terminals, but nowhere really exciting, and hardly anywhere will be open if you arrive late.

Accommodation

Hotel Los Arcos, Allende Sur 534 at Castro (ⓣ668/812-3253; ❸), is still the cheapest option, and you can see why as there is little going on here in terms of comfort. The *Hotel Hidalgo*, on Hidalgo Poniente 260 between Prieto and Zaragoza (ⓣ668/818-3453, ⓔhhidalgo@imm.megared.net.mx; ❹), is slightly more put-together and worth the extra cost, especially for two or more (up to four) sharing. Another notch up is the *Lorena*, Obregón at the corner of Prieto (ⓣ668/812-0239; ❺), with fifty mid-sized rooms with a/c and TV; if you ask, they will fix you a lunch for the train ride packed, and they also have a good, cheap Mexican restaurant upstairs. Similar is the tidy *Beltran* (ⓣ668/812-0710; ❺), at Hidalgo and Zaragoza, and the *Montecarlo*, Flores at Independencia (ⓣ668/812-1818; ❺), where plain, clean rooms are set around a colonial-style courtyard; make sure that you get one of the larger rooms as their rooms vary in size, but not in price. You can also try the renovated *Hotel Fénix* (ⓣ668/812-2623, ⓔhotelfenix@email.com; ❺), which has a café inside and is a great alternative if the others in this range are full. The luxury option is the modernish and rather bland *Hotel Santa Anita* on the southwest corner of Leyva and Hidalgo (ⓣ668/818-7046, ⓦwww.mexicoscoppercanyon.com; ❽), owned by the same people who operate many of the fancier lodges along the Copper Canyon line. The rooms themselves are nice but bland, predictable international hotel-style. The hotel also offers a rather expensive restaurant, a bar with live music and a travel agency, which is good for information. They should give you a slight discount in the off-season, but they can be full with tour groups during the high season.

Eating and drinking

You're not going to do much gourmet dining in Los Mochis. *La Cabaña*, on the corner of Obregón and Allende, serves excellent tacos and burritos; there's a second branch on Zaragoza and Obregón. For particularly good breakfasts and light meals in clean surroundings, head to the *Restaurante Patelería León*,

Moving on from Los Mochis

Buses

Tres Estrellas and Elite **buses** (leaving from Santos Degollado) have more first-class departures than the other services; finding a seat on mostly *de paso* buses can be a problem, but with departures north and south every thirty minutes or so you shouldn't have too long to wait. Buses cost US$23 to Mazatlán, US$50 to Guadalajara, US$7 to Navojoa, US$13 to Guaymas, US$20 to Hermosillo and US$70 to Tijuana.

Trains

Trains are far less convenient than buses and their rates have increased significantly. Moreover, the Nogales–Guadalajara train line is no longer in commercial service, and the only route open to passengers runs between Los Mochis and Chihuahua. Two trains leave for **Chihuahua** each day, the *Primera* (or *Estrella*, *Vista* or plain no. 73) at 6am (arrives Creel 2.30pm, Chihuahua 8pm) and the second-class *Económica* (or *Mixto* or no. 75) at 7am (arrives Creel 5pm, Chihuahua midnight), though remember that this line works on **Chihuahua time** – an hour later than local time in Los Mochis – so printed timetables will be one hour ahead of the times quoted here. Also note that the second train passes through some of the most beautiful terrain in the dark, so it might be worth forking out the extra cash for the earlier train. Fares on the *Primera* are currently US$58 to Creel and US$107 to Chihuahua; on the second-class train it costs US$31 to Creel and US$57 to Chihuahua. The **ticket office** at the station opens at 5am for same-day sales for both trains; tickets for the *Primera* can also be bought the previous day at Viajes Flamingo (Ⓣ668/812-1613, Ⓦwww.mexicoscoppercanyon.com), under the *Hotel Santa Anita* in town (see "Accommodation", opposite), or at the Viajes Aracely travel agent (see "Practicalities", opposite).

Ferries

Buses for the forty-minute journey to Topolobampo, from where the ferries leave, operate every fifteen minutes from Cuauhtémoc, between Zaragoza and Prieta. Departures for the 9–10hr **crossing to La Paz** are daily at 10pm, except Sunday; you can buy tickets as you board, but as ever it's safest to purchase tickets and check the timetable in advance. Currently, this route is covered only by Bajaferries. Tickets cost US$23 for a reclining seat, US$69 for a cabin and US$180 for a small car; the office is at Topolobampo port (Ⓣ668/862-0503).

Obregón 419 between Leyva and Flores, which also serves decent coffee and has a/c. The reliable Mexican-Spanish *Restaurante España*, Obregón 525 (Ⓣ668/812-2335), has international pretensions and prices to match. *El Taquito*, just over a block up Leyva from here, near the *Hotel Santa Anita*, is less expensive though on the bland side, but it's clean, safe and is open 24 hours. *El Farallon*, on the corner of Obregón and Flores, has a seafood-based menu, but is quite pricey.

Culiacán

Some 200km south of Los Mochis, **CULIACÁN**, the capital of Sinaloa, is a prosperous city with a population of more than a million, surrounded by some of the richest arable land in Mexico. The urban sprawl along the highway appears horribly ugly, but at its heart it's not too bad – mostly modern, but not unattractive. There's a lot more life in the streets, too, than in any of its near neighbours – probably thanks to the State University in the centre of town. Buses on the main road directly opposite the *Camionera* will take you to the **cathedral**, from where you can head three blocks downhill to the **market**. You could pass an hour or so inspecting the artworks in the local **Centro Cultural**, or get to local **beaches** at Atlata or El Tambor, about an hour away by bus. None of this, however, adds up to a very compelling reason to stop, especially as Mazatlán is only another 200km further south. In any case, it's often extremely hard to get back on a bus, all too many of which are *de paso*.

The several **hotels** right by the Central Camionera all seem to charge the same rate – the best of the bunch is the *Salvador*, Leyva Solano 297 (☎667/713-7462; ❺), directly opposite the station. There's better value, and more interesting surroundings, downtown. The *Hotel San Francisco* (☎667/713-5863; ❺), Hidalgo Pte 227, just by the market, is the best downtown choice, with TV and a/c in all the rooms; you could also try the *Hotel El Mayo* (☎667/715-2220; ❹), at Madero 730, the *Hotel Santa Fe* (☎667/716-0140; ❹), at Hidalgo Pte 243, or the slightly more upmarket, modern and airy *Santa Fe II* (☎667/716-0140; ❺), Hidalgo Pte 321.

There's **street food** aplenty round here, and several pizza places, but otherwise not too many restaurants in the centre – the terraced *Restaurant Santa Fe*, Hidalgo Pte 317, isn't bad, while the *Agualoha*, Insurgentes Norte 999, is favoured by the locals and is known for its steak *cabrería*, a regional specialty garnished with six different toppings and side dishes; or simply stick with the bus station's restaurant.

Mazatlán

About 20km from **MAZATLÁN** you cross the Tropic of Cancer. The transformation seems sudden: while Culiacán lies in a temperate agricultural zone, Mazatlán is a tropical town with a humid airlessness about it.

Primarily, of course, Mazatlán is a resort, and a burgeoning one at that, with hotels stretching further every year along the coast road to the north, flanking a series of excellent sandy beaches. The new avenues of hotels may be entirely devoted to tourism, but that said, on the whole Mazatlán seems far less dominated by its visitors than its direct rivals Acapulco or Puerto Vallarta. Most holiday-makers stay in the **Zona Dorada**, the "Golden Zone", and penetrate the town itself only on brief forays.

Mazatlán has been able to maintain much of its identity thanks in part to its status as Mexico's largest Pacific port. Also, with its location on a relatively narrow peninsula, the centre of town has preserved much of its old, cramped and traditional atmosphere. There are not many activities or sights in Mazatlán – you certainly wouldn't come here for the architecture – but it is a pleasant enough place and the separation of town and tourism means that you can find some remarkably good-value hotels on the streets just a few blocks inland. Mexican families mostly stay here, making the beachfront developments almost exclusively foreign preserves. There's an excellent bus service out along the coast road, so staying in town doesn't mean sacrificing the beach-bum lifestyle: with discretion, non-guests can use the hotel pools and the beaches in front of them. Remember to book accommodation well ahead if you are planning to be here around **Semana Santa**, when Mexicans descend on the city for massive celebrations.

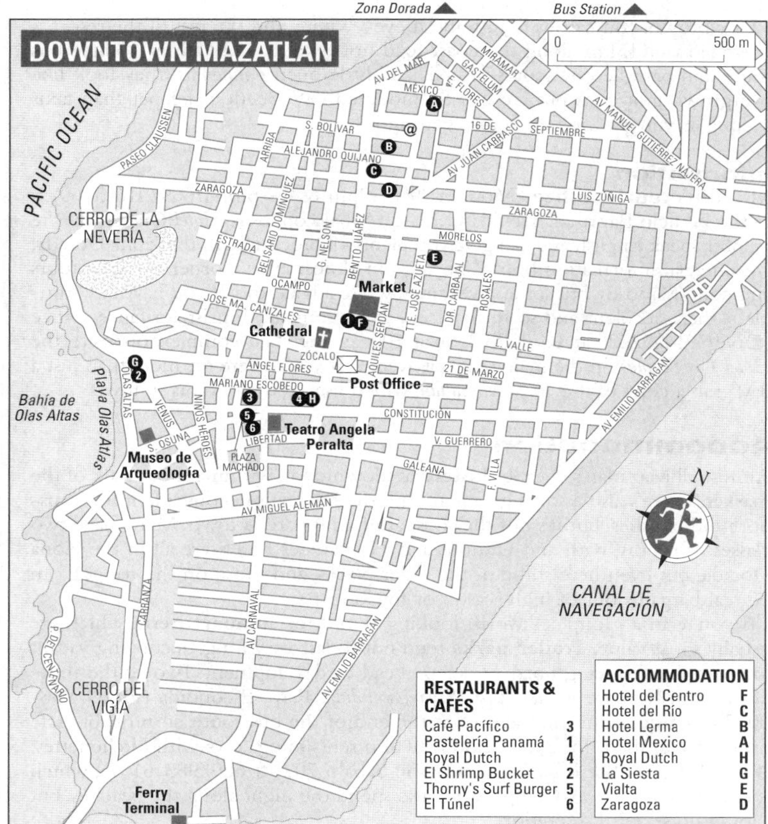

Arrival and information

The **bus station** lies on the main west coast route linking Tijuana and Mexicali in the north with Guadalajara and Mexico City in the south. The station has all facilities, including guardería and long-distance phones, and there are constant arrivals and departures to and from all points north and south. From the bus station, head up the hill to the main road and get on just about any bus heading to the right – they'll get you, by a variety of routes, to the **market**, very central and effectively the terminus for local buses. For the Zona Dorada, walk downhill from the bus station and catch a "Sábalo" bus heading to the right along the coast road.

Arriving by **ferry** you'll be at the docks, south of the centre: there are buses here, but getting an entire ferry-load of people and their baggage onto two or three of them always creates problems. Taxis (US$3 to the old town) are in demand, too, so try to be among the first off the boat. If you do get stranded, don't despair: the 1km walk to the centre of the old town isn't too bad. Mazatlán **airport** is some 20km south of town, served by the usual system of fixed-price vans (US$22) and taxis (about US$20).

Downtown, you can walk just about everywhere, and the rest of the resort is stretched out 15km along the coast road northwards – linked by a single bus route and patrolled by scores of taxis and little open *pulmonías* (they look like overgrown golf carts but are usually modified VW Beetles; cheaper than taxis as long as you fix the fare before getting in).

Information

Mazatlán's **tourist office** (Mon–Fri 9am–2pm & 4–7pm; ⓣ669/916-5160) is in the Edificio Banrural, Avenida Camarón Sábalo opposite *Hotel Quijote*; they're helpful, speak English and can give you plenty of brochures. In the Zona Dorada, commercial information booths pop up on almost every corner – selling tours and condos, mostly, but some give friendly, free advice, too. If you have any trouble – theft, accident and so forth – seek help from the Tourist Assitance Office (ⓣ669/914-3222) at Rodolfo Loaiza 100, in the mall complex opposite the *Hotel Los Sébalos* on the main seafront avenue. If you're here for more than just a day, grab a copy of the *Viejo Mazatlán*, which lists cultural events in town.

Accommodation

Almost all Mazatlán's cheaper **hotels** are downtown, within a short walk of the market. There's also a small group around the bus station, convenient for transport and beaches, but it's not the most appealing part of town. Many have two classes of rooms, with and without a/c. The fancier hotels are all in the Zona Dorada, but even here some of the older places, and those on the fringes, can be real bargains out of high season or for longer stays.

If you're in a group, it's worth looking round for an **apartment**, which are usually great value. **Trailer parks** tend not to last very long, occupying vacant lots and then moving north to keep ahead of development. Two of the more permanent sites are *Trailer Park Playa Escondida*, Playa Escondida (ⓣ669/988-0077), in a quiet location almost at the end of the bus route, so probably safe from development for a few seasons (it also rents bungalows with kitchenettes; ④), and *Trailer Park Rosa Mar*, Camarón Sábalo 702 (ⓣ669/983-6187), which is closer to the action. Campers can also spend the night along the beaches, but should do so with discretion.

The old town

Hotel del Centro Canizales 705 Pte, opposite the cathedral ⓣ669/981-2673. Large, clean rooms all with private bath, close to the centre. ④

Hotel del Río Juárez and Quijano (no phone). Attractive and tidy, though some rooms are not much larger than the bed. ③

Hotel Lerma Bolivar, between Serdán and Juárez ⓣ669/981-2436. Still the best deal in town. Sizeable, clean rooms around a very spacious courtyard with parking, and very hospitable staff. The café across the street has good, cheap breakfasts and comida corrida. ②

Hotel Mexico Mexico 201 and Serdán ⓣ669/981-3806. Friendly, clean and close to the sea. Rooms can be a bit small. Ask for a room facing away from the noisy street. ③

Royal Dutch Juárez, between Escobedo and Constitución ⓣ669/981-4396. What began as a café is now also a burgeoning B&B offering three clean, cozy rooms. Rates include a full breakfast, coffee and tea, as well as an afternoon tea and pastries. Reserve at least two weeks in advance, as they are almost always full. ⑥

La Siesta Olas Altas 11, between Ángel Flores and Escobedo ⓣ669/981-2640. Lovely old hotel with private balconies and great sea views (worth the extra money); drawbacks are small rooms and noise from *El Shrimp Bucket* restaurant next door. ⑤

Vialta José Azueta 2006, about three blocks north of the market ⓣ669/981-6027. Plain but acceptable rooms round a lovely courtyard; some with a/c. ③

Zaragoza Zaragoza 217, between Serdán and Juárez ⓣ669/912-5489. What you'd expect from almost the cheapest place in town, but the bare rooms are clean, with fan and bath, and the whole hotel feels spacious and cool. ③

Near the bus station

Emperador Río Panuco, right opposite the bus station ☎669/982-6724. Convenience is the main attraction, though rooms are sanitary and comfortable, with TV and a/c. ❸

La Fiesta Esperanza ☎669/981-7888. Big, well-kept rooms, but fairly basic. ❸

Motel Acuario Av del Mar 1196, near the Aquarium ☎669/982-7558. A short way down towards the Zona, the *Acuario*'s rooms are spartan, though there is a pool. ❹

Sands Hotel Av del Mar 1910 ☎669/982-0000. Facing the beach, straight down from the bus station. Comfortable, US-style motel with pool and sea views; very good value, especially off-season, when prices drop considerably. ❻

Santa María Ejército Mexicano ☎669/982-2304. Uphill from the station. Big and functional, but with good rooms, all with TV. ❸

Zona Dorada

Apartamentos Fiesta Río Ibis 502 ☎669/916-5355. Well into the Zona off Playa Gaviotas, three blocks inland from the *Hotel Balboa Towers*. Basic, good-value apartments and studios in garden setting for four or six people. Normally rented by the week, but in the off-season can be rented per night. ❸

Del Real Suites Av del Mar 1020 ☎669/983-1955. Well-appointed hotel with parking, a/c, cable TV and a pool. Accommodation (considerably cheaper by the week) is either in large suites with kitchenette (sleeping up to seven), smaller suites or kitchenless rooms. ❻

Los Girasoles Gaviotas 709 just next to the *Café Loma* ☎669/913-5288, ⓔmazatlanrental@hotmail.com. Huge, well-put-together rooms with kitchenettes on a quiet street off the strip. Pool and a/c. Prices are cut in half in the low season. ❼

Inn at Mazatlán Camarón Sábalo 6291 ☎669/913-5500. This classy hotel–timeshare complex oozes chic (or at least the Mazatlán equivalent thereof). Larger apartment units are excellent value for families or small groups. ❽

Las Jacarandas Av del Mar 2500, at entrance to the Zona ☎669/984-1177. Like the nearby *San Diego*, an older hotel with a pool that's been left behind by development and can no longer draw the crowds. Fading, but good value; some rooms with a/c and sea views. ❹

Motel Marley Gaviotas 226 ☎669/913-5533. Comfortable units in small-scale place with great position right on the sand, and a pool. Pricey, but you won't find a place on the water for much less. ❼

The Town

As befits a proper Mexican town, Mazatlán's **zócalo** is very much the commercial heart of the city, harbouring the eclectic and somewhat gaudy cathedral, the post office, government offices, main bank branches and travel agencies. Always animated, it's especially lively on Sunday evening (6–8pm), when there's a free *folklórico* show with singing and dancing.

Take time to stroll through the **market**, and in the other direction have a look round the newly restored **Plaza Machado**, surrounded by fine nineteenth-century buildings, including the **Teatro Angela Peralta**, which often hosts interesting events or exhibitions. Just off the plaza on Constitución is the **Casa Machado**, an interesting museum depicting life in nineteenth-century Mazatlán (daily 10am–6pm; US$2). Lesser attractions include the small **Museo de Arqueología**, Sixto Osuna 76 (Tues–Sun 10am–1pm & 4–7pm; US$1), just a couple of blocks towards Olas Altas, and the **Aquarium** (daily 9.30am–6.30pm; US$4), just off Avenida del Mar halfway between town and the Zona Dorada.

There are also some great **views** of town from the top of the **Cerro del Vigía** or **Cerro de la Nevería**; unless you're feeling very energetic, take a *pulmonía* or taxi up. Likewise, the top of the **Faro de Crestón** (unrestricted access) at the southern edge of town is a good vantage point, though you'll have to walk up. If you feel the need to take in a **bullfight**, head to the **Plaza de Toros**, Rafael Buelna; fights are held most Sundays in the winter at 4pm, and cost about US$5.

The beaches: Olas Altas, the Zona Dorada and Isla de la Piedra

Right in town, **Playa Olas Altas** is a great place to watch the sun go down or the local kids playing, but not the best place to swim – it's rather rocky and the waves tend to be powerful. Following the seafront drive from here around the rocky coast under the Cerro de la Nevería brings you to the **Mirador** – an outcrop of rock from which local daredevil youths plunge into the sea. At little over 10m, it's nowhere near as spectacular as the high-diving in Acapulco, but dangerous nonetheless. You'll see them performing whenever there are enough tourists to raise a collection, but generally starting at 10am or 11am – especially during the summer and Semana Santa – and again in the late afternoon (around 5pm) when the tour buses roll through.

To get to the **northern beaches** from here, you have to go back into the centre of town or continue all the way round to **Playa Norte**, as the buses don't follow the coast round the Cerro de la Nevería, though you can hop on some of the buses at Playa Olas Altas. Perfectly adequate though the Playa Norte may be, it's worth heading even further north to the **Zona Dorada**. The sands improve greatly around **Sábalo**, a short way into the Zona, where the first of the big hotels went up, many of which still remain. It really depends from here on what you want – the beaches right in front of the hotels are clean and sheltered by little offshore islands (boats sail out to these from various points along the beach), while further on they're wilder but emptier. The more populous area has its advantages – the beach never gets too crowded (most people stay by their pools and bars) and there's always a lot going on: water-skiing, sailing, parasailing behind speedboats, you name it. And if you get bored, there are the hotel pools and bars and any number of tourist watering holes and shops to pass the time. Among the dozens of artesanía markets and shopping malls, **Sea Shell City**, on Rodolfo Loaiza in the heart of the Zona, stands out as the kitschest of all – a two-storey emporium of seashells that describes itself as a museum and is definitely worth a look.

If you ride the bus past all this, though, you eventually get to an area where there's far less development. Along the way you can see just how quickly Mazatlán is spreading, and assess progress on the new marina development by the *Hotel Camino Real*. Towards the end of the bus line, make sure you get off somewhere you can reach the beach – often the only access is through villa or condo developments with gates and security. **Buses** (marked "Sábalo") leave from the market on the Juárez side, and run up Avenida del Mar and right through the Zona to the last hotel, where they turn around. Those marked "Cerritos" can be picked up on Avenida del Mar at *Fiestaland* and run north up along Avenida Camarón Sábalo. If your goal is to reach a beautifully serene beach, stay on the bus in this direction to either Playa Cerritos or Playa Bruja; these beaches have become popular with local surfers and those interested in horseback riding with Ginger's Bilingual Horses on Playa Bruja, (ⓣ669/922-2026; US$18/hr; closed Sun). There are also a few restaurants with great seafood, and the occasional spot for a post-beach drink. It is well worth enduring a few more minutes on the bus to reach these beaches.

Alternatively, south of the town centre, you can take a short and inexpensive boat trip (every 10min; 5am–7pm) from the beach next to the ferry docks to the **Isla de la Piedra** (or Stone Island), actually a long peninsula. There is a much more Caribbean feel here, with a very good palm-fringed beach that stretches for miles, excellent for swimming though keep an eye out for manta rays. It is possible to sleep out or sling a hammock on the terrace of one of the small restaurants – ask the owner first. Once a very basic community, the Isla is now included in many tour itineraries and can, at times, become crowded, especially on Sunday afternoons, when locals congregate here for live music and dancing under the beach palapas. Also from the ferry docks, the *Yate Fiesta* three-hour **harbour cruise** leaves daily (except Mon) at 11am (☎669/985-2237 or 2238; US$10).

Eating, drinking and nightlife

As a rule, Mazatlán's more authentic and lower-priced **restaurants** are in the old town. For rock-bottom prices, seek out the noisy and hectic restaurants on the upper floor of the **market** on the corner of Melchor Ocampo and Juárez. All along the Playa Norte are shacks selling freshly prepared fish at good prices. You can come across bargains in the Zona, too, as long as you don't mind the menu being in English and the prices in dollars. The sheer number of tourists there means lots of competition and **special offers**; breakfast deals are often the best of all.

The old town

Altazar Ars Café Constitución on the Plaza Machado. Serves burgers, tacos and other light fare. At night turns into a rock and blues club/bar, with live music every evening except Sundays.

Ambrosia Belisario Domínguez and Sixto Osuna just off Plaza Machado. A wide selection of reasonably priced vegetarian Mexican dishes. Reservations recommended at weekends.

Café Pacífico Constitución 501 at Heriberto Frías. Mexican and European mix of styles in a pub with a selection of beers and liquors, snacks, sandwiches and coffee. A relaxing place to drink (until 2am) without the macho overtones of many Mexican bars.

Jade Morelos and 5 de Mayo. About the only Chinese restaurant in the centre; not at all bad either.

El Jardín Right under the bandstand in the zócalo. Café with good coffee and breakfasts. Tables outside for watching the world go by.

Machado Sixto Osuna 34 in Plaza Machado. Superb fish tacos and a perfect setting for having a beer while looking out over Plaza Machado.

Marismeña Olas Altas, a block down from *El Shrimp Bucket*. Probably the best seafood restaurant in this part of town, but no outdoor seating.

Pastelería Panamé Juárez and Canizales, on the corner opposite the cathedral. Fast-food style restaurant/cafetería, good for breakfast but not cheap.

Royal Dutch Juárez, between Escobedo and Constitución. Great coffee, cakes, snacks and meals (until 8pm), in a relaxing atmosphere around an arcaded patio, marked by a windmill sign. Also offers eggs, hash and toast if you're not up for their fantastic apple strudel and cinnamon rolls. Some weekends they have live music. Closed July–Sept.

El Shrimp Bucket Next to the *Hotel La Siesta*, Olas Altas 11, between Ángel Flores and Escobedo. One of the oldest and best-known restaurants in Mazatlán and apparently the original of the *Carlos n' Charlie's* chain. Now in bigger, plusher premises, it still has plenty of atmosphere and decent if increasingly pricey food.

El Túnel directly across from the Teatro Angela Peralta. Perhaps the best Mexican food in all of Mazatlán, patronized by locals and tourists alike. Great specialties and coffee, but no beer (although you can bring your own). Open from noon to midnight daily. Also has a branch in the Zona Dorada on Sábalo near the *Holiday Inn*.

Zona Dorada

Anthony's Gaviotas L-39. A nice spot for some good Mexican food if you can bear the crowds in the surrounding area. Serves great seafood as well, and is reasonably inexpensive for the Zona Dorada.

Los Arcos Camarón Sábalo, across from the *Holiday Inn* ☎669/913-9577. Locals flock here for some of the best seafood in the city.

Arre LuLu De las Garzas 18. A not-so-crowded alternative for seafood and cheap drinks; they also offer a traditional Mexican menu. You can scoff a complete breakfast with eggs, beans, tortillas, juice and coffee for under US$3.

Casa Loma Gaviotas 104 ☎669/983-5398. For that perfect romantic – and expensive – evening, this secluded restaurant in a colonial setting has far more atmosphere than the big hotels. Reservations are recommended. Closed late Aug to Sept.

Coral Reef Terrace next to the *Coral Reef* hotel off Gaviotas, right on the beach. Very busy with tourists, but a fine place to have a meal, or perhaps just for a cocktail at sunset. Have a swim in the pool while you wait for your food.

Fiestaland Avenida del Mar and Buelna, at the far end of the coastal road. The Greco-Andalusian castle-like structure is a conglomeration of night-clubs, discos and bars, all centrally managed and charging fairly pricey covers.

No Name Café Gaviotas, a few steps down from the Sea Shell "Museum". Food and breakfast specials, but mainly a place for cold beer, party atmosphere, and big-screen TV sports.

Listings

American Express Camarón Sábalo, Plaza Balboa in the Zona (Mon–Fri 9am–1pm & 4–6pm, Sat 9am–1pm; ☎669/913-0600). Poor rates for cheques, but cardholders can receive mail.

Banks and exchange Citibank, Camarón Sábalo 1312, and Banamex, on Juárez at Ángel Flores by the zócalo, which has the longest hours (9am–2pm) and good exchange rates. Most places in the Zona accept dollars though often at a poor rate, so you may want to make use of Mazatlán's numerous casas de cambio.

Buses The region's major bus companies – Transportes Norte de Sonora, Tres Estrellas de Oro and Elite (☎669/981-3811, all), and Transportes del Pacífico (☎669/982-0577) – all have *de paso* services roughly hourly in both directions, beginning at 6.30am, and frequent local buses to Culiacán (4hr), Los Mochis (7hr), Tepic (4hr) and Guadalajara (4hr). In addition, two buses daily run direct to San Blas (currently 11am & 5pm; 4hr). Estrella Blanca (☎669/981-5381) and Transportes Frontera between them cover the route to Durango (13 daily; 6hr). To get to the bus station, take a "Sábalo" bus along the beachfront from Juárez near the market, then walk the 300m along Espinoza.

Car rental Dozens of outlets, including: Budget, Camarón Sábalo 402 ☎669/913-2000; Hertz, Camarón Sábalo 314 ☎669/913-6060; and National, Camarón Sábalo 7000 ☎669/913-6000.

Consulates Canada, *Hotel Playa Mazatlán*, Zona Dorada ☎669/913-7320; US (representative only), also at the *Hotel Playa Mazatlán*, call ☎669/913-4455 and ask for the representative.

Ferries Boats to La Paz (Sun–Fri 3pm Sept–June, plus Sat July & Aug; 18hr) leave the port at Playa Sur, 1km southeast of the centre; catch the "Playa Sur" bus from Juárez. Information and tickets are available from SEMATUR ☎669/981-7020 at the port: a *salón* class ticket (available on all boats) qualifies you for a reclining seat (US$60), a *turista* class ticket (daily except Wed) gets you a space in a four-berth cabin (US$170), *cabina* (US$208) in a two-berth cabin; a small car will cost around US$200, and bicycles go free. Food on board isn't great and, though there are signs prohibiting bringing your own, no one checks or seems to care. The travel agent Turismo Coral, listed below, can also arrange ferry tickets.

Flights Mazatlán airport (☎669/982-2399 or 2177) is 20km south of the city and only reachable by expensive taxi. Flights are run by Aeroméxico ☎669/914-1111, Alaska ☎669/985-2730, Delta ☎669/982-1349, Mexicana ☎669/982-7222, Noroeste ☎669/914-3855 and Saro ☎669/984-9768, but you'd do better booking through a travel agent (see opposite)

Internet access The cheapest are located in the old town, the best being Casa Mayte, Aquiles Serdán 2435, around the corner from *Lerma* hotel, which charges just over a US$1 per hour to surf the Net. Also try Juan Carlos Ríos at Ángel Flores 810. You will find many Internet places on the main drag in the Zona Dorada, though most are pricey, up to four times the cost of those in the old town (US$4–8/hr).

Laundry Lavafácil opposite the bus station by the *Hotel Fiesta*, and others at regular intervals throughout the Zona – in the Puebla Bonita complex, for example. There are also several downtown.

Medical emergencies Cruz Roja, Gutiérrez Najéra and Obregón (☎669/981-2225) runs free ambulance transport to local hospitals.

Phones You can make calls from any number of long-distance phones around the town (pick up a phonecard at a newsstand or kiosk) or in the *larga*

distancia places at Serdán 1512 (open 24hr), in the bus station or at several sites in the Zona.
Police ⓣ669/983-4510 or 066 for emergency assistance.
Post office Juárez and 21 de Marzo (Mon–Fri 8am–6pm, Sat 9am–1pm; ⓣ669/981-2121). They will accept your mail and hold it for ten days; have it sent to Lista de Correos, Administración Postal No. 1, Centro, Benito Juárez y 21 de Marzo, Mazatlán, Sinaloa, CP 82001, Mexico.
Spanish courses Centro de Idiomas, Belisario Domínguez 1908 (ⓣ669/982-2053, ⓔlanguagecenter@compuserv.com), offers courses from a week to a month, starting at around US$100; they can also arrange accommodation with Mexican families.
Tours and activities Pronatours, corner of Gaviotas and Sábalo (also in the *El Cid Hotel*), runs a host of nature, cultural, and adventure tours around the city and to the outlying islands. Prices average about US$35 for a tour (ⓣ669/913-3333 ext 3490, ⓦwww.elcid.com). Jet skis, catamarans and boats can usually be rented on the beach with no prior arrangement necessary. You can rent scooters and ATVs for riding around town (though not on the beaches) on Sábalo next to the *Hotel Palmas*. Prices run about US$60–100/day (daily 9am–8pm). Mazatlán Surf Center, Sábalo near Gaviotas, will rent you a surfboard for US$30/day (ⓣ669/913-1821).
Travel agent Turismo Coral, 5 de Mayo 1705 (Mon–Fri 8am–7pm, Sat 8am–2pm; ⓣ669/981-3290), northwest of the zócalo.

Mazatlán to Durango

Leaving Mazatlán, you have the choice of continuing **down the coast** to Tepic and from there along the main road to Guadalajara, or to more Pacific beaches at San Blas and Puerto Vallarta; or cutting **inland to Durango**, and the colonial cities of the Mexican heartland. This latter road, the first to penetrate the Sierra Madre south of the border, is as wildly spectacular as any in the country, twisting and clawing its way up to the Continental Divide at over 2500m. New vistas open at every curve as you climb from tropical vegetation, through temperate forests of oak, to the peaks with their stands of fir and pine. It can get extremely cold towards the top, so keep warm clothing on hand to cover the T-shirt and shorts you'll need for the first sweaty hour. Although it's little more than 300km long, the road is very slow, so reckon on six hours to Durango at the least.

Popular with tours from Mazatlán, but quiet otherwise, **CONCORDIA**, 42km inland, is an attractive colonial town with a reputation for making robust wooden furniture, examples of which are all over the region. The eighteenth-century Baroque **Church of San Sebastián**, overlooking the shady plaza, is unique in these parts but otherwise unexceptional, so you might as well press on towards the far grander edifices in the central highlands. For almost four hundred years, **COPALA**, a further thirty minutes on the bus towards Durango and a 1km walk down a side road, was Sinaloa's most important silver-mining town. But in 1933 Charles Butter's processing plant closed, putting six hundred people out of work; though the locals picked over the remains until the 1970s, the town's decline was already well advanced. The **jungle**, which has already engulfed the crushing mills and separation tanks, is nibbling at the edges of the village, which today largely relies on passing tourists from Mazatlán for its survival. Once the day-trippers leave, however, the place takes on a languorous air, making it a relaxing, and cool, place to **spend a night** or two. The *Copala Butter Company*, Plaza Juárez (ⓣ741/985-4225; ❸), has beautiful rooms with bath, and a balcony with views of the eighteenth-century church across the central plaza. It also offers **self-catering** bungalows (❹), sleeping up to four people. The restaurant here and the only other one in town, *Daniel's*, are both excellent and serve reasonably priced Mexican food, the latter in an open-air setting. Try the local speciality, coconut banana-cream pie.

South of Mazatlán: Tepic

Below Mazatlán the main road steers a little way inland, away from the marshy coastal flatlands. There are a few small beach communities along here, and deserted sands, but on the whole they're impossible to reach without transport of your own, and totally lacking in visitor facilities once you get there. The first town of any size, capital of the state of Nayarit and transport hub for the area, is **TEPIC**.

Despite its antiquity – the city was founded by Cortés' brother, Francisco Cortés, in 1544 – there's not a great deal to see in Tepic. Appealing enough in a quietly provincial way, for most it's no more than a convenient **stopover** before continuing across the mountains to Guadalajara, or a place to switch buses for the coast. This is probably the best way to treat it, for while the surrounding country is beautiful in parts, it's largely inaccessible and visited mainly by anthropologists for whom the mountains of Nayarit, homelands of the Huichol and Cora, are rich in interest.

The eighteenth-century **cathedral**, on the zócalo, is worth a look, as is the small **Museo Regional** (Mon–Fri 9am–7pm, Sat 9am–3pm; free), at the corner of México and Zapata, south from the zócalo, with a lovely collection of local pre-Columbian and Huichol artefacts. A couple of kilometres south on México, the **Ex-Convento de la Cruz de Zacate**, built in the sixteenth century to house a miraculous cross, has been restored for visitors. Plenty of places sell **Huichol "paintings"** (see box, opposite), one of the best being upstairs at Casa Arguet, Amado Nervo 132, west of the zócalo.

Tepic's **bus station** lies a couple of kilometres southeast of the centre on Avenida Insurgentes, but local buses shuttle in and out from the main road outside. Transportes del Pacífico (ⓣ311/213-2320) run buses to San Blas each hour for about US$4, as well as buses to Mazatlán (US$13), Los Mochis (US$34), Mexicali (US$65), Tijuana (US$85), Guadalajara (US$14) and beyond. Omnibus de México (ⓣ311/213-1323) also run services to Guadalajara and a less frequent service to Mexico City, which cost slightly more.

The main **tourist office** (Mon–Fri 9am–2pm & 4–7pm, Sat & Sun 10am–1pm; ⓣ311/214-8071) is at México Norte 178; there's a smaller branch in the Ex-Convento de la Cruz de Zacate. Should you need the **police** you can reach them at ⓣ311/211-5851; the **hospital** is contactable at ⓣ311/214-3291.

For just one night it's easiest to put up with the noise and stay by the bus station. Two cheap **hotels** with little to choose between them – the *Nayar* (ⓣ311/213-2322; ❸) and the *Tepic* (ⓣ311/213-1377; ❸) – stand immediately behind the terminal on Martinez. In the centre, try the *Hotel Sarita*, Bravo Pte 112 (ⓣ311/212-1333; ❸), north of the zócalo, or the *Cibrian*, Amado Nervo Pte 163 (ⓣ311/212-8698; ❹), slightly closer. For more comfort, the *Sierra de Alicia*, México Norte 180 (ⓣ311/212-0322; ❺), and the luxurious *Fray Junipero Serra*, Lerdo Pte 23 (ⓣ311/212-2525; ❻), right on the zócalo, are good choices. For **food**, there's plenty of choice around the zócalo and on México: *Pat Pac's*, upstairs at México Norte and Morelos, is good, popular and reasonably priced, offering an excellent breakfast buffet and Mexican menu; *Café Diligencias*, México Sur 29, is a good place to linger over a coffee; while *Acuarios*, Morelos Pte 139, serves simple vegetarian dishes. Fancier restaurants, other than those in the hotels, are west of here, near the open spaces of the Parque La Loma: try for example *Roberto's*, Paseo La Loma 472 at Insurgentes, which offers seafood and international fare.

The Huichol

The **Huichol**, some 10,000 of whom live in the isolated mountain regions around the borders of Nayarit, Jalisco, Zacatecas and Durango, are the indigenous people perhaps least affected by developments in the four and a half centuries since the Spanish invasion of Mexico. New roads are bringing inevitable pressure for "development" of their lands, but for now much of their territory remains accessible only by the occasional mule track or via one of many simple landing strips for light aircraft. In these fastnesses they have preserved their ancient beliefs, government and social forms.

Ritual and religion play such an intimate and essential role in Huichol life that it's almost impossible for an outsider to comprehend. Even the simplest action object or item of dress has ritual significance in a religion based on daily life: Mother Earth and Father Sun; the goddess of rain and the god of corn; the deer for hunters, and peyote for food gatherers. Peyote in particular, for which a group of Huichol have to make an annual cross-country pilgrimage to Real de Catorce (p.281), plays an important part in their ceremonies. The Huichol's brightly coloured woven "**paintings**" are rich in stylized symbols based in nature – animals, suns, moons – and traditional themes of fertility and birth. You can buy these paintings in Tepic and elsewhere. You may see traditionally dressed Huichol at the market or paying homage in the Church of Santa Cruz in Tepic (the missionaries did have some effect, and two Christs have been absorbed into the Huichol pantheon). There's more chance of seeing Huichol life at **religious festivals** in nearby villages, though you should consider whether you want to add your possibly unwelcome intrusion to that of many others.

Getting to Huichol territory is not easy, despite daily light planes from the airport in Tepic; you need permission from the authorities, and of course there are no regular facilities to feed or house visitors, little to see in the rustic villages and no guarantee that you'll be welcome.

San Blas

West of Tepic lies the coastal plain: sultry, marshy and flat, dotted with palm trees and half-submerged under lagoons teeming with wildlife. Through this you reach **SAN BLAS**, as godforsaken a little town as you could hope to see – at least on first impression. It was an important port in the days of the Spanish trade with the Orient, wealthy enough to need a fortress to ward off the depredations of English piracy, but though there's still an enviable natural harbour and a sizeable deep-sea fishing fleet, almost no physical relic of the town's glory days remains.

Life in San Blas is extremely slow. The positive side of this is an enjoyably laid-back travellers' scene, with plenty of people who seem to have turned up years ago and never quite summoned the energy to leave. For such a small town, though, San Blas manages to absorb its many visitors – who come mainly in winter – without feeling overrun, submissive or resentful. During the summer it's virtually deserted, save for legions of ferocious sand flies, but at the beginning of February the city hosts its biggest festival in recognition of San Blas – the week-long fiesta often actually begins before and stretches long after its set dates. Do not come here without insect repellent or you will be eaten alive: it is bearable by day, but the mosquitoes descend en masse at dusk.

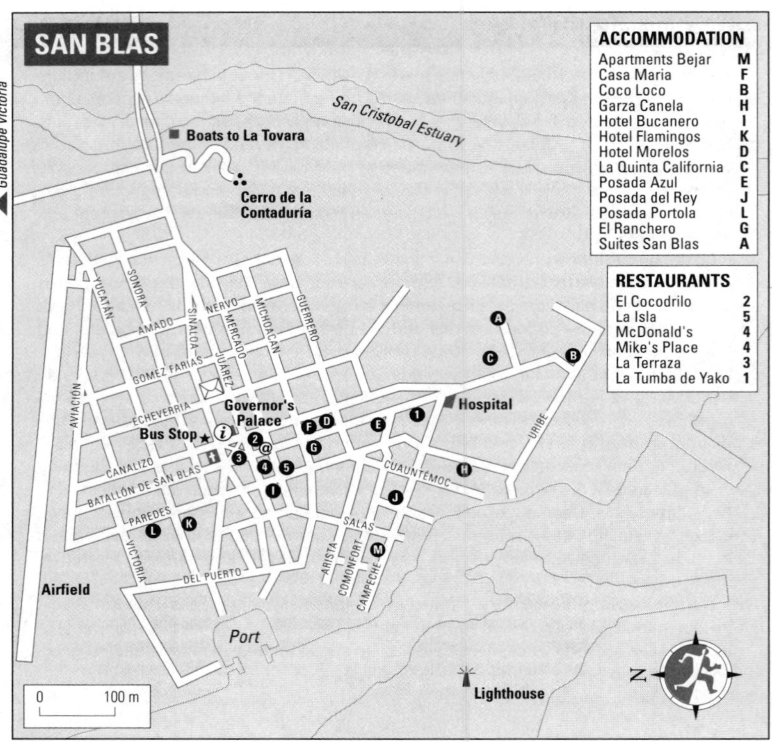

Arrival and information

The majority of the **buses** serving San Blas arrive from Tepic, 65km east, though if you're coming from neighbouring coastal resorts you can save time and hassle by catching either the direct bus from Mazatlán (twice daily) or the service from Puerto Vallarta (twice daily) via Las Varas along the coast. Transportes Norte de Sonora run these and a daily bus to Guadalajara via Tepic.

The **bus station** is on Sonora at the northeastern corner of the zócalo, right in the centre of town. Here Juárez crosses Heroico Batallón de San Blas, which runs 1km south to the town beach, Playa de Barrego. The very helpful **tourist office** (Mon–Fri 9am–3pm; ⓣ323/285-0221 or 0005) is located inside the Governor's Palace on the zócalo. Though the Banamex branch, on Juárez just east of the zócalo, cashes **cheques** (Mon–Fri 9am–2pm) and has an ATM, it is plagued by long queues, poor rates and an occasional lack of funds. Change money before you get here or, if pushed, see if the Pato Loco store on Mercado and Echevarría will change cheques. The **post office** is a block northeast of the bus station at Sonora and Echevarría, and long-distance **phones** can be found on the zócalo. There are a few places to log on to the **Internet** in town – try Café Net San Blas on Juárez and Batallón, around the corner from the creatively named *McDonald's* restaurant (daily 9am–11pm; US$1.50/hr) or San Blas en

Line, at *La Quinta California* (see below), a laid-back place with a coffee-house feel, and a good place to grab a book from their large secondhand collection.

Accommodation

Part of the appeal of San Blas is that there's plenty of choice of budget **hotels**. Most places are on Juárez or Heroico Batallón. The town is especially well geared to small, **self-catering** groups: "bungalows" and "suites" are apartments with up to six beds, a small kitchen and usually (though you should check) some cooking equipment. Wherever you stay, make sure that the screens are intact and the doors fit or you'll be pillaged by biting insects.

The *Coco Loco* **trailer park** (Ⓣ323/285-0820) is a shady and grassed camping area close to the beach, a kilometre down Batallón from the zócalo. There's also free camping on Playa de Barrego, but the bugs and the availability of good, cheap accommodation in town make this less than appealing.

Apartments Bejar 144 Salas, towards the estuary at Comonfort (no phone). Good deals on daily, weekly, and monthly rates, for fully furnished apartment/bungalows. ④

Garza Canela Paredes 106, follow signs from Batallón Ⓣ323/285-0112, Ⓦwww.garzacanela.com. Comfortable, if plain, a/c rooms, pool, garden, and some kitchenettes. Rates include breakfast. Significant discounts during low season. ⑧

Hotel Bucanero Juárez Ⓣ323/285-0101. Good, clean rooms surrounding an airy courtyard and fountain. A good spot if you are looking for a hotel within a stone's throw of the action; a/c available for an additional charge. ③

Hotel Flamingo Juárez 105 Ⓣ323/285-0485 or 0930. The nicest place in town: sleek, classy rooms around the perimeter of a wonderful garden courtyard with pool and ping-pong table. Also rents bikes for US$7/day. ⑦

Hotel Morelos opposite *El Ranchero* (no phone). Same family and set-up as *El Ranchero* (without the kitchen), and just as comfortable and clean. ③

Posada Azul Batallón, two blocks beyond *Casa María*. The cheapest in town. Basic, but safe and friendly. ②

Posada del Rey Campeche 10, not far from the water Ⓣ323/285-0123. Modern, plain and comfortable rooms with a/c and fans. Tiny pool and bar with views to the water. ⑤

Posada Portola Paredes 118, two blocks northeast of the zócalo Ⓣ323/285-0386. Exceptional value with immaculate rooms and good kitchenettes. Will also rent you bikes, resident or not. ④

La Quinta California Batallón Ⓣ323/285-0603. Amazingly good-value apartments with well-equipped kitchens, close to the beach behind *El Herradero Cantina*, amongst the trees. ③

El Ranchero Batallón at Michoacán Ⓣ323/285-0892. Friendly in the extreme; rooms with or without bath include use of kitchen; beds in communal rooms at peak times. Having become a popular budget choice, it's often full in winter, and can be a bit noisy. ③

Suites San Blas down by the beach Ⓣ323/285-0505. Especially good value for groups or families – units for up to six people with (ill-equipped) kitchen in quiet spot with a pool. Slightly faded rooms, cheaper without a/c. ④–⑥

The Town

Beyond lying on the pristine **beaches** to the south of San Blas or taking an excellent "jungle boat trip" to **La Tovara springs** (see overleaf, for both), most visitors seem content to simply relax or amble about town. A more focused hour can be spent at **La Contadoría**, the ruins of a late eighteenth-century fort which, with the vaulted remains of a chapel, crown the Cerro de San Basilio near the river, a kilometre along Juárez towards Tepic (US$0.60). From here you get great views over the town to the ocean, where, according to Huichol legend, the small white island on the horizon is said to represent peyote. It marks the symbolic starting point of their annual pilgrimage to the central highlands, the actual start being on the **Isla del Rey**, the lighthouse-topped peninsula across the Estero del Pozo channel from San Blas. The pilgrimage begins approximately two weeks before Easter, with feasts and elaborate ceremonies centred around a sacred **cave** below the lighthouse. Remains of the cave can still be seen, though most of it was recklessly destroyed by the government in the 1970s to provide rock for a jetty. You can catch a **boat** across to the Isla del Rey from the landing stage at the end of Héroes 21 de Abril.

San Blas is also an excellent place for both **fishing and whale-watching** trips, the latter in the winter months. Inexpensive as far as sport fishing goes, US$80–100 will get you a five- to seven-person boat for the morning, allowing you to troll for the abundant yellowfin tuna, as well as barracuda and others. You can spend half the morning fishing, half whale-watching, and you're bound to do quite well on both fronts – when grey whales are in the area (Dec–April), they show up just about everywhere. There are a number of guides in town who'll take you out, but two of the best around are Abraham Murillo (aka "Pipila") and Antonio Aguayo. If they don't find you first, walk down Paredes past the *Garza Canela* until you come to the inlet and small harbour of fishing *pangas*; there's a good chance either Pipila or Antonio will be there, but if not any of the men fixing their nets can point you in the right direction.

La Tovara and jungle boat trips

The **lagoons and creeks** behind San Blas are almost unbelievably rich in bird and animal life – the ubiquitous white herons, or egrets, and hundreds of other species too, which no one seems able to name (any bird here is described as a *garza* – a heron). The best way to catch a glimpse is to get on one of the three-hour boat trips "into the jungle", the *lancha* negotiating channels tunnelled through dense mangrove, past sunbaking turtles and flighty herons. The best time to go is at dawn, before other trips have disturbed the animals, when you might even glimpse a cayman along the way. Most trips head for **La Tovara**, a cool freshwater spring that fills a beautiful clear pool perfect for swimming and pirouetting off the rope swing – if you're not put off by the presence of crocodiles that is. Eat at the fairly pricey palapa restaurant or bring your own picnic.

Trips leave from the river bridge 1km inland from the zócalo along Juárez: get a group together for the best prices. Rates are fair and start at around US$20 for four, US$5 per extra person for two hours; US$30 for four and US$7 per extra person for three hours, including a trip to an alligator farm. You may also want to consider negotiating something longer, giving more time for swimming and wildlife-spotting en route. Shorter jungle boat trips leave from Matanchén (see below) but the longer boat ride from San Blas justifies the marginally higher cost.

The beaches

As well as the fine beaches right in town, there are others some 4km away around the **Bahía de Matanchén**, a vast, sweeping crescent of a bay entirely surrounded by fine soft sands. At the near end, the tiny community of **Las Islitas** on the Playa Miramar has numerous palapa restaurants on the beach, serving up grilled fish and cold beers and, on the point, a group of beautifully situated but relatively expensive cabins for rent; if you can swing it, it's well worth staying at this remote outpost. At the far end lies **Aticama** (with more basic shops and places to eat) and the disappointing Playa Los Cocos, where erosion is steadily eating away at what was once a pristine beach. In between, acres of sand are fragmented only by flocks of pelicans and the occasional crab. There are plenty of spots where you can camp if you have the gear and lots of repellent, as well as a trailer park at Los Cocos. The waves here, which rise offshore beyond Miramar and run in, past the point, to the depths of the bay, are in the *Guinness Book of Records* as the longest in the world: it's very rare that they are high enough for surfers to be able to ride them all the way in, but there's plenty of lesser **surfing** potential – surfboards and boogie boards can be rented in Las Islitas or in San Blas for a few dollars.

You can walk from San Blas to Matanchén, just about, on the roads through the lagoons – it's impossible to penetrate along the coast, which would be much shorter. Considering the sweltering temperatures in this area, it's far easier to make the trip on one of the **buses** ("El Llano") that leave several times daily from the station, or by **taxi** (bargain fiercely).

Eating and drinking

Seafood is big business in San Blas and you can buy it at beachfront palapas and street stands, as well as at the established **restaurants** in town. There's also plenty of fruit and other healthy offerings to cater for the tourists. At the beach most places close around sunset, and if you want to eat later you'll have to walk into town – a flashlight to guide your way is a worthwhile investment.

El Cocodrilo Juárez 1. A San Blas fixture with a great location on the zócalo. Travellers and locals alike come for the excellent if a bit pricey seafood, and to relax and drink long after the activity in the zócalo has died down.

La Isla Calle Mercado at Paredes. A must, if only to admire the astonishingly kitsch decor: draped fishing nets festooned with shell pictures, shell mobiles and shell lampshades. Moderately priced meat and seafood dishes of average quality. Also known as *Chief Tony's*.

McDonald's Juárez 36. No relation to Ronald's place, this unpretentious restaurant just off the zócalo is a prime meeting place, particularly among expats who gather here for breakfast. Broad menu and reasonable prices.

Mike's Place Juárez 36 above *McDonald's*. Quiet drinking midweek but livens up on Friday and Saturday with dancing and anything from Latin to classic rock.

La Terraza Batallón, right on the zócalo. Reasonably priced Mexican food and beer. A great place to sit and watch the world go by.

La Tumba de Yako Batallón at Querétaro. Kiosk run by the local surf team, popular for its banana bread and natural yogurt.

Around San Blas: Santiago Ixcuintla and Mexcaltitán

North of San Blas, from Hwy-15 you can take the turn-off for **SANTIAGO IXCUINTLA**, a market town where the only real interest lies in the **Huichol Centre for Cultural Survival and Traditional Arts** (approximately 1.5km from the central plaza towards Mexcaltitán at 20 de Noviembre and Constitución). This co-operative venture, aimed at supporting Huichol people and preserving their traditions, raises money by selling quality Huichol art and offering various classes. From Santiago a road leads straight down to the coast and the **Playa Los Corchos**, a perfect stretch of sand lined with palm trees, by the mouth of the Río Grande de Santiago. Santiago has a few cheap hotels, but no other formal facilities – you might, however, find someone prepared to rent you a room in their house, or else space to sling a hammock under the veranda of one of the beach bars.

To the right beyond Santiago, another road leads across the lagoon to the extraordinary islet of **MEXCALTITÁN**. The little town here must look something like a tiny version of Aztec Tenochtitlán before the Spanish arrived, laid out in radiating spokes from the centre of the round island; the name means "house of the Mexicans" in the Nahuatl language. Local transport is by canoe

Fiestas

JANUARY

Last week of the month ORTIZ TIRADO MUSIC FESTIVAL. Thousands descend upon **Alamos** for a week-long celebration in honour of Dr Alfonso Ortiz Tirado. Concerts, parades, cultural events and plenty of merrymaking.

FEBRUARY

3 DÍA DE SAN BLAS. The feria in **San Blas** (Nayarit) starts on January 30, with parades, dancing, fireworks and ceremonial, and ends a week or so later.

CARNAVAL (the week before Lent, variable Feb–March) is celebrated with particular gusto in **La Paz** (Baja California Sur), **Ensenada** (Baja California North) and **Culiacán** (Sinaloa). The best carnival in the north, though, is at **Mazatlán** (Sin).

MARCH

19 FIESTA DE SAN JOSÉ. Saint's day celebrations in **San José del Cabo** (BCS) with horse races, cockfights and fireworks, and in the hamlet of San José near **Guaymas** (Sonora), where the religious fervour is followed by a fair.

APRIL

Week before Easter PALM SUNDAY sees dramatizations of biblical episodes in **Jala** (Nay), an ancient little town between Tepic and Guadalajara.

HOLY WEEK is widely honoured. High points include Passion plays in **Jala** (Nay), processions and native dances in **Rosamorada** (Nay), north of Tepic on the main road, and, in the Yaqui town of **Cocorit** (Son) near Ciudad Obregón, pilgrimages and Yaqui dances including the renowned Danza del Venado. This can also be seen in **Potam** (Son), on the coast near here, along with curious ancient religious rites and the burning of effigies of Judas.

MAY

3 DÍA DE LA SANTA CRUZ. Celebrated in **Santiago Ixcuintla** (Nay), north of Tepic, a fiesta rich in traditional dances.

JUNE

1 Maritime celebrations in the port of **Topolobampo** (Sin) with parades and a fair.

24 DÍA DE SAN JUAN. **Guaymas** (Son), **Navojoa** (Son) and **Mochicahui** (Sin), a tiny village near Los Mochis, all celebrate the saint's day with processions and, later, with native dancing. In **Navojoa** there's a feria that carries on to the beginning of July.

29 In **Mexcaltitán** (Nay) a religious fiesta in honour of St Peter, with processions in boats round the islet.

JULY

First Sunday *Romería* in **Tecate** (BCN), extremely colourful, with cowboys, carnival floats and music.

along a series of tiny canals crossed by causeways, and indeed the place is one candidate for the site from which the Aztecs set out on their long trek to the Valley of México. Mexcaltitán sees very little tourism, but you should be able to find a guide to paddle you around the island, a room at the single **hotel**, *Ruta Azteca* (☎323/232-0211 ext 128; ④), offering four bare-bones rooms near the church, and somewhere to eat. If you're in the area around the end of June you should definitely try to visit the island fiesta, on June 28 and 29, when there are canoe races on the lagoons and rivers; be sure to make a reservation, too.

25 DÍA DE SANTIAGO. Celebrated in **Compostela** (Nay), south of Tepic, where the men ride around on horses all day – the women take over their mounts the following morning and then do the same. Also boasts a fair with fireworks.

SEPTEMBER

8 Formal religious processions in **Jala** (Nay) with traditional dress and regional dances.

16 INDEPENDENCE DAY is a holiday everywhere in the country, and especially lively along the border. **Tijuana** (BCN) has horse and motor races, *mariachi*, dancing, gambling and fireworks, as does **Ensenada**, while the much smaller crossing of **Agua Prieta** (Son) has a more traditional version of the same, with parades and civic ceremonies.

28 DÍA DE SAN MIGUEL. A pilgrimage to Boca, a community located very close to **Choix** (Sin), on the railway from Los Mochis. There's dancing and a number of parades in Choix, with a procession to Boca.

Late September to early October FIESTA DEL SOL. Music and arts, also commemorating **Calexico**'s founding.

OCTOBER

4 DÍA DE SAN FRANCISCO is the culmination of a two-week fiesta in **Magdalena** (Son), attended by many Indians (Yaqui and Sioux among them) who venerate this missionary saint. Traditional dances.

First Sunday In **Guasave** (Sin), between Los Mochis and Culiacán, a pilgrimage to the Virgen del Rosario, with many dance groups.

Last Sunday Repetition of events in **Guasave** and, in **Ixtlán del Río** (Nay), hundreds of pilgrims arrive to observe the DÍA DE CRISTO REY – more dancing.

NOVEMBER

2 DÍA DE LOS MUERTOS/DAY OF THE DEAD celebrations everywhere – **Navojoa** (Son) is one of the more impressive.

DECEMBER

First Sunday Lively festival honouring El Señor de la Misericordia in **Compostela** (Nay).

8 DÍA DE LA INMACULADA CONCEPCIÓN celebrated by the pilgrims who converge on **Alamos** (Son), and in **Mazatlán** (Sin), with parades, music and dancing. **La Yesca**, in a virtually inaccessible corner of Nayarit east of Tepic, has religious ceremonies and a feria attended by many Huichol people, which lasts till the 12th.

12 DÍA DE LA VIRGEN DE GUADALUPE. In **Navojoa** (Son), the climax of ten days of activities comes with a procession. **Tecate** (BCN) and **Acaponeta**, on the main road in northern Nayarit, both have lively and varied fiestas.

Tepic to Guadalajara: Ixtlán

Between Tepic and Guadalajara it's a long climb over the Sierra Madre, with an excellent new toll road much of the way. **IXTLÁN DEL RÍO** is the first place you might be tempted to stop – the only other is Tequila (see p.247). Ixtlán was made famous by Carlos Castaneda's *Journey to Ixtlán*, which is attraction enough for a few, though it's hard to believe that many find what they're after, as this is an exceptionally unattractive little strip development along the highway, beset by constant traffic noise from huge trucks and permanent jams. What it does offer is plenty of hotels and restaurants: if you do want to **stay**, try the *Hidalgo* (❹) or the *Santa Rita* (❹), two of the more central places on the highway. The *Río Viego*, very near the plaza, is a decent traditional Mexican **restaurant**.

Though it offers little spiritual diversion, Ixtlán does have one worthwhile attraction in its **archeological site**, a couple of kilometres east. The site is right by the highway and rail line: there are local buses, and second-class services on the main road should stop. Though not very impressive in comparison with the great sites in central and southern Mexico, this is one of the largest and most important in western Mexico, with numerous heavily restored buildings of plain, unadorned stone. Perhaps most striking is the sheer size of the place. What you can see is extensive, but the site in total is said to cover an area five times larger – and this is considered an "insignificant" culture of which relatively little is known. The site itself (dawn–dusk) has a series of rectangular buildings forming plazas, each centring on an altar. The finest structure, and the most thoroughly restored, is an unusual circular temple ringed by a wall. The sides, which now slope out slightly, were originally vertical, so that the cylindrical building looked like a brazier. Circular temples like this are usually associated with **Quetzalcoatl** in his guise of Ehecatl, God of Wind, but here the brazier shape may also refer to **Huehueteotl**, the Old God or God of Fire. Outside the site it's easy to spot piles of stones in the farm at the back and odd humps in the surrounding fields; at one point the site fence cuts through an obvious mound.

Travel details

Buses

Services on the main highways south from Tijuana or Nogales are excellent, with constant fast traffic and regular express services, if you want them, from the border all the way to Mexico City. Be warned, though, that *de paso* buses can be hard to pick up along the way, especially in Hermosillo, Culiacán and Los Mochis. Baja California has fewer services. Chief operators are Águila (Baja), Tres Estrellas de Oro – arguably the most reliable company – Transportes del Pacífico and Transportes Norte de Sonora (TNS), with dozens of second-class companies serving lesser destinations. For long distances and on the busiest routes you might consider one of the pullman services run by companies like Elite, with airline-style seats, drinks, video and icily effective air-conditioning. The following frequencies and times are for first-class services. Second-class buses usually cover the same routes, running ten to twenty percent slower. Keep in mind, too, that the Mexican bus service is always evolving and the number of departures can change overnight. The schedules below are approximate and should always be verified in person.

Alamos to: Navojoa (hourly; 1hr); Phoenix (1 daily; 13hr).

Cabo San Lucas to: La Paz via San José del Cabo (6 daily; 3–4hr); La Paz via Todos Santos (8 daily; 2hr); San José del Cabo (roughly hourly; 30min); Todos Santos (8 daily; 1hr).

Ensenada to: Guerrero Negro (7 daily; 8hr); La Paz (4 daily; 20hr); Loreto (4 daily; 15hr); Mexicali (4 daily; 4hr); San Felipe (2 daily; 3hr 30min); Tijuana (hourly; 1hr 30min).

Guaymas to: Hermosillo (every 30min; 1hr 30min); Los Mochis (every 30min; 5hr); Mexicali (every 30min; 11hr); Navojoa (every 30min; 3hr); Nogales (hourly; 5hr 30min); Tijuana (every 30min; 14hr).

Guerrero Negro to: Ensenada (7 daily; 8hr); La Paz (3 daily; 12hr); San Ignacio (7 daily; 3hr); Santa Rosalía (7 daily; 4hr); Tijuana (7 daily; 10hr).

Hermosillo to: Bahía de Kino (9 daily; 2hr); Guaymas (every 30min; 1hr 30min); Mexicali (every 30min; 9–10hr); Nogales (hourly; 4hr); Tijuana (every 30min; 12–13hr).

La Paz to: Cabo San Lucas via Todos Santos (8 daily; 2hr); El Rosario (2 daily; 16hr); Ensenada (4 daily; 20hr); Guerrero Negro (4 daily; 12hr);

Loreto (7 daily; 5hr); Mexicali (1 daily; 28hr); Mulegé (5 daily; 7hr); San Ignacio (3 daily; 9hr); San José del Cabo via eastern route (6 daily; 3–4hr); Santa Rosalía (5 daily; 8hr); Tijuana (1 daily; 22hr); Todos Santos (8 daily; 1hr).
Los Mochis to: Guaymas (every 30min; 7hr); Mazatlán (every 30min; 7hr); Navojoa (every 30min; 2–3hr); Tijuana (every 30min; 19hr); Topolobampo (every 15min; 40min).
Mazatlán to: Culiacán (every 30min; 4hr); Durango (13 daily; 6hr); Guadalajara (every 30min; 9hr); Los Mochis (every 30min; 7hr); San Blas (2 daily; 4hr); Tepic (every 30min; 4hr); Tijuana (every 30min; 26hr).
Mexicali to: Chihuahua (1 daily; 19hr); Ensenada (4 daily; 4hr); Guadalajara (1 daily; 34hr); Guaymas (every 30min; 11hr); Hermosillo (every 30min; 9–10hr); Los Mochis (every 30min; 17hr); Mazatlán (every 30min; 24hr); Mexico City (1 daily; 40hr); Monterrey (1 daily; 29hr); San Felipe (4 daily; 3hr); Tijuana (every 30min; 3hr).
Navojoa to: Alamos (hourly; 1hr); Ciudad Obregón (every 30min; 1hr 30min); Guaymas (every 30min; 3hr); Los Mochis (every 30min; 2–3hr); Tijuana (every 30min; 17hr).
Nogales to: Agua Prieta (2 daily; 3–4hr); Guaymas (hourly; 5hr 30min); Hermosillo (hourly; 4hr); Puerto Peñasco (1 daily; 5hr).
San Blas to: Mazatlán (2 daily; 4hr); Puerto Vallarta (2 daily; 3–4hr); Santiago Ixcuintla (3 daily; 1hr); Tepic (hourly; 1hr 30min).
Santa Rosalía to: Guerrero Negro (7 daily; 4hr); La Paz (5 daily; 8hr); Loreto (8 daily; 3hr); Mulegé (8 daily; 1hr); San Ignacio (7 daily; 1hr); Tijuana (4 daily; 14hr).
Tepic to: Guadalajara (every 30min; 5hr); Mazatlán (every 30min; 4hr); Puerto Vallarta (hourly; 3–4hr); San Blas (hourly; 1hr 30min); Tijuana (every 30min; 30hr).
Tijuana to: Culiacán (every 30min; 22hr); El Rosario (4 daily; 6hr); Ensenada (hourly; 1hr 30min); Guadalajara (every 30min; 35hr); Guaymas (every 30min; 14hr); Guerrero Negro (7 daily; 10hr); Hermosillo (every 30min; 12–13hr); La Pass (1 daily; 22hr); Los Mochis (every 30min; 19hr); Loreto (4 daily; 17hr); Los Angeles (12 daily; 4hr); Mazatlán (every 30min; 26hr); Mexicali (every 30min; 3hr); Mulegé (4 daily; 15hr); Navojoa (every 30min; 17hr); El Rosario (4 daily; 6hr); San Ignacio (4 daily; 13hr); Santa Rosalía (4 daily; 14hr); Tepic (every 30min; 30hr).

Trains

The main line through northwestern Mexico running from Nogales to Guadalajara no longer runs passenger services. The only train in the region that carries passengers is the amazing Los Mochis–Chihuahua Copper Canyon railway at Sufragio (Sinaloa). One train with first-class carriages and another with second-class run in each direction each day. Remember that timetables are confused by the hour's difference between the region covered in this chapter and the rest of Mexico. The Los Mochis–Chihuahua *primera clase* train departs Los Mochis daily at 6am, the regular (second-class) *económica* train at 7am local time.

Planes

Almost every town of any size has an airport, with flights, not necessarily direct, to Mexico City. Busiest are Tijuana – with half a dozen flights a day to the capital by a variety of routings and a couple direct to Guadalajara – and La Paz, with flights to Mexico City and many towns along the mainland coast. Mazatlán is the busiest of all. Aero California is the biggest of the local operators, though Mexicana and Aeroméxico operate flights to major Mexican cities, often at prices little higher than the equivalent cost of the bus.
La Paz to: Guadalajara (1 daily); Los Angeles via Loreto (1 daily); LA direct (2 daily); Mexico City (1 daily); Phoenix (1 daily); San Diego (1 daily); Tijuana (2 daily); Tucson (1 daily).
Mazatlán to: Denver (3 weekly); La Paz (1 daily); Los Angeles (3 daily); Mexico City (4 daily); Tijuana (2 daily).
San José to: Houston (2 daily); LA (many daily); Minneapolis (1 daily); Salt Lake City (1 daily); San Diego (many daily); San Francisco (2 daily); Tijuana (2 daily).

Ferries

All ferries linking Baja to the mainland were, until the 1990s, state-run and subsidized, their primary function being to help the development of the peninsula. As part of the government's privatization programme, they were sold off to a Japanese company that runs them on a commercial basis (under the name of SEMATUR). Accordingly, prices have risen for all users. Private vehicles do not have a high priority, and at times may have to wait days for space. Even foot passengers face extremely long queues: best arrive at the office well before it opens on the morning of departure (morning before for early ferries) – most offices are open 8.30am–1pm. In the past few years, Baja Ferries have also operated boats, but this line is geared towards vehicle transport and they do not allow more than one (male) person per vehicle. There are usually one or two others, also cargo-focused, though they will gladly sell you a ticket as a lone passenger.

Sematur services

Guaymas to: Santa Rosalía (10pm Mon, Thurs & Sat; 7hr).
La Paz to: Mazatlán (3pm daily except Sat/daily during holiday periods; 18hr); Topolobampo (10pm daily except Sun; 10 hr).
Mazatlán to: La Paz (2.30pm daily except Sat/daily during holiday periods; 18hr).
Santa Rosalía to: Guaymas (10pm Sun, Tues, & Fri; 7hr).
Topolobampo to: La Paz (10am Tues & Sat; 10hr).

Baja Ferries services

La Paz to: Topolobampo (3pm Mon–Sat; 6hr).
Topolobampo (Los Mochis) to: La Paz (10pm Mon–Sat; 6hr).

Between the sierras: northeast routes

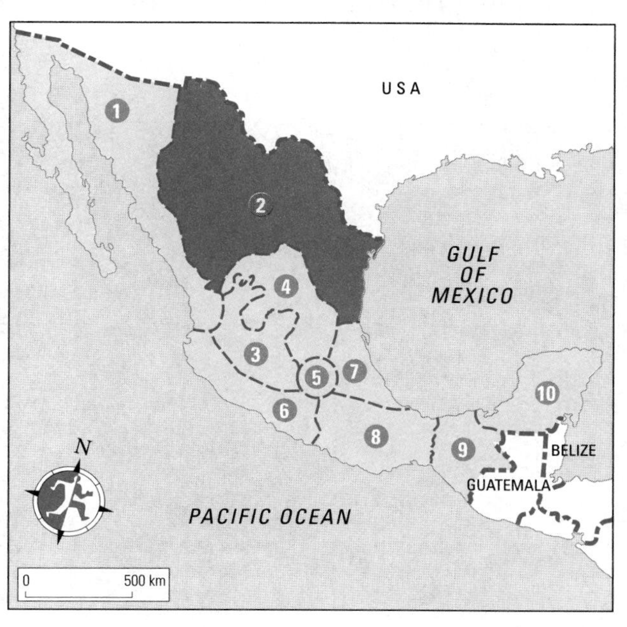

CHAPTER 2

Highlights

* **Paquimé** Fantastic ruins that are more than worth the five-hour trip from Chihuahua. See p.168
* **The Copper Canyon railway** The route from the west coast into the Sierra Madre offers perhaps the most dramatic and heart-stopping train experience in North America. See p.169
* **Creel** For some great adventure and a look into Mexico's past, hike to the Tarahumaran villages of the Copper Canyon around Creel, especially Batopilas. See p.174
* **Durango** Star in your own Wild West duel at the John Wayne film sets of Villa del Oeste. See p.184
* **Monterrey** The Barrio Antiguo and the museums of Monterrey are a must for their twin doses of art and culture. See p.203

△ Adobe foundations, Paquimé

Between the sierras: northeast routes

The **central and eastern routes into Mexico** are considerably shorter than the west coast road, and, though they don't have the beaches, they do offer direct access to the country's colonial heart and have much to see along the way. The high plain between the flanks of the **Sierra Madre** is also cool – even uncomfortably so in winter – and the highways crossing it are relatively modern and usually quite fast.

You'll find most interest heading down from **Ciudad Juárez**: highlights include the important archeological site of **Paquimé** at Casas Grandes, and in **Chihuahua** and **Durango** a foretaste of the majestic colonial cities to come in the country's heartland. If you happen to be passing through in March or April, you may be lucky enough to catch the desert in bloom – it's a riot of colour after a little rain.

There's a historic appeal, too: this was the country most fiercely fought for in the Revolution, and the breeding ground for Pancho Villa's División del Norte. The supreme attraction, though, must be the train journey through the **Copper Canyon** from Chihuahua to the Pacific coast: a thirteen-hour ride over soaring peaks and around the walls of vast canyons down to the steamy coastal plain. To the east, along the fastest route to the capital, **Monterrey** is a heavily industrialized city that has nevertheless managed to retain its finest sights; nearby **Saltillo** offers an escape into tranquil mountains.

Following the **Gulf coast** is less recommended – it's steaming hot in summer and not particularly interesting at the best of times. It is, though, the shortest way south, and if you stick it out past the refineries you'll reach the state of Veracruz (see p.549), with its fine beaches and wealth of archeological remains.

Border checks

Crossing the border, do not forget to go through **immigration and customs** checks. As everywhere, there's a free zone south of the frontier, and you can cross at will. Try to continue south, though, and you'll be stopped after some 30km and sent back to get your tourist card stamped (US$22).

The central corridor

Ciudad Juárez, the behemoth point of entry into the central corridor, offers little to detain most people heading south. If you have time, an excursion to the ruins at **Paquimé** near Nuevo Casas Grandes is worth the four-hour ride from the border, but those with less time should make for the rugged **Sierra Tarahumara** and the **Copper Canyon**. The town of **Creel**, on the Los Mochis–Chihuahua train line, is a great base for exploring the canyons and the many beautiful towns therein, such as **Batopilas**, which lies at the very bottom of a canyon. Allow plenty of time for Copper Canyon exploring; it's likely to be the best part of your trip through northern Mexico. The capital **Chihuahua** is interesting for a day but most come for the train or to catch a bus south.

Rapid and efficient bus services run throughout the central area, the best of the main lines probably being Transportes Chihuahuenses and Omnibus de México, with Estrella Blanca mounting a strong challenge as you head south. It can take as little as 25 hours to travel nonstop from the border to the capital.

Ciudad Juárez

CIUDAD JUÁREZ, just across the border from El Paso, Texas, is perhaps the least attractive of all the border towns – modern, sprawling and ugly, as well as extremely confusing to find your way around and, at times, positively intimidating. Sadly, there's little doubt that the best thing to do on arrival is to leave. In less than five hours you can reach Chihuahua or, rather closer, Nuevo Casas Grandes, the base for excursions to the archeological site at Casas Grandes.

Originally a small settlement on the Santa Fe Trail, known as Paso del Norte, Ciudad Juárez did have a brief moment of glory when Benito Juárez established his government here after he'd been driven out of the south by Maximilian – you can visit the **house** from which he governed, on Avenida 16 de Septiembre. The town changed hands frequently during the Revolution, most notably in 1913, when Pancho Villa, having stolen a train, managed to fool the local commander into expecting reinforcements and steamed into the middle of town with 2000 troops completely unopposed. Gaining access to the border and to arms from the north, this was one of the exploits that forged Benito's reputation.

During the 1990s, the town's reputation suffered from unsolved serial killings and its close ties to organized crime – having a role as the seat of the Juárez cartel, who, along with the Arellano Felix brothers in Tijuana, control much of Mexico's massive **drug-running** empire, masterminding cross-border trafficking of Colombian heroin and Andean cocaine.

Arrival, orientation and information

The two downtown **bridges over the Río Bravo** from El Paso to Ciudad Juárez are one-way for vehicles, those southbound taking Santa Fe Street, which crosses the border and becomes Avenida Juárez in Ciudad Juárez. Though you can enter by foot on either bridge, your best bet is to walk with the traffic, though visitors planning to push deeper into Mexico will need to

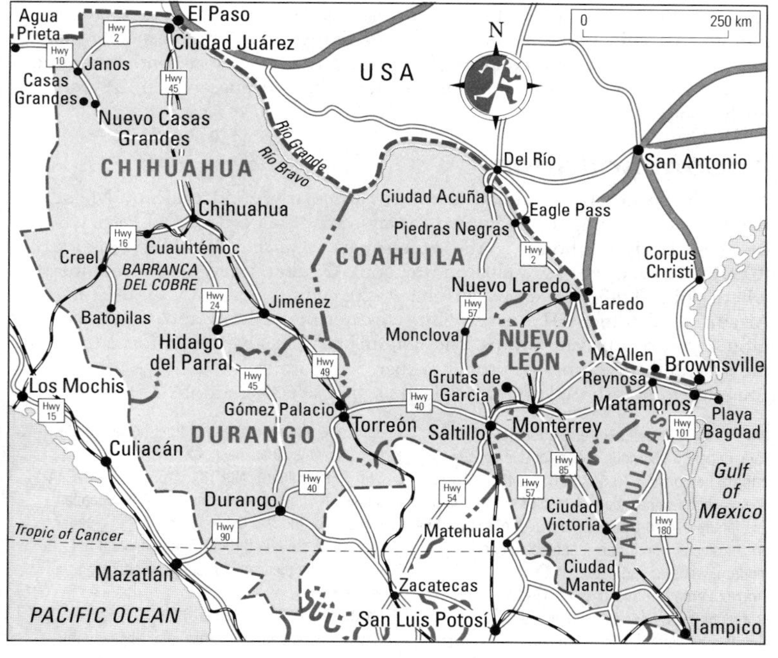

visit immigration close to the Mexican side of the northbound crossing. An alternative is to take a short hop on the frequent **El Paso–Juárez trolley** (US$1.50), which leaves from the bus stops in downtown El Paso and deposits you over the border on Avenida Juárez, the main drag. Ciudad Juárez enjoys excellent **bus** connections with the whole of north and central Mexico from its modern Central de Autobuses, at 4010 Oscar Flores (Ⓣ656/513-2083; 24hr guardería); local buses (#1A, #1B, or look for "C Camionera" on the windscreen) from there to the centre or the border generally take about thirty minutes (US$0.40), though a taxi (US$8) will get you there much more quickly. Likewise on your return, but if a bus is your only choice, get one from the corner of Guerrero and Villa by the market. You could also squeeze into one of the horribly cramped **shuttle vans** running to and from the border.

As soon as you cross the border the sordid nature of the place is immediately apparent: the blood banks and secondhand clothes emporia on the US side give way to seedy hotel lobbies, cheap bars and scores of cut-rate doctors and dentists on the Mexican side. However, if you're staying on this side, this is the place to be, in what's left of the old town. The **market** is a few blocks from the border straight up Lerdo, and the streets around it are home to most of the cheaper places to stay and eat.

If you **drive** across the border, you can avoid downtown Ciudad Juárez altogether by taking the Cordova bridge, a couple of kilometres east of the centre, or the new Zaragoza toll bridge, still further east, which directly connects the US and Mexican highway systems.

The Ciudad Juárez **tourist office**, Francisco Villa and Malecón (Mon–Fri 8am–2.30pm & 4–7pm, Sat & Sun 8am–2pm; Ⓣ656/615-2301 or 614-0607), currently only exists in an abbreviated form at the Chamizal bridge crossing, though the main office in the centre may reopen. The office can fill you in on details of rodeos, **charreadas** (April–Oct) and other local entertainment, as well as supply maps and information about things you'll be seeing further south.

Accommodation

None of the hotels in Ciudad Juárez is particularly good value by Mexican standards, so you might be tempted to stay across the border in El Paso, where the best **budget** choice is the atmospheric *Gardner*, 311 E Franklin St (Ⓣ915/532-3661, Ⓦwww.elpasohostel.com; ❹, discounted for HI members), where John Dillinger stayed in the 1920s while on his way to Tucson, Arizona – it's a nice **HI hostel** with self-catering facilities, and, if you please, more expensive private rooms. The helpful staff can give you information on the area, and sometimes run tours to Juárez and around.

Single women should take special care when selecting a hotel.

Del Prado in Pronaf centre Ⓣ656/616-8800. A safe, decent if luxurious option for Juárez. ❻

Impala Lerdo Nte 670 Ⓣ656/615-0431, Ⓦwww.hotel-impala.com. A block from the border, this family-owned place is the nicest of the slightly pricier places: comfortable, safe, clean and modern, with a/c and cable TV. ❺

Juárez Lerdo Nte 143 Ⓣ656/615-0358. Some of the cheapest beds in town. If you're willing to sacrifice a/c and stay in a room on the roof, you can save a few bucks more. Rooms are tidy, though the building itself has seen better days. ❷

Moran Juárez Nte 264 Ⓣ656/615-0862. A decent choice, though a little pricey for what you get: dank and dim rooms with little atmosphere and just passable cleanliness. ❺

San Carlos Juárez Nte 131 Ⓣ656/615-0419. A small cut above the local norm for the cheaper places. For the few extra pesos you get cleaner rooms, en-suite bathrooms with constant hot water, and a pleasant TV lounge overlooking the street. ❹

Santa Fe Lerdo Nte 675 Ⓣ656/615-1522, Ⓦwww.hotel-santafe-juarez.com. Opposite the *Impala* with nearly equal prices, though the rooms are slightly less attractive here. Quite nice, airy rooms, with a/c and TV with HBO, and a restaurant. Comfortable and convenient for late arrivals. ❺

The Town

If you decide to kill an hour strolling around the modest sights of downtown Juárez, be careful not to wander far off the main thoroughfares. Where 16 de Septiembre crosses Juárez, in the old customs building, the Aduana, there's a small, and mostly missable, **Museo Histórico** (Tues–Sun 10am–5pm; free), which traces the development of the town. A couple of blocks west of here on 16 de Septiembre you'll find a partly colonnaded square flanked by the cathedral and the seventeenth-century **Misión de Guadalupe**, around which the town grew up.

If you have more time, however, it's worth making for the **Museo de Arqueología del Chamizal** (Tues–Sun 10am–5pm; free) in the Parque Chamizal, east of the centre near the river, and the **Museo de Arte e Historia** (Tues–Sun 10am–5pm; free) in the **Pronaf tourist centre** – which also houses a huge, touristy craft market – not far from the bus station (local bus #8 runs there from the centre). Both museums offer limited introductions to Mexico; the former also has displays of some remarkable Paquimé pottery from the ruins at Casas Grandes (see p.168).

If you would like a guided tour of both Juárez and El Paso, the **border-jumper trolley** does just that, leaving hourly from the convention centre in El Paso (in the US Ⓣ915/544-0062; US$12). In El Paso itself, the **El Paso**

Museum of Art (Tues–Sat 9am–5pm, Sun noon–5pm; free; Ⓦwww.elpasoartmuseum.org) houses some five thousand European, North American and Mexican works of art from the fourteenth century onwards. You could also check out the murals painted by local youths and travellers alike, a couple of blocks west of the Greyhound station; what began as a vandalism problem is now positively encouraged by the town, and some of them are pretty good.

Eating and drinking

Places to eat are plentiful around the centre and border area, although new arrivals should probably take it easy on the street food. The fancier options line Juárez near the border. **El Paso** offers better value, however, and if you've been in Mexico some time, you may well want to rush across the border to the burger joints near the Greyhound station. The helpful staff at the *Camino Real* (see below) can also point you in the direction of any number of good restaurants within walking distance of the border.

Camino Real 101 S El Paso St, El Paso. Swanky hotel offering two restaurants: the *Azulejos*, a casual and relatively inexpensive alternative to the more international *Dome*, a fine-dining dinner-only restaurant.

El Coyote Inválido Juárez Nte 625 at Av Colon. Bright and breezy budget taco house that stays open late and serves up hearty chile relleno burritos and filling breakfasts.

La Nueva Central de Ciudad Juárez 16 de Septiembre Pte 322. Cavernous, cream-tiled and brightly lit place serving Mexican standards and basic Chinese specialities 24 hours a day.

Nuevo Restaurante Martino Juárez Nte 643. Classy, popular restaurant with high prices and varied cuisine, though the majority of the menu is traditional Mexican.

Restaurant Viva Juarez Juárez Nte 126, just before 16 de Septiembre (across from the *San Carlos* hotel). Good, inexpensive option for plain Mexican food.

Santa Fe Lerdo Nte 675. Fairly priced hotel restaurant, serving enchiladas and sandwiches.

La Seviliana Juárez behind the bullring. Juárez favourite that's been dishing out good Mexican fare for decades.

The Tap on Kansas and San Antonio. One of the spots near the Greyhound station, it has an inviting atmosphere with well-priced Mexican food and a jukebox playing *norteña*, classic rock, and American country music.

Listings

Banks and exchange It's easy enough to change money at casas de cambio and tourist shops along Juárez and 16 de Septiembre; most banks are on 16 de Septiembre, too, and you'll find ATMs at nearly all of them. Many places accept dollars, but make sure you know the current exchange rate before you do any such deals.

Buses There are constant departures with one company or another down the main highway to Chihuahua and points beyond, and every couple of hours for Nuevo Casas Grandes (via Janos). If you plan to head straight through, you should be able to get the hourly bus (US$5) direct to the Camionera Central from the El Paso Greyhound terminal at 1007 S Santa Fe St (and vice versa).

Car rental The only option is at the El Paso airport, though you'll need to purchase Mexican insurance if you're going to drive across. Dollar Ⓣ915/881-1500; Hertz Ⓣ915/775-6960.

Consulate US, López Mateos Nte 924 Ⓣ656/613-4050.

Internet access The public library across the border in El Paso (Mon–Thurs 8.30am–8.30pm, Fri & Sat 8.30am–5.30pm, Sun 1–5pm) has free Internet access. Walk north past the *Camino Real* hotel for about two blocks; it's on the corner of Franklin and Oregon. In Juárez, you can try Compu-Rent, 16 de Septiembre 372 at Lerdo (Mon–Sat 9am–9pm, Sun 10am–9pm; US$1.50/hr).

Post office At the corner of Lerdo and Peña, one block south of 16 de Septiembre.

Paquimé and Nuevo Casas Grandes

The only reason to stop in **Nuevo Casas Grandes** is to visit the nearby village of Casas Grandes and the adjacent archeological site of **Paquimé** (Tues–Sun 10am–5pm; US$1.30, free on Sun), the most important, and certainly the most striking, ruins in northern Mexico. Originally home to an agricultural community and comprising simple adobe houses (similar to those found in Arizona and New Mexico), it became heavily influenced by Mesoamerican, probably Toltec, culture. Whether this was the result of conquest or, more likely, trade is uncertain, but from around 1000 to 1200 AD, Paquimé flourished. **Pyramids** and **ball-courts** were constructed and the surrounding land irrigated by an advanced system of **canals**. At the same time local craftsmen were trading with points both south and north, producing a wide variety of elaborate ornaments and pottery. Among the finds on the site (many of them now in the National Museum of Anthropology in Mexico City) were cages that held exotic imported birds, whose feathers were used in making ornaments; necklaces made from turquoise, semiprecious stones and shells obtained from the Sea of Cortés; and other objects of copper, bone, jade and mother-of-pearl.

Much must have been destroyed when the site was attacked, burned and abandoned around 1340 – either by a marauding nomadic tribe, such as the Apache, or in the course of a more local rebellion. Either way, Paquimé was not inhabited again, its people abandoning their already depleted trade for the greater safety of the sierras. When excavation began in the late 1950s, there were only a few low hills and banks where walls had been, but by piecing together the evidence archeologists have partly reconstructed the adobe houses – the largest of which have as many as fifty interconnecting rooms around an open courtyard or **ceremonial centre**. The foundations of the houses, which were originally two or three storeys high, have been resconstructed to waist-height, with an occasional standing wall giving some idea of scale.

To fully appreciate the sophistication of this civilization, it pays first to pop into the somewhat new **Centro Cultural Paquimé** (Tues–Sun 10am–5pm; US$2.50, free on Sun), a beautifully laid-out, if thinly stocked museum, architecturally designed to mimic the ruins of the defence towers that once stood on the site. A large model of how Paquimé must have looked, interactive touch-screen consoles with commentary in Spanish and English, plus intelligent displays of artefacts aid interpretation. Modern examples of finds from the surrounding area – drums, dolls in native costume, ceramics and ceremonial masks – compete with the Paquimé artefacts, notably the beautiful pottery, its often anthropomorphic vessels decorated in geometric patterns of red, black and brown on a white or cream background. The cultural parallels are strongly evident though the jury is still out on whether descendants of Paquimé citizens number among the Tarahumara or other local indigenous people.

Practicalities

To **reach the site** you have first to travel 260km south of Ciudad Juárez through dusty chaparral and cotton country to Nuevo Casas Grandes. Travelling from Chihuahua is also an option as buses for the five-hour journey are equally frequent. Once in Nuevo Casas Grandes, take one of the frequent yellow buses ("Casas Grandes/Col Juárez") from the corner of Constitución and 16 de Septiembre to the plaza in Casas Grandes (about 15min), from where the site is signposted – it's a ten-minute walk.

Nuevo Casas Grandes itself is small and not especially interesting; if you leave Ciudad Juárez very early you can visit the site and continue to Chihuahua in the same day – a route that is longer but certainly more interesting than the main highway (though rains can take out the road south of Nuevo Casas Grandes). **Buses** arrive outside the adjoining Estrella Blanca and Omnibus de México offices on Obregón, just steps from the basic hotel *Juárez*, Obregón 110 (ⓣ636/694-0233; ❷), the cheapest place to **spend the night**, with small simple rooms and hot water on request. On the main street, a couple of blocks away, you'll find the hotel *California*, Constitución 209 (ⓣ636/694-1110; ❺), clean, though in dire need of central heating. Best of all, however, is the local-flavoured *Motel Piñón*, Juárez Nte 605 (ⓣ636/694-0655; ❻), a couple of blocks beyond the *California*, which boasts TV, reliable hot water and a swimming pool, and occasionally gives tours of the ruins – it even has a small museum of Paquimé clay pots.

Eating is a fairly basic affair in town, with a number of simple *taquerías* dotted around and slightly more upscale places such as *Dinno's Pizza* at the corner of Constitución and Minerva, which does small but tasty pizzas for US$4 as well as reliable burrito and enchilada staples. In Casas Grandes, you can have fantastic tortas and quesadillas at *La Michoacana*, the ice-cream store off the main square, just near the bus stop for Nuevo Casas Grandes.

If you need **Internet** access, there are a couple of places in Nuevo Casas Grandes located on Juárez: Versailles and La Playa both charge about US$2 per hour.

Los Mochis to Chihuahua: the Copper Canyon Railway

The thirteen-hour **train trip** that starts on the sweaty Pacific coast at Los Mochis, fights its way up to cross the Continental Divide amid the peaks of the Sierra Madre, then drifts down across the high plains of Chihuahua must rate as one of the world's most extraordinary rail journeys. Breathtaking views come thick and fast as the line hangs over the vast canyons of the **Río Urique**. Chief of these is the awesome rift of the **Barranca del Cobre**, with a depth, from mountain top to valley floor, of more than 2000m, and breadth to match – by comparison, the Grand Canyon is a midget. Scenically, however, there's no comparison with the great canyons of the southwestern US, and if you've visited them you may find the canyons here a little disappointing. Part of the difficulty is in getting a true sense of their enormity and beauty: there are none of the well-marked hiking tracks and official campsites that might tempt casual exploration north of the border, and serious hikers really need to devote the best part of a week to their endeavours.

The dream of the original builders, the Kansas City, Mexico and Orient Railway Company, was to carve a new route from the American Midwest to the Pacific, and in the early part of the twentieth century they had made it right across the plains, but were defeated by the sheer technical complexity of crossing the mountains. And it's easy to see why. Only in 1953 did the Mexicans start work on the final link, an engineering feat demanding the construction of 73 tunnels and 28 major bridges, which took a further eight years to complete.

Even when the bare mountain peaks here are snow-covered, the climate on the canyon floors is semitropical – a fact that the indigenous **Tarahumara**,

△ Aerial view of the Copper Canyon

who were driven into these mountain fastnesses after the Spanish Conquest, depend on, migrating in winter to the warmth of the deep canyons. The Tarahumara, whose population totals some 50,000, live in isolated communities along the rail line and in the stretch of mountains known as the Sierra Tarahumara, eking out an existence from the sparse patches of cultivatable land. Although as everywhere their isolation is increasingly encroached upon by commercial forestry interests, ranchers and growing numbers of travellers, they remain an independent people, close to their traditions. Their religious life, despite centuries of missionary work, embraces only token aspects of Catholicism and otherwise remains true to its agrarian roots – their chief deities being the gods of the sun, moon and rain. Above all, the tribe are renowned as runners: a common feature of local festivals are the foot races between villages that last at least a day, sometimes several on end, the runners having to kick a wooden ball ahead of them as they go.

The route

The train timetable (see box on p.173) more or less dictates that you tackle the journey eastbound from the coast to the mountains, otherwise you may well find yourself travelling along the most dramatic stretch of the line in the dark. The start of the journey is an inauspicious grind across the humid coastal plain, with passengers in the air-conditioned carriages settling back in their reclining seats while the rest just sweat.

The first-class cosseting becomes less of a benefit as the line breaks into the mountains and you start climbing into ever-cooler air. It was this section that defeated the original builders and from the train fanatic's point of view, this is the bit you've been waiting for. For six hours, the train zigzags upwards dizzily, clinging to the canyon wall, rocking across bridges, plunging into tunnels blasted through the rock, only to find itself constantly just a few metres above the track it covered twenty minutes earlier. Eventually, you arrive at **Divisadero**, where there's a halt of about fifteen minutes to marvel at the view. At first it seems a perverse choice for a stop, with nothing around but the mountain tops and crowds of Tarahumara hawking their crafts and food, including delicious *gorditas*. But walk a little way down the path and you're suddenly standing on the edge of space, on the lip of a vast chasm. Below you are the depths of the **Barranca del Cobre** and, adjoining it, the Barranca de Balojaque and the Barranca de Tararecua. There are a couple of absurdly expensive places to stay here and a few bare-bones cheaper ones as well, but for most people it's all too rapidly back on the train, which clanks on for an hour to **Creel**, just past the halfway stage and, at 2300m, close to the highest point of the line. This is the place to stop if you want seriously to explore the Sierra Tarahumara and the canyons; it gives easy access into some remarkable landscapes, and boasts the only reasonably priced hotel options en route (see p.174 for details of staying in Creel and exploring the Sierra Tarahumara).

From Creel, the train takes a further six hours to reach Chihuahua – though beautiful, it's not a truly spectacular run. In fact, if the train timetable doesn't suit, there's no reason why you shouldn't take the **bus** from Creel to Chihuahua: it costs about the same as the second-class train fare, is quicker, and covers much the same ground. East of Creel both bus and train begin to leave the Sierra Tarahumara behind as the route runs through gentle, verdant grazing land that wouldn't look out of place in some romantic Western film. In many ways, this is pioneer ranching country, centred on the town of **CUAUHTÉMOC**, 70km from Creel and 130km from Chihuahua. This is also

one of the chief centres for **Mennonites**, people you'll come across throughout northern Mexico – the men in their bib-and-tucker overalls and straw stetsons, as often as not trying to sell the excellent cheese that is their main produce; the women, mostly silent, wrapped in long, black nineteenth-century dresses with maybe a dash of colour from a headscarf. The sect, founded in the sixteenth century by a Dutchman, Menno Simonis, believe only in the Bible and their personal conscience: their refusal to do military service or take national oaths of loyalty has led to a long history of persecution.

The Mennonites arrived in Mexico in the early twentieth century, having been driven from Frisia to Prussia, thence into Russia and finally to Mexico by way of

Canada – each time forced to move on by the state's demand for military tribute or secular education. These days many are returning to Canada as impoverished emigrants, forced out of Mexico by limited land and a growing population – one lasting legacy is that they are credited with introducing the accordion to Mexican music. Among themselves the Mennonites still speak a form of German, although so divergent as to be virtually unintelligible to a modern German-speaker.

Rail practicalities

The Copper Canyon line is operated by the Ferrocarril de Chihuahua al Pacífico (CHP, pronounced SHAY PAY). There are two **trains**: the first-class **Primera** (also known as *Estrella* or simply no. 73), which is primarily a tourist service; and the second-class **Económica** (also known as *Mixto* or no.75), half the price but considerably slower and less comfortable. If you have the money, you're better off taking the *Primera* service, not only because it has air-conditioning and reserved, reclining seats, but also because the *Económica* tends to run late, so that particularly if you're travelling from Chihuahua out to the coast, you may pass many of the best sections in the dark.

Tickets for the *Económica* can only be bought from the station on the morning of departure, but *Primera* tickets can be prebooked either at the station or with any travel agency in Mexico City – to be sure of a first-class seat reserve early, especially from May to September and during Semana Santa. **Prices** for the whole journey from Los Mochis to Chihuahua have risen dramatically in the past few years – nearly US$57 on the *Económica* and about US$107 on the *Primera*. Tickets are available from travel agents, or Ferrocarril Mexicano directly (Ⓣ1614/439-7212, Ⓕ439-7208, Ⓦwww.chepe@ferromex.com.mx).

It's advisable to break up the journey, not only to get the most out of it, but also because the trip, even travelling first-class, is very exhausting. Section costs are based on a per kilometre rate, so you'll pay hardly any more no matter how often you break the journey; if you're travelling in the *Estrella* and want to maintain your reservation throughout the entire journey, however, you'll have to front the money at either Los Mochis or Chihuahua and ask for an *escala* ticket, which, for a fifteen percent surcharge, allows you to make up to two overnight stops along the way.

The CHP timetable

Currently the *Primera* and *Económica* travel daily in both directions, but always check to see if the service is running. Second-class carriages have been spotted tagged onto the first-class train, and it seems only a matter of time before there is only one train a day in each direction. The official times below are not entirely reliable, and trains (particularly the *Económica*) frequently run late – check with your travel agent (or other train ticket vendors) for information on delays, which may affect your schedule.

	Primera (no.73)		*Económica* (no.75)	
Los Mochis	6am	7.50pm	7am	10pm
El Fuerte	7.25am	6.30pm	8.40am	8.40pm
Bahuichivo	11.10am	2.45pm	12.45pm	3.45pm
Divisadero	12.35pm	1.05pm	2.25pm	1.55pm
Creel	2.15pm	11.30am	3.45pm	12.35pm
Cuauhtémoc	5.25pm	8.25am	7pm	9.35am
Chihuahua	7.50pm	6am	9.30pm	7am

The *Económica* is subject to seemingly random **cancellation** at any time, but both services may be cancelled due to derailed freight trains, or landslides, which plague the track during the rainy season.

You'll save money by taking along your own **food and drink**, but it's not essential; both are available on the train (though not cheaply), and throughout the journey people climb on board or stand on the platforms selling tacos, chiles rellenos, fresh fruit, hot coffee and whatever local produce comes to hand.

Creel and the Sierra Tarahumara

CREEL is a dusty little place with echoes of the Old West in its log cabins and its street scenes: you'll see Tarahumara people arriving on foot for supplies, ranchers on horseback, park rangers cruising in shiny new pick ups. The town was named after the state governor, Enrique Creel, son of the US ambassador to Mexico in the 1930s, who founded timberworks in the area. Now just one sawmill remains, but with the town's ideal location as a base for exploring the Sierra Tarahumara, tourism is fast becoming the main source of income. The main street, López Mateos, is increasingly being taken over by hotels, and even American franchises – Best Western and the like – are moving in, but it remains an attractive escape nonetheless, friendly and still relatively quiet. Remember that this is a mountain town at an altitude of 2300m, making the evenings cool year-round, with the occasional snowfall in the winter.

There isn't a great deal to do in the town itself, other than enjoy the refreshing cool mountain air; pretty much everything of interest is either on Francisco Villa, along the north side of the train lines, or López Mateos, which runs west from the zócalo, also parallel to the tracks. You can pass half an hour in the **Museo de la Casa de las Artesanías**, on the zócalo (Tues–Fri 9am–1pm & 3–6pm, Sat 10am–6pm, Sun 9am–1pm; US$1), which displays some fine examples of local handicrafts – including Tarahumara baskets woven from the long needles of the Apache pine – and panels on Enrique Creel and the construction of the railway, as well as some stunning black-and-white photos of the people.

There's an easy **hike** up the shrine-topped cliff face in town, which offers splendid bird's-eye views. Walk through the car park of the *Motel Parador de la Montaña* towards the rear field, and carry on towards the barbed-wire fence by the large boulder. Simply follow the steps carved into the rock face and you quickly reach the top of the cliff. To your right you'll see the train station, to your left the beginnings of the Copper Canyon and the Tarahumara lands, scattered with **rock formations** that locals insist include frogs, mushrooms, a nativity scene and even the eagle on the cactus of the Mexican flag.

Arrival and information

The train is obviously the way to **arrive** but, wonderful though it is, the vagaries of the timetable may induce you to catch one of the frequent daily buses that run between Creel and Chihuahua (US$16) – no great loss as the road pretty much follows the rail line. Both train station and bus stop are by the zócalo in the centre of town, where there's a less-than-reliable **tourist office** of sorts in the Jesuit mission shop, Artesanías Misión (Mon–Sat 9.30am–1pm & 3–6pm, Sun 9.30am–1pm), with limited information and local topographical maps. They also sell Tarahumara **crafts** – blankets, wooden dolls and drums – and photos of the Tarahumara, who on the whole dislike being photographed by tourists. If you want to be sure, however, that what you spend actually goes to the people who make the items themselves, buy directly from the women who sell the goods on the street. In front of the shop there is a plan of the town showing pretty much everything you're likely to need: a **bank** with ATM (dollar and travellers' cheque exchange and cash advances Mon–Fri 9am–1.30pm) and **post office** on the zócalo, long-distance **telephones** all over town, and a **laundry** (Mon–Fri 9am–2pm & 3–6pm, Sat 9am–2pm) in the two-storey house on Calle Villa, opposite the zócalo. For **Internet**, you're best off at Compucenter, Mateos 33 (daily 8.30am–11pm; US$2/hr).

Accommodation

The number of good **places to stay** in Creel grows every year, and most either meet the train with courtesy buses or dispatch small children to drum up business. Alternatively, take advantage of the courtesy buses that run to one of the luxury **lodges** out in the nearby countryside. RV drivers might fancy the clean KOA campsite (US$5 per person) on the edge of town, but **campers** are better off beside Lago Arareco, 7km south of Creel. Camping is also possible 4km closer at *Complejo Ecoturistico Arareko* (within the Tarahumara *ejido* of San Ignacio de Arareko), but you may find little privacy here.

Casa Margarita López Mateos 11 on the zócalo ⓣ635/456-0045. One of the better deals around, this hostel-like hotel is typically bursting at the seams with backpackers and a few better-heeled travellers. Rooms have a rustic, log-cabin feel, but are well heated, with local pine and oak for the flooring and walls. Also serves simple, but delicious breakfasts and dinners, which are included in the room price. Dorms ❷ (mattresses on the floor ❶), rooms ❹

Casa Valenzuela López Mateos 68 ⓣ635/456-0104. Less backpacker-oriented than the *Casa Margarita* and extremely quiet. It's cheap, relatively clean, has hot water all day, and feels like a home, though there is no heat in the rooms – a significant drawback during the winter months. Usually has vacant rooms even in peak season. ❸

Hotel Korachi just next to the bus station before the train station ⓣ635/456-0207. Bland, spartan and small rooms, it's still a decent alternative to either *Casa Margarita* or *Casa Valenzuela.* ❹

The Lodge at Creel López Mateos 61 ⓣ635/456-0071, from the US ⓣ1-877/844-0409, ⓦwww.thelodgeatcreel.com. Creel's best-known luxury lodging run by Best Western offers cabin-style rooms with spa, sauna, jacuzzi, and full restaurant. The wood-trimmed, rustic huts are ample and full of amenities, including coffee-makers, purified water and telephones. ❽

Margarita's Plaza Mexicana on Elfida Batista Caro off López Mateos ⓣ635/456-0245, ⓔalcalamsp@terra.com.mx. The fancier sibling of *Casa Margarita* has spacious heated rooms set around a courtyard, each decorated with murals. Popular bar on site; again the price includes breakfast and dinner. Discounts are possible in the low season, depending on demand. ❹

Motel Parador de la Montaña López Mateos 44 ⓣ635/456-0075, ⓦwww.members.tripod.com/copperinn.TV, tastefully decorated, tiled rooms and plenty of hot water make this the pick of the mid-range places, though you don't get nearly the same comfort, amenities and setting as you would at the *Lodge at Creel* for a bit more. ❻

Nuevo "Barrancas Del Cobre" Francisco Villa 121, right across from the train station; look for the "Nuevo" sign ⓣ635/456-0022. Slightly upmarket hotel with pleasant enough old rooms (some considerably better than others) and much nicer, newer a/c suites in log-cabin style, with TV and rooms sleeping up to four. ❺

Sierra Bonita Carretera Gran Visión about 1km out of town ⓣ635/456-0615. Perched on a hill overlooking Creel, the new "modern rustic" rooms, decked out with fireplaces and great views, are the most expensive in town; a taste of four-star Creel luxury nonetheless. Hotel also hosts one of the more popular discos in town. ❾

Los Valles Elfida Batista Caro s/n, next to *Margarita's Plaza Mexicana* ⓣ635/456-0075. This newly built motel off the main drag has small, clean rooms for decent prices; one of the better mid-range bargains in town. ❹

Eating and drinking

Almost all Creel's **restaurants and bars** are along López Mateos. The tiny *Mi Café*, at no. 21, serves bargain tortas, burritos and burgers (US$1), as well as hotcake and cornflake breakfasts (US$3) and real coffee; *Restaurant Verónica* and the simpler *Restaurant Lupita*, adjacent eateries a block down from *Mi Café*, are the most basic, and both serve reliable Mexican staples at modest prices; *The Lodge at Creel* hotel (see p.175) dishes up quality meals with a more American flavour that won't break the bank. Another option for antojitos is *Tío Molcas*, popular with both tourists and locals, with lots of plush seating and a small bar in the back. There are several other bars lining López Mateos: many foreigners gravitate to *Laylo's Lounge*, at no. 54, to keep up with the latest US sports via satellite. Backpackers are usually drawn by the drink specials in the bar at *Margarita's Plaza Mexicana* (see p.175).

The Sierra Tarahumara

Just about every hotel in Creel runs **organized trips** into the surrounding country or further afield to the canyons – enquire at *Margarita's*, the *Nuevo*, the *Motel Parador*, or try the tour booth on the zócalo. Keep in mind that tours leave in groups of at least four. All companies run much the same set of tours with little to choose between them; for the lengthier tours, remember to take your own lunch along. Most only give the faintest impression of what the canyons are like, but if you've only got a day or two and want to get out of town, then you've little choice but to take one; the best is probably the trip to Batopilas, easily arranged at *Casa Margarita* (see p.175). With more time you should definitely arm yourself with a topographic map, camping gear and set out to explore independently. You can get help with this from Three Amigos Canyons Expeditions on Mateos 46 next to the tourist office (daily 9am–8pm; Ⓣ635/456-0546, Ⓦwww.the3amigoscanyonexpeditions.com). They'll rent you a five-person-capacity double-cab pickup truck and arm you with food, cooler, maps, and all the information you might need to get out on your own (US$100/day). **Public transport** is highly irregular at best, but **hitching** is surprisingly easy to the places that are accessible by road. Don't venture off the beaten track alone, however, as this can be harsh and unforgiving country, and you don't want to stumble across illicit marijuana plantations. Again *Casa Margarita* is a good place to meet up with fellow travellers and get fixed up with inexpensive local guides.

You can also rent out **mountain bikes** from Umárike Expediciones, on Calle Ferrocarril, 500m west of the station, for around US$13 a day, though the building rarely seems open; they also give **rock-climbing** instruction. You might also try talking to Norberto at El Aventurero (Ⓔelaventurero@hotmail.com), who leads some guided hikes. Rather more expensive, but definitely worth it if you can afford it, is **horseback riding** in the vicinity – the staff at *Casa Margarita* can point you to the current outfitters (even if you are not a paying guest at the hotel). Or, less formally, you can hire horses from a stable about 50m from Expeditiones Umárike, which runs about US$8 per hour.

Perhaps the most popular of the tours is the four-hour spin (US$12) around a few minor local sights along the road south towards Guachochi. The usual itinerary includes a less-than-thrilling weathered boulder known as **Elephant Rock**; the pretty mountain lake **Arareco**, 7km from Creel; and **Cusárare**, about 10km further on, where there's an attractive 35-metre waterfall and an almost entirely original seventeenth-century Jesuit mission church with Tarahumara wall paintings. Hours are erratic, so if you are heading out to Cusárare on your own, enquire first in your accommodation at Creel as you're likely to find the church locked.

A full-day tour in the same direction heads to the organ-pipe formations of **La Bufa** (US$25), the canyon of the Río Batopilas on the road to Batopilas.

The trip claims to visit four of the region's canyons, though it turns out to be just a long drive through some admittedly impressive scenery – much of it not unlike the stratified towers and buttes of Arizona – turning back well short of Batopilas. Some of the best of the views can also be seen on the ride from Creel to Guachochi (see p.178). If you're driving on your own and need to spend the night here, *Juanita's* in La Bufa can give you a bed for the night for US$15; Juanita also makes great home-cooked meals.

There's also a full-day tour (US$25) away from the canyonlands, to the famous 254-metre **Basaséachic Falls**, protected in the Parque Nacional de Basaséachic. Said to be the highest single cascade in North America, this makes a long, but spectacularly rewarding, day's excursion – about four hours' driving followed by almost two hours on foot. Unfortunately the falls are virtually impossible to reach except as part of an organized excursion, and these only set off when there are enough takers to justify them. Tours also run to the **Recohuata hot spring** (7hr; US$18), where you can bathe in three pools of steamy and clean sulphurous water, and the Jesuit Mission shop in Creel run trips to the mission at **San Ignacio de Arareco**, a Tarahumara reserve run by the Jesuits, just ten minutes' drive from Creel. There are plenty of crafts on sale here; if you insist on taking photos, make sure you give your subjects a small tip or gift. Around the mission are superb pine forests, Indian cave dwellings and a set of odd rock formations known as the "valley of the mushrooms".

Batopilas, Guachochi and the lodges

Though Creel is the longest-established and best-known place to stay in the sierra, there are a number of alternative bases, which some feel offer better opportunities for exploring the deep canyons. One of the best is the former mining town of **BATOPILAS**, some 150km southwest of Creel, tucked right into the bottom of the canyon and stretching for about a mile along the side of the river of the same name – it's larger than you might expect for a place only connected by dirt road pushed through at the end of the 1970s. The Spanish found silver here in 1632 and mined it for centuries, the industry continuing until shortly after the Revolution. Today, it's a peaceful, subtropical place – resplendent with bougainvillea, palms and citrus trees – that can be hard to tear yourself away from. Mostly the pleasure is in just being in the canyons and lazing around, but there are a couple of specific **hikes** you can make. The best of these is to the restored "**Lost Cathedral**", a huge mission church 7km south of Batopilas at Satevo, standing in splendid isolation in a canyon bottom. The Tarahumara congregation just about prevent it from crumbling away completely, and the dry climate has kept the eighteenth-century murals in surprisingly good condition. Another track follows the Camino Real for three or four hours to the village of Cerro Colorado. Locals will point you to other trails, often best tackled with a guide; ask locally.

Buses and Suburbans leave Creel six times a week (buses: Tues, Thurs & Sat 7.30am; Suburbans: Mon, Wed & Fri 9.30am; both US$15) for the six-hour journey to Batopilas (they leave for the return trip to Creel Mon–Sat at 5am). Tickets are available from *Hotel Los Pinos* at López Mateos 39 (☎635/456-0044), from where the buses depart. On even the swiftest visit you'll have to **stay** here at least one night, and you'll find a host of budget accommodation. You're probably best at the *Hotel Palmera* (☎649/456-0633; ❸), about a kilometre out of town along the river, or at the considerably more basic *Hotel Batopilas* (no phone; ❷), two blocks north of the plaza just before the Dolores tributary empties into the river. The newly built *Hacienda Río Batopilas*

(Ⓣ635/456-0245: reservations need to be made through *Margarita's Plaza Mexicana*; ❾) has elegant rooms done in tile and brass and occupies the former hacienda and vault of a nineteenth-century mining magnate. It's located on your way into town along the river. Another luxury option is *Copper Canyon Riverside Lodge* (see opposite), an elegant, restored nineteenth-century hacienda where you're likely to want to stay for weeks. Dining in Batopilas is easy and cheap; try *Doña Mica*'s, near the plaza, which serves great dinners for about US$5; the *Hotel Mary*, opposite the church in town, also has a restaurant with good, inexpensive food.

Note that the drive down the canyon is not for the faint of heart: a narrow single-lane winding dirt roads snakes its way down over the ravine below. If you do decide to make a go of it alone, be sure to leave early enough to arrive by sundown and make certain that the brakes on your vehicle are in top shape, as you'll be using them for much of the three-hour descent.

An alternative is to head directly south towards Parral and Durango via the cowboy town of **GUACHOCHI**, 130km south of Creel, a disappointing destination, but reached along a dramatic and newly tarmacked mountain highway skirting the top edge of the great canyons and passing much of the best of the scenery seen on the tour to "La Bufa". If current schedules hold, the noon Estrella Blanca **bus** from Creel will get you to Guachochi in time to briefly tour the dusty streets, grab a bite to eat and catch the 4.45pm bus onwards for 190km to Parral – another dramatic ride, this time through magnificent cactus-strewn mountain scenery. The Estrella Blanca bus station is in a hidden yellow building at the northern end of town, almost a kilometre from the Transportes Ballezanos station, which also runs several buses a day on to Parral. If you get stuck, you'll find the very basic *Hotel Orpimel* (no phone; ❷), immediately above the Transportes Ballezanos station, and, around 300m north, the superior *Hotel Melina* (Ⓣ649/543-0340; ❺), which has a/c rooms with TV, and a decent restaurant, or the chartreuse *Las Cumbres Hotel* (Ⓣ649/543-0200; ❺) on the edge of town as you enter from Creel. The *Hotel Mansión* (Ⓣ649/543-0089; ❸), on 20 de Noviembre at no. 41, is clearly low-budget, but at least it's clean. Committed hikers can even use Guachochi as a base for exploring the remote **Sinforosa Canyon**. You can sometimes find a small **Internet** café open here at Aldana and Mateos, east of the zócalo (US$1/hr). For a quick, tasty bite, try *El Taco Movil*, on the corner of Malcovro and Herrera just west of the zócalo; they have decent tacos and good hamburgers for a few dollars.

For a chance to experience the canyons that's both more accessible than Batopilas and more appealing than Guachochi, you may want to consider the pricey **lodges** overlooking the canyons near stations along the rail line, all of which offer a variety of organized excursions; as the region begins to see more tourism, however, a number of smaller, more budget-minded places are being built around here. At **DIVISADERO**, the *Cabañas Divisadero Barrancas* (Ⓣ614/415-1199; ❾) are perched right on the canyon lip, and the *Posada Barranca del Cobre* (reservations in Los Mochis Ⓣ668/818-1630, from the US Ⓣ1-800/896-8196; ❾ with all meals), has rooms with terraces that have breathtaking views. The best hotel in the area, even if its rooms lack canyon-front views, comes just before the Divisadero stop, at **BARRANCA DIVISADERO**, where a bus takes you to the *Hotel Mansión Tarahumara* (in Chihuahua Ⓣ614/415-4721, Ⓕ416-5444; ❾), something resembling a medieval castle smack in the middle of the canyon; rates include all meals, and they have a pool. If you're in the mood for expensive aerial adventure, a local pilot runs helicopter tours of the canyons from the hotel's helipad; prices start at US$75/person for a fifteen-minute ride, minimum three persons. *Cabañas*

Diaz (Ⓣ635/578-3008), a few kilometres or so up the road in **POSADA BARRANCAS**, has small rustic rooms ranging in price from US$10 to US$25 and meals for US$5.

At **BAHUICHIVO**, on the rail line 50km west of Divisadero, buses will pick you up to take you to the extremely attractive *Hotel Misión* (reservations in Los Mochis Ⓣ668/818-1630, Ⓕ812-0046, from US Ⓣ1-800/896-8196; ❽ including all meals), in the mountain village of **CEROCAHUI**.

Two other possibilities, best organized before you arrive in Mexico, are the *Copper Canyon Lodges* (in the US Ⓣ248/340-7230 or 1-800/776-3942, Ⓕ248/340-7212, Ⓦwww.coppercanyonlodges.com), with a lovely small hotel at Cusárare and another at Batopilas (see opposite). They normally offer all-inclusive multi-day packages combining both hotels and starting from Chihuahua. Summer rates work out to around at least US$1400 a week for two, but booking in advance and accepting certain conditions can halve this.

Chihuahua

You're unlikely to see any of the little bug-eyed dogs in **CHIHUAHUA**, the capital of the largest state in the republic. They do come from here originally, but their absence is presumably because the vicissitudes of a dog's life in Mexico are too great for so fragile a creature. Perhaps, too, because few could stand the fumes of this transport hub and industrial centre, which marshals the state's mineral and agricultural wealth.

Though the gloom in poor weather is generally depressing – and a stay of a night or two is ample for most – Chihuahua can have some appeal, with its colonial centre and suburbs of grandiose nineteenth-century Gothic-style mansions built when silver brought wealth to the region. This is also *vaquero* heartland and one of the best places in the country to look for **cowboy boots**: you're spoiled for choice in the centre, especially in the blocks bounded by Calle 4, Juárez, Victoria and Ocampo.

Arrival, orientation and information

Transport in and out of Chihuahua is not well co-ordinated, frustrating the many travellers who come here only to take the Copper Canyon rail line. The **Central Camionera** (with guardería 9am–11pm and long-distance phone offices; Ⓣ614/429-0230) is miles out, near the airport on Avenida Aeropuerto; local buses (US$0.40) from the main road outside run to and from Avenida Juárez in the centre, and there are plenty of taxis (US$5). From the **airport**, the usual system of official transport operates – buy your voucher as you leave the terminal.

Arriving by **train** from the Copper Canyon at the CHP station (Ⓣ614/410-0514), you're 2km southeast of the centre at Mendez and Calle 24. You can take a bus into the centre, but you'll probably want to take a taxi; indeed you may have little choice, since you and your luggage will be grabbed by eager drivers the minute you step out. The Ciudad Juárez–Mexico City train no longer carries passengers.

Central Chihuahua is compact enough for you to **get around** everywhere on foot, but bear in mind that addresses can initially be confusing. Even-numbered cross streets lie to the south of the central Plaza de Armas and odd numbers to the north, with shop or hotel numbers taking their initial digit from the associated street; thus, Allende 702 is between calles 7 and 9 north of

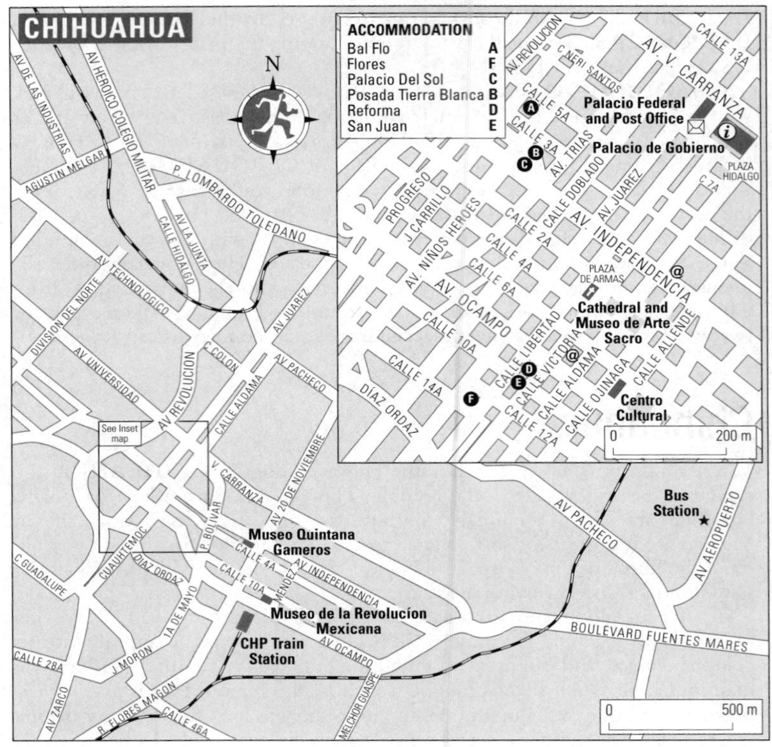

the centre, but Allende 607 will be south of the centre between calles 6 and 8.

There's a small, helpful English-speaking **tourist office** (Mon & Tues 9am–5pm, Wed–Fri 9am–7pm, Sat & Sun 9am–5pm; ⓣ614/410-1077 or 01-800/508-0111, ⓦwww.chihuahua.gob.mx/turismoweb) on the ground floor of the Palacio de Gobierno.

Accommodation

If you're arriving from the north you'll find Chihuahua's **hotels** wonderfully economical, with the cheaper examples lying southwest of the Plaza de Armas along Victoria and Juárez. Those a street or two further west may be a few pesos cheaper, but they're right in the heart of Chihuahua's small and tame, but nonetheless seedy, red-light district: Calle 10, especially, has a fair number of extremely cheap dives, though the city appears to be tearing down a number of these edifices. All the places listed have 24-hour hot water; at the cheaper places, a/c is only available in summer.

Bal Flo C 5a no.702 at the junction with Niños Héroes ⓣ614/416-0300. The bunker-like exterior softens within to reveal one of the better middle-range choices, featuring slightly poky but neat rooms with TV and phone. Winters at *Flo*'s are BYOB (bring your own blanket, as they've yet to install any heating here). ❺

Flores C 12a no.218 ⓣ614/416-0639. Small but relatively clean rooms and cheap rates are about all this hole-in-the-wall has to offer, but it may be enough. A bargain if you don't mind the red-light location. ❷

Palacio del Sol Independencia 116, five blocks west of centre ☎614/416-6000 or from US ☎1-800/852-4049. Top-notch, multistorey luxury, though somewhat of a monolithic eyesore; most of the large international-standard rooms offer expansive views over the city and come with satellite TV. Gymnasium, pricey cafeteria and restaurant/bar round out the package, and rooms are discounted at weekends. ❾

Posada Tierra Blanca Niños Héroes 100, beside the *Palacio del Sol* ☎614/415-0000. Spacious, open motel-style place right in the heart of the city with an open-air pool, gymnasium and tidy and spacious, if not exactly tasteful, rooms, plus on-site restaurant and bar. ❼

Reforma Victoria 809 ☎614/410-3998. Old hotel arranged around a massive, covered courtyard, which all suggests a *fin de siècle* European train station. For a few more pesos it's better than its neighbour, the *San Juan*, though the rooms are still a bit tatty and overall the place is pretty run-down. ❸

San Juan Victoria 823 ☎614/410-0035. Simple, old-fashioned hotel is usually friendly, though the interior could use a face-lift. Has some rooms off a courtyard and newer wooden-floored ones in a block behind, some with TV; ask for one of the courtyard ones if you can, as the ones upstairs give the vague sense that you're in a gymansium locker room. They also have Internet for guests at US$1/hr. ❷

The Town

Chihuahua centres on the teeming **Plaza de Armas**, where the city's fine **Cathedral** stands opposite a wonderfully camp statue of the city's founder in the very act of pointing to the ground, as if to say "Right lads, we'll build it here". The Baroque, twin-towered temple was begun in 1717 but took more than seven years to complete: work well worth it, though, since for once the interior detail is the equal of the facade. In a modernized crypt beneath the cathedral the small **Museo de Arte Sacro** (Mon–Fri 10am–2pm & 4–6pm; US$1.50) displays some fine examples of Mexican religious art from the eighteenth century, notably a selection of sombre saints by Francisco Martinez, and a collection of dark and forbidding images in which Christ is pushed, pulled, stabbed and punched.

Also on the Plaza de Armas is the imposing, but relatively modern, **Palacio Municipal**; follow Victoria down past this and you'll come to the Plaza Hidalgo, dominated by the **Palacio de Gobierno**. Now lined with bold murals of scenes from Mexico's colonial past painted by Aarón Piña Mora, this was originally a Jesuit College, and later converted to a military hospital after the expulsion of the Jesuits – here Padre Miguel Hidalgo y Costilla and Ignacio Allende, the inspiration and early leaders of the Mexican War of Independence, were executed in 1811, their severed heads sent for public display in Guanajuato. The site of the deed is marked (despite the fact that the building has been reconstructed several times since) and, by crossing the road to the adjacent Palacio Federal, you can visit the **Calabozo de Hidalgo**, at the corner of Juárez and Guerrero (Tues–Sun 9am–6.30pm; US$0.50), "Hidalgo's dungeon", where they were all held beforehand. The museum has on display various relics of Hidalgo and the Revolution, including his pistol, chest, crucifix and a number of personal letters. A golden eagle marks the entrance.

More recent history is commemorated in Chihuahua's premier sight, the **Museo de la Revolución Mexicana**, Calle 10 at no. 3010 (Tues–Sat 9am–1pm & 3–7pm, Sun 9am–5pm; US$1.50), which occupies Pancho Villa's former home. This enormous mansion was inhabited, until her death in the early 1980s, by Villa's "official" widow (there were allegedly many others), who used to conduct personal tours; it has now been taken over by the Mexican army and put on a more official footing. The collection is a fascinating mix of arms, war plans and personal mementoes, including the bullet-riddled 1922 Dodge in which Villa was assassinated in 1923 and a funerary mask clearly showing the bullet wound in his forehead. Quite apart from the campaign memories, the superbly preserved old bedrooms and bathrooms give an interesting insight into Mexican daily life in the early twentieth century.

The museum is some 2km east of the centre. To get there, walk along Ocampo, or take a bus (marked "Ocampo"), and continue two blocks past the huge church and two blocks to the left along Mendez. You may well want to break the journey at the extraordinarily elaborate **Museo Quinta Gameros** (Tues–Sun 11am–2pm & 4–7pm; US$2), at the junction of Calle 4 and Paseo Bolivar. Just the sort ostentatious display of wealth that Villa and his associates were hoping to stamp out in their battle against the landed elite, the building was designed by a successful mine owner as an exact replica of a Parisian home. The interior is sumptuously decorated, with magnificent Art Nouveau stained glass and ornate woodwork, and, curiously, scenes from *Little Red Riding Hood* are painted on the children's bedroom wall.

On the way back, call in at the **Centro Cultural de Chihuahua**, Aldama 430 at Ocampo (Tues–Sun 10am–2pm & 4–7pm; free), which puts on concerts and exhibitions from time to time and has a small but briefly diverting permanent display on the ruins at Paquimé (see p.168) with some nice pots.

Eating, drinking and entertainment

There's no shortage of good **places to eat** in Chihuahua, from basic cafés around the **market** (west of Juárez between calles 4 and 6), through taco stalls nearer the centre, to fancier steak houses and American burger restaurants around the main plazas. The southern end of Calle Victoria has some of the best options, and tends to stay open late.

For traditional, back-slapping cantina **drinking**, pick one of the swing-door places at the southern end of Juárez, though take care. If you're after something a little more upmarket, rub shoulders with Chihuahua's more moneyed set at the bars and clubs along Juárez's northern reaches, close to its junction with Colón. Alternatively, you can always see a subtitled American **movie** (around US$2) at Sala 2001, Guerrero at Escorza, and Cinema Revolución, where Doblado meets Calle Neri Santos.

Café Irene across from Mercado Chihuahua. The best of the market cafés with excellent comidas for US$3.

Café Merino Juárez 616 at Ocampo. A traditional-style place, they've been around for over seventy years, serving a full menu of antojitos, tortas and burgers at reasonable prices. Their specialty, the *menudo*, is beef doused with corn and *pozoles*.

La Calesa 3300 Juárez at Colón ☎1/416-0222. One of Chihuahua's fanciest restaurants, all dark wood panels, crisp linen tablecloths, sparkling wine glasses and waistcoated waiters. Northern-style steaks are the house speciality. Expect to pay US$8 for *chiles rellenos de camarón* and up to US$13 for a massive plate of succulent *mariscos*. Bookings recommended at weekends.

Casa de los Milagros Victoria 810, opposite *Hotel Reforma*. Casual restaurant and bar comprising a beautiful colonial courtyard with fountain, surrounded by numerous small rooms. Here, Chihuahua's well-groomed meet for margaritas (US$2), one of forty brands of tequila (US$1–5 a shot), real coffee and light snacks such as *quesadilla de flor de calabaza* (squash flower; US$4), burgers and salads.

Dino's Pizza Doblado 301, north of Independencia. Delicious pizzas made with an interestingly sweet dough ($8 buys one big enough for two) and with an excellent range of toppings. Also sandwiches and spaghetti dishes. Stays open late.

Mi Café Victoria 1000, almost opposite the *Hotel San Juan*. Reliable American-style diner with prices and quality both a little above average. The US$4 breakfast menu is in English and Spanish and extends from *norteño* and ranchero dishes to hotcakes and syrup. Come here later for burgers, sandwiches and steak and seafood mains.

El Vegetariano Libertad 1703. Chihuahua's only vegetarian restaurant, which is light on atmosphere but serves a US$3 daily buffet of soup, salad and soya-based dishes (1–4pm), and also sells veggie burgers, yogurt and granola, wholemeal bread and hearty cakes. Closed evenings and Sun.

Listings

Banks Most banks are centrally located, and nearly all have ATMs, with branches on Victoria and Libertad around the Plaza de Armas.

Buses The Central Camionera (see p.179) has representatives from Estrella Blanca, Transportes Chihuahuenses, Omnibus de México, plus a Greyhound one for buses to Denver, Los Angeles, Phoenix, Dallas and a few other US cities. Between the bus companies there are hourly buses to Juárez, frequent buses to Creel, a handful of buses for the 5hr jaunt to Nuevo Casas Grandes. The buses south are equally frequent, with hourly buses to Parral, at least ten buses to Durango, and every other hour to Mexico City and Guadalajara.

Internet access You're best bets in town are Int@rnet at Victoria and C 6 by *Mi Café*, or Acesso, Aldama 109 at Independencia (both US$1/hr).

Phones There's a good long-distance phone booth in the pharmacy at Independencia 808, east of Aldama (Mon–Sat 8am–8pm), though you can easily find Telmex phone booths all over town.

Post office Opposite the Palacio de Gobierno, in the Palacio Federal on Plaza Hidalgo (Mon–Fri 8am–7pm, Sat 9am–1pm).

Trains The only passenger train that services Chihuahua is the Copper Canyon line (see p.173), from the CHP train station. You can catch the buses marked "Sta Rosa" or "Col Rosalia", which run along Ocampo. Get out a couple of blocks past the big church (impossible to miss) and walk a couple of blocks to the right down Mendez to the station. There are occasional cancellations so it's a good idea to visit the station ticket office a day ahead; it's even now possible to buy tickets the morning of departure, assuming you make it there early enough (Mon–Fri 6am–5.30pm, Sat & Sun 6am–12.30pm).

Travel agent Rojo y Casavantes, Guerrero 1207 at Allende ⓣ614/439-5858, ⓦwww.rojoycasavantes.com (Mon–Fri 9am–7pm, Sat 9am–1pm).

South to Durango

Below Chihuahua sprawls a vast plain, mostly agricultural, largely uninteresting, broken only occasionally by an outstretched leg of the Sierra Madre Occidental. The freight train crosses at night, buses hammer through relentlessly and you'd be wise to follow their lead. At **Jiménez** the road divides, with Hwy-49 heading straight down through Gómez Palacio and Torreón, while Hwy-45 curves westwards to Durango. The nonstop route for Zacatecas and Mexico City is quicker, but if time is not your only consideration the Durango route offers far more of interest.

Torreón and **Gómez Palacio**, on the faster of the two routes, are virtually contiguous – there would be only one city were it not for the fact that the state border runs through the middle: Torreón is in Coahuila, Gómez Palacio in Durango. They're as dull as each other – modern towns anyway, both were devastated by heavy fighting in the Revolution. There's no need whatsoever to stop, though one consolation if you do is that they mark the start of wine-growing country, and you can sample the local produce (not the country's best) at various *bodegas*. On the longer route, **Durango** is the first of the Spanish colonial towns that distinguish Mexico's heartland, and while it's not a patch on some of those further south, it will certainly be the most attractive place you will have come to. That said, it's a good eight to ten hours on the bus from Chihuahua, so you might consider breaking the journey in **Hidalgo del Parral**.

Parral

PARRAL, or "Hidalgo del Parral" as it's officially known, is fixed in the Mexican consciousness as the town in which General Francisco "Pancho" Villa was assassinated, but the town's history goes back much further. Much of it is linked with the metal-rich stubby hills all around, where, in the early years after the Conquest, the Spanish set up a mine in the little town of **Santa Barbara**, 25km away, to extract silver above all, but also lead, copper and some gold. Santa Barbara soon became the capital of the province of Nueva Viscaya, a territory that stretched as far north as Texas and southern California; the capital was transferred to Parral after its foundation in 1638.

Once you have figured out the river-dictated street grid, you'll likely find a charming little town thoroughly unaffected by tourism. You could do worse than stay in Parral and explore the streets for an afternoon and visit the numerous churches, among them the **Catedral de San José**, which houses the remains of the town's founder Don Juan Rangel de Viesma. Although mining is still Parral's chief activity and its outskirts are grubbily industrial, at the centre the tranquil colonial plaza features a couple of remarkable buildings put up by prospectors who struck it rich. Chief of these are the **Palacio Pedro Alvarado**, an exuberantly decorated folly of a mansion built in the eighteenth century by a successful silver-miner, and, a few minutes' walk across the river, the **Iglesia de la Virgen del Rayo**. Legend has it this was constructed by an Indian on the proceeds of a gold mine he had discovered and worked in secret; the authorities tortured him to death in an attempt to find the mine, but its location died with him. There's also a small museum in the house from which Villa and his retinue of bodyguards were ambushed, located on Avenida Juárez.

Practicalities

Parral's compact colonial heart is around twenty minutes' walk from the main **bus terminal** (daytime luggage storage) – turn left, then left again onto Independencia – or take a bus or taxi (US$2) from just outside. There are buses almost hourly to both Durango and Chihuahua, and frequent buses to Juárez and Torreón. The cheapest acceptable **hotel** in town by far is the basic, if slightly untidy, *Hotel Zaragoza*, 115 Zaragoza (Ⓣ627/522-6590; ❷), especially cheap for groups. If that's full, there's the clean and simple *Hotel Fuentes* Maclovio Herrera 79 (Ⓣ627/522-0016; ❸). If you can pay a few pesos more, head to *Hotel Acosta*, near the main plaza on Agustín Barbachano 3 (Ⓣ627/522-0221; ❹), a pleasant old establishment with excellent rooms that overlook the city, a rooftop terrace and 1950s atmosphere. For a touch more luxury, only a stone's throw from the bus station, stroll to the *Hotel Los Arcos*, Dr Pedro de Lille 5 (Ⓣ627/523-0597, Ⓕ523-0537; ❺), where rooms front onto a modern courtyard and come with satellite TV and a VCR with choice of English-language videos; there's also a restaurant. For **eating**, in the centre just off the plaza the bright and cheery 24-hour *Restaurant Morelos*, Coronado 22, serves *pozole de puerco* for US$4 and excellent *enchiladas suizas*, made with chicken, guacamole and green chile. If you've a taste for a torta or burger, stop off at the *OK Parral*, Independencia 47, on your walk from the bus station into town. The popular *Chagos* makes a good dinner spot, with filling, though slightly pricey, steak filets; it's off Coronado. Ciber World is a good **Internet** spot at Bartolomé de las Casas 15 (near Juárez) and charges US$1.50 per hour.

Durango

Although the Sierra Madre still looms on the western horizon, the country around **DURANGO** itself is flat – with just two low hills marking out the city from the plain. The **Cerro del Mercado**, a giant lump of iron ore that testifies to the area's mineral wealth, rises squat and black to the north, while to the west a climb up the **Cerro de los Remedios** provides a wonderful

panorama over the whole city. Officially named Victoria de Durango, the city, with its nearly 600,000 inhabitants, sits between the two hills in the Valle del Guadiana. The newer development has sprouted eastwards and southwards. Highways 45 and 40 intersect at Durango, making it an important transport junction between the coast and the interior cities of Torréon, Saltillo and Monterrey, but the town is worth a visit in its own right, a national monument and with colonial architecture that is worth at least a day or two of your time. The people, too, are a charismatic and gregarious bunch whose hospitality comes as a charming respite from the north.

Durango's **fiesta**, on July 8, celebrates the city's foundation on that day in 1563 by Francisco de Ibarra. Festivities commence several days before and run right through till the fiesta of the Virgen del Refugio on July 22 – well worth going out of your way for, though rooms are booked solid.

Arrival and information

Since passenger trains no longer run here, you'll be arriving at the **Central de Autobuses** (guardería, 7am–11pm) over 4km out of town; to get to town, take one of the off-white buses marked "Centro" or "Camionera" from in front of the station. These will drop you right at the Plaza de Armas near the cathedral. Facing the cathedral, turn left along 20 de Noviembre (as it runs into Florida) just past Independencia to reach the second-floor **tourist office**, 1106 Florida, where the charming Beatriz should be able to help you out with whatever you need to find, see, or do in town (Mon–Fri 9am–6pm, Sat & Sun 10am–6pm; ⓣ618/811-2139, ⓦwww.turismodurango.com). Despite its compact, grid-plan centre, getting your bearings in Durango can initially be a little tricky, so it's as well to know that addresses south of Aquiles Serdán (two blocks north of the cathedral) are appended "Sur", and those west of Zarco (six blocks east of the cathedral) are tagged "Ote".

For **currency exchange**, there's a convenient branch of Bancomer right by the plaza at the corner of 20 de Noviembre and Constitución, in addition to several other banks nearby. The **post office** is at 20 de Noviembre Ote 500b, some twelve blocks east of the cathedral, and **American Express** operates from 20 de Noviembre Ote 810 (Mon–Fri 9am–7pm, Sat 10am–5pm; ⓣ618/817-0083), a further three blocks east of the post office; catch "Tecno" buses along 20 de Noviembre. The handiest booth for **long-distance calls** is at Bruno Martínez Sur 206 at Negrete (Mon–Sat 8am–9.30pm, Sun 8am–3pm). There are several inexpensive and good **Internet** cafés in Durango, among them the brand-new *El Cactus*, on the corner of Constitutión and Negrete (Mon–Sat 8am–9pm; US$1/hr). For **laundry**, there's a *lavandería* on Zarco at Negrete, where you can get 3 kilos washed and dried for US$3.

Accommodation

There's no shortage of **rooms** in Durango, though you should book ahead if you want to visit during the fiesta. Cheaper places are mostly pretty grim: if price is your only concern, try around the market, though even here the better places charge heavily. If you're willing to spend a little more, Durango has a couple of very fine places worth splashing out on.

Casablanca 20 de Noviembre Pte 811 at Zaragoza ⓣ618/811-3599. Big, old-fashioned colonial hotel. Spacious and comfortable if unexciting. ❺

Hotel Plaza Cathedral Constitución 216, beside the cathedral ⓣ618/813-2480, ⓕ813-2660. Excellent value for such a charming, historic and centrally located hotel. Hot water and cable TV; big rooms with high ceilings – everything is comfortably large here. Best deal in town, considering it's got great ambience and is very quiet yet still just a block from Durango's central plaza. ❹

María del Pilar Pino Suárez 410 ⓣ618/811-5471. Newly renovated and very clean, the rooms inside this pink building come with private bath and phone. ❸

Oasis Zarco 317 at 5 de Febrero ⓣ618/811-4561. Small, barely clean rooms with shower, near the market. A good value, given the location and rock-bottom price. ❷

Posada San Jorge Constitución Sur 102 at Serdán ⓣ618/813-3257, ⓕ811-6040. The best of the pricier places, a gorgeous and recently remodelled hotel in a colonial house, with a two-storey courtyard alive with caged birds and chatter from the Brazilian restaurant within. Rooms, all with cable TV, are individually decorated in rustic fashion, with tiled floors, wood beams, bold paintwork and potted cacti. Prices drop by about US$20 off-season. ❻

The Town

Almost all the monuments in downtown Durango cluster in a few streets around the Plaza Principal and the huge covered market nearby. On the plaza itself is the **cathedral**, its two robust domed towers dwarfing the narrow facade. It's a typical Mexican church in every way: externally imposing, weighty and Baroque, with a magnificent setting overlooking the plaza, and yet ultimately disappointing, the interior dim and by comparison uninspired. Facing it from the centre of the plaza is a bizarre little two-storey bandstand from the top of which the town band plays on Sundays; underneath, a small shop sells expensive local crafts.

Following Avenida 20 de Noviembre down from the cathedral (stretching away to the left as you face it) brings you to the grandiose Porfiriano **Teatro**

Ricardo Castro. Several blocks further, you will come to the new **Museo de Cine** (Mon–Fri 9am–6pm, Sat & Sun 10am–6pm; US$0.50), next door to the tourist office at Florida 1106, a fairly interesting tribute to the films created around Durango, including over a hundred Westerns. You can view the pictures of the sets, some old cameras and recording equipment.

Head back east on Avenida 20 de Noviembre and turn south onto Bruno Martínez, past the Teatro Victoria, and you come out in another plaza, its north side dominated by the porticoed facade of the **Palacio de Gobierno**. Originally the private house of a Spanish mining magnate, this was taken over by the local government after the War of Independence. The stairwells and walls of the two-storey, arcaded patio inside are decorated with murals by local artists depicting the state's history. On the east side of the square, an ancient **Jesuit monastery** now houses the offices of the Juárez Autonomous University of Durango.

From here Avenida 5 de Febrero leads back to the **Casa de los Condes**, the most elaborate of the Spanish-style mansions. Built in the eighteenth century by the Conde de Suchil, sometime Spanish governor of Durango, its exuberantly carved columns and wealth of extravagant detail are quite undamaged by time. History has given the mansion some strange functions, though: it was the seat of the local Inquisition for some time – and a more inappropriate setting for their stern deliberations would be hard to imagine – while nowadays it operates as a bank, having had a brief spell as a sort of upmarket shopping mall. A little further along 5 de Febrero, you reach the back of the **market**. It covers a whole block on two storeys and has just about everything anybody could want here, from medicinal herbs to farm equipment to small food stalls, as well as a couple of *bodegas* upstairs which serve beer to a primarily local crowd.

Back at the plaza, you can stroll up Constitución, a lively shopping street with several small restaurants, to the little church and garden of Santa Ana, much more peaceful than the plaza for an evening *paseo*. On the east side lies the **Museo de la Cultura** (Tues–Fri 9am–6pm, Sat & Sun noon–6pm; US$1), an old converted mansion with separate rooms dedicated to local, native styles of weaving, ceramics, basketware and mask-making. Enthusiastic guides explain all, and there are often interesting temporary exhibitions.

Parque Guadiana and Cerro de los Remedios

If you have kids in tow, or just fancy a break from bus diesel fumes, make for the prominent Cerro de los Remedios, 2km west of the city centre, or more particularly, **Parque Guadiana** on its northern flanks – take a bus marked "Remedios/Parque Guadiana" from outside the cathedral – a vast area of fragrant eucalyptus and shady willows, dotted with fountains and kids' playgrounds, and with a **miniature train** (Fri 3–7pm, Sat & Sun 11am–6pm; US$0.40). On the western side of the park, on Anillo de Circunvalación, is the **Zoológico Sahuatoba** (Tues–Sat 11am–6pm, Sun 10am–7pm; free), a collection of lions, tigers, hippos, monkeys and the like that's surprisingly well presented considering the free entry. Buses marked "Tierra y Libertad" come directly here from the corner of Serdán and Victoria.

The **Cerro de los Remedios**, rising immediately above the park and the zoo, is home to Durango's moneyed classes, and expensive modern homes are climbing inexorably towards the hilltop **Iglesia de los Remedios**, which commands a wonderful view over the entire city. The most direct way to walk up here from the city is to take the steps at the western end of Juan García.

Eating, drinking and entertainment

It isn't difficult to find great **places to eat** in Durango, among them – and for no apparent reason – a proliferation of reputable Italian places. Your cheapest eating options are the stalls upstairs in the **market**, some of which serve excellent food. Adjacent streets, and those off the main plaza, are also good hunting grounds, but the greatest concentration is along the first half-dozen blocks of Constitución going north from the plaza, where both fashionable and more modest eating and drinking places fill the gaps between the boutiques. Apart from Sunday evening, when the streets around the plaza are blocked off for the weekly free **entertainment** – mainly *norteña* and *ranchera* bands – nightlife revolves around the restaurants. For **live music**, try *Sloan's*, or better still, *Todos Santos*, listed below. If you want to see a **film**, there's a multiplex cinema in the shopping centre just across from the bus station. You can buy **books** and magazines at Sanborn's, next door to the cathedral, which also has a café upstairs that serves good coffee and has an extensive menu, including a filling egg and pancake breakfast for US$4.

El Agave Negrete 905 at Zaragoza. New spacious restaurant with a tasty nouveau Mexican menu that pours over thirty types of tequila. Until 6pm, with every drink you buy, you get a free *botana* off their tapas menu.

Corleone Pizza Constitución Nte 110 at Serdán. Straightforward and dimly lit place serving good slightly sweet pizzas and an admirable range of cocktails.

La Esquina del Café the southwest corner of Nogal and Florida. Tiny coffeeshop (it's all they sell) with real coffee, something of an anomaly in northern Mexico.

La Fogata Cuauhtémoc at Negrete. Moderately priced restaurant, serving mostly Mexican food, though they have a full bar and a wide selection of choice steaks.

Fonda de la Tía Chonda Nogal 110. A Durango dinner favourite, the elegant interior is often packed with locals; serves very good traditional Mexican cuisine at high prices.

La Granola corner or Negrete and Victoria. Small health-food store with a good selection of nuts, dried fruit, and other snacks.

Pampas in the *San Jorge* hotel. US$10 all-you-can-eat menu of huge Brazilian cuts of grilled steak, in something resembling churrascuria-style eating.

Samadhi Vegetarian Negrete Pte 403 between Madero and Victoria. Small, brightly coloured joint, which serves a bargain veggie comida for US$2, yogurt, salads and vegetable-filled enchiladas.

Sloan's Restaurant Bar Negrete 1003. Popular with Durango's upper class; continental menu, steaks are the speciality. The bar and live music kicks off around 11pm at weekends.

La Terraza 5 de Febrero 603, on the first floor overlooking the plaza opposite the cathedral. Only worthwhile for drinks or a pizza if you can get a window seat to watch the world go by. Deafeningly loud *norteña* and *mariachi* music at night.

Todos Santos Nogal 108 just west of Florida. Appealing to Durango's young elite and music-loving crowd, this two-floor bar was built around the stage and is lit accordingly. The owners are musicians and you're likely to hear some truly excellent blues here; the crowds are biggest from Thursday to Saturday.

Around Durango

The full title of Durango's tourist office is the Dirección de Turismo y Cinematografía del Estado de Durango. Not so long ago they spent much of their time organizing the vast number of **film** units that came to take advantage of the surrounding area's remarkably constant, clear, high-altitude light, the desert and mountain scenery (Westerns were the speciality), and the relatively cheap Mexican technicians and extras. Although only half a dozen movies have been shot here over the last decade, you can still see the paltry remains of the permanent sets at Chupaderos and Villa del Oeste. The main road from Parral runs within a few hundred metres of the movie towns, so it's easy enough to get there by bus, and to flag one down when you leave – alternatively you get a pretty good, if fleeting, view as you pass by.

Parral-bound buses departing from Durango's main bus station will drop you 12km north at **Villa del Oeste** (Tues–Fri 11am–7pm, Sat 11am–3am, Sun 11am–7pm; US$1.50), a kind of small theme park comprising the hundred-metre-long street of Bandido, which looks straight out of the Wild West until you realize the saloons and shops have been refashioned into a themed restaurant, music hall, and a bar and grill. You can show off your horseback skills (US$8/hr), and there's even a disco until late on Saturday nights.

If all this sounds too cheesy, stay on the bus to the dusty village of **CHUPADEROS**, 2km further north, where the villagers have pretty much taken over the set: the church and "Prairie Lands Hotel" are lived in, one house is a grocery store, and the livestock exchange has been commandeered by Alcoholics Anonymous. A good way to link the two towns is to catch the bus out to Chupaderos, then follow the track past the lived-in church, across the train tracks and through scrubby, cactus-strewn desert 2km to a kind of back entrance to Bandido in Villa del Oeste, where you may or may not be charged entry. It is a particularly nice walk in the late afternoon, past the heat of the day.

An alternative day out is to head 35km south to **El Saltito**, a waterfall surrounded by bizarre rock formations, which has itself been a recurrent film location; the bus can drop you on the road 4km away. On any of these trips, watch out for **scorpions**: there's a genus of white scorpion unique to this area, which, though rare – the only place most people see one is encased in the glass paperweights on sale all over the place – has a sting that is frequently fatal.

On **leaving Durango** you face a simple choice: **west** to the Pacific at Mazatlán, over an incredible road through the Sierra Madre (see p.163), which is itself a worthwhile journey; **east** towards Torreón, Saltillo and Monterrey; or **south** to Zacatecas (p.292), among the finest of Mexico's colonial cities.

Monterrey and the northeast routes

The **eastern border crossings**, from Ciudad Acuña to Matamoros, are uniformly dull – dedicated solely to the task of getting people and goods from one country to the other. In this they are at least reasonably efficient, with immigration officials on both sides well used to coping with mass cross-border traffic. In most, Mexican tourist cards are routinely issued at the border, while Mexican consulates in the Texan towns across the Río Grande can handle any problems. If you're walking over the bridges, there's a small toll to pay: keep a selection of US coins for the turnstiles.

Once across the border, you're faced with the choice of pressing on south (invariably the best option) or choosing a suitable hotel from the dozens on offer. If you're eager to head on from the border towns of **Nuevo Laredo**, **Reynosa** or **Matamoros** there are frequent city bus services to the main bus

Border checks

Crossing the border, do not forget to go through **immigration and customs** checks. As everywhere, there's a free zone south of the frontier, and you can cross at will. Try to continue south, though, and you'll be stopped after some 30km and sent back to get your tourist card stamped.

stations, though you have to walk a few blocks to catch them. The bus stations in **Ciudad Acuña** and **Piedras Negras** are in town, within walking distance of the border crossing.

Once through the border towns, you could be forgiven for hot-footing straight to the Bajío (Chapter Four) or even Veracruz (Chapter Seven), but you're talking at least twelve hours on the bus besides it would be a pity to miss **Monterrey**, Mexico's industrial dynamo and home to a few essential sights. Neighbouring **Saltillo** is also worthwhile, if only as a pleasant place to break a long journey. Direct buses from the border to Monterrey, Mexico City and most of the major northern cities are frequent and efficient. There are no more passenger trains from Nuevo Laredo to the capital.

The Lower Río Grande Valley: Ciudad Acuña to Matamoros

The **Río Grande**, known to Mexicans as the **Río Bravo del Norte**, forms the border between Texas and Mexico, a distance of more than 1500km. The country through which it flows is arid semi-desert, and the towns along the lower section of the river are heavily industrialized and suffer from appalling environmental pollution. This is the **maquiladora** zone, where foreign-owned assembly plants produce consumer goods, most of them for export to the States (see the box on p.198 for more on this). There are few particular attractions for tourists, however, and most visitors are here only for cheap bric-a-brac shopping or simply passing through on their way south.

Ciudad Acuña and around

The smallest of the border towns, **CIUDAD ACUÑA** (setting of the low-budget Mexican thriller *El Mariachi* and its sequel *El Regreso del Mariachi*) is quiet, relaxed and intensely hot. The zócalo has a small **museum** on one side, with a tiny collection of fossils and artefacts, in addition to rows and rows of deathly dull photographs of local dignitaries. Given that there's little to do in the town itself, the best idea is to press on south, unless you're drawn by the offerings around Acuña: water-sports enthusiasts are amply catered for at the **Presa Amistad**, a huge artificial lake straddling the border, while to the west the starkly beautiful mountains, canyons and desert of the interior of Coahuila state invite cautious exploration. The huge and scarcely visited **Parque Internacional del Río Bravo**, opposite Big Bend National Park in Texas, is a protected area offering superb wilderness, but you'll need a well-equipped vehicle to cope with the rugged terrain; there's no public transport, nor is there any real tourist infrastructure, though you might be able to wheedle some information out of someone at Big Bend (Ⓣ432/477-2251, Ⓦwww.nps.gov/bibe).

Arriving over the bridge from Del Rio, Texas, the bus drops you at the **border** post, where there's a map of the town in the modern customs building, together with some limited tourist information. A full-fledged **tourist information** office is at the end of Lerdo where it meets Hidalgo (ⓣ8/772-4692, ⓔturismo_acuna@terra.com.mx). The **bus station**, at the corner of Matamoros and Ocampo, is just five blocks from the border and one from the plaza. Most shops and restaurants are glad to change your dollars, at a fairly good rate for small amounts, but for proper exchange there's a choice of banks and **casas de cambio**. Of the **banks**, Bancomer, Madero 360, off Juárez, has a 24-hour ATM, as does Scotiabank at the corner of Guerrero and Madero. The **post office** is at Hidalgo 320, past Juárez. You'll pass several **hotels** as you walk down Hidalgo from the border: none is especially good value, but if you have to stay try the just renovated *San Jorge*, Hidalgo 165 (ⓣ8/772-5070; ⑤), which has tile, brick and stucco rooms with sparkling-clean bathrooms, or the more spacious *San Antonio*, corner of Hidalgo and Lerdo (ⓣ8/772-5108; ⑤). Also good for one night, especially if you're very tired, is the *Coahuila*, Lerdo 160, one block off Hidalgo (ⓣ8/772-1040; ④); if you're desperately poor, the less-than-spotless *Alfaro*, Madero 240, between Juárez and Lerdo (no phone; ②), will do; if you're lucky you might even be able to get in on a bingo game with some of the hotel's long-term residents out back. You may prefer not to stay in town at all: 30km south of Acuña the road to Piedras Negras (see below) passes through **JIMÉNEZ**, where there are plenty of tranquil spots for **camping**, and the new *Hotel Río San Diego* (ⓣ8/786-0045; ④) occupies a relaxing position overlooking the river; if the hotel looks dark or empty, try enquiring at the convenience store a block away on Hwy-2.

Back in Acuña, the biggest **bars** and **restaurants** – the ones which cater to dollar-toting border-crossers – are located around Hidalgo and Madero. Try the gargantuan early twentieth-century *Crosby's*, on Matamoros and Hidalgo, a restaurant/bar with a plaque posted on the door wisely allowing entry to "members and non-members only". Good-value **cafés** and *loncherías* line Matamoros – the *Café Garcia* has an unusual no-smoking policy – and the decent *Pappa's Pizza* at the corner of Madero and Matamoros has American deep-dish pizza at American prices.

Onward transport is more frequent from towns further south, and it may be easier to head to Piedras Negras, ninety minutes away, and change **buses** there; however, there are a few daily services to **Saltillo** (7hr) and **Monterrey** (8hr) via Monclova, and a couple to Mexico City and Torreón. In addition El Águila buses go to **Guadalajara** (1 daily), **Zacatecas** (2 daily) and **Chihuahua** (1 daily). The airline-style Expresso Futura buses (a/c, reclining seats, toilets and videos) have one daily service each to Mexico City, Querétaro and San Luis Potosí.

Piedras Negras and Monclova

Quaint, friendly and hassle-free, with the most laid-back immigration officers you're likely to encounter anywhere in Mexico, **PIEDRAS NEGRAS** is the ideal border town. The unpretentious main square is directly opposite the international bridge, and hotels and restaurants aren't far away. Nonetheless, there's no reason to stay longer than it takes to catch the first bus south, which traverses a parched plain before cutting through gaps in the mountains past **Monclova**, some four hours from Piedras Negras. Now little more than the site of a vast steelworks, Monclova can make a useful staging point, but you wouldn't go out of your way to visit.

Piedras Negras' extremely helpful **tourist office** (Mon–Fri 9am–5pm; ⓣ878/782-8424), by the main square as you enter Mexico from the US, has free maps of the town and Eagle Pass on the other side, as well as of other cities in Coahuila. From the customs post Allende runs straight ahead towards the bus station, while Hidalgo heads left past one of the better-value **hotels**, *Hotel Santos*, Hidalgo 314 at the corner of Matamoros (ⓣ878/782-4775; ❹), though like almost all the others in town it seems to be suffering from years of neglect and border-town overpricing. Alternatively, continue a couple of blocks along Hidalgo to the market square, where *Hotel del Centro*, Allende 510 (ⓣ8/782-8395; ❸), and the similarly priced *Muzquiz* next door, are best ignored in favour of the *Torreón*, Zaragoza and Dr Coss (ⓣ878/782-5043; ❹), which is newer and less dingy but don't expect much. Better still, stretch for the nearby and comfortable *Hotel Santa Rosa*, Guerrero 401 Ote, on the corner of Morelos (ⓣ878/782-0400; ❹), with bright rooms set around a plant-filled, tiled courtyard, or the luxurious Best Western-owned *Autel Río*, Padre de las Casas Nte 121, at Teran (ⓣ878/782-7064, ⓕ782-7304; ❻), with a TV in every room, a swimming pool and plenty of parking space; they also offer guests free Internet access in the lobby.

For a great introduction to cheap Mexican **food**, head straight for the *taquería Cerna*, in the marketplace just after the border crossing; they have delicious hard-shell bean, meat and veggie tacos for less than US$1 apiece. You could also check out *Sam's Bar and Grill*, across from the *Autel Río*, which makes cheap sandwiches and Mexican dishes in a diner-like environment. For **currency exchange**, head for one of the numerous stalls around the bus station, as rates here are generally very good; also try the market at Zaragoza 107. Bancomer (Mon–Sat 9am–5pm), one block from the main plaza on Morelos and Abasolo, has a 24-hour ATM. If you need access to the **Internet**, head to *Café Internet*, at Padre de las Casas and Allende (Mon–Fri 9.30am–9.30pm, Sat 10am–8pm, Sun 1–5pm; US$1.50/hr).

The **bus station** (ⓣ878/782-7484) is a fifteen-minute walk from the main plaza along Allende. The main companies, Blancos and Águila, operate a decent second-class service, with frequent departures to all the major points south. Expresso Futura buses run to **Mexico City**, **Aguascalientes** and **Monterrey**, while Turistar Ejecutivo luxury buses serve **Mexico City**, **Monclova** and **Querétaro**. Frontera second-class buses have frequent departures to **Nuevo Laredo**, three hours away. The Coahuilense service to **Saltillo** takes around seven hours.

If you're headed **Stateside**, cross the border to Eagle Pass, Texas, and walk 200m north to the Greyhound station, which has four direct departures to San Antonio daily, and one a day to Dallas.

Nuevo Laredo

The giant of the eastern border towns, **NUEVO LAREDO** is alive with the imagery and commercialism of the frontier. It doubles as the transport hub for the whole area, with dozens of departures to Mexico City and all major towns in the north. Cross-border traffic, legal and illegal, is king here, and both bridges from the Texan town of Laredo are crowded with pedestrians and vehicles 24 hours a day. The Mexican side greets you with insurance offices and sleazy cantinas, while tired horses hitched to buggies wait dispiritedly for their next load of pasty, overweight tourists.

You'll do best to head straight out: the road **south from Nuevo Laredo** – towards the vibrant northern capital, Monterrey – at first crosses a flat, scrub-covered, featureless plain, but after an hour the scenery begins to improve as far to the west the peaks of the **Sierra Madre** rise abruptly. Easily the most noticeable plants are the giant yuccas known as **Joshua trees**; to the early settlers their upraised, spiky branches brought to mind Joshua hands raised in supplication.

Arrival, orientation and information

As a tourist, entering or leaving Mexico, you'll take Puente Internacional no.1; there's a small toll, payable in dollars or pesos if you're heading north, but in US currency only (US$0.35) when Mexico-bound. Despite the crush, immigration usually proceeds smoothly, though expect long queues crossing to the US in the mornings and on Sunday evenings.

Nuevo Laredo's huge **Central Camionera** (24hr guardería) is some distance south of town on Romo and Melgar, but battered city buses (marked "Puente"/"Centro") run frequently between here, the border crossings and Plaza Hidalgo; it's about a 25-minute journey. Nuevo Laredo is serviced by buses from Monterrey (3hr) and Mexico City (15hr) day and night. Other buses come from and go to Saltillo, Ciudad Victoria, Guadalajara and Zacatecas; there are even a couple of services to Acapulco. Greyhound, Turismos Rapidos, El Espresso and Azabache all offer identically priced direct services between the Central Camionera and San Antonio (US$15), Austin (US$25), Houston (US$25) and Dallas (US$30).

The **Nuevo Laredo International Airport** is a long taxi ride (about US$12) out of town. There's actually nothing international about it, as the only two (very expensive) flights available are between here and Guadalajara or Mexico City (both on Mexicana).

Coming from Laredo, head up Guerrero, past the curio shops and dozens of casas de cambio, and you'll find everything you're likely to need within seven or eight blocks of the border. Walk past the first square, **Plaza Juárez**, home to the cathedral and Nuevo Mercado de la Reforma craft market, and head for the main square, the palm-shaded **Plaza Hidalgo**, easily the most pleasant spot in Nuevo Laredo. It's a pity there are no pavement cafés on the plaza, but pretty much everything else you'd want is nearby.

The helpful **tourist office** (Mon–Fri 8am–8pm, Sat 10am–1pm; Ⓣ867/712-7397, Ⓦwww.nuevolaredo.gob.mx) is about twenty blocks from the border in the Palacio Federal just alongside Plaza Hidalgo; you may also be able to pick up leaflets and a useful map of the town from lobbies of the larger hotels, theoretically for guests only. The Central Camionera has the cheapest **Internet** connection (US$1.50/hr), though only one computer. The town itself has a number of cybercafés, none right near the border: *Talamas* is located inside a music store about a ten-minute walk from the border down Guerrero at no.1729 where it meets Washington (Mon–Sat 9am–11pm, Sun 11am–10pm; US$2.50/hr), while *ISIC*, González 2807 above the Sandy Disco music shop at Plaza Hidalgo (Mon–Fri 8am–9pm; US$2/hr), has a few terminals.

Buses to the Central Camionera (marked "Carretera") leave from outside the Palacio Municipal – which houses the **post office** – tucked around the back on Camargo. Bancomer and Serfin **banks**, both with ATMs, are around the corner at the junction of Reforma and Canales, which is also a good area to begin looking for a hotel if you need one.

Accommodation

Although there's no shortage of inexpensive **hotels** in the city centre – especially along Hidalgo – many of them are extremely run-down, and frequented by prostitutes and their clients, so check what you're getting very carefully before parting with any money. Nonetheless, against the admittedly low standard of hotels in Mexican border towns in general, Nuevo Laredo's are decent value and in reasonable condition. If you arrive late, however, you will likely find most of the cheaper rooms taken.

Don Antonio González 2435 at Camargo ☎867/712-1876. Clean and comfortable, but a step below *La Finca*. ❹
Los Dos Laredos Matamoros 108 ☎867/712-2419. Simple, plain rooms with bathrooms and fairly plentiful hot water, and evening accompaniment from the local clubs. Only one block from the border; turn right along C 15 de Julio. ❸
Fiesta Ocampo 559 ☎867/712-4737. Relatively modern place with unrealized pretensions to grandeur but comfortable a/c rooms all with telephone, some larger and with TV ($35). ❺
La Finca Reynosa 811 ☎867/712-8883. Modern motel-style place with a/c, TV-equipped rooms that are always clean and in good condition. Excellent value with ample parking. ❺
Motel Romanos Doctor Mier 2420, one block east from Plaza Hidalgo ☎867/712-2391. Though it's seen a rather substandard remodelling job, this is particularly good value, all rooms being spacious with big beds and TV. ❺
Regis Pino Suárez 3013 ☎867/712-9845. A good but pricier alternative if everything else is full. Don't be put off by the smell of urinal mints in the lobby: the rooms are adequate and don't share the same fine aroma. ❺

Eating

There are plenty of decent places to eat around town: try the air-conditioned, reasonably priced and friendly *Café Almanza*, González 272, on the south side of Plaza Hidalgo, and the slightly upmarket restaurant in the *Hotel Reforma*, around the corner at Guerrero 806. *El Dorado Bar & Grill*, on the corner of Belden and Ocampo, serves fairly pricey seafood and meat dishes and attracts a lot of day-tripping Texans.

Reynosa

A very easy border crossing and excellent transport connections combine to make **REYNOSA** a favourite point to enter Mexico. A sprawling industrial city, filled with car repair shops and Pemex plants, it in fact holds little to detain you, but the centre is compact, people are generally friendly – and coming and going is simple. Crossing the international bridge over the Río Bravo from McAllen, Texas (US$0.25 coin-op pedestrian toll), don't forget to call in at the *migración* office (assuming you're headed south) and perhaps the small **tourist office** (Mon–Fri 9am–3pm; ☎899/922-5184, Ⓦwww.tamaulipas.gob.mx;), though don't expect too much enlightening information. The **bus station** is probably your first priority, and though buses do run into the centre and out again to the Central Camionera, it's probably easier simply to tackle the twenty-minute walk. Immediately off the bridge, head straight on along Lerdo de Tejada, which soon becomes Zaragoza, to the Plaza Principal, about five blocks down, where you'll find a couple of **banks** with ATMs. From here the bus station can be reached by following Hidalgo, the pedestrianized main street, for a few blocks and then turning left into Colón. Your best bet for **Internet** access is *Cybertel* off the plaza at Zaragoza and Hidalgo, where upstairs you'll find a dozen new computers with fast connections (daily 10am–10pm; US$1.50/hr).

Hotels here aren't great value for money, but *Hotel Avenida*, Zaragoza 885 Ote (☎899/722-0592; ❺), and the comparable *Hotel Internacional*, Zaragoza 1050 (☎899/922-2318, Ⓔexportadores@aol.com; ❺), both a five-minute walk to the centre from the border, are certainly comfortable enough, the latter having the edge, just. *Hotel Comfort*, Hidalgo 325 about six blocks south of the plaza (☎899/922-8910; ❹), has reasonable, if aging, rooms as well as some newer, pricier ones; *Hotel Estación*, Hidalgo Sur 305, across from the *Comfort* (☎899/922-7302; ❸), is a less than appealing, and not wonderfully clean, introduction to Mexican hotels, but it's at least cheap. Opposite the bus station there's the luxurious *Grand Premier Hotel*, Colón 1304 (☎899/922-4850, Ⓕ922-1150; ❼).

There are a number of inexpensive **food stalls** and a Gigante supermarket by the bus station, and a well-stocked **market** on Hidalgo, midway between the train station and the plaza. For a proper meal, you can't fault *Café Paris*, Hidalgo Nte 873, which serves great, inexpensive breakfasts (US$3) and comidas (US$5) in comfortable surroundings – occasionally someone wheels past a trolley full of cakes for your delectation.

For **moving on** from Reynosa, the Valley Transit Co operates buses between Reynosa and McAllen, Texas, roughly every fifteen minutes until 11.30pm (US$2). The nine-kilometre journey takes about forty minutes, including immigration. Autobuses Americana (☎899/922-0705) run two services daily to Houston and San Antonio (both $26), with connections beyond. Buses to the rest of Mexico include services to Matamoros and Ciudad Victoria; Tampico, Tuxpán and Veracruz on the Gulf coast; and even an overnight bus to Villahermosa (24hr). There is no longer a passenger train service from Reynosa.

Matamoros

MATAMOROS, across the Río Grande from the southernmost point of Texas, at Brownsville, is a buzzing, atmospheric town with more history than its brothers strung out to the west. What began in the mid-eighteenth century as a cattle-ranching colony eventually became known – with the introduction of the port of Bagdad – as "La Puerta México", and in the nineteenth century Matamoros (along with Veracruz) became the main port of entry for foreign immigrants. At the turn of the nineteenth century, rail lines from both sides of the border were directed through Matamoros, and again the city found itself as the necessary link in the trade crossroads. And since the passage of **NAFTA** in 1992, Matamoros has become an increasingly important point for trade.

Arrival and information

Stateside, Brownsville **Chamber of Commerce**, two blocks from the border at 1600 E Elizabeth St (in the US ☎956/542-4341, Ⓕ504-3348; Mon–Fri 8am–5pm), has leaflets on the valley of the Río Grande, and has a Matamoros-knowledgeable staff. The Matamoros **tourist office** (Mon–Fri 9am–7pm; ☎871/812-3630) right at the Mexican border post, is worthwhile for the latest Matamoros info, or for any destinations further south. Having paid your quarter toll, walked across the bridge and dealt with immigration, you'll be wanting the casa de cambio at the border before boarding the fixed-price *peseros*, known here as "maxi taxis", which run frequently along Obregón to the centre and the **Central Camionera** (☎871/812-2777; restaurant and guardería, 6.30am–10.30pm), a long way south (look for "Centro" for Plaza Allende, "Puente Internacional" for the border, or "Central" for the bus station). If heading into the Mexican interior, don't forget to have your tourist card stamped at the border (US$22).

Accommodation

Staying in Matamoros is no problem, with hotels in all price categories, including several good budget choices on Abasolo, the pedestrianized street

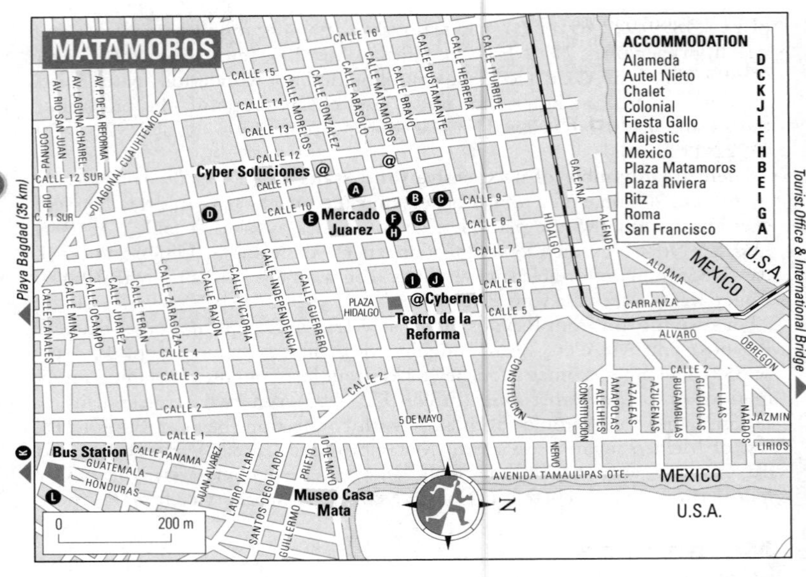

between C 6 and C 11, a block north of Plaza Hidalgo. There are also a number of **more expensive** hotels in the same area; if you're in a large group, it can be worthwhile asking for a suite.

Alameda Victoria 91 at C 10 T 868/816-7108. Lovely, clean and well-furnished rooms with TV, either in the main hotel (US$21) or across the road where they are larger and newer, a/c affairs (US$32). A great deal for Matamoros. 4

Autel Nieto C 10 no. 1508, between Bravo and Bustamante T 868/813-0857, E autelnieto@hotmail.com. Well-kept, carpeted rooms all with cable TV and telephone. There's a two-bedroom master suite that sleeps nine. Parking space and very kitschy lounge/lobby. 5

Chalet near the bus station at Aguilar 7 T 868/812-5975. Newer and cleaner rooms than the *Los Lirios* next door, and priced about the same. Best bus station hotel option. 4

Colonial corner of C 6 and Matamoros T 868/816-6606, W www.hcolonial.com. This is your best mid-range choice. Loaded with Mexican style and colour, the clean rooms are done in tile and brick, with small balconies. Recommended. 6

Fiesta Gallo very near the bus station at Aguilar 10 T 868/813-4406. If you're only interested in a comfortable bed for the night, then this fits the bill and they also have a decent restaurant. 4

Majestic Abasolo 131 between C 8 and C 9 T 868/813-3680. Best value among the budget hotels; staff are friendly, rooms are clean, spacious and have ample hot water. 3

México Abasolo between C 8 and C 9 T 868/812-0856. Simple, comfortable and the price is right. 3

Plaza Matamoros at C 9 and Bravo T 868/816-1696, W www.bestwestern.com/mx/hotelplazamatamoros. Best Western-owned; clean and safe, with somewhat predictable decor. Restaurant, parking and rooms with a/c and cable TV. 7

Plaza Riviera corner of Morelos and C 10 T 868/816-3998, F 816-4299. Very comfortable refurbished hotel split into two buildings, though one costing US$5 more for little apparent reason. Good value for the price: rooms are light and spacious and the hotel offers free Internet access for guests in the lobby. 6

Ritz Matamoros 612 and C 5 T 868/812-1190. Comfortable a/c hotel, whose rates include buffet breakfast. There's a suite available for six people, plus plenty of safe parking, and it's US$10 cheaper at weekends. 7

Roma at C 9 and Bravo T 868/813-6176. Nearly as nice as the Best Western across the street, and half the price (run by the same family). A considerable saving for groups up to five. 5

San Francisco C 10 between Abasolo and González ☎868/813-7110. Among the better central budget hotels with basic and clean rooms with shared showers, though be aware that it attracts its share of the one-hour crowd. ❸

The Town and Playa Bagdad

Orientation is not all that difficult even for those with little experience of Mexican street grids. The streets around the centre, about 1.5km from the border crossing, are easily understood: numbered streets run north–south and named streets run east–west. The busy but compact centre, focused on **plazas** Hidalgo and Allende and the **Mercado Juárez**, on Calles 9 and 10, is an accurate introduction to Mexican cities further south. It's also a surprisingly youthful place, with an enlivened entertainment scene: the plazas and shopping streets seem to be almost entirely filled with teenagers, their numbers swollen by Americans beating the Texan age limit on drinking.

If you've got an hour to kill, pop along to the **Museo Casa Mata**, Santos Degollado at Guatemala (Tues–Fri 8am–4pm, Sat & Sun 9am–2pm; free), a collection of memorabilia from the Revolution, in addition to a selection of Huastec ceramics, housed in a fort begun in 1845 to repel invaders from north of the border. When Zachary Taylor stormed in the following year, however, the building was still unfinished. Near the centre at the northeast corner of Abasolo and Calle 6, is the historic **Teatro de la Reforma**, originally built in 1864, and in 1881 the site of a festival honouring General Porfirio Díaz and his first four years as president (he would remain president until 1911). In 1992 the theatre was restored at the request of the town mayor, and now hosts drama and ballet performances, and various local entertainment.

Playa Bagdad (formerly "Playa Lauro Villar"), Matamoros' pleasant beach 35km east of town, was renamed after the US port of Bagdad, which stood at the mouth of the Río Grande and was at one stage the only port supplying the Confederates during the Civil War. Clean (though watch out for broken glass), and pounded by invigorating surf, it offers the chance for a first (or last) dip in the surf off Mexico's Gulf coast, and is very popular at weekends with Mexican families, who gather in the shade of the palapas that stretch for miles along the sand. There are lots of **seafood restaurants**, but few actually seem to offer much worth eating, so most locals bring picnics or cook on the public barbecues. You'll need half a day to make a worthwhile trip out to the beach, though you can **camp** for free in the sandhills. To get there, take a *combi* marked "Playa" from the Plaza Allende, which drops you off in the car park by the Administración. It takes about an hour, and the office has showers (small charge) and lockers where you can safely store your clothes while you swim.

Eating

Although most **restaurants** in Matamoros are fairly expensive – lots cater for cross-border trade – there are plenty of places for cheap, filling meals lining Calle 10, just off Plaza Allende, Calle 9 between Matamoros and Bravo, and a few *taquería* stands on the pedestrian *peotonál*, Abasolo.

Caféteria Natalia's C 5 between Abasolo and González, at Matamoros. Great diner-style place offering well-priced Mexican staples. Open until late, this makes a great pre-theatre stop if you're thinking of catching a performance at the *teatro* a block away.

El Chinchonal C 9 at Matamoros. A good lunch place serving a wide range of inexpensive dishes. They close early, though, so don't plan to be eating here after about 4pm or so.

Las Dos Repúblicas C 9 off Abasolo. Nice colonial-style restaurant, dishing up mammoth plates of

NAFTA, Mexico and the maquiladora debate

NAFTA (North American Free Trade Agreement), or **TLC** (El Tratado de Libre Comercio) in Mexico, went into effect on January 1, 1994, and created the largest free-trade area in the world. The comprehensive agreement sought to improve virtually all aspects of trade between its three partners – Mexico, the US and Canada – with many trade duties immediately cut and the rest to be phased out by 2009. Ever since, however, the benefit of NAFTA has been widely contested and remains a hot subject for debate among the three countries involved.

At the epicentre of this debate sits Mexico's blossoming **maquiladora** programme, with the dramatic population increase and the host of environmental and humanitarian problems it has brought to Mexico's borderlands. *Maquiladora*, from the Spanish *maquilar* (to perform a task for another), today refers to a Mexican corporation, entirely or predominantly owned by foreigners, which assembles products for export to the US or other foreign country. Sometimes referred to as "production sharing" or "the global assembly line", the programme was touted as a win-win situation for all – foreign businesses could reduce overheads and enjoy larger profits, giving Mexicans more labour opportunities and less reason to cross the border, and thus earning Mexico the foreign exchange while retaining its citizens.

With the passage of NAFTA in 1994, scores of US companies rushed to Mexican border towns to capitalize on cheaper labour and less stringent environmental laws, as well as to outsource more of their raw materials and, in most cases, only pay customs duties on any non-US portion of their products. The *maquiladora* plants now employ millions of people in Mexico, about seventy percent of whom are located in the border area. After petroleum and tourism, the *maquiladora* programme is the third most important source of foreign exchange.

But the picture is not entirely rosy. In the richest-ever manifestation of US financial spillover (except, perhaps, the drug industry), Mexican migrants now crowd the border towns in search of employment, and the area lacks the necessary infrastructure to sustain such numbers. Moreover, numerous **environmental studies** assert that *maquiladoras* (also known as *maquilas*) have dumped everything from raw sewage to toxic metals into the local land. Children have been poisoned by toxins at dump sites and defunct *maquiladoras* have left behind drums of hazardous waste in their adandoned factories. Lab samples from waterways in several borderlands, too, have revealed abnormal deposits of **industrial chemicals**, petroleum and various industrial solvents. In 1995 the Mexican Federal Attorney for Environmental Protection declared that a shocking 25 percent (13,000 tons) of hazardous and toxic wastes produced by the *maquiladora* industry had not been accounted for. What's more, *maquila* worker **abuses** have also entered the picture, and employees have come forth with horrific tales of unjust working conditions and treatment. Fortunately, third-party coalitions have sprung up to improve the working and living conditions of workers in the industry along the border and forced the governments to take note.

While Mexican policy-makers originally proclaimed the *maquiladora* industry as the necessary, temporary evil to aid Mexico's troubled economy, it now seems part of the backbone of the country's long-term economic strategy. And though Mexico has perhaps the strongest anti-NAFTA following of the three countries involved, pro-NAFTA devotees are equally abundant, especially in the north, where new fortunes can and have been made. Unfortunately for this new wealthy management class, Mexico is losing business at an alarming rate to other parts of the world with even lower-cost labour, especially China and Southeast Asia. The proposed FTAA (Free Trade Area of the Americas) would also give Mexico more labour competition for the North American market from smaller, impoverished Latin American nations. NAFTA and regional free trade remain hotly contested issues, but for the time being are here to stay.

tortillas, tacos, quesadillas and the like until around 7pm; everything on the menu costs about US$4.
Los Feroles Matamoros across from the *Ritz Hotel*. Though plainly decorated, they offer well-priced continental dishes like cheese sandwiches (US$3) and steak filets (US$6) as well as local *norteña* cuisine.
Los Panchos Plaza Allende at Guerrero. Popular local café serving great coffee and breakfasts. Simply sit down and the waiter will bring coffee and a basket of *pan dulce*; pay at the counter for what you've eaten from the basket.

Listings

Banks and exchange There are branches of Bancomer, at the corner of Matamoros and C 5, on the plaza itself, and Serfin (all operate Mon–Fri 9am–3pm). There are decent currency exchange facilities in the centre: head for Banorte, on Morelos between C 6 and C 7.
Buses The Central Camionera is well served by buses to the US and to the interior of Mexico. Greyhound has representatives in both Matamoros and Brownsville (in the US ⓣ956/546-7171), and has buses that cross the border to Brownsville for US$4, and they run all night. US-bound buses are frequent: Greyhound (cheaper than El Expresso) ventures to Houston (US$25), San Antonio (US$25), Dallas (US$40), and offers brave souls a 48-hour journey to New York (US$99). El Expresso will take you to Miami for US$119. Reynosa, Monterrey, Ciudad Victoria and Mexico City have frequent departures, and there is also a bus to Puebla. Heading west, Transportes Estrella de Oro serves Mexicali, Guadalajara and Mazatlán, while Autotransportes de Oriente covers the coast route, with buses to Tampico (7hr), Tuxpán (11hr), Veracruz (16hr) and Villahermosa (24hr).
Internet facilities There are a few places off lower Abasolo. Try *Cybernet*, Abasolo between C 5 and C 6 (Mon–Sat 10am–10pm, Sun 2–6pm; US$1.50/hr) or *Cyber Soluciones*, C 11 at Morelos (Mon–Sat 9am–9pm, Sun 10am–9pm; US$1/hr).
Post office In the Central Camionera (see p.195).

The coastal route

The eastern seaboard has so little to recommend it that even if you've crossed the border at Matamoros, you'd be well advised to follow the border road west to **Reynosa** and then cut down to Monterrey (see p.203). Unless you're determined to go straight down through Veracruz to the Yucatán by the shortest route, avoiding Mexico City altogether, there seems little point in coming this way. Even the time factor is less of an advantage than it might appear on the map – the roads are in noticeably worse repair than those through the heartland, and progress is considerably slower. Beyond Tampico, it's true, you get into an area of great archeological interest, with some good beaches around Veracruz, but this is probably best approached from the capital. Here in the northeast there's plenty of sandy beachfront, but access is difficult, beaches tend to be windswept and scrubby, and the whole area is marred by the consequences of its enormous oil wealth: there are refineries all along the coast, tankers passing close offshore, and a shoreline littered with their discards and spillages. It's also very, very hot.

At the time of the Spanish Conquest this area of the Gulf coast was inhabited by the **Huastecs**, who have given their name to the region around Tampico and the eastern flanks of the Sierra Madre Oriental. Huastec settlement can be dated back some three thousand years; their language differs substantially from the surrounding native tongues, but has close links with the Maya of Yucatán. **Quetzalcoatl**, the feathered serpent god of Mexico, was probably of Huastec origin.

The Huastecs were at their most powerful between 800 and 1200 AD – just before the Aztecs rose to dominance – and were still at war with the Aztecs when the Spanish arrived and found willing allies here. After the successful campaign against Tenochtitlán, the Aztec capital, the Spanish, first under Cortés and later the notorious Nuño de Guzmán, turned on the independent-minded Huastecs, decimating and enslaving their former allies.

Ciudad Victoria

CIUDAD VICTORIA, capital of the state of Tamaulipas, is little more than a place to stop over for a night. It's not unattractive but neither is it interesting, and while the surrounding hill country is a paradise for hunters and fishing enthusiasts, with a huge artificial lake called the **Presa Vicente Guerrero**, others will find little to detain them. The **bus station** (guardería daily 7am–10.30pm) is a couple of kilometres out of town and, if you arrive late, the *Hotel Colonial* (☎834/316-7707; ❸), left out of the station and then first left, is shaded, cool, and probably the cheapest place you'll find; avoid the noisy front rooms if you can. Local buses run frequently into the centre, where most of the town's facilities are concentrated around the zócalo, Plaza Hidalgo, but aside from the rather bland church, there isn't a whole lot going on. You've got several **hotels** to choose from here, including the excellent *Los Monteros*, Hidalgo 962 (☎834/312-0300; ❹), a lovely old colonial building with large rooms that are much cheaper than you might expect, and *Hostal de Escandón*, Juárez 143 at Hidalgo (☎834/312-9004; ❹), which offers good, clean rooms and food for US$2 or so per meal. Almost equally high standards and similar prices are maintained by a couple of places a block or so away: *Hotel Posada Don Diego*, Juárez Nte 814 (☎834/312-1279; ❹), has some nice large rooms (❺), all with TV and a/c. For **food**, the zócalo has a few options serving typical Mexican food at good prices – a full plate of chicken with vegetables and rice runs about US$4. A block away on Juárez is *Santa Elena*, which has fixed-price lunches for US$2.50. You can check the **Internet** at *El Portal*, Hidalgo 990 (daily 8am–11pm; US$1/hr).

Tampico

Along the 200km of road southeast from Ciudad Victoria to **TAMPICO**, the country's busiest port, the vegetation becomes increasingly lush, green and tropical – the Tropic of Cancer passes just south of Ciudad Victoria, and the Río Pánuco forms the border with the steamy Gulf state of Veracruz. As a treasure port in the Spanish empire, Tampico suffered numerous pirate raids and was destroyed in 1684. The rebuilding finally began in 1823, the date of the cathedral's foundation, and in 1828 Spain landed troops in Tampico in a vain and short-lived attempt to reconquer its New World empire. The discovery of oil in 1901 sparked Tampico's rise to prominence as the world's biggest oil port in the early years of the twentieth century.

The older parts of town, by the docks and former train station, have a distinct Caribbean feel, with peeling, ramshackle clapboard houses and swing-door bars: boisterous and occasionally gloomy. Yet Tampico is actually booming again, riding the oil surge with a welter of grand new buildings founded on the income from a huge refinery at the mouth of the Río Pánuco. Many campesinos and unskilled labourers have moved to town from the surrounding rural areas in search of work, contributing to a visible homelessness problem.

Downtown, the city's dual nature is instantly apparent. Within a hundred metres of each other are two plazas: the grandiose **Plaza de Armas**, rich and formal, ringed by government buildings, the cathedral (built in the 1930s with money donated by American oil tycoon Edward Doheny) and the smart hotels; and the **Plaza de la Libertad**, which is raucous, rowdy – there's usually some form of music played from the bandstand each evening – and peopled by wandering salesmen. Ringed by triple-decker wrought-iron verandas, it has been spruced up in recent years to form an attractive square, almost New Orleans in flavour. Also worth a look is the new **Casa de la Cultura**, formerly the town slaughterhouse and now home to an archeology and painting exhibition, with the second floor holding much of the town's archives and historic records. It's a bit of a hike to reach it (where Altamira runs into Hidalgo), so catch the "Águila" bus from the Plaza for US$0.40. To return, simply walk a block east until you reach Hidalgo, where you can jump on any number of buses headed into the centre.

Sadly, the docks pretty much cut off the centre of town from the water, so there's little to do here outside the centre, though you could head north to **Ciudad Madero**, Tampico's growing twin town, or onwards to **Playa Miramar**. The journey out is best made by bus or one of the lumbering 1970s Chevy colectivos (marked "Playa"; find them on Lopez de Lara, three blocks east of the Plaza de Armas), which will take you past the graceful arc of the new harbour-mouth bridge some 7km to the affluent, new and neatly planned suburbs of Ciudad Madero. Here it's worth calling in to see the Huastec artefacts at the small but excellent **Museo de la Cultura Huasteca** (Mon–Fri 10am–5pm, Sat 10am–3pm; free) in the Tecnológico Madero; get out at the Madero's central plaza, turn left along 1 de Mayo, and the museum is about 1km along, two blocks past the telecom tower. Playa Miramar, Tampico's town beach, lies a further 8km out (same buses and colectivos). Be warned that the water, so close to the refinery and the mouth of the river, is **heavily polluted**, and swimming is not recommended. That said, during the summer months, Semana Santa and weekends year-round, it seems that all Tampico is out here; at other times it's a little dispiriting with only a few run-down hotels, though there are a couple of little restaurants serving good fresh fish and offering showers for a small fee. This is also good **camping** territory, with a stand of small trees immediately behind the beach, and if you have your own transport you can drive miles up the sand to seek out isolation. In fact that's one other disadvantage out here – everyone insists on driving their cars around the beach, most local learners seem to take their first lessons here, and even the bus drives onto the sand to turn round.

Accommodation

One thing you can say for Tampico is that there's no shortage of **hotels**, though most are either expensive or very sleazy. If you don't want the hassle of carrying your bags downtown and searching for a room, then try either of the hotels opposite the bus station: *Hotel La Central,* Rosalio Bustamante 224 (Ⓣ833/217-0388; ❸), which offers probably the best value in town for your peso, and *Hotel Santa Helena*, Rosalio Bustamante 303 (Ⓣ/Ⓕ 833/213-3507; ❹), which offers less value, though you do get a/c rooms with TV and there's a good, if pricey, restaurant. Downtown, many of the cheaper hotels around the docks, train station and market area operate partly as brothels.

For the cheaper acceptable rooms, a good choice is the central and bright *Capri*, Juárez Nte 202 (Ⓣ/Ⓕ833/212-2680; ❸), about four blocks north of the plaza; its small rooms are some of the better bargains you'll find in town. Better still, on the Plaza de la Libertad is the comfortable *Posada del Rey*, Madero Ote 218 (Ⓣ833/214-1024, Ⓕ212-1077; ❺). The aged *Impala*, on Díaz Mirón (Ⓣ833/212-

0990; ⑤), has been renovated and is exceptionally clean, perhaps even elegant. The *Regis*, a a five-minute walk from the plaza to Madero Ote 605 (Ⓣ833/212-0290; ④), has plain, high-ceiling rooms that are carpeted and clean, but shouldn't be anyone's first choice. The more luxurious option, however, would be the *Best Western Inglaterra*, Díaz Mirón 116 (Ⓣ833/219-2857, Ⓦwww.bestwestern.com; ⑦), with a restaurant and small pool, near the plaza. Equally upmarket, but less expensive, the *Gran Hotel Sevilla* is at the southwest end of Plaza de Armas; some of the sleek rooms with wood floors come with great views onto the plaza (Ⓣ833/214-3833, Ⓔrecepcion@granhotelsevilla.com.mx; ⑥).

Practicalities, arrival and information

Tampico's modern **bus station** (guardería 6am–midnight) is in an unattractive area some 10km north of the city, though waiting for buses here can be one of northern Mexico's little pleasures, as the waiting hall offers comfortable couches. To get downtown, take a bus, a rattling colectivo, or one of the shared *perimetral* taxis (all US$0.40). Buses back to the *camionera* leave from the Plaza de la Libertad, at the corner of Olmos and Carranza. The grid-plan downtown area centres on the Plaza de Armas, where the junction of Carranza and Colón marks the point at which the cardinal suffixes on street names change.

The town's **tourist office**, Díaz Mirón 203 (Mon–Sat 8am–7pm; Ⓣ833/212-2668, Ⓦwww.tamaulipas.gob.mx), across from the *Hotel Impala*, can offer you a map and a pamphlet on the town, but little else. The **post office** at Madero 309 is easy to find, upstairs in the Correos building on the north side of the Plaza de la Libertad, and there are **banks** on the Plaza de Armas and all through the central area. Numerous cybercafés line Avenida 20 de Noviembre near the plaza: try *SCACT*, 20 de Noviembre 108 (daily 7am–11pm), or *Club Mita Net* at Carranza 106 (daily 8am–9pm), both of which charge US$1 per hour.

There are more than enough good **places to eat** to keep you happy for the day or so you might spend here. Across from the bus station there is the simple and fabulous *Comedor Silvina y Lorena*, which serves unbeatable comidas 24 hours a day. The town's market, a block south of the Plaza de la Libertad, has numerous excellent food stalls: the giant *Cafe y Nevería Elite*, Díaz Mirón Ote 211, serves good Mexican staples and offers a quiet haven in this noisy town. *Super Cream "La Parroquia"*, Olmos 301, is a Tampico standby, a quick diner-style joint that is hard to beat. There's also *Naturaleza*, Altamira Ote 412, serving buffet breakfasts and comida corrida lunches from 8am to 8.30pm; they also run the large health-food store next door. But the best dining, if only for the location, is at *La Troya*, in the *Hotel Posada del Rey*, which has a great veranda overlooking the Plaza de la Libertad, a strong Spanish and seafood menu and two-for-one drinks from 6pm to 8pm.

The road to San Luis Potosí

It is a seven-hour run from Tampico to San Luis Potosí (see p.285) – ideal for a sleep-over on a night bus you might think, but there are a couple of places along the way you could consider breaking the journey for. The town of **Río Verde**, surrounded by lush fields of maize, coffee and citrus fruit, is ringed by thermal springs and has the benefit of a small lake, the **Laguna de la Media Luna**, which is popular with snorkellers and divers. Further east still, the highway comes to **Ciudad Valles**, a busy commercial town some 140km from Tampico and the coast. The frequent **buses** to San Luis Potosí, Mexico City and Monterrey will set you back about US$28.

Monterrey and around

Third city of Mexico, capital of Nuevo León and the nation's industrial stronghold, **MONTERREY** is a contradictory place. The vast network of factories, the traffic, urban sprawl, pollution and ostentatious wealth that characterize the modern city are relatively recent developments; the older parts retain an air of colonial elegance and the setting is one of greaty beauty. Ringed by jagged mountain peaks – which sadly serve also to keep in the noxious industrial fumes – Monterrey is dominated above all by one, the Cerro de la Silla or "Saddle Mountain". But what makes Monterrey really outstanding are its most recent developments: the modern architecture and the bold statuary sprouting everywhere, expressions of Mexico at its most confident. Even if it's not to your taste, there is nowhere better to set yourself up for the dramatic contrast of the colonial heartland to come.

In addition to the national and religious holidays, autumn in Monterrey plays witness to a number of local festivals. There's a weekend-long, brewery-sponsored **Fiesta de la Cerveza**, in early October. The **Festival Alfonso Reyes**, with plenty of music and theatre, is held in the last week of October and the first week in November. The **Festival Cultural Barrio Antigua** (Nov

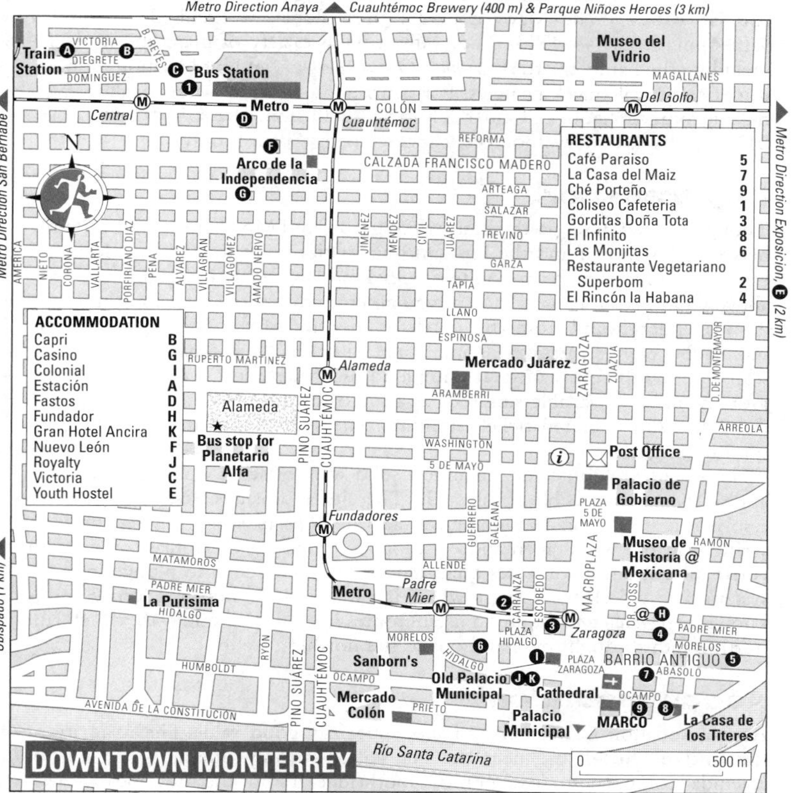

15–25) is relatively new on the festival list but easily the city's favourite – cafés, galleries and restaurants open their doors to the teams of people strolling through the streets, with concerts, films, art exhibitions and the like.

Arrival and information

Monterrey is the transport hub of the northeast, with excellent national and international connections. Flights from the rest of Mexico and from several points in the US (served by Continental, Delta, and Northwest) arrive at Mariano Escobedo **international airport** (Ⓣ81/345-4432), 6km or so northeast of the city, only accessible by taxi for around US$14–17. On arrival you'll find pricey luggage storage and somewhere to change money.

Scores of **buses** pull into the enormous Central Camionera, northwest of the centre on Avenida Colón, complete with its own shopping centre, 24-hour guardería (though it is closed from Fri 9pm until Sat 6.30am) and post office. To get from the **bus station** to the central Macroplaza, turn left towards the Cuauhtémoc metro station (see below) and take Line 2, or pick up a #1, #7, #17 or #18 bus heading down Pino Suárez and get off at a suitable intersection: Ocampo, Zaragoza or Juárez, for example. Or you can get just about anywhere by **taxi** for US$2 or less; bargaining is generally in order here.

There's usually someone who can speak English at the helpful Infotur **tourist office**, 5 de Mayo no. 525 (third floor), at Escobedo (Mon–Fri 9am–6pm; Ⓣ83/344-4343). They offer a wide variety of maps and leaflets – including the handy quarterly *What's On Monterrey* – and information on hotel prices and local travel agencies. For tourist information when dialling from outside Nuevo León, call Ⓣ01-800/832-2200; from the US Ⓣ1-800/235-2438; or check Ⓦwww.monterrey-mexico.com (Spanish only).

City transport

Though limited in scope, the best way to get around Monterrey – and certainly between downtown and the bus and train stations – is to take the clean and efficient **metro**, which runs on two lines: Line 1 is elevated and runs east–west above Colón (you see it as soon as you emerge from the bus station); and Line 2 runs underground from the north of the city to the Macroplaza (at the station General I. Zaragoza), connecting with Line 1 at Cuauhtémoc metro stop, right by the bus station. It's simple to use: tickets cost about US$0.40 per journey and are available singly or as a multi-journey card (at a small saving) from the coin-operated ticket machines. The system runs from around 5am until midnight.

The streets of Monterrey are almost solid with **buses**, following routes that appear incomprehensible at first sight. The city authorities have taken steps to resolve the confusion by numbering all the stops (*paradas*), having the fares written on the windscreen and occasionally providing the tourist office with **route plans**, but it still takes a fair amount of confidence to plunge into the system. The old clangers are slowly being replaced by more modern versions known as *panorámicos*, found on useful routes like #1, #17 and #18, which run north–south through town and out to the northern sights.

Accommodation

Accommodation in Monterrey is not especially good value. The majority of the **budget hotels** are near the bus station, mainly on the other side of Avenida Colón, safest crossed on the footbridge. It's not the most pleasant part of town, permanently noisy and crowded, a touch seedy and some way from the centre, but it's reasonably safe and the metro will whisk you into town in ten minutes. Amado Nervo, heading south off Colón immediately opposite the bus station, holds several possibilities, but it's best to penetrate a little further if you want to avoid the worst of the noise. Even so, you're unlikely to find anything half-decent under US$15.

Further **downtown** rooms are of a different class altogether, in modern and "international" hotels, all with a/c and many with a pool. Geared up for business travellers, they lower their prices slightly at weekends. There's a good concentration in the so-called "zona hotelera" around Plaza Hidalgo.

Capri Victoria Pte 1402 ⓣ81/375-0052, ⓕ372-9164. Best of the middle-market places in this area, although there seems to be some hourly-rates action around lunchtime. Modern and well-kept with a small restaurant and bar, off-street parking, and bright, spacious rooms with TV and a/c. ❺

Casino Arteaga 816 ⓣ81/372-0219. Another hourly-rental, though it's relatively new and clean, with TV and a/c in the rooms. One of the better-value options among the bus station hotels. ❺

Colonial Hidalgo Ote 475 ⓣ81/343-6791, ⓦwww.hotelcolonialmty.com. The small, ageing TV- and a/c-equipped rooms are much less expensive than anything else in the area, but still fairly poor value for your money. Includes continental breakfast. ❻

Estación Victoria Pte 1450 ⓣ81/375-0755. One of the nicest in the area with simple, comfortable and clean rooms arranged around a central courtyard. From the train station, turn right and then left at *Restaurant Hernandez*; from the bus station turn right, then right up Bernardo Reyes for two blocks, then left into Victoria. ❺

Fastos Colón Pte 956, right opposite the bus station ⓣ81/372-3250, in the US 1-800/839-2400, ⓕ81/372-6100. Comfortable, modern hotel with large rooms all featuring a/c and satellite TV. Not bad value for Monterrey if you don't mind being so far from downtown. ❻

Fundador Montemayor 802 at Matamoros ⓣ81/342-0121, ⓦwww.travelbymexico.com.mx. Colonial tile meets wood panelling. About the best value for money of all the hotels, and for now the only hotel in Barrio Antiguo, with comfortable and clean, if boring, a/c rooms, all with local TV. Fancy and nominally atmospheric restaurant in the same building. ❻

Gran Hotel Ancira Hidalgo and Escobedo, on Plaza Hidalgo ⓣ81/150-7000, from the US 1-800/333-3333, ⓦwww.hotel-ancira.com. Built as a grand hotel before the Revolution and full of period elegance, including a winding marble staircase, this is an outstanding (though very pricey, as rooms *start* at US$150) upmarket option; owned and operated by Radisson. ❾

Nuevo León Amado Nervo 1007 Nte ⓣ81/374-1900. About the best value of several places on this street (but only just), and the cheapest rooms for lone travellers. Fans, TVs and cheap underground parking. ❺

Royalty Hidalgo Ote 402 ⓣ81/340-9800, in the US 1-800/830-9300, ⓦwww.royaltyhotel.com. Straightforward, middle-of-the-road business-style hotel with a/c rooms, cable TV, gym, jacuzzi and a tiny pool. ❼

Victoria Bernardo Reyes 1205 Nte ⓣ81/375-4833. Slightly faded hotel that's a good bargain (though not the cheapest). Friendly, safe and only a block from the bus station, with some central rooms that aren't too noisy. From the bus station, turn right along Colón and then right onto Bernardo Reyes. ❹

Youth Hostel Madero 3500 Ote, at the Parque Fundidora ⓣ81/355-7380, ⓦwww.parquefundidora.org/hospedaje.htm. Huge and soulless but well-maintained place with dorms of differing sizes. There is even the possibility of gratis camping in the central garden, though you have to get permission beforehand. Call ahead to reserve a bed and take note of the 11.30pm curfew. Take Line 1 east to Y Griega metro station, walk 300m west along Colón, then left into Prisciliano Elizondo, and the *Villa Deportiva Juvenil* is the white building straight ahead (across the traffic). If you're coming by taxi, just tell the driver to take you to the "Parque Acero". ❷

The City

First impressions of Monterrey are unfavourable – the highway roars through the shabby shantytown suburbs and grimy manufacturing outskirts – but the **city centre** is quite a different thing. Here, colonial relics are overshadowed by the office blocks and expensive shopping streets of the "zona comercial", and by some extraordinary modern architecture – the local penchant for planting buildings in the ground at bizarre angles is exemplified above all by the **Planetario Alfa** (see p.209) and the **Instituto Tecnológico**. The city in general rewards a day of wandering, but there are three places specifically worth going out of your way to visit – the old **Obispado**, on a hill overlooking the centre, the giant **Cervecería Cuauhtémoc** to the north, and the magnificent **Museo de Arte Contemporáneo** (MARCO).

At the heart of Monterrey, if not the physical centre, is the **Macroplaza** (officially the Plaza Zaragoza, and sometimes known as the "Gran Plaza"), which was created by demolishing some six complete blocks of the city centre, opening up a new vista straight through from the intensely modern City Hall to the beautiful red-stone Palacio de Gobierno on what used to be Plaza 5 de Mayo. This is Mexican planning at its most extreme: when the political decision comes from the top, no amount of conservationist or social considerations are going to stand in the way, especially as the constitution's "no re-election" decree makes every administrator determined to leave some permanent memorial. The result is undeniably stunning, with numerous lovely fountains, an abundance of striking statuary, quiet parks and shady patios, edged by the cathedral, museums and state administration buildings. There are frequent concerts, dances and other entertainments laid on; in the evenings people gravitate here for no better reason than to stroll, and to admire the laser beam that flashes out across the city from the top of the tall, graceful slab of orange concrete known as the **Faro del Comercio**.

The **cathedral**, with its one unbalanced tower, is a surprisingly modest edifice, easily dominated by the concrete bulk of the new **City Hall**, squatting on stilts at the southern end of the square. Inside there's a small archeological collection, while in the **Palacio de Gobierno** at the other end of the square is a room devoted to local history. Between the two lie the city's newest and most celebrated museums.

The real star here is the wonderful **Museo de Arte Contemporáneo**, or **MARCO**, at the junction of Zuazua and Ocampo by the cathedral (daily 10am–6pm, Wed until 8pm; US$3.20, free on Wed; Ⓦwww.marco.org.mx). You're greeted by Juan Soriano's *La Paloma*, an immense sculpture of an obese black dove whose curvaceous lines stand in dramatic contrast to the angular terracotta lines of the museum building. It was built in 1991 to a design by Mexico's leading architect, **Ricardo Legorreta**, whose buildings are all highly individual but share common themes: visitors from the southwest of the US may recognize the style from various buildings dotted around Texas, Arizona and New Mexico. Inside, none of the floors and walls seems to intersect at the same angle. The vast, at times whimsical, open plan centres on an atrium with a serene pool into which a pipe periodically gushes water: at the sound of the pump gurgling to life, you find yourself drawn to watch the ripple patterns subside. You might imagine that such a courageous building would overwhelm its contents, but if anything the opposite is true.

Apart from a couple of monumental sculptures tucked away in courtyards, there is no permanent collection, but the standards maintained by the temporary exhibits are phenomenally high. A key factor in this is undoubtedly the bias towards Latin American (particularly Mexican) artists, who are currently producing some of the world's most innovative and inspiring work. The quality art bookstore and fancy café are both worth visiting, but don't fail to stop by the lovely bar, right by the central pool.

Several blocks north of MARCO lies one of the city's best new museums, the **Museo de Historia Mexicana**, Dr Coss 445 Sur (Tues–Sun 11am–8pm; US$1, free on Tues), another bold architectural statement, though save for the double-helix staircase, a less successful one. All the ingredients appear to be there, though – displays on Mexico's ancient, colonial and modern civilizations, an extensive array of traditional costumes, interactive computer consoles and the story of the Revolution, along with associated paraphernalia. Should your patience for Mexican history wear thin, you might rent one of the roofed paddleboats (US$3.50/hr) below the museum's plaza to saunter about the huge fountain pool, or buy some bread and feed the schools of rather large fish which swim therein.

Around the Macroplaza

West of the Macroplaza are smart shops, multinational offices and swanky hotels, centred on the little **Plaza Hidalgo** – a much more traditional, shady place, with old colonial buildings set around a statue of Miguel Hidalgo. The original Palacio Municipal, now superseded by the modern building, is here, acting today as an occasional cultural centre. Otherwise, the pavement cafés make a pleasant stop-off – though food is expensive. Pedestrianized shopping streets fan out behind, crowded with window-gazing locals.

Another part of the old centre survives to the east and has even grabbed the "**Barrio Antiguo**" tag, which seems appropriate for this increasingly gentrified district populated by chichi little galleries, appealingly laid-back cafés and, once the sun has gone down, the city's best nightlife opportunities. The city authorities are even playing ball, installing old-fashioned street lamps and taking measures to calm the traffic. There's usually a host of artistic goings-on here: check out the Centro Cultural Santa Lucía, Montemayor 510, for frequent photography, theatre and dance events, or have a glance at the bulletin boards posted in many of the local cafés and bars. There's also **La Casa de los Titeres** at Jardón 968 (Mon–Fri 9am–noon & 2–6pm, Sun 2–6pm; US$1.50; Ⓦ www.baulteatro.com). This small museum has a rather extensive & odd collection of puppets displayed behind glass. At 4pm on Sundays the owners put on a puppet show (US$5) based on anything from *Little Red Riding Hood* to García Lorca, which usually attracts a fair-sized crowd.

To the south is the dry bed of the Río Santa Catarina, now largely given over to playing fields, overlooked by the first slopes of the Cerro de la Silla, which rise almost immediately from its far bank.

Of Monterrey's two main **markets** – Juárez and Colón – the latter, on Avenida de la Constitución, south of the Macroplaza, is more tourist-oriented, specializing in local artesanía. Incidentally, the best of Monterrey's **flea markets** (*pulgas*; literally fleas) is also held on Constitución: market days are irregular, but ask any local for details.

El Obispado

The elegant and recently renovated **Obispado**, the old Bishop's Palace, tops Chepe Vera hill to the west of the centre, but well within the bounds of the city. Its commanding position – affording great views when haze and smog allow – has made it an essential target for Monterrey's many invaders. Built in the eighteenth century, it became in turn a barracks, a military hospital and a fortress: among its more dramatic exploits, the Obispado managed to hold out for two days after the rest of the city had fallen to the Texan general Zachary Taylor in 1846. The excellent **museum** inside (Tues–Sun 10am–5pm; US$2) records the city's long history with a little of everything: religious and secular art, arms from the War of Independence, revolutionary pamphlets and old carriages.

You get to the Obispado along Padre Mier, passing on the way the monumental modern church of **La Purísima**. Take the R4 bus, alighting where it turns off Padre Mier, then continue to the top of the steps at the end of Padre Mier and turn left; it's a ten-minute walk in all. Return to the centre using any bus heading east on Hidalgo.

North of the centre

If you're thirsty after all this, a visit to Monterrey's massive **Cervecería Cuauhtémoc** (Cuauhtémoc Brewery) is all but compulsory. This is where they make the wonderful Bohemia and Tecate beers you'll find throughout Mexico (as well as the rather bland Carta Blanca), and somehow it seems much more representative of Monterrey than any of the city's prouder buildings. Free guided tours of the brewery run almost constantly throughout the day, and you may be rewarded afterwards with free beer amidst strutting peacocks in the pleasant gardens outside – note the blackened tree trunks there which bear witness to the city's industrial pollution. Tours start across the road from the brewery at Alfonso Reyes Nte 2202, 1km north of the bus station (Mon–Fri 10am–5pm, Sat 10am–3pm; free; English-speaking tours given, though only a few per day). Connected to the brewery is the **Salón de la Fama**, Sporting Hall of Fame, commemorating the heroes of Mexican baseball; entry is free. To get there take Line 2 to its northern terminus (General Anaya station) and walk 300m south.

Some 3km north of the brewery lies the vast **Parque Niños Héroes** (Tues–Sun 9am–6pm; US$0.70), chiefly a gentle retreat from the city, best visited at weekends when the throng of Mexican families enjoying themselves goes some way towards masking the slightly run-down nature of the place. Among the semi-formal gardens and boating lake are minor sights (some have nominal entrance fees) such as the spherical aviary, a transport museum with fifty-odd vintage and classic cars and trucks, and the **Pinacoteca**, a small art gallery featuring mostly missable oils and sculpture by Nuevo León artists. The main attraction here are some fine pieces by Fidias Elizondo, notably the arching female nude *La Ola*.

Architecturally more compelling is the **Biblioteca Magna Universitaria**, Alfonso Reyes 4000 (Mon–Fri 8am–8pm, Sat 9am–8pm; free), in the northern end of the park but only accessible from the street. This is another fine example of the work of Ricardo Legorreta (see p.206), and though the design is completely different, the parallels to the MARCO building are strong: in fact it sometimes feels more like an art gallery than a library, and does generally have a couple of modern works on display near the lobby. Again, it is a constantly surprising building, with squares within circles and sudden courtyards, but with an overall sense of space and fun.

The park and library entrances can be reached on **buses** #17 and #18 from Padre Mier or on Cuauhtémoc outside the Cuauhtémoc metro station. To get back, take the same bus from Barragan on the western side of the park: the exits on this side are only sporadically open and you may have to make a long detour right round the park.

For decades, glass production has been one of Monterrey's industrial strengths (for one thing, it has to provide all the beer bottles), and to tap into the long history of Mexican glassware, pop along to the **Museo del Vidrio**, at the corner of Zaragoza and Magallanes (daily except Mon 9am–6pm; US$1, free on Sun; Ⓦwww.museodelvidrio.com). A small but select display of pieces over the centuries and a mock-up of a nineteenth-century apothecary's only act as a prelude to the attic, where modern, mostly cold-worked glass sculpture is shown to advantage: Raquel Stolarski's *Homage to Marilyn* is particularly fine. To get there take Line 1 to Del Golfo station, walk two blocks west and then two blocks north up Zaragoza.

South of the centre

Like some vision from H.G. Wells' *The War of the Worlds*, the cylindrical form of the **Planetario Alfa**, Roberto Garza Sada 1000, 8km south of the city centre (Tues–Fri 3–8.30pm, Sat 2–8.30pm, Sun noon–8.30pm; US$5; Ⓦ www.planetarioalfa.org.mx), rises out of the ground at a rakish angle, providing an unusual venue for Omnimax films. If you've never seen one of these super-wide-vision movies before, or have kids to entertain, it may be worth the trip out here. Otherwise, the few science demonstrations and hands-on experiments aren't really worth the bother. If you do come, don't miss Rufino Tamayo's stained-glass opus, outside the main complex, in the Universe Pavilion. The only way to get here is on the **free shuttle bus**, which leaves from a dedicated stop at the western end of the Alameda on Washington. Times vary, but it runs roughly on the hour from 3pm to 7pm and also on the half-hour at weekends.

Eating, drinking and nightlife

Monterrey's **restaurants** cater to hearty, meat-eating *norteños*, with *cabrito al pastor* or the regional speciality *cabrito asado* (whole roasted baby goat) given pride of place in window displays. You'll find scores of tiny bars and rather sleazy places to eat near the bus station – especially at the little market just south of Colón – but up here your best bet is to stick to one of the safer-looking fast-food joints. For fresh produce you could do worse than join the locals at the **Mercado Juárez**, north of the Gran Plaza on Aramberri. In the **centre** you can do a lot better, but you also pay more, especially at the dozens of places around the Gran Plaza.

After dark, the place to head is the Barrio Antiguo, five square blocks of cobbled streets bounded by Dr Coss, Matamoros and Constitución. On Thursday, Friday and Saturday evenings (9pm–2am), the police block off the junctions, leaving the cobbled streets – especially Padre Mier and Madero – to hordes of bright young things surging back and forth in search of the best vibe. You're best off taking their lead, but among specific recommendations try *El Rincón La Habana*, Morelos 887 near Montemayor, for nightly live Cuban music (see below), or *Reloj*, Padre Mier Ote 860, very popular and charging US$2–5 entry (less or nothing at all on Wed and Thurs). *Antropolis*, Montemayor and Padre Mier, is a dark, left-wing favourite among students and revolutionary types, while *Río Latino*, at the eastern end of Padre Mier, currently houses the bilingual jet-set crowd. *Cadaques*, Morelos 905, is a minimalist, white-leather-clad lounge that occasionally showcases European DJs for pricey covers. *La Tumba,* Padre Mier Ote 827 (5pm–2am; US$2–5 cover), is a large semi-outdoor bar whose main draw is live acoustic music on the large stage Thursday, Friday and Saturday nights. In the Barrio, too, are a few late-closing cafés (see below), which make the best destinations for a quieter evening.

Restaurants, cafés and bars

Café Paraíso Morelos Ote 958, Barrio Antiguo. Late-closing multi-roomed café and bar with local artwork on the walls, serving a fabulous range of coffees, delicious and huge tortas with fries (US$4) and fairly pricey drinks, though beers are two-for-one (US$3) round-the-clock.

La Casa del Maíz Abasolo Ote 870b at Dr Coss, Barrio Antiguo. Airy, modern place taking its decorative cues from MARCO down the street, and serving unusual Mexican dishes, either with or without meat. Try the *memelas la maica*, a kind of thick tortilla topped with a richly seasoned spinach and cheese salsa. Closed Sunday evenings and all day Monday, opens at 6pm other days. Have a look at the funky *Akbal* (Mayan for "night") *Lounge* upstairs.
Che Porteño Jardón Ote 814, Barrio Antiguo. Serving authentic Argentine cuisine, it shares the building with the Italian restaurant *Iannilli* (same owner, different chef). US$4 empanadas and US$12 *asado de tira,* plus a number of South American wines.
Coliseo Cafetería Colón 235. Clean and cheerful 24hr place near the bus station, serving regular Mexican staples at low prices; quesadilla (US$2.50), bean tacos (US$2), and passable café con leche (US$0.70).
Gorditas Doña Tota Escobedo near Morelos. This fast-food-like chain serves up delicious little gorditas for under a buck and has many outlets throughout the city. Beware, you might become a regular.
El Infinito Jardón Ote 904, Barrio Antiguo. A surprising little find, with sofas and a small lending library (some English books), serving some of Monterrey's best espressos and lattes. Cakes and sandwiches, too, and a few times a month they have live acoustic music.
Las Monjitas Morelos Ote 240 at Galeana. Waitresses dressed as nuns dish up Mexican steaks and a catholic selection of quality antojitos, including house specialities such as *Father Chicken*, *The Sinner* and *Juan Pablo II*, the last an artery-hardening concoction combining salami, pork, bacon, peppers, grilled cheese and guacamole. Beautiful azulejos on the walls make the slightly elevated prices worthwhile. There's a second branch a couple of blocks along at Escobedo Sur 913. Open daily 8am–11pm.
Restaurante Vegetariano Superbom upstairs at Padre Mier 300, near Galeana, Zona Centro. Excellent vegetarian comidas (US$4.50), and an all-you-can-eat buffet (US$6.50) from noon until 5pm; mornings the food is à la carte. Closed Sat.
El Rincón La Habana Morelos 887 near Montemayor, Barrio Antiguó. The combination of Cuban menu and nightly live music is hard to resist (the music begins after 10pm), though they only open Thurs, Fri and Sat.
Sanborn's Morelos near the Plaza Hidalgo, Zona Centro. As safe a bet as ever for sandwiches and snacks: great if your stomach's feeling homesick for more continental-style fare.

Listings

Airlines Aero California ☎81/345-9700; Aeroméxico ☎81/343-5560; American Airlines ☎81/340-3031; Continental Airlines ☎81/369-0838.
American Express American Express Travel Service, San Pedro 215 Nte, Colonia del Valle (Mon–Fri 9am–6pm, Sat 9am–noon; ☎81/318-3382 or 3369), holds clients' mail, and replaces and cashes travellers' cheques.
Banks and exchange You can change money at any of the several casas de cambio on Ocampo, between Zaragoza and Juárez (Mon–Fri 9am–1pm & 3–6pm, Sat 9am–12.30pm), and change travellers' cheques at banks (almost all with ATMs), most of which are on Padre Mier, right downtown – Banamex, Pino Suárez 933 Nte, which changes money until 1pm, is one example.
Bookstores Sanborn's, on Morelos near the Macroplaza (daily 9am–10pm), holds a rather poor selection of English-language novels, though they do sell numerous magazines and some guides. You're probably better off at Cristal, located at Padre Mier and Paras, or the American Bookstore, Roberto Garza Sada 2404a (Mon–Fri 9am–7pm, Sat 10am–7pm, Sun 10am–3pm).
Buses You'll have no trouble getting an onward bus from the Central Camionera at almost any time of day or night; as well as the border destinations (including Ciudad Juárez) and Mexico City, there are buses to points all around the country, including Guadalajara and Mazatlán. The bus station is divided into six "salas", or halls, each broadly serving different points of the compass; just ask at the first one you come to and someone will direct you to the right sala. Monterrey is also a good place to pick up transport into Texas: Transportes del Norte has direct connections with the Greyhound system with transfers in Nuevo Laredo; and Americanos run direct to San Antonio (7hr; US$28), Houston (10hr; US$32), Dallas (12hr; US$40), and Chicago (28hr; US$120).
Car rental If you fancy renting wheels to get out to the sights immediately around Monterrey, or to explore the mountains, head for Plaza Hidalgo where all the main agencies have offices. Advantage Rent-A-Car, Ocampo a block west of Zaragoza (☎81/345-7374), is among the cheapest at US$60 a day; if you rent for a week you only pay for six days. Alamo, Ocampo and Carranza (☎81/340-4600), charge around US$65 per day

with unlimited mileage. Two other options are Budget (☎81/369-0819) and Alal (☎81/340-7611), both off Plaza Hidalgo on Hidalgo.

Cinema There are handy mainstream showings at Cuauhtémoc 4, corner of Cuauhtémoc and Washington, close to the Alameda.

Consulates Canada, ground floor, Zaragoza 1300, Zona Centro (Mon–Fri 9am–1pm & 2.30–5.30pm; ☎81/344-3200); US, Constitución 411 Pte (Mon–Fri 8am–2pm; ☎81/345-2120).

Emergencies Angeles Verdes (☎81/340-2113); Cruz Roja (☎81/342-1212); Cruz Verde (☎81/371-5050); police (☎066 or ☎81/151-6001); Hospital Muguerza, Hidalgo 2525 (☎81/399-3400).

Internet access The best Internet facilities in town are offered by *Ships 2000*, Escobedo 819 Sur (daily 10am–10pm; Ⓦwww.ships2000.com.mx), which charges about US$3/hr. Also try *K'Fé*, Montemayor 713 at Allende in the Barrio Antiguo; it has a good connection and also houses a small cultural centre with art exhibitions and occasional poetry readings (Mon–Sat 11am–11pm; US$1/hr); in the same neighborhood is Ciber Cafe, upstairs at Dr Coss 843F at Padre Mier. Perhaps the handiest option is the communication centre at the bus station – it has one computer and a fast connection for US$1.50/hr (6am–10pm).

Laundry Lavandería Automática, Padre Mier 1102 Ote at Antillón (Mon–Sat 8am–7pm).

Photographic supplies There are photo-developing places selling print film all over the place, but for specialist needs head for Photos de Llano, Padre Mier 565 (Mon–Sat 9am–8pm).

Post office In the Palacio Federal at the north end of the Macroplaza (Mon–Fri 8am–7pm, Sat 9am–1pm).

Travel agents Several local agents offer tours of the city and to surrounding attractions: try Cantera Travel (☎4/922-9065) in the Mercado Gonzales Ortega mall.

Around Monterrey

After a day or two the bustle of Monterrey can get to you, but you can escape to the surprisingly wild and beautiful surrounding countryside. Without your own vehicle, however, getting around the sights in the vicinity can be awkward. An exception is getting out to the subterranean caverns of **Grutas de Garcia**, which, despite some impressive stalactites and stalagmites and an underground lake, have lost some of their appeal through overdevelopment. Only 40km west of Monterrey near the village of **VILLA GARCIA**, they are a popular outing from Monterrey, especially at weekends, when hundreds cram onto the funicular tram (US$5) from the village; you can walk from the end of the tram to the caverns in about thirty minutes. Buses run several times daily to Villa Garcia from outside the *camionera*, about a block and a half towards the train station; buy your ticket either from the Transportes Monterrey–Saltillo office or on the bus.

There's wilder country to the south in the **Parque Nacional Cumbres de Monterrey**, centred on the **Cañon de la Huasteca**, about 20km southwest of Monterrey, an impressive mountain ravine some 300m deep with vertical cliffs that have become a playground for committed rock climbers. Within it is **La Huasteca** "Ecological Park" (daily 9am–6pm; cars US$1, pedestrians US$0.15) with barbecue pits, picnic areas and a pool for children, all designed to cope with the weekend influx from the city.

The trip to the **Cascada Cola de Caballo** (Horsetail Falls), 35km south of Monterrey, is only really worthwhile after the rains – you can hire horses and burros to ride in the hilly Parque Nacional Cumbres de Monterrey, where there are views from the top of the falls and plenty of opportunity for hiking and camping. To get here by bus, take a Lineas Amarillas service to **El Cercado**, where colectivos wait to take you to the falls: once there, horse-buggy rides are available, and there are lovely swimming spots. You can camp for free with permission from the Administración.

Another option is to head up to the **Mesa Chipinque**, a mountain plateau just 18km from Monterrey with famous views back over the city. Here again you can hire horses (from the enormously flash *Motel Chipinque*) to explore the hinterland. If you want an **organized trip** to the caves or falls, try

Fiestas

Carnaval (the week before Lent, variable Feb–March) is at its best in the Caribbean atmosphere of **Tampico** (Tamaulipas) – also in **Ciudad Victoria** (Tam) and **Monterrey** (Nuevo León).

MARCH

19 FESTIVAL DE SAN JOSÉ. Celebrated in **Ciudad Victoria** (Tam).

21 Ceremonies to commemorate the birth of Benito Juárez in **Matamoros** (Coahuila), near Torreón.

APRIL

12 Processions and civic festival in honour of the nineteenth-century resettlement of **Tampico** (Tam), with dress of that era. Celebrations continue for two weeks.

27 FERIA DEL AZÚCAR. In **Ciudad Mante** (Tam), south of Ciudad Victoria; very lively with bands, dancing and fireworks.

MAY

2–5 FERIA DE LA RAZA. In **Monterrey** (NL), music and arts culminating with Cinco de Mayo festivities held along Calle Juárez.

3 DÍA DE LA SANTA CRUZ. **Tula** (Tam), between Ciudad Victoria and San Luis Potosí, stages a fiesta with traditional dance. In **Gómez Palacio** (Durango), the start of an agricultural and industrial fair that lasts two weeks.

15 DÍA DE SAN ISIDRO. Observed in **Guadalupe de Bravos** (Chihuahua), on the border near Ciudad Juárez, with dances all day and parades all night. Similar celebrations in **Arteaga** (Coah), near Saltillo.

JUNE

13 DÍA DE SAN ANTONIO DE PADUA. Marked in **Tula** (Tam) by religious services followed by pastoral plays and traditional dances. Colourful native dancing, too, in **Vicente Guerrero** (Dgo), between Durango and Zacatecas.

25 DÍA DE SANTIAGO. The start of a week-long fiesta in **Altamira** (Tam), near Tampico.

JULY

4 DÍA DE NUESTRA SEÑORA DEL REFUGIO. Marked by dancing and pilgrimages in **Matamoros** (Coah).

JEMA (☎8/373-6350), whose very reasonably priced day-excursions depart from Ocampo behind the *Gran Hotel Ancira* in Monterrey.

Saltillo

SALTILLO, capital of the state of Coahuila, is the place to head for if you can't take the hustle of Monterrey. Lying just 85km to the southwest, down a fast road that cuts through the Sierra Madre Oriental and a high desert of yucca and Joshua trees, it's infinitely quieter,much smaller than Monterrey and, at 1600m above sea level, feels refreshingly cool and airy.

There's not a great deal to do in Saltillo, but it's still a great place to stroll around admiring the smattering of beautiful buildings and soaking up some

8 Durango (Dgo) celebrates its founders' day, coinciding with the feria and crafts exhibitions.

23 FERIA DE LA UVA. In **Cuatro Cienegas** (Coah), a spa town near Monclova.

AUGUST

6 Fiesta in **Jiménez** (Chih) with traditional dances, religious processions and a fair. Regional dancing, too, in **Saltillo** (Coah).

9 Exuberant FERIA DE LA UVA in **Parras** (Coah), between Saltillo and Torreón.

13 Saltillo (Coah) begins its annual feria, lively and varied.

SEPTEMBER

8 DÍA DE LA VIRGEN DE LOS REMEDIOS celebrated with parades and traditional dances in **Santa Barbara** (Chih), near Hidalgo del Parral, and **San Juan del Río** (Dgo), between here and Durango.

10 Dancing from before dawn and a parade in the evening mark the fiesta in **Ramos Arizpe** (Coah), near Saltillo.

11 Major feria on the border at **Nuevo Laredo** (Tam).

15–16 INDEPENDENCE. Festivities everywhere, but the biggest in **Monterrey** (NL).

OCTOBER

25 Joint celebrations between the border town of **Ciudad Acuña** (Coah) and its Texan neighbour Del Rio. Bullfights and parades.

NOVEMBER

3 DÍA DE SAN MARTIN DE PORRES is the excuse for a fiesta, with native dances, in **Tampico** (Tam) and nearby **Altamira** (Tam).

15–25 FERIA DE LA CULTURA BARRIO ANTIGUO in **Monterrey** (NL), one of its leading festivals; throngs of people come for the music and food when the many cafés and cocinas open to the street.

DECEMBER

4 Santa Barbara (Chih) celebrates its saint's day.

12 DÍA DE NUESTRA SEÑORA DE GUADALUPE. A big one everywhere, especially in **Guadalupe de Bravos** (Chih), **El Palmito** (Dgo), between Durango and Parral, **Ciudad Anahuac** (NL) in the north of the state, and **Abasolo** (NL), near Monterrey. **Monterrey** itself attracts many pilgrims at this time.

atmosphere. Two contrasting, and almost adjoining, squares grace the centre of town: the **Plaza Acuña**, surrounded by crowded shopping streets, marks the rowdy heart of the modern city, while the old **Plaza de Armas** is formal, tranquil, illuminated at night and sometimes hosts music performances. Facing the Palacio de Gobierno across a flagged square, the magnificent eighteenth-century **cathedral** is one of the most beautiful in northern Mexico, with an elaborately carved churrigueresque facade and doorways, an enormous bell tower and a smaller clock tower. On the south side of the square the **Instituto Coahuilense de Cultura** (Tues–Sun 9am–7pm; free) hosts often diverting temporary exhibits by Coahuila artists.

The town's oldest streets fan out from the square, with some fine old houses still in private hands. One historic building worth seeking out is the carefully preserved old **Ayuntamiento** (town hall) on the corner of Aldama and Hidalgo. The walls of the courtyard and the staircase are adorned with murals depicting the history of Saltillo from prehistoric times to the 1950s. Calle Victoria spurs west off the square, passing a few hundred metres of the city's major shops and cinemas, on the way to the **Alameda**, a shaded, tree-lined park, peopled with students looking for a peaceful spot to work: there are several language schools in Saltillo as well as a university and technical institute, and, in summer especially, numbers of American students come here to study Spanish.

Saltillo is famous, too, for its **sarapes**, and there are several small shops where (at least on weekdays) you can watch the manufacturing process – the best is tucked at the back of the artesanía shop El Sarape de Saltillo, Hidalgo Sur 305 (Mon–Sat 9am–1pm & 3–7pm). Sadly the old ways are vanishing fast, and most now use artificial fibres and chemical dyes: all too many of those on sale in the market are mass-produced in virulent clashing colours.

Birders should head to **Museo de las Aves de México**, at the intersection of Hidalgo and Bolívar (Tues–Sun 10am–6pm), where you'll find a large collection of birds on exhibit throughout various themed rooms.

Practicalities

City buses (marked "Centro/Camionera") run from Saltillo's main **bus station** (no guardería), 3km southwest of the centre, to the cathedral on the Plaza de Armas, and onwards a couple more stops to the Plaza Acuña, right at the heart of things. The small **tourist office** is in a red-brick building just a few blocks north of the action at the intersection of Francisco Coss and Acuña (Mon–Sat 9am–6pm; ⓣ844/412-5122, ⓔprotursa@coah1.telmex.net.mx). Strategically positioned **maps of the city** – at the bus and train stations and on both squares – help orientation. The **post office** is at Victoria 453 and there are long-distance **phones** and **banks** with ATMs all over the centre of town. At Padre Flores 159, Cyberbase has **Internet** access for US$1/hr (Mon–Sat 8am–10.30pm, Sun noon–8pm). In the centre try Jack Designs, upstairs at Victoria 573 (Mon–Sat 9am–10pm, Sun 11am–10pm; US$1.50/hr).

Most of the better-value **hotels** are in the side streets immediately around Plaza Acuña, but have a tendency to fill up each night. Both *Hotel Jardín* (or *de Avila*), Padre Flores 211 (ⓣ844/412-5916; ❸), and *Hotel Bristol*, Aldama Pte 405 (ⓣ844/410-4337; ❸), are good-value budget places, the latter having the edge with cable TV. If you can spend a little more and want to savour some colonial atmosphere, have a look at the *Urdiñola*, Victoria Pte 207 (ⓣ844/414-0940; ❺), with its tiled open lobby dominated by a wide staircase flanked by suits of armour, and fountains playing amidst the greenery of the courtyard. If these are full, you might try the unremarkable *Saade* at Aldama 397 (ⓣ844/412-9120; ❺).

Restaurants in Saltillo tend to close early, and the ones in the centre mainly cater for office workers and students. There are, as always, plenty of cheap places to eat around the **Mercado Juárez**, beside the Plaza Acuña, which is a decent market in its own right – tourists are treated fairly and not constantly pressed to buy. The *Café Victoria*, on Padre Flores just south of Plaza Acuña, is good for breakfasts, bulging tortillas and comidas corridas. At the western end of Victoria by the Alameda, *Terrazza Romana* serves up toothsome pasta dishes for around US$6 and fine pizzas for a dollar or two more. If you're stocking up for a journey, pick up wholemeal bread, great carrot cake and the like from *Trigo Limpio*, Victoria 670; *Natura Es* across the street has good, healthy frozen yoghurt for US$1.50 and up.

From Saltillo you can head **southeast to Zacatecas** or follow the direct route **to Mexico City** via San Luis, passing through Matehuala (with the possibility of branching off to the mountain ghost town of Real de Catorce) and Querétaro. Going through Zacatecas, though slower, gives you the chance to visit more of the beautiful colonial cities north of the capital.

Travel details

Trains

The Copper Canyon railway (see p.169) is the big attraction in this region – one of the few train journeys in Mexico that you might want to take simply for the experience. Even though this region has a number of train stations and track running across the land, the two main lines heading south from the border to Mexico City are no longer available to passengers.

Buses

Services on the chief routes to and from the frontier (Ciudad Juárez– Chihuahua–Torreón/Durango and from the border to Monterrey– Saltillo–San Luis Potosí/Zacatecas) are excellent, with departures day and night. There are also direct services to Mexico City from just about everywhere. The best lines are generally, on the central route, Omnibus de México and Transportes Chihuahuenses, and in the east Frontera, Transportes del Norte and Autobuses del Oriente (ADO). Estrella Blanca, ostensibly a second-class company, often beats them all for frequency of services and efficiency. What follows should be taken as a minimum.

Chihuahua to: Ciudad Juárez (at least hourly; 5hr); Creel (every 2hr; 4hr); Jiménez (roughly hourly; 3hr); Mexico City (every 2hr; 18hr); Nuevo Casas Grandes (5 daily; 4hr 30min); Zacatecas (every 2hr; 12hr).

Ciudad Acuña to: Monterrey (4 daily; 8hr); Piedras Negras (hourly; 1hr 30min); Saltillo (8 daily; 7hr).

Ciudad Juárez to: Chihuahua (at least hourly; 5hr); Durango (at least hourly; 16hr); Jiménez (at least hourly; 8hr); Mexico City (10 daily; 24hr); Nuevo Casas Grandes (hourly; 4hr); Parral (at least hourly; 10hr); Torreón (at least hourly; 12hr); Zacatecas (hourly; 16hr).

Ciudad Victoria to: Matamoros (hourly; 4–5hr); Monterrey (hourly; 4hr); Reynosa (9 daily; 4–5hr); Tampico (hourly or better; 3hr).

Creel to: Batopilas (1 daily, 6hr); Chihuahua (9 daily; 4–5hr); Guachochi (2 daily; 3hr).

Durango to: Aguascalientes (20 daily; 6hr); Ciudad Juárez (at least hourly; 12–14hr); Fresnillo (11 daily; 3hr); Mazatlán (9 daily; 7hr); Mexico City (14 daily; 12–13hr); Monterrey (20 daily; 9hr); Parral (9 daily; 6hr); Torreón (6 daily; 4hr 30min); Zacatecas (roughly hourly; 4hr 30min).

Guachochi to: Chihuahua (5 daily; 7–9hr); Creel (2 daily; 3hr); Parral (6 daily; 4hr).

Matamoros to: Chicago (2 daily; 36hr); Ciudad Victoria (hourly; 4–5hr); Dallas (2 daily; 12hr); Houston (3 daily; 5hr); Monterrey (hourly; 4hr); Reynosa (every 45min; 2hr); San Antonio (3 daily; 6hr); Tampico (hourly; 7–8hr).

Monterrey to: Ciudad Victoria (hourly; 4hr); Dallas (3 daily; 12hr); Guadalajara (15 daily; 12hr); Houston (3 daily; 10hr); Matamoros (hourly; 4hr); Matehuala (12 daily; 4–5hr); Mexico City (hourly; 12hr); Nuevo Laredo (every 30min; 3hr); Piedras Negras (7 daily; 5–7hr); Reynosa (every 30min; 3hr); Saltillo (constantly; 1hr 30min); San Antonio (4 daily; 7hr); San Luis Potosí (12 daily; 7hr); Tampico (12 daily; 7–8hr); Zacatecas (hourly; 6hr).

Nuevo Casas Grandes to: Chihuahua (hourly; 4hr 30min); Ciudad Juárez (hourly; 4hr).

Nuevo Laredo to: Acapulco (2 daily; 20hr); Austin (14 daily; 7hr); Chicago (2 daily; 36hr); Dallas (14 daily; 9hr); Guadalajara (5 daily; 14hr); Houston (9 daily; 7hr); Mexico City (5 daily; 15hr); Monterrey (every 30min; 3hr); Piedras Negras (5 daily; 3hr); Reynosa (8 daily; 4hr); Saltillo (8 daily; 4–5hr); San Antonio (hourly; 4hr); San Luis Potosí (8 daily; 12hr); Tampico (2 daily; 10hr); Zacatecas (5 daily; 8hr).

Parral to: Chihuahua (roughly hourly; 4hr); Durango (9 daily; 6hr); Guachochi (6 daily; 3hr 30min).

Piedras Negras to: Ciudad Acuña (hourly; 1hr 30min); Mexico City (3 daily; 18hr); Monterrey (7 daily; 5–7hr); Nuevo Laredo (5 daily; 3hr); Saltillo (12 daily; 7hr).

Reynosa to: Ciudad Victoria (9 daily; 4–5hr); Matamoros (every 45min; 2hr); Mexico City (6 daily; 14–16hr); Monterrey (every 30min; 3hr); Nuevo Laredo (8 daily; 4hr); San Luis Potosí (9 daily; 9–10hr); Tampico (hourly; 7hr); Zacatecas (10 daily; 9hr).

Saltillo to: Ciudad Acuña (8 daily; 7hr); Guadalajara (13 daily; 10hr); Matehuala (8 daily; 2hr 30min); Mazatlán (4 daily; 12hr); Mexico City

(8 daily; 12hr); Monterrey (constantly; 1hr 30min); Nuevo Laredo (8 daily; 4–5hr); Piedras Negras (12 daily; 7hr).
Tampico to: Ciudad Victoria (hourly or better; 3hr); Matamoros (hourly; 7–8hr); Mexico City (every 1–2hr; 8hr); Monterrey (12 daily; 7–8hr); Nuevo Laredo (2 daily; 10hr); San Luis Potosí (11 daily; 7hr); Veracruz (8 daily; 9hr).
Torreón to: Ciudad Juárez (at least hourly; 12hr); Zacatecas (10 daily; 6hr).

Flights

There are frequent flights from most of the major cities to the capital – Chihuahua, Monterrey and Tampico all have several a day. From Monterrey you can also fly to Guadalajara and Acapulco, and there are international services to Dallas, Houston, San Antonio and Chicago. From Ciudad Juárez and Nuevo Laredo you can get to the capital and Guadalajara.

Northern Jalisco and Michoacán

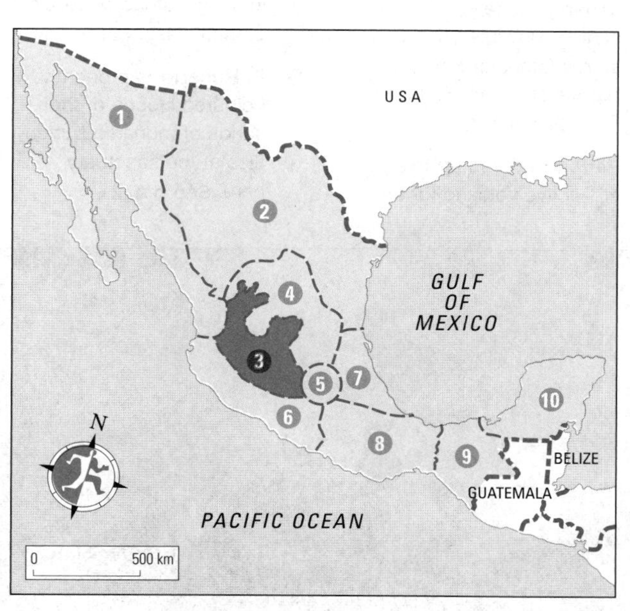

CHAPTER 3

Highlights

* **Guadalajara** Experience the drama of *mariachi* music in Mexico's most "Mexican" city, the capital of Jalisco. See p.222

* **Tequila** Visit a tequila distillery and, more importantly, sample the legendary spirit in a café on the town's plaza. See p.247

* **Uruapan** Take in the cascading waterfalls and lush surroundings of the Parque Nacional Eduardo Ruiz. See p.251

* **Paricutín** Climb up this still-active volcano for an unforgettable experience. See p.254

* **Pátzcuaro** One of the best places in Mexico for seeing the spectacular and moving Day of the Dead celebrations. See p.255

* **Morelia** Enjoy *dulces*, wine and classical music in one of the cafés overlooking historic Morelia's central plaza. See p.264

* **El Rosario** See brightly coloured clouds of thousands of monarch butterflies at the sanctuary here. See p.272

△ Lago de Chapala fishermen

Northern Jalisco and Michoacán

Separated from the country's colonial heartland by the craggy peaks of the Sierra Madre, the land that stretches from Guadalajara to Mexico City, through the semitropical states of **Jalisco** and **Michoacán**, has an unhurried ease that marks it out from the rest of the country. The area contains a complex landscape of lofty plains and rugged sierra, blessed with supremely fertile farms, fresh pine woods, cool pastures and lush tropical forest. Both states stretch all the way to the ocean and boast beaches that include the sophistication of Puerto Vallarta and the simplicity of Playa Azul: this coastal strip is covered elsewhere in this book, starting on p.469.

Something of a backwater until well into the eighteenth century, the high valleys of Michoacán and Jalisco were left to develop their own strong regional traditions and solid farming economy. There is a wealth of local commercial goods, both agricultural and traditionally manufactured items, from avocados to tequila, glassware to guitars. Relative isolation has also made the region a bastion of conservatism – in the years following the Revolution, the Catholic *Cristero* counter-revolutionary guerrilla movement enjoyed its strongest support here.

Easygoing **Guadalajara**, Mexico's second largest city, is packed with elegant buildings and surrounded by scenic country. Further afield the land is spectacularly green and mountainous, studded with volcanoes and lakes, most famously **Lago de Chapala**, where D.H. Lawrence wrote *The Plumed Serpent*. There are also some superb colonial relics, especially in the towns of **Morelia** and **Pátzcuaro**, although in the latter it's the majestic setting and the richness of Indian traditions that first call your attention. This powerful indigenous culture still in evidence more than compensates for the paucity of physical remains from the pre-Hispanic era, though the ruins of **Tzintzuntzán** on Lago de Pátzcuaro are certainly impressive. Local **fiestas** – and there are many – are among the most vital in Mexico, and the legacy of village handicrafts has survived since the earliest days of the Conquest.

Jalisco and Michoacán are among the most serene states in the country: relaxing, easy to get about, and free of urban hassle. Add the fact that Jalisco is the home of **mariachi** and of **tequila** and you've got a region where you could easily spend a couple of weeks exploring without even beginning to see it all.

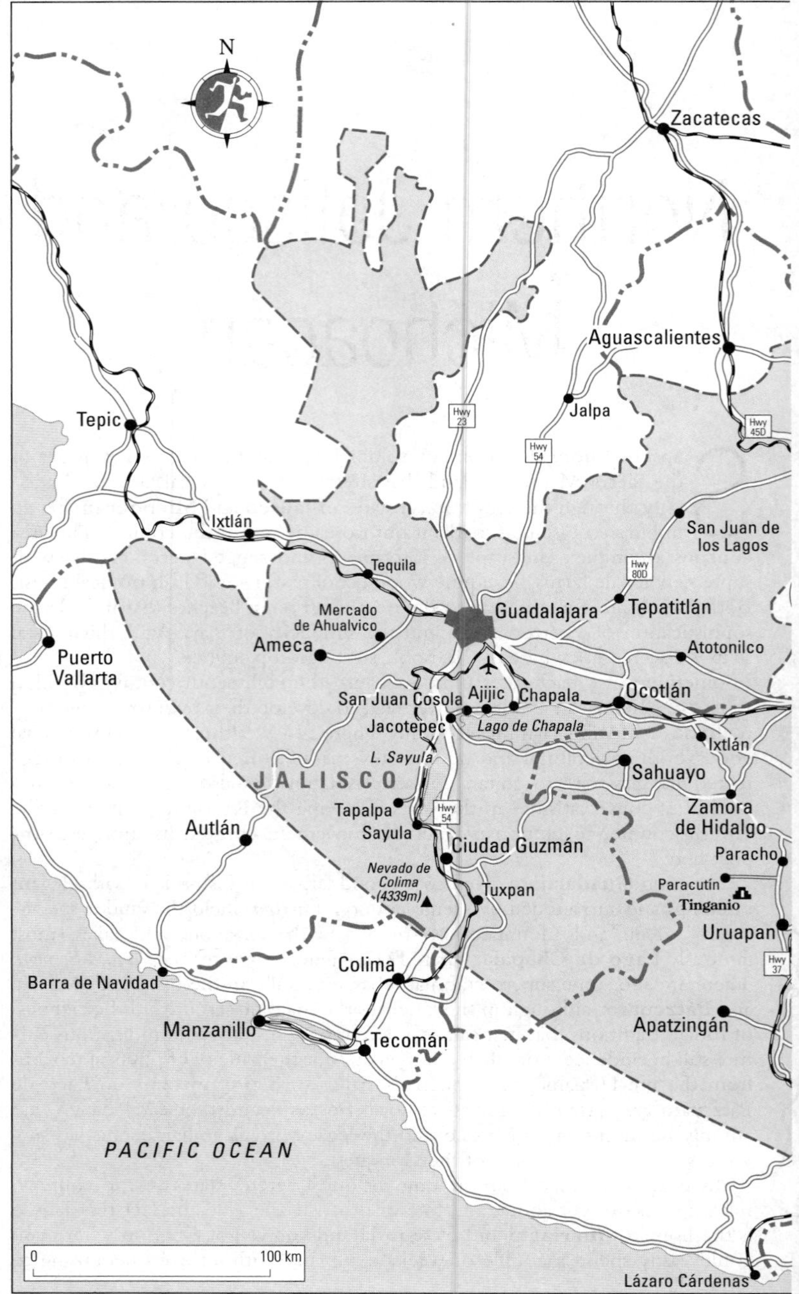

N
Zacatecas
Aguascalientes
Jalpa
Hwy 23
Hwy 54
Hwy 45D
Tepic
Ixtlán
Tequila
San Juan de los Lagos
Hwy 80D
Mercado de Ahualvico
Guadalajara
Tepatitlán
Ameca
Puerto Vallarta
Atotonilco
San Juan Cosola
Ajijic
Chapala
Ocotlán
Jacotepec
Lago de Chapala
Ixtlán
L. Sayula
Sahuayo
JALISCO
Tapalpa
Hwy 54
Zamora de Hidalgo
Autlán
Sayula
Ciudad Guzmán
Paracho
Nevado de Colima (4339m)
Tuxpan
Paracutín
Tinganio
Uruapan
Colima
Hwy 37
Barra de Navidad
Manzanillo
Tecomán
Apatzingán
PACIFIC OCEAN
0
100 km
Lázaro Cárdenas

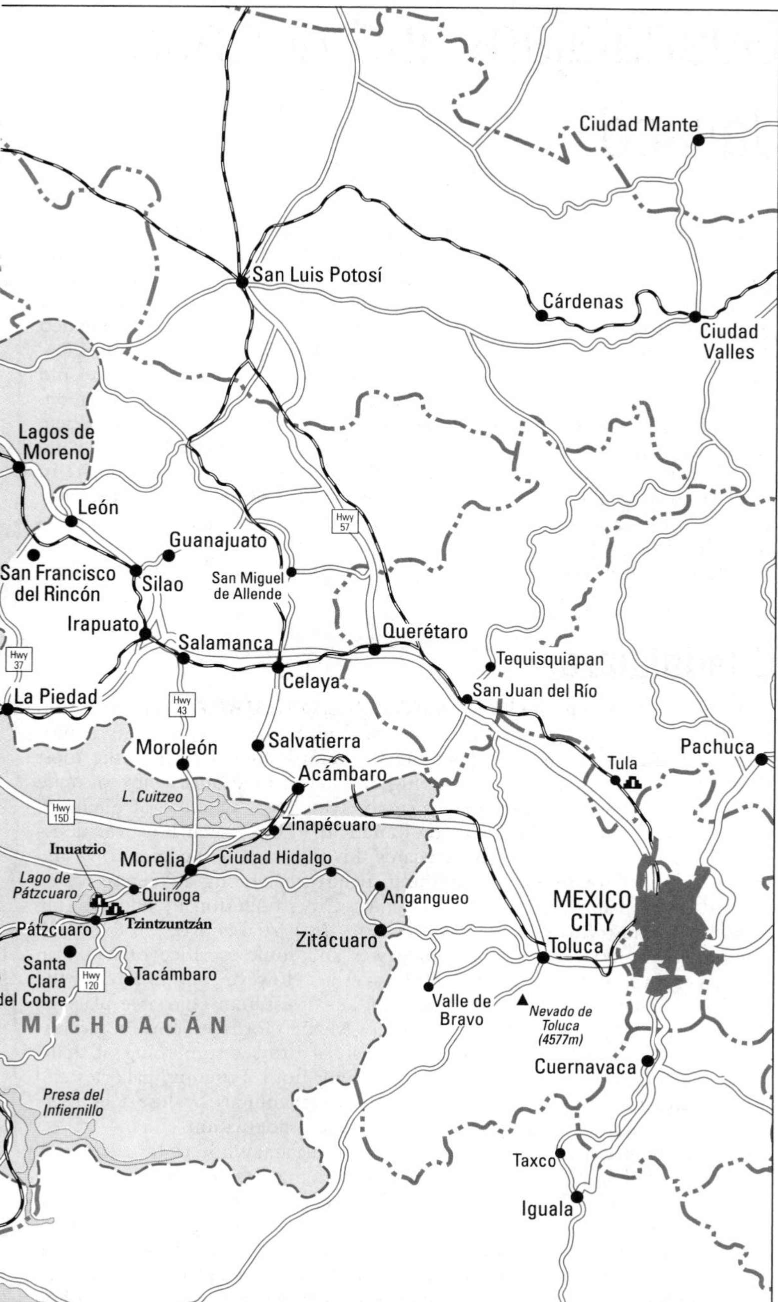
Ciudad Mante
San Luis Potosí
Cárdenas
Ciudad Valles
Lagos de Moreno
León
Guanajuato
San Francisco del Rincón
Silao
San Miguel de Allende
Hwy 57
Irapuato
Salamanca
Querétaro
Hwy 37
Celaya
Tequisquiapan
San Juan del Río
La Piedad
Hwy 43
Moroleón
Salvatierra
Acámbaro
Pachuca
Tula
L. Cuitzeo
Hwy 15D
Zinapécuaro
Inuatzio
Morelia
Ciudad Hidalgo
Lago de Pátzcuaro
Quiroga
Angangueo
Tzintzuntzán
Pátzcuaro
Zitácuaro
MEXICO CITY
Toluca
Santa Clara del Cobre
Hwy 120
Tacámbaro
Valle de Bravo
Nevado de Toluca (4577m)
MICHOACÁN
Cuernavaca
Presa del Infiernillo
Taxco
Iguala

Guadalajara and northern Jalisco

Guadalajara dominates the state of **Jalisco** in every way. It is not just the capital city, but is quite simply the main attraction. If you spend any time in the region, you're inevitably going to spend much of it here: it's also very much a transport hub, and would be almost impossible to avoid, even should you wish to. Here the road routes from the northwest meet the onward routes to Mexico City and the country's central highlands, with a growing web of expensive new *cuota* roads to speed you on your way. To see only Guadalajara, however, would be to miss the real nature of the state, which away from the capital is green, lush and mountainous. **Lago de Chapala**, south of the city, offers easy escape and tranquil scenery; in mountain villages like Tapalpa, there's fresh air and rural life still lived at the old tempo. **Tequila** offers . . . well, tequila. The climate in Guadalajara is delightfully temperate, save for the peak of the dry season in May when the city sizzles. Although its reputation as the "city of eternal spring" is somewhat exaggerated, Guadalajara is almost always warm – on much the same latitude as Bombay, yet protected from extremes by its altitude, around 1600m.

Guadalajara

The second city of the Mexican Republic, **GUADALAJARA** has a reputation as a slower, more conservative and traditional place than Mexico City, somewhere you can stop and catch your breath. Many claim that this is the most "Mexican" of big Mexican cities, having evolved as a regional centre of trade and commerce, without the imbalances of Monterrey's industrial giants or Mexico City's chaotic scale. Being less frenetic than the capital, however, doesn't make it peaceful, and by any standards this is a huge, sprawling, noisy and energetic city. Growth has, if anything, been accelerating in recent years, boosted by the campaign to reduce Mexico City's pollution by encouraging people and industry to relocate to other cities. Its partial conversion to a sleek metropolis has resulted in a hike in prices and some sacrifice of Mexican mellowness in favour of a US-style business ethic. However, enthusiasm for the new has not replaced affection for the old and it's still an enjoyable place to visit, with the edge on all other big cities of Mexico for trees, flowers, cleanliness and friendliness. It also remains a great place to see something of traditional and modern Mexico, offering everything from museums, galleries and colonial architecture, to magnificent revolutionary murals by José Clemente Orozco, to a nightlife enlivened by a large student population.

Parks, little squares and open spaces dot Guadalajara, while right downtown around the cathedral is a series of plazas unchanged since the days of the Spanish colonization. This small colonial heart of the city can still, especially at weekends, recall an old-world atmosphere and provincial elegance. The centre is further brightened by the **Plaza Tapatía**. It takes its name from *tapatío* – an adjective used to describe anything typical of Guadalajara, supposedly derived from the capes worn by Spanish grandees. Guadalajarans themselves are often referred to as *Tapatíos*. Although the plaza was only constructed in the late nineteenth century (by demolishing some of the city's oldest neighbourhoods), it manages to look as if it has always been there. It creates new sightlines between some of Guadalajara's most monumental buildings and opens out the city's historical core to pedestrians, as well as *mariachi* bands and street theatre. Around this relatively unruffled nucleus revolve raucous and crowded streets typical of modern Mexico, while further out still, in the wide boulevards of the new suburbs, you'll find smart hotels, shopping malls and modern office blocks.

Some history

Guadalajara was founded in 1532, one of the fruits of the vicious campaign of Nuño de Guzmán at the time of the conquest – his cruelty and corruption were such that he appalled even the Spanish authorities, who threw him into prison in Madrid, where he died. The city, named after his birthplace, thrived, was officially recognized by Charles V in 1542 and rapidly became one of the colony's most Spanish cities – in part because so much of the indigenous population had been killed or had fled during the period of conquest and suppression by the Spaniards. Isolated from the great mining industry of the Bajío, Guadalajara evolved into a regional centre for trade and agriculture. The tight reins of colonial rule restrained the city's development, and it wasn't until the end of the eighteenth century that things really took off, as the colonial monopolies began to crumble. Between 1760 and 1803 the city's population tripled to reach some 35,000, and a new university was established, as the city became famous for the export of wheat, hides, cotton and wool.

When the empire finally fell apart, Guadalajara supported Hidalgo's independence movement and briefly served as the capital of the nation when Mexico finally split with Spain. By the beginning of the twentieth century it was already the second largest city in the Republic, and in the 1920s the completion of the rail link with California provided a further spur for development. More recently, the exodus from Mexico City and attempts at industrial decentralization have continued to swell the population.

Arrival

Guadalajara's **airport** is some 17km southeast of the city on the road to Chapala. Facilities include money exchange and car rental, and there's also the usual system of fixed-price taxis and vans to take you downtown (around US$15 for a car with 3–4 people and US$25 for a van with 5–9 people – vouchers are sold inside the terminal and the ride takes 45min). A much cheaper bus service (every 15min 6am–9pm; US$1) also runs to and from the old bus station – the Camionera Vieja (see p.225) – from where you can hop on another bus, or walk, to the centre.

Right out in the city's southeastern suburbs, Guadalajara's **Central Camionera**, also known as the Camionera Nueva, is one of Mexico's newest and largest bus terminals, comprising seven buildings strung out in a wide arc, with its own shopping centre (Nueva Central Plaza) and hotel (see "Accommodation", p.227). Very broadly, each building serves a different area, but since they're organized by bus company rather than route, it's not quite that simple – there are buses to Mexico City from just about every building, for example. However, each has an extremely helpful information desk where staff will advise exactly which bus to take to get to where you're going, and can also book accommodation. Local bus #644 ("Centro") and the slightly dearer turquoise TUR bus stop outside each terminal, both of them taking you to Avenida 16 de Septiembre, within walking

△ Cathedral at Morelia

distance of the cathedral if not right past it. The last city buses between the terminal and the centre leave at around 10pm. Bus #275 from behind Building 1 also runs to the centre until around 10.30pm. For details of how to reach the terminal from the centre, and of long-distance buses running from it, see p.241.

Some second-class buses from local destinations, including Tequila, Tapalpa, Ciudad Guzmán and the villages on the shores of Lago de Chapala, as well as the airport service, use the **Camionera Vieja**, the old downtown terminal, surrounded by cheap hotels and only a short bus ride (#174) up Calzada Independencia from the centre. If you're coming from somewhere only an hour or two away, it can be worth the slightly less comfortable second-class journey for the convenience of this much more central point of arrival. The two *camioneras* are connected by the #616 bus.

The **train station**, a couple of kilometres south of the centre at the bottom of Calzada Independencia, has not functioned as a commercial train station for the last five years. Instead, the line is used for the touristy *Tequila Express* (see p.241).

Orientation

The centre of the old city is a relatively compact grid around the junction of **Morelos** and **16 de Septiembre**, by the huge bulk of the **cathedral**; east of here Morelos leads to the **Plaza Tapatía** and the **Mercado Libertad**, while to the west are busy shopping streets. **Juárez**, a couple of blocks south, is actually the main east–west thoroughfare in the centre, heading out to the west past the **university** (where it becomes Vallarta), and crossing avenidas **Chapultepec** and **Américas** in an upmarket residential area. Further west still, it crosses **López Mateos**, a main through route, which heads south past the **Plaza del Sol**, a shopping centre surrounded by big hotels, restaurants and much of Guadalajara's best, but expensive, nightlife, and eventually heads out of the city as the main road towards Colima and the coast.

The main north–south arteries in the centre are the **Calzada del Federalismo**, along which the *tren ligero*, the city's metro, runs and **Calzada Independencia**, which runs from the train station, up past the **Parque Agua Azul**, the old bus station, the market and Plaza Tapatía, and eventually out of the city to the **Parque Mirador**. Finally, **Revolución** leads off Independencia towards the southeast – to Tlaquepaque, the new bus station and Tonalá. If you fancy taking a **city tour** to get your bearings, try Panoramex (Ⓣ333/810-5109; US$13 for 5 hours, offered Mon–Sat).

Information

The helpful state **tourist office** is at Morelos 102 (Mon–Fri 9am–8pm, Sat & Sun 9am–1pm; Ⓣ333/668-1600 or 668-1601, Ⓕ333/668-1606, Ⓦhttp://visita.jalisco.gob.mx), off Plaza Tapatía, where there is also a tourist information booth run by the city council. In addition, there are information booths at the Central Camionera and the airport, as well as a free tourist information phone line from elsewhere in the country (Ⓣ01-800/363-2200).

Although any of the banks throughout the centre – the cluster including Banamex and Bancomer around Corona and Juárez, for example – offer **currency exchange**, casas de cambio, many of them around the corner of Maestranza and López Cotilla, are quicker, open slightly longer and offer almost identical rates. After hours, the bigger hotels will usually change money at a considerably worse rate. Most banks have **ATMs**.

Guadalajara's main **post office** (Mon–Fri 8am–7pm, Sat 9am–1pm) is at Venustiano Carranza 16, the junction with Independencia. *Casetas* for

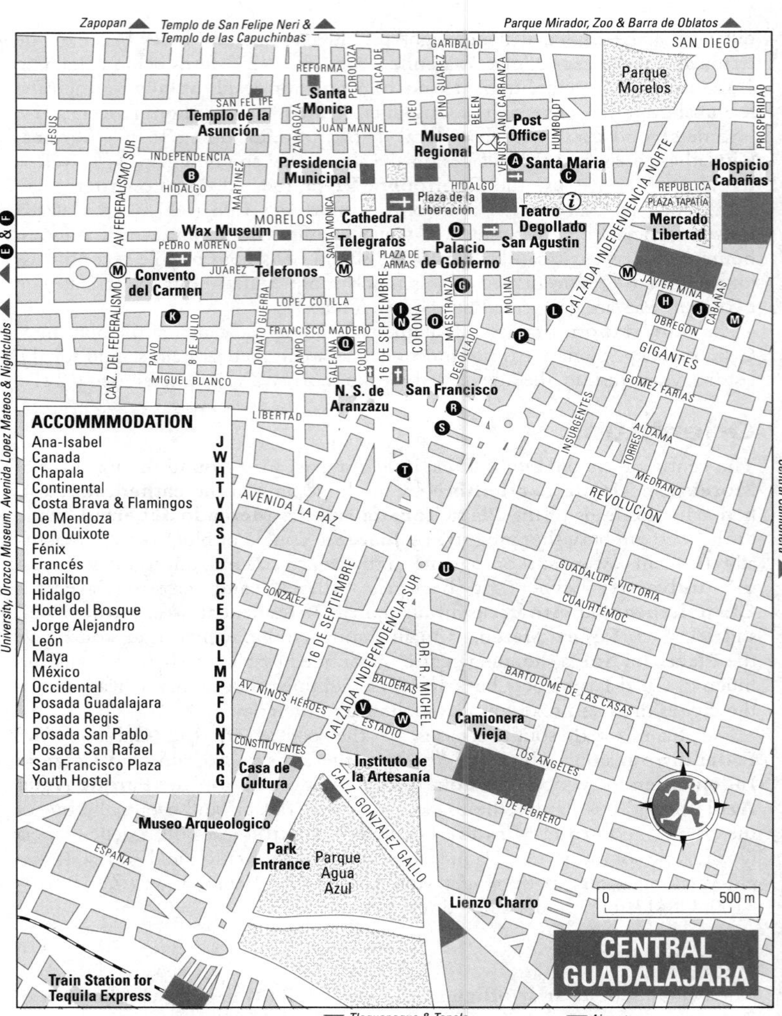

long-distance **phone** calls include Computel, in the Edificio Mulbar at Corona 181 and Madero, and also in the Camionera Vieja (Sala B and outside) and the Camionera Nueva (Building 2), and Telefónica Digital, at Sanchez 375 between Ocampo and Galeana. There are also plenty of public phones, including some relatively quiet ones around Plaza Tapatía.

City transport

Guadalajara is a very big city, but getting around is not too difficult once you've got the hang of the comprehensive system of public transport. In the centre, most of the main attractions are within walking distance of each other, and

Useful bus routes

All of these also run in the opposite direction: the #600 numbers are minibuses.

#60 Calzada Independencia–Soccer stadium and bullring–Camionera Vieja

#142 Centro–FFCC (train station)

#176 Centro–airport

#190 Centro–Zapopan-Tuzania

#275 Nueva Camionera–Tonalá–Tlaquepaque–Centro–Zapopan

#603-A Cabañas - Barranca de Huentitan

#616 Nueva Camionera–Camionera Vieja–Centro

#621 Centro–FFCC (train station)

#629 Centro–Morelos (westbound)/Pedro Moreno (eastbound)–Minerva Circle

#639 Centro–Colonia Jalisco

#707 TUR turquoise bus Nueva Camionera–Tonalá–Tlaquepaque–Centro–Zapopan

Trolleybus Independencia Centro–Soccer stadium and bullring–Zoo

elsewhere using public transport is relatively straightforward. Almost all **buses** are funnelled through the centre on a few main roads and have their destinations written on the windscreen. The sheer number of buses and the speed at which they move can make things slightly more difficult, however, especially at peak hours when you may have to fight to get on: if possible, get a local to show you exactly where your bus stops. The **tren ligero**, or metro system, with one north–south and one east–west line, is designed for local commuters, and you're not likely to use it.

Taxis are also reliable if you're in a hurry, and for a group they don't work out too expensive as long as you establish a price at the outset; many downtown taxi ranks post a list of fixed prices. From the centre to the Plaza del Sol, Nueva Camionera or Zapopan should cost around US$4.50, slightly less to Tlaquepaque and US$10 to the airport.

The best way to get around, however, is **on foot** – Guadalajara's streets are even more pleasant if you appreciate them slowly. If you stop to get your shoes cleaned too, you'll make somebody very happy.

Accommodation

Most of Guadalajara's **cheap hotels** are around the old bus station or in the streets south of the Mercado Libertad, areas that are noisy and none too appealing. The more **expensive** establishments, meanwhile, tend to be a long way out to the west of the city. In either case there are alternatives in the centre, within walking distance of the historical heart of the city, and if you can find space this is definitely the place to be. Finally, there's Avenida López Mateos, 2km to the west of the centre, which is Guadalajara's motel row.

Guadalajara's **youth hostel**, *Hostel Guadalajara Centro*, is at Maestranza 147 at the corner of López Cotilla (Ⓣ333/562-7520, Ⓦwww.hostelguadalajara.com; ❷). This spanking new establishment offers Internet access, laundry and cooking facilities, private lockers and discounts to ISIC members. A friendly staff, convenient location and US$10 beds make it a choice pick for budget travellers. If you arrive late at night at the **Camionera Nueva** and all you want to do is sleep, there's a hotel right by the entrance: *Hotel Serena* (Ⓣ333/600-0910, Ⓕ600-1774; ❹) is modern and soulless, but has two pools and reasonably soundproof rooms with TV.

In the centre

Continental Corona 450 ⓣ333/614-1117. Modern 1960s hotel with antique phones; smaller and cheaper than many of the business hotels, and just down the road from the fancy, high-rise *Aranzazu*. ❺

De Mendoza Carranza 16, at Hidalgo ⓣ333/613-4646, ⓕ613-7310, ⓦwww.demendoza.com.mx. Attractive establishment in a refurbished colonial convent; all amenities including pool and loads of towels shaped like swans. A central location makes this an ideal base for sightseeing. ❽

Don Quixote Héroes 91 at Degollado ⓣ333/658-1299, ⓕ614-2845. Friendly, small hotel with rooms around a colonial-style courtyard. ❻

Fénix Corona 160 ⓣ333/614-5714, ⓕ613-4005, ⓔ reservaciones@fenixhl.com.mx. Large, modern building in the centre of things: it's a Best Western and sometimes offers promotional deals. Rooms are impeccably clean and its breakfast buffet earns rave reviews. ❼

Francés Maestranza 35 ⓣ333/613-1190, ⓕ658-2831, ⓔreserva@hotelfrances.com. Just off the plaza behind the cathedral, this beautiful colonial building, founded in 1610 as an inn, is much the most atmospheric and appealing of Guadalajara's more expensive hotels. It's popular, so reserve in advance. At the very least stop by for a superb margarita — happy hours daily 1pm–8pm. ❻

Hamilton Madero 381, between Galeana and Ocampo ⓣ333/614-6726. Clean and friendly, this is a popular spot with backpackers and young Mexican couples, with private bath and TV. ❷

Hidalgo Hiladgo 14 ⓣ333/613-5067. Two blocks from the Teatro Degollado, a good budget option for travellers looking for something cheap, clean and central. ❷

Jorge Alejandro Hidalgo 656 ⓣ333/658-1051. The spotless rooms in this recently renovated central hotel, which was once a convent, have a large blue cross hung on the wall above each bed. The rooms with four beds are good for families or groups. ❺

Posada Regis Corona 171, near López Cotilla ⓣ/ⓕ333/614-8633, ⓔposadaregis@usa.net. Bizarre, ramshackle old building locked away from the world with an iron gate, with high-ceilinged rooms around a peaceful, covered courtyard (cheapest rooms are on the roof). Nylon sheets are the minus here. ❺

Posada San Pablo Madero 429 ⓣ/ⓕ333/614-2811. Hard to spot (there's no sign – ring the bell at the front door); clean rooms around a dark, covered courtyard replete with flowers and birds. ❷

Posada San Rafael López Cotilla 619 ⓣ333/614-9146, ⓦhttp://sanrafael1.tripod.com. A pleasant, friendly little place in a prettily decorated, recently renovated old house. Some rooms are brighter than others. Price decreases by twenty percent if you stay for three or more days. ❺

San Francisco Plaza Degollado 267 at Héroes ⓣ333/613-8954, ⓕ613-3257. Nice old place around a series of courtyards. ❻

Around the Mercado Libertad

Ana-Isabel Javier Mina 164 ⓣ/ⓕ333/617-7920. Simple but clean rooms, TV and parking. Worth bargaining if they're not full, though bear in mind this is a very noisy area. ❹

Chapala José María Mercado 84 ⓣ333/617-7159, ⓕ617-3410. Around the corner from the *Ana-Isabel*, neat and basic, but a touch dark. ❷

Maya López Cotilla 39 at Huerto ⓣ333/614-5454, ⓕ658-4641. Bare but decent rooms with TVs in a rough, noisy area, but better than on Javier Mina, with parking facilities. ❹

México Javier Mina 230 ⓣ333/617-9978. Near the *Ana-Isabel*, on the same noisy main road, but with tidy rooms with two or more beds – all with TV and private bath. ❺

Occidental Villa Gómez 17 at Huerto, just off Independencia ⓣ333/613-8406. Plain, good-value rooms with showers. ❸

South of the centre: Calzada Independencia and the Camionera Vieja

Canada Estadio 77 ⓣ333/619-4014, ⓕ619-3110. One of dozens surrounding the Camionera Vieja, this large place is pretty good value with the bonus of the excellent *Restaurante Ottawa*. Some better, pricier rooms available. ❺

Costa Brava Independencia Sur 739, near Los Angeles ⓣ333/619-2324 or 619-2327. New, friendly hotel. The slightly more expensive rooms have TV. ❸

Flamingos Independencia Sur 725 ⓣ333/619-8764. Next door to the *Costa Brava*: bigger, rougher and cheaper. ❸

León Independencia Sur 557 ⓣ333/619-6141. Basic, stark and the least expensive of all. ❷

West of the centre: Avenida López Mateos Sur

Hotel del Bosque López Mateos Sur 265 ⓣ333/121-4700, ⓦwww.hoteldelbosquegdl.com.mx. Modern motel with modern conveniences, featuring a restaurant with an international menu, single and double rooms, all with TV, and an attractive centre-courtyard pool. ❻

Posada Guadalajara López Mateos Sur 1280 ⓣ333/121-2022, ⓦwww.posadaguadalajara.com.mx. Rooms arranged over seven floors around a surprisingly charming open courtyard. Jacuzzis are included in top-floor baths, and there's a pool in the centre. ❽

The City

Any tour of Guadalajara inevitably starts at the **cathedral**. With the Sagrario, or sacristy, next door, it takes up an entire block at the very heart of the **colonial centre**, which is bordered by four plazas that form the shape of a Latin cross. At weekends and on warm evenings the plazas are packed, the crowds entertained by an array of street performers and wandering musicians; there are frequently bands playing during the day, too. All around is the traffic, noise and bustle of the busiest commercial areas of downtown Guadalajara: to the east the crowds spill over into Plaza Tapatía and its upmarket shops, beyond which is the complete contrast of the old market; unmodernized shopping streets to the west are no less busy.

Venture a little further and the atmosphere changes again. Guadalajara's rapid expansion has swallowed up numerous communities that were once distinct villages but are now barely distinguishable from the suburbs. Heading **west**, the university area blends into chic suburbia and some of the city's most expensive real estate. **East**, Tlaquepaque and Tonalá are the source of some of the area's finest handicrafts. And finally to the **north**, Zapopan has a huge, much revered church and a museum of indigenous traditions, while the Barranca de Oblatos offers stunning canyon views and weekend picnic spots.

The Cathedral

With its pointed, tiled twin towers, Guadalajara's **Cathedral** (daily 8am–8pm; free) is a bizarre but effective mixture of styles. Building work began in 1561 and wasn't finished until more than a century later – since then, extensive modifications, which effectively disguise the fact that there was probably never a plan behind the original design, have included a Neoclassical facade and new twin yellow-tiled towers (the originals collapsed in an 1818 earthquake). The interior is best seen in the evening, when the light from huge chandeliers makes the most of its rich decoration; the picture of the Virgin in the sacristy is attributed to the Spanish Renaissance artist **Murillo**.

Flanking the cathedral is a series of bustling plazas, often the scene of demonstrations and impromptu street performances. The **Plaza de los Laureles**, planted with laurel trees and with a fountain in the centre, faces the main west entrance, while to the north, by the porticoed **Presidencia Municipal** (less than fifty years old, though you wouldn't know it), lies the **Rotonda de los Jaliscienses Ilustres** in the centre of another plaza. This Neoclassical circle of seventeen Doric columns is the latest architectural expression of Jaliscan pride and commemorates the state's martyred heroes. Around the cathedral and departing regularly from in front of the Museo Regional, Mercado de San Juan de Dios, and the Jardín de San Francisco are *calandrias*, or elegant **horse-drawn covered carriages**. Most drivers are knowledgeable (and entertaining) city guides and charge around US$12 for a half-hour tour, and US$20 for a full hour and a half.

The Museo Regional

Across the plaza north of the cathedral, the **Museo Regional** (Tues–Sat 9am–6pm, Sun 9am–3pm; US$3.60, free Sun) is housed in an eighteenth-century colonial mansion: originally a religious seminary, later a barracks and then a school. It's a supremely elegant setting for an extensive and diverse collection. Downstairs, exhibits start with a section devoted to regional **archeology** and range from stone tools and the skeleton of a mammoth to the finest achievements of western Mexican pottery and metalworking. The peoples of the west developed quite separately from those in southern and central Mexico, and there is considerable evidence that they had more contact with South and Central American cultures than with those who would now be regarded as their compatriots. The deep **shaft tombs** displayed here are unique in Mexico, but were common down the Pacific coast in Peru and Ecuador. Later the Tarascan kingdom, based around Pátzcuaro (see p.262), almost came to rival the strength of the Aztecs – partially due to their more extensive knowledge and use of metals. Certainly the Aztecs tried, and failed, to extend their influence over Tarascan territory, though following Cortés' destruction of Tenochtitlán, the Tarascans submitted relatively peacefully to the conquistadors.

Upstairs, along with rooms devoted to the state's **modern history** and ethnography, is a sizeable gallery of colonial and modern art. Most remarkable here is the large collection of **nineteenth-century portraiture**, a local tradition that captures relatively ordinary Mexicans in a charmingly naive style. The modern equivalent of these portraits would be posed informal snapshots for the family album.

The Palacio de Gobierno and the Orozco murals

On the other side of the cathedral, south of the Sagrario, the **Plaza de Armas** centres on an elaborate kiosk – a present from the people of France – where the state band plays every Thursday and Sunday evening. Dominating the eastern side of the square is the Baroque frontage of the **Palacio de Gobierno** (daily 9am–5pm; free). Here Padre Miguel Hidalgo y Costilla (the "father of Mexican Independence") proclaimed the abolition of slavery in 1810 and in 1858, Benito Juárez was saved from the firing squad by the cry of "Los valientes no asesinan" – "the brave don't murder". The overwhelming reason to penetrate the arcaded courtyard, however, is to see the first of the great **Orozco murals**.

José Clemente Orozco

José Clemente Orozco (1883–1949) was a member, along with Diego Rivera and David Siqueiros, of the triumvirate of brilliant Mexican artists who emerged from the Revolution and transformed painting here into an enormously powerful and populist political statement, especially through the medium of the giant mural. Their chief patron was the state – hence the predominance of their work in official buildings and educational establishments – and their aim was to create a national art that drew on native traditions. Almost all their work is consciously educative, rewriting – or, perhaps better, rediscovering – Mexican history in the light of the Revolution, casting the Imperialists as villains and drawing heavily on pre-Hispanic themes. Orozco, a native of Jalisco (he was born in Zapotlan, now Ciudad Guzmán), was perhaps the least overtly political of the three: certainly his later work, the greatest of which is here in Guadalajara, often seems ambiguous. As a child he moved to Guadalajara and then Mexico City, where he was influenced by the renowned engraver **José Guadalupe Posada**, and most of his early work is found in the capital, where he painted murals from 1922 to 1927. There followed seven years in the US, but it was on his return that his powers as an artist reached their peak, in the late 1930s and 1940s, above all in his works at the Hospicio Cabañas and the University of Guadalajara.

The mural is typical of Orozco's work (see box, opposite) – Hidalgo blasts triumphantly through the middle, brandishing his sword against a background of red flags and the fires of battle. Curving around the sides of the staircase, scenes depict the Mexican people's oppression and struggle for liberty, from a pre-Conquest Eden to post-revolutionary emancipation. Upstairs in the domed Congress hall a smaller Orozco mural also depicts Hidalgo, this time as *El Cura de Dolores* (the priest from Dolores), legislator and liberator of slaves.

Plaza de la Liberación

The largest of the four squares is the **Plaza de la Liberación**, where the back of the cathedral looks across at the **Teatro Degollado** (daily 1–3pm; free to view, tickets to performances vary in price). Built in the mid-nineteenth century and inaugurated during the brief reign of Maximilian, the theatre is an imposing, domed Neoclassical building, with a Corinthian portico on whose pediment is a frieze depicting the Greek Muses. It still stages a programme of drama and concerts, mostly in October during the fiesta, and sporadically throughout the rest of the year, as well as the Sunday morning *folklórico* dances – details are posted up around the entrance. The impressively restored interior, most notably the frescoed ceiling illustrating scenes from Dante's works, warrants at least a visit.

On either side of the theatre are two small churches, **Santa María** and **San Agustín**, each all that remains of a former monastery. San Agustín has a fine Baroque facade; relatively plain Santa María is one of the oldest churches in the city, built in the seventeenth century on the site of Guadalajara's first cathedral. Guadalajara's new and outrageously popular **Wax Museum** is also near the Teatro Degollado, at Morelos 217 (daily 11am–8pm; US$3). It offers an interesting visual introduction to Mexico's presidents, artists and sports personalities, whose wax models are set alongside international figures such as US President Bill Clinton.

East along the Plaza Tapatía: the Hospicio Cabañas

Behind the theatre is the beginning of **Plaza Tapatía**, with a view all the way down to the Hospicio Cabañas. The plaza is almost entirely lined with swish department stores and glossy office buildings, but for all that the pedestrianized area, dotted with modern statuary and fountains, is an undeniably attractive place to wander and window-shop.

At the far end of the plaza, the **Instituto Cultural-Hospicio Cabañas** (Tues–Sat 10am–6pm, Sun 10.15am–2.45pm; US$1 plus US$1.25 for a camera, free on Sun) was founded as an orphanage by Bishop Juan Cabañas y Crespo in 1805 and took nearly fifty years to complete, during much of which time it operated as a barracks. It was an orphanage again, however, when **Orozco** came to decorate the chapel in 1939. The Hospicio is a huge, beautiful and tranquil building, with no fewer than 23 separate patios surrounded by schools of art, music and dance; an art cinema/theatre; various government offices; and a small cafeteria. The chapel, the **Capilla Tolsa**, is a plain and ancient-looking structure in the form of a cross, situated in the central patio right at the heart of the building. The **murals**, in keeping with their setting, are more spiritual than those in the government palace, but you certainly couldn't call them Christian: the conquistadors are depicted as the Horsemen of the Apocalypse, trampling the native population beneath them. The Man of Fire – who leads the people from their dehumanizing, mechanized oppression – has a symbolic role as liberator, which is clearly the same as that of Hidalgo in the palace murals. In this case, he is a strange synthesis of Christian and

Mexican deities, a Christ-Quetzalcoatl figure. There are benches on which you can lie back to appreciate the murals, and also a small museum dedicated to Orozco, with sketches, cartoons and details of the artist's life.

Almost alongside the Hospicio is the vast **Mercado Libertad**, which Guadalajarans claim is the world's largest indoor market. Although the building is modern, much of what's inside is thoroughly traditional, and it's one of the few places in the city where you can still haggle over prices. Beyond the touristy souvenir stalls, you'll find *curanderas* offering herbal remedies, dried iguanas (for witches' brews) and the renowned Paracho guitars. There are also countless stalls selling all manner of regional food and vast piles of colourful fruit, vegetables, chocolate and spices and traditional leather goods from saddles to clumpy working boots. The market is huge, chaotic and engrossing, but before you buy crafts here, it's worth paying a visit to the **Instituto de la Artesanía** in the Parque Agua Azul (see below), or to the expensive boutiques in Tlaquepaque (see p.234), to get some idea of the potential quality and value of the goods.

South of the Plaza de Armas

South of the Plaza de Armas, the churches of **San Francisco** and **Nuestra Señora de Aranzazu** face each other across Avenida 16 de Septiembre. San Francisco lies on the site of what was probably Guadalajara's first religious foundation, a Franciscan monastery established in the years just after the Conquest. The present church was begun in 1684 and has a beautiful Baroque facade. Aranzazu, by contrast, is entirely plain on the outside, but conceals a fabulously elaborate interior, with three wildly exuberant, heavily carved and gilded churrigueresque retables. The **Jardín de San Francisco**, which would be pleasantly peaceful were it not for the number of local buses rattling by, lies across from these two.

Parque Agua Azul

Several different buses (marked "Parque Agua Azul") run down from the Plaza de Armas to the **Parque Agua Azul** (Tues–Sun 10am–6pm; US$0.40). You couldn't really describe the park as peaceful: there's always some kind of activity going on and the green areas are permanently packed with kids enjoying the zoo, miniature train rides and playgrounds. An outdoor concert shell (*la concha*) hosts popular free performances on Sundays, and weekends see football games and constant crowds. Nonetheless, by Guadalajara standards, it's a haven of calm, especially during the week, and the entrance fee includes attractions such as a dome full of butterflies; exotic caged birds, including magnificent toucans; a palm house also full of tropical birds; and a strange, glass-pyramid orchid house.

Perhaps the greatest attraction of the park, however, is the **Instituto de Artesanía Jalisciense** (Mon–Fri 10am–6pm, Sat 10am–5pm, Sun 10am–3pm; free; entered from Calzado González Gallo 20). A showcase for regional crafts that is as much a museum as a shop, its collection is ambitious if a bit dusty, with examples of all sorts of local artesanía – furniture, ceramics, toys, glassware, clothing – all of the highest quality. Many of the items are expensive, but are worth it when you consider the fine worksmanship. Across the road, the **Casa de la Cultura** (Mon–Fri 9am–9pm; US$0.50) is by contrast a disappointment: extensively covered in ultramodern murals and frescoes, it houses a permanent exhibition of modern art, the State Library, and an information service about cultural events in the city. Despite its efforts, the exhibitions come across as stagnant and the information service is not always up to date or helpful. Equally a letdown is the nearby **Museo de Arqueología** (Tues–Sun 10am–2pm & 5pm–7pm; US$0.30), a low, modern building opposite the park entrance. It rarely seems to be open even when it's meant to be, and the small collection of relics of western cultures inside is really only of specialist interest.

West of the Plaza de Armas

The area to the west of the cathedral is a great part of the city for aimless meandering. There has been far less modernization in this direction, and the busy shopping streets, many of them closed to traffic, turn up fascinating glimpses of traditional Mexican life and plenty of odd moments of interest. There's a small general **market** at Santa Monica and Hidalgo. A little further out, the university area is quieter than the centre, the streets broader, and there's also a younger atmosphere, with plenty of good restaurants and cafés, while further out still are expensive residential areas, interesting in their own way for the contrast to crowded downtown.

The old **Telégrafos** building – also known as the "Ex-Templo de la Compañía" or the Biblioteca Pública del Estado (Mon–Fri 9am–9pm, Sat 9am–5pm; free) – lies just west of the Plaza de Armas at the junction of Pedro Moreno with Colón. Originally a church, the building later became a university lecture hall, during which time the nineteenth-century Neoclassical facade was added and it was decorated with **murals** by **David Siqueiros** and **Amado de la Cueva**. It later earned its name by housing the telegraph offices and is currently a library. The dramatic crimson-hued murals, depicting workers, peasants and miners in a heroic-socialist style, provide an interesting contrast to Orozco's work. Outside there's an attractive little plaza, and the pedestrianized streets make a pleasant escape from the traffic, if not the crowds.

Immediately to the north are several examples of the beautiful, little-known Baroque churches that stud Guadalajara. The closest is the **Templo de Santa Monica**, on Santa Monica between San Felípe and Reforma, with fabulously rich doorways and an elegant, stone interior. The nearby **Templo de San Felípe Neri**, San Felípe at Contreras Medellin, is a few years younger – dating from the second half of the eighteenth century – and more sumptuously decorated, with a superb facade and lovely, dilapidated tower overgrown with a tangle of plants. Both of these churches have rain-spouts that are extravagantly decorated – in the form of dragons on San Felípe. A block along Contreras Medellín, at the corner of Juan Manuel, the **Templo de las Capuchinas** is conversely a plain, fortress-like structure; inside, though, it's more interesting, with paintings and a lovely vaulted brick roof. Between these two, Contreras Medellín is lined with old printing shops (*imprentas*), where you can see the clanking, ancient presses at work. Back on the main route west, at Juárez and 8 de Julio, the ex-**Convento del Carmen** was one of the city's richest monasteries, but its wealth has largely been stripped, leaving an austere, white building of elegant simplicity. Modern art exhibitions, dance events and concerts are regularly staged here.

West to the University and the Plaza del Sol

The **University** is within easy walking distance (15min) of the centre, but if you're heading any further west, you may want to take a bus or taxi (anything heading for the Plaza del Sol should pass all the areas below, or look for "Par Vial"). At the university you can see more of **Orozco**'s major murals, among the first he painted in Guadalajara, in the **Museo de las Artes**, at Juárez 975 (Tues–Sun 10am–6pm; free), opposite the modern main university building at

Juárez and Díaz de León (aka Avenida Tolsa). Head for the main hall (*paraninfo*) to see the frescoed dome and front wall. Again, the theme fits the setting: in this case the dome shows the glories and benefits of education, while the wall shows the oppressed masses crying out for books and education, which are being denied them by fat capitalists and the military. Behind the university buildings, across López Cotilla, the **Templo Expiatorio**, a modern neo-Gothic church, features some innovative stained glass and an attractive altar. Across Díaz de León a block south at no. 300, you'll find the **Instituto Cultural Norteamericano**. Basically a language school, the institute has English-language magazines lying around and a café at the back. You are probably not supposed to wander in off the streets, but no one seems to mind.

Beyond the university, Juárez changes its name to Vallarta, and the character of the street changes rapidly, too. Within ten blocks, around the major junction of **Vallarta and Chapultepec**, you find yourself in a very different city, a far quieter place of broad avenues, expensive shops and pleasant restaurants, with drive-in burger joints and big houses in the back streets. Many of the airlines have their offices out here, along with American Express and several consulates; there's a large branch of Sanborn's at Vallarta and General Martín. Further out, Vallarta crosses the major artery of López Mateos at the Minerva Circle, an intersection marked by a triumphal arch.

Most buses turn left at the Minerva Circle down López Mateos Sur towards the **Plaza del Sol**, a vast commercial development said to be one of the largest in Latin America. There's an enormous shopping centre, as well as administrative offices, and inside a couple of good cafés, an ice-cream parlour and, in the evenings, several disco-clubs. Also on López Mateos are numerous big hotels and themed restaurants – all very much the modern face of suburban Mexico.

San Pedro Tlaquepaque and Tonalá

The most celebrated of Guadalajara's suburbs, **SAN PEDRO TLAQUEPAQUE** is famous for its artesanías and for its **mariachi** bands. Once a separate town, some 5km southeast of the centre, it has long since been absorbed by urban sprawl, and its traditional crafts taken over almost entirely by tourism. The streets are lined with shops selling, for the most part, pretty tacky goods at thoroughly inflated prices. Nevertheless, it's worth seeing and there are still quality pieces among the dross, notably some of the ceramics and glassware on which the area's reputation was founded.

Tlaquepaque centres around a pleasantly laid-back main square complete with bandstand, on whose northern side is the tangerine-roofed church of San Pedro. To its west, the three-domed Sanctuario de la Virgen de la Soledad is an almost equally distinctive landmark. Along the square's southern side runs Independencia, Tlaquepaque's main street. The #275 or TUR **bus** from the centre will drop you three blocks south on Porvenir, and can be picked up for the return journey two blocks north of Independencia on Constitución. You can also get on or off on General Marelino García Barragán at the western end of Independencia and Constitución, by a brick pedestrian overbridge and traffic circle. The **tourist office** is at Juárez 238 (Mon–Fri 9am–9pm; ⓣ333/635-1220); it organizes many free, guided local tours.

To see some of the best artesanías, visit the small **Museo Regional de la Cerámica** (Mon–Sat 10am–6pm, Sun 10am–3pm; free), at Independencia 237, which has displays of pottery not only from Tlaquepaque but from all over the state, and especially Tonalá (see opposite). Most of what's on show is for sale – the place is more store than museum. Beyond the individual works of some of the finest craftsmen, there's a traditional kitchen on display, complete with all its plates, pots and pans; and the building is a fine old mansion in its own right. Almost all of the fancier **shops** are nearby on **Independencia**, many of them again occupying colonial-era houses that are interesting in and of themselves. Closed to traffic, it's a pleasant street along which to window-shop. Among the more worthwhile stores are Sergio Bustamante, at no. 238, opposite the museum, where there are flamingos and peacocks in the patio to go with Sergio's famous fantastical figures in papier-mâché and bronze. They are worth looking at, even if the price and size are such that you won't be buying. Opposite each other a block west of the museum are La Casa Canela, at no. 258 (Mon–Fri 10am–2pm & 4pm–7pm, Sat 10am–6pm, Sun 11am–3pm), and Antigua de México, at no. 255 (Mon–Fri 10am–2pm & 3–7pm, Sat 10am–4pm), two more lovely houses that sell upmarket fabrics, furniture and antiques to a mainly Mexican clientele. Juárez, one block south of Independencia, has fewer – but slightly less touristy – stores and, at no. 317, a workshop where you can see glass being blown.

An equally compelling reason to make the trip out to Tlaquepaque, though, is to stop off at **El Parian**, an enclosed plaza that is, in effect, the biggest bar that you've ever seen. Since the shops all close down for a siesta anyway, you have every excuse to hang out here for a couple of hours. There are actually a dozen or so separate establishments around this giant courtyard, but since everyone sits outside, the tables tend to overlap and strolling serenaders wander around at random, it all feels like one enormous place. They all charge much the same, too, and offer the same limited range of food – basically birria, quesadillas and queso fundido – plus lots to drink: prices seem reasonable on the menu, but make sure to check the bill for added service charges. At the weekend, particularly Sunday afternoons, you'll see *mariachi* at its best here, when the locals come along and offer their own vocal renditions to the musicians' backing. On weekdays it can be disappointingly quiet.

You'll find El Parian on Independencia, just east of the main square. There are a couple of fine colonial churches here, too, and several **banks** in case you've been carried away by the shopping experience. And if you've had too good a time to struggle home, or you really take the purchasing seriously, you can **stay** right here at the *Posada en el Parian*, Independencia 74 (Ⓣ333/659-2511; ❹). There's a small local **Mercado Municipal** behind Independencia opposite El Parian (entrance by the posada), and numerous fine **restaurants** on Independencia. *Adobe*, at Independencia 195 (Ⓣ333/657-2792, Ⓔadobe-fonda@yahoo.com), flaunts stylish and unusual touches that include distinctive handcrafted furniture and a parade of creative dishes that exemplify Mexico's small but growing *nueva cocina*. It is very popular and run by a celebrity chef couple, so be sure to make reservations ahead of time. *Hotel Casa Campos* at Francisco de Miranda 30-A just off Independencia (Ⓣ333/838-5296, Ⓦwww.casa-campos.com; ❽) is the most charming place to lay your head in town. The recently remodelled B&B's rates include breakfast in the adjacent and colourful restaurant *Fonda Margarita*. Be sure to visit the family of palm-size marmoset monkeys in the garden.

Tonalá

Pottery is slightly cheaper at **TONALÁ**, a ceramics manufacturing centre some 8km beyond Tlaquepaque, but the trip is really only worthwhile if you are seriously planning to shop. However, you might also like to visit the **Museo Nacional de la Cerámica**, Constitución 104 (Tues–Fri 10am–5pm, Sat 10am–3pm; free), which has contemporary and a few antique pots from every

Mexican state. Market days are Thursday and Sunday, when things are considerably more animated and the village is crammed with sales people and shoppers. Be warned that ceramics sold at stalls tend to be rejects from the shops. Tonalá's **tourist office**, at Tonaltecas Sur 140 in the Casa de Artesanos (Mon–Fri 9am–3pm, Sat 9am–1pm; ⓣ333/284-3000 ext 09, or 683-0047), gives out free maps, useful for locating the various artisan workshops, and also organizes free craft and historical tours.

To get to San Pedro Tlaquepaque from the centre of town, take a #275 or TUR bus heading south on 16 de Septiembre, or a trolley bus south on Federalismo. Some of these buses continue to Tonalá, and both Tlaquepaque and Tonalá are on the route taken by many of the buses that run between the new bus station and the centre.

Zapopan

ZAPOPAN, some 6km northwest of the city centre, is the site of the **Basílica de la Virgen de Zapopan**, one of the most important churches in the city, much revered by the Huichols. Pope John Paul II gave a mass in the giant plaza in front of the church during a visit to Mexico in 1979; a statue commemorates the event. The Baroque temple houses a miraculous image of the Virgin that was dedicated to the local Indians by a Franciscan missionary, Antonio de Segovia, after he had intervened in a battle between them and the conquistadors. Since then, it has been constantly venerated and is still the object of pilgrimages, especially on October 12, when some 200,000 people march the Virgin back to the Basílica after an annual tour of all the churches in Guadalajara. This massive procession, which begins at the cathedral, the Virgin's final stop on the tour, is one of the highlights of the city's Fiestas de Octubre.

Beside the church, a small **museum** (Mon–Sat 10am–1.30pm & 3–6pm; US$0.10) exhibits clothes and objects relating to Huichol traditions, as well as a photographic display of their modern way of life. They also sell Huichol crafts, including psychedelic yarn paintings (*cuadros de estambre*) and beadwork.

Zapopan is served by the #275 and TUR **buses** at the opposite end of their routes from Tlaquepaque and has its own **tourist office**, at Av Vallarta 6503, two blocks behind the church in the Casa de Cultura (Mon–Fri 9am–3pm; ⓣ333/110-0754 or 0759, ⓦwww.zapopan.gob.mx), with further information about what to see and do in Zapopan and the surrounding area.

Barranca de Oblatos

Also to the north of the city, out at the end of Calzada Independencia, the **Barranca de Oblatos** is a magnificent 600-metre-deep canyon, along the edge of which a series of parks offer superb views and a welcome break from the confines of the city. The **Parque Mirador** (take buses marked "Parque Mirador" north along Independencia) is a popular family spot with picnic areas and excellent views, while the **Parque Barranca de Oblatos** (bus #603 from Vicente Guerro at the southwest corner of the Hospicio Cabañas) is more of a student haunt with a swimming pool, picnic areas and plenty of young couples. Also near the edge of the canyon, the city **zoo** (daily 10am–6pm; US$2.50; bus #60 or trolley bus north on Independencia) has superb views from its northern end, along with a relatively well-kept selection of Mexican and international wildlife. Opened in 1988, the modern zoo also features an ecological centre that works to preserve a range of endangered species through education and reproduction intitiatives. World-renowned artist Sergio Bustamante created the monkey sculptures that greet visitors at the zoo's entrance.

Eating and drinking

As a rule, *Tapatíos* take their food seriously and Guadalajara boasts literally hundreds of **places to eat**, ranging from elegant restaurants to unpretentious cafés, and from *loncherías* (cafés with more emphasis on short orders) to *neverías* (with ice cream and fresh-fruit drinks). Among the local specialities dished up at street stalls, bars and the markets are **birria**, consisting of stewed beef or mutton in a spicy but not particularly hot sauce, served with tortillas or in tacos; roast goat; and **pozole**, a stew of pork and hominy (ground maize). Don't pass up the **street vendors** either – their fresh tacos and bags of spiced fruit are delicious and make a cheap, healthy snack.

In the centre, there seems to be more choice west of the cathedral, where traditional cafés and restaurants line **Juárez**; the **university** area also offers good food, especially during the university session. For cheap, basic meals, the area around the old bus station is crowded with possibilities, none wildly exciting, while upstairs in the **Mercado Libertad** seemingly hundreds of little stands each display their own specialities. Though there are plenty of more **expensive** places round the centre, they tend to be rather dull: in the evenings, locals are far more likely to be found out in the suburbs, or enjoying a raucous night at one of many themed restaurants on López Mateos Sur, a US$4 taxi ride from the centre.

Where Galeana and Calle Colón meet, at Calle 2, there's a good selection of restaurants dotted around a pretty square with a fountain adorned with frog sculptures. Try any of the birrias around the square, such as *Birria de Chivo*, Colón 384, for traditional Mexican mutton dishes. Good **panaderías**, for bread and cakes for a picnic, are Danes, at the corner of Madero at Donato Guerra; Pan Estilo México, Santa Monica 96 at Independencia; and Pastelería Luvier, Colón 183 at Madero.

Downtown cafés and licuaderías

Café D'Val Pedro Moreno 690 between Pavo and 8 de Julio. Strong coffee in a relaxing atmosphere.

Café Madoka Gonzalez Martínez 78 between Pedro Moreno and Juárez. Big, traditional café, serving medium-priced good breakfasts, soups and antojitos. You can also just sip a coffee and play a game of dominoes.

Café Madrid Juárez 264 near Corona. A smallish Fifties-style diner and coffee bar, good for moderately priced breakfasts, comidas corridas at lunchtime, and sandwiches from 8am to 10pm.

Café Oasis Morelos 435 between Colón and Galeana. Bustling place handy for the centre – tacos, sandwiches and egg dishes.

Cafetería Restaurant Málaga 16 de Septiembre 210–214 between Madero and Prisciliano. Large café-restaurant with a moderately priced comida corrida, breakfasts, snacks, coffee and even tarot readings.

Jarro Café López Cotilla 1885. The self-proclaimed "casa del mejor café" lives up to the name, offering hot and cold combinations.

Nectar Hidalgo 426. Juice, ice-cream and yogurt bar dishing up instant refreshment, including tortas, tacos and fruit salads, close to the cathedral.

La Terraza Juárez 442 at Ocampo, upstairs. Bar with beer and tacos. Tables on balcony overlooking the street.

Villa Madrid López Cotilla 533 at Gonzalez Martínez. Great *licuados*, fruit salads and yogurt, as well as more substantial dishes.

Downtown restaurants

Alta Fibra Sanchez 370 between Ocampo and Galeana. Reasonably priced vegetarian restaurant with a wholemeal bakery next door.

La Chata Corona 126, between López Cotilla and Juárez. Excellent medium-priced Mexican dishes, including mole and *platillo jalisciense* (chicken with side snacks). Hugely popular with local families.

Chong Wah Juárez 558 at Enrique Gonzalez Martínez. Moderately priced Cantonese food to eat in or take away.

Devechan López Cotilla 570. Vegetarian restaurant with good-value buffet on Saturdays and decent breakfasts.

Egipto al Natural Sanchez 416 between Ocampo

and Donato Guerra. Friendly vegetarian restaurant with tasty and cheap comidas, vegetable and fruit drinks, soy-based dishes and a health-food store attached.

El Faro Moreno 466 between Galeana and Ocampo, upstairs. Pleasant, reasonably priced old restaurant with good tamales and tacos – try for a table by the window.

La Gran China Juárez 590 between 8 de Julio and Gonzalez Martínez, near the *Chong Wah*. Chop-suey house with good-value lunchtime set menu.

Guisitos Grill Degollado 230. Spanish and Mexican restaurant with tables in a covered forecourt. Cheap and tasty comidas corridas and homemade chocolate cake.

Lido Colón 294, at San Miguel Blanco. Spanish-style bar and restaurant, serving good, moderately priced Mexican moles, sandwiches, snacks and a reasonably priced set menu. Open 24 hours.

Mariscos Galeana Galeana 154 at López Cotilla. Reasonably priced, delicious seafood restaurant with prawn and octopus dishes (US$5) accompanied by live music at lunchtime.

Nuevo Faro López Cotilla 24. Simple restaurant with great-value, cheap comidas corridas.

La Rinconada Morelos 86 at Callejón del Diable, Plaza Tapatía ⓣ333/613-9914. In a glorious colonial setting, an expensive restaurant serving seafood, US-style steaks and a range of Mexican specialities, including birria and ox tongue in a spicy Veracruz sauce.

Sanborn's 16 de Septiembre 127 at Juárez. Plush restaurant with a wide selection of international and Mexican food, and a more informal café on the opposite corner across 16 de Septiembre. A great stand-by.

Sandy's Colón 39 at Moreno. Mezzanine-floor tables overlook the crowds of shoppers; simple Mexican food served. The US$3 buffet breakfast and set lunches attract shoppers, office workers and tourists alike.

Tacos El Pastor Juárez 424, between Galeana and Ocampo. Fast, flavoursome tacos; popular and cheap though some choices (like *oreja* – pig's ear – or *cabeza* – head) are not for the timid.

Taquería Los Faroles Corona 250 at Sanchez. Popular taco and torta joint with a wide range of tacos served till midnight daily.

University and further out

La China Poblana Juárez 887, by the university between Camarena and Escorza. Reasonably priced, traditional Puebla dishes, including mole and *chiles en nogada*.

La Choza Grill Calzada Federalismo 176 at López Cotilla. Smaller version of the big places out on López Mateos, and not so far from the city centre. Pricey meat and seafood dishes.

Corporales Pablo Neruda 2759 at Rubén Darío ⓣ333/585-7301. A bit unimagintive and commercial in its decor but you will find succulent *arranchera* steaks, tasty tamarind margaritas and lively *mariachi* music. Reserve in advance.

La Destilería Mexico 2916 ⓣ333/640-3440. Top-shelf tequilas, superb Mexican classics and a charming hands-on owner. Reserve ahead as it's a popular feeding and watering hole with the city's young professionals.

Guadalajara Grill López Mateos Sur 3771 ⓣ333/631-5622. Part of the *Carlos'n'Charlie* chain: Tex-Mex food, loud music, party atmosphere and dancing. It's a good idea to reserve in advance.

Los Itacates Chapultepec Norte 110 at Sierra, four blocks north of Vallarta ⓣ333/825-1106. Traditional Mexican food with live-music evenings. Best booked in advance.

Mesón de Sancho Panza Castellanos 112, on the west side of the Parque de la Revolución between Juárez and López Cotilla. Classy but not outrageously expensive Spanish restaurant, with a good-value, moderately priced Sunday menu (US$6). Photos on the wall commemorate a visit by Pope John Paul II.

Entertainment and nightlife

Though it has perked up in recent years, Guadalajara's nightlife is still less than hot. There are clubs springing up around the cathedral area, a district that appears tame on the surface but can be dicey after dark. Most of the fashionable, younger-crowd places tend to be a long way out in the more monied suburbs – the **Plaza del Sol complex**, for example, houses a couple of clubs, as do many of the big hotels out that way. Any of them will knock a sizeable hole in your wallet. There are more clubs where Avenida Juárez becomes **Avenida Vallarta** (most of which enforce the "no jeans or sneakers" policy typical at Mexican nightspots). **Avenida López Mateos** has a number of trendy pubs with live music and a younger crowd. Some have open bars on certain nights of the week in exchange for a cover charge of around US$5 for men, US$2.50 or less for women.

You needn't spend anything at all in the **Plaza de Mariachis**, a little area hard by the Mercado Libertad and the church of San Juan de Dios, where *mariachi* bands stroll between bars, playing to anyone prepared to cough up for a song. If they play for you personally, you'll have to pay (check how much before they start), but there are usually several on the go nearby. You'll also find *mariachi* bands out in Tlaquepaque, and theatre and dance performances, including *ballet folklórico*, in town at the Teatro Degollado.

Some of the downtown **bars** are a tad sleazy, although more trendy and stylish ones continue to open up all the time. Those listed below are worth a try.

Bars and clubs

Baron first floor above ground, Edificio Mulbar, Corona 181. Bar-restaurant with Latin music, including live acts. Daily 7pm–5am. No cover.

Casa Bariachi Vallarta 2221. Loud and colourful restaurant-bar, with *mariachis*. Daily 1pm–3am. No cover.

Coco & Coco Corona 160. Popular downtown nightclub, playing mixed music but mainly Latin. Mon–Sat 10pm–3am, Sun 5pm–midnight. Cover US$3.

Duran Duran Madero 273. Dark disco-bar that fills up at weekends but is dead on other nights, though it does a good-value set menu. Daily 9pm–3am. No cover.

Feria Corona 219. Central and popular restaurant with both tourists and locals, featuring various singers and *mariachis* from around 9pm. Daily 1.30pm–2am. No cover.

Maestranza Maestranza 179. Trendy bar with cheap beer, upbeat music, and a mostly straight young crowd. Daily 8pm–2am. Cover US$2.

Maskara Maestranza 238. Gay bar with special drink offers on various nights of the week. Daily 9pm–3am. No cover.

Moresca López Cotilla 1835. Good place for a bottle of house wine and a bruschetta. Mon–Fri 6pm–1.30am. No cover.

Musa Maestranza 86 at Juárez. One of the more stylish bars. Thurs–Sat 9pm–4am. Cover US$3.

Performing arts

There's an impressive range of traditional Mexican and classical concerts and contemporary gigs, opera, classic and modern film, theatre and art exhibitions in town, and you can see some kind of performance most nights of the week. For international and classic **films**, try Cine Charles Chaplin, López Mateos Norte 873 or Cine Cinematógrafo, Vallarta 1102 and Mexico 2222. For **listings** information, try the *Guadalajara Colony Reporter,* an English-language daily newspaper, or the Spanish-language *Público* (Friday edition).

There is a regular programme of **theatre and dance** in the beautiful Teatro Degollado and a series of events put on by the state Fine Arts Department in the former Convento del Carmen and other sites around the city. You can pick up details from the tourist office. Guadalajara's **ballet folklórico** – two hours of impressive traditional dance performed by the university dance troupe – is staged in the Teatro Degollado every Sunday at 10am (except when the company's on tour) and is definitely worth getting up for: tickets are sold at the theatre ticket office (daily 10am–1pm & 4–7pm; ⓣ333/613-1115). The state dance company performs a similar ballet, though its reputation isn't as good, in the Cine-Teatro Cabañas in the Hospicio Cabañas every Wednesday at 8.30pm and Sunday at 10am. Tickets go for around US$3 from the Hospicio (details ⓣ333/668-1640).

Less formally, you'll find **bands** playing and crowds gathered somewhere round the central plaza complex every weekend and often during the week, too (generally Tues and Thurs), and there's always entertainment of some kind laid on in the Parque Agua Azul.

The entire month of October in Guadalajara is dominated by the famous **Fiestas de Octubre**, with daily events including *charreadas* (rodeos) and processions (the biggest on the twelfth), free entertainment such as modern Mexican music performances put on from noon till 10pm in the fairgrounds of the Benito Juárez auditorium and fireworks each night. The Instituto Cultural Mexicano Norteamericano de Jalisco (Ⓣ333/825-5838), Enrique Díaz de León 300, hosts classical music concerts year-round.

In **Tlaquepaque** the big day is June 29 (Fiesta de San Pedro): endless *mariachis*, dances and a mass procession.

Sport

Jaliscans pride themselves on their equestrian skills, and other entertainment includes regular *charreadas* every Sunday in the Lienzo Charro, at Dr Michel 577 near the Parque Agua Azul (for details call Ⓣ333/619-3232), and **bullfights** (considered to be a sport for connoisseurs) in the Plaza de Toros Nuevo Progreso (the city's largest bullring), a long way north on Calzada Independencia (Ⓣ333/637-9982), or at the Plaza de Toros (Ⓣ333/667-9982), Pirineos 1930. **Football** and **baseball** are more popular, however, and the mighty Estadio Jalisco (Ⓣ333/637-9808 or 637-0563) is the enormous football stadium at Colinas 1772 where FC Guadalajara (Las Chivas) play their home matches (usually Saturday nights and Sunday afternoons). Buses #52C, #60, #62 and the Independencia trolley run up Calzada Independencia past the bullring and football stadium.

Haciendas and overnight retreats

The tourist office of Guadalajara (Ⓣ333/668-1600 or 668-1601, Ⓦwww.visita.jalisco.gob.mx) is more than happy to provide information on well-preserved haciendas, rural homes and other relaxing retreats all within an hour's drive of city limits. These destinations provide an easy overnight escape from bustling Guadalajara and are ideal for those on shorter trips who want to quickly and comfortably experience a bit of the countryside. Hacienda El Carmen, 35km west of the city, Km 58 Carretera Gdl-Tala-Etzatlán (Ⓣ333/633-1771, Ⓕ656-9436, Ⓦwww.hdaelcarmen.com; ❾), originated as a family-owned estate, became a convent in 1722 and retains a traditional feel in its current incarnation as a luxury hotel. Colonially styled accommodation encircles a patio garden, full spa and Aztec sweat lodge. There's also horseback riding, mountain biking on country roads, and nearby you'll find the archeological ruins of Guachimontones (Teuchitlan, 300–900 AD). Numerous other haciendas and guesthouses in the Guadalajara area provide a nice change of pace and shed light on a different side of *Tapatío* lifestyle.

Listings

Airlines and flights Aerocalifornia, Av Vallarta 2440, Plaza los Arcos, Local 4-A (Ⓣ333/616-8527); Aeroméxico, Corona 196 (Ⓣ333/613-6990); American, Av Vallarta 2440, Plaza los Arcos, Local 15-D (Ⓣ333/616-4402); Continental, *Hotel Presidente Intercontinental*, Moctezuma 3515, Local 8 & 9, first level (Ⓣ333/647-4251); Delta, López Cotilla 1701 (Ⓣ333/630-3130); Mexicana, Mariano Otero 2353 (Ⓣ333/112-0011); United, Av Mexico 3370, Plaza Bonita, Local U-6 (Ⓣ333/616-4002). There are constant flights to Mexico City, as well as departures to most other Mexican cities, and direct connections to many US, Canadian and Central American destinations.

American Express Av Vallarta 2440 ☎333/818-2300.

Banks See p.225.

Bookstores For English-language books, try Sanborn's, Juárez between 16 de Septiembre and Corona, and at Vallarta 1600, or Sandi Bookstore, Tepeyac 718 in Colonia Chapalita; many of the larger bookstores around the centre also have a small selection of English-language books.

Buses Long-distance buses all leave from the Central Camionera, way out in suburbia (see p.225). To get there from the centre, take a #275, #275A or #644 from 16 de Septiembre, or one of the buses marked "Nueva Central" heading south along Independencia or 16 de Septiembre. In general, make for buildings 1 and 2 for destinations in Jalisco, Colima and Michoacán, plus many of the pullman services to Mexico City, Mexico City via Morelia and many towns in the Bajío; 3 and 4 for the north and northwest, with buses to the US border and up the Pacific coast, plus points en route; 5 for eastbound services towards San Luis Potosí and Tampico, as well as some more local services; 6 for the Bajío, the northeast and many local second-class buses; and 7 for the north and northeast again, as well as Mexico City. If you're heading for somewhere just an hour or so away – Chapala or Tequila, say – it's usually quicker and easier to take a second-class bus from the Camionera Vieja, downtown.

Car rental Agents can be found at the airport, as well as downtown where they're concentrated on Av Niños Héroes near the *Sheraton* (not far from the Parque Agua Azul); these include Alaniz, Niños Héroes 961-B (☎333/614-6393); Budget, Niños Héroes 934 (☎333/613-0027, or at the airport ☎333/688-5216); Hertz, at the airport (☎333/688-5633); National, Niños Héroes 961-C (☎333/614-4595, or at the airport ☎333/688-5522); and Quick Rent-a-Car, Niños Héroes 954 (☎333/614-6052).

Consulates Canada, *Hotel Fiesta Americana*, Local 30, Aurelio Aceves 225 (☎333/615-5642); Guatemala, Calle Mango 1440, Colonia del Fresno (☎333/811-1503); Honduras, Milan 2528, Colonia Providencia (☎333/817-4482); UK, Plaza Bonita, Calle Jesús de Rojas 20 (☎333/343-2296); and the US, Progreso 175 (☎333/825-2700). The tourist information office (see p.225) has a complete list of addresses for all consulates.

Exchange American Express (see above); Thomas Cook, Circunvalación Agustín Yañez 2343-D ☎ 333/669-5507.

Internet facilities There are several Internet cafés in central Guadalajara, many within easy walking distance of the cathedral, including one at Moreno 413 (US$2 per hr), and Morelos 1245 (US$2.50 per hr).

Laundry Aldama 125, off Independencia a few blocks south of the Mercado Libertad (Mon–Sat 9am–8pm); and Juárez 323 (Mon–Fri 10am–2pm & 4–8pm).

Markets and shopping The giant Mercado Libertad is just one of Guadalajara's markets – every city barrio has its own. They include the very touristy Mercado Corona near the cathedral, and craft markets and upscale boutiques in Tlaquepaque and Tonalá. The Sunday flea market El Baratillo is vast, sometimes stretching a mile or more along Javier Mina, starting a dozen blocks east of the Mercado Libertad. The city is also big on nutritionists, and health-food/aromatherapy stores; head for López Cortilla if you're after some echinacea, green tea or muscle-building protein powder.

Pharmacy Farmacia Guadalajara (☎333/656-2931), in the centre at Corona 22 (daily, 24 hours).

Police ☎333/617-0920. The police station is way out to the east of the city, and it's easier to report a crime or accident at the Procuraduría de Justicia (Justice Department), Av la Paz 2873 (☎333/688-5588).

Spanish courses As well as Guadalajara University (☎333/616-4399, ⓦwww.cepe.udg.mx), a number of colleges offer Spanish courses here, costing from US$322 to US$965 for 5 weeks of instruction – for more information, contact the tourist office (see p.225).

Tours The *Tequila Express* train tour leaves the train station and runs through blue agave fields to Tequila train station, where there's a toast and a demonstration of the harvest process, alongside a contrived fiesta. While the outfit is commercial it is the best way for short-term visitors to learn about tequila production and offers a safe way to get from Guadalajara to Tequila and back. The train leaves at 10am, returning at 7pm and costs US$55 for adults, a steep US$40 for children under 12. Children under 6 go free. Tickets can be bought from the Chamber of Commerce cashier department Av Vallarta 4095 at Av Nino Obrero (☎333/880-9090 or 122-9020, ⓦwww.tequilaexpress.com.mx).

Travel agents There are plenty of travel agents around the centre, including in the lobbies of all the big hotels, or head for American Express or Thomas Cook (see "Exchange", above).

Lago de Chapala and around

At around 34km wide and 119km long, **Lago de Chapala**, just over 50km south of Guadalajara, is the largest lake in Mexico. These days, however, the water is murky and only around 8m deep: its level has dropped significantly in recent years, as the government has used it as a freshwater supply for Mexico's larger cities, and it now holds only around twenty percent of its potential capacity. Not only is there concern about this for environmental reasons but a knock-on effect is that hotels that claim "proximity" are actually watching the shoreline retreat further into the distance. The lake is not as scenic as it once was and offers diminished vistas these days, but vistas nonetheless.

It's said that some 30,000 (mostly retired) North Americans, the majority of whom are Canadian, live in and around Guadalajara, and a sizeable proportion of them have settled on the lakeside – particularly in **Chapala** and in the smaller village of **Ajijic**. In fact, during the 1990s, Lago de Chapala was spoken of locally as being in the "gay 90s" – the joke being that anyone who lived there was either gay or 90. English is spoken widely, and there's even an English newspaper produced there, appropriately called the *Lake Chapala Review*. This mass presence has rendered the area rather expensive and in many respects somewhat sanitized and stratified, but it cannot detract from the allure of the deep-red sunsets that fall over the lake. Whether the intense colour is the result of pollution remains a hot-button issue with locals. At weekends and holidays, day-trippers from the city help to create a party atmosphere, joining with local yahoos to tipple and whoop it up late into the weekend nights. Panoramex (see p.225) run a day-trip to Chapala and Ajijic from Guadalajara (US$15).

Chapala

CHAPALA, on the shore of the lake, is a sleepy community most of the time, and has a quiet charm and relaxed pace that you can easily get used to. However, it becomes positively festive on sunny weekends, when thousands come to eat, swim or take a boat ride, visiting one of the lake's islands. Shoreline restaurants all offer the local specialty, *pescado blanco*, famous despite its almost total lack of flavour and muddy origins, and street vendors sell card-board plates of tiny fried fish from the lake. Head to the left along the prom-enade, past streets of shuttered nineteenth-century villas, and you'll find a small **crafts market**. There's a flat *ciclopista* (cycle path) running along the lakeside between Chapala and Ajijic for easy cycling and walking, with nice views of the lake.

Buses leave the old bus station in Guadalajara for Chapala throughout the day (Sala A; every 30min; 6am–8.30pm). From Chapala, regular services run on to Ajijic (all of five minutes away) and from there back to Guadalajara by a more direct route along the highway to the coast – you can hail them in the street. From the bus station, the main street, Madero, heads six blocks down to the lakeside. The main square is halfway along it, with Hidalgo, the road to Ajijic, branching off right after five blocks. While Ajijic tends to offer better hotel options, Chapala does possess some decent accommodation. The moder-ately priced *Hotel Candilejas*, López Cotilla 363, just off the main square and up a steep hill (Ⓣ376/765-2279; ❹), welcomes guests like one of the family. *Casa de Huéspedes Las Palmitas* at Juárez 531 (Ⓣ376/765-3070; ❹) has slightly cheaper rooms with private baths, and is clean and comfortable. Past the *Candilejas*, halfway up López Cotilla on the opposite side of the street between house nos. 316 and 318, you'll find a pathway leading up to the cross on the top of the hill, where you get excellent views over the lake, if the weather is clear. *Villa Montecarlo,* Hidalgo 296 (☎376/765-2120; ❼), is a plush motel located on the outskirts of town offering tennis, pool, lake views, airy rooms and occasional holiday and weekend specials.

For **places to eat**, the *Café París* and *Restaurant Superior* on Madero have reasonably priced comidas and are great for people-watching. Also, *Casadores Casa Braniff*, Ramon Corona 18, which has been in operation since 1956, serves hearty surf-and-turf dinners amid the faded elegance of a grand mansion. There are more restaurants along Madero, along with some good **juice bars**. A plastic bag of juice is a healthy bargain at US$0.50. Terrific taco and torta stands dot the main square and a row of fish restaurants compete for custom along the lakefront, though this is more mud and sand than water these days. Note also that most of the fish served up is now brought in from elsewhere, due to depleted stock and lake contamination.

There is a **casa de cambio** (Lloyd's) and a **caseta telefónica** on the corner of Madero and Hidalgo, and a bookstore stocking books and magazines in English at Madero 230-B. The post office is a couple of blocks along Hidalgo, and there's a **laundry** on the corner of Zaragoza and López Cotilla. It's slightly cheaper to check your email here than in Ajijic – Computer Center, just off the main plaza near Juárez, charges US$1.50 per hour.

Ajijic

Though just 6km west of Chapala, **AJIJIC** has a decidedly more quaint atmosphere. Undeniably picturesque, it's even smaller, quieter and a more self-consciously arty place, with numerous little crafts shops. You get the distinct feeling that the expats here resent the intrusion of additional outsiders, regarding themselves as writers or artists *manqués*, hoping to pick up some of the inspiration left behind by **D.H. Lawrence** and more recent residents like Ken Kesey. In truth, there's little evidence that Lawrence liked the place at all (though he may have disliked it less than he did the rest of the country), but then he can't have had much time to appreciate it, since in just eight weeks here he turned out an almost complete 100,000-word first draft of *The Plumed Serpent* (or *Quetzalcoatl* as it was then titled). It may be a wonderful place to write a book or retire, with a thriving expat social and cultural life, but as a visitor you're likely to have exhausted its charms in a couple of hours, which is quite long enough to have wandered by the lake, seen the little art galleries, read the notice boards and been shocked by the prices of everything.

The **bus** drops you where the Carretera Chapala meets Colón, which runs six blocks southward to the lake, with the main square (where you'll find a **map** of the village) halfway along it. There are a number of fine but rather expensive **hotels** in Ajijic, as well as **apartments** and **houses** to rent for longer stays; check out the notice boards in shops, galleries and the **post office**, which is at Colón 4. The new *Mis Amores*, Hidalgo 22 (☎376/766-4640; ❼), is Ajijic's answer to a contemporary boutique hotel with tasteful decor, individual terraces shaded by banana trees and a warm proprietor – one of the best picks in town. The *Nueva Posada*, at Donato Guerra 9 (☎376/766-1444, Ⓔnuevaposada@laguna.com.mx; ❼), by the lake three blocks east of Colón, is an eclectically decorated, welcoming place with lovely gardens, small pool and distant water views. The recently renovated *Hotel Italo*, off the main square at Guadalupe Victoria 10 (☎376/766-2221, Ⓔmarianabrandi@hotmail.com; ❹), is a decent bet even though the bells of the church next door ring every hour. Each room at the romantic if slightly run-down *Salamandra*, Donato Guerra 10

(Ⓣ376/766-0689, Ⓦwww.hotelmex.com; ❺), has its own distinct character, and access to a sauna and jacuzzi. Some rooms have kitchens, and there are weekly and monthly discounts. Massages are offered by appointment.

There's also good **food** in town: the *Nueva Posada* (see above) offers pricey but excellent international fare and generous salads in a green lakeside setting, and *Hotel Italo* (see above) serves up a full Italian feast for US$6. The best place to dine is at *Mis Amores* (see above); its creative menu overtly appeals to sophisticated palates with an inventive use of chiles and local ingredients; its happy hour lasts all afternoon from noon to 7pm. Numerous places in the village cater to expat appetites with healthy sandwiches, fresh fish and juices, especially around the plaza, and at night keep your eyes peeled for makeshift family-run *sopes* stands, where you can eat heartily for US$2.

If you pass through Ajijic in mid-November, you'll catch its **film festival** (dates vary), which features a selection of international and Mexican films. The Casa de Cultura, on the north side of the plaza, also hosts regular performances and year-round exhibitions of history, art and photography.

San Juan Cosola and Jocotepec

Five kilometres or so along the lakeshore to the west, **SAN JUAN COSOLA** is a resort of a different kind, where a small cluster of hotels offers visitors the chance to bask in natural thermal waters said to have healing properties. The *Motel Balneario* (Ⓣ376/761-0222; ❻), right beside the lake, is the cheapest, most popular, and the only one to offer day-trippers the use of its pools (US$8); it also offers massages for US$20–25. Next door and also operated by the owners of the *Motel Balneario*, is the newer *Villa Bordeaux* (Ⓣ376/761-0222; ❼); this spiffy hacienda-style hotel features a thermal pool, sauna, steam room, reasonable dinners (US$8), and massages for US$10-22. Opposite, *Condominias Cosala* (Ⓣ376/761-0321; up to four people sharing; ❼) has rooms with TV, around a pool, plus rooms with jacuzzi that cost more. On the main road, the *Villas Buenaventura* (Ⓣ376/761-0303, Ⓕ761-0364; ❽) offers upmarket suites with two bedrooms and a kitchen (US$20 more), and some with a naturally heated jacuzzi.

The last major community along the north shore of the lake, **JOCOTEPEC** draws fewer tourists and foreign residents than the others, and doesn't really try to. Its lone claim to fame is the manufacture of **sarapes** with elaborately embroidered motifs, but you'll be hard-pressed to find any for sale these days.

Buses between Jocotepec and Guadalajara run on two routes, either along the lakeshore via Chapala, or more directly via the highway from the coast (every 30min).

South towards the coast: Tapalpa

Some of the most delightful alpine scenery in the country lies southwest of Lago Chapala, on the road to Colima. You'll miss much of it if you stick to the super-efficient new toll road, though even that has its exciting moments in the mountains: the following places are all reached from the far slower, far more attractive old road. For a few days of relaxation amid upland pastures and pine forests, the town of **TAPALPA** makes an ideal base. The climate changes dramatically when you reach Tapalpa, and when its ancient, wooden-balconied houses and magnificent surroundings of ranch country and tree-clad hills are covered in a rainy mist, you can easily feel that you're in Switzerland or Austria.

It's beginning to be discovered as a weekend escape from the city and can get quite crowded, but for the moment its charm is little affected (although some hotels are rather pricey). It's a place to appreciate the cool, fresh air, to walk and to wind down.

Though there's a village feel around the plaza, with its eighteenth-century wooden *portales* and two impressive **churches**, this is actually a fair-sized place, and messy development on the outskirts reflects rapid growth. The best **walks** are out on the road towards Chiquilistlán (signed as you enter Tapalpa). Here you quickly escape into fresh-scented pine forest, passing the romantic ruins of a *fábrica* – an old water-driven paper mill – and climb towards a gorgeous valley of upland pasture, studded with wild flowers and with huge boulders, Las Piedrotas, that look as if they've been dropped from the sky.

In fact there's good walking in almost any direction from Tapalpa, with plenty of wildlife, especially birds, to spot; you can also hire **horses** (look for the signs) for the popular ride to the local waterfall. Be warned that it's very cold in winter, and even the summer nights can become chilly. Locals brew their own *mescal* in the village, which may help warm you; it's sold from the barrel in some of the older shops and is extremely rough (but also very cheap). Alternatively, at any of the bars around the zócalo you can enjoy a shot of tequila, well regarded by the locals and sipped slowly with a complimentary glass of sweet sangrita to take away the bitter aftertaste.

Practicalities

Second-class **buses** run from Guadalajara's old bus station to Tapalpa (Sala B; hourly 6.30am–5.30pm; 3hr 15min); it's advisable to book your return as soon as you arrive, as the late buses are often full. In Tapalpa they stop near the ticket office, which is at Matamoros 135, just southwest of the Jardín Principal below the red church. Four daily services go direct to Ciudad Guzmán (2hr), but many more pass by the junction of the main road (El Crucero, some 20km away); it's easy enough to catch a bus, or even hitch, down there, but if you do hitch, go during the day and leave yourself plenty of time. Locals consider the route dangerous after dark.

For most things, head for Tapalpa's main plaza, where several of the old buildings have been refurbished as restaurants and hotels, and there's even an efficient branch of Ban Crecer where you can **exchange money** (Mon–Fri 9am–1pm). The municipal **tourist office**, on the north side of the plaza, does not seem to have fixed hours or a telephone, but you may be lucky and arrive when it's open. The cheapest **place to stay** is the *Hotel Tapalpa* (no phone; ❹), above the *Restaurante Tapalpa* on the southern (lower) side of the plaza, with simple rooms that smell a bit damp and have warm showers – expensive for what you get, but there's little competition. The *Posada la Hacienda*, a few doors to its left at Matamoros 7 (ⓣ343/432-0193; ❺), offers little more for a rather higher price, though the rooms are a bit airier. Far nicer – indeed a world apart – is the *Casa de Maty*, a few doors the other way at Matamoros 69 (ⓣ/ⓕ343/432-0189; ❻), a beautiful place with comfortably rustic rooms. Also offering luxury with country-style charm is the *Villa de San José*, two blocks southeast of the plaza at Ignacio López 91 (ⓣ343/432-0451; ❻). At some weekends all the rooms can be taken, but during the week you'll often be the only outsider.

Numerous **restaurants** around the main plaza serve plain country food – you get good steaks and dairy products up here – though many are open weekends only. One of the best is *Paulinos*, with balcony seats over the plaza and simple but excellent food; affordable food can be found in simple restaurants below the plaza's red church opposite the bus ticket office. Be on the lookout for places serving *poche*, a local wine made from an unusual concoction of pomegranate, peanuts, coffee, and guava.

Sayula, Ciudad Guzmán and the road to Colima

Beyond the turn-off for Tapalpa, the old main road starts to climb in earnest into the Sierra Madre, passing though **SAYULA** (the name chosen by Lawrence for his town on Lago de Chapala) and the sizeable city of Ciudad Guzmán. Sayula itself has an interesting enough history, relating to indigenous tribes that fought over production of salt from the nearby lake, and the development of the town as a commercial centre. There's little to see, however, apart from a thriving market and some old convents that have been converted into basic **hotels** – *Hotel Meson del Anima,* at Avila Camacho Oriente 171 (Ⓣ342/422-0600; ❹), and *Hotel Díaz,* a little bit further away from the main highway, at Portal Galeana 5 (Ⓣ342/422-0633; ❸). The area around the lake has been made into an ecological conservation zone for migratory birds.

Birthplace of José Clemente Orozco, **CIUDAD GUZMÁN** is a busy little city thoroughly steeped in local culture, with attractive colonnaded streets in the centre, though there seems little reason to stop except to break a journey. If you do visit, don't miss the lovely **Museo de las Culturas de Occidente** (Tues–Sun 10am–4pm; US$1.50) on Dr Angel Gonzalez, just off Reforma one block from the plaza – Reforma is the street that leads from the highway and bus station eastwards into town. It's just one room, but there are some lovely figures and animals in the collection of local archeology, and often an interesting temporary display that may include early works by **Orozco**. As ever, almost everything else is on or around the plaza, where you'll find banks, money changers, phones and **places to stay**. The *Hotel Zapotlan*, at Federico del Toro 61 (Ⓣ341/412-0040, Ⓕ412-4783; ❹), on the west side of the square, has a beautiful old wrought-iron courtyard, which the rooms sadly don't live up to. There's a variety of rooms at a variety of prices, so take a look around and see which one best fits your budget and taste. A block to the south, the *Hotel Flamingos*, at Federico del Toro 133 (Ⓣ341/412-0103; ❸), has less character but is clean and quiet. The cheapest place to stay is the *Hotel Morelos*, off the southwest corner of the square at Refugio Barragán del Toscano 20 (no phone; ❷), whose rooms are basic but tidy.

Back on the plaza are a few *taquerías* and a couple of **restaurants**: the *Juanito*, at Portal Morelos 65, a few doors from the *Hotel Zapotlan*. One block to the south, the attractive *Los Portales*, at Refugio Barragán del Toscano 32, has delicious, reasonably priced breakfasts and Mexican main dishes. There's also *Romances*, a bar-restaurant in the arcade at Portal Morelos 85, which serves excellent basics – enchiladas and the like. You can have an inexpensive and healthy breakfast, with cereal and fresh juice, at the stands behind the church in the main square. The local salty cheeses are a treat and can be bought at the **market** near the stalls. Cheap food and drink can also be found at the bus station.

Buses to Ciudad Guzmán stop at a station ten minutes' walk from the plaza (local bus #6 will drop you very closeby), though most people will find it quicker to walk into town than to wait for a bus. There are buses almost hourly to Guadalajara's Camionera Nueva (2hr), and cheaper but slower buses every hour to the Camionera Vieja (3hr 30min). There are also hourly buses the other way to Colima (1hr) and Manzanillo (3hr), and three daily services direct to Mexico City (9hr).

The road from Ciudad Guzmán to Colima

Between Ciudad Guzmán and Colima, the drive becomes truly spectacular, through country dominated by the **Nevado de Colima** – at 4335m the loftiest and most impressive peak in the west, which is snowcapped in winter. The new road slashes straight through the mountains via deep cuts and soaring concrete bridges, while the old one snakes above and beneath it as it switchbacks its way through the hills. Both have great views of the Nevado, at least when it's not covered by clouds. If you're on the old road, close your windows as you pass through **Atenquique**, a lovely if odorous hidden valley some 25km from Ciudad Guzmán, which is enveloped in a pall of fumes from a vast paper works. Not far from here, off the road but on the main train line to the coast, and served by two buses an hour from Ciudad Guzmán, **Tuxpan** is a beautiful and ancient little town, with a few hotels – it's especially fun during its frequent, colourful fiestas. Do not confuse it with Tuxpán (p.572) in Veracruz, where the exiled Fidel Castro plotted, organized and set off for the Cuban Revolution.

Tequila

The approach to **TEQUILA**, some 50km northwest of Guadalajara, is through great fields of spiky blue agave, a species of the cactus-like maguey plant. It's from these rugged plants that they make the quintessentially Mexican liquor to which the town lends its name, producing it in vast quantities at a series of local distilleries (*pulque* and *mescal* are made from different parts of maguey, and by different, less refined distillation processes). More than 100 million litres of tequila are manufactured annually, and this product alone accounts for some three percent of Mexico's export earnings. The town itself is a rather dusty, but pretty, little place, whose scattering of bourgeois mansions and fine church are somewhat overwhelmed by the trappings of thriving modern business. But no matter: you don't come here to sightsee, you come to drink or at least to visit the distilleries.

They've made tequila here since the seventeenth century and probably earlier, but the oldest and most important surviving **distillery** is La Perseverancia, the **Sauza** operation founded in 1873, where tours are available in English or Spanish every hour and a half (Mon–Fri 9.30am–2pm, Sat 9.30–11am; US$4). To get there, follow Calle Ramon Corona from the plaza down beside the Banco Promex. If you'd like to learn more, Sauza also operate an experimental agave farm, again open to the public (same ticket as the distillery), on the edge of town at Rancho El Indio, where they have planted some 197 different varieties of maguey. The other main distillery, **José Cuervo**, also offer tours every hour (Mon–Sat 10am–2pm, tours in English are at 10am and noon; US$3), which can be arranged through the tourist desk just two blocks away in front of the town hall in the main square. Across the street from the main entrance to the Cuervo distillery is the small but proud **Museo de la Tequila** (Tues–Sun; US$1.50), where visitors can learn about the history of the popular drink and its crucial role in the town's development. There are plenty of cafés around the plaza in Tequila to sample the local goods, or enjoy less potent drinks. It's also worth a stop at the serene **Herradura** distillery (Hacienda San José del Refugio) in the small town of **Amatitán**, located just a few miles outside of Tequila on the main road from Guadalajara. The restaurant here offers a unique dining experience – gourmet food and gracious service in an early 1900's hacienda.

It's easy enough **to get to Tequila** on regular buses from Guadalajara's Camionera Vieja bus station (Sala B; every 20min; 1hr 45min). Unfortunately, the bus is pretty slow and it can be rather uncomfortable to return to Guadalajara after a few too many tequila samples. It is better to go on an organized tour or take the train. Numerous agencies arrange tours, including Panoramex (see p.225) for US$25. By far the easiest and most hassle-free way to get to and discover Tequila is by train on the *Tequila Express* (see p.241). Unless you work in the spirits business and are on a buying trip, there's little need to spend more than an afternoon in Tequila.

San Juan de los Lagos and Lagos de Moreno

Heading east and then northeast from Guadalajara towards León, Aguascalientes and the Bajío, the old highway runs through **SAN JUAN DE LOS LAGOS**. From its outskirts, about 150km from Guadalajara, San Juan seems like just another dusty little town, but in the centre you'll find an enormous bus station surrounded by scores of hotels. This is thanks to the vast parish church and the miraculous **image of the Virgin** that it contains, making it one of the most important pilgrimage centres in Mexico. The site's busiest dates are February 2 (**Día de la Candelaria**) and December 8 (**Fiesta de la Inmaculada Concepción**), when the place is crammed with penitents, pilgrims, those seeking miraculous cures and others who are just there to enjoy the atmosphere. The celebrations spill over to several lesser events throughout the year, notably the first fortnight of August and the entire Christmas period. There's little chance of finding a room at these times and little point in staying long at any other, so it's best to treat San Juan de los Lagos as a day-trip from - or stopover between - **Lagos de Moreno** and Guadalajara (less than an hour from the former, around three hours from Guadalajara).

Lagos de Moreno

Just 45km east of San Juan, **LAGOS DE MORENO** lies on the intersection where the road from Mexico City to Ciudad Juárez crosses the route from Guadalajara to San Luis Potosí and the northeast. Though the town has always been a major staging post, surprisingly few tourists stop here now and, despite the heavy traffic rumbling around its fringes, it's a quiet and rather beautiful little town, with colonial streets climbing steeply from a small river to a hilltop monastery.

Cross the bridge by the bus station and head to your left along the stream, away from the choking fumes of the main road, and it's hard to believe you're in the same place. The **zócalo** is the place to head, whether you plan to stay a couple of hours or a few days: in the streets around are a massive **Baroque church** and a scattering of colonial mansions and official buildings, including a forbidding-looking jail that's still in use. The **Teatro José Rosas Moreno** on the north side of the square, which opened in 1906 to stage opera performances, is worth a look for the beautiful mural on the dome, depicting the Revolution and Independence, with local hero José Rosas Moreno, a famous writer of tales and fables, as the centrepiece. Once you've seen the centre, you might want to embark on the long climb up to the **hillside church**. The monastery is inhabited by monks, so you can't visit, and the church itself is tumbling down, but it's worth the trek for the **view**, especially at sunset.

There are several run-down but comfortable **hotels** near the zócalo. On the square itself, the *Hotel París* (Ⓣ474/742-0200; ④) is a bizarre, stark building and a little overpriced for what you get; the slightly posher *Hotel Colonial*, Hidalgo 279 (Ⓣ474/742-0142; ⑤), has its own restaurant and a very friendly and helpful manager. The *Hotel La Troje* (Ⓣ474/742-6677; ⑤) has modern and reasonable rooms and the *Hotel Victoria* (Ⓣ474/742-0620; ④) is slightly cheaper, with basic but clean rooms. The zócalo also boasts a few good **bars** and **places to eat**.

Getting to and from Lagos de Moreno could hardly be easier: there are **buses** at least every thirty minutes from Guadalajara, León, Aguascalientes, Zacatecas and Mexico City.

Northern Michoacán

To the southeast of Jalisco, **Michoacán** state is one of the most beautiful and diverse in all Mexico, spreading as it does from a very narrow coastal plain, with several tiny beach villages (see Chapter Six), up to where the Sierra Madre Occidental reaches eastwards into range after range of wooded volcanic heights. Several of the towns, including the delightfully urbane capital, **Morelia**, are utterly colonial in appearance, but on the whole Michoacán's attractions are simple. The land is green and thriving - in **Uruapan** the lush countryside seems to press in on the town, and is certainly the main attraction – while throughout the state there is a very active native tradition and a strength of indigenous culture matched only in the state of Oaxaca. This is largely thanks to Michoacán's first bishop, **Vasco de Quiroga**, one of the few early Spanish colonists to consider the native population as anything more than an expendable slave-labour force. The fruits of Quiroga's efforts are most clear in and around **Pátzcuaro**, the beautiful lakeside town that was his base. Here and in the surrounding villages, traditional and introduced crafts from weaving to guitar-manufacture have flourished for centuries, and today this region is one of the most important sources of Mexican artesanías. Native traditions also draw large crowds to the lake for the **Day of the Dead** at the beginning of November, one of the most striking of Mexican celebrations.

However, Michoacán remains a region that people travel through rather than to. Morelia, Pátzcuaro, Uruapan and other towns lie conveniently on a direct route from Guadalajara to Mexico City. You could easily spend several days in each, or weeks trying to explore the state fully, but even in a couple of days passing through you can get a strong flavour of the area. If you're doing so between mid-November and the end of March, the orange, black and white markings of the **monarch butterfly** may catch your eye as they sporadically float across your path. They migrate here from northern America every year to hibernate and reproduce, covering a formidable 4000km and in doing so have been appropriated as a symbol of economic integration between the US and Mexico – look out for them on the side of Pátzcuaro's taxis.

Some history

When the Spanish first arrived here in 1519, they found the region dominated by the **Purépechan** people whom they named **Tarascans** and whose chief town, Tzintzuntzán, lay on the shores of Lago de Pátzcuaro. Their civilization, a serious rival to the Aztecs before the Conquest, had a widespread reputation for excellence in art, metalworking and feathered ornaments. The Tarascans submitted peaceably to the Spanish in 1522, and their leader was converted to Christianity, but this didn't prevent the massacres and mass torture that Nuño de Guzmán meted out in his attempts to fully pacify the region and make himself a fortune in the following years. Guzmán's methods were overly brutal, even by colonial standards, and **Quiroga** was appointed bishop in an attempt to restore harmony. He succeeded beyond all expectations and secured his reputation as a champion of the native peoples, a reputation that persists today. He encouraged the population down from the mountains whence they had fled, established self-sufficient agricultural settlements and set up missions to teach practical skills as well as religion. The effects have survived in a very visible way for, despite some blurring in objects produced for the tourist trade, each village still has its own craft speciality: lacquerware in Pátzcuaro and Uruapan, pottery in Tzintzuntzán, wooden furniture in Quiroga, guitars in Paracho.

Vasco de Quiroga also left behind him a deeply religious state. Michoacán was a stronghold of the reactionary Cristero movement, which fought a bitter war in defence of the Church after the Revolution. Perhaps, too, the ideals of Zapata and Villa had less appeal here as Quiroga's early championing of native peoples' rights against their new overlords meant that the hacienda system never entirely took over Michoacán. Unlike most of the country, the state boasted a substantial peasantry with land it could call its own and therefore it didn't relate to calls for land and labour reform.

Guadalajara to Uruapan

From Guadalajara, the direct route to Mexico City heads east through the major junction of La Piedad to join the superhighway outside Irapuato. If you can afford to dawdle a while, though, it's infinitely more rewarding to follow the slower, southern road through Zamora and Morelia, spending a couple of days in Uruapan and Pátzcuaro. From Uruapan, a reasonably good road slices south through the mountains to the Pacific coast at Lázaro Cárdenas (see p.525).

Leaving Guadalajara, you skirt the northeastern edge of Lago de Chapala before turning south, heading into Michoacán and reaching **ZAMORA DE HIDALGO**, some 200km away. Zamora has little intrinsic interest. However, if you're planning to head straight down to Uruapan you may want to change buses here. You can catch a direct bus from Guadalajara to Zamora, where there's a frequent service to Uruapan. Although not much to go out of your way for, the town boasts several small **restaurants** and a **market** very close to the bus station. The old **cathedral**, unusually Gothic in style, is ruined andoften closed, but you can while away some time on the pleasant grassy plaza in front.

If you're driving, there's no need to stop on the way, though some local buses call in at **Carapan**, around 40km before Uruapan; as an alternative to changing in Zamora, you could get off here and flag down a bus going south. The route, on a road winding through pine-draped hills, is beautiful. About halfway along you pass through the village of **PARACHO**, which has been famous for the manufacture of **guitars** and other stringed instruments since Quiroga's time. Every house seems to have either a workshop, a guitar shop or both. The guitars vary enormously in price and quality – many are not meant to be anything more than ornamental, but others are serious, handcrafted musical instruments. Though you'll find them on display and for sale in the markets and artesanías museums in Uruapan or Pátzcuaro, you should buy them here at the source. Paracho also hosts a couple of fascinating **fiestas**. On Corpus Christi (the Thurs after Trinity, usually late May/early June) you can witness the **dance of Los Viejitos**. This, the most famous of Michoacán's dances, is also one of its most picturesque, with the dancers, dressed in baggy white cotton and masked as old men, alternating between parodying the tottering steps of the *viejitos* they represent and breaking into complex routines. Naturally enough, there's a lot of music, too. August 8 sees an even more ancient ceremony, whose roots go back to well before the Spanish era: an ox is sacrificed and its meat used to make a complicated ritual dish – *shuripe* – which is then shared out among the celebrants.

Uruapan

URUAPAN, they say, means "the place where flowers bloom" in the Tarascan language, though *Appleton's Guide* for 1884 tells a different story: "The word Uruapan comes from *Urani*, which means in the Tarasc language 'a chocolate cup', because the Indians in this region devote themselves to manufacture and painting of these objects." Demand for chocolate cups, presumably, has fallen since then. Whatever the truth, the modern version is certainly appropriate: Uruapan, lower (at just over 1500m) and warmer than most of its neighbours, enjoys a steamy subtropical climate and is surrounded by thick forests and lush parks.

It's a prosperous and growing town, too, with a thriving commerce based on the richness of its agriculture (particularly a vast export market in **avocados** and **macadamia nuts**) and on new light industry. To some extent this has come to overshadow the old attractions, creating ugly new development and displacing traditional crafts. But it remains a lively place with a fine market, an abiding reputation for **lacquerware**, and fascinating surroundings – especially the giant waterfall and "new" volcano of Paricutín (see p.254).

Arrival and information

Most visitors arrive at Uruapan's modern **bus station**, the Central Camionera, 3km from the centre; a local bus (marked "Centro") from right outside will take you down to the Jardín Morelos, the plaza in the heart of town, or back again from there. There's also a domestic airport with daily connections from Mexico City.

Uruapan's **tourist office** (Casa Regional del Turista), Carranza 20 (daily 9am–7pm; ⓣ452/524-0667), not only gives away a good **map** of town but also showcases and sells local crafts and comestibles. If you need to withdraw or change money, there are numerous **banks** with ATMs in the streets around the plaza and **casas de cambio** at: Portal Matamoros 18 on the south side of the plaza; Portal Degollado 15 in the northeast corner; Carranza 14D, just west of the plaza and Obregón 1D to its east. The **post office** (Mon–Fri 8am–7pm, Sat 9am–1pm) is at Reforma 11, three blocks south of the plaza. Long-distance **casetas telefónicas** include Computel at Ocampo 3 on the west side of the plaza and at the bus station, and Telmex at 5 de Febrero 12A, just south of the plaza. There is an **Internet** café at Independencia 33 (US$1.50 per hr). If you're interested in taking a **taxi tour** of the area, call ⓣ452/519-0480.

Accommodation

Uruapan lures visitors with its proximity to breathtaking natural beauty, which is why **camping** is an excellent idea if you plan to stay in the area. *Campamento Regional* (ⓣ452/524-0197, ⓦwww.parquenacional.org) makes nearly five square kilometres of protected pine and semi-tropical forest available to those wanting to sleep under the stars. For just US$3.60, campers can pitch a tent, or lay their heads in a basic cabin, which comes with a full kitchen and bath. Some units accommodate as many as 24 people. The town also seems to have more than its fair share of **hotels**, most of them conveniently sited around – or at least within walking distance of – Jardín Morelos.

Capri Portal Degollado 10, at the eastern end of the plaza (no phone). Basic, busy and right in the heart of town – the action of the plaza often spills over into the lobby. A much better bet than other hotels on the same block. ❹

Concordia Portal Carillo 8 ⓣ/ⓕ 452/523-0400, ⓔinfo@hotelconcordia.com.mx, ⓦwww.hotel-concordia.com.mx. On the plaza, modern, clean and efficient: all rooms with TV and phone. Parking facilities. ❹

Continental Nicolas Bravo 33 ⓣ452/523-9793, ⓦwww.hotelessucasa.com.mx. Friendly hotel with modern, clean rooms with TV and phone, parking facilities and a restaurant. ❻

Gran Hotel Acosta Filomena Mata 325 ⓣ452/523-4564. Opposite the bus station, this is hardly an ideal spot, but if you're passing through it does offer clean, simple, reasonably priced rooms. ❹

Hotel del Parque Independencia 124, near the Parque Nacional ⓣ452/524-3845. Best deal of the cheapies: clean and friendly, with large rooms (those at the front are nicest but a bit noisy), en-suite bathrooms and parking facilities. ❹

Mansión del Cupatitzio at the north end of the Parque Eduardo Ruíz ⓣ452/523-2100, ⓦwww.mansioncupatitzio.com. Uruapan's finest hotel, with superb service, pool, terrace restaurant and beautiful grounds full of all manner of flora. Located away from the fray, the hotel is conveniently adjacent to the entrance to the Parque Nacional. ❼

Plaza Uruapan Ocampo 64 ⓣ452/523-3599, ⓕ523-3980. Big, modern hotel at the western end of the plaza, with good views from the rooms and the second-floor restaurant. ❽

Posada Morelos Morelos 30 ⓣ452/523-2302. Secure, family-run hotel set around a lovely yellow courtyard. Clean and reasonably priced singles plus rooms for groups. ❸

Real Uruapan Nicolas Bravo 110 ⓣ452/527-5900. One block south of the plaza and hence a bit more peaceful, with good panoramic views from the top-floor restaurant. ❼

Regis Portal Carillo 12 ⓣ452/523-5844. Friendly place in a central location with its own car park; rooms have TV and some overlook the plaza. ❻

Victoria Cupatitzio 11 ⓣ452/523-6700, ⓦwww.hotelvictoriaupn.com.mx. Another fine, modern hotel with a garage and good restaurant. ❻

Villa de Flores Carranza 15 ⓣ452/524-2800. Clean, simple rooms around a beautiful little courtyard filled, as the name suggests, with flowers, though it does have a rather lurid colour scheme throughout. ❻

The Town

The **Jardín Morelos**, a long strip of tree-shaded open space, is in every sense the heart of Uruapan. Always animated, it's surrounded by everything of importance: shops, market, banks, post office, principal churches and most of the hotels. This is the place to head first, either to find a hotel or simply to get a feel for the place. On the plaza, too, is the town's one overt tourist attraction, **La Huatapera**. One of the oldest surviving buildings in Uruapan, it has been exquisitely restored to house the fascinating **Museo Regional de Arte Popular** (Tues–Sun 9.30am–1.30pm & 3.30–6pm; free), an impressive display of crafts from the region, especially Uruapan's own lacquerwork. The small courtyard with its adjoining chapel was built by Juan de San Miguel, the Franciscan friar who founded the town itself, and later it became one of Bishop Quiroga's hospitals and training centres. The carving around the windows bears a marked Arab influence, as they were crafted by Christianized Moorish artisans from Spain (Mudéjares). The wares shown are of the highest quality, and are worth close inspection if you plan to go out hunting for bargains in the market or in the shops around the park. The art of making lacquer is complex and time-consuming, involving the application of layer upon layer of different colours, with the design cut into the background. All too many of the goods produced for tourists are simply given a couple of coats (one for the black background with a design then painted on top), which is far quicker and cheaper but does not result in a comparable product.

The **Casa de la Cultura** (daily 8am–9pm; free), to the left of the museum on the north side of the plaza, hosts regular cultural events, exhibitions, concerts and dance performances. You'll find a bulletin board of upcoming events in the entryway. Walk round to the back of the museum and you come to the start of the **market**, first up the **Mercado de Antojitos**, a large open section just half a block south of the plaza, where women serve up meals for stallholders and visitors alike at a series of long, open-air tables. You'll find the cheapest, and very often the freshest and best, food in town. This is a great place to sample the salty regional cheese called *adobada*. The rest of the market sprawls along Corregidora and Constitución – replete with herbs, fruit, trinkets, shoe stalls and hot-dog stands. It's not a particularly good place to buy **native crafts** like pottery or wood furniture. Instead, look to the concentration of shops along **Independencia**, which leads up from the plaza to the Parque Nacional, for such items. At the top of this street are several small places where you can watch the artisans at work – some are no more than a single room with a display of finished goods on one side and a worktable on the other, while others are more sophisticated operations. Opposite the entrance to the park is a little "craft market", mostly selling very poor souvenirs.

The Río Cupatitzio and the Parque Nacional Eduardo Ruíz

The **Parque Nacional Eduardo Ruíz** (daily 8am–6pm; US$0.60) is perhaps Uruapan's proudest asset, a spectacular and luxuriant tropical park in which the Río Cupatitzio rises and through which it flows in a little gorge via a series of man-made cascades and fountains. The river springs from a rock known as *La Rodilla del Diablo* ("the Devil's knee"), according to legend, because water gushed forth after the Devil knelt here in submission before the unswerving Christian faith of the drought-ridden population. Alternatively, it is said that the Devil met the Virgin Mary while out strolling in the park, and dropped to his knees in respect. *Cupatitzio* means "where the waters meet", though it's invariably translated as "the river that sings" – another appropriate, if not entirely accurate, tag. If you don't feel like walking to get here, take a bus up Independencia.

Some 12km out of Uruapan, the Cupatitzio crashes over the **waterfall of La Tzaráracua**, an impressive 25-metre plunge amid beautiful forest scenery. This is a popular outing with locals, especially at weekends, and hence easy enough to get to – take one of the buses (marked "Tzaráracua") from Madero at Cupatitzio, a block south of the plaza, or share a taxi. If it seems too crowded here, make for the smaller fall, **Tzararacuita**, about 1km further downstream.

Eating and drinking

The best place to sample local delights at low prices has to be the **Mercado de Antojitos**; otherwise there are several good, cheap cafés on Independencia, just off the plaza, all serving a selection of hamburgers, tacos, pizzas, sandwiches and superb *licuados*.

Antojitos Yucatecos Carranza 37. Mexican breakfasts and good-value comidas. Open every day.
Café Sol y Luna Independencia 15. Arty café with antojitos and refreshments, and jazz some nights.
Café Tradicional de Uruapan Carranza 5. Great breakfasts, superb local coffee, ice cream, cakes and antojitos. Open-air seating.
La Casa Revolución 3. Charming interior courtyard café-cum-cocktail lounge good for coffee and tequila drinks.
Colibrí Independencia 19. Gourmet café selling flaky pastries and strong coffee, closed Sundays.
Comedor Vegetariano Morelos at Aldama. Cheap and cheerful restaurant serving veggie food to eat-in or take away.
Comida Económica Mary Independencia 59. Wholesome homestyle cooking at low prices; great for breakfast and lunch.
Hotel Real de Uruapan Nicolas Bravo 110. Top-floor restaurant with a beautiful view, where you can eat a reasonably priced evening meal while being serenaded by live music.
Jugos California Independencia 7. Myriad juices, ice creams and some snacks.
La Lucha Portal Matamoros 15, on the south side of the plaza. A small café basically serving only coffee, but it's a good place to sample the local hearty brews.
La Pergola Portal Carrillo 4, on the south side of the plaza. Reasonably priced, popular restaurant serving a good comida corrida, local coffee and a selection of regional and national dishes.
El Portal Madero 12. Serves reasonably priced dinners and regional specialties such as *cabrito* (goat) and rabbit. There's even a dance floor.
Restaurant Urani at the entrance to the Parque Nacional Eduardo Ruíz, next to *Mansión Cupatitzio*. Simply a delight. Enjoy avocado cocktail (US$2), grilled trout (US$6) and heavenly *aguas frescas* while overlooking the park's waterfalls and giant banana trees. Daily 9am–7pm.

Paricutín

An ideal day-trip from Uruapan, which gives you an unusual taste of the surrounding countryside, is to the "new" **Volcano of Paricutín**, about 20km northwest of town. On February 20, 1943, a peasant working in his fields noticed the earth rumble and then smoke. The ground soon cracked and lava began to flow to the surface. Over a period of several years, it engulfed the village of Paricutín and several other hamlets, forcing the evacuation of some seven thousand inhabitants. The volcano was active for eight years, producing a cone some 300m high and devastating an area of around twenty square kilometres. Now there are vast fields of cooled lava, black and powdery, cracked into harsh jags, along with the dead cone and crater. Most bizarrely, a church tower – all that remains of the buried hamlet of San Juan Parangaricutiro – pokes its head through the surface. During its active life, the volcano drew tourists from around the world, and indeed it's partly responsible for the area's current development; less exciting now, it continues to get a fair number of visitors, though as the years pass the landscape is sure to soften. Sightings of burgeoning volcanoes are not altogether unprecedented. Alexander von Humboldt devoted more than ten pages of his book on New Spain to the volcano of Jorullo, south of Pátzcuaro, which appeared equally suddenly in September 1759 – this was still hot enough, he reported, that "in the year 1780, cigars might still be lighted, when they were fastened to a stick and pushed in". Jorullo is no longer the subject of any interest, indeed no one seems to know quite where it is.

To get to the volcano, start early. By car, simply take the main road to Los Reyes and look for signs for **ANGAHUAN** – there are many. By bus, hop aboard Autotransportes Galeana's "Ruta Paraíso" headed toward Los Reyes or Zicuicho from the Central Camionera in Uruapan to the village of Angahuan (half-hourly 5am–7pm; about 40min; US$1.30); to avoid the trek to the bus station, flag down any bus marked "Los Reyes" near the Calzada de San Miguel traffic circle. The bus drops you on the highway outside the village, and from there you should walk to the **plaza**, where the **church** warrants a second glance. Built in the sixteenth century, its doorway was carved in the largely Arab Mudéjar style by Andalucian artisans (Andalucia was the centre of fine arts in the Arab empire until the fall of Granada in 1492). The cross in the courtyard, on the other hand, is most definitely Mexican, complete with serpents, a skull and other pre-Hispanic motifs. In the street to the right of the church (as you look at it), across from the side gate of the courtyard, a door carved in more modern style recounts the history of the volcano from its first appearance to the arrival of tourists seeking it out.

From the plaza turn right down Juárez for about 200m until you pass a superbly carved wooden house on the left; there take a left turn (signposted) and head straight on for a kilometre. You eventually arrive at the **Centro Turístico de Angahuan** (Ⓣ452/523-3934), which offers superb views of the volcano from its *mirador* with diagrams (explained in Spanish only) of the volcano and local plate tectonics. The Centro also has cabins (US$50), each with an open fire. Alternatively, you can **camp** on the grounds (US$10 for two people).

Though the trip to the Centro Turístico and the half-buried church can be done in a morning, the journey to the crater is more complicated. In Angahuan you should have no problem finding a **guide**, whether you want one or not. It's not really necessary if you're just going up the hill for a look, but it seems harsh not to allow the locals some profit from their misfortune (although the volcano was not all bad news, its dust proving a fine fertilizer on the fields that escaped the full flow). For the longer journey to the centre you do need a guide, and probably a horse, too; it's not an outrageous expense, and certainly well worth it. A short ride out to the buried church takes just thirty minutes, while a full ascent of the volcano is a day-trip, so take some provisions.

Tinganio

The pre-Hispanic ruin of **TINGANIO** (daily 10am–5pm; US$2.70, free Sun) is situated roughly halfway between Uruapan and Pátzcuaro in a town that is now called **Tingambato**. This was first inhabited around 450–600 AD and greatly expanded between 650 and 900 AD. The site is small but pretty and well restored, with a combination of influences: that of Teotihuacán is prevalent and evident in the pyramid that dominates the religious area, overlooking a plaza with a cruciform altar, beyond which is a ball-court, suggesting Toltec influence. Beyond the ball-court, an unexcavated pyramid lies under a grove of avocado trees. In the residential area just to the north, a sunken plaza with two altars and five stairways, each to a separate residence is very much in the style of Teotihuacán, but the tomb under the largest residence, (which the caretaker will open on request) has a false dome suggestive of Maya influence. Surrounded by beautiful countryside, the site is best appreciated from atop the pyramid. Except on Sundays, you are not likely to see many foreigners here. If you're going by car, take the *cuota* highway from Uruapan towards Pátzcuaro and take the Zirahuén exit and follow the *libre* road past Ajuno to Tingambato. It lies approximately 30km west of Pátzcuaro.

Pátzcuaro and around

Pátzcuaro is almost exactly halfway between Uruapan and Morelia, some 60km from both, yet strikingly different from either. Basically a village swollen by the tourist trade, Pátzcuaro is far more colonial than Uruapan and infinitely

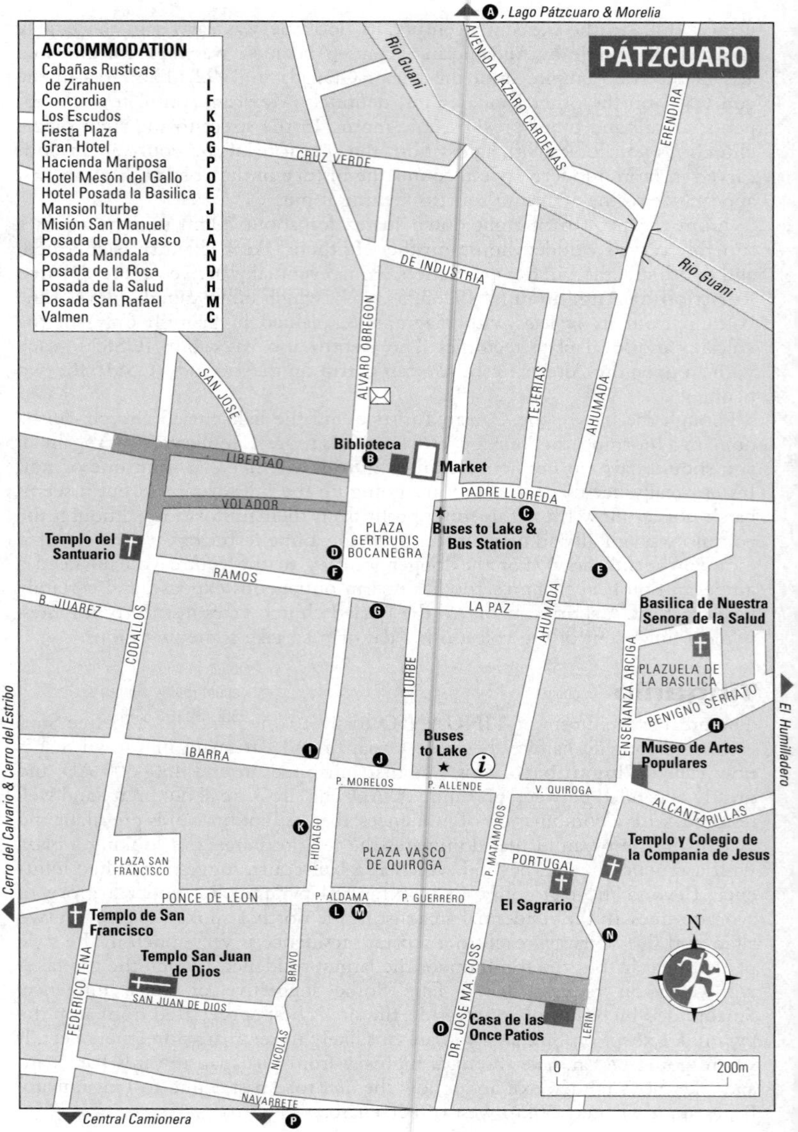

PÁTZCUARO

ACCOMMODATION

Cabañas Rusticas de Zirahuen	I
Concordia	F
Los Escudos	K
Fiesta Plaza	B
Gran Hotel	G
Hacienda Mariposa	P
Hotel Mesón del Gallo	O
Hotel Posada la Basilica	E
Mansion Iturbe	J
Misión San Manuel	L
Posada de Don Vasco	A
Posada Mandala	N
Posada de la Rosa	D
Posada de la Salud	H
Posada San Rafael	M
Valmen	C

more Indian than Morelia. It boasts both fine colonial architecture and a rich indigenous culture. Add to that the fact that it sits by the shore of **Lago de Pátzcuaro** (see p.261), probably the most beautiful lake in Mexico – certainly the most photogenic, especially during Pátzcuaro's famed **Day of the Dead** celebrations (see p.261) – and it's hardly surprising that it acts as a magnet for tourists, Mexican and foreign alike. In the vicinity, you can take trips around the lake, visit other, less developed villages, and see the site of **Tzintzuntzán**, one-time capital of the Tarascan kingdom.

Arrival, information and accommodation

Buses arrive at the **Central Camionera** in the south of town, about a fifteen-minute walk or a brief bus ride from the centre (take services marked "Centro" or "Col Popular"). Buses back to the bus station can be picked up in Plaza Bocanegra. Although the outskirts of Pátzcuaro straggle a kilometre or so down to the lakeshore, and some of the more expensive hotels are strung out along this drive, the centre of town is very small indeed, focusing on the two main squares, **Plaza Vasco de Quiroga** (or Plaza Grande) and **Plaza Bocanegra** (Plaza Chica).

The **tourist office** (Mon–Sat 9am–2pm & 4–8pm, Sun 9am–2pm; ⓣ434/342-1214) is located on the north side of Plaza Quiroga at 50A.

Accommodation

Few of Pátzcuaro's many **hotels** are cheap, but it does have some of the best mid-range places you'll find anywhere, and if you're prepared to pay a little extra, you'll get a lot more elegance. Most are on one or other of the plazas, with the ritzier establishments surrounding Plaza Vasco de Quiroga and a more basic selection around the Plaza Bocanegra. Wherever you stay, check that there will be an adequate **water supply** – Pátzcuaro suffers regular shortages.

During the first two days of November, when the town celebrates the **Day of the Dead** on the lake, there is little chance of getting a room anywhere near Pátzcuaro without prior booking.

Concordia Portal Juárez 31, Plaza Bocanegra ⓣ434/342-0003. Large, chilly place but a decent bargain. Simple clean rooms, some without bathrooms. ⑤

Los Escudos Portal Hidalgo 73, west side of Plaza Vasco de Quiroga ⓣ/ⓕ434/342-1290, ⓔhescudos@ml.com.mx. Beautiful colonial building with rooms around two flower-filled courtyards; all have carpet and TV, some their own fireplaces. There's also a dependable restaurant. Ask for a room in the original hotel and not the extension. ⑤

Fiesta Plaza Plaza Bocanegra 24 ⓣ/ⓕ434/342-2515. Big, simple new hotel with three floors of rooms set around a colourful open courtyard. ⑦

Gran Hotel Plaza Bocanegra 6 ⓣ434/342-0443, ⓦwww.mexonline.com/granhotel.htm. Clean, friendly hotel with small rooms and a good restaurant. ⑤

Hacienda Mariposa Carretera Pátzcuaro-Santa Clara del Cobre, km 3.5 ⓣ434/342-4728, ⓦwww.haciendamariposas.com. This comfortable upscale oasis outside of town offers pony treks, eco-tours and vegan cuisine in serene wooded surroundings. ⑨

Hotel Mesón del Gallo Dr Coss 20 ⓣ434/342-1474, ⓦwww.mexonline.com/mesondelgallo.htm. One of the oldest hotels in town. Attractively rustic common spaces, decent rooms and an excellent restaurant (see p.260). ⑦

Hotel Posada la Basílica Arciga 6 ⓣ434/342-1108, ⓔhotelpb@hotmail.com. Up the hill opposite the basilica. Sweet rooms, some with fireplaces, in an eighteenth-century building with superb views across the town's red rooftops. ⑧

Mansión Iturbe Portal Morelos 59, on Plaza Vasco de Quiroga ⓣ434/342-0368, ⓦwww.mexonline.com/iturbe.htm. Once a seventeenth-century muleteer's house and a now an architectural family jewel, this small luxury inn is run by a hands-on mother-daughter team and features work by local artists, a library, superb dining, and attractive bedrooms with soaring ceilings and down duvets. Rates are lower out of season, and every fourth night is free. ⑧

Misión San Manuel Portal Aldama 12 ⓣ434/342-1313. The great colonial front hides a modern interior; nevertheless this ex-convent offers comfortable rooms, all with fireplaces. ⑥

Posada de Don Vasco Av Lázaro Cárdenas 450 ⓣ434/342-0227. This tastefully decorated colonial-style hotel was built in 1938 on the outskirts of town. Now a Best Western, it boasts a modern exterior, swimming pool, tennis court and gardens filled with fruit trees. ⑨

Posada Mandala Lerin 14 ⓣ434/342-4176, ⓔmatiasag@hotmail.com. B&B near the Casa de los Once Patios, with a groovy proprietor and comfortable rooms with handwoven grass mats and exquisite rooftop views. ❺

Posada de la Rosa Portal Juárez 29, Plaza Bocanegra ⓣ434/342-1276. Next door to the *Concordia*; smaller, with stark, dark rooms around an upstairs courtyard, and some of the lowest prices in town. ❹

Posada de la Salud Serrato 9 ⓣ434/342-0058, ⓔposadadelasalud@hotmail.com. Behind the basilica, a short walk from the centre. Beautiful little budget hotel, peaceful and spotless and run by two sisters; some rooms have fireplaces. Probably the best value in town. ❹

Posada San Rafael Plaza Vasco de Quiroga 16 ⓣ434/342-0770. One of the largest hotels, with a long modern extension in colonial style behind the genuinely colonial front. Rooms tend to be dark but comfortable. ❹

Valmen Padre Lloreda 34 ⓣ/ⓕ434/342-1161, ⓦwww.mexonline.com/valmen.htm. Candy-green walls, large clean rooms with bathrooms and low prices, but an 11.30pm curfew. ❹

The Town

More than anywhere in the state, Pátzcuaro owes its position to Bishop Vasco de Quiroga, whose affection for the indigenous peoples (you'll find his statue in the centre of the plaza that bears his name) led him to settle in the Purépechan heartland on the shores of Lago de Pátzcuaro. It was he who decided, in the face of considerable opposition from the Spanish in Morelia (then known as Valladolid), to build the cathedral here, where it would be centrally located near the region's great source of water and accessible to many. Although subsequent bishops moved the seat of power back to Morelia, a basis had been laid. It's the fact that Pátzcuaro enjoyed a building boom in the sixteenth century and has been of secondary industrial and political importance ever since that creates much of its charm. Throughout the centre are old mansions with balconies and coats of arms, barely touched since those early years. Today, quaint Pátzcuaro has developed into an upmarket and artistically inclined town with numerous boutiques. You can spend hours wandering around the beautiful – and expensive – arts, crafts and antique shops, aimed mainly at visitors from Mexico City and abroad.

The plazas

Nothing much worth seeing in Pátzcuaro lies more than a few minutes' walk from **Plaza Gertrudis Bocanegra**, named after a local Independence heroine, and **Plaza Vasco de Quiroga**. The finest of Pátzcuaro's mansions are on the latter, especially the seventeenth-century **Casa del Gigante**, with its hefty pillars and crudely carved figures, and another nearby said to have been inhabited by Prince Huitzimengari, son of the last Tarascan king. Both are privately owned, however, and not open to visitors. There are more mansions on the Plaza Bocanegra, but the most striking thing around here is the **Biblioteca** (Mon–Fri 9am–7.30pm, actually located just off the plaza on Calle Obregón), with its stunning wooden barrel ceiling. The former sixteenth-century church of San Agustín, it has been converted into a library and decorated with **murals** by **Juan O'Gorman** depicting the history of Michoacán, and of the Tarascans in particular. O'Gorman (1905–82) possessed a prodigious talent, and is one of the muralists who inherited the mantle of Rivera and Orozco: his best-known work is the decoration of the interior of Chapultepec Castle in Mexico City. The paintings here couldn't be described as subtle, and he certainly ensures that the anti-imperialist point is taken. However, even O'Gorman manages to find praise for Vasco de Quiroga.

The Basílica

East of the Plaza Bocanegra, Quiroga's cathedral – the **Basílica de Nuestra Señora de la Salud**, or **Colegiata** – was intended by Quiroga to be Pátzcuaro's masterpiece, with space for 30,000 worshippers, a massive structure for such a small town. It was never completed and the existing basilica, finished in the nineteenth century, is only the nave of the original design. Even so, it is often full, for local people continue to revere Don Vasco's name and the church possesses a miraculous healing image of the Virgin, crafted in the traditional Tarascan method out of *pasta de caña*, a gum-like modelling paste made principally from maize. Services here, especially on saints' days, during fiestas (when the scrubby little **park** around the church becomes a fairground) or on the eighth of each month, when pilgrims gather to seek the Virgin's intercession, are extraordinary: you'll witness the worshippers in an intense, almost hypnotic fervour.

Museo de Artes Populares

The **Museo de Artes Populares**, at the corner of Quiroga and Lerin, south of the basílica (Tues–Sat 9am–7pm, Sun 9am–3pm; US$3.20, free on Sun), occupies the ancient Colegio de San Nicolas. Founded by Quiroga in 1540, the college is now devoted to a superb collection of regional handicrafts: local lacquerware and pottery; copperware from Santa Clara del Cobre; and traditional masks and religious objects made from *pasta de caña*, which, apart from being easy to work with, is also very light, and hence easily carried in processions. Some of the objects on display are ancient, others the best examples of modern work, and all are set in a very beautiful building. Almost opposite, the church of **La Compañía** was built by Quiroga in 1546 and later taken over by the Jesuits. Quiroga's remains and various relics associated with him are preserved here.

Casa de los Once Patios

A short walk south of the art museum, on Lerin, the **Casa de los Once Patios** (daily 10am–7pm, though individual stores may keep their own hours) is an eighteenth-century convent converted into a crafts showhouse, full of workshops and moderate to expensive boutiques. As its name suggests, the complex is set around a series of tiny courtyards, and it's a fascinating place to stroll through even if you can't afford the goods. You can watch restored treadle looms at work, admire the intricacy with which the best lacquerware is created, and wander at liberty through the warren of rooms and corridors.

El Humilladero and Cerro del Estribo

In the other direction, a thirty-minute walk from the basílica up Serrato, lies the church known as "**El Humilladero**" ("The place of humiliation"); frequent buses, marked "El Panteón", also run here. Probably the oldest church in Pátzcuaro, it stands on the site where the last Tarascan king, Tanganxoan II, accepted Spanish authority – hence the humbling name. Such a tag may seem appropriate with hindsight, though a more charitable view suggests that Tanganxoan was simply hoping to save his people from the slaughter that had accompanied resistance to the Spanish elsewhere.

The chapel itself offers little to see, so you might be better saving your hiking energies for a climb up the **Cerro del Calvario**, the tiny hill just west of town. A few minutes' walk will reward you with a great view of the lake, which is invisible as long as you stay in town. Leave the Plaza Vasco de

Quiroga on Ponce de León, pass the old customs house and a little plaza in front of the church of San Francisco, and keep straight on until you start climbing the hill. At the top is the little **chapel of El Calvario**, and if you take the road to the right here you can carry on to the much higher **Cerro del Estribo** (Stirrup Hill), about an hour's walk. For the better view with less effort, you could take a taxi, which leaves you at the bottom of 417 steps that climb to the summit.

Eating and drinking

Most of Pátzcuaro's hotels have their own **restaurants**, with fairly standard menus throughout: lots of good-value, if unexciting, comidas corridas. One feature of virtually all menus is *pescado blanco*, the rather flabby whitefish from the lake, and *sopa tarasca* – a tomato-based soup with chile and bits of tortilla in it that's usually very good. Cheap eats are hard to come by, but there are a few basic food stalls in the **market**. This used to operate just one day a week in the streets leading up from the Plaza Bocanegra, but nowadays there is some activity every day, though Monday and Wednesday tend to be slow. It is at its most colourful and animated on Friday, when the *indígenas* come in from the country to trade and barter their surplus. Most evenings you can also get basic food from the stalls set up in the Plaza Bocanegra. For the best **fish**, head to the lake, where a line of restaurants faces the landing jetty (see opposite). Stalls outside the *Hotel los Escudos* in Plaza Quiroga sell good **ice cream**, including tamarind, tequila and corn flavours.

Restaurants and cafés

Cafetería Betafumerio Portal Aldama 10. Fresh cakes and good coffee.

Cafetería La Compañía Hidalgo 70. Choice spot for coffee and elaborate desserts.

Cafetería La Escelera Chueca Plaza Quiroga 26. On the plaza, with local dishes and fish comidas.

Campana Portal Rayon 26. Reasonably priced regional dishes, including fish.

Casa de las 11 Pizzas Plaza Quiroga 33. Tasty pizza restaurant in a small courtyard off the Plaza Quiroga. It occasionally hosts plays.

Casona Plaza Quiroga 65. A good place to have a coffee and watch the world go by, or to have breakfast, on the plaza.

Don Rafa Mendoz 30. Cheap comidas in a cheerful joint whose friendly staff offers up tourist info for free.

Dona Paca Portal Morelos 59. Attached to the *Mansión Iturbe* hotel, with comfortable, elegant dining. Regional dishes include a rare selection of creative salads with local ingredients, triangular Purépechan tamales (*corundas*), hearty Tarascan soup, *churipo de carne* (beef stew), and fish with a sprightly coriander sauce.

Misión del Arriero in the *Hotel Mesón del Gallo* on Lerin near the basilica. Considerably more expensive than most, but with a successful colonial atmosphere and a menu of interesting local and national dishes.

Mistongo Dr Coss 4. Inviting restaurant with pared-down traditional Mexican decor serving fajitas and full Tarascan dinners for under US$10.

El Monge Portal Aldama 14 on Plaza Quiroga. Good restaurant with reasonably priced breakfasts and lunchtime menu.

El Patio Plaza Quiroga 19. Quite a chic little restaurant offering good coffee, reasonably priced breakfasts, Mexican antojitos, steaks, sandwiches and, of course, fish.

Premier Piso Plaza Quiroga 29. Gourmet restaurant mixing Tarascan, French and Italian flavours. Definitely worth splashing out, with romantic first-floor balcony views.

Restaurante los Escudos Portal Hidalgo 73, Plaza Quiroga. Hopping spot with live music and US$4 comidas corridas.

Tekare Arciga 6. Inside the *Posada la Basílica*, panoramic restaurant serving regional cuisine. Try the house specialty *kurucha urapiti*, or battered whitefish with chiles.

Listings

Banks and exchange There are banks with ATMs on both plazas and casas de cambio at Plaza Quiroga 67 on the north side of the plaza, at Ibarra 2 just off the plaza, and at the corner of Padre Lloreda and Ahumada near the *Hotel Valmen*.
Courier If you need to send packages home, there's a DHL service at the store Artesanías La Mojiganga in the Casa del Naranjo, Plaza Quiroga 29-2.
Internet access There are Internet cafés at Plaza Quiroga 33 (US$2 per hr) and Benito Mendoza 8 (US$2.50 per hr).
Laundry Lavandería San Francisco, Teran 16, is in front of the Templo San Francisco (Mon–Sat 9am–8pm).
Post office Obregón 13 (Mon–Fri 8am–4pm, Sat 9am–1pm).
Spanish courses The Centro de Lenguas y Ecoturismo de Pátzcuaro, Navarette 47A (ⓣ434/342-4764, ⓔcelep@rds2000.crefal.edu.mx), runs courses for US$250 a week.
Telephones You can phone and fax from Computel on the north side of Plaza Bocanegra, or *casetas* at Portal Hidalgo 67 on the west side of Plaza Quiroga, Dr Mendoza 21 between the plazas, or in the entrance to the *Posada de la Rosa* on Plaza Bocanegra; cardphones are virtually nonexistent.
Tours A number of companies offer guided day and half-day trips around Lago de Pátzcuaro and to local villages, such as the Instituto de Planificación Ecológica (ⓣ434/344-0167, ⓔfrancis_eronga@hotmail.com), headed by Francisco Castilleja, a self-styled veterinarian-philosopher-tour guide, who's based out of Erongaricuaro on the west side of the lake. His day-trips (US$35) concentrate on local ecology and include a traditional indigenous lunch. Ask at the tourist office for information on this and other tours.

Lago de Pátzcuaro

Pátzcuaro's other great attraction is, of course, **Lago de Pátzcuaro**. It's less than an hour's **walk** down to the jetty (follow the "embarcadero" signs), while **buses** and minibuses leave from the Plaza Bocanegra – those marked "Lago" will drop you right by the boats, while "Santa Ana" buses pass close by.

With the completion of several new roads, the lake itself is no longer the major boat thoroughfare it once was. Most locals now take the bus rather than paddle around the water in canoes, but there is still a fair amount of traffic and regular trips out to the closest island, **Janitzio**. **Fares** are fixed (get your ticket before you board) but there are almost always sundry "extras". Chief of these is a chance to photograph the famous butterfly nets wielded by indigenous fishermen from tiny dug-out canoes. It's hard to believe that anyone actually uses these nets for fishing any more, as they look highly impractical, but there's almost always a group of islanders lurking in readiness on the far side of the island, only to paddle into camera range when a sufficiently large collection of money has been taken. Longer trips around the lake and visits to the other islands, or private rental of a boat and guide, can be arranged at the embarcadero, either through the office there or by private negotiation with one of the boatmen; prices start at around US$3 and boats leave every thirty minutes from 9am to 7pm. Alternatively, ask at the tourist office about arranging a guided tour.

The **Day of the Dead** (Nov 1, and through the night into the next day) is celebrated in spectacular fashion throughout Mexico, but nowhere more so than on Lago de Pátzcuaro. Although many tourists come to watch, this is essentially a private meditation, when the locals carry offerings of fruit and flowers to the cemetery and maintain a vigil over the graves of their ancestors all night, chanting by candlelight. It's a spectacular and moving sight, especially earlier in the evening as indigenous people from the surrounding area converge on the island in their canoes, each with a single candle burning in the bows.

Janitzio

From the moment you step ashore on the island of **Janitzio**, you're besieged by souvenir hawkers, whose only possible source of income apart from fishing is tourism. At a distance the island looks quaint, but as you get closer it's easy to see that this crop of dry land is almost entirely impoverished. It's worth the trip only if you're in the mood for variety in the form of a boat ride, or to see the expansive views from the top of the island, which rises steeply from the water to a massive statue of Morelos at the summit. Up the single steep street, between the stalls selling pottery and crude woodcarvings, a series of little restaurants display their wares out front – most have good fish and bubbling vats of *caldo de pescado* in the cooler months.

Tzintzuntzán

The remains of **TZINTZUNTZÁN** (daily 10am–5pm; US$2.80, free on Sun), ancient capital of the Tarascans, lie 15km north of Pátzcuaro on the lakeshore. The site was established around the end of the fourteenth century, when the capital was moved from Pátzcuaro, and by the time of the Conquest the Spanish estimated that there were as many as 40,000 people living here, with dominion over all of what is now Michoacán and large parts of the modern states of Jalisco and Colima. Homes and markets, as well as the palaces of the rulers, lay around the raised **ceremonial centre**, but all that can be seen today is the artificial terrace that supported the great religious buildings (*yacatas*), and the ruins, partly restored, of these temples.

Even if you do no more than pass by on the road, you can't fail to be struck by the scale of these buildings and by their elliptical design, a startling contrast to the rigid, right-angled formality adhered to by almost every other major pre-Hispanic culture in Mexico. Climb up to the terrace and you'll find five *yacatas*, of which two have been partly rebuilt. Each was originally some 15m high, tapering in steps from a broad base to a walkway along the top less than 2m wide. Devoid of ornamentation, the *yacatas* are in fact piles of flat rocks, held in by retaining walls and then faced in smooth, close-fitting volcanic stone. The terrace, which was originally approached up a broad ceremonial ramp or stairway on the side furthest from the water, affords magnificent views across the lake and the present-day village of Tzintzuntzán. Tzintzuntzán means "place of the hummingbirds"; you're unlikely to see one nowadays, but the theory is that there were plenty of them around until the Tarascans – who used the feathers to make ornaments – hunted them to the point of extinction.

Down in the **village**, which has a reputation for producing and selling some of the region's best ceramics, you'll find what's left of the enormous **Franciscan Monastery** founded around 1530 to convert the Tarascans. Much of this has been demolished, and the rest substantially rebuilt, but there remains a fine Baroque church and a huge atrium where the indigenous people would gather for sermons. Vasco de Quiroga originally intended to base his diocese here, but eventually decided that Pátzcuaro had the better location and a more constant supply of water. He did leave one unusual legacy, though: the olive trees planted around the monastery are probably the oldest in Mexico, since settlers were banned from cultivating olives in order to protect the farmers back in Spain.

To **get to Tzintzuntzán**, take a Quiroga-bound bus from Pátzcuaro's Central Camionera. Second-class **buses** between Pátzcuaro and Uruapan (every 15min each way) stop in Tzintzuntzán, from where you follow the main street (signposted "Zona Arqueológica" or with a pyramid symbol) south through town, under a bridge, and then turn right by a school after a few hundred metres to reach the site. A new road from Pátzcuaro to Uruapan, still due to open at the time of writing, will bypass the village and probably reduce the number of buses.

Ihuatzio

If Tzintzuntzán has piqued your interest, then you might also want to check out the older, pre-Tarascan ruins of **IHUATZIO** (daily 10am–5pm; US$2.70, free on Sun), located on a remote road that traverses a cow pasture. Often referred to as the "Place of the Coyote", these strategically located ruins near the shores of the Lago de Pátzcuaro, which were once used for water defence and enemy lookout, are only partitially excavated, and therefore only partially open to the public, but are worth a peek if you have the time. Ihuatzio is essentially divided into two sections: one older (900–1200 AD) thought to have been constructed by the Náhuatl, and the other constructed in 1200–1530 AD during the Tarascan occupation. What can be visited are the two **squared-off pyramids**, which were once considered a sort of Plaza de Armas. Buses leave regularly from the Plaza Bocanegra in Pátzcuaro; expect to pay US$0.50 for the twenty-minute ride. You'll be dropped at the end of a cobblestone road and will have to walk 2km to the site's entrance.

Santa Clara del Cobre

Approximately 32km south of Pátzcuaro, via a serpentine country road, lies **Santa Clara del Cobre**, long celebrated for the **copper crafts** on which it continues to thrive. There are no fewer than 200 family-run studios (*talleres*) and shops, many of which line the quaint town's arcades and side streets selling everything from hammered sinks to sparkling *carnitas* caldrons.

Much more of the metal is on display at the town's **Museo del Cobre**, Morelos 263 at Pino Suarez (Tues–Sat 10am–3pm & 5–7pm, Sun 10am–4pm; US$0.20), which exhibits a small but impressive collection of decorative and utilitarian copper crafts. Sadly, only a handful of these intricate old designs are still being incorporated into the production of modern copper crafts. An annual **Copper Fair**, combined with the **Fiesta de la Virgen del Sagrario**, is held in Santa Clara del Cobre from August 9 to 17. Festivities include exhibits and sales of hand-worked copper, music and dance.

While the town is a quick day-trip from Pátzcuaro, you may be moved to spend the night, if not to shop, then to enjoy the clear vistas and mountain air. *Hotel Oasis* (☎434/343-0040; ❹) is serviceable and centrally located on the main plaza. Be sure to ask for a room with mountain views. For a more rustic experience, inquire in Pátzcuaro about **cabins** for rent near Santa Clara del Cobre at *Cabañas Rústicas de Zirahuen*, Calle Obregón 19 (☎434/342-0280; ❹). Restaurant *El Portal*, Portal Matamoros 18, overlooks the main plaza and serves good comidas corridas (US$3) and hamburgers (US$0.80). Driving time to Santa Clara del Cobre from Pátzcuaro is about twenty minutes (follow signs for Opopeo), taxis cost US$10, and buses (Autotransportes Galeana) leave the central station in Pátzcuaro every thirty minutes throughout the day, charging US$1 for the forty-minute trip.

Quiroga

Thanks to its position at the junction of the roads from Pátzcuaro and Morelia to Guadalajara, **QUIROGA**, 10km beyond Tzintzuntzán from Pátzcuaro, is another village packed with craft markets, but the only genuinely local products seem to be painted wooden objects and furniture. Really it's no more than a stopover, but if you find yourself waiting here, do take time to wander down to the **market**, which spreads on side streets in all directions from the main plaza. There's a regular bus service between Quiroga and Pátzcuaro, and if you're coming **direct from Guadalajara** to Pátzcuaro, this is the most straightforward route (don't miss the views over the lake from the north, shortly before you reach Quiroga). Logically, this would also be the quickest way of doing the journey in reverse, **from Pátzcuaro to Guadalajara**, but things aren't always that simple: there's no guarantee that you're going to be able to get onto one of the fast buses along the main road – most pass through Quiroga full, without stopping. So you may be forced to go from Quiroga to Morelia or back to Pátzcuaro, and take a bus to Guadalajara from there – that way you're guaranteed that the bus will at least stop.

Morelia

The state capital, **MORELIA**, is in many ways unrepresentative of Michoacán. It looks Spanish and, despite a large indigenous population, it feels Spanish – with its broad streets lined with seventeenth-century mansions and outdoor cafés sheltered by arcaded plazas, you might easily be in Salamanca or Valladolid. Indeed, Valladolid was the city's name until 1828, when it was changed to honour local-born Independence hero José María Morelos.

Morelia has always been a city of Spaniards and was one of the first they founded after the Conquest. It was two Franciscan friars, Juan de San Miguel and Antonio de Lisboa, who settled here among the native inhabitants in 1530 and first laid claim to the city. Ten years later, they were visited by the first

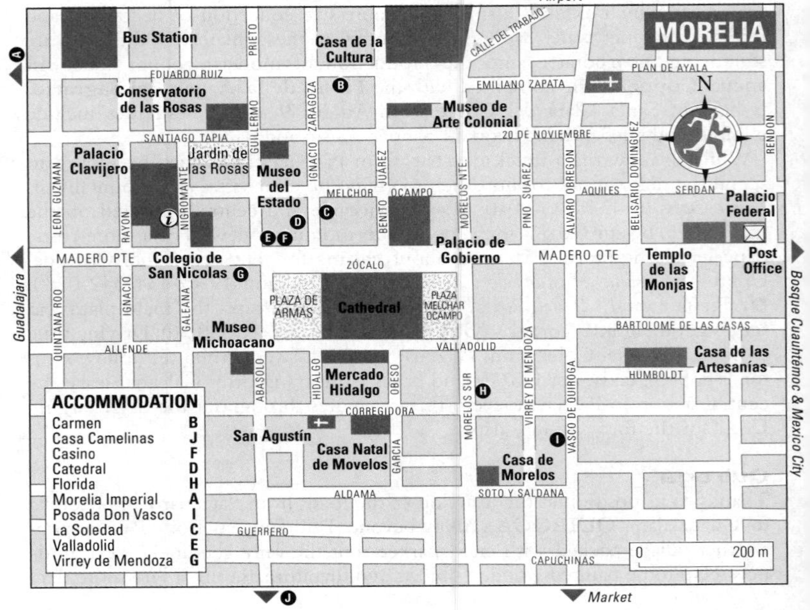

Viceroy of New Spain, Antonio de Mendóza, who was so taken by the site that he ordered a town to be built, naming it after his birthplace and sending fifty Spanish families to settle it. From the beginning, there was fierce rivalry between the colonists and the older culture's town of Pátzcuaro. During the lifetime of Vasco de Quiroga, Pátzcuaro had the upper hand, but later the bishopric was moved here, a university founded, and by the end of the sixteenth century there was no doubt that Valladolid was predominant.

There are specific things to look for and to visit in present-day Morelia, but the city as a whole outweighs them: it's been declared a "national monument", which allows no new construction that doesn't match perfectly with the old, such that it preserves a remarkable unity of style. Nearly everything is built of the same faintly pinkish-grey stone (trachyte), which, being soft, is not only easily carved and embellished but weathers quickly, giving even relatively recent constructions a battered, ancient look.

Arrival, information and accommodation

Morelia's Central Camionera is one of the few **bus** stations in Mexico to remain within walking distance of the city centre; the Plaza de Armas lies just four or five blocks southeast. The train service to Morelia no longer operates.

Between the bus station and the centre, the **tourist office**, located in the Palacio Clavijero, at Nigromante 79, just off Madero Poniente (Mon–Fri 9am–7pm, Sat 9am–6pm, Sun 9am–3pm; ⓣ443/312-8081, or toll-free from out of state ⓣ01-800/450-2300), has a few maps, leaflets, information about exhibitions, festivals and films, and the staff are friendly and mostly helpful. Plenty of **local buses** ply up and down Madero, though getting around town is easy enough without them.

Accommodation

Though there are plenty of inexpensive hotels scattered around the **bus station**, it's worth splashing out a little more to stay closer to the centre, where you have the choice of some wonderful fading, colonial hotels.

Carmen Eduardo Ruíz 63 ⓣ443/312-1725, ⓕ314-1797. Friendly budget hotel on a pretty square, with clean rooms, some with bathroom, some without, and TV. ❹

Casa Camelinas Jacarandas 172 ⓣ443/324-5194, ⓦwww.cimarron.net/mexico/camelinas.html. Friendly B&B a mile from the centre (a short taxi or bus ride away – take the orange "combi" bus #3 from in front of the cathedral), with light, spacious rooms, each with private bath and decorated with work by local artisans. Be sure to call before your arrival, as it's not near much. ❻

Casino Portal Hidalgo 229, on the Plaza de Armas ⓣ443/313-1328, ⓦwww.hotelcasino.com.mx. All rooms with carpet, TV and hot water, set around a covered courtyard. ❼

Catedral Ignacio Zaragoza 37 ⓣ443/313-0783, ⓔhotel_catedral@infoset.net.mx. Rooms around a restaurant in another covered colonial courtyard, although here you certainly pay for the atmosphere. Continental breakfast included. ❻

Florida Morelos Sur 161, southeast of the Plaza de Armas ⓣ443/312-1819. Comfortable and tidy rooms, all rooms with TV and phone, some newly renovated. ❻

Morelia Imperial Guadalupe Victoria 245 ⓣ443/313-2300, ⓕ317-0171. The broad colonial front conceals a modernized interior: all rooms have phone and TV. Popular with Mexican business people. ❺

Posada Don Vasco Vasco de Quiroga 232 ⓣ443/312-1484, ⓔposada_don_vasco@hotmail.com. Reasonably priced colonial-style hotel. Some rooms are nicer than others, so have a look around. ❹

La Soledad Ignacio Zaragoza 90, just off the Plaza de Armas ⓣ443/312-1888, ⓦwww.hsoledad.com. Spectacular colonial building that is the city's oldest running inn, with breezy rooms set around a beautiful open courtyard (❽), or lower-priced ones in the less attractive back courtyard (❻).

Valladolid Portal Hidalgo 245, on the Plaza de Armas ⓣ443/312-0027, ⓕ312-4663. Great position under the colonial arches, though rooms are dark and in need of facelifts. ❻

Virrey de Mendoza Madero Pte 310 ⓣ443/312-0633, ⓦwww.hotelvirrey.com. Fantastic colonial grandeur: even if you can't afford to stay it's worth dropping by to take a look. The rooms are not as impressive as the lobby and there is little ventilation, but a lovely spot just the same for its history, majestic public spaces and fine service. ❾

The Town

Avenida Francisco Madero, which runs along the north side of Plaza de Armas and the cathedral, is very much the main street of Morelia, with most of the important public buildings and major shops strung out along it. Everything you're likely to want to see is within easy walking distance of the Plaza de Armas.

Around the Cathedral

At the heart of the city, Morelia's massive **Cathedral** boasts two soaring towers that are said to be the tallest in Mexico. Begun in 1640 in the relatively plain Herrerian style, the towers and dome were not completed for some hundred years, by which time the Baroque had arrived with a vengeance; nevertheless, component parts harmonize remarkably, and for all the cathedral's size and richness of decoration, perfect proportions prevent it from becoming overpowering. The interior, refitted towards the end of the nineteenth century, after most of its silver ornamentation had been removed to pay for the wars, is simple and preserves, in the choir and sacristy, a few early colonial religious paintings.

Flanking the cathedral, the **Plaza de Armas** (or de los Martíres) is the place to sit around in the cafés under its elegant arcaded *portales*, with a coffee and a morning paper (you can buy the *Mexico City News* from the stands here), revelling in the city's leisurely pace. On the southwestern edge of the plaza, at the corner of Allende and Abasolo, the **Museo Michoacáno** (Tues–Sat 9am–7pm, Sun 9am–2pm; US$3, free on Sun) occupies a palatial eighteenth-century mansion. Emperor Maximilian lodged here on his visits to Morelia, and it now houses a collection reflecting the state's diversity and rich history: the rooms devoted to archeology are, of course, dominated by the **Tarascan culture**, including pottery and small sculptures from Tzintzuntzán, but also display much earlier objects, notably some obsidian figurines. Out in the patio are two magnificent old carriages, while upstairs the colonial epoch is represented in a large group of religious paintings and sculptures and a collection of old books and manuscripts.

A smaller square, the **Plaza Melchor Ocampo**, flanks the cathedral on the other side. Facing it, the **Palacio de Gobierno** was formerly a seminary – Independence hero Morelos and his nemesis Agustín Iturbide studied here, as did Ocampo, a nineteenth-century liberal supporter of Benito Juárez. It's of interest now for the **murals** adorning the stairway and upper level of the patio: practically the whole of Mexican history, and each of its heroes, is depicted. A little further down Madero are several **banks** that are among the most remarkable examples of active conservation you'll see anywhere: old mansions that have been refurbished in traditional style, and somehow manage to combine reasonably efficient operation with an ambience that is wholly in keeping with the setting.

West and north of the plaza

One block west of the Plaza de Armas, the **Colegio de San Nicolas** is part of the University of Morelia. Founded at Pátzcuaro in 1540 by Vasco de

Quiroga, and moved here in 1580, the college is the second oldest in Mexico and hence in all the Americas – it now houses administrative offices and various technical faculties. To the side, across Nigromante, is the public library in what was originally the Jesuit church of **La Compañía**, while next to this is the beautiful **Palacio Clavijero**, converted into government offices. At the bottom of Nigromante, on another charming little plaza, you'll come across the Baroque church of **Santa Rosa** and, beside it, the **Conservatorio de las Rosas**, a music academy founded in the eighteenth century. From time to time it hosts concerts of classical music – the tourist office should have details.

Also here, at the corner of Santiago Tapia and Guillermo Prieto, is the **Museo del Estado** (Mon–Fri 9am–2pm & 4–8pm, Sat & Sun 9am–2pm & 4–7pm; free). Inside, the complete furniture and fittings of a traditional *farmacia* have been reconstructed, after which you move, somewhat incongruously, to the prehistory and archeology collections. This is mostly minor stuff, though there's some fine, unusual Tarascan jewellery, including gold and turquoise pieces, and necklaces strung with tiny crystal skulls. Upstairs, there's one room of colonial history and various ethnological exhibits illustrating traditional local dress and lifestyles.

East of here, or north from the Plaza de Armas on Juárez, is the **Museo de Arte Colonial** (Tues–Fri 10am–2pm & 5–8pm, Sat & Sun 10am–2pm & 4.30–7pm; free), lying adjacent to the Plaza de Carmen. Its collection of colonial art is almost entirely regional, and not of great interest. Of greater interest on the north side of the plaza, entered from Morelos, the beautiful old Convento del Carmen now houses the **Casa de la Cultura** (open all day, but museum and most exhibits Mon–Fri 9am–6pm, Sat & Sun 10am–6pm; free). It's an enormous complex, worth exploring in its own right, with a theatre, café, space for temporary exhibitions and classes, and the fascinating little mask museum, **Museo de la Máscara** (Mon–Fri 10am–2pm & 4–8pm, Sat & Sun 10am–6pm; free), scattered around the former monastic buildings. On Sunday evenings at 6pm, there's usually a performance of music, dance or theatre in the front patio.

South and east of the plaza

Six blocks south of the Casa de la Cultura, or two blocks south of Plaza Melchor Ocampo, on Morelos Sur, the **Museo Casa Morelos** (daily 9am–7pm; US$3, free Sun) is the relatively modest eighteenth-century house in which Independence hero José María Morelos y Pavón lived from 1801 (see box overleaf). It's now a museum devoted to his life and the War of Independence. Nearby, at the corner of Corregidora (the continuation of Alzate) and García Obeso, you can see the house where the hero was born, the **Casa Natal de Morelos** (daily 9am–7pm; free), which now houses a library and a few desultory domestic objects. This in turn is virtually next door to the church of **San Agustín**, from where pedestrianized Hidalgo runs up one block to the Plaza de Armas, and opposite whose attractive facade is a tiny market area, the **Mercado Hidalgo**.

Walk a couple of blocks in the other direction – or take Valladolid directly from the Plaza Ocampo – to find the **Casa de las Artesanías** (Mon–Sat 10am–8pm, Sun 10am–3.30pm; free), possibly the most comprehensive collection of Michoacán's crafts anywhere, almost all of them for sale. The best and most obviously commercial items are downstairs, while on the upper floor are a series of rooms devoted to the products of particular villages, often with craftspeople demonstrating their techniques (these are staffed by villagers and hence not always open), and a collection of historic items that you can't buy

José María Morelos y Pavón

A student of Hidalgo, **José María Morelos** took over the leadership of the Independence movement after its instigators had been executed in 1811. While the cry of Independence had initially been taken up by the Mexican (Creole) bourgeoisie, smarting under the trading restrictions imposed on them by Spain, it quickly became a mass popular movement. Unlike the original leaders, Morelos (a *mestizo* priest born into relative poverty) was a populist and genuine reformer; even more unlike them, he was also a political and military tactician of considerable skill, invoking the spirit of the French Revolution and calling for universal suffrage, racial equality and the break-up of the hacienda system, under which workers were tied to an agricultural system. Defeat and execution by Royalist armies under Agustín de Iturbide came in 1815 only after years of guerrilla warfare, during which Morelos had come close to taking the capital and controlling the entire country. When Independence was finally gained – by Iturbide, now changed sides and later briefly to be emperor – it was no longer a force for change, rather a reaction to the fact that by 1820 liberal reforms were sweeping Spain itself. The causes espoused by Morelos were, however, taken up to some extent by Benito Juárez and later, with a vengeance, in the Revolution – almost a hundred years after his death.

It's all housed in what used to be the monastery of **San Francisco**, whose church, facing onto the little plaza next door, can also be visited.

Finally, in the far east of the city, about fifteen minutes' walk along Madero from the Plaza de Armas, past the Baroque facade of the **Templo de las Monjas**, is an area of tree-lined walks and little parks on the edge of town, through the middle of which runs the old **aqueduct**. Built between 1785 and 1789, these serried arches brought water into the city from springs in the nearby hills. On the right is the largest of the parks, the **Bosque Cuauhtémoc**, in which there are some beautifully laid-out flower displays and, 300m along Avenida Acueducto, a small **Museum of Contemporary Art** (Tues–Sun 10am–2pm & 4–8pm; free), featuring a variety of Latin American work. To the left, Fray Antonio de San Miguel (named for the bishop who built the aqueduct) runs down to the vastly overdecorated **Santuario de Guadalupe**, where market stalls, selling above all the sticky local *dulces*, set up at weekends and during fiestas.

Eating and drinking

For a reasonably priced sit-down meal, the area around the bus station is the best bet – most of the hotels there also have **restaurants** that serve a fairly standard comida corrida. Eating a full meal in any of the cafés on the Plaza de Armas will prove expensive, but they're good for snacks or for a breakfast of coffee and *pan dulce*. In the evening you can eat outdoors at places set up along traffic-free Hidalgo (between the plaza and San Agustín) and around the Mercado Hidalgo.

Chief of Morelia's specialities are its **dulces**, sweets made of candied fruit or evaporated milk – cloyingly sweet to most non-Mexican tastes, they're very popular here. You can see a wide selection at the **Mercado de Dulces y Artesanías**, up Gomez Farias from the bus station and on the left-hand side, around the back of the Palacio Clavijero. As its name suggests, there's a repetitive selection of local sweets, and they also sell handicrafts here, but on the whole nothing of much quality. Morelians also get through a lot of *rompope* (a drink that you'll find to a lesser extent all over Mexico) – again, it's very sweet, an egg-flip concoction based on rum, milk and egg with vanilla, cinnamon or almond flavouring. Finally, as always, there are food stalls and plenty of raw ingredients in the **market**, but Morelia's big Mercado Independencia is on the whole a disappointment, certainly not as large or varied as you'd expect. On Sunday, the main market day, it perks up a little. Get there by going towards the Plaza San Francisco and then a long six or seven blocks south on Vasco de Quiroga.

Acuarius Hidalgo 75. Vegetarian restaurant – pleasant location in a courtyard off the street, but unadventurous food.

Café del Conservatorio Santiago Tapia 363. A peaceful place to enjoy local *dulces* and reasonably priced wine while being lulled by classical music, facing the pretty Jardín de las Rosas.

Café del Teatro in the Teatro Ocampo, on Ocampo and Prieto. Its lush interior makes this one of the most popular spots in town for good coffee and people-watching – try and get a table overlooking the street.

Los Comensales Zaragoza 148. Pretty courtyard setting complete with caged birds. The comida corrida is good value at US$5; a bit more for elaborate Mexican specialties, including a tasty chicken in rich, dark mole.

Copa de Oro Juárez 194B at Santiago Tapia. Simple place for fresh *jugos* and tortas.

Del Olmo Juárez 95. Sophisticated but relaxed café-bar, set around a pretty interior courtyard, with good coffee, and eggs with ham for breakfast.

Dulces Morelianas de la Calle Real Madero Oriente 440. Magnificent old-fashioned candy store with a café serving decadent coffees with drizzles of *cajeta*. The staff even sport colonial dress, and there's a microscopic Museo del Dulces in the back.

Las Mercedes Leon Guzmán 47. Upscale Tarascan and Mexican dishes in a swanky setting accented by giant rocks. Surprisingly reasonable.

Los Mirasoles Madero Poniente 549 ⓣ443/317-5777, ⓦwww.losmirasoles.com. Inventive Mexican and international cuisine in a plush contemporary setting, which includes an enchanting courtyard. Some of the dining room music choices are odd but there's an impressive wine list. Reserve ahead.

Panadería & Charcutería Trico Valladolid 8. A well-stocked deli with an upstairs café serving up delicious breakfasts. Lines form around the block for its roasted chickens.

El Rey Tacamba Madero Poniente 157, Portal Galeana, opposite the cathedral. Small, bustling restaurant favoured by townspeople for its reliably good, local food.

San Miguelito Camelinas opposite the Centro Convenciones Fracc. La Loma ⓣ443/324-2300, ⓦwww.sanmiguelito.com.mx. Superb and unpretentious Mexican dishes. Bar is a recreated bullring. Be sure to sit in the room filled with 300 effigies of St Anthony and say a prayer for a good spouse.

Super Cucina La Rosa Santiago Tapia at Prieto. Filling comidas at unbeatable prices.

El Tragadero Hidalgo 63. A good place for breakfast or an inexpensive lunch, such as tacos or the daily special.

Vegetariano Hindÿ Madero Ote 549. Good, inexpensive (but not very Indian) vegetarian salads, soups, veggie burgers and breakfasts – opens at around 9.30am.

Woolworth Mendoza 60. Excellent selection of celestial hamburgers in the superb setting of a former church.

Listings

Banks and exchange There are plenty of very grand banks with ATMs along Madero Oriente, open for exchange on weekday mornings. Casas de cambio can be found at Nigromante 132, Valladolid 22, 137-A and 150; Morelos Norte 50-B and 328-A; Aquiles Serdan 30; and 20 de Noviembre 110.

Buses There are buses to just about anywhere in the state and to most other conceivable destinations elsewhere in the country: very frequently to Guadalajara, Pátzcuaro, Uruapan and Mexico City; regularly north to Salamanca, for Guanajuato and Querétaro. The shortest route to Mexico City, via Zitcuaro and Toluca, is very beautiful – passing through the Mil Cumbres (Thousand Peaks) – but mountainous and slow. Some buses go round by the faster roads to the north. If only for the scenery, you should try to take the former route – these mountains are the playground of Mexico City's middle classes, and there are a couple of places of interest along the way.

Entertainment International films are shown at the Museo Regional Michoacáno, the Casa Natal de Morelos and the Casa de la Cultura, several

Fiestas

Both Jalisco and Michoacán preserve strong native traditions and are particularly rich in fiestas: the list below is by no means exhaustive, and local tourist offices will have further details.

JANUARY

1 AÑO NUEVO (New Year's Day). In Uruapan and Pátzcuaro the new year is celebrated with the dance of the Viejitos, or elders.

2 AÑO NUEVO PURÉPECHO (Purépecho New Year). Native celebrations in a host of Purépechan communities (Mich).

6 DÍA DE LOS SANTOS REYES (Twelfth Night). Many small ceremonies: **Los Reyes** (Michoacán), south of Zamora and west of Uruapan, has dancing and a procession of the Magi; **Cajititlán** (Jal), on a tiny lake near Guadalajara, also has traditional dances.

8 San Juan de las Colchas (Mich) commemorates the eruption of Paricutín with a dance contest and traditional dress. Many of the homeless villagers moved to this village near Uruapan.

15 In **La Piedad** (Mich), traditional dances and a major procession for local saint's day.

20 DÍA DE SAN SEBASTIAN. **Tuxpan** (Jal), a beautiful village between Ciudad Guzmán and Colima, has traditional dances including the unique Danza de los Chayacates. Start of the mass pilgrimages to **San Juan de Los Lagos** (Jal), which culminate on February 2.

All month long in **Zitácuaro** region, you'll find celebrations of the Monarch Butterfly Festival.

FEBRUARY

1 In **Tzintzuntzán** (Mich), the start of a week-long fiesta founded in the sixteenth century by Vasco de Quiroga.

2 Celebrated in **Lagos de Moreno** (Jal) with pilgrimages, but much more so in nearby **San Juan de Los Lagos** (Jal), where it's one of the largest such celebrations in Mexico.

CARNIVAL (the week before Lent, variable Feb–March) is particularly good in **Zinapecuaro** (Mich), near Morelia, with pretend bulls chasing people through the streets; **Copandaro** (Mich), also near Morelia on the shores of Lago Cuitzeo, has similar fake bullfights, rodeos and marathon dances; and in **Charapan** (Mich), near Uruapan, you can see the dance of Los Viejitos. All these are best on Carnival Tuesday.

MARCH

17–21 FESTIVAL INTERNACIONAL DE GUITARRA (International Guitar Festival). In **Morelia**, this is a fantastic gathering of musicians from around the world.

APRIL

PALM SUNDAY is the culmination of a week's celebration in **Uruapan** (Mich) – the *indígenas* collect palms from the hills and make ornaments from the leaves, sold here in a big market.

HOLY WEEK (Semana Santa) is observed everywhere. In **Copandaro** (Mich), they celebrate the whole of the week, especially on the Thursday with the ceremony of Washing the Apostles' Feet, and Good Friday when they act out more scenes from Christ's Passion. These Passion plays are quite common, for example at **Tzintzuntzán** (Mich) and the hamlet of Maya near **Lagos de Moreno** (Jal). In **Ciudad Hidalgo** (Mich), there's a huge procession.

MAY

CORPUS CHRISTI (variable: the Thurs after Trinity) is celebrated in the neighbouring villages of **Cheran** and **Paracho**, in Michoacán.

3 DÍA DE LA SANTA CRUZ. Native dances in **Ciudad Hidalgo** (Mich) and **Angangueo** (Mich), *mariachis*– and tequila – in **Tequila** (Jal).

Last Sunday DÍA DEL SEÑOR DE LA MISERICORDIA. A fiesta in honour of this highly venerated image in **Tuxpan** (Jal) – includes native dances.

Dates vary in May EXPO FERIA MICHOACÁN (Michoacán Expo Fair). In **Morelia**, celebrating the arts and industry of the region.

JUNE

24 DÍA DE SAN JUAN. **Purepero** (Mich), between Uruapan and La Piedad, starts a week-long fiesta.

29 DÍA DE SAN PEDRO. In **Tlaquepaque** (Jal) a highly animated festival with *mariachi*, dancing and processions.

JULY

First Sunday Torch-lit religious processions in **Quiroga** (Mich).

22 DÍA DE MARÍA MAGDALENA. Fiesta in **Uruapan** (Mich), featuring processions of animals.

26 Culmination of a week-long feria in **Acatlán de Juárez** (Jal), south of Guadalajara: regional dress, dances and fireworks.

28 FIESTAS DEL SEÑOR DEL CALVARIO in **Lagos de Moreno** (Jal) continue until August 6.

AUGUST

4–7 FERIA DEL MUEBLE RÚSTICO Y TEXTIL BORDADO (Rustic Furniture and Embroidered Textile Fair). In **Pichataro** near Uruapan.

8 Ancient Pre-Columbian fiesta in **Paracho** (Mich), also coincides with the National Guitar Fair (Aug 2–10).

9–17 FERIA NACIONAL DEL COBRE (National Copper Fair). In **Santa Clara del Cobre** (Mich) near Pátzcuaro, includes a copper-hammering competition and coincides with the DÍA DE LA ASUNCIÓN (Assumption) on the **15th**.

SEPTEMBER

8–12 A festival in **San Juan de las Colchas** (Mich), with its climax on the 14th.

30 In **Morelia** (Mich), celebrations for the birthday of Morelos.

OCTOBER

Guadalajara's FIESTAS DE OCTUBRE run throughout the month.

4 DÍA DE SAN FRANCISCO. Saint's day celebrations culminate in a week of pilgrimages to **Talpa** (Jal), near Guadalajara, where the faithful come bearing flowers and candles. Celebrated, too, in **Jiquilpan** (Mich), between Zamora and Lake Chapala, and in **Uruapan** (Mich), where it's one of the year's biggest.

12 DÍA DE LA RAZA commemorates Columbus's discovery of America. Feria in **Uruapan** (Mich) and, in **Guadalajara**, the highlight of the fiestas is an enormous pilgrimage to the Virgin of Zapopan.

16 Native dances and an all-night procession honour a much-revered image of Christ in **Cuitzeo** (Mich), on Lago Cuitzeo north of Morelia.

17–18 FESTIVAL DE LA RAZA PURÉPECHA (Festival of the Purépecha People). In **Zacán** in the Purépechan plateau.

Fiestas *Continued*

21 DÍA DE SAN JOSÉ. In **Ciudad Guzmán** (Jal), the climax of a lively feria that lasts from the 12th to the 23rd.

22 **Apatzingan** (Mich), in beautiful mountain country south of Uruapan, has a fiesta that includes dance competitions and rodeos, on the rather flimsy excuse of the anniversary of the 1814 Constitution.

24–26 The FESTIVAL DE COROS Y DANZAS in **Uruapan** (Mich) sees a competition between Tarascan choirs and dance groups.

Last Sunday DÍA DE CRISTO REY. An ancient series of dances in honour of Christ the King in **Contepec** (Mich), south of Querétaro, east of Morelia. Also processions in regional costume.

NOVEMBER

2 DÍA DE LOS MUERTOS (All Souls' Day). The famous Day of the Dead is celebrated everywhere, but the rites in **Pátzcuaro** (Mich) and on the island of **Janitzio** are the best-known in Mexico. Highly picturesque, too, in **Zitácuaro** (Mich).

15–30 THE ARRIVAL OF THE MONARCH BUTTERFLY. The winged migration starts to arrive in the east of **Michoacán**.

17–24 FESTIVAL INTERNACIONAL DE MÚSICA (International Music Festival). In **Morelia**, with concerts, recitals, operas and conferences.

DECEMBER

8 DÍA DE LA INMACULADA CONCEPCIÓN. In **San Juan de Los Lagos** (Jal), the high point of a massive feria that attracts thousands of pilgrims and boasts an enormous crafts market. **Sayula** (Jal), between Guadalajara and Ciudad Guzmán, also has impressive displays of native dance. In Tequila (Jal), not surprisingly, the celebrations are more earthy, with rodeos, cockfights and fireworks. On the same day Pátzcuaro (Mich) celebrates La Señora de la Salud, an event attended by many Tarascan pilgrims and the scene of Tarascan dances including Los Viejitos.

12 DÍA DE LA VIRGEN DE GUADALUPE. Large fiesta in **Jiquilpan** (Mich) with fireworks and a torch-lit procession in which locals dress in the Mexican colours, green, white and red. **Tapalpa** (Jal) attracts pilgrims from a wide area, with regional dances in front of the church.

23 In **Aranza** (Mich), a tiny village near Paracho, they perform pastoral plays on Christmas Eve. In **Tuxpan** (Jal), there are traditional dances and a large religious procession.

times a week. There are also regular organ recitals in the cathedral (check with the tourist information office), and on Sundays band concerts in the zócalo.

Internet access *Chat Room*, Nigromante 132 (US$1.80 per hr) has a cable connection, coffee bar and is open until 10pm daily; *El Jardín Internet Café*, Guillermo Prieto 157 (US$1.50 per hr) is a big university hang-out.

Post office Madero Oriente 369 (Mon–Fri 9am–5pm).

Telephones Telmex, in the post office, has phone and fax offices (Mon–Fri 9am–8pm). Computel also offers long-distance phone and fax from its offices at Madero Oriente 157 (daily 7am–10pm); other *casetas* are at Madero Oriente 398 opposite the post office, Zaragoza 101 at Ocampo and Juárez 39.

The Monarch Butterfly Sanctuary

From November to mid-April, more than 100 million monarch butterflies migrate from the US and Canada to the lush mountains of Michoacán in order to reproduce. It's an amazing sight: in the cool of the morning, they coat the trees, turning the entire landscape a rich, velvety orange, while later in the day the increased humidity forces them to the ground, where they form a thick carpet of blazing colour. Although the butterflies sometimes come as far down as the highway, the best place to see them is in the **butterfly sanctuary** (mid-Nov to mid-March, daily 9am–5pm; US$2, US$3 to park; ⓣ01-800/450-2300, ⓦwww.turismomichoacan.gob.mx) in the mountains above the small village of **El Rosario**, around 120km from Morelia. It's best to go early in the morning (on weekdays preferably to avoid the crowds), when the butterflies are just waking up and before they fly off into the surrounding woodlands. Following a study showing that 44 percent of the original habitat had been destroyed by logging since 1971, a rate that would consume the forest within fifty years, in 2000 the Mexican government more than tripled the size of the reserve. At the same time, the government used the expansion to assert that conservation was not contrary to the country's economic and social development. **Guides**, whose services are included in the entry fee, show you around the sanctuary and give a short explanation (some in English) of the butterflies' lifecycle and breeding habits. Other guides wait in nearby Angangueo (see below), but charge upwards of US$5 just to take you up to the sanctuary, a short climb that you can easily do by yourself.

To get there by public transport, take a bus from Morelia (20 daily; 2hr 30min), Toluca (5–6 per hour; 1hr 40min) or Mexico City (5–6 per hour; 3hr) to Zitácuaro, and from there another bus to the village of Ocampo (every 15min; 30min); coming from Morelia, you could change buses at San Felípe where the road turns off for Ocampo. From Ocampo, there are buses to the sanctuary itself (US$2.50); alternatively there are tours from Zitácuaro, and in season direct buses daily: Autobuses de Occidente, Zinacantepec, and Via 2000. For further **information**, ask at the tourist office in Morelia or the information booth on the highway outside Zitácuaro, towards Toluca.

Accommodation in El Rosario itself is fairly limited; by far the best place to stay is the mining town of **Angangueo** (whose name in the Tarascan means "Entrance to the Cave"), jammed into the narrow valley just below El Rosario, 10km beyond Ocampo (buses from Zitácuaro continue to Angangueo). Here you'll find the comfortable and very friendly *Hotel Don Bruno*, at Morelos 92 on the way into the village (ⓣ/ⓕ715/156-0026; ❼), which has its own restaurant. Closer to the sanctuary in Zitácuaro, the *Hotel Rancho Cayetano*, Carretera a Huetamo km 2.3, Zitácuaro (ⓣ715/153-1926, ⓦwww.ranchosancayetano.com; ❾), has a pool and good restaurant set in its private woodland and is an easy trek to see the butterflies.

The road up to the sanctuary, Calle Matamoros, branches off from Calle Morelos where it becomes Calle Nacional. There are no buses up from Angangueo, but regular trucks do the run; alternatively, you could walk – it's a scenic hike of one or two hours, but uphill all the way and so a better bet for the return journey. From Ocampo (where there are also hotels), four buses a day do the run up to El Rosario, as well as regular colectivos until about 5pm. If you're coming by car, you can drive straight up the hill on the new road that leads directly to the sanctuary car park.

Travel details

Buses

What follows is a minimum of routes covering the major stops only – it should be assumed that these buses also call at the towns en route.

In general the fastest and most efficient operators are Omnibus de Mexico and Tres Estrellas de Oro, though there's little to choose between the first-class companies. Flecha Amarilla covers many of the local runs and is fairly reliable; Estrella Blanca is better but less frequent.

Guadalajara (Camionera Nueva) to: Aguascalientes (buildings 2, 3, 6 & 7; 2–3 hourly; 4hr); Colima (building 2; 2–3 hourly; 3hr); Guanajuato (buildings 1, 2 & 6; 11 daily; 4hr); Lagos de Moreno (building 5; half-hourly); Manzanillo (building 2; 2 hourly; 6hr); Mazatlán (buildings 3 & 4; 2 hourly; 8hr); Mexico City (buildings 1, 2 & 3; 4 hourly; 7–9hr); Morelia (building 2; 2–3 hourly; 3–5hr); Pátzcuaro (building 2; 2 daily; 6hr); Puerto Vallarta (buildings 2, 3 & 4; 27 daily; 6hr); Querétaro (building 5; half-hourly; 5hr); San Luis Potosí (building 5; 25 daily; 5hr); Tepic (buildings 1, 2, 3, 4 & 6; 10 hourly; 4hr); Tijuana (building 4; 11 daily; 32hr); Uruapan (building 2; 18 daily; 5hr).

Guadalajara (Camionera Vieja) to: Ajijic (hourly; 1hr); Chapala (half-hourly; 50min); Jocotepec (half-hourly; 1hr); Tapalpa (hourly; 3hr 15min); Tequila (every 20min; 1hr 45min).

Morelia to: Aguascalientes (4 daily; 7hr); Guadalajara (hourly; 3–5hr); Guanajuato (hourly; 3hr 30min); León (every 20min; 4hr); Mexico City (at least half-hourly; 4hr); Pátzcuaro (every 10min; 1hr); Querétaro (every 40min; 4hr); Toluca (hourly; 4hr); Zitácuaro (20 daily; 3hr).

Pátzcuaro to: Guadalajara (2 daily; 6hr); Mexico City (hourly; 5hr); Morelia (every 15min; 1hr); Quiroga (every 15min; 30min); Uruapan (every 15min; 1hr).

Uruapan to: Guadalajara (18 daily; 5hr); Lázaro Cárdenas (every 30min; 6hr); Los Reyes (hourly; 1hr); Mexico City (half-hourly; 6hr); Morelia (every 15min; 2hr); Paracho (every 30min; 40min); Pátzcuaro (every 15min; 1hr).

Flights

Guadalajara to: Acapulco (5 daily; 3hr); Cancún (6 daily; 5hr); Ciudad Juárez (6 daily; 2hr); Dallas (3 daily; 4hr 30min); Durango (3 daily; 11hr); El Paso (1 daily; 6hr 30min); Hermosillo (7 daily; 2hr 20min); Houston (3 daily; 2hr 15min); Ixtapa (6 daily; 1hr); Kansas City (3 daily; 5hr); La Paz (1 daily; 1hr 30min); Los Angeles (3 daily; 7hr); Mancolova (1 daily; 5–6hr); Manzanillo (1 daily; 40min); Mazatlán (2 daily; 1hr 15min); Mexicali (2 daily; 2hr 30min); Miami (3 daily; 6hr); Monterrery (9 daily; 4hr); New York (1 daily; 8hr 30min); Oakland (2 daily; 7hr 15min); Oaxaca (4 daily; 4hr); Phoenix (3 daily; 7hr); Piedras Negras (2 daily; 4hr); Puebla (2 daily; 2hr); Puerto Vallarta (1 daily; 40min); Saltillo (2 daily; 4hr); San Diego (3 daily; 8hr); San Francisco (3 daily; 8hr); San José (1 daily; 9hr); San José del Cabo (1 daily; 1hr 30min); Tijuana (4 daily; 2hr 30min).

Morelia to: Chicago (4 daily; 5hr 15min); Guadalajara (1 daily; 45min); Los Angeles (4 daily; 11hr); Mexico City (5 daily; 55min); Oakland (3 daily; 13hr); San Francisco (1 daily; 6hr 15min); San José (4 daily; 9hr 15min); Tijuana (5 daily; 4hr 45min); Uruapan (1 daily; 30min); Zacatecas (6 daily; 55min).

Uruapan to: Mexico City (1 daily; 1hr 45min); Morelia (1 daily; 30min); Tijuana (1 daily; 7hr 30min).

The Bajío

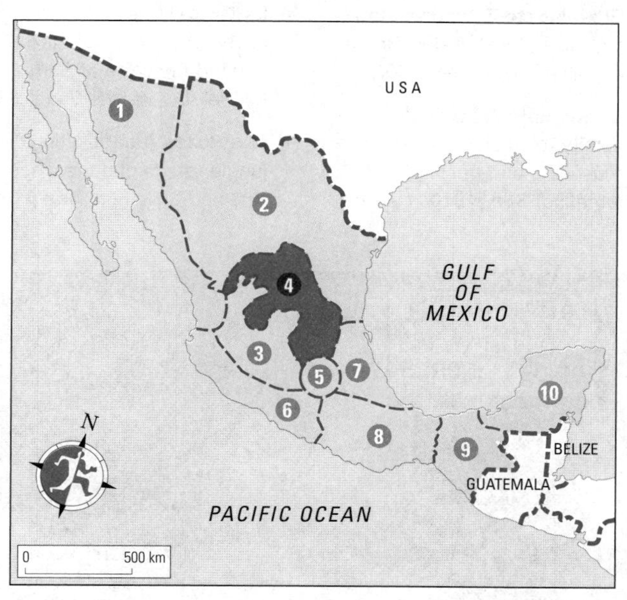
USA
1
2
GULF OF MEXICO
4
3
5
7
10
6
8
9
BELIZE
GUATEMALA
N
PACIFIC OCEAN
0 500 km

CHAPTER 4

Highlights

* **Real de Catorce** Good hotels, excellent Italian meals and desert scenery make this semi-ghost-town perfect for relaxing extended stays. See p.281
* **Zacatecas** Glorious former silver town located high up in the northern deserts and packed with great museums and buildings. See p.292
* **El Malacate** Zacatecas' top nightclub, located deep in an old silver mine. See p.302
* **Guanajuato** A fascinating university town studded with fine museums and bustling with streetlife. See p.310
* **San Miguel de Allende** Gorgeous colonial town with beautiful hotels and great food: Mexico's most appealing gringo enclave. See p.326
* **La Cucaracha** San Miguel de Allende's dim, seedy bar dripping with the spirit of Jack Kerouac and William Burroughs. See p.334
* **La Gruta** Mineral hot springs in verdant surroundings just beyond the edge of San Miguel de Allende. See p.335
* **Las Pozas** A captivating jungle village of surreal sculpture and buildings. See p.346

△ General store, Guanajuato

The Bajío

Richly fertile, rugged, and scattered with superb ancient towns, the twisting hills and beautiful valleys of the **Bajío** spread across the central highlands almost from coast to coast and as far south as the capital. This has long been the most heavily populated part of the country, providing much of the silver and grain that supported Mexico throughout the years of Spanish rule. As the colonial heartland, the legacy of Spanish architecture remains at its most impressive here, in meticulously crafted towns that – at their cores at least – have changed little over the centuries, while the surrounding country has been much the most consistently developed, both agriculturally and industrially.

Mexico's broad central plateau narrows and becomes hillier as it approaches the Valley of México. Here in the Bajío proper – the states of Guanajuato and Querétaro – are its finest colonial cities, founded amid barren land and grown rich on just one thing: silver. Before the arrival of the Spanish, this was a relatively unexploited area, a buffer zone between the more civilized heartland and the barbarian Chichimec tribes of the north. Though the Aztecs may have tapped some of its mineral wealth, they never began to exploit the area with the greed, tenacity and ruthlessness of the new colonists. After the Conquest, the mining cities grew rich, but in time they also grew restive under the heavy hand of control from Spain. The wealthy Creole (Spanish-blooded but Mexican-born) bourgeoisie were free to exploit the land and its people, but didn't control their own destinies and were forced to pay punitive taxes; lucrative government posts and high positions in the Church were reserved exclusively for Gachupines, those actually born in Spain, while the indigenous and poor *mestizos* were condemned either to landless poverty or to near-fatal labour. Unsurprisingly, then, the Bajío was fertile ground for revolutionary ideas. This land is La Cuna de la Independencia (the Cradle of Independence), where every town seems to claim a role in the break with Spain. In Querétaro the plotters held many of their early meetings, and from here they were warned that their plans had been discovered; in Dolores Hidalgo the famous grito was first voiced by Father Hidalgo, proclaiming an independent Mexico; and from here he marched on San Miguel de Allende, picking up more volunteers for his armed rabble as he continued towards a bloody confrontation in Guanajuato.

Approaching the Bajío from the north you cross several hundred kilometres of semi-desert landscape punctuated only by the occasional ranch, where fighting bulls are bred, or defunct mining towns, such as the wonderfully strange semi-ghost-town of Real de Catorce, its mines and mansions now totally deserted. Only then do you reach the colonial cities of Zacatecas and San Luis Potosí – both eponymous state capitals – that mark a radical change in

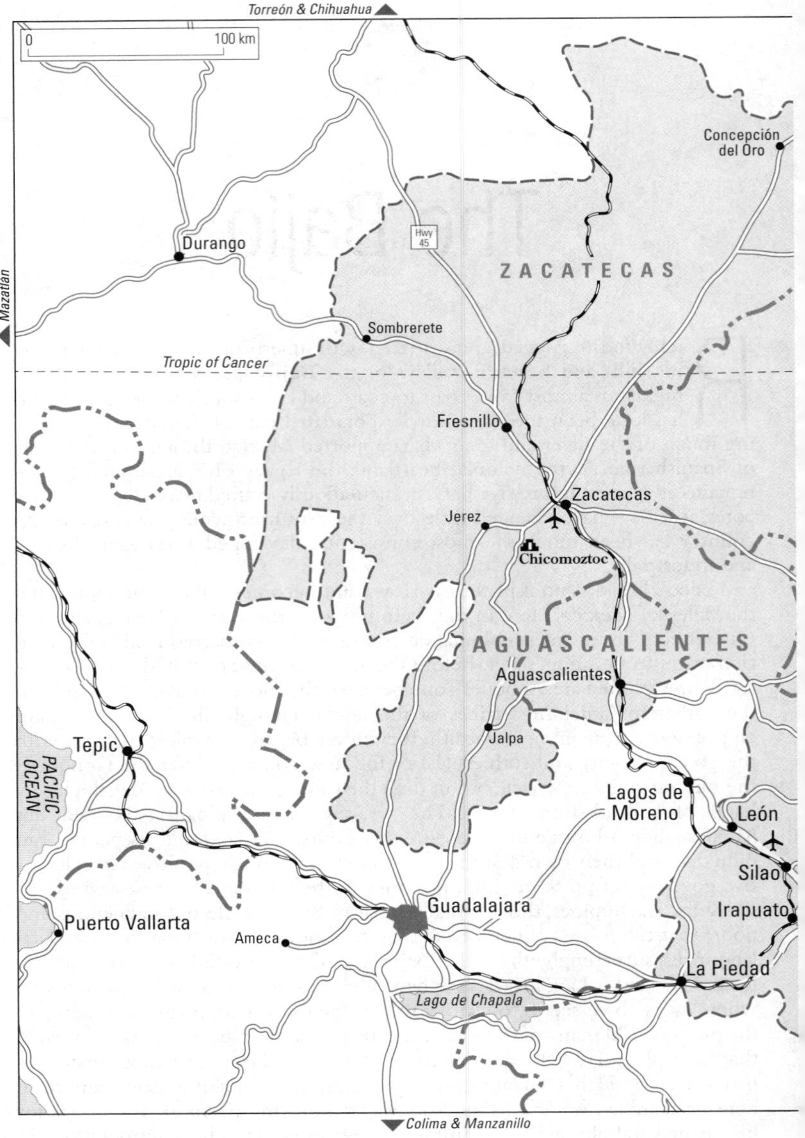

landscape and architecture. Though they're outside the Bajío proper, both are showcase examples of the region's architectural and historical heritage, sharing all the attributes of the towns further south. San Luis, a large modern metropolis, has its share of monuments, but Zacatecas is far more exciting, an oasis of culture and sophistication built in mountainous isolation on the bounty of the silver mines that riddle the landscape hereabouts. Some 300km south, beyond the modern town of **Aguascalientes**, you enter the green belt of the Bajío proper. Despite the total abandonment of its silver mines, this area continues to thrive, with centres of study, culture and tourism and thrusting modern cities benefiting from their proximity to the capital and the main transport routes.

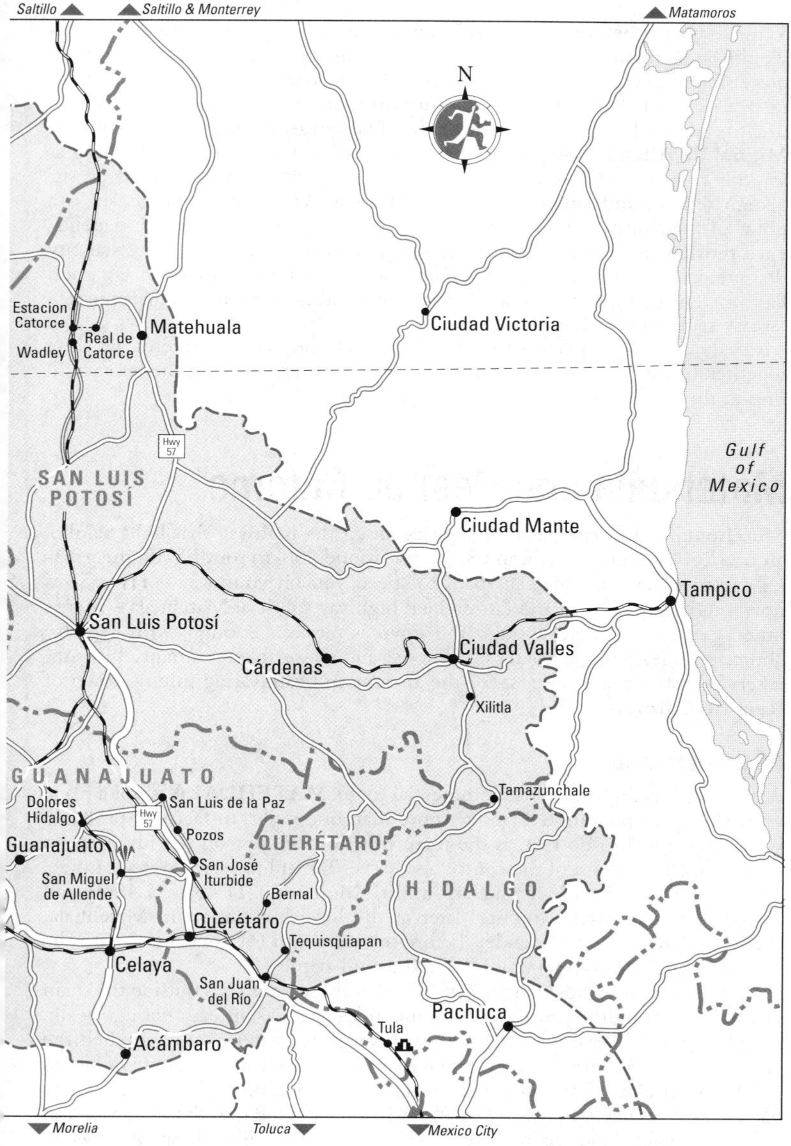

If you're heading straight for Mexico City, you'll bypass a number of places of interest, cutting through the industrial cities of **León** – famous for its leather

– and Irapuato before joining the highway past Celaya and Querétaro. This would be a mistake: crazily ranged up the sides of a ravine, **Guanajuato** is quite simply one of the country's richest and most scenic colonial towns, with one of its finest Baroque churches, a thriving student life, and, for good measure, the ghoulish Museum of Mummies. The gorgeous hillside town of **San Miguel de Allende** also has its advocates, as much for its wonderful setting as for the comforts of home, ensured by a large population of foreign artists, gringo retirees and language students. **Dolores Hidalgo**, in particular, is a point of pilgrimage for anyone with the least interest in Mexico's independence movement, as is, to a lesser extent, **Querétaro**, a large and industrial city that preserves a fine colonial quarter at its heart. Querétaro also serves as a good base for exploring the **Sierra Gorda mountains**, particularly the concrete fantasy sculptures of **Las Pozas**.

It's easy enough to **get around** the Bajío – all the towns of interest lie close together, bus services are excellent, and the **hotels** are some of the best you'll find in the entire country.

Matehuala and Real de Catorce

Matehuala is the only place of any size along the highway that links Saltillo, around 260km to the north, and San Luis, around 200km south. With the gradual improvement in Mexican roads to speed you on your way – Hwy-57 is now a relatively smooth and fast divided highway south of Matehuala – there's little need to stop here, though the town is pleasant enough, with a pretty church on a leafy plaza, several small hotels and reasonable restaurants. In truth, it serves best as a staging post for the ancient and captivating mining town of **Real de Catorce**.

Matehuala

A typically bustling, northern commercial town, **MATEHUALA** is not a place you're likely to be tempted to stay more than one night. In fact you probably won't even need to do that, as the main **bus station**, just off the highway on 5 de Mayo, 2km south of the centre, also serves Tamaulipas services to Catorce. These leave at 5.45am, 7.45am, 9.45am (Fri–Mon only), 11.45am, 1.45pm and 5.45pm and call fifteen minutes later at the local bus station in Matehuala, corner of Guerrero and Mendez, before the steep run (of 1hr 45min) into the mountains (US$3.90 one-way, US$7.80 round-trip).

If you do stay over, you can pick up "Centro" buses and taxis outside the main bus station, though if you don't have much luggage it's an easy enough walk, straight up 5 de Mayo and then left on Insurgentes when you've reached the centre – you can't miss the grey concrete bulk of the church a couple of blocks off the main plaza. The three main **hotels** are all within a block of the main plaza: *Hotel Alamo*, Guerrero 116 (Ⓣ488/882-0017; ❹), is the cheapest and quite acceptable, though an extra US$2 per person is well spent at *Hotel Matehuala*, at the corner of Bustamante and Hidalgo, a block north of the plaza (Ⓣ488/882-0680; ❺), where rooms surround a massive columned courtyard. Between the two, the new *Hotel de Valle*, Morelos 621 (Ⓣ488/882-3770; ❺), offers spacious, clean rooms if astonishingly ugly decor. There are several pricier motel-style places out on the main road. Local **restaurants** include: the *Fontella*, close to the *Hotel Matehuala*, at Morelos 618, which does excellent comida corrida for under US$5; and the *Santa Fe*, Morelos 709, on the plaza, which is strong on seafood. Food at the main bus station is also surprisingly good. There's also an ATM next to the bus station, which is a good place to stock up on cash for Real de Catorce, where many establishments don't accept credit cards. Be sure not to miss the Sevillanas candy store (also located next to the bus station), where you'll find a huge selection of Mexico's best and most beloved sweets, such as *Glorias*, or caramels made with goat's milk. On either side of this industrial town there are countless roadside stands selling rattlesnake skins for medicinal purposes.

Real de Catorce and around

REAL DE CATORCE (or "Villa Real de Nuestra Señora de la Concepción de Guadalupe de los Alamos de los Catorce", to give it its full title), west of Matehuala, is quite an extraordinary place. Its population of some 40,000 at the peak of its silver production early in the twentieth century – the hills around were reckoned to be the second-richest source of precious metals in Mexico, after Guanajuato – declined to virtually zero by the middle of the twentieth century, and mining operations ceased entirely in 1905. A few hundred inhabitants now hang on in an enclave at the centre, surrounded by derelict, roofless mansions and, further out, crumbling foundations and the odd segment of wall. Probably even before they were known to contain silver, the mountains around here were a rich source of **peyote**. Even now groups of Huichol Indians make the month-long annual pilgrimage on foot from their homelands in and around northeastern Nayarit to gather the precious hallucinogenic cactus, which they regard as essential food for the soul. Peyote also attracts a number of New Age tourists to Catorce, some of whom have moved in semi-permanently. The foreign contingent coexists amiably with locals who survive either digging for silver and hoping that the old veins can be reopened, or trusting in brighter prospects from tourism, which is now gathering pace. Every year a new restaurant or hotel opens up, catering as much to Mexican tourists as curious backpackers from further afield. The town even made its Hollywood debut as the picturesque setting for the decidedly mediocre Julia Roberts and Brad Pitt star-vehicle *The Mexican*.

Real de Catorce is built in a high mountain valley that you approach by road through the 2.3-kilometre-long Ogarrio tunnel (named after the founder's home town in Spain), which is only broad enough for one vehicle at a time. The bigger buses can't get through, so you'll probably have to change buses at the tunnel entrance. As you drive through, the odd mineshaft leads off into the mountain to either side – by one there's a little shrine to miners who died at work where a lone candle seems always to be burning. In the town, the austere, shuttered stone buildings blend with the bare rocky crags that enclose them. At 2700m the air is cool and clean, but you can't get away from the spirit of desolation that hangs over it all. The occasional pick up shoulders its way through the narrow cobbled streets, but most of the traffic is horses and donkeys. There's not much in the way of sights to visit – the big Baroque **church**, the **Museo Parroquial** and the **Panteón** – but simply wandering around, kicking up the dust and climbing up into the hills are big and worthwhile pastimes here. Lovers of high kitsch will also be pleased to find whole rows of stalls selling tacky icons and religious paraphernalia.

More ambitious explorers have the surrounding desert hill country virtually to themselves, and those looking for a destination can **hike** downhill through abandoned mine workings to the railway town of Estación Catorce, and its near neighbour Wadley, noted for its desert treats.

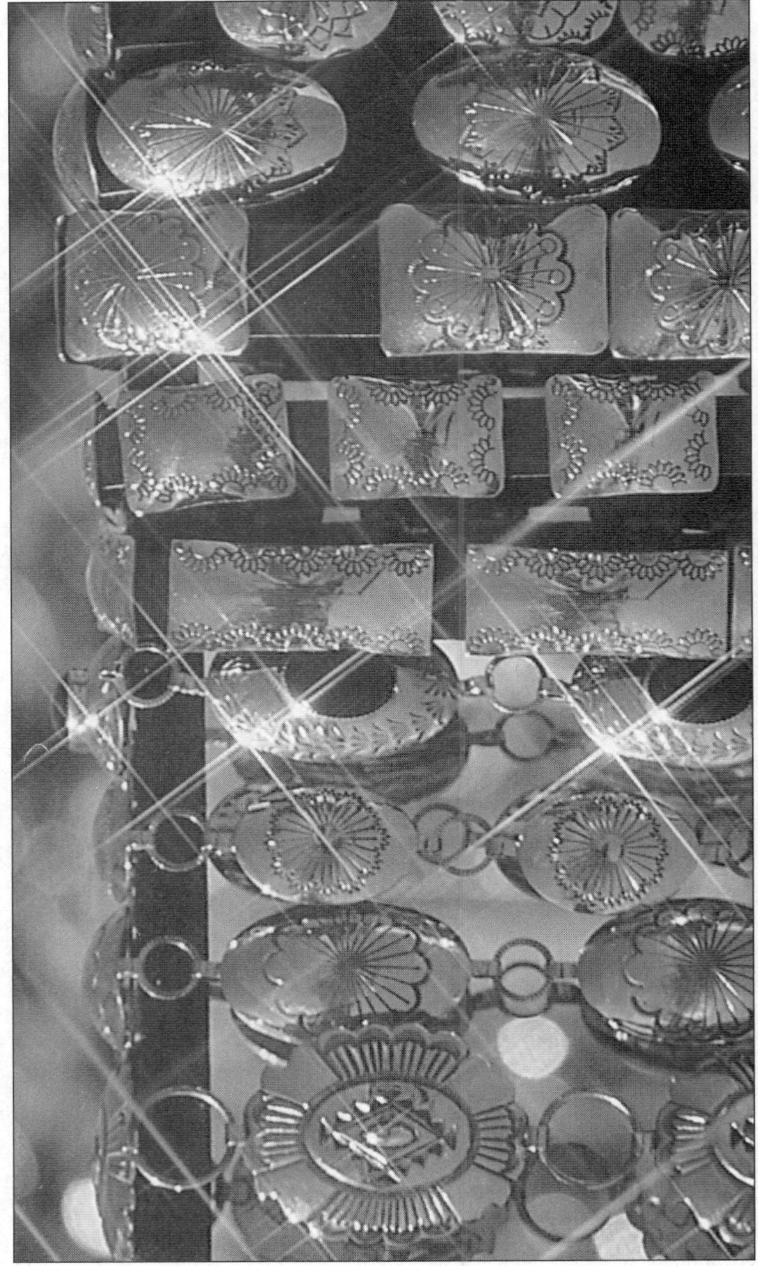

△ Silver jewellery from Taxco

The Town

The single main street, **Lanzagorta**, runs down through the town past the **Church of San Francisco** with its square, shaded plaza, and unusual removable wooden floorboards (for cleaning), and on down to the Jardín Hidalgo (aka Plaza de Armas), with its central bandstand. It's the church that attracts most Mexicans to Catorce, or rather the miraculous figure of St Francis of Assisi (known as Panchito, Pancho being a diminutive of Francisco) housed here. You'll soon spot the shrine by the penitents kneeling before it, but take time to head through the door to the left of the altar, where the walls are covered with hundreds of handmade *retablos* giving thanks for cures or miraculous escapes effected by the saint. They're a wonderful form of naive folk art, the older ones painted on tin plate, newer examples on paper or card or even photographs, depicting events that range from amazing to mundane – last-second rescues from the paths of oncoming trains, or simply the return of a stolen vehicle – all signed and dated with thanks to Panchito for his timely intervention. October 4, the saint's day, sees thousands of pilgrims crammed into Catorce, and the general festivities two weeks before and a week afterwards are also busy.

The church's **Museo Parroquial** (Sat & Sun 10am–4pm; US$0.20) has a small collection of old coins, rusting mine machinery, dusty documents – anything, in fact, found lying among the ruins that looks interesting. Across the square, the **Casa de Moneda** is a magnificent old mansion whose sloping site means that it has two stories on one side, three on the other. This is where Catorce's silver was minted into coin, and as if to retain the memory there's a small silver workshop inside. Heading north out of town along Libertad (which becomes Zaragoza), duck a few metres up Calle Xicotencatl to the lovely old **Palenque de Gallos**, where cockfights were once held (daily 9am–dusk; free), then continue out along Zaragoza to the ruinous Plaza de Toros, opposite the **Panteón** (daily except Tues 9am–5pm, hours can vary depending on mood of gatekeeper; free) where Catorce's dead lie covered by rough piles of dirt all around the mouldering church.

Practicalities

Real de Catorce tends to be much busier at weekends, for a week or two either side of October 4, Semana Santa and at Christmas when the better hotels put up their prices by around twenty percent. Currently there are **no banks** or ATMs in town, and few places take credit cards: bring plenty of cash. When it's time to leave, it always pays to ask about the latest **bus** timetables, but currently there are departures to Matehuala at 8am, noon, 2pm, 4pm and 5.45pm. You may choose to hike down to Estación Catorce and catch a bus from there: see p.285 for details. If you want to stay in touch with civilization, head to the Internet café *El Sótano del Real*, located at Constitución 6-A. Before, or during, your stay you can get acquainted with the town by visiting its superb website (Ⓦ www.realdecatorce.net).

On arrival, as likely as not, you'll be accosted by a knot of small boys eager to carry your bags and guide you to their favoured *casa de huéspedes* in return for a small *propina*. Ensure you've some pesos handy, if you decide to follow their lead. You're not obliged to accept what they show you but chances are you'll get a plain and small but clean **room**, which at least claims to have 24-hour hot water, for US$8–12: make sure there are plenty of blankets as it can be very cold here at night. Or, if you mention the name of your desired hotel, they'll guide you. If you're driving, don't be surprised if they hitch a ride on the bonnet of your car.

The best budget **hotels** are *Hospedaje Familiar*, Constitución 21 (no phone; with or without bath: ❸–❹), at the top end of the church square, with comfortable enough cells; and *Casa de Huéspedes San Francisco*, Terán 3, off Constitución (Ⓣ488/887-5009; with or without bath: ❷–❸), where an extra two dollars affords slightly more comfortable rooms – rooms 8 and 9 are particularly good, coming with bath and a sunny terrace. If you just need to use the facilities, *Casa de Huéspedes San Francisco* charges US$0.30 for the use of its bathroom, and US$1.80 for showers. *El Portón Azul*, at Lanzagorta 25 (Ⓣ488/877-5013; ❹), consists of comfortable rooms in the home of Sr Jorge Quijano, who is also a fine local guide.

At the other end of the scale, Real de Catorce is blessed with some wonderful hotels in converted mansions, often at very reasonable prices. The best of the lot is the friendly *Mesón de la Abundancia*, Lanzagorta 11 (Ⓣ488/887-5045; ❻–❽), just past the church, remodelled from the ruins and full of masks and huge stone-built rooms with beamed ceilings, rug-covered brick floors and ancient doors with their original hefty keys. A close contender is *Hotel Corral del Conde*, Constitución 17 at Morelos (Ⓣ488/887-5048 – doesn't accept reservations; ❻), where you get a whole suite of attractively furnished rooms, and Internet access for US$1.20 per half-hour. The *Hotel El Real,* Morelos 20, behind the Casa de Moneda (Ⓣ488/887-5058, Ⓔhotelelreal@yahoo.com.mx; ❻), is a charmingly converted old house (that's reputed to be haunted) with clean, airy rooms with native decoration, TVs, fireplaces and views galore. The modern *Quinta la Puesta del Sol* (Ⓣ488/882-3733; ❺), Calle del Cementerio 16, on the way to the Plaza de Toros, offers less atmosphere; it does, however, have satellite TV and great views down the valley to the plains.

Most of the fancier hotels serve **food**, and again *Mesón de la Abundancia* is the pick of the bunch with Mexican and Italian food that's superbly cooked and presented, and worth every peso: expect to pay US$10–12 for a full meal including a slice of torte and espresso. Curiously, many of the best eateries in Real de Catorce are the Italian-oriented restaurants: *Malambo*, Constitución 6 (open Wed–Sun), is the exciting newcomer serving pizza with *cabuches*, or the pickled bud of cactus flower, homemade pastas and divine puffed pastries with stewed fruits. *El Real* is a more expensive spot but does good pizza and hearty breakfasts, while *El Cactus*, by the plaza, does a fine cannelloni, great tortas and a huge range of fancy teas. Cheaper food can be found at the fairly basic stalls along the main street. Around the corner from *Hotel Corral del Conde* you'll find the Cine Club Ogarrio, at Constitución and Morelos, which is a not-for-profit theatre that shows foreign **films** in all languages (many in English) for US$0.50.

Around Real de Catorce: Estación Catorce and Wadley

The specific sights in town are soon exhausted, but you could spend days here making forays out into the mountains all around exploring any ruins you find, or heading downhill to the altiplano (high plain) of the desert below. One of the most relaxing ways to go is on **horseback**: horses are usually available around the Plaza de Armas and in front of the Mesón de la Abundancia, from where **guides** will take you out across the hills, perhaps visiting a Huichol ceremonial site, though this can seem unpleasantly voyeuristic if any Huichols are around. Since your group will have to pay for the guide's time, better deals can be struck by rounding up a ready-to-go group, and then haggling hard. Midweek you should get something for around US$12 for three hours, though you will have to pay more at weekends when demand is higher. For multiple-day guided horseback riding tours of the mountains and the pueblos, contact Ted Douglas at Buenos Paseos (Ⓦhttp://home.att.net/~buenos_paseos; US$79–100 for 5 days of riding). You really don't need any guidance for **short hikes**: just grab some water, food, good shoes, and something to protect you from the sun and go. About the best nearby destination is the **Pueblo Fantasma** "Ghost Town", an extensive set of mine ruins reached in an hour or so by following the winding track uphill just to the left of the tunnel entrance as you face it.

The most rewarding **longer hike** leads downhill from the Plaza de Armas (with the stables on your left), then forks right after 50m and follows a 4WD track towards the small dusty trackside town of Estación Catorce, about three hours (10km) away. There's no need to go all the way as you soon find yourself among mine ruins, passing a dam built to provide water and power for the mines, and even a tall chimney from one of the smelters. After about an hour you pass through the small village of **Los Catorces**, and beyond its cemetery, a second settlement known as **Santa Cruz de Carretas** (about 2hr from Real).

At this point you can turn around, satisfied that you've had the best of the hike, but it is possible to continue to **ESTACIÓN CATORCE** an hour further on. If hiking back seems too daunting, try flagging down the occasional vehicle, and be prepared to pay for your ride. A 4WD vehicle also plies the road a couple of times a day (charging under US$3 for the journey), though its timing is erratic and dependent on numbers: ask locally to find the vehicle. Estación Catorce itself is not a place to linger, though if you get stuck, there are a couple of fleapit hotels and a couple of places to eat, including a decent **restaurant**, located where **buses** depart for Saltillo (8am, 2pm & 6pm) and San Luis Potosí (6am & 7.45am). Estación Catorce is served by regular buses from the same places (San Luis Potosí 3 daily, 4hr; Saltillo 2 daily, 4hr) and fit hikers with relatively light packs might like to do the journey in reverse as a way of reaching Real de Catorce. It won't save you any money travelling this way, but from here you can walk up the road in a little over three hours, climbing all the while as you head deeper into the hills with no visible indication of what lies ahead. Just as you convince yourself there can be nothing but mountains in front, you round a corner and the town reveals itself.

Around 10km south of Estación Catorce along the asphalt road (and on the bus route from San Luis Potosí) lies **WADLEY** (or Estación Wadley), a small village that at first acquaintance seems less appealing. It has, however, garnered a devoted following, chiefly for its proximity to a section of desert renowned for its abundant **peyote**. Most people rent a room for a few days, usually choosing a place with a kitchen as restaurants here are very limited: ask around and you should get something for around US$5 each per day, especially if you are staying a few days. There are a couple of **hotels** behind the station on Calle Carranza, *Hotel Monis* (❹), and a nameless place opposite (❷), above a *comedor*.

San Luis Potosí

Situated to the north of the fertile heartland, the sprawling industrial centre of **SAN LUIS POTOSÍ** owes its existence and architectural splendour to a wealth of mineral deposits. Though it can by no means equal the beauty of Zacatecas, it does have a fine colonial centre and makes a good stopoff if you're

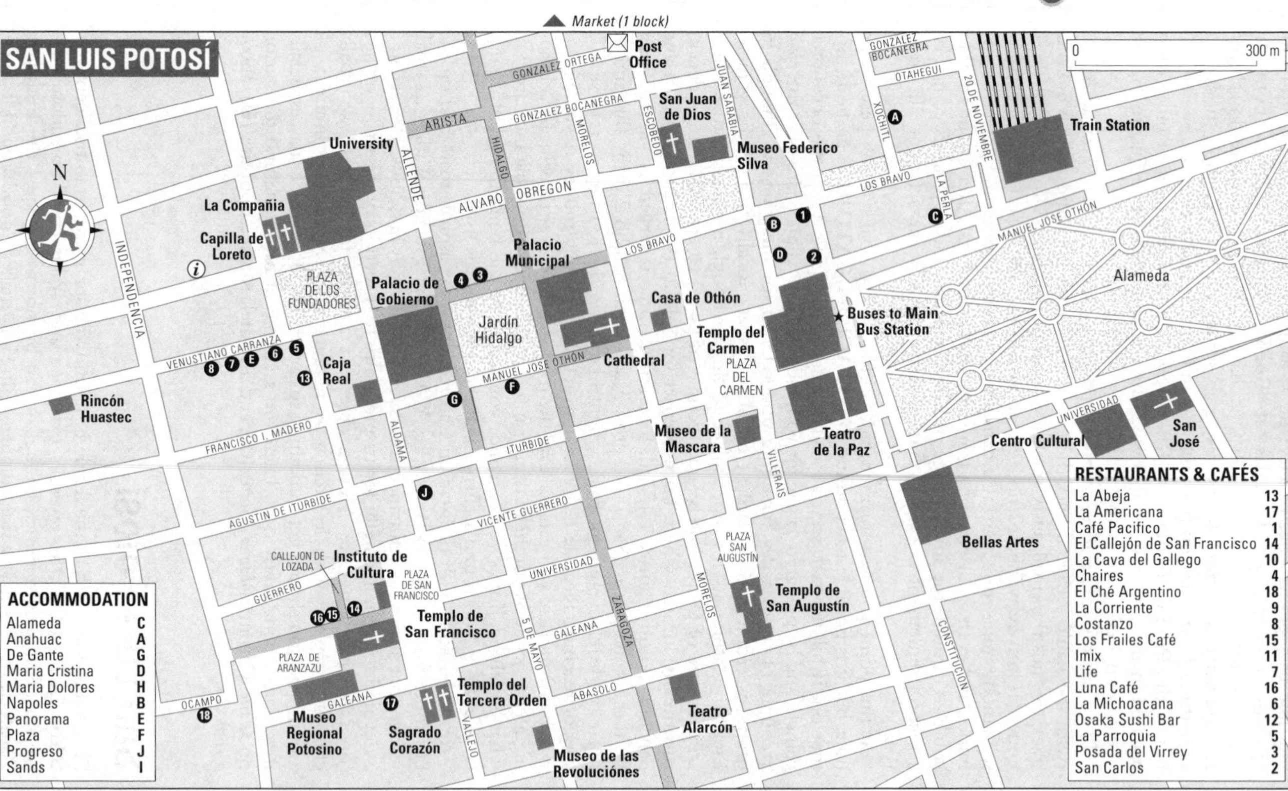
SAN LUIS POTOSÍ
Market (1 block)
Bus Station (3 km), Museo Taurino (500 m), H & I (3 km)
Hipo Campo (50 m), 9 (50 m), Zona Rosa (500 m), 10 (500 m), 11 (700 m), 12 (1 km) & Praque Tangamanga (4 km)
0 300 m
N
Post Office
San Juan de Dios
Museo Federico Silva
Train Station
University
La Compañia
Capilla de Loreto
Palacio Municipal
Palacio de Gobierno
Jardín Hidalgo
PLAZA DE LOS FUNDADORES
Caja Real
Casa de Othón
Templo del Carmen
PLAZA DEL CARMEN
Cathedral
Buses to Main Bus Station
Alameda
Rincón Huastec
Museo de la Mascara
Teatro de la Paz
Centro Cultural
San José
Bellas Artes
CALLEJON DE LOZADA
Instituto de Cultura
PLAZA DE SAN FRANCISCO
Templo de San Francisco
PLAZA DE ARANZAZU
PLAZA SAN AUGUSTÍN
Templo de San Augustín
Templo del Tercera Orden
Museo Regional Potosino
Sagrado Corazón
Teatro Alarcón
Museo de las Revoluciónes
GONZALEZ ORTEGA
GONZALEZ BOCANEGRA
OTAHEGUI
ARISTA
ALLENDE
HIDALGO
MORELOS
ESCOBEDO
JUAN SARABIA
XOCHITL
20 DE NOVIEMBRE
LOS BRAVO
LA PERLA
ALVARO OBREGON
MANUEL JOSE OTHÓN
INDEPENDENCIA
VENUSTIANO CARRANZA
FRANCISCO I. MADERO
ALDAMA
ITURBIDE
AGUSTIN DE ITURBIDE
VICENTE GUERRERO
GUERRERO
UNIVERSIDAD
5 DE MAYO
GALEANA
ZARAGOZA
VILLERAIS
ABASOLO
OCAMPO
VALLEJO
CONSTITUCIÓN
ACCOMMODATION
Alameda C
Anahuac A
De Gante G
Maria Cristina D
Maria Dolores H
Napoles B
Panorama E
Plaza F
Progreso J
Sands I
RESTAURANTS & CAFÉS
La Abeja 13
La Americana 17
Café Pacifico 1
El Callejón de San Francisco 14
La Cava del Gallego 10
Chaires 4
El Ché Argentino 18
La Corriente 9
Costanzo 8
Los Frailes Café 15
Imix 11
Life 7
Luna Café 16
La Michoacana 6
Osaka Sushi Bar 12
La Parroquia 5
Posada del Virrey 3
San Carlos 2

heading south from Monterrey towards the Bajío proper; from here most traffic is heading south on Hwy-57 towards Mexico City, along a fast divided highway all the way. Unless you're in a crazy hurry, though, you should definitely turn off into the Bajío proper, to Guanajuato, San Miguel or Dolores Hidalgo, some of the most fascinating towns in the whole of the republic. Hwy-70, the route east to Tampico and the Gulf of Mexico, can hardly compete for interest, but it does run through a few towns of minor interest along the way.

San Luis itself was founded as a Franciscan mission in 1592, but it wasn't long before the Spanish discovered rich deposits of gold and silver in the country round about and began to develop the area in earnest. They added the name Potosí (after the fabulously rich mines in Bolivia) in the expectation of rivalling the original, and though this was a thoroughly wealthy colonial town, that hope was never fully realized. Unlike its erstwhile rivals, however, San Luis is still prosperous – most of the silver may have gone but working mines churn out zinc and lead – with a considerable modern industrial base. As a result, San Luis, while preserving a little-changed colonial heart, is also a large and lively modern city.

Arrival and information

Long-distance buses arrive at the main suburban **bus station** (officially Terminal Terrestre Potosina, with a pricey 24-hour guardería), around 3km east of the centre on Hwy-57; for downtown and the Alameda walk outside and board Ruta 6. It appears to be heading out of town but doubles back: get off at the now disused train station and walk from there. For general information, head for the helpful **tourist office** (Mon–Fri 8am–8pm, Sat 9am–1pm; ⓣ444/812-9906, ⓕ812-6769), Alvaro Obregón 520, a block west of the Plaza Fundadores. They hand out a detailed **map** of the town and *San Luis Sensational*, a fairly comprehensive guide to the city.

Accommodation

The cheapest **rooms** are to be found in the slightly run-down area near the old train station close to the **Alameda**. Places on the back streets can be quieter than the generally more atmospheric spots closer to the main plazas, where the **Jardín Hidalgo** is the focus. Even here, though prices are good, there are few truly outstanding options, and for a little luxury you may prefer some of the more modern places around the long-distance bus station. It should be noted that these areas are not the wisest choice for women at night.

Alameda La Perla 3, behind the Pemex station on the north side of the Alameda ⓣ444/814-8901. Fairly basic and sometimes noisy, but clean and inexpensive. The best of a number of similar places in this area. ❸

Anahuac Xochitl 140 at Los Bravo ⓣ444/812-6505, ⓕ814-4904. Bright, clean and cheery rooms make this friendly and comfortable hotel about the best in the train station area, provided you can stomach the sappy photos emblazoned with scripture extracts. Some rooms with TV, for US$3 more, and there's safe parking. ❺

De Gante 5 de Mayo 140, corner of Jardín Hidalgo ⓣ444/812-1492, ⓔhoteldegante@prodigy.net.mx. Central and comfortable but with little atmosphere; chiefly of interest if you can get a room overlooking the Jardín Hidalgo. ❺

Maria Cristina Juan Sarabia 110 between Othón and Los Bravo ⓣ444/812-9408, ⓦwww.mariacristina.com.mx. Carpeted rooms with heavy wooden furniture distinguish this large, modern hotel, which is popular with hurried Mexican business people. Don't get stuck in a windowless interior room. Restaurant and bar on site. ❻

Maria Dolores Hwy-57 (Carretera Central) km. 1, Zona Hotelera at Benito Juárez, opposite the Central de Autobuses ⓣ/ⓕ444/822-1882. One of the swankiest of San Luis' hotels, all low-rise and set around attractive gardens studded with palms and swimming pools. Restaurants, bars and nightclubs fill ancillary buildings, and rooms, all with cable TV and minibars mostly have direct access to lawns. There are almost always sizeable reductions from the rack rate if you ask. ❽

Napoles Juan Sarabiá 120 ⓣ444/812-8418, ⓔhnapoles@prodigy.net.mx. Modern and well-maintained business hotel with parking, cable TV and phone in all rooms. One of the best in this price range. ❻

Panorama Venustiano Carranza 315, west of Plaza Fundadores ⓣ444/812-1777 or 800/480-0100, ⓔhpanorama@avantel.net.mx. Slick, upmarket business hotel – the plushest in the centre of town with pleasant breezy rooms, Moderne furniture, comfortable public areas, an outdoor pool, restaurant and piano bar. At the time of writing it was renovating rooms and adding a rooftop restaurant to capitalize on the towering building's breathtaking views. The minus here: noise from a nearby disco. Rates include dinner. ❼

Plaza Jardín Hidalgo 22, on Madero ⓣ444/812-4631. Very run-down but friendly hotel in a fading beauty of a building in the heart of the city with a pitch-black lobby and basic but comfortable rooms, some more expensive ones with TV. Still good value due to the smack-dab centre location. ❺

Progreso Aldama 415, at Iturbide ⓣ444/812-0366. One of the cheapest deals downtown, this somewhat dilapidated property does display some unusual details such as rare ceramic tiles. While rooms are strictly no-frills, they surprisingly have TVs. Ask for a streetside room. Breakfast available. ❹

Sands Hwy-57 km. 423, 100m east (right) of the Central de Autobuses ⓣ/ⓕ444/818-2436. Excellent-value hacienda-style motel set around a pool and shaded lawns. High-standard rooms all have cable TV, fans and adjacent parking. ❻

The City

Despite its uninviting industrial outskirts, the centre of San Luis Potosí is calm and beautiful, set on a tidy grid of largely pedestrianized streets around a series of little colonial plazas, chief among which is the **Jardín Hidalgo**, the old Plaza de Armas, surrounded by state and city government offices and overlooked by the cathedral. North of the plaza, pedestrianized Hidalgo, and the streets around it, comprise the city's main shopping area; the department stores near the plaza give way to smaller, simpler shops as you approach the **Mercado Hidalgo**, a good place for souvenirs and fresh produce. Further up, continuing along Alhóndiga, the street stalls and stores become increasingly basic until you reach another, much larger produce and clothing market, beyond the main road that delineates the edge of the centre. Hidalgo's southern continuation, Zaragoza, is also traffic-free and heads through a more up-and-coming area, while to the west lies swanky Avenida Carranza, which, five blocks from Jardín Hidalgo, becomes a fully fledged *zona rosa*, the fancy restaurants and designer boutiques running for perhaps a kilometre to the leafy square of Jardín Tequis.

Jardín Hidalgo and around

Certainly not the most elegant of the city's churches, the **cathedral** dominates the east side of the **Jardín Hidalgo**. Built in the early eighteenth century, successive generations have ensured that little remains of the original. Facing the cathedral across the square is the long facade of the **Palacio del Gobierno** (Mon–Fri 8am–3pm; free), with its balustraded roof. This, too, has been substantially refurbished over the years, but at least alterations have preserved the harmony of its clean Neoclassical lines. Inside, you can visit the suite of rooms occupied by Benito Juárez when San Luis became his temporary capital in 1863: head up either set of stairs and turn left. French troops supporting Emperor Maximilian soon drove him out, but Juárez returned in 1866, and in this building confirmed the death sentence passed on Maximilian. There's an absurd waxwork model of Juárez with the Princess Salm Salm, one of Maximilian's daughters, kneeling before him pleading for the emperor's pardon. He refused, "thus ending the short-lived empire," according to the state government's leaflet, "and strengthening, before all peoples and the entire world, Mexico's prestige as a liberty loving nation". Just behind the cathedral lies **Casa de Othón**, Othón 225 (Tues–Fri 10am–2pm & 4–6pm, Sat & Sun 10am–2pm; US$0.20), a pretty and well-tended museum, though a rather lifeless tribute to Manuel José Othón, San Luis' most famous poet, mainly comprising some of his furniture.

Plaza de San Francisco and Plaza de los Fundadores

Immediately behind the Palacio de Gobierno you can admire the ornate Baroque facade of the **Caja Real** – the old mint – one of the finest colonial mansions in San Luis. It is now owned by the university, which sometimes holds temporary exhibitions here: you can usually walk in and take a look during the day to see the gentle gradient of the stairway, supposedly to make it easier to lug boxes full of gold and silver up and down. Take a left turn from here, along Aldama, and you come to the quiet **Plaza de San Francisco**, a lovely shaded area redolent of the city's colonial history. It's named after the Franciscan monastery whose church, the **Templo de San Francisco**, towers over the west side and features a magnificent ship chandelier. The monastery itself now houses the **Museo Regional Potosino** (Tues–Sat 10am–7pm, Sun 10am–5pm; US$2.70, free on Sun), an excellent collection of pre-Hispanic sculpture and other archeological finds, displays of local Indian culture and traditions, and articles relating to the history of the state of San Luis Potosí. In addition to a fine cloister, there's access, upstairs, to the lavish Baroque chapel, **Capilla de Aranzazú** – said to be the only chapel in Latin America located on an upper floor – with exceedingly rich and enthusiastically restored churrigueresque decoration. Inside and through the side chapels lies a miscellaneous collection of religious paintings and artefacts. At the back of the museum, the **Plaza de Aranzazú** is another pleasant open space.

At the far end of the Plaza de San Francisco, two more tiny and elaborate churches, **Sagrado Corazón** and the **Templo del Tercera Orden**, stand side by side, with a small, plain Presbyterian chapel, seeming terribly incongruous amid all this Baroque grandeur, facing them across Galeana. On the plaza to the right of San Francisco, the **Instituto de Cultura** (Mon–Sat 10am–2pm & 4–7pm; free) is worth a quick look as much for its attractive architecture as the high-class artesanía shops and galleries that surround the courtyard. Also in the area, just southeast of the plaza, is the small **Museo de las Revoluciones**, 5 de Mayo 610 (Tues–Fri 10am–2pm & 4–6pm, Sat 9am–3pm, Sun 10am–2pm; free), with usually worthwhile photographic and fine-art exhibits displayed in the house where Independence hero José Mariano Jiménez was born.

Aldama runs four blocks north from the Plaza de San Francisco to the paved **Plaza de los Fundadores**, a much larger and more formal open space than the Jardín Hidalgo. Nothing much seems to happen here, though, despite the fact that it's dominated by the enormous Neoclassical **State University**. Alongside are two more small churches, **Capilla de Loreto** and **La Compañía**, while the fine arcaded portals of the square continue around the corner into Avenida Venustiano Carranza. Although not yet open at the time of writing, the **Museo Federico Silva Escultura Contemporánea** (Alvaro Obregon 80, Plaza San Juan de Dios (℡444/812-3848) will be housed in a fifteenth-century convent and will be the only museum in Latin American dedicated to contemporary sculpture.

Plaza del Carmen, San Agustín and the Alameda

The **Templo del Carmen**, on the little Plaza del Carmen up towards the Alameda, is the most beautiful and harmonious of all San Luis' churches. Exuberantly decorated with a multicoloured tiled dome and elaborate Baroque facade, it has an equally flashy interior: in particular, a fantastically intricate *retablo* attributed to eighteenth-century eccentric and polymath Francisco Tresguerras. Next to the abandoned Teatro Alameda, where once stood the monastery, is the bulky columned **Teatro de la Paz** (Tues–Fri 10am–2pm & 5–8pm, Sat 10am–2pm; free for viewing), built in the nineteenth century under Porfirio Díaz and typical of the grandiose public buildings of that era, though its modern interior fails to live up to the extravagance of the exterior. Directly opposite the theatre, you'll find the **Museo Nacional de la Máscara**, Villerias 2 (Tues–Fri 10am–2pm & 5–7pm, Sat & Sun 10am–2pm; US$0.50), a compulsive and fascinating place, exhibiting everything from pre-Hispanic masks to costumes that are still worn for fiestas and traditional dances. Included are the so-called "giants of San Luis", eight enormous models representing four royal couples (from Africa, Europe, Asia and America), which are flaunted in the streets during the festival of Corpus Christi in May. Look out too for the funerary mask made from a skull inlaid with a mosaic of turquoise and black stone. Displays instruct (in Spanish) as to the meaning and continued significance of many of the dances.

South of the museum, another magnificent Baroque exterior, that of the **Templo de San Agustín**, faces out onto the tiny Plaza San Agustín – there's little to offer if you venture inside, however. East on Universidad from here, you reach the southern side of the Alameda, where the **Centro de Difusión Cultural** (Tues–Sun 10am–2pm & 5–8pm; free) occupies a concrete building that looks like a modern church. It holds temporary exhibitions, which may be anything from modern art to stamp collections. The **Alameda** itself, ringed by heavy traffic, is crowded with strolling families, photographers, candy-sellers and people waiting for local buses.

Beyond the Centro Cultural lies the Plaza de Toros. If you're fascinated by "La Corrida" but would never attend, do so vicariously at the adjacent **Museo Taurino**, at the corner of Universidad and López Hermosa (Mon–Sat noon–2.30pm & 5.30–8pm; free), where, if you can rouse the custodian (buzz the second door on the left), you'll be shown ranks of dramatic promotional posters dating back to the glory days, elaborate blood-encrusted suits of lights and an array of stuffed heads all missing at least one ear.

Parques Tangamanga

If urban life is getting you down, the green expanses of the **Parques Tangamanga I** and **II** (open daily 6am–6pm) beckon. **Parque Tangamanga I** has considerably more amenities and recreation options: the entire vast acreage is piped for muzak and offers picnic spots, fitness circuits and a couple of small lakes. Joggers, soccer players and cyclists come here, and you can rent **bikes** for US$4 an hour from the kiosk here (daily except Mon). Founded in the early 1980s, the parks still lack maturity, as there are great stretches that remain undeveloped, but they makes a pleasant weekend outing nonetheless, with the added attraction of the **Museo de Arte Popular** (in Parque Tangamanga I, Tues–Fri 10am–2pm & 4–6pm, Sat 10am–2pm; free), a showcase museum-shop of local crafts, at the bottom of Tatanacho opposite the main park entrance. You can walk to the parks in an hour and a half through the shopping district to the south, or catch buses marked "Ruta 32" or "Parques del Sur" from the Alameda.

Eating, drinking and nightlife

The centre of San Luis has several **cafés** and simple **restaurants** offering good-value *menús del día*, though little that's more exciting. Local specialties to look out for include deep-fried enchiladas and *tacos Potosinos* (or *Huastecas*), dripping with salsa and cheese, and *cecina*, a thin cut of marinated and dried steak. The **Mercado Hidalgo** includes a host of food stalls, but the place is too packed and noisy for anything other than a hurried snack.

For anything more than good filling food in humdrum surroundings you're going to have to wander along Carranza (affectionately known as **La Avenida**) into what is effectively San Luis' *zona rosa*, starting half a kilometre west of Plaza Fundadores. Within half a dozen long blocks are some of the best boutiques the city has to offer, usually quite expensive and not entirely impressive. This has also traditionally been the place to head for **nightlife**, which, at weekends anyway, is pretty lively with many places staying open until the wee hours. Most of the nightclubs play a mix of the latest US and European club grooves and Latin beats, and generally charge little or no money to get in midweek and only a minimal entry at weekends: US$5 maximum, and less for women. In the last couple of years several new bars have opened up around the Plaza Aranzazú and many revellers start their evening off here before heading to La Avenida.

Central San Luis

La Abeja Díaz de León 104, around the corner from *La Parroquia* off Plaza Fundadores. Serves natural yogurts and fruit smoothies. Also sells healthy foods and vitamins.

La Americana Galeana 433. One of the best and most varied of the town's *panaderías*.

Café Pacífico Los Bravo and Constitución, with another location around the corner. A bustle of gossip, action and moderately priced food. Open 24hr, this very popular café-restaurant even has a nonsmoking section.

El Callejón de San Francisco Callejón de Lozada 1, just west of the Plaza de San Francisco ☎444/812-4508. Enchanting, quiet beam-and-stone restaurant, with a gorgeous rooftop terrace for sipping an afternoon beer while taking in the assorted spires and domes of the San Francisco church. Antojitos such as chicken fajitas and *tacos Potosinos* are served at surprisingly modest prices. Booking advised for dinner, especially at weekends, as this is one of the city's most charming eateries. Closed Mon.

Chaires next to the *Restaurante Posada del Virrey* on Jardín Hidalgo. Bustling with families, friends and canoodling couples sipping java and tucking into elaborate pastries.

El Ché Argentino Melchor Ocampo 135. A delightful smoke scent greets you at this excellent Argentine steak restaurant, whose specialties (*bife de chorizo* and *bife de lomo*) are both under US$10. The gracious owner also speaks English.

Costanzo Carranza 325 at Plaza Fundadores. A confections chain, with all manner of tempting chocolates and sweet things in shiny paper. No seating, but there's a café next door.

Los Frailes Café Universidad 165 by Plaza de San Francisco. Youthful evening café with occasional live acoustic music at weekends.

Life Carranza 333, next to *Hotel Panorama*. San Luis' hottest nightspot and concert hall. The meat market begins after midnight.

Luna Café Universidad 155, next to *Frailes Café*. Slightly more upscale than its neighbour, offering gourmet coffees and cocktails.

La Michoacana on Plaza Fundadores at Carranza. Extremely popular ice cream, popsicle and *aguas frescas* joint serving great traditional flavours such as horchata and original combinations such as mango-chile.

La Parroquia Carranza at Plaza Fundadores. Comfortable middle-of-the-range café, where crusty rolls replace the traditional stack of tortillas. Excellent breakfasts and comida corrida – a firm favourite with local office workers.

Restaurante Posada del Virrey Jardín Hidalgo 3, on the north side. Fine food in the fine surroundings of the former home of the wife of the Spanish viceroy. A mildly Mexican menu that includes great seafood. Mains mostly US$6–8.

Rincón Huastec Carranza 447. Traditional native Indian dishes in an attractive but somewhat commercial setting. Still, the *cecina* and tangy chorizo (which is also sold by the kilo to go) are very good, as are the prices.

San Carlos Othón at the corner of Constitución, right by the Alameda. The best breakfast deal in town: an all-you-can-eat US$4 buffet comprising juice, coffee, half a dozen cereals, yogurt, burritos, egg dishes and bread rolls. The antojito and mainstream Mexican mains – served all day – are comparable good value.

La Avenida

La Cava del Gallego Carranza 1040. No sign. Spanish-style bar that's fine for a quiet drink or as a place to practise your Spanish by discussing the football or the bulls on TV.
La Corriente Carranza 700, right at the start of the avenue. Lovely restaurant centred on a shaded courtyard and specializing in Mexican steak dishes (US$8–10) but also offering a wide range of enchiladas, chilequiles and a good comida corrida (US$5) at prices that are modest for this part of town.
Hipo Campo Carranza 725. Local casual hangout with fresh tortas, *aguas frescas* and rare sidewalk seating. Exceptionally clean.
Imix Carranza 1137. There's a small, dim and amiable bar with a trendy crowd and big-screen MTV. Get there before midnight and there are often drink specials and no cover.
Osaka Sushi Bar Carranza 1405, beyond Jardín Tequis. Reasonably priced sushi, *teppanyaki* and Mexican *botanas* (bar snacks), along with fairly pricey sashimi, served in numerous small rooms off a fern-filled courtyard.

Listings

Banks and exchange There are banks with ATMs all around the main plazas, including Banamex at Allende and Obregón, and several casas de cambio in the same area.
Books and newspapers The newsstands on Los Bravo, just off the Jardín Hidalgo, are good for English-language publications, and it might be worth trying Librerías Gonvil, Carranza 500. Sanborn's, in the Plaza Tangamanga shopping centre, close to the Parques Tangamanga, has a slightly wider selection, though unless you are desperate it may not be worth the journey.
Buses Ruta 6, from the northwest corner of the Alameda on Constitución, runs straight to the bus station, from where most traffic heads south on Hwy-57 towards Mexico City. Hwy-70 heads east to Tampico and the Gulf of Mexico. Buses cover every conceivable route, with departures for Mexico City and Monterrey every few minutes, for Guadalajara, Tampico and the border at least hourly. Flecha Amarilla has excellent second-class services to the Bajío: Dolores Hidalgo fourteen times daily, San Miguel every couple of hours, Guanajuato slightly less frequently. Northbound, there are very frequent services to Saltillo and beyond to the US border towns, most calling at Matehuala, where you change for buses to Real de Catorce.
Cinemas Cinema Alfa, Carranza 307, just off the Plaza de Fundadores, has just one screen; Avenida Cinemas, Carranza 780, ten minutes' walk west of the centre, has eight; and Multicinemas (Ⓣ444/817-5556), out in the Plaza Tangamanga shopping centre, has another three.
Emergencies For medical emergencies, the handiest clinic is Beneficencia Española, Carranza (Ⓣ444/811-5694), or just call the Cruz Roja on Ⓣ444/815-3635; for the judicial police call Ⓣ444/814-8493; and for the highway police call Ⓣ444/824-08891.
Internet access *Café Plaza*, 5 de Mayo 103-A (upstairs) charges $1.50 per hour, and has a coffeeshop and wonderful views to boot.
Pharmacy Farmacia Perla, Escobedo at Los Bravo (Ⓣ444/812-5922) and Farmacia Guadalajara, at Carranza 100, are always open, while Farmacia Avenida, Carranza 783 (Ⓣ444/812-3228), operates long hours.
Post office A little way north of the centre at Morelos 235, near where it crosses Gonzales Ortega.
Telephones *Larga distancia* phones are becoming rarer with the use of phone cards, but there is still one at Carranza 360 (Mon–Sat 7.30am–9pm), opposite the *Hotel Panorama*.

Zacatecas

ZACATECAS, almost 2500m up and crammed into a narrow gully between two hills, packs more of interest into a small space than almost anywhere in Mexico and ranks, alongside Guanajuato, as one of the Bajío's finest colonial cities. Its beauty enhanced by the harshness of the semi-desert landscape all around, it remains much as the British Admiralty's *Handbook of Mexico*

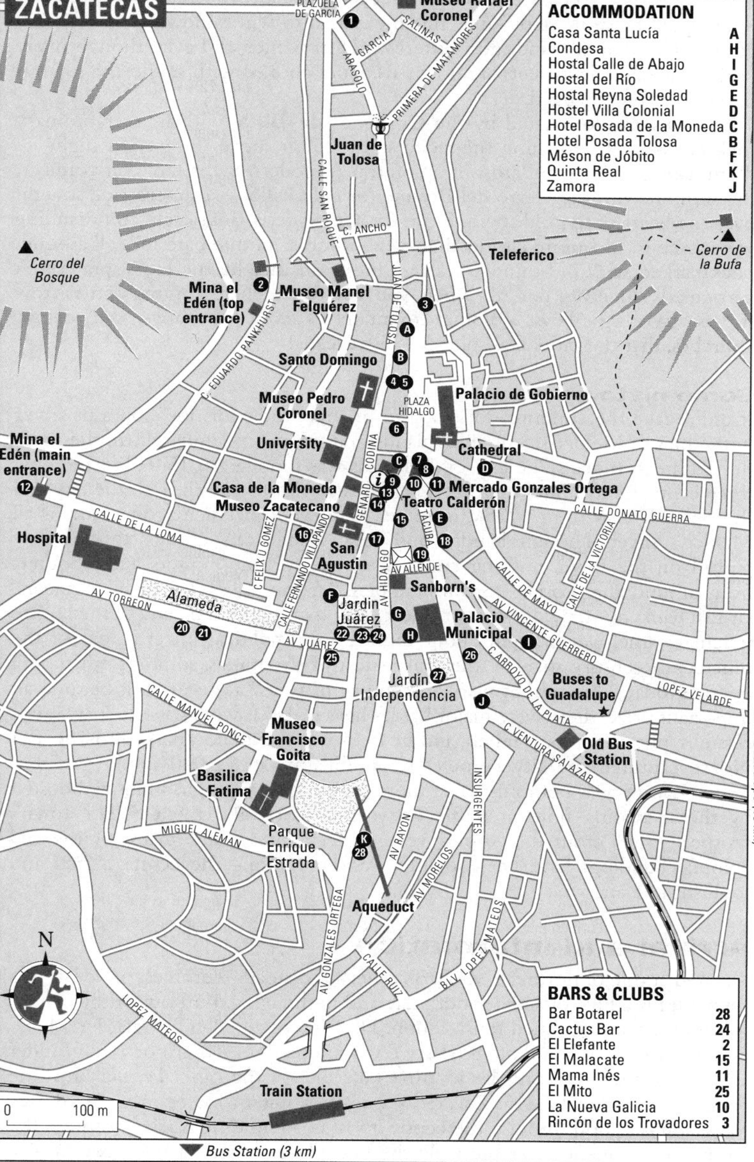

RESTAURANTS & CAFÉS

Acrópolis	7
Birrierias Jaramillo	5
Café Anis	14
Café la Colonial	8
Los Dorados de Villa	1
Garufa	23
Gorditas Doña Julia	9,18 & 20
Hong Kong	19
Il San Particio Café	12
Mi Viejo	16
La Plaza	28
El Raspanieve	4
El Recoveco	21
Restaurante la Bodeguilla	13
Restaurante el Tragadero	22
Rosticería el Pastor	27
Sanborn's	17
La Única Cabaña	26
Viva Pizza	6

described it in 1905: "irregular", its streets "very narrow, steep, and frequently interrupted by stone steps" and "much exposed to winds blowing through the gorge". Those same winds gust bitterly cold in winter, and even though many of the once cobbled streets are now paved and choked with traffic, the town is otherwise little changed.

All views are dominated by the **Cerro de la Bufa**, with its extraordinary rock cockscomb crowning the ridge some 150m above the city; at night it's illuminated, with a giant cross lit up on top. A modern Swiss cable car connects the summit with the Cerro del Bosque (or del Grillo) – a superb ride straight over the heart of the old town. From the Cerro de la Bufa itself, commanding views take in the entire city, its drab new suburbs and the bare hills all around, pockmarked with old mine-workings. From this height, the city's sprawl isn't particularly inviting, but it's when you get down there, among the narrow streets, twisting alleys, colonial fountains, carved doorways and ornate churches, that the city's real splendour is revealed.

Some history

It didn't take the conquistadors long to discover the enormous lodes of **silver** in the hills of Mexico's central highlands, and, after some initial skirmishes with the Zacateco Indians, the city of Zacatecas was founded in 1546. For the next three centuries its mines disgorged fabulous wealth to enrich both the city and the Spanish crown; in 1728 the mines here were producing one-fifth of all Mexico's silver. Though bandits and local indigenous groups continuously preyed on the town, nothing could deter the fortune-hunters and labourers from around the world – Spanish nobles, African slaves, German engineers, British bankers – drawn by the prospect of all that wealth. The end of the boom, when it came, was brought about more by the political uncertainties of the nineteenth century than by the exhaustion of the mines, some of which still operate today. Throughout nearly a century of war, Zacatecas itself became an important prize: there were major battles here in 1871, when Benito Juárez successfully put down local rebels, and in 1914 when Pancho Villa's **División del Norte** captured the city, completely annihilating its 12,000-strong garrison. Today Zacatecas is booming once more, its business and light industry boosted by the increasing flow of traffic between Mexico and the US. The town's prosperity has ensured a strong vein of civic pride, and many of the old colonial buildings have been lovingly restored, giving the centre a rich and sophisticated air.

Arrival and information

Situated at one of northern Mexico's crucial crossroads, Zacatecas' modern **bus terminal** is a hive of activity both day and night, lying 4km out of the centre, south of the now disused train station. There's a small 24-hour guardería here. To get into town take Ruta 8 (every few minutes 7am–10pm) or a taxi (under US$5) downtown. From the **airport** take one of the official *combis* into the centre, for around US$15. Zacatecas' one-way system forces most **local bus** routes onto a loop through the centre, most at some time passing through the Jardín Independencia. It's probably the best place to get off the bus if you've come from the bus station – wherever you're heading, you're almost certain to be able to get there from here, and it's within reasonable walking distance of most of the accommodation.

Barely marked, the **tourist office** hides away upstairs off a courtyard at Hidalgo 403, beside the Teatro Calderón (daily 9am–8pm; ⓣ492/922-4047 or

01-800/712-4078, Ⓦwww.turismozacatecas.gob.mx); they provide a smattering of leaflets, a poor street map, and informative, friendly advice.

Accommodation

Once you're in the middle of town, finding a **hotel** is no problem; there's a great hostel, and excellent mid-range and top-line places abound, though genuine budget hotels are rare. Most low-cost options are around the old bus station on López Mateos, south of the centre, and a couple aren't bad value. If you've a little more money to spend, head straight for the superbly elegant establishments in the centre. Nights are cold in Zacatecas, so check that you have enough blankets.

It is worth noting that accommodation is hard to come by around Semana Santa, the week leading up to Easter, and during the main fiesta in late August and the first half of September.

Casa Santa Lucía Hidalgo 717 Ⓣ492/924-4900, Ⓔmazzocco@prodigy.net.mx. Decent value among the more upmarket hotels, making attractive use of the beautiful ancient structure but still providing comfortable rooms with high ceilings, big tiled bathrooms, exposed stonework and simple but tasteful decor. Dotted with terracotta angels. ❼

Condesa Juárez 102 Ⓣ/Ⓕ492/922-1160. Good-value recently remodelled hotel with huge lobby exhibiting old photos. Fantastic central location amid the action of Jardín Independencia. Modern rooms with TV, cherry furniture, cheery linens; some with jacuzzis. Ask for a room with a view of the jardín. There's also a spiffy café and serviceable hotel bar. ❺

Hostal Calle de Abajo Victor Rosales 160 Ⓣ492/925-1255, Ⓔhostalcalledeabajo@hotmail.com. Situated on a quiet street, this friendly hostel has a dramatic arched entrance and antique reception desk. Rooms here are simple but comfortable, and breakfast is included in the rates. ❻

Hostal del Río Hidalgo 116 Ⓣ492/924-0035, Ⓕ922-7833. Rambling colonial place full of character and right in the heart of things. All rooms are whitewashed and come with simple decor and TV, and the gargantuan ones sleep up to five (great for families). Though it's a climb, ask for an upstairs room. Unlimited purified water available. ❺

Hostal Reyna Soledad Calle Tacuba 170 Ⓣ492/922-0790, Ⓦwww.hostalreynasoledad.com.mx. Clean-smelling, friendly hostal with rustic ceilings, rooftop terrace, courtyard fountain, colourful rooms, and tons of flowers. ❼

Hostal Villa Colonial corner Primero de Mayo and Callejón Mono Prieto Ⓣ/Ⓕ492/922-1980, Ⓦwww.hostels-zacatecas.com. A dream hostel located in the thick of it and enthusiastically run by Zacatecan locals. There are comfortable four-bed dorms (US$8) and three double and twin rooms (US$18), sunny rooftop terrace, Internet access, laundry facilities, cable TV, book exchange, and a genuinely sociable atmosphere. A new extension adds a large communal kitchen, where informal cooking classes are offered. Also organizes excursions. English spoken. ❷–❹

Hotel Posada de la Moneda Hidalgo 413, opposite the Mercado Gonzales Ortega Ⓣ/Ⓕ492/922-0881. Brilliant location for a pleasant but unspectacular hotel popular with Mexican business people. Ask for an outward-facing balcony room to avoid the darkness. ❻

Hotel Posada Tolosa Juan de Tolosa 811 Ⓣ492/922-5105, Ⓦwww.hotelposadatolosa.com.mx. Kitschy hotel on a quiet street. Halls and rooms can be dim, so ask for accommodation with a view. Restaurant (open all day) with light and bright tablecloths helps to balance things out. ❻

Mesón de Jóbito Jardín Juárez 143 Ⓣ/Ⓕ492/924-1722, reservations Ⓣ01-800/021-0040, Ⓔhmjobito@.logicnet.com. An entire colonial street converted into a superb luxury hotel that sits on the city's most enchanting jacaranda-laden square. Pretty, plush, and private, all rooms come with a/c, some with jacuzzis. There are two formal restaurants, and depending on the night, a lively bar – just what you'd expect in a top hotel, though at US$130 it's a good bit cheaper than the *Quinta Real*. ❾

Quinta Real Gonzalez Ortega, by the aqueduct Ⓣ492/922-9104 or 01-800/457-4000, Ⓦwww.quintareal.com. Gorgeous and outrageously luxurious hotel in the shadow of the colonial aqueduct, which beautifully incorporates what was once Zacatecas' bullring, the oldest in Latin America. Every comfort is taken to the *extreme* degree (there's even a "pillow menu"), and at almost US$200, this is certainly a place worth saving up for, not to mention one of the most distinctive properties in the Americas. ❾

Zamora Plaza Zamora, top of Calle Ventura Sálazar, by Jardín Independencia Ⓣ492/922-1200. Cheap, central, no-frills option. ❹

The Town

Although it can be tiring if you're not used to the altitude, the most rewarding way to enjoy Zacatecas is by aimless wandering, particularly in the cool of the evening, when the streets are filled. This is a city of constant surprises, with narrow alleys crowding in on each other as they scramble about the steep-sided ravine, revealing a series of little plazas and glimpses of tiny hidden courtyards. In the beautifully preserved town centre the highlight is undoubtedly the ornate **cathedral**, from where all other main sights are within walking distance.

Though the cathedral is the formal heart of the city, and the adjacent **Plaza Hidalgo**, in front of the Palacio de Gobierno, is where formal events take place, life for locals revolves more around the **Jardín Independencia**. Just a few paces from the market and from the important junction of Juárez and Hidalgo, this is in effect the city's main plaza, where people gather in the evenings, hang out between appointments and wait for buses. For a true glimpse of local life, poke your nose in El Montecarlo billiards hall, on the Jardín Independencia. The only place to really challenge the Jardín Independencia is the **Alameda**, a thin strip of stone benches, splashing fountains and a bandstand. Always full of students from the nearby university, it makes both a cool retreat from the heat of the day and a popular spot for the evening paseo. Adjacent, you'll find the charming oasis **Jardín de las Madres**, distinguishable by its fountain featuring a beatific maternal figure and well-tended flora.

Around the cathedral

Zacatecas' flamboyant **Cathedral** is the outstanding relic of the city's years of colonial glory: built in the pink stone typical of the region, it represents one of the latest, and arguably the finest, examples of Mexican Baroque architecture. It was completed in 1750, its facades carved with a wild exuberance unequalled anywhere in the country. The interior, they say, was once at least its equal – furnished in gold and silver, with rich wall hangings and a great collection of paintings – but as everywhere, it was despoiled or the riches removed for "safe-keeping", first at the time of Juárez's reforms and later during the Revolution; only the structure itself, with its bulky Doric columns and airy vaulting, remains to be admired. On each side of the cathedral there's a small plaza: to the north the formal Plaza Hidalgo, to the south a tiny paved *plazuela*, **Plaza Huizar**, which often hosts lively street theatre and impromptu musical performances.

The **Plaza Hidalgo** is surrounded by more colonial buildings. On the east side, the eighteenth-century **Palacio de Gobierno** was built as a home by the Conde Santiago de la Laguna and subsequently bought by the state government. In keeping with local fashion, a modern mural depicting the city's history embellishes the interior courtyard. Opposite, along with what is now the *Hotel Continental Plaza*, lies the Palacio de Justicia, known locally as the **Casa de la Mala Noche**. According to legend, its builder, Manuel de Rétegui, was a mine-owner down to his last peso, which he gave away to a starving widow to feed her family. He then spent a long night of despair in the house ("la mala noche"), contemplating bankruptcy and suicide, until at dawn his foreman hammered on the door with the miraculous news that a huge vein of silver had been struck, and they were all to be rich.

On the other side of the cathedral, the **Mercado Gonzales Ortega** is a strikingly attractive market building, built at the end of the nineteenth century.

It takes advantage of its sloping position to have two fronts: the upper level opening onto Hidalgo, the lower floor with entrances on Tacuba. Converted into a fancy shopping mall, it's now filled with tourist shops and smart boutiques, as well as a superb wine store, and a couple of cafés. On Hidalgo opposite the Mercado, the **Teatro Calderón** is a grandiose nineteenth-century theatre. Below the Mercado, head to the right down Tacuba past another delightful square, **Plazuela Goyita**, and you'll come to the real **market**, tucked in behind the Palacio Municipal.

Santo Domingo and the Museo Pedro Coronel

Climbing up from the west side of Plaza Hidalgo towards the Cerro del Bosque are streets lined with more mansions – some restored, some badly in need of it, but all deserted now by the mining moguls who built them. The church of **Santo Domingo** stands raised on a platform above the plaza of the same name, just up from the Plaza Hidalgo – its hefty, buttressed bulk a stern contrast to the lightness of the cathedral, though it was built at much the same time. In the gloom of the interior you can just make out the gilded churrigueresque *retablos* in the chapels.

Next door, the **Museo Pedro Coronel** (daily except Thurs 10am–5pm; US$2) occupies what was originally a Jesuit monastery attached to the church. Pedro Coronel Rivera was a local artist, brother of Rafael Coronel (see overleaf) and a son-in-law of Diego Rivera, which perhaps explains how he managed to gather an art collection that reads like a Who's Who of modern art: you'll find paintings here by Picasso, Kandinsky, Chagall, Dalí and Miró among others, as well as sketches by Goya, architectural drawings by Piranesi, Hogarth engravings and a few of Pedro's own works. It's undeniably an amazing collection – astonishing that one person could create it – but it's not as good as the roll call makes it sound. With the exception of a few of the Mirós, these are all very minor works, not particularly well lit or displayed. Some of the peripheral collections are more interesting, those of West African and Oriental art, and some pre-Columbian antiquities in particular. The building itself was converted into a hospital, a barracks and a prison before its recent restoration, and one of the grimmer dungeons is also preserved as an exhibit.

On the same street, in another converted mansion, is the main building of the Universidad Autónoma de Zacatecas, the **University Rectory** – a good place to check the notice boards for details of local events – and below this, on Calle Dr Hierro, is the **Casa de la Moneda**, Zacatecas' mint in the days when every silver-producing town in Mexico struck its own coins. Further along you come to the **Museo Zacatecano**, Dr Hierro 301 (daily except Tues 10am–5pm; US$1.20), where some superb and wonderfully natural 1940s' photos of Huicholes lead to a room chock-full of some two hundred Huichol embroideries, incorporating an amazing range of geometric designs, as well as maize symbols, deer and butterflies, all executed in black, red and green (for death, life and prosperity respectively). It should come as no surprise that peyote features in a big way, usually depicted by eight diamonds, a logo strangely adopted by the VIPS chain of pharmacies and restaurants. Nothing is labelled but one of the attendants may well give you an unbidden guided tour. Most of the rest of the museum is given to a display of religious iconography: a couple of hundred wonderfully naive hand-painted *retablos*, including a couple of sixteenth-century examples, depicting just about every saint, martyr and apostle going.

Across the street lies the church of **San Agustín** (Tues–Sun 9am–9pm; free), an early eighteenth-century temple that, after the Reform Laws, was converted into a casino, while the adjoining monastery became a hotel. It has been under restoration for more than twenty years, and though it's essentially complete, there are still chunks of statuary piled up with apparently nowhere to go. It must have been very beautiful once, and there's still a very un-Mexican simplicity and charm to the place. A series of before-and-after photographs in the nave chronicle the restoration work, and there are often interesting exhibits in a back room.

Museo de Arte Abstract Manuel Felguérez

Moving north along Genaro Codina and Juan de Tolosa you'll find **Museo de Arte Abstract Manuel Felguérez** (daily except Tues 10am–5pm; US$2), an extensive gallery recently and imaginatively converted from a prison and its associated church. In places the cells have been turned into mini-galleries where the intimacy of the space draws you into the works. Elsewhere several levels have been ripped out to leave huge rooms with floor-to-ceiling art viewed from steel walkways that gradually take you higher. Half of what's on show is by **Manuel Felguérez**, a native of Zacatecas state and an approximate contemporary of the Coronel brothers. Within the field of abstract art he is almost as highly regarded, though it can take a bit of effort to fully appreciate his work, particularly that of the early 1980s when he developed an obsession with male reproductive anatomy. He is perhaps most successful in his sculpture, notably 1995's *Arco del Día*, a huge bronze tripod that looks like it has just landed in a side chapel off the church. Nearby his huge canvas entitled *Dehumanized Technology* is also particularly striking. Elsewhere within the museum there is work by the **Coronel brothers** and several other Mexican artists, as well as an excellent art bookstore, though almost everything is in Spanish.

North along Calle de los Bolos towards Museo Rafael Coronel, take a quick look at the **Plazuela de García**, with its modern central feature based around a stone column sculpted with scenes from Mexican history.

Museo Rafael Coronel

Pedro Coronel may have amassed a spectacular art collection, but his brother Rafael has a far more beautiful museum, the centrepiece of which is a huge collection of traditional masks, possibly the finest in Mexico. The wonderful **Museo Rafael Coronel** (daily except Wed 10am–5pm; US$2) occupies the ex-Convento de San Francisco, on the north side of town. Founded in 1593 as a Franciscan mission (the facade is said to be the oldest in the city), it was rebuilt in the seventeenth century and started to deteriorate after the Franciscans were expelled in 1857, the damage completed by bombardment during Villa's assault. The building and gardens have now been partially but beautifully restored, and the museum brilliantly integrated with the ruins. There are more than five thousand masks on display, which makes taking it all in a bit overwhelming. The masks trace the art's development in what is now Mexico from some very ancient, pre-Columbian examples to contemporary masks: often there are twenty or more variations on the same theme, and one little room is entirely full of the visages of Moors and Christians from the *Danza de los Moros y Cristianos*. As well as the masks, you can see Coronel's impressive collections of ceramics and puppets, the town's original charter granted by Philip II in 1593, and sketches and drawings connected with his wife Ruth Rivera, architect and daughter of Diego. There's also a bookstore and spiffy café. If you don't fancy the pleasant walk to or from town, several bus routes, including #5, #8 and #9, pass close by.

The aqueduct and Museo Francisco Goitia

In quite the other direction, in the south of the city you can follow the line of the **aqueduct** that used to carry water to this area. Not much of it remains, but what there is can be inspected at closer quarters from the little **Parque Enrique Estrada** on Gonzales Ortega – the continuation of Hidalgo up the hill from the centre. At the back of the park, in what was once the governor's residence, stands a third local artist's museum, the **Museo Francisco Goitia** (Tues–Sun 10am–5pm; US$2). Goitia was one of Mexico's leading painters early in the twentieth century, and this enjoyable little museum houses a permanent exhibition of his work and that of more modern local artists (including Pedro Coronel), as well as hit-or-miss temporary displays and travelling art shows. Further behind the park sits the towering terracotta-coloured **Basílica Fátima,** which looks more impressive from a distance. There's not much historical significance here; only a few decades old, it's one of the city's most recent large-scale constructions, but it's worth trekking to its doors for a spectacular view of the city.

Mina El Edén

The **Mina El Edén**, or Eden Mine (daily 10am–6pm; US$2.50) is perhaps the most curious and unusual of all Zacatecas' attractions. The entrance to the old mine is right in the west of the city, up a road behind the modern hospital, from where a small train takes you to the beginning of the sixteenth-century shafts in the heart of the Cerro del Bosque, some 300m below the summit. Those who are claustrophobic be forewarned – the tunnels get tight at points. The forty-minute guided tour (roughly every 15min) – which takes in only a fraction of the workings and is only available in full-speed-ahead Spanish – involves being herded into an underground shop selling rocks from the mine, viewing a pathetic artificial waterfall and being fed all sorts of stupefying statistics, but is done with boundless charm. Some of the numbers are terrifying: if the guide is to be believed, fatalities among the workers ran to eight every day at the height of production. It seems perfectly possible when you're down there as level upon level of old galleries fall away for some 320m beneath you, inaccessible since the mine flooded when production stopped in the mid-1960s. Inside now are diverting subterranean pools, chasms crossed on rickety wooden bridges and, of course, a ghost. The entire hill is honeycombed with tunnels, and in one of them a lift has been installed that takes you up to the slopes of the Cerro del Bosque, about 200m from the lower station of the cable car (you can also enter the mine from this end, though you may have a longer wait for a guide).

To reach the mine, take a bus from the Jardín Independencia up Juárez to the hospital (buses marked "IMSS"), or walk, taking in a pleasant stroll along the Alameda followed by a brief climb.

The cable car and Cerro de la Bufa

The lower station of the **cable car** (daily 10am–6pm; US$2 each way; services can be disrupted by strong winds) is on the slopes of the Cerro del Bosque, near the back entrance to El Edén. Once you're used to the altitude, it's an easy climb up from San Agustín, or bus #7 will bring you right to the door. Out from the station the views down on the houses as you pass right over the city centre are extraordinary. Most people make a return trip across the city from Cerro del Bosque to the top of the Cerro de la Bufa, but walking back down is no great strain.

At the summit of the Cerro de la Bufa, after you've taken in the superb panorama of Zacatecas and its surroundings, visit the little **Capilla del**

Patrocinio, an eighteenth-century chapel with an image of the Virgin said to perform healing miracles, and stroll around the observatory, on the very edge of the crags. Also up here, the **Museo de la Toma de Zacatecas** (daily 10am–5pm; US$1.20), full of revolutionary arms and memorabilia, honours Pancho Villa's spectacular victory in the town, also commemorated with a dramatic equestrian statue outside.

Behind, hunkered below that great crest of rock, the **Mausoleo de los Hombres Ilustres** is where *Zacatecanos* who have made their mark on history are buried, or at least have their memorials. There are still a few empty places, and it would be a magnificent place to end up – as close to heaven as you could wish, with great views while you're waiting.

Eating, drinking and entertainment

For a relatively small town, Zacatecas is well served with good **restaurants** around the centre, and has a tolerably wide variety. Cheaper places are less abundant, but for inexpensive tacos, tostadas and burgers, head away from the centre towards the old bus station: Ventura Sálazar is lined with places serving quick snacks. While in Zacatecas, you should sample *tunas*, the succulent green or purple fruit of the prickly pear cactus. In season, they're sold everywhere, ready-peeled, by the bucketload, or if you go out into the country you can pick your own, though a pair of heavy gloves is a distinct advantage.

Nightlife, especially at weekends while the university is in session, is livelier than you might expect, much of the early evening action happening on the streets where there always seems to be some procession or a band playing, usually in the small plazas at either end of the Mercado Gonzales Ortega. On Friday and Saturday evenings (and sometimes Thurs and even Sun) you may well encounter a *callejóneada*, where musicians – usually with several big drums and a brass section – promenade around the back alleys followed by whoever wants to tag along. There's often a donkey bearing carafes of tequila, and you may be offered some, though it is as well to come equipped with your own tipple. Tag on as you hear them go by or head to the Alameda in the early evening to catch the start. Either way it is a great start to an evening on the town, visiting some of the numerous bars and clubs that dot the downtown landscape.

If you can, try to make it here for one of the town's two major celebrations. The principal **fiesta** – at the end of August and straying into the first two weeks in September – is the regional Feria de Zacatecas, which you should definitely try to get to if possible. The highlight is the battle between Moors and Christians acted out on the Cerro de la Bufa (an import from Spain, where this type of stylized fighting is more common). August 27 is the main day, but festivities spill over several days before and after, with **bullfights** (the fiercest fighting bulls in all Mexico are bred around Zacatecas) and plenty of traditional carousing.

The last decade or so has seen the ascendancy of Zacatecas en la Cultura, an enormous citywide celebration of all strands of culture that's something akin to Guanajuato's Cervantino festival. It lasts for two weeks around Semana Santa, with daily events all over town from high-quality Mexican rock acts and even a few foreign bands to folkloric dance, opera and ballet. It seems to get bigger each year, which is hardly surprising considering the overall quality and the fact that most events are free. For some of the more formal events there may be a small fee, and tickets can be obtained from a booth in Teatro Calderón and from the tourist office.

Restaurants and cafés

Acrópolis beside the cathedral in the corner of the Mercado Gonzales Ortega. Very popular café serving excellent but quite pricey breakfasts from 8.30am, ice cream, fruit juices, good coffee and main meals until 10pm. Most locals go for the burgers. English menus are available.

Birrierias Jaramillo Hidalgo 729. Relaxed and friendly with family-style birria for US$3–5. A terrific place to sample this regional dish.

Café Anis Hidalgo 306. Low-key place that's good for breakfast, and coffee and cakes all day.

Café la Colonial Mercado Gonzales Ortega. Overlooking Tacuba, with great views of the passing action (it gets the sun until mid-afternoon), this is a favourite spot for watching the world go by while drinking beer, sipping on *licuados* or snacking on sandwiches and ice cream. It's not as expensive as you'd expect, but the food isn't as good as you'd expect either.

Los Dorados de Villa Plazuela de García 1314 ⓣ492/922-5722. Delicious little restaurant a short walk from the centre with a cozy atmosphere thanks to Pancho Villa-themed decorations ("Los Dorados" were his young followers). Exotic birds fly free in the entrance and the excellent traditional menu, mostly moles, keeps people coming back for more. Mains are US$4–5 and it is so popular you must reserve in advance.

Garufa Jardín Juárez 135. Argentinian restaurant specializing in gargantuan and super-succulent steaks imported from the pampas (US$14–20), along with much cheaper salads and pasta dishes, served in attractive rustic surroundings.

Gorditas Doña Julia Hidalgo 409. A one-trick pony, only serving gorditas (US$0.80 each) stuffed with either various cuts of meat, refried beans, shredded nopal cactus in a hot salsa, or mole and rice, either to go or to eat in this cheerfully bright, open-fronted restaurant. Now with additional branches at Tacuba 110 and Torreón 601.

Hong Kong Allende 117. Attractive Cantonese restaurant and bar upstairs in the colonial surroundings of the bishop's former residence. All the expected foo yung, chow mein and fried rice dishes are here, mostly for US$3–4, and there's a daily special with several filling plates for US$7.

Il San Patricio Café Hidalgo 403. The best coffee in town, but also the highest prices, justified by the use of Italian espresso, the peaceful courtyard setting and a number of magazines to browse, some in English.

Mi Viejo Fernando Villapando 319. Cosy little café away from the bustle of town and with a great selection of coffees and sweet and savoury crepes at fairly high prices. Closed Mon.

La Plaza inside the *Quinta Real* (see p.295). Pick of the bunch for an expensive, formal meal, if only for the setting overlooking the former bullring. Expect to spend around US$35 a head for a full meal of nopal stuffed with shrimp, chicken in a tamarind sauce, dessert, coffee and something from the wine list – which includes a good Mexican selection.

El Raspanieve Hidalgo 805. Traditionally from the neighbouring town of Jerez, a *raspanieve* is ice cream served with crushed ice and mixed with either fruit syrups, chocolate or burnt sugar coating. This popular parlour has been in operation since 1940, and has sticky surfaces to prove it.

El Recoveco Torreón 513. One of the better bargains around with all-you-can-eat buffet of over 30 dishes for under US$4. Open daily 8am–7pm.

Restaurante la Bodeguilla Callejón de San Agustín 103. Small, sophisticated, Spanish-style tapas bar with a smartish, student atmosphere, freshly baked empanadas on the counter every afternoon and surprisingly modest prices. A popular evening hangout, too.

Restaurante el Tragadero Juárez 232, by the Alameda. Inexpensive and reliable traditional Mexican restaurant with delicious and piquant *enchiladas Zacatecas* for under US$4.

Rosticería el Pastor Calle Independencia 14. The scent of roasted chicken wafts to the street from this inexpensive, family-friendly joint. US$5 buys you a generous chicken dinner with all the fixings.

Sanborn's Hidalgo 212. Festooned with ferns, this department store/restaurant standby serves an all-you-can-eat buffet for US$7.50, which includes homemade pastries.

La Única Cabaña Jardín Independencia. Always alive with activity, this is one of the town's cheapest and most popular taco restaurants. Good, basic food served with a wide selection of salsas and beer at bargain prices in clean surroundings. Tacos are US$0.50 and full chicken dinner runs US$2.80. Wonderfully fruity and thirst-quenching aguas are also sold to go. Try the sprightly *chía* flavour (a local herb, also famously grown on Chia Pets). Live acoustic guitar in the afternoon too.

Viva Pizza Callejón de Venya 105, opposite the cathedral. US-style pizzas served in a small cheery room or to go, from around US$3 for a personal one. For delivery call ⓣ492/922-7965.

Bars and clubs

Bar Botarel *Quinta Real* hotel. Gorgeous bar built under the seating of what used to be the bullring. Arrive soon after 6pm to get one of the intimate booths from where you can look out at the plaza and the rest of the hotel. Prices are almost twice what you'd pay elsewhere but nowhere has this atmosphere. Live music Fridays and Saturdays until midnight.

Cactus Bar Hidalgo 111. Lively and popular nightclub with pool and table football upstairs, and two-for-one drink specials on Wed and Thurs. Small cover charge for men on Fri and for all on Sat. Closed Sun.

El Elefante Díaz Ordaz 717, by the lower cable-car station ⓣ492/922-7194. The main competition for *El Malacate* and with great views over town. While cheaper, it has less atmosphere and a 2am closing time, but it's not bad once it hots up after around 11.30pm. US$6 entry.

El Malacate main entrance to Mina El Edén (see p.299) ⓣ492/922-3002. Zacatecas' major club, right in the heart of the mountain and accessed on the same train used in the mine tour, with a lively atmosphere from around 11pm. Some Latin numbers, US and European dance tunes, but mostly cheesy electronic techno music. More pomp and circumstance than its reputation deserves but a novelty just the same. If you don't enjoy being trapped in an enclosed space, then this is not for you. Thurs–Sat 10pm–2.30am, reservations essential Fri and Sat; US$6 entry.

Mama Inés in bottom portion of the Mercado Gonzales Ortega. Kicking with Cuban flavour, live music and a long list of cocktails (US$4). Go late.

El Mito Juárez 108, opposite *Restaurante el Tragadero*. Black lighting, good dance music, and decked-out regulars make this a fun after-hours spot. US$4 entry. Open 10pm–2am.

La Nueva Galicia Plaza Goitia. Restaurant and glossy bar that's good for drink to get the evening going. Recently it's enjoyed a surge in popularity.

Rincón de los Trovadores Hidalgo 802. Very agreeable, mostly acoustic venue and bar where local musicians play every night except Monday (7pm–2.30am), the more exalted players at weekends and there's a looser, jamming atmosphere earlier in the week. Bring your instrument if you have one. No cover.

Listings

American Express Viajes Mazzocco, Fatima 115, Col. Sierra de Alilca, opposite Basílica Fátima, behind Parque Enrique Estrada (Mon–Fri 9am–7pm, Sat & Sun 9am–2pm; ⓣ492/922-0854, ⓔmazzocco@prodigy.net.mx), and another smaller more central location in the *Hotel Casa Santa Lucía*, Hidalgo 717 (Mon–Sat 9am–8pm, Sun 9am–4pm; ⓣ492/924-0050, same email). Hold mail, cash and replace travellers' cheques, and organize city tours (see below).

Banks and exchange Plenty of banks are situated along Hidalgo, including Banamex, Bancomer, Bital and Banorte, all between Juárez and Allende and all offering currency exchange (Mon–Fri 9am–1pm). All have 24-hour ATMs.

Books and newspapers The best (though still limited) source of English-language books, magazines and papers is Librería Páginas, Hidalgo 114.

Buses To get to the bus terminal, take Ruta 8 services marked "Central", which run frequently along Fernando Villapando and past the Jardín Independencia. There are frequent long-distance bus services to all parts of northern Mexico, including hourly buses to Durango and Chihuahua, some of which push on through to the border at Ciudad Juárez. There are also direct buses running to Torreón and Monterrey hourly and a couple daily to Mazatlán; you could also catch the first bus to Durango and get a connection to Mazatlán from there. Heading south, the highway to Mexico City splits, with hourly buses along either route – the faster, western route runs via Aguascalientes and León, while the eastern route runs via San Luis Potosí – the two roads meeting again at Querétaro. There are also hourly buses to Guadalajara. If you're headed to Real de Catorce, you'll need to change at both San Luis Potosí and Matehuala: make an early start to be sure of getting there in a day.

Cinema Salas 2000, López Mateos 430 (ⓣ492/922-6011), just uphill from the old bus station, and Nova Cinemas on Constituyentes 300 up from the Alameda (ⓣ492/922-5404) show mostly first-run Hollywood movies for around US$3. The Cine Club Universitário, Alameda 414, currently shows more art-house movies every second Thursday for next to nothing; check the monthly *Agenda Cultural* leaflet available from the tourist office.

Emergencies For tourist emergencies call ⓣ492/922-3426; open 24 hours a day 365 days a year. Especialidades Médicas, Vincente Guerrero 143 (ⓣ492/924-2928) handles medical emergencies and dental care.

Flights You can fly to Mexico City on a daily service: the local airport (some 20km to the north of the centre, reached by taxi) has regular connections to Tijuana and Morelia, too, as well as international services to Chicago, Dallas, Los Angeles, and Oakland.

Internet access Numerous businesses around town, mostly competitively priced around US$1.50

an hour. Try Optimus Prime, Tacuba 118 (daily 10am–10pm), or Cyber Central, Hidalgo 304 (daily 10am–9pm).

Laundry Fast Clean, Fernando Villapando 203 (Mon–Sat 9am–7pm), wash and dry for US$1.20 per kilo.

Post office Allende 111 (Mon–Fri 9am–5pm, Sat 9am–1pm).

Travel agencies and tours Several local agencies handle general travel requirements and offer tours of the city and to surrounding attractions: try Viajes Mazzocco (see above under "American Express"); and Operadora Zacatecas, Hidalgo 630 (Ⓣ492/924-0050 or 01-800/714-4150), opposite the *Hotel Casa Santa Lucía* (Mon–Sat 9am–8pm, Sun 9am–4pm; Ⓣ492/924-4900, Ⓔop-zacatecas@wspanmex.com.mx). All the bigger hotels stock leaflets detailing tours to Guadalupe (US$15) and to Chicomoztoc (US$22), among other destinations.

Around Zacatecas: the Centro Platero de Zacatecas, Guadalupe and Chicomoztoc

It's well worth basing yourself in Zacatecas to explore the immediate surroundings, not least the **Centro Platero de Zacatecas**, where the Zacatecan tradition of silver-working reaches is highest expression. Those with no interest in buying should definitely continue to **Guadalupe** – virtually a suburb of Zacatecas – to see the Convento de Guadalupe, a rich, sumptuously decorated monastery, rare in that it has survived the centuries more or less unscathed, and for that reason is one of the most important such buildings in Mexico. Further out (you'll need to allow the best part of a day), the ruins of the great desert fortress town **Chicomoztoc** are by contrast quite unadorned, but enormously impressive nonetheless. You can venture out to either place independently, though several travel agents in Zacatecas offer tours to the sites (see above).

The Centro Platero de Zacatecas

Galleries in town sell stacks of jewellery, but the quality is often low and the designs unimaginative and poorly executed. There are good places to be found, but if you are serious about buying silver, or just seeing artisans at work, devote a couple of hours to visiting the **Centro Platero de Zacatecas** (Mon–Fri 10am–6pm, Sat 10am–2pm; free), located about 5km south of the centre in the former Hacienda de Bernárdez, within the exclusive gated community of Club de Golf de Zacatecas. Ruta 11 from outside Sala 200 on López Mateos, runs to the gate, where you can ask directions and walk the last kilometre; alternatively take a taxi to the door for US$3–4.

Within the ex-hacienda, students and recent graduates of the on-site silversmith school maintain a series of small workshops where you can see them creating original designs, many influenced by pre-Columbian images, or iconography associated with Zacatecas. Of course, everything is for sale, often at very reasonable prices, though the very best work commands a high price tag.

Guadalupe

Local buses run out to **GUADALUPE**, 10km southeast of Zacatecas' centre, every few minutes from a little bus station on Callejón de Barra, just east of the old bus terminal. Once there, you can't miss the enormous bulk of the **church**, with its dome and asymmetric twin towers. You enter through a flagged, tree-studded courtyard; the entry to the church is through the elaborate Baroque facade straight ahead, while the entrance to the **monastery** (daily 10am–4.30pm; US$3, free on Sun) is to the right. The monastery, founded in 1704, is a vast and confusing warren of a place, with seemingly endless rows of cells opening off courtyards, stairways leading nowhere and mile-long corridors lined with portraits of monks and vast tableaux from the life of St Francis. There are guided tours in Spanish, but it's more enjoyable to wander alone, viewing the paintings – which cover every wall – at your own pace, and possibly tagging on to a group for a few minutes when your paths cross. You'll have to time your visit to arrive after 2pm on Sunday to gain access to the monastery's two highlights: the **Coro Alto**, the raised choir at the back of the church, with its beautifully carved and painted wooden choir stalls, and the **Capilla de Napoles**, whose Neoclassical domed roof is coated in elaborately filigreed gold-leaf. Presumably, 150 years ago, such sights were not altogether unusual in Mexican churches – today it's the richest you'll see anywhere. You can look into the chapel from the Coro Alto and any time from an entrance at the side of the main church, but the gates are officially only opened on special occasions.

Next door to the monastery, the **Regional History Museum** (Tues–Sun 10am–4.30pm; free) houses a collection of indigenous art and a marginally interesting transport exhibition with a reconstructed pre-Hispanic stone-wheeled cart, sumptuous horse-drawn carriages and nice bits of antique railway rolling stock.

Chicomoztoc

The ruins of **CHICOMOZTOC** (daily 10am–4.30pm; US$3.20, free on Sun), also known as **La Quemada**, lie some 40km south from Zacatecas on the road to Villanueva and Guadalajara. The scale of the complex isn't apparent until you're inside – from the road you can vaguely see signs of construction, but the whole thing, even the huge restored pyramid, blends so totally into the mountain behind as to be almost invisible. No two archeologists seem to agree on the nature of the site, its functions or inhabitants, even to the extent that many doubt it was a fortress, despite its superb natural defensive position and hefty surrounding walls. Most likely it was a frontier post on the outskirts of some pre-Aztec sphere of domination – probably the Toltecs – charged with keeping at bay the southward depredations of the Chichimeca. Alternatively, it could simply be the work of a local ruling class, having exacted enough tribute to build themselves these palaces, and needing the defences to keep their own subjects out. Huichol legend seems to support the second theory: there was an evil priest, the story runs, who lived on a rock surrounded by walls and covered with buildings, with eagles and jaguars under his command to oppress the population. The people appealed to their gods, who destroyed the priest and his followers with "great heat", warning the people not to go near the rock again. Chicomoztoc was in fact destroyed by fire around 1300 AD and was never reoccupied; even today, the Huichols, in their annual pilgrimage from the Sierra Madre in the west to collect peyote around Real de Catorce to the east, take a long detour to bypass this area.

In addition to the reconstructed temple, you'll see here a large hall with eleven pillars still standing, a ball-court, an extensive (if barely visible from the ground) system of roads heading out into the valley, and many lesser, ruinous structures all listed for eventual reconstruction. Much of the restoration work is based on drawings produced over the course of ten years from 1825 by a German mining engineer, Carlos de Burghes. Copies are on show in the superb **museum** at the site (daily 10am–4pm; US$0.70), which makes a masterful job of bringing the place alive with a select display of artefacts, a detailed model of the area and several explanatory videos (in Spanish only).

Most visitors get to the site by car (a half-hour drive on Ruta 54), by taxi (US$50), or on a tour, but **getting to Chicomoztoc** is easy enough by public transport with Villanueva-bound Perzona buses leaving every half-hour or so from the old bus station in Zacatecas. They're usually happy to drop you at the start of the two-kilometre access road (ask for "las ruinas"); the ride to this point takes about an hour, from where you've got a 25-minute walk to the entrance. To get back, hike to the highway and either flag down the first bus you see, or try to hitchhike while you're waiting.

Aguascalientes

The lively industrial town of **AGUASCALIENTES**, 100km south of Zacatecas, is an important and booming provincial capital with some fine colonial monuments in among its newer buildings. A couple of excellent **museums**, in addition, make this a good place to stop over for a day or two, especially when you take into account the town's reputation for some of the finest **fiestas** in Mexico – rarely a week goes by without celebration, or at least a band playing in one of the plazas at the weekend – and for the manufacture of excellent **wines** and **brandy**.

Arrival, orientation and information

The **bus station** is around 4km from the centre on the city's ring road (Avenida de la Convención), from where there's a frequent bus service into the **Plaza de Armas** ("Centro"), at the heart of town. Here, and on the adjoin-

ing **Plaza de la República**, also known as the **Plaza de la Patria**, are all the important public buildings, the cathedral, government offices, the fancier hotels and a handful of banks; many of the streets around here are pedestrianized, and most things you'll want to see are in easy walking distance.

The **tourist office** is also in the plaza, on the ground floor of the Palacio de Gobierno (Mon–Fri 9am–8pm, Sat & Sun 10am–6pm; ⓣ449/910-2088, ⓦwww.turismoags.com.mx or www.aguascalientes.gob.mx); if they've run out of maps, neighbouring Turiste, at the corner of Nieto and the plaza, sell an excellent one.

Accommodation

Budget accommodation in Aguascalientes is located mostly around the market area, while some of the **hotels** on and around the Plaza de la Patría offer real luxury. During the ferias, rooms are almost impossible to obtain at short notice and are likely to cost at least fifty percent more.

Colonial 5 de Mayo 552 ⓣ/ⓕ449/915-3577. Comfortable hotel with car park and a small restaurant on site. All rooms with TV, phone and large windows letting in plenty of light. ❺

Don Jesús Juárez 429 ⓣ449/915-5598. Basic, big and bare, very near the market, but fairly quiet and OK for the price, though you might prefer to pay the extra US$5 for a newer, carpeted room. ❸

Gomez Avenida Circunvalación, beside the bus station ⓣ449/978-2120. Not bad if you arrive late or plan to push on early. ❹

Holiday Inn Nieto 102, corner of José María Chavez, Plaza Principal ⓣ449/916-1666. Modern, luxury hotel, offering bags of comfort though little soul. To get a plaza view you'll have to go for a suite (❾). Rooms ❼

Hotel Posada San Rafael Hidalgo 205 ⓣ449/915-7761. Plain, good-value rooms with fans, TV and plenty of parking. ❹

Imperial 5 de Mayo 105 ⓣ/ⓕ449/915-1650. Very faded elegance in a fine colonial building, but the best-value place on the plaza, particularly if you can get a room with a balcony. ❺

Maser Juan de Montoro 303 ⓣ449/915-9662. Attractive and well-cared-for budget hotel with airy rooms around a central courtyard, and parking available. Rooms with TV cost US$3 more. ❹

Roble 5 de Mayo 540 ⓣ/ⓕ449/915-3994. One of the best-value places in town; big-clean and relaxed, with friendly management, rooms with cable TV, and plenty of parking. ❻

Rosales Guadalupe Victória 104 ⓣ449/915-2165. A bargain for the location, right by the north side of the plaza, with pleasantly furnished rooms around a central courtyard. Hot water only in the morning. ❸

Señorial Colón 104, south side of the Plaza Principal ⓣ449/915-1630. Simple carpeted rooms, but decent value for the location, particularly the corner rooms overlooking the plaza. ❺

Youth Hostel (CREA), in a sports complex at Avenida de la Convención and Jaime Nunó, in the suburb of Colonia Héroes ⓣ449/918-0863. Single-sex dorms (bunks under US$4) and an 11pm curfew; to get there, take bus #20 from outside the bus station. ❺

The City

The entire centre of Aguascalientes is undermined by a series of tunnels and catacombs carved out by an unknown civilization; unfortunately these are all closed to the public, and the most ancient constructions you'll see here are the colonial buildings around the central Plaza de la Patria, notably the cathedral, and the Palacio de Gobierno with its impressive murals. Fanning out from there are a few worthwhile museums, chief among them the **Museo José Guadalupe Posada**, dedicated to Mexico's most famous engraver. If you want to visit one of the **hot springs** from which the city takes its name, head for the Balneario Ojocaliente, which has a series of not-so-hot pools and bathing chambers, just outside town on the road to San Luis Potosí. To get there, take "Ruta 12" along López Mateos.

Around the Plaza de la Patría

The **Plaza de la Patria** is the place to start any exploration of Aguascalientes. In the centre of this enormous area is the **Exedra**, an amphitheatre-shaped space for performances, overlooked by a column topped with a Mexican eagle. Chief of the buildings around it is the **Palacio de Gobierno**, a remarkably beautiful Neoclassical structure, built in the seventeenth century from reddish volcanic rock, formed around an arcaded courtyard with a grand central staircase, and decorated with four marvellous **murals** by the Chilean Oswaldo Barra Cunningham, who learnt his trade from the greatest muralist of them all, Diego Rivera. The first of these, at the back on the ground floor, were painted in 1962, and others span the years since: the most recent (from 1992) are at the front of the building.

Next door, the modern **Palacio Municipal** is bland in comparison, while down the other side of the plaza, the eighteenth-century **cathedral** has recently been refurbished to reveal its full glory, in an over-the-top welter of gold and polished marble. The **Pinacoteca Religiosa**, in an annex, has a collection of eighteenth-century religious paintings that is well worth a look.

Venustiano Carranza leads down beside the cathedral to the **Casa de la Cultura** (daily 7am–9pm; free), a beautiful old mansion given over to music and dance classes and the occasional exhibition. The notice board here is an excellent place to find out what's on around town, and in the patio there's a small café (see "Eating", overleaf) – a tranquil spot to have a drink and a rest. A little further down Carranza, on the opposite side, the **Museo Regional de Historia** (Tues–Sun 10am–7pm; US$2.80, free on Sun) chronicles local history, from a fossilized mammoth tusk and traditional crafts to the Revolution. There's also material on local composer and pianist Manuel Ponce, who in the first half of the twentieth century ranked alongside the three great muralists as Mexico's artistic culture took its place on the world stage. The **Museo de Arte Contemporáneo**), at the corner of Morelos and Primo Verdad (Tues–Sun 11am–6pm; US$1, free on Sun), is little over a decade old and home to some of the most interesting and provocative art from the region. What's more, all the works were created by artists under 35 years of age.

Escape from the sun a little further west on Carranza in the shady **Jardín San Marcos**, a long, beautifully manicured park that runs down to the **Templo del San Marcos**. Turning left here you're on the pedestrianized **Paseo de la Feria**, which cuts through to López Mateos, its modern buildings in complete contrast to what went before. On your left is the **Casino de la Feria** with its giant palenque, where cockfights are staged – this is the site of the city's famous fiestas. It is worth taking a walk around the area just to see what wealthy, modern Mexico can look like: here there are numerous upmarket restaurants and clubs, the *Hotel Fiesta Americana*, Canal 6 TV headquarters and the Expo Plaza by the bullring, with plenty of greenery and postmodern neo-colonial architecture to boot. **Calle Nieto**, extending for several blocks between **Plaza de la Patria** and **Paseo de la Feria**, is lined with boutiques selling one of the city's most recognized crafts: **lace**.

The Museo Posada and the Museo Aguascalientes

Though it only occupies a couple of rooms in a small building about 1km south of the centre, the **Museo José Guadalupe Posada** (Tues–Sun 11am–6pm; US$1) is one of the main reasons to visit Aguascalientes, almost a place of pilgrimage for devotees of this influential printmaker, who is best known for his political satire and criticism of the Catholic Church expressed in dark but humorous scenes featuring costumed skeletons. Two rooms, plus

Posada – the most Mexican artist

The frequently macabre work of **José Guadalupe Posada** is familiar even if his name is not: Diego Rivera was not so wrong when he described the prolific Posada as "so outstanding that one day even his name will be forgotten". He was born in Aguascalientes in 1852, a baker's son later apprenticed to a lithographer. In 1888 he moved to the capital (having meanwhile lived in León for some time), and started to create in earnest the thousands of prints for which he soon became known. He mainly worked for the editor and printer Vanegas Arroyo, and his images appeared on posters and, mostly, in the satirical broadsheets that flourished despite – or more likely because of – the censorship of the Porfiriano era. Some of Posada's work was political, attacking corrupt politicians, complacent clergy or foreign intervention, but much was simply recording the news (especially disasters, which so obsess the Mexican press to this day), lampooning popular figures, or observing everyday life with a gleefully macabre eye. Later, the events and figures of the Revolution, grotesquely caricatured, came to dominate his work.

Although the *calaveras*, the often elegantly clad skeletons that people much of his work, are best known, the museum devoted to him in Aguascalientes covers the full range of his work. It all bears a peculiar mix of Catholicism, pre-Columbian tradition, preoccupation with death and black humour that can only be Mexican – and that profoundly affected all later Mexican art. Rivera and Orozco are just two of the greats who publicly acknowledged their debt to Posada. Technically, Posada moved on from lithography to engraving in type metal (producing the characteristic hatched effect seen in much of his work) and finally to zinc etching, an extremely rapid method involving drawing directly onto a zinc printing plate with acid-resistant ink, and then dipping it until the untouched areas corroded.

another for temporary exhibitions, contain scores of nicely pressed lithographs, along with the original plates, contemporary photos and biographical information in Spanish. A few poorly pressed prints are for sale. The museum occupies the former priest's house of the **Templo del Señor del Encino**, an elegant colonial church of pinkish stone with a pretty tiled dome; inside is the miraculous and much venerated "black Christ" of Encino. To get there, head east from the plaza and take the first right, Díaz de León, south for about seven blocks. In front of the church and museum there's a pleasant, quiet square, at the heart of a peaceful old neighbourhood.

The **Museo Aguascalientes** (Tues–Sun 11am–6pm; US$1, free on Sun) lies in the opposite direction, east from the plaza, then north on Zaragoza. Its art collection, mostly modern, is mostly of interest for its works by Saturnino Herrán, a local who was a contemporary and friend of Diego Rivera but who died young and never really achieved much recognition. Note his large stained-glass panel, and also rooms full of charcoal drawings, block prints and paintings by Gabriel Fernández Ledesma, another local son of some note. Opposite the museum, the over-the-top **Templo de San Antonio**, built around 1900, has a muddled facade with some vaguely discernible Neoclassical elements. Inside, murals provide a blaze of colour.

Eating, drinking and entertainment

Ordinary **restaurants** are surprisingly thin on the ground in Aguascalientes, though all the large hotels on the plaza have their own. In addition, plenty of simple places along **Juárez** serve good, tasty barbecued chicken, and there are taco and seafood places in the **market** itself, between Juárez and 5 de Mayo at Alvaro Obregón; the smaller Mercado de Artesanías, on Obregón, doesn't have much in the way of decent crafts, but it does have more eating places without the frenzy of the main market. Fancier places to eat line **López Mateos**, especially just west of the centre towards the Paseo de la Feria. While you're in town you should try some of the local **wine** (not always easy except in the more expensive restaurants) or at least the **brandy**: San Marcos is the best-known, made here and sold all over the republic.

The most important fiesta in the city – famous throughout Mexico – is the nearly two-centuries-old **Feria de San Marcos**, celebrated in the Jardín San Marcos during the month of April and the first week of May with every manner of cultural and now commercial event.

Restaurants, bars and cafés

Los Antojos de Carranza Carranza 301. Plenty of traditional, well-presented Mexican dishes, most under US$4, but more a place to stop in for a beer and top up on all manner of *botanas*. Always thick with roving minstrels eager to serenade you.

Los Arquitos Café inside Casa de la Cultura on Carranza. Serene spot for top-quality quiche, salads and that Mexican rarity, a strong espresso; not exactly cheap.

Café La Parroquia Correa 128. Cool, student café offering mainly sandwiches and burgers, along with the obligatory cappuccino.

El Infierno Paseo de la Feria 114, near Nieto. A video bar serving imbibers late into the night.

Jugos Acapulco Allende 106, between 5 de Mayo and Juárez. Incredibly clean juice bar that also serves hamburgers and more substantial meals; good for breakfast (US$2.50).

Kiko's Merendero Paseo de la Feria 132 (aka Arturo Pani), at Jardín San Marcos. More bar than restaurant, but food is served to soak up the drinks.

Mitla Restaurante Madero 222. Popular, old-fashioned Mexican restaurant that has been operating since 1938, with white-jacketed waiters serving a good selection of national and local dishes, including seafood and very reasonable comidas corridas. There's also an impressive US$6 Sunday buffet.

La Saturnina Carranza 12. Lovely and colourful courtyard café that's great for breakfast of just coffee and cake until around 3pm.

Listings

Banks and exchange Banamex and Bancomer are on 5 de Mayo on the north side of Plaza de la Patria, both with 24-hour ATMs. Casas de cambio are mostly clustered around the post office on Hospitalidad (see below).

Buses Aguascalientes is situated on Hwy-45 between Zacatecas and León, and there are hourly buses in either direction, many continuing as far as Chihuahua to the north and Mexico City to the south (via Irapuato and Querétaro). There are also slower services to Guadalajara and San Luis Potosí. For Guanajuato, you'll probably be quicker taking a bus first to León and getting a connection from there. To get to the station from the centre, catch a bus marked "Central" from beside the cathedral on Calle Matamoros.

Internet access Ciber Café La Web, Nieto 528. US$1 per hour.

Post office The main post office is on Hospitalidad, a block north of the plaza and reached by following Morelos and then turning right.

León

Heading south from Aguascalientes, the highway and near-constant buses pass through the town of Lagos de Moreno (see p.248) to **LEÓN**, a teeming, industrial city 60km away. There's a long tradition of **leatherwork** here – reflected today in the scores of shoe factories and, in the centre, hundreds of shoe shops: it's a good place to buy hand-tooled cowboy boots, leather jackets, belts or just about anything else made of leather.

The **bus station** is around 3km from the centre, and most people take one look and get no further, but if you're changing buses here it's well worth taking an hour to wander round the immediate vicinity. This area has the highest concentration of leather and shoe shops, most of which have very reasonable prices, although there are also some higher-class and pricier boutiques. Even if you only spend ten minutes in the bus station you'll see stacks of shoeboxes being loaded into just about every waiting bus. León also has the region's main **airport**, the nearest to both Guanajuato and San Miguel de Allende, with flights from all over Mexico and Houston, Dallas, LA, Chicago and more. On arrival, many just grab a cab direct to their destination, but there are also very infrequent buses and colectivos (around US$12) to León, and second-class buses ply the highway outside between León and Guanajuato; wave madly and you may be able to flag one down.

If you're determined to explore the town, stash your bag at the bus station's guardería and head for the partly pedestrianized Centro Histórico: walk left out of the bus station, pick up a city bus ("Centro") headed to the right along López Mateos and get off at Hidalgo. In town, the **Plaza de los Fundadores** is not at all what the rest of the city would lead you to expect – spacious, tranquil and elegant, with a fine eighteenth-century cathedral built by the Jesuits and a typically colonial palacio municipal. Little else survived a disastrous flood in 1883, but the plaza is surrounded by broad boulevards lined with shops, and there are a couple of other churches that deserve a look: the Baroque **Templo de los Angeles** and the extraordinary marble **Templo Expiatorio** on Madero, where you can visit a series of underground chambers.

Should you need a place to stay here, you'll find a number of cheapish **hotels** in the streets immediately opposite the bus station: try the pleasant, clean TV-equipped *Niza*, Nuevo Vallarta 213 (Ⓣ477/763-3557; ❹), or the simple but well-kept *Blanquita*, Tasco 150 at La Luz (Ⓣ477/763-1909, Ⓕ771-3303; ❺).

Guanajuato

Shoe-horned into a narrow ravine, **GUANAJUATO** was for centuries the wealthiest city in Mexico, its mines pouring out silver and gold in prodigious quantities. Today it presents a remarkable sight: emerging from the surrounding hills you come upon the town quite suddenly, a riot of colonial architecture dominated by the bluff (and rather ugly) bulk of the university, tumbling down hills so steep that at times it seems the roof of one building is suspended from the floor of the last. Declared a UNESCO World Heritage Zone in 1988, Guanajuato is protective of its image: there are no traffic lights or neon signs here, and the topography ensures that there's no room for new buildings.

This is an extremely enjoyable place to visit, peaceful, yet with plenty of life in its narrow streets (especially during term-time), lots of good places to eat and drink, and plenty to see – it's never dull and always surprising. There's an old-fashioned, backwater feel to the place, reinforced by the students' habit of going serenading in their black capes, the brass bands playing in the plazas, and the general refusal to make any special effort to accommodate the flood of tourists – who thankfully never really manage to disturb the daily ebb and flow.

Orientation

It's not difficult to find your way around Guanajuato and **maps** are rarely, if ever, necessary. The streets run in close parallel along the steep sides of the valley, while almost directly beneath the town's main thoroughfare, **Avenida**

Juárez, passes an underground roadway: the **Subterráneo Miguel Hidalgo**. It was built as a tunnel to take the river under the city and prevent the periodic flooding to which it was liable – and in the process to provide a covered sewer. The river now runs deeper below ground, and its former course, with the addition of a few exits and entrances, has proved very handy in preventing traffic from clogging up the centre entirely; more tunnels have since been added to keep the traffic flowing. If you're interested, some bus routes go through the tunnels, or you could duck down one of the many stairways and wander through a short section: it is especially dramatic at night, though fumey during rush hour. When walking – the best way to get around the city – it's enough to know that Avenida Juárez runs straight through the heart of town along the ravine floor and that everything of interest is either on it, or just off it on the lower slopes. Should you get lost, simply head downhill and you'll get back to Juárez. The town has two alternative centres: the western end is somewhat rougher, focused on the plaza outside the **Mercado Hidalgo**, where there is always plenty of action in the bars and cheap cafés; to the east, where Juárez becomes Sopeña, the city is calmer, focusing on the **Jardín de la Unión**, with its shaded restaurants, happy tourists and neatly clipped trees.

Arrival and information

The **bus station**, with a small tourist information booth, guardería and long-distance phones, lies 6km west of the city. Regular local buses ("Centro–Central") shuttle into town in about fifteen minutes, usually terminating outside the Mercado Hidalgo, leaving a ten-minute walk if you're staying close to the Jardín de la Unión. Alternatively, hop aboard one of the Panteón–Presa buses that run the length of town (partly through the tunnels) and ask to get dropped near the Jardín. The nearest **airport** is 30km west of Guanajuato and closer to León (see p.309); taxis direct to Guanajuato should cost around US$20, and if you're prepared to schlep a few hundred metres from the airport out to the highway you can flag down second-class buses north to León or south to Silao and Guanajuato.

It's worth checking out the **tourist office** at Plaza de la Paz 14 (Mon–Fri 9am–7pm, Sat 10am–5pm, Sun 10am–2pm; Ⓣ473/732-0397 ext 107 or 01-800/714-1086, Ⓔinformacion@guanajuato-travel.com), at least for the **free map**; there are also lots of private **information booths** throughout town, including at the bus station, offering tours and hotel reservations.

Accommodation

Rooms in Guanajuato can be hard to come by during certain times of the year, especially on Mexican public holidays, at Christmas, Semana Santa and during the **International Cervantes Festival** (two or three weeks in Oct). If your trip coincides with one of these holidays (see p.321) it's worth trying to book a room several weeks, if not months, in advance. If you can get a room on such occasions, you'll pay around a fifty percent premium on the rates quoted here, which are already fairly high by Mexican standards. By far the best place to stay in the centre of town is around the **Jardín de la Unión**, even if plaza-view rooms come with a sizeable premium and, at weekends, *mariachi* accompaniment until well past midnight. There are several budget options in the same area, which are generally preferable to the other main concentration of cheap hotels around the Mercado Hidalgo. In recent years there has been an increase in the number of quality mid-range places dotted all over town – often worth the few extra pesos.

Near the Mercado Hidalgo

Casa de José Callejón del Patrochino 1 (no phone). The cheapest beds in town; just eight beds in one room of a small house with a pleasant rooftop terrace, and charged at under US$10 a person. It is the first door on the right as you leave Plazuela de los Angeles. ❸

Casa las Manrique Juárez 116 Ⓣ473/732-7678, Ⓕ732-8306. Eight large suites, very nicely decorated and all with TV and minibar. No premium for those fronting the street with views over the town, but they're popular, so reserve early. ❽

Central Juárez 111 Ⓣ473/732-0080. The best of the cheap hotels around the Jardín Reforma, comprising simple rooms with TV. ❺

Hacienda de Cobos Padre Hidalgo 3 Ⓣ/Ⓕ 473/732-0143. Great-value hotel with a pool, and comfortable, attractive motel-style rooms around a large central plaza. There's a restaurant on site, parking, and a back entrance that means you're only five minutes' walk from the Mercado Hidalgo. Prices rise dramatically during popular times. ❻

El Insurgente Juárez 226 Ⓣ473/732-3192, Ⓕ732-6793. Central hotel with many clean, carpeted, comfortable rooms, but overpriced unless you get one on the top floor, which has by far the best views. ❻

Parador San Javier Plaza Aldama 92, 1km from centre on the road to Valenciana Ⓣ473/732-0626, Ⓕ732-3114, Ⓔhpsjgto@redos.int.com.mx. Beautiful hotel set in the magnificent manicured grounds of a former colonial hacienda, complete with lovely pool, posh bar and flash restaurant. Everything to the highest standard and wall-to-wall service staff. ❾

Posada San Francisco Juárez 178 and Gavira, beside the market Ⓣ473/732-2467. Central and large; the simple, spotless rooms all have private bathrooms. ❺

Socavón Alhóndiga 41-A Ⓣ/Ⓕ 473/732-4885, Ⓔhotelsocavon@hotmail.com. A dark tunnel opens into the sunny courtyard of this small, friendly place,

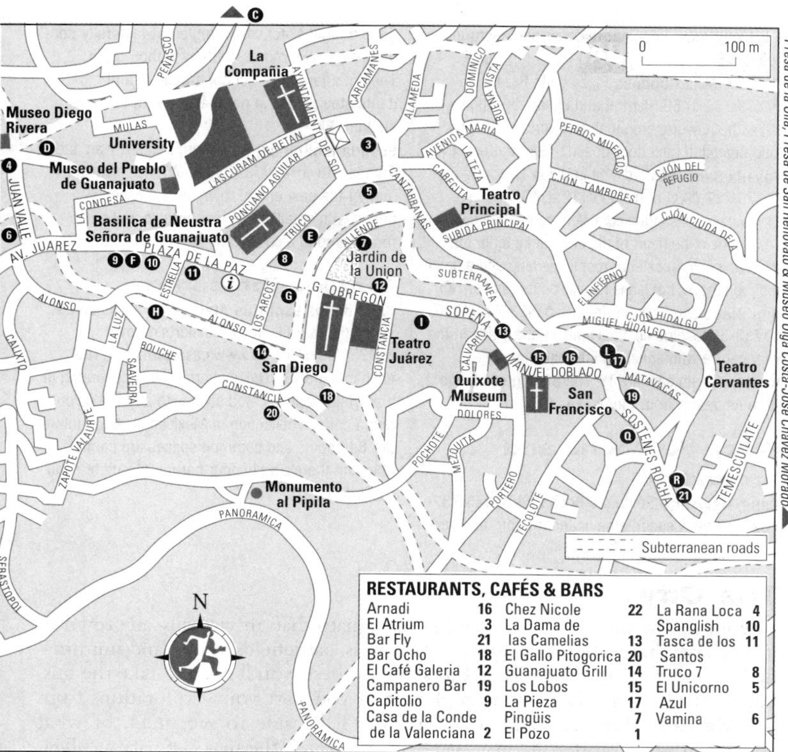

well cared for and with attractive brick-ceilinged rooms, all with TV. A short walk from the centre but worth it, and there's a restaurant on site. ❻

The Jardín de la Unión and around

Casa Kloster Calle de Alonso 32 Ⓣ/Ⓕ473/732-0088. One of the better budget deals in town and hugely popular with backpackers. Clean, simple rooms – avoid those by the street – around a flower-filled courtyard alive with caged birds. There are communal bathrooms with good hot showers, and rates are per person (US$10) in mostly dorm-style rooms with mix-matched decor, making this a steal for singles. Management prefers couples to be married, though they seldom ask, and they enforce a no-smoking rule. ❹

Hostal Cantarranas Cantarranas 50, half a block from the Teatro Principal Ⓣ473/732-5241, Ⓕ732-1708. A great, friendly and clean little place tucked away in the back streets, which doesn't look like much from the outside but features a wonderful rooftop terrace with views of the Pípila. Rooms have king-size beds, and the suites all come with a kitchen stocked with utensils. There's even a three-room suite sleeping six. ❺

Hostería de Frayle Sopeña 3 Ⓣ/Ⓕ473/732-1179. The nicest place near the Jardín in a lovely colonial-style building right in the heart of things with bougainvillea-draped courtyards, spacious common areas, and rooms that feature beautifully tiled bathrooms. Rooms vary, so look at a few first. ❽

Mesón de los Poetas Positos 35 Ⓣ/Ⓕ473/732-0705, Ⓦwww.mexonline.com/poetas.htm. A warren of very comfortable rooms (with cable TV) all painted in blues, yellows and reds, and lined with decorative tiles, while shady interior patios provide respite from the heat and noise of the day. Prices rise substantially from January to mid-March. ❽

Parador del Convento Calzada Guadalupe 17 Ⓣ/Ⓕ473/732-2524, Ⓔhconv@prodigy.net.mx. An attractive hotel on the slopes above the university, with decent rooms, though if you can afford it go for one of the *cuartos rústicos*, rooms which have a balcony, more imaginative decor and a lot more space. ❻

Posada de la Condesa Plaza de la Paz 60 ⓣ473/732-1462. Central and cheap, but rooms (all with showers) are small and scruffy, and the loud nightclub next door doesn't help matters. ❹

Posada Santa Fé Jardín de la Unión 12 ⓣ473/732-0084 or 01-800/112-4773, ⓦwww.posadasantafe.com. Very comfortable old hotel right in the heart of the city, with interior and (more expensive) exterior rooms, parking and a good rooftop terrace, but leans heavily on its location. ❼

San Diego Jardín de la Unión 1 ⓣ473/732-1300, ⓕ732-5626. Fine colonial warren of a place in the very centre with spacious international-style rooms, all with satellite TV. There are great views from its dearer front rooms. ❼–❽

Plaza de Rocha and around

Casa Mexicana Sóstenes Rocha 28 ⓣ473/732-7393, ⓦwww.escuelamexicana.int.com.mx. Very good budget hotel with simple but tastefully decorated modern rooms, with or without bath. There's a language school attached, and students staying at the hotel also get to use the kitchen. ❸

Posada Molino del Rey Padre Belaunzavan and Campanero ⓣ473/732-2223, ⓔmach1@avantel.net. At the east end of town, very reasonably priced with smallish but comfortable and quiet rooms around a courtyard. ❻

Outside the centre

Casa de los Espíritus Alegres Ex-Hacienda La Trinidad 1, Marfil, on the outskirts of town ⓣ473/733-1013, ⓦwww.casaspirit.com. This enchanting B&B exudes charm and is decorated in a playfully sophisticated style with a riot of colour and a curious collection of Mexican skeleton folk art. Bedrooms and common spaces are comfortable and there's an honour bar for late-night patio tippling. ❾

The City

There must be more things to see in Guanajuato than in virtually any town of its size anywhere: churches, theatres, museums, battlefields, mines and mummified corpses to name a few. To get to some of these, you'll need to take the bus, but most places are laid out along Juárez. If you start your explorations from the **Mercado Hidalgo** and walk east, you'll be able to see much of what Guanajuato has to offer in a day. Wandering through the maze of narrow alleys that snakes up the side of the ravine is a pleasure in itself, if only to spot their quirky names like Salto del Mono (Monkey's Leap) or Calle de las Cantarranas (Street of the Singing Frogs). Incidentally, references to **frogs** crop up everywhere around town – in sculpture, artesanías and T-shirts. The valley once had so many of the amphibians that the original name of the city was Quanaxhuato, meaning "Place of Frogs".

Mercado Hidalgo to the Plaza de la Paz

The first building of note as you head east up Juárez from where buses stop is the **Mercado Hidalgo**, a huge iron-framed construction reminiscent of British Victorian railway-station architecture, crammed with goods of every description. Beyond the market, to the left and through the **Jardín de la Reforma**, with its fountain and arch, you get to the lovely, quiet **Plaza San Roque**. A small, irregular, flagged space, the plaza has a distinctly medieval feel, heightened by the raised facade of the crumbling church of **San Roque** that towers above. It's a perfect setting for the city's lively annual International **Cervantes Festival** (see p.321). The Callejón de los Olleros leads back down to Juárez, or you can cut straight through to the livelier **Plazuela San Fernando**, with its stalls and restaurants. Return to Juárez from here and you emerge more or less opposite the **Plazuela de los Angeles**. In itself this is little more than a slight broadening of the street, but from here steps lead up to some of Guanajuato's steepest, narrowest alleys. Just off the plazuela is the **Callejón del Beso** (20m up Callejón del Patrimonio and turn left), so called because at only a little over half a metre wide, it is slim enough for residents to lean out of the upper-storey balconies and exchange kisses across the street – naturally enough there's a *Canterbury Tales*-style legend of star-crossed lovers associated with it. To learn more, join one of the *callejóneadas* (see p.321) that pass this way, or engage the services of one of the small children who hang around eager to tell a tale. To experience one balcony firsthand, come in the evening and walk through the strategically located gift shop.

The **Plaza de la Paz** lies east of the Jardín de la Reforma, beyond a number of banks on Juárez. For a distance here, Juárez is not the lowest road – Alonso cuts down to the right, to rejoin Juárez a little further along. Plaza de la Paz itself boasts some of the town's finest **colonial buildings**, among which the late eighteenth-century mansion of the Condes de Rul y Valenciana (then owners of the richest mine in the country) stands out as the grandest. It was designed by Eduardo Tresguerras, undoubtedly the finest Mexican architect of his time, and played host briefly to Baron Alexander von Humboldt, the German naturalist and writer on Mexico, an event commemorated by a plaque. The **Casa de Gobierno**, a short way down towards the Jardín de la Unión (see below), is another fine mansion, this time with a plaque recording the fact that Benito Juárez lived there in 1858, when Guanajuato was briefly his provisional capital. On the far side of the plaza stands the honey-coloured **Basílica de Nuestra Señora de Guanajuato**, the Baroque parish church that houses an ancient image of the Virgin, patroness of the city. This wooden statue, which now sits amidst silver and jewels, was given to Guanajuato in 1557 by Philip II, in gratitude for the wealth that was pouring from here into Spanish royal coffers. At the time it was already old and miraculous, having survived more than eight centuries of Moorish occupation hidden in a cave near Granada in Spain.

Around the Jardín de la Unión

From the Plaza de la Paz, you can cut up to the university, but just a short distance further east on Juárez is the **Jardín de la Unión**, Guanajuato's zócalo. It's a delightful little square – or rather triangle – set back from the street, shaded with trees, surrounded by cafés, tables spilling outside, and with a bandstand in the centre from which the town band regularly adds to the early evening atmosphere. This is the best time to sit and linger over a drink, enjoying the passing spectacle of the evening *paseo*.

Facing the Jardín across Juárez stands the Baroque church of **San Diego**, inside which are several old paintings and interesting chapels. One altar in particular is dedicated to the infant Jesus and mawkishly filled with toys and children's tiny shoes left as offerings. Next door is the imposing Neoclassical frontage of the **Teatro Juárez** (Tues–Sun 9am–1.45pm & 5–7.45pm; US$1), all Doric columns and allegorical statuary. The interior of the theatre is fabulously plush – decked out in red velvet and gilt, with chandeliers and a Moorish proscenium – as befits its period. Built at the end of the nineteenth century, it was opened in 1903 by the dictator Porfirio Díaz himself.

Beyond the Jardín, Juárez becomes Sopeña, lined by fancy boutiques, restaurants and bars as far as the pretty pink church of San Francisco, which marks the Plazuela San Francisco. Here, too, is the **Museo Iconográfico del Quijote** (Tues–Sat 10am–6pm, Sun 10am–3pm; free), an extraordinary little collection devoted entirely to Don Quixote. The museum contains mainly paintings of the don – including some by Pedro and Rafael Coronel – but also a couple of Dalí prints, a copy of a Picasso drawing, a Posada engraving of our hero as a *calavera*, murals, tapestries, sculptures, busts, miniatures, medals, plates, glassware, chess sets, playing cards, pipes and cutlery – you name it, it's here.

Pípila

The **Monumento al Pípila**, on the hillside almost directly above the Jardín de la Unión, affords fantastic views of Guanajuato. You seem to be standing directly on top of the church of San Diego, and if there is a band playing in the plaza it can be clearly heard up here. It's an especially wonderful spot for the 45 minutes or so during which the sun sets behind the hills and the electric lights start to come on in town. The steep climb takes about twenty minutes going up and ten minutes coming down: the bottom half is lit but the top isn't, so don't wait for total darkness before you descend. There are several possible routes up through the alleys – look for signs saying "al Pípila" – including up the Callejón del Calvario, to the right off Sopeña just beyond the Teatro Juárez, from the Plazuela San Francisco, or climbing to the left from the Callejón del Beso; the signs run out, but if you keep climbing as steeply as possible you're unlikely to get lost. Along the way there are various viewpoints and romantic nooks. There's also a bus ("Pípila") that takes you round the scenic Carretera Panorámica, and if plans ever come to fruition there'll be a kind of cliff railway up the steep valley side from behind the church of San Diego. Pípila was Guanajuato's own Independence hero (see opposite), and you can climb up inside his statue (daily 7.30am–8pm; US$0.10) to a point immediately behind his shoulder – from where you unfortunately can't see very much at all.

Around the university

At the back of the Jardín de la Unión and on the left, the **Plaza del Baratillo** is a small space with a quiet café and a clutch of crafts shops. From here the Teatro Principal is down to the right, while if you follow the curve on round to the left you find the church of **La Compañía**. The highly decorated monumental Baroque church is just about all that's left of a Jesuit seminary founded in 1732; step inside to admire the unusually light interior afforded by the clear glass in the dome. At the back in the sacristy is a small museum or *pinacoteca* (daily 10am–2pm; US$0.50) with a few seventeenth- to nineteenth-century oils including four images of saints by Miguel Cabrera.

The seminary was an educational establishment that eventually metamorphosed into the **State University**, now one of the most prestigious in Mexico. The university building is in fact quite modern – little more than four decades old – but designed to blend in with the town, which, for all its size, it does surprisingly effectively. There's not a great deal of interest inside to the casual observer, but wander in anyway: notice boards detail local cultural events, and there's often a temporary exhibition of some kind. High on the fourth floor you'll find the **Museo de Historia Natural Alfredo Dugés** (Mon–Fri 10am–6pm; US$0.70), a small collection of beetles, butterflies and assorted beasts, including a small two-headed goat. Next door to the university building, the **Museo del Pueblo de Guanajuato** (Tues–Sat 10am–6.30pm, Sun 10am–2pm; US$1.50) is a collection of local art and sundry oddities, housed in the seventeenth-century home of the Marqués de San Juan de Rayas. It's an attractive building with a nice little Baroque chapel, where much of the decoration has been replaced by modern murals painted by one of the current standard-bearers of the Mexican muralist tradition, José Chávez Morado.

Positos leads west from the front of the university to the fascinating **Museo Casa Diego Rivera**, Positos 47 (Tues–Sat 10am–6.30pm, Sun 10am–2.30pm; US$1.50), which occupies the birthplace of Guanajuato's most famous son. For most of his life Rivera, the ardent revolutionary sympathizer and Marxist, went unrecognized by his conservative home town, but with international recognition of his work came this museum, in the house where he was raised until he was 6. Until 1904, the Rivera family only occupied the lower floor, which is now furnished in nineteenth-century style, though only the beds and a cot actually belonged to the Rivera family. The place is far bigger than it looks from the outside, and the extensive upper floors contain many of Rivera's works, especially early ones, in a huge variety of styles – Cubist, Pointillist, Impressionist – showing the influences he absorbed during his years in France and Spain. Although there are no major works on show, the many sketches and small paintings are well worth a look, particularly those showing his fascination with all things pre-Columbian. There's also a large temporary exhibition space which often captures major international exhibitions as they pass through Mexico.

The Alhóndiga and the Museo de la Mineralogía

The **Alhóndiga de Granaditas**, the most important of all Guanajuato's monuments, lies west of the Museo Diego Rivera, more or less above the market. Originally a granary, later a prison, now a very good regional museum, this was the scene of the first real battle and some of the bloodiest butchery in the long War of Independence. Just thirteen days after the cry of Independence went up in Dolores Hidalgo, Father Hidalgo approached Guanajuato at the head of his insurgent force – mostly peons armed with nothing more than staves and sickles. The Spanish, outnumbered but well supplied with firearms, shut themselves up in the Alhóndiga, a redoubtable fortress. The almost certainly apocryphal story goes that Hidalgo's troops could make no impact until a young miner, nicknamed **El Pípila** ("the Turkeycock"), volunteered to set fire to the wooden doors – with a slab of stone tied to his back as a shield, he managed to crawl to the gates and start them burning, dying in the effort. The rebels, their path cleared, broke in and massacred the defenders wholesale. It was a short-lived victory – Hidalgo was forced to abandon Guanajuato, leaving its inhabitants to face Spanish reprisals, and was eventually tracked down by the royalists and executed in Chihuahua. His head and the heads of his three chief co-conspirators, Allende, Aldama and Jiménez, were suspended from the four corners of the Alhóndiga as a warning to anyone tempted to follow their example, and there they stayed for over ten years, until Mexico finally did become independent. The hooks from which they hung are still there on the outside walls.

Inside, there's a memorial hall devoted to the Martyrs of Independence and a **museum** (Tues–Sat 10am–1.30pm & 4–5.30pm, Sun 10am–2.30pm; US$3, free for students and for all on Sun; entry ceases 30min before closing). On the staircases are **murals** by local artist José Chávez Morado (see overleaf), depicting scenes from the War of Independence and the Revolution, as well as native folklore and traditions. The collection, mostly labelled in Spanish only, spans local history from pre-Hispanic times to the twentieth century: the most interesting sections cover the Independence battle and everyday life in colonial times. There are the iron cages in which the rebels' heads were displayed and lots of weapons and flags, as well as a study of Guanajuato's mining industry. There's also plenty of art, especially a wonderful series of portraits by Hermengildo Bustos; and don't miss the small artesanías section by the side door, which displays a bit of everything from fabrics and clothes to saddles and metalwork.

Only real rock enthusiasts will want to trek half a kilometre from here up Calle Alhóndiga to the **Museo de la Mineralogía** (Mon–Fri 10am–2.30pm;

free), which houses some 20,000 rock samples. The museum is in the "Escuela de Minas y Metalurgia" of the university, in a building on your left as you head out of town towards Valenciana: look for the broad set of steps about 200m past the *Hotel Socavón*.

Museo de las Momias

Halfway up the hill going west along Juárez from the Alhóndiga, the ghoulish Panteón, or **Museo de las Momias** (daily 9am–6pm; US$2), holds a very different sort of attraction. Here, lined up against the wall in a series of glass cases, are more than a hundred mummified human corpses exhumed from the local public cemetery. All the bodies were originally laid out in crypts in the usual way, but if after five years the relatives were unable or unwilling to make the perpetuity payment, the remains were removed. Many are found to have been naturally preserved, and the "interesting" ones are put on display – others, not properly mummified or too dull for public titillation, are burned or transferred to a common grave. The wasted, leathery bodies vary from some more than a century old (including a smartly dressed mummy said to have been a French mining engineer) to relatively recent fatalities, who presumably have surviving relatives. The burial clothes hang off the corpses almost indecently – others are completely naked – and the guides delight in pointing out their most horrendous features: one twisted mummy, its mouth opened in a silent scream, is the "woman who was buried alive"; another, a woman who died in childbirth, is displayed beside "the smallest mummy in the world". It's all absolutely grotesque, but nevertheless with a macabre fascination. You'll be admitted to the **Salón del Culto a la Muerte** (same hours), a house-of-horrors-style extension, with an array of holographic images, jangly motorized skeletons and yet more mummies. Fans of kitsch will be delighted with the hawkers outside selling mummy models and shards of rock in the shape of mummies. To get to the museum, either catch a bus ("Panteón" or "Momias") anywhere along Alonso or Juárez, or walk about 500m west of the Mercado Hidalgo along Juárez, then left into Calzada del Panteón.

Presa de la Olla and the Museo Olga Costa-José Chávez Morado

East of the centre of town, Sangre de Cristo (later Paseo de la Presa) runs gradually uphill for a couple of kilometres through some of Guanajuato's fancier residential districts before ending up at the **Presa de la Olla** and the Presa San Renovato, two dams with small green and rather unimpressive reservoirs. This is a popular picnic spot, and you can rent rowing boats or sit out at a restaurant by the Presa de la Olla. A number of buses run out here (look for "Presa"), heading through town on the underground street – steps near the church of San Diego will take you down to a subterranean bus stop. Off Sangre de Cristo, Calle Pastita runs northeast through the suburb of Pastita past a decayed section of an old aqueduct to the **Museo Olga Costa-José Chávez Morado** (Thurs–Sun 9.30am–4pm; US$1.50). The museum was formerly the Hacienda de Guadalupe residence and is where Mexican muralist Chávez Morado and his German painter wife spent much of their married life. He moved out and donated the building to the city of Guanajuato on his wife's death in 1993: her ashes fertilize a succulent prominently displayed on the patio outside. The house has been left largely as it was when they lived here, an eclectic mix of styles explained (in Spanish) by the guide: eighteenth-century majolica ceramics, seventeenth-century French chairs, Dutch porcelain, Iranian wall hangings and a fine collection of ex-votos. There's little of their work on show, but notice Morado's blue and white lamp, and his stained-glass windows – all blotches in red, yellow, blue and black – on the way up to the studio, now given over to temporary exhibitions. The museum is less than half an hour's walk from the Jardín de la Unión or you can flag down any bus marked "Pastita" at the eastern end of town.

The Ex-Hacienda de San Gabriel de Barrera

If the crush of Guanajuato gets too much for you, head 2km west of it (either by foot or take any bus going to the Central de Autobuses) to the **Ex-Hacienda de San Gabriel de Barrera** (daily 9am–6pm; US$2.20, students US$1.10), a colonial home now transformed into a lovely little museum. The beautifully restored **gardens** of the hacienda range through a bizarre selection of international styles – including English, Italian, Roman, Arabic and Mexican – and make a wonderful setting for the house, which has been restored with a colonial look. Cool rooms evoke daily life among the wealthy silver barons of nineteenth-century Guanajuato, but include numerous fine pieces of furniture dating back several centuries: grand and opulent on the ground floor, rich in domestic detail upstairs. It's a great place to wander at ease and brings home the sheer wealth of colonial Guanajuato.

La Valenciana

From close by the Alhóndiga on Calle Alhóndiga, buses ("Valenciana"; infrequent enough to make a short taxi ride a worthwhile investment) wind their way 4km uphill to the mine and church in **La Valenciana**. Near the top of the pass here, overlooking Guanajuato where the road to Dolores Hidalgo and San Miguel heads off north, you'll see the elaborate facade of the extraordinarily sumptuous **Templo de San Cayetano de Valenciana** church with its one completed tower. Built between 1765 and 1788, it's the ultimate expression of Mexico's churrigueresque style, with a profusion of intricate adornment covering every surface – even the mortar, they say, is mixed with silver ore. Inside, notice especially the enormous gilded *retablos* around the main altar and in each arm of the cross, and the delicate filigree of the roof vaulting, especially around the dome above the crossing.

The church was constructed for its owner, the Conde de Rul y Valenciana, who also owned La Valenciana **silver mine** – for hundreds of years the richest in Mexico, tapping Guanajuato's celebrated Veta Madre (Mother Lode). The mine still operates on a vastly reduced level, but exploitation continues apace with a clutch of ways to lure tourists to the associated silver shops, rock-sellers and restaurants. Beside the church, the original mine entrance now operates as the **Bocamina San Cayetano** (daily 10am–6pm; US$1.50), the name commemorating the saint who gets credit for the Mother Lode's discovery. Donning a hard hat fails to lend credibility to a brief tour of the upper 50m of tunnels, which end in a shrine to the mine's patron.

A road running west from beside the church leads 400m to the **Mina La Valenciana** (Tues–Sun 11am–6pm; US$1.50), where guides stationed outside charge a small fee to show you around the surface workings: essentially winding gear and a few decaying buildings mostly of interest to minings buffs. A visit to the excellent and expensive *Casa del Conde del la Valenciana* **restaurant** (see overleaf), opposite the church, makes the journey up here much more worthwhile.

Cerro de Cubilete and the statue of Cristo Rey

If you approached Guanajuato from León, you'll already have seen the huge statue of **Cristo Rey** crowning the 2661-metre **Cerro de Cubilete**. Variously claimed to occupy the geographical centre of the republic or just the state of Guanajuato, it seems a neat coincidence that it should be on the highest hill for miles. Nevertheless, the complex of chapels and pilgrims' dormitories is without question magnificently sited with long, long views across the plains. At its heart is the twenty-metre bronze statue – erected in 1950 and ranking as the world's second largest image of Christ, just behind Rio de Janeiro's Cristo Redentor – standing on a golden globe flanked by cherubs, one holding a crown of thorns, the other the golden crown of the "King of Kings".

The easiest way to get up here is on one of the US$10 tours advertised all around Guanajuato, though you can do the same for less than half the price by nipping out to the Central de Autobuses and picking up one of ten daily Autobuses Vasallo de Cristo, which run up there in around thirty minutes.

Eating

Finding something to eat in Guanajuato is easy as it's nearly impossible to walk more than a few yards down Juárez without passing some kind of café or restaurant. At the eastern end of **Juárez**, a whole series of very plain little places serve the standard Mexican staples, many of them also offering inexpensive comidas corridas; the **university area**, too, has plenty of choice. Rather more adventurous, and cheaper still, are the stalls in the modern annexe of the **Mercado Hidalgo**: two floors of delights (and horrors), where you'd be advised to take a careful look at what's on offer before succumbing to the frantic beckoning of the stallholders – some stalls are distinctly cleaner and more appetizing than others. Up around the **Jardín de la Unión**, the pricey outdoor restaurants are well worth visiting; in fact many people seldom stray from the excellent range of places all within five minutes' walk of each other along **Sopeña** and the surrounding streets. For bread and cakes, try *Panadería la Purísima*, Juárez 138.

Arnadi Plazuela de San Francisco 12. Eat-in *pastelería* with window seats that catch the afternoon sun.

El Atrium Plaza del Baratillo. One of Guanajuato's cooler cafés, serving probably the best coffee in relaxed surroundings. Great place for postcard writing.

El Café Galería Sopeña 10, right by the Teatro Juárez. Fashionable hangout with eating inside and a very popular outdoor terrace across the road where prices are high and the service slow.

Casa del Conde de la Valenciana at La Valenciana, 4km from town (see p.319). Beautifully set restaurant in the courtyard of a former hacienda with vines growing up the walls. The Mexican food is nicely prepared and presented, and you should leave room for the ice creams scooped out of the shells of the fruits they are flavoured with. Roughly US$15–20 for a full meal. Closed Sun.

Chez Nicole Arcos de Guadalupe 3 ⓣ473/733-1148, ⓔhdamarf@int.com.mx. One of the city's best restaurants with gorgeous garden dining, refined service and a mouthwatering Mexican-French menu. Its heaping plate of buttery *setas*, or mushrooms, for US$7 is reason alone to visit Guanajuato. Reservations recommended.

El Gallo Pitogorica Constancia 10 ⓣ473/732-9489. One of Guanajuato's best restaurants, predominantly Italian but with eclectic decor and a fabulous location high on the valley slopes right behind the San Diego church. Dine on prosciutto and melon followed by a tasty arrabiata as the sounds of the Jardín de la Unión waft up through the open windows. US$15–20 for a full meal.

La Pieza Cantarranas 52. Casual tapas bar with shaded outdoor tables and two-for-one happy hours. Next to the *Hostal Cantarranas*.

Pingüis northeast corner of Jardín de la Unión. The best bargain in the Jardín: a little faded, but still a buzzing, friendly place for good breakfasts, comidas corridas and a fair choice of Mexican and international main meals.

Pizza Piazza branches throughout town, including Plazuela San Fernando, Juárez 69, Calle de Cantarranas 14 and Hidalgo 11. Spaghetti, hamburgers and, as you might expect, pizza, and all pretty reasonable.

La Rana Loca Positos 7. The slightly sterile atmosphere won't encourage you to linger, but the food is great value, especially the comida corrida (a bargain at under US$3), and comes with a bottomless jug of *agua de fruta*.

Tasca de los Santos Plaza de la Paz 28. Smart Spanish restaurant with outdoor tables, serving European delights such as paella, chicken in white wine and jamón serrano. Moderate to expensive.

Truco 7 Truco 7. Beautiful little café with a convivial, student atmosphere, comfy chairs and all manner of artworks covering the walls. Great moderately priced breakfasts, comidas, salads, steaks and wonderful garlic soup with an egg poached in it. To avoid a dollop of corn syrup in your cappuccino, ask for it *sin miel*.

El Unicornio Azul Plaza del Baratillo 2. Tiny vegetarian restaurant selling wholewheat breads to go and soya burgers and juices to have inside.

Vamina Juan Valle 4, around the corner from the Diego Rivera museum. Indian-influenced vegetarian with US$4 comidas corridas and US$1.50 soya burgers. Adjacent Internet café.

Nightlife and entertainment

Guanajuato is a great town for sitting around knocking back coffee or bottles of beer, with a host of superb cafés and bars in which to do just that. Things are especially jumping at weekends, when refugees from the bigger cities, including Mexico City and León, come here to enjoy themselves. The rougher bars and clubs are down on Juárez around Mercado Hidalgo, where the cantinas are generally reserved for men and prostitutes. An excellent way to pass an hour or so is to follow one of the organized **callejóneadas** – walking tours that wind through the side streets and back alleys following a student minstrel group known as Estudiantinas. They're aimed at Mexicans, so without fluent Spanish and some local knowledge you'll miss most of the jokes and risqué tales, but they're great fun all the same. You can get details of these from any of the information booths, and at Juárez 210 where they'll sell you tickets entitling you to some wine as you promenade, but it's easier just to tag along. In high season, there's something happening most nights of the week, but at other times of the year Friday and Saturday nights are your best bet. Buy something to drink as you walk, then hang around the Jardín de la Unión near 8.30pm and just follow the crowd.

During the **International Cervantes Festival** (frequently referred to as the Cervantino; ⓣ473/731-1150 or 800/714-1086, ⓦwww.festivalcervantino .gob.mx) over the course of two and a half weeks in mid-October you can enjoy opera, dance, literature readings, music performances and the famous *entremeses* – swashbuckling one-act plays from classical Spanish theatre performed outdoors in Plaza San Roque. You don't need good Spanish to work out what's going on as they're highly visual and very entertaining. There's a grandstand for which you have to book seats, but it's easy enough to join the crowds watching from the edges of the plaza for free. Groups of students (who perform the *entremeses*) will quite often put on impromptu performances outside festival times, so it's worth wandering up here in the early evening just to see if anything is happening, especially on Saturday nights. During the festival itself the town, and just about every imaginable performance space, is alive with music and cultural events of every stripe; it is a great time to be here, though you'll need to book accommodation well (read: months) in advance.

For a more sedate evening, Guanajuato also has a **cinema,** Cine Años, tucked up a side street behind the university showing first-run movies several times a day from around US$3. On Friday nights (at 8.30pm) you can watch the town turn out in its finery for the **Orquestra Sinfónica de la Universidad de Guanajuato**, at the Teatro Principal; it has an enviable reputation throughout Mexico and only costs about US$6.

Learning Spanish in Guanajuato

Guanajuato is becoming a popular place to spend a couple of weeks while learning Spanish. The longest-standing **language school** is the Centro de Idiomas at the University of Guanajuato (ⓣ473/732-0006, ⓦwww.ugto.mx), which runs exchange programmes with universities around the world and accepts other students for their courses. They're aimed more at improvers than beginners, concentrating on Mexican and Latin American culture and costing US$600 for a four-week full-time programme. Students are encouraged to live with Mexican families; board is an additional US$20 or so per day with three meals. There's an altogether more informal feel to courses at other language schools in town, most letting you combine lessons with learning something of Mexican cooking, pottery, dance and so on. Check the web sites to see which suit you and your budget; rates vary considerably with number of contact hours and length of the programme, and most offer homestay for around US$20. Recommended language schools include: Academia Falcon, Paseo de la Presa 80 (ⓣ/ⓕ473/431-0745, ⓦwww.institutofalcon.com), who have reasonably priced classes beginning regularly; Escuela Mexicana, Sóstenes Rocha 28 (ⓣ473/732-5005, ⓦwww.escuelamexicana.int.com.mx), who offer week-long courses with four hours a day plus homestay for US$250.

Bars and clubs

Bar Fly Sóstenes Rocha 30. Tiny, sociable bar with folk, jazz or acoustic music most nights from 9pm, and seldom any cover.

Bar Ocho Constancia 8. Youthful bar set up with sofas for intimate conversation, and a pool table upstairs. A good place to wind down after the clubs. The name is a play on the word *borracho*, Spanish for "drunk".

Campanero Bar Campanero 4. Reached by a small bridge over a pedestrian alley, this quiet bar is a favourite of intellectuals looking to wax philosophical over their beer. Open 4pm–midnight.

Capitolio Plaza de la Paz 62. One of the town's premier clubs, thumping the night away from Wednesday to Saturday. Don't expect music anywhere close to cutting-edge, but it can be fun. US$3 cover.

La Dama de las Camelias Sopeña 34, opposite Museo Iconográfico. Great atmospheric bar, which stays open until dawn and comes with imaginative decor that incorporates evening dresses, high-heeled shoes and smashed mirror fragments. There's dancing most nights and great salsa late on Fridays. Closed Sun.

Guanajuato Grill Alonso 4. Guanajuato's other main club, fairly cheesy and usually packed with local teenagers doing very little but sweating and listening to the music.

Los Lobos Manuel Doblado 2. Dim and often crowded bar that resounds nightly to thumping rock classics. Low-cost two-for-one beers all night.

El Pozo at the *Parador San Javier*. Elegant bar at the entrance to the hotel, built around a large open well with water cascading into it. Perfect for a couple of quiet (and fairly expensive) drinks to start the evening.

Spanglish Plaza de la Paz 56, third floor. An unlikely combination of bookstore, dimly lit café and cool bar that is invisible from the street and frequented largely by those in the know. Early evening drink specials.

Listings

American Express Viajes Georama, Plaza de la Paz 34, operates as a travel agency (Mon–Fri 9am–8pm, Sat 10am–2pm; ⓣ473/732-5101, ⓔgeorama@redes.int.com.mx), and also has all the usual Amex services (Mon–Fri 9am–2.30pm & 5–6.30pm, Sat 10am–1pm).

Banks and exchange Banks can be found along Juárez: Bancomer at no.9, Bital on the Plaza de la Paz, and a convenient branch of Banorte between the Plaza de la Paz and the Jardín Unión. Outside bank hours, try Divisas Dimas, an exchange office at Juárez 33 (daily 9am–3pm & 4–7pm).

Books and newspapers *Spanglish* (see above; Mon–Sat from 2pm) has a reasonable stock of new and used books in English.

Buses Heading through the hills to Dolores Hidalgo couldn't be simpler, with half-hourly departures from Calle Alhóndiga, right in town just below the Alhóndiga. For other destinations, make for Guanajuato's Central de Autobuses (via local buses marked "Centro–Central" from Juárez), where there are regular services to Guadalajara, Mexico City, San Luis Potosí and Aguascalientes, and almost constant departures for León and San Luis de la Paz. There are relatively few buses direct to San Miguel de Allende, for which it's sometimes quicker to change in Dolores; if you have any problem getting anywhere else, head for León (see p.309), which is on the main north–south highway and has much more frequent services. Viajes Frausto, Juárez 10, close to the Jardín de la Unión (☎473/732-3580), have the timetables, fares and booking facilities for all first-class companies operating from the bus station.

Emergencies Police ☎473/732-0266; Cruz Roja ☎473/732-0487; for emergency medical attention visit Centro de Salud Urbano de Guanajuato, Pardo 5 (☎473/732-1467).

Flights Guanajuato state airport, 30km west, between Silao and León, has daily flights to major Mexican cities and the US. To get there, catch a second-class bus to León and get off as you pass the airport (or fork out US$25–30 or so for a taxi).

Internet access There are about thirty Internet businesses in town all offering access for around US$1.50 an hour, including one across from *El Atrium* on the Plaza Baratillo. There are several others near the tourist office (see p.311) and more up by the university (see p.316).

Laundry Lavandería del Centro, Sopeña 26 (Mon–Sat 9am–8pm; ☎473/732-0436). $US4.70 for up to 7kg.

Pharmacy El Fénix, Juárez 106.

Post office Located at the eastern end of Positos, behind the Jardín de la Unión (Mon–Fri 9am–5pm, Sat 9am–1pm).

Taxis Radio Taxis ☎473/732-6534 or 01-800/667-0682.

Telephones Computel, at the eastern end of Positos behind the Jardín de la Unión (Mon–Fri 9am–8pm, Sat 8am–1pm), has phone and fax services; there are several other *larga distancia* places, including one at Juárez 110.

Tours Kiosks mainly around the Mercado Hidalgo offer a fairly standard package of bus tours, all for around the same price and usually with at least a couple of departures daily. You're unlikely to get much from the City Tour (3hr; US$7), or those to Dolores Hidalgo and San Miguel de Allende (8hr; US$15), or León and around (8hr; US$15), but you might be interested in one to the Cristo del Rey statue (3hr; US$8).

Dolores Hidalgo and around

Fifty kilometres or so from both Guanajuato and San Miguel de Allende, **DOLORES HIDALGO** is as ancient and as historically rich as either of its southern neighbours. This was Father Hidalgo's parish, and it was from the church in the main plaza here that the historic **Grito de la Independencia** ("Cry of Independence") was first issued. Perhaps because of its less spectacular location or maybe because there is no university or major language school, Dolores hasn't seen a fraction of the tourist development that has overtaken other places. It's a good bet, though, for a one-night stopover, and certainly if you can't find accommodation in Guanajuato or San Miguel, this is the place to head; you'll get a better room here for appreciably less. True, there is less to see, but it's an elegant little town and thoroughly Mexican; it's busy, too, as it sits on a traditionally important crossroads on the silver route from Zacatecas.

Just a block or two from the bus station as you walk towards the central plaza, the **Casa Hidalgo** (Tues–Sun 10am–5.45pm; US$3.30, free on Sun), Hidalgo's home, has been converted into a museum devoted to his life, very much a point of pilgrimage for Mexicans on day-trips. It's a bit heavy on written tributes from various groups to the "Father of Independence" and on copies of other correspondence he either sent or received – but it's interesting nonetheless and includes a few highlights such as his letter of excommunication from the Inquisition less than a month after the Grito. Continuing in the same direction, you come to a beautifully laid-out plaza, overlooked by the exuberant facade of the famous church, where a left turn takes you to the **Museo de la Independencia Nacional**, Zacatecas 6 (daily 8am–5pm; US$1, free on Sun). Inside, vibrant, graphic murals depict significant scenes from Mexican history

The Grito de la Independencia

On the night of September 15, 1810, **Padre Miguel Hidalgo y Costilla** and some of his fellow plotters, warned by messengers from Querétaro that their intention to raise a rebellion had been discovered, decided to bring their plans forward. At dawn on the 16th, Hidalgo, tolling the church bell, called his parishioners together and addressed them from the balcony of the church with an impassioned speech ending in the **Grito de la Independencia**,"¡Mexicanos, Viva México!" That cry is repeated every year by the president in Mexico City and by politicians all over the country at midnight on September 15, as the starting point for Independence Day celebrations. September 16 remains the one day of the year when the bell in Dolores Hidalgo's parish church is rung; however, the bell in place today is a copy of an original that was either melted down for munitions or hangs in the Palacio Nacional in Mexico City, depending on which story you believe.

from the Aztec perception of the world through to the life of Hidalgo. Don't miss the glass cabinets filled with record sleeves and cowboy boots that pay homage to the greatest *ranchera* singer of all time, José Alfredo Jimenez, another of Dolores' native sons.

Besides a couple of other graceful churches, there's little else but the attraction of the dilapidated old streets themselves. As you wander around, look out for the locally made **ceramics**. They're on sale everywhere and are an ancient tradition here. The bigger shops are near the Casa Hidalgo, but the best deals are found on the outskirts of town.

Practicalities

Dolores is connected to both San Miguel and Guanajuato by regular, rapid **buses** to and from the Flecha Amarilla terminal, on Hidalgo beside the river. Herradura de Plata also has a terminal at the corner of Chiapas and Yucatán, from where buses run every thirty minutes south to San Miguel de Allende and Mexico City. There's little need to visit Dolores' small **tourist office** (daily 10am–7pm; Ⓣ/Ⓕ418/182-1164), on the main plaza by the church, but they can give advice on where to buy ceramics.

Local **hotels** are all reasonable: try the recently remodelled *Hotel Posada Hidalgo*, Hidalgo 15 (Ⓣ418/182-2683, Ⓕ182-0477; ❺), near the bus station; *Hotel Caudillo*, Querétaro 8, beside the church (Ⓣ/Ⓕ418/182-0198; ❺); and the *Posada Dolores*, Yucatán 8, past the Independence Museum and then left (Ⓣ418/182-0642; ❹), easily missed behind a small doorway, which charges by the person making it especially good value for lone travellers. The *Posada Cocomacan*, Plaza Principal 4 (Ⓣ418/182-6149, Ⓦwww.posadacocomacan.com; ❺), is the best bet in town, with its cool interior, intricate wood floors, new baths, cable TV and restaurant serving US$4 chicken mole. For those with a sweet tooth, Dulcería el Cubilete is a wonderful candy store right next door that sells all sorts of sugary regional delicacies. You can also eat well around the plaza at *Hotel Caudillo*, which has a good **restaurant**.

The tiny restaurant adjacent to *Posada Dolores* serves heavenly tacos made with freshly pressed corn tortillas and comidas corridas for just US$2.20, though for good, if pricey, espresso you'll need to head to *El Cafécito* two blocks east of the Casa Hidalgo at the corner of Puebla and Nuevo León. Some of the country's most unusual **ice creams** are sold in and around the Plaza Principal. Mexicans come in droves to lick creamy alfalfa, mole, *cerveza*, shrimp and avocado-flavoured scoops (fortunately most vendors let you sample before committing to a full cone).

East of Dolores: San Luis de la Paz, Pozos and San José Iturbide

If you carry straight on through Dolores, after 40km you hit the road between San Luis Potosí and Querétaro at **SAN LUIS DE LA PAZ**. Though of little interest in itself, a minor road runs south from here, parallel to the main Hwy-57, through the intriguing half-deserted town of **Pozos**, 50km to the historic town of **San José Iturbide**. There are frequent bus services between the three towns, and on south to Querétaro or San Miguel de Allende. San Luis de la Paz is the largest of this string of three towns, a typically Mexican provincial settlement with one main street, a colonial plaza, and horses tied up alongside farmers' pickup trucks outside the market. It's a good place to buy rugs and *sarapes* at reasonable prices, though most of what is made here is sent off to the markets in larger towns. If you need to stay, there are a couple of small, cheap hotels on the main street just up from the bus terminal.

Pozos

Twenty minutes south of San Luis, the road to San José passes through what was once a rich and flourishing mining community called Real de Pozos. Now just known as **POZOS** (or, officially, Mineral de Pozos), it is often referred to as a ghost town but is far from dead, with several hundred people living clustered around the gaping maw of half a church. Don't expect swing doors flapping in the breeze and tumbleweed gusting through the streets, but you will find vast areas of crumbling masonry inhabited only by the odd burro. In fact, the place seems to be in the throes of a small revival in its fortunes with low rents attracting a number of artisans, many of whom produce high-quality **pre-Columbian instruments** for sale – mostly drums, flutes, stone xylophones and slit gongs, and not cheap. The **Sala de Cultura** (daily 10am–2pm & 4–6pm) on Ocampo, is poorly marked and offers a lightweight introduction to the local culture. If you continue west from the main (and only) square, a vast area of harsh agave desert opens up, dotted with old mine shafts and perfect for a couple of hours' hiking: take water, sun screen and a hat and see where the road takes you.

If the prospect of moody walks isn't enough to entice you to **stay**, you might just be tempted by *Casa Mexicana*, Juárez 2 on the Plaza Principal (Ⓣ/Ⓕ442/293-0014; ❼), an attractive five-bedroom B&B with exquisite and highly individual rooms set around an attractive garden, and with an on-site art gallery. Nicely prepared meals are also served to non-guests, or you could just drop in for a margarita. A step up is the *Casa Montana*, Plaza Principal 4 (Ⓣ442/293-0032, Ⓦwww.casamontanahotel.com; ❽–❾), next door, offering luxury accommodation, lush terraces, and a laundry list of amenities. There is also an art gallery and they can arrange for private tours and horseback-riding treks. It may be best to visit on a day-trip from San Miguel de Allende (see p.326) if you're not able to secure a reservation at one of the two places to stay or if you've had enough of the town after a few hours' visit. In addition to the B&B restaurants, there are several **comedores** that sell tacos and comidas corridas sprinkled around the tiny town.

San José Iturbide

Further south, **SAN JOSÉ** is an immaculate town centred on a tidy plaza, chiefly distinguished by the behemoth of a Neoclassical **church**, dedicated to Agustín de Iturbide, a local opportunist who started the War of Independence as a general loyal to Spain – inflicting major defeats on Morelos – only to change sides later. Having helped secure Mexico's Independence without any concomitant reform, he briefly declared himself emperor in 1822. The plaque reads, accurately enough, "from one of the few towns which have not forgotten you".

There's little reason to stay, but if you just fancy a night in a small ordinary Mexican town with good **accommodation**, then try the excellent *Hotel Los Arcos*, Plaza Principal 10, right by the church (Ⓣ419/198-0330, Ⓦwww.hotellosarcossji.com; ❹), with large, modern rooms, the nicer ones going for a little more (❻). There's also the convenient, comfortable but basic *Hotel Posada Unión*, Callejón Olivera 10, two blocks west along Allende near the temple (Ⓣ419/198-0071; ❺). The best meals are in the **restaurant** at *Los Arcos*, and there are good **snacks** and espresso at *Casas Viejas*, just steps away on the main plaza.

San Miguel de Allende

Set on a steep hillside overlooking the Río Laja, **SAN MIGUEL DE ALLENDE** seems at first sight little different from any other small colonial town, dominated by red rooftops and domed churches. Its distinct character, though, is soon apparent: it's home to a very high-profile colony of artists and writers, fleshed out with less ambitious retirees from the US and by flocks of students drawn to the town's several language and arts schools. Like such a community anywhere it's inward-looking, often pretentious and gossip-ridden, but it's also extremely hospitable and much given to taking newcomers under its wing. The town's increase in popularity in recent years, which has resulted in the influx of expats and tourists, can be, in part, attributed to the popular book *On Mexican Time*. The colourful story, written by Tony Cohan, tells of a writer and his artist wife who abandon smog-ridden Los Angeles for a quieter life in San Miguel, where they restore an old house, learn the local lifestyle and are slowly seduced by the colonial city's unique charm.

There are many good reasons for the popularity of San Miguel – chiefly that it's a very picturesque town with a perfect climate and, for artists, good light throughout the year. What got it started, though, was the foundation in 1938 of the **Instituto Allende**, an arts institute that enjoyed an enormous boost after World War II when returning American GIs found that their education grants could be stretched much further in Mexico. With its fame established, San Miguel has never looked back. For all its popularity, the town remains one of the most pleasant places you could pick to rest up for a while in comfort, with luxurious hotels (and a couple of excellent ones), great restaurants, and some of the most vibrant nightlife in the interior. Having said that, you may find yourself blowing your budget in double-time.

There are few major sights, but the whole town (which has been a national monument since 1926, hence no new building, no flashing signs and no traffic lights) is crowded with old seigneurial mansions and curious churches. It was founded in 1542 by a Franciscan friar, **Juan de San Miguel**, and as "San Miguel El Grande" became an important supply centre for the big mining towns, and a stopover on the main silver route from Zacatecas. The name was later changed to honour **Ignacio Allende**, a native who became Hidalgo's chief lieutenant. The country hereabouts is still ranching territory, though increasingly being taken over by the tourists and foreigners: attractions include hot springs, a golf course nearby, horse riding at a couple of dude ranches and mountain biking.

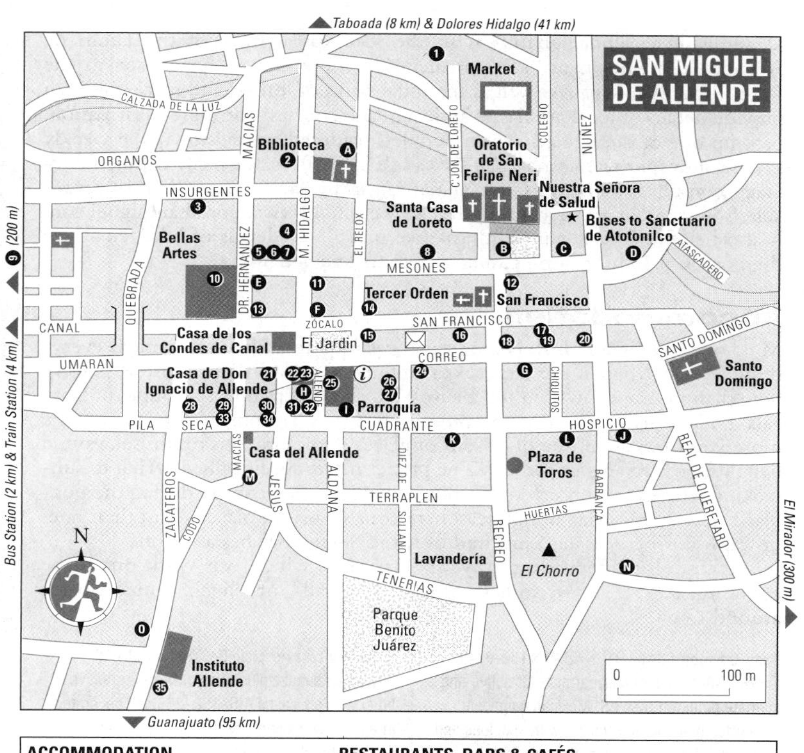

ACCOMMODATION	
Casa Carmen	G
Casa de Huéspedes	B
Casa de Liza	N
Casa de Sierra Nevada Quinta Real	K
Casa Quetzal	L
Casa Schuck	J
Hostal Alcatraz	A
Hotel Posada Carmina	H
Hotel Posada de San Francisco	F
Mesón de San Antonio	E
Parador San Sebastian de Aparicio	C
Posada Cholita	M
Posada de la Aldea	O
Vianey	D
Villa Rivera	I

RESTAURANTS, BARS & CAFÉS	
Apolo XI	8
Aqui es México	4
Azafrán	33
Los Burritos	7
Bugambilia	2
Café de la Parroquia	30
La Capilla	25
El Catrín	9
Char Rock	24
La Coronela	14
La Cucaracha	28
En Agua Pulquería	34
La Finestra Caffé	13
La Fragua	23
El Gato Negro	17
La Grotta	31
El Harem	20
L'Invito	19
Mama Mia	22
Mesón de San José	12
Las Musas	10
Olé Olé	1
El Pegaso	18
Petit Bar	29
El Petit Four	6
La Piñata	21
Rincón de don Tomás	15
San Augustín	16
Taquería los Faroles	3 & 35
El Ten Ten Pie	32
Tío Lucas	5
El Tomato	11
La Ventana	26
Chamonix	27

Arrival and information

Although San Miguel has a surprisingly poor bus service, this is still the easiest way to arrive, perhaps expedited by a change at Guanajuato or Querétaro if you're coming from some distance. The **bus station** (no guardería) is about 2km west of the centre, from where there are taxis and regular local buses (marked "Central") that run in along Calle Canal. San Miguel's nearest **airport** is near León (see p.309), from where Viajes San Miguel, Sollano 4 (Ⓣ415/152-2537, Ⓔtravelsm@prodigy.net.mx) run a shuttle van (US$27 one-way; reserve in advance) meeting most flights. They also run a US$50 shuttle service to Mexico City airport.

San Miguel's helpful **tourist office** (Mon–Wed 8.30am–5pm, Thurs & Fri 8.30am–7pm, Sat & Sun 10am–5pm; Ⓣ/Ⓕ415/152-0900, Ⓔinfo

@sanmigueldeallende.gob.mx) is in the southeast corner of the Jardín de Allende (also known as "Plaza Principal"), more or less next door to the Presidencia Municipal. As well as the usual ranks of leaflets and maps, they can provide details of local art classes and language courses. For more information, pick up one of the free ad-driven booklets scattered around town, the weekly gringo **newspaper** *Atención San Miguel* (US$0.70) or, for really detailed coverage, consult *The Insider's Guide to San Miguel* by Archie Dean (US$18), available from the library or at Lagundi. The website Ⓦwww.portalsanmiguel.com is also helpful. Check our "Listings" (see p.335), for details of bike rental; see the box on p.333 for horse riding, and tours and activities.

Accommodation

Most of San Miguel's **hotels** are near the Jardín and, like pretty much everything in San Miguel, the large expat influence makes them more expensive here than in other towns in the Bajío. With the exception of a couple of **hostels**, budget places are hard to come by, but if you're prepared to pay a little more you can stay in one of dozens of places with gorgeous rooms set around delightful courtyards or gardens. The pricier places specifically catering to sun-seeking retirees from north of the border tend to charge more during the popular December to March high season; reasonably priced places adjust their rates upwards during Semana Santa and over the September fiesta season.

The city also offers **long-stay apartments**, which can work out to be economical; ask at the tourist office for details, or check notice boards around town.

Casa Carmen Correo 31 Ⓣ/Ⓕ415/152-0844, Ⓦwww.infosma.com/casacarmen. Attractive and intimate hotel run by a US–Mexican couple. Comfortable and totally secure, with spacious and well-appointed rooms, each different. Rate includes breakfast and lunch. ❼

Casa de Huéspedes Mesones 27 Ⓣ415/152-1378. Quaint little second-floor hotel: friendly and relaxed, with clean, well-kept rooms – some with balconies – fluffy towels and fresh flowers. An especially good deal for singles. ❹

Casa de Liza Bajada de Chorro 7 Ⓣ415/152-0352, Ⓦwww.casaliza.com. One-of-a-kind B&B on Benito Juárez park. Each exquisite room is individually decorated with a variety of artwork. There's a pool, rambling patios, massage therapy, and a bilingual staff. The gracious mother-daughter owners live by the *mi casa es su casa* motto and are all too happy to tell you about their most famous guest: Antonio Banderas. ❾

Casa de Sierra Nevada Quinta Real Hospicio 35 Ⓣ415/152-7040, from US Ⓣ1-888/341-5995, Ⓦwww.quintareal.com. Luxury hotel with spacious rooms around a beautiful colonial courtyard, built in 1580 and lush with greenery. They've now taken over half a dozen houses in the vicinity and have also opened an equally sumptuous outpost at Santa Elena 2, at the north end of the Benito Juárez park. Pool and restaurant on site. ❾

Casa Quetzal Hospicio 34 Ⓣ415/152-0501, Ⓦwww.casaquetzalhotel.com. Quiet, attractive hotel with six suites (US$150–265), all decorated in a casually elegant style. Some have kitchenettes, fireplaces, and private terraces with rooftop views of the centre of town. ❾

Casa Schuck Bajada de Garita 3 Ⓣ/Ⓕ415/152-0657, Ⓦwww.casaschuck.com. Splendidly styled and colourful hotel with antiques, amply sized rooms, pool, leafy nooks, and personal touches. Welcoming owners make this one of San Miguel's best bets. ❾

Hostal Alcatraz Relox 54 Ⓣ415/152-8543, Ⓔalcatrazhostel@yahoo.com. The only true hostel in town. Fairly central location with a good kitchen, patio and barbecue area, but it often seems lifeless and is not especially welcoming. Bunks in dorms for under US$10 with a dollar discount for HI members. ❹

Hotel Casa Linda Mesones 101 Ⓣ415/154-4007, Ⓦwww.hotelcasalinda.com. Eclectic, inviting property with busy but attractive rooms, gym, jacuzzi, and video library. This lush oasis has loads of character and quiet charm. Breakfast included. ❾

Hotel Posada Carmina Cuna de Allende 7, a few metres south of the Jardín Ⓣ415/152-0458, Ⓦwww.posadacarmina.com. Large rooms with brick floors, high ceilings and white walls are set amid yet more colonial splendour around a beautiful courtyard; and there are cheaper but still very nice rooms in an adjacent wing. The staff are gracious. A shade pricey for what you get, but you can't beat its location, one block from the Jardín and one half-block from the town's best restaurant, *La Capilla*. ❽

Hotel Posada de San Francisco Plaza Principal 2 Ⓣ/Ⓕ415/152-0072, Ⓦwww.naftaconnect.com/hsanfrancisco. Aging but comfortable rooms in a lovely and sedate colonial building at surprisingly reasonable prices for its location right on the Jardín. ❼

Mesón de San Antonio Mesones 80 Ⓣ415/152-0580, Ⓔmsanantonio@cybertmatsa.com.mx. Modern and reasonably spacious carpeted rooms set around a small garden with a swimming pool; continental breakfast included. The extra US$15 for a two-level suite is money well spent. ❼

Parador San Sebastian de Aparicio Mesones 7 Ⓣ415/152-7084. Cool and tranquil, with simple rooms around a colonial courtyard, make this a huge bargain. ❹

Posada Cholita Hernández Macías 114 Ⓣ/Ⓕ415/152-2898. A cheery paint job enlivens spacious rooms in this small hotel. A good price for the location. ❺

Posada de la Aldea Ancha de San Antonio 15 Ⓣ/Ⓕ415/152-1022, Ⓦwww.naftaconnect.com/hotellaaldea. Clean and comfortable rooms all have modern amenities in this enormous hotel popular with Mexican tourists – with pool, tennis courts and parking – but its main virtue is being opposite the Instituto Allende. ❼

Vianey Aparicio 18 Ⓣ415/152-4559. Modern and spotless rooms lacking character, but a decent fallback if others are full. ❸

Villa Rivera Cuadrante 3 Ⓣ415/152-2289, Ⓦwww.villarivera.com. Another fine colonial establishment with a pool and gardens overlooking the back of the Parroquia, with very comfortable modern rooms. ❾

The Town

Head first to **El Jardín**, the name by which San Miguel's **zócalo** is best known, within walking distance of almost everything you'll want to see and the main focus of activity in the town's compact centre. The **Instituto Allende**, south of the centre and a fairly easy walk from there, is an alternative hub, and an especially useful source of information for anyone who wants to stay longer than a couple of days.

Wherever you go in town, it seems that any place that's not a café or restaurant is operating as some kind of gallery or **artesanía** shop. The stores offer a bewildering array of top-notch goods from all over Mexico – prices are correspondingly high, some even bordering on extortionate. There are really too many quality places to be very specific, but as a starting point, try the streets immediately south and west of the Jardín.

El Jardín

The most famous of the city's landmarks, **La Parroquia de San Miguel Archángel** – the parish church – takes up one side of the Jardín. This gloriously over-the-top structure, with a towering pseudo-Gothic facade bristling with turrets and spires, was rebuilt towards the end of the nineteenth century by a self-taught Indian stonemason, Zeferino Gutiérrez, who supposedly learned about architecture by studying postcards of the great French cathedrals and then drew diagrams in the dust to explain to his workers what he wanted. Inside, the patterned tilework of the floor, the azulejos along the walls and the pure semicircular vaulting along the nave exhibit distinct Moorish influences.

Opposite the church is a block containing the **Palacio Municipal** and the **Galería San Miguel**, one of the most prestigious of the many galleries showing local artists' work. Here also you'll find the *Hotel Posada de San Francisco*, where it is worth nipping in for a few minutes and asking to see **El Loco**; it's free, and will be better appreciated if your Spanish is reasonable, but to say more would give the game away.

The remaining two sides of the square are lined with covered *portales*, under whose arches vendors of drinks and trinkets shelter from the sun, with a row of shops behind them. On the Jardín, too, are some of San Miguel's most distinguished mansions, all of them – like almost every home in San Miguel – built in the Spanish style. The **Casa de Don Ignacio de Allende**, on the corner of Allende and Umarán, was the birthplace of the Independence hero: a plaque notes *Hic natus ubique notus* – "here was born he who is famous everywhere". The house now operates as the **Museo Histórico de San Miguel de Allende** (Tues–Sun 10am–4pm; US$3.20, free on Sun), with two floors of fossils, pots and diagrams exploring Mexico's pre-Hispanic and colonial past, naturally concentrating on the San Miguel area. The collection is well presented but fairly small and mostly of interest to history buffs. On the next corner, Hidalgo and Canal, you can see the **Casa de los Condes de Canal**, with an elaborately carved doorway and elegant wrought-iron grilles over the windows. Near here, too, just half a block down Umaran, is the **Casa de los Perros**, its central balcony supported by little stone dogs. Forbidding, even grim, from the outside, these mansions mostly conceal patios decked with flowers or courtyards with fountains playing.

East and north of El Jardín

Leave the Jardín eastwards and uphill on San Francisco, and the streets seem less affected by outsiders – Spanish or *norteamericano*. The architecture is still colonial, but the life that continues around the battered buildings seems cast in a more ancient mould. A block along San Francisco, the elaborate churrigueresque facade of the church of **San Francisco** contrasts sharply with its Neoclassical towers, tiled dome, plain interior, and quite overshadows the modest simplicity of its smaller neighbour, **Tercer Orden**. Behind, to the north, San Miguel's old market area has been refurbished to create a plaza complete with a huge equestrian statue of Allende. Here you'll find a little group of churches and chapels including the **Templo de Nuesta Señora de la Salud**, with its unusual concave facade topped by a scallop-shell pediment. To the left sits the **Oratorio de San Felipe Neri**, its Baroque facade showing signs of native influence – presumably the legacy of indigenous labourers – but the main interest lies in a series of paintings, among them a group depicting the life of San Felipe, attributed to Miguel Cabrera. One of its chapels, the **Santa Casa de Loreto** (entered from next door), is a copy of the Holy House at Loreto in Italy, and was put up by the Conde Manuel de la Canal; he and his wife appear as statues above their tombs in its gilded octagonal interior.

The town's **market** lies north of here and has managed to remain almost entirely traditional with fruit, vegetables, medicinal herbs, pots and pans all on display, though little exists specifically for the tourist among the cramped tables with their low canvas awnings. Official market day is Sunday, but no one seems to have told the locals, and it's pretty busy all week. Behind the regular market along **Andador Lucas Balderas** lies the **Mercado de Artesanías**, full of the sort of stuff you see all over Mexico, though little of what's here seems especially good value. You'll find much more exciting goods in the many crafts shops around town.

From the Oratorio you can head down Insurgentes to the **Biblioteca Pública**, Insurgentes 25 (Mon–Sat 10am–2pm & 4–7pm), which lends a substantial collection of books in English (see "Listings", p.335, for more details). They also sell a number of cheap secondhand books – either duplicates or those deemed too lightweight for preservation in the library. Inside the library, the *Café Santa Ana* offers a quiet space to sit down and read.

Bellas Artes

The Centro Cultural "El Nigromante" (also known as **Bellas Artes**) is on Hernández Macías, just one block downhill from the Jardín. Housed in the beautiful cloistered courtyard of the old **Convento de la Concepción**, it's an arts institute run by the state fine arts organization, concentrating on music and dance, but to a lesser extent teaching visual arts, too. Mexicans can take courses here for virtually nothing; foreigners pay rather more. Around the courtyard there are various exhibitions, and several murals, including an entire room covered in one by David Siqueiros, devoted to the life and works of Allende. There's also the lovely *Las Musas* café (see p.334). The church of **La Concepción**, part of the complex, is lovely, too, and noted mainly for its tall dome raised on a drum, again said to be the work of the untrained Zeferino Gutiérrez.

Instituto Allende and around

The **Instituto Allende** lies down at the bottom of the hill following Hernández Macías south from La Concepción. On the way, at the corner of Cuadrante, you pass the **Casa del Inquisidor**, at Cuadrate 36, an eighteenth-century mansion with a particularly fine facade, and opposite, the old building that served as a jail for the Inquisition. The Instituto itself, on the edges of the old town, occupies a former hacienda of the Condes de la Canal – it was moved here in 1951 when the government recognized its success and it was

Learning Spanish in San Miguel de Allende

For many, the reason to be in San Miguel is to learn Spanish. Notice boards around town advertise private lessons, but most people end up taking one of the courses run by the main **language schools**, each of which offers a range of courses taught by professional Mexican teachers. Instruction is almost entirely in Spanish, with the focus on practical usage rather than academic theory, and students usually stay with a local family (count on US$18–22 a day for full board, or three meals a day) to consolidate the instruction. The most prestigious of the schools is the Instituto Allende, Ancha de San Antonio 20 (Ⓣ415/152-0226, Ⓦwww.instituto-allende.edu.mx), which conducts university-credited four-week courses (from US$125 for an hour a day to US$470 for the full six hours to US$890 for four weeks of five hours of private classes a day) throughout the year at all levels. There are also intensive one-to-one classes (roughly US$13 an hour), less demanding monthly courses, and classes for you to apply your new-found skills to studying Mexican history, ceramics, paper making, photography and so on. With the institute's long-standing reputation, the other schools have to compete on both price and quality, and do both admirably. The Academia Hispano Americana, Mesones 4 (Ⓣ415/152-0349, Ⓦwww.ahaspeakspanish.com), also operates four-week sessions (US$450), with discounts for enrolling in more than one course, as well as more intensive courses and extension courses in Mexican folklore among other subjects. Another contender is the Centro Mexicano de Lengua y Cultura, Orizaba 15 (Ⓣ/Ⓕ 415/152-0763, Ⓦwww.infosma.com/centromexicano), with the option of taking as little as an hour's instruction a day (US$30 a week) and which will also organize conversational exchanges to bolster practical usage. Finally, the Instituto Habla Hispana, Calzada de la Luz 25 (Ⓣ415/152-0713, Ⓦwww.mexicospanish.com), runs month-long courses for US$380 with around twenty contact hours per week; alternatively, you can just do a week for US$100. They'll also organize homestays for around US$17 a day for a double, and US$20 for a private room.

accredited by the University of Guanajuato. It offers courses in all kinds of arts from painting to sculpture to photography, in crafts like silverwork and weaving, and Spanish-language instruction at every level (see box, p.331), all within beautiful, park-like grounds. There's a café down here, too, and the notice boards are covered with offers of long-term accommodation, requests for and offers of rides throughout Mexico and up to the States, and information about what's going on in San Miguel.

Parque Benito Juárez, El Chorro and El Mirador

Ten minutes' walk immediately south of town, the refreshing, shaded **Parque Benito Juárez** was created out of the fruit orchards that belonged to many of the city's old families. The homes round about are still some of the fanciest in town. From here it's an uphill walk to **El Chorro**, the little hill whose springs supply the city with water, and the site of the town originally founded by Juan de San Miguel. Here you'll find **La Lavandería**, a series of twenty old-fashioned tubs where locals still come to do their washing. To get the best views over town you'll have to climb higher (follow Bajada de Charro) to **El Mirador**, the viewing point on the road to Querétaro, where there's a little belvedere, a small café, and San Miguel spread out below, with the broad plain and a ridge of mountains behind.

Eating, drinking and entertainment

Eating in San Miguel can be an expensive business; even local staples such as cappuccinos and margaritas are likely to cost half as much again as they would in, say, Querétaro, or even touristy Guanajuato. Though there are **restaurants** where you can get a standard comida or a plate of tacos for little more than you would pay elsewhere – the daytime *menú del día* is usually a good bet – you'll generally find yourself giving in to temptation and gravitating to places serving anything from sushi to fondue and more besides. It can be a tremendous relief for long-term travellers, with loads of stuff you may not have tasted for weeks and a suprising array of **vegetarian** options. The plentiful **cafés** are alive with students and expats who often seem to do little but hang out in such places all day – which is not a bad idea. The food quality is excellent, and with delicate gringo stomachs in mind, many places prominently advertise their assiduous use of sanitized water.

Nightlife here can come expensive too, but there is a wide range to choose from, a refreshing change in itself. Your best bet is to gather with everyone else in the Jardín – to take the air, stroll around and check out what's going on. It is also worth seeing if there is anything on at Teatro Angela Peralta, Mesones 82 (Ⓣ415/152-2200), which typically hosts **ballet**, **theatre** and occasional performances of **classical music**. The quarter-century-old, two-week long **Chamber Music Festival** (Festival de Música de Cámara; Ⓣ415/154-5141, Ⓦwww.chambermusicmexico.org) usually takes place in early August and features a range of performances by internationally acclaimed musicians. There's also an **International Jazz Festival** that happens each November Ⓦwww.unisono.net.mx/jazz). The Film Commission of Guanajuato's **annual short film festival**, Expresión en Corto, (Ⓦwww.expresionencorto.com) takes place in July (in San Miguel de Allende and Guanajuato) showing nearly two weeks of short-film programming from around the globe, and is rapidly gaining recognition from the worldwide filmmaking community. **Cinemas** include one in the *Hotel Villa Jacaranda*, Aldama 53, at Terraplen (Ⓣ415/152-1015), which hosts English-language movies every night at 7.30pm (US$6

Tours and activities in and around San Miguel de Allende

The expat community runs a couple of **tours around town**, including the Historic Walking Tour (Mon, Wed & Fri 9.30am; US$10), which meets in the Jardín across from the Parroquia at 9.15am; all the proceeds go towards medical care for underprivileged children. There's also the House and Garden Tour (Sun at noon; US$15), which leaves from the Biblioteca Pública (see p.335) and typically visits three different homes – mostly owned by expat Americans – each week. All money is donated to the public library. Numerous companies around town offer day-trips and longer excursions to towns and sites of interest in the region. Look for their posters if you're interested; some of the most adventurous and fun are those with an outdoor emphasis organized by Aventuras San Miguel, Recreo 10 (Ⓣ415/152-6406, Ⓔadventurassma@yahoo.com), who organize custom tours along with **guided biking trips** to places such as Pozos and archeological sites (half-day US$25, full day US$50), **horse riding** (US$40 per half-day) and excellent **hiking and camping** trips, usually with donkeys to carry much of the load and the tequila. Coyote Canyon Horseback Adventures (Ⓣ415/154-4193, Ⓦwww.coyotecanyonadventures.com) run group and private riding trips, lessons and even moonlit excursions at all levels at their ranch 16km southwest of town and all give a great insight into **charro** life; they run half-day outings (US$60) as well as full-day (US$100) and overnight excursions (US$150). Full-day trips might also include hiking, camping, hot-air ballooning and ultra-lite plane rides (US$150).

including a drink and popcorn): a new film starts each Tuesday. Cinemateca also has occasional showings; check in the library foyer (see "Listings", p.335) for details of upcoming screenings. A couple of kilometres to the southeast by the Gigante supermarket there's Cine Gemelos, which shows first-run movies on two screens for around US$3.20.

Restaurants

Apolo XI Mesones 43. Head upstairs here for ultra-casual, cheap *carnitas* (sold by the kilo) served on an open-air terrace. The hot and vinegary house pickles will curl your toes.

Aqui es México Hidalgo 28. Cheerful and attractive upstairs dining area with a wide range of Mexican favourites, though the best value is one of the two comidas corridas (US$4–5).

Azafrán Hernández Macías 97. Trendy new eatery featuring health-conscious gourmet dishes (many that actually taste good); its fun somewhat nostalgic decor gives a nod to the sleeker styles of the 1980s.

Bugambilia Hidalgo 42 Ⓣ415/152-0127. Long-standing, charming courtyard restaurant usually with live acoustic guitar music as you tuck into beautifully prepared Mexican dishes such as warm goat's cheese topped with toasted almonds (US$7) followed by steak fillet slow-cooked in butter (US$15) or an excellent chicken and vegetable casserole (US$10). Some daily discounts if you pay in cash.

Los Burritos Mesones 86. Super-popular and super-cheap spot for burritos made with flour tortillas and stuffed with savoury, soupy mixtures. Try the *tinga* and mole flavours, and ask for extra napkins. Open only for lunch.

Café de la Parroquia Jesús 11, at Cuadrante. A great little place with seats inside or in the courtyard, justly popular with expats for breakfasts of hot-cakes or yogurt and fruit. Good Mexican food served as well – tamales, chilaquiles and the like – and coffee all day long. Closed Mon.

La Capilla Cuna de Allende 10, steps from the Jardín Ⓣ415/152-0698, Ⓔcapilla@unisono.net.mx. San Miguel's most spectacular dining experience. Housed in what was once part of the town's main chapel, this lovingly restored two-storey restaurant has a thoughtful menu featuring international and local specialties made with seasonal ingredients, and rooftop dining under the cathedral spires. Estudiantinas perform several times a week, and there's even a boutique selling handmade chocolates in creative flavours such as peanut-curry. It's not cheap but it's worth every peso. Reservations recommended. Closed Tues.

El Catrín Canal 154. Succulent BBQ served with organic veggies in a restored 1926 Pullman rail car. It's not cheap, but you're sure to rave.

La Finestra Caffé Plaza Colonial, opposite Bellas Artes. Another popular and relaxed breakfast café with sun streaming in through the windows, delicious *huevos a la cazuela* (baked in a pot with a hot sauce and cheese), and top-class coffee and pastries all day. Closed Tues.

La Grotta Cuadrante 5. Great pasta and pizza joint, now expanded to a cosy room with red-washed walls and kitchen pans hanging from the ceiling. The homemade pasta dishes (US$7–9) are great but no match for the crispy pizza and calzone (in four guises including a vegetarian one). Also fresh salads and a small selection of secondi piatti. No credit cards.

El Harem Murillo 7. Arabic restaurant serving hummus with pitta bread (US$2), lamb brochettes (US$5) and stuffed vine leaves. Coffee grounds "readings" a bonus. Closed Tues.

L'Invito Umarán 19 ⓣ415/152-7333. About the best Italian restaurant in town with wonderfully tasty US$6–7 pasta dishes such as fusilli al fungo, plus a couple of set menus: US$10 for those with small appetites, and a more substantial four-course one for US$14.

Mesón de San José Mesones 38 at Juárez. Lovely patio-restaurant serving quality Mexican mains for US$6–7 and several cheaper vegetarian choices.

Las Musas in the Bellas Artes complex. Beautifully sited café away from the traffic noise, where students take a break over coffee, sandwiches, ice cream and croissants.

Olé Olé Loreto 66-A. Decked out in antique posters of bullfights, this festive spot features fajitas (beef, chicken or shrimp) for US$10, but closes early at 9pm.

El Pegaso Corregiadora 6. Where *norteamericanos* and well-off San Miguel youth come for gazpacho, chicken burgers, pastrami sandwiches and great seafood. Closed Sun.

El Petit Four Mesones 99. Delightful little French patisserie with a few tables where you can tuck into a pain au chocolat or a slice of tarte aux pommes with your espresso. Closed Sun.

La Piñata Umarán 10. Unpretentious and excellent-value café that's perfect for tacos, tostadas and tortas at a price unmatched around the Jardín, just a block away. Closed Tues.

Rincón de Don Tomás Portal de Guadalupe at the corner of San Francisco on the Jardín. Fantastic place for breakfast. Authentic Mexican dishes at wallet-friendly prices.

San Augustín San Francisco 21. Run by a retired Mexico City *telenovela* star, this pleasant restaurant is especially known for its sugary, fried *churros*.

Taquería Los Faroles Insurgentes 178 and Ancha San Antonio (no number, just past the Instituto). A few pesos buy amazingly delicious tacos at this local favourite. Try the *tacos al pastor* and be sure to sample the colourful array of homemade salsitas. Open 7.30pm–midnight, closed Sun.

El Ten Ten Pie Cuna de Allende 21. Small café with walls covered in the work of local artists, serving good Mexican staples and an extensive US$6 comida.

Tío Lucas Mesones 103. Some of the most succulent steak in town – US$10 for a New York strip, or beef medallions baked in red wine and served with peppers and Roquefort — comes in generous portions and is served on a verdant patio to the strains of quality live jazz. The chicken and seafood dishes are equally memorable, and they serve excellent margaritas.

El Tomato Mesones 62, east of Hidalgo. Mostly healthy, mostly vegetarian place for lunch and dinner with soya- and spinach-based burgers, exotic salad concoctions and a US$6 three-course *menú*.

La Ventana Sollano 11. Window-service coffeeshop featuring dark roasts from Chiapas and all manner of java concoctions. Best bet in town for a caffeine fix.

Bars and clubs

Chamonix Sollano 17-A. Buzzing, chic cocktail lounge with live music. A better bet for drinks than its eclectic fusion dining. Closed Mon.

Char Rock Correo 7. Mostly cheesy cover bands, but can be fun if the 7–9pm happy hours manage to pack people in. Closed Tues.

La Coronela San Francisco 2. Dependable cocktail lounge decorated with old Mexican cinema posters featuring 2 for 1 beers on Mon and Tues.

La Cucaracha on Zacateros, between Umarán and Pila Seca. Dim and fairly seedy late-night bar where Jack Kerouac and William Burroughs knocked back titanic amounts of booze in the 1950s. Reputedly the location has changed, but the spirit and tenor remains with a great jukebox, cheap but very rough margaritas and plenty of offbeat company.

En Agua Pulquería Jesús 19. Funky, ultra-hip (and diminutive) *boîte* with tart margaritas, baby-blue leather banquettes and tables made from BBQ grills.

La Fragua Cuna de Allende 3, just off the Jardín. Terrific local stand-by featuring a tapas menu, expansive cocktail lounge, and live music Fri and Sat.

El Gato Negro Mesones 10. Tiny and hip swing-door cantina (women welcome) absolutely plastered in photos of Marilyn Monroe– plus a couple of Jim Morrison and John Lennon – with nightly live music from funk to flamenco. The drinks are cheap by San Miguel standards, and there's no cover. There's also an old-fashioned *pissoire*.

Mama Mia Umarán 8. Probably the most happening nightspot in town, with restaurant, superb terrace bar with great views over the rooftops, and the adjacent after-hours *Mama's Bar*. You can count on good DJs, live bands and a US$3 cover. Happy hour 7–9pm, and free salsa classes on Wed nights.

Petit Bar at *El Market Bistro*, Hernández Macías 95. Just a couple of small rooms (one with sofas and imaginative decor) attached to this French restaurant. Low-cost drinks and sometimes poetry readings earlier in the evening. Closed Tues.

Listings

American Express Viajes Vertiz, Hidalgo 1, just north of El Jardín (Mon–Fri 9am–2pm & 4–6.30pm, Sat 10am–2pm; ⓣ415/152-1856, ⓕ152-0499), hold mail and reissue stolen or lost cheques, and cash them if they have enough money.

Banks and exchange Banamex, at the northwest corner of the Jardín on Canal; and Banorte, half a block east of Banamex along San Francisco. Casas de cambio include Deal at Calle San Francisco 1 (Mon–Fri 9am–6pm, Sat 9am–2pm).

Bicycle rental Bici-Burro, Hospicio 1 (ⓣ415/152-1526, ⓦwww.bici-burro.com), will rent you a good front-suspension machine for around US$25 a day and point you in the right direction, or you can join one of their van-supported tours either to the Santuario de Atotonilco (5–6hr; US$55), or to Pozos (5–6hr; US$120).

Books and newspapers Purchase international weeklies from newspaper vendors around the Jardín. Airport novels and weightier fiction along with hardbacks, magazines and art supplies are all stocked by El Colibrí, Sollano 30 (Mon–Sat 10am–3pm & 4–7pm), a block or so south of El Jardín, and there's a good stock of magazines among other things at Lagundi, Umarán 17 (Mon–Sat 10am–2pm & 4–8pm, Sun 11am–3pm).

Consulates US, Hernández Macías 72, opposite Bellas Artes (Mon–Fri 9am–1pm; ⓣ415/152-2357, for emergencies ⓣ415/152-0068).

Emergencies General emergencies ⓣ415/152-0911; Cruz Roja ⓣ415/152-4121; Police ⓣ415/152-0022.

Internet access Unisono, Hernández Macías 72B Altos (Mon–Fri 9am–2pm & 4–6pm; ⓔunisono@unisono.net.mx); Cyber Café, Mesones 57 (daily 10am–10pm), cable modem for $1.50 per hour.

Laundry Lavamagico, Pila Seca 5 (Mon–Sat 8am–8pm), offers a same-day service at low prices if dropped off before noon.

Library The Biblioteca Pública, Insurgentes 25, allows visitors to borrow books after obtaining a library card (two passport photos and US$3; valid one year) and leaving a US$10 deposit.

Pharmacy Farmacia Agundis, Canal 26 (daily 10am–midnight). English spoken.

Post office and couriers Correo 16 (Mon–Fri 9am–5pm). There are numerous express postal services, including DHL, at Correo 19 and opposite the post office through the *Bagel Café*, and UPS, which has an agency next door.

Tours Instituto Allende Tours (ⓣ415/152-0226, ⓦwww.instituto-allende.edu.mx). Many full-fledged, well-organized and informatively led regional tours that range in focus from ecotourism to historic Mexico. Prices vary.

Around San Miguel: hot springs and Atotonilco

One of the easiest and most enjoyable outings from San Miguel is to spend a good part of the day at one of the **hot springs**, where the warm thermal waters are ideal for soaking your bones. There are numerous hotels and mini-resorts with geothermal pools all around the area, but the best and easiest to reach are clustered around 9km to the northwest on the road to Dolores Hidalgo. The most popular (certainly with San Miguel's wintering Americans) is **La Gruta** (daily 8am–5pm; US$5) right by the highway and with a series of outdoor mineral pools at different temperatures all surrounded by lawns and banana trees. There's even a little grotto you can swim into with an artificial waterfall, and a small and reasonably priced restaurant on site with snacks and

US$4 fajitas. The best bet, though, is to pack some food from town and plan to spend the best part of the day here. If you can round up a group it is also possible to rent the place for the evening (US$105 for up to ten people, then US$5 for each extra); Aventuras San Miguel (see box, p.333) organize private group trips here on Wednesday and Friday evenings for US$35 per person, US$15 per person during the day. Around 500m before La Gruta, a side road leads just over a kilometre to **Escondido** (daily 8am–5.30pm; US$5), an equally appealing proposition, with small lily-filled lakes all around, cool outdoor pools and a series of small indoor ones linked by little tunnels and cascades. It can be quiet here midweek, but comes alive at weekends. Second-class **buses** to Dolores Hidalgo from San Miguel's bus station will all drop off on the highway near both sets of pools; to get back just flag down any bus you see.

A day at the hot springs can be conveniently combined with a worthwhile outing to **SANTUARIO DE ATOTONILCO** (easily confused with the larger Atotonilco el Grande in Jalisco state), 5km further in the same direction, then 3km down a side road. This is a dusty, rural indigenous community, whose church has come to be a centre of pilgrimage for two reasons – it was founded by Padre Felipe Neri, later canonized, and it was from here that Padre Hidalgo, marching from Dolores to San Miguel, took the banner of the Virgin of Guadalupe that became the flag of the Mexicans in the War of Independence. Allende was married here, too. The six chapels of the church (now under extensive restoration but mostly open to the public), liberally plastered with murals and freely interspersed with poems, biblical passages and painted statues, demonstrate every kind of Mexican popular art, from the naive to the highly sophisticated. Direct **buses** to the "Santuario" leave every hour from beside the market in San Miguel and spend ten to fifteen minutes in Atotonilco, giving you just enough time for a quick look before the run back, possibly getting dropped off at the hot springs.

Querétaro and around

Most people seem to hammer straight past **QUERÉTARO** on the highway to Mexico City, catching sight of only the expanding industrial outskirts and the huge modern bus station. Yet of all the colonial cities in the Bajío, this is perhaps the most surprising, preserving a tranquil historical core that boasts magnificent mansions and some of the country's finest ecclesiastical architecture. Little more than two hours from Mexico City, and at the junction of every major road and rail route from the north, it's also a wealthy and booming city, one of the fastest-growing in the republic thanks to industrial decentralization and its close proximity to the capital. This vibrancy, along with a series of pretty plazas linked by narrow alleys all lined with restaurants and bars, makes this a wonderful place to spend a couple of evenings simply lingering over a meal, and perhaps seeking out some live music around the bars and cafés.

There's interest, too, in the surrounding hills of the Sierra Gorda, notably the small towns of **Bernal** and **Tequisquiapan**, and much more distant charms of Edward James' jungle "sculpture garden" at **Xilitla**.

Some history

There's a history as rich and deep here as anywhere in the republic, starting before the Conquest when Querétaro ("rocky place") was an Otomí town subject to the **Aztecs**; many Otomí still live in the surrounding area. In 1531

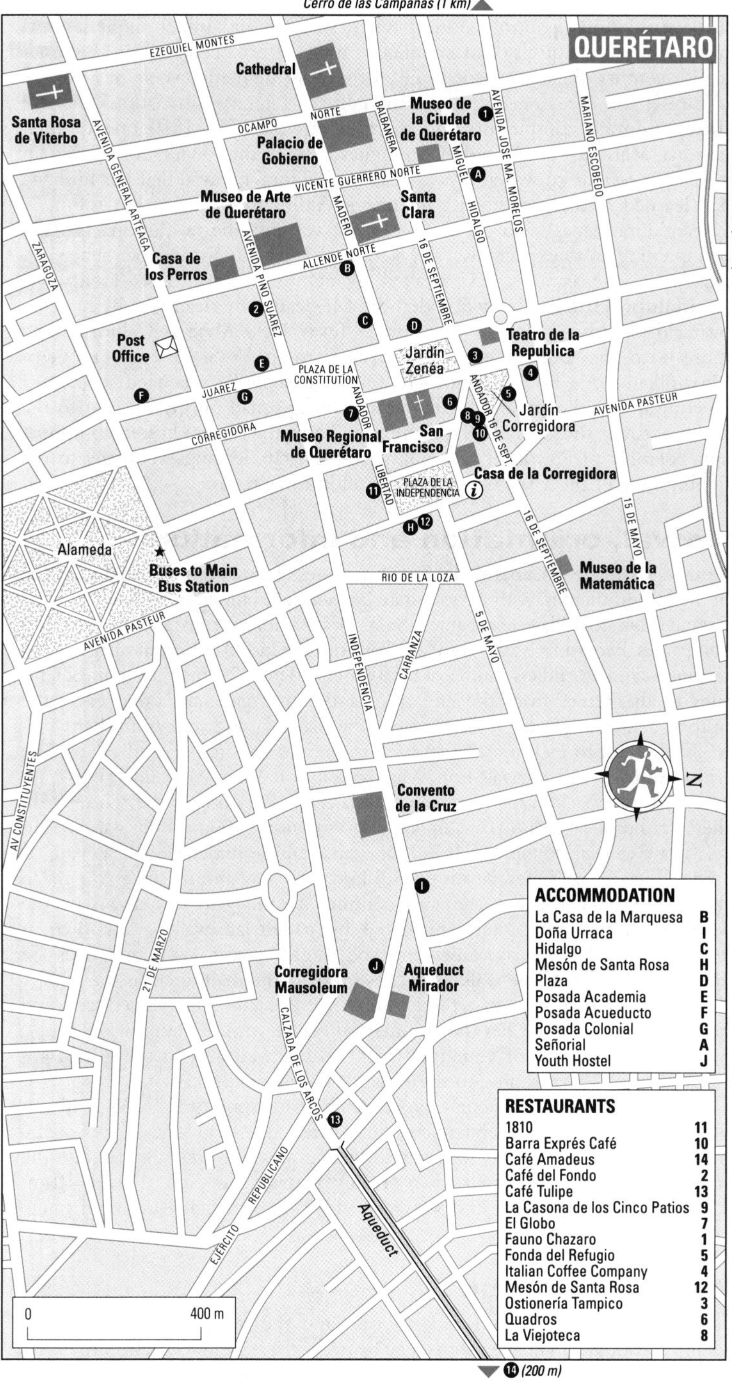
QUERÉTARO
Cerro de las Campañas (1 km)
Train Station (600 m)
Bus Station (5 km)
(200 m)
EZEQUIEL MONTES
OCAMPO
NORTE
VICENTE GUERRERO NORTE
ALLENDE NORTE
ZARAGOZA
AVENIDA GENERAL ARTEAGA
AVENIDA PINO SUÁREZ
MADERO
BALBANERA
16 DE SEPTIEMBRE
MIGUEL HIDALGO
AVENIDA JOSE MA. MORELOS
MARIANO ESCOBEDO
JUAREZ
CORREGIDORA
PLAZA DE LA CONSTITUTION
ANDADOR
ANDADOR 16 DE SEPT.
AVENIDA PASTEUR
LIBERTAD
PLAZA DE LA INDEPENDENCIA
15 DE MAYO
RIO DE LA LOZA
INDEPENDENCIA
CARRANZA
5 DE MAYO
AV CONSTITUYENTES
21 DE MARZO
CALZADA DE LOS ARCOS
REPUBLICANO
EJERCITO
Aqueduct
Cathedral
Santa Rosa de Viterbo
Palacio de Gobierno
Museo de la Ciudad de Querétaro
Museo de Arte de Querétaro
Santa Clara
Casa de los Perros
Post Office
Teatro de la Republica
Jardín Zenéa
Jardín Corregidora
Museo Regional de Querétaro
San Francisco
Casa de la Corregidora
Alameda
Buses to Main Bus Station
Museo de la Matemática
Convento de la Cruz
Corregidora Mausoleum
Aqueduct Mirador
N
0
400 m
ACCOMMODATION
La Casa de la Marquesa B
Doña Urraca I
Hidalgo C
Mesón de Santa Rosa H
Plaza D
Posada Academia E
Posada Acueducto F
Posada Colonial G
Señorial A
Youth Hostel J
RESTAURANTS
1810 11
Barra Exprés Café 10
Café Amadeus 14
Café del Fondo 2
Café Tulipe 13
La Casona de los Cinco Patios 9
El Globo 7
Fauno Chazaro 1
Fonda del Refugio 5
Italian Coffee Company 4
Mesón de Santa Rosa 12
Ostionería Tampico 3
Quadros 6
La Viejoteca 8

the Spanish took control without much struggle and under them it grew steadily into a major city and provincial capital before becoming, in the nineteenth century, the setting for some of the most dramatic events of Mexican history. It was here, meeting under the guise of Literary Associations, that the **Independence** conspirators laid their earliest plans. In 1810 one of their number, María Josefa Ortiz de Dominguez, wife of the town's Corregidor (or governor – she is known always as "La Corregidora"), found that her husband had learned of the movement's intentions. Although locked in her room, La Corregidora managed to get a message out warning the revolutionaries, thus precipitating an unexpectedly early start to the struggle for independence.

Later in the century, less exalted events took place. The **Treaty of Guadalupe Hidalgo**, which ended the Mexican–American War by handing over almost half of Mexico's territory – Texas, New Mexico, California and more – to the US, was signed in Querétaro in 1848. In 1867, Emperor Maximilian made his last stand here. Once defeated, he was tried by a court meeting in the theatre and finally faced a firing squad on the hill just to the north of town, the Cerro de las Campañas. The same theatre hosted an important assembly of Revolutionary politicians in 1916, leading eventually to the signing here of the 1917 Constitution, still in force today.

Arrival, orientation and information

Querétaro's massive **Central de Autobuses** lies 6km south of town and is one of the busiest there is, with two separate but adjacent buildings: **Sala A** for long-distance and first-class companies; **Sala B** for shorter runs and second-class companies. Fixed-price taxis (buy a ticket from the kiosk) run from outside both terminals, and an endless shuttle of local buses ("Ruta 8" is the most convenient) runs to the centre from the end of Sala B. Buses generally don't enter the historic centre, so get off at Zaragoza, by the Alameda, and walk from there. This is also the spot to pick up services back to the bus station: #36 and others. The **train station** (with arrivals from Mexico City on Mon, Wed and Fri at 1pm, and departures back to the capital an hour later) is 1km north of the centre; again there are buses ("Ruta 8" runs up Ocampo to within 100m of the station), but it's as easy to walk straight up Juárez, or grab a cab for under US$3.

For all its sprawl, Querétaro is easy to find your way around once you get to the centre, since the core remains confined to the grid laid down by the Spanish: all tiny plazas interconnected by pedestrian walkways known as *andadores*. Local buses run anywhere you might want to visit, and taxis are cheap, but on the whole walking proves simpler. The main focus is the zócalo, the **Jardín Zenéa**, with its typical triumvirate of bandstand, clipped trees and bootshines. To the west lies the commercial centre with the bulk of the shops, but you'll find much of your time spent to the west among the gift shops, restaurants and bars leading to the Plaza de la Independencia.

The **tourist office**, Pasteur 4 Norte (daily 9am–8pm; ⓣ442/238-5067 ext 5069, ⓦwww.turismo.queretaro.com.mx), offers free maps and copies of the monthly *Tesoro Turístico* newspaper, with listings of local events, and is also the starting point for hour-long town **trolley tours** (Tues–Sun at 9am, 10am, 11am, 4pm, 5pm & 6pm; US$3), which visit the main sights and might help you get your bearings.

Accommodation

For **hotels**, head straight for the zócalo and the streets in the immediate vicinity. Though streetside rooms may be noisy, there's a fair selection of places in this area, three of them particularly gorgeous (and expensive), in addition to several at the budget end of the range, some very basic. Where Querétaro trips up is in the mid-range, with few decent choices in the centre: if you can't stretch to the pricier places, go for the better rooms at, say, the *Hidalgo* or *Posada Acueducto*.

La Casa de la Marquesa Madero 41 ⓣ442/212-0092, ⓔreserv@casadelamarquesa.com. Very central and housed in a mansion with a gorgeous Moorish courtyard. The antique-furnished rooms are also magnificent, though for something truly special you'll want a suite (US$280–460). While its appearance is beautiful, service can be hit or miss, and the restaurant and lobby may be too staid for some. Breakfast included. ❾

Doña Urraca 5 de Mayo 17 ⓣ442/238-5400 or 01-800/021-7116, ⓦwww.donaurraca.com.mx. The city's newest (and best) hotel. Each room is named for a bird and features stone, wood and gorgeous natural-fibre linens. Spa rates are surprisingly reasonable. An excellent alternative to the *Casa de la Marquesa*. ❾

Hidalgo Madero 11 Pte, just off Jardín Zenéa ⓣ442/212-0081, ⓦwww.hotelhidlago.com.mx. Simple but clean rooms set around an open courtyard, all with bath and cable TV, and some of the larger rooms with balconies for a couple of dollars more. Good budget option. ❺

Mesón de Santa Rosa Pasteur 17 Sur ⓣ442/224-2623, ⓦmesondesantaroasa.com.mx. Superb luxury hotel, very quiet and beautiful, in an old colonial mansion on the Jardín Independencia and with a great restaurant to boot. ❾

Plaza Juárez Nte 23, on the Jardín Zenéa ⓣ/ⓕ 442/212-1138. On the zócalo; clean, but a touch faded and impersonal. All rooms with bath, TV and phone. ❺

Posada Academia Pino Suárez 3 ⓣ442/224-2739. Clean and basic rooms are nothing special but cheap and have TV. ❹

Posada Acueducto Juárez 64 Sur, at Arteaga ⓣ442/224-1289. Attractively decorated and well-cared-for hotel, right in the centre, with modern rooms all with cable TV. The large suites are particularly nice. ❺

Señorial Guerrero 10a Nte ⓣ442/214-3700, ⓔhotelsenorial@prodigy.net.mx. About the only decent mid-range place in the centre with comfortable carpeted rooms, cable TV, parking and some larger rooms with a/c. ❺–❻

Youth Hostel (CREA) Avenida Ejército Republicano, behind the ex-Convento de la Cruz, about a fifteen-minute walk from the centre ⓣ442/223-4350. This Villa Juvenil is one of Mexico's better; relatively helpful and with clean, if cramped, single-sex dorms and 24-hour hot water, but an inconvenient 10.30pm curfew. ❷

The City

Dominating the **Jardín Zenéa**, Querétaro's main square, the church of **San Francisco** was one of the earliest founded in the city. Its beautiful facade incorporates a dome covered in azulejos – coloured tiles imported from Spain around 1540 – but for the most part San Francisco was rebuilt in the seventeenth and eighteenth centuries. Adjoining, in what used to be its monastery, is the **Museo Regional de Querétaro** (Tues–Sun 10am–7pm; US$3.20, free on Sun). The building alone is reason enough to visit. Built around a large cloister and leading back to a lovely chapel, it's far bigger than you imagine from the outside. Inside the displays are eclectic: the keyhole through which La Corregidora passed on her news; early copies of the Constitution; the table on which the Treaty of Guadalupe Hidalgo was signed; and quantities of ephemera connected with Emperor Maximilian, whose headquarters were here for a while. There are also the more usual collections relating to local archeology, and a sizeable gallery of colonial art – altogether well worth an hour or two.

South of the museum lies the **Plaza de la Constitución**, a former market square now transformed into an attractive modern plaza with a central fountain mimicking the domed roof of the building on the south side. There's more interest a couple of blocks north at the **Teatro de la República**, at the junction of Juárez and Peralta (Tues–Sun 10am–2pm & 5–8pm; free), a grand nineteenth-century structure, which has played a vital role in Mexican history:

here a court met to decide the fate of Emperor Maximilian, and the 1917 Constitution was agreed. A small exhibition celebrates these events, though the main reason to go in is to take a look at the theatre itself. The guards sometimes let visitors slip in to hear the philharmonic orchestra practice for free.

Around the Plaza de la Independencia

The little pedestrianized alleys that lead up to the east of the Jardín are some of the city's most interesting. They are crammed with ancient houses, little restaurants, art galleries and shops selling junky antiques and the opals and other semiprecious stones for which the area is famous. If you decide to buy, double-check the stone for authenticity. The first of several little plazas, almost part of the Jardín Zenéa, is the **Jardín Corregidora**, another beautiful square, with an imposing statue of La Corregidora and several restaurants and bars where you can sit outside. The pedestrianized Andador Libertad runs past art galleries and boutiques from the Plaza de la Constitución to the **Plaza de la Independencia**, or Plaza de Armas, a very pretty, arcaded open space. In the middle of the plaza stands a statue of Don Juan Antonio Urrutia y Arana, Marques de la Villa del Villar del Aguila, the man who built Querétaro's elegant aqueduct, providing the city with drinking water. Around the square is the **Casa de la Corregidora**, now the Palacio Estatal (Mon–Fri 9am–9pm, Sat 9am–3pm; free). It was here, on September 14, 1810, that La Corregidora was locked up while her husband made plans to arrest the conspirators. She managed to get a message to Ignacio Perez, who carried it to the leaders Allende and Hidalgo in the towns of San Miguel and Dolores. The house is an attractive building, but there's not a great deal to see inside.

Immediately to the north, the **Museo de la Matemática**, 16 de Septiembre 63 Oriente (Mon–Fri 10am–2pm & 4–8pm, Sat 10am–2pm; US$1), may be of interest to visitors with an interest in geometry and mathematical phenomena, especially those who also have a good command of technical Spanish.

The commercial centre: Avenida Morelos and around

The more interesting restaurants and bars remain around the eastern plazas, but the commercial centre of Querétaro lies west of the zócalo, on and around **Avenida Morelos**. This is where you'll find most of the shops, on formal streets lined with stately mansions. At the corner of Madero and Allende, the little Jardín de Santa Clara features a famous **Fountain of Neptune**, designed by Tresguerras in 1797. **Francisco Eduardo Tresguerras** (1765–1833) is rightly regarded as one of Mexico's greatest architects – he was also a sculptor, painter and poet – and was almost single-handedly responsible for developing a native Mexican architectural style diverging from (though still close to) its Spanish roots. His work, seen throughout central Mexico, is particularly evident here and in nearby Celaya, his birthplace. Beside the fountain rises the deceptively simple church of **Santa Clara**, once attached to one of the country's richest convents. Inside it's a riot of Baroque excess, with gilded cherubs and angels swarming all over the profusely decorated altarpieces.

Carry on west down Madero and you get to the **Palacio de Gobierno** and the **cathedral**, eighteenth-century buildings, neither of which, by Querétaro's standards, is particularly distinguished. Cut north along Guerrero, however, and you'll come to the new **Museo de la Ciudad de Querétaro**, Guerrero 27 Norte (Tues–Sun 11am–7pm; US$0.50), which fills a huge colonial building with temporary exhibitions, predominantly contemporary painting, sculpture and photography. There's almost always something worth half an hour of your time.

Convento de la Cruz

There's more to see a short walk east from the centre at the **Convento de la Cruz** (daily 9am–2pm & 4–6pm; small donation requested), built on the site of the battle between the Spanish and the Otomí in which the conquistadors gained control of Querétaro. According to legend, the fighting was cut short by the miraculous appearance of St James (Santiago – the city's full name is Santiago de Querétaro) and a dazzling cross in the sky, which persuaded the Indians to concede defeat and become Christians. The **Capilla del Calvarito**, opposite the monastery entrance, marks the spot where the first mass was celebrated after the battle. The monastery itself was founded in 1683 by the Franciscans as a college for the propagation of the faith (Colegio Apostólico de Propaganda Fide) and grew over the years into an important centre for the training of missionaries, with a massive library and rich collection of relics. Because of its hilltop position and hefty construction, the monastery was also frequently used as a fortress. Functioning as one of the last redoubts of the Spanish in the War of Independence, it was Maximilian's headquarters for the last few weeks of his reign and he was subsequently imprisoned here to await execution – nowadays you can take guided tours (ask if there is an English one available). The greatest source of pride is the **Árbol de la Cruz**, a tree whose thorns grow in the shape of little crosses. The tree grew, so the story goes, from a walking stick left behind by a mysterious saintly traveller who slept here one night. It certainly does produce thorns in the form of crosses, but that may not be so rare. The monks, however, appear very excited by the phenomenon and point out that an additional five percent of the thorns grow with extra spikes to mark the spots where nails were driven through Christ's hands and feet; look for the framed collection in the entrance foyer.

Come up to the monastery in the late afternoon, then wander 200m beyond along Avenida Ejército Republicano to the **Mausoleo de la Corregidora** (daily 9am–5pm; free), where the heroine's remains, along with those of her husband, are surrounded by statues of illustrious *Querétanos*. Across the road a *mirador* provides a superb sunset-view of the city's early eighteenth-century **aqueduct**, a beautiful 1.3-kilometre-long series of 74 arches up to 23m high, which once brought water into the city from springs nearly 9km away. Spotlit at night, it looks magnificent, especially as you drive into town. *Café Tulipe* and *Café Amadeus* (see p.343) are both a short stroll down the hill from here.

The Museo de Arte de Querétaro and around

A couple of blocks south of the Museo de la Ciudad lies the **Museo de Arte de Querétaro**, Allende 14 Sur (Tues–Sun 11am–7pm; US$2, free on Tues) occupying the former Palacio Federal, by the church of San Agustín. Originally an Augustinian monastery (it has also been a prison and a post office in its time), it is one of the most exuberant buildings in a town full of them. In the cloister, every surface of the two storeys of portals is carved with grotesque figures, no two quite alike, and with abstract designs. The sculptures, often attributed to Tresguerras though almost certainly not by him, are full of religious symbolism, which you should try to get someone to explain to you. The large figures supporting the arches, for example, all hold their fingers in different positions: three held up to represent the Trinity, four for the Evangelists and so on. The contents of the museum are good, with galleries devoted to sixteenth- and seventeenth-century European painting downstairs, along with temporary exhibition spaces usually featuring quality contemporary Mexican art. The collection of Mexican painting upstairs is mostly from the seventeenth and eighteenth centuries, with a room full of works attributed to Tresguerras and

Manuel Cabrera and a fine series of nine (out of an original fourteen or fifteen) portraits of saints by Cristóbal de Villalpando.

A few metres south along Allende lies the **Casa de los Perros**, Allende 16 at Pino Suárez, a mansion named after the ugly canine gargoyles that line its facade. The church of **Santa Rosa de Viterbo** sits further out in this direction, at the junction of Arteaga and Montes. Its interior rivals Santa Clara for richness of decoration, but here there is no false modesty on the outside either. Two enormous flying buttresses support the octagonal cupola (remodelled by Tresguerras) and a blue and white tiled dome. The tower, too, is Tresguerras' work, holding what is said to be the first four-sided public clock erected on the American continent.

Cerro de las Campañas

Further out to the west, and a little to the north, the gentle eminence of the **Cerro de las Campañas** ("Hill of Bells") commands wide, if less than scenic, views over Querétaro and its industrial outskirts. Maximilian and his two generals, Miguel Miramón and Tomás Mejía, faced the firing squad here. The hill is dominated by a vast stone statue of the victor of that particular war, Benito Juárez, glaring down over the town from its summit. In order to reach the summit, avoid the parts of the new university campus sprawling up one slope, follow Hidalgo west, turn right onto Tecnológico and then left after 400m into Avenida Justo Sierra where there's the entrance to the neatly tended Parque Municipal del Cerro de las Campañas (daily dawn–dusk; US$0.50).

Eating, drinking and entertainment

There's plenty of good food in Querétaro, and some delightful places to sit outside amid the alleys and plazas east of the **Jardín Zenéa**. The **zócalo** itself has plenty of rather cheaper places. If you want to get together something of your own, head for the **market**, sprawled across several blocks just off Calzada Zaragoza, not far from the Alameda. While in Querétaro look out for a couple of **local specialities**, particularly a hearty lentil soup laced with chunks of dried fruit (usually just called "sopa regional"): it sounds odd but is delicious, though vegetarians won't appreciate the pork-broth base. Also try *enchiladas Queretanas*, tortillas fried in a chile sauce and stuffed with onions and cheese. In fancier places they may come topped with potatoes and carrots.

Evening entertainment tends to involve a couple of beers in one of the restaurants or an hour or two lingering in one of the cafés. More lively nightlife is harder to find, with the key **bars and clubs** scattered around the suburbs, a taxi ride apart. Most places have some sort of **live music** on Thursday, Friday and Saturday nights, when you can expect to pay US$2–5 to get in. Perhaps the best starting point is Bernardo Quintana (go to the eastern end of the aqueduct and then south), where *J.B.J. O'Briens* bar, at no. 109, and an outpost of the *Carlos 'N Charlie's* chain, at no. 160, prove popular with the richer local youth. Across from the latter, at no. 177, *Los Infiernos* is open primarily for hot salsa from Wednesday to Sunday. Elsewhere the club scene centres on *Qui*, Monte Sinai 103, and *La Iguana*, inside the *Hotel Santa María* on Universidad.

There are no centrally located **cinemas**. The ten-screen Cinepolis is behind the bullring on Constituyentes, almost 3km southeast of the centre. Buses run along Constituyentes but a taxi is a lot easier. Local daily papers list what's playing.

1810 Jardín Independencia Street/Number?. Excellent sidewalk restaurant that does regional specialities to perfection and seems less afflicted by cheesy crooners than other places on the Jardín. Expect to pay US$3–4 for Mexican staples, US$6–12 for meat and fish dishes.
Barra Exprés Café Andador 16 de Septiembre 40. A relaxed stop for the best coffee in town. Closed Tues.
Café Amadeus corner Calzada de los Arcos and Puente de Alvarado, halfway along the aqueduct. Good place for coffee and cake, but also serving fine breakfasts and antojitos, all to the strains of Mozart.
Café del Fondo Pino Suárez 9. Airy multi-roomed café serving bargain breakfasts from 7.30am, with fresh juice, espresso and a plate of eggs, enchiladas or hot-cakes for under US$2. There's also tasty food through the day, and good coffee and cakes all day until around 10.30pm. One room is often devoted to board games, particularly chess.
Café Tulipe Calzada de los Arcos 3, near the west end of the aqueduct. A definite favourite for its French-tinged menu, coffee and cakes, all at surprisingly modest prices. The delicious fondue and *caldo conde* (a black bean, cream and herb soup) are especially good.
La Casona de los Cinco Patios Andador 5 de Mayo 39. Run by the same owners as *La Viejoteca*. A shade pricey but you're guaranteed an impressive selection of delicious regional, national and international dishes in eclectic surroundings. This unique spot has earned a reputation as one of the city's best.
Fauno Chazaro Morelos 49-B. Fairly priced Mediterranean restaurant serving everything from *taramasalata* to a small, but choice selection of wines. Tranquil courtyard dining, but slightly out of the way.
Fonda del Refugio Jardín Corregidora, behind the statue. Not-too-expensive, very elegant place to sit outside, drink, and watch the world go by.
El Globo Corregidora 41. About the best *pastelería* in town, with lots of French pastries – croissants, pain au chocolat and so on – big sticky cakes and even Häagen Dazs ice cream, all to take out.
Italian Coffee Company Plaza de la Independencia. Good espresso served inside or out on a small plaza by a fountain. A shady spot in the heat of the day.
Mesón de Santa Rosa Pasteur 17 Sur, Plaza de la Independencia. Superb restaurant serving Mexican specialities and Spanish food in a beautiful setting, with correspondingly high prices.
Ostionería Tampico Jardín Corregidora. Top-notch seafood at moderate prices, best selected from one of three daily comidas at US$5–8. Their seafood cocktails should be eaten the traditional Mexican way: with a squirt of ketchup.
Quadros Andador 5 de Mayo 16. Light snacks are available, but this is primarily a café and bar with several intimate rooms off the central well of a colonial mansion. There's some form of live entertainment (usually folk or jazz) most nights of the week, especially Thursday to Saturday when there is a cover charge of a couple of dollars. The work of local artists adorns the walls. Closed Mon.
La Viejoteca Andador 5 de Mayo 39. Pricey piano bar in a large high-ceilinged room with interesting decor – anything from old jukeboxes to an entire wall of old pharmacy shelves – that's bustling most evenings and often has live music.

Listings

American Express Turismo Beverly Querétaro, Tecnológico 118 (Mon–Fri 9am–2pm & 4–6pm, Sat 9am–noon; ⓣ442/216-1049), has all the usual services. It's around 2km southwest of the centre, reached by buses running west along Zaragoza to Tecnológico, then 200m south.
Banks and exchange There are several banks around the Jardín Zenéa that will change currency (Mon–Fri 9am–3pm), and a couple of casas de cambio south along Juárez, such as Casa Acueducto at no. 58.
Books and newspapers International weeklies can usually be found at the newspaper stands around the Jardín Zenéa. Beyond that, Sanborn's, on Constituyentes, 2km southeast of the centre, have a wide range of magazines.
Emergencies For general emergencies call ⓣ066; Cruz Roja ⓣ442/229-0505.
Internet access There are several fairly low-cost Internet places in the centre: try Inteligencia Informática, second floor, 5 de Mayo 8, or Naftis, 16 de Septiembre 8, off Juárez.
Laundry Lavandería Verónica, Hidalgo 153 at Ignacio Pérez (Mon–Fri 9am–2.30pm & 4.30–8pm, Sat 9am–3pm), lies less than 1km west of the centre.
Pharmacy There are dozens of pharmacies around the centre, including the large Farmacia Guadalajara at Madero 32 just west of the Jardín Zenéa.
Post office Arteaga 5.

Around Querétaro

From Querétaro you can race straight into the capital on Hwy-57, and if you are not reliant on public transport, then there are a couple of places that might be visited en route: the ancient Toltec capital of Tula, and Tepotzotlán, with its magnificent Baroque architecture, both of which are covered in Chapter Five.

Before charging south, consider exploring something of the **Sierra Gorda** mountain range to the east of Querétaro, where the foothills are home to **Bernal**, **San Juan del Río** and **Tequisquiapan**, where you could easily spend a pleasant few days exploring one or all of the towns. More ambitious travellers should press on through the mountains to the wonderfully bizarre concrete fantasy of **Las Pozas** near **Xilitla**.

Bernal

The pretty village of **BERNAL**, 45km east of Querétaro, hunkers under the skirts of the monolithic Peña de Bernal, a 450-metre-high chunk of volcanic rock which towers over the plains and is the third largest boulder of its kind in the world. By wandering towards the rock you'll soon pick up a rough but clearly marked path about two-thirds of the way to the top (the ascent takes up to an hour, half that to get down), where there's a small shrine and long views stretching out below. Only appropriately equipped rock climbers should continue up the metal rungs to the summit, passing a memorial plaque to an earlier adventurer along the way.

At weekends, half of Querétaro seems to come out here, making for a festive atmosphere, but midweek it is an altogether more peaceful place: the mountain is likely to be deserted and you'll be about the only thing disturbing the lovely village plaza with its attractive church and terracotta-washed buildings, sumptuous in the afternoon light. Be forewarned, however, that many businesses are only open at the weekends and many more shut for the month of May.

The centre is ringed by narrow streets full of shops selling handicrafts, and there's even a small and sporadically open **tourist office** on Hidalgo, which runs west from the plaza, though there isn't much they can tell you that you can't discover for yourself in ten minutes. Also on Hidalgo is one of the nicest **places to eat**, in the shaded courtyard of *Mesón de la Roca*, at no. 5, serving moderately priced and well-presented Mexican dishes along with a US$6.50 comida corrida and grasshopper tacos for the daring. There are also several cheap *comedores*, and at weekends perhaps a dozen restaurants to choose from. Flecha Amarilla and Flecha Azul combine to offer hourly **buses** from Querétaro's bus station (Sala B) which drop you on the highway five minutes' walk from Bernal centre; it's worth remembering that the last bus back passes at around 6pm. If you get stuck, or just fancy a night here (not a bad thing), there are clean, comfortable and excellent-value **rooms** at *Posada Peña*, Iturbide 3, behind the church (Ⓣ441/296-4149; ⑤).

San Juan del Río

Though **SAN JUAN DEL RÍO**, 50km south of Querétaro, looks like nothing at all from the highway, it is in fact a major market centre, and a popular weekend outing from Querétero and the capital. Among the goods sold here are **gemstones** – mostly local opals, but also imported jewels, which are polished and set in town – as well as baskets, wine and cheese. Once again, if you're going to buy gems, be very careful: it's easy to get ripped off without expert advice. Other purchases are safer, though not particularly cheap on the whole. The best-known local wine is Hidalgo, a brand sold all over the country and usually reliable.

Most Mexico City-bound buses no longer call here, but direct buses from Querétaro (Flecha Azul from Sala B among others) take forty minutes to get to San Juan del Río's **bus station**, a couple of kilometres south of town. A local bus will run you up Hidalgo and drop you on a broad section of **Avenida Juárez**, where there's a central fountain, manicured trees and an attractive arcade on one side. Here you'll find a small **tourist office**, at Juárez 30 Oriente (Mon–Fri 10am–8pm; ⓣ427/272-4179).

The Mercado Reforma and the twin central squares of the Jardín Independencia and Plaza de los Fundadores are a couple of long blocks north of Avenida Juárez, up Hidalgo, but there is more interest a couple of blocks south of the tourist office at **Museo de la Muerte**, 2 de Abril 42 (Tues–Sun 10am–2pm & 4-7pm; free), where the former cemetery, on a hill overlooking town behind the church of Santa Veracruz, conveys the different ways Mexicans express their connectedness with the dead.

If you decide that you'd like to stay a while to enjoy San Juan's unhurried atmosphere, take your choice of several good **hotels**, on or just off Juárez: the simple and inexpensive *San Juan*, Hidalgo 4 Sur (no tel; ❸); the friendly, pleasant and comfortable *Portal Royalty*, Juárez 20 Oriente (ⓣ/ⓕ 427/672-0038; ❺); or, best of all, *Layseca*, across from the latter at Juárez 9 Oriente (ⓣ/ⓕ 427/272-0110; ❺), an old colonial house with rooms set around a beautiful open courtyard. In summer you might appreciate the pool at *Hotel Colonial*, Juárez 30 Poniente (ⓣ/ⓕ427/272-4022; ❺), where the older and somewhat darker rooms are more characterful.

For something to **eat**, choose from several restaurants along Juárez, many with outdoor seating, or head a few metres down Hidalgo to *El Encanto*, Hidalgo 8 Sur, which has attractive wooden tables, a tiled fountain and good value comida corrida for around US$4.

Tequisquiapan

Some 20km north of San Juan, along a road lined with factories and workshops, **TEQUISQUIAPAN** is a former Otomí village that developed in viceregal times primarily on account of its warm springs. Exclusive villas each with beautifully tended walled gardens are set around the central Plaza Santa María, itself ringed by arched *portales* on three sides, the church on the fourth, all painted in soft tones of orange, red and azure. It is very popular with wealthy Mexicans up from the capital, but has never really caught on with *extranjeros*. Although perfect as a weekend escape from the city, there's little to do other than bathe in your hotel pool, dine in one of many restaurants around the plaza and nose around the boutiques, some of which are cheap, many expensive and almost all of the highest standard. Like San Juan del Río, Tequisquiapan has a big **crafts market** – especially active on Sundays – one block from the main plaza. At the end of May running into June, Tequisquiapan hosts a major wine and cheese festival, the **Feria Internacional del Queso y del Vino**, which is well worth the visit. There's plenty of free food and drink and no shortage of other entertainment, including music and dancing. If you miss the festival and still have a taste for wine, Freixenet, the Spanish producer of bubbly, has a nearby cava with tastings at Carretera San Juan del Río km 40.5 (Sat & Sun 11.30am–1pm & 2–3pm; free tours; ⓣ414/277-0147).

Free town maps are available from the **tourist office** (Tues–Thurs 9am–2pm & 4–7pm, Fri–Sun 9am–7pm; ⓣ414/273-0295) on the main square. When the attraction of artesanía-shopping begins to pale, you'll probably want to press on, but if you decide to stay you can choose from the thirty-odd **hotels** packed into this tiny place, most ranged around bougainvillea-draped courtyards, many with pools fed by springs. Prices are relatively high, though lone travellers get a reasonable deal at *Hotel Posada San Francisco*, Moctezuma 2 (ⓣ414/273-0231; ❻), where plain but comfortable rooms have access to the lush garden and pool. Couples may prefer *Posada Los Arcos*, Moctezuma 12 (ⓣ414/273-0566; ❺), which lacks a pool but has more comfortable rooms; or even *La Plaza*, on the plaza at Juárez 10 (ⓣ414/273-0005, ⓦwww.tequisquiapan.com.mx/la_plaza; ❼), a perfect luxury hotel, very relaxed, with its own pool and some very attractive suites (❽). Best of all is *Hotel El Relox*, Morelos 8 (ⓣ/ⓕ 414/273-0006, ⓦwww.relox.com.mx; ❽), a vast complex of outdoor and indoor private pools, luxuriant gardens, gym, sauna, games areas, and a selection of gorgeous rooms and even more impressive suites (❾) that bills itself as an "ecological paradise", which is an overstatement. Massages average US$25.

Restaurants abound, though many only really come to life at the weekend. The place is so small that you can walk around them all in ten minutes and see what appeals on the day, though it is worth wandering along Morelos to *La Capilla*, an authentic Italian restaurant serving delicious arrabbiata, seafood risotto and tiramisú, all at low to moderate prices (closed May).

Hourly Flecha Azul **buses** from Querétaro (Sala B) run direct to Tequisquiapan, and there's a bus every half-hour from San Juan del Río. From the bus station, turn right and walk the ten minutes into the plaza, passing an ugly concrete tripod said to mark the geographical centre of the country.

Xilitla and Las Pozas

You'll have to travel considerably further afield, and set aside a couple of days, to reach and really appreciate the picturesque town of **XILITLA**, some 320km northeast of Querétaro. Little more than a large village, Xilitla perches on a hillside with tremendous views over the surrounding temperate rainforest thick with waterfalls, birdlife and flowers, particularly wild orchids. It is mainly of interest as a place to relax, though you might devote a few minutes to admiring the beautifully preserved interior of the sixteenth-century **Templo de San Agustín** which overlooks the central plaza, Jardín Hidalgo.

The real justification for the lengthy journey to Xilitla is to visit **Las Pozas** (roughly 9am–6pm; US$2), some 2km east of town along a dirt road: ask locally for directions or grab a taxi for around US$6. Here, English eccentric **Edward James** (see box, opposite) spent the 1960s and 1970s creating a surreal jungle fantasy full of completely useless concrete buildings that are full of imagination and whimsy. Sprouting beside the nine pools ("pozas") of the cascading jungle river you'll find a spiral staircase that winds up until it disappears to nothing, stone hands almost 2m high, thick columns with no purpose, a mosaic snake and buildings such as the "House With Three Stories That Might be Five" and "The House Destined To Be a Cinema". Only one is in any sense liveable, a hideaway apartment four stories up where James spent much of his time.

Mildew now ages the concrete beyond its years, and in places it is crumbling away revealing the reinforcing steel beneath, but it all adds to the enchanting quality of the place. You could see everything in an hour or so, but plan to spend the better part of a day here bathing in the pools and soaking up the atmosphere; best bring your own lunch.

Xilitla isn't really on the way to anywhere, over six twisting and winding hours through the Sierra Gorda from Querétaro and perhaps most easily accessed from the unexciting but sizeable town of **Ciudad Valles**, on the highway between San Luis Potosí and Tampico. You might need to change at Ciudad Valles for one of the regular buses for the sixty-kilometre journey south to Xilitla, though there are tolerably frequent direct services from Querétaro, Tampico and San Luis Potosí: all pull in at the bus station close to Jardín Hidalgo. There's no tourist office, but everything (including several **banks** with ATMs, and the **post office**) is easy to find on the streets nearby. Here, too, you'll find simple and clean **accommodation** at *Hotel Ziyaquetzas*, Jardín Hidalgo (Ⓣ489/365-0081; ❹), and nearby at *Hotel María* (Ⓣ489/365-0049; ❹), but *the* place to stay is definitely *Posada El Castillo*, Ocampo 105 (Ⓣ489/365-0038, Ⓦwww.junglegossip.com/castillo.html; no credit cards, ❼), half a block down from the plaza. It's highly recommended that you secure a reservation before making the long steep trek to Xilitla, especially at the popular *El Castillo*, where making contact can prove challenging. *El Castillo* is where James lived when he wasn't ensconced in his hut or apartment at Las Pozas, and his spirit still inhabits the eight highly individual guestrooms, designed by Esquer and harmoniously blending Mexican, English and Moorish styles. There's a pool, meals are served, and the hosts not only speak English but have produced a documentary on James' life and work which they screen for guests. There are several simple **restaurants** close to the Jardín Hidalgo.

Edward James

Born in 1907 to a second-rank British aristocrat and the scion of a wealthy American mining family, **Edward James** grew up cosseted by an Eton and Oxford education, and with no lack of money set about a life as a poet and artist. After limited success he became a patron of the arts, partly in an attempt to prolong his waning marriage to Hungarian dancer, Tilly Losch. Despite bankrolling ballets as a vehicle for her talents (notably those by George Balanchine's first company), she eventually left him, whereupon he retreated from London society to Europe where he befriended Salvador Dalí and agreed to buy his entire output for a year. Picasso and Magritte also benefited from his patronage as James increasingly aligned himself with the Surrealists. Indeed, Picasso is reputed to have described James as "crazier than all the Surrealists put together. They pretend, but he is the real thing." During Word War II, James moved to the US, where he partly funded LA's Watts Towers and made his first visit south of the border. After falling in love with Xilitla, he moved here in the early 1950s and experimented with growing orchids and running a small zoo. In later years he was often seen with a parrot or two in tow as he went about building his fantasy world. Aided by local collaborator and long-time companion, **Plutarco Gastelum Esquer**, and up to 150 workers, James fashioned his world, continually revising and developing, but never really finishing anything. He died in 1984 leaving his estate to Esquer and his family, though without making any provision for the upkeep of his work.

Fiestas

The Bajío is one of the most active regions in Mexico when it comes to celebrations. The state of Guanajuato is especially rich in fiestas: the list below is by no means comprehensive and local tourist offices will have further details.

JANUARY

1 NEW YEAR'S DAY widely celebrated. Fiesta in **Dolores Hidalgo** (Guanajuato).

6–15 Feria in **Matehuala** (San Luis Potosí).

20 DÍA DE SAN SEBASTIAN. In **San Luis Potosí** (SLP) the climax of ten days of pilgrimages; in **León** (Gto) the religious festival coincides with the agricultural and industrial fair.

21 San Miguel de Allende (Gto) honours Ignacio Allende with a parade, dances and bullfights.

FEBRUARY

1 Cadereyta (Que), northeast of Querétaro, holds a festival famous for its cockfights – also religious processions, dancing and *mariachi*.

February–March (variable) CARNIVAL, the week before Lent. On the Sunday **Yuriria** (Gto), between Celaya and Morelia, has real bullfights, processions and dances.

MARCH

Middle week FERIA DEL TORO DE LIDIA. Bull fights in **Tequisquiapan**.

17 St Patrick's Day has made it to Mexico. Music and carousing in **San Miguel de Allende.**

Week before Easter PALM SUNDAY is the culmination of a week's celebration in **San Miguel de Allende** (Gto), with a pilgrimage to **Atotonilco**.

Holy Week is observed everywhere. There's a huge procession, while in **San Miguel de Allende** families construct elaborate altars, proudly displayed in their homes. Semana Santa is a big deal in **San Luis Potosí** (SLP), particularly Good Friday's "Procession of Silence", when an effigy of Christ's dead body is paraded through the streets. On the Friday before Good Friday, **Guanajuato** (Gto) erects altars to the Virgen de los Dolores, the patron saint of miners.

APRIL

Early April (variable) **Irapuato** (Gto) holds its FERIA DE LA FRESA (Strawberry Fair) in honour of the region's principal cash crop.

25 FERIA DE SAN MARCOS in **Aguascalientes** (Ags) runs for around a week either side of this date. One of the largest and most famous in Mexico, there's dancing, bullfights, music and great wine.

MAY

24 Empalme Escobeda (Gto), near **San Miguel de Allende**, has a fiesta lasting until the next Sunday, with traditional dances including that of Los Apaches, one of the few in which women take part.

Thursday after Trinity CORPUS CHRISTI is celebrated in **San Miguel de Allende** (Gto). The following Wednesday sees a very ancient fiesta in **Juchipila** (Zac), between Zacatecas and Guadalajara, with flowers and dances including the famous Jarabe Tapatío, the Mexican Hat Dance. In **San Luis Potosí** (SLP), Corpus Christi sees the giant puppets (see p.290) out on parade.

Late May to early June FERIA NACIONAL DE QUESO Y VINO in **Tequisquiapan** (Que).

JUNE

13 San Miguel de Allende (Gto) holds a fiesta for one of its patron saints, San Antonio de Padua, involving a procession of crazily dressed revellers known as "Los Locos".

29 DÍA DE SAN PEDRO. **Chalchihuites** (Zac), between Zacatecas and Durango, stages a "Battle of the Flowers" in which local kids take part in parades of flower-covered floats.

Last half of June Artistic and cultural events surrounding the FIESTA DE SAN JUAN in **Guanajuato** (Gto).

JULY

First Monday FESTIVAL DE LA PRESA DE OLLA with local dances and serenading on the narrow streets of **Guanajuato** (Gto).

4 Acambaro (Gto), an ancient town between Celaya and Morelia, has a fiesta with religious processions, music and many traditional dances.

16 DÍA DE LA VIRGEN DEL CARMEN in **Celaya** (Gto) honours the Virgin with traditional food and festival games.

25 DÍA DE SANTIAGO widely observed. Mass pilgrimages to **San Luis Potosí** (SLP); saint's day celebrations in **Santiago Maravatio** (Gto), near Irapuato; stylized battles between Moors and Christians in **Jesús Mará** (Ags), near Aguascalientes.

AUGUST

15 DÍA DE LA ASUNCIÓN (Assumption) coincides with the FERIA DE LA UVA in **Aguascalientes** (Ags) and the FERIA DE LA CAJETA in **Celaya** (Gto), celebrating the syrupy confection made here.

25 DÍA DE SAN LUIS hugely enjoyed in **San Luis Potosí** (SLP) – giant procession and fireworks.

27 In **Zacatecas** (Zac), battles between Moors and Christians on the Cerro de la Bufa are the highlight of several days' celebrations.

SEPTEMBER

1 DÍA DE LA VIRGEN DE REMEDIOS justifies a fiesta in **Comonfort** (Gto), near **San Miguel de Allende**. Traditional dances.

8 In **Jerez** (Zac), the start of a festival lasting till the 15th.

14 Ten days of pilgrimages to the Señora del Patrocinio start in **Zacatecas** (Zac), coinciding with the FERIA NACIONAL and all sorts of secular entertainments, especially bullfights.

15–16 INDEPENDENCE CELEBRATIONS everywhere, above all in **Dolores Hidalgo** (Gto) and **Querétaro** (Que), where they start several days early. In **San Miguel de Allende** (Gto), the re-enactment of the "Grito" on the night of the 15th is followed by fireworks and parades.

Third Saturday San Miguel de Allende (Gto) has bull-running in its main streets, known as the SANMIGUELADA or PAMPLONADA.

28 Start of the three-day festival of San Miguel in **San Felipe** (Gto), north of Dolores Hidalgo, with Otomí dances and battles between Moors and Christians.

29 DÍA DE SAN MIGUEL, the most important of **San Miguel de Allende**'s (Gto) many fiestas: two days of processions, concerts, dancing, bullfights and ceremonies.

OCTOBER

4 DÍA DE SAN FRANCISCO DE ASIS. Culmination of two weeks of pilgrimage to **Real de Catorce** (SLP) and festivities in the town.

Fiestas *Continued*

4 DÍA DE SAN FRANCISCO. **Nochistlán** (Zac), between Aguascalientes and Guadalajara, holds a feria lasting to the end of the month. In San Miguel de Allende (Gto), a huge firework display at 4am commemorates San Miguel's fight with the devil, a battle known as the Alborada.

Middle two weeks FESTIVAL INTERNACIONAL CERVANTINO in Guanajuato (Gto) with all manner of cultural events.

23 Coroneo (Gto), south of Querétaro, begins a three-day feria.

NOVEMBER

2 DÍA DE LOS MUERTOS (All Souls). The famous Day of the Dead is celebrated country-wide.

7–14 FIESTA DE LAS ILUMINACIONES in **Guanajuato** (Gto).

Last Sunday Fiesta and crafts markets in **Comonfort** (Gto).

DECEMBER

1–17 FERIA INTERNACIONAL QUERÉTARO. Huge fair with rides and associated events, especially around Dec 12, GUADALUPE'S DAY.

8 DÍA DE LA INMACULADA CONCEPCIÓN. **Dolores Hidalgo** (Gto) combines a religious festival with a feria and traditional dancing.

12 FIESTA PATRONAL EN HONOR DE SANTA MARÍA. Various events in Tequisquiapan, also coinciding with Guadalupe's Day.

16–25 The traditional CHRISTMAS POSADAS are widely performed. Particularly good in **Celaya** (Gto). In **Querétaro** (Que), on the 23rd, there's a giant procession with bands and carnival floats.

Travel details

There's generally little to choose between the many excellent first-class services, which are a better bet (and only a few pesos more expensive) than the occasionally ropey, and slower, second-class buses. What follows is a minimum, covering the major stops only – it should be assumed that these buses also call at the towns en route.

Buses

Aguascalientes to: Guadalajara (9 daily; 6hr); Guanajuato (5 daily; 4hr); León (hourly; 2hr); Matehuala (at least hourly; 2hr); Mexico City (hourly; 7hr); Querétaro (hourly; 6hr); San Luis Potosí (hourly; 2hr 30min); San Miguel de Allende (4 daily; 4hr 30min); Zacatecas (every 30min; 2hr).

Dolores Hidalgo to: Guanajuato (every 20min; 1hr); Mexico City (every 40min; 5hr); Querétaro (every 40min; 2hr); San Luis de la Paz (every 20min; 1hr); San Luis Potosí (10 daily; 2hr 30min); San Miguel de Allende (every 15min; 50min).

Guanajuato to: Aguascalientes (4 daily; 4hr); Dolores Hidalgo (every 20min; 1hr); Guadalajara (5 daily; 6hr); León (constantly; 40min); Mexico City (7 daily; 4hr); Querétaro (8 daily; 3hr); San Luis de la Paz (5 daily; 2hr 30min); San Luis Potosí (10 daily; 3hr); San Miguel de Allende (10 daily; 1hr 30min).

León to: Aguascalientes (hourly; 1hr); Guadalajara (hourly; 4hr); Guanajuato (constantly; 40min); Mexico City (hourly; 5hr); Querétaro (hourly; 2hr); Zacatecas (hourly; 4hr).

Matehuala to: Real de Catorce (6 daily; 2hr); Saltillo (hourly or better; 2hr); San Luis Potosí (every 30min; 2hr).

Pozos to: San José Iturbide (every 30min; 40min); San Luis de la Paz (every 30min; 20min).

Querétaro to: Aguascalientes (hourly; 6hr); Bernal (hourly; 1hr); Dolores Hidalgo (every 40min; 2hr); Guadalajara (hourly; 6hr); Guanajuato (8 daily; 3hr); León (hourly; 2hr); Mexico City (every 10min; 3hr); San Juan del Río (every 15min; 45min); San Luis Potosí (hourly; 2hr); San Miguel de Allende (every 40min; 1hr 15min); Zacatecas (hourly; 5hr).

San José Iturbide to: Pozos (every 30min; 40min); Querétaro (every few min; 1hr 10min); San Luis de la Paz (every 30min; 1hr).

San Juan del Río to: Mexico City (every 15min; 2hr); Querétaro (every 15min; 45min); Tequisquiapan (every 20min; 30min).

San Luis de la Paz to: Dolores Hidalgo (every 20min; 1hr); Pozos (every 30min; 20min); San José Iturbide (every 30min; 1hr).

San Luis Potosí to: Aguascalientes (hourly; 2hr 30min); Dolores Hidalgo (14 daily; 2hr 30min); Guadalajara (13 daily; 5hr); Guanajuato (10 daily; 3hr); Matehuala (every 30min; 2hr 30min); Mexico City (hourly or better; 5hr); Monterrey (hourly; 7hr); Nuevo Laredo (hourly; 10hr); Querétaro (hourly; 10hr); San Miguel de Allende (8 daily; 3hr); Tampico (hourly; 7hr); Zacatecas (10 daily; 3hr).

San Miguel de Allende to: Aguascalientes (2 daily; 4hr); Dolores Hidalgo (every 15min; 50min); Guanajuato (10 daily; 1hr 30min); Mexico City (every 40min; 4hr); Querétaro (every 40min; 1hr 15min); San Luis Potosí (8 daily; 3hr).

Tequisquiapan to: Mexico City (every 40min; 2hr); Querétaro (every 30min; 1hr); San Juan del Río (every 20min; 30min).

Xilitla to: Ciudad Valles (hourly; 1hr 30min); Querétaro (8 daily; 6–7hr); San Luis Potosí (3 daily; 6–7hr); Tampico (7 daily; 4–5hr).

Zacatecas to: Aguascalientes (every 30min; 2hr); Chihuahua (hourly; 12hr); Ciudad Juárez (hourly; 18hr); Durango (hourly; 5hr); Guadalajara (hourly; 6hr); León (hourly; 4–5hr); Mazatlán (2 daily; 12hr); Mexico City (roughly hourly; 8hr); Monterrey (hourly; 6hr); Nuevo Laredo (5 daily; 8hr); Puerto Vallarta (3 daily; 12hr); Querétaro (hourly; 6hr); San Luis Potosí (10 daily; 3hr); Tijuana (4 daily; 36hr); Torreón (hourly; 6hr).

5

Mexico City and around

CHAPTER 5 Highlights

* **The Zócalo** Mexico City's huge central square, surrounded by the cathedral, Aztec ruins, and the Palacio Nacional. See p.376

* **Plaza Garibaldi** The frenetic site of massed *mariachi* bands. See p.393

* **Museo Nacional de Antropología** The country's finest museum covering all of Mexico's major pre-Columbian cultures. See p.401

* **Museo Dolores Olmedo Patiño** A huge collection of works by both Diego Rivera and Frida Kahlo. See p.421

* **Xochimilco** Ride the ancient waterways on flower-festooned boats. See p.421

* **La Merced** Mexico City's largest and most vibrant market. See p.437

* **Teotihuacán** The largest pre-Hispanic site in the country, dominated by the Pirámide del Sol. See p.446

* **The Great Pyramid of Cholula** Mexico's most massive pyramid ruin. See p.469

* **Taxco** This whitewashed hillside town makes a welcome stop on the road to Acapulco. See p.480

△ Mariachi performance

5

Mexico City and around

Since long before the Mexican nation actually existed, The **Valley of México** has been the country's centre of gravity. Located in this mountain-ringed basin – 100km long, 60km wide and over 2400m high, dotted with great salt- and fresh-water lagoons and dominated by the vast snowcapped peaks of Popocatépetl and Ixtaccíhuatl – were some of the most powerful civilizations the country has seen. Today the lakes have all but disappeared, and the mountains are shrouded in smog, but it continues to be the heart of the country, its physical centre and the generator of its political, cultural and economic pulse.

At the crossroads of everything sprawls the vibrant, elegant, frenetic and fascinating **Mexico City**. In population one of the largest cities in the world, with more than twenty million inhabitants, its lure is irresistible. Colonial mansions and excavated pyramids vie for attention with the city's fabulous museums and galleries, while above them tower the concrete and glass of thrusting development. But above all, the city is alive – exciting, sometimes frightening, always bewildering, but boldly alive. You can't avoid it, and if you genuinely want to know anything of Mexico you shouldn't try.

Round about there's escape and interest in every direction. To the north, and the most obvious destinations for day-trips, are the magnificent pyramid sites of **Teotihuacán** and **Tula**, the more dramatic legacies of the region's ancient peoples. The road to Tula passes **Tepotzotlán**, a weekend retreat from the city centred on a magnificent Baroque complex built by the Jesuits and filled with ornate treasures. To the east lies the small city of **Pachuca**, capital of Hidalgo state and a springboard for the hill country to the north, notably the attractive mountain village of **Real del Monte** with its Cornish connections.

East of Mexico City lies the region's second largest city, the thriving and ultra-colonial **Puebla**. This city probably only warrants a day or two of your time, but does work as a great base for forays north to more tranquil **Tlaxcala**, and west to **Cholula** with its enormous ruined pyramid. The ancient site here offers one of the best views of central Mexico's twin volcanoes, **Popocatépetl** and **Ixtaccíhuatl**, both currently off limits after Popo's recent eruptions.

Immediately south of the capital you climb over the mountains and descend to **Cuernavaca**, full of ancient palaces, and handy for the hilltop pyramid sites

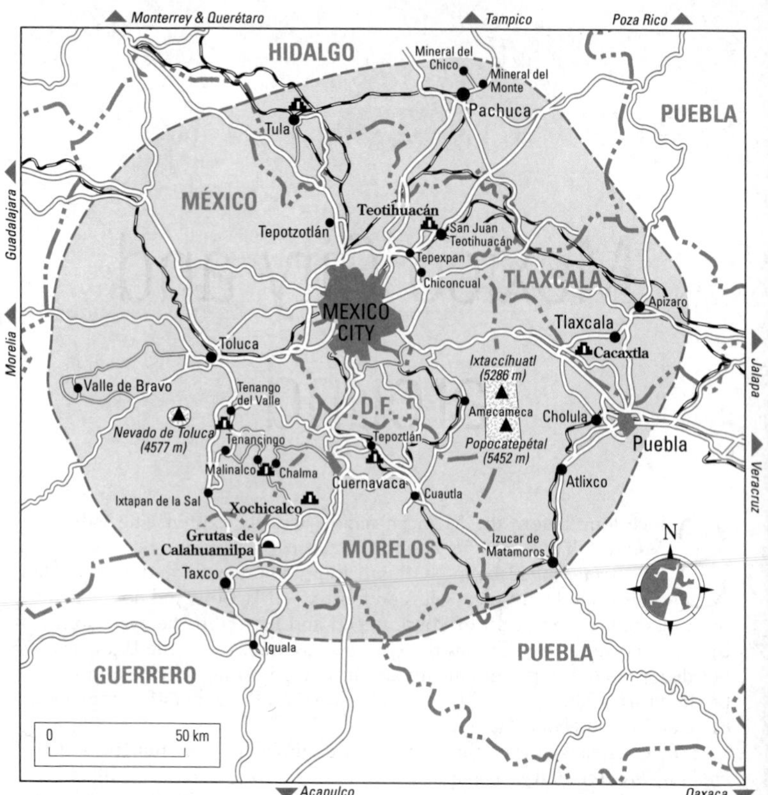

of **Tepoztlán** and **Xochicalco**. An hour further south the silver town of **Taxco** straggles picturesquely up a hillside, making it one of the most appealing destinations hereabouts. Possibly the least-visited quarter of Mexico City's environs is the west, where the city of **Toluca** offers only modest rewards, acting as a staging post for the lakeside resort town of **Valle de Bravo** and some small towns to the south, the most interesting being **Malinalco**, with yet more ancient pyramids.

All these ruins owe their existence to a long succession of pre-Columbian rulers, above all the **Aztecs**, whose warrior state was crushed by Cortés. But they were relative newcomers, forging their empire by force of arms in less than two centuries and borrowing their culture, science, arts and even language from the Valley societies that had gone before. **Teotihuacán**, whose mighty pyramids still stand some 50km northeast of the modern city, was the predominant culture of the Classic period and the true forebear of the Aztecs, a city of some 200,000 people whose influence spread throughout the country, south to the Maya lands in the Yucatán and beyond into Guatemala and Central America. Their style, though never as militaristic as later societies, was adopted everywhere: Quetzalcoatl, the plumed serpent, and Tlaloc, the rain god, were Teotihuacán deities.

For all its pre-eminence, though, Teotihuacán was neither the earliest, nor the only settlement in the Valley: the pyramid at **Cuicuilco**, now in the south of the city, is probably the oldest stone structure in the country, and there were small agricultural communities all around the lakes. The Aztecs, arriving some five hundred years after the destruction of Teotihuacán, however, didn't acknowledge their debt. They regarded themselves as descendants of the **Toltec** kingdom, whose capital lay at **Tula** to the north, and whose influence – as successors to Teotihuacán – was almost as pervasive. The Aztecs consciously took over the Toltec, military-based society, and adopted many of their gods: above all Quetzalcoatl, who assumed an importance equal to that of their own tribal deity, Huitzilopochtli, the god of war, who had brought them to power and demanded human sacrifice to keep them there. In taking control of the society while adopting its culture, the Aztecs were following in the footsteps of their Toltec predecessors, who had arrived in central Mexico as a marauding tribe of Chichimeca ("Sons of Dogs") from the north, absorbing the local culture as they came to dominate it.

Mexico City

Set over 2400m up in its shallow mountain bowl and crammed with over twenty million people (from fewer than five million in 1960), **MEXICO CITY** is one of the world's most densely populated urban areas, said to receive a thousand immigrants each day from the rest of the country. At times frustrating, the longer you spend there the more rewarding it can become, with unstructured wandering throwing up all sorts of surprises, and in a few days you can get around the main sights and soak up a good deal of the vibrant atmosphere. Despite a certain seediness found amidst the elegance of the new quarters and the genteel decay of the older parts of the city, the capital is nowhere near as intimidating as you might expect (see box, overleaf). Nonetheless, you may still prefer to take in the city a couple of days at a time, taking off in between to the smaller neighbouring colonial cities to recharge. You'll also find the city easier still if you acclimatize to the country first – if at all possible try not to spend too long here when you first arrive.

As you fly in or arrive by bus over the mountains, you'll catch glimpses of Popocatépetl and Ixtaccíhuatl, the volcanoes which every visitor used to admire, and which Sybille Bedford, author of a book on Mexico in the early 1950s, described as "Japanese-contoured shapes of pastel blue and porcelain snow, and thin formal curls of smoke afloat in a limpid sky". These days, "Popo" is more often perceived as a threat, with the international press depicting its recent activity as a serious menace to the capital. In reality, the volcano is 65km away, and though dust may temporarily close the airport during major outpourings, the city is highly unlikely to get smothered. The volcanoes are now rarely visible from the centre, courtesy of the city's pollution, which compensates by diffracting the light and producing wonderful golden sunsets.

Health and safety in Mexico City

Mexico City comes with an unenviable reputation for overcrowding, grime and crime. To some extent this is deserved, but things are improving and the city has gone as far as to consult with New York's sometimes draconian Rudy Giuliani about fighting street crime and stemming police corruption. Overall, Mexico City is no worse than you might expect of a city of the same size and population elsewhere in the developing world, and often a lot better. Certainly none of these issues is reason enough not to visit, and the frenzied atmosphere is part of what makes it such a fascinating city.

Certainly there is **pollution**. The whole urban area sits in a low mountain bowl that tends to deflect smog-clearing winds away from the city, allowing a thick blanket of haze to build up through the day. It is particularly bad in winter when there is no rain to wash the skies clean and pollution levels (reported daily in the English-language newspaper *The News*) tend to peak in the early afternoon. However, even at its worst, the sky overhead is almost always blue and the haze only apparent as you look towards the horizon. Couple this with the capital's altitude, and those prone to **respiratory problems** will sometimes have difficulty on arrival, though most suffer no ill effects. The city's stringent anti-emission regulations mean you'll be spared the clouds of black diesel smoke found in less developed countries all over the world. The **Hoy No Circula** ("Don't drive today") law prohibits **car use** from 5am to 10pm for one day in the working week for vehicles built before 1994, the day depending on the car's number plate; newer vehicles and rentals are exempt. On particularly high pollution days, the city government may declare a Doble Hoy No Circula day, on which two sets of cars are not permitted to drive. As an indication of the success of such anti-pollution measures, only one Doble Hoy No Circula day has been declared since 1999.

Mexico City newspapers take pleasure in reporting the city's **crime** in grisly detail. Much of what is reported is gang- or drug-related and takes place far away from anywhere you are likely to be. The capital is also where the Mexican extremes of wealth and poverty are most apparent, with shiny, valet-parked SUVs vying for space with pavement vendors and beggars. Such financial disparity fuels **theft**, but you only need to take the same precautions you would in any large city, and there is no need to feel particularly paranoid: keep your valuables – especially credit or debit cards – in the hotel safe (even cheap hotels often have somewhere secure), don't flash large wads of money around, and keep an eye on your camera and the like when in busy market areas. At night, avoid the barrio known as Doctores (around the Metro station of the same name, so called because the streets are named after doctors), and the area around Lagunilla market, both of which are centres of the street drug trade, and therefore of opportunist crime too. The ubiquitous green-and-white **taxis** found cruising the streets have a bad reputation and, though drivers are mostly helpful and courteous, there are reports of people being robbed at knife-point by drivers on occasion (often in taxis that have been stolen). It is best if possible to get your hotel to call you a cab (more expensive), or to call one yourself from one of the firms listed on p.371. If you do have to hail one in the street, always take a cab whose registration, on both the number plate and the side of the vehicle, begins with an L (for "libre" – to be hailed while driving around), and which has the driver's identification prominently displayed within. Better still, find a taxi rank and take a *sitio* taxi that can be tied down to it (with a number beginning in R, S or T, and again with the driver's ID prominently dispayed). Do not take taxis from the airport or bus terminals other than prepaid ones, and also avoid taking those waiting outside tourist spots. For further advice on taxi security, see Ⓦwww.mexicocity.gob.mx/taxis2.html.

Some history

And when we saw all those cities and villages built in the water, and other great towns on dry land, and that straight and level causeway leading to Mexico, we were astounded. These great towns and cities and buildings rising from the water, all made of stone, seemed like an enchanted vision from the tales of Amadis. Indeed, some of our soldiers asked whether it was not all a dream.

Bernal Díaz, *The Conquest of New Spain*

It's hardly surprising that Cortés and his followers should have been so taken by their first sight of **Tenochtitlán**, capital of the Aztecs. For what they found, built in the middle of a lake traversed by great causeways, was a beautiful, strictly regulated, stone-built city of 300,000 people, easily the equal of anything they might have experienced in Europe. The Aztec people (or, as they called themselves, the Mexica) had arrived at the lake, after years of wandering and living off what they could scavenge or pillage from settled communities, in around 1345. Their own legends have it that Huitzilopochtli had ordered them to build a city where they found an eagle perched on a cactus devouring a snake, and this they duly saw on an island in the middle of the lake; this is the basis of the nopal, eagle and snake motif that forms the centrepiece of the modern Mexican flag and appears everywhere, from coins and official seals to woven designs on rugs. The reality was probably more desperate – driven from place to place, the lake seemed a last resort – but for whatever reasons it proved an ideal site. Well stocked with fish, it was also fertile, once they had constructed their *chinampas*, or floating gardens of reeds, and virtually impregnable, too: the causeways, when they were completed, could be flooded and the bridges raised to thwart attacks (or to escape, as the Spanish found to their cost on the Noche Triste; see p.809).

The island city eventually grew to cover an area of some thirteen square kilometres, much of it reclaimed from the lake, and from this base the Aztecs were able to begin their programme of expansion: first, dominating the valley by a series of strategic alliances, war and treachery, and finally, in a period of less than a hundred years before the Conquest, establishing an empire that demanded tribute from and traded with the most distant parts of the country.

The Conquest

This was the situation when **Cortés** landed on the east coast in 1519, bringing with him an army of only a few hundred men, and began his long march on Tenochtitlán. Several key factors assured his survival: superior weaponry, which included firearms; the shock effect of horses (never having seen such animals, the Aztecs at first believed them to be extensions of their riders); the support of tribes who were either enemies or suppressed subjects of the Aztecs; and the unwillingness of the Aztec emperor to resist openly.

Moctezuma II (Montezuma), who had suffered heavy defeats in campaigns against the Tarascans in the west, was a broodingly religious man who, it is said, believed Cortés to be the pale-skinned, bearded god Quetzalcoatl, returned to fulfil ancient prophecies. Accordingly he admitted him to the city – fearfully, but with a show of ceremonious welcome. By way of repaying this hospitality the Spanish took Moctezuma prisoner, and later attacked the great Aztec temples, killing many priests and placing Christian chapels alongside their altars. Meanwhile, there was growing unrest in the city at the emperor's passivity and at the rapacious behaviour of his guests. Moctezuma was eventually killed – according to the Spanish, stoned to death by his own people while trying to quell a riot – and the Spaniards driven from the city with heavy losses. Cortés, and a few of his followers, however, escaped to the security of Tlaxcala, most loyal of his native allies, there to regroup and plan a new assault. Finally, rearmed and reinforced, their numbers swelled by indigenous allies, and with ships built in secret, they laid a three-month siege, finally taking the city in the face of suicidal opposition in August 1521.

The city's defeat is still a harsh memory: Cortés himself is hardly revered, but the natives who assisted him, and in particular Moctezuma and Malinche, the woman who acted as Cortés' interpreter, are non-people. You won't find a monument to Moctezuma in the country, though Cuauhtémoc, his successor who led the fierce resistance, is commemorated everywhere; Malinche is represented, acidly, in some of Diego Rivera's more outspoken murals. More telling, perhaps, of the bitterness of the struggle, is that so little physical evidence remains: "All that I saw then," wrote Bernal Díaz, "is overthrown and destroyed; nothing is left standing."

Spanish and post-colonial Mexico City

The victorious Spanish systematically smashed every visible aspect of the old culture, as often as not using the very stones of the old city to construct the new, and building a new palace for Cortés on the site of the Aztec emperor's palace. A few decades ago it was thought that everything was lost; slowly, however, particularly during construction of the Metro and in the remarkable discovery of remains of the **Templo Mayor** beneath the colonial Zócalo, remains of Tenochtitlán have been brought to light.

The **new city** developed slowly in its early years, only attaining the level of population that the old had enjoyed at the beginning of the twentieth century. It spread far wider, however, as the lake was drained, filled and built over – only tiny vestiges remain today – and grew with considerable grace. In many ways it's a singularly unfortunate place to site a modern city. Pestilent from the earliest days, the inadequately drained waters harboured fevers, and the native population was constantly swept by epidemics of European diseases. Many of the buildings, too, simply began to sink into the soft lake bed, a process probably accelerated by regular earthquakes. You'll see old churches and mansions leaning at crazy angles throughout the centre, and though repairs to buildings damaged by the disastrous **earthquake** of September 1985 are long complete, several empty shells remain standing.

By the third quarter of the nineteenth century, the city comprised little more than the area around the Zócalo and Alameda. Chapultepec Castle, Coyoacán, San Ángel, and the Basilica of Guadalupe – areas now well within city limits – were then surrounded by fields and the last of the basin's former lakes. Nonetheless, the city was beginning to take its present shape: the Paseo de la Reforma already linked Chapultepec with the city, and the colonial core could no longer accommodate the increasing population. From late 1870 through to 1911 the dictator Porfirio Díaz presided over an unprecedented, and self-aggrandizing, building programme which saw the installation of trams, the expansion of public transport and the draining of some of the last sections of the Lago de Texcoco which had previously hemmed in the city. Jointly these fuelled further growth, and by the outbreak of the Revolution in 1910, Mexico City's residents numbered over 400.000.

The modern city

As many as two million Mexicans died during the Revolution and many more lost their property, or livelihood or both. In desperation thousands fled to the rapidly industrializing capital in search of jobs and a better life. Between 1910

México, Mexico City and el DF

For clarity, we've referred to Mexico's capital as **Mexico City** throughout this guide, though Mexicans frequently refer to it simply as **México**, in the same way that Americans often refer to New York City as New York. It's a source of infinite confusion to visitors, but the country took its name from the city, so "México" can mean either, and in conversation it most often means the latter. To avoid misunderstanding, the nation may be referred to as La República Mexicana, or occasionally in speeches La Patria, while Mexico City may be referred to as **el DF** ("el day effay"), short for "Distrito Federal", the administrative zone that coincides with the city boundaries and contains most of the urban areas. Much less commonly, and usually only in an official context, is it called **La Ciudad de México**.

and the mid-1940s the city's population quadrupled and the cracks in the infrastructure quickly became gaping holes. Houses couldn't be built quickly enough to cope with the seven-percent annual growth, and many people wouldn't have been able to afford them anyway, so up sprung **shantytowns** of scraps of metal and cardboard. Most neighbourhoods had little or no water supply and sanitation was an afterthought. Gradually, civic leaders tried to improve the lot of its citizens by improving the services and housing in shantytowns, but a new ring of slums mushroomed even more quickly just a little further out. As the city expanded, transport became impossible and the city embarked on building the **Metro** system in the late 1960s. In 2000, the 175th and most recent Metro station was completed, but plans for new stations are purportedly in the works.

Urban growth continues today: some estimate that there are a thousand new arrivals each day, and the city now extends beyond the limits of the Distrito Federal and out into the surrounding state of México. Despite the spread, Mexico City remains one of the world's densest and most populated cities, with an unenviable list of major social and physical problems, and no sign of major improvement in the near future.

Orientation

The traditional centre of the city is the **Zócalo**, or Plaza Mayor; the heart of ancient Tenochtitlán and of Cortés' city, it's surrounded by the oldest streets, largely colonial and unmodernized. To the east, the ancient structures degenerate rapidly, blending into the poorer areas that surround the airport. Westwards, avenidas **Madero** and **Juárez** lead to the **Alameda**, the small park that marks the extent of the old city centre. Here is the Palacio de las Bellas Artes, the main post office and the landmark Torre Latinoamericana. Carry straight on past here and you get into an area, between the ugly bulk of the **Monumento a la Revolución** and the train station, where you'll find many of the cheaper hotels. Turn slightly south and you're amid the faded elegance of the **Paseo de la Reforma**, which leads down to the great open space of **Chapultepec Park**, recreation area for the city's millions, and home of the Museo Nacional de Antropología and several other important museums. Off to the right as you head down Reforma is a sedate, upmarket residential area, where many of the long-established embassies are based, while on the left is the **Zona Rosa** with its shopping streets, expensive hotels and constant tourist activity. To the south, the Zona bleeds into **Condesa**, which in recent years has

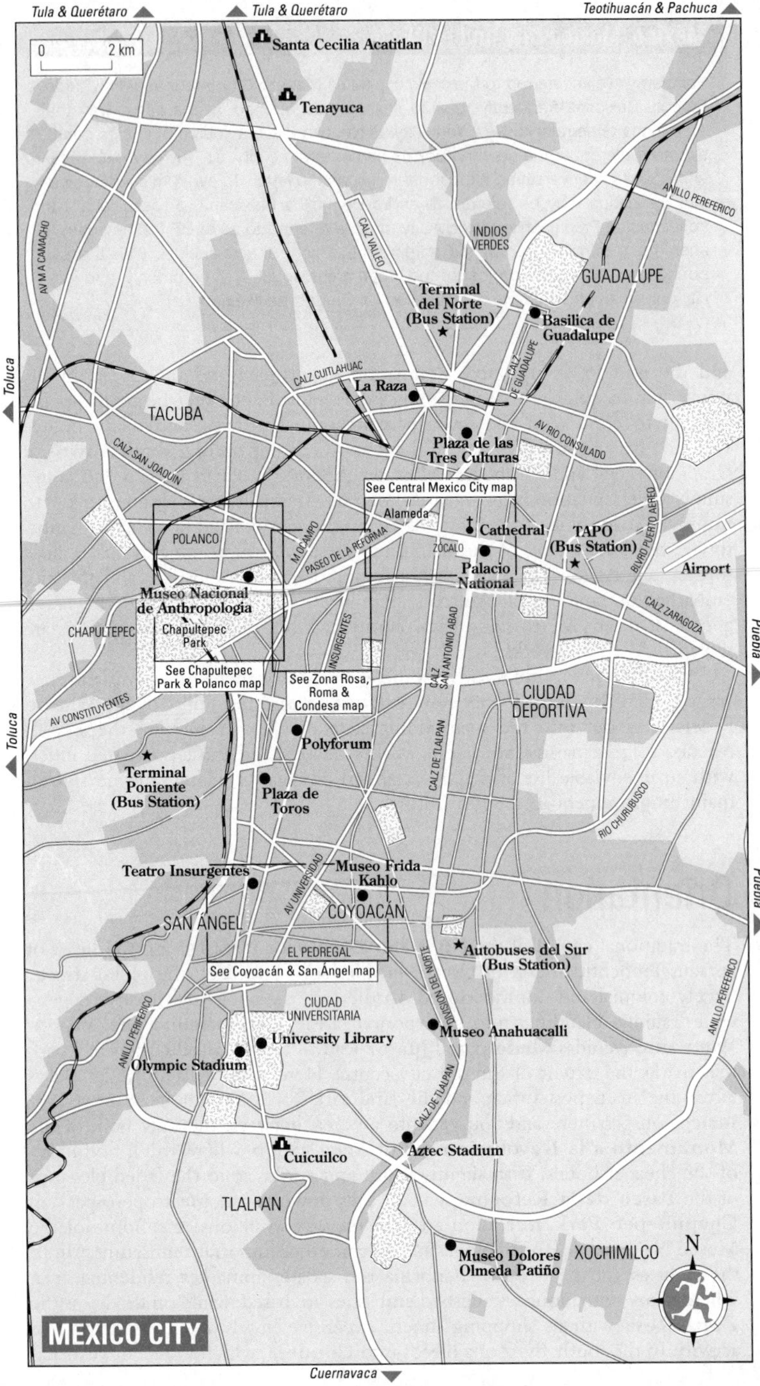
Tula & Querétaro
Tula & Querétaro
Teotihuacán & Pachuca
0 2 km
Santa Cecilia Acatitlan
Tenayuca
ANILLO PEREFERICO
CALZ VALLEJO
INDIOS VERDES
AV M A CAMACHO
GUADALUPE
Terminal del Norte (Bus Station)
Basilica de Guadalupe
Toluca
CALZ CUITLAHUAC
CALZ DE GUADALUPE
La Raza
TACUBA
AV RIO CONSULADO
Plaza de las Tres Culturas
CALZ SAN JOAQUIN
See Central Mexico City map
Alameda
Cathedral
TAPO (Bus Station)
POLANCO
M OCAMPO
PASEO DE LA REFORMA
ZOCALO
BLVRD PUERTO AEREO
Airport
Palacio National
Museo Nacional de Anthropologia
CALZ ZARAGOZA
CHAPULTEPEC
Chapultepec Park
INSURGENTES
CALZ SAN ANTONIO ABAD
Puebla
See Chapultepec Park & Polanco map
See Zona Rosa, Roma & Condesa map
CIUDAD DEPORTIVA
AV CONSTITUYENTES
Toluca
Polyforum
CALZ DE TLALPAN
Terminal Poniente (Bus Station)
Plaza de Toros
RIO CHURUBUSCO
Teatro Insurgentes
Museo Frida Kahlo
AV UNIVERSIDAD
Puebla
COYOACÁN
SAN ÁNGEL
Autobuses del Sur (Bus Station)
EL PEDREGAL
DIVISION DEL NORTE
See Coyoacán & San Ángel map
CIUDAD UNIVERSITARIA
ANILLO PERIFERICO
ANILLO PERIFERICO
University Library
Museo Anahuacalli
Olympic Stadium
CALZ DE TLALPAN
Aztec Stadium
Cuicuilco
TLALPAN
N
Museo Dolores Olmeda Patiño
XOCHIMILCO
MEXICO CITY
Cuernavaca

become *the* fashionable place to eat, drink and party. To the west, the northern flank of Chapultepec Park is lined by the flashy high-rise hotels of **Colonia Polanco**, among the city's chicest districts and home to many of the finest shops and restaurants.

The **Avenida de los Insurgentes** crosses Reforma about halfway between the Alameda and Chapultepec Park. Said to be the longest continuous city street in the world, Insurgentes bisects Mexico City more or less from north to south. It is perhaps the city's most important artery, lined with modern commercial development. In the south it runs past the suburb of **San Ángel** and close by **Coyoacán** to the **University City**, and on out of Mexico City by the **Pyramid of Cuicuilco**. Also in the southern extremities of the city are the waterways of **Xochimilco**, virtually the last remains of the great lagoons. In the outskirts Insurgentes meets another important through route, the **Calzada de Tlalpan**, which runs due south from the Zócalo past the eastern side of Coyoacán and past a couple of fine museums – Diego Rivera's Anahuacalli, and the wonderful Museo Dolores Olmedo Patiño.

To the north, Insurgentes leaves the centre past the train station, and close by the northbound bus station, to sweep out of the city via the basilica of **Guadalupe** and **Indios Verdes**. The northern extension of Reforma, too, ends up at the great shrine of Guadalupe, as does the continuation of the Calzada de Tlalpan beyond the Zócalo.

Remember that many **street names** are repeated over and over again in different parts of the city – there must be dozens of streets called Morelos, Juárez or Hidalgo, and a good score of 5 de Mayos. If you're taking a cab, or looking at a map, be clear which area you are talking about – it's fairly obvious in the centre, but searching out an address in the suburbs can lead to a series of false starts unless you know the name of the official **colonia**, or urban district (abbreviated "Col" in addresses outside the centre), that you're looking for.

Arrival

Arriving unprepared in the vastness of Mexico City may seem daunting, but in fact it's not hard to get into the centre, or to a hotel, from any of the major points of arrival. The only problem is likely to be hauling large items of luggage through the invariable crowds – take a taxi if you are at all heavily laden. The airport and all four major bus terminals have a system of **authorized taxis** designed to avoid rip-offs, particularly prevalent at the airport where people will offer rides at anything up to ten times the going rate to unsuspecting newcomers. The authorized system is the same wherever it operates from – you'll find a large map of the city marked out in zones, with a standard, set fare for each; you pick where you're going, buy a ticket at the booth, then walk outside and present the ticket to one of the waiting cabs. One ticket is good for up to four people to one destination. The driver may drop you a block or two from your hotel rather than take a major detour through the one-way systems (best to accept this unless it's very late at night), and he may demand a large tip, which you're in no way obliged to pay. Most hotels are used to late arrivals, so don't be overly concerned if your flight gets in late at night, though it would be wise to have somewhere booked in advance for your first night.

By bus

There are four chief **long-distance bus stations** in Mexico City, one for each point of the compass, though in practice the northbound terminal handles far more than its share, while the westbound one is tiny. All have **guarderías**, and **hotel reservation desks** for both the capital and the major destinations served, all have **Metro stations** pretty much right outside, and all have authorized taxis (see below). Each terminal also has a tourist information kiosk either in the termnal itself or just outside.

Apart from the major terminals listed below, there are large open-air bus stops at the end of all the Metro lines, with slow services to places up to an hour or so outside the city limits. For destinations in the capital's hinterland it can be quicker to leave from these.

Terminal del Norte

With all the direct routes to and from the US border, and services to every major city **north** of Mexico City (including the fastest services from and to Guadalajara and Morelia), the **Terminal del Norte**, Avenida de los Cien Metros 4907, is by far the largest of the city's four stations. There's a **Metro** station right outside the entrance (Metro Autobuses del Norte; line 5), and city buses head south from here along Insurgentes, about four blocks to the east – anything that reads "Metro Insurgentes" will take you down Insurgentes, past the train station, across Reforma, and on to the edge of the Zona Rosa.

In the vast lobby, and mostly in the centre of it, you'll find cafés, shops, a post office, telephone and Internet offices, a tourist information booth, a pharmacy, a 24-hour area for **left luggage** (US$1–2 a day), and kiosks selling tickets for authorized **taxis**: current fares from the terminal to the Zócalo and Alameda are US$5.50, to the Zona Rosa US$7, and Polanco US$6.50 (all plus US$1.30 10.30pm–6.30am).

TAPO

Eastbound services use the most modern of the terminals, the Terminal de Autobuses de Pasajeros de Oriente, always known as **TAPO**. Buses for Puebla, for Veracruz, and for places that you might think of as south – Oaxaca, Chiapas and the Yucatán, even Guatemala – arrive (and leave from) here. It is also the most central of the bus stations, located on Avenida Ignacio Zaragoza, towards the airport, and has a **Metro** station (Metro San Lazaro; lines 1 and B) just down a connecting tunnel, which also leads you to the stops for city buses and colectivos plying Zaragoza towards the Zócalo and the Alameda. In the same tunnel, opposite the Metro entrance, is the sales desk for the authorized **taxis**, which cost US$4.50 to the Zócalo and Alameda, US$5.50 to the Zona Rosa, and US$7.50 to Polanco (all plus US$1.50 10.30pm–6.30am). There's a tourist information kiosk in the terminal, and **left luggage** facilities (open 7.30am–10.30pm), but no telephone *caseta*, though there are plenty of cardphones.

Central de Autobuses del Sur

Buses **towards the Pacific coast** – Cuernavaca, Taxco, Acapulco and Ixtapa in particular – leave from the **Central de Autobuses del Sur**, Av Tasqueña 1320, where there's the usual selection of shops and snack bars, a telephone *caseta*, and an expensive **guardería**. There's a tourist information booth right outside the exit, and also outside is a big terminus for local buses and *peseros* (see p.370) to the centre and points around the south of town, and a **Metro** station (Metro Tasqueña; line 2). To find the Metro on arrival at the bus terminal, head right as you leave the terminal, and you'll see the sign; arriving by Metro, take the exit signposted "Autobuses del Sur", and the terminal is over to your left as you leave the station. Authorized **taxis** cost US$7 to the Zócalo (US$8.30 at night), US$8 (US$9.30) to the Alameda and Zona Rosa, and US$10 (US$11.30) to Polanco.

Terminal Poniente

Finally, for the **west**, there's the **Terminal Poniente**, at the junction of calles Sur and Tacubaya. The smallest of the terminals, it basically handles traffic to Toluca, but it's also the place to go for the slower, more scenic routes to Morelia, Guadalajara and other destinations in Jalisco and Michoacán, via Toluca. Aside from the **Metro** (Metro Observatorio; line 1), there are also buses (signed "Metro Observatorio") heading south on Reforma or from the stands by the entrance to Chapultepec Park. Authorized **taxis** cost US$4.50 to Polanco, US$6.50 to the Zona Rosa, and US$8.50 to the Alameda and Zócalo; from 9pm to 6am you pay US$1.30 more.

By plane

The **airport** (Metro Terminal Aérea; line 5; ⓣ55/5571-3600 ext 2208 for international arrivals and departures, or ext 2259 for domestic flights) is 5km east of the Zócalo and still very much within the city limits – you get amazing views as you come in to land, low over the buildings. It is an initially confusing place, with several **arrival** halls (Sala A–Sala F) arranged along a broad concourse, with the bulk of the **departure** lounges on the upper floor, poorly signposted above Salas E and F.

Most international arrivals reach the concourse on the ground floor at Sala E1 or Sala E3. Here you'll find numerous **ATMs** and several **casas de cambio**, open 24 hours a day and with reasonable rates for US dollars (rates vary, so shop around), though not always such good rates for travellers' cheques or other currencies (they'll usually take Canadian dollars, pounds sterling, euros, Swiss francs and Japanese yen, but nothing else). There are also plenty of pricey restaurants and snack bars, **car rental** agencies (see p.443), a post office (in Sala A), a telephone *caseta* (in Sala E2), Internet offices, a few bookshops and 24-hour **left luggage** lockers (in Sala A and Sala E3; US$5–7.50 a day). There are several airport enquiry desks dotted around, and a small **tourist office** in Sala A (7am–9pm; ⓣ55/5786-9002), with a limited range of city information.

As you emerge from Customs and Immigration, or off an internal flight, you'll be besieged by offers of a taxi into town. You are strongly advised not to take them (tourists arriving with all their baggage and valuables have been robbed by unauthorized taxi drivers on occasion); instead, by the main exit doors in Sala A you'll find a booth selling tickets for **authorized taxis** (see above), with a scale of fares posted according to where you want to go: bank on roughly US$11 to the Zócalo and Alameda, US$13 to the Zona Rosa and US$14.70 to Polanco.

If you're travelling reasonably light you could also go in on the **Metro** (out the doors at the end of Sala A, then follow the covered walkway for 200m) or continue past the Metro station out to Bulevar Puerto Aéreo and catch a city-bound **bus**.

If you don't fancy heading straight into the city so soon after arrival, you can get a **direct transfer to nearby cities**. There's a bus stop right outside Sala D where you can pick up first-class buses to Cuernavaca, Pachuca, Puebla,

Buses to and from Mexico City

Mexico City's **bus stations** are used by hordes of competing companies, and the only way to get a full idea of the **timetable** to and from any given destination is to check each one individually – different companies may take different routes and you can sometimes waste hours by making a faulty choice, though staff are generally very helpful. The following is a list of the main services including departure and arrival times. You may find that less frequent services use other terminals.

City/town	Bus terminal	
Acapulco	Sur, Terminal del Norte	half-hourly 6am–11.30pm from Sur; hourly 6am–1am from Norte
Aguascalientes	Terminal del Norte	17 daily
Amecameca	TAPO	every 20min 5am–11pm
Campeche	TAPO	3 daily
Cancún	TAPO	3 daily
Chetumal	TAPO	3 daily
Chihuahua	Terminal del Norte	hourly 7am–11pm
Chilpancingo	Sur	hourly 6.30am–11.30pm
Ciudad Juárez	Terminal del Norte	hourly 6.30am–11.30pm
Ciudad Obregón	Terminal del Norte	hourly 6am–8pm
Colima	Terminal del Norte	13 daily
Córdoba	TAPO	hourly 6.45am–12.45am
Cuautla	Sur, TAPO	every 15min 5.45am–11pm from Sur; 14 daily from TAPO
Cuernavaca	Sur	every 15min 5.30am–midnight
Dolores Hidalgo	Terminal del Norte	every 40min 6.30am–8.30pm
Durango	Terminal del Norte	9 daily
Fortín de las Flores	TAPO	2 daily
Guadalajara	Poniente, Terminal del Norte	5 daily from Poniente; hourly 5.30am–11.30pm from Norte
Guanajuato	Terminal del Norte	20 daily
Guaymas	Terminal del Norte	10 daily
Hermosillo	Terminal del Norte	hourly 7am–10pm
Iguala	Sur	half-hourly 6.30am–10.30pm
Ixtapa	Sur	7 daily
Ixtapan de la Sal	Poniente	hourly 7am–7pm
Jalapa	TAPO	21 daily
León	Terminal del Norte	half-hourly 6.30am–10pm
Los Mochis	Terminal del Norte	hourly 7am–10pm
Malinalco	Poniente	3 daily
Manzanillo	Terminal del Norte	3 daily
Matamoros	Terminal del Norte	7 daily
Matehuala	Terminal del Norte	10 daily
Mazatlán	Terminal del Norte	hourly 7am–10pm
Mérida	TAPO	3 daily
Mexicali	Terminal del Norte	hourly 6am–11pm
Monterrey	Terminal del Norte	hourly 6am–10pm

Morelia	Poniente, Terminal del Norte	42 daily from Poniente; every 40min 6.20am–7pm from Norte
Nuevo Laredo	Terminal del Norte	hourly 6am–10pm
Oaxaca	TAPO	38 daily
Oaxtepec	Sur	every 15min 5.45am–11pm
Orizaba	TAPO	24 daily
Pachuca	Terminal del Norte	every 10min 5.30am–10.30pm
Palenque	TAPO	2 daily
Pátzcuaro	Poniente, Terminal del Norte	10 daily from Poniente; 5 daily from Norte
Playa del Carmen	TAPO	3 daily
Puebla	Sur, TAPO	hourly 6.30am–9.30pm from Sur; every 12min 6am–2am from TAPO
Puerto Escondido	Sur, TAPO	5 daily from Sur; 1 daily from TAPO
Puerto Vallarta	Terminal del Norte	4 daily
Querétaro	Terminal del Norte	every 20min 4.50am–11.40pm
Saltillo	Terminal del Norte	17 daily
San Cristóbal de las Casas	TAPO	6 daily
San Luis Potosí	Terminal del Norte	40 daily
San Miguel de Allende	Terminal del Norte	every 40min 5.20am–6pm (last departure 12.45am)
Taxco	Sur	hourly 7am–8pm
Tehuacan	TAPO	hourly 7am–11pm
Tehuantepec	TAPO	3 daily
Teotihuacán	Terminal del Norte	every 15min 7am–3pm
Tepic	Terminal del Norte	18 daily
Tepoztlán	Sur	every 15min 6am–10pm
Tijuana	Terminal del Norte	hourly 6am–11pm
Tlaxcala	TAPO	every 20min 6am–10pm
Toluca	Poniente	every 5min 5.30am–10.30pm (last departure 11.30pm)
Torreón	Terminal del Norte	9 daily
Tula	Terminal del Norte	every 30–60min 7am–9.30pm
Tuxpan	Terminal del Norte	24 daily
Tuxtla Gutiérrez	TAPO	14 daily
Uruapan	Poniente, Terminal del Norte	9 daily from Poniente; 5 daily from Norte
Valle de Bravo	Poniente	15 daily
Veracruz	TAPO	35 daily
Villahermosa	TAPO	24 daily
Zacatecas	Terminal del Norte	24 daily
Zempoala	TAPO	2 daily
Zihuatanejo	Sur	7 daily

Toluca and Querétaro. There are also luxury car and van services, but they're almost ten times the price of the buses.

City transport

For all its size and frantic pace, once you're used to the city, it is surprisingly easy to get around, with an efficient and very cheap public transport system as well as reasonably priced taxis.

You'll want to **walk** around the cramped streets of the centre, but remember the altitude – walking gets tiring quickly, especially for the first day or so. If you're heading for Chapultepec or the Zona Rosa, you're better off taking the **bus** or **Metro** – it's an interesting walk all the way down Reforma, but a very long one. As for the outer suburbs, you've got no choice but to rely on taxis or public transport. You'll save a lot of hassle if you avoid travelling during **rush hour** (about 7–9am & 6–8pm).

Tours that take in the city and often include the surrounding area are available from most of the more expensive hotels, and from specialist operators such as Gray Line, Londres 166 (ⓣ55/5208-1163), and American Express, with various locations around the city (ⓣ55/5207-7049). One of the best city tours is with Turibus, whose open-top double-deckers run roughly every thirty to forty minutes (9am–9pm) and can be hailed at the Zócalo, the Benito Juárez monument on the south side of the Alameda, El Ángel on Reforma, or other stops along its route. The tour takes two and three-quarter hours, and costs US$10 weekdays, US$11.50 at weekends; you pay on board.

Driving

Rental cars (see p.443 for agents' details) are available from the airport and elsewhere, but it is generally better to wait until you are ready to leave the city before renting. If you already have a car, choose a hotel with secure parking and leave it there for the duration of your stay, except possibly to do a tour of the south of the city. Driving in the city is a nightmare, compounded by confusing one-way and through-route systems, by the impossibility of finding anywhere to park and by traffic police who can spot foreign plates a mile off and know a potential "fine" when they see one. If you insist on driving, note that the "Green Angels" that operate throughout the rest of the country (see p.43) do not operate within Mexico City: for **breakdown help** call the AMA (equivalent of the AA or the AAA) on ⓣ55/242-0262.

The Metro and Tren Ligero

Mexico City's superb modern **Metro** system (enquiries on ⓣ55/5709-1133, online information at ⓦwww.metro.df.gob.mx) is French-built, fast and quiet. It is crowded and at peak hours stations designate separate entries for women and children (look for the "Mujeres" signs). However, it is honestly no more crowded than its New York or London counterparts. **Tickets** (US$0.20) are sold individually and there is no discount for bulk purchases, though to save a lot of queueing and messing about with tiny quantities of change it makes sense to buy several at a time. In theory you're not allowed **luggage** of any size on the Metro (the official limit is 80cm x 50cm x 30cm), but in practice you can if you board at a quiet station at a quiet time, and these days even a backpack seems to be tolerated at busy times. The last train leaves from each end of

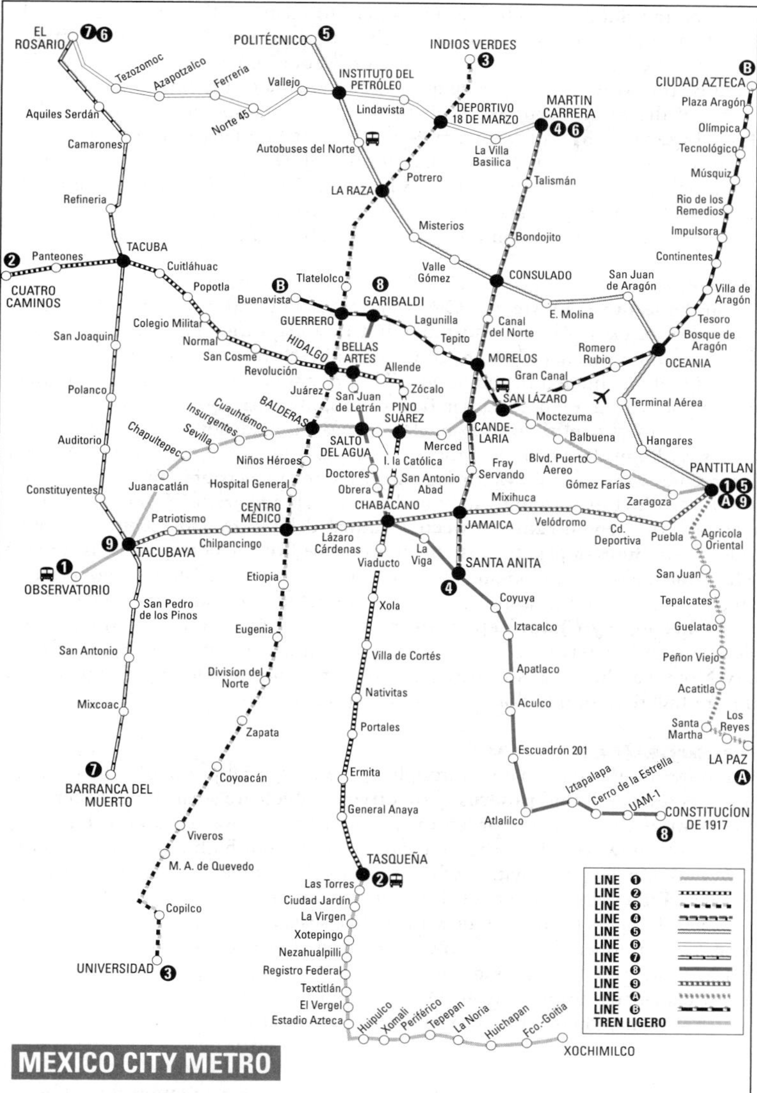

the line at midnight, with the first train at 4.50am Monday–Friday, 5.50am on Saturday and 6.50am on Sunday.

In general, there are no maps of the system on Metro platforms, and certainly not on the trains, just pictographic representations of the line you are on, along with the stations where you can transfer to other lines. The map above details the system, otherwise you'll need to work out before you set off which way you'll be travelling on each line, and where to change. Direction is indicated by the last station at either end of the line (thus on line 2 you'll want either "Dirección Cuatro Caminos" or "Dirección Tasqueña"); interchanges are indicated by the word "Correspondencia" and the name of the new line.

One of the most recent additions to the public transporation system is the **Tren Ligero** (light rail), which runs south from Tasqueña (the southern terminus of line 2) as far as Xochimilco, entirely above ground. It requires a different ticket from the Metro system. When you change at Tasqueña you'll need to buy a Tren Ligero ticket (good for any one-way journey) from the ticket window or the machines on the concourse (US$0.20).

City buses

At one time **buses** in Mexico City were beaten-up old bone-shakers trailing plumes of black smoke behind them, but nowadays they have smartened up their act and are generally large and reasonably clean, and may sometimes be two-unit affairs hinged in the middle. They're also very efficient, if you know where you're going. There's a flat **fare** of roughly US$0.20 per journey.

The two most **useful routes** are along Reforma, and along Insurgentes from Indios Verdes in the north, past the Terminal del Norte, the train station, Metro Insurgentes and eventually on to San Ángel and the university in the south. There are also **trolleybuses** running in both directions along Lázaro Cárdenas (the "Eje Central", or Central Axis) between Terminal del Norte and Central del Sur (Tasqueña). Buses display their destinations in the front window, which is somewhat more helpful than looking for route numbers, since the latter are not posted up and rarely used, and some buses terminate before the end of the route.

The area just by **Chapultepec Metro station** at the entrance to the park is also a major bus terminus, from where you can get to almost any part of the city. Note that during **rush hour** it can be almost impossible to get a bus: once they're full, they simply don't stop to let passengers on.

Peseros (colectivos)

Running down the major through routes, especially on Reforma and Insurgentes, you'll find **peseros** (**colectivos**), which are smaller and faster but charge more than the bus (far less than a regular taxi, however) and will let you on and off anywhere along their set route. They're mostly thirty-seater buses or VW vans, usually green with a white roof, and have their destination displayed on the windscreen – drivers of the smaller vehicles may sometimes hold up a number of fingers to indicate how many free seats they have. Like buses, *peseros* have route numbers, but routes often have branches, and a vehicle may start or finish in the middle of a route rather than at the end, so again it's more helpful to check the destination in the window. One of the most **useful routes** runs from Chapultepec Park via Avenida Chapultepec to the Zócalo.

Taxis

Ordinary **taxis** come in a variety of forms and have a reputation for robbery at the hands of the drivers (see p.358). You should think twice before taking one, especially if you are on your own. The most economical are the green-and-white cabs (using unleaded petrol) or, increasingly rarely, yellow-and-white cabs (using leaded) that cruise the streets looking for customers. Both are usually VW Beetles, and legitimate taxis should have a meter (make sure it's switched on). The cabs that wait at *sitios* (taxi ranks), and the red-and-white radio taxis, which you have to call by phone, charge slightly more, but in general work the same way. Watch out, though, for *turismo* taxis, which lie in wait outside hotels for unsuspecting tourists and charge rates at least triple those of ordinary taxis. In the normal course of events you should avoid them, but they do have a couple of advantages, namely that they're almost always around and that many of the drivers speak some English. They can be worth it if, for example, you need to get to the airport in a hurry (for which they charge no more than an authorized airport cab would) or if you want to go on a tour for a few hours. In the latter case, with some ferocious haggling, you might even get a bargain. If you need to **phone a taxi**, try Servitaxis (Ⓣ55/5516-6020) or Taximex (Ⓣ55/9171-8880) or, to the airport, ProTaxi (Ⓣ55/2599-0333). It can be difficult to get a taxi in the rush hour.

Information

Visitors arriving at the airport can pick up limited **tourist information** on the city at the booth in Sala A (7am–9pm), and those arriving by bus will find tourist information kiosks inside or just outside the terminals. Similar kiosks are dotted around town, none of which has much printed material to take away, though the staff are usually well versed in the ways of the city. The most central is in the **Zócalo** between the cathedral and Monte de Piedad (daily 10am–6pm; Ⓣ55/5518-1869; Metro Zócalo). The main SECTUR office at Presidente Mazaryk 172, Polanco (Mon–Fri 8am–6pm, Sat 10am–3pm; call 24hours daily in town on Ⓣ55/5250-0123 or 0151, or from elsewhere in the country toll-free on Ⓣ01-800/903-9200; Metro Polanco), is perfectly helpful – and flush with handouts about Mexico City and the country as a whole – but inconveniently sited a long way from where you are likely to spend your time. Apart from that, the largest and most useful tourist office is in the **Zona Rosa**, Amberes 54 at Londres (daily 9am–7pm; Ⓣ55/5525-9380; Metro Insurgentes). The government of the DF also runs a tourist information **website** (Ⓦwww.mexicocity.gob.mx/mexcity.html), with excellent background information, advice, tips, and patchy listings.

Useful local **guidebooks**, city **maps** (the best produced by Guia Roji), English-language magazines and pulp paperbacks are sold at Sanborn's, street newsstands, the airport, and many big hotels.

Accommodation

On any street, in any unlikely corner of the city, there seems to be one of Mexico City's thousands of hotels. They range from a few budget **hostels** to some of the swankiest and most expensive **hotels** in the country. In between those extremes there is bound to be something to suit, though the best-value places can fill up quickly, so **booking ahead** is always a good idea. The area of the city you choose to stay can easily influence your experience, and if you are spending a few days here or visiting more than once, it's a good idea to lodge in a couple of different places. For example, find a hotel for a night or two near the Zócalo in order to see the historic sights, and then spend some nights in the Zona Rosa where it is easier to get back to your hotel after an evening around the clubs of the Zona or the bars of Condesa.

The avenues around the **Zócalo** are awash with accommodation. Avenida 5 de Mayo is as good a place as any to begin, with a dozen or so fairly good options in close proximity. The hotels in this area are generally older and more established than elsewhere; high ceilings and internal courtyards are common. The cheaper places often have a lot of dark rooms, but most are comfortable and, considering the location – right in the heart of the sightseeing zone – excellent value. Here, too, are the city's large backpacker hostels. The area's main drawback is its distance from any good nightlife and the better places to eat, though there are new places opening all the time.

To the west is a sprawling area centred on the **Alameda** and the **Revolución monument**. Hotels here are a mixed bag, mostly rather humdrum and often very cheap, though you will find some luxury places at lower rates than in the rest of the city. The location is reasonably central to both the sights and the best nightlife, but neither is right on the doorstep. Hotels **north of the Alameda** are very convenient in the unlikely event of your arriving by train, but this is a rather less attractive area to stay on the whole, and can be a little intimidating at night, especially for women as this is something of a red-light area.

Accommodation in the **Zona Rosa** tends towards the expensive end of the market, though if you look hard you can find luxury accommodation at moderate prices. Here you'll be spoilt for choice with cafés, posh restaurants, bars and clubs, and you're also within twenty minutes' walk of the heart of Condesa. There's even more upmarket accommodation north of Chapultepec Park in **Polanco**, mostly high-rise but with a couple of smaller (and very expensive) boutique hotels.

Most places have 24-hour reception desks and are geared for late arrivals and early departures, and with reasonably cheap taxi fares into the Zócalo or Zona Rosa it seldom makes financial sense to stay near the bus stations or airport. However, if you arrive especially late or are just in transit and need a place to rest up for a while, there are places to stay that are very handy for the **airport** and **Terminal del Norte**.

Hostels

Casa de los Amigos Ignacio Mariscal 132 ⓣ55/5705-0521, ⓦwww.avantel.net/~friends. Involved in various community activities, the Quaker-run *Casa*, located on a quiet street in a house where José Clemente Orozco spent the last decade of his life, pitches itself as a guesthouse, though it still has eight- and four-bed dorms (US$8) as well as a few singles (US$10) and doubles (US$18). Clean and comfortable with a good kitchen (breakfast available), it is popular with people staying in the city for a few weeks, and has a two-night minimum stay. House regulations include no alcohol and no smoking. Metro Revolución. ④

Hostal Moneda Moneda 8 ⓣ55/5522-5821, ⓦwww.hostalmoneda.com.mx. Convivial, if a little threadbare, hostel with nearly 100 beds (US$10–11) arranged in rooms with their own bathroom. There's also a couple of lounges (one with TV), a decent kitchen and a panoramic rooftop terrace where a buffet breakfast (included) is served. There are also a few doubles. Make a reservation if you are to arrive after 11pm. Metro Zócalo. ④

Hostel Catedral Guatemala 4 ⓣ55/5518-1726, ⓦwww.hostelcatedral.com. Large, secure and efficiently run modern place in a former office right behind the cathedral, that's open 24hr, has spotless four- or six-bunk rooms, most with their own bathroom (US$12, HI members US$10; buffet breakfast included) and some private rooms. There's an on-site travel agency, Internet access, a café and bar and a great rooftop terrace with fabulous views. About the only drawbacks are a small kitchen (though it seems little used), limited communal areas and the noise that travels through the central well: bring earplugs and a lock for the lockers. Metro Zócalo. ④

Hostel Home Tabasco 303, Roma ⓣ55/5511-1683, ⓦwww.hostelhome.com.mx. The perfect antidote to the large-scale hostels downtown, this friendly twenty-bunk place (with more under construction) may be a little distant from the main sights, but has, as it advertises, a "chilled atmosphere" and 24hr access. Sleep in six- and eight-bunk rooms (US$9, HI members US$8), hang out in the sunny lounge (which has a small library, a stock of music and a TV), surf the Net at reasonable rates and cook in the smallish but well-equipped kitchen. Metro Sevilla. ④

Hotels

Around the Zócalo

Azores Brasil 25 ⓣ55/5521-5220, ⓦwww.hotelazores.com. Recently remodelled, fairly modern hotel with small but clean and comfy rooms around a central well, each with TV and bath. Metro Allende or Zócalo. ❹

Buenos Aires Motolinia 21 ⓣ55/5518-2104 or 2137. A friendly place and one of the cheapest in the centre, with rooms arranged around a central patio, pretty basic but with TV and en-suite bathroom; avoid the windowless ones on the ground floor. Metro Allende. ❸

Catedral Donceles 95 ⓣ55/5518-5232, ⓦwww.hotelcatedral.com. Very presentable mid-range place, all rooms having TV, FM stereo and telephone, and some with jacuzzi. Also has Internet access, a good restaurant and a terrace overlooking the cathedral. Quite popular. Metro Zócalo. ❻

Gillow Isabel la Católica 17 ⓣ55/5518-1441 to 6, ⓔhgillow@prodigy.net.mx. Highly recommended mid-priced hotel with large, if unimaginatively decorated, rooms (some with a small patio), in-house travel agency, and leather sofas in the public areas. Cable TV and the expected facilities. Metro Allende. ❺

Gran Hotel Ciudad de México 16 de Septiembre 82 ⓣ/ⓕ55/1083-7700, ⓔgranhotelmexico_ventas@yahoo.com.mx. Large hotel right on the Zócalo with sumptuous public areas but beware: some of the older rooms don't match the impression given by the lobby. The remodelled suites are nice, but cost US$150. Metro Zócalo. ❽

Isabel Isabel la Católica 63 ⓣ55/5518-1213, ⓦwww.hotel-isabel.com.mx. Good-value hotel with services such as taxis and laundry that are normally offered only at much larger hotels, plus an associated restaurant and bar. Rooms (with or without bath), though a little bit sombre, are very spacious with TV and safe, making this an especially good deal. Metro Isabel la Católica. ❸–❹

Juárez 1o Callejón de 5 de Mayo 17 ⓣ55/5512-6929. Not the cheapest, but about the best value of the budget hotels near the Zócalo. It's always spotlessly clean, there's a no-guest policy that keeps it safe, and all rooms have bath, phones, TV and bottled water; those without windows tend to be quieter. Checkout is a convenient 2pm and they'll store luggage free of charge while you're out of town. Avoid room no. 4, which is next to the hotel's main water pump. Metro Allende or Zócalo. ❸

Majestic Madero 73 ⓣ01-800/528-1234 (toll-free in Mexico outside the DF) or 55/5521-8600, in the US ⓣ1-800/528-1234, ⓦwww.majestic.com.mx. Luxury Best Western hotel on the Zócalo that has bags of character, is considerably cheaper than many of the places in the Zona Rosa and has many of the same facilities. Zócalo views from some rooms. Metro Zócalo. ❾

Montecarlo Av Uruguay 69 ⓣ55/5518-1418, ⓕ5510-0081. Originally an Augustinian monastery and later lived in briefly by D.H. Lawrence. Quiet and comfortable with a garage and a beautiful inner courtyard that is a little out of keeping with the rather small and dark rooms (with or without bath). Metro Zócalo. ❹

República Cuba 57 ⓣ55/5512-9517. Old and fairly grotty hotel on a quiet street with each room having a bathroom and TV. The price is right for two people sharing a bed, but it is poor value for those requiring two. ❷

San Antonio 2o Callejón de 5 de Mayo 29 ⓣ55/5512-1625 or 6, ⓕ5512-9906. Quiet, friendly place hidden away in a side street between 5 de Mayo and La Palma. Standards are high considering the price, with light, airy, spotless rooms, good firm beds, decent sheets and free bottled water. Metro Allende or Zócalo. ❹

Washington 5 de Mayo 54 ⓣ/ⓕ55/5512-3502. Good-value though not especially friendly hotel with clean, pleasant rooms all with nicely tiled bathroom, cable TV, phone and free water. Metro Allende or Zócalo. ❹

Zamora 5 de Mayo 50 ⓣ55/5512-8245. One of the most basic of the downtown hotels, the low prices making the noise, threadbare towels and marginal cleanliness acceptable. Very popular so you may have to book ahead at busy times. Rooms are with or without bath. Metro Allende or Zócalo. ❷–❸

North of the Alameda

Buenavista Bernal Díaz 34 ⓣ55/5535-5704. Bottom-of-the-barrel option in a red-light district, where you'll need to watch your luggage and not be too picky about cleanliness. It is incredibly cheap, though, and even cheaper if you do without bathroom and TV. Metro Revolución. ❷

Hotel de Cortés Hidalgo 85 ⓣ55/5518-2184 or 01-800/528-1234, in the US ⓣ1-800/528-1234, ⓦwww.albec.net.mx/hoteldecortes. A Best Western hotel that manages to rise above the corporate formula, mostly because of its wonderful setting. The cool, central patio houses a restaurant and a coffee house seemingly a million miles from the bustle of the Alameda. Facilities are good and the decor is sensitively done throughout, though maintenance sometimes lets them down. Avoid rooms 105 and 106, which are noisy. In quiet times rates may drop a couple of price bands. Metro Hidalgo. ❾

Managua Plaza de San Fernando 11 ⓣ55/5512-1312, ⓕ5521-3062. Good-value, clean and quiet place with a cafeteria that does room service, and rooms with TV, bathroom and free bottled water, all in a restful location facing the Jardín de San Fernando, just north of the Alameda. Metro Hidalgo. ❹

Polly Orozco y Berra 25 ⓣ55/5535-8881. A well-cared-for hotel with clean and reasonably sized, carpeted rooms each with bathroom, TV and writing desk. Metro Hidalgo. ❸

South of the Alameda and around

Bamer Juárez 52 ⓣ55/5521-9060 to 70, ⓔhbamer@prodigy.net.mx. Built in the 1950s, it retains enough period furnishing and good artworks to be charming rather than just old, and its massive double rooms, some overlooking the Alameda, make it one of the best mid-range places in the vicinity, with TV, phone and the expected facilities, plus a few suites. Metro Juárez. ❻

Casa Blanca Lafragua 7 ⓣ55/5705-1300 or 01-800/702-9800, in the US ⓣ1-800/972-2162, ⓦwww.hotel-casablanca.com.mx. Attractive but rather impersonal modern high-rise hotel with perfectly decent rooms at prices a good deal lower than a lot of the Zona Rosa places. There's even a rooftop pool, a gym, business facilities and a restaurant. Metro Revolución. ❾

Fleming Revillagigedo 35 ⓣ55/5510-4530 or 35, ⓔhotelfleming@prodigy.net.mx. Modern business-style hotel with little imagination to the decor but good facilities – comfortable, carpeted rooms, cable TV, etc – at moderate prices. Metro Juárez. ❺

Mayaland Antonio Caso 23 ⓣ55/5566-6066, ⓔhotelmayaland@hotmail.com. Squat and ugly from outside but tastefully decorated within. Good-value rooms all come with cable TV and purified water piped in, though you might want to spend US$7 extra for a more spacious double (with the standard two double beds) or US$4 for a jacuzzi. Metro Revolución. ❺

Pánuco Ayuntamiento 148 ⓣ55/5521-2916. Good-value and spotlessly clean hotel with carpeted rooms each with writing desk and TV – and a lot of fake marble – located in a drab part of town a little away from the most popular tourist areas, though tolerably close to the Zona Rosa. Parking and a restaurant on site, condoms available in reception. Tends to be full Fridays and Saturdays. Metro Juárez. ❸

Royalty Jesús Terán 21 ⓣ55/5566-9255. Very reasonable rates for rooms (some rather dark) with their own bathroom, TV and phone. Metro Revolución. ❷

The Zona Rosa and Roma

Calinda Geneve Londres 130 ⓣ55/5080-0870 or 01-800/900-0000, in the US ⓣ1-877/657-5799, in Canada ⓣ1-877/609-6940, ⓦwww.hotelescalinda.com.mx. A large, century-old, but thoroughly modern hotel right in the heart of the Zona with an understated but elegant feel. Rooms are comfortable if unspectacular with cable TV, minibar and the like, but the hotel excels in its facilities including the lovely Salon Jardín with its stained-glass-and-iron roof, restaurant, gym, spa, and on-site *Sanborn's* restaurant. Rooms start at US$230. Metro Insurgentes. ❽

La Casona Durango 280 at Cozumel, Roma ⓣ55/5286-3001, ⓕ5211-0871, ⓦwww.yellow.com.mx/casona. Set on the edge of the Zona Rosa in a listed early twentieth-century building, *La Casona* has an understated if slightly quirky European-style elegance, with polished wooden floors and antique furniture, a piano in its cosy lounge, and quite a collection of art – including masks and original cartoons as well as paintings. All rooms are different, with an aesthete's attention to detail. On-site restaurant. Metro Sevilla. ❾

Century Liverpool 152 ⓣ55/5726-9911 or 01-800/701-1100, from abroad ⓣ01-800/448-8355, ⓕ55/5525-7475, ⓦwww.century.com.mx. Five-star hotel with all the mod cons you would expect including a 22nd-floor outdoor pool. Decent but unimaginative decor. Metro Insurgentes. ❽

Del Principado Londres 42 ⓣ55/5533-2944 to 8, ⓦwww.hoteldeprincipado.com.mx. Comfortable hotel with debateable decor, but it is well kept, with largish rooms, all with TV and phone. Laundry service and parking available. Metro Insurgentes. ❻

Marco Polo Amberes 27 ⓣ55/5511-1839 or 01-800/900-6000, from abroad ⓣ01-800/310-9693, ⓦwww.marcopolo.com.mx. Beautiful and stylish, this small luxury hotel caters for an artistic

Mexican clientele. Standard double rooms are all attractively furnished and come with tasteful artworks and all the amenities you'd expect and then some, including a fitness apparatus in your room. Complimentary fruit, coffee and purified water supplied. Metro Insurgentes. 9

Posada Viena Marsella 28 at Dinamarca ⓣ55/5566-0700 or 01-800/849-8402, in the US ⓣ1-888/698-0690, ⓦwww.posadavienahotel.com.mx. A comfortable but unpretentious four-star with rooms nicely done out in rustic Mexican style, ceiling fans but no a/c. Metro Insurgentes. 6

Segovia Regency Chapultepec 328 ⓣ55/5208-8634, ⓦwww.naftaconnect.com/segovia. Reliable high-rise hotel with parking facilities that's often fully booked with business regulars, so it's best to reserve ahead, especially during the week. Metro Insurgentes. 6

Colonia Polanco

Casa Vieja Eugenio Sué 45 ⓣ55/5282-0067, ⓦwww.casavieja.com. Very chic ultra-deluxe small hotel in a suburban house with ten suites (from US$456), each with the best of everything: supremely comfortable beds, jacuzzi, kitchenette, phone and high-speed Internet line, fax machine, VCR, stereo, video and music library, and stacks of books and magazines. Decor is rich with mosaics, quality paintings, and every detail is taken care of. There's a superb restaurant and bar on site, and should you need even more space there are master suites (US$702). Metro Polanco. 9

Nikko Mexico Campos Elisos 204 ⓣ55/5280-1111, in US and Canada ⓣ1-800/NIKKO US, ⓦwww.nikkohotels.com, reservations through any Japan Airlines office. Not the most expensive high-rise business hotel in the city but as luxurious as you could want, with indoor pool, rooftop tennis courts, gym and acres of glass and marble. Rooms (some with a view over Chapultepec Park) come with TV/VCR, data ports and considerable comfort, and cost US$328 during the week but drop to US$155 on Friday and Saturday nights. Suite prices reach for the stratosphere – up to US$2106. Metro Polanco. 9

The airport and around

Aeropuerto Blv de Puerto Aéreo 380 ⓣ55/5785-5888 or 5851, ⓕ5784-1329. The cheapest of the hotels near the airport with well-maintained, carpeted rooms; all have TV and phone, plus there's room service from the on-site restaurant. Some (well-soundproofed) rooms have a view of the airport runway. The hotel is three minutes' walk from the airport terminal: follow signs from Sala A to the Metro, from whose entrance you can see the hotel across the busy road (use the footbridge). Metro Terminal Aérea. 5

Hilton in the airport ⓣ55/5133-0505 or 01-800/003-1400, in the US ⓣ1-800/HILTONS, ⓦwww.hilton.com. An elevator from Sala G takes you up to this swanky hotel which takes up much of the airport's third floor with its restaurants, bars, gym and very well-appointed, though not especially large, rooms (some with runway views). The multichannel TV even has in-house movies and flight information screens. Rack rates start at US$205 though weekend and off-peak discounts can bring it down to US$181. Metro Terminal Aérea. 9

JR Plaza Blv Puerto Aéreo 390 ⓣ55/5785-5200 or 01-800/702-4200, ⓦwww.hoteljrplaza.com.mx. Attractive business hotel with lower prices than the big airport hotels but still with most of their features and facilities. Located next to the *Hotel Aeropuerto* (see above), so it is barely worth using the hotel's free airport transfer. Metro Terminal Aérea. 8

Marriott opposite the airport terminal and linked by an enclosed footbridge from Sala A2 ⓣ55/3003-0033 or 01-800/888-0888, in US and Canada ⓣ1-866/401-8907, ⓦwww.marriott.com. Large and flashy hotel with rooftop pool, gym, numerous restaurants and bars, business centre and luxurious rooms with all the facilities you would expect for the midweek price of US$200 (reduced to US$138 at weekends). Metro Terminal Aérea. 9

Around Terminal del Norte

Acuario Poniente 112 #100 ⓣ55/5587-2677. Far inferior to the *Brasilia*, but cheaper and still decent despite the shabby exterior. Leaving the bus station turn left, then at the major junction (after 100m) turn right and the hotel is straight ahead. Metro La Raza. 3

Brasilia Av de los Cien Metros 4823 ⓣ55/5587-8577, ⓦwww.come.to/mexhotels. Particularly good-value business-style hotel just 150m east of the bus station where you can get a peaceful sleep in comfortable, carpeted rooms which all have cable TV and phone. There's a decent restaurant on site, car parking facilities, and even room service. Turn left as you exit and it's straight ahead of you. Metro La Raza. 5

Central Mexico City

The beating heart of Mexico City pumps strongest around the Zócalo, built by the Spanish right over the devastated ceremonial centre of the Aztec city of Tenochtitlán. Extraordinary uncovered ruins – chief of which is the **Templo Mayor** – provide the Zócalo's most compelling lure, but there's also a wealth of great colonial buildings, among them the huge **cathedral** and the **Palacio Nacional** with its striking **Diego Rivera murals**. You could easily spend a couple of days in the tightly packed blocks hereabouts, investigating the dense concentration of museums and galleries, especially notable for more works by Rivera and his "Big Three" companions, David Siqueiros and José Clemente Orozco.

West of the Zócalo the *centro histórico* stretches through the main commercial district past the **Museo Nacional de Arte** to the sky-scraping **Torre Latinoamericana** and the **Palacio de las Bellas Artes** with its gorgeous Art Deco interior. Both overlook the formal parkland of the **Alameda**, which is in itself another focus for museums, principally the **Museo Franz Mayer** which houses an excellent Alameda-related arts and crafts collection, and the **Museo Mural Rivera** with his famed *Dream of a Sunday Afternoon in the Alameda*. Further west, the **Revolution monument** heralds the more upmarket central suburbs, chiefly the **Zona Rosa**, long known as the spot for plush shops and restaurants, though that title has largely been usurped by swanky **Polanco** and hipper **Condesa**.

As a backdrop to Mexico City's quite remarkable sightseeing is a diverse, dynamic **street life** unequalled in Latin America – people hawking goods from streetside stalls, performers enacting Aztec dances, healers offering smoke cures for a few pesos, organ grinders panhandling, and much more. There's tremendous art, and not just in galleries, but everywhere you go. **Murals** adorn public buildings, abandoned churches are given over to contemporary installations, and even the Metro stations (Zócalo in particular) have free displays along the corridors of a standard you might pay to see elsewhere.

The Zócalo

The vast paved open space of the **Zócalo** (Metro Zócalo) – properly known as the Plaza de la Constitución – is said to be the second largest such city square in the world after Moscow's Red Square. The city's political and religious centre, it takes its name from part of a monument to Independence that was planned in the 1840s for the square by General Santa Ana. Like most of his other plans, this went astray, and only the statue's base (now gone) was ever erected: *el zócalo* literally means "the plinth". By extension, every other town square in Mexico has adopted the same name. Here stand the great **cathedral**, the **Palacio Nacional** with the offices of the president, and the city administration – all of them magnificent colonial buildings. But the area also reflects other periods of the country's history. This was the heart of **Aztec Tenochtitlán** too, and in the **Templo Mayor** you can see remarkable remains from the magnificent temples on this site. It is a constantly animated place: groups celebrating pre-Hispanic traditions dance and pound drums throughout the day, sometimes there may be street stalls and buskers in the evening, stages are set up for major national holidays and, of course, this is the place to hold demonstrations. In one of the best-supported expressions of solidarity in recent years, over 100,000 people massed here in March 2001 to support the Zapatistas after their march from Chiapas in support of indigenous people's rights.

Among the more certain entertainments is the ceremonial **lowering of the national flag** from its giant pole in the centre of the plaza each evening at sundown (typically 6pm). A troop of presidential guards march out from the palace, strike the enormous flag and perform a complex routine at the end of which the flag is left, neatly folded, in the hands of one of their number. With far less pomp, the flag is quietly raised again around half an hour later. You get a great view of this, and of everything else happening in the Zócalo, from the rooftop *La Terraza* restaurant/bar in the *Hotel Majestic* at the corner of Madero (see p.428).

The Zócalo does, of course, have its less glorious side. Mexico City's economic plight is most tellingly reflected in the lines of unemployed who queue up around the cathedral looking for work, each holding a little sign with his trade – plumber, electrician or mechanic – and a box with a few tools.

The Cathedral

The **Catedral Metropolitana** (daily 7.30am–7.30pm, must be discreet during services, mass on Mon–Fri at 9.30am, 10.30am, noon, 5pm, 6pm and 7pm, Sat same times plus 1pm, Sun 8am, 9.30am, 10.30am, noon, 1.30pm, 4pm, 5pm, 6pm and 7pm; free; Metro Zócalo) holds the bragging rights as the largest church in Latin America. It is flanked by the parish church of El Sagrario which actually first draws the eye, with its heavy, grey Baroque facade and squat, bell-topped towers. Like so many of the city's older, weightier structures, the cathedral has settled over the years into the soft wet ground beneath – the tilt is quite plain to see, despite extensive work to stabilize the building. The first church on this site was constructed only a couple of years after the Conquest using stones torn from the Temple of Huitzilopochtli, but the present structure was begun in 1573 to provide Mexico City with a cathedral more suited to its wealth and status as the jewel of the Spanish empire. The towers weren't completed until 1813, though, and the building incorporates a plethora of architectural styles throughout. Even the frontage demonstrates this: relatively austere at the bottom where work began in the years soon after the Conquest, flowering into full Baroque as you look up, and topped by Neoclassical cornices and clock tower.

Although the size of the cathedral is striking, the chief impression is of a rather gloomy space, with rows of side chapels so dimly lit it is hard to see much within. It is enlivened mostly by the **Altar de los Reyes**, a vast gilt reredos behind the main altar built of wood between 1718 and 1737 and featuring effigies of European kings and queens as well as two oil paintings, the *Assumption of the Virgin* and *Adoration of the Kings*. Fans of ornate handiwork will also appreciate the detailed work in gold and wood on the central *coro* (choir).

Next door, the **Sagrario Metropolitano** (daily 7.30am–7.30pm; free) feels bother lighter and richer inside, with its exuberant churrigueresque facade and liberal use of gold paint in the interior. It was originally built as the parish church, and performs most of the day-to-day functions of a local church, such as baptisms and marriages.

Templo Mayor

Just off the Zócalo, down beside the cathedral, lies the entrance to the site where the **Templo Mayor** (Tues–Sun 9am–5pm; US$3.70, plus US$3 to use a video camera; Metro Zócalo) has been excavated. What you see are the bare ruins of the foundations of the great temple and one or two buildings immediately around it, all highly confusing since, as was normal practice, a new

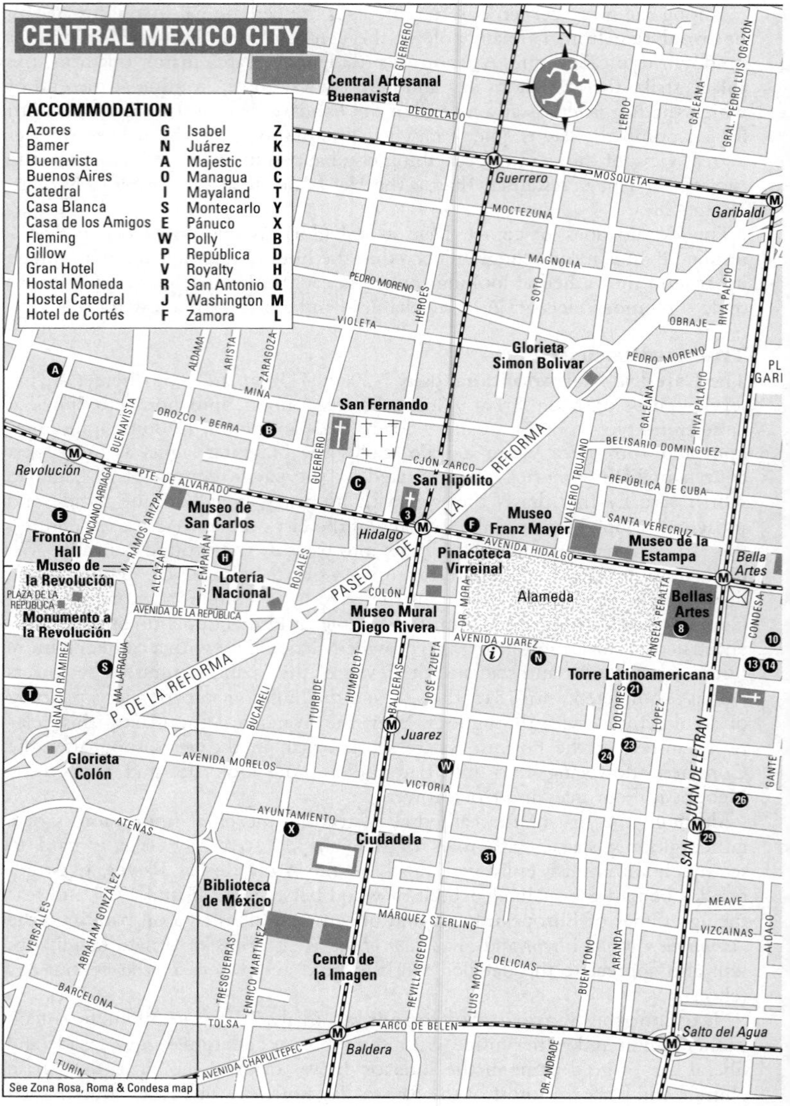

temple was built over the old at the end of every 52-year calendar cycle (and apparently even more frequently here), resulting in a whole series of temples stacked inside each other like Russian dolls. Look at the models and maps in the museum first (see p.380) and it all makes more sense.

Although it had been known since the beginning of the twentieth century that Tenochtitlán's ceremonial area lay under this part of the city, it

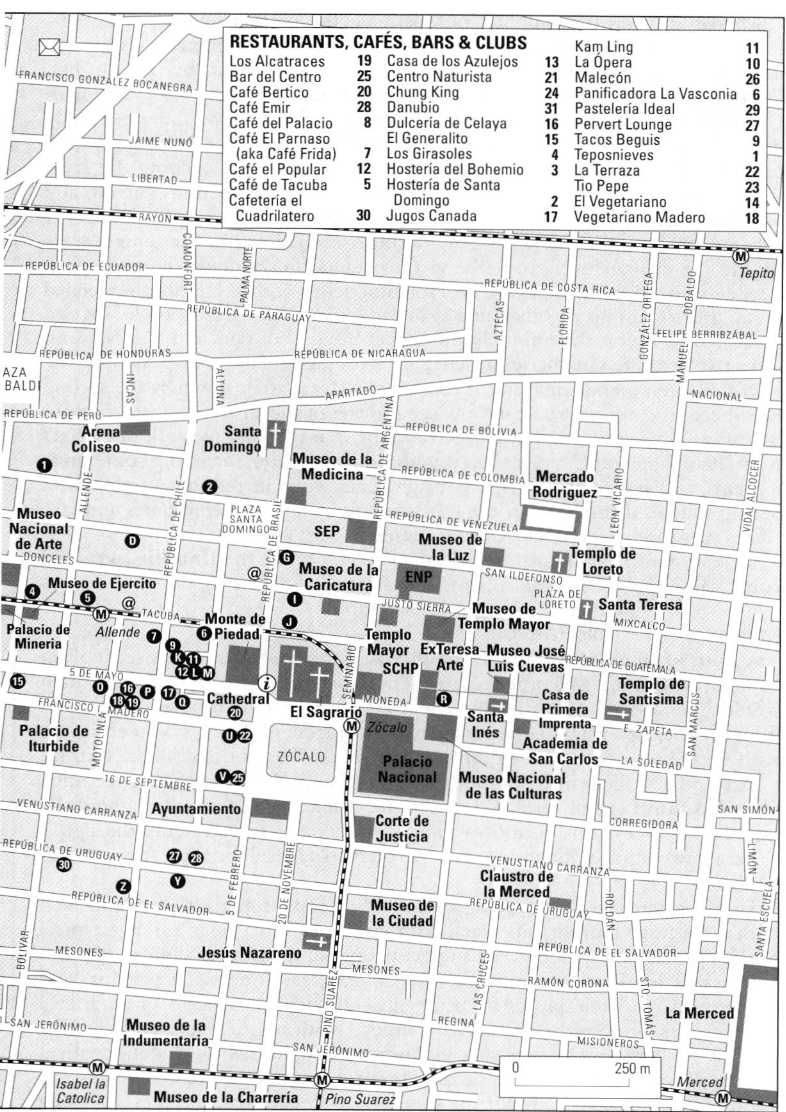

was generally believed that the chief temple, or Teocalli, lay directly beneath the cathedral. Archeological work only began in earnest in 1978 after workmen uncovered a vast stone disc in what were then colonial streets, weighing about eight tonnes and depicting Coyolxauhqui, goddess of the moon. Logic demanded that this must lie at the foot of the temple of Huitzilopochtli, and so the colonial buildings were cleared away and excavation began.

Coyolxauhqui was the daughter of Coatlicue, the mother goddess who controlled life and death; on discovering that her mother was miraculously pregnant, Coyolxauhqui vowed to wipe out the dishonour by killing her. Huitzilopochtli, however, sprang fully armed from the womb (like Athena in Greek mythology), decapitated and dismembered his sister and threw her body down a mountain. He then proceeded to drive off the four hundred other brothers who had gathered to help her: they scattered to become the stars. Coyolxauhqui is thus always portrayed with her head and limbs cut off, and was found here at the foot of the Temple of Huitzilopochtli symbolizing her fall from the mountain. The human sacrifices carried out in the temple were in part a re-enactment of this – the victims being thrown down the steps afterwards – and in part meant to feed Huitzilopochtli with the blood he needed as sun god to win his nightly battle against darkness. The Great Temple was also dedicated to Tlaloc, the infinitely more peaceful god of rain, and at its summit were two separate sanctuaries, reached by a monumental double stairway.

Of the seven reconstructions of the temple, layers as far down as the second have been uncovered. You can only see the top of the structure as the bottom is now well below the water table. Confusing as it is trying to work out what's what, it's a fascinating site, scattered with odd sculptures, including some great serpents, and traces of its original bright paintwork in red, blue and yellow. Seeing it here, at the heart of the modern city, brings the ceremonies and sacrifices that took place rather close to home.

It is also worth calling past here in the evening when the **floodlit pyramid ruins** can be seen from the surrounding streets.

Museo del Templo Mayor

The **museum**, entered through the site on the same ticket, helps set it all in context, with some welcome reconstructions and models of how Tenochtitlán would have looked at its height. There are some wonderful pieces retrieved from the site, especially the replica **tzompantli** (wall of skulls) as you enter, the eagle in Room 1 with a cavity in its back for the hearts of sacrificial victims, a particularly beautiful pulque god statue and of course the huge **Coyolxauhqui stone**, displayed so as to be visible from points throughout the museum. The design is meant to simulate the temple, so you climb through it to reach two rooms at the top, one devoted to Huitzilopochtli, the other to Tlaloc.

The best items are towards the top, including some superb stone masks such as the one from Teotihuacán, black with inset eyes and a huge earring, typical of the objects paid in tribute by subject peoples from all over the country. On the highest level are two magnificent, full-size terracotta eagle warriors and numerous large stone pieces from the site. The descent back to ground level concentrates on everyday life in Aztec times – with some rather mangy stuffed animals to demonstrate the species known to the Mexica – along with a jumble of later items found while the site was being excavated. There are some good pieces here too. Look for the superb turquoise mosaic, little more than a handspan across, but intricately set with tiny pieces forming seven god-like figures; and the two large ceramic sculptures of Mictlantecihtli, the god of death, only unearthed in 1994 from tunnels excavated below the nearby Casa de las Águilas.

Palacio Nacional and the Rivera murals

The other dominant structure on the Zócalo is the **Palacio Nacional** (daily 9am–5pm; free, bring ID; Metro Zócalo), its facade taking up a full side of it –

more than 200m. The so-called New Palace of Moctezuma stood here, and Cortés made it his first residence too, but the present building, for all its apparent unity, is the result of centuries of agglomeration and rebuilding. Most recently, in 1927, a third storey was added. From 1562 the building was the official residence of the Spanish viceroy, and later of presidents of the republic. It still contains the office of the president, who makes his most important pronouncements from the balcony – especially on September 15, when the Grito de Dolores signals the start of Independence celebrations around the country.

The overriding attraction is the series of **Diego Rivera murals** that decorate the stairwell and middle storey of the main courtyard. Begun in 1929, the murals are classic Rivera, ranking with the best of his work. The great panorama of Mexican history, *México a Través de los Siglos*, around the **main staircase**, combines an unbelievable wealth of detail with savage imagery and a masterly use of space. On the right-hand wall Quetzalcoatl sits in majesty amid the golden age of the Valley of México surrounded by an idealized vision of life in Teotihuacán, Tula and Tenochtitlán. The main section depicts the Conquest, oppression, war, Inquisition, invasion, Independence and eventually Revolution. Almost every major personage and event of Mexican history is here, from the grotesquely twisted features of the conquistadors, to the national heroes: balding, white-haired Hidalgo with the banner of Independence; squat, dark Benito Juárez with his Constitution and laws for the reform of the Church; Zapata, with a placard proclaiming his cry of "Tierra y Libertad"; and Pancho Villa, moustachioed and swaggering. On the left are post-revolutionary Mexico and the future, with Karl Marx pointing the way to adoring workers. Businessmen stand clustered over their tickertape in front of a somewhat ironic depiction of the metropolis with its skyscrapers and grim industrial wastes. Rivera's wife, the artist Frida Kahlo, is depicted, too, behind her sister Cristina (with whom Rivera was having an affair at the time) in a red blouse with an open copy of the Communist Manifesto.

A series of smaller panels was intended to go all the way round the upper (now middle) storey, an over-ambitious and unfinished project. The uncoloured first panel lists the products that the world owes to Mexico, including maize, beans, chocolate, tobacco, cotton, tomatoes, peanuts, prickly pears and chicle (the source of chewing gum). The remainder of the paintings that were completed reach halfway around and mostly depict the idyll of various aspects of life before the Conquest – market day, dyeing cloth, hunting scenes and so on. The last (completed in 1951) shows the arrival of the Spanish, complete with an image of La Malinche (the Indian woman widely perceived to have betrayed native Mexicans) bearing the blue-eyed baby sired by Cortés – the first Mexican *mestizo*.

Also on the middle storey is the chamber used by the Mexican Legislature from 1845 to 1872, when it was presided over by Benito Juárez, who lived in the palace until his death. The room houses the original copy of the 1857 Constitution, which was drawn up there, but is frequently closed for renovations.

Before leaving, take a moment to wander around some of the other **courtyards** (there are fourteen in all), and through the small floral and cactus **gardens**.

Ayuntamiento and Nacional Monte de Piedad

Clockwise round the Zócalo from the Palacio Nacional, the third side is taken up by the city and Federal District administration, the **Ayuntamiento**, while just along from there it is well worth visiting the *Gran Hotel*, 16 de Septiembre

Diego Rivera

Diego Rivera (c.1886–1957), husband of **Frida Kahlo** (see box, pp.412–413), was arguably the greatest of Los Tres Grandes, the "Big Three" Mexican artists who interpreted the Revolution and Mexican history through the medium of enormous murals, and put the nation's art onto an international footing in the first half of the twentieth century. His works (along with those of **José Clemente Orozco** and **David Siqueiros**) remain among the country's most striking sights.

Rivera studied from the age of 10 at the San Carlos Academy in the capital, immediately showing immense ability, and later moved to Paris where he flirted with many of the new trends, in particular Cubism. More importantly, though, he and Siqueiros planned, in exile, a popular, native art to express the new society in Mexico. In 1921, Rivera returned from Europe to the aftermath of the Revolution, and right away began work for the Ministry of Education at the behest of the socialist Education Minister, poet and presidential hopeful José Vasconcelos. Informed by his own Communist beliefs, and encouraged by the leftist sympathies of the times, Rivera embarked on the first of his massive, consciousness-raising **murals**, whose themes – Mexican history, the oppression of the natives, post-revolutionary resurgence – were initially more important than their techniques. Many of his early murals are deceptively simple, naive even, but in fact Rivera's style remained close to major trends and, following the lead of Siqueiros, took a scientific approach to his work, looking to industrial advances for new techniques, better materials and fresh inspiration. The view of industrial growth as a panacea (particularly in the earlier works of both Rivera and Siqueiros) may have been simplistic, but the artists' use of technology and experimentation with new methods and original approaches often have startling results – this is particularly true of Siqueiros' work at the Polyforum Siqueiros (p.410).

Communism continued to be a major source of motivation and inspiration for Rivera, who was a long-standing member of the Mexican Communist Party. When ideological differences caused a rift in Soviet politics, Rivera supported **Trotsky**'s "revolutionary internationalism", and in 1936, after Trotsky had spent seven years in exile from the Soviet Union on the run from Stalin's henchmen and was running out of countries that would accept him, Rivera used his influence over Mexican President Lázaro Cárdenas to get permission for Trotsky and his wife Natalia to enter the country. They stayed with Diego and Frida rent-free at their Coyoacán house before Trotsky moved down the road to what is now the **Museo Casa de León Trotsky**. The passionate and often violent differences between orthodox Stalinists and Trotskyites spilled over into the art world, creating a great rift between Rivera and ardent Stalinist Siqueiros, who was later jailed for his involvement in an assassination attempt on Trotsky (see box, p.417). Though Rivera later broke with Trotsky and was eventually readmitted to the Communist Party, Trotsky continued to admire Rivera's murals, finding them "not simply a 'painting', an object of passive contemplation, but a living part of the class struggle".

82, to admire the opulent lobby with its intricate ironwork, cage-lifts and wonderful Tiffany stained-glass dome.

Around the corner, on the fourth side of the Zócalo, arcades shelter a series of shops, almost all of which sell hats or jewellery. For strange shopping experiences, though, you can't beat the **Nacional Monte de Piedad** at the corner of the Zócalo and 5 de Mayo (Mon–Fri 8.30am–6pm, Sat 8.30am–1pm; Metro Zócalo). This huge building, supposedly the site of the palace in which Cortés and his followers stayed as guests of Moctezuma, is now the National Pawn Shop, an institution founded as far back as 1775. Much of what is put in hock here is jewellery, but there's also a wide variety of fine art and sculptures, and just about anything that will command a

Following the Rivera trail

There is a huge amount of Rivera's vast output accessible to the public, much of it in Mexico City, but also elsewhere around the country. The following is a rundown of the major Rivera sites organized by region and approximately ordered in accordance with their importance within that area.

Near the Zócalo, the Alameda and Chapultepec

Palacio National (p.380). Major murals abound right in the heart of the capital.

SEP (p.384). Acres of early murals around the courtyards of the Ministry of Education.

Palacio de las Bellas Artes (p.390). Rivera's monumental *Man in Control of the Universe* (and others) set among murals by his contemporaries.

Museo Mural Rivera (p.394). One of Diego's most famous murals, *Dream of a Sunday Afternoon in the Alameda*, on display.

Antiguo Colegio de San Ildefonso (p.385). One relatively minor Rivera mural.

Museo de Arte Moderno (p.406). Several quality canvases by Rivera and his contemporaries.

Museo Nacional de Arte (p.392). A handful of minor canvases.

The southern suburbs

Museo Dolores Olmedo Patiño (p.421). A massive collection of Rivera works from almost every artistic period.

Museo Frida Kahlo (p.416). Just a couple of Diego's works displayed in the house where he and Frida spent some of their married life.

Museo Casa Estudio Diego Rivera y Frida Kahlo (see p.411). Diego and Frida's pair of houses designed by Juan O'Gorman.

Museo Anahuacalli (p.420). Large Mayan-style house built by Rivera and housing his collection of pre-Columbian sculpture.

Museo de Carillo-Gil (p.411). A couple of paintings from Rivera's Cubist period.

Teatro de los Insurgentes (p.410). Rivera mural depicting the history of Mexican theatre.

Outside the capital

Palacio de Cortés, Cuernavaca (p.474). Early murals on a grand scale.

Museo Robert Brady, Cuernavaca (p.475). A few paintings each by both Frida and Diego.

Museo Diego Rivera, Guanajuato (p.316). Relatively minor works and sketches in the house where Diego was born.

reasonable price. From time to time they hold major auctions to clear the place out, but it's worth coming here just to take in the atmosphere and watch the milling crowds.

North of the Zócalo

Just a couple of blocks north of the centre the vast openness of the Zócalo gives way to a much more intimate section of small colonial plazas and mostly eighteenth-century buildings. It is still an active commercial area, and is packed with a mixed bag of ornate churches, small museums and some very fine Rivera and Siqueiros **murals**, all of which can be seen in a few hours.

Santo Domingo and the Museo de la Medicina

Beside the cathedral, Calle Monte de Piedad runs three blocks north (becoming República de Brasil) to the little colonial plaza of **Santo Domingo** (Metro Allende). In the middle, the gently playing fountain honours La Corregidora, here raised on a pedestal for her decisive role in Mexico's Independence struggle. Eighteenth-century mansions line the sides of the square along with the fine Baroque church of Santo Domingo on the site of the country's first Dominican monastery. Under the arcades you'll find clerks sitting at little desks with aging electric typewriters, carrying on the ancient tradition of public scribes. It's a sight you'll find somewhere in most large Mexican cities – their main function is to translate simple messages into the flowery, sycophantic language essential for any business letter in Spanish, but they'll type anything from student theses to love letters. Alongside them are street printers, who'll churn out business cards or invitations on the spot, on antiquated hand presses.

On the east side of the plaza the **Museo de la Medicina** (daily 9am–6pm; free; Metro Allende) occupies grand rooms around a courtyard that was once the headquarters of the Inquisition in New Spain. It was here that heretics were punished, and although the cruelty of the Inquisition is often exaggerated, it was undoubtedly the site of some gruesome scenes. The extensive museum itself kicks off with interesting displays on indigenous medicine, religion and herbalism, often with reference to infirmity in sculpture. It is surprising how often skin diseases, humped backs and malformed limbs crop up in pre-Columbian art: note the terracotta sculpture bent double from osteoporosis. The progress of Western medicine from colonial times to the present is also well covered, with an intact nineteenth-century pharmacy, a complete radiology room from 1939, and an obstetrics and gynecology room filled with human embryos in bottles. A "wax room" shows full-colour casts of various skin ailments, injuries and infections, the diseased genitalia always a hit with local school kids.

SEP and Colegio de San Ildefonso

From the Plaza de Santo Domingo, República de Cuba runs a block east to the Secretaría de Educación Pública or **SEP**, its entrance being round the corner at Argentina 28 (Mon–Fri 9am–5pm, Sat & Sun 9.30am–4pm; free; Metro Zócalo), the Ministry of Education building where, in 1923 and 1924, Rivera painted his first **murals** on returning from Paris. Note that the upper floors are only open Monday to Friday.

The driving force behind the murals was **José Vasconcelos**, revolutionary Minister of Public Education but better known as a poet and philosopher, who promoted educational art as a means of instilling a sense of history and cultural pride in a widely illiterate population. He is the man most directly responsible for the murals in public buildings throughout the country. Here, three floors of an enormous double patio are entirely covered with frescoes, as are many of the stairwells and almost any other flat surface. Rivera's work is very simple compared with what he later achieved, but the style is already recognizable: panels crowded with figures, drawing inspiration mainly from rural Mexico, though also from an idealized view of science and industry. The most famous panel on the ground floor is the relatively apolitical *Día de los Muertos*, which is rather hidden away in a dark corner at the back. Continuing clockwise, there are equally striking images, *Quema de Judas* and *La Asamblea Primero de Mayo*, for example, and the lovely *El Canal de Santa Anita*. On the first floor the work is very plain, mostly in tones of grey – here you'll find the shields of the states of Mexico and such general educational themes as *Chemistry* or *Physics*, mostly the work of Rivera's assistants. On the second floor are heroes and heroic themes from the Revolution. At the back, clockwise from the left-hand side, the triumphant progress of the Revolution is traced, culminating in the happy scenes of a Mexico ruled by its workers and peasants.

More murals, for which Vasconcelos was also responsible, adorn the eighteenth-century **Antiguo Colegio de San Ildefonso** (also called the "Escuela Nacional Preparatoria", or "ENP"; Tues–Sun 10am–6pm; US$3.50, free Tues; Metro Zócalo), nearby at Justo Serra 16, with an imposing facade that fills almost a whole block. Many artists are represented, including Rivera and Siqueiros, but the most famous works here are those of **José Clemente Orozco**, which you'll find on the main staircase and around the first floor of the main patio. As everywhere, Orozco, for all his enthusiasm for the Revolution, is less sanguine about its prospects, and modern Mexico is caricatured almost as savagely as the pre-revolutionary nation. *The Trench* depicts three Revolutionary soldiers resigning themselves to death in the battlefield, while *The Destruction of the Old Order* seems to suggest a return to a state of authoritarianism following the Revolution, rather than the ascent of any kind of free or just society.

Museo de la Caricatura and Museo de la Luz

Half a block west of ENP, Justo Serra becomes Doncelos, home to the **Museo de la Caricatura**, Donceles 99 (Mon–Fri 10am–6pm, Sat & Sun 10am–5pm; US$1.50; Metro Zócalo), located in a particularly fine example of an eighteenth-century nobleman's dwelling complete with central courtyard. It exhibits a limited selection of work from Mexico's most famous caricaturists, but without a strong sense of Mexican history and a comprehensive grasp of Spanish much of the impact is lost. It is still worth nipping in to see a small selection of bizarre nineteenth-century prints of skeletal *mariachis* by José Guadalupe Posada, a great influence on the later **Muralist movement**, and to take a break in the museum coffeeshop in the central patio. The most recent cartoons, many of which focus on world affairs rather than just Mexico, are also extremely sharp, and well worth a look.

A couple of minutes' walk to the northeast stands the ex-Templo de San Pedro y San Pablo, built for the Company of Jesus between 1576 and 1603. Later used as a library, military college and correctional school, it was eventually taken over by the university, and again Vasconcelos influenced its decoration: here plain white, with the arches and pilasters painted in floral designs by Jorge Enciso and Roberto Montenegro. The church has since been turned into the **Museo de la Luz** (Mon–Fri 9am–4pm, Sat & Sun 10am–5pm; US$1.50; Metro Zócalo), a kind of hands-on celebration of all facets of reflection, refraction, iridescence, luminescence and so forth. Good Spanish is essential if you want to learn anything, but it is fun just playing with the optical tricks and effects, and exploring the use of light in art.

Plaza de Loreto and around

Just along from the Museo de la Luz, and three blocks northeast of the Zócalo, the **Plaza de Loreto** (Metro Zócalo) feels a world apart. It is a truly elegant old square, entirely unmodernized and flanked by a couple of churches. On one side is the **Templo de Loreto** with its huge dome leaning at a crazy angle: inside, you'll find yourself staggering across the tilted floor. **Santa Teresa**, across the plaza, has a bizarre cave-like chapel at the back, entirely artificial. North of the Templo Loreto is a large and rather tame covered market, the **Mercado Presidente Abelardo Rodriguez**, inside most entrances of which are a series of large murals dating from the 1930s by an assortment of artists including Antonio Pujol and Pablo O'Higgins.

East of the Zócalo: along Calle Moneda

Calle Moneda, running east from the centre, is one of the oldest streets in the city, and it's fascinating to wander up here and see the rapid change as you leave the immediate environs of the Zócalo. The buildings remain almost wholly colonial, prim and refurbished around the museums, then gradually becoming shabbier and shabbier, interspersed with buildings abandoned after earthquake or subsidence damage. Within four or five blocks you're into a very depressed residential area, with street stalls spreading up from the giant market of La Merced, to the south.

Most of the appeal is in just wandering through and soaking up the atmosphere, but be sure not to miss the **Museo de la SHCP** and the **Museo Nacional de las Culturas**.

Museo de la SHCP and the Casa de la Primera Imprenta

Just a few steps from the Zócalo, the **Museo de la SHCP**, Moneda 4 (Tues–Sun 10am–5pm; US$0.80), occupies the former archbishop's palace and presents Mexican fine art from the last three centuries in rooms surrounding two lovely open courtyards. The building was constructed over part of Tenochtitlán's ceremonial centre, the *teocalli*, and excavations have revealed a few foundation sections for the Templo de Tezcatlipoca pyramid which once stood here. Notice the short flight of stairs, a jaguar carved in high relief and a series of anthropomorphic sculptures. In the galleries, accomplished eighteenth-century canvases by Juan Correa are a nice counterpoint to the small but wonderful collection of Russian icons of the same era. Other highlights include works by Diego Rivera and the stairway mural by José Gordillo, a follower of Siqueiros and Rivera, whose influence shows.

On the corner of Licenciado Primo Verdad, the **Casa de la Primera Imprenta** (Mon–Sat 10am–5pm; free) occupies the house where the first printing press in the Americas was set up in 1535, though the only indication of this is the model of the press that sits close to the entrance. Archeological finds unearthed during restoration work are displayed in one room; other rooms house temporary exhibits.

Temporary displays are also the stock in trade next door at the **Centro Cultural Ex-Teresa Arte**, Licenciado Primo Verdad 8 (daily 10am–6pm; free), in the former temple of Santa Teresa la Antigua, which has subsided so much that false floors are needed. You can wander around the mainly video and film installations put on by a nonprofit organization funded by the National Institute of Fine Arts.

Museo Nacional de las Culturas and beyond

Behind the Palacio Nacional, at Moneda 13, is the **Museo Nacional de las Culturas** (Tues–Sun 10am–6pm; free), a collection devoted to the archeology and anthropology of other countries. The museum occupies the sixteenth-century Casa de la Moneda, the official mint until 1848 and later the National Museum, where the best of the Aztec artefacts were displayed until the construction of the Museo Nacional de Antropología (see p.401). Now immaculately restored, with rooms of exhibits set around a quiet patio, it is more interesting than you might guess, though still somewhat overshadowed by so many other high-class museums in the city. One of the more intriguing aspects of the museum is the information on Mexico's historical alignment on the trade routes between Europe and Asia. Every continent is covered, with everything from Korean china to slit gongs from the Marwuasas Islands, and even a reclining nude by Henry Moore.

Just a block beyond the museum, the orange dome of the church of **Santa Inés** stands out a mile off. This, though, is its most striking feature, and there's little else to admire apart from the delicately carved wooden doors. Painters Miguel Cabrera and José Ibarra are both buried somewhere inside but neither is commemorated in any way. Around the corner, the church's former convent buildings have been transformed into the **Museo José Luis Cuevas**, Academia 13 (Tues–Sun 10am–5.30pm; US$1, free on Sun), an art gallery with changing displays centred on the eight-metre-high bronze *La Giganta* (The Giantess), designed by Cuevas. The only permanent collection is one room full of erotica ranging from pre-Hispanic sculpture to line drawings, some by Cuevas.

A few metres south is the **Academia de San Carlos**, Academia 22 (Mon–Fri 9am–7pm; free), which still operates as an art school, though on a very reduced scale from its nineteenth-century heyday; inside are galleries for temporary exhibitions and, in the patio, copies of classical sculptures. Further up Moneda, which by this time has become Emiliano Zapata, the **Templo de la Santísima Trinidad** boasts one of the city's finest Baroque facades. Again, the church's soft footing has caused it to slump, and plumb lines inside chart its continuing movement.

South of the Zócalo

The area immediately south of the Zócalo is perhaps the least rewarding in the centre, but still warrants a brief foray, particularly if you are en route to the wonderful **La Merced** market. Leaving the Zócalo to the south, Pino Suárez heads off from the corner between the Palacio Nacional and the Ayuntamiento towards the **Museo de la Ciudad**. First, though, right on the corner of the square, is the colonial-style modern building housing the **Suprema Corte de Justicia** (Mon–Fri 9am–2pm; free but must show ID; Metro Zócalo). Inside are three superb, bitter murals by Orozco named *Proletarian Battles*, *The National Wealth* and *Justice*. The last, depicting Justice slumped asleep on her pedestal while bandits rob the people of their rights, was not surprisingly unpopular with the judges and powers that be, and Orozco never completed his commission here.

Museo de la Ciudad de México and around

A couple of blocks south of the Zócalo, the **Museo de la Ciudad de México**, Pino Suárez 30 (Tues–Sun 10am–5.45pm; US$1.40, bring ID; Metro Zócalo), is housed in the colonial palace of the Condes de Santiago de Calimaya. This is a fabulous building, with carved stone cannons thrusting out from the cornice, magnificent heavy wooden doors and, on the far side, a hefty plumed serpent obviously dragged from the ruins of some Aztec temple to be employed as a cornerstone. The rooms are mostly given over to temporary exhibits on all manner of themes, but on the top storey is the preserved studio of the landscape artist **Joaquín Clausell**, its walls plastered in portraits and little sketches that he scribbled between working on his paintings.

Diagonally across the road from the museum a memorial marks the spot where, according to legend, Cortés first met Moctezuma. Here you'll find the church and hospital of **Jesús Nazareno**. The **hospital**, still in use, was founded by Cortés in 1528, and as such it's one of the oldest buildings in the city, and exemplifies the severe, fortress-like construction of the immediate post-Conquest years. The **church**, which contains the remains of Cortés and a bronze plaque to the left of the altar with the simple inscription "H.C. (1485–1547)", has been substantially remodelled over the years, its vaulting decorated by Orozco with a fresco of the Apocalypse.

More or less opposite is a small open space and an entrance to a bookstore-lined subterranean walkway between the Zócalo and **Pino Suárez Metro station**, where an Aztec shrine uncovered during construction has been preserved as an integral part of the concourse. Dating from around the end of the fourteenth century, it was dedicated to Quetzalcoatl in his guise of Ehecatl, god of the wind.

Heading east from here along Salvador or Uruguay takes you to the giant **market** area of La Merced (see p.437), passing, on Uruguay, the beautiful cloister that is all that remains of the seventeenth-century **Convento de la Merced** (currently closed to the public).

Westwards you can stroll down some old streets heading towards the Zona Rosa, passing several smaller markets. Though still only half a dozen blocks south of the Zócalo, you're well outside the tourist zone down here, and it is instructive to spend a little time watching the city life go by. There's not a great deal to see but you could call in to see if there any interesting temporary exhibitions at the **Museo de la Indumentaria Mexicana**, José María Izázaga 92 (Mon–Fri 10am–5pm; US$0.50; ⓣ55/5130-3300, ext 3415; Metro Isabel la Católica), a former convent. Across the road, a handsome colonial building holds the **Museo de la Charrería**, Isabel la Católica 108 (Mon–Fri 11am–5pm; free; Metro Isabel la Católica), dedicated to all things cowboy, including old photographs, some of them inevitably rather camp, as well as sketches and watercolours, costumes, spurs and brands.

West to the Alameda

The streets that lead down from the Zócalo towards the Alameda – **Tacuba**, **5 de Mayo**, **Madero**, **16 de Septiembre** and the lanes that cross them – are the most elegant in the city: least affected by any modern developments and lined with ancient buildings and traditional cafés and shops, and with mansions converted to offices, banks or restaurants. Few of these merit any special attention, but it's a pleasant place simply to stroll around. At the end of Madero, you're at the extent of the colonial city centre, and standing between two of the most striking modern buildings in the capital: the **Torre Latinoamericana** and the **Palacio de las Bellas Artes**. Though it seems incredible to draw any comparison, they were completed within barely 25 years of each other.

Along Madero

On **Madero** you'll pass several former aristocratic palaces given over to a variety of uses. First stop, though, is **Museo Serfin**, Madero 33 (Mon–Sat 9am–6pm; free), comprising just one room of usually interesting temporary exhibits. At no. 27, on the corner of Bolivar, stands the slightly dilapidated mansion built in 1775 by mining magnate José de la Borda (see p.480) for his wife, with a magnificent balcony. Still further down Madero, at no.19, you'll find the **Palacio de Iturbide** (Metro Allende), occupied by Banamex and thoroughly restored – the banks seem able to afford the best restoration work. Originally

△ Rivera mural at the Palacio Nacional, Mexico City

the home of the Condes de Valparaiso in the eighteenth century, it was from 1821 to 1823 the residence of the ill-fated "emperor" Agustín de Iturbide. Nowadays it periodically houses free art exhibitions laid on by the bank. In the next block, the last before you emerge at Bellas Artes and the Alameda, the churrigueresque church of **San Francisco** (Metro Bellas Artes) stands on the site of the first Franciscan mission to Mexico.

Opposite is the sixteenth-century **Casa de los Azulejos** (Metro Bellas Artes) – currently a branch of Sanborn's – its exterior swathed entirely in blue and white tiles from Puebla which were added during remodelling in 1737. The building survived a gas explosion in 1994, which did quite a bit of structural damage; luckily no one was hurt, and one of the most famous features of the building, the giant Orozco mural on the staircase, suffered few ill effects. Inside you'll find a restaurant in the glassed-over patio, as well as all the usual shopping.

The Torre Latinoamericana

The distinctly dated steel-and-glass skyscraper of the **Torre Latinoamericana**, Lázaro Cárdenas 2 (daily 9am–10pm; US$4; Metro Bellas Artes), was completed in 1956 and until a few years ago was the tallest building in Mexico and, indeed, the whole of Latin America. It has now been outdone by the World Trade Center (formerly the *Hotel de México*, on Insurgentes Sur) and doubtless by others in South America, but it remains the city's outstanding landmark and a point of reference no matter where you are. By world standards it is not especially tall, but on a clear day, the views from the 139-metre observation deck are outstanding; if it's smoggy you're better off going up around dusk, catching the city as the sun sets, then watching as the lights delineate the city far more clearly. Having paid the fee, you're whisked up to the 36th floor where, bizarrely, there are steps up to a small **aquarium** (US$2.80), and another lift to "El Mirador" on the 42nd floor. Here there is a glassed-in **observation area**, a small **café** on the level above, and a series of coin-operated telescopes on the outdoor deck a further level up. Plans in the observation area illustrate how the tower is built, proudly boasting that it is the tallest building in the world to have withstood a major earthquake (which it did in 1985, though others may now rival the claim). The general principle appears to be similar to that of an angler's float, with enormously heavy foundations bobbing around in the mushy soil under the capital, keeping the whole thing upright.

Bellas Artes

Diagonally across the street there's an equally impressive and substantially more beautiful engineering achievement in the form of the **Palacio de las Bellas Artes** (Metro Bellas Artes). It was designed in 1901, at the height of the Díaz dictatorship, by the Italian architect Adamo Boari and constructed, in a grandiose Art Nouveau style, of white marble imported from Italy. Building wasn't actually completed, however, until 1934, with the Revolution and several new planners come and gone. There are some who find the whole exterior overblown, but whatever your initial impression it does nothing to prepare you for the magnificent interior – an Art Deco extravaganza incorporating spectacular lighting, chevron friezes and stylized masks of the rain god, Chac.

Much of this can be seen anytime by wandering into the foyer (free) and simply gazing around the lower floor where there is a good arts bookstore and *El Café del Palacio* restaurant (see p.429). But Bellas Artes is also a major art museum: the **Museo del Palacio de las Bellas Artes** (Tues–Sun 10am–6pm; US$3, free on Sun or when there is no special exhibition on) is on the middle two floors. In the galleries you'll find a series of exhibitions, permanent displays of Mexican art and temporary shows of anything from local art-school graduates' work to that of major international names. Of constant and abiding interest, however, are the great **murals** surrounding the central space. On the first floor are *Birth of Our Nationality* and *Mexico Today* – dreamy, almost abstract works by **Rufino Tamayo**. Going up a level you're confronted by the unique sight of murals by **Rivera**, **Orozco** and **Siqueiros** gathered in the same place. Rivera's *Man in Control of the Universe* (or *Man at the Crossroads*), celebrating the liberating power of technology, was originally painted for the Rockefeller Center in New York, but destroyed for being too leftist – arch-capitalist Nelson Rockefeller objected to Rivera's inclusion of Karl Marx, even though he was well aware of Rivera's views when he commissioned him. This is Rivera's own copy, painted in 1934, just a year after the original. It's worth studying the explanatory panel, which reveals some of the theory behind this complex work, particularly the principal division between the capitalist world on the left, symbolized by war, disease and famine, and the socialist world on the right, all health and peace.

Several smaller panels by Rivera are also displayed; these, too, were intended to be seen elsewhere (in this case on the walls of the *Hotel Reforma*, downtown) but for years were covered up, presumably because of their unflattering depiction of tourists. Themes include *Mexican Folklore and Tourism*, *Dictatorship*, the *Dance of the Huichilobos* and, perhaps the best of them, *Agustín Lorenzo*, a portrayal of a guerrilla fighter against the French. You get the impression, though, that none of these was designed to be seen so close up, and you're always wanting to step back to get the big picture. *Catharsis*, a huge, vicious work by Orozco, occupies almost an entire wall, and there are also some particularly fine examples of Siqueiros' work: three powerful and original panels on the theme of *Democracy* and a bloody depiction of *The Torture of Cuauhtémoc* and his resurrection. The uppermost floor is devoted to the **Museo de la Arquitectura** (same ticket and hours), which has no permanent collection, but frequently has interesting exhibits.

Some of the finest interior decor in the building is generally hidden from view in the main theatre, so it is worth catching a performance if only to see the amazing Tiffany glass curtain depicting the Valley of México and the volcanoes. The whole interior, in fact, is magnificent, with a detailed proscenium mosaic, and more stained glass in the ceiling. Bellas Artes is the headquarters of the National Institute of Fine Arts, venue for all the most important performances of classical music, opera or dance, but the performance you should try to see here is the **Ballet Folklórico** – see "Entertainment and nightlife", p.432.

The Correo Central and Palacio de Minería

Around the back of Bellas Artes, at the corner of Tacuba and Lázaro Cárdenas, you'll find the **Correo Central** (Metro Bellas Artes), the city's main post office. Completed in 1908, this too was designed by Adamo Boari, but in a style much more consistent with the buildings around it. Look closely and you'll find a wealth of intricate detail, while inside it's full of richly carved wood. On the first floor is the small **Museo Postal** (Mon–Fri 10am–5.30pm, Sat & Sun 10am–3.30pm; free but bring ID), housing a rather uninspiring collection of old mailboxes, a few old documents and objects relating to the postal service, and a giant picture made of postage stamps.

Directly behind the Correo on Tacuba is the **Palacio de Minería**, a Neoclassical building completed right at the end of the eighteenth century and designed by Spanish-born Manuel Tolsá, who is the subject of the devotional

Museo Manuel Tolsá (daily 10am–6pm; US$1) within – just a couple of rooms of paintings and architectural drawings, strictly for fans only. The palacio also houses another museum, the more macabre **Torture Museum** (daily 10am–7pm; US$3.50), illustrating instruments of torture and execution from the time of the Inquisition onward. The Palacio de Minería makes an interesting contrast with the post office and with the Museo Nacional de Arte (formerly the Palacio de Comunicaciones) directly opposite, the work of another Italian architect, Silvio Contri, in the first years of the twentieth century.

Around the corner on Filomeno Mata is the small Convento de las Betlemitas, a seventeenth-century convent that now houses the **Museo del Ejército y Fuerza** (Tues–Sat 10am–6pm, Sun 10am–4pm; free), with a small exhibition of antique arms, and explanations mostly in Spanish – strictly for weaponry enthusiasts.

The Museo Nacional de Arte

The **Museo Nacional de Arte**, Tacuba 8 (Tues–Sun 10.30am–5.30pm; US$3, free on Sun), is set back from the street on a tiny plaza in which stands one of the city's most famous sculptures, **El Caballito**, portraying Carlos IV of Spain. This enormous bronze, the work of Manuel Tolsá, was originally erected in the Zócalo in 1803. In the intervening years it has graced a variety of sites and, despite the unpopularity of the Spanish monarchy (and of the effete Carlos IV in particular), is still regarded affectionately. The latest setting is appropriate, since Tolsá also designed the Palacio de Minería (see above). The open plaza around the sculpture is now often the scene of intense pre-Columbian drumming and dancing, which usually draws an appreciative crowd.

The museum itself has undergone a major refit that has brought its rooms and facilities up to international standards. Yet despite being the foremost showcase of Mexican art from 1550 until 1954, the interest here is mainly historical, even with over a thousand works and most of the major players represented – essentially mediocre examples spiced only occasionally with a more striking work. Come here to see something of the dress and landscape of old Mexico, and also some of the curiosities.

Temporary displays take up the lower floor (along with a good bookstore and café), leaving the two floors above for the permanent collection. To follow the displays in chronological order, start on the **upper floor** which covers work up to the end of the eighteenth century. Vast religious canvases take up whole walls, but seldom hold your interest for long, though Miguel Cabrera is particularly well represented with half a dozen works, notably *La Virgen del Apocalipsis*. In the same room there are some fine polychrome sculptures, particularly the diminutive nativity scene in the glass case. You could hardly miss eighteenth-century painter Francisco Antonio Vallejo's masterwork, the four-canvas *Glorificación de la Inmaculada*, with the heavenly host borne by clouds above the court of Carlos IV.

The museum really comes to life, and modern Mexico begins to express itself, on the **middle floor**, where traditional oils are supplemented by lithographs, sculpture and photography: note the images of nineteenth-century Mexican railways, *pulqueros* tapping the maguey cactus, and cattle grazing in the fields of Chapultepec Park. Elsewhere there are a couple of photos by Henri Cartier-Bresson and several by Hungarian-born Katy Horna, who worked in Mexico from 1939 until her death in 2000. The half-dozen Diego Riveras are mostly minor, though it is instructive to see early works such as *El Grade de España* from 1914 when he was in Braque mode. Notice too how Rivera's technique influenced many of the other painters of the time, especially

Saturnino Herrán and Olga Costa. Look too for the landscapes of the Valley of México by José María Velasco (one of Rivera's teachers).

The Alameda

From behind Bellas Artes, Lázaro Cárdenas runs north towards the **Plaza Garibaldi** (see p.432) through an area crowded with seedy cantinas and eating places, theatres and burlesque shows. West of the Palacio de Bellas Artes lies the **Alameda**, first laid out as a park in 1592, and taking its name from the *alamos* (poplars) then planted. The Alameda had originally been an Aztec market and later became the site where the Inquisition burned its victims at the stake. Most of what you see now – formally laid-out paths and flowerbeds, ornamental statuary and fountains – recalls the nineteenth century, when it was the fashionable place to stroll. It's still popular, always full of people, the haunt of ice-cream and sweet vendors, illuminated at night, and particularly crowded at weekends, but it's mostly a transient population – office workers taking lunch, shoppers resting their feet, messengers taking a short cut and Zapatista supporters selling Subcomandante Marcos T-shirts. The Alameda was one of the areas worst hit by the 1985 earthquake, and a number of buildings are still shored up, while others (on the south side) have been cleared, but not yet replaced.

Museo de la Estampa and Museo Franz Mayer

On the north side of the Alameda, Avenida Hidalgo traces the line of an ancient thoroughfare, starting from the Teatro Hidalgo, right opposite Bellas Artes. To the west, the church of Santa Vera Cruz marks the **Museo de la Estampa** (Tues–Sun 10am–5.45pm; US$1, free on Sun), which concentrates on engraving, an art form that is taken seriously in Mexico, where the legacy of José Guadalupe Posada (see p.308) is still revered. There is no permanent collection, but you may expect anything from engravings and printing plates from pre-Columbian times to the modern age, including works by Posada.

Immediately next door, the **Museo Franz Mayer**, Hidalgo 45 (Tues–Sun 10am–5pm; US$2, free on Tues), is dedicated to the applied arts, and occupies the sixteenth-century hospital attached to the church of San Juan de Dios. It's packed with the personal collection of Franz Mayer, a keen hoarder of Mexican arts and crafts who settled here from Germany: colonial furniture, textiles and carpets, watches, Spanish silverwork, religious art and artefacts, a valuable collection of sculpture and paintings, and some fine colonial pottery from Puebla. There is also much furniture and pottery from Asia, reflecting Mexico's position on the trade routes, as well as a library with rare antique editions of Spanish and Mexican authors and a reference section on applied arts. Even if this doesn't sound like your thing, it's well worth seeing. It is a lovely building, beautifully furnished, and offers a tranquil escape from the crowds outside. The coffee bar, too, is a delight, facing a courtyard filled with flowers and a fountain – there's a charge of US$0.50 for those not visiting the museum.

Laboratorio Arte Almeda and Museo Mural Rivera

Almost at the western end of the Alameda, duck down Calle Dr Mora to the **Laboratorio Arte Almeda**, at no. 7 (Tues–Sun 9am–5pm; US$1.50, free on Sun), an art museum built into the glorious seventeenth-century monastery of San Diego. The cool, white interior is filled with temporary exhibitions of challenging contemporary art. They're all superbly displayed around the church, chapel and cloister of the old monastery, a space also occasionally used for evening concerts – mostly chamber music or piano recitals.

One of the buildings worst hit by the 1985 earthquake was the *Hotel del Prado*, which contained the Rivera mural *Dream of a Sunday Afternoon in the Alameda*. The mural survived, was picked up in its entirety and transported around the Alameda, and can now be seen in the **Museo Mural Diego Rivera** (Tues–Sun 10am–6pm; US$1, free on Sun), at the western end of the Alameda, at the corner of Balderas and Colón. It's an impressive work – showing almost every famous Mexican character out for a stroll in the park – but one suspects that its popularity with tour groups is as much to do with its relatively apolitical nature as with any superiority to Rivera's other works. Originally it included a placard with the words "God does not exist", which caused a huge furore, and Rivera was forced to paint it out before the mural was first displayed to the public.

A leaflet (available at the entrance; US$0.50) explains every character in the scene: Cortés is depicted with his hands stained red with blood, José Guadalupe Posada stands bowler-hatted next to his trademark skeleton, *La Calavera Catrina*, who holds the hand of Rivera himself, portrayed as a 9-year-old boy. Frida Kahlo stands in motherly fashion, just behind him. There's a rather unenlightening **sound-and-light show** (*luz y sonido*; Tues–Fri 11am & 4pm, Sat & Sun 11am, 1pm, 4pm & 5pm), narrated in Spanish by voices representing Rivera, Kahlo and the *Calavera*. Around the walls there are also displays on the history of the Alameda and its place within the city as a whole.

Centro de la Imagen and Biblioteca de México

A short detour south of the Alameda takes you past the excellent **artesanía market** of Ciudadela to a shady open space of the same name. Along the south side are the **Centro de la Imagen** (Tues–Sun 11am–6pm; free), with changing photographic exhibits and, next door, the **Biblioteca de México** (daily 8.30am–7.30pm; free), an extensive library also containing rooms where touring art shows are displayed.

Around the Monumento a la Revolución

Beyond the Alameda, avenidas Juárez and Hidalgo lead towards the Paseo de la Reforma. Across Reforma, Hidalgo becomes the **Puente de Alvarado**, following one of the main causeways that led into Tenochtitlán. This was the route by which the Spanish attempted to flee the city on the Noche Triste (Sad Night), July 10, 1520. Following the death of Moctezuma, and with his men virtually under siege in their quarters, Cortés decided to escape the city under cover of darkness. It was a disaster: the Aztecs cut the bridges and, attacking the bogged-down invaders from their canoes, killed all but 440 of the 1300 Spanish soldiers who set out, and more than half their native allies. Greed, as much as anything, cost the Spanish troops their lives, for in trying to take their gold booty with them they were, in the words of Bernal Díaz, "so weighed down by the stuff that they could neither run nor swim". The street takes its name from Pedro de Alvarado, one of the last conquistadors to escape, crossing the broken bridge "in great peril after their horses had been killed, treading on the dead men, horses and boxes". Not long ago a hefty gold bar – exactly like those made by Cortés from melted-down Aztec treasures – was dug up here.

Puente de Alvarado: San Fernando and the Museo San Carlos

The church of **San Hipólito**, at the corner of Reforma and Puente de Alvarado, was founded by the Spanish soon after their eventual victory, both as a celebration and to commemorate the events of the Noche Triste. The present building dates from 1602, though over the years it's been damaged by earthquakes and rebuilt, and it now lists to one side. West along Puente de Alvarado is the Baroque, eighteenth-century church of **San Fernando**, by the plaza of the same name. Once one of the richest churches in the city, San Fernando has been stripped over the years like so many others. Evidence of its former glory survives, however, in the highly decorative facade and in the *panteón*, or graveyard, crowded with the tombstones of nineteenth-century high society.

At Puente de Alvarado 50 you'll find the **Museo Nacional de San Carlos** (daily except Tues 10am–6pm; US$2.50, free on Mon), which houses the country's oldest art collection, begun in 1783 by Carlos III of Spain, and comprising largely European work of the seventeenth and eighteenth centuries with some notable earlier and later additions. Major names are largely absent, but look for the delicate *San Pedro, San Andrés y San Mateo* by fifteenth-century Spanish painter Maestro de Palaquinos, portraits by Reynolds, Rubens and Hals, and a luminous canvas of Breton women by the sea (*Mujeres Bretones a la Orilla del Mar*) by another Spaniard, Manuel Benedito y Vives. Travelling exhibitions are also frequently based here.

The building itself is an attractive Neoclassical design by Manuel Tolsá, with something of a bizarre history. Its inhabitants have included the French Marshal Bazaine, sent by Napoleon III to advise the Emperor Maximilian – who presented the house to him as a wedding present on his marriage to a Mexican woman – and the hapless Mexican general and sometime dictator Santa Ana. Later it served for a time as a cigarette factory.

Along Juárez to the monument

Leaving the Alameda on Juárez, you can see the massive, ugly bulk of the Monumento a la Revolución ahead of you. The first couple of blocks, though, are dull, commercial streets, heavy with banks, offices and travel agents. The junction with Reforma is a major crossing of the ways, and is surrounded by modern skyscrapers and one older one – the marvellous Art Deco **Lotería Nacional** building. In here, you can watch the winning tickets being drawn each week, although the lottery offices themselves have been moved to an ordinary-looking steel-and-glass building opposite. Beyond Reforma, Juárez continues in one long block to the **Plaza de la República** and the vast **Monumento a la Revolución**. Originally intended to be a new home for the Cortes (or parliament), its construction was interrupted by the Revolution and never resumed – in the end they buried a few heroes of the Revolution under the mighty columns (including Pancho Villa and presidents Madero, Carranza and Cárdenas) and turned the whole thing into a memorial. More recently the **Museo Nacional de la Revolución** (Tues–Sun 9am–5pm; US$1.20, free on Sun) was installed beneath the monument, with a history of the Revolution told through archive pictures, old newspapers, films and life-size tableaux. Somehow the whole area seems sidelined by the mainstream of city life and is often all but deserted.

Reforma, Zona Rosa, Condesa, Roma and Polanco

West of the Alameda and Revolution monument the tenor of the city changes, particularly along the grand avenue of **Reforma**, lined by tall buildings, including Mexico's stock exchange. South of here is the tight knot of streets that make up the **Zona Rosa**, one of the city's densest concentrations of

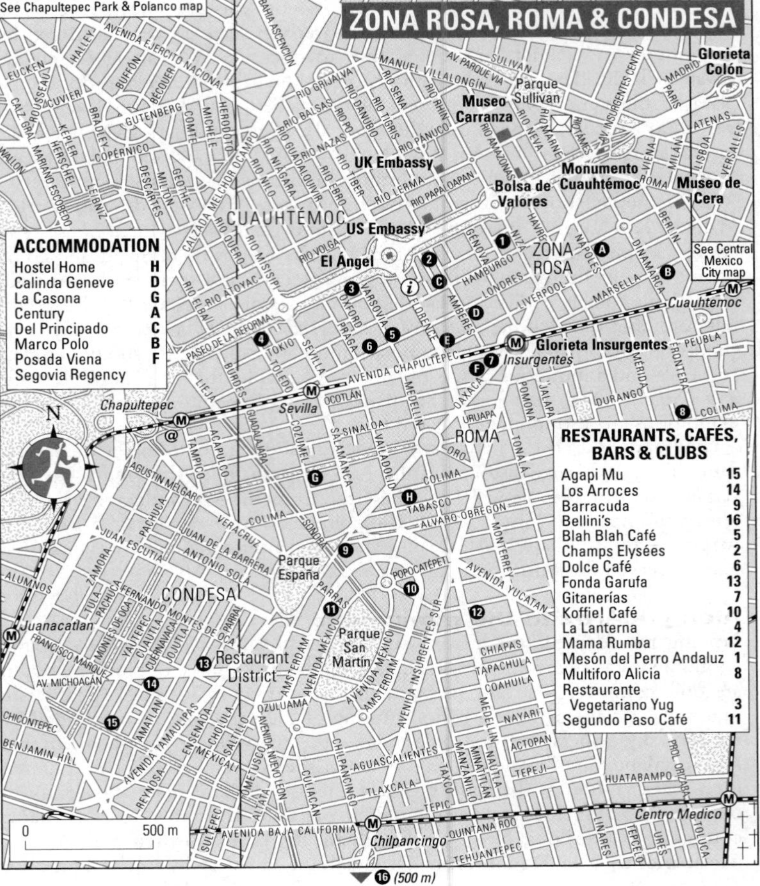

hotels, restaurants and shops. The residential districts of **Condesa** and **Roma** warrant attention for their numerous small-time art galleries and particularly for Condesa's restaurant district. The Paseo de la Reforma runs direct to Chapultepec Park, on the north edge of which lies **Polanco**, home to wealthy socialites and the stylish youth.

Paseo de la Reforma

The **Paseo de la Reforma** is the most impressive street in Mexico City. Laid out by Emperor Maximilian to provide the city with a boulevard to rival the great European capitals – and doubling as a ceremonial drive from his palace in Chapultepec to the centre – it also provided a new impetus, and direction, for the growing metropolis. The original length of the broad avenue ran simply from the park to the junction of Juárez, and although it has been extended in both directions, this stretch is still what everyone thinks of as Reforma. "**Reforma Norte**", as the extension towards Guadalupe is known, is just as wide (and the traffic just as dense), but is almost a term of disparagement. **Real Reforma**, though, remains imposing – ten lanes of traffic, lines of trees, grand statues at every intersection and perhaps three or four of the original French-style, nineteenth-century houses still surviving. Twenty or thirty years ago it was the dynamic heart of the growing city, with even relatively new buildings being torn down to make way for yet newer, taller, more prestigious towers of steel and glass. The pulse has since moved elsewhere, and the fancy shops have relocated, leaving an avenue now mostly lined with airline offices, car rental agencies and banks, and somewhat diminishing the pleasure of a stroll.

It's a long walk, some 5km from the Zócalo to the gates of Chapultepec, and you'd be well advised to take the bus – they're frequent enough to hop on and off at will. The *glorietas*, roundabouts at the major intersections, each with a distinctive statue, provide easy landmarks along the way. First is the **Glorieta Colón**, with a statue of Christopher Columbus. Around the base of the plinth are carved various friars and monks who assisted Columbus in his enterprise or brought the Catholic faith to the Mexicans. The Plaza de la República is just off to the north. Next comes the crossing of Insurgentes, nodal point of all the city's traffic, with **Cuauhtémoc**, last emperor of the Aztecs and leader of their resistance, poised aloof above it all in a plumed robe, clutching his spear, surrounded by warriors. Bas-relief engravings on the pedestal depict his torture and execution at the hands of the Spanish, desperate to discover where the Aztec treasures lay hidden. **El Ángel**, a golden winged victory atop a forty-metre column, is the third to look out for – the place to get off the bus for the heart of the Zona Rosa. Officially known as the **Monumento a la Independencia** (daily 9am–6pm; free), and finished in 1910, the column stands atop a room containing the skulls of Independence heroes Hidalgo, Aldama, Allende and Jiménez.

Zona Rosa

To the south of Reforma lies the **Zona Rosa** (Metro Insurgentes) – a triangular area bordered by Reforma, Avenida Chapultepec, and the park to the west. You'll know you're there as the streets are all named after famous cities. Packed into this tiny area are hundreds of bars, restaurants, hotels and above all shops, teeming with a vast number of tourists and a cross-section of Mexico City's aspiring middle classes. Until recently this was the city's swankiest commercial neighbourhood, but the classiest shops have moved to Polanco (see p.398) and many of the big international chains have relocated to the out-of-town malls that have sprung up around the *periférico*. It is a process that has left the Zona Rosa in an odd situation. There's no shortage of good shopping, and the selection of restaurants, cafés, clubs and bars is respectable (see p.429 & p.435), but it has lost its exclusive feel. You're as likely to spend your time here buying cheap knick-knacks at market stalls and watching street entertainers as admiring the remaining fancy store windows. Nevertheless, the presence of numerous hotels and a certain natural momentum mean that tourists still flock here and can be seen milling around being collared by English-speaking tourist-taxi drivers keen for a good fare.

You might visit during the day to eat well, then return at night for the clubs, or may choose to stay here, but you certainly wouldn't make a special journey for the sights unless you've got kids with you. The only real attraction is the **Museo de Cera**, or Wax Museum (daily 11am–7pm; US$4; Metro Cuauhtémoc), on the fringes of the Zona, at Londres 6. Thoroughly and typically tacky, with a basement chamber of horrors that includes Aztec human sacrifices, it shares its site with the **Museo de lo Increíble** (same hours and prices; joint ticket for the two museums US$6.50), which displays such marvels as flea costumes and hair sculpture.

The northern side of Reforma, where the streets are named after rivers (Tiber, Danubio and the like), is a much quieter, posh residential area officially known as **Colonia Cuauhtémoc**, though usually just bundled in with the Zona Rosa. Here you'll find some of the older embassies, notably the US embassy, on Reforma, bristling with razor wire and security cameras. Near the much more modest British embassy is the **Museo Venustiano Carranza**, Río Lerma 35 (Tues–Sat 9am–6pm, Sun 10am–4pm; US$2.80, free on Sun; Metro Insurgentes). Housed in the mansion that was the Mexico City home of the revolutionary leader and president who was shot in 1920, it contains exhibits relating to his life and to the Revolution. Not far away, just north of the junction of Reforma and Insurgentes, the **Parque Sullivan** hosts free open-air exhibitions and sales of paintings, ceramics and other works of art every Sunday (roughly 10am–4pm); some of them are very good, and a pleasant holiday atmosphere prevails.

Condesa and Roma

South of the Zona Rosa lie the residential districts of Roma and Condesa, full of quiet leafy streets once you get away from the main avenues that cut through. Both suburbs were developed in the 1930s and 1940s, but as the city expanded they became unfashionable and run-down. That all changed about a decade back when artists and the bohemian fringe were drawn here by low rents, decent housing and proximity to the centre of the city. Small-time galleries sprang up and the first of the bars and cafés opened. **Condesa**, in particular, now has perhaps the greatest concentration of good eating in the city and is definitely the place to come for lounging in pavement cafés or dining in bistro-style **restaurants** (for a rundown, see p.429). The greatest concentration is around the junction of Michoacán, Atlixco and Vicente Suárez, but establishments spread out into the surrounding streets, where you'll often find quiet neighbourhood places with tables spilling out onto the pavement. Sights in the usual sense are virtually nonexistent, but you can pass a few hours just walking the streets keeping an eye out for interesting art galleries, which seem to spring up all the time. A good starting point is **Parque México**, officially Parque San Martín, a large green space virtually in the heart of Condesa that was set aside when the owners of the horse track sold it to developers back in 1924. The streets around the park, especially Calle México, are rich in buildings constructed in Mexico's own distinctive version of Art Deco.

The Metro system gives Condesa a wide berth, with line 1 skirting the north and west while line 9 runs along the south side. Nonetheless, it is easy enough to **walk to Condesa** south from the Zona Rosa (Metro Insurgentes, Sevilla or Chapultepec); for more direct access to Condesa's main restaurant district take line 1 to Juanacatlán, and cross the Circuito Interior using the nearby footbridge. This brings you onto Francisco Marquez, which leads to the restaurants – ten minutes' walk in all.

Polanco

High-priced high-rise hotels line the northern edge of Chapultepec Park, casting their shadow over the smart suburb of Colonia **Polanco**. Unless you've got brand-name shopping in mind or need to visit one of the district's embassies, there's not much reason to come out this way, though it is instructive to stroll along **Presidente Masaryk**, the main drag, watching the beautiful people drive by in their Porsches and Lexus SUVs on their way to the Fendi or Ferragamo stores. Polanco also has great dining and we've recommended a few places on p.430, but bad restaurants don't last long here and you can do just as well strolling along and picking any place you fancy.

The only specific destination is the **Sala de Arte Público David Siqueiros**, Tres Picos 29 (Tues–Sun 10am–6pm; US$1, free on Sun; Metro Polanco), a small but interesting collection of the great muralist's later work, including sketches he made of the Polyforum murals (see p.410). They're all displayed in his former residence and studio, donated (along with everything in it) to the people of Mexico just 25 days before his death in 1973. If it is not already playing, ask to see the hour-long **video** (in English) on his life and work made just before his death, and watch it surrounded by his murals which cover just about every piece of wall space.

The Bosque de Chapultepec and the Museo Nacional de Antropología

Chapultepec Park, or the **Bosque de Chapultepec** (Tues–Sun 5am–4.30pm; free), is a vast green area, some 400 hectares in all, dotted with trees, scattered with fine museums – among them the marvellous **Museo Nacional de Antropología** – boating lakes, gardens, playing fields and a zoo. Ultimately, it provides an escape from the pressures of the city for seemingly millions of Mexicans: on Sundays, when at least a visit is all but compulsory for locals and many of the museums are free, you can barely move for the throng. They call it the lungs of the city, and like the lungs of most of the city's inhabitants its health leaves a lot to be desired, though it still manages to look pretty good and remains one of Mexico City's most enduring attractions. The most visited areas get a heavy pounding from the crowds and some areas are occasionally fenced off to allow the plants to recover their equilibrium. There has even been talk of sealing the whole place off for three years to give the grass a chance to grow back, but that is never likely to happen – public outrage at the very suggestion has seen to that. However, the entire park and many of the museums are closed on Mondays.

The park is divided into three sections, the first and easternmost containing the bulk of the interest, including the Anthropology, Modern Art and Rufino Tamayo museums and the zoo. The second section is mostly aimed at kids, with an amusement park, technology museum and natural history museum, while section three contains aquatic and marine parks open at weekends.

The rocky outcrop of **Chapultepec** (Nahuatl meaning "Hill of the Locust"), which lends its name to the entire area, is mentioned in Toltec mythology, but first gained historical significance in the thirteenth century when it was no more than another island among the lakes and salt marshes of the valley. Here the Mexica, still a wandering, savage tribe, made their first home – a very temporary one before they were defeated and driven off by neighbouring cities, provoked beyond endurance. And here they returned once Tenochtitlán's power was established, channelling water from the springs into the city, and turning Chapultepec into a summer resort for the emperor, with plentiful hunting and fishing around a fortified palace. Several Aztec rulers had their portraits carved into the rock of the hill, though most were destroyed by the Spanish soon after the Conquest.

Park practicalities

Chapultepec is a big place with a lot to see. You could easily spend a couple of days here and still not see it all, but if you are selective you can see the best of it in one tiring day. It is tempting to visit on Sunday when a lot of the museums are free and the park is at its vibrant best, but expect the Museo Nacional de Antropología and the zoo to be packed.

How you approach the park depends on what you want to see first, but the easiest access is via the Chapultepec Metro station, from where you follow the crowds over a broad bridge across the Circuito Interior (inner ring road). Straight ahead you'll see the Niños Héroes monument and the Castillo containing the Museo Nacional de Historia. The entrances to the Museo Nacional de Antropología and its acolytes are all grouped together along Paseo de la Reforma, less than a fifteen-minute walk from the Metro station, but if that is where you are headed first it is faster to catch a *pesero* ("Auditorio", "Reforma Km 13" and others) anywhere along Reforma. Visitors with kids may want to head straight for the Second Section, either picking up a *pesero* along Avenida Constituyentes (Routes 2, 24 and others) from Metro Chapultepec, or going direct to Metro Constituyentes and walking from there.

Wherever you go in the park there'll be someone selling **food and drink**, and the Museo Nacional de Antropología has a good (if pricey) **restaurant**. Nonetheless, it is as well to take some snacks (or an entire picnic lunch) and a big bottle of water: museum hopping can be thirsty work.

Chapultepec Hill

As you approach the park from the Chapultepec Metro station you're confronted by Chapultepec Hill, crowned by Maximilian's very peaceful-looking "castle". In front of it stands the strange, six-columned monument dedicated to the **Niños Héroes**, commemorating the cadets who attempted to defend the castle (then a military academy) against American invaders in 1847. According to the story, probably apocryphal, the last six flung themselves off the cliff wrapped in Mexican flags rather than surrender. The **Castillo** itself was built only in 1785 as a summer retreat for the Spanish viceroy – until then it had been the site of a hermitage established on the departure of the Aztec rulers. Its role as a military school followed Independence, but the present shape was dictated by Maximilian who remodelled it in the image of his Italian villa. Today it houses the National History Museum.

First, though, as you climb the hill – and for the less able-bodied, there are land trains that'll take you up and bring you back for US$1 – you pass the modern **Museo de Caracol** (Tues–Sun 9am–4.15pm; US$3.20, free on Sun), devoted to "the Mexican people's struggle for Liberty". It's full name is the Museo Galería de la Lucha del Pueblo Mexicano por su Libertad, but it's colloquially known as the "shell museum" for the snail-like spiralling route through the displays. These trace the history of the constant wars that have beset the country – from Independence, through the American and French interventions to the Revolution – and after the recent renovation look pretty good.

Spread over two floors of the castle, the **Museo Nacional de Historia** (Tues–Sun 9am–5pm; US$3.70, free on Sun) is a more traditional collection. The setting is very much part of the attraction, with many rooms retaining the opulent furnishings left behind by Maximilian and Carlota, or by later inhabitants with equally expensive tastes – notably Porfirio Díaz. Rivalling the decor is a small collection of carriages, including the fabulously pompous Cinderella-goes-to-the-ball state coaches favoured by Maximilian. A collection of furniture,

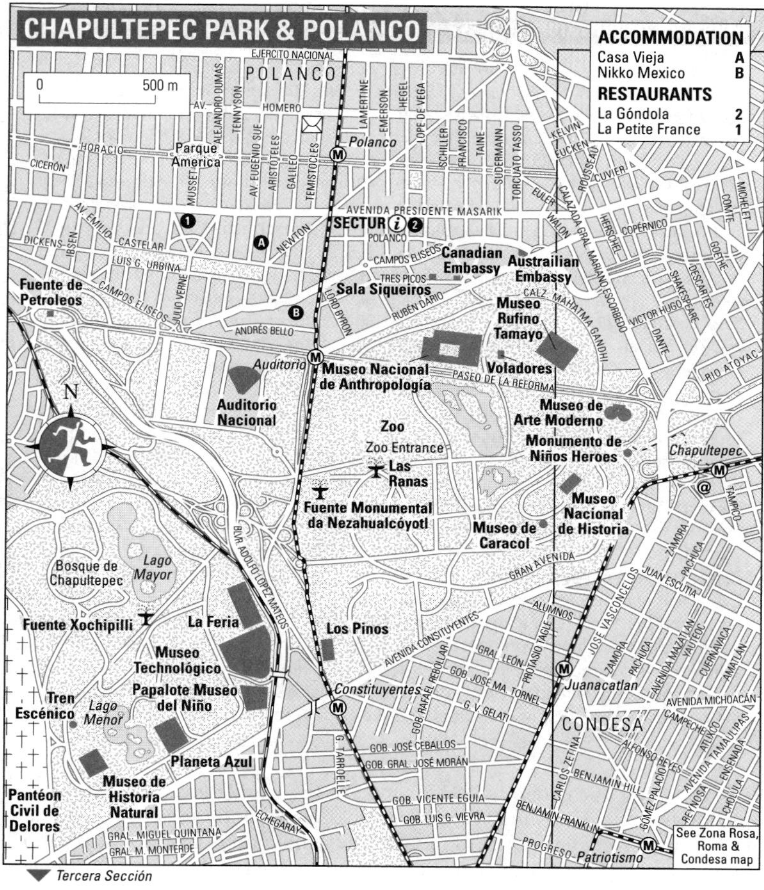

glassware and medals leads on to the main attraction of the lower floor, a series of ornate rooms viewed from a black-and-white tiled terrace which affords great views over the park and city. Peer into Maximilian's office, games room and drawing room, all gilt and rich dark woods, then move on to Carlota's bedroom and a gorgeous tiled bathroom.

The upper floor is arranged around a formal rooftop garden off which you can visit yet more sumptuous rooms and a magnificent Parisian stained-glass wall imported by Díaz and depicting five goddesses in a Greco-Roman setting. There are several murals here as well, including a number of works by **Orozco** and **Siqueiros**, but the ones by **Juan O'Gorman** most directly attract attention for their single-minded political message.

Museo Nacional de Antropología

The park's outstanding attraction – for many people the main justification for visiting the city at all – is the **Museo Nacional de Antropología** (Tues–Sat

Museum orientation

The museum's rooms, each devoted to a separate period or culture, are ranged chronologically in an anticlockwise pattern around the central courtyard. As you come into the **entrance hall** there's a small circular space with temporary exhibitions, usually very interesting and devoted to the latest developments in archeology; here too is the small **Sala de Orientación**, which presents an audiovisual overview of the major ancient cultures. Off to the left you'll find the **library** and a **shop** selling postcards, souvenirs, books in several languages on Mexican culture, archeology and history, and detailed **guidebooks** (in English, French and German US$5.50), which provide full descriptions of most of the important pieces. The **ticket office**, and the **entrance** to the museum proper, is by the huge glass doors to the right, where you can also rent headsets which effectively take you on a **tour** of the museums highlights – US$5 in Spanish, US$6 in English. They're very rushed, but you do get around the whole thing with some form of explanation: labelling of individual items is mostly in Spanish, though the general introduction to each room is accompanied by an English translation.

The full tour of the museum starts on the right-hand side with three **introductory rooms** explaining what anthropology is, the nature of and relationship between the chief Mesoamerican cultures, and the region's prehistory. It's worth spending time here if only to note the clear acknowledgement of the continuing discrimination against Mexico's native people. They're followed on the right-hand side by halls devoted to the **pre-Classic**, **Teotihuacán** and **Toltec** cultures. At the far end is the vast **Mexica** (Aztec) room, followed around the left wing by **Oaxaca** (Mixtec and Zapotec), **Gulf of Mexico** (Olmec), **Maya** and the cultures of the north and west. Every hall has at least one outstanding feature, but if you have limited time, the Aztec and the Maya rooms are the **highlights**; what else you see should depend on what area of the country you plan to head on to. The upper floor is given over to the **ethnography collections** devoted to the life and culture of the various indigenous groups today; stairs lead up from each side. Downstairs, behind the hall devoted to the cultures of the north and west, is a very welcome **restaurant**.

9am–7pm, Sun 10am–6pm; US$3.70), one of the world's great museums, not only for its collection, which is vast, rich and diverse, but for the originality and practicality of its design. Opened in 1964, the exhibition halls surround a patio with a small pond and a vast, square concrete umbrella supported by a single slender pillar around which splashes an artificial cascade. The halls are ringed by gardens, many of which contain outdoor exhibits. If you're rushed it can all be taken in on one visit, but it is far more satisfactory to spread your visit over two days. As stated before, the museum can get rather crowded on Sundays when admission is free.

The entrance from Reforma is marked by a colossal statue of the rain god Tlaloc – the story goes that its move here from its original home in the east of the city was accompanied by furious downpours in the midst of a drought. The museum is entered from a large open plaza, at one end of which is a small clearing pierced by a twenty-metre pole from which **voladores** "fly". This Totonac ceremony (see box on p.569 for details) is performed several times a day, and loses a lot of its appeal through its commercial nature – an assistant canvasses the crowd for donations as they perform – but it is still an impressive spectacle.

Pre-Classic

The **Pre-Classic** room covers the development of the first cultures in the Valley of México and surrounding highlands – pottery and clay figurines from these early agricultural communities predominate. Notice especially the **small female figures** dated 1700–1300 BC from Tlatilco (a site in the suburbs), probably related to some form of fertility or harvest rites. Later the influence of the growing Olmec culture begins to be seen in art, including the amazing **acrobat**, also from Tlatilco. With the development of more formal religion, recognizable images of gods appear: several of these, from Cuicuilco in the south of the city, depict **Huehueteotl**, the old god or god of fire, as an old man with flames on his back.

Teotihuacán

The next hall is devoted to **Teotihuacán** (see p.446), the first great city in the Valley of México. Growing sophistication is immediately apparent in the more elaborate nature of the pottery vessels and the use of new materials, shells, stone and jewels. There's a full-scale reproduction of part of the **Temple of Quetzalcoatl** at Teotihuacán, brightly polychromed as it would originally have been. It contains the remains of nine sacrificial victims dressed as warriors and complete with their funerary necklaces: a relatively recent confirmation of human sacrifice and militarism at Teotihuacán. Nearby is a reconstruction of the inside courtyard and central temple of an apartment complex bedecked in vibrant murals representing ritual life in the city, including *The Paradise of Tlaloc*, a depiction of the heaven reserved for warriors and ball-players who died in action. Many new gods appear, too – as well as more elaborate versions of Huehueteotl, there are representations of Tlaloc, of his companion Chalchiutlicue, goddess of rivers and lakes, of Mictlantecuhtli, god of death (a stone skull, originally inlaid with gems), and of Xipe Totec, a god of spring, clothed in the skin of a man flayed alive as a symbol of regeneration.

Toltec

The **Toltec** room actually begins with objects from Xochicalco, a city near modern Cuernavaca (see p.479), which flourished between the fall of Teotihuacán and the heyday of Tula. The large stone carvings and pottery show distinct Maya influence: particularly lovely is the stylized stone **head of a macaw**, similar to ones found on Maya ball-courts in Honduras. Highlights of the section devoted to Tula are the weighty stone carvings, including one of the Atlantean columns from the main temple there, representing a warrior. Also of note are the **Chac-mool**, a reclining figure with a receptacle on his stomach in which sacrificial offerings were placed, symbolizing the divine messenger who delivered them to the gods; and the **standard bearer**, a small human figure that acted as a flagpole when a standard was inserted into the hole between its clasped hands. This is found high up, above a large frieze. Down and to the left is the stone relief of a **dancing jaguar**; and the exquisite sculpture of a **coyote's head** with a bearded man emerging from its mouth – possibly a warrior in a headdress – inlaid with mother-of-pearl, and with teeth made of bone.

Also here are reproductions of seventh-century frescoes of a birdman and jaguar from Cacaxtla (see p.462), found by a campesino tending his fields in 1975; and an extensive collection of rings, which serve as goals in the ancient ball-game.

Mexica

Next comes the biggest and richest of them all, the **Mexica Gallery**, characterized above all by massive yet intricate stone sculpture, but also displaying pottery, small stone objects, even wooden musical instruments. Two of the finest pieces stand at the entrance: the **Ocelotl-Cuauhxicalli**, a jaguar with a hollow in its back in which the hearts of human sacrifices were placed (it may have been the companion of the eagle in the Templo Mayor museum; the two were found very close to each other, though over eighty years apart); and the **Teocalli de la Guerra Sagrada** (Temple of the Sacred War), a model of an Aztec pyramid decorated with many of the chief gods and with symbols relating to the calendar. There are hundreds of other powerful pieces – most of the vast Aztec pantheon is represented – and everywhere snakes, eagles, and human hearts and skulls are prominent. Among them is a vast statue of **Coatlicue**, goddess of the earth, life and death, and mother of the gods. She is shown with two serpents above her shoulders representing the flow of blood; her necklace of hands and hearts and pendant of a skull represent life and death respectively; her dress is made of snakes; her feet are eagles' claws. As a counterpoint to the viciousness of most of this, be sure to notice **Xochipilli**, the god of love and flowers, dance and poetry (and incidentally featured on the hundred-peso bill). You'll come across him wearing a mask and sitting cross-legged on a throne strewn with flowers and butterflies, to the left of the entrance as you come in. Also impressive is a reconstructed version of **Moctezuma's headdress**, resplendent in bright blue Quetzal feathers.

The undoubted highlight, though, is the enormous 24-tonne **Piedra del Sol**, the Stone of the Sun or Aztec Calendar Stone. The latter, popular name is not strictly accurate, for this is much more a vision of the Aztec cosmos, completed under Moctezuma only a few years before the Spanish arrived. The stone was found by early colonists, and deliberately reburied for fear that it would spread unrest among the population. After being dug up again in the Zócalo in 1790 it spent years propped up against the walls of the cathedral. You'll pick up the most detailed description on a guided tour, but briefly: in the centre is the sun god and personification of the fifth sun, Tonatiuh, with a tongue in the form of a sacrificial knife and claws holding human hearts on each side, representing the need for human sacrifice to nourish the sun; around him are symbols for the four previous incarnations of the sun – a jaguar, wind, water and fiery rain; this whole central conglomeration forms the sign for the date on which the fifth world would end (as indeed, with defeat by the Spanish, it fairly accurately did). Encircling all this are hieroglyphs representing the twenty days of the Aztec month and other symbols of cosmic importance, and the whole thing is surrounded by two serpents.

Oaxaca

Moving round to the third side of the museum you reach the halls devoted to cultures based away from the highlands of the centre, starting, in the corner of the museum, with the **Zapotec** and **Mixtec** people of **Oaxaca**. Although the two cultures evolved side by side, the Zapotecs flourished earliest (from around 900 BC to 800 AD) as accomplished architects with an advanced scientific knowledge, and also as makers of magnificent pottery with a pronounced Olmec influence. From around 800 AD many of their sites were taken over by the Mixtecs, whose overriding talents were as craftsmen and artists, working in metal, precious stone and clay. The great site for both is Monte Albán (see p.603).

The Zapotec collection demonstrates a fine sense of movement in the human figures: the reproduction of part of the carved facade of the Temple of the Dancers at Monte Albán; a model of a temple with a parrot sitting in it (in the "Monte Albán II" case); vases and urns in the form of various gods; and the superb jade mask representing the bat god. Among the Mixtec objects are many beautifully polychromed clay vessels, including a cup with a humming-bird perched on its rim, and sculptures in jade and quartz crystal. Reproductions of Zapotec and Mixtec tombs show how many of the finer small objects were discovered.

Gulf of Mexico

Next is the **Gulf of Mexico** room, in which are displayed some of the treasures of **Olmec** art as well as objects produced in this region during the Classic period. The Olmec civilization is considered the mother culture of Mexico for its advanced development as early as 1500 BC, which provided much of the basis for the later Teotihuacán and Maya cultures. Olmec figures are delightful, but have many puzzling aspects, in particular their strikingly African features, nowhere better displayed than in some of the famed **colossal heads** dating from 1200–200 BC, long before Africa is supposed to have had any connection with the Americas. Many of the smaller pieces show evidence of deliberate deformation of the skull and teeth. The statue known as "the wrestler", with arms akimbo as if at the point of starting a bout, and the many tiny objects in jade and other polished stones are all outstanding. The later cultures are substantially represented, with fine figures and excellent pottery above all. The two most celebrated pieces are a statue of **Huehueteotl**, looking thoroughly grouchy with a brazier perched on his head, and the so-called **Huastec Adolescent**, a young Huastec Indian priest of Quetzalcoatl (perhaps the god himself) with an elaborately decorated naked body and a child on his back.

Maya

The hall devoted to the **Maya** is perhaps the most varied of all, reflecting the longest-lived and widest-spread of the Mesoamerican cultures. In some ways it's a disappointment, since their greatest achievements were in architecture and in the decoration of their temples – many of which, unlike those of the Aztecs, are still standing – so that the found objects seem relatively unimpressive. Nevertheless, there are reproductions of several buildings, or parts of them, friezes and columns taken from them, and extensive collections of jewellery, pottery and minor sculpture. Steps lead down into a section devoted to burial practices, including a reproduction of the Royal Tomb at **Palenque** (see p.685) with many of the objects found there – notably the prince's jade death mask. Outside, several small temples from relatively obscure sites are reproduced, the Temple of Paintings from **Bonampak** among them. The three rooms of the temple are entirely covered in frescoes representing the coronation of a new prince, a great battle, and the subsequent punishments and celebrations. They are much easier to visit than the originals and in far better condition.

Northern and western societies

As a finale to the archeological collections on the ground floor, there's a large room devoted to the north and the west of the country. **Northern** societies on the whole developed few large centres, remaining isolated nomadic or agricultural communities. The small quantities of pottery, weapons and jewellery that have survived show a close affinity with native tribes of the American Southwest. The **west** was far more developed, but it, too, has left relatively few traces, and many of the best examples of **Tarascan culture** (see p.250) remain in Guadalajara. Among the highlights here are some delightful small human and animal figurines in stone and clay, a Tarascan Chac-mool, the jade mask of Malinaltepec inlaid with a turquoise and red-shell mosaic, and a two-storey reconstruction of the houses at Paquimé in the Chihuahua desert.

The Ethnography Section

The **Ethnography Section** is on the upper floor. You must cross the courtyard back towards the beginning of the museum before climbing the stairs – otherwise you'll go round in reverse order. The rooms relate as far as possible to those below them, showing through photographs, models, maps and examples of local crafts the lifestyle of surviving indigenous groups in the areas today. Regional dress and reproductions of various types of hut and cabin form a major part of this inevitably rather sanitized look at the poorest (and most oppressed) people in Mexico, and there are also objects relating to their more important cults and ceremonies.

Around the Museo Nacional de Antropología

The enormous success of the Museo de Antropología has led to a spate of other audacious modern **exhibition halls** being set up in the park. Two are very close by, and with the adjoining **zoo**, make this one of the finest concentrations of diversion in the otherwise sprawling city.

Museo de Arte Moderno

Some 300m east of the Museo Nacional de Antropología on Paseo de la Reforma lies the **Museo de Arte Moderno** (Tues–Sun 10am–6pm; US$1.50, free on Sun). This consists of two low circular buildings devoted to twentieth-century Mexican and Latin American art. The majority of the galleries, along with a separate gallery reached through the **sculpture garden**, are devoted to temporary and touring exhibitions, which are usually well worth inspection. The **permanent collection** is housed on the ground floor of the Sala Xavier Villaurrutia, to the right as you enter, and should not be missed.

All the major Mexican artists of the twentieth century are well represented. Among several works by Siqueiros, the most powerful is *Madre Campesina*, whose peasant woman carries her child barefoot through an unforgiving desert of cacti. There's a whole corner devoted to Orozco, and oils by Diego Rivera, notably a portrait of his second wife, Lupe Marín, painted in 1938, long after their divorce. Look too for Olga Costa's *Vendedora de Frutas*, whose fruit-seller surrounded by bananas, sugar cane, watermelons, pumpkins, pawpaws, soursops and *mameyes*, all painted in vibrant reds and yellows, is about as Mexican a subject as you could want. The star attraction is Frida Kahlo's *Las Dos Fridas*, which stands out even among the museum's selection of haunting and disturbing canvases by Kahlo. It is one of her earliest full-scale paintings, and one whose theme she was constantly to return to. In it, Frida is depicted on the left in a white traditional dress, her heart torn and wounded, and her hand being held by a stronger Frida on the right, dressed in modern clothes and holding a locket with a picture of her husband Diego Rivera as a boy. Alongside these great paintings are works by less well-known Mexican luminaries: José Chávez Morado with his beautiful *Plantas y Serpientes*, and an intriguing multiple self-portrait by Juan O'Gorman.

Museo Rufino Tamayo

Hidden among trees across the street from the Museum of Modern Art is the **Museo Rufino Tamayo** (Tues–Sun 10am–6pm; US$1.50, free on Sun; Ⓦwww.museotamayo.org), another fine collection of modern art – this one with an international focus. The modernist structure was built by the artist Rufino Tamayo, whose work in murals and on smaller projects was far more abstract and less political than the Big Three, though he was their approximate contemporary and enjoys a reasonable amount of international fame. There is much of his own work here, and exhibits of his techniques and theories, but also a fairly impressive collection of European and American twentieth-century art – most of it from Tamayo's private collection. Artists represented may include Picasso, Miró, Magritte, Francis Bacon and Henry Moore, though not all of these are on permanent display. First-rate contemporary international exhibits usually find their way here and sometimes take over the space of parts of the permanent collection.

Lago Chapultepec and the Parque Zoológico de Chapultepec

On the south side of Reforma, opposite the Museo de Antropología lies **Lago Chapultepec**, where you can rent **boats** and while away a leisurely afternoon. At the western side of the lake is the main entrance to the **Parque Zoológico de Chapultepec** (Tues–Sun 9am–4.30pm; free; Ⓦwww.cnf.org.mx), which occupies a large section in the centre of the park and is divided up into climatic zones – desert, tropical, temperate forests, etc – some of which work better than others. Enclosures are mostly open-air and are tolerably large, though the animals still look bored and confined, and you wonder about their sanity on a Sunday afternoon when half of Mexico City's children seem to be here vying for the animals' attentions. Probably the most satisfying sections are the most archetypally Mexican, the desert zone, and the enclosure of **Xoloitzcuintle**, the hairless dogs that represent the last surviving of four pre-Columbian breeds.

All the big beasts are here too: tigers, bears, lions, bison, camels, giraffes, hippos, elephants and the ever-popular **giant pandas**. The zoo is inordinately proud of these, evidenced by the posters around town which advertise new baby bears when they are born – in fact, it was the first place in the world to breed giant pandas in captivity.

The Auditorio Nacional and Los Pinos

Continuing west from the zoo, Reforma crosses Calzada Chivatito at Metro Auditorio, beyond which is the **Auditorio Nacional**, a major venue for dance, theatre and music events, with a couple of small theatres and the enormous auditorium. Further out Reforma leaves the park via the Fuente de Petróleos, a complex of modern skyscrapers surrounding a monument to the nationalization of the oil industry, and heads into Las Lomas, an expensive suburb whose luxury villas are mostly hidden behind high walls and heavy security gates.

Heading south from Metro Auditorio, Calzada Chivatito becomes Molino del Rey, a street named after the major battle here during the Mexican–American War. There are still barracks here, along with **Los Pinos**, the president's official residence, which is strictly off limits. A couple of footbridges lead from outside the barracks across the *periférico* (Bulevar Lopez Mateos) to the park's second section.

The Nuevo Bosque de Chapultepec: Segunda and Tercera secciónes

Over the years, new sections of parkland have been added to the west of the original Bosque de Chapultepec. These are occasionally still referred to as the **Nuevo Bosque de Chapultepec**, but are more commonly known as the

Segunda Sección, or Second Section (marked on signs and maps as "2a Sección") and **Tercera Sección**, or Third Section (3a Sección). With very few places to cross the *periférico*, it is difficult to reach the newer parts of the park from the old. It is far better to make a separate visit (see "Park practicalities", p.400) to these sections, epecially if you've got kids, who will appreciate the child-friendly museums, boating lake and the city's major amusement park, La Feria. There are fewer genuinely compelling reasons to visit either section for adults, though the second section is an enjoyable area to stroll about, and a good deal quieter than the main section of the park.

Segunda Sección

Approaching the second section from Metro Constituyentes, follow Avenida Constituyentes west for a few metres and then cross it on a footbridge. Follow a short street to the *periférico*, also crossed by a nearby footbridge, to bring you to the **Museo Tecnológico** (daily 9am–5pm; free), entered on its west side, with its central building surrounded by outdoor exhibits. Many are sponsored by some of Mexico's biggest companies but remain unengaging affairs, at odds with the professionalism evident in the displays in most of Mexico City's museums. You can walk around a model of a geothermal power plant, another of a hydro project, and assorted bits of machinery and railway rolling stock all too static or inaccessible to really arouse much interest. Inside it is more accomplished, with hands-on displays, flight simulators and collections of models. It's fun for kids to play, but only educational if their (or your) Spanish is fairly good.

Right next door is **La Feria** (Semana Santa, July, Aug & Dec daily 10am–9pm; rest of the year Mon–Fri 10am–6pm, Sat & Sun 10am–9pm; US$1), the city's premier fun park complete with assorted rides and sideshows, easily the best being the old-fashioned wooden roller coaster (*montaña rusa*). A US$6 pass gives you access to most of the rides, but not the roller coaster (US$1).

On the other side of the Museo Tecnológico lies **Papalote Museo del Niño**, Constituyentes 268 (Mon–Fri 9am–1pm & 2–6pm, Sat & Sun 10am–2pm & 3–7pm; US$6), a kind of cross between an adventure playground and a science experiment, with loads of fascinating hands-on experiments, plus an IMAX cinema (US$7; combined ticket US$11). It can have the atmosphere of a psychotic kindergarten, but if you have kids, it will keep them entertained.

Heading west from Papalote you pass the rather tacky **Planeta Azul** fun park (daily 9am–6pm; US$2, US$4 or US$5, depending on what attractions are included) en route to the **Museo de Historia Natural** (Tues–Sun 10am–5pm; US$1.75, free on Tues), ten interconnecting domes filled with displays on nature and conservation, biology and geology, including rundowns on Mexico's mineral wealth, flora and fauna. Modern and well presented – and with the obligatory dinosaurs – it is again particularly popular with children.

Running north from here is the **Tren Escénico** (Tues–Sun 10am–4.30pm; US$0.50), a mini railway that will take you on a short loop around the park through some gum trees, and the ceremonial Fuente Xochipilli. From the fountain, a long pool gradually descends to a spot where you can double back past La Feria and the Museo Tecnológico, where you started.

Tercera Sección

The newest section of the park, the **Tercera Sección**, lies yet further west, beyond the **Panteón Civil de Dolores** cemetery (daily 6am–6pm), where Diego Rivera, José Clemente Orozco and other illustrious Mexicans are buried. To get there catch a *pesero* (route #24 to "Panteón Dolores", "Rollo" or "Atlantis") from Metro Chapultepec or along Avenida Constituyentes.

In this section, the main draws – open to the general public only on weekends and public holidays – are **El Rollo** (Sat & Sun 10am–6pm; US$8.50; Ⓦwww.elrollo.com.mx), a water park with all manner of chutes, slides and wave generators; and **Atlantis** (Sat & Sun 10am–6pm; US$4.50), a kind of zoo-cum-circus with marine mammals and assorted birds, some of them trained to take part in various performances, for some of which there is an additional fee.

South of the centre

Mexico City spreads itself furthest to the south, where a series of old villages swallowed up by the urban sprawl harbour some of the most enticing destinations outside the centre. The colonial **suburbs** of **Coyoacán** and **San Ángel**, each with a couple of worthwhile museums, make a tranquil respite from the

Getting to the southern suburbs

It's not at all difficult to get out to any of the sights on **public transport**, but getting from one to the other can be tricky if you're cutting across the main north–south routes. In fact, there is easily enough to see to justify a couple of separate trips out this way, thereby avoiding the slightly complicated matter of traversing the southern suburbs – and while none of the connections you have to make is impossible, it's worth taking a few short taxi rides between them, from San Ángel to Coyoacán, for example, or from Coyoacán to Rivera's Anahuacalli Museum.

If you want to see as much as possible in a day or even an afternoon, you might consider getting a **tourist taxi** (see p.370) to take you round the lot. If you bargain furiously, this may not be as expensive as it sounds; indeed it sometimes seems that you can barely be paying for the fuel used. Alternatively there are **coach tours** run by several of the bigger travel agencies in the Zona Rosa.

For **San Ángel and the University City**, the best approach is along Insurgentes Sur, where you'll find a constant stream of buses and *peseros*. Their main destinations should be chalked up, or displayed on a card, on the windscreen – look for "San Ángel", "Ciudad Universitaria", "CU", or "UNAM" for Universidad Nacional Autónoma de México. Other terminals for heading south are the bus stands by Metro Chapultepec or at Metro Tasqueña for services along the Calzada de Tlalpan and to the southwest of the city, above all to Xochimilco. If you'd rather stick to the **Metro**, take line 3 to Miguel Ángel de Quevedo.

To get to Coyoacán from San Ángel, buses head down Altavista by the *San Ángel Inn*; from the centre, buses leave from Metros Chapultepec, Insurgentes or Cuauhtémoc. In each case look for "Coyoacán" or "Colonia del Valle/Coyoacán". There's also a trolleybus that runs down Lázaro Cárdenas against the flow of traffic from a stop close by Bellas Artes. Metro line 3, too, passes close by, though note that Viveros station is considerably closer to the action than Coyoacán: from here walk south on Avenida Universidad, then turn left (east) to reach the centre. If you're coming straight from the centre of town down Avenida Cuauhtémoc or Avenida Lázaro Cárdenas, it makes sense to visit the Kahlo and Trotsky museums first, in which case you'll want to get off the bus immediately after passing under Avenida Río Churubusco. The Metro stops are slightly more distant, but a good approach is to take line 2 to General Anaya and walk west from there past the Museo de las Intervenciones and the Trotsky and Frida Kahlo houses.

city centre's hustle, and a startling contrast to the ultramodern bravado of the architecture of the nearby National Autonomous University of Mexico (UNAM).

There are echoes of ancient Mexico, too, in the archeological site of **Cuicuilco** and in the canals of **Xochimilco** – all that remains of the great valley lakes – and a couple of stations on the Diego Rivera trail, his remarkable collection of antiquities in the **Museo Anahuacalli**, and a very fine collection of paintings by him and Frida Kahlo in the Museo Dolores Olmeda Patiño.

Out here too is the residential area of **El Pedregal**, which gets its name from the vast lava flow that spreads south of San Ángel through the University City and on to the south of Coyoacán. Craggy and dramatic, it was regarded as a completely useless stretch of land, the haunt of bandits and brigands until the early 1950s when architect Luis Barragan began to build extraordinarily imaginative houses here, using the uneven lava as a feature. Now it's filled with the most amazing collection of luxury homes, though even if you drive around you'll unfortunately see little of what is behind the high walls and security fences.

Insurgentes

Insurgentes, the most direct approach to the suburbs, is interesting in its own right: leaving behind the Glorieta de Insurgentes (the roundabout at Insurgentes Metro station), it runs almost perfectly straight all the way out to the university, lined the whole way with huge department stores and malls, cinemas, restaurants and office buildings. A little under halfway to San Ángel, you pass on the right the enormous **World Trade Center**, the tallest building in the city and topped by *Bellini's*, an expensive revolving restaurant (see p.430).

Just south of the World Trade Center, and on the right (if heading south) is the garish **Polyforum Siqueiros** (daily 9am–6pm; US$1.50; ⓣ55/5536-4520 to 23, ⓦwww.polyforumsiqueiros.com) designed and decorated by David Siqueiros, its exterior plastered in brash paintings by Siqueiros and some thirty other artists. Inside, it contains what is allegedly the world's largest mural (about 4500 square metres), painted by Siqueiros alone, entitled *The March of Humanity on Earth and Towards the Cosmos*. For the full impact of the changing perspectives and use of sculptural techniques, try to see the **sound-and-light show** show (in principle Sat & Sun 10am, noon & 1.30pm; US$3) with taped narration by Siqueiros. Elsewhere, the building houses visiting art exhibitions and a sizeable display of expensive crafts for sale.

Beyond this monster you shortly pass close by the **Plaza México**, the largest bullring in the world, with a capacity of 48,000. You can't actually see it from Insurgentes, but it's only a ten-minute walk along Avenida San Antonio, hard by the **Estadio Azul**, a 65,000-seat soccer stadium that is home to Cruz Azul. Finally, just before San Ángel comes the **Teatro de los Insurgentes**, its facade covered in a huge mosaic designed by Diego Rivera depicting the history of Mexican theatre, and assorted historical figures. At the top are Los Insurgentes of Mexico's War of Independence: Hidalgo, Morelos and Benito Juárez on the left, and Zapata on the right.

San Ángel

The upmarket colonial suburb of **San Ángel** lies 12km southwest of central Mexico City, clustered around the point where Insurgentes Sur and Revolución almost meet, linked by the 200-metre-long Avenida La Paz. With its markets and ancient mansions around flower-draped patios, San Ángel is a very exclusive place to live, underlined by the high-priced shops – Cartier,

Italian designer furniture and the like. It makes an inviting place to visit, packed with little restaurants and cafés where you can sit outside and watch the crowds go by, and is especially appealing on Saturdays when the delightful **Plaza San Jacinto** is taken over by **Bazar Sábado**, a lively outdoor art market. Initially, the Saturday market was based in one of the mansions on the square, which still opens every weekend selling upmarket crafts and artworks, but nowadays there are stalls in all the surrounding streets, with fairground rides and freak shows. The plaza is surrounded by San Ángel's oldest mansions, notably the eighteenth-century **Casa del Risco**, at no. 15 (Tues–Sun 10am–5pm; free), housing a collection of antique furniture and paintings, with an extraordinary fountain in the patio made from old porcelain plates and cups, broken and unbroken.

Whether you choose to visit on Saturday or one of the quieter days of the week, consider sticking around until evening to blow an appreciable wad of cash on some of the finest dining in the city (see p.430).

Museo del Carmen

San Ángel takes its name from the former Carmelite Convent of San Angelo Mártir, on Avenida Revolución just south of its junction with Avenida La Paz, which is now run as the **Museo del Carmen** (Tues–Sun 10am–4.45pm; US$3.20, free on Sun). Its three tiled domes, brightly coloured predominantly in yellow, still preside over this part of town and add the final touch of grace to this lovely example of early seventeenth-century architecture. The church is still used but the rest of the convent has become a museum where just walking through the maze of monks' cells, rooms and courtyards is pleasure enough, though there's also an extensive collection of colonial religious paintings and furniture. Just about everyone wants to make their way to the crypt to see the dozen **mummies**, found here by troops during the Revolution and thought to be eighteenth-century nuns and monks, now displayed behind glass. Elsewhere, check out the extensive displays on daily life in New Spain and a collection of eighteenth-century oils by Cristóbal de Vallalpando.

Museo de Arte Carrillo-Gil

Heading north along Avenida Revolución, past a small flower market, you reach the **Museo de Arte Carrillo-Gil**, Revolución 1608 (Tues–Sun 10am–6pm; US$1.50, free on Sun), a surprisingly good museum of modern art that seems a little incongruous in old colonial San Ángel. The museum was built in 1974 to house the collection of skilled painter, art critic and friend of Siqueiros, Dr Alvaro Carrillo, a long-time supporter of the avant-garde who had been amassing works since the 1930s. Three airy and spacious floors feature works by Mexicans including Rivera (a couple of Cubist canvases), Siqueiros, and most importantly, Orozco, of whose work *Zapata* and *Christ Destroying His Cross* are the most striking examples here. There's also a smattering of international big names, but many are out on loan or stored away to make space for the numerous temporary exhibits and contemporary installations.

Museo Casa Estudio Diego Rivera y Frida Kahlo and the San Ángel Inn

From the Museo de Arte Carillo-Gil it's just over half a kilometre along Avenida Altavista to the **Museo Casa Estudio Diego Rivera y Frida Kahlo**, Calle Diego Rivera 2 (Tues–Sun 10am–6pm; US$1, free on Sun), a pair of modernist houses built for Diego Rivera and Frida Kahlo in 1931–32 by the leading architect of the time, Juan O'Gorman. On what was once a quiet corner and tucked behind an organ cactus fence sits a small compound with a large maroon-coloured house (Diego's) and a much smaller blue abode (Frida's) connected by a rooftop causeway. From 1933 to 1941 they both stayed here, living and working apart yet still near enough to visit each other and for Frida to deliver Diego's meals. In both buildings, walls are concrete, floors are wooden and many of the windows, especially in Diego's studio, go from floor

Frida Kahlo

Since the 1970s, the work of **Frida Kahlo** (1907–54) has progressively been re-assessed to the point where she is Mexico's most internationally renowned artist. Her reputation now outshines that of her muralist husband, Diego Rivera (see box, p.382), who recognized her talent as "the first woman in the history of art to treat, with absolute and uncompromising honesty, one might even say with impassive cruelty, those general and specific themes which exclusively affect women". Julie Taymor's biopic *Frida*, starring Selma Hayek in the title role, has further consolidated her role as something of a twentieth-century feminist icon, a position earned as much through her life as through her art. Her work is certainly deeply personal, centred on herself, her insecurities and her relations with family, her country and her politics. "I paint myself," she said, "because I am so often alone, and because I am the subject I know best."

The daughter of a *mestizo* Mexican mother and Hungarian Jewish father, Frida was born in the Blue House in Coyoacán (now the **Museo Frida Kahlo**, see p.416) in 1907. She always claimed she was born in 1910, symbolically uniting her birth with the start of the Mexican Revolution and the dawning of modern Mexico. The deceit wasn't entirely fatuous, as themes of rejuvenation and Mexican life pervade her work in a way impossible to imagine in Mexican art just a couple of decades earlier. To get a sense of her life you'll need to visit the Museo Frida Kahlo and perhaps Kahlo and Rivera's pair of houses in **San Ángel** (see overleaf), but you can't really understand her life without seeing her art. Frida's relatively short painting career was never prolific and her total output was small. By far the largest collection of her work – something like a third of her total output – is at the **Museo Dolores Olmedo Patiño** (see p.421).

At 6 she suffered a bout of polio that left her right leg withered, something she tried to hide for the rest of her life. She rebounded and, as a precocious 14-year-old at Mexico City's top school, first met Diego Rivera (twenty years her senior) who was painting a mural there. She shocked her friends by declaring that she wished to conceive his child "just as soon as I convince him to cooperate". Such an opportunity never presented itself, and they didn't meet again for many years.

Meanwhile, Frida was already breaking free of the roles preordained for women in early twentieth-century Mexico, and was just beginning to pursue a career in medicine when, aged 18, she suffered a gruesome **accident**. The bus she was riding in was struck by a tram, and it was while bedridden for months – recovering from multiple fractures and a pelvis skewered by a steel handrail – that she first took up a paintbrush. Later in life, she reflected "I had two accidents in my life. One was the bus, the other Diego", and it was after her recovery that she fell in with a left-leaning bunch of artists, free-thinkers and Communists where she again met Rivera. Within a year they were married: she a striking, slender woman of 21; he a massively overweight man twice her age with a frog-like face and a womanizing reputation few could match. Diego went about his affairs quite publicly (including briefly with Frida's sister, Cristina), though with true macho jealousy he was furious when Frida took up with other men, occasionally brandishing his pistol to ward them off. Frida's several affairs with women seemed to delight him. Nonetheless, she was completely to ceiling – all very advanced for the early 1930s and especially so for Mexico. Indeed, the whole set-up is in such contrast to the Blue House in Coyoacán (see p.416) that it is hard to imagine that the houses were inhabited by the same people.

Diego's studio contains some of his materials along with personal items, reproductions of some of his work and some large papier-mâché skeletons. Temporary exhibits take up much of Frida's house, though there are a couple

devoted to Diego and dependent on him, emotionally and often financially. He was almost equally dependent on her though he didn't admit it, either to himself or publicly, until after her death when he wrote "Too late now, I realized that the most wonderful part of my life had been my love for Frida."

With encouragement from Diego, Frida pursued her painting career. Her early portraiture flowered into her distinctive style particularly in the early 1930s when she and Diego spent four years in the United States while he was feted and paid handsomely for large mural projects. Over half of Kahlo's canvases are self-portraits: an unsmiling face with dark monobrow and a moustache she never tried to conceal above a body often sliced open and mutilated. Increasingly her self-portraits were imbued with sophisticated personal symbolism, with themes of abortion, broken bones and betrayed love explored through the body set in an unlikely juxtaposition of elements. Frida was soon embraced by the Surrealists – the dominant artistic wave in Europe at the time – and while she appreciated the exposure it gave her work, she always hated the comparison. Her work is quite different, shorn of overarching Freudian subconsciousness, with Frida always there to edit her own emotions.

In 1932, Frida miscarried and was hospitalized in Detroit where she painted *Henry Ford Hospital*. This disturbing portrayal of a woman's grief, shows her naked body lying on a bed in an industrial wasteland surrounded by a foetus, pelvic bones and surgical implements all umbilically tied back to the bleeding Frida. After returning to Mexico, their circle of friends expanded to include Trotsky (with whom she had a brief affair), Cuban Communist Julio Antonio Mella and muralist David Siqueiros (who was later implicated in an attempt to kill Trotsky, see box, p.417). By now Frida and Diego were living in paired houses in San Ángel, a situation which allowed them to maintain relatively separate lives. During this period, Kahlo had an abortive affair with photographer Nikolas Muray. In 1939, Frida and Diego divorced, a devastating event Frida recorded in *Self-Portrait with Cropped Hair*, in which her trademark long tresses and indigenous Tehuana dresses (both much loved by Diego) are replaced by Diego's oversized suit and cropped hair. They remarried a year later with Frida insisting on financial independence and a celibate relationship. In more upbeat mood she then painted *Self-Portrait with Plait*, the shorn locks braided together and piled precariously on the head.

The injuries she sustained from her accident continued to dog her throughout her life, and as of her physical condition worsened she continued to find solace in her work (as well as drink and pain-killing drugs), painting *The Broken Column*, in 1944, with her crushed spine depicted as an Ionic column. Despite increasing commercial and critical success, Frida only had one solo exhibition of her work during her lifetime, in Mexico City just a year before she died. In her later years she was wheelchair-bound, but continued the political activism she had always pursued, and died after defying medical advice and taking part in a demonstration against American intervention in Guatemala while she was convalescing from pneumonia in July 1954. By this stage, she knew she was dying, and her painterly control was going. On her last work, of sliced watermelons, she daubed "Viva la Vida" – "Long Live Life", signing off with a degree of positivity and optimism.

A walk from San Ángel to Coyoacán

The most enjoyable way to take in San Ángel and Coyoacán on the same day is to put an hour or so aside and **walk** between the two through quiet streets past some of the city's prime real estate and a few minor sights. The most pleasant route (marked on the map opposite) starts at the main junction in the centre of San Ángel where Avenida Revolución passes the Museo del Carmen (see p.411). From here, follow Avenida La Paz towards the northeast and cross Insurgentes to reach the **Jardín de la Bombilla**, a small park centred on a blockish concrete monument to General Alvaro Obregón who was assassinated here in 1928 soon after being re-elected as president. Revolutionary workers (corn cob in one hand, hammer and sickle in the other) flank the monument, and you can duck inside to see the bronze statue of Obregón. On the east side of the park, cross Calle Chimalistac and walk through the tiny Plaza Frederico Gamboa. On the east side of Plaza Frederico Gamboa, take a left and cross Miguel Ángel de Quevedo, passing **Parque Tagle** on your left, and turning right into Arenal. This leads you across Avenida Universidad to the **Capilla de San Antonio Panzacola**, a little red chapel sited attractively next to a small stone bridge.

Continue east on the peaceful, cobbled Avenida Francisco Sosa, one of the most beautiful streets in the city, and also one of the oldest. Peer over the high walls to catch a glimpse of some gorgeous residences, but the only way to get inside one of these houses is to visit the **Museo Nacional de la Acuarela**, Calle Salvador Nova 88 (Tues–Sun 11am–6pm; free). This small museum is devoted to watercolour painting but includes some architectural and graphic art as well. Look for work by Saturnino Herrán and don't miss the temporary exhibits in a separate gallery reached through a small sculpture garden.

Ten minutes' walk further along Avenida Francisco Sosa you reach **Plaza Santa Caterina**, a tranquil square overlooked by its mustard-yellow church and with a couple of restaurants. From here it is a short walk to Coyoacán's Plaza Central reached through a twin-arched gateway.

of fine portraits of her taken by Nikolas Muray, with whom Frida had an affair in the late 1930s, and some of Frida's own ex-voto paintings of her debilitating accident.

Just around the corner from the twin houses is the famous **San Ángel Inn**, a former Carmelite monastery built in the late seventeenth century which, since 1915, has operated as an elegant restaurant (see p.430). It is expensive, the food is superb, and when you factor in the sumptuous garden setting it is no surprise that Mexico City's elite and just about every visiting dignitary comes here. Such is its reputation, though, that it is also packed with tourists (it is included on many day-trip itineraries), but is nevertheless worth visiting.

Coyoacán

Around 3km east of San Ángel lies **COYOACÁN**, another colonial township that has been absorbed by the city. Even before the Conquest it was a sizeable place, the capital of a small kingdom on the shores of the lake subjugated by the Aztecs in the mid-fifteenth century. Cortés based himself in Coyoacán during the siege of Tenochtitlán, and continued to live here while the old city was torn down and construction began on the capital of Nueva España. It remains far less touristed than San Ángel, although the plazas are pretty lively, especially so at weekends. The focus of the area is the spacious **Plaza Central**.

Nearby, in the small Plaza la Conchita, the Capilla de la Concepción has a wonderful Baroque facade. Overlooking the square, the distinctive red Casa de

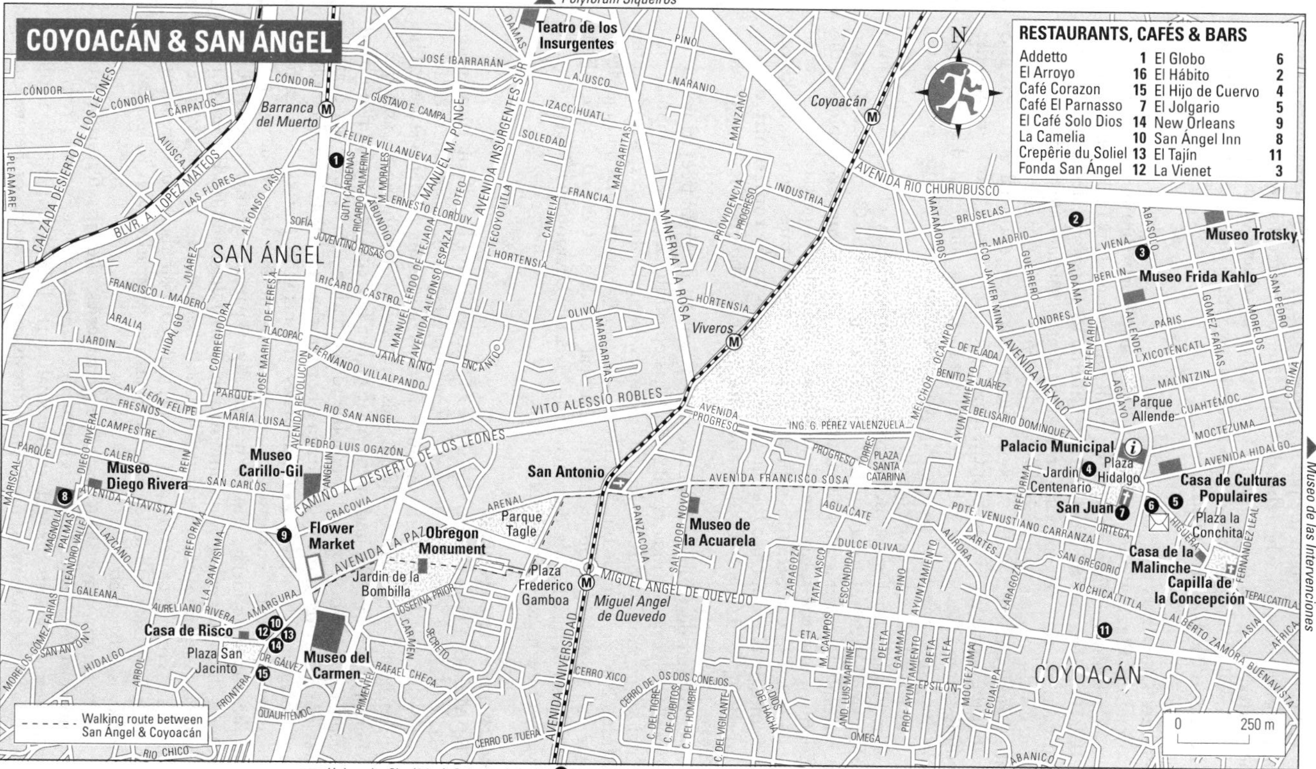
COYOACÁN & SAN ÁNGEL
RESTAURANTS, CAFÉS & BARS
Addetto 1
El Arroyo 16
Café Corazon 15
Café El Parnasso 7
El Café Solo Dios 14
La Camelia 10
Crepêrie du Soliel 13
Fonda San Ángel 12
El Globo 6
El Hábito 2
El Hijo de Cuervo 4
El Jolgario 5
New Orleans 9
San Ángel Inn 8
El Tajín 11
La Vienet 3
Polyforum Siqueiros
Teatro de los Insurgentes
Museo de las Intervenciones
University City (2 km), Cuicuillo (5 km) & 16 (6 km)
SAN ÁNGEL
COYOACÁN
Barranca del Muerto
Coyoacán
Viveros
Miguel Angel de Quevedo
Museo Trotsky
Museo Frida Kahlo
Parque Allende
Palacio Municipal
Plaza Hidalgo
Jardín Centenario
San Juan
Casa de Culturas Populaires
Plaza la Conchita
Casa de la Malinche
Capilla de la Concepción
Museo de la Acuarela
San Antonio
Parque Tagle
Plaza Frederico Gamboa
Obregon Monument
Jardin de la Bombilla
Flower Market
Museo Carillo-Gil
Museo Diego Rivera
Casa de Risco
Plaza San Jacinto
Museo del Carmen
Walking route between San Ángel & Coyoacán
0 250 m

la Malinche (not open to the public) is the house in which Cortés installed his native mistress – and where he allegedly later murdered his wife shortly after her arrival from Spain. No visit to Coyoacán is complete without strolling out to the northern reaches of the suburb to the two main sights, the **Frida Kahlo and Leon Trotsky museums**.

Plaza Central

Coyoacán's **Plaza Central** is one of the city's main stomping grounds for artists, artisans and musicians. It is actually made up of two adjoining plazas – **Plaza Hidalgo** and the **Jardín del Centenario**. Bars and cafés ring the plaza, with activity centred especially around the *Café el Parnaso*, attached to a bookstore on the corner of the square, and the *Hijo del Cuervo* bar at the opposite side – both are good places to check out the local scene, as well as to relax and watch the world go by. On Sunday, there's a market in the Plaza Central – the whole area is taken up by stalls and various rock, folk and reggae bands. It's far and away the most fun place to buy your souvenirs, though most of the stuff can be found cheaper elsewhere.

The Plaza Central is also home to the sixteenth-century church of San Juan and a small Palacio Municipal (also known as the Casa de Cortés) said to have been built by Cortés himself. Inside are two Rivera **murals** depicting the Conquest and the torture of Cuauhtémoc. The latter is particularly apposite since it was in Coyoacán that the Aztec leader was tortured and finally killed. The murals aren't open to the public, but if you ask at the **tourist office** (daily 9am–8pm; ⓣ55/5659-6009) in the same building they might let you take a peek.

The Museo de Culturas Populares (Tues–Sun 10am–8pm; free), close to the Plaza Hidalgo at Avenida Hidalgo 289, has colourful displays on popular cultural forms, mostly dolls, masks and costumes. Avenida Hidalgo also leads to the Museo Nacional de las Intervenciones (see p.419) – to find it, continue down Avenida Hiadalgo for about 300m, and bear left down General Anaya, which leads directly to the museum (crossing Avenida División del Norte on the way), a fifteen- to twenty-minute walk.

Museo Frida Kahlo

The **Museo Frida Kahlo**, Londres 247 at Allende (Tues–Sun 10am–6pm; US$3; Metro Coyoacán) is just a few minutes' walk from the centre of Coyoacán, and about twenty minutes from General Anaya Metro station. The appropriately named Blue House was the Kahlo's family home and this is where Frida was born and spent most of her life, sporadically with husband Diego Rivera, who donated the house to the nation shortly after her death. It was during Frida and Diego's tenure here in the late 1930s that they played host to the newly arrived **Leon Trotsky** and his wife. Trotsky, ever fearful of assassins, apparently expressed his concern about the ease of access from a neighbouring property, and in a typically expansive gesture Diego simply bought the other house and combined the two. Diego and Frida were continually at the centre of the capital's leftist bohemian life. D.H. Lawrence was among a coterie of artists and intellectuals to visit the house frequently – though Lawrence had little political or artistic sympathy with Kahlo, or with Trotsky for that matter.

Several rooms have been set aside as galleries, the first featuring around twenty relatively minor (and less tortured) examples of Frida's work, from some of her early portraits through to her final work, 1954's *Viva la Vida*, a still life of sliced watermelons painted when the pain and trauma of her recent leg

The assassination of Trotsky

The first attempt on Trotsky's life, in his house at Coyoacán, left more than seventy scars in the plaster of the bedroom walls. At 4am on May 24, 1940, a heavily armed group led by the painter David Siqueiros (who had been a commander in the Spanish Civil War and was working under the orders of the Stalinist Mexican Communist Party) overcame the guards and pumped more than two hundred shots into the house. Trotsky, his wife and son survived by the simple expedient of hiding under their beds. After this the house, already heavily guarded, was further fortified, but the eventual assassin had already inveigled his way into the household, posing as a businessman being converted to the cause. Although he was never fully trusted, it seemed unsuspicious enough when he showed up on the afternoon of August 20, with an article that he wanted Trotsky to look over. Trotsky invited him into the study and moments later the notorious **ice pick** (the blunt end), which had been concealed under the killer's coat, smashed into Trotsky's skull. He died some 24 hours later, in the hospital after an operation failed to save his life. The killer, who called himself Frank Jackson and claimed to be Belgian, served twenty years in jail, though he never explained his actions or even confessed to his true identity, Jaime Ramón Mercader del Río.

amputation had taken their toll on her painterly control, if not her spirit. Look too for a beautiful charcoal self-portrait from 1932 and the more political *Marxism Gives Health to the Sick* from 1954.

A room full of Frida's signature **tehuana dresses** leads on to more paintings, over a dozen by Rivera including *Paisaje de la Quebrada*, which shows a rock face at Acapulco into which Diego has painted his own face in purple. Alongside are several works by Velasco and Orozco, a Klee and a Tanguy.

Other sections of the house faithfully show the artesanía style that Frida favoured. Witness the blue-and-yellow kitchen with "Diego" and "Frida" picked out in tiny ceramic mugs on the wall. Its extraordinary decoration continues with bizarre papier-mâché animals and figures, and an impressive collection of *retablos* around the stairway. This leads up to Frida's airy studio where her wheelchair is artfully set next to an easel and, of course, a mirror.

In one of the bedrooms Diego's large work-overalls and trademark hat give a sense of ownership, but his influence is seen more through his interest in Mexico's pre-Hispanic culture. Artefacts are scattered throughout the house and a small collection is displayed on the courtyard on a small two-step pyramid he had constructed there.

Museo Casa de León Trotsky

Trotsky's House, or the **Museo Casa de León Trotsky**, Río Churabasco 410 (Tues–Sun 10am–5pm; US$3; Metro Coyoacán), where the genius of the Russian Revolution and organizer of the Red Army lived and worked in exile, is about four blocks away and represents virtually the only memorial to Trotsky anywhere in the world – his small tomb and ashes stand in the gardens. After Lenin's death, Trotsky was forced into exile and condemned to death, and as increasing numbers of countries refused him asylum he sought refuge in Mexico in 1937, aided by Diego Rivera (at the time an ardent Trotskyite) who petitioned President Lázaro Cárdenas. Here Stalin's long arm finally caught up with him (see box, above), despite the house being reinforced with steel gates and shutters, high walls and watchtowers. The fortified building seems at first a little incongruous surrounded by the bourgeois homes of a prosperous suburb, but inside it's a human place, set up as he left it, if rather dustier: books on the shelves, his glasses smashed on the desk, and all the trappings of a fairly comfortable ordinary life – except for the bullet holes.

The University, Olympic Stadium and Cuicuilco

Around 2km south of San Ángel, Insurgentes enters the great lava field of the Pedregal, an area partly given over to plush housing, but also home to the **university campus**, the **Olympic Stadium** (Estadio Olímpico), and **Cuicuilco**, the oldest pyramid in central Mexico.

Getting to the area is easy, as it's reached from San Ángel by just about any bus or *pesero* heading south along Insurgentes. All stop outside the Olympic Stadium, right opposite the university library, and many (try those marked "Villa Olímpica", "Cuicuilco" and "Tlalpan") continue on to the pyramid at Cuicuilco, visible on the left just after you pass under the *periférico*. The university can also be reached by Metro (line 3): Copilco is the most convenient station, Universidad much less so as it brings you out at the back of the campus, from where you have to walk all the way through – past the *frontón* courts and medical faculty – to reach the library.

University City

To the east of Insurgentes Sur is the **University City**. The campus is dominated by the astonishing, rectangular twelve-storey **Library**, each face of which is covered in a mosaic designed by **Juan O'Gorman** – mostly natural stone with a few tiles or glass to supply colours that would otherwise have been unavailable. Representing the artist's vision of the country's progression through history, the focus of the larger north and south faces is on pre-Hispanic and colonial Mexico; on the west wall are the present and the university coat of arms; on the east, the future is ranged around a giant atom. It's remarkable how this has been incorporated as an essential feature of the building – at first it appears that there are no windows at all, but look closely and you'll see that in fact they're an integral part of the design, appearing as eyes, mouths or as windows of the buildings in the mosaic.

More or less beside this are the long, low **administration buildings** (*rectoría*) with a giant mural in high relief by Siqueiros (or a "sculptural painting", as he called it), intended to provide a changing perspective as you walk past or drive by on Insurgentes. At the front here, too, are the University Theatre and the **Museo Universitario de Ciencias y Artes** (Mon–Fri 9am–6pm, Sat & Sun 10am–6pm; free), the latter a wide-ranging general collection, with interactive scientific exhibits, plus exhibitions on contemporary art and culture. Behind them spread out the enormous grounds of the main campus, starting with a large esplanade known as the Plaza Mayor, with sculptural groups dotted around a shallow artificial pond. Towards the back are more murals, adorning the **Faculties of Science and Medicine**; continue past these to reach another grassy area with the **Botanical Gardens** and several large walls against which the students play *frontón*.

After almost fifty years of use, parts of the campus are beginning to show their age, but while it's no longer the avant-garde sensation it was when it opened it remains a remarkable architectural achievement. The whole thing was built in just five years (1950–55) under the presidency of Miguel Alemán, and is now one of the largest universities in the world with some 300,000 students and staff. It's also the oldest on the American continent: granted a charter by Philip II in 1551, the University of Mexico occupied a succession of sites in the city centre (including the Hospital de Jesús Nazareno and what is now the Escuela Nacional Preparatoria), was closed down several times in the nineteenth century and was finally awarded its status as the Universidad Nacional Autónoma de México (UNAM) in 1929.

Estadio Olímpico

Directly across Insurgentes from the university library is the sculptured oval of the 100,000-seat **Estadio Olímpico**, its main facade decorated with a mosaic relief by Diego Rivera representing the development of human potential through sport. Most taxi drivers will tell you that the stadium was deliberately designed to look like a giant sombrero, but this, sadly, is not the case; it's undeniably odd, though, half sunk into the ground as if dropped here from a great height and slightly warped in the process.

Cuicuilco

The **Pirámide de Cuicuilco** (daily 9am–4.45pm; free) is dominated by the circular temple clearly visible from Insurgentes around 3km south of the Estadio Olímpico and opposite the former Olympic Village, now a housing complex. This is much the oldest construction of such scale known in central Mexico, reaching its peak around 600–200 BC before being abandoned at the time of the eruption of Xitle (the small volcano that created the Pedregal, which took place around 100–300 AD) just as Teotihuacán was beginning to develop. Not a great deal is known about the site, much of which has been buried by modern housing (completing the work of the lava). The pyramid itself, approached by a ramp and a stairway, is about 25m high by 100m in diameter and is composed of four sloping tiers (of a probable original five), the lowest one made visible only by digging away 4m of lava. A small **museum** displays objects found here and at contemporary settlements.

Calzada de Tlalpan

Along with Insurgentes Sur, the other main approach to the south is the **Calzada de Tlalpan**, running south from the Zócalo more or less in parallel with Metro line 2 (initially underground, then running down the middle of the road) and subsequently the Tren Ligero, almost all the way to Xochimilco.

The two train lines provide the easiest access to some fine museums – including Diego Rivera's **Anahuacalli** and the wonderful **Museo Dolores Olmedo Patiño** – and passes the giant **Estadio Azteca** football stadium on its way to the canals of Xochimilco. This is also provides alternative access to the eastern end of Coyoacán.

Museo Nacional de las Intervenciones

Travelling south on Metro line 2, the first station worth stopping at is General Anaya, from where it is a five-minute walk along 20 de Agosto to the **Museo Nacional de las Intervenciones**, 20 de Agosto and General Anaya (Tues–Sun 9am–6pm; US$3.20, free on Sun). This occupies the old Franciscan **Convento de Churubusco**, which owes its present role to the 1847 battle in which the invading Americans, led by General Winfield Scott, defeated a Mexican force under General Anaya – another heroic Mexican effort whereby the outnumbered defenders fought to their last bullet.

On arrival, you'll notice the building first of all – a stunner, especially if you arrive at the darkening of day as the lights are coming on in the gardens. The exhibits, all on the upper floor, may not mean a great deal unless you have a reasonable grasp of Mexican history; they're labelled only in Spanish and not very fully at that. They're devoted to the history of foreign military adventures in Mexico, and skeletons in the cupboards of Britain, Spain, France and the US are all loudly rattled. One section is devoted largely to the Mexican–American wars – with a very different perspective from that of the Alamo. Much of what's on show, however, comprises paintings of generals and flags, and unless you're a history buff you might better spend your time in the pleasant surrounding gardens. Apart from the Metro, the museum is also accessible by *pesero* ("Gral Anaya") from Coyoacán: pick it up by the market at the junction of Allende and Xicoténcatl.

The Trotsky and Frida Kahlo museums, and central Coyoacán are about a fifteen-minute walk from the Museo Nacional de las Intervenciones. To reach them, take Calle General Anaya, opposite the museum entrance, cross División del Norte and go straight ahead for about 500m, by which time General Anaya has merged into Calle Hidalgo. For central Coyoacán and the Frida Kahlo Museum, continue straight on (see map, p.415). For the Trotsky Museum, take a right down Madero (signposted, but not easy to spot) opposite Hidalgo 62.

Museo Anahuacalli

Metro line 2 finishes at Tasqueña, where you can transfer to the Tren Ligero and continue four stops to Xotepingo, a ten-minute walk from the bizarre **Museo Diego Rivera Anahuacalli**, Museo 15 (Tues–Sun 10am–6pm; US$3; Tren Ligero Xotepingo), designed and built by Diego Rivera to house his own huge collection of pre-Hispanic artefacts. It's an extraordinary blockish structure, started in 1933 and worked on sporadically until Rivera's death, then finished off by Juan O'Gorman and opened in 1963. Inspired by Maya and Aztec architecture, this sombre mass of black volcanic stone is approached through a courtyard reminiscent of a Maya ball-court. The exquisite objects in the collection often form part of a thoroughly imaginative exhibit: one small chamber contains nothing but a series of **Huehueteotls**, all squatting grumpily under the weight of their braziers, and the studio has ball-player and animal displays.

The **ground floor** is devoted to objects from the main cultures of the Valley of México – Teotihuacán, Toltec and Aztec – which provided Rivera with an important part of his inspiration. On the **middle floor**, rooms devoted to the west of Mexico (arguably the best such collection in the country) surround the huge airy room that Rivera, had he lived, would have used as a studio. It's been fitted out as if he had anyway, with portraits and sketches including preliminary studies for *Man in Control of the Universe*, his massive mural in the Palacio de las Bellas Artes. On the **top floor** are more Aztec objects, along with pottery and small figures from Oaxaca and the Gulf coast. Up here you can also get out onto the **rooftop terrace**, for the magical views to Popocatépetl and Ixtaccíhuatl, both seeming really close here, their snowy peaks glistening on less smoggy days.

Walking through the dark recesses of the museum, note the ceilings, each with individual mosaic designs, and even the floor of the rooftop terrace which is inlaid with snake, dog and frog forms, distinct but barely noticeable if you're not looking for them. As you leave the main museum, you'll see a low building diagonally to the left, which houses temporary exhibitions and is worth a visit if only to get a sense of the underlying volcanic rock – part of El Pedregal (see p.410) – which was hewn away to provide building materials for the museum.

To get here from the Xotepingo Tren Ligero station, follow the signs to the Calle Museo exit, double back at the bottom of the steps and take the first left down Calle Museo. After 100m, cross División del Norte, and it's about 500m ahead on your right. On the way, *Antojito Berenice* at Museo 71 is a good little place to stop for a comida corrida.

Museo Dolores Olmeda Patiño

To see a good deal more of Rivera's work (the largest private collection anywhere), and to experience one of the city's finest museums, head ten stops further along the Tren Ligero line to the **Museo Dolores Olmeda Patiño** (Tues–Sun 10am–6pm; US$3; Tren Ligero La Noria). The museum sits amid peaceful and beautifully tended grounds where peacocks strut, oblivious of the busy streets outside. It is built into a seventeenth-century mansion, donated in 1994 by the elderly Dolores Olmedo, a wealthy collector, and longtime friend and patron of Diego's. Over the years she amassed over 130 of his works, all on display here, spanning his career from Cubist experimentation in the late 1910s through self-portraits (exhibiting varying degrees of flattery) to 25 sunsets painted in Acapulco from the balcony of his patron's house. His body of work is immensely varied and this is perhaps the best place to get a true sense of just how versatile the master was. Look particularly for three large and striking nudes from the early 1940s, and sketches for his famous paintings of calla lilies.

Diego's work is reason enough to come here, but the museum also has an outstanding collection of two dozen paintings by **Frida Kahlo**. Arranged in approximate chronological order, it is easy to see her development as an artist from the Riveraesque approach of early works such as 1929's *The Bus*, to her infinitely more powerful self-portraits. Many of her finest works are here including *Henry Ford Hospital*, *A Few Small Pricks*, *The Broken Column* and *Self-Portrait with Monkey*, the latter featuring a Xoloitzcuintle, one of the pre-Columbian grey-skinned, hairless dogs. To see them in the flesh, wander out into the garden where a few are still kept. There's also a portrait of Kahlo by Rivera elsewhere in the museum in a pastiche of her own style.

Though easily outshone by Diego and Frida, it is also worth looking at the wood-block prints done by **Angelina Beloff**, Diego's first wife, featuring scenes from Mexico and her native Russia.

To get to the museum from La Noria Tren Ligero station, go straight ahead from the exit and take the first left. The museum is a couple of minutes' walk on your left.

Xochimilco

The so-called "**floating gardens**" adjoining the suburb of **Xochimilco** (Tren Ligero Xochimilco) offer an intense carnival atmosphere every weekend and are likely to be one of your most memorable experiences of the city. Considerable effort has been expended in recent years to clean up the canals and maintain the water levels that had been dropping here , so Xochimilco ("place of the flower fields" in Nahuatl) looks set to remain the most popular Sunday outing for thousands of Mexicans. It's also the one place where you get some feel for the ancient city and its waterborne commerce, thriving markets and dazzling colour – or at least an idealized view of it. Rent any of the colourful boats and you'll be ferried around miles of canals, continually harangued by women selling flowers, fruit and hot food from tiny canoes, or even by larger vessels bearing marimba players and entire *mariachi* bands in their full finery who, for a small fee, will grapple alongside you and blast out a couple of numbers. The "floating gardens" themselves are no more floating than the *Titanic*: following the old Aztec methods of making the lake fertile, these *chinampas* are formed by a raft of mud and reeds, firmly rooted to the bottom by the plants. The scene now appears no different from a series of canals cut through dry land, but the area is still a very important gardening and flower-producing centre for the city. If you wander the streets of Xochimilco town you'll find garden centres everywhere, with wonderful-looking flowers and fruit in the **market** (though whether it's healthy to eat food raised on these dirty waters is open to question) which enlivens the town centre for much of Saturday.

What you pay for your **boat rental** depends on the size of the *trajinera* (skiff), how long you want to go for, and most importantly your skill at bargaining. If you can get a boatload together (a small skiff seats twelve, but twenty-seaters are also possible), you should be able to get a deal, but there's a long tradition of milking tourists here and you want to be certain of what you've agreed on before parting with any money. Remember that there are likely to be sundry **extras**, including the cold beers thoughtfully provided by the boatman, and any flowers, food or music you find yourself accepting on your way. Expect to pay US$8–10 per person per hour depending on the size of your group. You'll be encouraged to go for two hours, but try to avoid paying upfront or you're likely to get only an hour and a half, which will include a visit to the garden centre of their choice. The boatman won't like it, but you can always take your business elsewhere. Also, be clear which boat you are getting or you are liable to be shuffled to an inferior and less attractive model. You can rent a boat on any weekday for a little less-crowded cruising, but Sunday is by far the most popular and animated day; Saturdays are lively, too, partly because of the produce market. Off the huge central plaza is the lovely sixteenth-century church of **San Bernardino**, full on Sundays with a succession of people paying homage and leaving offerings at one of its many chapels; in the plaza itself there are usually bands playing, or mime artists entertaining the crowds.

For the easiest **approach to Xochimilco**, take the Metro to Tasqueña station (line 2) and from there the Tren Ligero to Xochimilco (end of the line); there are also buses and *peseros* from Tasqueña as well as buses direct from the centre, down Insurgentes and around the *periférico* or straight down the Calzada de Tlalpan. On Sundays many extra services are laid on. To get a boat, go straight ahead from the Tren Ligero station exit and follow the "Embarcadero" signs (about a 10min walk).

North of the centre

Compared to the southern suburbs, the area north of the city centre has less to offer, but two sites of compelling interest – the emotive **Plaza de las Tres Culturas** and the great **Basilica of Guadalupe** – well deserve the afternoon it takes to cover both. Further out, and harder to get to, you'll find the pyramids of **Tenayuca** and **Santa Cecilia**, the two most dramatically preserved remains of Aztec architecture in the city.

Plaza de las Tres Culturas

Site of the ancient city of **Tlatelolco**, the **Plaza de las Tres Culturas** will be your first stop. Today, a lovely **colonial church** rises in the midst of the excavated ruins, which are in turn surrounded by a **high-rise housing complex**: all three great cultures of Mexico side by side.

Although there is a Tlatelolco Metro station (line 3), the easiest way **to get to the Plaza** de las Tres Culturas is to take Metro lines 8 or B to Garibaldi and then walk for ten minutes northwards along Lázaro Cárdenas. Alternatively catch one of the buses headed north along Lázaro Cárdenas from near Bellas Artes, or take "La Villa" buses and *peseros* which pass within about three blocks along Reforma on their way to Guadalupe.

The ruins

The site of the ancient ruins of **Tlatelolco** (daily 9am–7pm; US$3.50, free on Sun; Metro Garibaldi – from the exit, cross Reforma and head north up Lázaro Cárdenas, where you'll find it after 400m on your right) represents just the core of a city that was considerably more ancient than Tenochtitlán, based on a separate but nearby island in the lake. For a long time, under independent rule, its people existed in close alliance with the Mexica of Tenochtitlán and the city was by far the most important commercial and market centre in the Valley – even after its annexation to the Aztec empire in 1473 Tlatelolco retained this role. By the time the Spanish arrived, much of the swampy lake between the two had been filled in and built over. **Cortés** and his troops marvelled at the size and order of the Tlatelolco market. He estimated that 60,000 people, buyers and sellers, came and went each day, and Bernal Díaz wrote (after several pages of detailed description):

We were astounded at the great number of people and the quantities of merchandise, and at the orderliness and good arrangements that prevailed . . . every kind of goods was kept separate and had its fixed place marked for it . . . Some of the soldiers among us who had been in many parts of the world, in Constantinople, in Rome, and all over Italy, said that they had never seen a market so well laid out, so large, so orderly, and so full of people.

In 1521 the besieged **Aztecs** made their final stand here, and a plaque in the middle of the plaza recalls that struggle: "On the 13th of August 1521," it reads, "defended by the heroic Cuauhtémoc, Tlatelolco fell under the power of Hernan Cortés. It was neither a triumph nor a defeat, but the painful birth of the mixed race that is the Mexico of today." The ruins are a pale reflection of the original, whose temples rivalled those of Tenochtitlán itself, and some idea of their scale can be gained from the size of the bases. The chief temple, for example, had by the time of the Conquest reached its eleventh rebuilding – what you see now corresponds to the second stage, and by the time nine more had been super-imposed it would certainly have risen much higher than the church that was built from its stones. On top was likely a double sanctuary similar to that on the Great Temple of Tenochtitlán. The smaller structures include a square **tzompantli**, or Wall of Skulls, near which nearly two hundred human skulls were discovered, each with holes through its temples – presumably the result of having been displayed side by side on long poles around the sides of the building.

The church and other buildings around the plaza

The adjacent **church** (still used and not considered part of the ruins) on the site was erected in 1609, replacing an earlier Franciscan monastery. Parts of this survive, arranged about the cloister. In the early years after the Conquest, the friars established a college at which they instructed the sons of the Aztec nobility in European ways, teaching them Spanish, Latin and Christianity. Bernardino de Sahagún was one of the teachers, and it was here that he wrote down many of the customs and traditions of the natives, compiling the most important existing record of daily Aztec life in the process.

The modern buildings that surround the plaza – mostly a rather ugly 1960s housing project but including the Ministry of Foreign Affairs – represent the third culture. The contemporary state of Mexico was rather more brutally represented on October 2, 1968, when troops and tanks were ordered to fire on an almost 250,000-strong **student demonstration** here. It was the culmination of several months of student protests over the government of the day's social and educational policies, which the authorities were determined to subdue with only ten days left before the ceremonial opening of the Olympic Games in the city. Estimates of deaths vary from an official figure at the time of thirty to student estimates of more than five hundred, but it seems clear that hundreds is more accurate than tens. The Mexican philosopher Octavio Paz saw it all as part of the cycle of history – a ritual slaughter to recall the Aztec sacrifices here – but it's perhaps better seen as an example of at least one thread of continuity between all Mexico's civilizations: the cheapness of life and the harsh brutality of their rulers.

Basílica de Nuestra Señora de Guadalupe

The **Basílica de Nuestra Señora de Guadalupe** (Metro La Villa Basílica, line 6) is in fact a whole series of churches, chapels and shrines, set around an enormous stone-flagged plaza and climbing up the rocky hillock where the miracles that led to its foundation occurred. It can be reached by Metro, by **buses** and **peseros** north along Reforma ("Metro La Villa"), or by **trolleybus** from Metro Hidalgo ("Indios Verdes").

The Virgin of Guadalupe, Mexico's first indigenous saint, is still the nation's most popular – the image recurs in churches throughout the country, and the Virgin's banner has been fought under by both sides in almost every conflict the nation has ever seen, most famously when Hidalgo seized on it as the flag of Mexican Independence. According to the legend, a Christianized native, **Juan Diego**, was walking over the hill (formerly dedicated to the Aztec earth goddess, Tonantzin) on his way to the monastery at Tlatelolco one morning in December 1531. He was stopped by a brilliant vision of the Virgin, who ordered him, in Nahuatl, to go to the bishop and tell him to build a church on the hill. Bishop Juan de Zumarraga was unimpressed until, on December 12, the Virgin reappeared, ordering Diego to gather roses from the top of the hill and take them to the bishop. Doing so, he bundled the flowers in his cape, and when he opened it before the bishop he found the image of the dark-skinned Virgin imprinted into the cloth. The cloak today hangs above the altar in the gigantic modern basilica, which takes its name from the celebrated (and equally swarthy) Virgin in the monastery of Guadalupe in Spain.

The first church was built in 1533, but the large Baroque basilica you see now – mostly impressive for its size – was completely reconstructed in the eighteenth century and again remodelled in the nineteenth and twentieth. Around the back, the **Museo de la Basílica de Guadalupe** (Tues–Sun 10am–6pm; US$0.50) contains a large collection of ex-votos and some of the church's many treasures of religious art, including a series of slightly insipid early eighteenth-century canvases by José de Ibarra and more powerful oils by Miguel Cabrera and Cristóbal de Villalpando.

To the left of the great plaza is the modern home of the image – a huge **church** built in 1976 with space inside for 10,000 worshippers and for perhaps four times that when the great doors all round are thrown open to the crowds, as they are pretty much every Sunday. Whenever you visit, it's always crowded and there seems to be a service permanently in progress. The famous cloak, framed in gold and silver, hangs above the main altar, and to avoid constant disruption there's a passageway round the back. To prevent anyone lingering too long at the spot right underneath you must board a travelling walkway and admire the image as you glide respectfully by.

From the plaza you can walk round to the right and up the hill past a series of little chapels associated with the Virgin's appearance. Loveliest is the **Capilla del Pocito**, in which is a well said to have sprung forth during one of the apparitions. Built in the eighteenth century, it consists of two linked elliptical chapels, a smaller and a larger, with colourful tiled domes and magnificently decorated interiors. On the very top of the hill, the **Capilla de las Rosas** marks the spot where the miraculous roses grew.

Around all this, there swirls a stream of humanity – pilgrims, sightseers, priests and salesmen offering candles, souvenirs, pictures of the Virgin, snacks, and any number of mementoes. On **December 12**, the anniversary of the second apparition, their numbers swell to hundreds of thousands (newspaper reports claim millions). For several days before you see them on the approach roads to the capital making their pilgrimage on foot, many covering the last kilometres on their knees in an act of penance or devotion. For others it is more of a vast fiesta, with dancing, singing and drinking throughout the day.

Tenayuca and Santa Cecilia

In the extreme north of the city, just outside the boundaries of the Distrito Federal, lie the two most wholly preserved examples of **Aztec**-style architecture. They're a little hard to reach by public transport, but can thoroughly repay the effort involved if you've an interest in the Aztecs. **Tenayuca** is just off the Avenida de los Cien Metros, some 6km north of the Terminal del Norte. Take the Metro to 18 de Marzo (five blocks west of the Basílica de Nuestra Señora de Guadalupe) or La Raza and catch the "Ruta 88" *pesero* to Tenayuca (though be warned that not all "Ruta 88" *peseros* go to Tenayuca, so check first). There are also "Tenayuca" *peseros* plying Lázaro Cárdenas anywhere north of Bellas Artes: ask the driver to drop you at the *pirámide*. *Peseros* take around thirty to forty minutes from downtown.

Route #88 continues to **Santa Cecilia**; there are also *peseros* there from Metro Rosario, and it's a twenty-minute walk, or short taxi ride, from Tenayuca. Some bus tours take both in on their way to Tula and Tepotzotlán. To return to the city from here, catch a *pesero* to Metro Rosario (lines 6 and 7) or 18 de Marzo (lines 3 and 6).

Tenayuca

The twenty-metre-high **Pirámide de Tenayuca** (Tues–Sun 10am–4.45pm; US$2.80), plonked right in the main square of the suburb of the same name, is another site that predates Tenochtitlán by a long chalk – indeed there are those who claim it was the capital of the tribe that destroyed Tula. In this, its history closely mirrors almost all other Valley settlements: a barbarian tribe from the north invades, conquers all before it, settles in a city and becomes civilized, borrowing much of its culture from its predecessors, before being overcome by the next wave of migrants. There's little evidence that Tenayuca ever controlled a large empire, but it was a powerful city and provides one of the most concrete links between the Toltecs and the Aztecs. The pyramid that survives dates from the period of Aztec dominance and is an almost perfect miniature replica of the great temples of Tlatelolco and Tenochtitlán. Here the structure and the monumental double stairway are intact – only the twin sanctuaries at the top and the brightly painted decorations would be needed for it to open for sacrifices again tomorrow. This is the sixth superimposition; five earlier pyramids (the first dating from the early thirteenth century) are contained within it and are revealed in places by excavations which took place in the 1920s. Originally there was a seventh layer built on top, of which some traces remain.

The most unusual and striking feature of Tenayuca's pyramid is the border of interlocking stone **snakes** that must originally have surrounded the entire building – well over a hundred of them survive. Notice also the two coiled snakes (one a little way up the north face, the other at the foot of the south face) known as the "turquoise serpents". Their crests are crowned with stars and aligned with the sun's position at the solstice.

Santa Cecilia Acatitlán

A road leads north from Tenayuca to **Santa Cecilia Acatitlán** (Tues–Sun 10am–5pm; US$2.80), where there's another pyramid – much smaller and simpler but wholly restored and remarkably beautiful with its clean lines. When first encountered by the Spanish, this was a temple with a double staircase very similar to the others, but the outer structure was stripped away during excavation to reveal an earlier, well-preserved building inside. It's a very plain structure, rising in four steps to a single-roofed shrine approached by a broad ramped stairway. The studded decorations around the roof represent either skulls or stars. You approach the pyramid through a small museum in a colonial house, whose displays and grounds are both well worth a look.

Eating

Eating out seems to be the main pastime in the capital, with reasonably priced restaurants, cafés, *taquerías* and juice stands on every block, even in the heart of the Zona Rosa, along Reforma or just off the Zócalo. As throughout the country, those on a tight budget wanting to eat well should make their main meal a late lunchtime comida. Lunch is still the biggest meal for working people and more expensive evening dining is the habit of the upper classes.

Costs vary enormously. You can get a decent **comida corrida** (cheap set menu) pretty much anywhere in town, even in the fancier neighbourhoods (though not in Polanco or Condesa), for US$2–3 including soup, rice, main course and usually a token dessert, and you won't need to look far to find it. Otherwise, there are excellent bargains to be found all over the city in small restaurants and *taquerías*, but as you move up into the mid-range places you'll be paying something approaching what you would at home. At the top end you can soon find yourself paying big money, especially if you order something decent from the wine menu.

The choice of where to eat is almost limitless in Mexico City, ranging from traditional coffeehouses to fast-food lunch counters, and taking in **Japanese**, **French**, **Spanish**, expensive **international** and rock-bottom **Mexican** cooking along the way. There's even a small Chinatown of sorts where a cluster of **Chinese** restaurants line Calle Dolores, just south of the Alameda. There are also the traditional food stalls in **markets** throughout the city. Merced is the biggest, but not a terribly pleasant place to eat. At the back of the Plaza Garibaldi, however, there's a market hall given over to nothing but food stands, each vociferously competing with its neighbours. Mexico City also abounds in **rosticerías**, roast chicken shops, serving tasty set meals and crispy chicken with beer, in a jolly atmosphere. There are quite a few good choices on Avendia 5 de Febrero. For lighter, sweeter fare try a **jugería**, juice bar, or a **pastelería**, cake shop, for everything from *licuados* to fresh-baked pastries. Both are a good bet for a flavourful and inexpensive breakfast.

More so than anywhere else in the country, Mexico City is flooded with **chain restaurants**. American franchise establishments are well represented downtown and in the wealthier suburbs, but they're not especially cheap by Mexican standards. Slightly classier Mexican chains are found in many of the same areas. The best-known is *Sanborn's*, also not particularly inexpensive, but good for a light breakfast or reasonably authentic Mexican food tailored to foreign tastes: the most interesting by far is the flagship *Sanborn's* at *Casa de los Azulejos* (see overleaf). *VIPS* is another widely scattered chain restaurant that serves somewhat sanitized Mexican dishes in an American diner atmosphere. On the whole, you're better off with a comida corrida.

The area **around the Zócalo** and west through to the **Alameda** is packed with places to eat, many catering to office workers (which often close by early evening) and to tourists, the latter staying open later. The selection is fine for grabbing something while you're seeing the sights but, with a few notable exceptions, you're better off elsewhere for serious dining. Most visitors seem to end up eating in the **Zona Rosa** where there's a huge stock of more upmarket places wedged into a few blocks. The standard is high and new places open all the time, but by far the most active area for cafés and mid-range restaurants is **Condesa**, about twenty minutes' walk south of the Zona. We've mentioned a few in this area, but they are really just starting points, and the real pleasure is in simply wandering around and seeing what grabs your fancy. Top-class restaurants are mostly concentrated in **Polanco**. The southern suburbs of **San Ángel** and **Coyoacán** are also good hunting grounds and it is worth sticking around for your evening meal after a day's sightseeing.

Dress standards are mostly casual, but the better the restaurant the more out of place you'll feel in sneakers and a T-shirt. A few of the very best restaurants require jacket and tie, something we've mentioned where appropriate.

Something else to look out for that is becoming common in the better restaurants is a **cover charge** of US$1–3 per head that is automatically added to the bill.

Around the Zócalo: cafés and restaurants

Los Alcatraces Madero 42. Daytime cafetería and restaurant with outdoor seating in a plant-filled, though noisy, recess off Madero. It catches the midday sun, making it a good spot for their three-course lunches (US$3.50–5, or US$7.50–8 if you have a steak). Metro Zócalo.

Café Bertico Madero 66. Spacious and friendly café specializing in pasta dishes (US$6.20), gelati (US$1.50) and even sushi (from US$3.30). Also good for breakfast and great coffee. Metro Zócalo.

Café de Tacuba Tacuba 28. Good coffee and excellent food at a price, though this doesn't deter the folk who've been packing it out since 1912. One of the country's top rock bands is sponsored by the café and thus bears its name. Metro Allende.

Café Emir Uruguay 45. Modernized café that's been operating since 1936 and serves good espresso, empanadas and a Mexican variation on baclava. Metro Zócalo.

Café el Popular 5 de Mayo 52. Cheap place serving simple food 24hr a day and almost always crowded despite the perennially surly service. It's a little cramped with a fast turnover, but great for breakfast (US$2–3.35), coffee and snacks. There is a second branch called *Café la Pagoda* at 5 de Mayo 10. Metro Allende.

Casa de los Azulejos Madero 4. Flagship *Sanborn's* restaurant in a wonderful sixteenth-century building (see p.390) with prime seating around a fountain in an enclosed three-storey courtyard. Food comprises *Sanborn's* stock in trade of well-prepared Mexican staples, though a little overpriced of course for what you get. Breakfasts go for US$4.50–5.50, chicken fajitas for US$7.50, and comidas corridas for US$12. Metro Bellas Artes.

Danubio Uruguay 3 ⓣ55/5512-0912, ⓦwww.danubio.com. Established restaurant that has specialized in seafood in all its guises since 1936. As ever, the best deals are the set lunches, in this case a full six courses for US$14, though you can also order from the menu, with most dishes priced at US$8–15. Metro San Juan de Letrán.

El Generalito Filomeno Mata 18. A small diner but nicely done out, with breakfasts (US$1.80–2.60) and comidas corridas (US$3.50) in pleasant surroundings. Metro Allende.

Los Girasoles Xocoténcatl 1 ⓣ55/5510-3281. One of the most appealing restaurants in the centre, with Mediterranean decor, a casual atmosphere and great food served up at moderate prices. Start with the blue corn quesedillas (US$3.70) and perhaps follow with the trout (US$10) served up on an ornate pewter platter bursting with sunflowers, then finish with a rose-petal pie and espresso. Closes 8pm on Sun, 1am other days. Metro Allende.

Hostería de Santo Domingo Belissario Dominguez 72 ⓣ55/5510-1434. Highly atmospheric, this moderately priced restaurant in part of a former convent really looks the part, with decorations hanging from the ceiling, artesanía all over the walls and, usually, a pianist and singer in the corner. The food, though good, isn't quite as good as they seem to think it is; even their signature *chiles en nogada* (US$13.50) is better done at a few other places. Note that a compulsory tip is added to the bill. Metro Allende.

Kam Ling 1a Cerrada de 5 de Mayo 14 ⓣ55/5521-5661. Straightforward Chinese food in seriously large proportions to eat in or take away. Set menus go from around US$4 to US$8.80, and there are individual dishes (US$4–6.40) such as squid and green pepper in oyster sauce, and chicken and vegetables, all washed down with huge pots of jasmine tea (US$1.50). Metro Allende.

Tacos Beguis Isabel la Católica 10. Bustling little restaurant serving a great range of tacos (from US$0.70), tortas, tostadas and breakfasts. Metro Allende.

La Terraza 7th floor of *Hotel Majestic*. Restaurant with a great terrace that's perfect for watching the Zócalo life go by over a coffee or a beer (US$2–3). The buffet breakfast (7–11am; US$15) and buffet *menú comercial* (Mon–Fri 1–5pm; US$10) are also both good, and in the evening there's à la carte dining with well-prepared Mexican standards for US$20–30, with a barbecue *buffet ranchero* for lunch at weekends (Sat & Sun 1–5pm; US$20). Metro Zócalo.

El Vegetariano Filomeno Mata 13. Healthy and nonsmoking vegetarian restaurant that's inexplicably decorated with mountain photos. The best deal is usually the four-course *menú del día* (US$4.50). Metro Zócalo.

Vegetariano Madero upstairs at Madero 56. This sunny, spacious vegetarian restaurant lurks behind an unprepossessing stairway entrance but offers some of the best-value vegetarian food around, usually with piano accompaniment at lunchtime. The best deal is usually the four-course US$4.20 *menú del día*, though they also do great breakfasts (from 8am). Metro Zócalo.

Around the Zócalo: bakeries and snack bars

Dulcería de Celaya 5 de Mayo 39. A wonderful stop for those with a sweet tooth: a sweet shop, with candied-fruit *comates* and *dulce de membrillo*. Metro Allende.

Jugos Canada 5 de Mayo 49. Very good torta and juice bar, and at regular juice-bar prices, despite its central location. Metro Allende.

Panificadora La Vasconia Tacuba 73. One of the best bread and cake shops in the centre with a huge range of Mexican staples at low prices. Metro Allende.

Pastelería Ideal Uruguay 74. Bakery with a good range of pastries, but worth a special visit to see the huge array of outrageously ornate wedding cakes. Metro San Juan de Letrán.

Teposnieves Donceles 4. Local firm selling delicious sorbets in a range of fruit flavours, plus some unlikely ones, such as peanut, rice and *mescal*. Metro Bellas Artes.

Around the Alameda

El Café del Palacio inside Bellas Artes. An elegant restaurant in Art Deco surroundings with limited views of Tamayo's murals as you dine amid business lunchers and pre-theatre diners. Meals are moderately priced especially if you go for the two-course *menú del Palacio* (available 2–5.30pm; US$13–18.50 depending on the main course). Dishes include Waldorf salad, smoked turkey breast sandwich, duck in hibiscus sauce, and almond and pear tart, plus there's a decent wine list. Closes 6pm. Metro Bellas Artes.

Cafetería El Cuadrilatero Luis Moya 73. Like Mexico City's other wrestling cafés, *El Cuadrilatero* – "The Ring" – is owned and run by an ex-wrestler whose old masks are framed on the walls along with photos of his glory days. The food's good too, including standard Mexican mains, burgers and tortas (US$2–10) that are big enough for a wrestler or two mere mortals (the biggest of all comes free if you can eat it single-mouthed in fifteen minutes). Metro Balderas.

Centro Naturista Dolores 10, south of the Alameda. Macrobiotic canteen with soups and juices, tortas and quesadillas, and set menus US$2.80–3.10. Also offers tarot readings, holistic massages and meditation classes. Metro Bellas Artes.

Chung King Dolores 27. Reasonable Cantonese and Szechuan restaurant, one of several in this mini-Chinatown, serving the usual chop suey house standards. Set meals US$6.50–13.50. Metro Bellas Artes.

Zona Rosa

Restaurants in the Zona Rosa are shown on the map on p.396. Though the area does tend to be full of pricey tourist traps, budget eats can also be found here, especially on Londres west of Florencia, and along Avenida Chapultepec.

Blah Blah Café Londres 171 at Florencia. Café, bar and Argentinian grill, where an executive steak lunch will set you back around US$10. Metro Insurgentes.

Champs Elysées Reforma 316 ⓣ55/5514-0450. One of the capital's finer French restaurants that's been reliably feeding the Mexico City elite for almost forty years. Look out on El Ángel as you feast on truly excellent food, complemented by something from the extensive wine list, delicate desserts and a great cheeseboard. Reservations required and expect to pay US$40 for a full meal. Closed Sun. Metro Insurgentes.

Dolce Café Londres 211. Small and peaceful café a little away from the main bustle of the Zona, serving good coffee, baguettes, croissants and assorted salads and pastries at prices that are modest for the area. Metro Insurgentes.

La Lanterna Reforma 458 at Toledo ⓣ55/5207-9969. Long-standing and convivial trattoria with an intimate and suitably Italian feel, enhanced by pasta freshly made in-house and combined with some delicious sauces (US$9). The *segundi piatti* (US$12.50–14) are equally wonderful. Pizzas go for US$10.80. Metro Insurgentes.

Mesón del Perro Andaluz Copenhague 26 ⓣ55/5514-7480. Very popular Spanish restaurant with a lively atmosphere. Choices include chilled gazpacho soup (US$3), squid stewed in its ink (US$7.50), Madrid-style tripe (US$7) and paella alla Valenciana (US$11). Alternatively, go for a US$7.50 lunchtime menu. Metro Insurgentes.

Restaurante Vegetariano Yug Varsovia 3 ⓦwww.yug.com.mx. Worthy contact point for vegetarians and vegans, with set breakfasts, salads and antojitos in bright cheery surroundings. There's a particularly good buffet lunch upstairs 1–5pm for US$6.50 weekdays, US$7 at weekends, and a great comida corrida (US$5.20–5.70). Weekdays 7am–9pm, Saturdays 8.30am–8pm, Sundays 1–8pm. Metro Insurgentes.

Condesa and Roma

Restaurants in Condesa and Roma are shown on the map on p.396.

Agapi Mu Alfonso Reyes 96 ⓣ55/5286-1384. About the best Greek restaurant in the city, but very low-key and affordable as long as you don't go too mad on the retsina and Hungarian wines. It's especially fun from Thursday to Saturday when there's live music and Greek dancing. Closed Sun. Metro Juanacatlán or Patriotismo.

Los Arroces Michoacán 126 ⓣ55/5286-4287. The title defines the essence of this fashionable rice restaurant where every imaginable species of rice (and many you'd never dreamed of) is put to work in almost every dish, from soup to dessert, on a multinational menu. Most dishes are in the US$5–10 range. Metro Juanacatlán.

Bellini's 45th floor, World Trade Center, Avenida de las Naciones at Insurgentes Sur ⓣ55/5628-8304 or 5. Revolving restaurant at the top of the city's tallest building (see p.410), where business people come to impress their clients, and pick of the crop for a romantic candlelit dinner. Dishes from an international menu are prepared to the highest standards and service is impeccable. Obviously it isn't the cheapest place in town, but it isn't stupidly expensive: even at the top end of the menu, you can start with smoked salmon, caviar and avocado for US$15.70, followed by red snapper in lobster and brandy sauce for US$13.60.

Fonda Garufa Michoacán 93 ⓣ55/5286-8295. Popular Argentine and Italian restaurant with plenty of streetside tables where you can tuck into their excellent steaks or something from their extensive range of inventive pasta dishes, all at moderate prices. Metro Juanacatlán.

Koffie! Café Amsterdam 308 at Celaya. Modern café spilling out onto a quiet leafy street, making it a great spot for a US$4–5 weekend breakfast, especially if you like good strong coffee. Later on, Italian salads, pasta dishes and stuffed baguettes all come in at around US$4 and an international selection of mains mostly cost under US$7. Metro Sevilla.

Segundo Paso Café Amsterdam 76 at Parras. Relaxed low-lit corner restaurant and café, open on both sides to pavement seating. Salads, pasta dishes and mains such as chicken breast served with al dente vegetables are all well prepared and complement Iberian dishes such as Spanish tortilla and Serrano ham served with black olives and cheese. Most mains US$6–7.50. Metro Juanacatlán.

Polanco

Restaurants in Polanco are shown on the map on p.396.

La Góndola Hegel 406 at Presidente Masaryk ⓣ55/5255-0612 or 0912. Modern Italian restaurant with floor-to-ceiling windows and polished wooden floors and serving well-prepared Italian staples at moderate prices. Try the *pollo diabla*, chicken marinated in olive oil, garlic and herbs, the osso bucco on fetuccini, or the Roquefort and spinach ravioli, which all go for US$8.80–12.50. Metro Polanco.

La Petite France Presidente Masaryk 360 ⓣ55/5281-0327. Swanky French restaurant whose starters include no less than four different snail dishes (US$9.50–10.50), with main courses such as coq au vin (US$8.80), fondue (US$13.80) or roast duck in hibiscus sauce (US$12.80), but no frogs' legs. Metro Polanco.

San Ángel and south

San Ángel is most easily reached by bus or colectivo down Insurgentes – see p.410. The nearest Metro is Miguel Ángel de Quevedo. Restaurants in San Ángel are shown on the map on p.415.

Addetto Revolución 1382 ⓣ55/5662-3363. Smart modern Italian establishment combining a deli and spacious dining areas. It is a little inconveniently sited, but worth the journey for delightfully sticky risotto dishes (US$7.60–8.40), pasta (US$5.60–8.40), and a wide range of mains (US$8.40–12.50). There's a US$1.60 per head cover. Metro Barranca del Muerto.

El Arroyo Insurgentes Sur 4003, Tlalpan, 6km south of San Ángel ⓣ55/5573-4344. Well off the beaten path but worth the journey, this unusual restaurant comes complete with its own small bullring (used by novice bullfighters in bloodless *corridas* from April to Oct) and has almost a dozen dining areas that can jointly serve over 2500 diners. As you'd imagine, there's always a lively atmosphere, helped along by *mariachis*, but the Mexican food is good too, and they usually keep at least four types of flavoured pulque.

El Café Solo Dios Plaza San Jacinto 2. Popular take-away spot for good, low-cost espresso made from Chiapas beans. Flavours available.

Crepêrie du Soliel Madero 4c. Small and peaceful café that's good for an espresso, cakes and, of course, crepes.

Fonda San Ángel Plaza San Jacinto 3 ⓣ55/5550-1641, ⓦwww.fondasanangel.com.mx. Moderately priced restaurant specializing in contemporary Mexican cuisine.

San Ángel Inn Diego Rivera 50 at Altavista ⓣ55/5616-2222. Very popular, upmarket restaurant surrounded by the gardens of a beautiful old hacienda, with linen tablecloths, heavy wooden furniture and a restrained but elegant air (jackets required for men). The menu has some European overtones, but is predominantly Mexican with some slightly less common dishes such as huitlacoche, a kind of fungus that grows on corn, which is here served in crepes. Expect to pay at least US$25 per head plus wine (US$5 a glass). Reservations required.

Coyoacán

Restaurants in Coyoacán are shown on the map on p.415.

Café El Parnaso (aka *Café Frida*) Carillo Puerto 2. Predominantly sidewalk café with attached bookstore; a good spot for light snacks or just a coffee.

El Globo corner Hidalgo and Caballocalco. Local outpost of this excellent chain of French-inspired bakeries. Pricey but very good.

El Jolgario Higuera 22. Excellent modern restaurant with an avant-garde menu, almost half of it meat-free. The imaginative combinations aren't always a success but try one of their excellent salads (US$5.50, half-portion US$3), or one of the US$5–8 mains, including chile stuffed with spinach and mushrooms, or some strange interpretations of Indian dishes, such as "tandoori rice" (rice with apple sauce and cashews, which are considered Indian because they're called *nueces de la India* in Spanish), or chicken breast with apple chutney, curried carrots, and apple and raisin sauce. Wash it down with one of their "spiritual" non-alcoholic cocktails.

El Tajín Centro Veracruzano, Miguel Ángel de Quevedo 687 ⓣ55/5659-4447. Veracruz specialities at medium to high prices; the fish dishes, such as *Huachinango a la Veracruz* and *Mojarra al mojo del ajo*, are exquisite. Expect to pay around US$20 per head plus wine.

La Vienet Viena 112 at Abasolo. A good place for refreshments in between visits to the Kahlo and Trotsky houses, this small daytime café serves great coffee and cakes as well as antojitos, and paella on Sunday. Closed lunchtime and weekends.

Entertainment and nightlife

There's a vast amount going on in Mexico City, which is the nation's cultural and social centre as much as its political capital. **Bars** are dotted all over the city and range from dirt-cheap dives to upscale lounges, but there's unfortunately little in the way of mid-range bars. The bottom rung is occupied by **pulquerías** and **cantinas**, from where it is a major step up to the fancy **hotel bars** (most of which are in the centre) or to the established nightspots in well-touristed enclaves.

A lot of the obvious **nightlife**, especially in the larger hotels, is rather tame in its attempt to be sophisticated, but in recent years the **live music** scene has broadened appreciably. Finding what you want can still be hit and miss, a process full of disappointments but with occasional delights. Sometimes the genuinely appealing stuff is tucked away in less visited parts of the city, but by assiduous trawling of the listings magazine (see overleaf) and following our recommendations, there's no shortage of diverting stuff to do in tried and tested areas. Rock and Latin music are common, with US chart music and Europop filling in around that, but you'll also come across Cuban grooves, deep trance beats and even live jazz. Many of the best venues are to be found in the south, towards Coyoacán and San Ángel, but the Zona Rosa and Condesa are also good stomping grounds, and if you are looking for luxury, there are several classy joints in Polanco.

Two attractions stand out from the crowd and shouldn't be missed: the *mariachi* music in the **Plaza Garibaldi**, a thoroughly Mexican experience; and to a lesser extent, the **Ballet Folklórico**, which is unashamedly aimed at tourists but has an enduring appeal, too, for Mexicans.

While Mexican **theatre** tends to be rather turgid, there are often excellent **classical music** concerts and performances of **opera** or **ballet** by touring companies. Bellas Artes and the Auditorio Nacional are the main venues, but other downtown theatres, as well as the Polyforum and the Teatro de los Insurgentes, may have interesting shows. On most Sundays, there's a free concert in Chapultepec Park near the lake.

Cinemas are scattered all over the city, though there are very few within easy walking distance of anywhere you are likely to be staying. We've mentioned several opposite: some are in the Zona Rosa, but the greatest concentration is along Insurgentes. Most show all the latest releases, usually very soon after release in the US and typically in their original language with subtitles. If you go to the cinema arrive early, as popular screenings frequently sell out.

Listings for current cinema, theatre and other cultural events can be found in the weekly magazine *Tiempo Libre* (Ⓦwww.tiempolibre.com.mx), available at most newsstands.

Plaza Garibaldi

Plaza Garibaldi (Metros Bellas Artes and Garibaldi) is the traditional final call on a long night around the capital's bars, and as the night wears on and the drinking continues, it can get pretty rowdy. The plaza is on Lázaro Cárdenas, five blocks north of Bellas Artes in a thoroughly sleazy area of cheap bars, streetwalkers, grimy hotels and several brightly lit theatres offering burlesque and strip shows. Despite a high-profile police presence, **pickpockets** are always a threat and you'd be better off not coming laden down with expensive camera equipment or an obviously bulging wallet.

Hundreds of competing **mariachi** bands gather here in the evenings, all in their tight, silver-spangled *charro* finery and vast sombreros, to play for anyone who'll pay them among the crowds wandering the square and spilling out of the surrounding bars. A typical group consists of two or four violins, a brass section of three trumpeters standing some way back so as not to drown out the others, three or four men on guitars of varying sizes, and a vocalist, though the truly macho man will rent the band and do the serenading himself. *Mariachis* take their name, supposedly, from the French *mariage*, it being traditional during the nineteenth-century French intervention to rent a group to play at weddings. You may also come across **norteño** bands from the border areas with their Tex-Mex brand of country music, or the softer sounds of **marimba** musicians from the south. Simply wander round the square and you'll get your fill – should you want to be individually serenaded, pick out a group and negotiate your price.

At the back of the square is a huge market hall in which a whole series of stalls serve simple food and vie furiously for customers. Alternatively, there is at least one prominent *pulquería* on the square (see box, p.434), and a number of fairly pricey restaurant-bars, which try to drown out the *mariachi* bands with their own canned music, and tempt customers with their "No Cover" entry. The last Metro leaves at midnight.

Ballet Folklórico

The **Ballet Folklórico** (Ⓣ55/5529-9320, Ⓦwww.balletamalia.com.mx/eng) is a total contrast: a long-running, internationally famed compilation of traditional dances from all over the country, elaborately choreographed and designed, and interspersed with Mexican music and singing. That said – and despite the billing – there's nothing very traditional about the Ballet. Although it does include several of the more famous native dances, they are very jazzed up and incorporated into what is, in effect, a regular musical that wouldn't be out of place on Broadway.

The best place to see the Ballet Folklórico is in the original setting of the **Palacio de Bellas Artes** (see p.390), where the theatre is an attraction in itself; pressure of other events, however, occasionally forces a move to the Auditorio Nacional in Chapultepec Park (see p.399). There are usually performances on Sunday at 9.30am and 8.30pm, and Wednesday at 8.30pm. You should try to book at least a couple of days in advance – **tickets** (US$24 for the cheap seats, US$40 for something really good) are available either from the Bellas Artes box office direct (Mon–Sat 11am–7pm, Sun 9am–7pm) or through Ticketmaster (☎55/5325-9000), or arrange to go with an organized tour, for which you'll pay a considerable premium.

Cinema

Mainstream Hollywood movies make it to Mexico just a few weeks after their release in the US and often before they get a British or European release. With the exception of movies for kids, they're almost always in their original language with subtitles, and since you'll usually only pay around US$3–4 (often half price on Wed), a visit to the flicks can be a cheap and entertaining night out. Movies are **listed** every week in *Tiempo Libre*, as well as in most of the Spanish-language dailies.

There are **cinemas** scattered all over the city though none anywhere near the Zócalo. One of the largest concentrations is along the length of Insurgentes Sur where there are half a dozen multiplexes adding up to perhaps fifty screens in all. Well off the Metro system, they are not particularly convenient and you might prefer the handier places in the Zona Rosa such as Ramírez Diana, Reforma 423 (☎55/5511-3236), Lumière Reforma, Río Guadalquivir 104 at Reforma (☎55/5514-0000); or in Polanco where there is Cinemex Casa de Arte, Anatole France 120 (☎55/5280-9156) and Sala Maria Félix, Socrates 156 at Homero (☎55/5557-4101).

Bars, clubs and live music venues

Bars where you might sit around and chat are relatively thin on the ground in Mexico City, that function more often filled by restaurants. There are a few, but most of these still concentrate on music or bill themselves as **antros**, a relatively modern creation somewhere in between a bar and club where you can sit and talk (just about) or dance if the Latin pop hits get you going. As elsewhere in the country, **cantinas** and **pulquerías** are very much a male preserve, but here at least things are beginning to change. Despite the signs above the doors banning *mujeres*, there'll often be a few women inside braving the back-slapping camaraderie. Even so, it's safer for unaccompanied women to stick to hotel bars.

Live music venues are dotted all over town, offering anything from old-fashioned romantic ballads to cutting-edge alternative rock bands. Cuban music is particularly fashionable at the moment, and with Cuba just a short flight away, Mexico City provides a local but international proving ground for the island's talent. Elsewhere you'll find *trova*, often played by an acoustic guitarist flexing his songwriting skills, and leavened with reliable standards known to all (tourists excepted). A curiosity of the underground rock scene here at the moment is a wave of home-grown punk and ska-rock bands, a strange echo of 1970s Britain.

Club-oriented nightlife starts late, with live acts often hitting the stage after 11pm and few places really getting going before midnight. Entry can be expensive, ranging up to US$20 for men (women often get in for much less or

Pulque

Pulque is the fermented sap of the maguey cactus, a species of agave that grows in the countryside north and east of Mexico City. Production continues much as it has done for centuries, with barrels being shipped daily to the **pulquerías** of the capital, of which there were over 1400 during pulque's heyday in the first half of the twentieth century. It has always been considered a poor man's drink, and as beer and other drinks have become more affordable, pulque's stock has gone down. *Pulquería* owners estimate there are now only around a hundred left and with no new ones opening up that number looks set to decline further.

Unless you are looking for them, *pulquerías* are hard to spot; they're concentrated in less salubrious areas of town mostly unvisited by tourists and often have no sign, just a pair of swinging doors guarding a dark interior. Like cantinas, they are macho territory and women are more likely to receive a respectful welcome when accompanied by a male friend. That said, most drinkers will be so surprised to see a foreigner in there that you'll immediately strike up a friendly conversation.

These places are not set up for anything much more sophisticated than knocking back large glasses of this slightly astringent opaque white beverage, usually ladled out of barrels behind the bar. Among the aging clientele the emphasis is as much on socializing as drinking, which is a good thing since most pulque is only 2–4 percent alcohol and getting drunk requires considerable commitment. The task is made easier when pulque is blended with fresh fruit juices – pineapple, apricot, guava and many others – to form a weaker but more palatable cocktail. The least intimidating hunting ground is the **Plaza Garibaldi** where *La Hermosa Hortensia* is always brightly lit and usually has several good flavours served up to a cross-section of men and women, locals and foreigners. During the day you are better off exploring the district south of the Zócalo where Calle Mesones is home to a couple of early-closing establishments: *La Elegancia*, at no.51, on the corner of Isabela la Católica; and *La Risa*, at no.71, on the corner of Callejón de Mesones (both daily 9am–9pm).

free), though this is likely to include *bar libre*, where your drinks are free for at least part of the evening. If you stray far from your hotel and stay out after the Metro has closed for the night, be sure to get the bar or club to order a **sitio cab** for you; flagging down a cab late at night is not generally considered safe, especially if you are lost and drunk.

Around the Zócalo and the Alameda

Bar del Centro inside the *Gran Hotel* by the Zócalo. Relaxed atmosphere that is comfortable for female patrons, although lone women will still attract attention. Metro Zócalo.

La Hostería del Bohemio Hidalgo 107. An alcohol-free café set around a large open courtyard of the former San Hipolito convent. Smooching couples sit at candlelit tables half-listening to romantic ballads emanating passionately from the live band in the corner. Metro Hidalgo.

La Ópera 5 de Mayo 10, near Bellas Artes. The best watering hole downtown, in the grand tradition of upmarket cantinas with magnificent *fin-de-siècle* decor – ornate mahogany panelling, a brass-railed bar, gilt-framed mirrors in the booths – and a bullet hole in the ceiling reputedly put there by Pancho Villa. You can dine here too but most people come for a fairly pricey beer or cocktails in the booths or at the bar. Metro Bellas Artes.

Pervert Lounge Uruguay 70 ⓣ55/5518-0976. One of the centre's more cutting-edge clubs and nowhere near as sleazy as it might sound. From Wednesday to Saturday the beautiful people flock to hear funky beats and Latin grooves, paying about US$7 for entry. *Club 69*, next door, is similar and equally good. Metro Allende.

Tio Pepe Independencia 26 at Dolores. Convivial cantina with moulded ceilings and wooden bar. Minstrels frequently drop in to bash out a few numbers, and despite the sign on the door, women are allowed in. Metro Bellas Artes.

Zona Rosa and Polanco

Afrika Genova 40, Zona Rosa ☎55/5208-9551. Despite its name, this regular discotheque plays commercial house and dance music, with an admissions policy that proudly proclaims no bar to anyone on grounds of race, religion, clothing, hairstyle, hair colour, social status, or sexual, political or cinematic preference. Wed–Sat 9pm–4am. Metro Insurgentes.
Fiera Café Presidente Masaryk 107, Polanco ☎55/5282-635. A favourite among the young and trendy, playing lounge music and electronic pop, with a restaurant attached – open late. Metro Polanco.
Fonda Av Chapultepec 311, Zona Rosa. Basic, traditional Mexican restaurant and bar (one of several adjacent places) that's good for cheap straightforward boozing to get you primed before the clubs. Metro Insurgentes.
Salon 21 Andromaco 115, Polanco. A popular venue for all kinds of visiting bands, foreign or home-grown, playing rock, reggae, hip-hop or anything else. Metro Polanco.

Condesa and Roma

Barracuda Nueva León 4A at Sonora, Condesa ☎55/5211-9346. Hip venue with different styles of music each night, ranging from deep blues and ambient to live Latin jazz. Open Tues–Sat with bands and things beginning to hot up around 11pm. Metro Sevilla.
Gitanerías Oaxaca 15, Roma ☎55/5514-2027. Flamenco club with Spanish dancer, complete with frilly skirt and castanets. Tues–Sat from 9pm. US$10 entry. Metro Insurgentes.
Mama Rumba Querétaro 230 at Medellin, Roma ☎55/5564-6920 or 7823. Reservations are advised for this dance bar with Afro-Antilles rhythms pumped out by the Cuban house band. They get the small dance floor packed in no time, so come prepared to move your feet even if you don't know the steps. Open Thurs–Sat from 9pm, bands come on at 11pm. Wheelchair access. Metro Insurgentes.
Multiforo Alicia Cuauhtémoc 91, between Colima and Durango, Roma ☎55/5511-2100. "He who hasn't been to Alicia, doesn't know rock music", they claim, which may be an exaggeration, but this is definitely the place to catch Mexico's latest rock *ondas*. Most of the action is on Fri & Sat from 8.45pm, with some early shows at 6.30pm. Expect to pay US$5–6. Metro Cuauhtémoc.

Coyoacán and San Ángel

La Camelia Plaza San Jacinto, San Ángel. Early evening boozing to recent US and Latin pop hits, either inside or out on the street.
El Hábito Madrid 13, Coyoacán ☎55/5659-6305. Small and quirky fringe theatre and music club, mainly jazz.
El Hijo de Cuervo Jardín Centenario 17, Coyoacán ☎55/5659-5196. Dark and hip bar with seats overlooking the square and music that ranges from Latin rap to rock. There's no cover charge, and a lively evening atmosphere that runs through to 2.30am Friday night/Saturday morning and Saturday night/Sunday morning.
New Orleans Revolución 1655, San Ángel ☎55/5550-1908. Excellent jazz venue-cum-restaurant with very good food at moderate prices and a classy Cuban house band. Open Tues–Sun from 8pm (band on at 9pm), but weekends are much the liveliest unless there is some international jazz act playing. Entry costs US$5 (US$3.50 on Sun), and is well worth it.

Markets and shopping

The big advantage of **shopping** in the capital is that you can get goods from all over the country and, if you are flying out of here, you don't have to lug them around the country. For **crafts** and traditional goods don't miss the markets and artesanía shops listed below, though they will usually be more expensive than at source.

One fascinating (and occasionally frustrating) facet of shopping in the capital is the practice of devoting a whole street to one particular trade, something found to some extent throughout the city. There are blocks where you can buy nothing but stationery, other areas packed exclusively with shoe shops and still others full of musical instruments. Due to the lack of variety in a given place – and without some luck or good directions – you can spend all day walking through markets without ever finding the item that you seek. This is a hang-over from Aztec life, as their well-regulated markets were divided up according to the nature of the goods on sale, and the practice was continued by colonial planners.

Every area of the city has its own **market** selling food and essentials, and many others set up stalls for just one day a week along a suburban street. Less formal **street stalls** spring up all over the city and can be just a sheet on the pavement with some New Age devotee selling cheap jewellery, to a relatively sophisticated stand selling anything from pens and watches to computer hard drives and fake designer clothing and bags. The **Centro Histórico** and **Zona Rosa** are good hunting grounds, though the concentration of stalls in these areas is influenced by occasional crackdowns on this illegal but widely accepted trading. At more sensitive times you'll notice vendors alert to the presence of the authorities, and occasionally catch them packing up and sprinting off.

For anything you really need – clothes and so on – a good starting point is El Palacio de Hierro at 20 de Noviembre 3, just south of the Zócalo, one of several big **department stores** in the area; another is Liverpool, opposite. It is also worth trying one of the many **Sanborn's** branches, which sell books, maps and quantities of tacky souvenirs. Every location also has a sizeable pharmacy.

If you've a taste for **designer clothing**, quality **jewellery** or genuine Mexican **antiques**, the Zona Rosa has traditionally been the place to go. There are still classy shops there, but in the last few years many have moved out to Polanco. **T-shirts** and replica Mexican football shirts can be found in the *tianguis* (street stalls) on San Juan Letrán between Bellas Artes and Salto del Agua, or those in the streets north and east of the Zócalo. In the Zócalo itself, EZLN supporters usually have a stall in front of the cathedral selling T-shirts with portraits of Zapata, Marcos, or even Maria Sabina (the *curandera* who introduced magic mushrooms to the West).

If you have been in Mexico for a while you'll be desperate for **English-language books** and magazines. Sadly the capital isn't much better than the rest of the country. *Time* and *Newsweek* are available all over the place, but for anything else you'll have to seek out the places we've listed opposite, none of which has a huge range. For art and architecture books, most of the major art galleries have good selections. Postcards of course are widely available, but one place with a selection of Revolution-era photos and Kahlo and Rivera artworks in the form of postcards is at Donceles 87 by Avenida República de Brasil.

Haggling for a bargain is no longer the thrilling (or daunting) prospect it once was in Mexico City. The nation's increasing prosperity and sophistication means that most things are fixed-price. As a tourist (and especially if your Spanish is poor) you can expect people to try to bump up the price occasionally, but on the whole what you see is what you pay. If times are quiet some hotels (particularly large business hotels) might drop the prices if you ask, but hostels and budget hotels seldom do the same. The best hope for reductions is with crafts and artesanía goods, but even here fixed prices are becoming more common.

Markets

Bazar Sábado Plaza San Jacinto, San Ángel. Very popular open-air art and sculpture market takes place pretty much all day Saturday. On Sunday it moves to Parque Sullivan, just north of the Zona Rosa (see p.398).
Central Artesanal Buenavista Aldama 187, just east of the train station. Handicrafts from around the country in what is claimed to be Mexico's largest shop. Rather pricey compared to the Ciudadela and less characterful. Daily 9am–6pm. Metro Buenavista.
Centro Artesanal de San Juan (Mercado de Curiosidades Mexicanas) about five blocks south of the Alameda along Dolores. Modern tourist-oriented complex that's possibly the least appealing of the major artesanía markets, though there are still deals to be had (particularly in silver) provided you haggle. Mon–Sat 9am–7pm, Sun 9am–4pm. Metro San Juan de Letrán.
Ciudadela corner of Balderas and Emilio Donde. The best place in the capital to buy regional crafts and souvenirs from every part of the country. If you forgot to pick up a hammock in the Yucatán or some Olinalá lacquerwork in Guerrero, fear not: you can buy them here for not a great deal more. Bargaining has limited rewards. Mon–Sat 11am–7pm, Sun 11am–5pm. Metro Balderas.
Coyoacán markets There are two interesting markets in Coyoacán: the daily markets three blocks up from Plaza Hidalgo are typically given over to food, while on Sunday a craft market converges on the plaza itself. There you can buy any manner of *típico* clothing and that essential souvenir, the Marcos doll, made in Chiapas by the Maya. Metro Viveros.
La Lagunilla spreading along Rayon, a couple of blocks north of the Plaza Garibaldi. Comes closest to rivalling La Merced in size and variety, but is best visited on a Sunday when the *tianguis* expands into the surrounding streets, with more stalls selling stones, used books, crafts and bric-a-brac. Get there on buses ("La Villa") heading north on Reforma, or walk from Metro Garibaldi.
Mercado de Sonora three blocks from La Merced on Avenida Fray Servando Teresa de Mier. This market is famous for its sale of herbal medicines, medicinal and magical plants and the various *curanderos* (indigenous herbalists) who go there. Metro La Merced.
La Merced corner Izazaga San Pablo and Eje 1 Ote. The city's largest market, a collection of huge modern buildings, which for all their size can't contain the vast number of traders who want to set up here. Sells almost anything you could conceive of finding in a Mexican market (and much more you'd never thought of), though fruit, vegetables and other foods take up most space. Even if you're not buying you could easily spend half a day here browsing metre-diameter columns of nopal leaves as high as a man, the stacks of dried chiles and all manner of hardware from juice presses to volcanic-stone mortars known as *molcajetes*. The Metro takes you right into the heart of things. Daily 6am–6pm. Metro La Merced.
Palacio de Las Flores corner of Luis Moya and Ernesto Pugibet. A small market selling nothing but flowers – loose, in vast arrangements and wreaths, growing in pots, even paper and plastic. Similar markets can be found in San Ángel and Xochimilco. Metro Salto de Agua or Balderas.

Artesanía shops

Artesanías del Centro Palma Norte 506-F at Cuba. Small shop conveniently sited near the Zócalo and stocking a small but select range of metalwork, replica icons, scented candles and the like. Metro Allende.
FONART Juárez 89 ⓣ55/5521-0171, ⓦwww.fonart.gob.mx. A reasonable crafts shop run by FONART, the government agency that promotes quality arts and crafts and helps the artisans with marketing and materials. The fixed prices are usually higher than elsewhere, but it is worth visiting to check price and quality before venturing to the markets. Metro Hidalgo. There's another FONART outlet at Reforma 116.

English-language books and newspapers

International weeklies are available downtown from **newspaper stands** (especially along 5 de Mayo), but for most other items you'll need to head to the Zona Rosa or Colonia Polanco. Sanborn's, dotted all over town, usually have a modest supply of English-language material, much of it business-oriented. The **airport** has numerous small shops partly stocked with English-language magazines and airport novels, plus a few foreign newspapers. The best bets are the Cenca store in Sala E2, and Libros y Arte between Salas C and D.

American Book Store Bolivar 23, Centro Histórico ⓣ55/5512-0306. Despite the name, their stock of books in English is limited and mostly business- or computer-oriented. OK for a few paperbacks, magazines and newspapers. Mon–Sat 10am–7pm.
Casa de la Prensa Hamburgo 141 at Amberes, Zona Rosa ⓣ55/5208-1419. A good source of magazines and newspapers in English, German and French. Mon–Fri 8.30am–10pm, Sat 8.30am–9pm, Sun 8.30am–8pm.
Cenca Temistocles 73, near corner of Mazaryk and Arquimedes, Polanco ⓣ55/5280-1666, has a good selection of magazines, novels and even a few guidebooks, plus a good café next door for reading them all. Mon–Fri 8am–10pm, Sat & Sun 9am–9pm. Metro Polanco.
La Torre del Papel Callejón de Betlemitas 6a, beside the Museo del Ejército y Fuerza, near Bellas Artes. Stocks up-to-date newspapers from all over Mexico and Latin America with a good showing of US, British, Spanish and Italian newspapers, plus magazines such as *National Geographic, The Economist, Entertainment Weekly* and *Paris Match*. Mon–Fri 8am–7.30pm, Sat 8.30am–2.30pm.

Sport

Sport is probably the city's biggest obsession, and while **football**, **wrestling** and **bullfighting** are the three leading lights, the sporting calendar doesn't stop there. In years gone by, you could spend a moderately interesting evening watching **frontón** (pelota vasca, or *jai alai*) right in the city centre at the Frontón México on the Plaza de la República. With the players on strike since 1993, in a dispute that shows no signs of being resolved, some wonder whether the sport will ever regain its former following, especially since it is a pretty dull game (unless you're betting) and was already losing popularity when play was suspended. There's **horse racing**, too, throughout the year (afternoons, especially Sat) at the Hipodromo de las Americas on Avenida Industria Militar (ⓣ55/5387-0600, ⓦwww.hipodromo.com.mx; Metro Cuatro Caminos); buses and *peseros* heading west on Reforma will take you there – look for "Hipodromo". More exciting horse action is involved in the *charreadas*, or **rodeos**, put on by amateur but highly skilled aficionados most weekends, primarily at the Rancho del Charro, Constituyentes 500 (ⓣ55/5277-8706), close to the third section of Chapultepec Park; call to find out what's going on.

Football

Fútbol (football, meaning soccer) is undoubtedly Mexico's most popular sport. The big games are held at the 114,000-seat Estadio Azteca (see p.419), which hosted the World Cup finals in 1970 and 1986, and is home to América (Las Águilas, or The Eagles), the nation's most popular and consistently successful club side. Elsewhere in the city, the university side, UNAM (Las Pumas), have a strong following at the Estadio Olímpico across the road from the university (see p.419); and Cruz Azul (known as Los Cementeros for their long-time sponsorship by a cement company) pack out Estadio Azul right by the city's main bullring. There are two other major teams, Necaxa (Los Rayos), who share the Estadio Azteca with América, and Atlante (Los Potros, "the Colts"). There are usually at least two **games** every Sunday afternoon from August to May – check local papers for fixture details – and you can almost always get a **ticket** (US$2–10) at the gate. The exceptions are the big games such as major local derbies, and "El Clásico", when América host Chivas from Guadalajara, the biggest team from the country's second largest city. Estadio Azteca can be reached by Tren Ligero or Ruta #26 ("Xochimilco") colectivo, both from Metro Tasqueña; Estadio Olímpico is reached by "Tlalpan" bus from

Metro Chilpancingo; Estadio Azul is reached on foot from Metro San Antonio or from any bus running along Insurgentes Sur.

Wrestling

Though its popularity has waned in recent years, *lucha libre*, or **wrestling**, remains one of Mexico's most avidly followed spectator sports. Over a dozen venues in the capital alone host fights several nights a week for a fanatical public. Widely available magazines, comics, photonovels and films recount the real and imagined lives of the rings' heroes and villains, though the once nightly telecasts are now a thing of the past.

Mexican wrestling is generally faster, with more complex moves, and more combatants in the ring at any one time than you would normally see in an American or British bout. This can make the action hard to follow for the uninitiated. More important even than the moves is the maintenance of stage personas, most of whom, heroes or villains, wear masks. The *rudos* tend to use brute force or indulge in sneaky, underhand tactics to foil the opposition, while the *técnicos* use wit and guile to compensate for lack of brawn. This faux battle, not at all unlike the WWE on-screen antics, requires a massive suspension of disbelief – crucial if you want to join in the fun.

One of the most bizarre features of wrestling was the emergence of wrestlers as political figures – typically still in costume. Perhaps the most famous of all, **Superbarrio** ("Superneighbourhood") arose from the struggle of Mexico City's tenant associations for fair rents and decent housing after the 1985 earthquake. He has since become part of mainstream political opposition, regularly challenging government officials to step into the ring with him, and acting as a sort of unofficial cheerleader at opposition rallies. Other wrestlers have espoused political causes, such as Jalapa's Superecologista Verde ("Green Superecologist") who campaigns on environmental issues, including the demanded closure of Laguna Verde nuclear power station.

The most famous wrestler of all time, however, was without doubt **El Santo** ("the Saint"). Immortalized in more than twenty movies, with titles such as *El Santo vs the Vampire Women*, he would fight, eat, drink and play the romantic lead without ever removing his mask, and until after his retirement, he never revealed his identity. His reputation as a gentleman in and out of the ring was legendary, and his death in 1984 widely mourned. His funeral was allegedly the second best-attended in Mexican history after that of President Obregón.

Fights can be seen, particularly on Fridays and Sundays, at the Arena Coliseo, Peru 73 (Metro Allende) and the Arena México, Dr Río de la Loza 94, Colonia Doctores (one block south and one east of Metro Balderas, but not a good area to be in at night).

Bullfighting

Soccer and wrestling may be more popular, but there is no event more quintessentially Mexican than the **bullfight**. Rooted in Spanish machismo and imbued with multiple layers of symbolism and interpretation, it transcends a mere battle of man against animal. Many visitors arrive in Mexico revolted by the very idea of what may appear to be a one-sided slaughter of a noble beast, and there are certainly elements of cruelty in the proceedings. But spend an hour watching on TV and you may well find yourself hooked; if nothing else, it is worth attending a *corrida de toros* to see this integral part of the Mexican experience. It is a sport that transcends class barriers, something that is evident every Sunday afternoon during the winter season when men and women from all walks of Mexican society file into the stadium – though some admittedly

Football in Mexico

As in much of Latin America, *fútbol* in Mexico is a national addiction, if not an obsession. Turn on the TV and often as not you'll come across a match: every league game is televised, usually with delayed transmission, while the national team always seems to be in the midst of a lengthy qualifying stage for an international competition, not to mention frequent friendly matches. Still, if you can get to see a live game, it's a different experience entirely.

The game was introduced to Mexico in the early twentieth century, when a group of Cornish miners in Hidalgo formed the team Pachuca, and it was to take more than ninety years for them to win their first and, as yet, only league championship. The **league** follows a ladder system: the first division is divided into four tables of five teams each, which are decided by the previous season's placings, with the league champions placed first in table one, second placed top of table two and so on. Each team plays each other team in the table only once, and then the top two teams of each table compete in a play-off for the league championship. However, if any third-placed team has more points than a second-placed team, there is a play-off between them to see who goes forward to the finals. As this system means only nineteen league games to a season, there are two seasons each year, summer (Jan–May) and winter (July–Nov). While some believe this makes the lead-up games less exciting, local rivalries and old scores tend to add some intrigue. At the end of the winter season, the two seasons' winners (if they are different) compete to decide that year's champion of champions, though this is more of a show match than anything, with no trophy or official title attached to winning. The top teams aren't necessarily the safe bet that they are in most European leagues, this unpredictability due in part to the draft system, where out-of-contract players meet managers every June to organize new contracts, thus ensuring more of a balance between the teams over a year.

Relegation to a lower division is decided over a two-season (yearly) loss average so it is, in fact, technically possible to come first in the league and be relegated in the same season (although relegation means immediate disqualification from the play-offs). However, relegation need not be the disaster that it might seem. Take, for example, Puebla C.F., who when relegated in 1999 simply bought the team promoted from Primera B (Curtodores), changed their name to Puebla and relocated them, which is perfectly legal under Mexican financial regulations. Similarly, there are no regulations preventing anyone from owning more than one team, which can lead to a clash of interests that are never more than speculated upon; suspicion of corruption is rife but rarely, if ever, investigated. Another way of avoiding relegation is if the team that have won promotion from the Primera "B" are owned or sponsored by one of the top league clubs. They cannot be promoted and the relegated team

end up in plush *sombre* (shade) seats while the masses occupy concrete *sol* (sun) terraces.

During the **season** (late Oct to early April) fights take place every Sunday at 4pm at the giant 48,000-seat Plaza Mexico, the largest bullring in the world. Each corrida lasts around two hours and involves six bulls, all from one ranch, with each of three matadors taking two bulls. Typically there will be two Mexican matadors and one from Spain, which still produces the best performers: Enrique Ponce and Julian Lopez (always referred to as "El Juli") are currently the two top Spanish names, and if you see them billed you should definitely try to get along.

Each **fight** is divided into three *suertes* (acts) or *tercios* (thirds), each announced by a trumpet blast. During the first tercio, several *toreros* with large need not go down, all of which means that promotion and relegation are by no means certain in any given season.

Away from the Machiavellian machinations of the league system, **matches** themselves are almost always exciting and enjoyed by even the most diehard "anti-futbolistas". Music, dancing and, of course, the ubiquitous Mexican Wave make for a carnival atmosphere, enhanced by the spectators dressing up and wearing face paints. It's usually very much a family affair, with official sales people bringing soft drinks, beer and various types of food at fixed prices to your seat. **Stadiums** tend to be mostly concrete, all-seater affairs – though standing isn't prohibited – and can sometimes be dangerously overcrowded, though accidents are thankfully rare. Attendances vary depending on which team is playing, since support is less locally based than you might expect and the more successful teams naturally have the edge, to the detriment of smaller, local sides. The bigger clubs are those of Mexico City (América, Cruz Azul, Pumas – the national university side, Necaxa and Atlante) and Guadalajara (Chivas, Atlas and Tecos) and the games between any of these can draw crowds of up to 80,000, while smaller clubs like those of Puebla, Irapuato and Celaya may get no more than 10,000 or 15,000 spectators per game. The vast distances between clubs makes travelling to away games impossible for many fans, another reason why smaller, more out-of-the-way clubs don't get as much support. Passion for the game means that emotions run high, but this very rarely translates into violence. Opposing fans aren't generally separated, but there's a good relationship between them and an atmosphere of self-policing prevails – part of what makes it an ideal family occasion. The greatest risk is often to the referee, who is frequently escorted from the pitch by armed riot police. The players, on the other hand, are accorded a great deal of respect and the more popular ones tend to pick up nicknames, such as El Tiburón (Cardozo – the Shark), El Matador (Hernandez – the Killer) and El Ratón (Zarate – the Rat).

For **national games**, of course, the whole country is united and football has many times been shown to rise above the partisan politics of the country. In 1999, despite being outlawed by the government of Zedillo, the EZLN football squad even played an exhibition match against the national side in Mexico City's Estadio Azteca. The national side play frequently in both friendlies and small competitions on top of qualifiers (which may account for their high standing in FIFA rankings). Many of these games, even against South American sides, are played in southwestern US states but still achieve high attendances from the local Mexican population. Sometimes friendly matches will even draw capacity crowds and are an excellent opportunity to enjoy the spectacle of Mexico's premier sport.

For **up-to-date information** on Mexican league teams, fixtures and tables, visit Ⓦwww.futmex.com or Ⓦwww.megasoccer.com/main/world/ame/mex.

capes tire the bull in preparation for the *picadores* who, from their mounts atop heavily padded and blindfolded horses, attempt to force a lance between the bull's shoulder blades to further weaken him. The *toreros* then return for the second *tercio*, in which one of their number (and sometimes the matador himself) will try to stab six metal-tipped spikes (known as *bandilleras*) into the bull in as clean and elegant a manner as possible.

Exhausted and frustrated, but by no means docile, the bull is now considered ready for the third and final tercio, the *suerte de muleta*. The matador continues to tire the bull while pulling off as many graceful and daring moves as possible. By now the crowd will have sensed the bravery and finesse of the matador and the spirit of the bull he is up against, and shouts of "¡Olé!" will reverberate around the stadium with every pass. Eventually the matador will entice the bull to challenge him head-on, standing there with its hooves together. As it charges he will thrust his sword between its shoulder blades and, if it is well executed, the bull will crumple to the sand. However barbaric you might think it is, no one likes to the see the bull suffer and even the finest performance will garner the matador little praise without a clean kill. Successful matadors may be awarded one of the bull's ears, rarely two, and perhaps two or three times a season the tail as well. An especially courageous bull may be spared and put out to stud, a cause for much celebration, but this is a rare spectacle.

Elaborate posters around town advertise **upcoming events**, as do most of the major newspapers. Look out too for the weekly coverage of the scene in the press during the season. **Tickets** can be bought at the gate and you can expect to pay as little as US$4 for general admission to sunny concrete benches far from the action. Fifty cents more and you'll have the luxury of some shade, and from there prices rise rapidly the closer you get to the ring, often reaching US$40 for a front-row seat: something in the *primera tenida* (US$20–30) is close enough for most first-timers. To get there, pick up any bus heading south on Insurgentes and follow the crowds, or walk ten minutes east from Metro San Antonio.

Listings

Airlines The main ones are Aerocalifornia, Reforma 332 at El Ángel ⓣ55/5207-1392; Aerocaribe, Xola 535, 28th floor, Col del Valle ⓣ55/5448-3000; Aerolineas Argentinas, Xola 535, 4th floor, Col del Valle ⓣ55/5523-7097; Aerolitoral, Reforma 445, 10th floor ⓣ55/5513-4026; Aeromar, airport Sala B ⓣ55/5784-1139 or 01-800/704-2900; Aeroméxico, Reforma 445 ⓣ55/5514-9736 or 01-800/021-2622; Air Canada, Reforma 389, 14th floor ⓣ55/5208-1883 or 01-800/719-2827; Air France, Edgar Allen Poe 90, Polanco ⓣ55/5627-6000 or 01-800/006-7700; America West, Río Tiber 103, 6th floor, Zona Rosa ⓣ55/5511-9779 or 01-800/533-6862; American, Reforma 314 at Amberes ⓣ55/5209-1400 or 01-800/904-6000; Aviacsa, Reforma 107, local B ⓣ55/5705-2825; British Airways, Polanco Plaza, Calle Jaime Balmes 8 ⓣ55/5387-0300; Canadian, Reforma 389, 14th floor ⓣ55/5208-1691; Continental, Andrés Bello 45, 18th floor, Polanco ⓣ55/5283-5500 or 01-800/706-6800; Cubana, Temístocles 246, Polanco ⓣ55/5255-3776; Delta, Reforma 381 near El Ángel, Zona Rosa ⓣ55/5279-0909 or 01-800/902-2100; Iberia, Reforma 24 ⓣ55/5130-3030; LACSA, Reforma 509 ⓣ55/5211-6604; Lufthansa, Paseo de las Palmas 391, Lomas de Chapultepec ⓣ55/5230-0000; Mexicana, handiest offices at Juárez 82 at Balderas, and Reforma 312 at Amberes ⓣ55/5448-0990 or 01-800/501-9900; Northwest/KLM, Paseo de las Palmas 735, 7th floor, Lomas de Chapultepec ⓣ55/5279-5390; Qantas, Reforma 10, 14th floor ⓣ55/5628-0547; United, Hamburgo 213 ⓣ55/5627-0222.

Airport To get to the airport, either take the Metro (Metro Terminal Aérea, line 5), or phone ProTaxi the day before (ⓣ55/2559-0333) or one of the firms listed on p.371 to arrange a cab from your hotel. For flight enquiries, call ⓣ55/5571-3600 – you'll be offered a choice of languages, and then given the option of dialling an extension number: dial ⓣ2208 for international flight enquiries, or ⓣ2259 for domestic. For details of airport facilities, see p.365.

American Express Central office and clients' mail service at Reforma 350 by El Ángel (Mon–Fri 9am–6pm, Sat 9am–1pm; ⓣ55/5207-7049). Several other offices throughout the city.

Banks and exchange ATMs are everywhere and with the appropriate credit or cash cards you can get money throughout your stay without ever visiting a bank. Besides, many banks will only change money in the morning, and many are unhelpful for currencies other than US dollars: Banamex is your best bet. Most large hotels and shops will change travellers' cheques and cash dollars, but the quickest and easiest places to change money are casas de cambio, scattered all over town. In the Centro Histórico try Casa de cambio Puebla, Madero 27 at Bolivar (Mon–Fri 9am–5pm, Sat 10am–2.30pm) or Cambios Exchange, at Madero 113 near Filomena Mata (daily 9.30am–7pm). You'll find several in the Zona Rosa, especially on Amberes, Londres and Liverpool, and a couple on the south side of Reforma, just south of the Monumento a la Revolución.

Buses There's a checklist of the main destinations from each bus station on p.366. It's rare not to be able to get on a bus at short notice, but it can be worth booking in advance for long-distance journeys or for express services to popular destinations at busy times – that way you'll have a choice of seat and be sure of getting the fastest service. If you're uncertain which bus station you should be leaving from, simply get into a taxi and tell the driver what your ultimate destination is – he'll know where to take you. You'll find places to eat, and stalls selling food and drink for the journey in all the terminals along with ATMs and newsstands.

Car rental There are thousands of agencies throughout the city, and the small local operations are often cheaper than the big chains. Either way, renting a car isn't going to be cheap, and a car can be more of a liability than a help while you're in the city. Expect to pay US$50–75 a day for the cheapest car with tax, insurance and unlimited mileage, more in July and August; the usual deal for a week is that you pay for six days and get the seventh free. The major operators all have offices at the airport and in the Zona Rosa, and some of the smaller companies do too, a major boon as it saves you trawling around the city for the best deals. The best airport deals are with Kim Kar (Ⓣ55/2599-0267) who are marginally cheaper than Gold Car Rental (Ⓣ55/2599-0090 or 91, Ⓦwww.gold.com.mx) or EconoMovil (Ⓣ55/2599-0147), and somewhat cheaper than Royal Rent A Car (Ⓣ55/2599-0147, Ⓦwww.royalrent.com). Current best prices among the multinational firms are from Hertz (Ⓣ55/5783-7400 or 01-800/709-5000, Ⓦwww.hertz.com.mx) and National (Ⓣ55/5786-8228, Ⓦwww.national-car.com.mx); others represented (in ascending price order) include Thrifty (Ⓣ01-800/800-2382, Ⓦwww.thrifty.com.mx), Alamo (Ⓣ55/1101-1100 or 01-800/849-8001, Ⓦwww.alamo-mexico.com.mx), Budget (Ⓣ55/5271-4322 or 01-800/700-1700, Ⓦwww.budget.com.mx) and Avis (Ⓣ55/5588-8888 or 01-800/288-8888, Ⓦwww.avis.com.mx). Note that rental cars are exempt from the one day a week driving restriction.

Courier services DHL at Madero 70, Centro Histórico (Mon–Fri 9am–6pm) and other locations (Ⓣ55/5345-7000); FedEx at Reforma 308, Zona Rosa (Mon–Fri 9am–7pm, Sat 9am–2pm) and other locations (Ⓣ55/5228-9904 or 01-800/900-1100).

Cultural institutes Several countries maintain cultural institutes and libraries for their nationals within Mexico City, often allowing short-term visitors to use some of their facilities. They can also be useful places for contacts, and if you're looking for work, long-term accommodation or travelling companions their notice boards are good places to start. The US has the Biblioteca Benjamín Franklin, Liverpool 31 at Berlin (Mon–Fri 11am–7pm; Ⓣ55/5080-2000, Ⓦwww.usembassy-mexico.gov/biblioteca; Metro Cuauhtémoc); the UK has the British Council, Lope de Vega 316 (Mon–Fri 8am–3pm; Ⓣ55/5263-1930; Metro Polanco); Canadians can use the Canadian Embassy Library (see below; Mon–Fri 9am–12.30pm).

Embassies and consulates Australia, Rubén Darío 55, Polanco (Mon–Thurs 8.30am–5.15pm, Fri 8.30am–2.15pm; Ⓣ55/5531-5225, Ⓦwww.mexico.embassy.gov.au; Metro Auditorio); Belize, Bernardo de Gálves 215, Lomas de Chapultepec (Mon–Fri 9am–1.30pm; Ⓣ55/5520-1274, Ⓔembelize@prodigy.net.mx); Canada, Schiller 529, Polanco (Mon–Fri 9am–1pm & 2–5pm; Ⓣ55/5724-7943, toll-free emergency number for Canadians Ⓣ01-800/706-2900, Ⓦwww.canada.org.mx; Metro Polanco); Costa Rica, Río Po 113 at Río Lerma, Zona Rosa (Mon–Fri 9am–5pm; Ⓣ55/5255-7764 to 6, Ⓔconsulg@podernet.com.mx; Metro Insurgentes); Cuba, Presidente Masaryk 554, Polanco (Mon–Fri 10am–2pm; Ⓣ55/5280-8039, Ⓔcancilleria@embacuba.com.mx; Metro Polanco); El Salvador, Temístocles 88, Polanco (Mon–Fri 9am–4pm; Ⓣ55/5281-5723 or 5, Ⓔembesmex@webtelmex.net.mx; Metro Polanco); Guatemala, Explanada 1025, Lomas de Chapultepec (Mon–Fri 9am–2pm & 3–5pm; Ⓣ55/5540-7520, Ⓔembaguate@mexis.com); Honduras, Alfonso Reyes 220 at Ometusco (Mon–Fri 9am–1.30pm; Ⓣ55/5211-5250, Ⓔemhonmex@mail.internet.com.mx; Metro Patriotismo); New Zealand, J.L. LeGrange 103, 10th floor, Polanco (Mon–Thurs 8.30am–2pm & 3–5.30pm, Fri 8.30am–2pm; Ⓣ55/5283-9460, Ⓔkiwimexico@compuserve.com.mx); Panama, Horacio 1501, Polanco (Mon–Fri 8.30am–3.30pm; Ⓣ55/5557-6159, Ⓦwww.embpanamamexico.com; Metro Polanco); UK, Río Lerma 71 at Río Sena, Zona Rosa (Mon–Fri 9am–3pm; Ⓣ55/5207-2089, Ⓦwww.embajadabritanica .com.mx; Metro Insurgentes); US, Reforma 305 at Danubio, Zona Rosa (Mon–Fri 8.30am–5.30pm; Ⓣ55/5080-2000, Ⓦwww.usembassy-mexico.gov; Metro Insurgentes).

Emergencies All emergency services (police, fire, ambulance) Ⓣ080; fire department Ⓣ068; Red Cross ambulance Ⓣ065; rabies prevention Ⓣ55/5796-3790; forest fire Ⓣ55/5554-0612;

Locatel, which gives information on missing persons and vehicles, medical emergencies, emotional crises and public services ☎55/5658-1111; police ☎060.

Hospital The American-British Cowdray Hospital (ABC) is at Av Constituyentes 500, Col Lomas Altas (☎55/5230-8000). Embassies should be able to provide a list of multilingual doctors if necessary and American Express cardholders can make use of their Global Assist medical referral service.

Internet access Numerous cybercafés all over the city generally charge around US$1.50–2 per hour, but shop around as there are often special offers (two hours for the price of one, etc). In the centre, the best deal at last check (two hours for US$1.50) was with *Internet*, #110, 1st floor, Tacuba 40 (Mon–Fri 10am–9pm, Sat 10am–3pm; Metro Allende). Otherwise, try: *Hostel Catedral* (see p.372; Metro Zócalo); Lafoel Internet Service, 1st República floor, Doncelos 80 at República de Brasil (Mon–Fri 9am–8pm, Sat 10am–8pm; ☎55/5512-3584; Metro Allende). In the Zona Rosa, there are several inside the roundabout at Glorieta Insurgentes, or try Java Chat, Génova 44 (Mon–Fri 8am–11.30pm, Sat & Sun 10am–11.30pm; Metro Insurgentes).

Language schools Many places run Spanish courses in the city, though most people prefer to study away from the capital in such places as Cuernavaca, San Miguel de Allende and Guanajuato. For those who prefer the metropolis, the two main language schools in town are Alliant International University, Álvaro Obregón 110, Roma (☎55/5264-2187, ⓦwww.usiumexico.edu), and the University's Centro de Enseñanza para Extranjeros, Avenida Universidad 3002, Ciudad Universitaria (☎55/5622-2470, ⓦwww.cepe.unam.mx), and it is also worth checking out ⓦwww.planeta.com/mexico.html which has good links to Mexican language schools.

Laundry Self-service launderettes are surprisingly rare in Mexico City, but most hotels should be able to point one out for you. Options include Lavandería Automática Lavajet, Danubio 123b at Lerma (Mon–Fri 8.15am–6pm, Sat 8.15am–5pm), close to the Zona Rosa; and Lavandería Automática Edison, Edison 91 at Arriaga near the Plaza de la República (Mon–Fri 9.30am–7pm, Sat 10am–6pm; Metro Revolución).

Left luggage Most hotels will hold your bags for the rest of the day after you've checked out, and some will allow you to leave excess luggage for several days, sometimes for a small charge. At the airport there are lockers at two locations (Sala A and Sala E3) for US$5–7.50 a day. All four main bus terminals have left luggage facilities, but only the one at Terminal del Norte is open round the clock (US$1–2 a day depending on the size of your bag).

Opening hours Hours for most businesses in Mexico City are from 10am until 7pm. Very few now close for the traditional 2pm to 4pm siesta.

Pharmacies Sanborn's offers a wide range of products at most branches, as well as dispensing some prescription drugs. Other options include El Fénix, Madero 41 at Motolinia. There are homeopathic pharmacies at Mesones 111-B at 20 Noviembre, and República Guatemala 16, behind the cathedral.

Photographic supplies Film is available almost everywhere – pharmacies, tourist locales and so on – at reasonable prices, but for specialist needs head to one of several large shops on Avenida Juárez, along the south side of the Alameda, such as Foto Imagen at no.56 (☎55/5510-0240).

Post office The main post office is on Lázaro Cárdenas at Tacuba, across the street from Bellas Artes (Mon–Fri 8am–8pm, Sat & Sun 8am–4pm). Branch offices (Mon–Fri 9am–3pm, Sat 9am–1pm) can be found at Ponciano Arriaga 11 near the Revolution Monument, and Río Lerma at Río Marne, just north of the Zona Rosa, among other places.

Telephones Local, domestic long-distance and international phone calls can be made from any public phone with a phonecard. Cheaper international calls can be made via the Internet, though only a few Internet locales are offering this service as yet – Java Chat at Génova 44 is one that does. Otherwise, a number of shops have public phones (for international services look for the blue "Larga Distancia" signs). You can dial direct from most big hotels, but it will cost much more. *Casetas de larga distancia* are closing down in the face of widespread use of cardphones, but you'll find them at all the bus terminals except TAPO, at the airport, Sala E2 (all hours), and at Amberes 62 in the Zona Rosa.

Tourist cards Should you lose yours, or want an extension, you apply, when your original length of stay is almost finished, to the Instituto de Migración, Ejército National 862, at the western end of Polanco (Mon–Fri 9am–1pm; ☎55/2581-0164 or 5; *peseros* from Chapultepec to Toreo run along Ejército Nacional). Extensions are pretty much routine if the period is two weeks or less, and should take around half an hour; go to desk D23 – "Ampliación de Estancia". Longer extensions will require copies, form filling and possibly an onward ticket or proof of sufficient funds. For anything other than a straight extension to your duration of stay as a tourist (such as residence or a student visa), you may need to go to the main immigration office at Homero 1832, at the very far western end of Polanco (Mon–Fri 9am–1pm; ⓣ55/5387-2400), where you can expect to spend a fair time waiting in line.

Trains Following privatization, all passenger train services out of Mexico City have ceased to run, and the only indication that they ever did is an old steam locomotive standing outside what used to be the terminus on Buenavista.

Travel agencies A particularly good firm for youth and student fares is Mundo Joven (ⓦwww.mundojoven.com), with offices at Guatemala 4 behind the cathedral (ⓣ55/5518-1754 to 5), Homero 342 in Polanco (ⓣ55/5250-7191), and Sala E3 in the airport (ⓣ55/2599-0155).

Women's groups *La Casa de los Amigos* (see p.372) have details of women's groups and support general social development projects.

Work Very hard to come by – there's some chance of finding a job teaching English, or maybe au pair-type work. Language teachers could advertise private lessons in one of the Spanish papers, but remember that it is illegal to work if you are in the country as a tourist.

Around the city

Breaking out of the capital in any direction, you'll find targets of interest within a couple of hours' drive. First, and the one day-trip that everyone seems to take, are the massive pyramids and ancient city of **Teotihuacán**, about 50km northeast. Though the setting isn't as stunning as some of the southern Mexican sites, this is easily the largest, and there's enough to see to occupy a full day. Directly north, on the road to Querétaro, lies **Tula**, the centre that succeeded Teotihuacán as the Valley's great power, with its striking large statues atop the main pyramid. On the way out to Tula you can stop at **Tepotzotlán**, which holds some of the finest Baroque and colonial art in the country and has a relaxed feel enlivened by an influx of day-trippers from Mexico City at weekends.

To the east, **Pachuca** is a fairly workaday town that's home to the national photography museum and is made more interesting by the nearby presence of **Real del Monte**, where Cornish miners introduced soccer to Mexico in the nineteenth century. Moving clockwise around the capital, **Tlaxcala** and **Cholula** were important allies of the Aztecs when Cortés marched this way from the coast. Tlaxcala is now a wonderfully quiet colonial town, while at Cholula is the rubble of the largest pyramid in Mexico. Here the conquistadors claimed to have erected a church on the site of each pagan temple, and there's said to be a chapel for every day of the year. Between these two stands **Puebla**, a crowded industrial centre with aspects of colonial charm. Puebla and Cholula provide the region's best views of the twin volcanoes, **Popocatépetl** and **Ixtaccíhuatl**, both currently off limits after Popo's sporadic eruptions.

South of Mexico City, **Cuernavaca** has long been a sought-after refuge from the capital. Brimming with attractive colonial mansions and gardens, it also draws visitors on account of its proximity to several important archeological sites – while beyond it lies the road to Acapulco and the tourist haven of **Taxco**, renowned for its silver jewellery. **Toluca**, on the old road to Morelia, hosts a colossal market every Friday, and the surrounding country is full of mountain retreats where Mexicans go to escape city life, notably the small town of **Malinalco** with its ancient hillside ruins, and the water-sports destination of **Valle de Bravo**.

Teotihuacán and around

It seems that every visitor to Mexico City at some stage heads out to the pyramids at **Teotihuacán** (daily 7am–6.30pm, last ticket sold at 6pm; US$3.70, camcorder US$3): there's a constant stream of tours, buses and cars heading this way, and the site itself can be crawling with people, especially on Sunday. It is an extensive site that can easily take up the majority of a day, and it makes sense to plan ahead. The best bet is to head out here as early as you can manage and do most of your exploration in the cool of the morning before the crowds arrive. From 11am to 3pm it can be very busy, and there is little shade, so it is best to spend that time at a restaurant or in the **museum**, and return refreshed for the photogenic light of the late afternoon. Visitors with limited Spanish will be pleased here – the majority of explanatory signs are also in English.

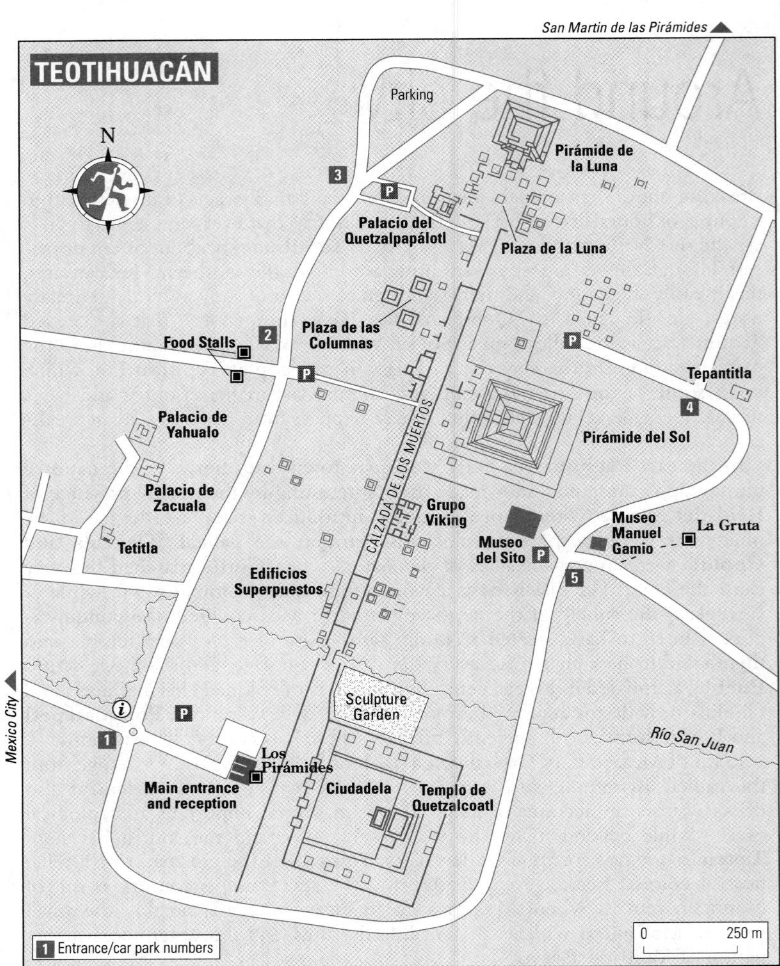

Site practicalities

To get to Teotihuacán you can catch one of the buses that leave every fifteen minutes or so (6am–3pm; 1hr) from the Terminal del Norte. Go to the second-class (left-hand) side of the bus station and look for the Autobuses Teotihuacán stand in Sala 8; be aware that these buses have from time to time been targeted by bandits, so make sure you're not carrying a lot of cash. A slightly quicker alternative is to catch the Metro to Indios Verdes (line 3) and head to the northern end of Platform J, from where buses leave frequently for "Las Pirámides". A road, the Carretera de Circunvalación, provides access to the main structures through one of six gates (each with parking and lines of souvenir stalls): buses might arrive at any *puerta* (gate), though Puerta 1 and Puerta 4 are the most common. These are the best places to wait for the frequent **buses back to Mexico City**, but late in the day most of them make a full circuit of all gates before departing the site.

If you are on a budget it's best to bring all your **food and drink** with you as anything bought at the site is going to be expensive. The main **restaurant** and bar, *Las Pirámides*, is at the principal entrance at Puerta 1, and has an all-you-can-eat buffet for US$9.20. Prices are high considering the quality of the food, but the view of the site from the top-floor restaurant is great. Cheaper food (including comidas corridas for as little as US$3) is most easily found at the handful of small restaurants beside the ring road at Puerta 2, whose representatives will be

The rise and fall of Teotihuacán

The rise and fall of Teotihuacán is almost exactly contemporary with Imperial Rome. From around 600 BC, there was evidence of small agricultural communities in the vicinity and by 200 BC a township had been established on the present site. From then until 1 AD (the period known as the **Patlachique** phase) the population began to soar, and the city assumed its most important characteristics: the great Pyramids of the Sun and Moon were built, and the Calzada de los Muertos laid out. Development continued through the **Tzacualli** and **Miccaotli** phases (1–250 AD) with more construction and the blossoming of artistic expression, then through the **Tlamimilolpa** phase (250–450 AD) there is evidence of the city's influence (in architecture, sculpture and pottery) occurring at sites throughout modern Mexico and into Guatemala and Honduras. From 450 to around 650 (**Xolalpan** phase) it reached the peak of population and power, with much new building and addition to earlier structures. Already by the end of this period, however, there were signs of decline, and the final period (**Metepec** phase) lasted at most a century before the city was sacked, burnt and virtually abandoned. This, presumably, was the result of attack by northern tribes, probably the Toltecs, but the disaster may in the end have been as much ecological as military. Vast forests were cut down to build the city (for use in columns, roof supports, door lintels) and huge quantities of wood burnt to make the lime plaster that coated the buildings. The result was severe soil erosion that left the hillsides as barren as they appear today. In addition, the agricultural effort needed to feed so many people (with no form of artificial fertilizer or knowledge of crop rotation) gradually sapped what land remained of its ability to grow more.

Whatever the precise causes, the city was left, eventually, to a ruination that was advanced even by the time of the Aztecs. To them it represented a holy place from a previous age, and they gave it its present name, which translates as "The Place Where Men Became Gods". Although Teotihuacán features frequently in Aztec mythology, there are no written records – what we know of the city is derived entirely from archeological and artistic evidence, so that even the original name remains unknown.

on your case as soon as you set foot outside the gate. For something a little special, head for *La Gruta*, 200m west of Puerta 5 (☎595/956-0104), a fancy restaurant set deep in an open-sided cave, with white-jacketed waiters and a live show Saturday and Sunday at 3.30pm. At around US$10–15 for a main course it isn't that much more expensive than *Las Pirámides* and is much more satisfying.

The site

Teotihuacán is not, on first glance, the most impressive site in Mexico – it lacks the dramatic hilltop setting or lush jungle vegetation of those in the south – but it reveals a city planned and built on a massive scale, the great pyramids so huge that before their refurbishment one would have passed them by as hills without a second look. At its height this must have been the most imposing city ever seen in pre-Hispanic America, with a population thought to have been around 80,000 (though 200,000 is suggested by some sources) spread over an area of some 23 square kilometres (as opposed to the four square kilometres of the ceremonial centre). Then, every building – grey hulks now – would have been covered in bright polychrome murals.

Calzada de los Muertos

From the main entrance, you emerge at the bottom of the two-kilometre-long **Calzada de los Muertos** (Causeway of the Dead), which originally extended 1.5km further south, and formed the axis around which the city developed. A broad roadway some 40m wide linking all the most significant buildings, it was conceived to impress, with the low buildings that flank most of its length serving to heighten the impact of the two great temples at the northern end. Other streets, leading off to the rest of the city, originally intersected it at right angles, and even the Río San Juan was canalized so as not to disturb the symmetry (the bridge that then crossed it would have extended the full width of the street). Its name is something of a misconception, since it isn't a simple street but more a series of open plazas linked by staircases rising about 30m between the Citadel and the Pyramid of the Moon. Neither is it in any way linked with the dead, although the Aztecs believed the buildings that lined it, then little more than earth-covered mounds, to be the burial places of kings. They're not, and although the exact function of most remains unclear, all obviously had some sacred significance. The design, seen in the many reconstructions, is fairly uniform: low three- or four-storey platforms consisting of vertical panels (*tableros*) supported by sloping walls. In many cases several are built on top of each other – nowhere more clearly demonstrated than in the **Edificios Superpuestos** (superimposed buildings) on the left-hand side shortly beyond the river. Here you can descend a metal staircase to find excavated structures underneath the present level – these may have been the living quarters of Teotihuacán's priests.

La Ciudadela

Directly opposite the main entrance lies **La Ciudadela**, the Citadel. This enormous sunken square, surrounded by stepped platforms and with a low square altar in the centre, was the city's administrative heart, with the houses of its chief priests and nobles arranged around a vast meeting place. Across the open space stands a tall pyramid construction inside which, during excavation, was found the **Templo de Quetzalcoatl**. With the back of the newer pyramid demolished, the elaborate (Miccaotli phase) temple structure stands revealed. Pyramids aside, it is one of the most impressive sections of the whole site, rising in four steps (of an original six), each sculpted in relief and punctuated at intervals by the stylized heads of Quetzalcoatl, the plumed serpent, and **Tlaloc**, the rain god. Traces of the original paint can be seen in places. This theme – with the goggle-eyed, almost abstract mask of Tlaloc and the fanged snake Quetzalcoatl, its neck ringed with a collar of feathers – recurs in later sites throughout the country.

Pirámide del Sol

The great **Pirámide del Sol** (Pyramid of the Sun) is Teotihuacán's outstanding landmark, a massive structure 70m high and second in size only to Cholula of Mexico's ancient buildings (and Cholula is a total ruin). Its base is almost exactly the same size as that of the great Pyramid of Cheops in Egypt, but the lower-angled sides and its stepped nature make it very much lower. There are wonderful views from the top nonetheless, and the bulk is all the more remarkable when you consider the accuracy of its alignment: on two days a year (May 19 and July 25), the sun is directly over the pyramid at noon, and the main west facade faces the point at which the sun sets on these days. This alignment just off the cardinal points determined the line of the Calzada de los Muertos and of the entire city. Equally remarkable is the fact that the 2.5 million tonnes of stone and earth used in its construction were brought here without benefit of the wheel or any beast of burden, and shaped without the use of metal tools. The pyramid you see was reconstructed by Leopoldo Batres in 1908, in a thoroughly cavalier fashion. He blasted, with dynamite, a structure that originally abutted the south face, and stripped much of the surface in a search for a more complete building under the present one. In fact, the Pirámide del Sol, almost uniquely, was built in one go at a very early stage of the city's development (about 100 AD), and there is only a very small older temple right at its heart. As a result of Batres' stripping of the stone surface, the temple has eroded considerably more than it might otherwise have done. He also added an extra terrace to the original four.

You approach by a short staircase leading to the right off the Calzada de los Muertos onto a broad esplanade, where stand the ruins of several small temples and priests' dwellings. The main structure consists of five sloping layers of wall divided by terraces – the large flat area at the top would originally have been surmounted by a sanctuary, long disappeared. Evidence of why this massive structure came to be raised here emerged in 1971 when archeologists stumbled on a tunnel (closed to the public) leading to a clover-leaf-shaped **cave** directly under the centre of the pyramid. This, clearly, had been some kind of inner sanctuary, a holy of holies, and may even have been the reason for Teotihuacán's foundation and the basis of its influence. Theories abound as to its exact nature, and many fit remarkably with legends handed down through the Aztecs. It's perhaps most likely that the cave was formed by a subterranean spring, and came to be associated with Tlaloc, god of rain but also a bringer of fertility, as a sort of fountain of life.

Alternatively, it could be associated with the legendary "seven grottos", a symbol of creation from which all later Mexican peoples claimed to have emerged, or to have been the site of an oracle, or associated with a cult of sacrifice – in Aztec times the flayed skins of victims of Xipe Totec were stored in a cave under a pyramid.

Pirámide de la Luna

At the end of the Causeway of the Dead rises the **Pirámide de la Luna** (Pyramid of the Moon), a smaller structure built slightly later (but still during the Tzacualli phase), whose top, thanks to the higher ground on which it's built, is virtually on a level with that of the Pirámide del Sol. The structure is very similar, with four sloping levels approached by a monumental stairway, but for some reason this seems a very much more elegant building: perhaps because of the smaller scale, or perhaps as a result of the approach, through the formally laid-out **Plaza de la Luna**. The top of this pyramid offers the best overview of the site's layout, looking straight back down the length of the central thoroughfare. It is perfect for sunset, though as it is close to closing time the guards will soon chase you down.

The Palacio de Quetzalpapálotl and the Palacio de los Jaguares

The **Palacio de Quetzalpapálotl** (Palace of the Quetzal-butterfly) lies to the left of the Plaza de la Luna, behind the low temples that surround it. Wholly restored, it's virtually the only example of a pre-Hispanic roofed building in central Mexico and preserves a unique view of how the elite lived at Teotihuacán. The rooms are arranged around a patio whose elaborately carved pillars give the palace its name – their stylized designs represent birds (the brightly coloured quetzals, though some may be owls) and butterflies. In the galleries around the patio several frescoes survive, all very formalized and symbolic, with the themes reduced almost to geometric patterns. **Mural art** was clearly very important in Teotihuacán, and almost every building has some trace of decoration, though much has been removed for restoration. Two earlier buildings, half buried under the palace, still have substantial remains. In the **Palacio de los Jaguares**, jaguars in feathered headdresses blow conch shells from which emerge curls of music, or perhaps speech or prayers to Tlaloc (who appears along the top of the mural); in the **Templo de los Caracoles Emplumados** (Temple of the Plumed Shells), you see a motif of feathers and seashells along with bright green parrots. Other murals, of which only traces remain, were found in the temples along the Calzada de los Muertos between the two pyramids.

Tepantitla, Tetitla and Atetelco

Mural art was not reserved for the priests' quarters – indeed some of the finest frescoes have been found in outlying apartment buildings. At **Tepantitla**, a residential quarter of the old city across the road from the back of the Pirámide del Sol, the famous *Paradise of Tlaloc* mural (reproduced in the Museo Nacional de Antropología, see p.401) was discovered. Only a part of it survives here, but there are others in the complex depicting a procession of priests and a ball-game. All have great vitality and an almost comic-strip quality, with the speech bubbles emerging from the figures' mouths, but their themes always have a religious rather than a purely decorative intent. More can be seen at **Tetitla**, to the west of the main site, and **Atetelco**, a little further west, just off the plan (on p.446).

Museo del Sitio

Plan to spend at least some of your time in Teotihuacán's excellent **Museo del Sitio** (site hours; entry included in site fee) situated behind the Pirámide del Sol and surrounded by a lovely sculpture and botanical garden. In the cool interior artefacts from the site are well laid out and effectively lit to highlight the key features of each item. There's just about everything you would expect of a ritual site and living city from sharp-edged obsidian tools and everyday ceramics to some fine polychrome vessels decorated with animal and plant designs, and a series of five ceremonial braziers or censers ornamented with appliqué flowers, butterflies and shields.

Vast windows framing the Pyramid of the Sun take up one entire wall of the next room where you walk across a glass floor below which there's a huge relief map of the entire city as it might once have been. This area leads to a second section mostly comprising larger sculptural pieces depicting assorted gods, often bottom-lit to accentuate the gruesome features. There are some superb masks too, along with a couple of funerary sites modelled on those found under the Templo de Quetzalcoatl.

Nearby, just outside the gate, the **Museo Manuel Gamio** (daily 7am–7pm; free) houses interesting temporary exhibitions, and is worth a look if you're passing.

Around Teotihuacán

On the way to the pyramids you pass a couple of places that, if you're driving, are certainly worth a look, but barely merit the hassle involved in stopping over on the bus, though they can both be accessed easily by *combi* from a junction 500m beyond Puerta 5. At the village of **TEPEXPAN**, is a **museum** (Tues–Sun 10am–5pm; free) housing the fossil of a mammoth dug up in the surrounding plain (then marshland). There's also a skeleton known as the "Tepexpan Man", once claimed to be the oldest in Mexico but now revealed as less than 2000 years old. This whole area is a rich source of such remains – the Aztecs knew of their existence, which is one of the reasons they believed that the huge structures of Teotihuacán had been built by a race of giants. The museum is a fifteen-minute walk from the village, near the motorway toll booths, where any second-class bus will drop you; the village itself is attractive, with a good café on Calle de los Reyes, just off the main square. Buses to Metro Indios Verdes and *combis* to Teotihuacán can be picked up at the junction just outside the museum.

A few kilometres towards Teotihuacán (ten minutes by *combi* from Tepexpan, twenty from Teotihuacán) is the beautiful sixteenth-century monastery of **San Agustín Acolman** (daily 9am–6pm; US$2.70). Built on a raised, man-made terrace (probably on the site of an earlier, Aztec temple), it's a stern-looking building, lightened by the intricacy of its sculpted facade. In the nave and around the cloister are preserved portions of early murals depicting the monks, while several of the halls off the cloister display colonial religious painting and pre-Hispanic artefacts found here. If you turn right out of the gate, *combis* for Teotihuacán or Tepexpan can be picked up after 100m at the main road. **CHICONCUAC** to the south is rather more of a detour, but on Tuesdays, when there's a large market that specializes in woollen goods, sweaters and blankets, it's included in the itinerary of many of the tours to the pyramids. Again, this is hard to get to on a regular bus, and if you want to visit the market it's easier to do so as an entirely separate trip – buses, again, from the Terminal del Norte.

Tepotzotlán

TEPOTZOTLÁN lies en route from the capital to Tula, and while you'll have to take a couple of buses, it is quite possible to visit the two on one long day from the metropolis. Having said that, Tepotzotlán is easily close enough to the city to be a morning's excursion, though once you're there you may find the place seduces you into staying longer. The town is small and thoroughly Mexican-colonial, and the trees, hills and slow pace make a wonderful antidote to the big-city blues. Though it's somewhat touristy, commercialization is still low-key, and the majority of visitors are Mexican: the festive atmosphere on Saturdays is particularly enjoyable; that on Sundays less so as the crafts market draws large crowds. In the week before Christmas, the *pastorelas*, or **nativity plays**, staged here are renowned – and booked up long in advance; at other times, you may well catch a concert in the church or cloisters.

Museo Nacional del Virreinato

Atmosphere apart, the reason people come to Tepotzotlán is to see the magnificent Baroque **Colegio de San Francisco Javier** and the **Museo Nacional del Virreinato** (Viceroyalty Museum; Tues–Sun 9am–6pm; US$3.70, free on Sun) that it houses. These, though, are attraction enough. The church was founded by the Jesuits, who arrived in 1580 with a mission to convert the Otomí locals. Most of the huge complex you see today was established during the following century but constantly embellished right up to the expulsion of the Jesuits in 1767. The facade of the church – considered one of the finest examples of churrigueresque architecture in the country – was completed barely five years before this. The wealth and scale of all this gives some idea of the power of the Jesuits prior to their ousting; after they left, it became a seminary for the training of regular priests until the late nineteenth century, when the Jesuits were briefly readmitted. The Revolution led to its final abandonment in 1914.

Iglesia de San Francisco Javier

The main entrance to the Colegio de San Francisco Javier leads into the **Claustro de los Aljibes**, with a well at the centre and pictures of the life of Ignatius Loyola (founder of the Jesuits) around the walls. Off the cloister is the entrance to the church, the **Iglesia de San Francisco Javier**. If the facade is spectacular, it's still barely preparation for the dazzling interior. Dripping with gold, and profusely carved with a bewilderment of saints and cherubim, it strikes you at first as some mystical cave of treasures. The main body of the church and its chapels house five huge gilded cedarwood *retablos*, stretching from ceiling to floor, each more gloriously curlicued than the last, their golden richness intensified by the soft yellow light penetrating through the alabaster that covers the windows. Much of the painting on the main altar (dedicated to the church's patron saint) is attributed to Miguel Cabrera, sometimes considered to be Mexico's Michelangelo, whose talents are also on display towards the main church door, which is framed by two large oils, one depicting worshippers bathing in the blood from Jesus' crucifixion wounds.

All this is only the start, for hidden to one side is arguably the greatest achievement of Mexican Baroque, the octagonal **Camarín de la Virgen**. It's not a large room, but every inch is elaborately decorated and the hand of the native craftsmen is clearly evident in the exuberant carving – fruit and flowers, shells and abstract patterns crammed in between the angels. There's a mirror angled to allow visitors to appreciate the detail of the ceiling without straining their necks. The Camarín is reached through the **Capilla de la Virgen de Loreto**, inside which is a "house" tiled with eighteenth-century azulejos – supposedly a replica of Mary's Nazareth house, in which Jesus grew up. Legend claims the original house was miraculously lifted by angels to save it when Muslims invaded the Holy Land, then deposited in the Italian town of Loreto in 1294.

The rest of the Colegio de San Francisco Javier

Directly off the Colegio's central cloister are rooms packed with a treasure of beautiful silver reliquaries and crucifixes, censers, custodia, vestments and even a pair of silver sandals; notice too the painted panel depicting the spiritual conquest of New Spain and showing the relative influence of the Franciscans, Augustinians and Dominicans in the sixteenth century, and above it the diagram of churches liberally dotted among the lakes of the Valley of México.

The **upper storey** around the cloister contains more religious painting than anyone could take in on one visit, including portraits of the Society of Jesus and others of beatific eighteenth- and nineteenth-century nuns. Here too is the **Cristo del Árbol**, a crucifix carved beautifully from a single piece of wood towards the end of the seventeenth century.

Stairs descend to the **Claustro de los Naranjos**, planted with orange and lemon trees and with a fountain in the middle. Around it are displays of wooden religious statuary – Balthazar and Caspar, two of the three kings, are particularly fine. Other rooms contain more colonial miscellany – lacquerwork, furniture (notably an inlaid wooden desk) and clothes – and some temporary exhibition space. Outside extends the walled **Huerta**, or garden, some three hectares of lawns, shady trees and floral displays, as well as vegetables and medicinal herbs cultivated as they would have been by the monks. It is not as well tended as it could be, but makes a break from the museum and has a few architectural pieces and large sculptures dotted around, including, at the far end, the original eighteenth-century **Salto del Agua** that stood at the end of the aqueduct carrying water from Chapultepec into Mexico City (a replica of the fountain stands in the capital now, near Metro Salto del Agua).

Returning to the main cloister, you find a mixed bag with pre-Hispanic statuary leading on to details of Spanish exploration, suits of armour, exquisite marquetry boxes and a sequence of rooms, one filled with ivory statues, another laid out for Spanish nobles to dine, and then the **Botica**, or pharmacy, with bottles, jars, pestles and mortars, and all the other equipment of an eighteenth-century healer. The **Capilla Doméstica** also opens off the cloister, a whirl of painted and gilded Rococo excess, with a magnificent gilded *retablo* full of mirrors and little figures.

Practicalities

To get to Tepotzotlán from Mexico City, take a bus from Metros Cuatro Caminos or Rosario. The buses are slow, rattling their way round the suburbs for what feels like hours (though the total journey is actually little over an hour) before finally leaving the city. Alternatively, you can take an indirect ("via Refinario") Tula bus or a second-class service to Querétaro, both of which depart from the Terminal del Norte, and get off at a road junction about 200m before the first motorway tollbooths, Caseta de Tepotzotlán. From here it's about a twenty-minute walk west along a minor road to the town of Tepotzotlán, but there's a good chance of being able to hitch, and plenty of local buses. The same road junction by the tollbooths is also the place to pick up buses on to Tula or back to Mexico City.

Tepotzotlán's only central **hotel**, the *Hotel Posada San José*, Plaza Virreynal 13 (Ⓣ55/5876-0835; ❸), has some fairly poky cells at the back and some much more appealing rooms with plaza views (❹). There's a good deal more choice when it comes to **eating and drinking**, with cheap eats around the Mercado Municipal, just west of the plaza, and numerous places around the plaza, most with outdoor seating and many hosting *mariachi* musicians at weekends. They're all pretty good, so peruse the menus and take your pick: favourites include *Pepe's*, below the hotel, and the slightly more expensive *Restaurant Virreyes*, on the north side of the main square, which serves a wide range of dishes for around US$8, special barbecues at weekends (US$10) and a Sunday paella (US$10).

Less visible, but still noteworthy, is the fairly pricey *Hostería del Convento*, set beautifully in the seminary's grounds and serving excellent Mexican food for US$6–8 a dish, or US$8.40 if you go for the trout. Not far away, the tiny Plaza Tepotzotlán shopping courtyard contains *Los Miralos*, on the corner of Pensador Mexicano and Calle Zaragoza, a lovely spot to while away half an hour over a coffee and pastry.

Tula

The modern city of **TULA DE ALLENDE** lies on the edge of the Valley of México, 85km north of Mexico City. A pleasant enough regional centre, it's worth taking a few minutes to look over the impressive, fortress-like **Franciscan monastery and church** (built around 1550), but most likely you'll want to grab a meal and move on, most notably to the wonderful pre-Hispanic pyramid site of **Tula**, 2km north of the centre on a small hill.

In legend at least, the mantle of Teotihuacán fell on Tollan, or Tula, as the next great power to dominate Mexico. History, legend and archeological evidence, however, are here almost impossible to disentangle and often flatly contradictory. The Aztecs regarded their city as the descendant of Tula and hence embellished its reputation – the streets, they said, had been paved with gold and the buildings constructed from precious metals and stones; the Toltecs, who founded Tula, were the inventors of every science and art. In reality it seems unlikely that this was ever as large or as powerful a city as Teotihuacán had been – or as Tenochtitlán was to become – and its period of dominance (about 950–1150 AD) was relatively short. Yet all sorts of puzzles remain about the Toltec era, and in particular the extent of their influence in the Yucatán – at Chichén Itzá much of the architecture appears to have been influenced by the Toltecs (see p.806). Few people believe that the Toltecs could actually have had an empire, or an influence, that stretched so far: however warlike (and the artistic evidence is that Tula was a grimly militaristic society, heavily into human sacrifice), they would have lacked the manpower, resources or any logical justification for such expansion. Nevertheless, they were there.

The answer lies, perhaps, in the legends of **Quetzalcoatl** that surround the city. Adopted from Teotihuacán, the plumed serpent attained far more importance here in Tula, where he is depicted everywhere. Again the facts and legends are almost impossible to extricate, but at some stage Tula certainly had a ruler regarded as Quetzalcoatl who was driven from the city by the machinations of the evil god Texcatlipoca. In legend, Quetzalcoatl fled to the east where he either burnt himself to become the morning star or sailed across the ocean on a raft of snakes, promising one day to return (a prophecy that Cortés turned skilfully to his advantage). One theory was that the ruler, defeated in factional struggles within Tula, fled with his followers, eventually reaching Maya territory where they established a new Toltec regime at Chichén Itzá, a theory now out of fashion following finds there that seem to undermine it (see p.754).

△ Statues at Tula

The site

Only a small part of **the site** itself (daily 10am–5pm; US$3.20, plus US$3 for a camcorder, free for students and free on Sun) is of interest: though the city spreads over some considerable area only some of it has been excavated, and the outlying digs are holes in the ground, meaningful only to the archeologists who created them. The ceremonial centre, however, has been partly restored. Centrepiece is the low five-stepped pyramid of the **Templo de Tlahuizcalpantecuhtli** (Temple of the Morning Star, or Pyramid B), atop which stand the famous **Atlantes**. These giant, five-metre-tall basalt figures originally supported the roof of the sanctuary: they represent Quetzalcoatl in his guise as the morning star, dressed as a Toltec warrior. They wear elaborately embroidered loincloths, sandals and feathered helmets, with ornaments around their necks and legs – for protection, each bears a sun-shaped shield on his back and a chest piece in the form of a stylized butterfly. Each carries an *atlatl*, or spear-thrower, in his right hand and a clutch of arrows or javelins in his left.

Other pillars are carved with more warriors and gods, and these reliefs are a recurrent theme in Tula: the entire temple was originally faced in sculpted stone, and although this was pillaged long ago you can see some remnants from an earlier incarnation of the temple – prowling jaguars and eagles, symbols of the two great warrior groups, devouring human hearts. In front of the temple is a great L-shaped colonnade, where the partly reconstructed pillars originally supported a huge roof under which, perhaps, the priests and nobles would review their troops or take part in ceremonies in the shade. Part of a long bench survives, with its relief decoration of a procession of warriors and priests. More such benches survive in the **Palacio Quemado** (Burnt Palace – it was destroyed by fire), next to the temple on the western side. Its three rooms, each a square, were once roofed, with a small central patio to let light in. The middle one is the best-preserved of them, still with much of its original paint, and two Chac-mools.

The main square of the city stood in front (south) of the temple and palace, with a low altar platform in the centre and the now ruinous pyramid of the Templo Mayor on the eastern side. The larger of two **ball-courts** in the central area is on the western side of the square: although also largely ruined, this is one of the closest links between Tula and Chichén Itzá, of identical shape and orientation to the great ball-court there and displaying many of the same features. To the north of the temple stands the **Coatepantli** (Serpent Wall), elaborately carved in relief with images of human skeletons being eaten by giant rattlesnakes; beyond this, across an open space, there's a second ball-court, smaller but in better order.

The whole significance of the site is made much clearer if your Spanish is up to translating all the information presented in the **museum** (daily 10am–5pm; free) located by the entrance, and filled with fragments of Atlantes, Chac-mools and basalt heads along with assorted bits of sculpture and frieze.

Practicalities

Buses run from Mexico City's Terminal del Norte (Autobuses del Valle de Mezquital; every 40min, 30min morning and evening, 60min late night; less than 1hr 30min; slower services via a refinery – "via Refinario" – run every 15min), and frequently from Querétaro (18 daily; 2hr 30min). As you approach town, ask to be dropped off beside the train track by the *Hotel Sharon*, from where you should be able to walk (1km), pick up a local bus to just outside the site, or get a taxi (around US$2). Buses from Mexico City and Querétaro terminate at the bus station on Calle Xicohténcatl close to the centre of town. From there, the **entrance to the site** is at least a thirty-minute walk: turn right out of the bus station to the main road (Ocampo), where you turn right again, over the river and left before the train tracks (by the *Hotel Sharon*), following signs to "Zona Arqueológica".

To get to the town centre from the bus station, turn right as you leave, take the first left (Calle Rojo del Rio) to the end, where a right turn into Calle Hidalgo brings you to the **cathedral** and main square (Plaza de la Constitución). On the corner of the square with Calle Zaragoza, a small local museum, the **Sala Histórica Quetzalcoatl** (daily 9am–5pm; free), has a small display of archeological finds including a mammoth tusk and some Toltec artefacts. There are several reasonably priced **hotels** nearby, including the *Catedral*, Zaragoza 106 (Ⓣ773/732-0813, Ⓕ732-3632; ④), with fairly characterful old rooms all with bathroom and 24-hour hot water, but mostly without outside windows. Two other good bets are the *Auto Hotel Cuellar*, behind the cathedral on 5 de Mayo 23 (Ⓣ773/732-0442, Ⓕ732-0170, Ⓔhotcuellar@prodigy.net.mx; ④), with frumpy rooms and parking; and the *Casa Blanca*, Pasaje Hidalgo 11, off Calle Hidalgo by no.129 (Ⓣ773/732-1186, Ⓔcasablancatul@yahoo.com.mx; ④), with small but comfortable rooms, off-street parking and bottled water, plus TV for an extra US$4.

There are several good **cafés and restaurants** around the main square, particularly *La Pergola*, at no.10 on the north side, where you can get an excellent comida corrida for US$2. A few steps up Calle Hidalgo the restaurant *Casa Blanca*, Hidalgo 114, has a buffet and salad bar for US$7, with breakfasts at US$4–6; and *Cafetería Nevería Campanario*, beside the *Catedral*, is good for burgers, quesadillas and coffee.

Pachuca and around

In recent years, **PACHUCA**, the capital of Hidalgo state, has burst out of the ring of hills that once hemmed in the town, its expansion fuelled by the desperate need to move industry away from Mexico City. By Mexican standards, though, it remains a fairly small city, its centre easily walkable and full of colonial mansions built on the profits of the rich silver-mining country all about. Stick around just long enough to see the photography museum, but it is worth venturing to nearby towns where the mining heritage is more apparent and the clean mountain air provides a refreshing break.

Arrival and accommodation

The **bus station** is about 5km south of the centre and sees both second-class Flecha Roja and first-class ADO arrivals from Mexico City's Terminal del Norte every ten to fifteen minutes. Colectivos outside run frequently to Plaza de la Constitución, one of two main squares in the town centre. The other, two blocks away, is Pachuca's zócalo, the **Plaza de la Independencia**, where most of the action happens. From here, Matamoros runs south past a couple of hotels, becoming Mariano before reaching the Glorieta Revolución. There's a small **tourist office** (Mon–Fri 9am–6pm, Sat & Sun 10am–6pm; Ⓣ771/715-1411) in the base of the **Reloj Monumental** on the zócalo (see below).

Of Pachuca's **hotels**, there's nowhere especially classy anywhere near the centre but several reasonable places. The best value is the colonially styled and plant-filled *Noriega*, a block south of the zócalo at Matamoros 305 (Ⓣ771/715-1555 or 715-1569, Ⓕ715-1844; ❹), with a one-dollar saving if you can manage without TV. Somewhat cheaper but not as nice is *América*, Victoria 203 (Ⓣ771/715-0055; ❷), almost opposite, which has slightly dingy rooms with bath (❸) and some with bath and TV (❹). More characterful is *Hotel de los Baños*, just off the zócalo at Matamoros 205 (Ⓣ771/713-0700 or 01, Ⓕ715-1441; ❹), with carpeted rooms, each with TV and bathroom around a central, enclosed courtyard. Standard rooms have attractively carved wooden furniture, though in the superior rooms (❺) the craftsmanship is decidedly over the top. For a slightly higher standard of comfort, there are two almost identical modern hotels facing each other across the zócalo, both with rooms that have plaza views: *Ciro's* (Ⓣ771/715-5351; ❺), which has pleasantly furnished rooms with phone and TV; and *Emily* (Ⓣ771/715-0828 or 0849, Ⓦwww.hotelemily.com.mx; ❺), much the same but also with some suites (❻).

The Town

Nestled below the hills, which once provided such a bounty, Pachuca's zócalo is dominated by the 1910 **Reloj Monumental**, a forty-metre French Neoclassical clock tower. There's a good deal more interest at the late sixteenth-century Ex-Convento de San Francisco, reached by walking three blocks south along Matamoros, then left for 300m along Revolución (which becomes Arista). The ex-convent now operates as the **Centro Cultural Hidalgo**, which contains the **Museo de la Fotografía** (Tues–Sun 10am–6pm; free). Drawing on over a million photographic works stored here as the national archive, the museum does a great job of showcasing both Mexican and foreign photographers and foreigners working in Mexico. Early photographic techniques are illustrated before you move on to the gallery space, where displays change constantly but almost always include images from the Casasola Archive. The pre-eminent Mexican photojournalist of his day, **Agustín Casasola** chronicled both the Revolution itself and everyday life in its wake, forming an invaluable record of one of Mexico's more turbulent periods. Look too for work by Guillermo Kahlo, father of Frida, stereoscopic plates of early railway construction, and photos by Tina Modotti, an Italian-born American who worked here in the 1930s and was part of the Kahlo/Rivera set.

Pachuca's other museum is the mildly diverting **Museo de Minereía** (Wed–Sun 10am–2pm & 3–6pm; US$1.50), which is one block south and two blocks east of the zócalo at Mina 110 (that's Calle de Javier Mina, not Calle de la Mina), and full of mineral samples and mining equipment.

Eating and drinking

Pachuca is known in Mexico for **pastes**, which originated with the Cornish pasties once made by Cornish miners working in nearby Real del Monte (see opposite). They still come *tradicional* (or *tipo Inglés*), filled with ground meat, onion and potato, as well as with fillings such as chicken mole or *refritos*. Though they differ in shape, they're closely related to typical Mexican empanadas, which are usually sold in the same shops stuffed with tuna, pineapple or even rice pudding. You'll find bakeries selling *pastes* all over the region, and even at the bus station. These might sustain you for a short visit but on longer stays you'll want to visit **restaurants** such as *Reforma*, Matamoros 111, on the east side of the zócalo, which does good breakfasts (US$3–5) and typical Mexican antojitos (US$3.50–4). For espressos, croissants and burgers, pop down the street to *Mi Antiguo Café*, Matamoros 115; and for something classier in the evening make for either the family-style *Mirage*, Guerrero 1210 (a block west of the zócalo and 300m south), where you might try the local *tacos mineros* (chicken tacos with salsa and cheese), or *Alex Steak*, about 500m south of the zócalo at Glorieta Revolución 102 (ⓣ771/713-0056), where enormous and beautifully prepared steaks are served for around US$17. There's little in the way of diverting nightlife, but the *Mirage* does have a cozy **bar**.

Around Pachuca: Real del Monte and Mineral del Chico

Draped across pine-clad hills 14km north of Pachuca sits **REAL DEL MONTE** (aka Mineral del Monte), a formerly very wealthy silver-mining town high in the crisp clean air at over 2700m and a nice retreat from Mexico City. There's not a lot to do here, but it is a quietly appealing place to wander around the well-tended streets, and perhaps out into the hills all about to carefully explore mining relics. The town's architecture is largely Spanish colonial given an odd twist by the almost exclusive use of red corrugated-iron roofing, and the existence of Cornish-style cottages with their double-pitched rooflines. Some 350 Cornish miners moved here after 1824 when a British company operated mines that were first opened by the Spanish in the mid-sixteenth century. Most left after the mining company pulled out in 1848, but the Cornish influence remained through surprisingly authentic Cornish pasties and the introduction of *fútbol* (soccer) which, tradition has it, was played for the first time on Mexican soil here in Real. Some of the miners now rest in the British cemetery (Panteón Inglés) on the edge of town.

To reach Real del Monte from Pachuca, walk 200m north of the zócalo along Zaragoza to Calle de Julian Villagran (the northwest corner of Plaza de la Constitución) and pick up one of the very frequent **colectivos**, which drop you close to the centre of Real. Less convenient buses also run hourly from the bus station. Most likely you'll visit on a day-trip from Pachuca, but there is tempting **accommodation** in the form of *Hotel Monte del Real*, just off the main square on the corner of Iturbide and García (ⓣ & ⓕ 771/797-1202 or 3, ⓦwww.hotelsecoturisticos.com.mx; ❺ midweek, ❻ weekends), beautifully decorated and furnished, with wooden floors, antique-style furniture and heaters to ward off the chilly nights. The *Restaurant D'Karla* opposite also rents out rooms (ⓣ771/797-0709; ❺). Several other small **restaurants** are located along Avenida Hidalgo, off the central plaza. *La Central* has decent food and a US$2.50 comida corrida. *Real de Plateros*, right opposite, does the town's best *pastes* (Cornish-style potato, or Mexican-style bean) and empanadas.

Mineral del Chico

The road between Pachuca and Real del Monte passes a road junction, 10km north of Pachuca, from where a side road winds down towards **Parque Nacional El Chico**, which is noted for its impressive rock formations and good hiking. The tiny village of **MINERAL DEL CHICO**, 4km from the road junction, is the main base for exploring the park and offers a few restaurants and a couple of luxurious **hotels**: *Posada del Amencer*, right in town at Morelos 3 (ⓣ771/715-4812; ❼); and *Hotel El Paraíso* (ⓣ771/715-5654, ⓦwww.hotelesecoturisticos.com.mx; ❾), about 1km before town. There is no direct public transport from Real del Monte, but colectivos from Pachuca can be found on Calle Carranza, 300m north of Plaza de la Constitución.

Tlaxcala and around

TLAXCALA, capital of the tiny state of the same name, is 100km west of Mexico City and just 30km north of Puebla. As Cortés' closest ally in the struggle against the Aztecs, the town suffered a very different fate from that of Cholula, and one that in the long run has led to an even more total disappearance of its ancient culture. For although the Spanish founded a town here – now restored and very beautiful in much of its original colonial glory – to the Mexicans Tlaxcala was a symbol of treachery, and to some extent still is. Siding with Spain in the War of Independence didn't help greatly either, and whether for this reason, or because of its genuine isolation, development has largely passed by Tlaxcala.

The town sits in the middle of a fertile, prosperous-looking upland plain surrounded by rather bare mountains. At the centre you'll discover an exceptionally pretty and much rehabilitated colonial town, comfortable but in the final analysis fairly dull. Most of the interest lies very close to the zócalo, with its central bandstand, where the terracotta and ochre tones of the buildings lend the city its tag of "Ciudad Roja", the Red City. Its appearance, slow pace and proximity to the nation's capital have drawn a small but significant expat community, though the latter's impact on daily life is minimal.

Arrival and accommodation

Frequent **buses** from Mexico City, Puebla and surrounding towns arrive at the bus station on the edge of the centre. Colectivos parked outside run to nearby villages and the zócalo, though it's easy enough to walk in around ten minutes: exit the bus station and turn right downhill to the next main junction, then take a right down Avenida Guerrero for five blocks and left down Juárez. To return to the bus station, take the colectivo that stops on the corner by the church just off the zócalo.

Behind the Palacio de Gobierno, on the zócalo, there's a helpful **tourist office** on the corner of Juárez and Lardizábal (Mon–Fri 9am–6pm, Sat & Sun 10am–6pm; Ⓣ246/465-0968, Ⓦwww.tlaxcala.gob.mx/turismo), where you can pick up useful free maps and book guided tours. Most other facilities – banks, post office and the like – cluster round the zócalo and along Juárez.

Low-cost **accommodation** is limited to *Posada Mary*, Xicohténcatl 19 (Xicohténcatl runs parallel with Juárez one block to the east; Ⓣ246/462-9655; ❸), which is clean but basic, with rather meagre bed covers. For something better, follow Morelos east off the zócalo to *Hotel Alifer*, at no. 11, by the junction with Xicohténcatl (Ⓣ/Ⓕ246/465-0620 to 21, Ⓦwww.hotelalifer.com; ❺), which has carpeted rooms with TV. Best of all is the *Hotel Posada San Francisco*, on the southern side of the zócalo at Plaza de la Constitución 17 (Ⓣ246/462-6022, Ⓦwww.posadasanfrancisco.com; ❽), occupying a lovely old mansion on the zócalo with colonially furnished rooms, pool and tennis courts.

The Town

The entire north side of the zócalo is taken up by the **Palacio de Gobierno** (daily 8am–8pm; free; enter by westernmost door), whose patterned brick facade is broken by ornate windows and doorways. The building incorporates parts of a much earlier structure, erected soon after the Conquest, and inside boasts a series of brilliantly coloured **murals** by a local, Desiderio Hernandez Xochitiotzin, who began work on them in the early 1960s and can still occasionally be seen finishing off the stairway. Large sections have been restored in recent years, notably the panels depicting the history of the Tlaxcalan people from their migration from the north to their alliance with Cortés; the most spectacular are one on the stairs depicting the Spanish Conquest, and another at the bottom showing the Great Market.

To the west of the Palacio de Gobierno, and dominating a small square off the side of the zócalo, stands the tiled facade of the **Parroquia de San José**. It's an attractive building, but the inside is disappointing except for two fonts beside the door depicting Camaxtli, the Tlaxcalan god of hunting and war. Notice, too, the seventeenth-century painting beside the altar that depicts the baptism of a Tlaxcalan chief, as overseen by Cortés and his mistress, La Malinche.

At the opposite corner of the zócalo, the smaller Plaza Xicohténcatl holds the **Museo de la Memoria** (Tues–Sun 10am–5pm; US$1), a modern and spacious museum mostly devoted to the cultural history of the region. It is very light on artefacts, but makes up for that with imaginative modern displays (some interactive) illustrating pre-Hispanic *tianguis* (markets), Franciscan life under the Spanish, and a comparison of the ruling structures in Tlaxcala before and after Cortés.

At the southeastern corner of Plaza Xicohténcatl, a broad, tree-lined path leads up to a triple set of arches and beyond them to an open area, overlooking the city's pretty nineteenth-century bullring and flanked on one side by the Ex-Convento de San Francisco, started in 1537. Here, wrapped around the cloister, the **Museo Regional de Tlaxcala** (Tues–Sun 10am–5pm; US$3.20, free on Sun) covers local life from prehistoric times to the present day – an unexceptional collection but well displayed in a series of bare, whitewashed rooms. The **Catedral de Nuestra Señora de la Asunción** next door is also relatively plain, though it has a beautiful vaulted wooden ceiling decorated in Mudéjar style, the design elements harking back to the Moorish style then common in southern Spain. The Moors were expelled from Spain in 1492, and their influence continued for some decades, though this is only apparent in a very few Mexican churches started immediately after the Conquest. One large chapel, more richly decorated than the rest, contains the font in which Xicohténcatl and the three other Tlaxcalan leaders were baptized in the presence of Cortés in 1520. Opposite, the lower walls of another small chapel bear traces of ancient frescoes.

Tlaxcala's third museum is the **Museo de Artes y Tradiciones Populares**, corner of Mariano Sanchez and 1 de Mayo, three blocks west of the zócalo (Tues–Sun 10am–6pm; US$0.60), focusing on traditional crafts and customs, with sections on bell making (including an example cast on the site) and a fascinating room on the manufacture and consumption of pulque.

Santuario de Ocotlán

Approaching town you will almost certainly have noticed the twin wedding-cake towers of the **Santuario de Ocotlán**, overlooking Tlaxcala on a height to the east. There are great views over the surrounding countryside from up here, but the real interest is the church, its facade a riot of churrigueresque excess that ranks it alongside those at Tepotzotlán and Taxco. Inside, it is no less florid, the huge Baroque *retablo* seeming to spread seemlessly to the dome and along the transept in a frenzy of gilt woodwork. Such exuberance is justified by the miraculous legend of the Virgin, in which she is said to have appeared to a poor Indian in 1541 with instructions to cure an epidemic with waters from a stream that suddenly appeared. Naturally everyone recovered, after which the Virgin asked the Indian to bring the local Franciscan monks to a forest, though once there, ferocious flames suddenly raged without harming the trees. The monks returned the next day, to find that one pine tree (*ocotlán*) contained a wooden image of the Virgin. Now installed on the altar, what is truly remarkable is that it is carved and painted very much in the style of the times. All manner of fortuitous interventions are attributed to the statue, and the life of the Lady of Ocotlán is portrayed around the eight walls of the ornate **Camarín de la Virgen** (the Virgin's Dressing Room) behind the altar. In May, the church and surrounding streets host the procession of the Virgin, attended by thousands of pilgrims.

The church is about 1km from the zócalo, a fairly steep thirty minutes' walk north along Juárez, then right onto Avenida Guridi y Alcocer, which runs past the **Pocito**, a small octagonal shrine.

Eating and drinking

For a relatively small city, Tlaxcala seems particularly well stocked with **restaurants** and **bars**, generally around the zócalo and along Juárez. Some of the most inviting are those under the *portales* on the eastern and southern sides of the zócalo, where you can sit outside and watch life go by: try *Los Portales*, Plaza de la Constitución 8 (ⓣ246/462-5419), with its broad range of antojitos, burgers, salads, pasta dishes and the delicious *sopa tlaxcalteca* (US$2.80), made from black beans, tortilla chips, cheese, avocado and *chicharrón*. The *Italian Coffee Company* at no.4 has the best coffee and a lively atmosphere. Another place worth trying is *Mandukare*, Xicohténcatl 9 (closed Sun), a small café-restaurant serving healthy salads, pasta, and crepes both sweet and savoury, with a few vegetarian options.

The restaurants all serve alcohol, but for a more dedicated drinking experience visit *El Cantino de Marina*, a cowboy-themed **bar** at Avenida Guridi y Alcocer 50.

Around Tlaxcala: Cacaxtla and Xochitécatl

Some 17km southwest of Tlaxcala lies the ancient site of **Cacaxtla** (daily 9am–5pm; US$3.70, free on Sun), where a particularly fine series of murals depicting battle scenes was discovered in 1974. They are clearly Maya in style, and continue to baffle archeologists.

Two kilometres west of Cacaxtla, the ruins of **Xochitécatl** (same hours and ticket) have three impressive pyramids and monolithic stones. These can be reached by frequent colectivo ("San Miguel del Milagro") from Bulevar Mariano and Lardizábal, or by bus to the nearby village of Nativitas from either Tlaxcala or Puebla. Alternatively, every Sunday there are **guided tours** to both sites for US$5.70; you're picked up in Tlaxcala from outside the *Hotel Posada San Francisco* at 10am and dropped off at 1pm. They run a Saturday tour of Tlaxcala itself, too (US$2), also visiting the rather less impressive archeological site of **Tizatlán** (Tues–Sun 10am–5pm; US$3.20, free on Sun), 4km north of town; this can be reached independently by colectivo from 1 de Mayo and 20 de Noviembre.

Puebla

East of the capital, a fast road climbs steeply, with glorious views of the snowy heights of Popocatépetl and Ixtaccíhuatl, to **PUEBLA**. Little more than an hour on the bus from Mexico City, this is the republic's fifth largest city after

Mexico City, Guadalajara, Monterrey and Tijuana, and one of its hardest to pin down. On the whole it's a disappointment, with the initial impression of industrial modernity imparted by the huge Volkswagen factory on the outskirts compounded by the permanently clogged, raucous and rushed streets of the centre. Yet this is as historic a city as any in Mexico, and certainly in the centre there's a remarkable concentration of interest – a fabulous **cathedral**, a "hidden" **convent**, museums and colonial **mansions** – while the mountainous country round about is in places startlingly beautiful. Nevertheless, Puebla is unlikely to tempt you into staying particularly long and in a couple of leisurely days (or one packed day) you can see the best of the city and nearby **Cholula**.

The city itself was founded by the Spanish in 1531 and, rare for this area, was an entirely new foundation, preferred to the ancient sites of Cholula and Tlaxcala possibly because there the memories of indigenous power remained too strong. It rapidly assumed great importance as a staging point on the journey from the capital to the port at Veracruz and for the trans-shipment of goods from Spain's Far Eastern colonies, which were delivered to Acapulco and transported across Mexico from there. Wealth was brought, too, by the reputation of its ceramic and tile manufacture (still very much in evidence), which was due in part to the abundance of good clays and in part to its settlement by Spaniards from Talavera who brought traditional ceramic skills with them. The city did well out of colonial rule, and perhaps not surprisingly it took the wrong side in the War of Independence. As a result, it preserves a reputation for conservatism and traditional values, not dispelled even by the fact that the start of the

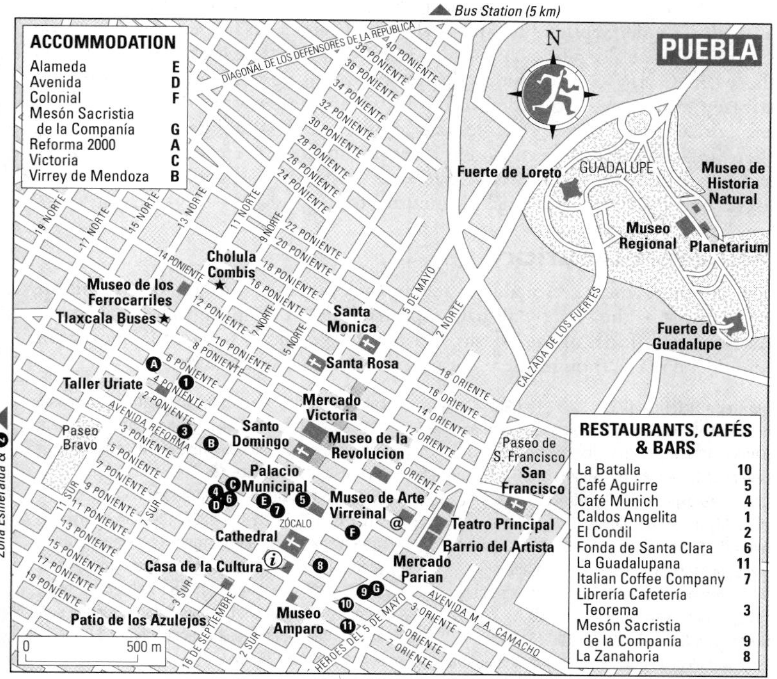

5

MEXICO CITY AND AROUND | Puebla

Revolution is generally dated from the assassination of Aquiles Serdán in his Puebla home.

Military defeat, too, seems to play an even larger part in Puebla's history than it does in most of Mexico – the city fell to the Americans in 1847 and to the French in 1863 – but what's remembered is the greatest victory in the country's history, when a force of some two thousand Mexicans defeated a French army three times its size in 1872. To this day, May 5 (**Cinco de Mayo**) is commemorated with a massive fiesta here, and with a public holiday throughout the country.

Arrival and information

Puebla's **bus station**, known by the acronym CAPU (Central de Autobuses de Puebla), lies 5km out in the northwest of the city and has a cheap guardería. There are **authorized taxis** to the centre of town for under US$3.50, or you can turn right outside and walk about 200m along the main road where you can hop onto one of the frequent local buses and colectivos that run to the centre. To get back to CAPU from town, buses can be picked up along 9 Norte or 9 Sur. You'll need to get back to CAPU for all except local destinations such as Cholula, which can be reached by *combi* from 14 Poniente at Calle 11 Norte, or Tlaxcala, which (in addition to buses from CAPU) is served by micros from a terminal on Calle 10 Poniente between Calle 11 Norte and Calle 13 Norte, by the railway museum.

At Calle 5 Oriente 3, near the corner of Calle 16 de Septiembre, the **tourist office** (Mon–Sat 9am–8.30pm, Sun 9am–2pm; ⓣ222/246-2044; ⓦwww.turismopuebla.com.mx) provides information and free maps; the same maps are available at many hotels and tourist sights around town. The **post office**, at Calle 16 de Septiembre and Calle 5 Oriente, has an efficient Lista de Correos; there's also a branch at Calle 2 Oriente 411. Banamex at Reforma 135 (between Calle 3 Norte and 5 de Mayo) is among banks that will **change money**, and there's a casa de cambio in the arcade between the north side of the zócalo and Calle 2 Oriente, and another at CAPU. For Internet access, there are a few places around Calle 2 Sur just south of the zócalo, but the office at Calle 4 Oriente 404–B (Mon–Sat 9am–9pm) has reasonable prices for web access and cheap international phone calls too.

Accommodation

Finding somewhere reasonable to stay in Puebla can be difficult, but **hotels** are easy to spot as they nearly all have a protruding "H" sign, and most are just to the west and north of the zócalo. On the whole, the closer to the zócalo, the higher the price, though there are good budget places close in.

Alameda Reforma 141 ⓣ222/242-0882. Good hotel mainly notable for its gorgeous tiled and painted stairway, though the rooms are also decent with modern bathrooms and TV. The prized (and more expensive) streetfront rooms are considerably more spacious and airy. ❹

Avenida 5 Pte 336 ⓣ222/232-2104. A basic place, but friendly, relatively clean and quiet, recently renovated, and with some extremely cheap rooms without bathroom. ❸

Colonial 4 Sur 105 ⓣ222/246-4612, ⓦwww.colonial.com.mx. Luxury in a beautiful colonial building next to the Autonomous University of Puebla. All rooms have TV and phone, and many have beautifully tiled bathrooms. There's also a fine restaurant on site. ❻

Mesón Sacristía de la Compañía 6 Sur 304 ⓣ01-800/712-4028 or 222/242-3554, ⓦwww.g-networks/sacristia/. Gorgeous hotel in a 200-year-old house with just nine spacious rooms and suites, each one different but all with heavy wood beams, furnished with antiques and elegantly decorated. Room and breakfast costs around US$150, suites are US$175. ❾

Reforma 2000 4 Pte 916, corner of 11 Nte ⓣ222/242-3363, ⓕ246-3073. Comfortable with carpeted, spacious rooms, TV and phone. Nice bar and restaurant, plus parking facilities. ❺

Victoria 3 Pte 306 ⓣ222/232-8992 or 01-800/849-2793. Basic but clean and quiet rooms each with bathroom and 24hr hot water. ❸

Virrey de Mendoza Reforma 538 ⓣ222/242-3903. Small hotel with big carpeted rooms around a verdant central courtyard with its own grand staircase. Good value and one of the best of the mid-range places. ❺

The Town

Puebla's **zócalo** is the centre of the numbering system for the ancient grid of streets (lowest numbers are nearest to the centre) and home to the great looming **Cathedral** (daily 7am–12.30pm & 4.15–7.30pm; free), second largest in the republic and under construction from 1562 until the middle of the following century. The exterior is ugly and grey, but inside it improves considerably with amazing ornamentation in onyx, marble and gilt, and a wonderful altar designed by Manuel Tolsá in 1797. The cathedral, and particularly the tower, was partly funded by Bishop Juan de Palafox y Mendoza, illegitimate son of a Spanish noble who grew up with his poor mother but inherited his father's wealth. Behind the cathedral, near the tourist office, lies the old Archbishop's Palace, converted to a library in the seventeenth century (the Biblioteca Palafoxiana, reputed to be the oldest library in the Americas), and now housing the original collection of ancient books and manuscripts on the upper floor. Downstairs there's the **Casa de la Cultura** (daily 10am–8pm; free), which hosts regular exhibitions of local arts and crafts.

Museo Amparo

The undoubted star in Puebla's museum firmament is the modern **Museo Amparo**, Calle 2 Sur 708 at Calle 9 Oriente (daily except Tues 10am–6pm; US$2.50, free on Mon, camcorder US$5; ⓦwww.museoamparo.com), which concentrates on art from pre-Hispanic Mesoamerica, with additional material from the colonial and more recent eras. Set in a pair of modernized colonial buildings with peaceful courtyards and piped classical music, the collection is the legacy of philanthropist Manuel Espinosa Iglesias, who set up the Amparo Foundation in honour of his wife.

The historical significance of the pieces isn't glossed over, but the focus is firmly on aesthetics, with well-presented cases displaying artefacts to their best advantage. To set the tone, the entrance features an impressive glass replica of a **Tzompantli skull-wall** with alternating Olmec and Totonac heads in each of the glass blocks. A room decorated with reproduction **cave paintings** from Altamira in Spain, Arnhemland in Australia, Utah, Norway and Baja California put Mexico's cultural development into some sort of context before you launch into the main collection. This is far smaller than that in Mexico City's anthropology museum, but is well chosen and a good deal more manageable. It is particularly strong on the Olmecs, a people who greatly influenced life around Puebla and left behind some strikingly beautiful pieces such as the half-metre-wide stone head. Elsewhere notice the exquisite Colima jaguar, the beautiful carved conch shell from the gulf coast and a kneeling woman from Nayarit with her distinctive face painting and chevron body painting.

The last section of the museum is devoted to **colonial painting** and rooms set with seventeenth- and eighteenth-century furnishings. Everything in the museum is thoroughly documented at strategically located computer consoles, so you probably won't need the rental **headsets** (US$2; available in Spanish, English, French, German and Japanese) with their relatively cursory commentary. Free guided tours in English and Spanish take place at noon on Sunday.

North of the zócalo

Head north from the zócalo along 5 de Mayo and you reach the church of **Santo Domingo** at the corner of 4 Poniente. Its Capilla del Rosario is, even in comparison to the cathedral, a quite unbelievably lavish orgy of gold-leaf and Baroque excess; a constant hushed, shuffling stream of devotees lights candles and prays to its revered image of the Virgin for miraculous cures. Three doors down, the **Museo José Luis Bello y Zetina**, 5 de Mayo 409 (Tues–Sun 10am–4pm; free), displays the paintings and furniture of the wealthy Bello household during the nineteenth century – everything from seventeenth-century Flemish masters to a Napoleonic bedroom suite. It somehow seems too comfortless for a home yet not formal enough for a museum, though the enthusiasm of your personal guide may rub off.

Nearby, a passage leads to the glass-and-iron **Mercado Victoria**, at the corner of 5 de Mayo and 6 Oriente, once Puebla's main market, but now a rather sanitized shopping centre. East of the market, candy stores along Calle 6 Oriente sell a regional speciality, *camotes*, gooey fingers of sweet potato and sugar flavoured with various fruits. If you're thinking of buying any to take home, however, note that they only last a couple of weeks. Further along the street, the devotional **Museo Regional de la Revolución Mexicana**, 6 Oriente 206 (Tues–Sun 10am–5pm; US$1, free on Tues) records the struggles for Liberalism of the Serdán family against the dictatorship of Porfirio Díaz. The assassination of Aquiles Serdán in this house was one of the most important steps in the fall of Díaz: the date of Serdán's death, November 18, 1910, is – in the absence of any firmer indicators – generally recognized as marking the start of the Revolution. In the house the bullet holes have been lovingly preserved, and a huge smashed mirror still hangs on the wall where it appears in contemporary photos of the carnage. Revolution buffs will also enjoy the biographies of key figures in the struggle, photos of the ragtag bands of wide-hatted revolutionaries with their bandoleers, and the trap door in the floor under which Serdán spent several fruitless hours trying to avoid his fate.

Nine blocks north of the zócalo you'll find the remarkable "hidden" convent now operating as the **Museo Religioso Santa Mónica**, at 18 Poniente 103, (Tues–Sun 9am–5.30pm; US$2.30, free on Sun). Here, from the suppression of the church in 1857 until their discovery in 1934, several generations of nuns lived hidden from the public gaze behind a smokescreen of secret doors and concealed passages. Just how secret they were is a matter of some debate – many claim that the authorities simply turned a blind eye – and certainly several lay families were actively supportive, providing supplies and new recruits. But it makes a good story, embellished by the conversion of the building into a museum that preserves the secret entrances along with many religious artworks and a beautiful seventeenth-century cloister. Several simple cells are also in evidence, and from the hidden chapel you can look down through a screen at the still-operating church next door.

In the same general direction lies the **Ex-Convento de Santa Rosa**, 14 Poniente 305 on the corner of 3 Norte (Tues–Sun 10am–5pm; US$1, free on Tues), whose main claim to fame is that the great *mole poblano* was invented here in its wonderful yellow-tiled kitchens. The kitchens are the highlight of the guided tour which includes rooms full of crafts and artesanía from the state of Puebla.

East of the zócalo

The rest of the interest is concentrated mostly to the east and northeast of the zócalo. First stop is the **Museo Poblano de Arte Virreinal**, at the corner of 4 Oriente and 6 Norte (Tues–Sun 10am–5pm; US$1.50, free on Sun), located in the Casa del Alfeñique, an elaborate old mansion covered in Puebla tiles. Within, you can see period furnishings, Puebla ceramics, a small archeological section and an excellent display of colonial art.

At the end of 4 Oriente lie the **Mercado Parian** – mostly given over to rather tawdry tourist souvenirs – and the **Barrio del Artista**, traditionally the artists' quarter, now selling work aimed squarely at the tourist market. The **Teatro Principal**, nearby, is a fine eighteenth-century theatre, said to be the oldest on the continent, which still hosts occasional performances.

West of the zócalo

Follow 4 Poniente west from the zócalo to reach **Taller Uriarte**, 4 Poniente 911 (Mon–Fri 9am–6pm, Sat 10am–5pm, Sun 11am–4pm, free half-hour tours Mon–Fri 11am, noon & 1pm; ⓣ222/232-1598), about the best-known of Talavera pottery factories. It is a small-scale affair shoehorned into what appears to be just another urban house, but it is well set up for visitors, letting them see every stage of the process from forming the plates and bowls to painting the intricate designs in paints whose colours are completely transformed during firing into the blues and yellows so distinctive of Puebla.

Press on a few blocks further out to the **Museo Nacional de los Ferrocarriles**, 11 Norte at 12 Poniente (Tues–Sun 10am–6pm; free), an open-air collection of Mexican railway rolling stock arranged around the old Puebla train station. Pride of place is given to some menacing-looking steam locomotives, including one 285-tonne monster built in 1946, which was so heavy it could only be run on the most robust lines from Mexico City to the US border. If your Spanish is up to it you can engage one of the old rail buffs hanging around and they'll tell you all you ever wanted to know about the varied array of carriages – everything from an old caboose to presidential carriages made for travel in a more gracious age.

Cerro de Guadalupe

Puebla's suburbs are less rewarding than the centre, and the same can be said for the **Centro Cívico 5 de Mayo**, a collection of museums that crown **Cerro de Guadalupe** to the northwest, the site of the constant battles and sieges of the nineteenth century. Neither of the two forts nor any of the museums are a match for sights in the centre, and even the views are partly blocked by mature gum trees. Nonetheless, it is a decent place to spend a couple of hours away from the fumes and the noise of the city centre. To get there take a Ruta #72 colectivo (marked "Centro Cívico") from Bulevar 5 de Mayo, three blocks east of the zócalo.

First stop should be the **Fuerte de Loreto** (Tues–Sun 10am–4.30pm; US$3.50, free on Sun), where the moat and high walls protect a large empty parade ground and a small church containing the Museo de la No Intervención. This focuses on the events surrounding the 1862 Battle of Puebla, celebrated on Cinco de Mayo, and records 150 years of the defence of the republic through replicated battle scenes. The views of Popo and Ixta from the battlements are some of the best in Puebla.

The best of the rest is the modern **Museo Regional de Puebla** (Tues–Sun 10am–4.30pm; US$3.50, free on Sun), largely devoted to the area's archeology and ethnology in the state. There's some exquisite Olmec jade sculpture and sculptural pieces along with a four-metre-high polychrome statue of San Cristóbal from the seventeenth century, and sections of wider relevance such as a detailed explanation of native migration from east Asia through Alaska. Readers with kids will want to traipse across the road to the **Museo Interactivo Imagina** (Mon–Fri 9am–1pm & 2–6pm, Sat & Sun 10am–2pm & 3–7pm; US$3.50, extra for some exhibits), a collection of educational interactive games; and the adjacent **Planetarium**, with its IMAX screen and shows (Tues–Sun 10am–noon & 4–6pm; US$3) throughout the day at weekends.

The highest point on the hill is occupied by the **Fuerte de Guadalupe** (Tues–Sun 9am–6pm; US$3, free on Sun), the meagre but well-tended remains of an 1862 fort – really just a few arches and roofless rooms.

Eating and drinking

As with any large Mexican city there's a huge range of **places to eat**, from cheaper places around the Mercado Victoria to good mid-range options around the centre, with better places tucked away in back streets. While here you should definitely check out a couple of **local specialities**, particularly *mole poblano*, an extraordinary sauce that's bursting with flavour and is made of chocolate, numerous varieties of chile, and any number of herbs and spices. Typically served over chicken, turkey or enchiladas, it is found all over Mexico, but is nowhere better than here where it was supposedly invented for the viceroy's visit to the Convento de Santa Rosa in colonial times. Should you want to buy some paste to take home and cook up a mole for yourself (the paste lasts for ages and doesn't need to be refigerated), a good place to buy it is Abarrotes Lulu at Calle 16 Poniente 304–A, by Mercado 5 Mayo.

Another taste sensation is *chiles en nogada*, a dish reputedly concocted in 1821 to celebrate Mexican Independence and made to resemble the colours of the Mexican flag. Green poblano chili is filled with ground meats, fruits and nuts, then covered with a creamy walnut sauce and doused with bright-red pomegranate seeds. It is best sampled from July to September, but can often be found at other times.

Central Puebla is mostly quiet at night and to find any bars you'll have to head a few blocks south to the Plazuela de los Sapos, near 6 Sur and 5 Poniente, where several lively bars face each other across a small square. Things don't really get going until Thursday night, when you might also head around six long blocks west of the zócalo to the Zona Esmeralda, where there's a string of bars and clubs to keep you going. Otherwise, many people head out to **Cholula** to join the lively, studenty atmosphere there, though you'll have to be prepared for a fairly expensive taxi ride back: buses stop running at around 11pm, just when the clubs start warming up.

La Batalla 6 Sur 506. Just one of a handful of similar bars and antros on the Plazuela de los Sapos mostly pumping out Latin and US pop hits. Take your pick from *La Boveda* at no.503, *El Reguardo de los Angeles* at no.504 or *D'Pasadita* at no.501, which is more of a drinkers' bar.

Café Aguirre 5 de Mayo 4. Predictable and safe restaurant that's a long-standing local favourite and is always popular with business people for its range of ten breakfast combos each with juice and coffee (US$3.20–4.70), lunchtime menus (US$5.50), antojitos (US$3.20–5.30) and tortas.

Café Munich corner 3 Pte and 5 Sur. Basic but reliable restaurant serving a wide range of soups and mains and a great comida in a room decorated with photos of Bavarian scenes and drawings of Einstein, Beethoven, Goethe and Wagner. Cheap (US$2.80) and pricier (US$7) menus are available at lunchtime.

Caldos Angelita corner 6 Pte and 9 Norte. A popular no-nonsense diner doling out hearty bowlfuls of chicken broth (US$1.70) and *mole poblano* (US$2.30), but only until 6.30pm.

El Condil Juárez 1305. Lively bar 2km west of the town centre in the Zona Esmeralda (Juárez is a continuation of Calle 7 Pte west of the Paseo Bravo) with music most nights from around 9pm and sometimes a guitarist.

Fonda de Santa Clara 3 Pte 307, a couple of blocks west of the zócalo ☎222/242-2659. The best-known – and most touristy – restaurant in town, which serves local food with an upmarket twist in a pretty room decorated with Mexican art. A good place to try the local specialities without breaking the bank. The weekend buffet breakfast is also worth investigating. There's a second branch at Calle 3 Poniente 920 (☎222/246-1952).

La Guadalupana 5 Ote 605, Plazuela de los Sapos ☎222/242-4886. One of Puebla's most celebrated restaurants in a beautiful colonial building and specializing in regional dishes, many served in a *molcajete*, a kind of volcanic-rock bowl.

Italian Coffee Company Reforma 107. Flavoured espresso coffees, teas, infusions and cakes in convivial surroundings. Other branches around town include one at Calle 4 Oriente 202, and one on Calle 2 Sur between the zócalo and Calle 5 Oriente.

Librería Cafetería Teorema Reforma 540 at Calle 7 Norte. Combined bookstore, café and live music venue with a relaxed bohemian atmosphere and food, beer and espresso coffees. Gigs usually start around 9.30pm, with acoustic *trova* from Sunday to Thursday and rock on Friday and Saturday. Cover US$1–2.50.

Mesón Sacristía de la Compañía 6 Sur 304 ☎222/242-3554. Fine dining in the lovely enclosed courtyard of this superb hotel where you really should try the house mole (US$7) preceded by their special soup made with fried tortilla chips, *chicharrón*, cheese and chipotle (US$3.40). Efficient, friendly service and a good wine list make this one of Puebla's best dining experiences.

La Zanahoria 5 Ote 206 ☎222/232-4813. A bustling vegetarian restaurant in Mexican style, with several meat dishes amid the vast array of wholesome vegetarian choices. Burgers and salads are good value though no match for the US$2.20–3.60 breakfasts and US$3.90 *menús del día* (replaced by a US$5.90 buffet on Sundays).

Cholula and around

The expansion of Puebla in recent years makes **CHOLULA**, 15km to the southwest, virtually a suburb. Nonetheless, it retains its small-town charm and has one abiding reason to visit: the **ruins of Cholula**, and especially the **largest pyramid in Mexico**. A rival of Teotihuacán at its height, and the most powerful city in the country between the fall of Teotihuacán and the rise of Tula, Cholula was at the time of the Conquest a vast city of some four hundred temples, famed as a shrine to Quetzalcoatl and for the excellence of its pottery (a trade dominated by immigrant Mixtecs). But it paid dearly for an attempt, inspired by its Aztec allies, to ambush Cortés on his march to Tenochtitlán: the chieftains were slaughtered, their temples destroyed and churches built in their place. The Spanish claimed to have constructed 365 churches here, one for each day of the year. Although there are a lot of churches, the true figure certainly doesn't live up to the claim. There may well be 365 chapels within the churches, though, which is already a few hundred more than the village population could reasonably need.

One side of Cholula's large zócalo – the Plaza de la Concordia – is taken up by the ecclesiastical buildings of the **Convento de San Gabriel**, built from 1529 on the site of the temple of Quetzalcoatl. The Gothic main church is of little interest, but behind it (access at Calle 4 Norte 401) is the great mustard-yellow **Capilla Real** (daily 10am–4.30pm), topped by 49 tiled cupolas. Moorish in conception, the interior comes with a forest of columns supporting semicircular arches and immediately recalls the Mezquita in Córdoba, Spain.

The site

Arriving in Cholula you can't miss the **church** picturesquely sited atop a hill with Popocatépetl in the background. What's not immediately apparent is that the hill is in fact the remains of the **Great Pyramid of Cholula** – the Pirámide Tepanapa – the largest pyramid ever constructed, now ruined, overgrown, and really not much to look at. At 66m high it is shorter than the largest of the Egyptian pyramids but with each side measuring 350m it is also squatter and bulkier. Typically the outer shell was built over a series of nested pyramids, constructed between 200 BC and 800 AD, something amply illustrated in the **site museum**. Cross the road to reach the **archeological site** (daily 9am–6pm; US$3.20, free on Sun, camcorder US$3; ticket includes both the museum and the site), accessed through a 400-metre-long series of tunnels dug by archeologists, just a fraction of the 8km of exploratory tunnels which honeycomb the pyramid. They're well lit and capacious enough for most people to walk upright, but there's still a palpable sense of adventure as you spur off down side tunnels, which reveal elements of earlier temples and steep ceremonial stairways that appear to go on forever into the gloom. Emerging at the end of one tunnel you'll find an area of open-air excavations, where part of the great pyramid has been exposed alongside various lesser shrines with explanations of their importance in English. The ruins are a good deal less impressive than some of the more famed sites around the Valley of México, though the ring of superimposed structures around the **Patio de los Altares** are worth a look and there are some fine **murals**, though these can be better appreciated in the site museum where replicas are kept.

As you leave the site, a road on the right winds up the pyramid/hill towards the church of **Nuestra Señora de los Remedios** (daily 8am–6pm; free). From the top, or from a viewpoint about halfway up, you can attempt to count the town's churches, and gaze across the countryside at Popocatépetl.

Detailed printed guides are available at the bookstore next to the museum, and human guides hang around the tunnel entrance trying to drum up customers: neither is necessary but can be useful if you have a deep interest in these ancient structures.

Practicalities

Buses for Cholula leave CAPU in Puebla every fifteen minutes or so, and there's a constant stream of colectivos from 14 Poniente, between 9 and 11 Norte. In Cholula, they run right by the archeological site, passing en route the Estrella Roja terminal at 12 Poniente and 5 de Mayo, from which there are services back to Puebla until 10.30pm, and to TAPO in Mexico City until 7.30pm. From the bus station, head down 5 de Mayo to get to the centre of town. From the zócalo, follow Morelos past the railway track to reach the pyramid.

There are a few **hotels** in Cholula, the most economical being the *Reforma,* Morelos and 4 Sur (Ⓣ222/247-0149; ❹), which has decent enough rooms, some with bath. Alternatively, *Hostal Chelollan*, Privada de Chelollan 2003, between 20 and 22 Oriente (Ⓣ222/247-7038, Ⓔhostalchelollan@hotmail.com; ❷), has affordable dorm beds. For large modern rooms with tiled floors and TV, try the central *Hotel Suites San Juan*, 5 Sur 103 (Ⓣ222/247-0278, Ⓕ247-4544; ❺), or the slightly more distant *Villas Arqueológicas*, 2 Poniente 601, just south of the pyramid (Ⓣ222/247-1966, Ⓕ247-1508; ❼), run by Club Med and featuring a pool, tennis courts and very comfortable rooms. If you are camping, head 2km out along 6 Norte to *Trailer Park Las Américas*, at 30 Oriente (Ⓣ222/247-0134), where you can pitch a tent or park a trailer for US$4 per person.

As the site of the Universidad de las Américas campus, Cholula is often packed with local and foreign students, a good number of them seemingly spending most of their time hanging out at the outdoor cafés and **restaurants** under Portal Guerrero along one side of the zócalo. This is the place to come for eating, with *Café Enamorada*, at no.1, eternally popular with coffee drinkers, diners and those here to drink while listening to the occasional band. Along the way at no.7, *Los Jarrones* has a wider menu, good food and a more rustic character.

Cholula has become the **nightlife** capital of the Puebla region, but while a few bars cluster around 14 Poniente and 5 de Mayo, most of the action has moved about 3km out to Recta a Cholula, the main highway between Cholula and Puebla – thoroughly inconvenient and making taxi rides essential. They're also far apart from each other, making it hard to find the hottest action. The best bet is to ask locally for the current favourite and commit yourself to just one place for the night – not a bad idea when entry can cost close to US$10.

Around Cholula

If you want to explore some of the churches round about, **ACATEPEC**, easily reached by local bus, is the place to head. The spectacular village church here, San Francisco, has a superb Baroque facade entirely covered in glazed bricks and azulejos of local manufacture. It's not particularly large but it is beautifully proportioned and quite unexpected in this setting.

Just a kilometre's walk to the northwest, in the village of **TONATZINTLA**, the plain facade of the church of Santa María conceals a remarkably elaborate Baroque treasury. Here local craftsmen covered every available inch in ornament, interspersing bird, plant and native life with the more usual Christian elements. "Chipilo" **buses** from the corner of 3 Norte and 6 Poniente run to both towns.

Popocatépetl and Ixtaccíhuatl

You get excellent views of the snow-clad volcanic peaks of **Popocatépetl** (5452m) and **Ixtaccíhuatl** (5285m) from almost anywhere west of the capital, but viewing from afar is all most people do these days. "Popo" has been rumbling and fuming away since September 1994, and for much of the time since then the region has been on Yellow Alert, with evacuation procedures posted throughout surrounding towns. Activity was renewed in December 2000, culminating in the largest eruption on record, outdoing the last really full-throated eruption of 1802. Hot rocks were spat out of the crater, dust fell on the capital and, on several occasions, Mexico City's airport (over 60km away) was closed for a few hours, but there were no devastating lava flows. Foreign media hyped the eruption excessively and fanned tourist anxiety, but the only real hardship was felt by the local villagers who were evacuated for weeks while their livestock trampled their fields trying to find enough to eat.

While the area within a two-kilometre radius of Popo remains closed to the public, the rest of the **Parque Nacional de Volcanes** (daily 7am–9pm; US$1), which surrounds both volcanoes has reopened – though for details on the latest situation, contact the park office in Amecameca at Plaza de la Constitución 9, (Ⓣ597/978-3830). Being in the park is an exceptional experience with the nation's second and third highest peaks (after the 5700m Pico de Orizaba) rising above the Paso de Cortés, the 3800-metre-high pass between the two volcanoes.

The names stem from an Aztec Romeo-and-Juliet-style legend. Popocatépetl (Smoking Mountain) was a warrior, Ixtaccíhuatl (White Lady) his lover, the beautiful daughter of the emperor. Believing Popocatépetl killed in battle, she died from grief, and when he returned alive he laid her body down on the mountain, where he eternally stands sentinel, holding a burning torch. From the west, Ixta does somewhat resemble a reclining female form and the various parts of the mountain are named accordingly – the feet, the knees, the belly, the breast, the neck, the head, the hair.

Practicalities

If you'd just like to get as close as possible to the mountains, visit **Amecameca** (usually just Ameca), a lovely little town an hour south of Mexico City, reached by "Servicio Volcánes" buses from TAPO (every 20min; 5am–11pm). Dramatic views of the mountain peaks are bizarrely framed by the palms of the zócalo, around which you'll find a couple of good, inexpensive hotels. If Popo quietens down you may again be able to drive or hitch, or get a taxi from Amecameca – there are no buses – along the good asphalt road up to the pine-dotted Paso de Cortés. Here there used to be a primitive refuge where people slept and rented crampons and ice axes for the physically challenging though technically easy one-day ascent of Popo. Ixta is a challenging climb for serious mountaineers only, involving a night or two with all your gear at very high altitude, and a technical three-kilometre-long ridge traverse (often requiring ropes) to reach the highest point.

Cuernavaca and around

CUERNAVACA has always been a place of escape from the city – the Aztecs called it Cuauhnahuac (Place by the Woods), and it became a favourite resort and hunting ground for their rulers. Cortés seized and destroyed the city during the siege of Tenochtitlán, but he too ended up building himself a palace here, the Spanish corrupting the name to Cuernavaca (Cow Horn) for no better reason than their inability to cope with the original. The fashion then established has been followed ever since: the Emperor Maximilian and the deposed Shah of Iran both had houses here, and the inner suburbs are now packed with the high-walled mansions of wealthy Mexicans and the expats who flock down here from the US and Canada each winter.

For the casual visitor the modern city is in many ways a disappointment. Its spring-like climate remains, but as capital of the state of Morelos, Cuernavaca is rapidly becoming industrialized and the streets in the centre permanently clogged with traffic and fumes. The gardens and villas that shelter the rich are almost all hidden behind high walls, or in districts so far out that you won't see them. It seems an ill-planned and widely spread city, certainly not easy to get about on foot, though much of what you'll want to see is close to the centre and accessible on foot. Food and lodging, too, come relatively expensive, in part thanks to the large foreign contingent, swelled by tourists and by students from the many language schools. On the other hand, the town is still attractive enough to make it a decent base for heading north to the village of **Tepoztlán** (see p.477), with its raucous fiesta, or south to the ruins of **Xochicalco**. If you are at all interested in Mexican history, it may also be worthwhile taking a trip to **Cuautla**, where Emiliano Zapata is buried in the Jardín Revolución del Sur.

Arrival and information

Cuernavaca is unusual in that it doesn't have a single main bus station. Instead, half a dozen companies have their own depots in different parts of town. Very frequent **buses** from Mexico City's Central del Sur mostly arrive close to the centre: Estrella Blanca services are probably the most convenient, with their Cuernavaca terminal easy to find on Morelos, just north of the centre. Pullman de Morelos buses also stop quite close to the centre, at the corner of Abasolo and Netzahualcoyotl; simply walk up the latter and you find yourself at the heart of things. The first-class Estrella de Oro terminus is around 2km south of the centre on Morelos. Estrella Roja coaches from Puebla pull in at a station three blocks south of the zócalo at Cuauhtémotzin and Galeana. The bus stations where you are most likely to arrive generally have someone handing out local **maps**, but their knowledge of the town is limited and for more detail you'll need to head 2km south to the very helpful and well-informed state **tourist office**, near the Estrella de Oro terminus, at Morelos Sur 187 (Mon–Fri 8am–5pm, Sat 10am–1pm; ⓣ777/314-3872, ⓦwww.morelostravel.com). They also have information on buses and excursions, plus leaflets on language schools in town and on other destinations around the state.

Accommodation

Cuernavaca has a reasonable range of **hotels** close to the centre but little that is particularly appealing in budget categories: many of the cheaper options are just north of the centre, on Matamoros and the streets that connect it with Morelos. Visitors looking for mid-range and top-end places are well served, with some occupying grand old mansions in the centre, and others spread around pools and lush gardens in the suburbs.

Cuernavaca's tourist office has a long list of contact addresses for families offering **private rooms**, a service aimed at students attending local language schools – the schools themselves and their notice boards are also good sources for such accommodation.

América Aragón y León 14 ⓣ777/318-6127. Basic but respectable place in a street mostly full of dives; all rooms have bath, but you pay US$3.50 to have a TV. ❸

Casa Colonial Netzahualcoyotl 37 ⓣ777/312-7033, ⓦwww.tourbymexico.com/colonial. Gorgeous historic rooms in a delightful eighteenth-century mansion close to the Museo Robert Brady (see p.475). With attractive colonial public areas and a pool, this is one of the most appealing places in the centre, and prices include breakfast. TV on request, no phones. As well as rooms, there are suites (US$138–155) and junior suites (US$107–121). Prices are about 15 percent higher at weekends. ❽

Colonial Aragón y León 104 ⓣ777/318-6414. Across the street from the *América* and a bit less basic; the most comfortable hotel in Aragón y León. ❺

Las Mañanitas Ricardo Linares 107 ⓣ777/314-1466 or 01-800/221-5299, ⓕ777/318-3672, in the US ⓣ1-888/413-9199, ⓦwww.lasmananitas.com.mx. One of the best luxury hotels in Cuernavaca, and conveniently sited within a ten-minute walk of the zócalo. The colonial street-front entrance gives little clue of the oasis within, where peacocks, flamingoes and African cranes strut around a pool and lush gardens. The tiled-floor rooms come with heavy wooden furniture and all the fittings, plus there's a superb restaurant on site. Suites range from US$270 to US$425; rooms start at US$220. ❾

Papagayo Motolina 13 ⓣ777/314-1711 or 1924, ⓦwww.tourbymexico.com/hpapagayo. Large hotel close to the centre with rooms in blocks set around spacious grounds and large pool. With a family atmosphere and children's area this place can get a bit raucous on occasion, but the rooms are good value and the price includes breakfast in the on-site restaurant/bar. The recently remodelled rooms and suites are a little nicer than the standard rooms. ❻

Roma Matamoros 17 ⓣ777/318-8778. Simple but clean budget option with parking space; all rooms have bathroom, overhead fan and TV. ❹

Royal Matamoros 11 ⓣ777/314-4018. One of a number of similar places along Matamoros; fairly shabby but with comfortable enough rooms with bath, and space for parking. ❺

The Town

The zócalo – as ever, the heart of the city – comprises the **Plaza de Armas** and the smaller Jardín Juárez, with its bandstand, to the northwest. Around the twin plazas you'll find a series of cafés where you can sit outdoors overlooked by the huge, black, volcanic-rock **statue of Morelos** which gazes across the plaza at the Palacio de Gobierno. The **Palacio de Cortés**, with its Rivera murals, is right behind the statue, and almost everything else of interest lies within a few minutes' walk of here, principally the understated **cathedral** and the flamboyant **Museo Robert Brady**. Beyond lie a handful of minor sights, the formal yet peaceful **Jardín Borda** and a few other botanical gardens, the Salto de St Anton waterfall, and a pair of minor **pyramids**.

Palacio de Cortés

At the eastern end of the Plaza de Armas, behind the statue of Morelos, is the **Palacio de Cortés**, which houses the **Museo Regional Cuauhnahuac** (Tues–Sun 9am–5pm; US$3.70, free on Sun). Building work began as early as 1522, when, although Tenochtitlán had fallen, much of the country had yet to come under Spanish control, and the fortress-like aspect of the palace's earlier parts reflects this period. Over the centuries, though, it's been added to and modified substantially – first by Cortés himself and his descendants, later by the state authorities to whom it passed – so that what you see today is every bit a palace. The museum is a good one, spacious and well laid out with a substantial section covering local archeology, including some fine examples of stelae and a lovely seated figure from Xochicalco. In fact, the building is partly constructed over the ruins of a small pyramid that can be seen in the courtyard and elsewhere. There's also a substantial collection of colonial art, weaponry and everyday artefacts, including the sixteenth-century clock mechanism from the cathedral, and a reproduction of a *cuexcomate*, a kind of thatched granary still found around the state.

The highlight, though, is the series of **murals** around the gallery, painted by Diego Rivera in 1929 and 1930. Depicting Mexican history from the Conquest to the Revolution, they concentrate in particular on the atrocities committed by Cortés, and on the revolutionary Emiliano Zapata, who was born in nearby Cuautla, raised most of his army from the peasants of Morelos, and remains something of a folk hero to the locals. From the balcony here, there are wonderful, though sometimes hazy, views to the east with Popocatépetl in the far distance.

The Cathedral

From the plaza, Hidalgo runs three blocks west to the **Catedral de la Asunción**, located on the south side of a grassy tree-shaded compound populated with a couple of other small churches. Founded by Cortés in 1529, the cathedral looks bulky and threatening from the outside (at one stage there were actually cannons mounted along the battlemented roof line), but it has been remarkably tastefully refurbished within. Stripped almost bare, the modernist approach is an enormous relief if you've grown tired of the churrigueresque and Baroque flamboyance elsewhere. Most of the decor is understated, but traces of murals discovered during the redecoration have been uncovered in places – they have a remarkably East Asian look and are believed to have been painted by a Christian Chinese or Filipino artist in the days when the cathedral was the centre for missions to the Far East. The main Spanish trade route then came through here, with goods brought across the Pacific to Acapulco, overland through central Mexico, and on from Veracruz to Spain.

If you need your fix of golden exuberance, pop into the **Capilla del Santísimo**, where there's a small gilt *retablo* and stations of the cross done in charcoal on paper.

Until his death in December 2000, Cuernavaca's bishop was **Luis Cervantes**, one of the country's most liberal and outspoken clergymen. Apart from doing up his cathedral, he was renowned for instituting the "Mariachi Mass", something continued by his disciples. Every Sunday, this service is conducted to the accompaniment of traditional Mexican music and usually attracts large crowds.

Museo Robert Brady

South of the cathedral, at the corner of Netzahualcoyotl and 20 de Noviembre, the **Museo Robert Brady** (Tues–Sun 10am–6pm; US$3) occupies a former convent built in the sixteenth century and holds the private collection of the Iowa-born artist, who moved to Cuernavaca in the 1960s and died in 1986. Filled with art from around the world and decorated in an intensely colourful artesanía style, it is a fabulous place, with rooms arranged aesthetically, without regard to history, geography or classification of artists' style. As a result, what you see is a beautiful home rather than a typical museum, and is well worth a visit.

Rooms, arranged around a couple of outside patios complete with sculptures and a delightful pool, are filled with most of the greats of twentieth-century Mexican art. Even the bathrooms contain works by Diego Rivera and Rufino Tamayo, and there are also pieces by Frida Kahlo, Graham Sutherland, and some particularly good entries by Rafael Coronel, including a portrait of Peggy Guggenheim. Everything is labelled in English.

Jardín Borda

Immediately west of the cathedral is the entrance to the **Jardín Borda**, Morelos 103 (Tues–Sun 10am–5.30pm; US$3, free on Sun), a large formal garden adjacent to the mansion of the Taxco mining magnate José de la Borda (see p.480). It falls short of the grandeur Borda dreamed of when he commissioned the garden in the eighteenth century – but both the garden and the mansion are a delightfully tranquil reminder of the haven Cuernavaca once was, and no doubt still is behind the walls of its exclusive residences. Maximilian and Carlota adopted Borda's legacy as their weekend home, but Maximilian also had a retreat in Cuernavaca that he shared with his native mistress, "La India Bonita". Officially named La Casa del Olindo, this second house was popularly known as La Casa del Olvido ("House of Forgetfulness") since the builder forgot to include quarters for Carlota.

Out from the centre

About twenty minutes' walk into the suburbs beyond the Jardín Borda is the **Salto de St Anton** (Tues–Sun 8am–6pm; free), a beautiful 36-metre cascade surrounded by vegetation and natural columns of crystallized basalt. Unfortunately the site has been overdeveloped and is marred by concrete walkways, litter and a faint stench from the polluted water, but it's still pretty and the road to the falls passes a number of flower shops and restaurants.

Rather more distant – 2km southeast of the centre, in the Colonia Acapantzingo – is the **Jardín Etnobotánico**, Matamoros 200 (daily 9am–5pm; free), whose grounds and collection of medicinal plants are just about worth taking a taxi (or a long walk) to see. As well as the labelled specimens – coffee, guava, roses and medicinal herbs – there is a small museum of traditional medicine.

Other sites scattered further out in the fringes of the city include the sole significant reminder of the pre-colonial period, the **Pyramid of Teopanzolco** (daily 9am–6pm; US$2.70, free on Sun). Even this was so effectively buried that it took an artillery bombardment during the Revolution to uncover it. To the northeast of the centre beyond the train station (which is what the gunners were aiming at), it's a small temple in which two pyramids can be seen, one built over the other. The pyramid can be reached by city bus #6 from Degollado and Reelección.

Eating, drinking and nightlife

You don't need to wander far from the centre to find good **places to eat**: there's a particularly fine group around the zócalo, and you can get juices and tortas at any time around the bandstand in the zócalo's Jardín Juárez. **Evening activity** mostly centres on the Plazuela del Zacate, just a couple of blocks south of the zócalo where the corner of Galeana and Hidalgo is intersected by Fray Bartolomé de las Casas. Most nights there are large groups hanging around a small triangular area, occasionally popping into one of the fashionable cafés and bars for a beer, or sitting outside listening to someone playing on the makeshift stage. There are also free concerts from the bandstand in the Jardín Juárez every Thursday evening at 6pm.

Los Arcos Jardín de los Héroes 4 ⓣ777/312-1510. Ever-popular restaurant and bar on the south side of the zócalo serving espresso coffee and a wide range of fairly pricey dishes catering to locals and foreign students. In the evening most people are here to drink and listen to the nightly live music, which comes in a variety of styles and abilities.

El Barco Rayon 5–F. A diner specializing in pozole (US$2.80–4) and seafood salads (US$4–8), but also serving tacos and tostadas.

Cafeona Morrow 6 ⓣ777/318-2757. Small and friendly café that promotes the culture and food of Chiapas, with native decor, salads, good low-cost breakfasts and dishes suchs as *tamales chiapanecos*. Comida corrida for US$2.50, and there is occasional live acoustic music in the evening.

La India Bonita Morrow 20, just off Morelos ⓣ777/312-5021. Lovely restaurant with a pleasant outdoor patio, excellent but moderately priced food (including set breakfasts) and impeccable service. Expect to pay around US$8 for delicious mains, or just drop in for a quiet drink at the bar.

Las Mañanitas Ricardo Linares 107 ⓣ777/314-1466 or 01-800/221-5299. The sort of place that people drive hours to visit, this well-known restaurant serves fine international cuisine in the sumptuous grounds of the hotel of the same name. You'll probably part with at least US$40 for a full meal but you won't regret it.

Pollo y Más Galeana 4. Opposite the zócalo, serving tasty roast chicken, enchiladas and antojitos.

Vienes Lerdo de Tejada 302. Austro-Hungarian café, patisserie and restaurant just a block from the zócalo; a great spot for Continental-style coffee and pastries.

Listings

Buses The first-class Estrella de Oro terminus, around 2km south of the centre on Morelos, has services to Acapulco and Iguala. Estrella Roja go to Puebla, Cuautla and Miacatlán (for the Crucero de Xochicalco) from their station three blocks south of the zócalo at Cuauhtémotzin and Galeana. The most frequent buses to Mexico City (every 15min) are provided by Pullman de Morelos, with fewer from Estrella Blanca and Estrella de Oro. Second-class buses to Tepoztlán and Cuautla leave from the local bus stand just south of the market (head east on Degollado to find it).

Exchange Casas de cambio include Gesta on the corner of Galeana and Lerdo de Tejada, plus more on Morrow at nos.7, 8 and 11.

Internet There are several places around the centre of town, and prices are low though connections are slow. Best rates are at Cyber Gasso, Hidalgo 22–D and Gutenberg 206 (Mon–Fri 7.30am–9.30pm, Sat 8.30am–9.30pm, Sun 9.30am–9.30pm), and Computación Cuernavaca, Gutenberg 26a (daily 7am–8pm).

Language schools The state tourist office has leaflets and brochures issued by several schools offering Spanish language courses.

Laundry Lavandería Morelos, Matamoros 28 (Mon–Sat 9am–8pm).
Pharmacy The handiest pharmacy is the 24hr Farmacia del Ahorro at the corner of Hidalgo and Galeana, just south of the zócalo.

Phone and fax services Next door to the post office (Mon–Fri 8am–7.30pm, Sat 9am–4.30pm, Sun 9am–12.30pm).
Post office At the southwest corner of the zócalo (Mon–Fri 8am–3pm, Sat 9am–1pm).

Tepoztlán

One of the most interesting side-trips from Cuernavaca is to **TEPOZTLÁN**, just 21km to the northeast, and dramatically sited in a narrow valley spectacularly ringed by volcanic mountains. Until recently this was an isolated agrarian community inhabited by Nahuatl-speaking people whose life could have changed little between the time of the Conquest and the beginning of the twentieth century. It was on Tepoztlán that Oscar Lewis based his classic study of *Life in a Mexican Village* and traced the effects of the Revolution on it: the village was an important stronghold of the original Zapatista movement. New roads and a couple of luxury hotels have changed things, and Tepoztlán has become a popular weekend retreat from the capital with a good selection of restaurants and quality arts and crafts shops springing up to cater to the visitors. Midweek, at least, it is still a peaceful spot, and the stunning setting survives, as does a reputation for joyously boisterous **fiestas** (especially the drunken revelry of the night of Sept 7).

Buses between Cuautla (see overleaf) and Cuernavaca or Mexico City (Autobuses del Sur) leave you at a *caseta* on the highway a kilometre west of town at the end of Calle 22 Febrero. Direct second-class buses from Cuernavaca drop you half a kilometre south of town at the end of the main street, Avenida 5 Mayo. One block north of the junction of Calle 22 Febrero and Avenida 5 Mayo is the zócalo, at whose northern end you'll be dropped if you arrive by slower second-class bus from Cuernavaca (there's a Bancomer for **currency exchange** on Avenida 5 Mayo near the bus stop). On Sundays and Wednesdays a **market** is held in the zócalo, on whose eastern side stands the massive, fortress-like **Ex-Convento Dominico de la Natividad**. It was indeed a fortress for a while during the Revolution, but is now in a rather beautiful state of disrepair with some attractive sections of mural still surviving in the cloister. Around the back and accessed off Calle Gonzales, part of the church has been given over to the **Museo de Arte Prehispánico** (Tues–Sun 10am–6pm; free) with a remarkably good archeological collection. Several pre-Hispanic temples have been found on the hilltops roundabout and you can see one to the north, perched high up in impossibly steep-looking terrain. This is the **Santuario del Cerro Tepozteco** (daily 9am–5.30pm; US$2.70, free on Sun), reached after an exhausting climb of an hour or so up what at times is little more than an upgraded dry streambed: follow the blue signs from the upper side of the zócalo. It is all worth it for the views from this artificially flattened hilltop, and the chance to inspect the site at close quarters. The small, three-stepped, lime-washed pyramid here was dedicated to Tepoztecatl, a god of pulque and of fertility, represented by carvings of rabbits. There were so many pulque gods that they were known as the four hundred rabbits: the drink was supposedly discovered by rabbits nibbling at the agave plants from which it is made. This one gained particular kudos when the Spanish flung the idol off the cliffs only for his adherents to find that it had landed unharmed – the big September fiesta is in his honour. Follow the example of Mexicans and reward your efforts with a picnic lunch (water and soft drinks are available at a price), but buck the trend and take your empty containers back with you.

Practicalities

Many people visit Tepoztlán as a day-trip since the **hotels** are all fairly expensive. The cheapest is *Posada Ali*, Calle Netzahualcoyotl 2 (Ⓣ739/395-1971; ❻), out towards the ruins and with its lower-cost rooms tucked under the eaves. Larger rooms have sunflower-carved headboards on the beds and wood-beamed ceilings, and everyone has access to the small pool and *frontón* court. If you can stretch to it, *the* place to stay is the elegant but unpretentious *Posada del Tepozteco*, at Paraíso 3 (Ⓣ739/395-0010, Ⓦwww.posadadeltepozteco.com; ❾), wonderfully sited above most of the town with views of the mountains from the manicured gardens and two outdoor pools. The rooms are simple but well equipped and the service of a standard you would expect when prices start at US$112 (US$135 on Fri and Sat); gorgeous suites go for US$182 (weekends US$205).

There are plenty of **restaurants** either close to the zócalo or out along the road towards the ruins. For cheap Mexican mains plus vegetarian dishes, salads, wholemeal bread and good coffee, visit *El Milenio* two blocks north of the zócalo on Avenida de Tepozteco (the continuation of Avenida 5 Mayo), or for something more upmarket get a table at *Los Colorines*, half a block south along the same street.

Cuautla

Some 42km southeast of Cuernavaca, and an hour and a half by bus, lies **CUAUTLA**, really just a small regional town of limited consequence except for being the burial place of **Emiliano Zapata**. The Plazuela de la Revolución del Sur, a block south of the zócalo, surrounds a huge bronze statue of him standing in heroic pose, moustachioed with broad-brimmed sombrero, a bandoleer across his shoulder and clutching a rifle in one hand and a proclamation in the other declaring "Tierra y Libertad" ("land and freedom").

Back on the zócalo, there's minor interest at the **Casa de Morelos** (Tues–Sun 10am–6pm; US$2.70, free on Sun), a beautiful colonial mansion and gardens, formerly the home of Independence leader and local boy José Maria Morelos (see p.268), containing archeological finds and items of local historical interest. Three blocks further north along Los Bravo, Cuautla's former train station is now home to the **Museo José Maria Morelos y Pavón** (Tues–Sun 10am–6pm; US$0.50) mainly tracing the life and times of Morelos, and the Independence movement in this state that bears his name. Of more interest to train buffs is the 1904 **steam locomotive** and carriages once used by the town's other great local hero, Emiliano Zapata. Until recently, you could ride on it along a kilometre-long section of track on Saturday and Sunday evenings, but services were suspended at last check, and may or may not resume in the near future.

Cuautla also has something of a reputation for its thermal **spas**, and there are several large complexes a little way out from the centre. The emphasis is more on swimming than luxuriating, but for around US$3 you could easily while away an hour or two at Agua Hedionda: look for the dedicated purple-and-white buses or yellow *combis* that rumble through town and jump aboard (around a ten-minute trip).

Practicalities

Cuautla has three **bus stations**, all close to each other a couple of blocks west of the zócalo. If you can't find a map at the bus stations, ask directions for the old train station where there's a small **tourist office** next to the museum

(Tues–Sat 9am–6pm; ⓣ735/352-5221, ⓕ352-8554). There is little enough reason to stay the night, though **hotels** are generally good value, the best being the motel-style *Madero*, Madero 27 (ⓣ735/352-6665; ❸), three long blocks south of the zócalo, with well-kept modern rooms all with TV and bathroom. Closer to the centre there's *España*, 2 de Mayo 22 (ⓣ735/352-2186; ❹), and the more upmarket *Defensa del Agua*, Defensa del Agua 34 (ⓣ735/352-1679; ❹), with a pool, parking and clean modern rooms with TV. The centre of town has numerous small cheap **restaurants**, but for something a little special make for *Las Golondrinas*, Nicolás Catalán 19A, a block north of the zócalo, where fountains splash as you sink back in comfy chairs and tuck into corn and *cuitlacoche* soup (US$2), *ranchera* fish kebabs (US$7.20) or regional specialities such as barbecued rabbit (US$5.40); there's also a lunchtime menu for US$6.

Xochicalco

Some 38km south of Cuernavaca lie the impressive hilltop ruins of **Xochicalco** (daily 9am–6pm; US$3.70). While not much is known of the history of this site or the peoples who inhabited it, it is regarded by archeologists as one of the most significant in central Mexico, forming as it does a link between the ancient culture of Teotihuacán and the later Toltec peoples. Xochicalco flourished from around 700 AD to 900 AD – thus overlapping with both Teotihuacán and Tula – and also shows clear parallels with Maya and Zapotec sites of the era.

The setting, high on a bare mountain top, is reminiscent of Monte Albán (see p.603), the great Zapotec site near Oaxaca and, like Monte Albán and the great Maya sites (but unlike Tula or Teotihuacán), Xochicalco was an exclusively religious and ceremonial centre rather than a true city. The style of many of the carvings, too, recalls Zapotec and Maya art. Their subjects, however, and the architecture of the temples, seem to form a transition between Teotihuacán and Tula: in particular, Quetzalcoatl first appears here in human guise, as he was to appear at Tula and almost every subsequent site, rather than simply as the feathered serpent of Teotihuacán. The ball-court is almost identical to earlier Maya examples, and similar to those that later appeared in Tula. For all these influences, however, or perhaps because there are so many of them, it's almost impossible to say which was dominant: some claim that Xochicalco was a northern outpost of the Maya, others that it was a subject city of Teotihuacán that survived (or perhaps precipitated through revolt) the fall of that empire.

Arriving at the site, first stop in at the **museum**, on a neighbouring hilltop, where you buy your entry **ticket**, and can take a look at some of the more portable pieces found at the site. A carved stele that once graced one of the lower courtyards (and has now been replaced by a concrete pillar) takes pride of place in the first room, and is followed by numerous slabs of carved stone, a delicate alabaster bowl, and some fine jade masks. From here it is a ten-minute walk to the site.

The site

Much the most important surviving monument here is the **Pirámide de Quetzalcoatl**, on the highest part of the site. Around its base are carved wonderfully elaborate plumed serpents, coiling around various seated figures and symbols with astronomical significance – all clearly Maya in inspiration. On top, part of the wall of the sanctuary remains standing, though it now surrounds a large hole. In 1993 the centre of the pyramid was excavated to reveal the remains of an earlier pyramid inside.

The other main point of interest is the **Solar Observatory** (nominally daily 11am–4pm, but hours are sporadic in practice) located to the northwest of the main pyramid and down the hill a little, accessed through the northern ball-court. Here, you'll find the entrance to some subterranean passages, a couple of natural **caves** augmented by steps and tunnels, one of which features a shaft in the roof that is oriented so as to allow the sun to shine directly in. At astronomical midday (midway between sunrise and sunset) for around five weeks either side of the summer solstice – May 14/15 to July 28/29 – the shaft casts a hexagonal patch of light onto the cave floor. At any time, the custodian should point out the remains of frescoes on the walls.

Practicalities

The quick and comfortable way to the site is by half-hourly first-class **bus** headed to Miacatlán from Cuernavaca's Pullman de Morelos terminal, which will take you to the Crucero de Xochicalco, 4km from the site. There is often a taxi waiting here to run you to the site for about US$2; otherwise you'll have to walk. There's also a very slow and circuitous second-class bus which leaves hourly from Cuernavaca's market bus station and takes you right to the site.

If you're **driving**, or if you go with a **tour**, you can continue another thirty-odd kilometres down the road beyond Xochicalco to the caves of Cacahuamilpa (see p.484), from where Taxco (see below) is only a short distance.

Taxco

Silver has been mined in **TAXCO** since before the Conquest, and although its sources have long been depleted it still forms the basis of the town's fame and its livelihood. Nowadays, though, it's in the shape of jewellery, made in hundreds of workshops to be sold throughout the country and in a bewildering array of shops (*platerías*) catering to the tourists in Taxco itself. It's an attractive place, a mass of terracotta-tiled, whitewashed houses lining the narrow cobbled alleys that straggle steeply up the hills like some Mexican version of a Tuscan village. At intervals the pattern is broken by some larger mansion, by a courtyard filled with flowers, or by the twin spires of a church rearing up – above all the famous Baroque wedding cake of **Santa Prisca**. Unfortunately, the streets are eternally clogged with VW Beetle taxis and colectivos struggling up the steep slopes, and forming an endless *paseo* around the central Plaza Borda. Once you've spent an hour or so in the church and a couple of museums there's really nothing to do but sit around the plaza cafés. Still, it is a pleasant enough place to do just that if you don't mind the relatively high prices, and the profusion of other tourists.

Though it might seem a prosperous place now, Taxco's development has not been a simple progression – indeed on more than one occasion the town has been all but abandoned. The Spaniards came running at the rumours of mineral wealth here (Cortés himself sent an expedition in 1522), but their initial success was short-lived, and it wasn't until the eighteenth century that French immigrant **José de la Borda** struck it fabulously rich by discovering the San Ignacio vein. It is from the short period of Borda's life that most of what you see originated – he spent one large fortune on building the church of Santa Prisca, others on more buildings and a royal lifestyle here and in Cuernavaca; by his death in 1778 the boom was already over. In 1929 a final revival started with the arrival of the American architect and writer **William Spratling**, who set up a jewellery workshop in Taxco, drawing on the local traditional skills and pre-Hispanic designs. With the completion of a new road around the same time, the massive influx of tourists was inevitable, but the town has handled it fairly well, becoming rich at the expense of just a little charm.

Arrival, orientation and information

Approaching Taxco, you'll arrive on Avenida Kennedy, the main road that contours around the side of the valley at the bottom of town. From Kennedy several streets wind through the houses, all more or less converging on Taxco's zócalo, the **Plaza Borda**, where Santa Prisca towers above all other buildings. Just below and east of Plaza Borda is the tiny **Plazuela de Bernal**, from where several streets fan out; to the west, the narrow Cuauhtémoc runs back to **Plazuela de San Juan**, where you'll find several hotels and restaurants.

Taxco has two **bus stations**, both on Avenida Kennedy and both with fairly frequent services to Mexico City, Cuernavaca and Acapulco. They're about 1km apart, but from either it is about a ten-minute steep walk or US$2 taxi ride from Plaza Borda. To get in from the Estrella Blanca terminal, cross the road and turn right up the hill and then left to climb even more steeply past the church of Santa Veracruz to the centre. Arriving at Estrella de Oro, head straight up Calle de Pilita, the steep alley directly across from you, until you come, on your right, to the Plazuela de San Juan, and from there go down Cuauhtémoc to the zócalo.

All the information you really need is a map of the town, which can be picked up at the bus stations, obviating the need to visit the small **tourist office** (daily 10am–7pm; ⓣ762/622-0798) inconveniently sited on Avenida Kennedy at the very northern end of town, where the remains of an aqueduct named Los Arcos cross the road (regular *combis* connect Los Arcos to the zócalo). There are several **banks** with ATMs on the streets surrounding the zócalo, along with numerous casas de cambio, including Argentu just off Plazuela de San Juan at Real de Cuauhtémoc 17, which offers good rates and civilized opening hours (Mon–Fri 9am–6pm, Sat 10am–2.30pm).

Accommodation

Taxco has some excellent **hotels**, and when the day-trippers have left the place settles into a calmer mode. There are plenty of inexpensive places near the zócalo, while at the higher end of the scale you're swamped with choices, in particular some lovely restored colonial buildings that now serve as comfortable, popular hotels.

Agua Escondida Plaza Borda 4, on the zócalo ⓣ762/622-0726 or 0736, ⓦwww.aguaescondida.com. The small Plaza Borda frontage gives little clue to the size of this rambling hotel which includes a pool, table tennis, and a choice of "economic" rooms hidden away down the back stairs, or "remodelled" rooms with TV and telephone, some with good views, but not really worth the price difference, since they cost almost twice as much, and those at the front can be noisy due to the night-time revelries on the square. ❺

Los Arcos Juan Ruíz de Alarcón 2 ⓣ762/622-1836, ⓔlosarcoshotel@hotmail.com. Good-value rooms, one with a little attic, a couple of blocks east of the zócalo in a pretty colonial building built in the seventeenth century as a monastery. Rooms around a pretty courtyard are simple and attractive. Book ahead if you plan to stay at a weekend. ❺

Casa Grande Plazuela de San Juan 7 ⓣ762/622-0969, ⓕ622-8316. One of the cheapest places in town with a slightly run-down charm, but friendly and functional. Cheerfully decorated rooms have bathroom but no TV, and those on the top floor have direct access to the rooftop terrace. ❹

Casa de Huéspedes Arellano Pajaritos 23 ☎762/622-0215. Good-value budget hotel by the market with three sun terraces and cheaper rooms the higher up you get. ❹

Posada de los Castillo Juan Ruíz de Alarcón 7 ☎762/622-1396. Lovely colonial hotel, near the zócalo, with rooms decorated in bright tiles and old wood. Rooms with TV cost ten bucks extra. ❺

Posada San Javier Estacadas 32 ☎762/622-3177, ⓔposadasanjavier@ hotmail.com. Central and spacious hotel arranged around a pool and attractive gardens. Rooms are large and simply but attractively decorated (and some have good views), though it is definitely worth stepping up to the junior suites with their terracotta-tiled floors and heavy wooden furniture. No credit cards. ❺

Santa Prisca Cena Oscuras 1 ☎762/622-0080 or 0980, ⓔhtl_staprisca@yahoo.com. Attractive converted colonial building just off the zócalo, with a pleasant flower-filled patio and a variety of rooms, some of which have their own terrace. ❻

The Town

The heart of town is the diminutive Plaza Borda, ringed by recently restored colonial buildings and dominated by Taxco's one outstanding sight, the church of **Santa Prisca**. The building is so florid and expensive that it tends to provoke extreme reactions, ranging from praise to downright criticism.

Its hyperelaborate facade towers over the zócalo, and displays a rare unity, having been entirely built between 1751 and 1759. Inside there's a riot of gilded churrigueresque altarpieces and other treasures, including paintings by Miguel Cabrera, a Zapotec native who became one of Mexico's greatest colonial religious artists. His work can be seen in the medallions of the altarpieces, lunettes of the martyrdom of St Prisca and St Sebastian, a series of fifteen scenes from the life of the Virgin in the Episcopal Sacristy behind the altar, and a collection of paintings of prominent townspeople of the age (including Borda) in a side chapel to the left. Note, too, the *manifestador*, a gilt construction immediately in front of the altar that was designed to display the Holy Sacrament and comes decorated with small statues of Faith, Hope and Charity. This was thought to have been lost until rediscovered in 1988 during renovations.

In the northeast corner of the zócalo, a doorway opens onto a courtyard packed with silver shops, which provides the approach to the **Museo de Platería**, Plaza Borda 1 (daily except Wed 10.30am–5pm; US$1). Turn left and down the stairs to reach this small but worthwhile collection of silver, including beautiful Art Deco cutlery, a coffee jug and a gorgeous teapot all from William Spratling's original workshop. The rest of what's on show spans the years since then: everything from a walking stick in the form of a snake to modern designs incorporating amethysts found in geodes hereabouts, and even one piece with a whole geode worked into the design. Almost next door, the **Centro Cultural de Taxco** (Mon–Sat 10am–3pm & 5–8pm, Sun 10am–4pm; free) is really just a showcase for local artists and is worth a quick visit if only for the views over the town from many of the windows.

William Spratling's personal collection of antiquities is contained in the **Museo Guillermo Spratling**, Porfirio Delgado 1 (Tues–Sun 9am–6pm; US$3, free on Sun), right behind Santa Prisca and reached down Calle del Arco at the right-hand side of the church. There are several good pieces, but overall it is disappointing, especially if you've just been to the Museo Nacional de Antropología in Mexico City (see p.401): if you've yet to go, save your money until then. Taxco's most interesting museum, the **Museo de Arte Virreinal** (Tues–Sat 10am–7pm, Sun 9am–3pm; US$1.50), is nearby at Calle Juan Ruíz de Alarcón 6, housed in the beautiful colonial Casa Humboldt, an old staging inn named after the German explorer-baron who spent just one night here in 1803. Labels in Spanish and English provide detailed and diverting background to the town, its religious art and history, partly focusing on Taxco's importance on the trade routes between Acapulco (where Manila galleons docked) and Veracruz (from where the booty was shipped to Spain). The life and works of José de la Borda and Humboldt both get extensive coverage too, and there's a good collection of ecclesiastical vestments and furniture, including a fine sacristy bench, a huge eighteenth-century candlestick, and a kind of early waffle iron for making communion wafers.

Beyond these few sights, the way to enjoy Taxco is simply to wander the streets, nosing about in the *platerías*, stopping occasionally for a drink. If you're buying **silver** you can be fairly sure it's the real thing here (check for the hallmark: ".925" or "sterling"), but prices are much the same as they would be anywhere and quality and workmanship can vary enormously: there's everything from mass-produced belt buckles and cheap rings to designer jewellery that will set you back thousands of dollars. Whatever you buy, the shops off the main streets will be cheaper and more open to bargaining. A section in the **market**, down the steps beside the zócalo, is given over to the silver-hawkers and makes a good place to start. The bulk of the market, however, seems to specialize in rather tacky tourist goods.

There is little of interest in the immediate vicinity, though to while away an afternoon you could follow Benito Juárez to Plazuela el Minero (a small square with a statue of a miner), then head left up Avenida Kennedy to the northern end of town (around 2km – alternatively take a *combi* from the zócalo to Los Arcos), from where you can catch the **teleférico** (daily 7am–7pm; US$3 round-trip) up to the hilltop *Hotel Monte Taxco* for the views.

Eating and drinking

Finding somewhere to **eat** in Taxco is no problem at all, with several enticing places around the zócalo that make wonderful spots to watch the world go by. They tend to be expensive, and by sacrificing a little atmosphere you'll do better along some of the streets which lead away from the centre. All except the cheapest of the hotels have their own dining rooms, and for rock-bottom prices, the **market** has a section given over to food stalls, which are better than they look. In the evening everyone gathers around the zócalo to see and be seen, to stroll or to sit outdoors with a coffee or a drink at one of the bars.

El Adobe Plazuela de San Juan 13. Atmospheric restaurant where excellent Mexican food is served for moderate prices either in the cozy interior or on a balcony overlooking the square.

Bar Berta Plaza Borda 2. Traditional meeting place almost next to the church, and one of several places in Mexico claiming to be the original home of the margarita. Here it is a tequila and lime mixture known as a Berta.

Bar Paco Plaza Borda 4. Directly opposite Santa Prisca and with excellent views, especially if you can get one of the prized window seats. It has been the place to come since 1937 and remains the spot for sipping a beer or dining on one of their fairly pricey but well-prepared meals.

Café Sasha Juan Ruíz de Alarcón opposite *Hotel Los Arcos*. Excellent upstairs café with no view to speak of, but an intimate atmosphere with comfy sofas, artesanía decor and even some English-language books for sale. Reliably good and modestly priced food, extending to pizzas, tortas, salads, falafel, garlic bread and daily specials (always including a vegetarian option), all washed down with speciality coffees. Local *músicos* turn up most evenings, making this a relaxed place to drink.

La Concha Nostra upstairs at Plazuela de San Juan 7. Primarily a bar with live rock on Saturdays (no cover), but also serving meals throughout the day and pizza at low prices.

West of Mexico City

The terrain west of Mexico City is varied: high and flat due west around Toluca and broken only by the occasional soaring peak, then dropping away on all sides, particularly to the south where as you descend the country becomes ruggedly hilly. It's also warmer, far more verdant and dotted with small towns of some interest. The main artery through the region is Hwy-55, superseded in places by a modern autopista, but still used by most of the buses you'll need to get to the small towns. Making a clockwise circuit, Taxco (see p.480) is the staging point for visits to the limestone formations inside the **Grutas de Cacahuamilpa**, a worthwhile stop en route to the spa town of **Ixtapan de la Sal**. Further north, the market town of **Tenancingo** provides access to the mountainous country to the east, principally **Malinalco** with its exquisite hill-side Aztec ruins and the neighbouring pilgrimage centre of **Chalma**.

The region's only large city is **Toluca**, worth a brief visit for its Friday market, the wonderful stained glass of its botanical gardens, and a couple of good art museums. You'll probably need to change buses here to get to **Valle de Bravo**, a small-town retreat brimming with aquatic diversions.

The Grutas de Cacahuamilpa

Just 20km north of Taxco on the highway to Ixtapan de la Sal and Toluca, you pass close to the vast complex of caves known as the **Grutas de Cacahuamilpa** (open daily for guided tours only: on the hour 10am–5pm; US$3). This network of caverns, hollowed out by two rivers, extends for some 70km – although the ninety-minute obligatory tour obviously takes in only a fraction, passing evocative rock formations, all illuminated to better illustrate their names, "the hunchback", "the bottle of champagne" and others. Among the graffiti you're shown a rather prim note from the wife of Maximilian "María Carlota reached this point". Alongside, Lerdo de Tejada, who became president in 1872, five years after Maximilian's execution, has scrawled "Sebastian Lerdo de Tejada went further". There's a restaurant and several food stalls by the entrance to the caves.

Buses running between Taxco and Ixtapan de la Sal pass within 1km of the entrance: ask to be dropped off at the junction and walk down the hill for fifteen minutes. Colectivos to the caves also leave hourly from opposite the Estrella Blanca bus terminal on Avenida Kennedy in Taxco.

Ixtapan de la Sal

Continuing north on Hwy-55, the next possible stop is **IXTAPAN DE LA SAL**, not a very attractive town by Mexican standards but a long-established spa whose mineral-rich waters are supposed to cure a plethora of muscular and circulatory ills. Bathing in Ixtapan's pools is really the only reason to stop, and this can be done either among the slides and fairground-style rides at the **Spa Ixtapan**, at the very top of Juárez (daily: pools 7am–7pm, spa 8am–7pm, aquatic park 10am–6pm; US$14), or more cheaply in the centre of the old town at the **Balneario Municipal**, corner of Allende and 20 de Noviembre (daily 7am–6pm; US$4), which is little more than a geothermally heated swimming pool.

The **bus station** (from where local buses run into town) is located in the middle of nowhere around 3km south of town on Hwy-55, connected to the centre by taxis (US$2) and *combis*; second-class buses may be prepared to drop you in town at the foot of Benito Juárez, which forms the main drag. The town gets pretty packed out at weekends, when it may be hard to find a room, but there are some very pleasant **hotels** to choose from, among them the excellent-value *Casa*

Sarita, three blocks east and one north of the Balneario Municipal at Obregón 512 (☎721/143-0172; ❹), where you get nicely decorated, carpeted rooms with TV. At weekends you must take full board (❺) and tuck into the hotel's good wholesome food. Almost opposite, at Obregón 6, *Casa de Huéspedes Francis* (☎721/143-0403; ❹) is a good budget option, with simple rooms with metal doors, tiled floors, TV and bathroom. For more luxury, try the *Avenida*, Juárez 614, near the Spa Ixtapan (☎721/143-0241, Ⓕ143-1039; ❻), a three-star hotel with swimming pool, whose rooms and suites all have cable TV, phone and FM radio. Alternatively, on Aldama, near its junction with Juárez, you'll find various casas de huéspedes with prices in the ❸ bracket. Some of these lock you in after 11pm (or out, if you stay out too late).

There are numerous **restaurants** along Juárez, though if you're just here briefly you may be happy with the juice bar under the central bandstand and the torta shops nearby.

Tenancingo

TENANCINGO is 33km north of Ixtapan de la Sal and is the next village of any size along Hwy-55. It is an attractive enough small town with a decent small hotel that makes it a quiet alternative to Toluca or Taxco. But the chief reason to be here is its proximity to the amazing Aztec ruins at **Malinalco** (see below), which can be reached by regular **buses** (every 15min; 30min), most of which continue on to Chalma. Liqueurs made from the fruit that grows in abundance on the plain surrounding Tenancingo, and finely woven traditional *rebozos* (shawls) are sold here, many of them produced at the lovely monastery of **El Santo Desierto**. This is also a big flower-growing region and as you pass through you'll see whole fields devoted to one bloom, and acres of land protected by plastic greenhouses.

Most **buses** stop around the corner of Victoria and Juárez, about five blocks south of the town's tiny zócalo. You can usually change straight onto a bus for Malinalco, but if you get stuck there is acceptable **accommodation** at *Hotel Lazo*, Victoria 100 (☎714/402-0083; ❹), where rooms are a bit rough and don't have TV, though there is always hot water. Several small **cafés** serve Mexican staples cheaply.

Tenango del Valle and Metepec

Half an hour north of Tenancingo you reach **TENANGO DEL VALLE**, from where you can visit the nearby excavated remains of the large fortified Malatzinca township of **Teotenango** (Tues–Sun 9am–5pm; US$1, free on Wed). It is a fifteen-minute flat walk to the entrance, then a steep ten-minute hike up to the site: to get there from the centre of the village, head north along Porfirio Díaz Norte, then take a left up Roman Piña Chan Norte. There's a small museum on site.

Some 25km further north you pass **METEPEC**, famed as a **pottery**-making centre. Brightly coloured local wares can be found at craft shops throughout the country; supposedly, the figures that characterize these pots were originally inspired by the saints on the facade of Metepec's sixteenth-century Franciscan monastery, and in the twentieth century Diego Rivera taught the villagers new techniques of colouring and design. There's a market here on Mondays. From Metepec it is less than 10km on to Toluca (see p.487).

Malinalco and around

The village of **MALINALCO**, 20km east of Tenancingo, is a lovely little place nestled in a fertile, alluvial valley at 1800m and surrounded by rich villas –

many of them, complete with swimming pools, the weekend retreats of the capital's privileged few. It is noticeably warmer than most of the towns hereabouts, making it a popular weekend retreat in winter. It centres on the huge Augustinian church of **Santa Mónica** and has a vibrant Wednesday morning **market**, but the real reason to come here is to see the exemplary **Aztec ruins**.

The site

The Aztec **site of Malinalco** (Tues–Sun 9am–5.30pm; US$3.20) sits high on a hill to the west of town (follow Guerrero west from the zócalo) and can be reached after a twenty- to thirty-minute walk up a very steep, stepped path. Having only been started in 1501, it was still incomplete at the time of the Conquest but it is undeniably one of the most evocative of its kind, carved in part from the raw rock hillside of the Cerro de los Idolos. This was the setting for the sacred **initiation ceremonies** in which Aztec youths became members of the warrior elite. Looking back over the village and valley, the ruins may be small, but they are undeniably impressive, the main structures and the stairways up to them partly cut out of the rock, partly constructed from great stone blocks. The most remarkable aspect is the circular inner sanctuary of the main temple or **Cuauhcalli** (House of the Eagle), hewn entirely from the face of the mountain. You approach up a broad staircase on either side of which sit stone jaguars – in the centre an all but worn-away human statue would have held a flag. To one side of the entrance, a broken eagle warrior sits atop Quetzalcoatl, the feathered serpent; guarding the other side are the remains of a jaguar warrior, representative of the second Aztec warrior class. The doorway of the sanctuary itself, cut through a natural rock wall, represents the giant mouth of a serpent – entrance was over its tongue, and around it traces of teeth are still visible. Right in the centre of the floor lies the figure of an eagle, and on the raised horseshoe-shaped bench behind are two more eagles and the pelt of an ocelot, all carved in a single piece from the bedrock. Behind the first eagle is a hole in the ground where the hearts of human sacrificial victims would be placed, supposedly to be eaten while still beating as the final part of the initiation into warriorhood.

Other structures at the site include a small circular platform by the entrance, unfinished at the time of the Conquest, and a low pyramid directly in front of the main temple. Beyond this lie two larger temples. The first, Edificio III, again has a circular chamber at the centre, and it is believed that here Aztec warriors killed in battle were cremated, their souls rising to the heavens to become stars. Edificio IV was originally a temple of the sun; much of it was used to construct the church in the village. Below the pyramids, visible from about halfway up the steps to the ruins, you can see another prehistoric building nestling among the mountains. It's still used by local residents as a place of pilgrimage each September 29: formerly a shrine to an Aztec altar-goddess, it is now dedicated to San Miguel.

Practicalities

The easiest way to reach Malinalco is by **bus** or shared taxi from Tenancingo. Most buses arrive in the central plaza in front of the church of Santa Monica, but those headed for Chalma sometimes hurtle straight down Morelos, which bypasses the centre: ask to be dropped at the end of Hidalgo, which runs 200m to the zócalo. Malinalco has a virtually useless **tourist office** in the town hall at the uphill end of the main plaza (Mon–Fri 9am–3pm, Sat 9am–1pm; ⓣ714/147-0111). **Banks** and ATMs are on Hidalgo.

Of the several **places to stay**, the best is the well-kept *Hotel Marmil*, Progreso 67 (ⓣ714/147-0916; ❹), with very pleasant country-style rooms, off-street parking, ceiling fans, a pool and cable TV. It is ten minutes' walk uphill from the zócalo (if coming by bus from Tenancingo, ask to be dropped near the hotel), and is almost always full at weekends. The best budget bet is *Hotel Santa Mónica*, Av Hidalgo 109 (☎714/147-0031; ❷), near the plaza on the way to the site; and you could also try *Posada Familiar Maria Dolores*, south of the main square at Juárez Norte 113 (☎714/147-0354; ❹), which has pleasant rooms beside a quiet garden, though maintenance and cleanliness leave something to be desired.

Come midweek and you'll find many of the **restaurants** closed but at weekends there are at least half a dozen places catering to the weekly influx from the capital and Cuernavaca. Everything is close by so you can walk around and take your pick. Options east of the main square on Hidalgo include *Ehecatl* for something relatively posh, or *Cocina Económica Ameyali* for something cheaper.

Around Malinalco: Chalma and Ahuehuete

Just 7km east of Malinalco, **CHALMA** is an important centre of pilgrimage, attracting vast crowds every Sunday and at times of special religious significance (especially the first Friday in Lent, Semana Santa and Sept 29): so many people converge here, in fact, that it's impossible to get anywhere near the church. At such times pilgrims camp out for miles around to take part in the rituals, a fascinating blend of Christian and more ancient pagan rites: the deity Oztocteotl, god of caves, was at one time venerated in a natural cave here, but he was "miraculously" replaced by a statue of Christ on the arrival of the first missionaries. In the seventeenth century, this crucifix was moved to a new church, the **Santuario de Chalma**, now the place of pilgrimage and of miraculous appearances of a Christ-like figure. As well as paying their devotions to Christ, the pilgrims bathe in the healing waters that flow from the cave. Despite all this, and the fact that the town is surrounded by impressive craggy peaks, it has to be added that Chalma is a complete dump, its filthy, muddy streets lined with stalls offering tacky souvenirs.

Colectivos leave Malinalco's zócalo every few minutes for Chalma, from where you can continue direct to Mexico City (Terminal Poniente) passing nearby **AHUEHUETE**, which also has a shrine visited by many pilgrims, at a spot where a miraculous spring issues from the roots of a huge old tree. Many people stop here before visiting Chalma and proceed the last few kilometres to Chalma on foot.

Toluca and around

The capital of the state of Mexico, **TOLUCA DE LERDO** is today a large and modern industrial centre, sprawling across a wide plain. At an altitude of nearly 2700m, it is the highest city in the country, and comes surrounded by beautiful mountain scenery, dominated by the white-capped **Nevado de Toluca**. With only a few minor attractions, it is not a place you'll want to linger. It is, however, the site of what is allegedly the largest single **market** in the country, despite being halved in size by the city's government. Held a couple of kilometres southeast of the centre, just east of the bus station, every Friday (and to a lesser extent throughout the week), the market constitutes the overriding reason to visit, and you may want to stop over on a Thursday night (book accommodation in advance) and then move on, or even make an early start from Mexico City on the Friday morning.

The market attracts hordes of visitors from the capital, but is so vast that there can be no question of its being overwhelmed by tourists; quite the opposite, many outsiders find themselves overwhelmed by the scale of the place, lost among the thousands of stalls and crowds from the state's outlying villages. Though increasingly dominated by cheap imported goods and clothing, there is still a substantial selection of **local crafts** – woven goods and pottery above all. For an idea of what quality and prices to expect, head first for the Casa de Artesanías, Paseo Tollocan 700 Ote, a few blocks east of the market.

Arrival and orientation

An almost uninterrupted stream of **buses** leaves Mexico City's Terminal Poniente for Toluca throughout the day; the journey takes a little over an hour. Toluca's modern bus station is right by the market and a local bus will take you the last 3km into the centre. *De paso* services from Mexico City to Zitácuaro and Valle de Bravo usually stop on the bypass 500m south of the bus station. To return to the bus station, pick up buses labelled "Terminal" on Juárez, just west of the *portales*. **Moving on** from Toluca, there are frequent buses from the terminal to Mexico City, Chalma, Cuernavaca, Morelia, Ixtapan, Malinalco, Querétaro and Taxco during the day (at night the terminal virtually closes and services are much less frequent).

Unusually for Mexico, the heart of the city is formed not by an open plaza but by a central block surrounded on three sides by the nation's longest series of arcades, built in the 1830s and known as *portales*, lined with shops, restaurants and cafés: **Portal Madero** is on the south along Hidalgo; **Portal 20 de Noviembre** is on the east along Allende; and **Portal Reforma** is on the west along Bravo. The fourth side is taken up by the nineteenth-century **cathedral** and, to its east, the mustard-yellow church of **Santa Cruz**.

Accommodation

In general, Toluca's **hotels** are poor value for money, with a number of fairly grotty places clustered around the market. Even these fill up by Thursday nights when **finding a room** can be difficult.

Colonial Hidalgo Ote 103 ⓣ722/215-9700, ⓕ214-7066. One of the better city-centre options, quiet and relatively cosy with a slightly old-fashioned feel. ❺

Rex Matamoros 101, opposite Portal Madero ⓣ722/215-9300 or 02. Clean, functional and relatively low-priced, with fairly well-maintained rooms, all with bathroom and TV. ❹

San Carlos Portal Madero 210 ⓣ722/214-4336 or 214-4343. Best value in the city centre: very central with friendly staff and large, comfortable, modernized rooms. ❺

San Francisco Rayon Sur 104 ⓣ722/213-4415. Modern luxurious hotel with its own pool, bar and restaurant. ❼

Terminal Felipe Berriázabal 101 ⓣ722/217-4588. Fairly decent hotel despite its grotty surroundings right by the bus station (and with access from inside the terminal). Carpeted rooms all have bathroom, 24hr hot water and TV. Those on the fifth floor upward have slightly higher rates. ❸

The Town

Most of the central sights are clustered north of the *portales* and the cathedral, close to the massive open **Plaza de los Mártires**, dominated on the north side by the Palacio del Gobierno. To the east is the **Plaza Garibay**, rather prettier with shrubbery and fountains stretching down to the **Jardín Botánico Cosmovitral** (Tues–Sun 10am–6pm; US$1), Toluca's botanical gardens housed in an enormous hundred-metre-long Art Nouveau greenhouse that was built in 1909 and served as the main market until 1975. With predominantly semi-tropical displays, small pools and even a well-tended Japanese corner, it is an attractive garden, but the highlight is undoubtedly the amazing stained-glass panels done in the Mexican muralist style by local artist Leopoldo Flores. Coloured glass covers almost every inch of the walls and roof, the red of the flaming human figure at the west end gradually fading to blue in the east. Come early or late to catch the low sun giving a coloured cast to the plants. The northwestern corner of Plaza Garibay is occupied by the **Museo de Bellas Artes**, on Santos Degollado (Tues–Sun 10am–6pm; US$0.50, free on Sun), which typically shows off some of the best fine arts in the state but is currently being renovated.

Back on Plaza de los Mártires, the **Museo José Maria Velasco** (Tues–Sat 10am–6pm, Sun 10am–4pm; free) occupies two floors of a colonial house and displays a good collection of nineteenth-century paintings, much of it by Velasco, who was born in the state of México in 1840, though he spent much of his life in Mexico City. There's a re-creation of his studio along with busts, portraits, and some delightful landscapes including a delicate rendering of the volcanoes and the Valley of México. Several rooms host temporary exhibits, often featuring work by his contemporaries from the San Carlos academy in the capital.

The state of México makes a point of honouring its artistic sons, and adjoining the Velasco museum (entrance round the corner on Nicolas Bravo) are two more museums dedicated to local painters. The **Museo Felipe Santiago Gutierrez**, Nicolas Bravo 9 (Tues–Sat 10am–6pm, Sun 10am–4pm; US$0.50), fills a colonial mansion with sketches, oils and portraits of prominent nineteenth-century Mexicans; but there is more interest next door at the **Museo Taller Nishizawa** (Tues–Sat 10am–6pm, Sun 10am–4pm; US$0.50), where large abstract landscape canvases by Mexican-Japanese Luis Nishizawa take pride of place alongside pen and ink drawings and some of his more recent portraiture.

The Centro Cultural Mexiquense

Some 8km west of Toluca, the **Centro Cultural Mexiquense** harbours several museums (all Tues–Sun 10am–6pm; US$2, free on Sun) scattered in park-like grounds. Among them are the **Museo Regional**, devoted to the archeology and history of the state, a small **Museo de Arte Moderno** and, perhaps the most interesting, the **Museo de Artes Populares**, a collection of local crafts, ancient and modern, in a restored hacienda. Although local buses run out there (look for "Centro Cultural Las Palomas" along Lerdo), you really need your own transport to explore the place fully.

Calixtlahuaca and Nevada de Toluca

While in Toluca put a couple of hours aside to visit the archeological site of **Calixtlahuaca** (daily 10am–5pm; US$3.20, free on Sun). This was the township of the Matlazinca people, inhabited from prehistoric times and later subjugated by the Aztecs, who established a garrison here in the fifteenth century. Calixtlahuaca was not a willing subject, and there were constant rebellions; after one, in 1475, the Aztecs allegedly sacrificed over 11,000 Matlazinca prisoners on the **Temple of Quetzalcoatl**. This, several times built over, is the most important structure on the site. Dedicated to the god in his role as Ehecatl, god of wind, its circular design is typical, allowing the breezes to blow freely around the shrine. See also the remains of the pyramid devoted to Tlaloc, and the nearby *tzompantli* (skull rack), both constructed of the local pink and black volcanic stone. Bring something to light your way in the short dark tunnels which reveal evidence of earlier constructions; and don't worry too much about the opening hours since the site is not fenced. A small **museum** is sporadically open.

Fiestas

JANUARY

6 DÍA DE LOS SANTOS REYES (Twelfth Night). The Magi traditionally leave presents for children on this date: many small ceremonies include a fiesta with dancing at **Nativitas** (Distrito Federal), a suburb near Xochimilco, and at **Malinalco** (México state).

17 BENDICIÓN DE LOS ANIMALES. Children's pets and peasants' farm animals are taken to church to be blessed. A particularly bizarre sight at the cathedral in **México** and in **Taxco** (Guerrero), where it coincides with the fiestas of Santa Prisca (Jan 18) and San Sebastián (Jan 20).

FEBRUARY

2 DÍA DE LA CANDELARIA is widely celebrated, especially in **Cuernavaca** (Morelos).

CARNAVAL (the week before Lent, variable Feb–March) is especially lively in **Cuernavaca** (Mor) and nearby **Tepoztlán** (Mor); also in **Chiconcuac** (Méx) on the way to Teotihuacán. In **Xochimilco** (DF), for some reason, they celebrate Carnaval two weeks after everyone else.

MARCH

On the Sunday following March 9, a large feria with traditional dances is held at **San Gregorio Atlapulco**, near Xochimilco (DF).

PALM SUNDAY (the week before Easter) sees a procession with palms in **Taxco** (Gro), where representations of the Passion continue through Holy Week.

HOLY WEEK itself is observed everywhere. There are very famous Passion plays in the suburb of **Itzapalapa** (DF), culminating on the Friday with a mock Crucifixion on the Cerro de la Estrella, and similar celebrations at **Chalma** (Méx) and nearby **Malinalco**. In **Cholula** (Puebla), with its host of churches, the processions pass over vast carpets of flowers.

APRIL

Cuernavaca's (Mor) flower festival, the FERIA DE LA FLOR, usually falls in early April.

MAY

1 May Day, a public holiday, is usually marked by large marches and demonstrations in the capital. In **Cuautla** (Mor), the same day sees a fiesta commemorating an Independence battle.

3 DÍA DE LA SANTA CRUZ is celebrated with fiestas, and traditional dancing, in **Xochimilco** (DF), in **Tepotzotlán** (Méx) and in **Valle de Bravo** (Méx).

5 Public holiday for the battle of Puebla – celebrated in **Puebla** (Pue) itself with a grand procession and re-enactment of the fighting.

15 DÍA DE SAN ISIDRO. Religious processions and fireworks in **Tenancingo** (Méx), and a procession of farm animals through **Cuernavaca** (Mor) on their way to be blessed at the church.

On the third Monday of May, there's a large religious festival in **Tlaxcala** (Tlax) as an image of the Virgin is processed around the town followed by hundreds of pilgrims.

CORPUS CHRISTI (variable – the Thurs after Trinity). Thousands of children, rigged out in their Sunday best, gather in **Mexico City**'s Zócalo to be blessed.

JUNE

29 DÍA DE SAN PEDRO observed with processions and dances in **Tepotzotlán** (Méx) and traditional dancing in **San Pedro Actopan** (DF), on the southern outskirts of Mexico City.

JULY

16 DÍA DE LA VIRGEN DEL CARMEN. Dancers, and a procession with flowers to the convent of Carmen, in **San Ángel** (DF).

25 DÍA DE SANTIAGO particularly celebrated in **Chalco** (Méx), near Amecameca. The following Sunday sees a market and regional dances at the **Plaza de las Tres Culturas** (DF) and dances, too, in **Xochimilco** (DF).

29 DÍA DE SANTA MARTA in **Milpa Alta** (DF), near Xochimilco, celebrated with Aztec dances and mock fights between Moors and Christians.

AUGUST

13 Ceremonies in **Mexico City** commemorate the defence of Tenochtitlán, with events in the Plaza de las Tres Culturas, around the statue of Cuauhtémoc on Reforma and in the Zócalo.

15 DÍA DE LA ASUNCIÓN (Assumption) honoured with pilgrimages from **Cholula** (Pue) to a nearby village, and ancient dances in **Milpa Alta** (DF).

SEPTEMBER

1 Massed processions with fireworks and dances in honour of the Virgen de los Remedios in **Cholula** (Pue).

8 A very ancient ceremony in **Tepoztlán** (Mor), a Christianized version of homage to the Pyramid of Tepozteco, and more usual candlelit religious processions in **Cuernavaca** (Mor).

15–16 INDEPENDENCE CELEBRATIONS everywhere, above all in the Zócalo in **Mexico City**, where the president proclaims the famous Grito at 11pm on the 15th, followed by the ringing of the Campana de Dolores and a huge firework display.

21 DÍA DE SAN MATEO celebrated in **Milpa Alta** (DF).

29 DÍA DE SAN MIGUEL provokes huge pilgrimages to both **Taxco** (Gro) and **Chalma** (Méx).

OCTOBER

4 DÍA DE SAN FRANCISCO sees a feria in **Tenancingo** (Méx), with much traditional music-making, and is also celebrated in **San Francisco Tecoxpa** (DF), a village on the southern fringes of the capital.

12 FIESTA DEL SANTUARIO DE LA DEFENSA is a street party that centres around an ancient church just outside of **Tlaxcala** (Tlax).

NOVEMBER

1–2 DÍA DE LOS MUERTOS (All Souls) is observed by almost everyone, and the shops are full of chocolate skulls and other ghoulish foods. Tradition is particularly strong in **San Lucas Xochimanca** (DF) and **Nativitas** (DF), both to the south of **Mexico City**.

First Monday following Día de los Muertos. DÍA DE JUMIL in **Taxco** (Gro), where the townsfolk climb the Cerro de Huixteco to collect *jumiles* and celebrate this small grub.

22 DÍA DE SANTA CECILIA. Santa Cecilia is the patron saint of musicians, and her fiesta attracts orchestras and *mariachi* bands from all over to **Santa Cecilia Tepetlapa** (DF), not far from Xochimilco.

DECEMBER

1 FERIA DE LA PLATA. The great silver fair in **Taxco** (Gro) lasts about ten days from this date.

Fiestas *Continued*

12 DÍA DE NUESTRA SEÑORA DE GUADALUPE – a massive pilgrimage to the **Basilica of Guadalupe** (DF) runs for several days round about, combined with a constant secular celebration of music and dancing.

25 CHRISTMAS. In the week leading up to Christmas, nativity plays – also known as *posadas* – can be seen in many places. Among the most famous are those at **Taxco** (Gro) and **Tepotzotlán** (Méx).

The site is on a hillside just outside the village of Calixtlahuaca, easily reached by **taxi** (roughly US$5) or by a circuitous local **bus** which takes half an hour from the stop on Santos Degollado, one block north of the main square at its junction with Nicolas Bravo.

If you've got your own vehicle – and a sturdy one at that – one trip you should make is to the crater of the extinct **Nevado de Toluca** (Xinantécatl, 4690m), which rises high enough above the surrounding plain for it to rank as Mexico's fourth highest peak. A rough dirt road – impractical during the rainy season or midwinter – leads all the way to the crater rim, from where there are numerous trails leading down to the sandy crater floor and two small lakes, the **Lagos del Sol** and **de la Luna**, right in its heart. From its jagged lip the views are breathtaking: below you the lakes; eastwards a fabulous vista across the valleys of Toluca and México; and to the west a series of lower, greener hills ranging towards the peaks of the Sierra Madre Occidental. If you do hike down into the crater, remember to take it easy in this thin, high-altitude air.

Eating and drinking

As usual, the markets and outlying areas are the places to go for budget **food**, while around the *portales* there are some good, pricier choices. For a selection of pastries and the best coffee in town visit *Caffé Espresso*, Portal 20 de Noviembre 109, and a few doors away *Hostería de las Ramblas*, Portal 20 de Noviembre 107, serves an excellent range of antojitos and local specialities for US$2–5 a plate, and breakfasts at US$5.20. On the other side of the *portales* block at Portal Reforma 108, *Las Ramblitas* has tasty and very reasonable set breakfasts (US$2.90–4), as well as pozole, enchiladas, *mole poblano*, and a US$3 lunchtime menu.

Valle de Bravo

West from Toluca, the road towards Morelia and the state of Michoacán is truly spectacular. Much of this wooded, mountainous area – as far as Zitácuaro – is given over to villas inhabited at weekends by wealthy refugees from the capital, and nowhere more so than the small colonial town of **VALLE DE BRAVO**, reached by turning off to the left about halfway. Set in a deep, pine-clad valley surrounded by low mountains, the town sits on the eastern shore of an artificial lake, **Lago Avandaro**. With terracotta-tiled roofs, iron balconies affixed to many of the older buildings, and a mass of whitewashed houses all huddled together, it is an immediately appealing place, something which has drawn a coterie of artistic refugees from the big city. They mostly keep to themselves, leaving the water's edge for weekenders who descend for upmarket relaxation: boat trips, sailing, swimming, water-skiing, riding, paragliding, hiking and golf. If you indulge, it can be an expensive place, but the town itself isn't that pricey and it does make for a very relaxing break provided you come during the week, when fewer people are about and some of the hotels drop their prices.

The zócalo, ringed with restaurants and centred on a twin-towered church, sits on a rise a ten-minute walk from the waterfront, where there's a small tourist office (weekends only), and a couple of wharves from which you can take boat rides: either rent one from US$30 an hour, or join a *lancha colectiva* for around US$3 an hour.

Practicalities

Buses from Toluca make a long circuit around town before depositing you at the **bus station** on Calle 16 de Septiembre (no guardería). Head downhill past a few cheap *comedores* to get to the centre. The best of the more reasonably priced **places to stay** is the *Posada Casa Vieja,* Juárez 101 (Ⓣ726/262-0318; ❹), with clean, bright rooms, ample hot water, a sunny veranda and the choice of more spacious rooms with TV (❺). Alternatives include *Posada Familiar*, 16 de Septiembre 417 (Ⓣ726/262-1222; Mon–Thurs ❹, Fri–Sun ❺), which is 100m downhill from the bus station and has plain but appealing rooms with TV; and *Posada Los Girasoles*, Plaza Independencia 1 (Ⓣ726/262-2967; ❺), right on the main square, clean and cool with firm beds.

Valle de Bravo has a wide range of **restaurants**, though many of the fancier places close midweek or operate limited hours. For good cheap eats, make for *Ranchita*, 16 de Septiembre 406, a *comedor* just below the bus station that serves flavourful comida corrida for US$2.50. Moving upmarket, go for *Restaurante Don Paraíso*, Calle Joaquín Payoza, which runs off the zócalo, where moderately priced Mexican dishes are served around a cool inner courtyard, or out on the sunny terrace.

Travel details

The capital is the centre of the nation to such an extent that any attempt at a comprehensive list of the comings and goings would be doomed to failure. What follows is no more than a survey of the major services on the main routes: it must be assumed that intermediate points are linked at least as frequently as those mentioned. Literally thousands of buses leave Mexico City every day, and you can get to just about any town in the country, however small, whenever you want. Even if there's not a bus leaving to your destination right away, there'll be one to an intermediate town, which will speed you on your way. Those we list are a bare minimum of the main road routes. Journey times given are for the fastest services.

Flights

Meanwhile, Mexico City's airport is the nation's largest hub by far with numerous international arrivals (mostly from the United States) and frequent flights to all points of Mexico with the main Mexican airlines – Aeroméxico and Mexicana – or one of the minor regional servers such as Aerocalifornia, Aerocozumel, Aeromar, Aerocaribe, Aviacsa and others. We've only listed direct non-stop flights but many more places are served, often without changing planes.

Mexico City to: Acapulco (8 daily; 45min); Aguascalientes (5 daily; 1hr); Bajío/León (6 daily; 50min); Campeche (2 daily; 1hr 10min); Cancún (19 daily; 2hr); Chetumal (2 daily except Sat; 1hr 50min); Chihuahua (6 daily; 2hr); Ciudad Carmen (3 daily; 1hr 25min); Ciudad Juárez (6 daily; 2hr 20min); Ciudad Obregón (2–3 daily; 2hr 15min); Ciudad Victoria (3 daily; 1hr 10min); Cozumel (1 daily; 2hr); Culiacán (7 daily; 1hr 45min); Durango (3 daily; 2hr); Guadalajara (hourly; 1hr); Hermosillo (12 daily; 2hr 30min); Huatulco (1–3 daily; 1hr 10min); Julapa (1 daily; 1hr); La Paz, Baja California Sur (3 daily; 2hr 5min); Laredo (6 weekly; 2hr 10min); Lázaro Cárdenas (2 daily weekdays only; 1hr 10min); Los Cabos (4–5 daily; 2hr); Los Mochis (2–3 daily; 2hr); Manzanillo

(4 daily; 1hr 40min); Matamoros (3 daily; 1hr 20min); Mérida (8 daily; 1hr 40min); Monterrey (hourly; 1hr 20min); Morelia (4 daily; 55min); Nuevo Laredo (1–2 daily; 1hr 35min); Oaxaca (8 daily; 55min); Puebla (6 weekly; 35min); Puerto Escondido (5 weekly; 1hr); Puerto Vallarta (6–7 daily; 1hr 20min); Querétaro (2 daily; 45min); Reynosa (4 daily; 1hr 25min); Saltillo (2 daily; 1hr 25min); San Cristóbal (1 daily; 2hr); San Luis Potosí (8 daily weekdays, 4–5 daily weekends; 1hr 15min); Tampico (4 daily; 55min); Tapachula (4 daily; 1hr 35min); Tepic (3 daily weekdays, 2 daily weekends; 1hr 55min); Tijuana (22 daily; 3hr 20min); Torreón (6 daily; 1hr 25min); Tuxtla Gutiérrez (11 daily; 1hr 20min); Uruapan (1 daily; 1hr 35min); Veracruz (8 daily; 50min); Villahermosa (10 daily; 1hr 20min); Zacatecas (4 daily; 1hr 15min).

Puebla to: Guadalajara (2 daily; 1hr 40min); Mexico City (4 daily; 35min); Monterrey (4 daily; 2hr).

Buses

Cholula to: Mexico City (every 20–30min; 2hr 30min); Puebla (buses every 10–15min; 20min; plus frequent colectivos).

Cuautla to: Cuernavaca (every 15min; 1hr 20min); Mexico City Autobuses del Sur (two every 15min; 1hr 40min); Mexico City TAPO (every 15min; 1hr 40min); Tepoztlán (every 15min; 40min).

Cuernavaca to: Acapulco (Estrella de Oro terminal, 23 daily; Estrella Blanca terminal, 9 daily; 5hr); Cuautla (Estrella Roja terminal and market terminal, every 15min; 1hr 20min); Iguala (Estrella de Oro terminal, 16 daily; Estrella Blanca terminal, 3 daily; 1hr 30min); Mexico City (Pullman de Morelos terminal, every 15min; 1hr 15min); Mexico City airport (Pullman de Morelos terminal, roughly hourly; 1hr 30min); Puebla (Estrella Roja terminal, hourly; 3hr 30min); Taxco (Flecha Roja in Estrella Blanca terminal hourly; 1hr 40min); Tepoztlán (market terminal, every 15min; 45min); Toluca (Flecha Roja in Estrella Blanca terminal, every 30min; 2hr 30min).

Ixtapan de la Sal to: Acapulco (3 daily; 6hr); Cuernavaca (6 daily; 3hr); Mexico City (indirect every 15min; 3hr; direct hourly; 2hr); Taxco (hourly; 1hr 20min); Tenancingo (every 15min; 45min); Toluca (every 20min; 1hr).

Mexico City (N = Terminal del Norte; S = Central de Autobuses del Sur; E = TAPO; W = Terminal Poniente) to: Acapulco (S, half-hourly, N, hourly; 5hr); Aguascalientes (N, 17 daily; 6hr); Amecameca (E, every 20min; 1hr 15min); Campeche (E, 3 daily; 17hr); Cancún (E, 3 daily; 24hr); Chetumal (E, 3 daily; 18hr); Chihuahua (N, hourly; 18hr); Chilpancingo (S, hourly; 3hr 30min); Ciudad Juárez (N, hourly; 24hr); Ciudad Obregón (N, hourly; 26hr); Colima (N, 13 daily; 11hr); Córdoba (E, hourly; 4hr); Cuautla (S, every 15min; E, 14 daily; 1hr 40min); Cuernavaca (S, every 15min; 1hr 30min); Dolores Hidalgo (N, every 40min; 4hr); Durango (N, 9 daily; 12hr); Fortín de las Flores (E, 2 daily; 4hr); Guadalajara (N, hourly; W, 5 daily; 7hr); Guanajuato (N, 20 daily; 5hr); Guaymas (N, 10 daily; 27hr); Hermosillo (N, hourly; 32hr); Iguala (S, every 30min; 3hr); Ixtapa (S, 7 daily; 10hr); Ixtapan de la Sal (W, hourly; 2–3hr); Jalapa (E, 21 daily; 5hr); León (N, every 30min; 5hr); Los Mochis (N, hourly; 21hr); Malinalco (W, 3 daily; 2hr 30min); Manzanillo (N, 3 daily; 12hr); Matamoros (N, 7 daily; 14hr); Matehuala (N, 10 daily; 7hr); Mazatlán (N, hourly; 15hr); Mérida (E, 3 daily; 28hr); Mexicali (N, hourly; 30hr); Monterrey (N, hourly; 12hr); Morelia (every 30min; 4hr); Nuevo Laredo (N, hourly; 15hr); Oaxaca (E, at least hourly; 6hr); Oaxtepec (E, every 15min; 1hr 30min); Orizaba (E, 24 daily; 4hr); Pachuca (N, every 10min; 1hr 15min); Palenque (E, 2 daily; 13hr); Pátzcuaro (W, 10 daily; N, 5 daily; 7hr); Playa del Carmen (E, 3 daily; 22hr); Puebla (E, every 12min; S, hourly; 2hr); Puerto Escondido (S, 5 daily; 15hr); Puerto Vallarta (N, 4 daily; 12hr); Querétaro (N, every 20min; 2hr 40min); Saltillo (N, 17 daily; 10hr); San Cristóbal de las Casas (E, 6 daily; 17hr); San Luis Potosí (N, 40 daily; 5hr); San Miguel Allende (N, every 40min; 4hr); Taxco (S, hourly; 2hr 30min); Tehuacán (E, hourly; 4hr); Tehuantepec (E, 4 daily; 10hr); Teotihuácan (N, every 15min; 1hr); Tepic (N, 18 daily; 12hr); Tepoztlán (S, every 15min; 1hr 15min); Tijuana (N, hourly; 42hr); Tlaxcala (E, every 20min; 1hr 40min); Torreón (N, 9 daily; 14hr); Tula (N, every 30–60min; 1hr 15min); Tuxpan (N, 24 daily; 4hr); Tuxtla Gutiérrez (E, 14 daily; 14hr); Uruapan (W, 9 daily; N, 5 daily; 5hr 30min); Valle de Bravo (W, 15 daily; 3hr); Veracruz (E, 35 daily; 7hr); Villahermosa (E, 24 daily; 11hr); Zacatecas (N, 24 daily; 8hr); Zempoala (E, 2 daily; 6hr 30min); Zihuatanejo (S, 7 daily; 9hr).

Pachuca to: Mexico City (every 10min; 1hr 15min); Mexico City airport (12 daily; 1hr 40min); Puebla (22 daily; 4hr); Real del Monte (frequent colectivos; 20min); Tlaxcala (22 daily; 3hr); Tula (every 15min; 1hr 30min).

Puebla to: Cholula (buses every 10–15min; 20min; plus frequent colectivos); Cuernavaca (hourly; 3hr 30min); Mexico City (every 12min; 2hr); Mexico City airport (hourly; 2hr 15min); Oaxaca (11 daily; 4hr 30min); Pachuca (22 daily; 4hr); Tlaxcala (every 8min; 40min; plus frequent micros); Veracruz (hourly; 4hr 30min).

Taxco to: Acapulco (4 daily; 5hr); Cuernavaca (hourly; 1hr 40min); Ixtapan (18 daily; 1hr 20min); Mexico City (hourly; 2hr 15min); Toluca (18 daily; 3hr 30min).
Tenancingo to: Ixtapan de la Sal (every 15min; 45min); Malinalco (every 15min; 30min; plus shared taxis); Toluca (every 30min; 1hr; plus shared taxis).
Tlaxcala to: Mexico City (every 20min; 1hr 40min); Pachuca (22 daily; 3hr); Puebla (every 8min; 40min; plus frequent micros).
Toluca to: Cuernavaca (every 30min; 2hr 30min); Ixtapan (every 20min; 1hr); Mexico City (every 5min; 1hr 30min); Morelia (hourly; 4hr); Querétaro (hourly; 3hr 30min); Taxco (18 daily; 3hr); Tenancingo (every 30min; 1hr); Tenango del Valle (every 5min; 30min); Valle de Bravo (every 20min; 2hr).
Tula to: Mexico City (every 30–60min; 1hr 30min); Pachuca (every 15min; 1hr 30min); Querétaro (18 daily; 2hr 30min); Tepotzotlán (Caseta de) (every 15min; 1hr).

6

Acapulco and the Pacific beaches

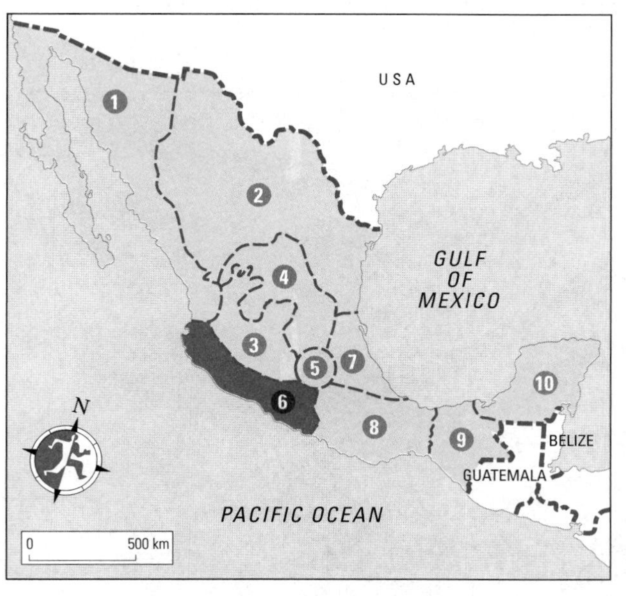

CHAPTER 6

Highlights

* **Yelapa beach** Accessible only by boat, it is the perfect spot for rest and relaxation. **See p.506**
* **Puerto Vallarta** Perhaps the best Asian food in the Americas, served up in an exquisite Zen garden at *Archie's Wok*. **See p.507**
* **Whale-watching** Watch the humpback whales frolic in the Bahía de Banderas from December to April. **See p.510**
* **Barra de Navidad** Relax in this gorgeous, laid-back beach village at one end of an enormous bay. **See p.511**
* **Comala** Sip a beer and feast on free snacks while *mariachis* compete for your attention in the town plaza. **See p.524**
* **Barra de Potosí** An untouched beach where you can eat fresh fish and row through a mangrove lagoon. **See p.530**

△ Whale-watching near Puerto Vallarta

6

Acapulco and the Pacific beaches

The 800-kilometre stretch of coast between Puerto Vallarta and Punta Maldonada, where the Sierra Madre reaches out to the ocean to form a string of coves, bays and narrow stretches of sand, is lined with some of Mexico's most popular resorts. **Acapulco** – the original, the biggest, and for many the best – is a steep-sided, tightly curving bay that for all its excesses of high-rise development remains breathtakingly beautiful, from a distance at least, and always at night. This is the stomping ground of the wealthy, whose villas, high around the wooded sides of the bay, offer isolation from the packaged enclaves below. It's pricey, but not ridiculously so, and despite the tourists, the city itself retains a local feel, with the coarse characteristics of a working port.

Puerto Vallarta, second in size and reputation, feels altogether smaller, more like the tropical village it claims to be, while in fact spreading for miles along a series of tiny beaches. More chic, younger, more overtly glamorous and certainly far more single-mindedly a resort, it lacks Acapulco's great sweep of sand but makes up for it with cove after isolated cove. South of here, **Barra de Navidad** is a lovely crescent of sand, backed for once by flatlands and lagoons, with a village at either end. By contrast **Manzanillo**, like Puerto Vallarta well connected with Guadalajara, is first and foremost a port and naval base – its pitch for resort status seems something of an afterthought. **Zihuatanejo** and its purpose-built neighbour **Ixtapa** are the most recently developed resorts, the latter so much so that there's nothing there but brand-new hotels. Zihuatanejo is more attractive: almost, to look at, a mini-Acapulco, with magnificent villas mushrooming on the slopes overlooking the bay, but lacking the high-rise development.

All along this coast, between the major centres, you'll find **beaches**: some completely undeveloped; others linked to a village with a few rooms to rent and a makeshift bar on the sand; and the odd few with an isolated, maybe even luxurious, hotel. The ocean breakers can be wild, positively dangerous at times, and there are minor discomforts – unreliable or nonexistent water and electricity supplies, vicious mosquitoes – but the space and the simplicity, often just an hour's drive from a packed international resort, are well worth seeking out.

Most people arrive on the new, fast – and expensive – **Autopista del Sol** from Mexico City to Acapulco, but the **coast road**, whatever some old maps

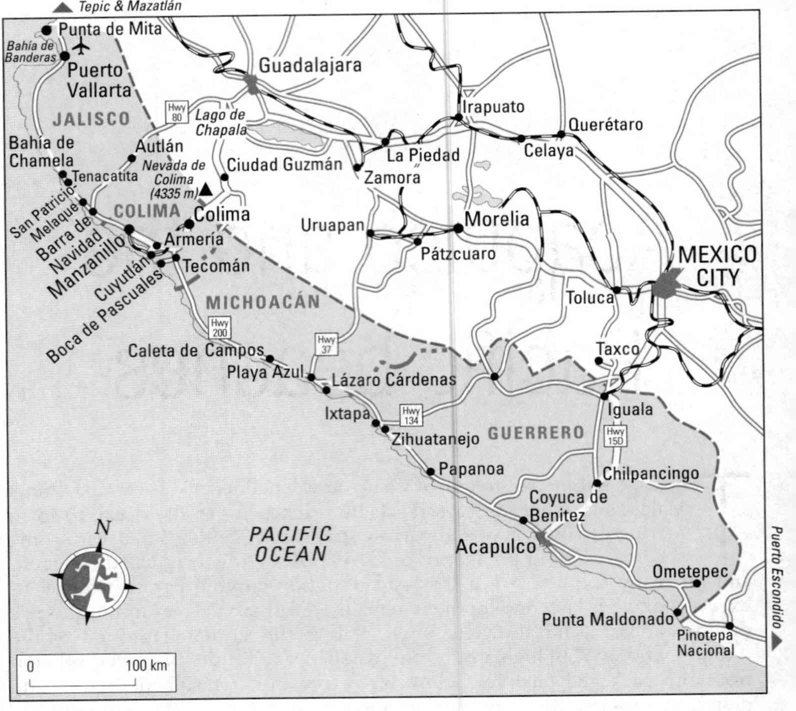

may say, is perfectly feasible (if a little rough in the final stretches) all the way from the US border to Guatemala. Between Puerto Vallarta and Acapulco, it's a good modern highway, unrelentingly spectacular as it forces its way south, sometimes over the narrow coastal plain, more often clinging precariously to the fringes of the sierra where it falls away into the ocean.

Most **buses** heading down from **Mazatlán** turn inland to Guadalajara, but many also continue to **Puerto Vallarta**, and from there on down Hwy-200 towards Acapulco. Guadalajara itself has very frequent bus connections with Puerto Vallarta, **Barra de Navidad** and **Manzanillo**, while from central Michoacán you can head down to the coast at **Lázaro Cárdenas**. **Zihuatanejo** has direct bus services from Mexico City, and hourly services to **Acapulco**. Plentiful buses also run between these resorts, though you may have to change if you're travelling long-distance. It's easy to get from Puerto Vallarta to Barra de Navidad, and from there to Manzanillo and from Manzanillo to Lázaro Cárdenas, but there are few direct services from Puerto Vallarta all the way down. In the state of Guerrero there are occasional **military checkpoints** on the roads, where all traffic is stopped and searched. Tourists usually assume that this is for drugs, which may be at least partly true, though the check rarely amounts to more than a peremptory prod at the outside of your case. More importantly the wild and relatively undeveloped hills retain a reputation for banditry and guerrilla activity. This is not something you need expect to come across, but travelling these roads you should keep your passport and papers handy and not carry anything you wouldn't want discovered.

Prices in the resorts, particularly for accommodation, are dictated largely by **season**. High season at the bigger destinations stretches from early or mid-December to after Easter or the end of April, during which time the swankier hotels can charge as much as double the off-season rates and need to be booked in advance. Budget hotels vary their prices less, but costs are still twenty to thirty percent down outside the peak season. Smaller beach towns catering exclusively to Mexicans have a shorter season, usually just December and Semana Santa (around Easter), but the same rules apply.

Puerto Vallarta and around

By reputation the second of Mexico's beach resorts, **PUERTO VALLARTA** is smaller, quieter and younger than Acapulco. In its own way, it is actually every bit as commercial – perhaps more so, since here tourism is virtually the only source of income – but appearances count for much, and Puerto Vallarta, while doing all it can to catch up with Acapulco, appears far less developed and retains a more Mexican feel, even though the resort attracts far more foreign visitors (mainly Americans) than does Acapulco. Puerto Vallarta has also emerged as one of the **gay** centres of Mexico, with a great deal more tolerance for – and entertainment geared towards – the gay scene than almost anywhere else in the country.

The town lies in the middle of the 22-kilometre-wide **Bahía de Banderas**, the seventh largest bay in the world, fringed by endless sandy beaches and backed by the jungle-covered slopes of the Sierra Madre. Its hotels are scattered along several miles of coast with the greatest concentration in **Nuevo Vallarta**, north of the town and sliced through by an eight-lane strip of asphalt. Just south of Nuevo Vallarta is the new **marina**, where you can stroll along the boardwalk and have a look at how the other half lives, on beautiful boats. Despite the frantic development of the last decade, the historic town centre, with its cobbled streets and white-walled, terracotta-roofed houses, sustains the tropical village atmosphere, an asset assiduously exploited by the local tourist authorities.

Until 1954 Puerto Vallarta was a small fishing village where the Río Cuale spills out into the Bahía de Banderas; then Mexicana airlines, their hand forced by Aeroméxico's monopoly on flights into Acapulco, started promoting the town as a resort. Their efforts received a shot in the arm in 1964, when John Huston chose Mismaloya, 10km south, as the setting for his film of Tennessee Williams' play **The Night of the Iguana**, starring Richard Burton. The scandalmongering that surrounded Burton's romance with Elizabeth Taylor – who was not part of the cast but came along – is often considered responsible for putting Puerto Vallarta firmly in the international spotlight: "a mixed blessing" according to Huston, who stayed on here until his death in 1987, and whose bronze image stands on the Isla Río Cuale in town.

The package tourists stay, on the whole, in the beachfront hotels around the bay, but are increasingly penetrating the town centre to shop in the pricey boutiques and shops that line the streets leading back from the beach, and to eat in some of the very good restaurants both on the malecón and downtown. Nevertheless, what could be a depressingly expensive place to visit turns out to be liberally peppered with good-value hotels and budget restaurants, especially during the low season (Aug–Nov).

Time zones

Remember that **if you've come south** from Tepic, San Blas, Mazatlán or points north along the coast, you need to advance your watch an hour: the time zone changes at the state border, just north of Puerto Vallarta's airport.

Arrival and information

The **Río Cuale**, spanned by two small road bridges and a couple of wobbly footbridges, divides Puerto Vallarta in two. The main square, official buildings, market and the bulk of the shops and many of the more upscale restaurants lie on the north side. South you'll find the town beach and the cheaper hotels. It's a very small place, hemmed in by the ocean and by the steep slopes behind – downtown, you can walk just about anywhere. Frequent local **buses** run around the edge of the Bahía de Banderas to the north, towards the hotel zone (buses marked "Hoteles"), and, slightly less frequently, south to smaller beaches such as Mismaloya and Boca de Tomatlán.

About 4km north of the town centre lies the sparkling clean, long-distance bus station, the **Central Camionera**, equipped with a guardería and long-distance telephones, and served by buses to and from the centre marked "Aeropuerto", "Ixtapa", "Juntas" or "Mojoneras". If catching a city bus from outside the entrance of the Central Camionera, be sure to ask the driver if the bus is going to the city centre, since many will be heading the other way. See p.545 for details of bus services out of town.

The **airport** (information on ⓣ322/221-1298) lies 2.5km north of the centre on the coastal highway, and is linked to the city by local buses that stop a few steps outside the perimeter fence. Airport taxis go right to the door and cost around US$12. If you can find a colectivo it should be around a third of the price, but local buses (marked "Olas Altas" or "Centro") provide an easy and far cheaper alternative. See p.545 for details of flights.

The reasonably helpful **tourist office** (Mon–Fri 8am–4pm; ⓣ322/221-8080) is in the Palacio Municipal on the zócalo. For up-to-date, if somewhat promotional, information on what's going on in town, pick up the English-language daily *Vallarta Today*, or the weekly *Vallarta Tribune* (both free, in gringo hangouts). Puerto Vallarta is also well represented on various **websites**: ⓦwww.puertovallarta.net is the Tourism Board's official site and contains comprehensive listings of what to do and where to stay, along with news and weather reports; ⓦwww.vallartaonline.com provides travel news as well as practical information on local bus routes, money exchange, Spanish schools and the like. If you find yourself in any sort of trouble or just need advice, approach one of the people dressed in white uniforms and blue caps – these are the **tourist police**.

Accommodation

With the exception of the long string of big package hotels along the beach, Puerto Vallarta's **places to stay** are within easy walking distance of each other. Most of the more affordable options lie south of the Río Cuale, though there are a couple of places worth considering north of the river. The **budget accommodation** is concentrated along Madero – slightly seedy at night – but remember, too, that the pricier places can transform into bargains during the low season, when prices can be as much as halved. The **youth hostel** is also located south of the river, at Aguacate 302-A (ⓣ322/222-2108). Closed for

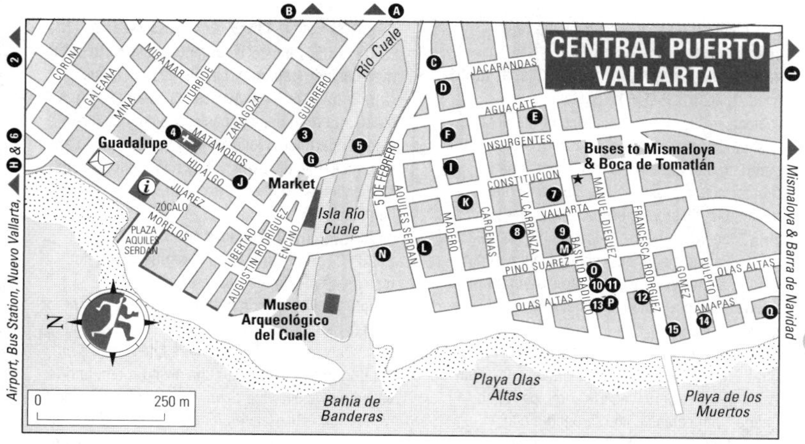

ACCOMMODATION				RESTAURANTS			
Azteca	C	Hotel Posada Río Cuale	L	Archie's Wok	15	Le Bistro Jazz Café	5
Blue Chairs Resort	Q	Lina	F	Café des Artistes	2	El Palomar de los Gonzáles	1
La Casa del Puente	G	Molino de Agua	N	Café de Olla	10	A Page in the Sun	7
Casa Kimberley	B	Playa Los Arcos	P	La Dolce Vita	6	The Pancake House	11
Escuela Cecattur	J	Posada de Roger	M	Fredy's Tucán	9	Planeta Vegetariano	8
Estancia San Carlos	K	Vientos del Río	A	Kaiser Maximilian	13	El Torito	12
Getaway Club	H	Villa del Mar	D	Karpathos Taverna	14	Las Tres Huastecas	3
Hortencia	I	Yasmin	O			Trio	
		Youth Hostel	E				

renovation at the time of writing, beds in single-sex dorms cost US$7.50 and there is a midnight curfew. For groups of up to six, fully equipped **apartments** can be very good value.

The closest formal **campsite** to town is the grassy *Puerto Vallarta Trailer Park* (Ⓣ322/224-2828; ❹), several kilometres north of the hotel zone. Free camping on any of the more popular beaches around the middle of the bay is out, but if you're reasonably well equipped and protected against mosquitoes, you could try **Punta de Mita** at the northern end of the bay or **Boca de Tomatlán** to the south (where the main road turns inland), each of which from time to time sees small communities establishing themselves on the sand. At **Yelapa**, a southern beach to which there are boat trips from town (see p.506), you might be able to rent a hut or find somewhere to sling a hammock; otherwise there is a good hotel.

South of the Río Cuale

Azteca Madero 473, at Jacarandas Ⓣ322/222-2750. Simple and clean, the lack of light in the rooms is compensated for by the attractive wrought-iron balconies, flourishing plants and peaceful atmosphere. ❹

Blue Chairs Resort Almendro 4, at Playa de los Muertos Ⓣ322/222-5040, Ⓕ222-2176, Ⓦwww.bluechairs.com. Gay visitors, even if not staying here, will inevitably gravitate to this gay owned and operated landmark on the town beach. This resort has suites with or without kitchens and ocean views, as well as a rooftop bar and pool. ❽

Estancia San Carlos Constitución 210, at Cárdenas Ⓣ322/222-6230. Spacious rooms with a/c and television, white walls and wooden furnishings, set around a mosaic-tiled swimming pool. Apartments with fully equipped kitchens, sleeping six, also available (US$84). On-site coin-operated laundry. ❻

Hortencia Madero 336, at Insurgentes Ⓣ322/222-2484, Ⓦwww.hotelhortencia.com. Spacious, light quarters with TV that justify the extra cash over the real cheapies. ❺

Hotel Posada Río Cuale Serdán 242, at Vallarta ⓣ & ⓕ 322/222-0450, ⓔriocaule@pvnet.com.mx. One of the best-designed of the central hotels, with rooms staggered around gardens to give an open feel. Comfortable a/c rooms with balconies and a decent bar-restaurant beside the pool. ❻

Lina Madero 376, east of Insurgentes ⓣ322/222-1661. Simple, clean, but slightly gloomy rooms around a courtyard. The on-site restaurant has a fresher feel, but can occasionally be noisy for guests at the hotel. ❹

Molino de Agua Vallarta 130 ⓣ322/222-1907, ⓕ222-6056, ⓦwww.molinodeagua.com. Fully in keeping with Puerto Vallarta's tropical village image, with cabins dotted around a pool in big, tranquil gardens where the Río Cuale meets the sea. ❽

Playa Los Arcos Olas Altas 380, at Diéguez ⓣ322/226-7102, ⓦwww.playalosarcos.com. The best of the beachfront hotels, with well-appointed a/c rooms and a large, frequently crowded pool. ❽

Posada de Roger Basilio Badillo 237 ⓣ322/222-0639, ⓕ223-0482, ⓦwww.posadaroger.com. Fairly modern, spacious hotel, whose attractive rooms overlook a shady courtyard, where excellent breakfasts are served. Only a couple of blocks from the beach, and with a small pool. ❻

Villa del Mar Madero 440, at Jacarandas ⓣ322/222-0785. Relaxed, long-time favourite of budget travellers. All rooms have bathrooms; the larger (slightly more expensive) ones also have small balconies. Some two-person apartments available (US$36). ❹

Yasmin Basilio Badillo 168 ⓣ322/222-0087. Reasonable mid-range option one block from the beach, although the clean rooms with fans are not radically different from the cheaper places along Madero. ❺

North of the Río Cuale

La Casa del Puente Insurgentes, just north of the river behind *Restaurant La Fuente del Puente* ⓣ322/222-0749, ⓦwww.casadelpuente.com. A real home from home: spacious, elegantly furnished apartments (overlooking the river), and an extremely friendly owner. Only two "suites" (with fully equipped kitchens), and one double room, so book early. ❼

Casa Kimberley Zaragoza 445 ⓣ & ⓕ 322/222-1336. Time-warped shrine which doubles as a hotel in the house Richard Burton bought for Liz Taylor's birthday in 1964. Except for the Liz memorabilia, the decor is little changed from when she sold it ten years later. Rooms are comfortable with a communal living room, unrivalled views over the town, a swimming pool and free breakfasts. Heaven for Liz freaks and lots of fun for everyone else. Prices drop by fifty percent in low season. ❾

Escuela Cecattur Hidalgo, at Guerrero ⓣ322/222-4910, ⓔcecati63@prodigy.net.mx. This hotel doubles as a school for those wishing to work in tourism and hospitality, where students take a part in the day-to-day running of the hotel. Rooms are large, if somewhat characterless. A good second choice if others are fully booked. ❻

Getaway Club Francisco Medina Ascencio, next to the *Sheraton* ⓣ322/226-3300, ⓕ223-3601, ⓦwww.getawayvallarta.com. If you want to stay at an all-inclusive resort, this is an excellent candidate: only thirty minutes' walk north from the zócalo, with spacious rooms, good food, two large pools and, with no children allowed, it is more relaxing than the other resort establishments. ❾

Vientos del Río Cuauhtémoc 460, at the end of Guerrero across the street from *Casa Kimberley* ⓣ322/222-1758. Two beautiful, fully furnished suites with a small pool and big views over the river. ❼

The Town

Apart from the **beaches**, and the tourist shops that pack the centre of town, there's not a great deal in the way of attractions in Puerto Vallarta. That said, you can still fill a very pleasant hour or two wandering along the malecón, the old seafront which runs adjacent to Morelos in the downtown area, and on the island in the river. The **zócalo**, where everyone gathers in the evenings and at weekends, is backed by the **Church of Guadalupe**, its tower a city landmark, topped with a huge crown modelled on that of Maximilian's wife, Carlota, in the 1860s. Just down from here on the malecón is the **Plaza Aquiles Serdán**, with a strange little amphitheatre and four arches looking out over the sea, like a lost fragment of the Roman Empire. A short stroll northwards brings you to another Puerto Vallarta icon, the **seahorse statue**. In between the plaza and the statue are many new, fantastical sculptures.

On the **Isla Río Cuale** a small park surrounds a clutch of shops and restaurants. At the seaward end there's a tiny, irregularly open, local **archeology museum** (Tues–Sat noon–2pm & 4–6pm), with half a dozen cases of local discoveries. Further inland, expensive restaurants and **galleries** line the middle of the island towards the Insurgentes Bridge. Beyond, past **John Huston's statue**, there's a park and a patch of river where women come to do the family washing, overlooked from the hillsides by the opulent villas of "Gringo's Gulch".

Beaches in and around Puerto Vallarta

Puerto Vallarta's **beaches** vary in nature as you move round the bay: those to the north, out near Nuevo Vallarta and the airport, are long, flat stretches of sand often pounded by surprisingly heavy surf; south, a series of steep-sided coves shelter tiny, calm strands. The town beach, **Playa de los Muertos** (Beach of the Dead), or "Playa del Sol" as the local tourist office would prefer it known, falls somewhere between the two extremes: not very large and reasonably calm, despite facing apparently open water. This is the most crowded beach of all, with locals, Mexican holiday-makers and foreign tourists, and in many ways it's the most enjoyable – plenty of people and activities on offer, food and drink close at hand. But don't leave anything of value lying about. The **gay** section of this beach is situated at its southern end opposite the *Blue Chairs Resort* (see p.503) – look out for the blue chairs.

To the **north** of the bay, the best beaches tend to front the big hotels, but beyond Nuevo Vallarta, where the landscape becomes drier and scrubbier, there are some lovely, deserted stretches of sand, pounded by heavy surf. If you decide to swim here, don't underestimate the strength of the undertow.

The smaller stretches of sand to the **south** are far more popular. Buses leave regularly from the junction of Constitución and Basilio Badillo and head south on Hwy-200. There are small beaches every few hundred metres, difficult to get to unless you're staying at one of the hotels or condos that back them, while 9km out of town towards Mismaloya (see below) is a **bungee-jumping** operation. For US$55 you can hurl yourself off a small platform and plunge 40m down to the swirling waters of the Pacific; head-dunking is optional (daily 10am–6pm).

Mismaloya

The best-known and most convenient beach is **Mismaloya**, some 10km out of Puerto Vallarta. Here John Huston filmed *The Night of the Iguana*, building his film set on the southern side of a gorgeous bay at the mouth of what was once a pristine, jungle-choked gorge. Plans to turn the set and crew's accommodation into tourist cabins never came to anything, and now the huge and expensive *La Jolla de Mismaloya* **hotel** (❾) completely dominates the valley. Crowded with sun-worshippers and enthusiastic vendors selling everything from coconuts to sarongs, Mismaloya is not a beach on which to relax. You can still wander out to the point and the ruins of the film set where a couple of expensive restaurants sell beer and seafood cocktails. Boats are on hand to take you snorkelling at **Los Arcos**, a federal underwater park and "eco-preserve" around a group of offshore islands, some formed into the eponymous arches. A superb array of brightly coloured fish – parrot, angel, pencil, croaker and scores of others – negotiate the rock walls and the boulder-strewn ocean floor 5m below. In addition to the scheduled ninety-minute trips from the beach, boats are rented to groups for unlimited periods. If you're feeling adventurous, you could even rent snorkelling gear in Puerto Vallarta beforehand, get off the bus almost as soon as you see Los Arcos, and swim out to the islands; they're less than 300m offshore.

From behind the beach, an unpaved road, accessible by car, foot or on horseback, leads up inland through a small village and after 2km arrives at *Chino's Paradise*, a **restaurant** serving seafood and steaks for lunch in a stunning setting next to a sparkling river. The prices are higher than usual but worth it as the tables, shaded under palapas, are dotted around a waterfall, overlooking natural swimming pools filled with crystal-clear, icy-cold water. A further 2km up the road is the town of **El Edén**, where the Arnold Schwarzenegger movie *Predator* was filmed. The *El Edén* **restaurant** enjoys a blissful riverside setting, but the food is overpriced and the buses ferrying tour groups and waiters clad in army fatigues are quite at odds with the natural tranquillity of the surroundings.

Boca de Tomatlán and beyond

If you're after peace and quiet, the best option is to continue along the highway for another 4km until you reach the sleepy village of **Boca de**

Trips from Puerto Vallarta

There are **boat trips** out to Mismaloya (see p.505) from Puerto Vallarta, and for the wonderful **beaches** further south – Playa Las Animas, Quimixto and Yelapa are the most common destinations – a boat is the only means of access. Travel agents all over town tout a variety of excursions, most of which leave from the marina. Miller Tours at Paseo de las Garzas 100, between *Hotel Krystle* and *Hotel Crown Paradise* in Nuevo Vallarta (Ⓣ322/224-0585), and Vallarta Adventure at the marina (Ⓣ322/221-0657, Ⓦwww.vallarta-adventures.com) both have good reputations, though compare prices and what's on offer in the way of food and drink – if meals are not included, it's worth taking your own food along.

A much cheaper way to travel is to jump on a **water taxi**. These depart from Playa de los Muertos for Quimixto, Las Animas and Yelapa at 11am, returning from all destinations at about 4pm. Alternatively, you can catch a **bus** to Boca de Tomatlán, from where about five taxis a day, starting at 10.30am, sail to all three destinations.

Quimixto and **Las Animas** are beaches pure and simple, while at **Yelapa** there's a small "typical" village not far from the white-sand beach, and a waterfall a short distance into the jungle. It's marketed as an "untouched paradise" but is more of a luxurious if rustic retreat – there's no electricity, but long-distance phone lines, sushi, and Reiki massages are all on offer. During the day Yelapa is a lively place with day-trippers enjoying all the usual beach activities including parasailing, horse riding and boat trips. If you've got the time and money, stay for the night, as the beach empties as the sun sets and becomes the perfect spot for total rest and relaxation. *Hotel Lagunita* (Ⓣ322/209-5055, Ⓦwww.hotel-lagunita.com; ❼) has beautiful **cabañas**, a pool and beachfront **restaurant** serving Mexican and international food, but it's easy to **camp** on the beach, or with luck you might be able to rent a **hut** for very little.

If you want to go **snorkelling** or **scuba diving** at the southern beaches, tours are led by Chico's Dive Shop, Díaz Ordaz 770-2, on the malecón (daily 8am–10pm; Ⓣ322/222-1895, Ⓦwww.chicos-diveshop.com). You can rent gear here, too (US$12 a day for the mask, snorkel and fins; US$40 for the full scuba rig, including tank). It is usually too stiflingly humid to consider anything as energetic as **mountain biking**, but Bike Mex, Guerrero 361, at Miramar, just north of the upper river bridge (Ⓣ322/223-1834), rents out bikes (US$20 a day, with maps of the surrounding area), but prefers you to take one of their organized tours into the jungly slopes behind the town and beyond (from US$40).

Tomatlán, which has a small but beautiful beach in a protected cove, dotted with fishing boats. The local speciality, cooked to perfection by the beachside *enramadas*, is *pescado de bara*: a fish impaled on a stick and slow-cooked over a barbecue. The Río Horcones, with its thickly forested banks, empties into the sea beside the beach, so there's a choice of fresh or salt water for swimming. From Boca de Tomatlán, the main road heads inland and passes another idyllically set, if expensive restaurant, *Chico's Paradise*. Below the restaurant, the Río Horcones tumbles over a jumble of smoothed rocks or, in drier periods, forms cool, clear pools perfect for whiling away an afternoon. There's no formal accommodation, but there are sites for fully equipped campers. Immediately upstream in the small village of **Las Juntas y Los Veranos**, you can take a **canopy tour**, where you slide along cables up to 60m high attached only by a body harness (vertigo sufferers beware). The cables link ten treetops and carry you past coffee trees, vanilla vines and the plant used to make tequila. Tours last from one and a half to two hours and cost US$66 (ⓣ322/223-6060, ⓦwww.canopytours-vallarta.com).

Eating

Finding somewhere **to eat** in Puerto Vallarta is no problem – tourist restaurants offering cocktails by candlelight abound – but eating inexpensively is somewhat harder. As usual, the **market** – on the north bank of the river by the upper bridge – has a few cheap *comedors* tucked away upstairs, overlooking the river, well away from the souvenir stalls that fill the rest of the building. **Taco and hot-dog stands** line the streets, while vendors on the beach offer freshly caught fish, roasted on sticks. Gutiérrez Rizo Supermarket, at Serdán and Constitución, sells **picnic** supplies. South of the Río Cuale along Olas Altas, and particularly on Basilio Badillo between Suárez and Insurgentes, several **restaurants** bridge the gap between out-and-out tourist traps and plainer eating houses. Of the more **expensive places**, most offering some form of music or entertainment, or at least a good view while you eat, you can really take your pick – there are also several mid-range options serving a variety of international cuisine at the marina.

South of the Río Cuale

A Page in the Sun Olas Altas 399, at Diéguez ⓣ322/222-3608. A nice little café, with tables in the sun, coffee, *licuados*, chess and magazines, which doubles as a used-book shop and is situated in a bustling part of town.

Archie's Wok Rodríguez 130 ⓣ322/222-0411. State-of-the-art Oriental cooking by the wife of John Huston's former personal chef. Delicious, healthy food in Filipino, Thai and Chinese sauces served in a serene Zen garden, expensive but considered one of the best Asian restaurants in the Americas. Closed Sun and all of Sept.

Café de Olla Basilio Badillo 168, at Olas Altas. Good traditional Mexican food delivered by cheerful, attentive waiters. Always popular and brimming with diners who come again and again. Closed Tues.

Fredy's Tucán Basilio Badillo 245, at Vallarta ⓣ322/223-0778. Popular spot for Mexican and continental breakfasts, omelettes and pancakes, served until 2.30pm in the cool courtyard of the *Posada de Roger* hotel. European football matches are screened in the bar on evenings and weekends.

Kaiser Maximilian Olas Altas 380-B, next to *Playa Los Arcos* hotel ⓣ322/223-0760. Elegant, expensive restaurant with traditional Austrian dishes (including many heavy pastries), along with other European and some Mexican offerings. Closed Sun.

Karpathos Taverna Gómez 110, at Playa de los Muertos ⓣ322/223-1562. Airy Mediterranean-style restaurant delivering a fairly standard Greek menu. The prices aren't too bad, though, and the food's great, though the service can be a bit slow.

El Palomar de los Gonzáles Aguacate 425 ⓣ322/222-0795. Elegant, mainly Mexican and seafood restaurant boasting a good wine list and exotic desserts, high on the hill to the south of the centre with stunning views over the city. The place to take your credit card for that romantic candlelit dinner. Evenings only, from 6pm.

The Pancake House Basilio Badillo 289. Marquee-like affair serving good pancakes, waffles, blintzes and all-you-can-drink coffee to a tourist crowd. Daily 8am–2pm.

El Torito Vallarta 291, at Carranza ⓣ322/222-3784. Reasonably priced bar and restaurant for sports jocks, with satellite coverage of everything from Serie A to the Super Bowl. Ribs are a speciality.

Las Tres Huastecas Olas Altas 444, at Rodríguez. Good-value restaurant right near Playa de los Muertos and specializing in seafood and classic Mexican dishes such as chicken in mole sauce.

North of the Río Cuale

Café des Artistes G. Sanchez 740 ⓣ322/222-3228. Gourmet restaurant where the quality of the French cuisine matches the fine surroundings: eat in the garden or dining room decorated with artwork. Live piano and flute music nightly adds to the refined atmosphere.

La Dolce Vita Malecón 674, at Dominguez ⓣ322/222-3852. Pizzas, pasta and other dishes such as beef carpaccio and chicken cacciatore at reasonable prices. Live jazz Thurs–Sun. Very popular.

Le Bistro Jazz Café Isla Río Cuale, just east of Insurgentes ⓣ322/222-0283. Sophisticated, predominantly seafood dining in classical surroundings or alfresco, soothed by cool jazz. On the expensive side but a great place to wind down. Open from 9am for breakfast, too. Closed Sun.

Planeta Vegetariano Iturbide 270, at Hidalgo ⓣ322/222-3073. All-you-can-eat vegetarian buffet with a choice of main courses, salads, soup, dessert and a soft drink. The walls are painted with fantastic frescoes, the food is reasonably priced and deliciously spiced.

Trio Guerrero 264 ⓣ322/222-2196. Top-quality Mediterranean cuisine prepared by a German and Swedish chef with Michelin credentials and served in an exquisite dining room filled with original art and hanging plants. A fabulous treat if you can afford the prices.

Nightlife and entertainment

The **malecón** is the obvious centre of night-time activity, lined with places that specialize in creating a high-energy party-time atmosphere. They are typically full of young Mexicans and, during March and April, American spring-breakers. This said, there is a good variety of music on offer, from techno to salsa, and some places are a lot less frenetic and rowdy than others. The highest concentration of **bars** and **clubs** is along the stretch of the malecón which runs about 400m north of the Plaza Aquiles Serdán. Most of these establishments are at ground level, making it easy to wander along and take your pick of the **happy hours** and compare **cover charges** – sometimes nonexistent, at other times around US$5–15 depending on the night and season, and almost always subject to a discount if you pick up one of the many coupons distributed liberally by the touts and tourist office. South of the river also has its share of clubs, which are generally more down-to-earth, more varied in character and atmosphere. This is also where you'll find most of the **gay nightlife**.

There are two **cinemas**: Cine Bahía is south of the river at Insurgentes 189; and Cine Luz Maria is north of the river at Avenida México 227. Both show predominantly Hollywood films in English with Spanish subtitles. Look for listings in *Vallarta Today* and other free handouts. Sunday tends to be quiet – some places close – except on the zócalo where, from around 6pm, huge crowds gather around the dozens of taco and cake stands and listen to the brass band. And there's always the **pool hall**, at Madero 279.

South of the Río Cuale

Club Roxy Vallarta 217, at Madero. A popular bar-club with bands playing blues, reggae and rock and a great atmosphere that attracts locals and tourists alike.

Paco Paco Vallarta 278. The largest and most popular gay club: a multifaceted venue with DJs playing the latest in techno, hip-hop and pop on the ground floor; Mexican music, a cantina and pool table on the first floor; a rooftop bar on the second; and strippers at "The Ranch", a smaller space connected to the main club by a passageway.

The Jazz House Rodríguez, at Olas Altas. Hosts first-class jazz in a tastefully decorated, sit-down venue that also serves good if slightly pricey food.

North of the Río Cuale

Los Balcones Juarez 182, at Libertad. Puerto Vallarta's oldest gay club, on three floors with balconies overlooking the street, a dance floor and strippers during high season.

La Bodeguita del Medio Malecón 858. Restaurant named after the famous Havana bar is as popular for its *mojitos*, *cuba libres* and live salsa bands as its Cuban and Mexican food.

Carlos O'Brian's Malecón 786. The most popular of the bar-restaurant chains. Serves American- and Mexican-style bar food day and night, with a dance floor and bar specializing in yards of alcoholic and non-alcoholic cocktails, both of which see an increasing trade as the night wears on.

Christine's at *Hotel NH Krystal Puerto Vallarta*, Av de las Garzas. Upmarket, expensive and slightly pretentious discotheque. It is smart, glitzy and convenient for those staying in the hotel zone north of the town centre.

Hilo Malecón. Huge out-of-place statues of Mexican peasants reverberate to the thumping techno music at this club with high ceilings and an energetic vibe.

The Zoo Malecón 630. Leopard- and zebra-skin chairs and plastic gorillas swinging from the rafters lend a kitsch element to this club where DJs play the latest dance tunes for a young, hip clientele.

Listings

Airlines Aeroméxico ⓣ322/224-2777; Air Canada ⓣ01-800/719-2827; Alaska ⓣ322/221-1350; American ⓣ322/221-1799; Continental ⓣ322/221-1025; Mexicana ⓣ322/224-8900.

American Express Morelos 660, at Abasolo ⓣ322/223-2955; holds mail and changes cheques (Mon–Fri 9am–6pm, Sat 9am–1pm).

Banks and exchange Banamex, on the zócalo, will change cheques (Mon–Fri 9am–4pm, Sat 10am–2pm) and also has an ATM. Other ATMs are plentiful, but if you're not travelling with plastic, you can change money at the numerous casas de cambio that line the nearby streets: rates tend to vary, so it's worth shopping around.

Buses Estrella Blanca, at the station, with an office at Basilio Badillo 11, at Insurgentes (ⓣ322/290-1014; closed Sun), have first-class services to a long list of destinations including Acapulco (2 daily; 18hr), Guadalajara (almost hourly; 5hr), Lázaro Cárdenas (1 daily; 12hr), Mazatlán (1 daily; 8hr) and Mexico City (3 daily; 13–14hr). Primera Plus (ⓣ322/290-0715) run first-class services to Barra de Navidad (2 daily; 4hr), Guadalajara (13 daily) and Manzanillo (1 daily; 5hr). They share their offices at Lázaro Cárdenas 268–9 with ETN (ⓣ322/290-0997), who operate super-deluxe services to Guadalajara and Mexico City. Pacifico, at the station, with an office at Insurgentes 160, at Carranza (ⓣ322/290-1008), also offer first-class services to a long list of destinations. For second-class buses to Manzanillo (8 daily) and Barra de Navidad (6 daily) try Servicios Coordinados (ⓣ322/221-0095).

Car rental Avis, at the airport ⓣ322/221-1112; Hertz, Francisco Medina Ascencio 1602 ⓣ322/222-0024; and Alamo, Díaz Ordaz 660A ⓣ322/221-3030.

Consulates Canada, Obelisco Condominio, Francisco Medina Ascencio 1951 ⓣ322/293-0098 (Mon–Fri 9am–3pm); US, Edificio Vallarta Plaza, Zaragoza 160 ⓣ322/222-0069 (Mon–Fri 10am–2pm, closed every third Wed).

Emergencies English-speaking medics at CMQ Clinic, Basilio Badillo 365, between Insurgentes and Aguacate ⓣ322/223-1919; and Cruz Roja, Río Balsas y Plata ⓣ322/222-1533.

Flights Puerto Vallarta is well served by flights to other Mexican cities, the US and Canada. Prices vary dramatically with season and availability, but tend not to be cheap if purchased in Mexico. Contact the airport (see p.502) for further details or call the airlines direct (see above). Travel agents (see below) or any of the numerous agencies north of the river can also provide up-to-date information and advice.

Laundry Lavandería Blanquita, Madero 407, east of Aguacate (Mon–Sat 8am–8pm). There's also a coin-operated laundry at hotel *Estancia San Carlos*, Constitución 210, at Cárdenas.

Pharmacy CMQ, Basilio Badillo 367 ⓣ322/222-2941, next to CMQ Clinic, is open 24hr; or try Lux, Insurgentes 169 ⓣ322/222-1909.

Phone and fax services There are various booths providing long-distance phone and fax services, such as the one on Cárdenas near Pino Suárez.

Post office The main post office is at Mina 188 between Juárez and Morelos (Mon–Fri 9am–5pm, Sat 9am–1pm).

Travel agents SAET Travel Service, in the Centro Comercial, corner of Morelos and Rodríguez ⓣ322/222-1886 (Mon–Fri 9am–7pm, Sat 9am–2pm).

Nuevo Vallarta, Bucerías and Punta de Mita

North of Puerto Vallarta, over the state line in Nayarit, the **Bahía de Banderas** arcs out to **Punta de Mita**, some 30km away. A summer preserve for Mexicans from Guadalajara and a winter retreat for motorhome vacationers from the north, these gorgeous beaches offer facilities in just a few spots – **Nuevo Vallarta, Bucerías** and **Punta de Mita** – leaving miles of secluded sand for camping. To get out there from Puerto Vallarta, the best bet is to catch any northbound local bus to the *Sheraton* hotel, then flag down an Autotransportes Medina "Punta de Mita" bus.

NUEVO VALLARTA, 12km north of the airport, is a mega-resort, an ever-expanding cluster of astronomically expensive hotels. Although the beaches here are great, they are all fronting ugly buildings and because the hotels tend to offer all-inclusive services to their guests, there's nothing much for the day-visitor to do, save **swimming with dolphins** at Dolphin Adventure (US$130; ⓣ322/297-1212 ext 25, ⓦwww.dolphin-adventure.com), a dolphin educational centre located at Paseo de la Palmas 39.

It's really better to push on to another great beach at **BUCERÍAS**, the last of the bay resorts on Hwy-200, which has a cheerful, laid-back atmosphere and wonderful views across the water to Puerto Vallarta from the seafront **restaurants**. *Adriano's* (ⓣ329/298-0088) with its bright-orange walls and extensive range of fresh fish, is superb, if pricey. For a tea-time treat visit the locally renowned *Pie in the Sky* **bakery** opposite the *De Camarón* hotel at Héroe de Nacozari 202, for heavenly chocolate brownies and exotic cheesecakes. If you want to stay, there are several **apartment**-type places such as *Motel Marlyn* (ⓣ329/298-0450; ❹) and the *Bucerías Trailer Park* (ⓣ329/298-0265; ❹).

Keeping to the coast, you leave the main highway for Punta de Mita, passing the beach-free fishing village of **Cruz de Huanacaxtle** and **Manzanillo** and **Piedra Blanca** beaches. The Punta de Mita road continues through increasingly rocky, arid terrain, with small roads dipping down to secluded beaches. The *enramada* (a **restaurant** under palapas) at **Destiladeras** is the only one in the area, which allows them to charge rather inflated prices for the usual fare. If you've brought a picnic, you can rent palapas, tables and chairs for the day and boogie boards are rented out for US$2 per hour. **Camping** on the beach is great, but you need to bring everything.

PUNTA DE MITA is more developed, with bars, cafés and seafood restaurants strung along the beach. Follow the road parallel to the beach and you'll find the Sociedad Cooperativa de Servicios Turísticos (ⓣ329/291-6298), which rents out **snorkelling** and **diving gear** and organizes two-hour *panga* trips to the offshore wildlife sanctuary **Las Islas Marietas**. The boats hold up to eight people and cost US$80 – this is probably the cheapest way to get close to the **humpback whales** present in the bay from around December to April, where they come to mate and give birth before returning to the polar waters of the north. Alternatively, book an organized whale-watching tour from Puerto Vallarta with an operator such as Open Air Expeditions, Guerrero 339 (ⓣ322/222-3310, ⓦwww.vallartawhales.com). You can **camp** on the beach or **stay** at the pretty *Hotel Punta Mita* (ⓣ329/291-6269; ❻) or the ultra-luxurious *Four Seasons Punta Mita* (ⓣ329/291-6000; ❾).

The Costa Alegre and Bahía de Navidad

The stretch of coast known as the **Costa Alegre** starts about 100km south of Puerto Vallarta. If you are heading down the coast and feel like breaking your journey, the **Bahía de Chamela** lies 130km south of Puerto Vallarta and comprises a huge, sweeping arc of superb beaches. Although large luxury hotels are cropping up with alarming frequency, you can still find long sections of untouched beach and cheap accommodation. To reach **Playa Perula**, at the northern end of the bay, it's a one-kilometre walk or drive down a dusty track from Hwy-200. There's a small village and you can stay at the average, fourteen-room *Hotel Punta Perula* (ⓣ315/333-9782; ❹), one block north of the main road. A little further down the highway there's another unpaved road which leads to **Playa Chamela**. The *Paraíso Costa Alegre* (ⓣ315/333-9778; ❺) has attractive oceanfront cabañas surrounded by palm trees as well as full hook-ups for RVs (❸). Otherwise, it's easy to camp on the beach.

Tenacatita, a further 40km south, is another gorgeous beach, with the added attractions of a mangrove lagoon teeming with birdlife and snorkelling in still, clear water, swarming with rainbow-hued fish. The **restaurant** on the beach organizes bird-watching boat trips and you can **stay** at the *Hotel Paraíso Tenacatita* (ⓣ314/353-9623; ❹), which also has a restaurant and simple rooms built round a courtyard. It's also possible to visit Tenacatita from Barra de Navidad.

Most people choose to press on to the twin towns of **Barra de Navidad** and **San Patricio-Melaque**, 30km further south and among the most enticing destinations on this entire stretch of coastline. They're not undeveloped or totally isolated – indeed, families from Guadalajara come here by their hundreds, especially at weekends – neither are they at all heavily commercialized: just small, simple and very Mexican resorts. The entire bay, the **Bahía de Navidad**, is edged by fine sands and, if you're prepared to walk, you can easily leave the crowds behind. Regular buses and colectivos connect the two communities, or you can walk it along the beach in around half an hour.

Barra de Navidad

Lying towards the southern end of the bay, where the beach runs out and curves back round to form a lagoon behind the town, **BARRA DE NAVIDAD** is easily the more appealing of the Bahía de Navidad communities. A couple of kilometres north, San Patricio-Melaque, at the other end of the same beach, is less attractive and more commercial, but if you can't find a room in Barra, it makes a good second choice, with a considerably wider range of hotels.

The much anticipated opening of the *Grand Bay* hotel, golf course and marina complex across the channel from Barra de Navidad has, as yet, changed things surprisingly little, not even spoiling the view from the beach. If you have time, it's worth taking a **boat** over to check it out. Catch one outside the restaurant *El Manglito* near the jetty; they run across the channel every half-hour from 6am to 6pm (US$0.70) and, less frequently, to the beaches on the other side. **Colimilla** (US$1.40 round-trip), across the Laguna de Navidad, is the most popular destination, chiefly for its seafood restaurants such as *Fortino's* (daily 9am–10pm; bring insect repellent if dining after dark) and as a base for the two- or three-kilometre walk over to the rough Pacific beach of Playa de Cocos. The *cooperativo* at the jetty also offers fishing trips, lagoon tours and day-trips to **Tenacatita**.

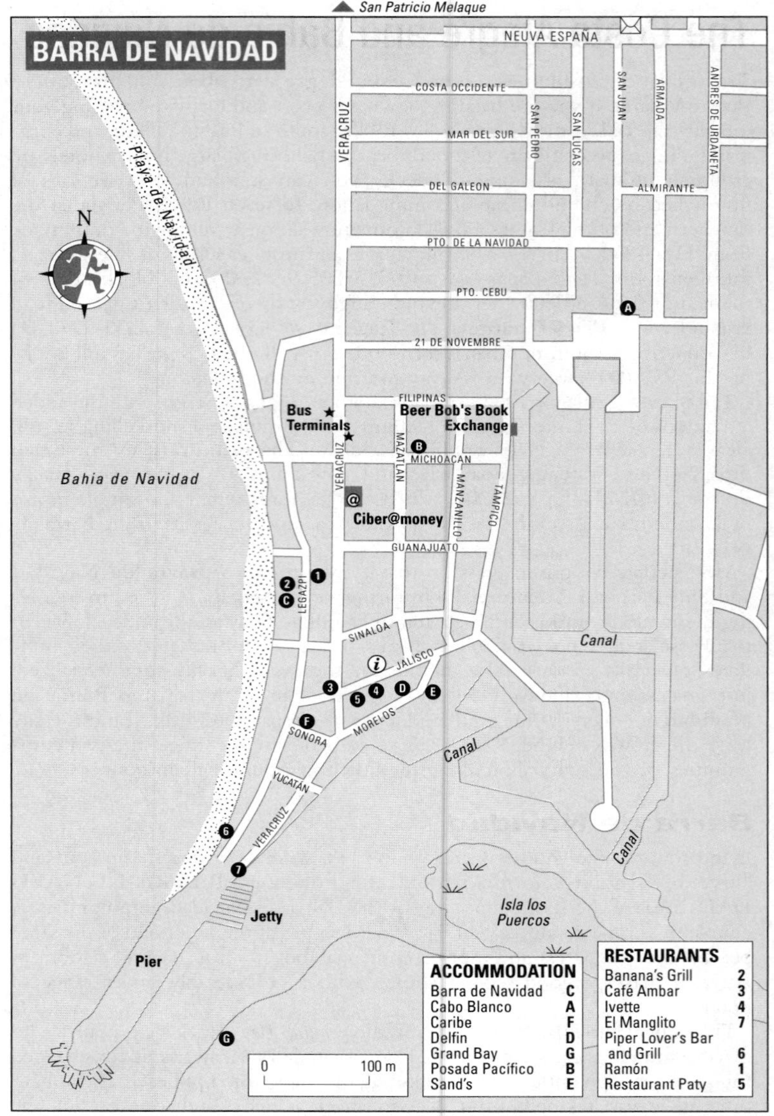

Practicalities

Buses arrive in Barra at either of two terminals almost opposite each other on Veracruz, the town's main drag. The services you are likely to need – post office, *larga distancia* phones and hotels – are all close by; in any case, it only takes twenty minutes to walk around the whole town. The one shortcoming is that there is **no bank** or casa de cambio (the nearest bank is in San Patricio-

Melaque; see overleaf), although you can **exchange** dollars and travellers' cheques at the Ciber@money **Internet** café at Veracruz 212 (Mon–Fri 9am–2pm & 4–7.30pm, Sat 9am–6.30pm). The **post office** is a few blocks north at Nueva España 37 (Mon–Fri 8am–3pm, Sat 9am–12.30pm).

The **tourist office** at Jalisco 67 (Mon–Fri 9am–5pm, Sat & Sun during high season; ⓣ315/355-5100) serves both Barra de Navidad and San Patricio-Melaque. They can advise on anything happening locally – usually not much – though you can probably obtain more useful information from the owner of Beer Bob's Book Exchange at Tampico 8 (Mon–Fri noon–3pm), two rooms absolutely packed with English-language paperbacks: bring one and take one, no charge.

Accommodation

Although Barra has enough hotels to suit all tastes and budgets, reservations are recommended should you plan on staying during high season (roughly Dec–April). Free **camping** is also a possibility along the beach to the north of town. It's easiest to follow the beach, rather than the road, up to a point where you feel comfortable, as beach access is limited.

Barra de Navidad Legazpi 250 ⓣ315/355-5122, ⓦwww.hotelbarradenavidad.com. The only beach hotel left standing after a devastating October 2000 hurricane is a good choice for its comfortable a/c rooms with great sea views and large pool. ❼

Cabo Blanco Armada, at the marina ⓣ315/355-6495 or 01-800/710-5690, ⓦwww.hotelcaboblanco.com. Occupying a quiet inland location next to the marina, a full-service hotel with its own restaurant, tennis courts, "Kid's Club" and accommodation in a/c rooms or one-, two- or three-bedroom suites. All-inclusive only during high season. ❻

Caribe Sonora 15 ⓣ315/335-5952. Reasonable budget option, with rocking chairs on a pleasant terrace, but rather gloomy rooms. ❺

Delfin Morelos 23 ⓣ315/355-5068, ⓦwww.hoteldelfinmx.com. Multi-storey hotel two blocks from the beach, with spacious, clean rooms, a tiny pool, and sea views from the upper floors. ❻

Grand Bay Circuitos de los Marinos, Isla Navidad ⓣ315/331-0500. Luxurious resort with a mountain backdrop, idyllic location on the bay, and a complete range of facilities for golfers, watersports enthusiasts and those simply in need of serious pampering. ❾

Posada Pacífico Mazatlán 136 ⓣ315/355-5359. A simple, friendly place with clean airy rooms, some with balconies, around a tree-shaded courtyard. The best budget option in town. ❹

Sand's Morelos 24 ⓣ315/355-5018. Decent rooms and a large garden overlooking the lagoon where you'll find a bar and a swimming pool – which non-residents can use for US$3. ❺

Eating and drinking

Of the many good **restaurants** in Barra, most are on Legazpi, or else at the junction of Veracruz and Jalisco, where *Restaurant Paty* (ⓣ315/355-5907) is the best of a number of similar budget places serving excellent *ceviche*, fresh fish and meaty Mexican staples. Next door, *Ivette* dishes up good pizza, while diagonally opposite at Veracruz 101, *Café Ambar* (ⓣ315/355-8169) is renowned for its crepes, salads and French dishes, including escargots; the same management operate a good Italian restaurant (again with some French dishes) in a cosy, beachfront location at Legazpi 158. Slightly pricier than most, *Banana's Grill*, upstairs at the *Barra de Navidad* hotel, offers very good breakfasts (but no other meals), while directly opposite at Legazpi 260, *Ramón* (ⓣ315/355-6435) has an extensive range of Mexican and international food, including some decent fish and chips. Exclusively **seafood restaurants** crowd Legazpi, Morelos and the southern end of Veracruz down towards the point: *El Manglito* is one of the best, and has tables overlooking the lagoon.

Nightlife is fairly limited, but you can play pool, drink, munch on snacks and listen to live rock, jazz and blues at *Piper Lover's Bar and Grill* by the beach on Legazpi, and there's dancing at *El Galeón* disco next to *Hotel Sand's*.

San Patricio-Melaque

SAN PATRICIO-MELAQUE seems much more of a typical Mexican town, with its central plaza, church, largish market, and substantial **bus station** at the junction of Carranza and Gómez Farías. Opposite, in the Pasaje Comercial, you'll find the town's only **casa de cambio** (which changes travellers' cheques), with a *larga distancia* **phone** and fax (Mon–Sat 9am–6pm); next door is an **Internet** café (daily 9am–2pm & 4–10pm; US$2 per hour). Half a block further down Gómez Farías there's a Banamex **bank** (Mon–Fri 9am–4pm, Sat 10am–2pm) with a 24-hour **ATM**; you can also **exchange** travellers' cheques here. The **post office** is hidden on Orozco, round the corner from *Hotel San Patricio*. There's no **tourist office**: the office in Barra de Navidad serves both towns (see p.513).

Very cheap **camping** is an option on the patch of land at the northern end of the beach beyond the restaurants. There's a full-facility campsite right by the beach, *Playa Trailer Park*, Gómez Farías 250, at López Mateos (ⓣ315/355-5065; ❹), which charges the same for RVs and tents, but if you want a roof over your head, walk for about 200m along Gómez Farías, parallel to the beach. Here, *Posada Pablo de Tarso*, Gómez Farías 408 (ⓣ315/355-5117; ❻), provides good mid-range accommodation, with comfortable, nicely furnished **rooms**, with TV and phone, around a verdant courtyard, and a good pool; apartments (❻–❼) sleep between three and six people. The cheaper *San Patricio*, opposite *Pablo de Tarso* at Gómez Farías 84 (ⓣ315/355-5244; ❺), has outside kitchens and a communal dining area; some apartments (sleeping up to eight) have kitchenettes. There's safe parking, too. At the northern end of Gómez Farías at no. 1, *Club Náutico El Dorado* (ⓣ315/355-5239, ⓦwww.eldoradoclubnautico.com; ❼), is more luxurious with its air-conditioned rooms with TV, phone and room service, and considerably more expensive. Note that during Semana Santa (Easter), even the high-season rates quoted here can double.

Eating options are fairly limited. *La Terraza*, upstairs in the courtyard of *Hotel Monterrey* on Gómez Farías, serves generous breakfasts, while *Koala's*, about five blocks south of the centre at Obregón 52, specializes in creative fusion cookery served in a romantic garden with light-bedecked trees. It is open from 6pm – the food is excellent but portions are quite small. Across the road at Obregón 8, the Canadian-run *Ava* has good ribs and hamburgers. Other than that you're limited to the identical restaurants along the northern end of the beachfront, the cheaper comidas on the streets beachside of the central plaza and the *licuado* stalls around the market on Hidalgo and Corona. Note that during the quieter summer months many restaurants will be closed.

Manzanillo and around

Two roads head **inland to Guadalajara** from this part of the coast. The direct-looking route from Barra de Navidad is indeed reasonably fast (although any route has to tangle spectacularly with the Sierra Madre), but it's also very dull, with just one town of any size, the dusty, provincial and

untempting community of Autlán. The journey along the coast to Manzanillo and inland via **Colima** is considerably more interesting, not only for the towns themselves but also for the spectacular snowcapped volcanoes that come beyond.

Just ninety minutes down the road from the Bahía de Navidad, **MANZANILLO** is a very different sort of place: a working port where tourism – although highly developed – very definitely takes second place to trade. Downtown, it has to be said, is not at all attractive: crisscrossed by railway tracks, rumbling with heavy traffic and surrounded by a bewildering array of inner harbours and shallow lagoons that seem to cut the place off from the land. You can easily imagine that a couple of hundred years ago plague and pestilence made sailors fear to land here, and it's not surprising to read in an 1884 guide to Mexico that "the climate of Manzanillo is unhealthy for Europeans, and the tourist is advised not to linger long in the vicinity". Although few tourists do stay even now – most are concentrated in the hotels and club resorts around the bay to the east – the town is healthy enough, and there's a certain shabby romance in staying in the centre. Certainly it's a lot more interesting than the sanitized resort area, and cheaper, too. Buses out to the beach are frequent and efficient, but if you're kicking your heels in the centre, you could climb one of the **hills** that rise in the heart of the town, causing streets to disappear for a few blocks to make way for them, in order to get a better view of the bay.

Practicalities

Half a dozen **bus** companies provide services along the coast, as well as inland to Colima and Guadalajara. The brand-new bus station, the **Terminal Autobuses Manzanillo** or TAMA, opened in September, 2003, and is located about 5km from the centre, roughly halfway between Manzanillo and the beaches on the eastern side of the bay. City buses to the zócalo (marked "Jardín") and the beaches (marked "Santiago") leave from the station entrance.

Manzanillo's commercial core centres on its zócalo, the **Jardín Alvaro Obregón**, right on the harbourfront opposite the main outer dock. All the hotels, restaurants, banks and offices are a very short walk away. Banamex and Bancomer **banks** (both with ATMs) are next to each other on México, at Bocanegra; there's a *larga distancia* office (Mon–Sat 8am–11pm, Sun 9am–2pm & 5–11pm; collect calls) on the Jardín Obregón at Dávalos 27; and the **post office** is a short distance south along México, at Galindo 30 (Mon–Fri 9am–3pm). One of the best and cheapest **Internet** cafés (US$1 per hour) is on the second floor of the Centro Comercial del Puerto, on México between Quintero and Galindo. The helpful **tourist office** is in the Palacio Municipal on the zócalo (Mon–Fri 9am–8pm, Sat 9am–1pm), while another office with more limited hours is at the beach several kilometres out of town, at Miguel de la Madrid 1033 (Mon–Fri 9am–2pm & 4–7pm).

For **moving on**, both Autotransportes del Sur de Jalisco and Sociedad Cooperativa de Transportes run second-class services to Colima (6 an hour between them; 1hr 30min), the former also serving Tecomán (every 20min; 1hr), Guadalajara (every 90min; 5–6hr) and Lázaro Cárdenas (4 daily; 6–7hr). La Linea runs first- and executive-class buses to Colima (every hour; 1hr 30min) and Guadalajara (every hour; 6hr). Primera Plus serves Barra de Navidad (11 daily; 1hr 30min) and Servicio Plus runs twelve buses daily to **Puerto Vallarta** (7hr). Estrella Blanca runs first-class to **Acapulco** (3 daily; 12hr), Mexico City (2 daily; 12hr) and all points to Tijuana (2 daily; 38hr).

Accommodation

Finding a **place to stay** is no problem in Manzanillo; there's a range of budget to moderately priced hotels, though nothing special, close to the centre. **Prices** at all but the cheapest drop by about 25 percent outside the high season (roughly December to May) and Semana Santa. In town, *Hotel Flamingos*, Madero 72 (☎314/332-1037; ⑤), is the best of the budget options, with fairly spacious rooms and chunky wooden furniture, though the service can be a little gruff. Just off the zócalo, the *Emperador*, Dávalos 69 (☎314/332-2374; ③), has decent, though smaller rooms with hot showers and fans, and a cheap *comedor*, too – far better value than some of the pricier places nearby. If you have the money, though, head straight for *Hotel Colonial*, Bocanegra 28, at México (☎314/332-1080; ⑤), where attractive rooms with TV are set around a Moorish-style courtyard with Andalucian azulejos and a cooling fountain. If you want to be by the sea, but still within walking distance of the zócalo, try *Hotel San Pedrito*, Azueta 3 (☎314/332-0535; ⑤), a rambling place around a pool and tennis court, backing onto **Playa San Pedrito**, about 1km east of the centre (twenty minutes' walk from the zócalo along the waterfront); spacious, kitchen-equipped apartments sleeping six (⑦) are also available. This beach is probably your best bet for camping, too: Manzanillo has no trailer park and all the other beaches are pretty built-up.

Eating and drinking

Places to eat are concentrated around the zócalo, with several good cafés overlooking the Jardín Alvaro Obregón itself. *Chantilly* on Juárez, at Madero

(Ⓣ314/332-0194; closed Sat), and *Roca del Mar* (Ⓣ314/332-0302), diagonally opposite, both serve a huge range of decent meals, top-value comidas corridas and good espresso and cappuccino. Another excellent, relaxing place for a coffee – or a frozen cappuccino – is *Café Costeño*, just off the zócalo at México 69. Heading east along Morelos, parallel to the waterfront, you come to *La Perlita*, which dishes up antojitos and seafood on shaded tables close to the water and, a little further along, *LyChee*, Niños Héroes 397 (Ⓣ314/332-1103; closed Mon), which serves acceptable, moderately priced Chinese food at tables with good views of the bay. If you head down Avenida México, Manzanillo's main commercial and shopping street, you'll find a whole series of other possibilities, from takeaway *taquerías* and the tiny vegetarian *Yacatecuhtli*, at no. 249 (Ⓣ314/332-5670), with its health foods, energy drinks, fruit salads and soya burgers, to the fancy restaurant at *Hotel Colonial*, where you can get a steak for around US$8. At the other end of the scale, there are several very cheap places – grimy and raucous on the whole – in the market area three blocks down México and at the bottom end of Juárez by the railway tracks.

The coast around Manzanillo

While locals might go **swimming** from the tiny harbour beach of San Pedrito and in the Laguna de Cuyutlán behind the town, both are polluted. Far better to head for beaches around the bay proper, where the tourist hotels congregate. The nearest of these, at **LAS BRISAS**, are in fact very close to town, just across the entrance to the inner harbour, but to get there by road you have to go all the way round the Laguna de San Pedrito, before turning back towards Manzanillo along the narrow strip of land that forms Las Brisas. Frequent **buses** from the centre (marked "Las Brisas") run all the way along the single seafront drive; it's a rather strange area, as much suburb as resort, and the beach, steeply shelving and often rough, is perhaps not as good as those round the bay in the other direction. As the original seaside strip, Las Brisas offers a number of older, and consequently cheaper, hotels and restaurants, but – except when it's flooded by holiday-makers from Guadalajara – the whole place has a quiet, slightly run-down feel. If you want to **stay** by the beach, take the bus out here and have a look around. *La Posada*, Lázaro Cárdenas 201, right at the end of the seafront drive towards Manzanillo (Ⓣ314/333-1899, Ⓦwww.hotel-la-posada.info; ❼), is by far the best choice – a delightful, 23-room hotel a few metres from the beach, excellent made-to-order breakfasts included in the price. Cheaper options include *Las Brisas*, Lázaro Cárdenas 1243 (Ⓣ314/333-2716; ❺), and the marginally better-equipped *Star*, Lázaro Cárdenas 1313 (Ⓣ314/333-2560; ❺), which is on the beach side of the street and has a pool.

Better and more sheltered swimming can be found along the coast further round, where the bay is divided by the rocky Peninsula de Santiago. "Miramar" **buses** run all the way to the far side of the bay, past the settlements of **Salahua** and **SANTIAGO** and a string of beaches. The best are around the far edge of the peninsula (get off the bus at Santiago). Here you'll find the reasonable **hotel** *Maria Cristina*, 28 de Agosto 36 (Ⓣ314/333-0966; ❺), two blocks inland from Santiago's zócalo, with a pool, a pleasant garden and some rooms that can take four (❻) and eight (❾) people. There are several restaurants here, too, both in the village and down on the beach: *Juanito's*, on the highway (Ⓣ314/333-1797), is a long-standing favourite with gringos and locals alike and has **Internet** access and *larga distancia* **phone and fax** facilities, as well as excellent **food**, mainly hamburgers and various Mexican snacks.

If you're prepared to walk a little way out onto the peninsula, you can reach the beautiful cove of **La Audiencia**, with its calm and tranquil water. From here, if you're feeling reasonably energetic and looking smart enough to get past the guards, you can climb over the hill to **Las Hadas** (ⓣ314/331-0101 or 01-800/713-3233, ⓦwww.brisas.com.mx; ❾) – the amazingly flashy, glistening, wedding-cake-style hotel complex where Dudley Moore and Bo Derek frolicked in the film *10*. It's worth seeing even if you can't afford a drink at any of the numerous bars. There's more flash and glitz at the all-inclusive *Club Maeva* (ⓣ314/331-0800 or 01-800/523-8450, ⓦwww.clubmaeva.com.mx; ❾), further round the bay on **Playa Miramar**, but on the whole the hotels in the vicinity are thoroughly average, and **nightlife**, such as it is, is confined to a few discos strung out along the coast road.

South from Manzanillo

If all you need is a heaving ocean and a strip of beach backed by a few *enramadas*, then you're better off skipping Manzanillo altogether in favour of a series of infinitely preferable, though tiny resorts that adorn the shoreline 50–80km beyond. Easily accessible by bus, Cuyutlán, Paraíso and Boca de Pascuales boast great beaches that draw Mexican holiday-makers, but none is in any way elaborate, each equipped with very few facilities. To get to Cuyutlán and Paraíso from Manzanillo, first catch a bus (every 15min) 50km to the inland market town of **ARMERÍA**. The town has a bank, post office and long-distance bus stop on the main street, and, should you need to stay, a clean, good-value **hotel**, *La Herradura* (ⓣ313/328-8027; ❹), at the entrance to town coming from Manzanillo. To catch buses to Cuyutlán (every 30min; 20min) and Paraíso (every 45min; 15min), a few kilometres further south, walk two blocks north from the long-distance bus stop, then two blocks east to the market. For buses to Boca de Pascuales (every 45min until 6pm; 25min), you'll need to take a direct bus from Manzanillo and change at the market town of Tecomán, 20km south of Armería. Buses also run from Tecomán to Colima and Lázaro Cárdenas.

Cuyutlán

CUYUTLÁN, the largest of the three coastal resorts some 12km southwest of Armería, is also the most appealing, backed by an immense coconut grove that stretches along a narrow peninsula from here almost to Manzanillo. The old town around the zócalo is sleepy, its inhabitants idling away the day on wooden verandas under terracotta roofs. Life in the hotels by the beachfront malecón isn't much faster, except around Christmas and Semana Santa, when things liven up considerably and you should book well ahead to secure a room.

If you're staying for a couple of days, it's worth taking a trip out to the **Centro Ecológico el Tortugario** (US$1.50; closed Mon) – catch a cab from the zócalo (US$3) or stroll southwards down the beach for about 45 minutes. From July to December, three **turtle** species visit the local beaches to lay their eggs and a team from the centre goes out every night to collect them before they end up as someone's dinner. The newly hatched turtles are then kept in tanks for a couple of days before being released back into the sea, normally at around 4.30pm. At other times of the year there's a resident turtle population and lots of information on hand – some of the staff speak English. The sanctuary has a swimming pool and boats used for the three-hour **tours** (US$5) to

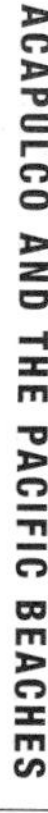

△ Acapulco cliff diver

Paraíso (see below) and back through the mangrove tunnels of the idyllic, jungly **Laguna Estero Palo Verde**, well known for its birdlife.

There's also a **Salt Museum** (daily 8am–6pm; donation) in town, two blocks east of the zócalo on Juárez, housed in an original, wooden salt *bodega*. Salt was worth more than gold in pre-Columbian times and if you're interested, the retired salt-workers who run the place will talk you through its long history.

In spring, the **coast** both here and further south is subject to the **Ola Verde**: vast, dark-green waves up to 10m high that crash down on the fine grey sand. Theories to explain their green hue vary widely – from the angle of the sun refracting off the wave to algal bloom – but whatever the reason, the Ola Verde has entered Cuyutlán mythology, ever since a huge tidal wave destroyed the town in 1932. At other times of the year the surf is impressive but easier to handle.

Outside the high season, **hotels** are affordable (in low season many places sell three nights for the price of two) and all clustered within a block or two of the junction of Hidalgo and Veracruz. The ones to go for are *Morelos*, Hidalgo 185 (Ⓣ313/326-4013; ❺), with good clean rooms, fans, hot water and the town's best swimming pool (US$1.50 for non-residents); the long-standing *Fénix*, Hidalgo 201 (Ⓣ313/326-4082, Ⓔhotelfenixcuyutlan@yahoo.com; ❹), which has some great old-fashioned rooms opening onto spacious communal verandas; and *San Rafael*, Veracruz 46 (Ⓣ313/326-4015; ❺), where some lovely rooms lead straight out onto the beach. All three hotels boast good **seafood restaurants**.

Paraíso and Boca de Pascuales

With your own vehicle you can reach **PARAÍSO** directly from Cuyutlán, or you could take the Laguna Estero Palo Verde boat tour (see above) and get off at the halfway point at Paraíso. However, by bus you'll have to return to Armería, from where it's 8km to this tiny place that consists of a few neglected buildings either side of the dust-and-cobble street. The beach is fun, though, with banks of crashing surf, and a few *enramadas* behind. Only at *Hotel Paraíso*, right on the seafront (Ⓣ in Colima 312/312-1032; ❺), is the feeling of dilapidation dispelled; the older rooms have character, but the new wing is more comfortable, and everyone uses the pool and watches the sunset from the bar. If you **camp** on the beach, they'll let you use a shower, especially if you buy a drink.

Smaller still, **BOCA DE PASCUALES**, 13km from Tecomán, is little more than a bunch of palapa restaurants and a beach renowned for huge waves and challenging surfing. Swimming can be dangerous, but otherwise it's a fine place to hang out for a few days. Beach **camping** is your best option; the uninspiring *Estrella del Surf* (no phone; ❸), on the way in, offers simple and somewhat overpriced rooms. The best **restaurant**, the expensive *Las Hamacas del Mayor* (Ⓣ313/324-3846), serves top-notch seafood and draws a large crowd despite its remote location.

Colima

Inland **COLIMA**, capital of the state of the same name, 100km from Manzanillo, is a distinctly colonial city, and a very beautiful one too, famed for its parks and overlooked by the perfectly conical **Volcán de Colima** and, in the distance, the Nevado de Colima. It doesn't offer a whole lot in the way of

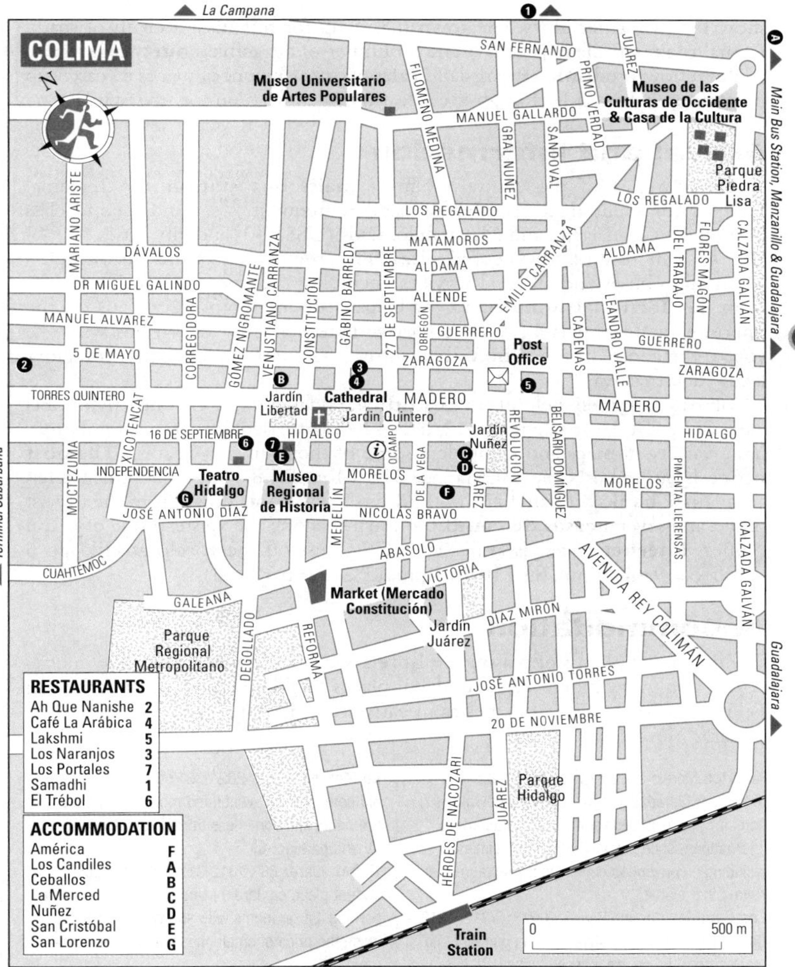

excitement, but it's a pleasant place to stop over for a night or two: cooler than the coast, but never as cold as it can get in the high mountains, and with some good-value hotels and restaurants to boot.

Archeological evidence – much of it explained in the city's museums – points to three millennia of rich cultural heritage around Colima, almost all of it wiped out with the arrival of Cortés' lieutenant Gonzalo de Sandoval who, in 1522, founded the city on its present site. Four years later Cortés decreed that Colima – named after Cilimán, a former ruler of the local Nahua people – should be the third city of New Spain after Veracruz and Mexico City. However, Acapulco's designation as the chief Pacific port at the end of the sixteenth century deprived Colima of any strategic importance and, combined with a series of devastating earthquakes, left it with few grand buildings to show for its former glory. The town makes up for this with a chain of shady formal **plazas** (called "jardíns") and a number of attractive **courtyards**, many of them now used as restaurants and cafés, wonderfully cool places to catch up on writing postcards – though the selection of these is uniformly awful.

Arrival and information

Some 2km east of the centre, Colima's **main bus station**, the Terminal Forañea (or Central de Autobuses) handles frequent first- and second-class buses from Guadalajara and Manzanillo. Taxis (US$1.40) and city buses #2, #4 and #5 run towards the central plaza from the station. Many second-class Manzanillo buses and all local services, including the one to Comala, operate from the **Terminal Suburbana** (or Central de los Rojos), 2km out on the opposite, western, periphery. If you arrive here, a #3, #4 or #6 bus will take you to the centre of town; from the centre, a #2 from Madero, at Revolucíon, leads back that way.

Colima's extremely helpful **tourist office**, Hidalgo 96, at Ocampo (Mon–Fri 9am–8pm, Sat 10am–2pm; ⓣ312/312-4360, ⓔturiscol@correo.col.gob.mx), has a variety of maps and pamphlets, some of them only in Spanish. The **post office** is on Jardín Nuñez, at Madero 247 (Mon–Fri 8.30am–5.30pm). There's a Banamex **bank** with an ATM on Hidalgo, a few doors down from the tourist office, and several **casas de cambio** on Juárez, along the western side of Jardín Nuñez. **Internet** access is available at CI@, just off the zócalo at Hildago 6 (Mon–Sat 9am–10pm, Sun 10am–4pm; US$1.50 per hour).

Accommodation

Colima boasts plenty of reasonable **hotels** within a few blocks of the centre. **Rates** don't vary much year-round, but places do fill up rapidly during the San Felipe and Todos los Santos fiestas in early to mid-February and late October to early November.

América Morelos 162 ⓣ312/312-0366, ⓔhameric@prodigy.net.mx. Colima's downtown hotel for business people, a fairly characterless, international-style place with all the facilities, including a convention centre, fancy restaurant and swimming pool. ❼

Los Candiles Camino Real 399 ⓣ312/312-3212. Comfortable, business-style hotel a couple of kilometres from the centre, passed by several bus routes (eg #10). Similar facilities to comparable spots downtown, but less expensive. ❻

Ceballos Portal Medellín 12 ⓣ312/312-4444, ⓦwww.hotelceballos.com. Colonial hotel right on the Jardín Libertad, with wonderfully spacious halls and high-ceilinged, attractive rooms with hand-painted furniture. Many have French windows and wrought-iron balconies. ❼

La Merced Juárez 282 ⓣ312/312-6969. Lovely old hotel with fan-ventilated rooms around a central patio, and some less attractive, newer rooms. TV and parking. ❹

Nuñez Juárez 88 ⓣ312/312-7030. Reliable budget place on Jardín Nuñez, again with private parking. Large rooms with showers are almost twice the price of small ones with shared bathroom. ❷

San Cristóbal Reforma 98, at Independencia ⓣ312/312-0515. Budget option offering clean, basic rooms, with or without a private bathroom and TV. ❷

San Lorenzo Cuauhtémoc 149 ⓣ312/312-2000. In a quiet part of town, but still reasonably central. Modern hotel with excellent, well-priced rooms. ❹

The Town

As in all these old cities, life in Colima centres on the **zócalo**, where you'll find the government offices (take a quick look at the distinctly second-rate murals in the Palacio de Gobierno) and the unimpressive Neoclassical cathedral. Quite out of character for this part of Mexico, however, the town actually boasts a couple of really good **museums**.

The most central of these, Colima's **Museo Regional de Historia** (Tues–Sat 9am–6pm, Sun 5–8pm; US$2.90), stands across the street from the Palacio de Gobierno in a lovely old building that also houses the university art gallery. Move swiftly through the stuff on **local crafts** – though the animal and diabolical masks used in traditional dances are interesting – and make for the later rooms, chock-full of **pre-Hispanic ceramics**: gorgeous figurines with superbly expressive faces, fat Izcuintli dogs and people working on mundane, everyday tasks. Though characteristic of western Mexican culture, these examples are specific to Colima, many of them found in *tumbas de tiro* – well-like tombs up to 16m deep, more commonly found in South America and the Pacific Islands. The cultural parallel isn't well understood, but explanatory panels (all in Spanish) show the different styles.

More widely trumpeted than the regional museum, the **Museo de las Culturas de Occidente** (Tues–Sun 9am–6.30pm; US$1.50), 1km northeast of Jardín Nuñez, holds another substantial collection of local archeology. You'll see the same kind of thing here as in the former, but more figurines: dogs with litters fighting, oversized frogs, surreal, serpent-headed deities, people blowing conch shells, playing musical instruments and dancing, even a man in a caiman mask whose dances were said to avert hurricanes. There's also a more detailed explanation of the rural agricultural society that produced such well-preserved tombs; again, all is in Spanish. In the same park as the museum, an auditorium hosts occasional concerts, plays and films. Look for posters advertising what's on.

Climbing the Nevado de Colima

The **Parque Nacional Nevado de Colima** comprises two beautiful volcanoes, snowcapped in winter, rising north of Colima. The **Volcán de Colima** (3900m), also known as Volcán de Fuego, is officially still active and smokes from time to time, though there seems little imminent danger. It is far less frequently climbed than its larger and less active brother, the **Nevado de Colima** (4335m), which, with its pine- and oak-forested slopes, is popular with local mountaineers during the clear, dry winter months. Unless there's a lot of snow – in December and January crampons and an ice axe are essential – and provided you are fit and can get transport high enough, it's a relatively easy **hike** up to the summit. The most popular option is to ascend the Nevado de Colima from the cabin at **La Joya** (3500m), but it's also possible to walk to the microwave station a little way beyond, from where it's a stiff but non-technical walk.

You'll need to set three days aside for the climb, take a sleeping bag and waterproofs, pack enough food and water for the trip, and walk from the village of El Fresnito. First, take a bus from Terminal Forañea in Colima to Ciudad Guzmán (about 90min) and from there catch a bus from stall #21 to **El Fresnito**, where there are very limited supplies. Ask for the road to La Joya, take this and keep right until the route becomes obvious. This rough service road for the microwave station leads up through cow pastures and goes right past the hut, about six to eight hours' walking (35km). You can tank up from the supply of running water here, but don't expect to stay in the hut, which is often locked, and even if open may be full as it only sleeps six. Plan on a day from La Joya to the summit and back, then another to get back to Colima, though a very fit walker starting before dawn could make the trip back to Colima, or at least Ciudad Guzmán, in a day. Note that **hitching** isn't an option as the logging roads up here are rough, requiring high clearance or 4WD vehicles, and see very little traffic.

With more time to spare, wander eight blocks north of the zócalo to the **Museo Universitario de Artes Populares** (Tues–Sat 10am–2pm & 5–8pm, Sun 10am–1pm; US$1), which has an eclectic but poorly explained collection of masks, traditional textiles and costumes, modelled by enormous papier-mâché figures, shoes, ceramics, images of the Virgin, toy aeroplanes and a small musical instrument collection including a violin made from scrap wood and a Modelo beer can.

The source of some of the museums' treasures is the **archeological site** at La Campana (Tues–Sun 9am–5pm; US$2.20, free on Sun), a couple of kilometres northwest of the centre, which dates to around 500 AD and contains some small pyramids, temple remains and one tomb. To get there, head north out of town along Gabino Barreda and take a left onto Avenida Tecnológico.

On a hot day, you can cool off in one of two parks: the **Parque Piedra Lisa** to the east – the "sliding stone" in the name referring to a rock that is said to ensure your return if you slide on it – and the **Parque Regional Metropolitano** (Wed–Sun 10.30am–5pm) to the southwest. The latter has a small, depressing zoo, a boating lake with boats for rent, and a swimming pool (closed for renovation at the time of writing).

Eating and drinking

For a town of its size, Colima has a great range of places to eat, from restaurants serving **Oaxacan** and local specialities to the region's best **vegetarian** food.

Ah Que Nanishe 5 de Mayo 267, west of Mariano Arista ☎312/314-2197. Surprisingly inexpensive courtyard restaurant specializing in dishes from the owner's native Oaxaca. The name means "how delicious" in Zapotec. Well worth the walk out from the centre. Closed Tues.

Café La Arábica Gabino Barreda, at Madero ☎312/307-0025. The smell of roasting Colimense beans heralds this tiny coffeeshop. Americano, espresso or cappuccino made from excellent locally grown, roasted and ground coffee – but little else – is served.

Lakshmi Madero, at Revolución ☎312/312-6433. Mainly a wholefood shop and bakery producing great banana and carrot bread, but with a restaurant area for veggieburgers and nutritious drinks.

Los Naranjos Gabino Barreda 34, north of Madero ☎312/312-0029. Slightly upmarket restaurant where you can get a substantial comida corrida for around US$6 and a good selection of meat dishes, especially beef.

Los Portales Hidalgo, on Jardín Libertad ☎312/312-8520. Nice place on the zócalo, great for sitting outside and watching the world go by. Reasonably priced antojitos and seafood dishes.

Samadhi Juan Rulfo 458 ☎312/313-2498. Despite its inconvenient relocation to a site about 2km north of the centre, the almost entirely vegetarian menu, featuring veggieburgers, crepes and delicious *licuados*, still justifies a visit.

El Trébol 16 de Septiembre, at Degollado ☎312/312-2952. Comfortable, cosy and inexpensive place, just off the zócalo, for egg dishes, snacks and light meals. Closed Sat.

Around Colima: Comala

The best time to be in Colima is on a clear winter day when the volcanoes in the **Parque Nacional Nevado de Colima** dominate the views to the north. Climbing them, while not that difficult, needs some planning (see box, p.523). You can get a closer look, however, by spending an afternoon at **COMALA**, 10km north of Colima. Not only do you get a fantastic view of the mountains from the town's colonial plaza, but you can sip a beer or margarita while competing *mariachi* bands pitch for your business. Four **restaurants**, huddled together under the zócalo's southern portal, each try to outdo the other by producing better *botanas* – plates of snacks, dips and tacos – free with drinks until about 6pm. Of course drinks are expensive (around US$2 for a beer or soft drink), but stay for an hour or so and you won't need a meal. There's little to choose between them, so, if you can face the roving *mariachis*, a restaurant crawl might be an idea. Find a place where one band dominates, otherwise you'll find yourself trying to disentangle the sound of three. Friday and Saturday are the liveliest times, when you can mingle with day-tripping, predominantly middle-class Mexicans from Guadalajara; on Sundays and Mondays there are craft markets in the square. **Buses** run frequently to Comala from Colima's Terminal Suburbana (every 15min; 20min).

South to Lázaro Cárdenas

Beyond the state of Colima you run into a virtually uninhabited area: there are occasional beaches, but for the most part the mountains drop straight into the ocean – a spectacular sight, but offering little reason to stop. Moving into Michoacán, **CALETA DE CAMPOS**, some 70km short of Lázaro Cárdenas, is the first and in many ways the best place to stop. It's a small village, barely electrified and with distinctly dodgy plumbing, but with two lovely beaches and an impressive ocean view. The streets are unpaved, and horses stand tied to hitching posts alongside the campers of dedicated American surfers and the fancy new cars belonging to visitors from the city. There are two **hotels** – *Yuritzi* (Ⓣ753/531-5010; ⑤), recommended, with its own generator and water supply, and the less expensive *Arcos de Guadalupe* (Ⓣ753/531-5038; ④) – and a string of makeshift bar-restaurants down at the beach. For much of the year the place is virtually deserted, but in winter, when the Californian beach boys come down in pursuit of sun and surf, and at weekends, when families pile in from Lázaro Cárdenas, it can take on some crowds. If both hotels are full, which at such times they can be, beg a hammock under the thatch of one of the beach bars: most are happy enough to have you as long as you eat there, too, though you may be bitten by voracious mosquitoes.

In any case the beach should definitely be seen at night, when, if the conditions are right, the ocean glows a bright, luminous green. This is not a product of the excellent local beer, or of the Acapulco Gold marijuana that allegedly grows in the surrounding mountains, but a naturally illuminated, emerald-green plankton: go swimming in it and you'll come out covered in green sparkles. The phenomenon is common to much of this coast, and also seen in Baja California – but is nowhere as impressive as here. One word of warning: the second beach, cut off by a narrow, rocky point, looks like an unspoilt paradise (which it is), but you can only get there by boat or a stiff climb over the rocks – try to swim round and you'll be swept out to sea by a powerful current. Locals are well used to picking up tourists who suddenly find themselves several hundred metres offshore.

In addition to the occasional long-distance services, local buses make the trip from Caleta de Campos to **LÁZARO CÁRDENAS** several times a day. But there's little reason to go there except to get somewhere else – it's strictly industrial, dominated by a huge, British-funded steelworks. If you get stuck for the night, you'll find several small **hotels** around the bus terminals, which are next to each other in the centre. *Hotel Veronica*, Javier Mina 7 (Ⓣ753/532-3409; ④), is a good budget option, with fan, TV and hot water, while *Hotel Casablanca*, one of the tallest buildings in town at Nicolas Bravo 475 (Ⓣ753/537-3480; ⑥), has air-conditioned rooms with phones and is a more upscale choice. There are three **bus stations**: the ones served by Sur de Jalisco and La Linea and Galeana, Ruta Paraíso and Parhikuni are opposite one another on either side of Avenida Lázaro Cárdenas; to get to the third, served by Elite, Estrella Blanca and others, walk out the front of the Galeana station, turn right, right again and second right. Buses to Caleta de Campos depart from the Galeana station. If you need information, the **tourist office** is at *Hotel Casablanca* (Mon–Sat 9am–2pm & 5–7pm, Sun 9am–2pm).

Playa Azul

Once a small-time, slow-moving beach not far removed from Caleta de Campos, **PLAYA AZUL** has been rather overrun by the growth of Lázaro Cárdenas, 20km away. However, there are still several reasonably priced hotels and a moderate beach, backed by scores of palapa restaurants. Aside from lying on the sand (the surf is too heavy for safe swimming), all there is to do is walk 2km north to see the rusting hulk of the *Betula*, a Norwegian sulphuric acid carrier that foundered in 1993 (all the acid has now disappeared into the sea).

Long-distance **buses** don't pass directly through Playa Azul, so ask to be dropped off at La Mira, the nearest town on the highway – from here, numerous local buses and *combis* run the remaining 7km down to Playa Azul. Coming from Lázaro Cárdenas, local buses direct to Playa Azul (marked "Playa") leave from along Avenida Lázaro Cárdenas. The road into town crosses four streets, parallel to the beach and running down to the vast plaza at the southern end. As you come in you'll pass *Hotel Playa Azul* (☎753/536-0024; ❻), where the best **rooms** have air-conditioning and a pool view. You can also **camp** here (❹), though the campsite is little more than a patch of dirt behind the hotel. The pool, though, is a better prospect (US$2 for non-guests), and at weekends their larger pool, El Balneario, complete with water slide, costs no more. For somewhere a little cheaper, try the friendly and comfortable *María Isabela* (☎753/536-0016; ❺), on the far side of the plaza, which also has a pool. The best and priciest accommodation is at *Hotel María Teresa*, also on the plaza (☎753/536-0005; ❻), which has attractive rooms, a decent pool and a garden bar-restaurant serving breakfast only (included in the price). **Beachfront restaurants** such as *El Pirata del Caribe* serve mainly seafood lunches and dinners, while the poolside restaurant at *Hotel Playa Azul* has a good range of international food, including pizzas and pasta dishes.

Zihuatanejo and on to Acapulco

Although it's only about 7km from Ixtapa to Zihuatanejo, the two places could hardly be more different. **IXTAPA**, a purpose-built, computer-planned "paradise" resort, is quite simply one of the most soulless towns imaginable – to say nothing of being one of the most expensive. Twenty-odd years down the line, it still hasn't begun to mellow or wear itself in, and its single coastal drive still runs past a series of concrete boxes of varying heights. These completely cordon off Ixtapa's admittedly lovely stretch of beach from the road, forcing those who can't afford the hotels' inflated prices to trespass, or even use the hotels' facilities. You might want to visit one of the clubs in the evening, but you will definitely not want to stay.

ZIHUATANEJO, on the other hand, for all its growth and popularity in recent years, has at least retained something of the look and feel of the village it once was – what building there has been is small-scale, low-key and low-rise.

ACCOMMODATION

Angela's Hotel and Hostel	B
Brisas del Mar	L
Bungalows Adelmar	M
Bungalows Sotelo	J
Los Cabañas Trailer Park	Q
Casa Bravo	D
Casa de Huéspedes Elvira	I
Casa Nancy	F
La Casa Que Canta	R
Palacios	N
Posada Michel	C
Raúl Tres Marias	G & K
Susy	E
Ulises	H
Villa del Sol	P
Villas Miramar	O
Villa Vera	A

RESTAURANTS

Bandidos	7
Las Brasas	5
Cafetería Nueva Zelanda	3
Cenaduria Antelia	6
Mariscos El Acacio	2
Pollos Locos	4
La Sirena Gorda	8
Splash Bar	1

Nevertheless, this is a resort town first and foremost: taxi drivers are forever touting for customers, trinket and tacky T-shirt shops are abundant, and as likely as not there'll be a cruise ship moored out in the bay. But at least here there are a fair number of small, reasonably priced hotels and some inexpensive restaurants. For some it's the ideal compromise – quiet, almost dead by night, yet with the more commercial excitements of Ixtapa within easy reach. The one real problem is its popularity – with strictly controlled development, rooms can be hard to find in the centre of Zihuatanejo, a region of barely ten small blocks hemmed in by the main roads into town, the yacht marina and the beach.

Arrival and information

Buses arrive at Zihuatanejo's Central Camionera, about twenty minutes' walk from the centre of town. There are plenty of taxis outside, and if you walk a couple of hundred metres to the left, you can pick up passing "Zihuatanejo" buses, which will generally drop you off at the top of Juárez, the place where the **Ixtapa minibuses** leave (6am–10pm; every 10min). Buses marked "Noria" go straight past the youth hostel and *Casa Nancy*. *Combis* making the thirty-minute run between Zihuatanejo and the **airport**, 20km south (and only 2km off the highway to Acapulco), also pass by the bus station, before dropping off (and picking up) just outside the market, at Gonzalez and Juárez. You can buy long-distance bus tickets at the downtown Estrella Blanca office on Alvárez, at Ramírez (Mon–Sat 9am–3pm & 4–8pm).

Zihuatanejo's facilities are widely scattered. The **tourist office** (Mon–Fri 8am–4pm; ⓣ755/554-2747) is inconveniently located about 2km out of town in the Ayuntamiento building, Paseo Zihuatanejo 21, near the Fuente del Sol fountain. The Ixtapa office is at Paseo de las Gaviotas 12, behind the cinema (Mon–Fri 9am–2pm & 4–7pm; ⓣ755/553-1270). The **post office** (Mon–Fri 8am–5.30pm, Sat 9am–1pm) is on Avenida Carteros at the northeastern corner of town; and the most useful **bank**, Banamex (Mon–Fri 9am–6pm; 24hr ATM), lies on Ejido, at Guerrero. The **casas de cambio** don't generally offer good rates, but Central de Cambios Guiball, on Galeana just south of Bravo, is open until 9pm daily and has a *larga distancia* **phone** for inexpensive collect calls. There are a handful of **Internet cafés** along Guerrero, most of which charge US$1 per hour.

Accommodation

Zihuatanejo's **high season** is fairly long, from mid-November or earlier to the end of April. Outside those times some of the slightly more expensive hotels drop their **rates** to those of the budget places – which tend to vary their prices less. Rates are generally charged per person, not per room, so there's little advantage for groups. Just ten minutes' walk from the centre, the **youth hostel**, Paseo de las Salinas (ⓣ755/554-2003; US$5 per person), has compact, four-bed, single-sex rooms – or you can camp in the garden and use all their facilities for US$2.50. Although a little more expensive, *Angela's Hotel and Hostel*, Ascencio 10 (ⓣ755/554-5084, ⓦwww.zihuatanejo.com.mx/angelas; US$8 per person), offers more appealing three-bed dorms, as well as some private rooms (❹).

You could also opt to stay at one of the **beaches**, covered opposite. **Playa la Madera**, while part of Zihuatanejo, has a different feel, slightly removed and a touch exclusive – though not necessarily more expensive. **Playa la Ropa**, more than a kilometre from the centre, feels a world apart; next to the *Villa del Sol* (see opposite), *Las Cabañas Trailer Park* (ⓣ755/554-4718; ❸) is a small, clean **campsite and trailer park** that is more like someone's back garden. You can also camp officially at the north end of Playa Linda, north of Ixtapa. The hotels in **Ixtapa** are all expensive: around US$80–100 in low season, US$120–200 in high season.

Central Zihuatanejo

Casa Bravo Nicolás Bravo 8 ⓣ755/554-2548. Comfortable, mid-range hotel where the rooms have TV, private bath and fans (or you can pay more for a/c). All-day hot water. ❺

Casa de Huéspedes Elvira Alvarez 109 ⓣ755/554-2061. Small rooms with basic bathrooms, attached to one of the seafood restaurants on Paseo del Pescador. Right by the beach. ❹

Casa Nancy Paseo del Cantil 6 ⓣ755/554-2123. Clean, tidy and cheap family-run guesthouse with hammocks on the roof and a peaceful location, but still only ten minutes' walk from the waterfront over the lagoon footbridge. Buses marked "Noria" pass the door. ❹

Posada Michel Ejido 14 ⓣ755/554-7423. Bright hotel right in the centre. Tastefully decorated, with a ground-floor corridor that resembles a railway carriage. ❺

Raúl Tres Marias Alvarez 214 ⓣ755/554-6706, ⓔgarroboscrew@prodigy.net.mx. Shiny and spotless, with some sea views from the top floor, a/c and bathrooms with hot water all day. Another, cheaper branch of the same hotel is at Noria 4, just across the lagoon footbridge (ⓣ755/554-2191; ❺). ❻

Susy Alvarez 2 ⓣ755/554-2339. Well-run hotel with modern, if slightly cheerless, rooms with small balconies, fans and shower. ❺

Ulises Armada de México 9 ⓣ755/554-3751. Budget option close to the sea. The box-like rooms with aluminium doors and shutters can appear somewhat dreary, but are good value. ❹

Villa Vera Morelos 165 ⓣ755/554-2920, ⓦwww.ixtapa-zihuatanejo.net/villavera. Not the cheapest in town, but very well run, decorated in soothing colours and equipped with a pool. ❻

Playa la Madera and Playa la Ropa

Brisas del Mar López Mateos, Playa la Madera ⓣ755/554-2142, ⓦwww.brisasdelmar.net. Spacious suites with private terraces complete with hammocks from which to enjoy the sea views. Other facilities include a fitness centre, and massages are available to ease the hammock cramp. ❾

Bungalows Adelmar Adelita 40, Playa la Madera ⓣ755/554-9190, ⓔbungalows_adelamar@hotmail.com. Immaculately clean, modern rooms, all with well-equipped kitchens – and some with small gardens – an excellent pool and tranquil location close to the beach. Up to four people in a room. Recommended. ❽

Bungalows Sotelo López Mateos, Playa la Madera ⓣ755/554-6307. Comfortable apartments with a/c, satellite TV, balconies, kitchens and great sea views. The most luxurious rooms have jacuzzis on the balcony. ❻

La Casa Que Canta Playa la Ropa ⓣ755/555-7030 or 01-800/710-9345, ⓦwww.lacasaquecanta.com. Luxury hillside hotel which winds down to the sea, featuring beautifully landscaped salt- and fresh-water swimming pools, breezy rooms with traditional Mexican decorations, spa and fitness centre. The cheapest rooms in low season start at US$360. ❾

Palacios Adelita 15, Playa la Madera ⓣ755/554-2055. Good, spacious and clean rooms, with tiled bathrooms and sea views from the balconies. Small pool, too. Rooms with a/c cost ten percent more. ❺

Villa del Sol Playa la Ropa ⓣ755/555-5500 or 01-888/389-2645, ⓦwww.hotelvilladelsol.net. Lush gardens of hibiscus and bougainvillea hide spacious luxury suites all with terraces and some with small private pools. Of course there's a big pool, too, a private patch of beach, spa, fitness centre and other creature comforts. Expensive even off-season (rooms start at US$240), and there's a US$60 minimum to be spent on food per day during the winter season. ❾

Villas Miramar Adelita, Playa la Madera ⓣ755/554-3350. Beautiful hotel with rooms on both sides of the road. Those with sea views and access to a small pool cost more than others set in luxuriant gardens around a larger pool. Also a penthouse suite with kitchen for four people (US$150). ❽

Activities

Zihuatanejo has a few things to distract you from lying on the beach. Quite apart from jet skiing, parasailing and getting dragged around on a huge inflatable banana, you could arrange to go **fishing** for dorado, yellowtail, bonito or big game. Trips, run by Lanchas de Pesca (ⓣ755/554-2056), leave from the pier in Zihuatanejo. Prices vary according to the size of your group: seven hours' fishing costs US$150 for four people, US$250 for six (in a bigger boat). **Scuba-diving** courses are organized by Whisky Water World (ⓣ755/554-0147, ⓦwww.ixtapa-sportfishing.com) on Paseo del Pescador, next to the pier. A half-day resort course with one dive costs US$50, and one-tank reef dives for certified divers will set you back US$45. Full PADI certification takes five to six days and costs US$400.

Just behind the beach you'll find the **Museo Arqueológico de la Costa Grande** (Tues–Sun 10am–6pm; US$0.60), a small and simple affair not deserving more than twenty minutes, though it does its best to tackle the history of what has always been a fairly insignificant region.

The beaches

Four beaches surround Bahía de Zihuatanejo. **Playa Principal**, in front of Zihuatanejo, is unspectacular, but interesting to watch when the fishermen haul in their catch early in the morning and sell much of it there and then. A narrow footpath heads east from the end of the beach across the normally dry outlet of a drainage canal, then winds around a rocky point to the calm waters of **Playa la Madera**, a broad, moderately clean strand with a couple of restaurants, and hotels and condos rising up the hill behind. Climb the steps between the condos to get to the road if you want to continue a kilometre or so over the headland, past the mirador with great views across the bay, to **Playa la Ropa**, which takes its name – "Clothes Beach" – from the silks washed up here when one of the *nao de China* (see p.532) was wrecked here. This is Zihuatanejo's finest road-accessible beach, palm-fringed for more than a kilometre, with a variety of beachfront restaurants and hotels. You can walk a further fifteen minutes beyond the end of Playa la Ropa to **Playa las Gatas**, the last of the bay's golden beaches, its crystalline blue water surrounded by a reef, giving it the enclosed feel of an ocean swimming pool. This makes it safe for kids, though the sea bottom is mostly rocky and tough on tender feet. Nonetheless, the clear waters are great for **snorkelling** – you can rent gear from vendors among the rather pricey palapa restaurants. Las Gatas is directly opposite the town and accessible by launches (daily 9am–5pm, last return 5.30pm; 10min; US$3 round-trip) run by Lanchas de Pesca (see p.529). Buy tickets at the entrance to the pier.

The long sweep of **Ixtapa**'s hotel-backed **Playa de Palmar** is fine for volleyball or long walks, but often too rough for easy swimming, and plagued by the inevitable jet skis. Powered water sports are also in evidence at the inappropriately named **Playa Quieta**, some 5km north of Ixtapa. The water here is wonderfully clear and the surrounding vegetation magnificent, but you won't get anything to eat or drink unless you pay handsomely to enter the confines of the three luxury resorts that dominate the beach. The next beach along, **Playa Linda**, is a huge sweep of greyish sand, with a cluster of *enramadas* at the pier end where the bus drops you off. Heading out along the beach, the restaurants are supplanted by coconut groves, which in turn give way to small cliffs. To find all the space you need, just keep walking away from the crowded pier end.

Boats leave from the pier at Playa Linda for **Isla Ixtapa** (9am–5pm; US$3.50 round-trip), a small island a couple of kilometres offshore with two swimming beaches, a spot reserved for diving, all the usual aquatic diversions and a few restaurants – but nowhere to stay. You can also get there on a daily launch from Zihuatanejo, which leaves at 11am (1hr; US$10). The boat returns at 5pm.

For absolute peace and quiet, the best idea is to take a day-trip out of Zihuatanejo to visit **Barra de Potosí**, a tiny community situated at one end of an expansive, postcard-perfect, golden sandy beach that curves steeply round the bay and keeps going as far as the eye can see. The inky-blue ocean is backed by gentle hills in a gorgeous patchwork of greens and browns. To get there, board a Petatlán-bound **bus** from the station on Calle Palmas and ask the driver to drop you off at the village of Los Achotes. From here, pickup trucks leave when full to run the final bone-rattling twenty minutes to the beach: you'll be dropped off at one end of the bay where a bunch of *enramadas* sell delicious seafood for half the price of the restaurants in town. There's not much to do here except relax in a hammock, but if you ask at the *enramadas*, fishermen will take you on a **boat trip** through the dense mangrove forests in the lagoon adjacent to the beach, home to innumerable exotic birds. If you want to stay, you can ask to pitch a tent under a palapa, head for the only **hotel**, the *Barra de Potosí* (Ⓣ755/554-8290; ❼), which drops its rates by over fifty percent in low season, or opt for one of a handful of **B&Bs**, including the four-room, disabled-accessible *Our House* (Ⓣ755/556-7310, Ⓦwww.ourhouse-zihua.com; ❽).

Eating, drinking and nightlife

You can barely move for **restaurants** in Zihuatanejo: the waterfront Paseo del Pescador is the place for fresh fish, expensive drinks and atmosphere; the cheapest place, as ever, is the **market** on Juárez. There isn't much **nightlife** in town, however: for that people head over the hill to Ixtapa, where a typical night out starts at *Señor Frog's*, in the shopping plaza opposite the *Presidente Inter-Continental* hotel, or *Carlos 'n Charlie's*, next to the *Posada Real Ixtapa* hotel, two bar-restaurant chains offering food, plenty of alcohol, loud music and dancing, before progressing to the flashy and expensive *Christine* nightclub at *Hotel Krystal*. Buses to Ixtapa run until about 10pm; after that you'll need to get a taxi (US$4 to Zihuatanejo).

Bandidos 5 de Mayo 8 ☎755/553-8072. Although a little touristy, with overpriced fish and steak dinners, this is one of the few places in Zihuatanejo with live music (mainly salsa) daily 9pm–2am.

Las Brasas Cuauhtémoc, at Bravo (no phone). Simple but very cheap breakfasts and comidas corridas served in this cavernous and friendly restaurant that runs through to Galeana.

Cafetería Nueva Zelanda Cuauhtémoc, at Ejido ☎755/554-2340. You pay slightly over the norm for the good *licuados*, tortas, breakfasts and cappuccinos in this diner-style café.

Cenaduría Antelia Nicolás Bravo 14 ☎755/554-3091. A great little spot to eat tacos, enchiladas and the like until midnight. The café next door has chairs and tables in a quiet alley off Nicolás Bravo.

Mariscos El Acacio Ejido, at Galeana ☎755/554-2087. Simple seafood restaurant, much cheaper than those on Paseo del Pescador, but still with a pleasant atmosphere as you eat at tables on a tree-shaded, pedestrianized street.

Pollos Locos Nicolás Bravo 15 ☎755/554-4044. Tasty wood-fired meals – chicken, pork ribs, steaks – served without ceremony. Not much ambience, but good for a quick bite.

La Sirena Gorda Paseo del Pescador ☎755/554-2687. Fairly expensive but well sited, right where evening strollers can watch you dine on succulent tuna steaks and seafood cocktails in the balmy night air. Creatively decorated with paintings of the eponymous Rubenesque mermaids. Closed Wed.

Splash Bar Guerrero, at Ejido. Coloured bulbs illuminate this dim bar, where people lurk in corners playing chess or backgammon to the accompaniment of constant surf, ski and snowboard videos. Open 7pm–2am.

On to Acapulco

From Zihuatanejo to Acapulco – along Hwy-200, a fast road with regular buses – the aspect of the coast changes again, becoming flatter, more heavily populated and regularly cultivated. At **PAPANOA**, 50km on, there's a beautiful beach, some 15km long, overlooked from the point at its far end by *Hotel Club Papanoa* (☎742/422-0150; ❻). Obviously someone's plan for a luxurious, Club Med-style development, it never quite panned out – there's still considerable comfort, a pool, and a stairway down to the beach through manicured gardens, but the place has a distinctly run-down air. It's not cheap, but nor is it in the high-luxury bracket, and a double **room** is easily large enough for four. You could also quite easily **camp** on this stretch of sand, getting supplies from the nearby village of Papanoa. The hotel restaurant is also good value, and the staff friendly.

Beyond Punta Papanoa the road again leaves the coast for a while – although with sturdy transport of your own, there are several places where you could find your way down to a surf-pounded beach – not to rejoin it until shortly before Acapulco itself. Of little interest otherwise, **Coyuca de Benitez**, the last village of any size, has some pleasant restaurants overlooking the Río Coyuca, and you can arrange boat trips downriver into the Laguna de Coyucán. Nearby you could certainly find somewhere to camp or sling a hammock at **Playas de San Jerónimo**, but again it's an exposed, windswept and wave-pounded stretch of sand. You could also get a minibus from Coyuca to the beach at **El Carrizol**, where it's possible to rent a reasonably priced bungalow.

Acapulco

Everyone – even if they've not the remotest idea where it is – has heard of **ACAPULCO**, yet few people know what to expect upon arrival. Acapulco lies 230km south of Mexico City, bordered by the rugged Sierra Madre to the east and beautiful Acapulco Bay to the west. Truth is, as long as you don't yearn to get away from it all, you'll find almost anything you want here, from magnificent beaches by day to clubs and discos by night. That said, the manicured and sanitized hotel zone, where everything is geared towards package tourists, can be thoroughly off-putting, as can some of the restaurants and clubs, which exhibit a snobbery seldom seen elsewhere in Mexico. In the old town, the grime, congestion and exhaust fumes are the most apparent aspects of the city's **pollution problem**, which peaks in the rainy season when everything from plastic bags to dead dogs gets washed off the streets and back alleys into the bay.

What Acapulco undoubtedly has going for it, however, is its stunning **bay**: a sweeping scythe-stroke of yellow sand backed by the white towers of the high-rise hotels and, behind them, the jungly green foothills of the sierra. And, even though there are hundreds of thousands of people here throughout the year – the town itself has a population approaching one and a half million – it rarely seems oppressively crowded. Certainly there's always space to lie somewhere along the beach, partly because of its sheer size, partly because of the number of rival attractions from hotel pools to parasailing and "romantic" cruises. **Hawkers**, too, are everywhere – there's no need to go shopping in Acapulco, simply lie on the beach and a string of goods will be paraded in front of you. Most of the hawkers are easy enough to handle, but they can become irritating and at times heavy. For women, and women alone in particular, the constant pestering of would-be gigolos can become maddening. For anyone, the derelict downtown back streets can be dangerous at night – remember that this is still a working **port** and, in the midst of all the tourist glitz, real poverty remains. It is best to not leave valuables lying about on the beach or temptingly displayed in hotel rooms.

The star-shaped Fuerte de San Diego and the several freighters tied up along the quayside are testament to Acapulco's sixteenth-century status as one of Mexico's most important ports, the destination of the famous *nao de China*, which brought silks and spices from Manila and returned laden with payment in Mexican silver. Most of the goods were lugged overland to Veracruz and from there shipped onwards to Spain. Mexican Independence, Spain's decline and the direct route around southern Africa combined to kill the trade off, but for nearly three hundred years the shipping route between Acapulco and the Far East was among the most prized and preyed upon in the world, attracting at some time or other (if you believe all the stories) every major pirate. In one such raid, in 1743, Lord Anson (the "Father of the British Navy") picked up silver worth as much as £400,000 sterling from a single galleon, and altogether, with the captured ship and the rest of its cargo and crew, collected booty worth over a million even then. With the death of its major trade, however, Acapulco went into a long, slow decline, only reversed with the completion of a road to

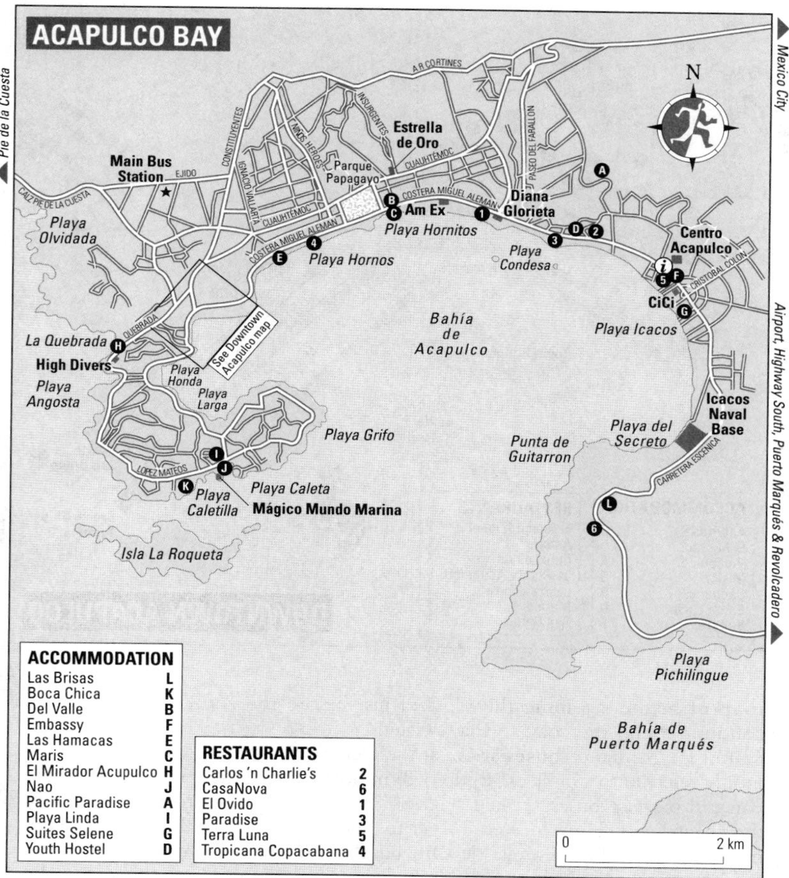

the capital in 1928. Today only a minor port compared with Veracruz, Tampico and Coatzacoalcos on the Gulf coast, Acapulco's economic mainstay is tourism.

Orientation, arrival and information

Acapulco divides fairly simply into two halves: the **old town**, which sits at the western end of the bay, with the rocky promontory of **La Quebrada** rising above it and curving round to protect the most sheltered anchorage; and the **resort area**, a string of hotels and tourist services following the curve of the bay east. A single seafront drive, the **Costera Miguel Alemán** – usually just "Costera" – stretches from the heart of the old town right around the bay, linking almost everything of interest. You can reach everywhere near the zócalo on foot, but to get further afield, frequent **buses** (look for "Caleta/Base", "Zócalo" or "Hornos") run all the way along Costera. From the east "C Río" buses travel past all the big hotels, then turn inland onto Cuauhtémoc, where they pass the Estrella de Oro **bus station** and the

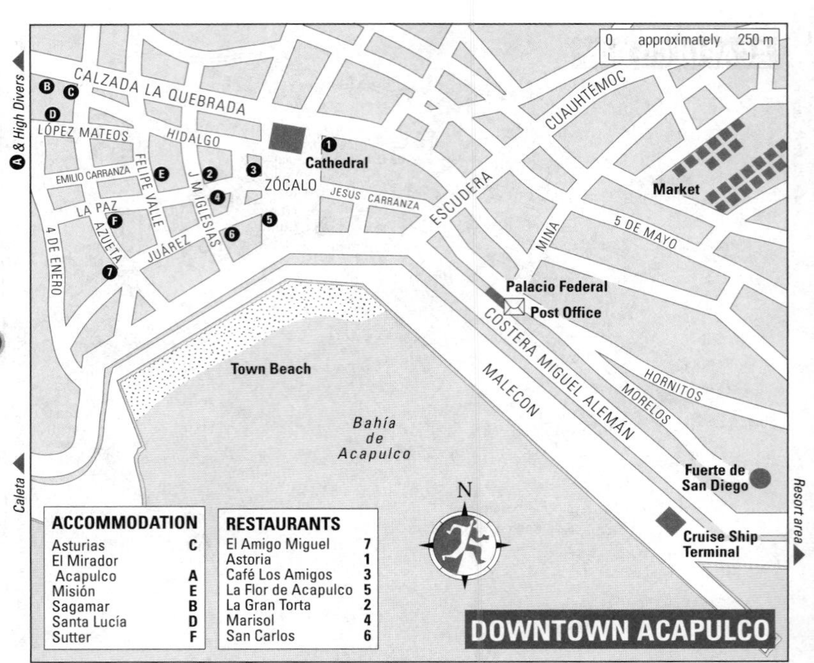

market before rejoining the Costera just before the zócalo. "Caleta" buses continue round the coast to Playa Caleta.

Most long-distance **buses** arrive at the Central de Autobuses on Ejido (commonly referred to simply as "Ejido"), 3km northwest of the zócalo, from where you can pick up buses marked "Centro" or "Caleta" to get to the area where the cheaper hotels are located. To get to Ejido from the zócalo, look for buses marked "Mocimba". Estrella de Oro buses from Mexico City arrive at their own terminal, 3km west of the zócalo, again connected to the centre by "Caleta" city buses, or to the hotels along Costera by "Río/Base" buses. Both stations have a guardería. The busy international **airport** (information on ⓣ744/435-2060), 23km southeast of the city, is linked only by expensive taxis (US$17–20 from most points) and the Transportaciones Aeropuerto shuttle service (US$7.50 one-way; will pick up from hotel; ⓣ744/462-1095). Cheaper still is to take a town bus to Puerto Marquéz, then another from there to the airport. Frequent flights leave Acapulco for numerous other domestic and international destinations. For flight details, contact any travel agent or the airlines (see "Listings", p.541).

Acapulco's **tourist office** (daily 8am–10pm; ⓣ744/484-4416) is located, in the Centro Acapulco complex, a block west of CiCi Waterpark (see p.539). Unless you strike lucky and encounter an enthusiastic staff member, you're likely to come away with little but an armful of brochures. For more edifying reading, try the **book swaps** at some of the budget hotels or browse through the selection of magazines at the bigger hotels and *Sanborn's*, two blocks west of the zócalo. For 24-hour tourist information and assistance, call the **toll-free phone number** (no charge if calling from Acapulco): ⓣ744/481-1100.

Addresses along Costera

Finding places along Costera can be tricky, as the numbering system is completely meaningless: 50 could be followed by 2010, which is next door to 403. The best **landmarks**, apart from the big hotels, are (moving east from the zócalo) **Parque Papagayo**, the roundabout with the **Diana Glorieta statue** and the **CiCi waterpark**.

Accommodation

As with everything in Acapulco, hotel rooms are far less expensive in the **old town**. Head for the streets immediately to the west and slightly inland of the **zócalo**, in the calles La Paz and Azueta, and particularly on Calzada La Quebrada where it leads up the hill. In contrast to most of Mexico, many hotels in this area charge by the person rather than per room.

You won't find places as cheap out along **Costera** but, if you want to stay by the tourist beaches and the clubs, there are a few reasonably priced options, especially off-season, when even some of the fancier hotels along Costera become quite competitively priced. A new and much needed **hostel** has opened in a good location on the Costera, at no. 116 opposite the *Fiesta Americana* hotel. *Hostal Juvenil K3* (Ⓣ744/481-3111, Ⓦwww.k3acapulco.com) is a clean, friendly place with small, air-conditioned four-bed dorms (US$17.50 per person), lockers, a kitchen and snack bar. The hotels at the smaller beaches of **Caleta** and **Caletilla**, a ten-minute bus ride from the centre, are rather older than those along Costera, mostly patronized by Mexican families, and often booked up in advance.

Still further out there's **Pie de la Cuesta**, a quiet alternative 15km north of Acapulco. This is the only place with official year-round **camping**, at *Acapulco Trailer Park* (Ⓣ744/460-0010; ❹).

Acapulco's **high season** lasts longer than most, from late November or early December through to the end of April.

In the centre

Asturias Calzada La Quebrada 45 Ⓣ744/483-6548, Ⓔgerardomancera@aol.com. Simple budget option, fractionally more expensive than the competition by virtue of its small pool. ❹

El Mirador Acapulco Plazoleta La Quebrada 74 Ⓣ744/483-1155 or 01-800/021-7557. Though you pay for the location – right above the rocks where the divers plummet – this is still a fine hotel, featuring cottage-like rooms with kitchenettes, ranged along the clifftop. Three pools. ❽

Misión Felipe Valle 12 Ⓣ744/482-3643. The best hotel in the centre. An old colonial-style house, formerly the American consulate and later a Wells Fargo office, with attractive rooms spread out around a mango-shaded patio. Continental or Mexican breakfasts, and book swap. ❻

Sagamar Calzada La Quebrada 51 Ⓣ744/483-5053. Despite the tatty exterior, the rooms aren't bad for the price. Ask for one of the five rooms with a balcony. ❹

Santa Lucía López Mateos 33 Ⓣ744/482-0441. The pick of the budget hotels: clean rooms with fans and private bathroom. Cheap and good value. ❸

Sutter Azueta 10 Ⓣ744/482-0209. Although more spacious than others of a similar price, the rooms are rather plain; the ones in the back are quieter. ❹

Along Costera

Due to the confusing nature of Costera's numbering system (see box, above), the following hotels are listed in order of their distance along Costera from the zócalo.

Del Valle Manuel Gómez 150, opposite the eastern entrance to Parque Papagayo ⓣ744/485-8336. Spacious, modern rooms (some with a/c), a pool and private kitchens (outside the rooms) which can be rented for US$6 a day. ❺

Embassy Costera 50, opposite CiCi ⓣ744/481-0881. Best value in this part of town, with a small pool and a/c rooms. Some have seen better days, so look at a couple before deciding. Convenient for the nightclubs. ❻

Las Hamacas Costera 239, 1km east of the zócalo ⓣ744/483-7709, ⓦwww.hamacas.com.mx. The closest international-standard hotel to the centre. Swimming pool, comfortable rooms, cable TV, although not located at the most attractive part of the beach. ❾

Maris Costera, at Wilfrido Massieu ⓣ744/485-8440. A good choice if you're looking for a high-rise on the beach with all the amenities, but not too expensive. Ideal location roughly halfway between the centre and Playa Condesa. ❾

Pacific Paradise Punta Bruja 1, near Playa Condesa ⓣ744/481-1413. Mediterranean-style resort with spotless, attractive rooms on three floors. Situated a few blocks back from the Costera, so night-times are quieter and it's better value than many of the beachside establishments. ❻

Suites Selene Cristóbal Colón 175, next to CiCi ⓣ744/484-2977. Cosy hotel with a pool, private parking, a/c rooms and kitchen-equipped suites for four people. ❻

Caleta and Caletilla

Boca Chica on the point at the western end of Caletilla ⓣ744/483-6601. Beautifully sited hotel with a pool and some great views of either Isla La Roqueta or the beach (cheaper). ❽

Nao east end of Caleta ⓣ744/483-8710. Faded but acceptable hotel with a pool; usually full of Mexican families. Fan-cooled rooms with shower, some much better than others. ❺

Playa Linda Costera 1, as you reach Caleta ⓣ744/482-0814. Renovated hotel with nicely decorated rooms, some with sea-view balconies. All rooms (sleeping up to four) have a/c, TV and fully equipped kitchenettes. ❻

Pie de la Cuesta

The following hotels are listed in order of distance from Hwy-200. All are right by the beach and reduce their prices dramatically out of season.

Bungalows María Cristina ⓣ744/460-0262. Good-value suites for up to five people with fully equipped kitchens, and balconies; the rooms are fine, too. ❺

Casa de Huéspedes Playa Leonor ⓣ744/460-0348. Simple but clean rooms, breezier on the upper floor. Not as good value as the other options. ❺

Villa Nirvana ⓣ744/460-1631, ⓦwww.lavillanirvana.com. Delightful retreat with spacious rooms painted in soothing pastels around an attractive garden and great pool. Rooms with kitchen facilities and a little beach cottage also available. ❺

The Town

No one comes to Acapulco for the sights. By day, if people aren't at the beach or asleep, they're mostly scouring the expensive shops. If you only do one thing in Acapulco, though, make sure you see its most celebrated spectacle, the leap of the daredevil **high divers** (see box, opposite).

About the only place in Acapulco that gives even the slightest sense of the historic role the city played in Mexico's past is the **Museo de Acapulco** in the old town (Tues–Sun 9.30am–6.30pm; US$3, free on Sun). It's situated inside the **Fuerte de San Diego**, an impressive, if heavily restored, star-shaped fort built in 1616 to protect the Manila galleons from foreign corsairs. The building's limited success is charted inside the museum, where displays also extend to the spread of Christianity by the proselytizing religious orders and a small anthropological collection. Air-conditioned rooms make this a good place to ride out the midday heat, and you can pop up on the roof for superb views over Acapulco. The only other cultural diversion in the centre is on Cerro de la

Pinzona, near La Quebrada, where a mural by famous Mexican artist **Diego Rivera** covers the entire outside wall of the house of his former model and partner, Dolores Olmedo. The work, made of seashells and coloured tiles, depicts various figures of Aztec mythology, although the hammer and sickle in the original (Rivera was a communist) was removed on government orders.

Along Costera, the **Centro Acapulco** is home to the convention centre and **Centro Cultural**, which has an art gallery, a crafts store and a theatre, and also hosts a regular programme of cultural events with a regional bias.

The beaches

To get to the best of the sands **around Acapulco Bay** from the centre of town, you're going to have to get on the bus; there is a tiny beach right in front of the town, but it's not in the least inviting, with grey sand made greyer by pollutants from the boats moored all around it.

Caleta, Caletilla and La Roqueta

Playas Caleta and **Caletilla** (any "Caleta" bus from Costera) have a quite different atmosphere from those in the main part of the bay. Very small – the two are divided only by a rocky outcrop and breakwater – they tend to be crowded with Mexicans (the foreign tourists who once flocked here have since decamped east), but the water is almost always calm and the beach is reasonably clean. Most enticingly, you can sit at shaded tables on the sand, surrounded by Mexican matrons whose kids are paddling in the shallows, and be brought drinks from the cafés behind; not particularly cheap, but considerably less than the same service would cost at the other end of the bay. There are showers here, too, and, on the rock, the **Mágico Mundo Marina** (daily 9am–6pm; US$3), a water park with a predictable aquarium and sea-lion show, decent water slides and a choice of the pool or the bay to swim in.

From outside the complex, small boats ply the channel to the islet of **La Roqueta**, where there are more and yet cleaner beaches, a small zoo (daily 10am–4pm; US$0.30) and beer-drinking burros, one of the town's less compelling attractions. Catch one of the glass-bottomed boats (frequent, daily 8am–6pm) and keep your ticket for the return journey: US$3 for the direct

Acapulco's divers

Acapulco's famed **clavadistas** plunge some 35m from the cliffs of La Quebrada into a tight, rocky channel, timing their leap to coincide with an incoming wave. Mistimed, there's not enough water to stop them hitting the bottom, though the chief danger these experts seem to face is getting back out of the water without being dashed against the rocks. It could easily be corny, but it's undeniably impressive, especially when floodlit at night. The times – 12.45pm, 7.30pm, 8.30pm, 9.30pm and 10.30pm – are rigidly adhered to. A typical display involves four exponents, three taking the lower (25m) platform with two diving simultaneously, the fourth diving from the upper level after first asking for the Virgin's intervention at the clifftop shrine. The final diver in the last show carries a pair of flaming torches. From the road you can see the spectacle for nothing, but you'll get a much better view if you go down the steps to a **viewing platform** (US$2.50) more or less opposite the divers. Get here early for a good position. Alternatively, you can sit in the bar at *El Mirador Acapulco* hotel (US$12.50 cover includes two drinks) or watch from their expensive *La Perla* restaurant. To get there, simply climb the Calzada La Quebrada from the town centre, about fifteen minutes' walk from the zócalo.

launch or US$5 for those that detour past the submerged one-tonne nickel and bronze statue of the Virgin of Guadalupe. Whether you are off to La Roqueta or only going to Caleta, leave early (especially at weekends) for the best of the sun and at least a sporting chance of getting a beach chair or a patch of sand. Behind the beach a group of moderately priced restaurants and cheaper *loncherías* offer good breakfasts and fish lunches.

Along Costera and on to Revolcadero

The main beaches, despite their various names – Hamacas, Hornos, Hornitos, Morro, Condesa and Icacos – are in effect a single sweep of sand. It's best to go some considerable distance round to **Playa Condesa** or **Playa Icacos**, in front of hotels (which make good points of reference) such as the *Hyatt Regency* and the *Casa Inn*, or opposite the Centro Acapulco, where the beach is far less crowded and considerably cleaner. It's easy enough to slip in to use the hotel showers, swimming pools and bars – there's no way they're going to spot an imposter in these thousand-bed monsters. The *Hyatt Regency*, at the very far end (Ⓣ744/469-1234, Ⓦwww.acapulco.regency.hyatt.com; ⑨), is the swankiest of the bunch. The beaches around here are also the place to come if you want to indulge in such frolics as being towed around the bay on the end of a parachute, water-skiing, or sailing. Outfits offering all of these are dotted at regular intervals along the beach; charges are standard though the quality of the equipment and the length of the trips can vary.

Beyond this end of the bay to the south are two other popular beaches: **Puerto Marqués** and **Revolcadero**. On the way you'll pass some of the fanciest hotels in Acapulco. *Las Brisas*, overlooking the eastern end of the bay (Ⓣ744/469-6900, Ⓦwww.brisas.com.mx; ⑨), is probably the most exclusive of all, its individual villas offering private swimming pools and pink jeeps to every occupant. Puerto Marqués (buses marked "Puerto Marqués") is the first of the beaches, a sheltered, deeply indented cove with restaurants and beach chairs right down to the water's edge, overlooked by two more deluxe hotels. You can continue by road to Revolcadero (though only an occasional bus comes this far) or get there by boat down a narrow inland channel. The beach, a long exposed stretch of sand, is beautiful but frequently lashed by a surf that makes swimming impossible.

Pie de la Cuesta

Pie de la Cuesta, around 15km north of Acapulco, is even more open to the vicissitudes of the ocean. It's definitely not for swimming – even if these weren't the massive waves that dump on the beach, there are said to be sharks offshore – but it's good a place, as you can imagine, to come and watch the sun sink into the Pacific or to ride horseback along the shore. The sand extends for miles up the coast, but at the Acapulco end, where the bus drops you, there are several rickety bars and some tranquil **places to stay**, away from the hubbub of the city.

Behind, and only separated from the ocean by a hundred-metre-wide sandbar on which Pie de la Cuesta is built, lies the **Laguna de Coyuca**, a vast freshwater lake said to be three times the size of Acapulco Bay, which only connects with the sea after heavy rains. Fringed with palms, and rich in bird and animal life, the lagoon is big enough to accommodate both the ubiquitous noisy jet skiers and the more sedate **boat trips** that visit the three lagoon islands. Various outfits along the hotel strip offer tours – prices hover around US$7.50 per person but it's worth checking what's on offer and how long the cruise is, as times tend to differ. Most boats stop on one island for lunch (not included in the price) and swimming. The bus ("Pie de la Cuesta") runs east every ten minutes or so past the zócalo along Costera. The last bus back leaves around 8pm.

Activities

Acapulco Bay has a multitude of water-sport activities on offer. You can go **sea fishing** and **scuba diving** – tours run by Fish-R-Us, Costera 100 (Ⓣ744/482-8282, Ⓦwww.fish-r-us.com) – or take a **boat trip** on the bay. Night-time excursions are particularly appealing, illuminated by the lights of the town shining out from all around the coast. After dark, too, most of the boats lay on some kind of entertainment as they cruise. Prices vary with the length of the trip and what's on offer, but US$10–20 for a couple of hours with a free bar is typical at night, US$8–12 with no free bar during the day. Thrill-seekers will appreciate the high-speed **jet-boat rides** through the mangrove lagoons at Puerto Marqués beach offered by Shotover Jet, Costera 121 (Ⓣ744/484-1154, Ⓦwww.shotoverjet-acapulco.com), the **bungy jumping** from a crane-like structure at Playa Condesa, just west of the *Fiesta Americana* hotel (US$60 per jump, including a free T-shirt and diploma) and, budget permitting, the **skydiving** (tandem jumps US$220 per person with Skydive Acapulco, Costera 130) Ⓣ744/484-6672, Ⓦwww.skydiveacapulco.com). You'd have to have a sadistic streak, however, to pay for the privilege of taking a **horse-drawn carriage ride** along the impossibly congested and noisy Costera. Going east along Costera, at Playa Icacos, the **CiCi Waterpark** (daily 10am–6pm; US$6 or US$7 with dolphin show; Ⓣ744/484-1970, Ⓦwww.cici.com.mx) makes for a welcome break from the beach, where you can splash around in swimming pools and on water slides and watch performing dolphins. The other amusement park along Costera, **Parque Papagayo**, at Playa Hornos (free entrance), attracts picnicking families with its green spaces, boating lake and fairground rides. Acapulco also boasts around fifty public **tennis** courts and four eighteen-hole **golf** courses.

Eating and drinking

Though it may not seem possible, there are even more **restaurants** than hotels in Acapulco. To eat cheaply, though, you're confined to the area around the **zócalo**. Places actually on the square tend to be quite expensive, but are great for lingering over breakfast at an outdoor table.

Eating by the **beach** – where there's some kind of restaurant at every turn – is of course very much more expensive, and increasingly so as you head east, although the food is normally very good. Throughout the tourist zone, especially along Costera, *100% Natural*, a chain of 24-hour "healthy" eating places, serves good salads, fruit shakes, burgers and the like at grossly inflated prices, and also offers home delivery (Ⓣ744/486-2033). Alternatively, you can choose from *McDonald's*, *KFC*, the *Hard Rock Café* and several raucous Mexican bar-restaurant chains such as *Carlos 'n Charlie's* and *Señor Frog's*.

One thing to keep an eye out for wherever you are is **pozole**, a hearty pork and vegetable stew traditionally served on Thursdays and Saturdays, but available every day.

In the centre

El Amigo Miguel Juárez 31 Ⓣ744/483-6981. Two locations at the junction of Juárez and Azueta, both serving good seafood at reasonable prices in clean, if harsh, surroundings.

Astoria inland end of the zócalo next to the cathedral Ⓣ744/483-2944. Quiet café, cheaper and classier than *La Flor de Acapulco*, tucked just off the plaza under the shade of a huge tree. Good coffee and light meals.

Café Los Amigos La Paz 10 Ⓣ744/482-2390. Popular shady spot just off the zócalo. Excellent breakfasts and tortas served all day, plus daily specials of spaghetti, pork chops and the like. Hawkers are actively discouraged, so it's relatively peaceful.

La Flor de Acapulco on the zócalo ☎744/421-7649. Good for Mexican dishes, cocktails or just a coffee. Not the cheapest on the square, but a pleasant spot to linger and a popular meeting place for travellers.

La Gran Torta La Paz 6, opposite the *Marisol* ☎744/483-8476. Considerably less choice than its neighbour – mainly tortas and tacos – but still inexpensive.

Marisol one block from the zócalo on La Paz ☎744/483-1475. Offers a terrific variety of tasty Mexican dishes, including plenty of breakfast menus, at bargain prices – understandably popular.

San Carlos Juárez 5, one block from the zócalo ☎744/482-6459. Another great budget restaurant in the centre, serving good *pozole* and comidas corridas all day for US$3.

Along Costera and beyond

CasaNova Carretera Escénica, south of *Las Brisas* hotel ☎744/446-6237. One of Acapulco's most highly regarded restaurants, as much for its spectacular location nestled in a hillside overlooking the bay as for its fine northern Italian cuisine.

El Ovido just west of Diana Glorieta ☎744/481-0203. Upscale nouvelle Mexican cuisine, combining traditional Mexican flavours with French and Italian dishes. Good *crema quemada* (Mexican-style *crème brûlée*) and dreamy views of the bay from the dual-level, open-air dining room.

Paradise next to the bungy-jumping tower, just west of the *Fiesta Americana* hotel ☎744/484-5988. Just one of many alfresco places in this area, serving expensive seafood which you can eat on the beachfront terrace or directly beneath the plummeting divers. Try also *Barbarroja*, *Baby Lobster*, *Bambu* and *El Sombrero* (slightly cheaper).

Terra Luna west of CiCi, opposite the *Hard Rock Café* ☎744/484-2464. Excellent crepes as well as French/Italian dishes and imaginative salads.

Nightlife

If you are so inclined, and perhaps more importantly, if you are extremely rich, you could spend several weeks in Acapulco doing nothing more than trawling its scores of nightclubs and bars, discos and dinner-dances. There are people who claim never to have seen the town during daylight hours. Anywhere with music or dancing will demand a hefty **cover charge** – usually not less than US$30 in high season, though often with a free bar – before they even consider letting you in. You can reduce prices by haggling, especially on weeknights and in the off-season when business is slow (this is particularly effective for larger groups), and by using the discount coupons distributed freely on the beach and along Costera. On "Ladies' Nights" women get a special discount.

The majority of the clubs and discos are out along **Costera** in the hotel district, beyond CiCi. They move in and out of fashion with bewildering rapidity; look for queues outside to see what's flavour of the month. If you're not easily intimidated, you could also try some of the **downtown bars and cantinas**: you'll find a couple that aren't too heavy around the bottom of Azueta – *La Sirena*, for example – but these aren't recommended for women on their own.

There are a number of **cinemas** along Costera, showing exclusively American films, in English with Spanish subtitles. More traditional entertainment can be found at the Fiesta Mexicana in the Centro Acapulco, which features two weekly performances by a troupe of the **Ballet Folklórico**. Although the admission is a bit steep, and the waiters persistent, the large-scale show – around sixty singers/dancers/musicians plus full regalia – is undeniably impressive.

Baby'O Costera, east of CiCi. One of the more consistently popular clubs, set in an imitation cave, though it does try to maintain a spurious exclusivity by turning people away at the door.

Carlos 'n Charlie's Costera, west of the Diana Glorieta. Very popular chain bar-restaurant to start the evening with a bite to eat (ribs a speciality), a few drinks and a shuffle on the small, invariably crowded dance floor before moving on to a nightclub.

Enigma Carretera Escénica, north of *Las Brisas* hotel. High-tech club complete with two waterfalls, 10m-tall statues and large windows overlooking the bay. Exclusive and luxurious, though the club's claim that "you will never have to light your own cigarette" overdoes it.

Relax Lomas del Mar 4, opposite *El Presidente* hotel. While not as gay-friendly as Puerto Vallarta (see p.501), Acapulco does have some gay bars and discos: this is one of the more reliable – small and a little claustrophobic, but featuring strippers and other live shows.

Salon Q Costera, west of CiCi. Live Latino music, a reasonable cover charge (US$10; no free bar) and a slightly older clientele.

Tropicana Copacabana Costero, Playa Hornos. One of a series of similar bar-restaurants that tend to play *cumbia*, merengue and salsa as much as American rock. Diners take to the dance floor later in the evening.

Listings

Airlines America West ⓣ744/466-9257; American ⓣ744/481-0161; Aviacsa ⓣ744/481-3240; Continental ⓣ744/466-9063; Mexicana ⓣ744/486-7585 or 466-9121.

American Express Costera, just east of the Diana Glorieta ⓣ744/469-1100 (Mon–Fri 9am–6pm, Sat 9am–1pm). Will hold mail and exchange money.

Banks and exchange Banks (particularly Banamex) and casas de cambio (slightly poorer rates) are numerous along Costera. In the centre, there's a Bancomer and Santander Serfin on the zócalo.

Buses The first-class Estrella de Oro terminal at the corner of Cuauhtémoc and Wilfrido Massieu (city buses marked "C Río" from opposite the zócalo) handles hourly buses to Mexico City (5hr). The much larger Central de Autobuses (aka Estrella Blanca or Ejido; ⓣ744/469-2028; city buses marked "Ejido" or "Mocimba") handles the unified services of several companies; don't be surprised if you find yourself on a bus that doesn't match the company named on your ticket. Buses to Mexico City leave continually day and night in five classes: *futuro* and *primera* are the ones to go for, as the spacious seating and free drinks of the expensive *ejecutiva* class fail to justify the extra expense. Second-class, avoiding the autopista, is very slow. You can also get to Chilpancingo and Taxco, while first- and second-class buses run to Zihuatanejo, many of them continuing on to Lázaro Cárdenas.

Car rental Alamo ⓣ744/484-3305, Avis ⓣ744/466-9190, Budget ⓣ744/481-2433 or Hertz ⓣ744/485-8947.

Consulates Canada, Centro Comercial Marbella, Diana Glorieta ⓣ744/484-1305; UK, Centro Acapulco ⓣ744/484-1735; US, next to *Hotel Continental Plaza*, Diana Glorieta ⓣ744/484-0300.

Emergencies Cruz Roja ⓣ744/485-4100; Emergency IMSS Hospital ⓣ744/445-5353; Police ⓣ744/485-0334 or 486-8220; Tourist complaints ⓣ744/484-4416.

Internet Ikernet, upstairs at Carranza 14, just off the zócalo (8.30am–12.30am; US$1.50/hr. There are a few Internet facilities along Costera, one of the best being on the first floor of La Gran Plaza shopping mall (US$1/hr; allows you to save your remaining time for another session).

Laundry Lavandería Coral, Juárez, at Felipe Valle (Mon–Fri 9am–2pm & 4–7pm, Sat 9am–5pm; US$1 per kilo).

Pharmacy Plenty of 24hr places in the hotel zone along Costero; plus Botica de Acapulco, Carranza 3, just off the zócalo.

Phones Long-distance and collect calls can be made from Caseta Alameda (Mon–Sat 9am–8pm), on La Paz, next to *Café Los Amigos*.

Post office On Costera, three blocks east of the zócalo (Mon–Fri 8am–5.30pm, Sat 9am–1pm).

Travel agents About the nearest to the zócalo is Las Hamacas (ⓣ744/482-4892), at the hotel of the same name. A number of other agents are interspersed between the hotels along Costera.

Chilpancingo

Nestled in a bowl in the Sierra Madre Occidental, 130km north of Acapulco, restful **CHILPANCINGO**, Guerrero's modest state capital, makes a cool stop-off – it's higher than 1000m – on the trip inland to the capital. Well off the tourist circuit and lent a youthful tenor by the large

Fiestas

JANUARY

NEW YEAR'S DAY is celebrated everywhere. In **Cruz Grande** (Guerrero), on the coast road about 120km east of Acapulco, the start of a week-long feria.

Second Tuesday DÍA DEL SEÑOR DE LA EXPIRACIÓN is marked in **Pueblo de Coquimatlán**, near Colima (Colima), by a mass pilgrimage to a nearby hacienda.

26 In **Tecomán** (Col), on the coast road, a colourful religious procession.

FEBRUARY

2 DÍA DE LA CANDELARIA (Candlemas) celebrated in **Colima** (Col) and **Tecomán** (Col) with dances, processions and fireworks. Similar events in **Zumpango del Río** (Gro), on the road from Acapulco to Mexico City, and particularly good dancing in **Atzacualoya** (Gro), off this road near Chilpancingo.

5 Fiesta Brava – a day of bullfights and horse races – in **Colima** (Col).

CARNIVAL (the week before Lent: variable Feb–March). **Acapulco** (Gro) and **Manzanillo** (Col) are both famous for the exuberance of their celebrations; rooms can be hard to find.

MARCH

6 Local fiesta in **Zumpango del Río** (Gro) lasts through the night and into the following day – traditional dances.

10 Exuberant FIESTA DE SAN PATRICIO in **San Patricio** (Jalisco) continues for a week.

19 DÍA DE SAN JOSÉ is the excuse for fiestas in **Tierra Colorada** (Gro), between Acapulco and Chilpancingo, and **San Jerónimo** just outside Acapulco.

HOLY WEEK is widely observed: the Palm Sunday celebrations in **Petatlán** (Gro), just south of Zihuatanejo, are particularly fervent.

MAY

3 DÍA DE LA SANTA CRUZ. Saint's day festival in **Cruz Grande** (Gro).

5 The victorious battle of Cinco de Mayo commemorated – especially in **Acapulco** (Gro).

8 In **Mochitlán** (Gro), near Chilpancingo, the Festival de las Lluvias has pre-Christian roots: pilgrims, peasants and local dance groups climb a nearby volcano at night, arriving at the summit at dawn to pray for rain. Also a local fiesta in **Azoyu** (Gro), just off the coast road south of Acapulco. **Manzanillo** (Col) celebrates its Founder's Day.

15 DÍA DE SAN ISIDRO provokes a week-long festival in **Acapulco**. Celebrations too in **San Luis Acatlán** (Gro), south along the coast, where you might see the rare Danza de la Tortuga (Dance of the Turtle), and in **Tierra Colorada** (Gro).

student population, it has a traffic-free zócalo, which is a good place to sense the town's vibe.

The modern **Ayuntamiento** and **Palacio de Gobierno** combine a harmonious blend of Neoclassical and colonial influences. The latter is adorned with a huge bronze sculpture, *El Hombre Hacia el Futuro*; there's more monumental metalwork, along with busts of famous Guerrerans, in the Alameda, three blocks east along Juárez.

Directly opposite its replacement, the former Palacio de Gobierno houses frequently changing exhibitions in the **Instituto Guerrerense de Cultura** and the excellent little **Museo Regional de Guerrero** (both Tues–Sun

31 Puerto Vallarta (Jal) celebrates its Founder's Day.

JUNE
1 DÍA DE LA MARINA (Navy Day) in the ports, particularly **Puerto Vallarta**, **Manzanillo** and **Acapulco**.

13 DÍA DE SAN ANTONIO. A feria in **Tierra Colorada** (Gro).

Third Sunday Blessing of the Animals at the church of Señor de la Expiración in **Lo de Villa**, outside **Colima** (Col).

JULY
25 At **Coyuca de Benitez** (Gro), very near Acapulco, festival of the patron saint. A colourful fiesta too in **Mochitlán** (Gro).

AUGUST
6 A fiesta in **Petatlán** (Gro) distinguished by dances and a mock battle between *indígenas* and Spaniards.

23 DÍA DE SAN BARTOLOMÉ. In **Tecpán de Galeana** (Gro), between Acapulco and Zihuatanejo, religious processions the preceding night are followed by dancing, music and fireworks.

SEPTEMBER
15–16 INDEPENDENCE CELEBRATIONS almost everywhere – rooms are hard to find.

28 DÍA DE SANTIAGO celebrated in several villages immediately around **Acapulco** (Gro).

29 DÍA DE SAN MIGUEL exuberantly celebrated in **Azoyu** (Gro) and **Mochitlán** (Gro).

NOVEMBER
First week Colima's major feria runs from the last days of October until November 8.

2 DAY OF THE DEAD is widely observed, with picturesque traditions in **Atoyac de Alvarez** (Gro), just off the Acapulco–Zihuatanejo road.

DECEMBER
12 DÍA DE NUESTRA SEÑORA DE GUADALUPE, patroness of Mexico. In **Atoyac de Alvarez** (Gro) and **Ayutla** (Gro), there are religious processions and traditional dances, while **Acapulco** enjoys more secular celebrations. In **Manzanillo** (Col) the celebrations start at the beginning of the month, while in **Puerto Vallarta** (Jal) they continue to the end of it.

9am–6pm; free). Well-laid-out displays – some labelled in English – record the history of the state's native peoples from their migration from Asia across the Bering land bridge thirty thousand years ago to the Maya and Teotihuacán influences on their pottery and stelae. With the coming of the Spaniards, the region benefited from the Manila galleons that put into Acapulco and from Chilpancingo's location on the *Camino de China* from the coast to Mexico City. But the city's most dramatic chapter – vividly depicted on murals around the internal courtyard – came with the Independence struggle. After Hidalgo's defeat in the central highlands it was left to the southern populist movement, fuelled by the spread of land-grabbing haciendas and led by the skilled tactician **José María Morelos**, to continue the campaign. With almost the whole country behind them, they forced the Spanish – who still held Mexico City – to attend the Congress of Chilpancingo in 1813, where the Declaration of Independence was issued and the principles of the constitution – chiefly the abolition of slavery and the equality of the races – were worked out. Ultimately the congress failed and within two years the Spanish had retaken Guerrero and executed Morelos.

Practicalities

Buses from Mexico City and Acapulco arrive at either the Estrella Blanca or Estrella de Oro terminals, opposite each other, 2km east of the zócalo on 21 de Marzo – turn right and then right again along Juárez. Minibuses run into town along Juárez and back out along the parallel Guerrero. Madero crosses these two streets just before the zócalo, and it's around here that you'll find all the essential services.

If you want to **stay** overnight, you'll be perfectly comfortable at *Hotel Paradis*, Guerrero, at 21 de Marzo, right next to the Estrella de Oro terminal (☎747/471-1122; ❻), which has spotless, modern rooms and tiled floors and bathrooms. There are a couple of less expensive places near the zócalo: the colonial *Hotel Cardeña*, Madero 13 (no phone; ❷), with plain, slightly musty, en-suite rooms and cheaper bathless ones around a courtyard, and the *Laura Elena*, Madero 1 (☎747/472-4880; ❹), which has pleasant enough rooms – some much lighter and airier than others.

You can **eat** light meals or cake with an espresso at *El Portal*, beside the cathedral on Madero, or find more substantial meals at *Martita*, Guerrero 6B, and *La Parroquia*, with shaded outdoor tables off the north side of the zócalo. The café in the Casino del Estudiantes, on Guerrero near Madero, serves good-value comidas corridas, and is the best place to ask if there is anything happening in the way of **nightlife**.

South of Acapulco: the Costa Chica

It's hardly surprising that most tourists zoom straight through the stretch of Hwy-200 south of Acapulco: there's little in the way of facilities between here and Puerto Escondido – a good seven hours on the bus. However, if you have your own transport, it's worth taking some time out to explore this occasionally bizarre coastline, not least for the few great **beaches**.

The people who inhabit the area towards the border of Oaxaca are for the most part either indigenous Amuzgo or black – the latter descendants of African Bantu slaves who escaped and settled here. In fact the look of the land is vaguely reminiscent of parts of Africa – flat grazing country, many of whose villages consist of thatched huts. In **Coajinicuilapa**, the impression is reinforced by the predominance of round constructions, though these are in fact as much a local *indígena* tradition as an African one. From here a road runs some 20km down to the coast at **Punta Maldonada**, which, along with nearby San Nicolas, has some beautiful beaches but virtually no facilities, and only one or two buses a day. These places are famed, above all, for glass-clear water and are perfect for skin diving and snorkelling – most people come down in campers to take advantage.

If you want to break your journey in rather more comfort, there are two possibilities. **Ometepec**, an old gold-mining town a few kilometres inland of the main road before it reaches Coajinicuilapa, has several small hotels. Although it's off the highway, there are hourly buses to Acapulco, so it's easy enough to get back to the junction and pick up transport heading south from there. The second option is **Pinotepa Nacional**, across the border in the state of Oaxaca, where again there are a number of basic places to stay. Pinotepa's Sunday market is one of the best in the region, a meeting place for local Amuzgo, Mixtec and Chatino Indians.

Travel details

Buses

Bus services all along the coast are frequent and fast, with the possible exception of the stretch between Manzanillo and Lázaro Cárdenas, and there are almost constant departures on the major routes heading inland. The southern sector – Acapulco and Zihuatanejo – is served largely by Estrella de Oro and Estrella Blanca (first-class) and Flecha Roja (second-class). In the north there's more competition: Primera Plus, Transportes del Pacífico and Elite are the first-class stand-bys, while Servicios Coordinados and Flecha Amarilla are the most widely seen second-class outfits. The following list covers first-class services and some local second-class services. On most routes there are as many, if not more, second-class buses, which take around twenty percent longer.

Acapulco to: Chilpancingo (every 30min; 2hr); Cuernavaca (4 daily; 4hr); Guadalajara (3 daily; 17hr); Lázaro Cárdenas (5 daily; 6–7hr); Manzanillo (1 daily; 12hr); Mexico City (frequently; 5–7hr); Puerto Escondido (5 daily; 7hr); Puerto Vallarta (2 daily; 18hr); Salina Cruz (5 daily; 12–13hr); Taxco (2 daily; 5hr); Tijuana (2 daily; 49hr); Zihuatanejo (hourly; 4–5hr).

Barra de Navidad to: Cihuatlán (every 15min; 30min); Guadalajara (22 daily; 6–7hr); Manzanillo (every 30min; 1hr 30min); Puerto Vallarta (17 daily; 5hr).

Chilpancingo to: Acapulco (every 30min; 2hr); Mexico City (hourly; 3hr 30min).

Colima to: Comala (every 15min; 20min); Guadalajara (hourly; 3hr); Lázaro Cárdenas (4 daily; 6–7hr); Manzanillo (every 15min; 1hr 30min); Mexico City (8 daily; 11hr); Puerto Vallarta (2 daily; 6hr); Tecomán (every 15min; 45min); Tijuana (1 daily; 38hr).

Lázaro Cárdenas to: Acapulco (hourly; 6–7hr); Colima (1 daily; 6–7hr); Guadalajara (2 daily; 9hr); Manzanillo (2 daily; 6hr); Mexico City (4 daily; 11–14hr); Morelia (2 daily; 7–8hr); Pátzcuaro (1 daily; 7hr); Puerto Vallarta (2 daily; 12hr); Uruapan (2 daily; 6hr); Zihuatanejo (every 30min; 2hr).

Manzanillo to: Acapulco (3 daily; 12hr); Barra de Navidad (every 30min; 1hr 30min); Colima (every 15min; 1hr 30min); Guadalajara (hourly; 5–6hr); Lázaro Cárdenas (7 daily; 6hr); Mexico City (5 daily; 12hr); Puerto Vallarta (13 daily; 5–7hr); Tijuana (2 daily; 38hr).

Puerto Vallarta to: Acapulco (2 daily; 18hr); Barra de Navidad (10 daily; 5hr); Colima (2 daily; 6hr); Guadalajara (at least hourly; 6hr); Lázaro Cárdenas (3 daily; 12hr); Manzanillo (13 daily; 5–7hr); Mazatlán (4 daily; 8hr); Mexico City (7 daily; 14hr); Tepic (every 30min; 2hr 30min).

Zihuatanejo to: Acapulco (hourly; 4–5hr); Ixtapa (continuously; 15min); Lázaro Cárdenas (every 30min; 2hr); Manzanillo (2 daily; 7–8hr); Mexico City (6 daily; 9hr); Morelia (2 daily; 8hr); Puerto Vallarta (2 daily; 12–13hr); Salina Cruz (1 daily; 17–18hr); Tijuana (2 daily; 40hr).

Trains

Both the main rail lines in the region, one linking Manzanillo to Colima and Guadalajara and the other connecting Lázaro Cárdenas and Morelia, have been indefinitely suspended.

Flights

This section of Mexico's coast is well served by **flights**, with international services to Acapulco, Puerto Vallarta and Zihuatanejo and domestic flights to various points in between. Guadalajara and Mexico City are accessible from Manzanillo, Ixtapa/Zihuatanejo and Acapulco; Acapulco also has flights to US cities including Los Angeles, New York, Chicago, Phoenix, Dallas and Houston.

Puerto Vallarta is one of the busiest air hubs in Mexico, with flights to: Acapulco (1 daily); Amsterdam (1 weekly); Calgary (1 weekly); Chicago (5 weekly); Dallas (1 daily); Denver (2 weekly); Fairbanks (1 daily); Guadalajara (3–5 daily); Houston (1–3 daily); León (6 weekly); London (1 weekly); Los Angeles (2–4 daily); Los Cabos (4 weekly); Mexico City (5–11 daily); Monterrey (3–5 daily); Montreal (1 weekly); Newark (1 weekly); Oakland (6 weekly); Phoenix (2–3 daily); Portland (7 weekly); San Francisco (2–3 daily); Seattle (1–3 daily); St Louis (2 weekly); Tijuana (2 weekly); Toronto (2 weekly); Vancouver (1 weekly).

7

Veracruz

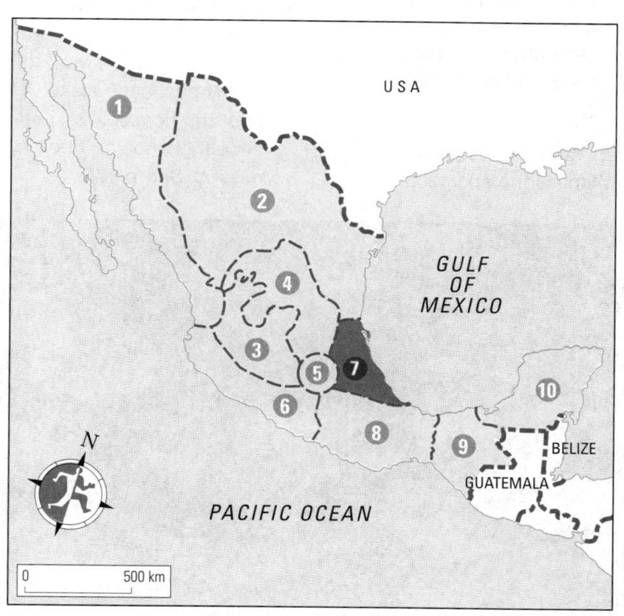

USA
1
2
4
3
5
6
7
8
9
10
GULF OF MEXICO
BELIZE
GUATEMALA
PACIFIC OCEAN
N
0
500 km

CHAPTER 7

Highlights

* **Xalapa** Enjoy the café culture in this university town surrounded by coffee fields. The Museum of Anthropology here is second only to Mexico City's. See p.552

* **Veracruz carnaval** Show your fiery side and salsa with divas wearing the most outrageous costumes in Mexico. See p.559

* **El Tajín and Papantla** Witness the spectacular Voladores dancers flying through the air. See p.569

* **San Andrés Tuxtla** The place for Mexican cigars – watch them being rolled and then smoke one of the freshly made *puros*. See p.574

* **Catemaco** Find peace in one of the last remaining tracts of jungle in Mexico, at this enchanting lake. A boat trip here is an experience that shouldn't be missed. See p.575

△ Café on the zócalo, Veracruz

7

Veracruz

The central Gulf coast is among the least-visited yet most distinct, atmospheric areas of Mexico. From the capital you descend through the southern fringes of the Sierra Madre Oriental, past the country's highest peaks, to a broad, hot and wet coastal plain. In this fertile tropical zone the earliest Mexican civilizations developed, and it remained densely populated throughout the pre-Hispanic era. Cortés himself began his march on the capital from Veracruz, and the city remains, as it was throughout colonial history, the busiest port in the country. Rich in agriculture – coffee, vanilla, tropical fruits and flowers grow everywhere – the **Gulf coast** is further enriched by oil and natural gas deposits.

The majority of the few tourists who find their way here are simply passing through. In part, at least, this is because the area doesn't especially need them and makes no particular effort to attract them; and in part the **weather** can be blamed – it rains more often and more heavily here than just about anywhere else. Yet even in the rainy season the torrential downpours are short-lived, and within a couple of hours of the rain starting, you can be back on the steaming streets in bright sunshine. Though there are long, windswept beaches all down the Atlantic coast, they are less beautiful than their Pacific or Caribbean counterparts, and many suffer pollution from the busy shipping lanes, the oil industry or even sewage outlets. Most of the coastal towns are commercial centres, of little interest to the visitor.

That said, the eastern slopes of the **Sierra Madre** hold a number of colonial cities worth a look at least in passing: **Xalapa**, seat of the state government, is worth a longer visit, with its balmy climate and superb archeological museum. **Veracruz** is among the most welcoming of all Mexican cities – too busy with its own affairs to create a separate life for visitors, you're drawn instead into the atmosphere of a steamy tropical port with strong echoes of the West Indies. Within a couple of hours lie **La Antigua**, where Cortés established the first Spanish government in the Americas, and **Cempoala**, ruined site of the first civilization he subdued. **El Tajín**, near the coast in the north of the state, is one of the most important archeological sites in the country, and **Filo Bobos**, only recently excavated, is also well worth a visit. Both sites are in an area where Totonac culture retains a powerful influence. To the south, **Catemaco** is a beautiful lake set in an extinct volcanic crater, where you can see the last remaining tract of Gulf coast **rainforest**. The area is renowned as a meeting place for native *brujos* and *curanderos*, witches and healers.

The state also has some great **food** – not only local coffee, fruit and vanilla (Mexicans inevitably take home a plastic bottle of vanilla essence as a souvenir), but also seafood. *Huachinango a la Veracruzana* (red snapper Veracruz-style) is

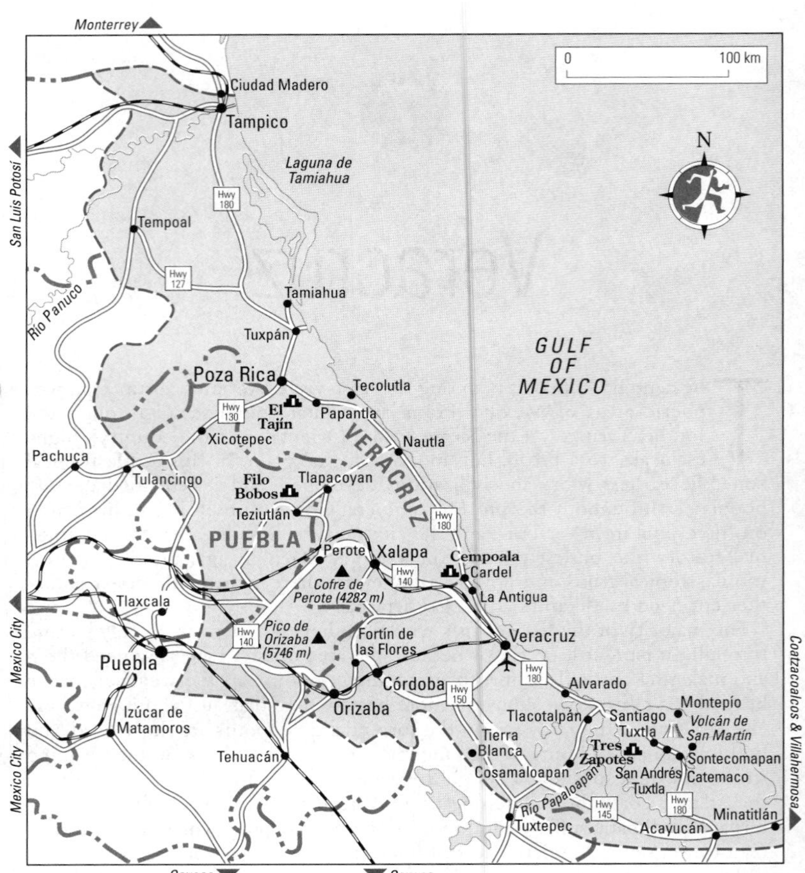

served across the country, and is of course on every menu here. But there are many more exotic possibilities, from langoustines and prawns to *jaiba*, a large local crab; look out for anything made with *chile chipotle*, a hot, dark-brown chile with a very distinctive (and delicious) flavour – *chilpachole de jaiba* is a sort of crab chowder that combines the two. Sweet tamales, too, are a speciality, and to wash it all down, the local brewery at Orizaba produces several distinctive beers – less expensive and better than the big national brands.

The route from Mexico City

If you take the direct bus **from Mexico City to Veracruz**, you'll bypass every major town en route on the excellent toll highway; if you're driving yourself, be warned that tolls are extremely high (about US$35 for the journey from Mexico City to Veracruz). For those pressed for time, the fast Hwy-150 is a blessing – Veracruz and the coast are very much the outstanding attractions –

but there are at least three cities in the mountains that merit a stop if you're in no hurry. This is, however, the rainiest area of all, and while it brings bounties in terms of great coffee and a luxuriance of flowers, downpours can become a problem. Particularly irritating – especially in October and November – is what the locals call *chipichipi*, a persistent fine drizzle caused by warm airstreams from the Gulf hitting cooler air as they reach the eastern face of the sierra. When it's not raining, though, this is among the most beautiful drives in Mexico. As Ixtaccíhuatl gradually disappears behind you, the snow on the **Pico de Orizaba** comes into view, and the plains of corn and maguey in the west are supplanted on the eastern slopes by woods of pine and cypress, and by green fields with fat and contented cows out to pasture.

Orizaba

ORIZABA, the first major town in the state of Veracruz, some 150km from Puebla, is largely an uninviting industrial city. What Orizaba lacks in charm, though, it makes up for in location, positioned at the foot of the **Pico de Orizaba** (or Citlaltépetl), a perfectly formed volcano and, at 5746m, the highest peak in Mexico.

There's further comfort in that the most important industry here is brewing, with the giant Cervecería Moctezuma producing some of the best **beer** in the republic – ask at the tourist office (see below) for details of tours. Seeing the town need only take a couple of hours even so, and there are more attractive places to spend the night further down the road at Fortín and Córdoba. If, however, you plan to tackle the Pico de Orizaba – and the **climb**, detailed in R.J. Secor's *Mexican Volcanoes*, is only for serious mountaineers – you should change here for the second-class bus to the villages of Serdán or Tlachichuca, from where the main trails start.

Orizaba's **tourist office** (Mon–Sat 8am–2pm & 4–9pm; Ⓣ272/726-5861), on the second floor of the Palacio Municipal, can help with further information and details of companies that arrange trekking and climbing activities in the area. Should you need **to stay**, *Hotel Trueba*, Oriente 6, at Sur 11, near the ADO bus station (Ⓣ272/724-2930, Ⓕ724-2744; ❺), is both comfortable and affordable. Similarly priced and on the same street is the colonial *Gran Hotel de France*, no. 189, at Sur 5 (Ⓣ272/725-2311, Ⓕ725-4444; ❺).

Fortín de las Flores

FORTÍN DE LAS FLORES, "Fortress of the Flowers", at a point where a beautiful minor route cuts across country to Xalapa, nearly 150km distant, lies on the old road to Córdoba, 15km northeast of Orizaba. Its name is singularly appropriate: here more than anywhere in the state you'll see flowers all over the place – in the plaza, at the hotels, on the hillsides all around. Rain, which is frequent from May to December, and the constant muggy warmth ensure their growth – in particular, with the coming of the rains in May, wild orchids bloom freely.

Here you can visit the **Hacienda de las Animas**, once a residence of Maximilian and Carlota, now part of the *Fortín de las Flores* hotel, on Avenida 2 between calles 5 and 7 (Ⓣ271/713-0055 or 0108; ❻). Rooms are somewhat musty, although there is a huge swimming pool set in attractive gardens. You can fully appreciate the luxuriance of the vegetation a couple of kilometres west of town at the **Barranca del Metlac**: above the ravine flourish plantations of coffee and fruit trees, while the banks of the torrent itself are thick with a stunning variety of wild plants, which attract hummingbirds and insects of all kinds.

Fortín is a small town, but with a number of good **places to stay**. *Hotel Posada Loma*, on the eastern edge of town opposite the market (Ⓣ271/713-0658, Ⓔposada66@prodigy.net.mx; ❼), has comfortable, air-conditioned rooms around a pretty garden. Also attractively situated, in dense vegetation overlooking the Córdoba Valley, roughly halfway between Fortín and Córdoba, are the two bungalows of *Las Magnolias B&B* (Ⓣ272/716-4908, Ⓔfrankania@yahoo.com; ❺) (the owners will pick you up at either bus station). Cheaper accommodation is available at the *Bugambilias* (Ⓣ272/713-1350; ❹), not far from the *Fortín de las Flores* hotel, on Avenida 1 between calles 7 and 9; several other inexpensive places to stay and **to eat** are nearby on Avenida 1 – there are several cheap cafés on the zócalo, too. Undoubtedly the best place to eat breakfast is at the *Posada Loma*, where you can enjoy sweet and savoury tortillas and views of the Pico de Orizaba. One block behind the zócalo, on Avenida 2, is an **Internet** café that charges US$1.50 per hour.

Córdoba

Second-class buses take the mountain road from Fortín to Xalapa fairly regularly, but it's only just over 100km further on towards the coast. A short local bus ride, meanwhile, **covers** the 7km to **CÓRDOBA**. At the centre of the local coffee trade, this is a busy modern town grown up around a somewhat decaying colonial centre. Founded in 1618 by thirty Spanish families – and so also known as the "City of the Thirty Knights" – its main claim to fame is that here, in 1821, the last Spanish viceroy, Juan O'Donoju, signed a treaty acknowledging Mexican Independence with General Iturbide, soon to become emperor. This took place in the Palacio de los Condes de Zevallos – known as the **Portal de Zevallos**, on the zócalo. The Portal is now filled with cafés and restaurants, where you can sit and sample Córdoban coffee or the local drink, *julep*, a cocktail of wine and mint. There's little else to do, but it's a pleasant enough place to while away an hour or two.

Practicalities

The smart **bus terminal** is located 3km south of the centre at Privada 4 between calles 39 and 41, a short taxi ride (US$1.50) from the zócalo, or take one of the buses marked "Centro". Buses to Fortín de las Flores leave every ten minutes or so from Calle 1, at Avenida 11, and take about fifteen minutes. The Palacio Municipal houses both the **tourist office**, on Avenida 1, at Calle 1 (Mon–Fri 9am–7pm, Sat 9am–1pm; Ⓣ271/717-1700, Ⓦwww.mpiocordoba.gob.mx), and the **post office**, on Avenida 3, half a block from the plaza (Mon–Fri 8am–4pm, Sat 9am–1pm).

The more pricey **hotels**, such as *Bello*, Avenida 2, at Calle 5 (Ⓣ271/712-8122; ❻), are located around the zócalo. Otherwise, you'll find plenty of cheap places scattered about, especially along Avenida 2. Closest to the action, overlooking the zócalo, are the *Virreynal*, by the side of the cathedral on Avenida 1, at Calle 5 (Ⓣ271/712-2377; ❺), which has been spruced up by recent renovation, and the quieter and marginally more expensive *Mansur*, in the same block of Avenida 1 (Ⓣ271/712-6000; ❺). The best of the budget hotels is the pleasant *Iberia*, slightly further out on Avenida 2 at no. 919 (Ⓣ271/712-1301; ❹). Around the zócalo, **places to eat** are good but pricey: *El Cordobés* (Ⓣ271/712-0798) has a varied menu with huge comidas, as does the cheaper *La Casa de la Abuela*, Calle 1, at Avenida 4 (Ⓣ271/712-0606), an ideal place for lunch, with street musicians serenading diners enjoying the comida corrida. Along Calle 15 there are some good seafood restaurants serving fresh fish in a variety of sauces, as well as some more unusual dishes such as black pepper casserole. Cheaper options offering traditional Mexican fare are along Avenida 2. For a break from Mexican food, try the sushi and other Japanese specialities at the comfortable *Mikasa*, Avenida 5 at no. 212-A (☎271/712-7613), or the excellent crepes at *Los 30's* on Avenida 9 between calles 20 and 22 (☎271/712-3379).

Xalapa

Although it's a slower route, a number of buses go from Mexico City to Veracruz via **XALAPA** (or Jalapa, as some locals and bus companies occasionally spell it). The state capital, Xalapa is remarkably attractive despite its relative modernity and traffic-laden streets, and is set in countryside of sometimes breathtaking beauty. The city sprawls across a tumbling hillside below the volcanic peak of the **Cofre de Perote** (4282m), and enjoys a richness of vegetation almost the equal of Fortín's (with which it also shares a warm, damp climate). In addition to these natural advantages, Xalapa has been promoted by its civic leaders as a cultural centre, and frequent music festivals, or other events, may well add to your stay. Home of the **University of Veracruz**, it's a lively place, enjoyable even if you do nothing more than hang out in one of the many wonderful cafés that pack the centre of town, sip the locally grown coffee and watch life pass by.

Arrival and information

Xalapa's modern **bus station** is a couple of kilometres east of the centre on 20 de Noviembre. You can get to town by either taxi or bus: the journey to the centre by regulated taxi, booked from a booth in the station, will cost about

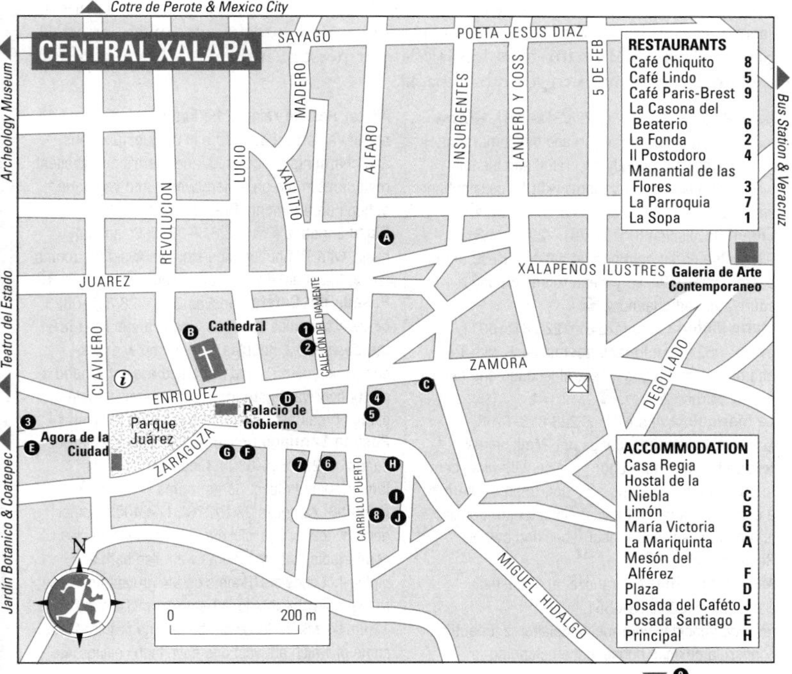

US$2.20. Buses marked "Centro" run along 20 de Noviembre; note that going back to the bus station, they're marked "CAXA" (Central de Autobuses de Xalapa). If you're heading on **from Xalapa to Veracruz**, you'll pass through Cempoala (see p.565), and it's well worth breaking the journey here to visit the ruins should you have a couple of hours to spare.

Xalapa's **tourist office** occupies a kiosk under the arches at the Palacio Municipal, near Parque Juárez (Mon–Fri 9am–3pm & 5–7pm; ⓣ228/842-1214) – for advice in English, ask to go to the administrative office inside the Palacio Municipal. To **change money**, try Bital bank on Zamora, at Mata (Mon–Fri 8am–7pm), or the casa de cambio one block north on Xalapeños Ilustres, at Mata (Mon–Fri 9am–3pm & 5–7pm, Sat 10am–3pm); there are also **ATMs** on Zamora. The **post office** (Mon–Fri 8am–7pm, Sat 9am–5pm, Sun 9am–noon) is on Zamora, at Diego Leño, and is also where you'll find a Western Union office. For **laundry**, head one block north of the post office to Lavandería Diamante, Rojano 21A. Several places have **Internet** access – for example, there are a couple of good ones (both US$1.50 per hour) on Carillo Puerto.

A number of ecotourism companies offering rafting, trekking and jungle **tours** operate from Xalapa. Try Amigos del Río, Chilpancingo 205 (ⓣ228/815-8817, ⓦwww.amigosdelrio.com.mx); Ecco Sports, 20 de Noviembre Ote 631 (ⓣ228/812-3954, ⓔinfo@eccosports.com.mx) or Veraventuras, Santos Degollado 81 (ⓣ228/818-9579, ⓦwww.veraventuras.com.mx). A half-day outing with any of these costs around US$50.

Accommodation

There are some truly charming hotels in Xalapa, often located in historic and atmospheric houses. The town has a recently opened **hostel**, *Hostal de la Niebla*, Zamora 24 (ⓣ228/817-2174 or 818-2842, ⓦwww.delaniebla.com), compensating somewhat for the rather meagre choice of budget accommodation. A place in a six-bed dorm costs US$10.50 per person, and there's hot water and lockers large enough to store backpacks.

Casa Regia Hidalgo 12 ⓣ228/812-0591, ⓦwww.posadacasaregia.com.mx. Around the corner from the *Principal*, this brightly decorated and friendly place has peaceful, cosy rooms with TV, constant hot water, plus a breakfast area near the lobby. ❺

Limón Revolución 8 ⓣ228/817-2204, ⓕ817-9316. One of the best budget options, close to the centre, with small, very clean rooms around a courtyard, and a laundry. ❷

María Victoria Zaragoza 6 ⓣ228/818-6011, ⓕ818-0521. Comfortable rooms, each with TV and phone, and a good, central location one block east of Parque Juárez. ❻

La Mariquinta Alfaro 12 ⓣ228/818-1158, ⓦwww.lamariquinta.xalapa.net. Meticulously restored eighteenth-century house with nice, comfortable rooms and long-stay apartments. There is a common room with a vast collection of books and an English- and French-speaking owner. Recommended. ❻

Mesón del Alférez Zaragoza, at Sebastian Camacho ⓣ228/818-6351, ⓦwww.geocities.com/mesondelalferez. Beautiful, converted colonial house, once belonging to Alférez Real de Xalapa, the former colonial governor of Veracruz. Each room is unique, luxurious and charmingly decorated, and there's an excellent restaurant in the basement with some vegetarian options on the menu. Breakfast included. ❻

Plaza Enriquez 4 ⓣ228/817-3310. Clean and basic, with TV and luggage storage. Avoid the rooms facing the street if you plan on getting any sleep. ❸

Posada del Caféto Canovas 8 ⓣ228/817-0023, ⓦwww.geocities.com/posadadelcafeto. Next to the *Casa Regia*, doubles here, some with balconies, all have TV and bath, and are set around a pretty courtyard garden. The on-premises café serves breakfast (only) and has books to read. ❺

Posada Santiago Úrsulo Galván 89, near Parque Juárez ⓣ228/818-6333. Clean and friendly, family-owned place. Some rooms with TV. ❸

Principal Zaragoza 28 ⓣ228/817-6400. Another good budget option, close to the zócalo, with clean, comfortable and light rooms with tiled bath and piping-hot showers. Rooms on the ground floor next to the main street tend to be noisy until around 10pm, so ask for those on the second or third floors, some of which are vast and have high ceilings. ❸

The Town

Downtown – the small colonial area around **Parque Juárez** (the zócalo) – is the main attraction. Here, the eighteenth-century **cathedral** and **Palacio de Gobierno** (with murals by the Chilean artist José Chaves Morado) both deserve to be seen, and, at dusk, the trees around the zócalo are filled with extraordinarily raucous birds. Xalapa's lively arts crowd meets up at the **Agora de la Ciudad**, a cultural centre in the parque; and just west on María Avila Camacho is the **Teatro del Estado**, home to the state orchestra – for more on both of these, see p.557. There is an **art museum** on the west side of the parque, on Herrera (Tues–Sun 10am–6pm; US$0.50), showcasing the work of artist Alfredo Zalse; about a kilometre east of the parque, the **Galería de Arte Contemporáneo** on Xalapeños Ilustres (daily 10am–7pm; US$1) also hosts regular temporary exhibitions.

At 1590m, the easily climbable **Macuiltepec** is the highest of the hills on which the town is built, and from its mirador – if you're lucky – you might catch a glimpse of the Gulf. About thirty minutes' walk from the centre (or a ride on the "Tepic" bus), Macuiltepec also boasts an Ecological Park at its base, with a specially designed barbecue and picnic area. Entrance is from calles Tepic or Volcán de Colima (Tues–Sun 6am–5pm). Another potential picnic spot is **Parque Los Tecajeto**, ten minutes' walk from the zócalo along María Avila Camacho (daily 6am–6pm), a very well-kept public park with lush vegetation and plenty of shaded seating areas.

Xalapa's outstanding sight, however, is the **Archeology Museum** (Tues–Sun 9am–5pm; US$3.75), also known (and signposted) as the **Museum of Anthropology**, located on the outskirts of town – take any bus marked "Xalapa" along Dr Lucio. Ranked by many as the second-best archeological museum in the country after the one in Mexico City, the collection itself can certainly rival any outside the capital in both extent and quality, and the building that houses it, flowing down the hillside in a series of spacious marble steps, may well be the finest in Mexico. It's a wonderful introduction to the various pre-Hispanic cultures of the Gulf coast. You start at the top of the hill, where the first halls deal with the **Olmecs**. There are several of the celebrated colossal stone heads, a vast array of other monumental statuary and some beautiful masks. Later cultures are represented mainly through their pottery – lifelike human and animal figurines especially – and there are also displays on the architecture of the major sites: El Tajín, Cempoala and so on. Finally, with the **Huastec** culture come more giant stone statues. Some of the larger, less valuable pieces are displayed in the landscaped gardens outside. There's a **café** on the first floor, and also a shop selling fantastic, though expensive, masks. Behind the museum, the woody **Parque Ecológico Macuiltépetl** has subalpine flora and great views of the city.

The **Museum of Science and Technology** (Tues–Fri 9am–6pm, Sat & Sun 10am–7pm; US$5 includes IMAX), near the Archeology Museum on Murillo Vidal, is a great place to take kids: along with a permanent outdoors exhibition of Mexican cars and planes, and an IMAX cinema – the largest in Latin American – the museum features a planetarium and rooms dedicated to different sciences, such as space exploration, with interactive displays and impressive models.

Around Xalapa

With time on your hands, a number of worthwhile excursions can be made into the jungly country around Xalapa. Just a couple of kilometres south of the city, on the road to Coatepec (local bus), is the **Jardín Botánico Francisco**

Clavijero (daily 9am–5pm; US$0.50), a collection of plants native to the state, from jungle to mountain forest. A few kilometres further out in the same direction, the villages of **Coatepec** itself and **Teocelo** are also worth a visit, mainly for their beautiful setting. The coffee consumed in the cafés of Xalapa is grown in Coatepec, and in May the Feria del Café celebrates this fact. Coatepec has a number of good **restaurants**, including *El Tío Yeyo* (☎228/816-3645), which specializes in fresh fish served in a variety of delicious sauces. Nearby is the spectacular **Cascada de Texolo**, a triple waterfall that can be admired from a modern bridge, a replacement for the crumpled ancient iron one alongside, which was wrecked by an earthquake. Many of the scenes in the film *Romancing the Stone* were shot around these villages and waterfalls, and there are more sets from the film near the village of **Naolinco**, 30km north of Xalapa. All can be reached by local bus; further details are available from the Xalapa tourist office (see p.554). To get to the Cascada de Texolo, take a bus from the ADO station to **Xico**, 19km from Xalapa (about 20min), and get off at the outskirts of the village, by a tiny church. Then ask the way – it's forty minutes' hot walk along a paved road through banana and coffee plantations, but worth it.

On the road to Veracruz, 10km outside the city, is the **museum of El Lencero** (Tues–Sun 10am–5pm; US$2.50), a colonial hacienda that was once the property of the controversial general and president, Antonio López de Santa Ana. It is preserved in its full nineteenth-century splendour, and the grounds and surrounding countryside are stunning, too. The Chilean poet Gabriela Mistral stayed here in 1949, and wrote about the fine view of the coast.

Eating and drinking

Good **food** is abundant in Xalapa; the city is home to the **jalapeño pepper**, which you'll probably taste in all main meals. Another of the great pleasures here is local **coffee** – actually grown in nearby Coatepec (see above) – consumed in great quantities in one of the city's numerous **traditional cafés**. A particularly high concentration of appealing ones are on Carillo Puerto, while those listed below also have full lunch and dinner menus. Meanwhile, several appetizing restaurants, and some good *jugo* and torta places, can be found on Enriquez and in the couple of blocks to the north and south of it. You can buy fresh food (and wine) for a picnic in the park at the **supermarket** on Lucio; the Rex Centro supermarket and pharmacy on Enriquez, at Carillo Puerto, is open 24 hours.

Café Chiquito Nicolás Bravo 3, at Dr Pedro Rendón (opposite the hospital) ☎228/812-1122. One of the larger cafés, with plenty of tables around a small garden and a fireplace right at the back. Reasonable menu, mostly of snacks and sandwiches, along with the usual range of caffeinated beverages.

Café Lindo Primo Verdad 21. Café with good sandwiches in addition to a full complement of Mexican-style snack foods. Lively, youthful atmosphere in the large, dimly lit dining and drinking area.

Café Paris-Brest Díaz Mirón 29, at the southern end of Parque Los Berros ☎228/818-1261. Main dishes cost US$6–10 at this French restaurant. Cheaper specialities include *croque monsieur*, quiche lorraine, a fine array of sweet and savoury crepes and some mouth-watering pastries.

La Casona del Beaterio Zaragoza 20 ☎228/818-2119. Hundreds of old photographs adorn the walls at one of the city's best eateries, which serves up fine and reasonably priced Mexican food. Live traditional music Thurs–Sun.

La Fonda Callejón del Diamante (aka Antonio Ma de Rivera) 1 ☎228/818-7287. Justifiably popular lunchtime spot (plenty of room upstairs if the street-level dining room is full), offering copious and very cheap comidas corridas or an à la carte choice of chicken, meat and even some seafood dishes for US$5 and up.

Il Postodoro Primo Verdad 11 ⓣ228/841-2000. All of the pasta is made on the premises – as are the several flavours of ice cream – at this welcoming Italian restaurant. Excellent wine list, dominated by Chiantis.

Manantial de las Flores Úrsulo Galván 102 (walk up the side street beside the church, roughly opposite *Posada Santiago*) ⓣ228/812-4557. Shop for natural products, pottery and the latest in hippie fashions at the adjacent eco-shop before sampling the mainly organic food at the restaurant. In a quiet spot 50m or so back from the main road.

La Parroquia Zaragoza 18 ⓣ228/817-4436. Venerable establishment best known for its breakfast menus starting at around US$3, but whose unpretentious and busy dining room is also open for lunch and dinner. Another branch at María Avila Camacho 42.

La Sopa Callejón del Diamante (also known as Antonio Ma de Rivera) 3A ⓣ228/817-8069. Popular for its no-nonsense enchiladas, tacos and soups, almost all for well under US$3, and its tranquil location – roaming *mariachi* bands notwithstanding – on a traffic-free street.

Nightlife and entertainment

Xalapa is a city of great creative energy, boosted by a large student community, a number of good theatres and an excellent orchestra. The **Teatro del Estado** on María Avila Camacho, at Ignacio de la Llave (box office ⓣ228/817-3210), hosts regular **concerts** by the Orquesta Sinfónica de Xalapa, in addition to dance and theatre. Tickets cost US$5 for the front section of the auditorium (best for watching) and US$4 for the back (best for listening). Meanwhile, the **Agora de la Ciudad** in Parque Juárez (variable opening times) is an **arts centre** with a cinema, theatre, gallery, bookstore and coffeeshop with fine views over the southern suburbs of the city.

A number of **bars** offer live music and occasional poetry readings or theatre, and there are numerous **nightclubs** catering to all tastes. The loudest and hippest places tend to be along María Avila Camacho, with the *Nyx Bar* at no. 84 good for dancing – to mainly techno music. There are also a couple of clubs opposite the CAXA bus terminal: *La Casona*, a chic establishment with live music and a US$5 cover, and *La Corte de los Milagros*, which is one of the few places in town where you can listen and dance to salsa music. Elsewhere, *Los Molinos*, Úrsulo Galván 57, is a restaurant-bar offering a wide selection of spirits and live entertainment, and appealing to an older clientele; *La Tasca* on Xicoténcatl has traditional acoustic music; and *La Muerte Chiquita*, Canovas 4, next to *Posada del Caféto*, is a mellow lounge-bar with candles and psychedelic art on the walls.

Veracruz

VILLA RICA DE LA VERACRUZ was the first town founded by the Spanish in Mexico, a few days after Cortés' arrival on Good Friday, 1519. The first development – little more than a wooden stockade – was in fact some way to the north, later being moved to La Antigua (see p.564) and subsequently to its present site in 1589. The modern city is very much the heir of the original; only recently, for the first time since its foundation, has Veracruz begun to lose its position as the most important port in Mexico (to Tampico and Coatzacoalcos), and its history reflects every major event from the Conquest onwards. "Veracruz," states author Paul Theroux, "is known as the 'heroic city'. It is a poignant description: in Mexico a hero is nearly always a corpse."

Though tranquil enough today, the port's past has been a series of "invasions, punitive missions and local military defeats . . . humiliation as history". The problems started even before the Conquest was complete, when **Pánfilo Narváez** landed here on his ill-fated mission to bring Cortés back under the

control of the governor of Cuba, and continued intermittently for the next four hundred years. Throughout the sixteenth and seventeenth centuries, Veracruz and the Spanish galleons that used the port were preyed on constantly by English, Dutch and French buccaneers. In the **War of Independence** the Spanish made their final stand here, holding the fortress of San Juan Ulúa for four years after the country had been lost. In **1838** the French occupied the city, demanding compensation for French property and citizens who had suffered in the years following Independence; in **1847** US troops took Veracruz, and from here marched on to capture the capital; in **1862** the French, supported by Spanish and English forces that soon withdrew, invaded on the pretext of forcing Mexico to pay her foreign debt, but ended up staying five years and setting up the unfortunate Maximilian as emperor; and finally, in **1914**, US marines were back, occupying the city to protect American interests during the Revolution. These are the "Cuatro Veces Heroica" of the city's official title, and form the bulk of the history displayed in the museums.

The first, and the lasting, impression of Veracruz, however, is not of its history but of its life now. The zócalo, a lively waterfront location and the relative absence of tourists make Veracruz one of the most enjoyable places in the republic in which simply to be, to sit back and watch – or join – the daily round. This is especially true in the evenings, when the tables under the *portales* of the plaza fill up and the drinking and the *marimba* music begin – to go on through most of the night. **Marimba** – a distinctively Latin-Caribbean sound based around a giant wooden xylophone – is *the* local sound, but at peak times there are also *mariachi* bands and individual strolling crooners, all striving to be heard over each other. When the municipal band strikes up from the middle of the square, confusion is total. Before Ash Wednesday every year (dates vary), Veracruz has a nine-day riotous **carnaval** that rivals the best in the hemisphere, while the **Festival del Caribe** is the highlight of the last two weeks of August, with many free dance and music performances, film showings and art exhibitions.

Arrival and information

As the train station is no longer functioning, you'll arrive here either by bus or by plane. The **bus stations**, both ADO first-class and AU second-class, are about 3km from the centre on Díaz Mirón (the entrance to second-class is actually on the street behind, La Fragua). Any bus heading to the right as you come out of the first-class terminal onto Díaz Mirón should take you to the centre – most will have "Díaz Mirón" or "Centro" on the windscreen; if not, ask. They head straight to the end of Díaz Mirón, round a confusing junction at Parque Zamora, and then take a variety of routes that mostly end up on Independencia as it runs past the zócalo. To get back, head for 5 de Mayo, parallel to Independencia, and take any bus marked "Camionera". The **airport** is 10km or so south of the city; taxis between here and the centre cost US$10–12.

Although Veracruz is a large and rambling city, the downtown area is relatively small and straightforward – anywhere further afield can be reached by local bus from somewhere very near the zócalo. This attractive plaza, shaded by trees and surrounded by the cathedral, the Palacio Municipal and various atmospheric colonial buildings that now mainly operate as bars, cafés and hotels, is, to an even greater extent than usual, the epicentre of city life – the place where everyone gathers, for morning coffee, lunch, afternoon strolls and night-time revelry.

The helpful **tourist office**, on the ground floor of the Palacio Municipal right on the zócalo (Mon–Sat 8am–8pm, Sun 10am–6pm; ⓣ229/989-8817 or 989-8800 ext 158), publishes an interesting guide to the city's history, arts and culture, written by Bernardo Lorenzo Camacho, who's usually on hand to answer any questions.

Accommodation

There's a **hotel** right next to the first-class bus station, and several very cheap and rather grim places around the back of the second-class bus terminal, but unless you've arrived late at night, there's no point staying this far out. The other cheap places are mostly within a couple of blocks of the zócalo, often around the market; they're nothing to write home about, and noise can be a real problem – from the prostitutes servicing the local sailors as much as from the road – but at least you should find a clean room with a fan. There are also a few more expensive options on the zócalo itself or not far from it. Alternatively, you could try staying out by the beach. There are some decent and not too expensive hotels along the malecón (María Avila Camacho) within walking distance of the zócalo, while plenty of luxurious establishments front the beaches of Villa del Mar, Mocambo and Boca del Río, which also has a number of campsites. A few blocks back from the waterfront before Boca del Río are various drive-in love motels with hourly rates and only recommended as a last resort (for more on accommodation at Veracruz's beaches, see p.562).

Amparo Serdán 482 ⓣ229/932-2738, ⓔamparohotelver@hotmail.com. The least sleazy of a cluster of cheap places and popular with backpackers, behind the zócalo near the market. ❸

Baluarte Francisco Canal 265, at 16 de Septiembre ⓣ229/932-5222. Well-kept hotel where the rooms have TV, a/c and, in some cases, views of the Baluarte de Santiago. Free parking for guests. ❻

Candilejas Juan Barragan 35, at M Avila Camacho ⓣ229/932-5880. Just past the *Royalty*,this friendly hotel has clean, though not particularly cheap, rooms with a/c and good views of the bay, as well as a garage. ❼

Cielo S Perez Abascal 580 ⓣ229/937-2367. Pleasant enough for a night or two, and convenient if you've arrived late at the second-class bus terminal. ❹

Colonial Miguel Lerdo 117 ⓣ/ⓕ229/932-0193, ⓦwww.hcolonial.com.mx. Comfortable rooms (some with balconies) at this good-value option on the zócalo, with a swimming pool, garage, a/c rooms and views over the square from selected rooms. ❻

Emporio Paseo de Malecón 244 ⓣ229/932-0020 or 2222, ⓕ931-2261, ⓦwww.hotelesemporio.com. Big, luxurious US-style hotel with all the associated amenities, including pool, gym and sauna, and slightly pricier rooms with a sea view. ❾

Holiday Inn Centro Histórico Morelos 225 ⓣ229/932-4550, ⓕ932-4255, ⓔhichvera@prodigy.net.mx. Smart hotel in a renovated building with all the modern conveniences, and a pretty pool enclosed by a courtyard. ❽

Imperial Lerdo 153 ⓣ229/932-1204, ⓕ931-4508, ⓦwww.hotelimperialveracruz .com. Although some rooms at the adjacent *Colonial* have unimpeded balcony views over the zócalo and cathedral, all of the best rooms here look right onto the square and church. Some of the suites are very large and decorated with colonial-style furniture. In a grand old 1794 building (note the stained-glass ceiling in the lobby). ❼

Mar y Tierra M Avila Camacho, at Figueroa ⓣ229/931-3866, ⓕ932/6096, ⓦwww.hotelmarytierra.com. One of the best mid-priced options on the seafront, and only ten minutes from the zócalo. A/c rooms in the old (at the front) and new buildings are very different, so look first: some have sea views. On a pleasant stretch of the malecón animated by divers street vendors. ❺

Rias Díaz Mirón 1242 ⓣ229/932-5399. The most upscale accommodation near the bus station, three blocks from the ADO first-class terminal. Clean, modern rooms with fan or a/c. ❺

Royalty Abasolo 34, at M Avila Camacho ⓣ229/932-2844, ⓕ932-7096. Clean, friendly, quiet and good-value seafront hotel close to the centre, with a/c rooms plus some cheaper ones with a fan, TV and small balcony. Accepts credit cards (not American Express). ❹

Ruíz Milán Paseo del Malecón ⓣ229/932-3777 or 1-800/221-4260, ⓦwww.ruizmilan.com. Comfortable hotel (especially if you get a room at the front) with all a/c rooms, a small indoor pool and hot-tub, plus a good restaurant. Close to both the zócalo and malecón. ❻

Santo Domingo Serdán 481 ⓣ229/931-6326. Opposite the *Amparo*, and slightly more expensive. Central and clean, with small rooms with private bath. ❹

The City

The outstanding sight in Veracruz is the **Castillo de San Juan de Ulúa**, the great fortress that so singularly failed to protect the harbour. In most cases this was hardly the fault of its defenders, since every sensible invader landed somewhere on the coast nearby, captured the town and, having cut off the fort by land and sea, called for its surrender. Prior to closing for refurbishment in 1997, the fortress was the thoroughly run-down and fitting location for the climactic chase scene in *Romancing the Stone*, with its unguarded ten-metre drops and dingy, dripping corridors, but now the renovated fort – the site of Cortés' 1519 landing – and **museum** are open to the public (Tues–Sun 9am–4.30pm; US$3, free on Sun). The main attraction of the fortress is its prison – three dark, unpleasant cells known as El Purgatorio, La Gloria and El Infierno (Purgatory, Heaven and Hell), where many political prisoners died during the rule of Díaz. Apart from the prison, the fortress is an empty ruin of battlements and stairways. To get here, take one of the buses marked "San Juan de Ulúa" from the Plaza de la República, which follow a meandering route from the centre.

Back in town, the first of some worthwhile museums occupies an old mansion on Zaragoza, about five blocks from the Palacio Municipal. The **Museo de la Ciudad** (Tues–Sun 10am–6pm; US$2.50; free on Sun) covers local history and folklore from the earliest inhabitants to the 1914 US invasion. Inevitably, given the scope of material to be covered, it's rather a potted version, and many of the exhibits go completely unexplained (and those that are are done so only in Spanish), but there's some beautiful Olmec and Totonac sculpture, including one of the giant Olmec heads; thought-provoking information on Mexico's African population, much of which was concentrated in this area after the slave trade; and relics of the city's various "heroic defenders". Just two blocks from the Museo de la Ciudad, towards the sea, the facades of **Las Atarazanas** are worth a passing look. These colonial warehouses once backed onto the sea and were built for the storage of arms and wares used by the troops that protected the city from pirates.

From here walk one block north to Mariano Arista, where the town's second museum, the **Museo Histórico Naval** (Tues–Sun 9am–5pm; free), has numerous interesting displays of weapons and model ships, along with information in Spanish about the US attacks on Veracruz in the late nineteenth and early twentieth centuries. In the same building, the **Museo Venustiano Carranza** is dedicated to Venustiano Carranza, who established his Constitutionalist government in Veracruz in 1915 (with the support of US President Woodrow Wilson, whose troops then occupied the town). Inside are gathered assorted memorabilia of his government's term here, and you can view Carranza's bedroom and living room. Carranza lived in the Castillo de San Juan while running his government – and the war against Villa and Zapata – from the old *faro* (lighthouse) alongside the huge Pemex Tower on the malecón. There's a fine statue of Carranza in front of the *faro*, looking exactly as John Reed describes him in *Insurgent Mexico*: "A towering, khaki-clad figure, seven feet tall it seemed . . . arms hanging loosely by his side, his fine old head thrown back."

Less impressive but much more central than the Castillo de San Juan de Ulúa, the **Baluarte de Santiago** is a seventeenth-century fort between 16 de Septiembre and Gómez Farías, two blocks south of the Museo Histórico Naval. Originally one of nine forts along a 2650-metre-long wall, the Baluarte is now the only survivor – it's hard to imagine that the sea reached this far when the fort was built in 1635 to fend off constant attacks by pirates and buccaneers. You can go inside for a wander around the small museum (Tues–Sun 10am–4.30pm; US$3.20, free on Sun), which has a few exhibits of exquisite pre-Columbian gold jewellery discovered in 1976 by a local octopus fisherman. Most of his find had been melted down and sold before the authorities got wind of it, and though only a fraction remains, it's still a significant contribution to what little remains from colonial times. Apart from this, there's not a great deal to see.

Well worth a visit is the **Acuario de Veracruz** (Mon–Thurs 10am–7pm, Fri–Sun 10am–7.30pm; US$5), in the shopping centre next to *Hotel Villa del Mar* on María Avila Camacho. Designed by a Japanese architect, this modern and well-run aquarium has some large ocean fish, including sharks, barracudas and huge tarpons, as well as smaller tanks filled with a variety of saltwater, brackish and freshwater fauna. There are also some interesting educational exhibits, in addition to skeletons of various marine mammals and turtles.

Back in the heart of town, on Francisco Canal, at Zaragoza, the **Instituto Veracruzano de Cultura** (Mon–Sat 9am–8pm; free) has regular art and photography exhibitions in its two-floor gallery.

Tours and trips around Veracruz

To see marine life at close quarters, head for Tridente, M Avila Camacho 165 (Ⓣ/Ⓕ229/931-7924), or Scubadiver, Hernandez y Hernandez 563 (Ⓣ229/932-3994, Ⓦwww.scubaver.net), both near the *Mar y Tierra* hotel, two of the city's best dive shops. They offer guided **dive trips** to a large number of little-visited **reefs** and **beaches**, including those around Veracruz's offshore islands, along with PADI certification at better rates than you'll find in the Caribbean. Fiesta Viajes, in the lobby of *Hostal de Cortés*, on M Avila Camacho, at Bartolomé de las Casas (Ⓣ229/935-3754, Ⓦwww.fiestaviajes.com), offers diving and **fishing** trips as well as **historical** tours. Kayak Mexico (Ⓣ229/913-0452, Ⓦwww.kayakmexico.com) runs day-trips in the **mangrove swamps**. The tourist office has details of other companies offering ecotours and rafting trips; count on spending US$50 for a half-day outing, US$70 for a full day.

The beaches

You wouldn't make a special trip to Veracruz for its **beaches** – although for Mexicans from the capital it's a relatively cheap and handy Florida-style resort, and there are hotels, however ugly, catering to them for miles to the south – but for an afternoon's escape to the sea, they're quite good enough. **Villa del Mar** is Veracruz's closest, most crowded and least clean beach, and also the location of a cluster of hotels, including the upmarket *Hostal de Cortés*, which has a pool, air-conditioned rooms with balconies and sea views. Rather than stop here, continue on to the beach at **Mocambo** (the locals' favourite and where most of the hotels are) or further along the coast to the village of **Boca del Río**, which also has a reasonable stretch of sand. **Buses** (marked "Boca del Río") head out to both from the corner of Gómez Farias and Serdán, arriving twenty minutes later at *Hotel Mocambo* (Ⓣ229/922-0200 or 01-800/290-0100, Ⓕ229/922-0212, Ⓔhmocambo@infosel.net.mx; ❽), a grand old **hotel** freshly renovated to compete with the comfortable but homogenous alternatives offered in these parts. For slightly cheaper lodgings, try the *Playa de Oro*, Paseo Ejército Mexicano 23, opposite the *Mocambo* (Ⓣ/Ⓕ 229/921-8805; ❻), where the rates include breakfast. The huge Las Américas shopping mall, 400m or so before the *Mocambo*, has all the **food** outlets, **shops** and **ATM** machines you might need. Buses to Mocambo take the quick route via Ruíz Cortínes; for the scenic route along the coastal road (María Avila Camacho), join the open-air **tour buses** which leave from in front of *Hotel Emporio* when they have at least ten passengers (US$3.50 round-trip). From the *Mocambo*, follow the street down to the wide sandy beach, where the water is warm and calm – though from time to time it can be pretty dirty (in which case consider paying the US$3 to use the public swimming pool next to the beach). As its name suggests, the small village of Boca del Río, twenty minutes or so further on by bus from Mocambo, is located at the mouth of a river. Apart from the persistent boat-trip touts, there is not much going on here.

Tridente (see box, above) have an ecotourism site, with camping and a restaurant, at **Antón Lizardo**, a small village beyond Boca del Río. From here they run boat trips to the best beaches and reefs near Veracruz, on the offshore coral islands. These have white sands, clean water and very few visitors. Tridente can help you get permission to stay on one of the islands if you have your own tent.

Eating and drinking

"**A la Veracruzana**" is a tag you'll find on menus all over the country, denoting a delicious sauce of onions, garlic, tomatoes, olives, chiles and spices, served with meat or fish. And not surprisingly, there are seafood restaurants all over Veracruz, although by no means is each one particularly good value. The zócalo itself is ringed by **bars** and **cafés**, but these are really places to drink, and though most do serve food, or at least sandwiches, it's generally overpriced and not up to much. Lots of people, locals and tourists alike, start their night off with a drink at "los portales", the arcades leading into the zócalo, where you can try traditional mint *julep* – prepared with dark rum, dry sherry, vermouth, sugar and mint – in bars like *La Tasca*, *Bar Palacio* or *Regis*. While nowhere near as prevalent as in Xalapa, there are some **coffeeshops** away from the zócalo, notably on Mario Molina between Independencia and 5 de Mayo, where you can enjoy the excellent coffee produced in this part of Mexico.

For more substantial meals, there are a whole series of small **fish restaurants** around the market, and the top floor of the market building itself is given over to cooked-food stalls. For seafood in slightly less frenetic surroundings, head up Zaragoza towards the museum, where you'll find several more fish restaurants.

Restaurants

El Cochinito de Oro Zaragoza, at Serdán ☎229/932-3677. This down-to-earth and friendly eatery has been around for fifty years, offering a reasonable selection of seafood dishes – fish, shrimp, octopus with onions – for not more than US$7. The menu is translated into English.

La Estrella del Sabor M Avila Camacho 281, between hotels *Mar y Tierra* and *Royalty*. Convenient if you're staying at a seafront hotel, this hole-in-the-wall grill and bar has nothing but seafood – shrimp, crayfish, octopus and various types of fish – which you can order by the plate (US$6) or in a taco (US$1).

La Gaviota Trigueros 21 ☎229/932-3950. Open 24 hours, so a useful address for nocturnal revellers. Offers fortifying, predominately meat dishes, snacks and a well-stocked bar should you wish to keep the party going.

Gran Café de la Parroquia Gómez Farias 34, at Paseo del Malecón ☎229/937-2584. The vast white dining rooms, occupying nearly a whole block on the malecón, are invariably full of hundreds of diners being served modest and comparatively pricey egg, meat and fish meals. Check out the vintage coffee machines.

Gran Café del Portal Independencia 1187, opposite the cathedral ☎229/931-2759. The coffee (which is roasted on the premises) is undeniably good, and you can order food from a varied menu until midnight, but the street terrace attracts rather too many street vendors and beggars.

Pink Panther's Food Plazuela La Lagunilla ☎229/931-7982. Bar-restaurant with a satisfactory, if not outstanding, menu, recommended for its pleasant tables on a small square free from the occasionally tiresome street vendors who inhabit the zócalo. You can also order food until the early hours of the morning.

Puerto Alegre at *Hotel Ruiz Milán* ☎229/932-3777. High-quality, well-presented buffet breakfasts and lunches. Tasty seafood salads, fruits and tempting desserts accompany the four or so meat and fish dishes at lunch.

Sanborn's Independencia 1069, at Lerdo ☎229/931-0219. The Veracruz branch of the 100-year-old national department store/restaurant chain. Offerings range from Mexican snacks to filet mignon, served in an a/c dining room or the much cosier adjoining café.

Nightlife and entertainment

You could start your night on the town at the zócalo, where there is often a marimba band playing. Alternatively, find a table at any of the café terraces around the zócalo, and in no time you'll have your very own entertainment/distractions in the form of grinning musicians or a bizarre selection of touts – from boys selling balsa toucans to fortune-tellers and uniformed nurses offering to take your blood pressure. The malecón is also worth a night-time stroll, when it's animated with street vendors and yet more entertainers, and the twinkling lights of the ships in the port add to the romantic atmosphere.

In the centre ofVeracruz, there are a couple of **bars** on the quiet Plazuela La Lagunilla where you can listen to **live music**. *El Rincón de la Trova* has excellent Afro-Cuban music (Thurs–Sat), and also serves food during the day. Next door, *Casona de la Condesa* opens at 10pm and has music every night (closed Mon). The best places for **dancing**, both to salsa music and electronic dance music, are out of the centre along Ruíz Cortínes, a main thoroughfare of strip malls. *Carioca*, Ruíz Cortínes 10, is a good place for salsa, as is *Kachamba*, María Avila Camacho, at Médico Militar, where a Cuban orchestra plays from Thursday to Saturday. One of the newest and flashiest techno clubs is *La Roka* at Ruíz Cortínes 8. The best **cinema** is the multi-screen complex at the Las Américas mall in Mocambo (see p.562).

Listings

Airlines Aerocaribe, Costa Dorada 500 ⓣ229/922-5205; Aeroméxico, M Avila Camacho ⓣ229/931-8460; American, Ruíz Cortínes 1111 ⓣ229/921-5929; Continental, at the airport ⓣ229/938-6066; Mexicana, 5 de Mayo 1266 ⓣ229/932-224.

Banks and exchange Branches of all the main banks, where you can change travellers' cheques and find ATM machines, are on Independencia, at Benito Juárez. The casa de cambio at Morelos 43A has longer opening hours than the banks (Mon–Sat 9am–11pm, Sun 10am–6pm).

Car rental Alamo, Ruíz Cortínes 3495 ⓣ229/922-9494; Avis, Collado 241 ⓣ229/932-6032; Budget, M Avila Camacho 3748 ⓣ229/937-5706; Fast Car, Miguel Lerdo 245 ⓣ229/932-7100; Hertz, M Avila Camacho 3797 ⓣ229/937-4776.

Consulates Cuba, Altamirano ⓣ229/921-4304; Denmark ⓣ229/937-5554; Finland, Emparan 251 ⓣ229/931-2437; France, Heriberto Jara 156 ⓣ229/935-0649; Germany ⓣ229/937-5611; Holland ⓣ229/923-0500; Italy, Chalehihuecan 316 ⓣ229/937-8676; Norway ⓣ229/923-0600; Spain, Francisco Canal 264 ⓣ229/932-5829; Sweden ⓣ229/934-5653; Switzerland ⓣ229/931-5535; UK, Independencia 1394 ⓣ229/931-6694.

Hospital ⓣ229/932-3690.

Internet Cafés near the zócalo include two on Miguel Lerdo, at 5 de Mayo (US$0.80 and US$1 per hour) and one at Mariano Arista 711, at Independencia (US$1 per hour).

Pharmacies Del Ahorro Home Delivery Service (7am–10.30pm; ⓣ229/937-3525); Torres Pharmacy, 20 de Noviembre 486 (ⓣ229/932-2885); Hospital Español, 16 de Septiembre 955 (open 24 hours; ⓣ229/932-0021).

Phones There are Ladatel phones throughout the city, and several fax and copy centres where you can make international calls – including one at Landero y Cos 41, near the zócalo.

Police ⓣ229/938-0664.

Post office On the Plaza de la República, a couple of blocks north of the zócalo (Mon–Fri 8am–4pm, Sat 9am–1pm).

Taxis Radio Taxi ⓣ229/938-2233; Vera Taxis ⓣ229/932-7368.

La Antigua and Cempoala

Heading north fromVeracruz, there's a short stretch of highway as far as Cardel, at the junction of the coastal highway and the road up to Xalapa. **LA ANTIGUA**, site of the first real Spanish town in Mexico, lies just off this road. Although it does see an occasional bus, you'll find it much easier and quicker to take one heading for Cardel (about every thirty minutes from the second-class terminal in Veracruz) and get off at the toll-booths. From here it's about twenty minutes' walk up a signed road.

For all its antiquity, there's not a great deal to see in La Antigua; however, it is a beautiful, broad-streeted tropical village on the banks of the **Río La Antigua** (or Río Huitzilapan). At weekends it makes a popular excursion for Veracruzanos, who come to picnic by the river and to swim or take boat rides – and there are lots of seafood restaurants catering to the visitors. In the semi-ruinous centre of the village stand a couple of the oldest surviving Spanish buildings in Mexico: the **Edificio del Cabildo**, built in 1523, housed the first ayuntamiento (local government) to be established; the **Casa de Cortés**, a fairly crude construction of local stone, was built for Cortés himself a few years later; and the parish church also dates from the mid-sixteenth century, though it's been altered and restored several times since. On the riverbank stands a grand old tree – the Ceiba de la Noche Feliz – to which, according to local legend, Cortés moored his ships when he arrived here. Its roots and vines now almost totally cover Cortés' house.

Cempoala

That Cortés came to this spot at all, after first landing near the site of modern Veracruz, was thanks to the invitation of the Totonac of **CEMPOALA** (or Zempoala), then a city of some 25,000 to 30,000 inhabitants. It was the first native city visited by the conquistadors and quickly became their ally against the Aztecs. Cempoala, which had existed in some form for at least eight hundred years, had been brought under the control of the Aztec empire only relatively recently – around 1460 – and its people, who had already rebelled more than once, were only too happy to stop paying their tribute once they believed that the Spanish could protect them from retribution. This they did, although the "Fat Chief" and his people must have begun to have second thoughts when Cortés ordered the idols of their deities smashed and replaced with crosses and Christian altars.

Cortés left Cempoala in August 1519 for the march on Tenochtitlán, taking with him two hundred Totonac porters and fifty of the town's best warriors. The following May he was forced to return in a hurry by the news that Pánfilo Narváez had come after him with a large force, on a mission to bring the conquistadors back under the control of the governor of Cuba. The battle took place in the centre of Cempoala, where, despite the fact that Narvaez's force was far larger and had taken up defensive positions on the great temple, Cortés won a resounding victory: many of Narváez's generals were captured and most of the men switched sides, joining in the later assaults on the Aztec capital.

The **archeological site**, near Cardel – (daily 8am–5.30pm; US$3, plus another US$3 for a video camera, free on Sun), dates mostly from the Aztec period, and although obviously the buildings have lost their decorative facings and thatched sanctuaries, it's one of the most complete examples of an Aztec ceremonial centre surviving – albeit in an atypical tropical setting. The pyramids with their double stairways, grouped around a central plaza, must have resembled those of Tenochtitlán, though on a considerably smaller scale. Apart from the main, cleared site, consisting of the **Templo Mayor** (the largest and most impressive structure, where Narváez made his stand), the Great Pyramid and the Templo de las Chimeneas, there are lesser ruins scattered throughout, and around, the modern village. Most important of these are the Templo de las Caritas, a small temple on which a few carvings and remains of murals can still be seen, in open country just beyond the main site, and the Templo de Ehecatl, on the opposite side of the main road through the village. You need a couple of hours to explore the site.

Practicalities: Cardel

There are **buses** (second-class) to Cempoala from both Veracruz and Xalapa, but it's quicker – certainly if you plan to continue northwards – to go to **Cardel** and change there for a first-class service. Coming **from La Antigua**, you can go back to the main road, get a bus to Cardel and go on from there. From Cardel there are plenty of green-and-white taxis to the site, but the buses marked "Cempoala" that leave from the bus station are cheaper. Cardel itself is not of much interest, but has several seafood restaurants and a couple of small **hotels** around the plaza. The mid-range *Plaza*, Independencia 25 Pte (☎296/962-0288; ❻), just opposite the ADO bus stop, may let you bargain off-season; *Hotel Cardel*, on the plaza itself (☎296/962-0014; ❹), is better value for money, though both have satisfactory rooms, some with air-conditioning and TV. From Cardel you can head down to a good beach at **Chachalacas** (another short bus journey), a small fishing village with a luxury hotel and some excellent seafood.

North to Tuxpán

Continuing north, there's very little in the long coastal stretch (about 4hr on the bus) from Cardel to Papantla. The village of **Quiahuitzlán**, about 70km from Veracruz, bears the name of a fortified Totonac town visited by Cortés, with some fairly unimpressive ruins nearby. At **Laguna Verde** there's an ugly nuclear-power station, which almost closed as a result of public pressure a few years ago. At **Nautla** you pass the largest town en route, surrounded by coconut groves. Although there are long, flat stretches of sand along much of the so-called "Costa Esmeralda", they are pretty uninviting – desolate, windswept and raked by grey surf. Only in the final stretch does the beach offer much temptation, with several (expensive) motels dotted between Nautla and **Tecolutla**, a low-key resort 8km off the main road. If you crave the beach you can stay here, and still get to Papantla and El Tajín with relative ease. Try *Casa Malena* (no phone; ❸) or the smarter *Ibatros* (☎766/846-0002; ❹), both on the main street; hotels on the beachfront are more expensive, though they do come with the required ocean views, like the *Mirador* (☎766/846-0200; ❺). There are plenty of places to eat, from hotel restaurants to palapas at the beach, most of which serve seafood.

Tlapacoyan

Some 50km southwest of Nautla, bounded to the south by the Río Bobos and to the north by the Río María de la Torre, **TLAPACOYAN** is surrounded by forested hills and pre-Columbian ruins. Most important of these are the massive undeveloped sites of **Filo Bobos**, inaugurated in 1994 as part of a plan to turn the area into a major tourist destination. The town itself is still largely unspoiled, a friendly place going about its main business as a centre of citrus fruit production. Captured on a raid from the port of Nauhtla (Nautla), Tlapacoyan was besieged by Austrian troops loyal to Emperor Maximilian back in 1865. One of the republican commanders, Colonel Ferrer, distinguished himself in the battle and today his statue stands in the main square.

Buses to Tlapacoyan run from Xalapa, Papantla, Veracruz, Puebla and Mexico City. ADO buses drop off in the centre of town. Turn left at 5 de Mayo and walk up Héroes de Tlapacoyan for the zócalo. Second-class services to Nautla leave from the terminal opposite ADO. **Hotels** are thin on the ground, but in the centre there are a few quiet, good-value choices. On the square itself, try the *Plaza* (☎225/315-0520; ❺) or the cheaper *San Agustín* (☎225/315-0291; ❹), the latter of which also has the best restaurant in town, and organizes river trips to Filo Bobos.

Filo Bobos

Work continues at the **Filo Bobos** archeological project, which opened to the public in 1994. Here you can visit two of the several pre-Hispanic sites so far identified along the Río Bobos valley. Both **El Cuajilote** and **Vega de la Peña** are well worth visiting as much for the beauty of their location, the birdlife and the serenity, as for the ruins themselves.

No one yet knows for certain who occupied the Filo Bobos sites. Signs of a fertility cult suggest a **Huastec** influence, yet the other sculpture found is more Totonac in style, and the earliest buildings at El Cuajilote, which may be as old as 1000 BC, are decidedly Olmec. Archeologists are now speculating that Filo Bobos was the centre of an as yet unknown, syncretistic Mesoamerican civilization, which provided an important trade link between the Gulf coast, its environs and the central valleys.

The **trail** that leads to and links the two sites cuts through ranch land running along the sides of the Río Bobos, with steep rainforested hills rising to either side. There are unexplored mounds of pre-Columbian rubble all along the way, and you're unlikely to see any other tourists. The first and most impressive site you come to is **El Cuajilote**, with platforms and pyramids arranged around a rectangular central plaza measuring 31,500 square metres. The surrounding buildings imitate the shape of the valley, and appear to be a series of temples dedicated to a fertility cult: a monolithic, phallic stele more than two metres tall and oriented to the stars stands in the middle of the plaza, and at Shrine A4 more than 1500 other phallic figurines were found, though none of these remains on site today. You can also make out a ball-court and some sculptures, including one of a giant frog – this may also be a fertility symbol.

The trail continues to the site of **Vega de la Peña**, 4km away, which covers some eight thousand square metres. There's little doubt that structures buried beneath the lush greenery extend beyond that; some archeologists believe they may have stretched as far as Nautla. If true, this would radically alter the accepted conception of Mexican and Mesoamerican pre-Columbian history, placing this coast in a far more prominent position than previously thought. What you see here today are small buildings, with more palatial dwellings than at El Cuajilote, and a small ball-court.

The complete **walk** takes about six hours and begins at a little village called **Santiago**, reached by bus from the Terminal Regional de Tlapacoyan on the

El Baile de los Negritos

Popular at festivals across the state of Veracruz, the frenetic **Baile de los Negritos** is a Totonac dance dating back to colonial times, when black slaves were imported in numbers to work on local plantations, often living and labouring alongside *indígenas*. Stories abound as to the origin of the dance: the most popular version has it that a female African slave and her child escaped from a plantation near Papantla, and lived in the dense jungle with the local indigenous groups. After her child was poisoned by a snake bite, the mother, using African folk medicine, began to dance herself into a trance. The Totonacs around her found the spectacle highly amusing and, it is said, began to copy her in a spirit of mockery.

The costumes of the dance are influenced by colonial dress, and the dancers wear a snake motif around the waist. The dance is directed by a "Mayordomo", the title given to plantation overseers in the colonial era. If you're in Tlapacoyan for the **Feast of Santiago** (July 24), dedicated to the town's patron saint, or the **Day of the Assumption** (August 16), you'll see the dance at its best and most spectacular; at other times it's held on a smaller scale in other village festivals in the area.

corner of 5 de Mayo and Valdez, two blocks from the zócalo in Tlapacoyan. The bus driver will drop you in the village at the start of the road that leads to El Cuajilote, some 8km away. The walk down this road takes about an hour, though you can cut through fields to make it a little quicker, along a steep, mossy and slippery path shown as "aceite vueltos". The path is not always clear, but there are ranches along the road, and locals will point you in the right direction, and those with transport may even take you as far as Rancho Nuevo, leaving only 2km to walk. From El Cuajilote, a path leads out of the back of the site towards Vega de la Peña, and from there another leads to a manned river crossing with a small restaurant. From here it's a straightforward walk up a road lined with banana plantations to the village of **Encanto**, where you can catch local buses to Tlapacoyan. The site wardens at both El Cuajilote and Vega de la Peña are very helpful and will ensure that you are on the right path, as will the locals.

Papantla

PAPANTLA, 227km from Veracruz, is by far the most attractive town on the route north, flower-filled and straggling over an unexpected outcrop of low, jungly hills. It's also one of the most important centres of the Mexican **vanilla** industry – the sweet, sticky odour frequently hangs over the place, and vanilla products are on sale everywhere – as well as being one of the surviving strongholds of **Totonac** life. There are Totonac murals in the zócalo – on the wall beneath the Iglesia de la Asunción, which is built on a terrace, and on the inside of the bandstand roof – and you'll see Totonacs wandering around barefooted in their loose white robes, especially in the market. You can also regularly witness the amazing dance-spectacle of the **Voladores de Papantla** here at Papantla and at El Tajín (see box, opposite), and at the top of the hill behind the cathedral is a monument paying tribute to them, showing one of the fliers playing his pipe. The best **views** across the city, however, are from the tower on the Santuario de Cristo Rey – the pretty church you pass as you enter the town by bus. The Casa de Cultura near the zócalo has regular dance and music performances – you can check what's on at the tourist office.

Practicalities

First-class **buses** use the ADO terminal on Juárez, a short distance from the centre; walk uphill along Juárez until you meet Enriquez, where you turn right for the zócalo (taxis cost around US$1.40). It can be hard to get a bus out, as most are *de paso*: book ahead for a local service, or take second-class, at least as far as Poza Rica, from where there's much more choice. The chaotic second-class Transportes Papantla terminal is more central on 20 de Noviembre – again, walk straight up (a couple of blocks) to the zócalo. Regular buses **to El Tajín and Poza Rica** run from behind *Hotel Tajín* on 16 de Septiembre.

There's a small **tourist office** down a winding staircase inside the Palacio Municipal (Mon–Fri 9am–3pm, Sat 9am–noon). Ask for a copy of the comprehensive and free *Guía Turística Veracruz Zona Norte*, which has commentary in Spanish and English on the major points of interest in the northern part of the state. All of the major **banks** are on Enriquez, a block or two south of *Hotel Provincia Express*, where you can change travellers' cheques and find ATM machines. Papantla has several **Internet** cafés – the one on the zócalo next to the Palacio Municipal charges US$1 per hour and is air-conditioned. Walk up the stairs to get to the entrance.

There are several reasonably priced **hotels** in Papantla. The *Provincia Express*, on the zócalo at Enriquez 103 (Ⓣ784/842-1645, Ⓕ842-4214; ❻), has pleasant modern rooms, while the *Tajín*, diagonally opposite and next to the cathedral (Ⓣ784/842-0121, Ⓕ842-0121; ❺), is just as comfortable, slightly cheaper, and has good views across the city (the three rooms with unobstructed views of the zócalo are usually rented out on a long-term basis to archeologists working at El Tajín). Ask at the hotel about guided tours to El Tajín. Cheaper options include the *Totonacapan* on Olivio, at 20 de Noviembre, near the second-class bus terminal (Ⓣ784/842-1220; ❺), which has a disco on Saturday nights, and the much more basic *Trujillo*, 5 de Mayo, at Artes (Ⓣ784/842-0100; ❷).

Restaurants are cheap and plentiful, though the selection of food differs only slightly from one place to the next. The *Plaza Pardo* on Enriquez (Ⓣ784/842-0059) has the best view over the zócalo from the prettiest terrace, good breakfasts and a reasonable menu with Mexican fare. Other options on the zócalo include *La Hacienda*, next to the Palacio Municipal (Ⓣ784/842-0633), the *Sorrento*, and next to it the *Plaza Pardo* (Ⓣ784/842-0067). *Café Catedral*, next door to *Hotel Tajín*, is a nice place for early morning coffee, hot chocolate and pastries. Vegetarians could try *Idea Pizza*, on Obispo, the street behind *Hotel Tajín*, while anyone on a tight budget should head for the eateries on José Azueta and around the market towards the second-class bus station.

El Tajín

However charming and peaceful Papantla may be, the main reason anyone goes there is to visit the ruins of **EL TAJÍN**, by far the most important archeological site on the Gulf coast, and a much more interesting and impressive collection of buildings than the more recent remains of Cempoala. The current opinion is that the principal architecture dates from the Classic period (300–900 AD), declining in the early Post-Classic (900–1100 AD). By the time of the Conquest it had been forgotten, and any knowledge of it now comes from archeological enquiries since the accidental discovery of the site in 1785. El

The Voladores de Papantla

The dance of the **Voladores** involves five men: a leader who provides music on flute and drum, and four performers. They represent the five earthly directions – the four cardinal points and straight up, from earth to heaven. After a few preliminary ceremonies, the five climb to a small platform atop a pole, where the leader resumes playing and directs prayers for the fertility of the land in every direction. Meanwhile, the four dancers tie ropes, coiled tightly around the top of the pole, to their waists and at a signal fling themselves head-first into space. As they spiral down in ever-increasing circles the leader continues to play, and to spin, on his platform, until the four hit the ground (hopefully landing on their feet, having righted themselves at the last minute). In all they make thirteen revolutions each, symbolizing the 52-year cycle of the Aztec calendar. Although the full significance of the dance has been lost – originally the performers would wear bird costumes, for example – it has survived much as the earliest chroniclers reported it, largely because the Spanish thought of it as a sport rather than a pagan rite. In Papantla (performances in front of the cathedral Sat & Sun) and El Tajín (regular performances outside the entrance to the ruins) it has become, at least partly, a tourist spectacle – though no less hazardous for that – as the permanent metal poles attest. If you can see it at a local village fiesta, there is still far more ceremony attached, particularly in the selection of a sufficiently tall tree and its erection in the place where the dance is to be performed.

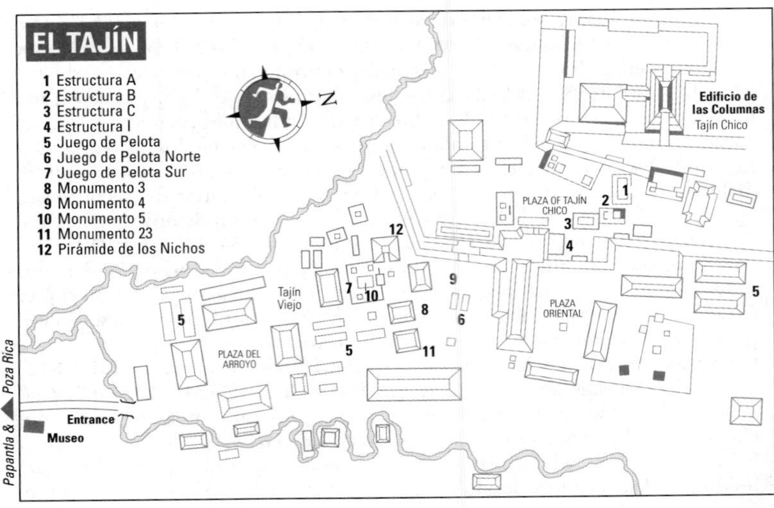

Tajín remains one of the most enigmatic and least understood of all of Mexico's ancient cities. No one even knows who built it. Some claim it was the Huastecs, others the Totonacs, but although "Tajín" means thunderbolt in Totonaca, experts consider it unlikely to have been built by their ancestors. Most archeologists prefer not to speculate too wildly, instead calling the civilization "Classic Veracruz" after its archeological hallmarks. You'll notice many of these at El Tajín, the most obvious of which are the niches and the complex ornamental motifs known as "scrolls", the latter of which are most prevalent on items and bas-reliefs associated with the ball-game, with which they were so obsessed (look at some of the stone "yokes" in the site museum). Classic Veracruz influence was widespread, and is strongly felt at Teotihuacán, such that some consider it may have been the Veracruzanos who built that city.

Despite many years of effort, only a small part of the huge site has been cleared, and even this limited area is constantly in danger of being once more engulfed by the jungle: stand on top of one of the pyramids and you see green mounds in every direction, each concealing more ruins.

The easiest way to **get to El Tajín** from Papantla is to take one of the *camionetas* that leave regularly from behind *Hotel Tajín*. There are also buses direct from El Tajín, or from Chote, to Poza Rica (marked "El Chote" and "San Andrés"), from where you can connect with services to Mexico City as well as up or down the coast. In itself, though, Poza Rica is not a place of any delights – a dull, oil-boom city with something of a reputation for violence. Continuing northwards, you'd be much better off in Tuxpán, about an hour up the coast.

The site

The site (daily 8am–6pm; US$3.70, plus US$3 for video cameras; free storage of bags and backpacks) divides broadly into two areas: **Tajín Viejo**, the original explored area centring on the amazing Pirámide de los Nichos, and **Tajín Chico**, a group of administrative buildings built on an artificial terrace. From the entrance (where, as well as the museum, there's a café and bar) a track leads through a small group of buildings, and into **Tajín Viejo**. Before you reach the square in front of the pyramid you pass several **ball-courts**, the most important, on your left, being the South Court, or **Juego de Pelota Sur**. There are seventeen such courts, possibly more, and the game must have assumed an importance here far greater than at any other known site. We know little of the rules, and courts vary widely in size and shape, but the general idea was to knock a ball through a ring or into a hole without the use of the hands. Clearly, too, there was a religious significance, and at El Tajín the game was closely associated with human sacrifice. The superb bas-relief sculptures that cover the walls of the South Court show aspects of the game, and include portrayals of a decapitated player, and another about to be stabbed with a ritual knife by fellow players, with Death waiting to his left. These bas-reliefs are a constant feature of the site, adorning many of the ball-courts and buildings, with more stacked in the museum, but those in the South Court are the most striking and best-preserved.

The unique **Pirámide de los Nichos** is the most famous building at El Tajín, and indeed one of the most remarkable and enigmatic of all Mexican ruins. It rises to a height of about 20m in six receding tiers, each face punctuated with regularly spaced niches; up the front a steep stairway climbs to a platform on which the temple originally stood. If you tally up the niches, including those hidden by the stairs and those, partly destroyed, around the base of the temple, there are 365 in all. Their exact purpose is unknown, but clearly they were more than mere decoration: perhaps each would hold some offering or sacrifice, one for each day of the year, or they may have symbolized caves – the dwellings of the earth god. Originally they were painted deep red, with a blue surround, to enhance the impression of depth. Niches predominate on other buildings at the site, and some bear the attribute of Quetzalcoatl, the plumed serpent, Tajín's most depicted god.

Around the plaza in front of the pyramid stand all the other important buildings of Tajín Viejo. Opposite is Monumento 3, a similar pyramid without the niches, and behind it **Monumento 23**, a strange steep-sided bulk, one of the last structures to be built here, and the only pyramid upon which you are allowed to climb – there are good views over Tajín Viejo from the top. To the right of the Pirámide de los Nichos, Monumento 2, a low temple, squats at the base of **Monumento 5**, a beautiful truncated pyramid with a high decorative pediment broken by a broad staircase; on the left, Monumento 4 is one of the oldest in El Tajín, and only partly restored.

From the back of Monumento 4 the path continues, past the **Juego de Pelota Norte** with its worn relief sculptures, up onto the levelled terrace of **Tajín Chico**. Originally this raised area was supported by a retaining wall, part of which has been restored, and reached by a staircase opposite the ball-court (which is no longer there). Only parts of the buildings now survive, making a rather confusing whole. **Estructura C**, and the adjoining Estructura B, are the most impressive remains: Estructura C has stone friezes running around its three storeys, giving the impression of niches. In this case, they were purely decorative, an effect that would have been heightened by a brightly coloured stucco finish. It has the remains of a concrete roof – originally a huge single slab of poured cement, unique in ancient Mexico. **Estructura A** also had a covered interior, and you can still get into its central terrace via a narrow staircase, the entrance covered by a false arch of the type common in Maya buildings. To the left of Estructura C, **Estructura I** features internal and external murals, and was probably the residence of some major political or religious figure. On the hill above Tajín Chico stood the **Edificio de las Columnas**, which must have dominated the entire city. El Tajín's governor, 13 Rabbit, lived here – bas-reliefs on columns recorded his exploits, and some of these are now on show in the museum. The building is little restored, and bits of broken, pre-Columbian pottery litter the area. This part of the site is closed to the public.

Tuxpán

Straddling the river of the same name, the town of **TUXPÁN** (or Tuxpam, pronounced "Toosh-pam") offers a far preferable overnight stay to its uglier southern neighbour, Poza Rica, on the journey up the coast to Tampico (see p.200). That said, it's still an unattractive place, with oblong concrete houses offering slim shade to barking dogs, in a landscape further marred by half-built oil platforms.

The zócalo and marketplace both spill out onto the north riverbank, although the town's most attractive spot is **Parque Reforma**, a square with plenty of trees about 200m west of the zócalo along Juárez. Small boats leave from in front of the zócalo, crossing the river to the town's single attraction, the **Museo de la Amistad Mexico–Cuba** (Mon–Sat 9am–8pm, Sun 9am–2pm; free). Occupying the house where Fidel Castro spent a year planning his revolutionary return to Cuba, the museum, comprising one small room of unlabelled photos, and another where a video is shown, focuses on Castro, Ché Guevara and Spanish imperialism in the Americas in general. There's usually somebody around who can give you a rundown on the displays, but ask the security guard at the gate if they're not immediately visible. The revolutionaries sailed from Tuxpán in December 1956 in the *Granma* yacht, almost sinking on the way, and arrived in Cuba to find Batista's forces waiting. A replica of the *Granma* stands on the riverbank. To get there, walk inland a couple of blocks to Obregón and then turn right, heading back to the river at the end of the street.

The only other reason to stick around is some long, if mediocre, beaches at **Barra de Tuxpán**, by the river mouth some 12km east of town. **Buses** (marked "Playa") run all day along riverside Reforma, past fishing boats and tankers, and arrive twenty minutes later at a vast stretch of grey sand. There are restaurants and changing rooms here and some palapas where you can sling a hammock.

Practicalities

The first-class ADO **bus** terminal lies at the junction of Reforma and Rodríguez, one block from the river and some 300m east of the zócalo – follow the river along Reyes Heroles to get to the centre. Omnibus de México (with both first- and second-class services) is not far away – 300m further east at the junction of Cuauhtémoc and 15 de Septiembre, beside the huge bridge across the river. For moving on, there are regular ADO buses to Tampico, Veracruz and Mexico City (direct and via Poza Rica), and several services daily to Papantla. Buses for the nearby village of Tamiahua leave every hour or so from the Omnibus de México terminal.

The helpful, well-stocked **tourist office** (Mon–Fri 9am–8pm, Sat 10am–6pm; ☎783/834-0177) is in the Palacio Municipal, at Juárez 20. There's a **laundry** at Ocampo 8. **Change money** or travellers' cheques at the Bancomer or Banamex, the former on Zapata two blocks west of the cathedral, the latter on Juárez at Parque Reforma. There is an **Internet** café next to Banamex, at Juárez 52.

Several of the town's **hotels** are found on Juárez between the zócalo and Parque Reforma. The best place to stay is the expensive *Reforma*, in a grand building opposite the cathedral at Juárez 25 (Ⓣ783/834-0210, Ⓕ834-0625; ❼), which has air-conditioned rooms with TV, as well as the best restaurant in town (see below). Cheaper options include the *Tuxpán*, Juárez, at Mina (Ⓣ783/834-4110; ❹), and *Posada San Ignacio*, Ocampo 26, one block north of Parque Reforma (no phone; ❹), where you can find simple rooms with fans around a quiet courtyard.

With its good steaks and live music on Fridays and Saturdays, *Antonios*, at *Hotel Reforma*, is the chicest **restaurant** in town. Otherwise, Parque Reforma is the best place to head for. Sip natural fruit juices on tables and chairs which fan out from the centre of the square, or sit at the terrace of *El Mejicano*, Morelos 49, and eat from its menu of Mexican food, including good guacamole. Alternatively, *Nuevo 303* on Pipila, leading down from Juárez to the river, is popular with locals and open 24 hours.

South of Veracruz

Leaving Veracruz to the south, Hwy-180 traverses a long expanse of plain, a country of broad river deltas and salt lagoons, for nearly 150km, until it hits the hills of the volcanic **Sierra Tuxtla**. This is one of the most beautiful stretches of Veracruz, boasting picturesque **fishing villages**, **volcanoes**, **waterfalls** and the idyllic **Lago de Catemaco**, around which the last expanse of Gulf coast **rainforest**, the Amazonia, is preserved. The region is most important, however, as the birthplace of Mexico's first civilization, the **Olmecs**. Here lies the sacred mountain – the **Volcán de San Martín** – which the Olmecs believed to be the place where the world was created; they built a replica "creation mountain" at their city, La Venta, on the border with Tabasco (see p.701). Although archeologically important, their second major city at **Tres Zapotes**, near Santiago Tuxtla, is little more than a mound in a maize field. Beyond the Tuxtla mountains, there's more low, flat, dull country all the way to Villahermosa (see p.693).

This part of southern Veracruz, around Lago Catemaco, is known as the "**Tierra de los Brujos**" (land of the witches or wizards), and every March a gathering takes place on Cerro Mono Blanco (White Monkey Hill). Mexico has thousands of practising witches, warlocks, shamans, herbalists, seers, healers, psychics and fortune-tellers, following a syncretic religion that blends Catholicism with ancient rites and practices. The thirteen *brujos* of Catemaco, however, who call themselves "the Brothers", are acknowledged as the high priests of the trade.

Alvarado and Tlacotalpan

ALVARADO is the first stop en route south from Veracruz, an extraordinary town on a narrow strip of land between the sea and the Laguna de Alvarado, some 40km from Veracruz. It's a working fishing port and is refreshingly traditional. There are plenty of hotels in sight, but it's not somewhere you'd want to stay long. You might, however, be tempted to stop for a meal – the fishing fleet is enormous and there are lots of good **fish restaurants** along the front. Alvarado's Port Authority restaurant, especially, is famed for its excellence and is also cheap, being genuinely used by port workers and fishermen.

If you want somewhere small, quiet and entirely off the tourist circuit to stay, try instead **TLACOTALPAN**, some twenty minutes away on the spectacular road that heads inland towards Tuxtepec. It's most famous for being where the musician and composer Agustín Lara, whose works have been interpreted by the likes of Pavarotti, Carreras and Domingo, spent his early childhood. On the edges of the Río Papaloapan, close to the lagoon, it's a very pretty village, and although there's absolutely nothing laid on, you can rent boats on the river, and fish or swim. Near the zócalo, you'll find a small **museum** (Mon–Fri 9am–5pm; US$1.50) with antique furniture and local artefacts, while the **Casa de Cultura** (Mon–Fri 9am–5pm; free) on Caranza also has displays of Lara memorabilia and, upstairs, modernist paintings by Alberto Fuster, another local.

The upmarket *Dona Lala* **hotel** (Ⓣ288/884-2580; ❻) by the river has lovely rooms and a smart restaurant serving good seafood. Otherwise, there are a couple of small hotels on the main street near where the **buses** stop, but avoid the posada, which doubles as a brothel. Alternatively, you can easily find a **room** in a local house for around US$10 – ask around in the restaurants and cafés near the zócalo. The **cafés** in front of the *Dona Lala*, near the river, have delicious, cheap seafood. Further items relating to the town's favourite son, Lara, are on show near the zócalo in the *Blancanieves* **bar**.

Los dos Tuxtlas

The two townships of **Santiago Tuxtla** and **San Andrés Tuxtla** together form the hub of the attractive, volcanic hill country – known as "La Suiza Veracruzana" (the Veracruz Switzerland) – that emerges beyond Alvarado. Things become much more interesting at this point, and the cooler climate is an infinite relief.

Santiago Tuxtla and Tres Zapotes

Before arriving at its larger brother, San Andrés Tuxtla, first-class buses from Veracruz pass the quiet and picturesque **SANTIAGO TUXTLA**, a place not inundated with facilities and attractions, but worth a stop nonetheless. A giant Olmec head stands in the centre of the zócalo, on one side of which is a small **museum of local archeology and ethnography** (closed for renovation at the time of writing; US$2.90). Although Santiago is itself a beautiful spot, the main reason people come here is to visit the important Olmec site of **Tres Zapotes**, a little less than an hour away by local bus (they leave from near the main highway, and are usually marked "3 Zapotes"). Frankly, the journey is barely worth it: a painfully slow ride to what is basically just a **museum** (daily 9am–6pm; US$2.50) containing little that is not duplicated elsewhere. Its main interest lies in a series of stelae inscribed with Olmec glyphs. Of the site itself, nearby, virtually nothing can be seen.

There are a couple of small **hotels** in town, including the remarkably good *Castellanos* (Ⓣ294/947-0300; ❺), in a distinctive circular building right on the zócalo, with 53 air-conditioned rooms and a good **restaurant** serving meat dishes, seafood and salads. There are a few other restaurants and cafés, again around the zócalo, such as *Super La Joya*, where you can eat standard Mexican fare at tables outside.

San Andrés Tuxtla

SAN ANDRÉS TUXTLA is the larger of the two Tuxtlas. The majority of **buses** stop at the top of the hill where the highway passes by – the first-class bus terminal is at the top of Juárez, which leads straight down to the zócalo. Other, second-class buses will drop you by the market, again within easy walking distance of the centre.

Surrounded by tobacco fields, San Andrés Tuxtla is home to several **cigar factories**, where you can watch *puros* being hand-rolled and then buy some. One of the top brands in Mexico, Matacapan Tobaccos, is produced here and has brought international fame to the town. The Santa Clara factory (Mon–Fri 8am–7pm, Sat 8–11am; free), on the highway one block from the ADO bus station, welcomes visitors. The tobacco export company Calidad Tobaccos (Ⓦwww.calidadtobaccos.com) runs full guided tours of the cultivation fields and factory, and even hands-on cigar-rolling workshops.

Local buses run from here to Santiago Tuxtla and Catemaco, but there are a couple of more local attractions. The **Laguna Encantada** is a volcanic lake about 2km from the town and a popular local swimming spot. Oddly, the water level falls when it rains, and rises when the weather is dry. It can be reached in less than an hour on foot – follow Belisario Dominguez to the top where it crosses the highway, turn right (towards Catemaco), and then take a signed path up to the left – though locals have recently been **warning** against visits, following assaults on both tourists and residents. The spectacular **Salto de Eyipantla** is a little further afield (about 9km from San Andrés), but safely reached by frequent local buses that leave from 5 de Mayo where it meets the market. This series of three waterfalls, accessed via 244 worn steps down from a car park, is a beautiful spot – not a place for swimming, but surrounded by lush vegetation and peaceful enough if you avoid the busy summer months.

Most **accommodation** and other facilities are very close to the zócalo or on Juárez. The *Catedral*, on Pino Suárez – reached via the alley beside the church (Ⓣ294/942-0237; ❷), is clean and friendly, while one block away at the corner of Suárez and Belisario Dominguez, you could try the very cheap and basic *Colonial* (Ⓣ294/942-0552; ❷) or the *Figueroa* (Ⓣ294/942-0257; ❸), the pick of the budget options, with charming rooms along a plant-strewn balcony and a good range of leaflets, brochures and maps about the region. A number of fancier hotels are visible from the square: the *San Andrés*, Madero 6 (Ⓣ294/942-0604; ❹), is the most reasonably priced, with *Hotel del Parque*, Madero 5 (Ⓣ294/942-0198, Ⓕ942-3050; ❺), a little classier and pricier.

Food and drink options include **cafés** on the zócalo – sip a coffee while people-watching at *Hotel del Parque*, for instance. The *San Andrés* café (attached to the hotel) has comidas corridas for under US$3 and *El Pequeño Archi*, next to the *Catedral* hotel (Ⓣ294/942-4796), is a good spot for breakfast. There's an excellent **market**, too, with some cheap food stands, where you can buy superb baked goods, locally grown tropical fruits and vegetables, freshwater fish and the best selection of medicinal herbs in the region. There are also a number of reputable fish and seafood restaurants, especially along Madero, past the *San Andrés* hotel – *Mariscos Chazaro*, at no. 12 (Ⓣ294/942-1379), has great prawn cocktails. For something more special, try the *Montepio*, at the end of the alley opposite the *San Andrés* hotel (Ⓣ294/942-1496), which has a steak menu, a good wine list and a bar that welcomes women.

There are several **banks** with ATMs around the zócalo; the best bank for **travellers' cheques** is Bital, 16 de Septiembre, at Carranza. For **Internet** access, try Café Virtual (US$1 per hour), one block west of the zócalo, or Actualis (US$1 per hour), two blocks down from the first-class bus station, on Juárez.

Catemaco and around

Squatting on the western shore of a large, mountain-ringed lake, the fourth largest inland body of water in Mexico and by tradition a centre of native witchcraft, **CATEMACO** is a much more picturesque spot to break the journey before the long leg south, with the nearby marshland and lagoon supporting large colonies of waterbirds including herons, cormorants, wintering ospreys and many other resident and migratory species. The surrounding mountains, which are volcanic in origin (though the most recent activity was in 1793), are unique on the Gulf coast as they descend right into the sea.

Veracruzanos arrive in force at weekends and holidays, when the main strip can get pretty busy – but it's little spoiled for all that, with development so far stretching just five blocks or so back from the waterfront, although hotels can be expensive. Watch out for the touts, who'll try and persuade you to attend a native spiritual purification ceremony or to visit the place where Sean Connery's *Medicine Man* was filmed: Playa Azul, one of the lake's several beaches and the location of a fancy resort-style hotel. A **boat trip** around the lake or to one of the islands within it, however, is one of the highlights of southern Veracruz. The Sociedad Cooperativa de Lanchas, on the lake opposite the *Julita* hotel, one block from the zócalo, runs ninety-minute trips to all of

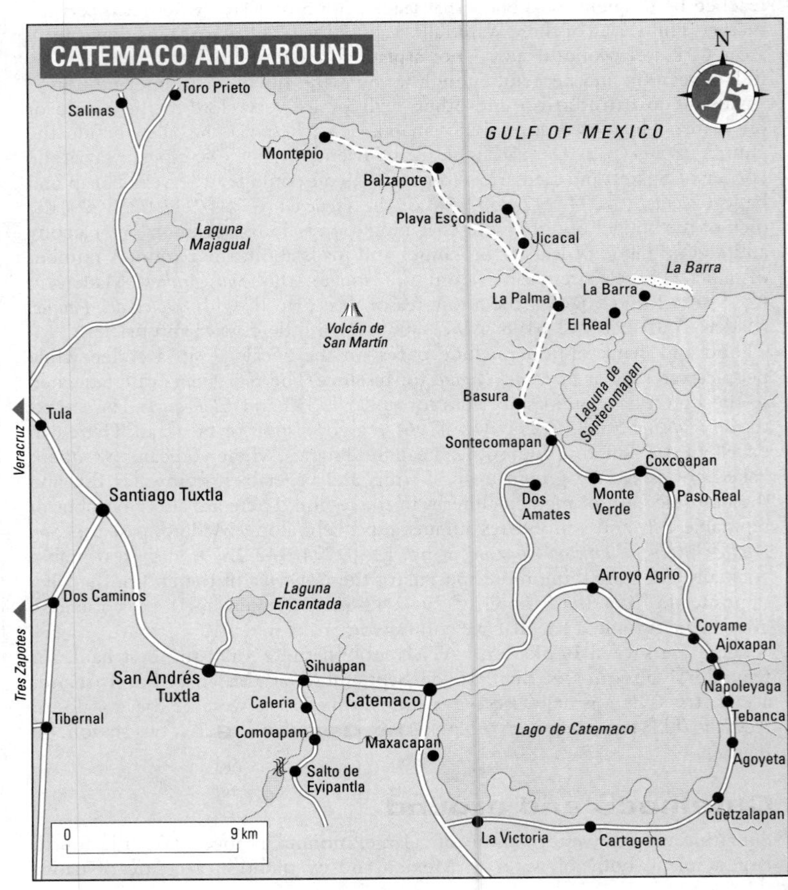

the lake's main sights and some of its beaches for US$35 for one to six people. On **Isla de los Changos** there are monkeys (actually mandrill baboons native to Thailand) that officially belong to Veracruz University – who have pleaded for them to be left alone – but boat operators continue to feed them so tourists can photograph them. Colectivos run from the zócalo to various nearby sights, including the waterfalls at **Salto de Eyipantla**, a few kilometres south of town, and Sontecomapan village, 18km north of town, where you can take a trip up the pretty **Sontecomapan canal**, which offers good **bird-watching** possibilities. For birding and eco-adventure trips up the Chuniapan River and to La Barra beach (see p.580), contact Operadora Turística La Continga at the *Playa Azul Resort* (Ⓣ294/943-0001). Conducted by renowned ornithologist William J. Schadlach, the tours cost around US$50 per day, plus launch expenses. Alternatively, just chill out on one of the lake **beaches**. There are crocodiles in the lake, but they are so well fed on left-over fish scraps from the lakeside restaurants, apparently, that they never attack.

Catemaco is also an important Catholic place of pilgrimage, thanks to its statue of the Virgin of Carmen, who is said to have appeared to a fisherman in 1714 in a narrow grotto in **El Tegal**, roughly twenty minutes' walk around the lakeshore. The only other tourist site is the **Basílica de Nuestra Señora del Carmen**, decorated with multicoloured tiles, and located on the eastern side of the lake. A local bus from the plaza (marked "La Margarita") goes round much of the shore, passing a couple of beaches and the beautiful Río Cuetzalpan. There is only one departure daily, at 2pm.

After all this activity, wind down with a *temazcal*, a traditional Mesoamerican sauna that purifies body and soul, available at *Nanciyaga* (see p.579) for US$15 or Ecoparque La Punta, near the bus terminal by the lakeshore (Ⓣ294/943-0456, Ⓔecoparque@hotmail.com), for US$30 per person (minimum of two; includes four treatments).

Practicalities

Catemaco is slightly off the main road, and although there are some direct **buses** from Veracruz, there's no need to make a special effort to get one, as regular local services from San Andrés Tuxtla make the short journey back and forth. Catch them in Catemaco from the plaza five blocks northwest of the zócalo. For moving on, second-class buses depart the AU terminal near the main highway for all the main towns in western Mexico; try to buy tickets a day in advance, since seats are numbered. The ADO first-class terminal is surely the most scenic in the country, facing the lake about a five-minute walk from the centre (walk to the lakefront from the zócalo and turn left). On the zócalo, which lies two blocks in from the waterfront, there's a **tourist office** in the Palacio Municipal (Mon–Fri 9am–3pm) and an **ATM** machine next to the *Catemaco* hotel – note that to change cash and travellers' cheques, you'll have to go to San Andrés Tuxtla. The **post office** is just off the zócalo towards the *Juros* hotel. Also just off the zócalo, on Carranza next to the cathedral, you'll find a couple of **Internet** cafés.

On the whole, **hotels** right on the lake are expensive, though out of season prices do drop. Otherwise, there are several places a couple of streets inland, just down from where the buses stop; people may try to accost you as you arrive to take you to a hotel, but rooms are easy enough to find without help. On the lakeside very close to the centre, *Julita*, Playa 10 (Ⓣ294/943-0008; ❸), offers simple, clean and bright rooms with fans and is the best value in town. Further along, at no. 14, *Juros* (Ⓣ294/943-0084; ❺) boasts a fantastic rooftop swimming pool, but rooms vary in quality. *Los Arcos*, next door to the *Juros* at

Fiestas

JANUARY

In the last week of January **Tlacotalpan** has a fiesta with dances, boat races and bulls let loose in the streets.

FEBRUARY

2 DÍA DE LA CANDELARIA. Colourful Indian fiesta in **Jaltipán** on the main road south of Catemaco, which includes the dance of La Malinche (Malintzin, Cortés' Indian interpreter and mistress, known to the Spanish as Malinche, is said to have been born here), re-creating aspects of the Conquest. Also the final day of celebrations in **Tlacotalpan**.

4 Agricultural festival in **Otatitlán**, near the Oaxaca border off the road from Alvarado to Oaxaca, where many Indians attend a midnight mass to bless their crops.

CARNAVAL (the week before Lent, variable Feb–March) is celebrated all over the region, most riotously in **Veracruz**.

MARCH

On the first Friday, the FERIA DEL CAFÉ in **Ixhualtán**, a coffee-growing town near Córdoba – both trade fair and popular fiesta.

18–19 FIESTAS DE SAN JOSÉ. In **Naranjos**, between Tuxpán and Tampico, a fiesta with many traditional dances celebrates the local patron saint. Similar events in **Espinal**, a Totonac village on the Río Tecolutla, not far from El Tajín and Papantla, where with luck you can witness the spectacular Voladores.

HOLY WEEK. Re-creations of the Passion are widespread in this area. You can witness them in **Papantla** – where you'll also see the Voladores – in **Coatzintla**, a Totonac village near Tajín, in **Cotaxtla**, between Veracruz and Córdoba, and in **Otatitlán**. **Naolinco**, a beautiful village near Xalapa, stages a mock Crucifixion on Good Friday. Also celebrations in **Catemaco** – and in the port of **Alvarado** – a far more ribald Fish Fiesta following hard on the heels of the Veracruz carnival.

APRIL

15–17 (approx) FERIA DE LAS FLORES. Flower festival in **Fortín de las Flores**.

MAY

3 Hundreds of pilgrims converge on **Otatitlán** to pay homage to the village's Cristo Negro.

27 DÍA DEL SAGRADO CORAZON. The start of four days of festivities in **Naranjos**.

CORPUS CHRISTI (variable, the Thurs after Trinity) sees the start of a major four-day festival in **Papantla** and, in particular, regular performances by the Voladores.

Madero 7 (ⓣ294/943-0003, ⓕ943-0773, ⓦwww.arcoshotel.com.mx; ❻), has pleasant, air-conditioned rooms with TV built around an attractive pool. Some of the higher rooms have lake views. On the zócalo, the *Catemaco* (ⓣ294/943-0203, ⓕ943-0045; ❻) has similar facilities, plus its own restaurant. Finally, *Hotel del Lago*, Paseo del Malecón, on the lakeshore at the edge of the village on the Tuxtla road (ⓣ294/943-0160, ⓕ943-0431; ❻), is a secure, friendly place with small, clean, air-conditioned rooms, a palm-ringed pool and restaurant.

By far the best place to stay if you want to appreciate the area's natural beauty,

JUNE

13 DÍA DE SAN ANTONIO. Fiesta in **Huatusco**, between Córdoba and Veracruz.

24 DÍA DE SAN JUAN is celebrated in **Santiago Tuxtla**, with dancing, and in **Martinez de la Torre**, on the road inland from Nautla, where the Voladores perform.

JULY

15 DÍA DE LA VIRGEN DEL CARMEN. A massive pilgrimage to **Catemaco**, accompanied by a fiesta which spills over into the following day.

24 DÍA DE SANTIAGO is celebrated with fiestas in **Santiago Tuxtla** and **Coatzintla**; each lasts several days. In **Tlapacoyan** you can see the bizarre Baile de los Negritos.

AUGUST

14 Teocelo, a village in beautiful country between Xalapa and Fortín, celebrates an ancient fiesta with dance and music.

15 In **Tuxpán**, a week-long feria begins, and includes dancing and Voladores.

16 In **Tlapacoyan**, the Baile de los Negritos is held to commemorate the Day of the Assumption.

24 Córdoba celebrates the anniversary of the signing of the Treaty of Independence.

SEPTEMBER

15–16 Independence celebrations take place everywhere.

21 DÍA DE SAN MATEO sees secular as well as religious celebration in **Naolinco**.

30 Coatepec, between Xalapa and Fortín, celebrates its patron's day – processions and dances.

OCTOBER

7 FIESTA DE LA VIRGEN DEL ROSARIO, patroness of fishermen. In **La Antigua** she is honoured with processions of canoes on the river, while **Alvarado** enjoys a more earthy fiesta, filling the first two weeks of the month.

NOVEMBER

2 DAY OF THE DEAD is honoured everywhere – the rites are particularly strictly followed in **Naolinco**.

30 Fiestas in **San Andrés Tuxtla**, carrying on into December 1.

DECEMBER

12 DÍA DE LA VIRGEN DE GUADALUPE is widely observed, especially in **Huatusco**, **Cotaxtla**, and **Amatlán de los Reyes**, near Córdoba.

24 Christmas, of course, celebrated in **Santiago Tuxtla** with a very famous festival that lasts until Twelfth Night, January 6.

however, is *Nanciyaga* (Ⓣ/Ⓕ 294/943-0199), an ecotourism facility on the far shore of the lake, little visited by Westerners and a great place to meet young Veracruzanos; **cabañas** in the jungle (US$25 Mon–Fri, US$50 Sat & Sun) have room for up to four people. The organizers rent canoes, arrange guided walks through the forest and teach traditional Mexican arts and crafts. It's only 7km by taxi to *Nanciyaga*; you can also get there by launch.

Seafood **restaurants** abound on the shore and around the zócalo, most offering the local speciality, *mojarra* (small perch from the lake), best sampled when cooked *a la tachagovi* – with a delicious hot sauce. Eateries popular with the locals include *Los Sauces* (ⓣ294/943-0548) and *El Pescador* (ⓣ294/943-0705), next to each other on Paseo del Malecón, and the restaurant at the *Julita* hotel. The best all-round eating option, however, is *La Casona*, on the zócalo at Aldama 4 (ⓣ294/943-0813), which has plenty for seafood- and meat-lovers alike, great breakfasts, an attractive dining room looking out onto a verdant garden and a talkative parrot to boot. Another good place for breakfast is *La Casita*, Ocampo 30, which also has reasonable Mexican fare and seafood.

Coastal beaches

From Catemaco a paved road with spectacular views of Lago Catemaco, the rainforest and the lagoon leads through sections of ranch land only recently hacked out of the rainforest, to the small fishing village of **Sontecomapan** (see p.577), after which it deteriorates into an appalling state as it continues on to some of Veracruz's best, least-visited beaches: at **Montepio** there are a couple of posadas (❸), the better of which, the *San José*, is nearer the sea; at **Playa Escondida**, a beautiful beach some 15km from Montepio, there's *Hotel Playa Escondido* (❸). *Camionetas* leave Catemaco from Calle Lerdo, at Revolución, five blocks from the lakeshore, every fifty minutes and take up to two hours to make the journey of 38km (about US$3.50) to Montepio. **La Barra** is another lovely stretch of sand and is often deserted: collective and private launches can be rented to here from the entrance to Sontecomapan canal (see p.577), for around US$2 each way (you may have to wait for a return launch) and around US$40 for a round-trip in a private launch (the boatman will wait for you at the beach or return at an appointed time). At La Barra, *Restaurant Juan Cruz* serves up tasty fresh seafood.

Coatzacoalcos and Acayucán

The **northern shore** of the Isthmus of Tehuantepec – the narrowest part of Mexico – is less attractive, with a huge industrial zone stretching from the dirty concrete town of Minatitlán to **COATZACOALCOS** (formerly Puerto México, the Atlantic railway terminus), dominated by a giant oil refinery. If you have to stop in this area, Coatzacoalcos is definitely the better choice: big enough to have a real centre and with plenty of hotels and restaurants around the *camionera*. Coatzacoalcos also boasts a spectacular modern bridge – known as Coatzacoalcos II – by which the main highway bypasses the town. If you're on a bus heading downtown you'll cross the Río Coatzacoalcos by an older, lesser suspension bridge. In legend, Coatzacoalcos is the place from which Quetzalcoatl and his followers sailed east, vowing to return.

Crossing the north of the isthmus you'll also inevitably pass through **ACAYUCÁN**, where the coastal highway and the trans-isthmus highway meet. The enormous bus station and equally giant market cater to all the passing travellers; there's little otherwise but mud, dust and noise, though the **market** stalls here can be a good place to stop off for provisions such as nuts, cheese, fresh pineapple and corn bread. Make your visit a short one and, if you have any choice at all, press straight on through to Villahermosa (see p.693). If you do need to **stay**, go for *Hotel Plaza* (ⓣ924/245-1344; ❹) or the *Joalicia* (ⓣ/ⓕ 924/245-0877; ❸), both on the zócalo, or the more luxurious *Kinaku*, just off it at Ocampo Sur 7 (ⓣ924/245-0410; ❻).

Travel details

Buses

First-class buses are mostly operated by Autobuses del Oriente (ADO) – remarkably slick and efficient. **Second-class** is dominated (at least on long hauls) by Autobuses Unidos (AU), more of a mixed bag. The following is a brief rundown of the routes, mainly taking into account the ADO services, and should be regarded as a minimum.

Papantla to: Mexico City (6 daily; 6hr); Poza Rica (frequently; 30min); Tlapacoyan (4 daily; 3hr); Tuxpán (3 daily; 1hr 30min); Veracruz (6 daily; 4hr); Xalapa (7 daily; 4hr).

Xalapa to: Fortín de las Flores (7 daily; 3hr); Mexico City (15 daily; 5hr); Papantla (7 daily; 4hr); Veracruz (frequently; 2hr).

Poza Rica to: Mexico City (8 daily; 5hr); Tuxpán (frequently; 1hr); Veracruz (frequently; 4hr 30min).

San Andrés Tuxtla to: Catemaco (frequently; 30min); Coatzacoalcos (9 daily; 2hr 30min); Veracruz (frequently; 3hr).

Tuxpán to: Mexico City (9 daily; 6hr); Poza Rica (frequently; 1hr); Tampico (10 daily; 3hr); Veracruz (6 daily; 5hr 30min); Xalapa (7 daily; 6hr).

Veracruz to: Cardel (frequently; 30min); Catemaco (9 daily; 3hr 30min); Coatzacoalcos (17 daily; 5hr 30min); Córdoba (frequently; 2hr); Mexico City (16 daily; 6hr); Oaxaca (3 daily; 7hr); Orizaba (frequently; 2hr); Papantla (6 daily; 4hr); Poza Rica (frequently; 4hr 30min); San Andrés Tuxtla (15 daily; 3hr); Tuxpán (11 daily; 5hr 30min); Villahermosa (14 daily; 7hr); Xalapa (frequently; 2hr).

Flights

There are regular flights to Mexico City from Veracruz, and also services to Poza Rica, Oaxaca and Cancún. The schedules change regularly, so check with the tourist office or travel agents in Veracruz (see p.559) or Xalapa (see p.554) for the latest information.

Oaxaca

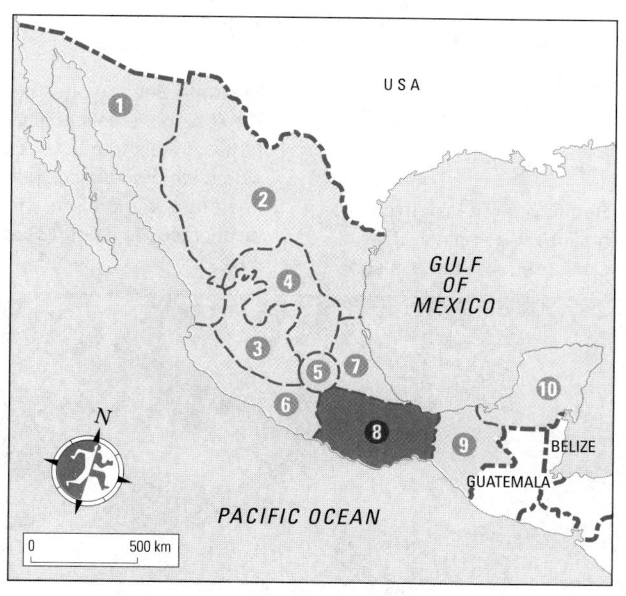
USA
1
2
4
3
5
7
6
8
9
10
GULF OF MEXICO
BELIZE
GUATEMALA
PACIFIC OCEAN
N
0
500 km

CHAPTER 8 Highlights

✱ **Oaxaca** This colonial city and artistic centre is home to the beautifully restored Museo de las Culturas, fantastic markets, and rich indigenous traditions. **See p.588**

✱ **Monte Albán** Once a potent symbol of Mixtec power, these ruins were an astounding ancient city with a population of over twenty thousand. **See p.603**

✱ **El Tule** Break your journey to marvel at what may be the oldest tree in the Americas. **See p.606**

✱ **Benito Juárez** Visit this quaint village named after Oaxaca's most famous son and walk along the footpaths in the beautiful mountain surroundings. **See p.608**

✱ **Hierve el Agua** Watch the sun set across the valley at this enchanting limestone waterfall. **See p.612**

✱ **Puerto Escondido** Ride the Mexican pipeline – or just watch – at this world-famous surfing spot and beach destination. **See p.616**

✱ **Mazunte** See the queens of the sea, the female golfina turtles, in this tranquil ocean-side town or increase your heart rate with a trip to the local crocodile lagoon. **See p.627**

△ Straw cowboy hats

8

Oaxaca

The state of **Oaxaca** marks the break between North American central Mexico and Central America. Here the two chains of the Sierra Madre converge, to run on as a single range, through the country's narrowest point, the Isthmus of Tehuantepec, right into South America and the Andes. The frequently barren landscapes of northern Mexico are left behind, replaced by thickly forested hillsides, or in low-lying areas by swamp and jungle. The striking differences of the region are compounded by the relative lack of development – the "Mexican economic miracle" has yet to reach the south.

Indigenous traditions remain powerful in this area, which is home to fifteen different indigenous groups. The old languages are still widely spoken, and there are scenes in the villages that seem to deny that the Spanish Conquest ever happened. Oaxaqueño resourcefulness, pride and craft skills are manifest everywhere. For the colour and variety of its markets, and the fascination of its fiestas, there is no rival in Mexico. One of Oaxaca's most rewarding and eye-opening experiences can be a stay in one of the central valleys' **Tourist Yú'ù** facilities, where you'll be a guest of the local indigenous community. Less enticingly, but arising out of the same traditions, the region has witnessed considerable **political disturbance** in recent years, though protest has never been as manifest as in its more troubled neighbour, Chiapas.

The relaxed city of **Oaxaca** itself is the prime destination, close enough to Mexico City and the mainstream to attract large numbers of tourists to its fine crafts stores, markets and seemingly constant fiestas, cobbled, gallery-lined walkways, sophisiticated restaurants and nearby indigenous villages and ancient ruins. Here you can see one of the region's – and the whole of Iberian America's – most magnificent **Baroque churches**, Santo Domingo, which fuses Spanish and native influences to spectacular effect. From the earliest times the valley of Oaxaca was inhabited by the same Zapotec and Mixtec peoples who comprise the bulk of its population now. Their ancient sites – at **Monte Albán**, **Yagul** and **Mitla** – are less well known than their contemporaries in central and eastern Mexico, but every bit as important and impressive.

The growing Pacific resorts of **Puerto Escondido**, **Puerto Ángel** and **Huatulco** are easily reached from the city. Their reputation for being unspoiled beach paradises is no longer entirely justified – Escondido in particular is a resort of some size, with an international airport, and there's another huge resort under construction at Huatulco. All along this coast you'll discover some of the emptiest and best **Pacific beaches** in Mexico, including the tranquil idyll of **Mazunte**, easily reached from the main centres. Be warned, however, that robberies have been reported on Hwy-131 and Hwy-175 to the

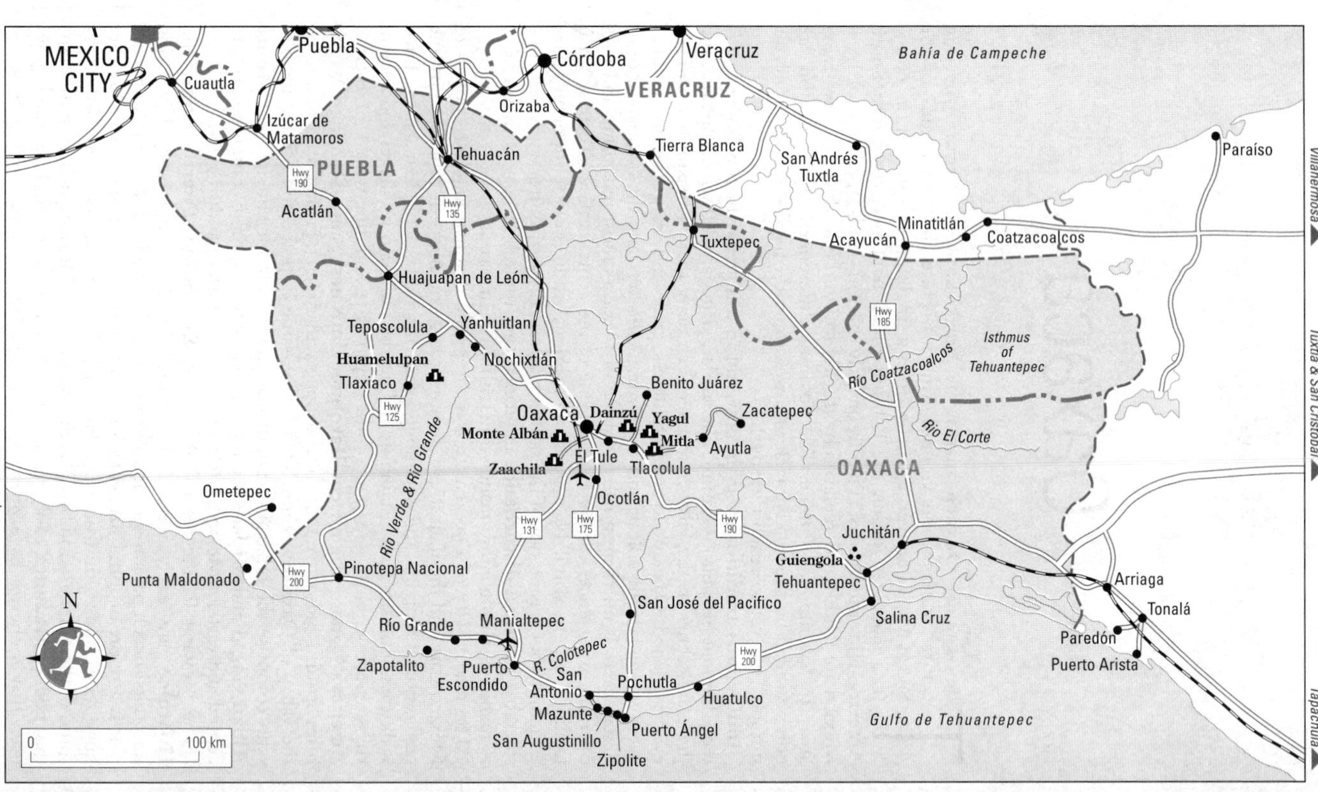
Villahermosa
Tuxtla & San Cristóbal
Tapachula
Acapulco
MEXICO CITY
Puebla
Córdoba
Veracruz
Bahía de Campeche
VERACRUZ
Cuautla
Orizaba
Izúcar de Matamoros
Tierra Blanca
San Andrés Tuxtla
Paraíso
Tehuacán
PUEBLA
Hwy 190
Hwy 135
Acatlán
Minatitlán
Acayucán
Coatzacoalcos
Tuxtepec
Huajuapan de León
Hwy 185
Teposcolula
Yanhuitlan
Nochixtlán
Isthmus of Tehuantepec
Huamelulpan
Tlaxiaco
Río Coatzacoalcos
Benito Juárez
Hwy 125
Oaxaca
Dainzú
Yagul
Zacatepec
Monte Albán
Mitla
Ayutla
Río El Corte
Río Verde & Río Grande
El Tule
Zaachila
Tlacolula
OAXACA
Ometepec
Ocotlán
Hwy 131
Hwy 175
Hwy 190
Juchitán
Guiengola
Punta Maldonado
Hwy 200
Pinotepa Nacional
Tehuantepec
Arriaga
N
San José del Pacifico
Salina Cruz
Tonalá
Río Grande
Manialtepec
Paredón
R. Colotepec
Hwy 200
Puerto Arista
Zapotalito
Puerto Escondido
San Antonio
Pochutla
Huatulco
Mazunte
Gulfo de Tehuantepec
0
100 km
San Augustinillo
Puerto Ángel
Zipolite

coast (from Oaxaca to Puerto Escondido and Pochutla), and the coastal Hwy-200, but only at night. The journey takes longer than it should too, as both roads to the coast are in a terrible state of repair, with enormous potholes.

The resorts are all around 250km from Oaxaca, reached via spectacular mountain roads that take a minimum of six hours to traverse. Although there are regular **buses** to **Pochutla**, just inland from Puerto Ángel, and then on to Puerto Escondido, it's a slow and occasionally heart-stopping journey along winding, mountainous highways. Many people prefer to **fly** down, either with Aerotucán from Oaxaca to Escondido – an experience in itself – or with Mexicana direct from Mexico City to Escondido or Huatulco. There are also regular bus connections along the coast, from Acapulco in the north or Salina Cruz in the south, and a direct overnight service between Mexico City and Puerto Escondido.

Getting there from Mexico City and Acapulco

There are two routes to Oaxaca **from Mexico City**. The first, via **Hwy-135**, which links to the Mexico City–Puebla–Córdoba autopista, takes only five hours and is the more travelled route. The slower, ten-hour, journey on **Hwy-190** passes through the spa town of **Cuautla**, remarkable only as the birthplace of Emiliano Zapata, and **Huajapan de León**, a town of little interest but marking the beginning of *mescal*-producing territory, with spiny, bluish-green maguey cactuses cultivated all along the road. This also marks the beginning of the **Mixteca**, one of the state's most interesting regions. On the side road that leads from here to the spa town of **Tehuacán**, you pass through one of the largest and most impressive **cactus forests** in the republic. Both routes take in some interesting mountain scenery (particularly the autopista), with cacti and scrub in the early stages giving way to thicker vegetation as you approach Oaxaca, and both are well served by buses.

To reach Oaxaca **from Acapulco**, it's probably quicker to go through Mexico City, but there are relatively frequent buses up from the Pacific coast at **Pinotepa Nacional**; and more frequently, and equally uncomfortably, from **Puerto Escondido** or Pochutla, the service town for **Puerto Ángel**. That said, if you are travelling along the Pacific coast, it seems a pity to miss out on the region's excellent beaches just to get to Oaxaca quickly.

Tehuacán

The only place that merits a stop as you speed down the autopista from Mexico City to Oaxaca is **TEHUACÁN**, the source of a good percentage of the bottled mineral water (Agua de Tehuacán) consumed throughout Mexico. A spa town of some antiquity, relaxing, easy-paced, temperate in every sense of the word, its centre is dotted with buildings from the town's early twentieth-century heyday. The tiled arcade-fronted house on the zócalo, with its Moorish flourishes, was obviously designed with Vichy or Evian in mind and bears a plaque to Señor Don Joaquim Pita, who first put the water in bottles. Take a look, too, at the underside of the colonnade for highly graphic murals depicting the five regions that make up Tehuacán district. A more pedestrian introduction to the region fills the halls of the **Museo del Valle de Tehuacán** (Tues–Sun 10am–6pm; US$1.50), in the elegant Ex-Convento de Carmen at

Reforma Norte 210, featuring a brightly coloured tiled dome that dominates the skyline in this part of town. A tiny collection of prehistoric relics shores up the thinly illustrated story of maize in Mesoamerica and particularly in the Tehuacán valley, which was the first place to truly cultivate (rather than simply harvest) the crop some six or seven thousand years ago – ample evidence that this was one of the earliest settled areas in Mexico.

All this can be seen in a couple of hours, but if you decide to stay in town you can fill the time by heading out to the **springs** on the outskirts to sample the clean-tasting water, or take a dip at **Balneario San Lorenzo** (daily 6.30am–6pm; US$3), a large complex of sun-warmed pools (including one Olympic-sized affair), most of which draw from the local springs. Catch a bus from the Autobuses Unidos bus station to San Lorenzo, a suburb 5km west of the centre. Alternatively, you can pamper yourself with a *temazcal* sauna and massage at the *Hotel Aldea Bazar* (Ⓣ2/382-2550; ❺), a five-minute taxi ride from the centre of town at Calzada Adolfo López Mateos 3351.

Practicalities

Most long-distance **buses** arrive at the ADO station on Independencia, two blocks west of the zócalo. Second-class buses from Mexico City, Oaxaca and elsewhere arrive at the Autobuses Unidos station near the junction of Calle 5 Oriente and Calle 5 Sur, on the opposite side of the centre. Independencia runs all the way out to the suburb of San Lorenzo, past ADO.

The most luxurious **place to stay** in Tehuacán is the *Hotel México*, Independencia at Reforma Norte, one block west of the zócalo (Ⓣ2/382-0019; ❻), which has a pool, parking and large, modern and clean rooms. Budget hotels can be found near the zócalo, including the *Hotel Monroy*, at Reforma Norte 217 (Ⓣ2/383-0491; ❹). **Banks** (with ATMs) and other services are mostly on Reforma.

Oaxaca

The state capital, **OAXACA** sprawls across a grand expanse of deep-set valley, 1600m above sea level, some 500km southeast of Mexico City. Its colour, folklore, numerous fiestas, the huge extent of its indigenous markets, which are known for being particularly diverse and traditional, and its thoroughly colonial centre combine to make this one of the most popular, and most rewarding, destinations for travellers, many of whom come here to study. Even the increase in package tourism and the pedestrianization of Macedonio Alcalá, the main thoroughfare from the zócalo to the cathedral – a street now lined with upscale handicraft and jewellery shops – have done little to destroy the city's gentle appeal. Furthermore, Oaxaca is also widely seen as the artistic centre of Mexico, with several state-run and private galleries, resident artists, art and jewellery master classes and regular exhibitions (including free ones in the zócalo). In the market and in shops everywhere, you'll find Oaxaca's trademark fantastical and fantastically coloured model animals.

Once central to the **Mixtec** and **Zapotec** civilizations, the city took a lesser role during the early years of the Spanish conquest of Mexico. **Cortés**, attracted by the area's natural beauties, took the title of Marqués del Valle de Oaxaca, and until the Revolution his descendants held vast estates hereabouts. But for practical purposes, Oaxaca was of little interest to the Spanish, with no mineral wealth and no great joy for farmers due to the rugged mountain terrain (though coffee was grown). Nevertheless, by 1796 it had become the third largest city in Nueva España, thanks to the export of cochineal and subsequently textile manufacturing. Meanwhile, the **indigenous** population was left to get on with life and did not have to deal with much outside influence beyond the interference of a proselytizing Church. An earthquake destroyed much of the city in 1854 and the slow rebuilding was shaken to pieces by another quake in 1931. The city's most famous son, **Benito Juárez**, is commemorated everywhere in Oaxaca, a privilege not shared by **Porfirio Díaz**, the second most famous Oaxaqueño, whose dictatorship most people choose to forget.

Benito Juárez

Despite the blunder and poor judgement of his later years, **Benito Juárez** ranks among Mexico's greatest national heroes. He was the towering figure of nineteenth-century Mexican politics, and his maxim "El respeto al derecho ajeno es la paz" ("The respect of the rights of others is peace") has been a rallying cry for liberals ever since. A **Zapotec**, he strove against nineteenth-century social prejudices and, through four terms as president, successfully reformed many of the worst social remnants of Spanish colonialism, earning a reputation for honesty and fair dealing.

Juárez was born outside the city, in **San Pablo Guelatao**, in 1806. His parents died when he was 3, and he grew up speaking only Zapotec; at the age of 12 he was adopted by priests and moved to Oaxaca, where he began to study for the priesthood, which included learning Spanish. Turning his talents to law, he provided his legal services free to impoverished villagers, and by 1831 had earned a seat on Oaxaca's municipal council, lending voice to a disenfranchised people. Juárez rose through the ranks of the city council to become **state governor** from 1847 to 1852, on a liberal ticket geared towards improving education and releasing the country from the economic and social stranglehold of the Church and the aristocracy. In 1853 the election of a conservative government under Santa Ana forced him into eighteen months of exile in the US.

Liberal victory in 1855 enabled Juárez to return to Mexico as minister of justice and lend his name to a law abolishing special courts for the military and clergy. His support was instrumental in passing the **Ley Lerdo**, which effectively nationalized the Church's huge holdings, and bills legalizing civil marriage and guaranteeing religious freedom. In 1858, President Ignacio Comonfort was ousted by conservatives enraged by these reforms, and Juárez, as **the head of the Supreme Court**, had a legal claim to the presidency. However, he lacked the military might to hold Mexico City and retired to Veracruz, returning three years later, victorious in the War of Reform, as constitutionally elected **president** for further attempts to reduce the power of the Church. Stymied by an intractable Congress and empty coffers, Juárez suspended all debt repayments for two years from July 1861. To protect their investments, the British, Spanish and French sent their armies in, but when it became apparent that Napoleon III had designs on the control of Mexico, the others pulled out, leaving France to install Hapsburg **Archduke Maximilian** as puppet emperor. Juárez fled again, this time to Ciudad Juárez (originally called Paso del Norte) on the US border, but by 1867 Napoleon III had buckled under Mexican resistance and US pressure, and Juárez was able to return to the capital and his army to round up and execute the hapless Maximilian.

Juárez was returned as president at the 1867 elections but alienated much of his support by unconstitutional attempts to use Congress to amend the constitution. Nevertheless, he was able to secure another term in the 1870 elections, spending two more years trying unsuccessfully to maintain peace before dying of a heart attack in 1872.

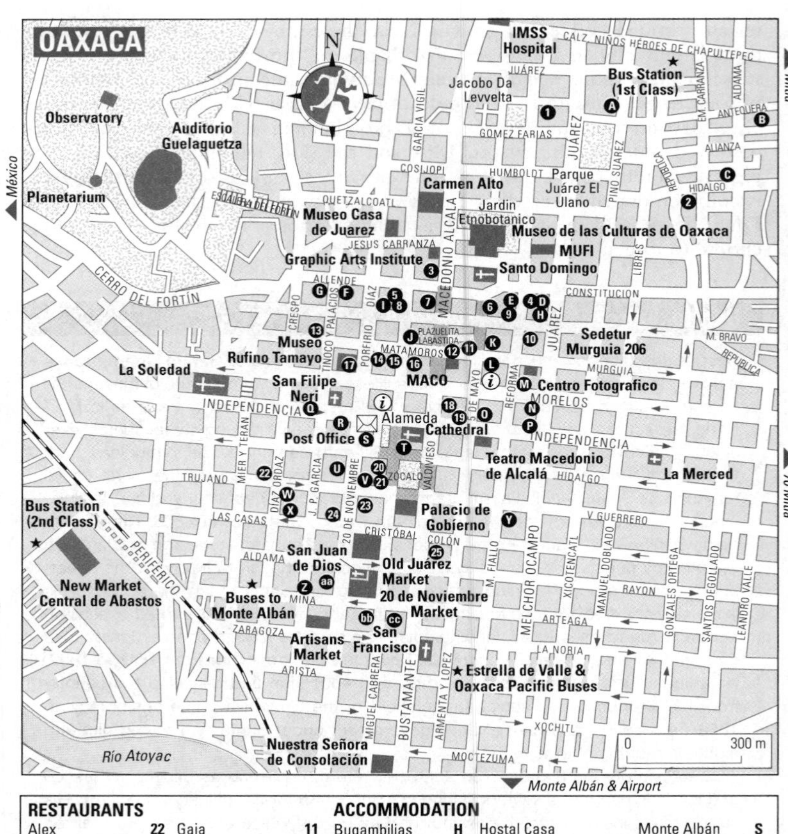

RESTAURANTS

Name	Key	Name	Key
Alex	22	Gaia	11
Antigua	9	Los Girasoles	25
El Biche Pobre	2	El Manantial Vegetariano	13
La Brew	5	Marco Polo	19
Café Gecko	6	El Naranjo	23
Cafetería Bamby	15	Osho Angel Gallery	1
Cafetería Royalty	16	La Olla	4
La Casa de la Abuela	20	Panini	14
Casa Oaxaca	I	Pizza Nostrana	3
Coffee Beans	5	Quince Letras	10
Los Danzantes	7	Red	24
Del Jardín	21	Restaurant Quickly	18
Flor de Loto	17	El Topil	12

ACCOMMODATION

Name	Key	Name	Key	Name	Key
Bugambilias	H	Hostal Casa Paulina	W	Monte Albán	S
Calesa Real	J	Hotel Francia	U	Plata Gelatina	R
Camino Real Oaxaca	K	Hotel Posada del Rosario	bb	Posada Catarina	Z
Casa Arnel	B	Hotel Santa Clara	N	Posada del Centro	Q
Casa de la Tía	O	Hotel Villa de León	E	Posada El Chapulín	aa
Casa Oaxaca	I	Lupita	X	Posada El Cid	A
Casa del Sótano	F	Luz de Luna	P	Principal	L
Cazomalli	C	Magic Hostel	Y	Reforma	M
Chocolate Posada	cc	Marques del Valle	T	Las Rosas	V
Las Golondrinas	G			Yagul	C
Hostal Guadalupe	D				

Oaxaca is becoming an industrial city – the population is well over 200,000 and the streets are choked and noisy, with large numbers of people choosing to retreat here from Mexico City – yet it remains easy to handle. In the **colonial centre**, thanks to strict building regulations, the provincial charm is hardly affected and just about everything can be reached on foot. It also remains provincial in its habits, as the big excitements are dawdling in a café or gathering in the famous **zócalo** to stroll and listen to the town band. By eleven at night much of the city is asleep, although late-night dancers keep going strong.

Surrounding Oaxaca is some fantastic topography, making an impressive backdrop to the city skyline at sunset. The Sierra Madre del Sur enters Oaxaca state from the west, while the Sierra Madre de Oaxaca runs down from Mexico's central volcanic belt. The two ranges meet in the centre of the state and between them, converging in Oaxaca town, lie the three Valles Centrales.

Arrival, information and city transport

Both **bus stations** in Oaxaca are a good distance from the centre – upwards of twenty minutes' walk. First-class (with guardería luggage storage) is on Calzada Niños Héroes de Chapultepec, northeast of the centre; from here your best bet is to find a taxi. If you prefer to walk, turn left along the main road for about three blocks to Avenida Juárez, left again for nine or ten blocks to Independencia, then right to the zócalo. Once you reach Juárez you can pick up city buses. The second-class terminal (also with guardería) is west of the centre by the *abastos* market buildings: walk west from the zócalo on Trujano or Las Casas, or north along the market.

From the **airport**, 5km south of the city, a colectivo service, Transportación Terrestre Aeropuerto (ⓣ9/514-4350) will drop you right by the zócalo for about US$2. On leaving, you should buy tickets in advance wherever possible – tickets are sold on the Alameda de León, next to the *Monte Albán Hotel.*

Information

Oaxaca's **tourist office** (daily 8am–8pm; ⓣ9/516-0123) is inside the Palacio Municipal, at Independencia 607 opposite the Alameda, with a second, larger branch at Murguia 206, west of 5 de Mayo (daily 8am–8pm; ⓣ9/516-0984 or 4828). Both are extremely helpful and have contacts for apartment rentals and homestays, as well as supplying piles of maps and other handouts. The free monthly **English-language newspaper**, the *Oaxaca Times,* and the monthly *Oaxaca* carry topical features, events listings and ads for apartments and houses to rent. The **Spanish-language newspaper** *Noticias* has rental ads too and can be bought from newspaper vendors around the zócalo. The Spanish schools (see "Listings") are another good source of rental and homestay information. You can find more on Oaxaca, including accommodation listings and language courses, **on line** at ⓦwww.oaxaca.com, ⓦwww.oaxaca.magazine.net, ⓦwww.oaxacatimes.com, and ⓦwww.oaxaca-travel.com.

City transport

Walking is by far the best way of getting around compact Oaxaca. The bus routes are Byzantine and, once you've hopped on the right one, the traffic is so slow that you could have taken a pleasant stroll to your destination in half the time. **Taxis** are a better bet; they can be found on Independencia near the cathedral, or flagged down anywhere.

Getting out to the sites around the valley by **public transport** is a different matter. While taxis charge around US$10 to most of the surrounding villages and archeological sites, buses from the second-class bus station are frequent and cheap. There are also vast numbers of **colectivos** heading for destinations all over the state. These depart, when full, from various points around the city (ask the tourist office), mostly from behind the *abastos* market, and are only a little more expensive. **Car rental** is as pricey here as anywhere in the country, but if you are planning extensive exploration of the valley may prove worthwhile, allowing you to trade a week of long waits for a couple of days of independence; see p.601 for details of agents offering car rental. **Bike rental** (see p.602) can also prove an effective means of exploring the city and some of the outlying villages. Several **tour** companies offer day-trips to Monte Albán and other places around the city that include bird-watching, hiking and mountaineering excursions; again, see p.602 for more details.

Accommodation

Although there are hundreds of **hotels** in Oaxaca, there are thousands of visitors, and if you arrive late in the day you may well have difficulty finding a room. Under such circumstances, it's best to take anything that's offered and look for something better the next morning. Alternatively, call at the main tourist office and consult their lists of families who take in guests on a daily basis (usually around US$15 per person), or apartments, many of them fairly central, which cost around the same.

The cheapest places tend to be **south of Independencia**, especially between the old market and Calle Trujano, and along Trujano, Díaz Ordaz, Garcia and Aldama, although they are dwindling in number as more upscale hotel offerings pop up in the more touristic zone near the zócalo and north of Independencia. Closer to the **zócalo** and to the **north**, both prices and quality tend to be higher, though there are some surprisingly good-value places. **Prices** in general drop by ten to thirty percent outside the Christmas, Semana Santa, July and August high seasons. It's often worth asking for a *descuenta* or discount – the worst they can say is no.

The only **campsite** anywhere near town is the barely functioning *Trailer Park Oaxaca* (❷), just over 3km north of the centre at Violetas 900, at the corner of Heroica Escuela Naval Militar: follow Niños Héroes east five blocks from the first-class bus station and turn left up Ruíz.

Tourist Yú'ù facilities are dotted around Oaxaca's valleys, offering a fascinating and economical alternative to staying in the city (see box on p.594). For visiting some of the artisan communities or the ruins at Mitla or Yagul, they're also more convenient than staying in the city. If you're really counting the pennies, you can even pitch a tent on their grounds.

Around the zócalo

Hotel Francia 20 de Noviembre 212 ⓣ9/516-4811. Somewhat overpriced colonial hotel, with gussied-up rooms with fans and TVs, where D.H. Lawrence stayed for a bit in 1925. ❺

Magic Hostel C Fiallo 305 ⓣ9/516-7667, ⓔmagichostel@backpacker.com. Lively hostel popular among backpackers and budget travellers, with a communal kitchen, bar, lounge area, hot showers, Internet access, baggage storage, hammocks on the roof and videos every night. Gets very busy around Christmas. ❷

Marqués del Valle north side of the zócalo at Portal de Claveria, ⓣ9/516-3677. Spacious, light, comfortable rooms, some with balcony, all with private bath and incomparable views over the zócalo – which is what you pay for. ❽

Monte Albán Alameda de León 1 ⓣ9/516-2777, ⓕ516-3265. Beautiful, if cavernous, colonial-style hotel right opposite the cathedral. Excellent value given the location, with some lovely external rooms and gloomier internal ones. Nightly *folklórico* dancing takes place in the main sala. ❹

Plata Gelatina Independencia 504 ⓣ9/514-9391. A stone's throw from the zócalo, this small but good-value hostel is decorated with art and photography and has a young and friendly atmosphere. It offers clean dorms or private rooms, hot showers, Internet access and a bar. ❷

Posada del Centro Independencia 403 ⓣ9/516-1874. Pleasant rooms around a tiled courtyard, most with shared bath and some with private bath; a good deal, although front rooms face a heavily trafficked street. ❹

Las Rosas Trujano 112 ⓣ9/514-2217. Surprisingly peaceful and spacious white rooms around a courtyard where tea and coffee are available and there are magazines to read. ❺

North of Independencia

Bugambilias Reforma 402 ⓣ/ⓕ 9/516-1165, ⓦwww.mexonline.com/bugambil.htm. Peaceful colonial house beside *La Olla* café, with eight beautiful, airy rooms (individually decorated with work by local artists) with private bath – perfect for honeymooning couples. Price includes a healthy, traditional breakfast. ❼

Calesa Real García Vigil 306 ⓣ9/516-5544. Azulejo-tiled corridors, a small pool and modern tile-floored rooms with locally made rugs make this one of the best values of the top-end places, although it has a slightly institutional feel. ❻

Camino Real Oaxaca 5 de Mayo 300 ⓣ9/516-0611, ⓕ516-0732, ⓦwww.camino-real-oaxaca.com. Oaxaca's priciest hotel (US$220), in the beautifully converted sixteenth-century Ex-Convento de Santa Catalina. Not particularly welcoming – money talks here – but worth the splurge if you have the cash. ❾

Casa Arnel Aldama 404 in Colonia Jalatlaco ⓣ9/515-2856, ⓕ513-6285, ⓦwww.oaxaca.com.mx/arnel. Between the zócalo and the first-class bus station, and within easy walking distance of both, the family-run *Casa Arnel* is a popular place, tucked away down a cobbled street. Reasonably priced rooms (with or without bath – some are smaller than others, so have a look around) are set around a leafy courtyard with parrots, with access to a roof top terrace bar. Internet, laundry, a library and tours offered. ❹

Casa de la Tía 5 de Mayo 109 (ⓣ9/514-1963, ⓦwww.prodigyweb.net.mx/latia. Friendly posada with rooms with thoughtful details, TV, private bathrooms and books to read, although not the bargain it once was. ❺

Casa del Sótano Tinoco y Palacios 414 ⓣ9/516-2494. Brand-new, elegant hotel with comfy rooms in earth tones and dark wood that evoke fancy monks' quarters. Its inviting terrace café has a fantastic view, and is run by a friendly character who also oversees the lovely art gallery on the premises. ❻

Casa Oaxaca García Vigil 407 ⓣ9/514-4173, ⓕ516-4412, ⓦwww.casa-oaxaca.com. If you are going to splurge, this is the place; seven spacious rooms around a pristine white courtyard, with a luxurious tiled pool and sumptuous restaurant. Breakfast included. ❾

Cazomalli Salto 104, near Aldama ⓣ9/513-3513. Quaint little posada with comfy rooms in a colonial house with a gorgeous rooftop breakfast area, and a helpful owner. ❺

Las Golondrinas Tinoco y Palacios 411 at Allende ⓣ9/514-3298, ⓕ514-2126. Charming rooms each with separate reception area and bathroom in an old colonial house with a gorgeous flower-filled courtyard. Very tranquil with a distinctly local flavour. ❺

Hostal Guadalupe Juárez 409 ⓣ9/516-6365. A short walk from the zócalo, this quiet little hostel has dorms and private rooms with tidy shared bathrooms. Luggage lockers are available. ❷

Hotel Villa de León Reforma 405 ⓣ9/516-1977. One of the cheapest places left in the neighbourhood, the three floors of rooms are clean and comfortable, albeit with long-outdated decor and soft mattresses. Upper floors have better air circulation and light. ❹

Luz de Luna Juárez 101 ⓣ9/516-9576. A hostel with a friendly vibe, workable bathrooms, coffee available all day and kitchen access. Men and women sleep in separate dorms. Breakfast included for US$2.50 more. ❷

Posada El Cid Pino Suárez 903 ⓣ9/515-1070. If you need to stay right near the first-class bus station, this fits the bill: clean, professionally run, although on a noisy intersection. ❺

Principal 5 de Mayo 208 ⓣ9/516-2535. Colonial-style place with a central courtyard and good rooms with private bathrooms, and a lovely garden that suggests something pricier than what it is. Good value considering the atmosphere and location. ❺

Reforma Av Reforma 102 ⓣ9/516-0939. Friendly and cheap, with a rooftop patio, although the rooms aren't much to speak of and there are sometimes problems with hot water. ❷

South of Independencia

Chocolate Posada Mina 212 ⓣ9/516-5760. Tidy rooms with shared bath, on a bustling street above a chocolate shop. ❷

Hostal Casa Paulina Trujano 321 ⓣ9/516-2005. Best hostel in town. Ultra-clean, breezy and open, with separate dorm rooms for men and women, clean bathrooms, and some private rooms. There are fountains, beer for sale in the lobby and a rooftop lounge. ❷

Hotel Posada del Rosario 20 Noviembre 508 ⓣ9/516-4112, ⓕ514-4911. Motel rooms come with or without TV and a/c. Those on the ground floor are not so hot – the best are at the front on the second floor. There's parking, and you can pay with credit cards. ❺

Lupita Díaz Ordaz 314 ⓣ9/516-5733. Very cheap, small, bare rooms with or without shower. ❷

Posada Catarina Aldama 325 ⓣ9/516-4270. Reasonably priced, charming rooms clustered around three gardens, a stone's throw from the market. ❹

Posada El Chapulín Aldama 317 ⓣ9/516-1646. Simple but adequate rooms with private baths, centrally located by the market. ❹

Yagul Mina 103 ⓣ9/516-2750. Pleasant, with a little garden and spacious clean rooms, but slightly pricey for what you get. ❹

The City

Simply being in Oaxaca, wandering through its streets and absorbing its life, is an experience, especially if you happen to catch the city during a **fiesta** (they happen all the time – the most important are listed at the end of the chapter), but you should definitely take time out to visit the State Museum and the Museo Tamayo, the market (shopping in Oaxaca is quite simply some of the best in the entire country), the churches of Santo Domingo and La Soledad, and to get out to Monte Albán and Mitla. All in all it could be a long stay.

Around the zócalo

The **zócalo**, closed to traffic, surrounded by *portales* sheltering cafés and constantly animated, sees a steady stream of beggars, hawkers, business people, tourists and locals. On Sundays and many weekday evenings there's a band playing in the centre, or else a performance or exhibition opposite the cathedral. On the south side, the Neoclassical, Porfiriano **Palacio de Gobierno** features a historical mural by Arturo García Bustos depicting Oaxacan history, second-rate by Mexican standards; at the top of the mural are the revolutionary Ricardo Flores Magon (left), Benito Juárez and his wife Margarita Maza (centre), and José María Morelos (right). Porfirio Díaz appears below Juárez, with a sword. At the bottom right, Vincente Guerrero's execution at Cuilapan is shown, and the left wall shows ancient Mitla.

You reach the rather clumsy cathedral, at the northwest corner, by crossing the square. Begun in 1553, its construction was only completed in the eighteenth century after several earthquakes, since when it has been repeatedly pillaged and restored; as a result, despite a fine Baroque facade, it's not the most

Staying in local communities around Oaxaca: Tourist Yú'ù

In 1994 SEDETUR and the Secretaría de Turismo opened the first batch of **Tourist Yú'ù** (pronounced YOU) – Zapotec for "house" – small self-contained houses scattered through the villages of the Oaxaca valleys. These help to bring income to the local villages while minimizing the disruptive effects of mass tourism. Visitors are shown around the village by the locals and are given the opportunity to view community life at close quarters.

Alternatively, SEDETUR can make reservations at a number of other locally built and run **cabins** for tourists. Some of these are equally charming and even more off the beaten track, though facilities tend to be a little more basic.

Either type of accommodation makes a convenient and economical base for exploring the communities and archeological sites of Oaxaca state. Many communities have their own particular handicraft tradition, such as carpet-weaving, wickerwork or pottery; others often have their own museum devoted to archeological finds from the area and the life of the villagers. Some are in areas of outstanding natural beauty, where locals will take you horseback riding, trout fishing, biking or caving.

The Tourist Yú'ù are designed to sleep six (the cabins sleep more), with a bedroom, a fully equipped kitchen with stove and refrigerator, and outside shower and toilets which can also be used by people camping in the grounds. Each facility has a custodian who collects US$9 per person, US$30 for groups of six, and US$5 for campers; some offer guides and camping equipment for rental.

Reservations can be made – ideally a few days in advance, especially for the more accessible sites – through Oaxaca's tourist office, preferably the Murguia 206 location (Ⓣ9/516-0984 or 4828, Ⓔsedetur3@Oaxaca.gob).

interesting of Oaxaca's churches. It is impressively big, though, with a heavy *coro* blocking the aisle in the heart of the church.

Walk past the cathedral and the Alameda, then right onto Independencia, and you reach the **Teatro Macedonio de Alcalá** in a couple of blocks, built in the French style fashionable under Díaz. Still operating as a theatre and concert hall, it's typical of the grandiose public buildings that sprang up across Mexico around 1900 – the interior, if you can see it (try going to a show, or sneaking in before one), is a magnificent swath of marble and red plush.

North of the zócalo

Heading north from the zócalo, Valdivieso crosses Independencia to become Macedonio Alcalá, the city's pedestrianized shopping street, a showcase for the best Mexican and Oaxacan crafts. This is the place to come for exquisitely intricate silver designs, finely executed, imaginative textiles, and the highest prices: check the quality here before venturing out to the villages where many of the crafts are made, and where the selection tends to include pieces of varying quality and lower prices. Halfway up Alcalá is **MACO**, the **Museum of Contemporary Art** (Mon & Wed–Sun 10.30am–8pm; US$1, free on Sun), housed in a colonial seventeenth-century building, widely regarded as Cortés' house although actually built after his death. Founded in 1992 with the intention of preserving Oaxaca's cultural heritage, the museum's permanent collection includes work by leading Oaxacan artists such as Rufino Tamayo, Francisco Toledo, Rodolfo Morales, Rodolfo Nieto and Francisco Gutiérrez. Regular exhibitions by local and international artists are also shown here.

A block further up Alcalá stands the church of **Santo Domingo** (daily 7am–1pm & 4–8pm; no sightseeing during mass; free). This sixteenth-century extravaganza is elaborately carved and decorated both inside and out, the external walls solid, defensive and earthquake-proof, the interior extraordinarily rich. Parts were damaged during the Reform Wars and the Revolution – especially the chapels, pressed into service as stables – but most have now been restored. Notice especially the great gilded main altarpiece, and, on the underside of the raised choir above you as you enter, the family tree of the Dominican order, in the form of a vine with leafy branches and tendrils, busts of leading Dominicans and a figure of the Virgin right at the top. The place drips with gold-leaf throughout, beautifully set off in the afternoon by the light flooding through a predominantly yellow window. Looking back from the altar end you can appreciate the relief scenes high on the walls, the biblical events depicted in the barrel roof, and above all the ceiling of the choir, a vision of the heavenly hierarchy with gilded angels swirling in rings around God. The adjoining Capilla del Rosario is also richly painted and carved: the Virgin takes pride of place in another stunning altarpiece, all the more startlingly intense in such a relatively small space.

Behind the church, the old Dominican monastery (the Ex-Convento de Santo Domingo) has been restored to house the **Museo de las Culturas de Oaxaca** (Tues–Sun 10am–8pm; US$3 50, free on Sun). The damage caused by its use as a barracks for years during the Revolution has finally been repaired and the exhibits reinstalled. As if the restoration work itself wasn't impressive enough, inside you can see the magnificent Mixtec jewellery discovered in Tomb 7 at Monte Albán (see p.603), which constitutes a substantial proportion of all known pre-Hispanic gold, since anything the conquistadors found they plundered and melted down. Highlights of the collection include a couple of superbly detailed gold masks and breastplates. The museum also owns smaller gold pieces, and objects in a wide variety of precious materials –

mother-of-pearl, obsidian, turquoise, amber and jet among them. An interesting video shows members of each of the state's fifteen indigenous peoples speaking their own language. Through the museum windows you'll see beautiful views of the mountains, plus you'll find another hidden artistic masterpiece – the cactus garden, or **Jardín Etnobotánico** (free guided tours in English, Tues & Thurs 11am and Sat 11am & 4pm; sign up in advance). There are strategically positioned cacti in front of the museum, which make striking patterns across the earth at sundown.

Across the road at Alcalá 507, the **Instituto de Artes Gráficas** (Mon & Wed–Sun 9.30am–8pm; donation), one of many cultural centres in the state sponsored by painter Francisco Toledo, displays changing exhibits of works by nationally renowned artists. It's worth popping in just to amble around the small rooms of what was once a rather grand colonial house and to spend an hour in the excellent art library and idyllic, leafy garden reading room. There are also evening music recitals.

The **Museo Casa de Juárez** (Tues–Sat 10am–7pm; US$3, free on Sun), a block to the west at García Vigil 609, is where the young Benito Juárez once worked for bookbinder Antonio Salanueva. The renovated house gives an impression of what life must have been like for the middle class in early nineteenth-century Oaxaca through exhibits and reconstructed rooms including the original binding workshop.

Oaxaca is also the proud mother of Mexico's only **philatelic museum**, east of here at Reforma 504 (Tues–Sat 10am–7pm; free), which has a respectable permanent exhibition of Mexican stamps. Just around the corner at Murguia 302 you'll find the **Centro Fotográfico Alvarez Bravo** (daily except Tues 10am–8pm; free), also established by Toledo, which has three exhibition rooms displaying historic and contemporary photographs, plus an excellent reference library.

West of the zócalo

Four blocks south along Alcalá from Santo Domingo, then three blocks west, at Morelos 503, lies the **Museo Rufino Tamayo** (Mon & Wed–Sat 10am–2pm & 4–7pm, Sun 10am–3pm; US$3), a private collection of pre-Hispanic artefacts, gathered by the Oaxaqueño abstract artist who ranks among the greatest Mexican painters of the twentieth century. Rather than set out to explain the archeological significance of its contents, the collection is deliberately laid out as an art museum, with the focus on aesthetic form, and includes some truly beautiful items from all over Mexico, with pottery and carvings from pre-Classic civilizations, including ceramic dog figurines from Colima. Aztec, Maya and western indigenous cultures all feature strongly, though there's surprisingly little that is Mixtec or Zapotec. There are also some contemporary works.

Around the corner at J.P. García and Independencia, the church of **San Felipe Neri** is mostly Baroque, with a richly decorated proliferation of statues on the plateresque facade and an equally ornate gilt altarpiece, but what really makes it unusual is its interior decor. The church was built in 1733 used as barracks during the Revolution and, by the 1920s, needed to be repainted, which it was in an unusual Art Nouveau/Art Deco style. Its other claim to fame is that it's the church in which Benito Juárez and Margarita Maza were married.

The **Basílica de Nuestra Señora de la Soledad**, not far to the west along Independencia, contains an image of the Virgen de la Soledad – not only Oaxaca's patron saint, but one of the most revered in the country. The sumptuously decorated church, late seventeenth-century with a more recent facade,

Market days in the villages around Oaxaca

Despite Oaxaca's many crafts stores, if it's quality you're after, or if you intend to buy in quantity, visiting the villages from which the goods originate is a far better bet. Each has a different specialty (Teotitlán del Valle, for example, for rugs, or San Bartolo Coyotepec for black pottery; see p.607 and p.612), and many have their own market each week. Though there's no guarantee that you'll be able to buy better or more cheaply, you will be able to see the craftspeople in action, you may be able to have your own design made up, and quite apart from all that, a village market is an experience in itself.

MONDAY **Miahuatlan**: *mescal*, bread, leather; **Ixtlan de Juárez**: flowers, produce.

TUESDAY **Santa Ana del Valle**: rugs; **Santa Maria Atzompa**: pottery.

WEDNESDAY **Etla**: cheese, flowers.

THURSDAY **Zaachila**: meat, nuts; **Ejutla**: *mescal*, embroidered blouses.

FRIDAY **Ocotlán**: flowers, meat, pottery, textiles.

SATURDAY **Oaxaca**: everything; **Tlaxiaco**: leather goods, blankets, *aguardiente*, baskets.

SUNDAY **Tlacolula**: *mescal*, ceramics, rugs, crafts.

is set on a small plaza surrounded by other buildings associated with the Virgin's cult. This is where the best ice cream in town, if not the whole of Mexico, is sold. The adjoining Plaza de la Danza is a setting for outdoor concerts, *folklórico* performances, or specialist craft markets. A line of ramshackle stalls behind the ice-cream vendors sells brightly coloured religious icons. Just in back of the church there's a small **museum** (daily 8am–2pm & 4–7pm, except Wed 8am–2pm only; US$0 20) devoted to the cult. It's a bizarre jumble of junk and treasure – native costumes displayed on permed blonde 1950s mannequins; ex-voto paintings giving thanks for miracles and cures – among which the junk is generally far more interesting. The museum also explains how the church came to be built here, after the image miraculously appeared in 1620, in a box on the back of a mule.

South of the zócalo

The only local church to compare with La Soledad, in terms of the crowds of worshippers it attracts, is the ancient **San Juan de Dios**, right in the heart of the old market area. Here villagers and market traders who've come to town for the day drop in constantly to pay their devotions.

Saturday, by tradition, is market day in Oaxaca, and although nowadays the markets operate daily, it's still the day to come if you want to see the old-style *tianguis* at its best. *Indígenas* flood in from the villages in a bewildering variety of costumes, and Mixtec and Zapotec dialects replace Spanish as the lingua franca. The majority of this activity, and of the serious business of buying and selling everyday goods, has moved out to the sprawling **Mercado de Abastos** by the second-class bus station. This is the place to go for fruit, vegetables, meat, herbs and spices, and a range of household goods from traditional cooking pots to wooden utensils and furniture. The **Mercado 20 de Noviembre** is lined with *comedores* serving inexpensive prepared food, such as chile rellenos and tamales, although the quality varies, so it's best to eat at one of the more popular spots. The old **Mercado Benito Juárez**, southwest of the zócalo, is the site for village handicrafts, such as *rebozas* (shawls), rag dolls, green china, plenty of fresh produce and flowers, and the infamous *chapulines* (see p.599). Be warned that it's very touristy – you're harassed far more by the vendors and have to bargain fiercely – and the quality of the goods is also often suspect. *Sarapes*, in particular, are often machine-made from chemically dyed artificial fibres: these look glossy, and you can also tell real wool by plucking out a thread – artificial fibres are long, thin and shiny, woollen threads short, rough and curly (and if you hold a match to it, a woollen thread will singe and smell awful; an artificial one will melt and burn your fingers). There are numerous **shops** around the zócalo and on Alcalá that will give you a good idea of the potential quality of items you can buy in the market, or try the Regional Association of Craftswomen of Oaxaca at 5 de Mayo 204 (daily 9am–8pm).

Out from the centre

Although it's fairly easy to find your bearings in the centre of town, to get a fix on Oaxaca's relation to the rest of the valley and Monte Albán, take a hike (about 45min from the zócalo) up Cerro del Fortín, on the northwestern edge of the city. It is steep, but the views are rewarding and in the evening you can call in on the **Planetario Nundehui** (25min shows on astronomy and the solar system in Spanish only: Mon–Fri 9am–9pm, Sat noon–8pm; US$2). The road up here passes the **Auditorio Guelaguetza**, the venue for the annual festival known as Lunes del Cerro ("Monday of the Hill"), primarily because the folk dances take place on the first two Mondays after July 16. Around Christmas, many of Oaxaca's boisterous celebrations also take place here.

Eating and drinking

Food is more than just good in Oaxaca, and it's readily available on almost every street corner. The cheapest places to eat are in the **markets**, either in a section of the main market around 20 de Noviembre and Aldama, with rows of *comedores* and choose-your-own grilled meats and veggies, or in the *abastos* market by the second-class bus station – where you'll find excellent tamales. More formal but still basic restaurants are to be found in the same areas as the cheaper hotels, especially along **Trujano**. The **zócalo** is ringed by cafés and restaurants where you can sit outside – irresistible as ever and not as expensive as their position might lead you to expect – and there are plenty of simple places for everyday meals in the streets round about. Try the excellent, inexpensive **licuado bar**, rarely frequented by travellers, on 20 de Noviembre, opposite the bus ticket office, or the gorgeous cakes at *Tartamiel* in front of the cinema on Trujano. Oaxaca also provides welcome relief for **vegetarians**, who have been restricted to endless huevos and quesadillas in other parts of the country.

Around the zócalo

La Casa de la Abuela Hidalgo 616. Touristy, but with a great view over the zócalo from the second floor, which is what you pay for. Serves classic local dishes.

Del Jardín Portal de Flores 10, on the zócalo. One of the best cafés for watching life go by, serving reliable, if not inspired, soups and snacks.

Los Girasoles 20 de Noviembre 102. Mid-priced food in generous portions, including some inexpensive options for vegetarians; especially good breakfasts and excellent *mescal*.

Restaurant Quickly Alcalá 100, just north of the zócalo. Touristy menu featuring burgers, shakes and some Oaxacan dishes. Nothing special, and slow, but inexpensive.

North of Independencia

Antigua Reforma 401. Gourmet café with liqueur coffees, pastries, sandwiches, wine and *mescal*; a lively evening after-dinner scene.

El Biche Pobre Calzada de la República 600 in Colonia Jalatlaco ☎9/513-4636. Long-standing, reasonably priced family restaurant, serving generous portions of local favourites.

La Brew García Vigil 409. Eclectic café owned by knowledgeable American, who serves delicious coffee and home-baked brownies, waffles and

Food and drink in Oaxaca

Oaxaca is a wonderful city for gourmands, and you don't have to go to one of the smart restaurants serving contemporary Oaxacan cuisine to sample local specialities: worth trying are **tamales** – in just about any form, and often better from street or market vendors than in restaurants – as well as **mole Oaxaqueño**, which is not significantly different from mole anywhere else, but good nonetheless, and **chapulines**, crunchy seasoned grasshoppers peddled around the market. **Tlayudas**, giant crisp tortillas dressed with beans and mild Oaxacan string cheese, called **quesillo**, are staples of cafés and street stands after dark.

The place to go for very special homemade **ice cream** is the plaza in front of the church of La Soledad, full of rival vendors and tables where you can sit and gorge yourself while watching the world go by. Flavours are innumerable and often bizarre, including *elote* (corn), *queso*, *leche quemada* (burnt milk – even worse than it sounds), *sorbete* (cinnamon-flavoured sherbet) and exotic fruits like *mamey*, *guanabana* and *tuna* (prickly pear, a virulent purple that tastes wonderful), as well as more ordinary varieties such as chocolate, peanut and coconut.

Mescal, the local drink of choice, is sold everywhere in bottles that usually have a dead worm in the bottom. Legend has it that the creature lives on the cactus-like maguey plant and is there to prove that the ingredients are genuine (although it is debatable if they are actually ever found in the plant and these days most of the worms are farm-raised and inserted as a marketing gimmick). You don't have to eat it, though few people are in any state to notice by the time they reach the bottom of the bottle, and no one seems to come to much harm, at least not from the worm. *Mescal* and tequila are similar drinks as tequila is simply a specialty type of the more varied *mescal.* True tequila is made only from the prized blue agave species, while *mescal* may be a combination of a number of types of maguey. Both alcohols are made from the sugary heart of the plant, which is baked, pulverized and then distilled through different processes. These liquors were developed around the same time, when the Spaniards introduced distillation after the Conquest. *Mescal* is drunk the same way as tequila, with a lick of salt and lime. Specialist shops all around the market – try El Fornoso, J.P. García 405, and El Flor de Maguey, 20 de Noviembre 606 – sell *mescal* in various qualities (including from the barrel), and most also sell it in souvenir pottery bottles, which are amazingly cheap.

On the south side of the market, your nose will lead you to Calle Mina, which is lined with **spice** vendors selling plump bags of the chile and chocolate powder that makes up Oaxacan mole. Cinnamon-flavoured chocolate powder is also available, for cooking or making into drinking chocolate.

smoothies – as well as organizing fascinating tours, sharing her expertise about the Oaxaca valley.

Café Gecko 5 de Mayo 412. Inexpensive omelettes, yogurt and granola, coffee and snacks, indoors or within a leafy courtyard. Open until 8pm weekdays, 11pm at weekends.

Cafetería Bamby García Vigil 205. Cafetería and *tortería* two blocks from the zócalo. Reasonably priced comida corrida that's hit or miss. The *panadería* next door has fresh, fragrant baked goods.

Cafetería Royalty Matamoros 100. Basic daytime eatery offering a *menú económico* with tacos, enchiladas and other staples for a few dollars.

Casa Oaxaca García Vigil 407 ⓣ9/514-4173. Sublime contemporary Mexican food with an international twist, served in the candlelit courtyard of the hotel of the same name. Reservations must be made in advance. Entrees are upwards of US$10.

Los Danzantes Alcalá 403 ⓣ9/501-1184. Contemporary Oaxacan food in a slick, nouveau-design setting; good cocktails and coconut shrimp. Prices range from US$6–12.

Flor de Loto Morelos 509 at Díaz, next to the Rufino Tamayo museum. Predominantly vegetarian restaurant catering to Westerners with a bland menu that includes pasta, pizza and some meat dishes. Filling comida corrida.

El Manantial Vegetariano Tinoco y Palacios 303. Vegetarian Mexican breakfasts, affordable veggie burgers and fruit shakes are the order of the day at this small but excellent wholefood restaurant. Bargain Sunday buffet.

Marco Polo 5 de Mayo 103 and Pino Suárez 806. Fresh daily seafood specials. While the 5 de Mayo location is open much later, the Pino Suárez version has a lovely outdoor patio, brick oven, and is right by the Parque Juárez (aka El Llano) – although it closes at 6pm.

La Olla Reforma 402. Pretty café-gallery with a tasty and reliable breakfast menu, generous fruit salads, vegetable salads, meat dishes and hot drinks.

Panini Matamoros 200. Tiny hole-in-the-wall that makes tasty sandwiches with a variety of fillings, on spongy ciabatta bread.

Pizza Nostrana Alcalá 501. Home-cooked Italian pastas with savoury sauces and pizza across from Santo Domingo. Tasty, but beware of the over-zealous musicians.

South of Independencia

Alex Díaz Ordaz 218, at Trujano. Pleasant place for good-value meals, especially the excellent breakfasts, huge licuados and US$3 comidas corridas.

El Naranjo Trujano 203 ☎9/514-1878. Delicious and creative contemporary Oaxacan cuisine, mixed delicately with international flavours (such as goat cheese.) The chile relleno is mouthwatering, as are the daily varying moles. The head chef also offers cooking classes.

Red Las Casas 101 ☎9/514-6853. Excellent, bustling fish restaurant serving enormous whole-fish dishes, mixed seafood soups, prawn cocktails and octopus.

Nightlife

If you're not content sitting around the zócalo over a coffee or a beer, whiling away a balmy night to the accompaniment of *mariachi* or brass bands, don't expect too much of evenings in Oaxaca. The *guelaguetza* **folk dances** at the *Camino Real Oaxaca* (Friday nights) and *Monte Albán* (nightly) hotels are another possibility, but there's nothing much more lively even at weekends, aside from a small handful of bars which can get packed and noisy. Weeknights are fairly quiet, though there is frequently some kind of cultural activity outside both the church of Santo Domingo and the cathedral, as well as the ubiquitous street musicians in the zócalo.

Caffe del Borgo Matamoros 100. Little Italian bar serving beer, aperitifs and European coffees.

Candela Murguia 413 ☎9/514-2010. Restaurant by day, this place comes alive after 11pm when the dance floor is packed with locals and tourists coming to practise their salsa, rumba and merengue, accompanied by a live band. The older generation flock here at weekends (US$3.50 cover).

Casa del Mezcal Flores Magon 209. Long-standing, classic Mexican cantina with cheap shots of *mescal* in the market district.

Chester's Bar Juárez 605. English-style pub with billiards and live music Fri–Sun, overlooking the Parque Llano.

Decano 5 de Mayo 210. A cozy café by day becomes a hopping bar full of young Oaxaqueños and foreigners at night with a hip, bohemian feel.

La Divina Gurrion 104. Funky bar decorated with masks and model animals in the setting of the Santo Domingo church. Unlike many other local bars, the music won't blow your ears off.

Freebar Matamoros 100. Packed madhouse on weekends, with locals and some foreigners dancing and spilling into the street, dancing and screaming.

Hipótesis Morelos 511. A romantic, intimate little piano bar, with the music starting around 10pm and small tables tucked in dark corners.

La Nueva Babel Porfirio Díaz 224. Loungey wine bar, also serving coffee and snacks, sometimes featuring live folk music and poetry readings. Closed Sun.

La Sol y La Luna Reforma 502. This restaurant by the cathedral has live jazz and occasional salsa dancing Thurs–Sat, from 9pm. US$2 cover.

Tabuko Porfirio Díaz 219. Three-for-one (junior-sized) beers in this dim bar that sometimes has good, loud rock music.

La Tentación Matamoros 101. Live Latin music and rock every night, 9pm to midnight – often packed with sweaty, gyrating gringos and Mexicans. Some nights there's a US$3 cover.

Listings

Airlines and flights Aerocaribe, Fiallo 102 at Independencia ☎9/516-6099; Aeroméxico, Hidalgo 513 ☎9/511-5044; Aerotucán, Alcalá 201 ☎9/501-0530; Aviacsa, Pino Suárez 604 ☎9/518-4577; Mexicana, Fiallo 102 ☎9/516-8414, Ⓦwww.mexicana.com; Aerovega, Alameda de León ☎9/516-2777. Prices increase dramatically during Mexican holiday times, but expect to pay around US$100 to Mexico City, US$90 to Puerto Escondido and US$200 to Mérida. Oaxaca's airport is about 10km south of the city on the road to San Bartolo Coyotepec and Ocotlán. Buses between Oaxaca and these two towns (from the second-class bus station) pass within a kilometre or so of the airport, but it is far easier to contact Transportación Terrestre Aeropuerto (Mon–Sat 9am–2pm & 5–8pm, ☎9/514-4350) on the Alameda de León across from the cathedral; if you book with them the day before your flight, they'll pick you up from your hotel and deliver you for around US$2.

American Express Valdivieso 2 inside Viajes Mexico, Mon–Fri 9am–5pm, ☎9/516-2700.

Banks and exchange Scotiabank, on Independencia at Alcalá, has 24-hour ATM and good rates (Mon–Fri 9am–5pm, Sat 10am–2pm); Banamex, in back of the cathedral, has ATM and Western Union service (Mon–Fri 9am–4pm, Sat 10am-2pm). Casas de cambio litter the centre of town – shop around, as rates vary.

Bike rental Several tour operators rent bicycles (see p.602).

Books and maps There are a number of bookstores selling Spanish and English titles, as well as museum shops and reference libraries. Amate, Alcalá 307, has an excellent selection of new English-language books (including literature, travel and cooking) and magazines. You can get new and secondhand English books about Oaxaca, Mexico and Latin America from Librería Universitaria, Guerrero 108, just off the zócalo (Mon–Sat 9am–2pm & 4–8pm), or try the main library, the Biblioteca Circulante de Oaxaca, Alcalá 305 (Mon–Fri 10am–1pm & 4–7pm, Sat 10am–1pm), between Matamoros and Bravo; the Instituto Welte de Estudios Oaxaqueños at 5 de Mayo 412 (for enthnography, archeology and geography); or the excellent, predominantly arts library at the Graphic Arts Institute, Alcalá 507.

Buses From the first-class station at Chapultepec 1036, bus companies Cristóbal Colón, ADO and UNO (☎9/515-1214) between them run regular first-class and pullman services to Mexico City, Puebla, Puerto Escondido, Pochutla, Huatulco, San Cristóbal, Tehuacán and Villahermosa. Ticketbus offices, one on Valdivieso by the cathedral (☎9/516-3820), another at 20 de Noviembre 103 (Mon–Sat 8am–10pm, Sun 9am–4pm; ☎9/514-6655, Ⓦwww.ticketbus.com.mx) sell tickets for first-class lines. Slower, cheaper, more frequent and less comfortable services leave from the second-class bus station near the new market, to Mexico City (mostly overnight), Puerto Escondido, Pinotepa Nacional, Pochutla, Salina Cruz, Tuxtla Gutiérrez and other destinations. Suburban and minivan taxis make many of the trips; inquire at the tourist office.

Car rental Alamo, 5 de Mayo 203-A (☎9/515-8534), Budget, 5 de Mayo 315-A (☎9/515-0330), and Hertz, Labastida 115-4 (☎9/516-2434), are all expensive, although the cheapest rates tend to be booked through their web sites (Ⓦwww.alamo.com, Ⓦwww.budget.com, Ⓦwww.hertz.com). VW Bugs start around US$40/day, including insurance.

Cinema You can see international and Mexican films for free at the Cine Pochote, García Vigil 817 (for listings see the *Oaxaca Times*). The Allianza Francesca at Morelos 306 has occasional French films.

Consulates Canada, Pino Suárez 700 (☎9/513-3777); US, Alcalá 407 (☎9/514-3054). Other consulates in Oaxaca move regularly – check the latest at the tourist information office.

Dentists English-speaking dentists are listed in the *Oaxaca Times*, or ask at the tourist information office (see p.591).

Doctors The Clínica Hospital Carmen, Abasolo 215 (☎9/516-2612) is open 24hr and has English-speaking doctors.

Emergencies Dial 066, or the Tourist Police are located at Independencia 607 (☎9/516-0123, ☎9/514-2155 or ☎1-800/903-9200).

Internet access Internet cafés are abundant; most have a copy and printing service, and some have long-distance call booths. Open latest is *C@fé Internet*, upstairs at Valdivieso and Independencia – it closes most nights at 11pm. *Café Punto*, at García Vigil 212, is good; towards the first-class bus station, Interactivando at Pino Suárez 804 is speeedy and cheap.

Laundry Azteca Laundry, 404B Hidalgo (Mon–Sat 8am–8pm, Sun 9am–2pm); Superlavandería Hildalgo, Hildalgo at J.P. García (Mon–Sat 8am–8pm); Clin Lavandería, 20 de Noviembre 605 (Mon–Sat 9am–8pm); and Lavandería Domar, Murguia 307 (Mon–Sat 9am–9pm, Sun 10am–3pm) is the cheapest.

Legal aid If you have a complaint, have lost important documents or have been robbed, go to the Centre for the Protection of Tourists, Independencia 607 (☎ 9/516-0123).
Massages and saunas Traditional *temazcal* sauna (US$20) and massage (US$20) are offered in a peaceful garden on the outskirts of town through *Bugambilias,* Reforma 402 (☎ 5/295-1165; reserve at least a day in advance), a short taxi or cheap bus ride away.
Phones Available in the post office (see below), with plenty more all over town.
Post and shipping services The post office is on Independencia by the Alameda (Mon–Fri 8am–7pm, Sat 9am–1pm), and has fax services and Ladatel phones for collect calls.
Study Language classes and courses in Latin American literature and Mexican civilization and culture can be arranged through the Centro de Idiomas at the Benito Juárez University of Oaxaca (☎/Ⓕ 9/515-3922; write to Centro de Idiomas, Burgoa s/n Oaxaca, Oaxaca 68000). Other courses are offered by the Instituto Comunicación y Cultura, in a restored sixteenth-century building near the zócalo at Macedonio Alcalá 307 (☎ 9/516-3443, Ⓦ www.iccoax.com); Amigos del Sol, Libres 109 (☎ 9/514-3484, Ⓦ www.oaxacanews.com/amigosdelsol.htm); Becari Language School, Plaza San Cristóbal, M. Bravo 210 (☎/Ⓕ 9/514-6076, Ⓦ www.becari.com.mx); the Instituto Cultural Oaxaca, Juárez 909 (☎ 9/515-3404, Ⓦ www.instculruraloax.com.mx) and Academia Vinigulaza, Abasolo 503 (☎ 9/513-2763, Ⓦ www.vinigulaza.com). If you're interested in Oaxacan cuisine, you can learn to cook while practising Spanish at the Seasons of My Heart cooking school, Rancho Aurora, Admon 3 (☎ 9/518-7726, Ⓦ www.seasonsofmyheart.com), at El Naranjo, Trujano 203 (☎ 9/514-1878), or through Milagros Para Ti, 5 de Mayo 412 (☎ 9/501-2009).
Tour operators Day-trips to Monte Albán and nearby villages (such as El Tule) cost around US$15. Operators include: Cantera Tours, Plaza Gonzalo Lucero, 5 de Mayo 412 (☎ 9/516-0512) and Turismo Marqués del Valle, *Hotel Marqués del Valle*, on the zócalo (☎ 9/514-6962). El Condor Jeep (no address; ☎ 9/514-3570) go slightly more off the beaten track. Bicicletas Bravo at García Vigil 409-C (☎ 9/516-0953, Ⓦ www.bikeoaxaca.com); Bicicletas Pedro Martinez, Hidalgo 100 in Colonia Jalatlaco (☎ 9/518-4452, Ⓦ www.bicicletaspedromartinez.com), and Turismo de Aventura Teotitlán, Juárez 59 (☎ 9/524-4103) all rent bikes and run day-trips from Oaxaca to places like Dainzú or Santa Cruz (prices vary); Pedro Martinez will design routes for those who want to ride solo, and he also runs a five-day trip to the coast. Tierra Dentro, Reforma 528 (☎ 9/514-9284, Ⓦ www.tierradentro.com), organizes more adventurous hiking, mountaineering and rock-climbing expeditions. Expediciones Sierra Norte, M. Bravo 210-I (☎ 9/514-8271, Ⓦ www.sierranorte.org.mx), and Tierraventura, Abasolo 217 (☎ 9/501-1363, Ⓦ www.tierraventura.com), lead treks to the Sierra Norte mountains outside Oaxaca City. Ecotourism companies run horse-riding, bird-watching and nature photography trips – ask at the tourist office (p.591) for more information.
Western Union A shop at Guerrero 112, as well as Banamex locations, including Valdivieso 116, in back of the cathedral, offer Western Union money transfer.
Work The Oaxaca Street Children Grassroots project (Centro de Esperanza Infantil) aims to bring a brighter future to Oaxaca's neediest children. You can contribute to their food and medical programme, or volunteer with them in Oaxaca by visiting or contacting the centre at Crespo 308 (☎ 9/502-2069, Ⓦ www.oaxacastreetchildren.org).
Yoga and meditation Classes offered several times a week at La Casa del Angel, Jacobo Dalevuelta 200 between Reforma and Juárez (☎ 9/545-3203). Listings for other alternative health practitioners can be found in the *Oaxaca Times*. Calypso Gym at Allende 211, and Aurobic's Fitness at Constitución 300, offer day-passes for aerobic and yoga classes and their weight rooms.

Around Oaxaca: the Zapotec and Mixtec heartland

The region around Oaxaca can be divided into two parts: the **central valleys**, which radiate from the state capital to the south and east, towards Mitla, Ocotlán and Zaachila; and the **Mixteca**, which extends northwest towards Puebla and arcs down to the Pacific coast via Tlaxiaco and Pinotepa Nacional. The central valleys include the state's most famous and frequented archeological centres, while the Mixteca, rich in ruined Dominican convents and ancient towns and villages, is less visited but well worth exploring.

This area saw the development of some of the most highly advanced civilizations in pre-Hispanic Mexico, most notably the Zapotecs and Mixtecs. Their craft skills – particularly Mixtec weaving, pottery and metalworking – were unrivalled, and the architecture and planning of their cities, especially at Zapotec-built **Monte Albán**, stand out among ancient Mexico's most remarkable achievements. The traditions, the village way of life and indigenous languages are all vigorously preserved by Mixtec and Zapotec descendants.

Note that many of the towns outside Oaxaca don't observe daylight-saving time, so your watch might be an hour off local time.

Some history

The Oaxaca valley is the cradle of some of the earliest civilizations in Mexico. The story begins with the **Zapotecs**, who founded their first city, San José Mogoté (now little more than a collection of mounds a few kilometres north of the state capital), some time before 1000 BC. As the city grew in wealth, trading with the Pacific coastal communities, its inhabitants turned their eyes to the stars, and by 500 BC they had invented the first Mexican calendar and were using hieroglyphic writing. At this time, San José, together with smaller villages in the area, established a new administrative capital at Monte Albán, a vantage point on a mountain spur overlooking the principal Oaxaca valley. By waging war on potential rivals, the new city soon came to dominate an area that extended well beyond the main valley – the peculiar *danzante* figures that you can see at the ruins today are almost certainly depictions of prisoners captured in battle. As the population expanded, the Zapotecs endeavoured to level the Monte Albán spur to create more space, essentially creating a massive plateau – the result was an engineering project that boggles the mind. Without the aid of the wheel or beasts of burden, millions of tons of earth were shifted to create a vast, flat terrace on which the Zapotecs constructed colossal pyramids, astronomical observatories and palaces. By the time of Christ, the city was accommodating some twenty thousand people, and Monte Albán not only controlled the smaller townships in the valley below, but had a sphere of influence as extensive as that of its great imperial trading partner, Teotihuacán, to the north.

Just like Teotihuacán, Monte Albán mysteriously began to implode from about 700 AD, and the Zapotec influence across the central valleys waned. Only Yagul and Mitla, two smaller cities in the principal valley, expanded after this date, though they never reached the imperial glory of Monte Albán. The gap left by the Zapotecs was slowly filled by the **Mixtecs**, pre-Hispanic Mexico's finest craftsmen, who expanded into the southern valleys from the north to occupy the Zapotecs' magnificent cities. Influenced by the Zapotec sculptors' abstract motifs on the walls at Mitla, the Mixtecs concentrated their artistic skills on metalwork and pottery, examples of which can be seen in the state capital's museums. By the fifteenth century, the Mixtecs had become the favoured artisans to Mexico's greatest empire, their conquerors, the **Aztecs** – Bernal Díaz recounts that Moctezuma only ate from plates fashioned by Mixtec craftsmen.

Monte Albán

Imagine a great isolated hill at the junction of three broad valleys; an island rising nearly a thousand feet from the green sea of fertility beneath it. An astonishing situation. But the Zapotecs were not embarrassed by the artistic responsibilities it

imposed on them. They levelled the hill-top; laid out two huge rectangular courts; raised pyramidal altars or shrines at the centre, with other, much larger, pyramids at either end; built great flights of steps alternating with smooth slopes of masonry to wall in the courts; ran monumental staircases up the sides of the pyramids and friezes of sculpture round their base. Even today, when the courts are mere fields of rough grass, and the pyramids are buried under an obscuring layer of turf, even today this high place of the Zapotecs remains extraordinarily impressive . . . Monte Albán is the work of men who knew their architectural business consummately well.

Aldous Huxley, *Beyond the Mexique Bay*

In the years since Aldous Huxley visited, little has changed at **MONTE ALBÁN**. The main structures have perhaps been cleared and restored a little more, but it's still the great flattened mountain-top (750m by 250m), the overall layout of the ceremonial precinct and the views over the valley that impress more than any individual aspect. Late afternoon, with the sun sinking in the valley, is the best time to see it.

It seems almost madness to have tried to build a city here, so far from the obvious livelihood of the valleys and without even any natural water supply (in the dry season water was carried up and stored in vast urns). Yet that may have been the point – to demonstrate the Zapotecs' mastery of nature. Certainly, the rulers who lived here must have commanded a huge workforce, first to create the flat site, later to transport materials and keep it supplied. What you see today is just the very centre of the city – the religious and political heart later used by the Mixtecs as a magnificent burial site. On the terraced hillsides below lived a bustling population of craftsmen, priests, administrators and warriors, all, presumably, supported by tribute from the valleys. Small wonder that so top-heavy a society was easily destabilized.

Getting there

Monte Albán (daily 8am–6pm; US$3.70, free on Sun) is just 9km from Oaxaca, up a steeply switchbacking road. Autobuses Turísticos, operating from the *Hotel Rivera del Ángel* at Mina 518, holds a monopoly on **buses from Oaxaca** to the site (US$2.40 round-trip). In peak season buses depart more frequently, but usually they leave at 8.30am (returning at 11am), 9.30am (back at noon) and hourly until 3.30pm (returning at 5.30pm), giving at best two hours at the site – barely enough to see it even quickly. If there's space, you can return on a later bus, but you may have to pay half the fare again. It's sometimes possible to hitch a ride or find a taxi (which for four or five people is not much more expensive than the bus), and walking back is also a realistic option: more than two hours, but downhill almost all the way – get a guard or one of the kids selling "genuine antiquities" to show you the path. The **bus from Zaachila** (see p.614) passes close to the front of the site, but it's a stiff walk (about 1hr) from there. There's a car park, restaurant and souvenir shop by the entrance, and a small **museum** in the same complex: the collection is tiny, but there are good photographs of the site and its surroundings before and after clearing and restoration.

The site

You enter the **Great Plaza** at its northeastern corner, with the ball-court to your left and the large northern platform to your right. Sombre, grey and formal as it all appears now, in its day, with its roofs and sanctuaries intact, the whole place would have been brilliantly polychromed. The **Plataforma Norte** may well have been the most important of all the temples at Monte

Albán, although now the ceremonial buildings that line its sides are largely ruined. What survives is a broad monumental stairway leading up to a platform enclosing a square patio with an altar at its heart. At the top of the stairs are the remains of a double row of six broad columns, which would originally have supported a roof to form a colonnade, dividing this plaza off from the main one.

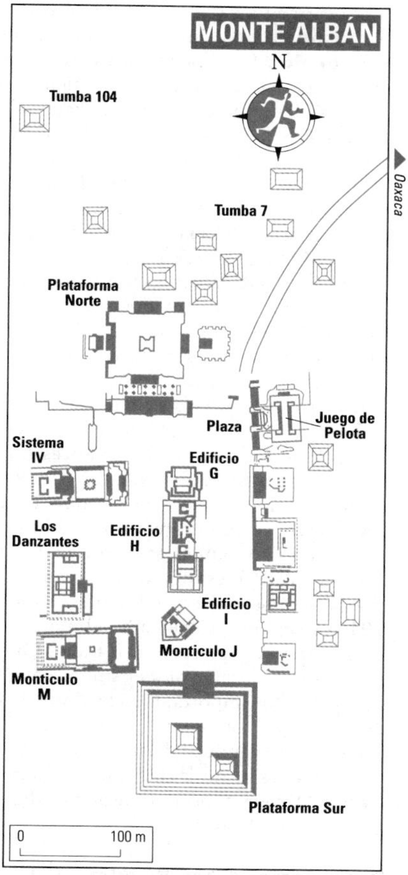

The eastern side of the Great Plaza consists of an almost continuous line of low buildings, reached by a series of staircases from the plaza. The first of them looks over the **Juego de Pelota** (ball-court), a simple I-shaped space with no apparent goals or target rings, obviously an early example. Otherwise, the platforms on the east side are relatively late constructions dating from around 500 AD onwards. Facing them from the middle of the plaza is a long tripartite building **(Edificios G, H** and **I**) that must have played an important role in any rites celebrated here. The central section has broad staircases by which it can be approached from east or west – the lower end temples have smaller stairways facing north and south. From here a complex of tunnels runs under the site to several of the other temples, presumably to allow the priests to emerge suddenly and miraculously in any one of them. You can see the remains of several of these tunnels among the buildings on the east side.

South of this central block, **Monticulo J**, known as the observatory, stands alone in the centre of the plaza – at 45 degrees to everything else – and its arrow-shaped design marks it out from its surroundings. Although the orientation is almost certainly for astronomical reasons, there's no evidence that this was actually an observatory; more likely it was built (around 250 AD, but on the site of an earlier structure) to celebrate an earlier victory. Relief carvings and hieroglyphics on the back of the building apparently represent a list of towns captured by the Zapotecs. In the vaulted passage that runs through the heart of the building, several more panels carved in relief show *danzante* figures (see overleaf) – these, often upside down or on their sides and in no particular order, may have been reused from an earlier building.

The southern end of the mountain-top is dominated by its tallest structure, the **Plataforma Sur**. Unrestored as it is, this vast square pyramid still offers the best overview of the site. Heading back from here up the western side of the plaza, you'll pass just three important structures – the almost identical **Monticulo M** and **Sistema IV**, with the great Dancers Group between them. Monticulo M and Sistema IV, which are probably the best-preserved buildings on the site, both consist of a rectangular platform reached by a stairway from the plaza. Behind this lies a small sunken square from which rises a much larger pyramid, originally topped by a roofed sanctuary.

The gallery and building of **Los Danzantes** (the Dancers) are the most interesting features of Monte Albán. A low wall extending from Monticulo M to the base of the Danzantes building forms the **gallery**, originally faced all along with blocks carved in relief of Olmec or African-featured "dancers". Among the oldest (dating from around 500 BC) and most puzzling features of the site, only a few of these *danzantes* remain *in situ*. What the nude male figures actually represent is in dispute. Many of them seem to have been cut open and may represent sacrificial victims or prisoners; another suggestion is that the entire wall was a sort of medical textbook, or that the figures really are dancers, or ball-players or acrobats. Whatever the truth, they show clear Olmec influence, and many of them have been pressed into use in later buildings throughout the site. The **Danzantes building** itself is one such, built over and obscuring much of the wall. It's a bulky, relatively plain rectangular platform with three temples on top – tunnels cut into the structure by archeologists reveal earlier buildings within, and more of the dancing figures.

Several lesser buildings surround the main plaza, and although they're not particularly interesting, many contained tombs in which rich treasures were discovered (as indeed did some of the main structures themselves). **Tumba 104**, reached by a small path behind the Plataforma Norte or from the car park area, is the best-preserved of them. One of several in the immediate vicinity, this vaulted burial chamber still preserves excellent remains of murals. **Tumba 7**, where the important collection of Mixtec jewellery now in the Oaxaca Museum was found, lies a few hundred metres down the main road from the site entrance. Built underneath a small temple, it was originally constructed by the Zapotecs towards the end of Monte Albán's heyday, but was later emptied by the Mixtecs, who buried one of their own chiefs here along with his magnificent burial trove.

The road to Mitla

Mitla (see p.611), some 45km from Oaxaca, just off Hwy-190 as it heads towards Guatemala, involves a slightly longer excursion. It's easy enough to do, though: buses leave from the second-class terminal every thirty minutes or so throughout the day. On the way are several of the more easily accessible **native villages**, some of which have community museums. Check with the tourist office for which one has a market on the day you're going – there will be more buses and much more of interest once you get there. Also en route are a couple of smaller, lonelier ancient sites. If you rent a car in Oaxaca, you can take in all of this in a single day. If you want to explore the valley further, it's a good idea to stay in one of the villages, some of which have self-catering **Tourist Yú'ù** facilities (see box, p.594), which are as comfortable as many of Oaxaca's budget hotels.

Santa María del Tule

At **Santa María del Tule**, a first stop on Hwy-190 as you head east out of Oaxaca, you pass the famous Árbol del Tule in a churchyard by the road. This mighty tree, said to be at least 2000 years old (some say 3000), is a good 58m round, slightly fatter than it is tall. A notice board gives all the vital statistics: suffice to say that it must be one of the oldest living (and flourishing) objects on earth, and it's a species of cypress (*Taxodium mucrunatum*) that has been virtually extinct since the colonial era. Sadly, the tree has recently come under threat from industry and housing sapping its water supply.

A tacky souvenir market takes advantage of the passing trade, and there are various food and drink stalls, but if you're on the bus (on the left-hand side heading for Mitla) you might get a glimpse as you pass. A close-up look provides a better view, for US$0.20; the tree is mightily impressive and worth a stop. **Buses** for El Tule depart from Oaxaca's second-class bus terminal every ten minutes.

Dainzú

Seven kilometres further on Hwy-190 from the turn-off for Abasolo, **DAINZÚ**, the first significant archeological site, lies about 1km south of the main road (daily 8am–6pm; US$2.30, free on Sun). A Zapotec centre broadly contemporary with Monte Albán, Dainzú stands only partially excavated in a harsh landscape of cactus-covered hills. The first structure you reach is **Edificio A**, a large and rambling construction, with elements from several epochs, set around a courtyard. The highlight of this building is a tomb with a jaguar doorway. Nearby is the ball-court, only one side of which has been reconstructed, and higher up the hill **Edificio B** is the best-preserved part of the site. Along the far side of its base a series of dancer figures can be made out, similar to the Monte Albán dancers except that these clearly represent ball-players.

Teotitlán del Valle

Just before the small Zapotec archeological site **Lambityeco** (daily 8am–6pm; US$2.30), a road leads 4km to **TEOTITLÁN DEL VALLE**, the most famous weaving town in Oaxaca. All over the village you see bold-patterned and brightly coloured **rugs** and **sarapes**, some following traditional designs from Mitla, others imitating twentieth-century designs, among them those of Escher. Most are the product of cottage industry: even if you're not buying, poke your head into the compounds with rugs hanging outside. When dropped off the bus, you'll probably be pointed along a street to the left, which leads to the **mercado de artesanías**. You'll see the widest range here – ask to rummage in the back and you'll find some especially nice deals – and prices are generally cheaper than in Oaxaca.

The village has an interesting **community museum** (Tues–Sun 10am–2pm & 4–6pm; US$0.50) with displays on pre-Hispanic artefacts, and information about carpet-weaving and life in the area. Inside the local **church**, whose walls are studded with bits of Zapotec temple, worship is a syncretic fusion of Catholic and indigenous ritual.

Teotitlán has a few worthy **restaurants**. *Tlamanalli*, Avenida Juárez 39 (Tues–Sun 2–5pm), serves delicious local classics, such as squash blossom soup and stewed chicken; the menu changes daily. The less expensive *La Cúpula*, on the road into town, offers authentic Zapotec food, including hearty *pozole* soup, adjacent to a fine weaving shop. About 3.5km outside, back towards Hwy-190, there's an inconveniently sited **Tourist Yú'ù** – check with the tourist office to see if it's open. If not, *El Descanso*, Juárez 51, offers **accommodation** (❹). There are direct **buses** out here every hour or so from Oaxaca, and frequent micros from Tlacolula, further east along Hwy-190.

Benito Juárez

Perched on a ridge and surrounded by pine trees at 3000m overlooking the Oaxaca valleys, the little village of **BENITO JUÁREZ** is known for spectacular sunsets – in clear weather from the mirador here you can see all the way to Mexico's highest mountain, Pico Orizaba. It's also the starting point for more than 100km of signposted rural **foothpaths and country roads** through the *pueblos mancomunados* (literally "joint villages") of the Sierra Norte towards Ixtlan (see below), suitable for hikers and mountain bikers of all abilities. The paths have been used for centuries by local people accustomed to sharing resources within the surrounding communities. The villages are an impressive example of community social organization in Mexico, with eight small towns perched on common land in mountains and woods, all of which have affordable cabañas if you plan a longer trek. The landscape is spectacular – some sections of the pine forest have been classified by the World Wildlife Foundation as being the richest and most varied on earth. The footpath between the villages of Latuvi and Amatlan is believed to be part of a larger pre-Columbian route that connected the Zapotec cities in the central valleys of Oaxaca with the Gulf of Mexico and you can still see remains of the old road along the trail. Bear in mind that this area has extremes of altitude and temperature – it's advisable to let your body acclimate before engaging in any strenuous physical activity, to drink plenty of water and wear sunscreen. If you ask around, or check with the tourist office (see below), locals can also take you on **horse** or **donkey rides**, and there's a river where you can **fish** for trout. All in all it's a relaxing place to spend a few days, enjoying nature and getting firsthand experience of rural Oaxacan life.

The small but extremely helpful **tourist information** office (Mon–Sat 9am–5pm; ☎9/545-9994) in Benito Juárez, next to the town square, has excellent maps which show the varying demands of each trek, and rents out reliable mountain bikes, but only with a guide (US$20 for bike and guide). Next door, the simple and friendly **restaurant** serves cheap breakfasts, comidas, hot drinks and sells sandwiches and water for those going on any of the walks.

Accommodation is limited to the pleasant Tourist Yú'ù (❷), which has bunk beds and family cabins with kitchens (make sure the caretaker switches on the hot water before he disappears for the night). You can reserve in advance through Oaxaca's tourist office (see p.591) although it's not strictly necessary in the low season. **Camping** is also an option in well-organized campgrounds (❶). Temperatures drop dramatically at night – take warm clothing and a sleeping bag (they can provide wool blankets) as it gets chilly up here and there's snow in winter. You can also indulge in *temazcal* in town for US$10, which can be arranged through the Tourist Yú'ù.

Ixtlan

Ixtlan, a pretty village near San Pablo Guelatao (the birthplace of Benito Juárez), is set in an area of great natural beauty, and its cloud forests, pine and oak woodlands are claimed to hold 500 bird varieties and 6000 species of plants. As such, the place is very much dedicated to ecotourism projects, and on the main plaza you'll find the **Museo de la Bioversidad** (Mon–Fri 9am–5pm; free), which has information on the local environment and related ecoprojects, as well as examples of butterflies and animals, including the ten local species of rat. Several companies offer **ecotours** exploring the region, including Viajes Ecoturisticos Shiaa Rua Via (☎9/553-6075,

Ⓦ www.oaxacamex.info/ixtlan). Like the other villages nearby, Ixtlan has basic cabin **accommodation** (❷), as well as the simple *Yu Yeeva Posada* (❸). Everyone will tell you that the best place to eat is *Las Truchas*, a trout farm just outside of town serving fresh (pellet-fed) fish. Ixtlan is accessible either by direct **bus** from the second-class station (2 per day), or by colectivo.

Tlacolula and Santa Ana del Valle

In the valley below Benito Juárez, just a few kilometres beyond Teotitlán del Valle, **TLACOLULA** is a scruffy and dirty village, but worth a stop to see the sixteenth-century **church**, about 1km to the south of the main road, its interior as ornate as Oaxaca's Santo Domingo, though less skillfully crafted. In the adjoining chapel, some gory carvings of martyrs include a decapitated St Paul. The best day to go is Sunday, when there's also a large **market**. **Buses** leave every twenty minutes for Tlacolula from Oaxaca's second-class bus station.

A road leading north from the junction at Tlacolula goes to **SANTA ANA DEL VALLE**, smaller than Teotitlán but with a fine selection of locally produced **rugs**. Lucio Aquino Cruz and his younger brother Primo, at Morelos 2, make some of the most exquisite rugs in Mexico – it's worth visiting their house just to see them, even if they are beyond your price range. Alternatively place orders with Lucio for your own designs – and you can see the production from beginning to end. One side of the small central square is devoted to the **Shan-Dany Community Museum** (Mon–Sat 10am–2pm & 4–6pm). Its name is Zapotec, meaning "foot of the hill", and it marks the exact spot where a couple of **tombs** were discovered in the 1950s and more recently excavated. Probably contemporary with Dainzú and Monte Albán, the Zapotec site here boasts some fine glyphs. Excavations have also been carried out beneath what are now basketball courts outside, enough pots and stones being recovered to fill the small but impressive co-operatively run museum. The local weaving industry is also covered and, though panels are all in Spanish, the gist is clear enough.

There's a tranquil, landscaped **Tourist Yú'ù** in Santa Ana if you want to stay. The local **baker** makes delicious bread, and there's a shop where you can buy basic **provisions**. **Buses** leave every ten minutes from Tlacolula.

Yagul

The site of **YAGUL** (daily 8am–6pm US$2.80, free on Sun) lies just to the north of the highway at about 35km – just a couple of kilometres uphill from where the bus from Oaxaca stops. Lightly touristed Yagul is situated on a large cactus-dotted plateau overlooking the spectacular Tlacolula valley. It is a large site, spread expansively across a superb defensive position, and although occupied by the Zapotecs from a fairly early date, its main features are from later on (around 900–1200 AD, after the fall of Monte Albán) and demonstrate **Mixtec** influence. On the lowest level is the **Patio de la Triple Tumba**, where the remains of four temples surround an altar and the entry to the **Triple Tomb**, whose three chambers show characteristically Mixtec decoration. Immediately above the patio, you'll see a large and elegantly simple ball-court, and a level above this, the maze-like **Palacio de los Seis Patios**. Probably a residential complex, this features six small courtyards surrounded by rooms and narrow passages. Climbing still higher towards the crest of the hill and the fortress, you pass several lesser remains and tombs, while from the fortress itself there are stunning views, and a frightening rock bridge to a natural watchtower.

△ Zapotec man, Tlacolula

Mitla

The town of **MITLA** ("Place of the Dead"), where the bus from Oaxaca finally drops you, is some 4km off the main road and just ten minutes' walk from the site of the famous ruins. It's an unattractive, dusty little place where you'll be harassed by would-be guides and vendors of handicrafts (there's also a distinctly second-rate crafts market by the ruins). **Accommodation** can be found at the *Hotel Mitla* (Ⓣ9/568-0112; ❹), or *La Zapoteca* (Ⓣ9/568-0026; ❹), in town on the way to the ruins.

The history of Mitla is a complicated one, and still far from agreed among archeologists. The abstract designs on the buildings seem to echo patterns on surviving **Mixtec** manuscripts, and have long been viewed as purely Mixtec in style. But more recent opinion is that the buildings were built by **Zapotecs** and that the city was a ceremonial centre occupied by the most important Zapotec high priest. This Uija-Tao, or "great seer", was described by Alonso Canesco, a fifteenth-century Spaniard, as being "rather like our Pope", and his presence here would have made Mitla a kind of Vatican City.

A few minutes by local bus from Mitla you'll find the small town of **Matatlan**, mostly dedicated to *mescal*, where you can visit the ateliers in which the drink is produced, enjoy free samples from the town stores, and eat the maguey plant itself. Be warned of what a few samples of home-made *mescal* can do to your senses.

The site

The **site** itself (daily 8am–6pm; US$2.80, free on Sun) may seem disappointing on first sight: it's relatively small, and in the middle of the day overrun with visitors. But on closer inspection the fame of the place becomes more justifiable. The palace complexes are magnificently decorated with elaborate stone mosaics. You'll see it at its best if you arrive towards closing time, when the low sun throws the patterns into sharp, shadowed relief, and the bulk of the visitors have left.

The **Grupo de las Columnas** is the best-preserved and most impressive of the palace complexes, and the obvious place to head for from the entrance. The only other sites that these long, low, fabulously decorated buildings recall in any way are the two post-Classic sites of El Tajín (see p.569) and Uxmal (see p.742), which, along with other evidence, suggests that there may have been some contact between these most influential groups.

The first large courtyard is flanked by constructions on three sides – its central **Templo de las Columnas** is magnificent, precision-engineered and quite overpowering in effect. Climbing the broad stairway and through one of three entrances in its great facade, you come to the **Salón de las Columnas**, named after the six monolithic, tapered columns of volcanic stone that supported its roof. A low, narrow passageway leads from here into the small inner patio (**Patio de las Grecas**), lined with some of the most intricately assembled of the geometric mosaics. Four dark rooms that open off it continue the patterned mosaic theme. It is here that the Uija-Tao would have lived. If the latest theory is correct, the Zapotec architects converted the inner room of the traditional Mesoamerican temple, in which priests usually lived, into a kind of exquisitely decorated "papal flat" arranged around a private courtyard. The second courtyard of the Columns group, adjoining the southwestern corner of the first, is similar in design though perhaps less impressive in execution. Known as the **Patio de las Tumbas**, it does indeed contain two cross-shaped tombs, long since plundered by grave-robbers. In one the roof is supported by the **Columna de la Muerte**; embrace this, they say, and the gap left between your outstretched hands tells you how long you have left to live: hand-widths translate into years remaining.

The **Grupo de la Iglesia**, a short distance north, is so called because the Spanish built a church over, and from, much of it. Two of its three original courtyards survive, however, and in the smaller one the mosaic decoration bears traces of the original paint, indicating that the patterns were once picked out in white from a dark-red background.

Three other groups of buildings, which have weathered the years less well, complete the site. All of them are now right in the modern town, fenced off from the surrounding houses: the **Grupo de los Adobes** can be found where you see a chapel atop a pyramid; the **Grupo del Arroyo** is very nearby; and the **Grupo del Sur** lies right beside the road to the main site.

Hierve el Agua

Before the environmental degradation worsens, you should visit **Hierve el Agua**. Some 25km east of Mitla, down a side road that leads to **San Lorenzo Albarradas** (Hierve el Agua lies just beyond), it's the site of the spectacular limestone **waterfalls** that you'll see in photographs all over Oaxaca city. Tourism here threatens to be more environmentally destructive than in the rest of the valley, the town can barely support the volume of visitors it receives, and the people running the little restaurants near the falls are a little less friendly than others in the Oaxaca villages. The area is beautiful, though, and the stars at night awe-inspiring – there's no electricity and the hills shield the glow from Oaxaca's populated valleys. There is a **Tourist Yú'ù** (check with the Oaxaca tourist office on the status, see p.591) and some **cabins**, as well as a few **restaurants**, which close after sunset. It's a two- to three-hour drive up here from Oaxaca through some beautiful countryside. One **bus** is scheduled to make the journey from Oaxaca every day, leaving the second-class bus terminal at 8am, and returning at 2.30pm, but the service is somewhat erratic.

The valleys south of Oaxaca

The two roads that run almost due south of Oaxaca don't have the same concentration of interesting villages and sites as the Mitla road, but poking through the villages or admiring the beauty of the valley by bike could easily occupy a day or so. Again, you can travel around the area by **public transport** on market days – by far the best time to go – but **cycling** on rented bikes from Oaxaca isn't as arduous as it might sound, especially if you are careful about the midday heat.

San Bartolo Coyotepec

Fifteen kilometres south of Oaxaca on the main highway to Puerto Ángel lies **SAN BARTOLO COYOTEPEC**, as unprepossessing a town as you could imagine. It is famed only for its shiny black, purely ornamental pottery **barro negro brillante**, which can be found in crafts shops all around Oaxaca state, but is only made in the small factory in this town. From the bus stop, a road, one side awash with black-pottery vendors, leads to the pottery where, in 1934, Doña Rosa developed the manufacturing technique. Her family still run the sole "factory", now very tourist-oriented, with pieces ranging from beautifully simple amphorae to ghastly clocks. Prices are supposed to be fixed, and at the factory they probably are, but places down the road will haggle; just remember your piece has to get home and the stuff is fragile. **Buses** to San Bartolo Coyotepec leave Oaxaca's second-class bus station every hour.

San Martín Tilcajete and Santo Tomás Jalieza

The same buses continue south, passing **SAN MARTÍN TILCAJETE**, a sleepy town whose main street is lined with family workshops carving, painting and polishing the bright wooden animal figurines known as *alejibres* – although not as famous as those in Arrazola (see below), there are still some nice examples. It's easy to wander through the workshops and observe the process.

To the east of the highway is **SANTO TOMÁS JALIEZA**, where women specialize in weaving cotton on backstrap looms. An all-women's co-operative market in the centre of town sells thick cotton tablecloths and placemats, backpacks, clothing and belts, at fixed (and generally reasonable) prices.

Ocotlán

The ride ends forty minutes from Oaxaca at **OCOTLÁN**, chiefly noted for the **clay** figures crafted by the Aguilar sisters. On the approach into town, look out on the right for the adjacent workshops of Guillermina, Josefina and Irene, and on the left for Constitución, each producing slightly different items, though the distinctive Aguilar style, originated by their mother, shows through them all. Again, you can find examples in Oaxaca, but a trip out here allows you to see the full range, including figures of animals, men and buxom women at work and play, and even nativity scenes (apparently no subject matter is off limits), all often gaudily decorated in polka dots or geometric patterns. Try to make it on a Friday when the weekly **market** takes place not far from the **Parroquia de Santo Domingo de Guzmán**, with its newly restored facade and multiple domes richly painted with saints. Take a peek in at the gilded south transept.

Ocotlán is also the birthplace of famous Oaxacan artist **Rodolfo Morales** (1925–2001), who set up the Fundación Cultural Rodolfo Morales here, at Morelos 108, which has provided the town with its first ambulance and computer centre, as well as establishing conservation and land-restoration projects. The former jail, for example, has been turned into an art museum and restaurant.

Arrazola, Cuilapan and Zaachila

The other major region of interest in this area is along, or beside, the road to Zaachila that runs southwest from Oaxaca past the foot of Monte Albán. **ARRAZOLA**, an easy cycle ride 5km off to the right from this road, is the home of the local woodcarvers and painters who produce many of the delightful boldly patterned animals from copal wood that you'll see for sale in Oaxaca and all over Mexico. Carvers from other villages are catching on to the popularity of these whimsical, spiky figures and producing the polka-dot, hooped or expressionist examples themselves, but few, if any, are better than in Arrazola.

The village of **CUILAPAN**, 14km from Oaxaca (frequent buses from the second-class bus station), seems insignificant beneath the immense sixteenth-century hulk of the Dominican **Ex-Convento de Santiago Apóstol**, which, though badly damaged, is still an impressive place to wander around, with a Renaissance twin-aisled nave and largely intact vaulting. One section is still roofed, and mass is said here amid the clangs and echoes of ongoing restoration work. The real interest, however, lies around the back in the **cloister** (daily 8am–6pm; US$2.30), which features a few faded frescoes on the wall. Look out for the sign pointing to the back wall, where **Vicente Guerrero** was executed by firing squad after spending his captivity here.

Buses from Oaxaca to Cuilapan continue 5km to **ZAACHILA**, which has a colourful Thursday market. Come here on that day and you've got the best chance of being able to get into the **zona arqueológica** (nominally daily 8am–6pm; US$2.30, free on Sun), up behind the multi-domed church. There's not a great deal to see, but you can step down into the two opened tombs – of what is probably a much larger site – and, when your eyes become accustomed to the gloom, pick out detailed bas-relief geometric figures on the lintel and owls guarding the entrance. Two marvellous glyphs show who was interred here: Señor 9-Flower, probably a priest, depicted carrying a bag of copal for producing incense.

The Mixteca

The two areas of Oaxaca's Mixteca region – the barren hills of the **Mixteca Baja** and the mountainous, pine-clad **Mixteca Alta** – are not as obvious tourist destinations as the Central Valleys. Although they hold some interesting colonial architecture, the pre-Hispanic sites here are far less spectacular, and there are no artisan centres to compare with Teotitlán or Arrazola. But fewer tourists mean that you are likely to have vast crumbling monasteries and little-visited Mixtec ruins to yourself, and though you'll pick up fewer trinkets at the colourful Mixtec markets, you'll know that you're witnessing a scene that has remained relatively unchanged since before Cortés.

Public transport through the region is fairly easy. Hwy-135, one of the country's best roads, cuts through the Baja's deforested hillsides, eventually reaching Mexico City. Hwy-125 leads off 135 to the south, traversing the steeper slopes of the Mixteca Alta, eventually arriving at Puerto Escondido via a long and circuitous route. There are frequent buses and *camionetas* from Oaxaca heading out to the monasteries and the major towns.

The Baja: Yanhuitlán, Teposcolula and Coixtlahuaca

Among the **Mixteca Baja**'s highlights are a trio of **Dominican monasteries** – Yanhuitlán, Teposcolula and Coixtlahuaca – once centres of mass conversion, but each now eerily deserted and in various stages of decay, although zealous restoration projects are under way. These vast and imposing relics of Mexico's imperial past are widely regarded as among the country's most important colonial buildings. All three can easily be visited as a day-trip from Oaxaca if you have your own transport; less easily so by public transport, though it's possible (see p.601).

Head out on Hwy-190 for about 120km to reach the first monastery, at **Yanhuitlán**, the permanent seat of the vicarage of the Mixteca during the sixteenth century. The church is massive, built on an enormous pre-Hispanic platform, no doubt intended to remind the Mixtecs of the supremacy of the new religion. Inside are many original paintings and sculptures – the principal altarpiece, dating to 1570, is the work of the Spanish artist Andrés de la Concha. **Teposcolula**, south on Hwy-125 in the village of the same name, has one of the finest *capillae abierta* in the Americas. These graceful open-air chapels were used for mass preaching and conversion, and are only found in the New World. The Ex-Convent of San Juan Bautista, at **Coixtlahuaca**, a couple of kilometres off Hwy-135, dates from 1576 and has some unusual sculpture on the facade, depicting grand rosettes, symbols of the Passion and John the Baptist flanked by saints Peter and James. There's an impressive churrigueresque altarpiece within.

To see all three monasteries in a single, if long, day-trip from Oaxaca, catch a **minibus** from Transportes Tlaxiaco, a small terminal on J.P. García, between Arista and Nuno del Mercado (if you do want to stay, there are plenty of basic hotels on the route). The minibuses leave when full, approximately every hour, and take about an hour and a half to reach Yanhuitlán. You can catch the next bus, or a taxi, to Teposcolula, less than 25km away. From Teposcolula, take a cab or catch a second-class bus to **El Crucero**, at the junction of Hwy-125, Hwy-190 and Hwy-135, only about 10km from the town. Frequent first- and second-class buses heading to Mexico City or Oaxaca stop here. Catch one going towards Mexico City and get off after about 20km at the turn-off to Coixtlahuaca. The monastery is about 1.5km up a side road.

Santiago Apoala

About 98km north from Oaxaca, reached by following Hwy-190 to the town of **Nochixtlán**, and then heading north on an unpaved road, is the rural village of **SANTIAGO APOALA**, tucked in a beautiful high valley. It's a wild place, ideally located for hiking, biking and various activities in the surrounding rivers, lagoons and falls. The comfortable **Tourist Yú'ù** (❷) can be reserved through the tourist office in Oaxaca, and the village ecotourism co-operative, Comité de Turismo de Santiago Apoala (ⓣ5/151-9154), can arrange meals, organize expeditions and guides and provide general information.

Apoala can be reached by a variety of means: second-class buses make the trip daily, and minivans go to Nochíxtlan, where taxi or microbus (Wed, Sat & Sun) can make the remaining climb into the mountains and into the village's lush, spring-fed valley.

The Alta: Tlaxiaco and around

Hwy-125 climbs into the **Mixteca Alta** after Teposcolula, entering some beautiful pine forest as it gets closer to Tlaxiaco. On the way, about 50km after Teposcolula, lies **Huamelulpan**, 2km up a side road. This tiny mountain village has an extensive and mostly unexplored Mixtec archeological site, with two large plazas cut out of a hill, a ball-court, and some temple complexes. Some of the sculptures found here have been embedded in the walls of the colonial church. Other artefacts from the ruins are displayed in the small community **museum** (Mon–Fri 9am–6pm), which also has information about indigenous medicines – these are still used by traditional healers in the local community. The surrounding countryside is picturesque, with deer and coyotes in the woodland, and the villagers are friendly. They administer a small, very basic **tourist lodge** here (book through the tourist office in Oaxaca, or just turn up as you're likely to be the only visitor; ❷); the grocery shop on the main square can prepare **food** for you.

Tlaxiaco, a fifteen-minute bus ride beyond Huamelulpan, is famed for its pulque, the lightly fermented drink made from cactus. The city once served as the economic heart of the Mixteca, and consequently its important Saturday market attracts indigenous people from across the region. An attractive town square and nearby good-value hotels could serve as a base for exploring the countryside and the Mixtec and Triqui villages nearby. The *Hotel del Portal* (ⓣ9/552-0154; ❺), in a converted colonial house on the main plaza, is a wonderful **place to stay**, especially if you make sure you get a room in the old building. The rather grandiose **restaurant** within serves fresh juices and special dishes such as *molcajete*, a hot stone bowl of stewed meat and vegetables. Slightly less expensive are the *Hotel Colón* (ⓣ9/552-0013; ❸), Colón 11, and the cheery *Hotel México* (ⓣ9/552-0086; ❸), Hidalgo 13. The *Rincón de Gon* restaurant, next door to the *México*, has a good menu, including some vegetarian options, and puts on live music most nights.

Camionetas for Tlaxiaco leave from Oaxaca's Transporte Tlaxiaco (hourly; 3hr). There are also two second-class **buses** per day. For moving on from Tlaxiaco, buses leave for **Pinotepa Nacional**, where you can change for

Puerto Escondido and the Pacific coast. There are also buses from Tlaxiaco to Mexico City and Puebla.

San José del Pacífico

On the route down to the coast from Oaxaca via Hwy-175, perched on the side of a pine-tree-clad mountain, you'll find **SAN JOSÉ DEL PACÍFICO**. It's a pleasant place to break the journey south, or to stay for a day or two if you want to enjoy the forest trails and cool mountain air. San José is also renowned for its hallucinogenic **mushrooms**, the season for which runs from July to October. Many people make the short trip from nearby Zipolite, just two hours away (see p.625) for a lovely overnight stay. The *Puesta del Sol* on the main road (Ⓣ/Ⓕ9/572-0111, Ⓦwww.sanjosedelpacifico.com) has a good **restaurant** serving comidas, *dulces* and *mescal*, plus you can stay here in wooden **cabañas** (❸) or bungalows (❹) with incredible views over the valley (try to get one of the cabañas furthest from the restaurant so that you get a clear view). Round the corner, in the centre of the village, the *Pacífico* (no phone) has equally nice cabañas that are slightly cheaper (❷), some of which also have good views, though they aren't as breathtaking as those at the *Puesta del Sol*. It gets chilly at night here in winter (although it heats up during the day), so bring warm clothing and a sleeping bag and indulge in some *mescal*.

Puerto Escondido

The journey to **PUERTO ESCONDIDO** ("Hidden Port") from Oaxaca is dramatic, passing through mountainous pine forests and descending into lush tropical lowlands. To the south, the air pushed in from the sea meets the air in the tropical forest, condenses and regularly rises in impressive, cold gusts up the mountainside.

No longer the tranquil hangout it was thirty-plus years ago – and with direct flights from the capital and an international reputation – Escondido has firmly established itself as a mainstream resort, with the standard strings of souvenir shops and constantly spiralling prices. It still has a lot going for it, with **beaches** stretched out around the bay for miles in each direction and an atmosphere that remains, against all the odds, somewhat small-town, bohemian, casual and free. While there is a tremendous number of hotels to choose from, the majority tend to be on the small side, and most of the visitors are young, with surfing high on their agendas.

Indeed, it is along the surf beach, **Zicatela**, less than a kilometre away from the centre, that most of the recent changes have taken place. Where once stood just a few weather-beaten huts, there's now a thriving community with several good hotels – most with pools, since the sea is almost always too rough for swimming – and great restaurants. Everything revolves around surfing and being outdoors: you can get your hair cut while watching the surfers on the boards, or watch a video of the morning's action in one of the hotels. Non-surfers have also latched on to the relaxed pace, and Zicatela is now as much a destination as Escondido town itself, especially between August and January when the weather is ideal. At either end of this season, Escondido is packed for the **surf tournaments**: a locally sponsored event in late August and two international ones, one in August and the other in late November. The town also has a cult reputation amongst Italians on the back of Gabriele Salvatores' travel and crime film *Puerto Escondido*; as a result, pasta is a staple on many restaurant menus.

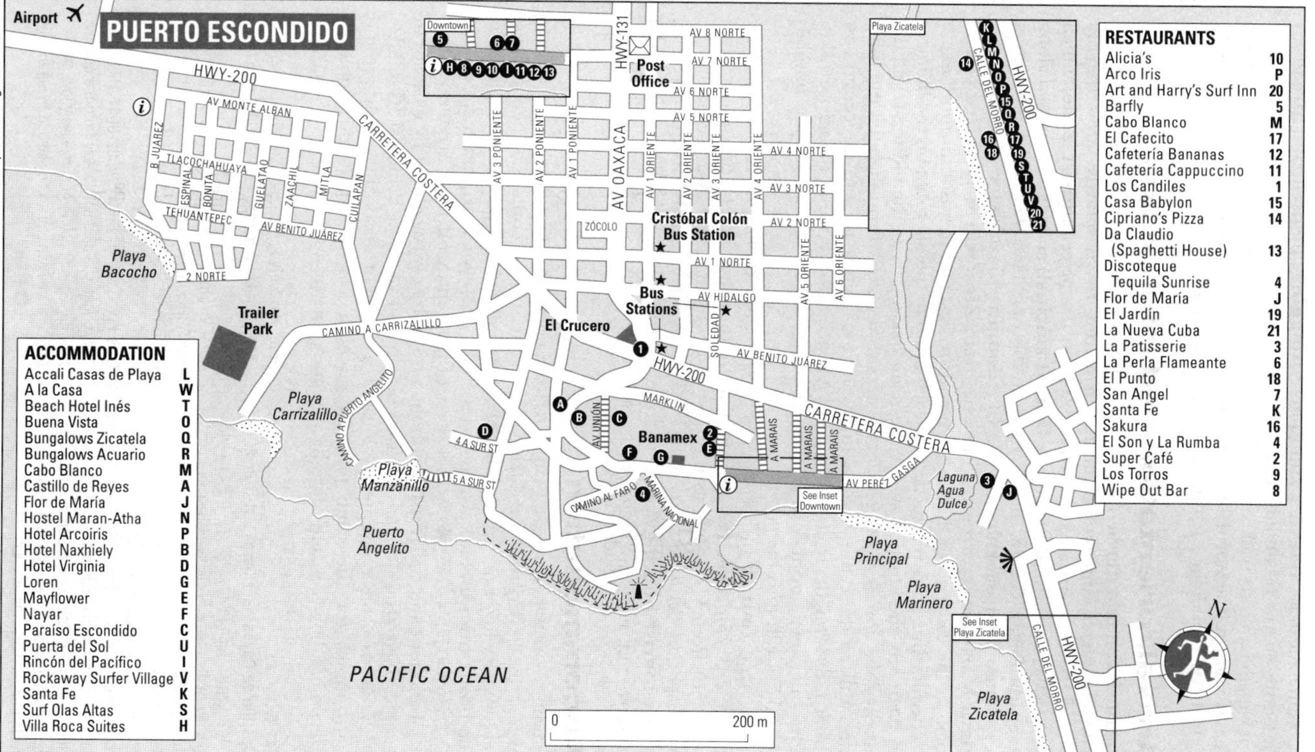
PUERTO ESCONDIDO
Airport
Oaxaca
Acapulco & Lagoons
HWY-200
HWY-131
CARRETERA COSTERA
AV OAXACA
Post Office
Cristóbal Colón Bus Station
Bus Stations
El Crucero
Banamex
ZÓCOLO
Trailer Park
AV 8 NORTE
AV 7 NORTE
AV 6 NORTE
AV 5 NORTE
AV 4 NORTE
AV 3 NORTE
AV 2 NORTE
AV 1 NORTE
AV HIDALGO
AV BENITO JUÁREZ
SOLEDAD
AV 1 ORIENTE
AV 2 ORIENTE
AV 3 ORIENTE
AV 4 ORIENTE
AV 5 ORIENTE
AV 6 ORIENTE
AV 1 PONIENTE
AV 2 PONIENTE
AV 3 PONIENTE
MARKLIN
AV UNIÓN
A MARAIS
AV PERÉZ GASGA
CAMINO AL FARO
MARINA NACIONAL
4 A SUR ST
5 A SUR ST
CAMINO A CARRIZALILLO
CAMINO A PUERTO ANGELITO
AV MONTE ALBAN
B JUAREZ
TLACOCHAHUAYA
ESPINAL
BONITA
TEHUANTEPEC
GUELATAO
ZAACHIL
MITLA
CUILAPAN
AV BENITO JUÁREZ
2 NORTE
CALLE DEL MORRO
Playa Bacocho
Playa Carrizalillo
Playa Manzanillo
Puerto Angelito
Playa Principal
Playa Marinero
Playa Zicatela
Laguna Agua Dulce
PACIFIC OCEAN
See Inset Downtown
See Inset Playa Zicatela
Downtown
Playa Zicatela
0
200 m
N
ACCOMMODATION
Accali Casas de Playa L
A la Casa W
Beach Hotel Inés T
Buena Vista O
Bungalows Zicatela Q
Bungalows Acuario R
Cabo Blanco M
Castillo de Reyes A
Flor de María J
Hostel Maran-Atha N
Hotel Arcoiris P
Hotel Naxhiely B
Hotel Virginia D
Loren G
Mayflower E
Nayar F
Paraíso Escondido C
Puerta del Sol U
Rincón del Pacífico I
Rockaway Surfer Village V
Santa Fe K
Surf Olas Altas S
Villa Roca Suites H
RESTAURANTS
Alicia's 10
Arco Iris P
Art and Harry's Surf Inn 20
Barfly 5
Cabo Blanco M
El Cafecito 17
Cafetería Bananas 12
Cafetería Cappuccino 11
Los Candiles 1
Casa Babylon 15
Cipriano's Pizza 14
Da Claudio (Spaghetti House) 13
Discoteque Tequila Sunrise 4
Flor de María J
El Jardín 19
La Nueva Cuba 21
La Patisserie 3
La Perla Flameante 6
El Punto 18
San Angel 7
Santa Fe K
Sakura 16
El Son y La Rumba 4
Super Café 2
Los Torros 9
Wipe Out Bar 8

Despite Zicatela's laid-back atmosphere, **muggings** do occur and have given the entire Puerto Escondido area a bit of an overblown reputation for thievery – it's inadvisable to walk on the beach at night, but the road by the hotels is fine. If you use the normal precautions, and are not lured into a false sense of security by the idyllic surroundings, there shouldn't be any problems.

Arrival, orientation and information

Puerto Escondido can be loosely divided into three zones, all contiguous but with completely different characters. The **old town** sprawls across the hill behind the bay, separated by Hwy-200 from the newer **tourist zone**, which spills down towards the water (the **Bahía Principal**) and is concentrated along **Avenida Peréz Gasga**, the town's main thoroughfare. Half of the latter street is pedestrianized and known as the **El Adoquín** – Spanish for "paving stone". **Playa Marinero** separates the main bay from **Zicatela** beach (hidden behind rocks at the east end of the bay), which runs east and then south from here.

The four **bus stations** are all near each other in the old town on the hill near **El Crucero**, the junction where the main road between the old town and the tourist zone crosses the Carretera Costera (Hwy-200). From here it's ten minutes' walk to the centre and about twenty to Zicatela; taxis to the centre cost about US$3. Flights from Oaxaca and Mexico City arrive at the airport 3km north of town, from where taxis (around US$8) and a cheaper minibus (US$3.50) run into the centre.

The main **tourist office** (Mon–Fri 9am–2pm & 4–7pm, Sat 10am–2pm; ⓣ9/582-0175) is on the turning off to the new hotel zone (near Playa Bacocho) from Hwy-200, to the west of town, and gives away copies of the free paper *El Sol de la Costa*, which has festival and event **listings**. There's a nearer **tourist booth** (Mon–Fri 9am–2pm & 4–6pm, Sat 10am–2pm) at the western end of the walking section of Adoquín.

Accommodation

Finding somewhere to stay in Puerto Escondido shouldn't be a problem, except over Christmas or during the major surfing contests, when **prices**, seldom very low, can rise considerably. Standards of hotel quality are high across the board, from simple cabañas to tasteful rooms. For **campers** there is *Villa Relax* (ⓣ9/582-2977; ❶), to the west of the centre, off the Carretera, with a pool and tent and trailer space, although it can be overwhelmed by busloads of people. *Trailer Park Neptune*, by the eastern end of Playa Principal (ⓣ9/582-0327; ❶), is more conveniently located, a tatty but reasonably shady ground with cabins for the same price as pitching a tent – rates quadruple in December, however, and there have been reports of robberies.

In town

Castillo de Reyes Peréz Gasga 201 ⓣ9/582-0442. Large, clean rooms with fan in a spacious, slightly castle-themed hotel a few blocks from the Adoquín. ❹

Flor de María 1a Entrada a Playa Marinero ⓣ9/582-0536, ⓦwww.mexonline.com/flordemaria.htm. One of the best-value places in town, its design and decor showing the mark of the Italian owner. Fan-cooled rooms with beautifully tiled bathrooms, and a rooftop pool with restaurant and great views. ❺

Hotel Naxhiely Peréz Gasga 301 ⓣ9/582-3075. Cheery posada with plain rooms, a little café and a sprinkling of potted plants. ❹

Hotel Virginia 4a Sur 504 ⓣ9/582-0176. Three blocks from the Adoquín, on a quiet street, with cheerful details, powerful fans and ocean views from the upper floor. ❹

Loren Peréz Gasga 507 ⓣ9/582-0057. High-standard, brightly painted hotel away from the ocean but with a good pool and impressively low off-season prices, which can be slashed by up to fifty percent. ❻

Mayflower Andador Libertad s/n ⓣ9/582-0367. Cheap and popular place on the flight of steps up from the Adoquín, with dormitories, a bar, communal kitchen and people lounging in ample common areas. Some upper rooms have little balconies where you can glimpse the Pacific. ❸

Nayar Peréz Gasga 407 ⓣ9/582-0113. Slightly institutional hotel, popular with Mexican tourists, that has a pool and pretty restaurant. Some of the rooms have spacious balconies with views of the water. ❺

Paraíso Escondido Unión 10 ⓣ9/582-0444. On a flight of steps on the hill before the Adoquín, an upscale motel decorated artistically with tiles and sculptures; rooms with balconies and a central, pretty pool, bar and restaurant area. ❽

Rincón del Pacífico Peréz Gasga 900 ⓣ9/582-0056. Can be a bargain in low season; slightly motel-like, but clean, decent-sized rooms overlooking the beach and its own stone courtyard. ❺

Villa Roca Suites Peréz Gasga 602 ⓣ9/582-3525. The fanciest place on the Adoquín strip, with white stucco walls, palapa roofs and slightly frilly rooms backing on the Playa Principal. ❽

Zicatela beach

The hotels below are listed in order of distance from Puerto Escondido.

Santa Fe Calle del Morro s/n ⓣ9/582-0170, ⓦwww.hotelsantafe.com.mx. Puerto Escondido's top hotel, catering to an older crowd, with comfortable balconied rooms. ❽

Accali Casas de Playa Calle del Morro s/n ⓣ9/582-0754. Little wooden cottages scattered around a pool with bath and ceiling fans – comfortable and pleasant. ❹

Cabo Blanco Calle del Morro s/n ⓣ9/582-0337. Rustic bungalows for rent at this friendly seafood restaurant and live music venue. It's bustling on Monday nights, when they host popular happy-hour parties. ❸

Hostel Maran-Atha Calle del Morro s/n. Relaxed little hostel with a lot going on: one cavernous room with dorm beds, hammocks, a couple of small private rooms, and books, arts and crafts, and many people lounging, in a lively, if somewhat cluttered, communal area. ❷–❸

Buena Vista Calle del Morro s/n ⓣ9/582-1474. Set slightly off the road behind the beach up the hill, these light, clean rooms have lovely terraces with a beautiful view over the bay. ❹

Hotel Arcoiris Calle del Morro s/n ⓣ9/582-1494, ⓦwww.oaxaca-mio.com/arcoiris.htm. One of the best and most relaxing places on the beach. Luxuriant gardens and a secluded pool hide behind a block of spacious, comfortable rooms, some with fully equipped kitchen, some without. The restaurant has good vegetarian selections. ❻

Bungalows Zicatela Calle del Morro s/n ⓣ9/582-0798. Modest rooms full of surfers and boards, scattered around a pool, some with kitchen; adjacent restaurant with bar. ❺

Bungalows Acuario Calle del Morro s/n ⓣ9/582-1027. A range of lodgings surrounding an attractive pool and bar, with access to a gym (US$1.50 per day for non-guests), and an Internet café with a/c. ❹–❻

Surf Olas Altas Calle del Morro 310 ⓣ9/582-2315, ⓦwww.surfolasaltas.com. Large, upmarket and slightly swanky hotel that seems incongruous with the surfer ethic. ❽

Beach Hotel Inés Calle del Morro s/n ⓣ9/582-0792. Varying prices depending on the kind of room you take, with bungalows and hotel rooms – a good place to share a cheap cabaña with a group, as you have access to the hotel pool and a pleasant, relaxed restaurant and poolside scene. ❸–❻

Puerta del Sol Calle del Morro s/n ⓣ9/582-2922. Slightly upscale mission-style bungalows clustered along a swimming pool. Laundry service and kitchen facilities available. ❻

Rockaway Surfer Village Calle del Morro s/n ⓣ9/582-0668. Aptly named hotel where dedicated surfers hole up for the entire season. Simple but nice dark-wood cabins (with hammocks but no showers) around the pool sleep up to four. Surf shop and volleyball court. Prices halved in the low season. ❹

A la Casa Bajada Las Brisas s/n ⓔalacasa@hotmail.com. Dorm beds with mosquito nets in a homely hostel with books, surfboard rentals (the cheapest on the beach), games and communal meals. ❷

The beaches

Apart from shopping for international surf designs, beachwear and crafts (some tacky, some classy), Escondido offers little beyond the standard beach activities of swimming, surfing, lazing on the sand, eating, drinking and watching beautiful sunsets. In most places you needn't move all day, as you'll be regularly approached by ice-cream carts, people trying to sell cold drinks or hot snacks, and vendors of T-shirts and trinkets. The choice of **beaches** even within a couple of kilometres of town is impressive. Take your pick from the town strand, with the convenience of shops and bars nearby, pounding surf beaches or secluded coves ideal for snorkelling. Note that the surf should be treated with respect – the waters along Zicatela, for example, have a lethal **undertow** and the sand gets drawn out from under your feet, which can make it doubly difficult to get back in. There are three main beach areas: the town beach (**Bahía Principal**), which stretches round to the east and south from the town centre; the surfing destination of Zicatela; and the trio of small coves to the west. The sand directly in front of town is perhaps a little overused, and shared, too, with the local fishermen and the activities of the port. A little to the east, beyond where the **Laguna Agua Dulce** occasionally reaches the sea, **Playa Marinero** is quieter, sometimes graced with gentle waves and so is a good place to play in the waves and to learn to surf. But the real big stuff is southeast, beyond the little headland, where **Zicatela** stretches for 2km. One of the world's top surf beaches, Zicatela ("place of big thorns") regularly receives beach breaks of around 4m and can maintain the surf swell for days on end. This spot is referred to as the "**Mexican pipeline**", because the breaking waves curl into perfect cylinders – permitting expert surfers to momentarily ride inside the "pipe-like" tube. Surfboards and boogie boards can be rented from a number of places along Zicatela beach. When it is pumping, consider your strength and swimming fitness (you can check the wave reports on line at one of the Internet cafés, or ask in one of the surf shops) before venturing into the waves: they're very powerful, and occasionally even experienced surfers drown, although there are *salvavidas* (lifeguards) patrolling the beach. If the Mexican Pipeline is too much for you to handle, head east for a little over a kilometre down the beach to La Punta (the point). La Punta is a much easier point break that can also be exceptional when the swell is up. It provides good, slower waves that are excellent for longboarding. The sheltered beach break inside of La Punta is recommended as a spot to learn to surf when the waves are smaller.

Everything is much calmer in the coves to the west of the town. **Puerto Ángelito** is the closest, divided in two by a rocky outcrop, with a second beach, slightly further inland from Ángelito, called **Manzanillo**. They're about twenty minutes' walk from town, either by a track that leads to the left off Peréz Gasga, or direct from the highway on a signed road leading down opposite *El Padrino* restaurant (the two paths meet above the beach). An alternative is the recently completed concrete footpath that sets out from the western end of the town beach, dipping and turning over the coastal rocks and eventually climbing up to a road. Follow this inland, then turn left along the road signposted for "Playa Manzanillo", which turns into steps going down to the beach. Both the little inlets have small beaches and excellent snorkelling among the rocks (if you can avoid the boats), but you'll have to bring your own gear or rent some at great expense from the makeshift restaurants lining the beach. You can also drive or get a taxi to drop you off at the top of the steps to the beach.

The next bay, **Carrizalillo**, is reached by continuing west along the same track. At the end you have to scramble down over the rocks to reach the sand, guaranteeing that there won't be too many other people around. **Bacocho Bay** is further, following the highway out towards the airport and then cutting through the new hotel zone. There aren't many hotels here yet, so Bacocho offers good, secluded sand, though swimming isn't considered safe as this beach is pounded by heavy surf and has a strong undertow. *Coco's Bar and Restaurant* serves decent, if pricey, **food**; you can use their pool for US$3.

You can also take a **boat** to the above beaches, and some further afield, from in front of the *Hotel Rincón del Pacífico* on the Adoquín, for around US$3, which will return to pick you up at an agreed time.

Eating, drinking and nightlife

It doesn't cost much to eat well in Escondido. Many of the restaurants and cafés are laid-back, low-key affairs with plenty of natural light and a cool breeze. The **seafood** is always fresh, and you can vary your diet with **vegetarian** food, excellent bread and cakes and **Italian** food from the inordinately large number of Italian restaurants. The classier restaurants on the Adoquín, such as the *Junto al Mar,* have terraces opening onto the main bay. There are more restaurants and several laid-back cafés along Zicatela beach and on the beach itself, serving cheap pasta, snacks and drinks.

Happy hours at the popular *Wipe Out Bar, 3 Diablos* and *Barfly* run between 5pm and 8pm, and most of the restaurants double as **bars** too, some even hosting **live music**. The Italian film *Puerto Escondido* – which is more about drug running from Real de Catorce than high intrigue in a beach resort – is shown nightly at 8.30pm in the *Spaghetti House* (also known as *Da Claudio*, see below). Otherwise, nightlife is concentrated in the bars along Peréz Gasga.

There are more **films** on show at *CineMar*, at the east end of Zicatela, this time art-house, usually in English or with subtitles. The schedule is on view at *El Cafecito* (see overleaf) in Zicatela – there are two showings nightly.

In town

Alicia's Peréz Gasga. Inexpensive, reliable little cafeteria with extensive menu including seafood and Mexican standards, and comida corrida options.

Barfly Peréz Gasga. Eclectic lounge-bar towards the western end of the Adoquín. Good music and comfy cushions to lie on while sipping a frosty cocktail.

Cafetería Bananas Peréz Gasga. Italian joint, with pizza, pasta and crepes; good for a quick snack.

Cafetería Cappuccino Peréz Gasga s/n. A good place for breakfast and coffee, light lunches, pasta and snacks.

Los Candiles 1a Poniente, at the Carretera. A well-priced restaurant decorated with hand-woven tablecloths and artesanía. The chef specializes in delicious Oaxaqueña dishes and fresh seafood; the fish special of the day is a good bet.

El Chubasco 2a Sur 8. Possibly the cheapest place in town to eat a full meal. A simple but appealing café with the TV blaring and frequently a group of men playing cards in the corner. Serves tacos, seafood and chicken dishes. Fried fish, rice and salad can be had for US$2.

Da Claudio (Spaghetti House) just off the eastern end of Peréz Gasga, towards the beach. About the best Italian place in town. Inexpensive and great food, with a tatty video of *Puerto Escondido* playing in the background.

Discoteque Tequila Sunrise just up the street from *Son y La Rumba*, open Friday and Saturday nights from 10pm. Upbeat music, but spotty attendance. US$1.50 cover.

Flor de María Playa Marinero. Attached to the hotel and a nice place for a quiet meal – with stuffed peppers, meat dishes and pasta.

La Patisserie Calle del Morro, Playa Marinero. Croissants and pastries from *Carmen's* at Zicatela, plus sandwiches, fruit salads and yogurt, served in a quiet palm hut with a book swap.

La Perla Flameante Peréz Gasga. Moderately priced sushi and seafood restaurant, on the second floor above the Adoquín, that will suffice if in the throes of a major sushi craving. It also delivers.

San Angel Peréz Gasga. Seafood, chicken, steak and the odd Thai dish opposite *Cafetería Bananas*. Try the mango flambée.

El Son y La Rumba Andador Mar y Sol, off Peréz Gasga. Salsa bar with a tiny dance floor where gringos inevitably fail to imitate the locals. Live *cumbia*, merengue and reggae. Opens around 10pm.

Super Café up the steps above Peréz Gasga at the western end of the Adoquín. Coffeeshop with scrumptious homemade breakfast specials and delicious Oaxacan bulk coffee for sale that smells divine.

Los Torros off west end of Adoquín around the corner from the tourist booth. Pinkish tube-lighting illuminates this cowboy bar, that offers cheap beer and a jukebox, and is low-key and friendly.

Wipe Out Bar Peréz Gasga. This is the favourite spot on the Adoquín for surfers and travellers, so don't come here looking for a quiet drink; it gets packed and rowdy.

Zicatela beach

The restaurants and bars below are listed in order of distance from Puerto Escondido.

Santa Fe Luxurious setting to tuck into chile rellenos, vegetarian fare and classic Mexican dishes at moderate to expensive prices.

Cabo Blanco The best seafood on the beach at reasonable prices. Fish or shrimp dressed with a choice of delicious sauces: Thai curry or lime, wine and cream. Live music most nights draws a lively crowd.

Cipriano's Pizza Thin, crispy, cheesy pizzas, served at romantic tables wedged into the sand.

Arco Iris Good traditional Mexican and international dishes, pasta, fresh fish and a happy hour – even has vegetarian comidas corridas.

Casa Babylon Busy, friendly late-night bar next door to the *Hotel Arcoiris*. Board games, mellow music and a useful reference library with travel books and *National Geographic* magazines.

Sakura A pleasant spot under an enormous palapa, facing out onto the pounding surf, serving authentic Japanese fare: sushi, sashimi, tempura and sake.

El Cafecito Rightly popular, open-fronted palapa restaurant. A great place for breakfasts, baked goods (from the adjacent bakery), burgers and burritos through the day, and seafood in the evening. Check out the daily specials and two-for-one drinks 5.30–7pm.

El Punto Late-night bar and disco right on the beach that gets going once the other places close. It's hit or miss.

El Jardín Pleasant palapa café in front of *Hotel Olas Altas* with an extensive menu including home-baked sourdough bread, yogurt, snacks and baked pizzas in the evening.

Art and Harry's Surf Inn Favourite evening spot where surfers and their acolytes come to watch the sun go down and drink two-for-one beers, staying on to play pool and look over that morning's surf photos on the notice board. Tasty, good-value salads, seafood and burgers served all day.

La Nueva Cuba Cozy, little bar and café, popular for night-time mojitos, tacos, burgers and assorted snacks.

Around Puerto Escondido: the lagoons

Though most people find it almost impossible to drag themselves off the beaches of Puerto Escondido, there are a couple of boat trips worth making. **Laguna Manialtepec**, about 15km west of Puerto Escondido, is cut off from the sea most of the year, forming a freshwater lake extraordinarily rich in **wildlife**. You can easily spot fifty-odd species in a day, among them several types of heron, ibis, egret, duck, cormorant and parrot. **Buses** run out here from El Crucero, or you can go with an organized tour through one of the travel agencies in Puerto Escondido.

With more time to spare – preferably a couple of days so you can stay over – the wildlife of the **Lagunas de Chacahua** and the beach at the far end make a more interesting venture. Catch a **bus** from El Crucero (every 20min) to **Río Grande**, 50km west of Puerto Escondido on Hwy-200, then change onto one of the frequent minibuses to the one-time cacao and cotton port of **Zapotalito**. The road does continue a short way from here to the beach and palapa restaurants at **Cerro Hermoso**, but it is better to take a *lancha* to **Playa Chacahua** – you could also rent one to tour the lagoon, but unless you have a special interest in tangled webs of mangroves you might as well make straight for the beach. There's a **restaurant** and some basic **rooms** (❷) by the water, and more just across the lagoon – cabañas (❸) – and a huge beach, calm enough in parts but with some good surf, though the currents are strong, so check where it's safe to swim. There's also space to **camp** and a row of outdoor seafood restaurants where you could hang a hammock.

An ecotourism project has been established in the **Barra de Navidad**, ten minutes east of Puerto Escondido on Hwy-200 (the turning, on the right, comes just after the bridge that crosses the lagoon). For US$6, locals will take you on a tour of the local **crocodile** lagoon, and nearby deserted beach – a haven for **birdlife**; ask for Galo when you arrive. **Colectivos** run here from the main bay at Escondido – you can get more information at the tourist booth on the Adoquín (see p.618).

Listings

Banks and exchange There's a casa de cambio on the Adoquín (Mon–Sat 9am–9pm, Sun 9am–5pm), although better rates are available just up the hill at the busy Banamex on Peréz Gasga near the *Paraíso Escondido* (Mon–Fri 9am–4pm, Sat 10am–2pm), which also has an ATM. There's also an ATM on the Adoquín. In Zicatela, there's an exchange in *Bungalows Acuario* (see p.619).

Buses Of the four bus stations, Estrella Blanca, at Oaxaca and Benito Juárez (☎9/582-0086), is the most useful, with first- and second-class buses to Acapulco, Huatulco, Mexico City and Salina Cruz. The next best is Cristóbal Colón at Calle 1 Oriente at Calle 1 Norte (☎9/582-1073), which has buses to Oaxaca, including one overnight. Estrella del Valle, Hidalgo at Calle 3 Oriente (☎9/582-0050), runs to Oaxaca in three classes: deluxe (at 10.30pm; 6hr), first-class (2 daily; 6hr) and second-class (6 daily; 8hr). Transportes Oaxaca Istmo, Hidalgo at Calle 1 Oriente, operates second-class to Salina Cruz (5 daily; 5hr), with one a day continuing to Tuxtla Gutiérrez (10hr). A new bus station is under construction in the centre of the city that will consolidate all the companies.

Flights You can get daily flights to Oaxaca with Aerotucán (☎9/582-1725); the approximate cost one-way is US$100. There's also a daily Aerocaribe (☎9/582-2023, ⓦwww.mexicana.com) flight to Mexico City, also about US$100. You can save money on taxis by engaging the services of Transportes Aeropuerto y Turístico (☎9/582-0123), whose office is in town at the foot of the hill of Peréz Gasga.

Internet access There are several slightly pricey Internet cafés in Zicatela and on Peréz Gasga charging around US$2 an hour. Venturing outside of the tourist zone around the Adoquín leads to cheaper, US$1/hour Internet access – head north of the Carretera on any major street.

Laundry There's the self-service Lavamatica del Centro next door to Banamex, on Peréz Gasga near the *Paraíso Escondido* (Mon–Sat 8am–8pm). A laundry service can be found towards the east end of the Adoquín.

Phones There are several Ladatel phones (free collect calls) on the Adoquín, where there's also a *larga distancia* office. There are also pay phones in Zicatela.

Post office In the old town at Av Oaxaca, Norte 7 (Mon–Fri 9am–3pm & 6–8pm, Sat 9am–1pm), though you can get stamps from postcard vendors (at a half-peso premium) and chance your luck with the mail boxes along Peréz Gasga.

Trips and activities Surfing lessons are offered at Central Surf and Mexpipe on Zicatela, and several outfits teach scuba diving, including Aventura Submarina (☎9/582-2353) on the Adoquín. Ecotourism is also being promoted here from lagoon trips to cycling, camping, rock-climbing, bird-watching , trips to coffee plantations in Nopala and hot springs in Atonillo; Turismo Dimar (☎9/582-1551), Ana's Ecotours (☎9/582-2954) and other agencies on the Adoquín can arrange them. Massage is offered at various places along Zicatela, including *Hotel Inés* and the gym at the *Acuario* (see p.619). Temazcalli, 10min out of town on Hwy-200 past Zicatela beach and over the bridge, at Av Infraganti and C Temazcalli (☎9/582-1023, ⓦwww.temazcalli.com), has a range of treatments, from shiatsu and aqua mystical to *temazcal* – the pre-Hispanic traditional bath with herbs that purify the body.

Puerto Ángel and around

Though it's pretty well known these days, **PUERTO ÁNGEL** still goes about its business as a small, scruffy fishing port with minimum fuss. Everything remains resolutely small-scale, and you might find pigs and chickens mingling with the visitors on the streets. Set around a sheltered bay ringed by mountains, it has two, rather dirty beaches: one right in front of town, the other opposite, beyond a rocky promontory and the mouth of a small stream. Small hotels, rooms and simple places to sling a hammock, however, are abundant, some of the most promising on the road between the main village and the second beach, Playa del Panteón. Locals fish off the huge concrete dock in Puerto Ángel – which never seems to be used for anything else – catching yellowtail tuna and other gamefish with a simple rod and line. Although the beaches are less than pristine, it is a pleasant place to spend a few days, meandering and sampling the superb local **seafood**, available at every turn.

Playa del Panteón, reached by road or a path around the base of the cliffs to the west, is the cleanest and quietest of the beaches, with interesting snorkelling round the rocks. By the afternoon, though, it's in shade, so most people wander round to the town beach. With just a little more effort you can visit one of the far better beaches either side of Puerto Ángel. To the west is the more primitive **Zipolite**, while to the east, about fifteen minutes' walk up the Pochutla road and then down a heavily rutted track to the right, you'll find **Estacahuite**. Here there are three tiny, sandy coves, divided by outcrops of rock. The rocks are close in, so you can't swim far, but there's wonderful **snorkelling** and rarely more than a couple of other people around. You can rent snorkelling gear here, or hire it from cafés on the Playa del Panteón and bring it with you. In a pleasantly breezy palapa overlooking the first of the coves, the *Club Playa Estacahuite* (fancy name, simple place) serves amazingly good seafood.

There are other lovely beaches near Estacahuite, including the idyllic Playa **Boquilla**, where you'll find the *Bahía de la Luna* **accommodation** and a **restaurant**, accessible by boat from Puerto Ángel. Boquilla is signposted from the main road to Pochutla, but it's inadvisable to drive down here, as the seven-kilometre road is in a terrible state. A better idea is to arrange a boat trip in advance to both beaches, turtle-spotting along the way.

Accommodation and information

There's no bank, a couple of **larga distancia** places, one just back from the pier, near the **post office**, no police, a few shops and **Internet** access (US$1.60 per hour) at Gel@Net (in Gambusino's travel agency, which also has a *larga distancia*). There is also a **tourist information booth** (Mon–Fri 10am–noon & 4–8pm, Sat–Sun 10am–noon). Puerto Ángel's **hotels** are a bit scattered but the village is small enough that you should be able to find someone to mind your bags while you look around. The places listed below represent only a fraction of the total, but you'll find little better.

Almendro Blv Uribe s/n ☎9/584-3068. Friendly place with simple, clean rooms (all with fan and private bath) and great food from the Swiss chef in the restaurant (who can also arrange Spanish lessons with his Mexican wife). ❹

Bahía de la Luna Boquilla beach ☎9/584-6186, ⓦwww.totalmedia.qc.ca/bahiadelaluna. With bungalows for two to five people set up the hillside, and a restaurant-café on the beach serving fresh fish. It also offers holistic therapy treatments, personal development workshops and yoga. ❻

Buena Vista ☎9/584-3104. A short walk along the footpath north from Blv Uribe, next to the Arroye river, after the fork to the left, you will find one of the nicest hotels in Puerto Ángel, set back from the main road, arranged over three floors, with an ocean view from the top-floor restaurant terrace and a rooftop swimming pool. Surrounded by plants, the quiet rooms (some with luxurious baths) have breezy balconies and hammocks. The *Alta Mira* in Mazunte (see p.628) has the same owners. ❺

Casa Arnel José Azueta 666 ☎9/584-3051. The sister hotel of the *Casa Arnel* in Oaxaca (see p.593) has clean rooms with fans, bathrooms, and a hammock area, in a homely environment. ❹

Casa de Huéspedes Gundí y Tomas Blv Uribe ☎9/584-3068. Up some steps opposite the naval base in the centre. Friendly atmosphere, open-sided lounge area with views of the bay, and decent meals. The cheaper rooms leave a bit to be desired. Hammock space for a few dollars. ❹

Casa Penelope Blv Uribe s/n ⓣ9/584-3073. The friendly owner offers four reasonably priced quiet, comfortable and safe rooms, with chilled-out music and laundry facilities. Try her secret-recipe margaritas. ❹

Posada Cañon Devata inland from the far end of Playa del Panteón ⓣ9/584-3137, ⓦwww.posadapacifico.com. Simple but beautifully furnished rooms spread through a jungly hillside behind Playa del Panteón. Rooms are barely visible from each other and you'd think you were miles from a beach. Nice view and relaxing location make it perfect for recharging your batteries. ❹–❻

Puesta del Sol Blv Uribe ⓣ/ⓕ 9/584-3096, ⓔgolfo52@hotmail.com. The pick of the cheaper hotels. Not much in the way of a view but spacious rooms around a garden, laundry, Internet access and communal space lined with photos. ❹

Rincón Sabroso Blv Uribe ⓣ9/584-3095. Pleasing, if dark, rough-tiled rooms with fans, *baños* and hammocks outside make this hotel a steal. ❸

Eating and drinking

Beto's Blv Uribe s/n, on the outskirts of town on the way to Zipolite, has high-quality seafood, and is a lively spot for drinks.

La Costenita on the pier, serves tasty antojitos, such as tamales, tacos and beer.

Hard Times Blv Uribe, just past *Puesta del Sol Hotel* on the way to Zipolite. Offers reliable seafood and Mexican dishes; the service is efficient and friendly.

Posada Cañon Devata at the hotel of the same name, inland from Playa Panteón, offers nightly vegetarian feasts in a romantic jungle setting.

El Rincón del Mar precariously balanced on a cliff between playas Principal and Panteón, has mouthwatering seafood, nightly specials based on the catch of the day and offers windy views of the ocean.

Susy's Playa Panteón, right on the beach, is reliable for snacks and drinks during a day at the beach, although better seafood platters can be found elsewhere.

La Villa Florencia Blv Uribe. Serves hearty Italian staples, antipasto and pasta with seafood, and tends to attract foreigners.

Zipolite

Though some people rave about Puerto Ángel, others are ecstatic about **ZIPOLITE**, 3km along the road north, whose reputation as the ultimate in relaxed beach resorts has become legendary. Referred to by some as "sexyport" because people either come here to get high or hook up, the travellers' grapevine is alive with tales of the widely available hallucinogens, low living costs and liberal approach to **nudity** – rumours that are largely well founded, much to the chagrin of the locals. Certainly, nude bathing – predominantly at the western end – is sanctioned by the local military; keep cover handy for trips to the restaurants, though. As for drugs, grass, mushrooms and acid are as illegal as – though more prevalent than – anywhere else in Mexico, and unscrupulous dealers are not above setting people up. **Theft**, too, particularly along the beachfront at night, can be a problem, but seems in no way to detract from the lure of a few days of complete abandonment.

The origin of the name Zipolite is uncertain – one theory is that it comes from the Nahuatl word meaning the "beach of the dead", hence the constant references to it as the "playa de los muertos". The **beach** itself is magnificent, long and gently curving, pounded by heavy surf with a riptide that requires some caution as drownings are depressingly common (although there are local lifeguards, as well as flags denoting danger levels up and down the beach). The beach is divided into three segments, Roca Blanca towards the western end, Centro in the middle, and Playa del Amor at the eastern end nearest Puerto Ángel. Palapa huts line all three, catering to visitors' needs, along with restaurants offering seafood and pasta. **Hammocks** (US$3–5) are strung from every rafter and many places rent basic **rooms**; it can be worth getting a room just to have a safe place to store your gear. **Hurricane Pauline** blew away many of the weaker structures in 1997, but since then Zipolite has grown markedly. New buildings towards the west end of the beach caused some fuss when they were built three or four stories high, and despite a severe fire in March 2001 that wiped out virtually all of the accommodation from the *Posada San Cristóbal*, in the middle of the beach, to the lagoon close to the western end, most of the buildings were rebuilt.

Zipolite is a good base for **trips** to nearby places such as Mazunte or Escondido, and the surrounding beaches, as accommodation is abundant and inexpensive. Taxis run up and down the road behind the beach, but a better and cheaper way of getting around is by colectivos, which also run along the same route. All of the palapas along the beachfront advertise **boat trips** out to sea for US$15, where you can snorkel and sometimes spot turtles, dolphins and, if you're really lucky, whales on their way up to Baja California. Scuba **diving** is also offered, but the reef isn't particularly impressive here.

Practicalities

The main road coming into Zipolite from Puerto Ángel runs east to west, and passes a grocery store and then the *Lyoban* (see below). A turn to the left takes you onto the road immediately behind the beach, which has a **laundry** and a few small shops with Internet access, long-distance phones, beach gear and other bare necessities, but for anything other than the simplest needs you'll have to catch the colectivos that run to Puerto Ángel and on to Pochutla (every 20min, until around 8pm; the trip is about 20min long). Follow the road to the end onto a dirt track to get to the more peaceful, western end of the beach.

One of the best **places to stay** is at the west end of the beach. The idyllic *Lo Cósmico* (ⓦwww.locosmico.com; ❸) has some beautiful cabañas with views of the coast and a delicious crepe restaurant, a peaceful atmosphere and secluded beach out front. Next door, the long-established and highly eccentric *Shambhala Posada* (❸) is tucked away by a rocky outcrop, up the side of a hill, with beautiful vistas, sharing the *Cósmico*'s beach area. It is, however, badly in need of repair, and has slightly tatty cabañas and terrace space for hammocks. The meditation spot, at the top of the hill behind the *Shambhala,* is a great place to watch the sun rise and set over the bay. Below the *Cósmico*, on the sand, is *El Alquimista*, one of the best restaurants in town, which gets packed in the evenings for oceanside seafood and pizza. It also offers five cabañas with bath and fan for rent (❺).

Working east down the beach, you'll find *Posada San Cristóbal* (ⓣ9/584-3191; ❸), with pleasant shared bath cabañas and rooms; the friendly American-run *Brisa Marina* (ⓣ9/584-3193; ❸), a more solidly built tall hotel with a range of rooms; *Tao*, with clean cabañas (❸); and *La Habana*, which offers a few rustic cabins raised on stilts (the closest thing to sleeping on the beach without actually doing it), with nets and shared bath. You can also try the cheap cabañas at *Palapa Katy* (❷) and *Palapa Aris* (❷) a little further east. The smarter *Lyoban* (ⓣ9/584-3177; ❸), after that, has space to lock luggage as well as pool and ping-pong in the lounge. At the far east end of Zipolite beach is *Castillo Oasis,* with four clean, beautifully designed rooms in a leafy green oasis (ⓕ9/584-3070; ❹) and *Solstice Yoga Center* (ⓦwww.solstice-mexico.com; ❺), with bungalows and accompanying yoga and meditation programmes. *Fernando's Trailer Park* (❷), on the road to Puerto Ángel, has electrical hook-ups under shady palm trees. A good bet among high-end accommodation is *Rancho Cerro Largo* (ⓕ9/584-3063, ⓔranchocerrolargomx@yahoo.com; ❼), perched on the ridge between

Zipolite and San Agustinillo, the next beach along, with one of the most spectacular views of the Mexican Pacific. The restaurant here is considered the best in the area, and the price of a double includes breakfast and dinner – guests and employees eat together in an open-air dining room. Catch any Mazunte-bound *camioneta* to get here, or walk – it's about 3km from Zipolite.

Zipolite is a great place for food, with most of the popular **restaurants** along the western beachfront, such as the *Eclipse*, which serves savoury pasta and pizza, *Posada San Cristóbal*, covering backpacker staples such as eggs, pancakes and salads, and *Tao* and *Nueva Sol*, both of which have seafood and Mexican dishes. *Chupón* (which has delicious crab ravioli) and *El 3 Diciembre* (pizzas, vegetarian Mexican dishes and homemade cheesecake, and also rooms to rent), at the start of the road behind the beach, are definitely worth the short walk. *El Hongo* has a happy hour and keeps going until late, and the popular but cheesy **disco** *La Puesta del Sol* kicks off around midnight.

Mazunte and San Agustinillo

Rounding the headland north of Zipolite you come to **San Agustinillo**, another fine beach graced with good surfing waves. The sand is backed by restaurants, which offer space for a hammock or small rooms for rent in addition to reasonably priced, fresh seafood. *Palapas Olas Altas*, *Palapa Jazmín* and *Palapa Lupita* all have simple cabañas (❷) and hammocks (❶), right next to the peaceful and breezy beach. *Posada Dona Sol*, across the street, has rooms with bath and fan (❷). The grand and slightly bizarre *Posada San Agustinillo*, set in impressive grounds at the east end of the village, looks like it has had better days, but offers reasonable rooms looking out to sea, with balcony space (❸).

Further on is the tiny village of **MAZUNTE**. It has grown in recent years, but remains an attractive place, with a beautiful beach and a natural, relaxed atmosphere, more peaceful than Zipolite and lacking its hippie-party vibe. The surf is less powerful here and at the western end of the beach, beyond the rocky outcrop, there's a smaller bay where the waves are more gentle and it's safer to swim.

The village's name is derived from the Nahuatl word "maxonteita", which means "please come and spawn", a reference to the **golfina turtles** that come here to breed, although it was once notorious as the site of an abattoir that at its most gruesome supposedly slaughtered three thousand of the creatures a day. In 1990, the Mexican government bowed to international pressure and effectively banned the industry overnight, removing in one fell swoop the livelihood of the villagers, who then turned to slash-and-burn agriculture. With help from national and international organizations, Mazunte was then declared a reserve and more sustainable, long-term programmes such as eco-tourism have been encouraged, including the **natural cosmetics** co-op (daily 9am–4pm), which you see as soon as you enter the village, set up with help from companies such as Body Shop and selling beauty products made from local ingredients. Poaching of turtles and their eggs remains a problem, however, in addition to the destruction of their environment and boat activity. The government-funded **turtle museum** (Tues–Sat 10am–4.30pm, Sun 10am–2.30pm; US$2), at the east end of the village, features an aquarium with some particularly large turtles and a turtle research centre. It's well worth the visit, especially as proceeds go towards the conservation of this majestic species. Although female turtles lay around one hundred eggs, which are the size of ping-pong balls, in their nest buried in the sand, it's been estimated that only one or two hatchlings will survive to maturity. First, the hatchlings emerge at night from the nest and make their crucial, manic scramble to the sea as crabs, birds and various mammals stand by to feed on them – and even if they make it to the water, numerous fish then await them. Second, beach traffic, especially people, can crush eggs in the nest or compact the sand so the hatchlings can't emerge from it. And third, hatchlings instinctively head for the sea by following the light reflected off the surf, but beachfront lighting can distract them into heading in the wrong direction. Most of the egg-laying takes place between May and August.

Don't leave Mazunte without following the trail next to the *Balam Juyuc* (see below), which runs past the remains of some unmarked **ruins** to **Punto Cometa** – a beautiful, natural park on top of the rocky headland next to Mazunte beach, the southernmost point in Oaxaca, where you get breathtaking views at sunset. The "Jacuzzi," a rocky pool that fills with foamy surf as the waves rush in, can be accessed by scrambling down the rocks at the south end of the pool. Another nearby treat is the crocodile lagoon at **Playa Ventanilla**, about 2km to the west, where you can test your heart rate by going out on the water in a shallow boat to navigate among the scaly inhabitants. The lagoon can be reached by colectivo, or by taxi (about US$3) and the boat trips are arranged by the village co-operative, for around US$4.

Practicalities

A makeshift tourist booth on the main street keeps erratic hours but is an excellent source of information on **accommodation** and activities – a guide named Markus mans the office, and also leads tours and boat rides to spot turtles and other wildlife. Rafting trips can be arranged at *La Empanada* restaurant, where they are a much better deal than in nearby Huatulco.

All of the palapas on the beach have **cabañas** and hammock space (❶), along with **restaurants** serving basic breakfasts, seafood and pasta. If you are equipped and feel so inclined, you can pitch your tent right along the beach. At the west end of the sandy stretch, pass the rocks to the second small bay for the area's best swimming, where the *Posada del Arquitecto* has hammocks (❶) and ecologically designed rooms with private bath (❹). Set discreetly up the hill, the *Alta Mira* (Ⓦwww.labuenavista.com; ❺) is the most elegant place in town, with smart bungalows with tiled bathrooms and beautiful views from the restaurant terrace. The rooms do not have electricity, but it is seldom missed, and in the evenings bungalows are lit with candles. The *Balam Juyuc* next door is a more chilled option, with an impressive view of the ocean, comfy shared-bath cabañas (❹), with massage offered as well as turtle-viewing trips and surfing lessons. In the middle of the beach, *Palapas El Mazunte* (❸) is a popular backpacker hangout, with cheap rooms, hammock and tent space, and a packed café. At the east end of the beach, the friendly *Cabañas Ziga* has a range of decent rooms with a glorious sea view from the patio restaurant (❹). You can rent modest rooms at a few places on the main road in the village too; these tend to be cheaper the farther they are from the ocean: *Aketzalli*, across from the turtle museum, has simple cabins (❷), and *Posada Lalo*, down a small track running into the village, has cabañas and camping (❷).

There are some appealing food options, including the excellent Italian-run restaurant *La Dolce Vita*, on the main road through town, which has brick-oven pizza, pastas with seafood and occasional movies in the evenings. *La Empanada*, also on the main road, has hearty sandwiches on homemade bread, and blended juices (try the delicious cucumber and lemon juice); *Tania*, farther along, has homely Mexican fare. *El Pescador* offers mouthwatering seafood close to the surf.

A **lavandería** can be found on Rinconcito (the street connecting the western end of the beach to the main street through town); a pricey **Internet** café, also on Rinconcito, is open until 10pm.

You can save time and money **getting to Mazunte** from Puerto Escondido by getting dropped off at **San Antonio**, a cluster of just a few houses and a restaurant, from where you can hitch or take a taxi the 5km to Mazunte. Otherwise the bus drags you through Pochutla and Puerto Ángel before arrival. **Colectivos from Mazunte** go to Zipolite, Puerto Ángel and Pochutla (every 30–40min), but if you can time it correctly, it makes sense also to return through San Antonio. There are no banking facilities in Mazunte, so make sure you withdraw enough money in Pochutla or Escondido (where there are ATMs) before coming here.

Pochutla

Anyone visiting Puerto Ángel and the beaches either way along the coast comes through **POCHUTLA**, a slightly dull place 2km north of Hwy-200, some 12km from Puerto Ángel. Apart from catching a bus to the coast there's no major reason to come here, though if you're staying on the coast for long you'll proably need to return here to change money – once again, there are no banks at the other beaches – and perhaps to visit the **market**, or one of the excellent **panaderías**, north of the bus station, for provisions. A good pit stop on the way, just north of Puerto Ángel on Hwy-175, is the *Finca de Vaqueros* outdoor barbecue restaurant, famous with locals for grilled meats of every kind. Two cowboy brothers pour draught beer, fresh tomato juice and keep the place open every day of the year.

Pochutla's centre is gradually being smartened up – the main street has recently been resurfaced and Internet cafés are springing up along it. Local artisans sell jewellery and other knick-knacks in the pedestrianized alley leading to the zócalo, opposite the *Café Café*, which has real **espresso** machines and delicious cold mocha cappuccinos.

The **bus stations** – the second-class Estrella Blanca (Ⓣ9/584-0380), Oaxaca Pacífico (Ⓣ9/584-0349) and the first-class Cristóbal Colón (Ⓣ9/584-0274) – are close to each other on Lázaro Cárdenas, which runs from Hwy-200 into the centre of town. Daily first-class services cover Huatulco, Juchitán, Mexico City, Oaxaca, Puerto Escondido and San Cristóbal; daily second-class class buses leave for the same destinations and more local routes.

Further along Cárdenas, Scotiabank (Mon–Fri 9am–5pm) or Bancomer (Mon–Fri 8.30am–4pm), both with ATM, will change **money**; the Bital nearby is also open Saturdays from 8am to 3pm. Of the **hotels**, *Hotel Pochutla*, Madero 102 (Ⓣ9/584-0033; ④), on the central plaza, is comfortable and spacious; the *Costa del Sol*, Cárdenas 47 (Ⓣ9/584-0049; ⑤), is a bit more luxe; while *Hotel Santa Cruz*, Cárdenas 88 (Ⓣ9/584-0116; ③), a little near the bus stations, is much poorer with noisy front rooms. The *Panificadora 7 Regiones*, a bakery across from the *Costa del Sol*, has delicious cookies and a fine selection of cheeses and groceries.

Buses head down frequently to Puerto Ángel and Zipolite, along with **colectivos** or *especial* **taxis**; one of these taxis may cost well over five times as much, so go colectivo – you should rarely have to wait long for fellow passengers. In Puerto Ángel, the taxis drop off at the rank by the dock. If you want to go further, over to Playa del Panteón for example, make this clear as you set out or you'll be charged an outrageous amount for the last part of the journey (you probably will be anyway, but at least you'll be prepared).

Huatulco and around

Heading **east from Puerto Ángel** towards Salina Cruz, there's 170km of coast that until recently was quite untouched. It's a slow, hot drive – but an enjoyable one – along a jungly coastal strip regularly cut by small rivers and giving frequent tantalizing glimpses of fabulous-looking beaches. Most of these are extremely tough to get to, however, and few are as idyllic as they appear: quite apart from the total lack of facilities, they're marred by strong winds, tricky currents, and, as you approach Salina Cruz, an increasing amount of oil pollution.

At **HUATULCO**, some 35km from Puerto Ángel, the latest of Mexico's purpose-built resorts is well under way. By the late 1980s there was an airport, four large hotels including a Club Med (now *Las Brisas*) and a Sheraton (now the all-inclusive *Gala*) and an expectation of rapid expansion. More recently, however, progress has slowed. This is probably a blessing as it gives FONATUR – the government tourist development agency – a chance to carry out its professed intention of preserving ecological zones among the hotels and ensuring that the infrastructure (especially sewage treatment plants) keeps pace with demand. For the moment, only two of the nine bays have been developed, though new roads mean that there is now automotive access to eight of them. The long-term effects of the tourism influx remain to be seen, but this is a large area, and it may be years before the outlying bays are developed. The lack of budget accommodation continues to be a problem for a number of visitors.

Huatulco is the all-encompassing name of the resort, with **Santa Cruz Huatulco**, the village on the coast, as its focus. It's been cleaned up in expectation of becoming an "authentic Mexican village", something it patently fails to be, comprising a marina, handicraft stalls, a few relatively inexpensive seafood restaurants and a handful of condos. There's no reason to stay here – and nowhere reasonably priced to do so – but at the embarcadero you can organize horseback rides to **Maguey Beach**, fishing and diving trips or catch boats (on demand) that ply the coast to the more remote bays. All of these have at least some sort of beach front business, and **San Agustín**, one of the most developed, is lined with seafood restaurants.

On the plus side, there are many nearly pristine beaches to be explored, including **Cacaluta Beach**, accessed by walking through the jungle from the coastal road, where the highly successful Mexican movie *Y Tu Mamá También* was filmed. Access to the beach at **Tangolunda**, 5km northeast over the headland, is almost completely cut off by the aforementioned international hotels, the swanky *Camino Real* and the homes of the likes of Julio Iglesias and ex-Mexican president Carlos Salinas de Gortari. The only public access is by the road near the *Quinta Real* and, of course, you can sneak into the *Gala* for a swim in the pool, but there's little else to do and the restaurants are grossly overpriced. The **tourist office** near the *Gala* in Tangolunda (Mon–Fri 9am–5pm & Sat 9am–1pm) has details of tours, rafting trips and more affordable local accommodation.

Crucecita

The purpose-built town of **CRUCECITA**, 2km inland from Santa Cruz Huatulco, serves both bays. Though designed to house the ten thousand locals needed to support and staff the bayside hotels, it is now becoming a tourist centre in its own right, probably helped along by the lack of hotels elsewhere. Certainly it boasts a **zócalo**, shops and various businesses, along with pizza joints, costly tourist shops and Internet cafés. Nevertheless, in its fifteen years of existence, it has matured well to become a thriving and enjoyable place.

Finding a budget **place to stay** in Crucecita, while easier than around the bays, is still a problem, though outside the high season (Dec, Semana Santa, July & Aug) prices drop by up to fifty percent. One of the cheapest options is the basic *Hospedaje Gloriluz* (Ⓣ9/587-0160; ❹), on Pochote 305 near the entrance to town, although *Hotel Benimar* (Ⓣ9/587-0447; ❹), on Bugambilia 1404, is much better. *Hotel Busanvi*, one block from the zócalo on Carrizal 601 (Ⓣ9/587-0056; ❺), is surprisingly decent value for motel-like rooms with TV that can fit up to four people. *Misión de los Arcos,* Gardenia 902 (Ⓣ9/587-0165; ❻), is the swankiest, with crisp, white stucco suites, while *Posada Michelle*, Gardenia 8 (Ⓣ9/587-0535; ❸–❺) has a range of cheap rooms in the low season, and can help arrange tours.

The majority of the **restaurants** surround the zócalo, among them *Oasis*, on the corner of Bugambilia and Flamboyan, which serves up reasonably priced tortas as well as excellent sushi. For something simpler, try the tacos at *Los Portales*, on the zócalo, or the burger stand on Bugambilia and Macuitle after 8pm. For more sophistication, the *Mambo Café* is just outside town beneath the *Hotel Edén Costa* (Ⓣ9/587-2480), at Calle Zapoteco 3, off Bulevar Chahué, and specializes in traditional Mexican and European dishes, including Swiss fondue. There are a few **bars and clubs** near the zócalo – the popular *Crema* is a good place to see a cross-section of people, and *Café Dublin*, a welcoming pub, serves giant, juicy grilled hamburgers; both are on Carrizal. All these places, and everywhere else in Crucecita, lie within easy walking distance of the **bus stations** that line Gardenia. The **post office** is a bit further out on the road to Santa Cruz Huatulco, where you'll also find a number of **banks** (with ATMs). Hurricane Divers (Ⓣ9/587-1107), on Santa Cruz beach, offers **dive trips** in the area, along with PADI and NAUI certification. They also speak English. Copalita River Tours run **rafting and kayaking trips** from their office in the *Posada Michelle* (see above); Explora Mexico also runs class 4 rafting trips, as well as less challenging excursions, out of Huatulco (Ⓣ9/587-2058).

On to the Isthmus of Tehuantepec

The **Isthmus of Tehuantepec**, where the Pacific and the Atlantic are just 210km apart and the land never rises to more than 250m above sea level, is the narrowest strip of land in Mexico. Prior to the completion of the Panama canal, there was talk about cutting a waterway through the isthmus. The coast-to-coast train (still a link in the railway to Guatemala) was, in the late nineteenth century, an extremely busy trade route, the chief communication link between the American continent's east and west coasts. It's a hot and steamy region, long run-down and not in any way improved by the trappings of the 1980s oil boom. The best, perhaps only, reason to stop is if there's a **fiesta** going on as they're among the most enthusiastic in the country. Otherwise, you can go straight through – from Oaxaca to **Tuxtla Gutiérrez** or **San Cristóbal** in Chiapas – in a single, very long, day. Only if you plan to go to the Yucatán is there any particular reason to cross the isthmus from the south to the north. To head into Chiapas it's considerably quicker to stick to the lowlands along the

Gulf of Tehuantepec, though the inland route (leading into the Chiapas highlands) is more scenic.

Historically, the *indígenas* of this region, especially in the south, have had a **matriarchal** society. Though you'll still find women dominating trade in the markets, this is a tradition that is dying faster than most others in macho Mexico. Nevertheless, some elements remain: the women exude pride and power dressed in spectacular colours and draped with gold jewellery; it's still the mother who gives away her child at a wedding (and occasionally still the eldest daughter who inherits any land); and on feast days the women prove their dominance by climbing to the rooftops and throwing fruit down on the men in the Tirada de Frutas.

Salina Cruz

SALINA CRUZ, 130km east of Huatulco on the coast, was the Pacific terminus of the trans-isthmus railway and the port through which everything was shipped. Nowadays it's exporting oil in large quantities, and is a sprawling, unattractive place with a reputation for crime and brawling violence; it also serves as a transportation link to and from the coast. **Buses** arrive and leave from a central terminal at 5 de Mayo 412. If you get stuck here and need a **place to stay**, head for the large zócalo, half a block north of the bus station, which has several decent hotels nearby. One block east, at Puerto Ángel 408, is the well-appointed *Hotel Calendas*, with TV and a/c (☎9/714-4574; ❺), while a block west is the bare-bones *Casa Ríos* (☎9/714-0337; ❸), at Wilfredo Cruz 405. At Camacho 108 lies the *Posada del Jardín* (☎9/714-0162; ❹), a clean little place with a courtyard.

La Ventosa, the nearby beach village, reached by bus from the side of the plaza, may once have been picturesque, but it's now spoilt by the oil refinery backdrop. As windy as its name implies, and polluted too, it's a run-down place, where most of the seafront restaurants seem in danger of dissolving into the sea. The best **hotel**, conveniently the first one you reach, is the *Posada Rustrián* (☎9/714-0450; ❹), which has a courtyard and a garden.

Tehuantepec

The modest town of **TEHUANTEPEC**, 14km north of Salina Cruz, visibly preserves many of the isthmus' local traditions, has some of the **best fiestas** in the region and is also an extremely pleasant place to stop, with a fine zócalo and several inexpensive hotels. In the evening, the zócalo really comes alive, with singing birds and people strolling and eating food from the many stalls set up by the townswomen, who proudly wear the traditional flower-embroidered *huipil* and floor-length velvet skirt of the Zapotec – a costume adopted by the artist Frida Kahlo in some of her self-portraits. Tehuantepec is a tiny place where a walk of ten blocks in any direction will take you out into the countryside. Perhaps because the town is so concentrated, it's extraordinarily noisy considering its size and remote location. The constant din of passing buses is made worse by the flatbed motor tricycles (*motos*) that locals use as taxis. There's really no reason to stay long, and the number of second-class buses makes it extremely easy to leave, but if you do stop awhile pop into the **Casa de Cultura** (Mon–Fri 9am–2pm & 5–8pm, Sat 9am–2pm; free), where sporadic dance, music and art workshops are held in the remains of the Dominican Ex-Convento Rey Cosijoní. Construction of the convent was begun in 1544 at the behest of Cortés and it was named after the incumbent Zapotec king. Now used as a school during the week, it also has museum exhibits, including archeological pieces, local costumes and modern art, locked up on the first floor – ask a member of the staff if you'd like to have a look around. You can see the few remaining frescoes by taking Hidalgo from the north side of the zócalo and following it right as it becomes Guererro.

The ruins of Guiengola

The hilltop fortress of **GUIENGOLA**, 15km north of Tehuantepec, was the Zapotec stronghold on the isthmus, and in 1496 its defenders successfully fought off an attempt by the Aztecs to gain control of the area, which was never fully incorporated into their empire. It continued to be a centre of resistance during the early years of the Conquest and was a focus of Indian revolt against Spanish rule throughout the sixteenth and seventeenth centuries.

At the site you'll see remains of pyramids and a ball-court, but the most striking feature is the massive **defensive wall**. By definition, Guiengola's superb defensive location makes it somewhat inaccessible and it's probably best to take a **taxi**, though **buses** to Oaxaca do pass the turn-off to the site, 8km from Tehuantepec on the main road (look out for the "Ruinas Guiengola" sign). From here it's a hot, seven-kilometre, uphill walk. The site is open daily, and if the caretaker is around you may be asked to pay a small fee, though you'll almost certainly have the place to yourself.

Tehuantepec practicalities

Buses stop at the northern edge of town on Hwy-190, a short *moto* ride or walk from the centre. There's a **post office** and bank on the north side of the square; on 5 de Mayo itself you'll find a **Bancomer** with good rates and an ATM, and a **caseta de larga distancia** (6am–9pm). **Hotels** aren't far away: *Donaji* (Ⓣ9/715-0064; ❹), at Juárez 10, two blocks south of the zócalo, is marginally the best, overlooking the Parque Juárez and with a rooftop view over the town. *Hotel Oasis*, Ocampo 8 (Ⓣ9/715-0008; ❹), is one block south of the zócalo and has breezy, clean rooms with a/c or fan. The *Casa de Huéspedes Istmo*, to the north of the zócalo at Hidalgo 31 (Ⓣ9/715-0019; ❷), is very basic, with shared-bath rooms set in a courtyard behind a storefront funeral parlour. Calle Juana, south from the zócalo, has one of the best **places to eat**: *Café Colónial*, at no. 66, which stays open till 10pm and dishes up good local food, including chicken prepared in almost every way imaginable. On the west side of the zócalo itself are stands offering shakes and snacks, with steaming taco carts lining the east side. *Mariscos Angel* at the entrance to town, is good for **seafood**, and be sure to try some of the **corn bread** that local women hawk to everyone arriving on the bus. For something more atmospheric, try *Scaru* (north of the square next to the *Donaji*), which has murals depicting Tehuantepec life and offers seafood, pasta and cocktails – open until 11pm.

While Tehuantepec is a major stopping point en route to Oaxaca or the Chiapas coast, few **buses** originate here, so moving on, you may find it easier to take one of the constant stream of buses to Juchitán, 26km away (see below), and continue from there. The main long-distance routes, operated by first-class Cristóbal Colón and Autobuses Unidos, serve Oaxaca, Mexico City, Tuxtla Gutiérrez, Coatzacoalcos and Villahermosa, and there are also buses to San Cristóbal and Puerto Escondido; you can buy **tickets** in advance. Several second-class companies also operate between the main towns on the isthmus, and there are constant departures for Salina Cruz.

Fiestas

JANUARY

1 NEW YEAR'S DAY is celebrated everywhere, but is particularly good in **Oaxaca** (Oaxaca) and **Mitla** (Oax).

14 Fiesta in **Niltepec** (Oax), on the Pacific coast road.

20 DÍA DE SAN SEBASTIÁN. Big in **Tehuantepec** (Oax), **Jalapa de Díaz** (Oax), near Tuxtepec, and in **Pinotepa de Don Luís** (Oax), near the coast and Pinotepa Nacional.

FEBRUARY

2 DÍA DE LA CANDELARIA. Colourful Indian celebrations in **Santa María del Tule** (Oax) and in **San Mateo del Mar** (Oax), near Salina Cruz.

22–25 Feria in **Matias Romero** (Oax), between Juchitán and Coatzacoalcos.

Week before Lent – variable Feb–March. CARNAVAL at its most frenzied in the big cities – especially **Oaxaca** (Oax) – but is also celebrated in hundreds of villages throughout the area.

25 Fiesta in **Acatlán** (Puebla), with many traditional dances.

MARCH

HOLY WEEK is widely observed – particularly big ceremonies in **Pinotepa Nacional** (Oax) and nearby **Pinotepa Don Luís** (Oax), as well as in **Jamiltepec** (Oax).

21 **Guelatao** (Oax), near Oaxaca, celebrates the birthday of Benito Juárez, born in the village.

MAY

3 DÍA DE LA SANTA CRUZ celebrated in **Salina Cruz** (Oax), the start of a week-long feria.

8 DÍA DE SAN MIGUEL. In **Soyaltepec** (Oax), between Oaxaca and Huajuapan de León, festivities include horse and dog races, as well as boating events on a nearby lake.

15 DÍA DE SAN ISIDRO sees peasant celebrations everywhere – famous and picturesque fiestas in **Juchitán** (Oax).

19 Feria in **Huajuapan de León** (Oax).

Thursday after Trinity CORPUS CHRISTI. A particularly good feria in **Izúcar de Matamoros** (Pue).

JUNE

24 DÍA DE SAN JUAN falls in the midst of festivities (22–26) in **Tehuantepec** (Oax).

JULY

First Wednesday **Teotitlán del Valle** (Oax), near Oaxaca, holds a fiesta with traditional dances and religious processions.

23 Feria in **Huajuapan de León** (Oax).

25 DÍA DE SANTIAGO provokes widespread celebration – especially in **Izúcar de Matamoros** (Pue), **Niltepec** (Oax) and **Juxtlahuaca** (Oax).

Last two Mondays In **Oaxaca** itself, the famous festival of GUELAGUETZA (or the Lunes del Cerro), a mixture of traditional dancing and rites on the Cerro del Fortín. Highly popular; tickets for the good seats are sold at the tourist office.

Juchitán

JUCHITÁN, just 26km east of Tehuantepec and the point where the road meets the railway to Guatemala, is a dusty commercial centre clogged

AUGUST

13–16 Spectacular festivities in **Juchitán** (Oax) and lesser fiestas in **Nochixtlán** (Oax), between Oaxaca and Huajuapan de León, and on the 15th in **Tehuantepec** (Oax).

24 Fiesta in **San Bartolo Coyotepec** (Oax), near Oaxaca.

31 Blessing of the animals in **Oaxaca** – locals bring their beasts to the church of La Merced to be blessed.

SEPTEMBER

3–5 Juchitán (Oax) once again hosts a series of picturesque celebrations.

8 Religious ceremonies in **Teotitlán del Valle** (Oax), in **Putla** (Oax), on the road inland from Pinotepa Nacional, and in **Tehuantepec** (Oax).

25 FIESTA DE SAN JERÓNIMO in **Ixtepec** (Oax) lasts until October 2.

29 DÍA DE SAN MIGUEL is celebrated in **Soyaltepec** (Oax).

OCTOBER

1 Several barrios of **Tehuantepec** (Oax) have their own small fiestas.

First Sunday DÍA DE LA VIRGEN DEL ROSARIO is celebrated in **San Pedro Amuzgos** (Oax).

Second Sunday Large feria in **Tlacolula** (Oax), near Oaxaca.

Second Monday FERIA DEL ÁRBOL, based around the famous tree in **Santa María del Tule** (Oax).

18 Indian fiesta in **Ojitlán** (Oax), near Tuxtepec, with a formal, candlelit procession.

24 In **Acatlán** (Pue), a fiesta with processions and traditional dances.

NOVEMBER

2 DAY OF THE DEAD is respected everywhere, with particularly strong traditions in **Xoxocotlán** (Oax) and in **Atzompa** (Oax).

25 Patron saint's day in **Mechoacán** (Oax), on the coast near Pinotepa Nacional.

29 DÍA DE SAN ANDRÉS celebrated in **San Juan Colorado** (Oax), on the coast road near Pinotepa Nacional.

DECEMBER

8 DÍA DE LA INMACULADA CONCEPCIÓN is widely observed – especially with traditional dances in **Juquilla** (Oax), not far from Puerto Escondido, and **Zacatepec** (Oax), on the road inland from Pinotepa Nacional.

16–25 The pre-Christmas period is a particularly exciting one in **Oaxaca**, with processions and nativity plays nightly. The 18th is the FIESTA DE LA VIRGEN DE LA SOLEDAD, patroness of the state, with fireworks, processions and music. The 23rd is the FIESTA DE LOS RABANOS (Radishes), when there's an exhibition of statues and scenes sculpted from radishes. On Christmas Eve there's more music, fireworks and processions before midnight mass. Throughout it all, *buñuelos* – crisp pancakes that you eat before smashing the plate on which they are served – are dished up at street stalls.

with traffic and somewhat lacking in tourist infrastructure. Despite this, the city is culturally fascinating, offering glimpses into the matriarchal society the region is known for, with widely observed native traditions and near-constant **fiestas**, also known as **velas**. In May there seem to be daily parties, although they take place throughout the year, where women dress in colorful *traje* and men in formal wear, for all night marathons of music and dancing that often wrap up late into the morning. The residents are also known for strong political views and socialist leanings. The town managed to elect a reforming socialist local government in the early 1980s, which the PRI didn't take kindly to. Eventually the state governor found a pretext to remove local officials from power and replace them with party faithfuls. The political trouble – and violence – that followed has largely blown over, but local tumult still occasionally makes the front pages, and Juchitán's fiestas have a tendency to develop into political demonstrations. Another claim to fame is the region's relatively tolerant attitude towards homosexuality; it's one of the few places in Mexico where gay men live openly, sometimes even attending *velas* in drag.

The **bus** stations line the highway and you won't have long to wait, whichever direction you're heading. Unfortunately, Juchitán doesn't offer much in the way of good-value **accommodation**, and therefore Tehuantepec makes a better base. Options in town include the ramshackle *Hotel La Mansión* (☎9/711-2055; ❺), at 16 de Septiembre 11, a couple of blocks towards the centre from where most of the buses stop. Better to press on 2km along 16 de Septiembre to the nicer *Hotel Lopez Lena*, 16 de Septiembre 70 (☎9/711-1388; ❺) or to the marginally better-value *Hotel Alex* (☎9/711-2055; ❺), which has institutional-feeling air-conditioned rooms and a handful of tiny rooms without a/c that are much cheaper, at 16 de Septiembre 48. The adequate *Casa de Huéspedes Echazarreta* (no phone; ❸) is the cheapest option, and is right on the zócalo. Here you'll also find the **post office**, a **Banamex** and some good **places to eat**, notably the *Casa Grande*, which serves moderately priced seafood in an elegant cool atrium. The **Casa de Cultura**, on Belisario Domínguez beside the church, was started by Francisco Toledo (who was born in Juchitán), and offers a tiny archeological display with pre-Hispanic stone carvings and pottery shards, an art library and occasional exhibitions of local artists.

A cooling day-trip from Juchitán is to the natural clear-water **spring** (US$1) in **Santiago Laollaga**, about 36km northwest of town. The concrete swimming pools by the car park can be overrun by kids, but a short walk upstream leads to natural pools by the spring's source, perfect for a refreshing dip followed by a beer in one of the streamside restaurants – although the occasional duelling stereos can mar the peaceful atmosphere. There is nowhere to stay in town, unless you want to camp. You can get to Santiago Laollaga quickly by car, north through **Ixtepec**, or by buses on the same route in about an hour. The spring is at the north edge of town.

Travel details

Buses

The following frequencies and times are for first-class services. Scores of second-class buses usually cover the same routes, taking ten to twenty percent longer.

Huatulco to: Oaxaca (4 daily, 7hr); Pochutla (hourly; 1hr); Puerto Escondido (hourly; 2hr 30 min); Salina Cruz (almost hourly; 3hr); San Cristóbal (2 daily; 10hr).

Oaxaca to: Mexico City (at least hourly; 6hr); Pochutla (5 daily; 6hr); Puerto Escondido (4 daily; 9.5hr); San Cristóbal (3 daily; 10–12hr); Tehuacán (3 daily; 3hr); Tehuantepec (hourly; 5hr); Veracruz (5 daily; 7hr); Villahermosa (5 daily; 12hr).

Pochutla to: Huatulco (hourly; 1hr); Oaxaca (14 daily; 7–8hr); Puerto Escondido (hourly; 1hr 30min); San Cristóbal (1 daily; 11hr).

Puerto Escondido to: Huatulco (hourly; 2hr 30min); Mexico City (2 daily; 16hr); Oaxaca

(2 daily; 9hr); Pochutla (hourly; 1hr 30min); Salina Cruz (8 daily; 5hr 30min); Tehuantepec (3 daily; 6hr).

Salina Cruz to: Huatulco (10 daily; 1hr); Oaxaca (2 daily; 5.5hr); Pochutla (5 daily; 1hr); Puerto Escondido (5 daily; 5hr 30min); Tehuantepec (every 30min; 30min).

Tehuacán to: Córdoba (3 daily; 2hr); Mexico City (hourly; 4hr); Oaxaca (5 daily; 4hr); Veracruz (3–5 daily; 3hr 30min).

Tehuantepec to: Coatzacoalcos (10 daily; 5hr); Mexico City (12 daily; 11hr); Oaxaca (hourly; 4hr 30min); Puerto Escondido (2 daily; 6hr); Salina Cruz (every 30min; 30min) Tuxtla Gutiérrez (4 daily; 5hr); Veracruz (2 daily; 7hr 30min).

Flights

Oaxaca to: Cancún via Tuxtla, Villahermosa and Mérida (daily); Huatulco (daily, through Mexico City); Mexico City (10 daily); Puerto Escondido (2 daily).

Puerto Escondido to: Mexico City (1 daily); Oaxaca (2 daily).

9

Chiapas and Tabasco

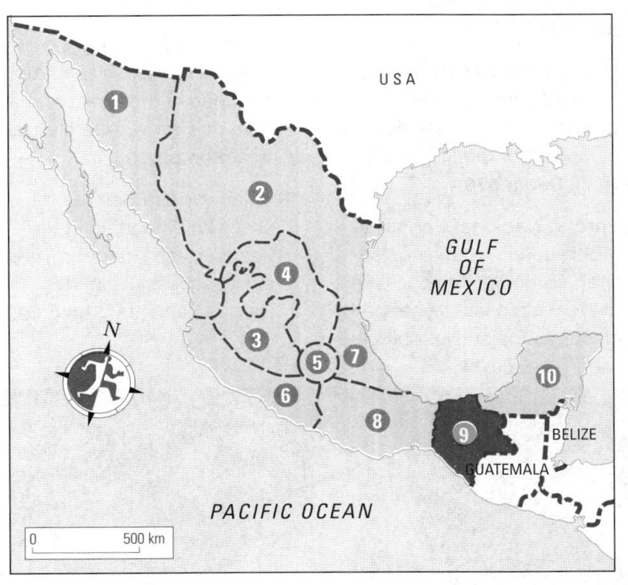

CHAPTER 9

Highlights

* **Tuxtla Gutiérrez** Home to ZOOMAT, the best zoo in the country, where you can see animals native to Chiapas at close quarters living in relatively natural surroundings. See p.654

* **San Cristóbal de las Casas** Ride on horseback through the hills and pine forests to the timeless villages nearby. See p.659

* **San Juan Chamula** Witness extraordinary displays of religious faith in the haunting surroundings of the Iglesia San Juan. See p.670

* **Parque Nacional Lagos de Montebello** A stunning, isolated corner of Chiapas where the mountain lakes change colour as the sunlight hits the water. See p.674

* **Palenque** Bathe in the crystal-clear cascades of the Río Otolum after visiting the tomb of a Maya ruler deep beneath the Templo de las Inscripciones. See p.680

* **Bonampak** Hike at first light along the forest trail to the site and be the first person that day to see the still beautiful murals. See p.688

* **Yaxchilán** For many the most magical of the Chiapas ruins, set deep in the forest and a boat ride away from civilization. See p.690

* **Villahermosa** See the massive, Olmec-carved stone heads at the site of La Venta, easily accessible in the Parque La Venta. See p.693

△ Church, San Juan Chamula

9

Chiapas and Tabasco

Endowed with a stunning variety of cultures, landscapes and wildlife, **Chiapas**, Mexico's southernmost state, has much to tempt visitors. Deserted Pacific beaches, rugged mountains and ruined cities buried in steamy jungle offer a bewildering choice of settings, and many **indigenous traditions** survive intact. Administered by the Spanish as part of Guatemala until the early nineteenth century, when it seceded to join newly independent Mexico, today it is second only to Oaxaca in terms of the proportion of Indians in its population.

The main tourist town is **San Cristóbal de las Casas**, in the geographic centre of the state, and the surrounding villages are a stronghold of **Tzotzil** and **Tzeltal** culture – the main indigenous groups. A visit to these villages is like an entry to another age, where ancient customs and religious practices survive against a backdrop of ever-present commercialism. There is, of course, a darker side to this: picturesque as their life may seem to tourists, the indigenous population has long been bypassed or ignored by the political system, their land and their livelihood under constant threat from modernization, or straightforward seizure. The **Zapatista rebellion** (see p.643), which broke out on New Year's Day 1994 and centred in this area, did not appear from nowhere.

One continuing legacy of the rebellion is a heavy **military** presence in what the Mexican authorities refer to as the "**conflict zone**", an area occupied (nominally at least) by the Zapatistas in the southeastern corner of the state. At its widest extent this could be anywhere east of the road from San Cristóbal via Ocosingo to Palenque, though in essence it means the **Lacandón forest region**, now encircled by the **Carretera Fronteriza** – The Frontier Highway, running roughly parallel with the Guatemalan border. Though you'll see signs announcing the fact that "you are entering Zapatista territory where the Mexican government is not obeyed", you are extremely unlikely to stumble into trouble when visiting the main attractions in this region, the **Parque Nacional Lagos de Montebello** or the ruins of **Yaxchilán** or **Bonampak**, and genuine tourists are always treated with respect.

The state of **Tabasco** is less obviously attractive than its neighbour state – steamy and low-lying for the most part, with a major oil industry to mar the landscape. Recently, however, the state has been seeking to encourage tourism, above all pushing the legacy of the **Olmecs**, Mexico's earliest developed civilization, as well as the boundless possibilities for adventure and eco-tourism. The vibrant, modern capital, **Villahermosa**, has a wealth of parks and museums, the best-known of which, the **Parque La Venta**, displays the original massive Olmec heads. In the extreme southwest, bordered by Veracruz and Chiapas, a section of Tabasco reaches into the mountains up to 1000m high.

Here, in a region almost never visited by outsiders, a low-impact tourism initiative allows you to splash in pristine rivers and waterfalls and explore the astonishing ruins of **Malpasito**, a city of the mysterious **Zoque** culture.

Chiapas

The terrain of **Chiapas** ranges from the Pacific coastal plain, backed by the peaks of the Sierra Madre de Chiapas, through the mainly agricultural Central Depression, irrigated by the Río Grijalva, rising again to the highlands, **Los Altos de Chiapas**. Beyond the highlands the land falls away again: in the

Visiting Chiapas: the legacy of the Zapatista rebellion

On **January 1, 1994**, the day that NAFTA came into effect, several thousand lightly armed rebels, wearing their uniform of green or black army-style tunics and black *pasamontañas* (Balaclavas), occupied San Cristóbal de las Casas, the former state capital and Chiapas' major tourist destination. When the Mexican army recovered from the shock, its immediate response was to launch a violent counter-attack. However, an unprecedented level of international solidarity with the rebels soon forced the Mexican government to halt a brutal counter-insurgency policy. Despite a cease-fire agreed in 1995, years of on/off negotiations, and with the PRI no longer in power, a lasting peace treaty was never signed. A series of violent evictions and attacks on Zapatista communities restarted the hostilities in July 2002, but things have been quieter since, though tensions are simmering beneath the surface. The Zapatista's leader, Subcomandante Marcos, retains his enigmatic charisma as champion of the underprivileged and the Zapatistas continue to benefit from immense popular support both at home and abroad.

Throughout the rebellion **tourists** have visited Chiapas without problems other than delays due to army checks. In San Cristóbal, Zapatista dolls and Marcos souvenirs, the latter emblazoned with his masked features, sell in their thousands. A word of **warning**, though, if your sympathies extend beyond giving economic assistance to the indigenous souvenir-makers – government officials, citing the "infestation of foreign activists who stir up and manipulate many indigenous groups contrary to constitutional order", claim that the presence of *simpático* foreigners influences and even controls political opposition in the state. Although there are foreign observers in "civil peace camps" in the Zapatista areas, they are not recognized as such by the Mexican authorities. Being in (or even near) the **conflict zone** invites suspicion of taking part in political activities – illegal for foreigners – and can lead to deportation.

If you do go, be as fully informed as you can: **SIPAZ**, the International Service for Peace, have a volunteer programme in Chiapas and their website – Ⓦwww.nonviolence.org/sipaz – provides more information. The extremely well-organized Zapatista website – Ⓦwww.ezln.org – has superb links, and is also an excellent source of information. Chiapaslink (Ⓦwww.chiapaslink.ukgateway.net/news) provides regular updates on the latest political developments.

north to the Gulf coast plain of Tabasco, while to the east a series of great rivers, separated by the jungle-covered ridges of the **Lacandón rainforest**, flow into the Río Usumacinta, which forms the border with Guatemala. The **climate**, too, can vary enormously. In one theoretical day you could be basking on the beach at Puerto Arista in the morning, and spending a chilly night by a fireside in the old colonial capital of **San Cristóbal de las Casas**. As a rule the lowlands are hot and humid, with heavy afternoon rainfall in summer, but while days in the highlands can also be hot, by evening you may need a sweater.

For its size Chiapas has the greatest **biological diversity** in North America. A visit to the **zoo** in the state capital of **Tuxtla Gutiérrez**, which houses only animals native to the state, will whet your appetite for the region's natural wonders. In the huge **Montes Azules Biosphere Reserve**, reached from Palenque, a section of the largest remaining rainforest in North America has been preserved. This is also the home of the **Lacandón Maya**, who retreated into the forest when the Spanish arrived, and shunned contact until fifty years ago. There's **cloud forest** in the south, protected in the **El Triunfo Biosphere Reserve** and, far easier to visit, the beautiful lakes and hills of the **Lagos de Montebello National Park**.

The Classic-period Maya site of **Palenque**, on the northern edge of the highlands, is one of Mexico's finest ancient sites and has been the focus of much recent restoration work. The limestone hills in this area are pierced by crystal-clear rivers, creating exquisite waterfalls – most spectacularly at **Agua Azul**. Palenque is also the best starting point for a trip down the **Usumacinta valley**, to visit the remote ruins of **Bonampak** and **Yaxchilán**. The Frontier Highway pushes on south beyond these sites, through the growing town of Benemérito, where you can get a boat to **Guatemala**, or visit **Ixcán**, on the **Río Lacantún**, where some new tourist accommodation (sponsored by the state government to encourage economic development) enables you to visit the southern edge of the Montes Azules Reserve. The highway is now served by buses day and night, enabling you to travel on to the **Lagos de Montebello** and back to San Cristóbal – passing frequent army checkpoints along the route.

Travelling around Chiapas is not difficult: the main cities are connected by a network of good, all-weather roads and the **Panamerican Highway** passes from west to east through some of the most spectacular scenery in the state. In the south the coastal highway offers a speedy route from **Arriaga**, near the Oaxaca border, to **Tapachula**, almost on the frontier with Guatemala. In the out-of-the-way places, particularly in the jungle, travel is by dirt roads, which, though generally well maintained, can cause problems in the rainy season. These more remote places are also fairly well served by public transport, though it's more likely to be *combis* and trucks taking people and produce to and from markets than the comfortable buses of the main roads.

The Chiapas coast

Hwy-200 provides a fast route from the Oaxaca border to Tapachula: if you plan on getting **to Guatemala** as quickly as possible, this is the road to take. It traverses the steamy coastal plain of the **Soconusco**, running about 20km inland, with the 2400-metre peaks of the **Sierra Madre de Chiapas** always in view. These little-visited mountains, protected by National and Biosphere Reserve status, are penetrated by roads only at their eastern and western extremities: **Puerto Arista** is the only place even remotely resembling a resort town on the Chiapas coast. The plain itself is a fertile agricultural area, mainly given over to coffee and bananas, though there are also many ranchos, where cattle grow fat on the lush grass; the excellent local **cheese** is celebrated in the Esposición de Quesos, held in Pijijiapan the week before Christmas. **Tapachula**, the "capital" of the Soconusco, which is cut off from the rest of Chiapas by the mountains, has frequent connections to the two southern border crossings into Guatemala, and on the way you can easily visit the ancient Olmec and Maya site of **Izapa**. From Tapachula you can also take a relaxing trip up to the delightful little town of **Unión Juárez**, the base for expeditions to **Volcán Tacaná**, the highest peak in Chiapas.

Arriaga and Tonalá

ARRIAGA, the first town on the Chiapas coast road, is a dusty, uninteresting place, but its location at the junction of Hwy-190 (the road over the mountains to Tuxtla) means you may have to change buses here. The **Central de Autobuses**, with plenty of first- and second-class connections, is just off the main road, six blocks from the zócalo. All southbound buses will also stop at **Tonalá**, a slightly better option if you have to spend the night, though it's better still to push on to the beach at **Puerto Arista**, where accommodation is cheaper and of a better standard.

Larger and marginally more inviting than Arriaga, **TONALÁ** is just a thirty-minute bus ride away down Hwy-200, which, as Avenida Hidalgo, forms the town's main street. Tonalá, which means "hot place" in Nahua, was the only city in Chiapas that fought for independence, with the help of Mario Matamoros. All the **bus** companies terminate along Hidalgo: the main first-class companies pull in about 1km west of the zócalo; second-class to the east.

Everything you need in Tonalá (including banks) is either on the **zócalo** – Parque Esperanza – or within a couple of blocks of it. The central feature of the park is the **Estela de Tlaloc**, a large, standing stone carved by the Olmecs, depicting the rain god Tlaloc and showing the influence of Teotihuacán. If you're stuck for something to do, you could always visit what's known as the **Museo Arqueológico** (no set hours; free), in the Casa de Cultura on Hidalgo, between the bus station and the plaza, though it's hardly worth it as the Olmec and Maya exhibits here appear to have been abandoned. The **Iglesia San Francisco**, a couple of blocks northeast of the zócalo, merits a quick peek inside for its rose-coloured font and colonial-style iron pews. Tonalá's **tourist office** (Mon–Fri 8am–7pm, Sat 9am–3pm; ⓣ966/663-2787), on the corner of 5 de Mayo and Hidalgo, two blocks east of the zócalo, is a good source of information about beaches nearby.

The heat and constant traffic noise make **staying** in Tonalá rather uncomfortable, and most of the hotels are overpriced. *Grajandra* (ⓣ966/663-0144, ⓕ663-2645; ❻) at Hidalgo 204, just along from the bus station, is not cheap but offers better value for money than most, with large, clean, comfortable en-suite rooms with cable TV. *Galilea* (ⓣ966/663-0239; ❺), is well located on the east side of the zócalo, and has clean, basic rooms with private bathrooms, a/c, TV, and parking. It also has a good **restaurant**. A few other restaurants and food stalls also ring the zócalo, perhaps the best being *El Tizoncíto*, near Hidalgo. There are plenty of **Internet** cafés as well along Hidalgo, including M&M (daily 10am–10pm; US$0.80 per hour), on the corner with 15 de Mayo.

Leaving Tonalá, Cristóbal Colón has hourly first-class departures to Tuxtla (1.55am–8.40pm; 3hr 30min) and Tapachula (1am–7.35pm; 3hr 30min) and some afternoon departures to Mexico City (2 daily) and Oaxaca (3 daily); there are at least as many second-class buses to Tuxtla and Tapachula. In the bustling market area a couple of blocks west of the tourist office, *combis* (from the corner of 5 de Mayo and Juárez) and red-striped taxis (a block away at the corner of 5 de Mayo and Matamoros) leave when full for **Puerto Arista** and **Boca del Cielo** (both US$1 per person). The green-striped **city taxis** charge considerably more for the journey to Puerto Arista (US$7 per car).

Puerto Arista

Although this quiet village may not be everyone's idea of a perfect beach resort, **PUERTO ARISTA**, with its miles of clean sand, patrolling flocks of frigate birds and invigorating surf, does offer a chance to escape the unrelenting heat of the inland towns. It's a bit run-down and there's little to see, but it's a worthwhile stop if you've been doing some hard travelling. While the waves are definitely refreshing, be aware of the potentially dangerous **riptides** that sweep along the coast – never get out of your depth.

The road from Tonalá joins Puerto Arista's only street, Avenida Matamoros, at the lighthouse. Get off here and you're in the centre of town: walk a couple of kilometres left or right and you'll be on a deserted shoreline; ahead lies the beach, with hotels and restaurants packed closely together. You won't feel crowded, though, unless you arrive at Christmas or Semana Santa, as there seem to be at least as many buildings abandoned or boarded up as there are occupied.

There are many **hotels** in Puerto Arista but few customers: bargain with a couple of the places below as some owners will initially quote prices higher than they are prepared to settle for – and you can always **camp** on the beach for free. There's a cluster of similar and reasonably priced places to stay on the seafront, a couple of blocks right from the lighthouse. The best of these is *La Puesta del Sol* (Ⓣ994/600-9047; ❺), with cool, dark rooms and TV. All of these options are clean and well run, with private bathrooms. Turn left at the lighthouse (with your back to the beach), and it's six blocks to the *Arista Bugambilias* (Ⓣ/Ⓕ 994/600-9044; ❻), a luxury option with rooms and suites around a pool and private garden right on the beach. Take a right and accommodation is rather thinner on the ground – you'll walk a long way before you find the first decent option. The *Lucero* (Ⓣ994/600-9042; ❼), just back from the beach, has tiled rooms decorated with wildlife murals, and suites with a/c, and a pool. Beyond here the tarmac is replaced by a dust track, and if you take the left before *Lucero* you'll soon come across signs for *José's Camping and Cabañas* (Ⓣ994/600-9048; ❸), the friendliest place in Puerto Arista and great for budget travellers. Accommodation is in sturdy thatched bungalows with electric lighting; some are en suite, but the shared bathrooms are very clean and have dependable water supplies. There's also a flower-filled patio with hammocks and a refreshing pool, and camping (❶) is also possible among the coconut trees. For food there are a couple of dozen beachfront palapa **restaurants**, serving basic seafood, but only five or six ever open at any one time and there's little that distinguishes them in terms of cost, menu, or quality; generally the best place to eat will be at your hotel.

You can easily get transport 15km along the coast to **Boca del Cielo**, a cluster of houses and fishing boats on the landward side of a lagoon, where you can board a *lancha* (US$8 round-trip) and speed across to a beautiful, deserted beach. If you're planning a visit, head back well before 7pm, as it can be almost impossible to find onward transport after dark. Some of the basic palapa restaurants will let you sling a hammock for a small fee. If you plan to sleep outdoors be prepared for mosquitoes.

All of the beaches along this stretch of coast are used by **turtles** for nesting. The peak of the season is October, when the turtles emerge during the early hours of the morning to deposit their eggs beneath the sand. In June and July, the hatchlings that managed to evade egg collectors struggle to reach the sea, desperately trying to avoid being picked off by gulls, frigate birds and other predators.

From Tonalá to Tapachula

With your own vehicle, you can explore some of the side roads leading from Hwy-200 in the 220km between Tonalá and Tapachula: either up into the mountains, where the heavy rain gives rise to dozens of rivers and waterfalls, or down to near-deserted beaches. Around **PIJIJIAPAN**, 75km from Tonalá along Hwy-200, a series of dirt roads leads down to unspoilt beaches and lagoons with opportunities for fishing, swimming, or merely relaxing in the sun. The best of these is **Playa Palo Blanco**, 20km due south of Pijijiapan. Most of the coastal villages are actually on the landward side of a narrow

△ Giant Olmec head, Palenque

lagoon, separated from the ocean by sand bars. These sand bars block many rivers' access to the sea, causing marshes to form and providing a superb wetland habitat, protected as the **Reserva de la Biosfera La Encrucijada**, 45km of coastline and an important wintering point for North American migrant birds. Travelling **by bus**, it's much more difficult (though still possible) to take in destinations off the main road, and you need to be prepared to hitch and camp. At **HUIXTLA**, 42km before Tapachula, Hwy-211 snakes over the mountains via Motozintla to join the Panamerican Highway near Ciudad Cuauhtémoc and the Guatemalan border at La Mesilla. This bone-shaking road offers stupendous mountain views and is covered by buses running between Tapachula and Comitán and San Cristóbal de las Casas.

Tapachula

Set in the imposing shadow of the 4000-metre Volcán Tacaná, **TAPACHULA** is a gateway to Guatemala and the Pacific coast. A busy commercial centre and the capital of the Soconusco, the southeastern region of the state, it grew in importance during the nineteenth century with the increasing demand for coffee and bananas. As a border city, it has a lively cultural mix, including not only immigrants from Central America, but also small German and Chinese communities. The **Museo Regional de Soconusco** (Tues–Sun 9am–5pm; US$0.50), in the same building as the tourist office, tells their story, as well as displaying scraps of excavated finds from local ruins. The centre of activity is the **zócalo**, a pleasant place to while away an afternoon in the shade of laurel trees, or an evening listening to the marimba bands. Look out for *cohetes*, strange green fruits resembling giant olives with the flavour of sour plums, pickled in rum and sold from street stalls around the zócalo.

Arrival, orientation and information

All the main **bus stations** are north of the centre; the various second-class companies have their terminals within walking distance of the zócalo, while first-class Cristóbal Colón (also the terminal for international buses from Guatemala) is further out at Calle 17 Ote between avenidas 1 and 3 Nte. A taxi to the centre costs US$1.50 and walking takes about twenty minutes. From Tapachula's **airport**, 18km south on the road to Puerto Madero, a colectivo from the airport into Tapachula costs US$5.50 per person and drops you at your hotel. Buy a ticket at the booth just outside the arrivals lounge. If you are in a group it works out cheaper to take a taxi for around US$8.

The town's **layout** is a little confusing, for while the streets are laid out in the regular numbered grid common in Chiapas, the zócalo, **Parque Hidalgo**, is not at its centre. It's not too far away, though: Calle Central meets Avenida Central three blocks east and a block south of the zócalo.

The **tourist office** (Mon–Fri 8am–8pm, Sat 8am–2pm; ⓣ962/626-1485 ext 116) is on the ground floor of the old Palacio Municipal, on the west side of the zócalo. They can provide city maps for most of the major destinations in Chiapas. The main **banks** are one block east of the zócalo, but for **changing cash** and travellers' cheques you'll get much quicker service from Casa de Cambio Santa, Avenida 2 Nte 9, between Calle Central and Calle 1 Pte (Mon–Fri 9am–5pm, Sat 9am–2pm); you can also get Guatemalan quetzales here. The **post office** (Mon–Fri 9am–3pm, Sat 9am–1pm) is a long way southeast of the zócalo at Calle 1 Ote, between avenidas 7 and 9 Nte. One block east of here the Guatemalan **consulate** is opposite the school on Calle Norte, between avenidas 5 and 7 Sur (Mon–Fri 9am–2pm & 3–5pm; ⓣ962/626-1252). **Visas** cost

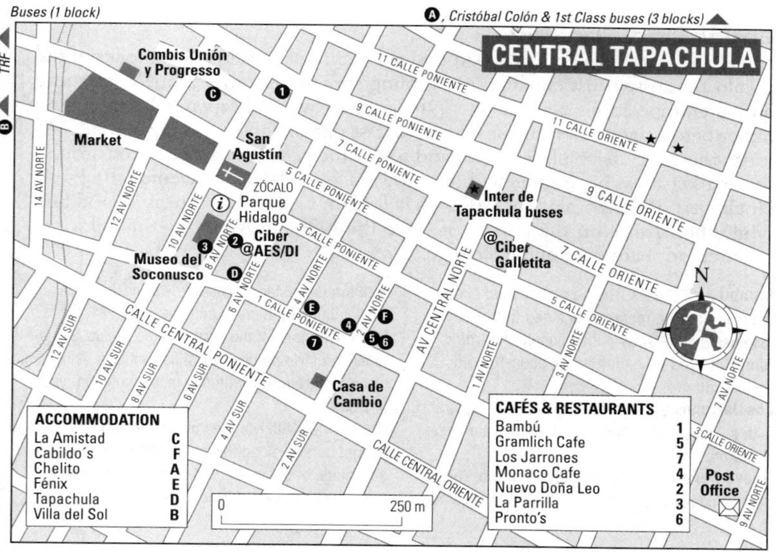

US$25 but are currently not required for citizens of Europe, North America, Australia and New Zealand. The most convenient **Internet** access is at *AES/DI* (daily 9am–11pm; US$1 per hour) on the south side of the zócalo.

Accommodation

There's no shortage of accommodation options in Tapachula, with most budgets well catered for. There is at least one **hotel** near any of the bus stations, but the ones around the second-class terminals are often sleazy. The best bet is to try the streets immediately east of the zócalo, where several good-value hotels can be found along avenidas 4 Norte and 1, 3, and 5 Poniente. The cheapest accommodation is located west of the zócalo, where the market straggles down the hill, and though most are rather desperate-looking there are one or two good budget options.

La Amistad C 7 Pte 34, between avenidas 10 and 12 Nte ⓣ962/626-2293. The best budget hotel in the city; clean, with colourful rooms around a flower-filled courtyard. Free drinking water. No a/c but rooms have fans. ❸

Cabildo's Av 2 Nte 17 ⓣ962/626-6606. Apartment-style accommodation in a central location. Huge airy rooms with all modern conveniences, plus a pool and secure parking facilities. Accepts Visa and MasterCard. ❻

Chelito Av 1 Nte at C 17 Ote ⓣ962/626-2428. Handy location just around the corner from the Cristóbal Colón buses (head left out of the terminal), and clean tiled rooms (some with a/c and cable TV) with private bathrooms. There's a small restaurant and parking for guests. ❹

Fénix Av 4 Nte 19, near C 1 Pte ⓣ962/625-0755, ⓦwww.fenix.com.mx. One of the better of the town's expensive options. Rooms have a/c and cable, and there's a cooling fountain in the courtyard plus leafy gardens complete with parrots. ❻

Tapachula Av 6 Nte 18 ⓣ962/626-4370. Entered through a little shop, with some rooms that are a bit shabby, but all are en suite and are the cheapest in town. Great location just off the zócalo. Rooms at the back are best. ❷

Villa del Sol Av 3a Pte 45 ⓣ962/626-6193. This clean and friendly option offers large, brightly coloured rooms with cable TV and telephone. Rooms without a/c are considerably cheaper. ❹–❺

Eating and drinking

There are more than enough inexpensive restaurants within a few blocks of the zócalo to satisfy most cravings, but finding something more refined is a more difficult proposition. Calle 1 Pte Nte is lined with cheap restaurants, some rather better than others, most with breakfast options and a comida corrida. As usual, there are cheap places to eat and some fine *panaderías* to be found around the market area, beginning with the row of juice bars on Avenida 10 Pte, a block west of the zócalo. For **cafés** *Gramlich*, on Calle 1 Pte Nte, is a good bet, while the *Monaco* on the corner of Calle Pte Nte and Avenida 4 Nte also has an international telephone exchange.

Bambú Av 7 Pte 23. The best of several economical Chinese restaurants along this street; also has a take-away option should the traffic fumes put you off eating in the open-fronted restaurant.

Los Jarrones C 1 Pte Nte. Classy hotel restaurant with a varied if slightly pricey menu. Try the *tacos camarón*.

Nuevo Doña Leo south side of the zócalo. The best-value breakfast and comida corrida, together with tortas and tacos. *Los Comales* next door is similar, but a bit more expensive.

La Parrilla just off the corner of the zócalo. South American style *parillas* (grills) as well as a delicious *taquiza mixta*, with five mouthwatering types of tacos.

Pronto's C 1 Pte Nte. One of several good-value budget options along this street, with the added advantage of being open 24 hours. Try *menudo sinaloense*, a typical Mexican *caldo* (broth).

Unión Juárez and Santo Domingo

The small town of **UNIÓN JUÁREZ**, 43km from Tapachula and perched on the flank of the Volcán Tacaná at a height of over 1100m, offers a welcome respite from the heat of the lowlands as well as some of the finest hiking in southern Chiapas. There are no direct buses from Tapachula, and you have to

Moving on from Tapachula

First-class buses for destinations throughout Mexico leave from the Cristóbal Colón terminal; any bus or *combi* from the centre to Talismán Bridge (see p.652) or the border (see p.653) passes the entrance. Some of the better second-class services also leave from here. If you're heading directly **to Guatemala City** you can take advantage of the daily luxury Galgos (6am & noon) or Linea Dorada (2pm) services, which leave from here and take you right across the border (US$20; 5–6hr); you'll have to get off the bus for Mexican immigration at the Talismán Bridge and walk across to the Guatemalan immigration post and then reboard. Any travel agent in the centre should be able to sell you tickets for these buses (or even for the Ticabus, connecting most Central American capitals); try Viajes Tapachula at Av Central Nte 42 (☎962/625-1345). First-class bus tickets can also be bought from Multi Pack, in the terminal; call ahead to reserve them (☎962/625-6259). All first-class and most second-class buses **to Tuxtla (for San Cristóbal)** head up the coast via Arriaga.

The main **second-class bus** operators are TRF, at the corner of Av 16 Nte Pte and C 3 Pte Nte, for the coast as far as Salina Cruz and Tuxtla; Inter de Tapachula, 7 Pte between C 2 and Central Nte, for the coast road and Ciudad Hidalgo on the Guatemalan border. Unión y Progreso, C 5 Pte between avenidas 12 and 14 Nte, runs frequent *combis* to Unión Juárez and to the Talismán Bridge for the Guatemalan border.

Tapachula's airport (see p.648) is served by **flights** operated by Aeroméxico (☎962/626-3921), Aviacsa (☎962/626-1439), and Aerocaribe (☎962/626-9872); to get to it, call Transporte Terrestre (☎962/626-1287).

change at the town of **Cacahoatán,** approximately halfway between the two. **Buses** and *combis* for Cacahoatán leave at least every twenty minutes from the Unión y Progreso terminal in Tapachula. As the road climbs up the lush green valley of the Río Suchiate, which forms the border with Guatemala, the bananas and cacao give way to coffee and you begin to enjoy good views of two majestic **volcanoes**: Tacaná, at 4092m the highest peak in Chiapas; and the 4220-metre peak of Tajumulco, the highest mountain in Guatemala. Cacahoatán Transportes Tacaná buses leave from the station across the street from the Unión y Progreso terminal. The whole journey takes around eighty minutes (each leg costs US$8), finally pulling in on the west side of the plaza in Unión Juárez. To get back to Tapachula again, take the *combis* departing for Cacahoatán from the east side of the plaza (every 15min until 8pm; last bus to Tapachula 9pm from Cacahoatán).

One of the main reasons for visiting Unión Juárez are the excellent **dayhikes** in the surroundings. There are countless waterfalls in the area and, with a guide, you can reach the volcano's summit, where a monument symbolizes the kinship between Mexico and Guatemala. Fernando Valera Saá (Ⓔfernandao772@hotmail.com), an excellent Spanish-speaking guide, leads three-day trips for about US$50; bring a warm sleeping bag.

Unión Juárez itself has two **hotels**: the budget but comfortable *Posada Aljoad*, half a block off the west side of the plaza (no phone; ❹), which has neat rooms with private bathrooms around a courtyard, and a good inexpensive restaurant; and the good-value *Hotel Colonial Campestre*, which you pass as you enter the town (Ⓣ/Ⓕ962/647-2015; ❺). Rooms and suites here are comfortable and spacious, with solid wooden furniture, en-suite bathrooms, and TV. The owner, José Antonio Valera Saá, has written two fascinating (and locally controversial) books, *Aroma de Café Amargo* (*Aroma of Bitter Coffee*) and the follow-up *Aroma de Café Dulce* (*Aroma of Sweet Coffee*) in Spanish – part autobiography, part local history – which he will be happy to discuss with you over coffee. Both books are available from the hotel.

The *Campestre* has a good **restaurant**, *La Suiza Chiapaneca*, and on the north side of the attractive plaza, the *Carmelita* and *La Montaña* are also good, inexpensive restaurants serving a standard menu of meat, chicken and tacos. You can sit outside and enjoy views of Pico de Loro, a steep, rocky outcrop that actually looks like its namesake – a parrot's beak.

The area around Unión Juárez is one of the best **coffee**-growing areas in Chiapas and on the way up from Tapachula, a few kilometres before Unión Juárez, the road passes a restored 1920s coffee-plantation house in the small village of **SANTO DOMINGO**. The three-storey wooden house, with balconies all around and set in beautiful gardens with a pool, was the home of Enrique Braun Hansen, whose German origins are reflected in the building's architectural style – early North American meets Alpine hotel, with predominately Art Nouveau interiors. Now part of a successful community-based tourism project, the house includes a good restaurant on the ground floor and a **museum of coffee** (free) above. Across the road the *Hotel Santo Domingo* (Ⓣ962/629-9073; ❹) is a good-value **place to stay**, where rooms with spacious, private bathrooms and comfortable beds are set around a patio garden.

The ruins of Izapa

The road to the border passes right through the archeological site of **IZAPA** (daily 9am–5pm), an interesting, if little-visited site. Entry is officially free, but the guard sees so few visitors that he may try to extract a small fee, or sell you an overpriced information booklet for US$3. Besides being easy to get to, the site is large – with more than eighty temple mounds – and important for its evidence of both the Olmec and early Maya cultures. Izapa culture, in fact, is seen as a transitional stage between the Olmecs and the glories of the Classic Maya period. Even though many of the best carved monuments have been removed to museums, including the Anthropology Museum in Mexico City (see p.401), you can still see early versions of the rain god Chac and others, many in rather sad-looking huts surrounded by barbed wire. From its founding before 1250 BC, Izapa flourished up to and throughout the Maya pre-Classic period, until around 300 AD; most of what remains is from the later period, perhaps around 200 AD, and the site continued to be occupied until the post-Classic.

The **northern side** of the site (left of the road as you head to the border) is more accessible than the southern half. There's a ball-court, and several stelae, which, though not Olmec in origin, are carved in a recognizable Olmec style, similar to monuments at other early Maya sites. The **southern side**, down a track about 1km back along the main road, is a good deal more overgrown, but you can spot altars with animal carvings – frogs, snakes, and jaguars – and several unexcavated mounds. To **get there**, take any bus or *combi* to the Talismán border and ask the driver to drop you at the site, which is signposted from the road.

The Guatemalan border: the Talismán Bridge and Ciudad Hidalgo

Both of these southern crossing points are easy places to enter Guatemala (see box opposite), but the **Talismán Bridge** is closer to Tapachula and better for onward connections. Apart from a few grubby hotels and unappealing *comedores* there is nothing at Talismán itself. From Tapachula, *combis* (operated by Unión y Progreso; US$0.80) leave when full (taking about 30min), passing the Cristóbal Colón bus station on the way. If you are **leaving Mexico** and don't plan to return you will have to pay the departure tax of US$21. You can pay at the border, though there is no telling where the money goes, and it may be wiser to pay at a bank in Tapachula. **Changing money** is best done in Tapachula; there's no shortage of moneychangers at the border but rates are unfavourable – ask around and make sure you have some idea of the official exchange rate beforehand.

If you're heading **onwards**, Guatemala City is about five to six hours away: there's usually a bus waiting, otherwise take a bus or van to **Malacatán** and continue from there. The best way, though, is to take one of the international bus services from Tapachula to Guatemala City (see p.709; you can pick them up here, though there may not be a seat). Travelling **into Mexico** you'll be given a tourist card at immigration and there's no shortage of *combis* to Tapachula and plenty of first-class buses from Tapachula onwards. You'll probably have your passport checked many times along Hwy-200, so be prepared.

Further south, the border town of **CIUDAD HIDALGO** is a very busy road crossing and the point where the railway enters Guatemala, but it's less convenient if you're travelling by bus. There are several **casas de cambio** and the freelance moneychangers generally give fair rates for Guatemalan quetzales. The Cristóbal Colón terminal is here too, one block from immigration, running a daily service to Mexico City at 6.45pm and shuttles to Tapachula every fifteen minutes (US$1). The best of the **hotels** is the homely *Hospedaje La Favorita*, Calle Central Oriente (☎962/628-0045; ❸), where you walk right through the owners' kitchen to get to the rooms. Plenty of willing locals offer

Crossing into Guatemala

There are two major crossings (Talismán Bridge and Ciudad Hidalgo) and three minor crossings (Frontera Corozal, Ciudad Cuauhtémoc, and La Palma; see p.709) from Chiapas into Guatemala. Crossings are relatively trouble-free at the larger points, though it is not uncommon for both sets of customs to solicit illegal entry and departure fees. Requesting a receipt is often a sufficient response to get them to waive the fee, but it may well be less hassle to pay. The only genuine tax is the Mexican **exit tax** (US$21), payable if you are leaving Mexico and do not intend to return before your tourist card expires. This is officially to be paid at a city bank before departure. If you will be returning to Mexico you will be allowed to proceed in possession of your current tourist card free of charge. Procedures at Frontera Corozal, Ciudad Cuauhtémoc, and La Palma are rather more unpredictable. These are notorious entry points for illegal immigrants and the *aduanas* consist of little more than armed soldiers manning riverside tables. The soliciting of illegal fees is almost standard at these crossings; best just to avoid the situation entirely.

Citizens of the US, Canada, the EU, Australia, and New Zealand **do not require visas** to enter Guatemala. Citizens of other countries should check with the Guatemalan embassy in Tapachula (see p.648). Bear in mind that Mexico observes daylight-saving time, making it one hour later here during the summer than it is in Guatemala.

to pedal you across the Puente Rodolfo Robles to **Ciudad Tecún Umán** in Guatemala (US$0.50), but it's an easy walk.

The Chiapas highlands

There is nowhere in Mexico so rich in scenery or indigenous life as **inland Chiapas**. Forested uplands and jungly valleys are studded with rivers and lakes, waterfalls, and unexpected gorges, and flush with the rich flora and fauna of the tropics – wild orchids, brilliantly coloured birds, and monkeys. For much of its history the isolation of the state allowed the **indigenous population** to carry on with their lives little affected, though the differing pressures brought by Catholicism and commercialism are slowly eroding the traditional way of life in all but the most isolated of communities.

Strong and colourful as the traditions are – away from the big towns, **Spanish** is still very much a second language – the economic and social lot of the *indígena* population remains greatly inferior to that of *ladinos*. The oppressive exploitation of the *encomienda* system remained powerful here far longer than in parts of Mexico more directly in the government eye (there were local rebellions, quickly suppressed, in the early eighteenth and late nineteenth centuries), and despite some post-revolutionary land redistribution, most small villages still operate at the barest subsistence level. Not surprisingly, many of the customs are dying fast, and it's comparatively rare to see men in traditional clothing, though many women still wear it. Conversely, such traditions as do survive are clung to fiercely by the older generations, and you should be extremely sensitive about **photography** – especially of anything that might have religious significance – and donning **native clothing**, the patterns on which convey subtle social and geographic meaning. It's worth noting that many indigenous communities and some local transport operators refuse to observe the **time change** in summer, preferring *la hora vieja* – the old time.

Tuxtla Gutiérrez

TUXTLA GUTIÉRREZ, the capital of the state, does its best to deny most of Chiapas' attraction and tradition – it's a fast-growing, modern, and crowded city. Though not actually in the highlands, it's the main gateway from central Mexico and a major transport hub; you may well end up having to stay the night. If you do, there's a fascinating **zoo** and some excellent **museums** to fill some time. Day-trips to surrounding attractions are better organized in San Cristóbal two hours further east (see p.659).

Arrival and information

Tuxtla has two airports. The **Aeropuerto San Juan**, near Ocozocautla on a hilltop often shrouded in fog, 28km to the west of town, is generally used only in summer; colectivos run from here into the city. The main airport is **Aeropuerto Francisco Sarabiá** (also called **Aeropuerto Terán**), 7km west of the city. To get there from the centre take *combi* route 81 from Calle 2 Pte between 8 and 9 Sur or get a taxi for around US$7. First-class **buses** pull into the ADO/Cristóbal Colón station (☎961/612-5122) on Avenida 2 Nte at Calle 2 Pte. To reach the centre, turn left from the entrance onto Calle 2 Pte Nte and left again when you reach Avenida Central. The main second-class terminal, used by Autotransportes Tuxtla Gutiérrez (ATG) and a couple of smaller companies, takes up half a block of 3 Sur Ote, near 7 Ote, 1km southeast of the centre: for the zócalo, follow Calle 2 Sur west past the market area until you hit Calle Central Sur, then turn right.

The **municipal tourist office** (Mon–Fri 8am–8pm, Sat 8am–2pm; ☎961/612-5511) is conveniently located in the underpass at Calle Central Nte and Avenida 2 Nte Ote. The Chiapas state **tourist office** is a good way west

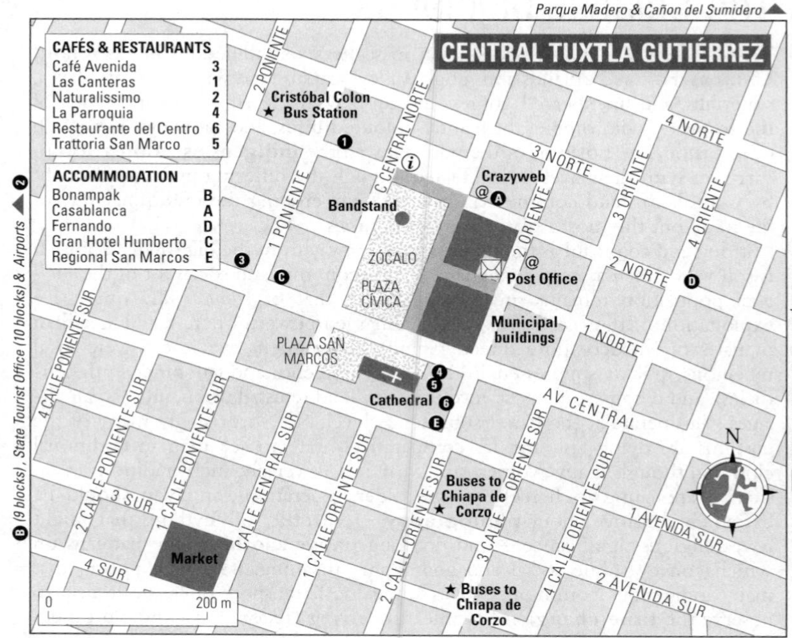

of the zócalo, across from the *Hotel Bonampak* in the Edificio Plaza de las Instituciones at Blv Belisario Domínguez 950 (Mon–Fri 9am–3pm & 6–9pm; ⓣ961/602-5127). You can obtain **topographic maps** of the state from the Hacienda and INEGI offices (government departments), on the fourth floor of the corner of Avenida Central and Calle 2 Ote Sur – useful if you're travelling in out-of-the-way places.

Accommodation

Tuxtla has no shortage of decent **places to stay**, with plenty of budget options. Though inexpensive, the hotels near the **bus stations** are noisy. Most hotels have hot water, but there are occasional shortages. Check, too, if your hotel has pure drinking water: the ones listed below do. If you want more convenience, with less noise, head a few blocks east (left out of the first-class bus station, crossing the zócalo by the underpass) to find a clutch of hotels in all price ranges along 2 Nte Ote.

Bonampak Belisario Domínguez 180 ⓣ961/602-5925, ⓕ602-5914, ⓔhotbonam@prodigy.net.mx. Fourteen blocks west of the zócalo, where Av Central becomes Blv Domínguez, this hotel belongs to the Best Western chain. Rooms all have a/c, and there's a pool, leafy gardens, restaurant, travel agency, and car hire. ❼

Casablanca Av 2 Nte Ote 251 ⓣ/ⓕ 961/611-0305, ⓔamhm@chiapas.net. Friendly place offering good-value blue-and-yellow rooms; those with a/c and TV almost double the rates. There's an attractive palm garden and luggage storage as well. ❹, with a/c and TV ❺

Fernando Av 2 Nte Ote 515 ⓣ961/613-1740. The best value of the options just east of the zócalo: large, comfortable rooms with en-suite bathroom, wooden furniture, and TV. All rooms have fans but no a/c. Parking available. ❸

Gran Hotel Humberto Av Central, one block west of the zócalo ⓣ961/613-6784, ⓔHotelHum@prodigy.net.mx. All rooms come with a/c, cable TV and a tiled bathroom; suites are available too, with separate bedroom and living area. The lobby features representations of the Bonampak murals (see p.688). ❻, suite ❼

Regional San Marcos C 2 Ote 176 at Av 1 Sur ⓣ/ⓕ961/613-1940, ⓔsanmarcos@chiapas.net. Popular and well-run modern hotel, a block south of the zócalo and a block east of the cathedral, with some air-conditioned rooms, plus there's a good restaurant and bar on site. ❹–❺

The City

Sights downtown are few: the **zócalo**, known as the "Plaza Cívica", is the chief of them, recently refurbished with much ostentatious marble, fountains and a statue of General Joaquín Miguel Gutiérrez Canales (1796–1838), former governor of Chiapas and campaigner for *indígena* rights. There's often free live music on the plaza, especially at weekends. On the other side of Avenida Central is the restrained, whitewashed **San Marcos Cathedral**. Its bell tower is one of the leading local entertainments: every hour a mechanical procession of the twelve apostles goes through a complicated routine accompanied by a carillon of 48 bells. Surrounding the cathedral, the **Plaza San Marcos** is a favourite spot for relaxing in the shade distinctly lacking on the Plaza Cívica. West of the centre, between calles 8 and 9, you pass the clean and very popular **Parque la Marimba**, a favourite evening gathering-spot for strolling and listening to the marimba bands.

Slightly further afield, you could head out to the **Parque Madero**, northeast of the centre, where the small **Museo Regional de Chiapas** (Tues–Sun 9am–4pm; US$3.50) details the history of pre-Hispanic Chiapas, and the results of the Conquest. The highlights are the intricately carved human fencers from the ruins of Chiapa de Corzo (see p.657). Botanical gardens and an Orquideario full of blooms native to the Chiapas jungle are in the same complex, reached along a shaded walkway. To get there, head north from the zócalo and then turn right onto Avenida 5 Nte Ote – about 1km in all; or take *combi* route 49 or 51, usually marked "Parque Madero" from Calle 2 Ote.

The zoo

If you have half a day to spare, it's definitely worth spending it at the recently renovated Zoológico Miguel Álvarez del Toro, or **ZOOMAT** (Tues–Sun 8.30am–5.30pm; free, but donations welcome), on a forested hillside south of the city. There's a **bus** out there, #60, marked "Cerro Hueco" or "Zoológico", which you can catch on Calle 1 Ote Sur between avenidas 6 and 7 Sur, a bit of a walk from the centre – it's very slow and roundabout, though, and a **taxi** (US$3) is a great deal easier.

Despite its inflated claims to have every species native to Chiapas, it does have quite a selection, including some of the more spectacular invertebrates. By any standards, it's an excellent zoo with good-sized cages, complete with natural vegetation, freshwater streams, and a conservationist approach. A number of animals, including *guaqueques negros* (agoutis) – rodents about the size of a domestic cat – and some very large birds, are free to roam the zoo grounds. People of a nervous disposition should avoid the *vivario*, which contains a vast and stomach-turning collection of snakes, insects, and spiders you might meet on your travels.

Eating and drinking

The centre of Tuxtla has dozens of **restaurants**, and you need never wander more than a block or so on either side of Avenida Central to find something in every price range. Juice bars are everywhere, and there are also some great bakeries along Avenida Central. The very **cheapest** places are between the second-class bus area and the centre, where several tiny, family-run restaurants each serve an excellent-value comida corrida, including *Restaurante del Centro* next to *Hotel Regional San Marcos* on Calle 2 Ote Sur. More cheap places to eat can be found in the Mercado Díaz Ordáz, Calle Central Sur, between avenidas 3 and 4 Sur.

Most popular for socializing and people-watching are the **restaurants** under the arches on Plaza San Marco behind the cathedral, all with outdoor seating and often packed with smartly dressed locals. Here prices for the Mexican food at *La Parroquia* are not too high, and there's a good breakfast buffet. Next door, the *Trattoria San Marco* serves good portions of pizza and Mexican food at slightly higher prices. For **vegetarian** food, try *Naturalissimo*, just off Avenida Central at Calle 6 Pte Nte, west of the zócalo. It's inexpensive, clean, and modern, and offers a great daily special. One block east of the Cristóbal Colón terminal, *Las Canteras* provides a more refined atmosphere in an open, airy restaurant serving traditional Chiapecan cookery. The *Café Avenida*, next to the *Hotel Avenida*, at Avenida Central 224, is an authentic Mexican coffeeshop, where old men sip black coffee to a background of *mariachi* music and slow service.

Listings

Airlines Aerocaribe ⓣ960/602-5651; Aviacsa ⓣ967/671-5246; Mexicana ⓣ960/602-5771. It's only a short taxi ride to the Aeropuerto Francisco Sarabia (approx US$7); if you're flying from the San Juan airport check with your airline about a *combi*.

Buses Cristóbal Colón, ADO and Maya de Oro buses all depart from the first-class station at the corner of Av 2 Nte Ote and C 2 Pte Nte; Rapidos del Sur (RdS), a good second-class line, is adjacent. Cristóbal Colón has frequent departures for San Cristóbal (15 daily; 2hr), some continuing to Comitán (7 daily; 4hr). Other destinations include Mexico City (7 daily; 16hr), Veracruz (2 daily; 11hr), Mérida (1 daily; 14hr), Cancún (2 daily; 18hr), and

Oaxaca (3 daily; 9hr). RdS serve the Chiapas coast of the other second-class terminals dotted around the city, the main one, at the junction of Av 3 Sur Ote and C 6 Ote Sur, is used by Autotransportes Tuxtla Gutiérrez (ATG), and serves San Cristóbal, Oaxaca, Villahermosa, Mérida and Palenque, and Cancún. Other local buses operate from the street outside.

Internet access Widely available, particularly along Av 2 Nte, and costs around US$0.80 per hour. MBI at C 2 Ote Nte 220, just off Av 2 Nte is open later than most, closing at midnight.

Travel agent Viajes Miramar, off the northeast corner of the zócalo at Av 1 Ote Nte 310 ⓣ961/612-3930.

Chiapa de Corzo and around

CHIAPA DE CORZO is an elegant little town overlooking the river, barely twenty minutes by bus east from Tuxtla. An important centre in pre-Classic times, this is the place where the oldest **Long Count date**, corresponding to December 7, 36 BC, has been found on a stele. The remaining ruins are on private land behind the Nestlé plant, beyond the far end of 21 de Octubre (see 000). To get to Chiapa, hop on one of the microbuses that leave every five minutes from the Transportes Chiapa–Tuxtla office at 3 Ote Sur and 3 Sur Ote in Tuxtla.

The most striking feature of the town is an amazingly elaborate sixteenth-century fountain, which dominates the plaza. Built of brick in the Mudéjar style, in the shape of the Spanish crown, the fountain is one of the most spectacular surviving early colonial monuments in Mexico – a tribute to the painstaking restoration. There are a couple of small museums: **Museo de Laca** (Tues–Sun 10m–5pm; free) on the second floor of the **Convento de Santo Domingo**, features the local painted and lacquered gourds, while **Casa Museo Ángel Albino Corzo** (daily 10am–2pm & 6–9pm; free) on the northwest side of the zócalo was the former residence of Ángel Albino Corzo, local and national reformer, after whom the town was named. Housing an interesting jumble of period furniture and local history, it features two cannons used in the so-called Pastry War against France in 1838. On the south side of the plaza, the huge tree bursting from its confines is **La Pochota**, a national monument to the suffering of the *indígenas* under the Spanish, and said to have been standing there when the town was founded in 1528.

There are two **hotels** in town: the centrally located *Los Angeles* (ⓣ961/616-0048; ④), on the southeast corner of the zócalo, which has small but comfortable en-suite rooms; and the newer, more upmarket **Hotel La Ceiba**, Domingo Ruíz 300 (ⓣ/ⓕ961/616-0389, ⓦwww.prodyweb.net.mx/hotellaceiba; ⑥), three blocks west from the plaza, which is very quiet and comfortable, with a/c rooms and a small pool. Several restaurants specialize in Chiapecan cuisine, including *El Campanario*, next to the municipal building on Avenida Coronel Urbina 5, and *Los Corredores* at the southwest corner of the plaza.

The ruins of Chiapa de Corzo

Strategically located on an ancient trade route high above the **Río Grijalva**, the ruins of **Chiapa de Corzo** comprise some two hundred structures scattered over a wide area of private property, shared among several different owners and sliced in two by the Panamerican Highway. This is the longest continually occupied site in Chiapas, beginning life as a farming settlement in the early pre-Classic period (1400–850 BC). By the late pre-Classic (450 BC–250 AD), it was the largest centre of population in the region, trading with all of Mesoamerica. What you see today are mainly low pyramids, walls, and courtyards.

To **get to the site** from town, take any microbus heading east, get off at the junction with Hidalgo and follow the signs. After about ten minutes, you'll come to an unmarked gate in a fence on the right; go to the house (officially closed Mon) and pay the US$1 **fee** to the family who farm among the ruins. **Walking**, it's about 3km northeast from the plaza in Chiapa de Corzo, passing the beautifully located sixteenth-century church ruin of **San Sebastián** on the way.

El Chorreadero, Tecpatán and Laguna Verde

Fourteen kilometres west of Chiapa de Corzo off the highway to Tuxtla, the 25-metre high **EL CHORREADERO** waterfall makes for a pleasant day-trip. The water cascades from a cave, filled with stalactites and stalagmites, down to the forest floor, where it forms a series of glistening pools, some of which are safe for swimming. Heading north along Hwy-195 you eventually reach the village of Soyaló, where Hwy-102 branches east towards **TECPATÁN**. A former Dominican covent, the sixteenth-century building is a fascinating blend of Mudéjar, Renaissance and Baroque styles with a Moorish tower, the only one of its kind in Mexico. Although partly ruined, the walls of the vestry still bear *ajaraca* decorations, a Moorish technique, and there are fantastic views of the surrounding countryside from the atrium. Just prior to Tecpatán, a road leads 10km or so northwest to **LAGUNA VERDE**, a jungle reserve and tourist centre. There's a restaurant, jungle trails, water-sports, swimming and horse-riding opportunities, and you can also stay in one of the thatched **cabañas** (❸).

Cañon del Sumidero

Driving east from Chiapa de Corzo towards San Cristóbal, you'll catch occasional glimpses of the lower reaches of the **Cañon del Sumidero**. Through this spectacular cleft the Río Grijalva runs beneath cliffs that in places reach almost 1000m in height. Another road running north from Chiapa de Corzo climbs rapidly, passing a series of miradors, in a national park that includes all the most scenic sections of the canyon. The best views are from the mirador known as La Coyota. There's no public transport (other than joining a tour), but to see at least the lower reaches you could take a "Km 4" *combi* from Tuxtla heading north along Calle 11 Ote Nte, past the Parque Madero, and get off at the turnaround point. From here, it's a 25-minute walk to the first mirador, **La Ceiba**, for stunning views of the canyon and river.

For better views still, take a **boat ride** through the canyon. Regular boat trips (7am–5pm; US$9.50 per person) run from Cahuaré, where the highway crosses the river, or Chiapa de Corzo. Trips last a couple of hours, passing several waterfalls including the remarkable El Árbol de Navidad, where bizarre calcareous formations covered with algae resemble a Christmas tree from a distance. Crocodiles are commonly seen here, as well as vast numbers of pelicans, egrets, and cormorants.

Bochil and Simojovel

Just beyond Chiapa de Corzo, Hwy-195 – winding spectacularly down to the Gulf plain – cuts off to the north. Few tourists take this route, since the Panamerican Highway continues to the far more enticing destination of San Cristóbal. The road climbs at first through mountains wreathed in cloud to **BOCHIL**, some 60km from Tuxtla, and if you have your own transport it makes an interesting stop on the route north to Villahermosa. Bochil is a pleasant small town, a centre for the **Tzotzil Maya**, and a good base from which to explore the surrounding hills and villages. Most people still wear the traditional dress, or *traje*: the women in white *huipiles* with red embroidery, pink ribbons in their hair, and dark blue skirts, and maybe a few men in the white smock and trousers rolled up to the knee. You'll be stared at, usually covertly, and, as always, should be *very* wary of **taking photographs**. There are a couple of simple **places to stay**, including the *Posada San Pedro* (no phone; ❷), whose basic rooms are set out around a courtyard on 1 Pte Nte, a block from the plaza: to get here, head for Banamex at the top of the plaza and turn right. For onward travel, Bochil has a frequent second-class **bus** service to Tuxtla, run by Autotransportes Tuxtla–Bochil.

Combis run regularly up the minor road to **SIMOJOVEL**, 40km away at the head of a spectacular valley, the source of most of the amber you'll find sold in local markets. Should you want **to stay**, the *Casa de Huéspedes Simojovel* (no phone; ❷) on Independencia, a block south of the plaza, has basic rooms round a flower-filled courtyard.

Jaltenango

Completely unused to visitors, the small town of **JALTENANGO**, the jumping-off point for the **Reserva de la Biosfera El Triunfo**, is just a three-hour bus ride south of Tuxtla. Also known as **Ángel Albino Corzo**, it lies at the junction of three rivers and is surrounded by coffee *fincas* on the slopes of the Sierra Madre de Chiapas. The highest peaks of the reserve, a refuge for Chiapas' tropical wildlife, are covered in dense **cloud forest**.

Of the three **hotels** here, the *Hotel Esperanza* (no phone; ❸), one block east of the plaza, is by far the best, with good clean, if basic rooms, comfortably furnished with fan; there are also a couple of basic **restaurants** and a bakery. Tracks lead up to the hills, and if you're a wildlife enthusiast you could easily spend a few days exploring the area, though to get the most out of a visit you need to camp and get the help of a local guide. Ask around at the hotels for where to find a guide. **Buses** leave Tuxtla several times a day from the Cuxtepeques y Anexas station at Calle 10 Ote and Avenida 3 Nte.

San Cristóbal de las Casas and around

Just 85km from Tuxtla Gutiérrez, **SAN CRISTÓBAL DE LAS CASAS** is almost 1700m higher – a cool place where low, whitewashed red-tiled houses huddled together on the plain give it an unrivalled provincial colonial charm. The town was designed as a Spanish stronghold among an often hostile indigenous population – the attack by Zapatista rebels in January 1994 was the latest in a long series of uprisings. It took the Spanish four years to pacify the area sufficiently to establish a town here in 1528. Officially named "Ciudad Real" (Royal City), it was more widely known as "Villaviciosa" (Evil City) for the oppressive exploitation exercised by its colonists. In 1544, Bartolomé de las Casas was appointed bishop, and he promptly took an energetic stance in defence of the native population, playing a similar role to that of Bishop Vasco de Quiroga in Pátzcuaro (see p.258). His name – added to that of the patron saint of the town – was held with something close to reverence by the *indígenas*. Throughout the colonial era, San Cristóbal was the capital of Chiapas, then administered as part of Guatemala, and it lost this rank in 1892 only as a result of its reluctance to accept the union with Mexico.

SAN CRISTÓBAL DE LAS CASAS

ACCOMMODATION

Barón de las Casas	J
Bungalows Posada Los Morales	Q
Casa Margarita	G
Casa Na Bolom	A
Ciudad Real	K
Don Quijote	F
Fray Bentos de las Casas	T
Parador Mexicanos	C
Posada Casa Blanca	N
Posada Casa Real	I
Posada Chilam Balam	R
Posada Diego de Mazariegos	E
Posada de Gladys	B
Posada Mayambé	H
Posada La Media Luna	P
Posada San Cristóbal	O
Real Jovel	V
Rincón del Arco	D
Santa Clara	L
Villa Real I and II	S & U
Youth Hostel/Albergue Juvenil	M

CAFÉS AND RESTAURANTS

Café El Kiosco	7
Café El Puente	8
Café Museo Café	6
Café San Cristóbal	12
Café La Terraza del Cerrillo	1
La Casa de Pan	2
Emiliano's Moustache	11
El Gato Gordo	10
Mandala Yam	3
Madre Tierra	15
El Mirador II	9
Normita	13
La Parrilla	4
El Teatro	5
Tuluc	14

Despite being the main focus of the Zapatista attack, the town was only occupied for thirty hours, and no tourists were harmed. Many, in fact, took advantage of the opportunity to be photographed with the rebels and San Cristóbal remains one of the most restful and enjoyable places in the republic to spend a few lazy days, its infrastructure catering mainly for its young, predominantly European visitors.

Despite a wealth of colonial churches and many interesting little museums to visit in San Cristóbal, the true pleasure lies in simply wandering the streets and absorbing the atmosphere, while it's also a great base for visiting nearby villages, buying inexpensive textiles, weavings and jewellery, and studying at one of the numerous Spanish-language schools.

Arrival and information

The road from Tuxtla Gutiérrez to San Cristóbal twists through the mountains and constantly climbs, breaking through the cloud into pine forests. First impressions of San Cristóbal itself, as the modern parts of the city sprawl unattractively along the highway, are not the best, but in the centre there is none of this unthinking development.

Whether you arrive by first- or second-class **bus**, you'll almost certainly be just off the Carretera Panamericana (Hwy-190) at the southern edge of town, though if you've arrived from Bochil, you'll be just north of the market area. For the centre, turn right out of the Cristóbal Colón **first-class terminal**, and it's seven blocks along Insurgentes to the plaza. There's no guardería at the bus station, but you can rent **lockers** at the Tienda El Paso, one block up Insurgentes on the left. Most **second-class** services stop along the Panamerican Highway on either side of Cristóbal Colón. The **airport** is 18km east of the town; a taxi into the centre costs US$10–15, while taxis within town cost US$1.50.

The helpful **state tourist office**, just off the southwest corner of the plaza at Hidalgo 1B (Mon–Fri 8am–8pm, Sat 9am–8pm, Sun 9am–2pm; ⓣ967/678-1467), is one of the best in the country, with good, free city maps, up-to-date lists of hotels in all price ranges, bus times, and event information. The staff know Chiapas well, and there's usually someone who speaks English. Free **listings** magazines with information on hotels, restaurants, and excursions are also usually available here. There are more bulletin boards in and around the **municipal tourist office** (Mon–Fri 8am–8pm, Sat 9am–3pm; ⓣ967/678-0665) in the Palacio Municipal, on the northeast corner of the zócalo. The excellent *Mapa Turístico de Chiapas* (1:400,000 scale, 1cm:4km) is available at most of the bookstores in town and some hotels, though not at the tourist offices.

Accommodation

Vast numbers of visitors and competition for business mean that San Cristóbal boasts some of the best-value **hotels** in Mexico. There are a few good places around the Cristóbal Colón terminal, but walking up Insurgentes to the plaza you'll pass more examples in all price ranges. Most of the best **budget options** are found in the streets east of the zócalo, particularly along Real de Guadalupe and in its vicinity. An ever-larger proportion of hotels here call themselves "**posadas**", and most live up to the convivial ambience this is presumably meant to convey, but it's always worth seeing your room before you pay. Even the most basic places now have hot water, though not necessarily all of the time. Nights can be pleasantly cool in summer, but cold in winter, so make sure there are enough blankets.

For **longer stays**, check out the many notice boards in the bus stations, language schools, and popular cafés, where you'll find rooms and even whole houses for rent. The closest official **campsite** is at *Rancho San Nicolás*, 2km east of the centre along the extension of Francisco León (ⓣ967/678-0057).

Barón de las Casas Belisario Domínguez 2 ⓣ/ⓕ 967/678-0881. Well-run, modern hotel one block east of the plaza. Each room has a TV and a spotless tiled bathroom with plenty of hot water. The owners speak English. ❹

Bungalows Posada Los Morales Ignacio Allende 17 ⓣ967/678-1472, ⓔpanchito-sc@hotmail.com. Whitewashed stone cabins each having a living room with fireplace, bathroom, and stove, and sprawling up the hillside garden four blocks west of the plaza. Wonderful views of the town. Some cabins are better-kept than others. ❹ with breakfast

Casa Margarita Real de Guadalupe 34 ⓣ967/678-0957. Long-standing budget favourite. Recently renovated to include some en-suite rooms, though the communal showers are clean and perfectly adequate. Good, inexpensive café in the blue-and-white tiled courtyard, and the more expensive restaurant (next door) has live music Wed–Sat. Good travel agency and luggage storage, too. ❸–❹ with bathroom

Casa Na-Bolom Vicente Guerrero 33 ⓣ/ⓕ 967/678-1418, ⓦwww.nobalom.org. Very comfortable rooms with fireplaces and private bathrooms around courtyards, and lovely private cottages in the tranquil gardens, all decorated with textiles, artefacts, and photos taken by Gertrude Blom in this famous museum and research centre (see p.665). Meals are served, using organically grown vegetables from the garden. ❻

Ciudad Real Plaza 31 de Marzo 10 ⓣ967/678-0464. Colonial mansion, superbly located overlooking the zócalo and popular with European tour groups. Most rooms rise above the covered courtyard (now a dining room, adorned with potted plants); quieter ones are at the back. Friendly, helpful staff, and rooms have cable TV, telephone, and room service, as you would expect for four-star prices. ❼

Don Quijote Cristóbal Colón 7, at Real de Guadalupe ⓣ967/678-0920, ⓦwww.hoteldonquijote.com.mx. Excellent-value hotel on a quiet street. Comfortable, well-lit, carpeted rooms with shower and constant hot water. The lobby is decorated with costumes from Chiapas villages collected by the owner, who speaks English and French. Free morning coffee. ❹

Fray Bentos de las Casas Niños Héroes 2, at Insurgentes ⓣ967/678-0932. Split into two sections, this hotel has an old part with more character, arranged around a pretty courtyard with a central fountain, though hot water is available only for three hours in the morning and three hours in the evening. The newer section has 24-hour hot water and TV, but lacks the same charm. ❹–❺

Parador Mexicanos 5 de Mayo 38 ⓣ/ⓕ 967/678-1515, ⓦwww.hparador.com.mx. Very reasonably priced option given the level of facilities, with 24 colourful and rustic en-suite rooms, restaurant, tennis court, and Internet access available to guests, as well as laundry and valet services. ❻

Posada Casa Blanca Insurgentes 63, no phone. A good budget option, in a convenient location just off the plaza. Rooms (some with private bathrooms) are basic but clean; shared showers have hot water. ❷

Posada Casa Real Real de Guadalupe 51 ⓣ967/678-1303. Large rooms with double beds, run by friendly Amparo Salazar. There's a *pila* for washing clothes on the sunny, flower-filled rooftop terrace. No private baths, but there is hot water. Price is 50 pesos per person, so very good value for singles. ❸

Posada Chilam Balam Niños Héroes 9 ⓣ967/678-4340. Very basic but as cheap as you'll find, run by the friendly Gutiérrez family. Single-storey red-tiled rooms are set around a courtyard, and there's a *pila* in the tiny garden. Mind your head on the way to the shared bathrooms. ❷

Posada de Gladys C Cintalapa 6-A ⓣ967/678-5775. A long way from the plaza and a little difficult to find at first, lost in a maze of little streets, this is a deservedly popular, well-run travellers' hangout with both dorm beds in small rooms (US$40 per person) and private rooms. The clean, tiled, shared bathrooms have hot water, and there's a communal area with TV and a kitchen for guests. ❸

Posada Diego de Mazariegos 5 de Febrero 1 ⓣ967/678-0833, ⓦwww.diegomazariegos.com.mx. San Cristóbal's top historic hotel, in two colonial buildings, on either side of General Utrilla. Spacious rooms – all featuring a fireplace, antique furniture, and beautifully tiled bathrooms – are arranged around attractive courtyards. Often busy with tour groups. ❼

Posada Mayambé Real de Guadalupe 66 ⓣ967/674-6278. Simple, but great-value rooms, plus kitchen and laundry facilities and a restaurant which serves Thai, Lebanese, and Indian food. Owners speak excellent English. ❸ including breakfast

Posada La Media Luna Felipe Flores 1 ⓣ/ⓕ 967/678-1658, ⓔpaint49@hotmail.com. Five simply but beautifully furnished rooms with bedside lights – some with private bath – around a shady courtyard. Run by artist Luciana Tamayo Lizama, who teaches art and Spanish, and also speaks French and English. Rates include breakfast. ❸–❹ with bath

Posada San Cristóbal Insurgentes 3 Ⓣ/Ⓕ967/678-6881. Charming wood-panelled three-star hotel with spacious rooms, *azulejo* bathrooms, excellent restaurant and leafy courtyard with fountain; the best value of the options around the plaza. ❺

Real Jovel Insurgentes 66 Ⓣ967/678-1668, Ⓔreal-jovel@hotmail.com. Adjacent to the Cristóbal Colón bus terminal and open into the early hours for late arrivals. Bright and airy rooms with tiled en-suite bathrooms. Good value. ❹

Rincón del Arco Ejército Nacional 66, at Vicente Guerrero Ⓣ967/678-1313, Ⓕ678-1568. Lovely, well-priced luxury hotel. The large rooms and suites, with antique furniture, fireplaces, and beautifully tiled bathrooms, are set around a courtyard or in delightful gardens. About 1km northeast from the plaza, it's just a block from *Casa Na-Bolom* and affords gorgeous views of the surrounding hills. Includes restaurant and parking. ❼

Santa Clara Insurgentes 1, corner of the plaza Ⓣ967/678-1140, Ⓕ678-1041, Ⓔhotelsantaclara@hotmail.com. A former colonial mansion, known locally as La Casa de la Sirena after the sixteenth-century carvings of a mermaid on the corners of the building. Rooms and suites surround a spacious, plant-filled patio and have antique furniture, and public areas are adorned with colonial artefacts. Facilities include a heated pool and good restaurant. ❻

Villa Real I and II two locations on Av Benito Juárez, 8 and 24-A I Ⓣ967/678-2930 & II Ⓣ967/678-4485. Comfortable, well-furnished, carpeted rooms all with private bathrooms, cable TV, and access to parking facilities. *Villa Real I* is the older but cheaper of the two. I ❹, II ❺

Youth Hostel/Albergue Juvenil Av Benito Juárez 2, near Madero Ⓣ967/678-7655, Ⓔyouth@sancristobal.com.mx. Offers dorm rooms of four beds (US$40 per person) and six beds (US$35 per person) as well as doubles. Not HI-affiliated. ❷

The City

In the centre, Plaza 31 de Marzo, usually referred to simply as *el parque*, is worth seeing, not so much for the relatively ordinary sixteenth-century cathedral (though it does have a nice *artesanado* ceiling and elaborate pulpit) as for some of the colonial mansions that surround it. The finest of the mansions is **La Casa de la Sirena**, now the *Hotel Santa Clara*, which was probably built by the Conquistador Andrés de la Tovilla in the mid-sixteenth century and has a very elaborate doorway around the corner on Insurgentes. In the middle of the plaza there's a bandstand and a café, which both provide piped music when no band is playing. For a full description of the city's colonial churches and monuments, pick up a copy of Richard Perry's excellent book *More Maya Missions: Exploring Colonial Chiapas* (see the bookstores listed on p.667). The most attractive new development in the centre is the **Andador Eclesiástico**, a tree-lined pedestrian walkway tiled with geometric designs, connecting the Templo del Carmen on Hidalgo, via the plaza, to Santo Domingo at the north end of 20 de Noviembre. From the plaza, Hidalgo leads south to the **Templo del Carmen**, by the Moorish-style (Mudéjar) tower and arch across the road, which once served as the gateway to the city. The church is not particularly inspiring architecturally, but you can pop in to see the adjoining cultural complex surrounding the peaceful formal gardens, with the **Casa de la Cultura** and **Instituto de Bellas Artes** (daily 9am–5pm). Considering the amount of artistic activity in and around San Cristóbal, these sights are pretty disappointing – especially since a serious fire in 1993 destroyed several eighteenth-century religious paintings – but sometimes there's an interesting temporary exhibition or concert on.

Santo Domingo

Santo Domingo, five blocks north of the plaza, is perhaps the most intrinsically interesting of San Cristóbal's churches. The complex was constructed between 1547 and 1551 and the church's lovely pinkish Baroque stucco facade combines Oaxacan and Guatemalan styles. Inside, it's huge and gilded

Local crafts

It's the local crafts and the indigenous way of life that draw visitors to San Cristóbal, an influx not always appreciated by the *indígenas* themselves. Nevertheless, the life of the town depends on the people from surrounding villages, who fill its streets and dominate its trade. Many of the sales people who set up shop around the market are *expulsados* – converts to evangelical Protestantism expelled by the village leaders and now living in shanties on the edge of town, unable to make a traditional living from farming. In an effort to eke out a living they have turned to craft-making, with tourists their main source of income.

The plaza in front of Santo Domingo church is filled with **craft stalls**, often the best place to buy souvenirs. Part of the former *convento* next door has been converted into a craft co-operative (**Sna Jolobil**) selling textiles and other village products. The quality here is generally good, but the prices higher than elsewhere. The Mercado de Artesanías y Dulces on Insurgentes is another good place to look for local crafts, although traders here are less willing to barter.

Other **crafts shops**, many specializing in amber and jade, are dotted around town, with the greatest concentration on Real de Guadalupe – those furthest from the plaza, like Artesanías Real at no. 44, and Artesanías Chiapanecas at no. 46C, are the best. La Pared (Ⓦwww.laparedmexico.com), on Hidalgo, which runs north from between the first- and second-class bus stations, also sells a very good selection of genuine, good-quality amber and silver jewellery at reasonable prices. A visit to Taller Leñateros, Flavio Paniagua 54, allows you to observe the fascinating process of making paper by hand from such diverse items as banana leaves, cornstalks, coconut fibre, and bamboo, mixed with waste paper and rags and coloured with natural dyes. The finished products are then printed with traditional indigenous and modern designs to become beautiful cards and notebooks. *Leñateros* is Spanish for "woodcutters" and many workers here formerly cut firewood from the pine forests surrounding San Cristóbal. Now, in addition to creative paper goods, they also produce *La jícara* (The Gourd) – a **literary magazine** in the folded-bark book design of a Maya codex; most of the original codices were destroyed by Spanish friars.

At the corner of Hidalgo and Niños Héroes, the **Tienda de los Artesanos de Chiapas** (Tues–Sun 9am–2pm & 5–8pm) is a state-sponsored venture that provides an outlet for Chiapas' textiles and crafts at fair prices. The weaving and embroidery exhibited here are as good as what you'll find in any museum.

everywhere, with a wonderfully ornate pulpit – see it in the evening, by the dim light of candles, and you can believe it's all solid gold. A block behind the church, in another part of the monastery, the **Museo Etnografía y Historia**, or Centro Cultural de los Altos de Chiapas (Tues–Sun 10am–5pm; US$3.20, free on Sun), tells the story of the city, with vivid painted portrayals of how the Indians fared under colonial rule. For scholars, the **library** at the rear is a fascinating place to study old books and records of Chiapas, and the gardens are a relaxing place to rest.

City museums

Three blocks west of the plaza, along Diego de Mazariegos, the **Museo del Ambar** (Tues–Sun 10am–2pm & 4–6pm; free; Ⓦwww.museodelambar.com.mx) is located in the former Convento de la Merced. The museum displays and sells authentic amber found in the Simojovel Valley. Amber was one of the most treasured decorative items in Maya society, valued both as a trade item and for its beauty and rarity. So, too was jade, something which can be found at the small **Museo del Jade** (Mon–Sat noon–8pm, Sun noon–6pm;

US$3), two blocks north of the plaza along 16 de Septiembre. Perhaps the most unusual of the city museums is the **Museo de Medicina Maya** (Mon–Sat 9am–6pm, Sun 9am–4pm; US$2), a long way north of the centre along 14 de Septiembre (taxi US$1.80). It offers a fascinating journey through the world of Mayan medicine, complete with medicinal plants growing in the gardens and a herbal pharmacy on site to dispense remedies.

The market

San Cristóbal's daily **market** lies beyond Santo Domingo along General Utrilla. It's an interesting place, if only because here you can observe indigenous life and custom without causing undue offence. What's on sale is mostly local produce and household goods, but you'll also find good tyre-soled leather *huaraches* and rough but warm sweaters, which you might well need. The market is far bigger than it first appears, so make sure you see it all; bear in mind that the main covered area is full of stomach-churningly vile butchers' stalls that are not for the faint-hearted. Wander through the market's other covered parts, including the section selling clothes, then up and down the hill behind.

Casa Na-Bolom

Behind Santo Domingo, Chiapa de Corzo leads east towards the **Casa Na-Bolom** at Vicente Guerrero 33, not only a private home and one of the best hotels in San Cristóbal (see p.662), but also a **museum and library** of local anthropology (library open daily 10am–2pm; free). This was the home of Danish explorer and anthropologist Frans Blom, who died in 1963, and his Swiss wife Gertrude (Duby), an anthropologist and photographer who died in 1993. Today it's renowned as a centre for the study of the region's indigenous cultures, particularly of the isolated Lacandón Maya, the "Hach Winik" (True People).

A tour of house, grounds, and **Museo Moxviquil** (daily 10am-5pm; tours in English or Spanish at 11.30am & 4.30pm; US$3.50, US$4.50 with tour), is the best way to learn about Na-Bolom and the story of its founders. The museum exhibits discoveries from the site of Moxviquil (see p.669) and explains the history and culture of the Chiapas highlands and the Lacandón forest. There's also a collection of items belonging to Frans Blom, including the detailed maps for which he is renowned. Beyond the main buildings, arranged around beautiful, flower-filled courtyards, is Na-Bolom's **garden**, lush with flowers and vegetables set among towering pine trees. After the tour, you can watch a film about the life of the Bloms and specific ecological, cultural, and political aspects of life in Chiapas, then stop by the small **café**, the *Jaguar Garden*, across the street from the entrance, set in a quiet garden. In one corner is a replica of a traditional house of the highlands, made with wooden walls covered with mud and a roof thatched with grass. There's also a **gift shop**, which sells the entrance tickets for the main museum.

The whole centre is overseen by the Asociación Cultural Na-Bolom, which arranges some small-scale volunteer cultural and agricultural projects, though you'll need to speak Spanish to participate; write or email for details – see the hotel review on p.662.

Guadalupe and San Cristóbal

Further afield, two churches dominate views of the town from their hilltop sites: **Guadalupe** to the east and **San Cristóbal** to the west. Neither offers a great deal architecturally, but the climbs are worth it for the views – San Cristóbal, especially, is at the top of a dauntingly long and steep flight of steps. Be warned, though, that women have been subjected to harassment at both of these relatively isolated spots (especially San Cristóbal): don't climb up here alone or after dark.

Eating and drinking

San Cristóbal has no lack of places to eat, with a huge variety of good **restaurants** in the streets immediately east of the zócalo, especially on Madero. Where the city really scores, however, is in lively places that cater to a disparate, somewhat bohemian crowd, made up of university and language-school students, a cosmopolitan expatriate population, and a constant stream of travellers. Many places are vaguely arty, with a coffee-house atmosphere and interesting menus that feature plenty of **vegetarian** options.

Cafés

Café El Kiosco in the zócalo. In a great location under the bandstand, where you can enjoy a coffee at the outdoor tables and watch the world go by.

Café El Puente Real de Guadalupe 55. Popular café serving inexpensive salads, soups, sandwiches, and cakes; also acts as a cultural centre, with Internet access, live music, lectures, film shows, and a good notice board. Closed Sun.

Café La Terraza del Cerrillo in the plaza on the hill behind the market. A great place to wind down after exploring the hustle and bustle of the market, with good coffee and light snacks.

Café Museo Café María Adelina Flores 10. Delicious coffee served in the café of a small museum, where the walls are adorned with beautiful illustrations depicting the history of the coffee trade in Mexico. The café also sells beans produced by a co-operative of local coffee producers (one of which you can visit – ask at the museum for information).

Café San Cristóbal Cuauhtémoc 2, near Insurgentes. Tiny old coffee house, subtly refurbished, and a popular spot to play chess and read the newspapers.

Restaurants

La Casa de Pan Dr Navarro 10. A superb range of vegetarian food and baked goods, made with locally grown organic ingredients and at very reasonable prices, are on offer here. A meeting place for expatriate aid-workers, and the owners are active in development projects for indigenous women and organic agriculture. Live music nightly, closed Mon.

Emiliano's Moustache Cresencio Rosas 7, near Cuauhtémoc. Vast range of authentic tacos – the *especial* is big enough for two – with some vegetarian chioces. Live music in the evening.

El Gato Gordo Madero 28. Inexpensive and deservedly popular backpacker place serving Mexican and international dishes with great-value specials. You can also read the newspapers, watch TV, and listen to music. Closed Tues.

Madre Tierra Insurgentes 19, opposite the Mercado de Artesanías. European-style restaurant in a colonial house with great, healthy food which includes homemade soup, salad, and pasta. The bakery and deli next door sell wholewheat bread and carrot cake until 8pm Mon–Sat. The upstairs terrace bar has good views of ancient walls and red-tiled roofs.

Mandala Yam Dr Navarro 1. Funky and colourful vegetarian restaurant with outdoor seating and a wide selection of tacos, salads, tortas, and full meals. Weekly programme of events includes live music and cinema shows. Closed Mon.

El Mirador II Madero 16. The best cheap Mexican restaurant on Madero, with good tortas and comidas corridas for US$3.

Normita corner of Juárez and José Flores. A great little restaurant, serving Jaliscan specialities and inexpensive breakfasts.

La Paloma Hidalgo 3, just south of the zócalo. Sophisticated restaurant in La Galería cultural centre, where international food is served in the refined atmosphere of an art-filled colonial mansion. Live music most evenings.

La Parrilla corner Belisario Domínguez and Dr Navarro, on a tiny square adjacent to *La Casa de Pan*. Specializing in grilled meats, including *alambres al queso*, similar to a kebab with melted cheese. Sit on one of the saddles used as bar stools to enjoy the atmosphere and great views. Closed Mon.

El Teatro 1 de Marzo 8 ☎967/678-3149. Superb, moderately priced French and Italian food. Boasts the only rooftop dining area in San Cristóbal – definitely the best place to enjoy the sunset as you eat. French and English spoken.

Tuluc Insurgentes 5. Justifiably popular, with a good comida corrida and dinner specials. This is the first place in town to open in the morning (6.30am), ideal if you have to catch an early bus.

Nightlife

Many of the cafés and bars host **live music** in the evenings, usually salsa or Latin, and only rarely impose a cover charge. *La Creación* on 1 de Marzo near 5 de Mayo has a DJ on weeknights and live jazz at weekends, while *Latinos* at the corner of Madero and Juárez plays a variety of music from salsa and reggae to jazz and rock. *Tequila Zoo Mariachi Bar* on General Utrilla, one block from the plaza, has more than a hundred varieties of tequila and screens frequently hilarious *mariachi* music videos. The only real disco in town is *Palacia Olimpio Club* (Ⓣ967/678 2230; Thurs–Sat) a long eight blocks south of the zócalo along Cresencio Rosas.

Listings

Banks and exchange Several bank branches (with ATMs) surround the zócalo; most will exchange dollars and give cash advances (mornings only). You'll get much quicker exchange, however, at good rates from Casa de Cambio Lacantún, Real de Guadalupe 12 (Mon–Sat 8am–2pm & 4–8pm, Sun 9am–1pm); they change most major currencies and also usually have Guatemalan quetzales.

Bike rental An enjoyable way to get out to the surrounding villages. Best rental is at Los Pinguinos, 5 de Mayo 10B (Ⓣ967/678-0202). Well-maintained bikes for about US$2 per hour, US$8 per day, and takes tours to local attractions. German and English spoken.

Bookstores Librería Chilam Balam, on General Utrilla near Dr Navarro, has a wide selection, including academic and educational books; also guides and topographic maps of Chiapas. Librería La Pared, Hidalgo 2, opposite the tourist office, has new guidebooks (including *Rough Guides*) and the largest selection of new and secondhand books in English and other languages in southern Mexico; you can rent, trade or buy books. Accepts Visa and MasterCard. Other useful bookstores are Librería Soluna, Real de Guadalupe 13B, with a fair choice of books, including guides, and Casa Na-Bolom, Vicente Guerrero 33, which has an excellent library (daily 10am–2pm; free) and sells some books and maps of the Lacandón forest.

Buses You can get directly to most destinations in the state and throughout the Yucatán; the tourist office (see p.661) maintains accurate and up-to-date timetables. Ticket queues are long, so buy them in advance; TRF (across the highway), running first- and second-class buses to most main destinations, often has faster queues. Tuxtla Gutiérrez (2hr) is served frequently by most companies, and in addition *combis* tout for customers outside the bus stations on the Carretera Panamericana. Villahermosa (2 daily; 7hr) is not so well served, though there are a few first-class services daily with Cristóbal Colón; it's easier to get any bus to Tuxtla and change there. For Palenque (9 daily; 5hr), there are plenty of first- and second-class departures, day or night. All buses going to Palenque call at Ocosingo (2hr 30min), and in addition there's ample passenger-van traffic: just go to the highway and someone will call out to you. Cristóbal Colón has the best service to Ciudad Cuauhtémoc (3hr 30min; all via Comitán; 2hr) on the Guatemalan border, and on the highway you'll also find any number of *combis* to Comitán. For Oaxaca (12hr) there are two overnight services at 5pm and 10pm; other departures are from Tuxtla. The first-class companies all have several daily overnight services to Mexico City (5 daily; 19hr). For Campeche (1 daily; 10hr) and Mérida (1 daily; 13hr), there's a first-class service at 5.30pm. For the Yucatán coast, Maya de Oro has a luxury service at 4.30pm, calling at Chetumal (10hr; for Belize), Playa del Carmen (14hr), Tulum (15hr), and Cancún (16hr).

Flights Currently there is only one daily flight from San Cristóbal on Aeromar to Mexico City at 1.25pm.

Immigration office Ⓣ967/678-7910. The office itself (Mon–Fri 9am–3pm) is a couple of kilometres west of the centre, at the junction of the Carretera Panamericana and Diagonal Centenario – best get a taxi.

Internet access It's scarcely possible to walk a block in the centre without coming across a place with Internet access. Most close around 10pm and the price is usually US$0.60 to US$0.80 per hour.

Language courses Centro Bilingüe, in Centro Cultural El Puente, Real de Guadalupe 55 (Ⓣ/Ⓕ 967/678-3723, Ⓦwww.sancristobalya.com/elpuente), is the longest-established language school in San Cristóbal. Instituto Jovel, María Adelina Flores 21 (Ⓣ/Ⓕ 967/678-4069, Ⓦwww.institutojovel.com), is newer but very highly recommended and gives a personal service. Both offer Spanish courses at various levels, and can arrange accommodation with local families.

Laundry Lava Sec, Cresencio Rosas 12; Lavorama, Guadalupe Victoria 20A; Lavandaría Mixtli, corner of 1 de Marzo and 16 de Septiembre; and many more, particularly along Real de Guadalupe and Domínguez.

Phones Librería La Pared, Hidalgo 2, across from the tourist office, has the cheapest long-distance and international rates at under US$0.80 per minute to North America, Europe, and Japan. There are Ladatel phones on the plaza, under the arches of the Palacio Municipal, and in the Cristóbal Colón terminal, but you need a phonecard to operate them.

Post office At the corner of Ignacio Allende and Diego Mazariegos three blocks southwest of the zócalo (Mon–Fri 8.30am–7pm, Sat 9am–1pm); in addition, most hotels have Mexipost boxes, and many of the larger ones sell stamps.

Travel and tour agencies San Cristóbal has dozens of tour agencies, most doing the same four standard tours to local villages, the Sumidero Canyon, Lagos Montebello, and Palenque. Easily the best horse-riding tours are provided by English-speaking Marcos Ruíz (Ⓣ967/698273; US$10). Call or turn up at the *Café del Centro* on Real de Guadalupe at 9am, where you're sure to find him. One of the best local tour agencies is Navarra, Real de Guadalupe 15D (Ⓣ967/678-1143, Ⓦwww.mundomaya.com.mx/tours). The best agent for international and domestic air tickets is Santa Ana Tours, Madero 9-A (Ⓣ967/678-0422). For local and national adventure tours try Viajes Pakal, Cuauhtémoc 6 (Ⓣ967/678-2818, Ⓔpakal@sancristobal.podernet.com.mx). City tours are organized by El Coleto (US$3), a bus-like contraption which leaves when required 10am–1pm and 4–7pm from outside the Mercado de Artesanías on Insurgentes.

Around San Cristóbal: Grutas de Rancho Nuevo, El Arcotete and Moxviquil

Some organized outings go to the popular **GRUTAS DE RANCHO NUEVO** (daily 9am–5.30pm; US$1), an enormous cavern extending deep into a mountain about 10km to the southeast of San Cristóbal. It's easy enough to visit it by bus or bike, though, since they're well signed, just off the main road to Comitán. A track leads for about 1km from the road through a pine-forested park with hiking trails often used by the army. By **bike**, it's about a fifty-minute ride, uphill most of the way from San Cristóbal. There's an average restaurant here for refreshment and you can hire

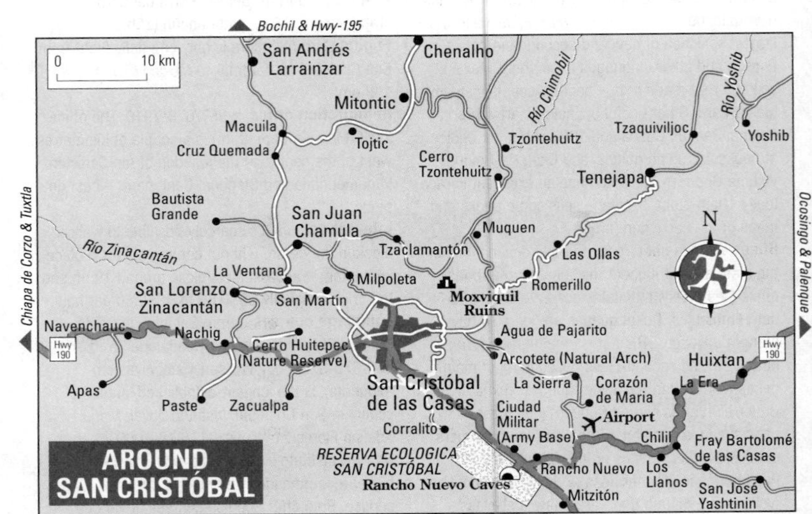

horses for US$5 per hour. Although the cave system is quite extensive, only 1km of pathway is open to the public.

Another favourite trip is to **EL ARCOTETE**, a large, natural limestone arch that forms a bridge over a river. To get there, follow Real de Guadalupe out of town, past the Guadalupe church, where it then becomes the road to Tenejapa; El Arcotete is down a signed track to the right about 3.5km past the church.

MOXVIQUIL, a completely deserted, ruined ancient site, is a pleasant excursion of a few hours on foot from San Cristóbal; it's best, however, to study the plans at the *Casa Na-Bolom* first (see p.665), as all you can see when you get there are piles of rough limestone. To reach the site, find Avenida Yajalon, a few blocks east of Santo Domingo, and follow it north to the end (about 30min) at the foot of tree-covered hills, in a little settlement called Ojo de Agua. Head for the highest buildings you can see, that is, two timber shacks with red roofs. The tracks are at times indistinct as you clamber over the rocks, but after about 300m a lovely side valley opens up on your left which is suitable for camping. The main path veers gradually to the right, becoming quite wide and leading up through a high basin ringed by pine forest. After 3km you reach the village of Pozeula; the ruins are ahead of you across a valley, built on top of and into the sides of a hill.

Chamula and Zinacantán

Despite the growing number of organized tours to the villages of **SAN JUAN CHAMULA** and **SAN LORENZO DE ZINACANTÁN**, visits should still be treated with extreme sensitivity. Ask permission before taking photographs (be willing to pay for the privilege) and certainly never do so inside the churches. Be careful about what you wear and don't wear native clothing – it may have some meaning or badge of rank for the people you are visiting.

If you do not intend to take a tour (though one is recommended), the best time to make your visit is on a Sunday (market day) or during a **fiesta** when the villages are full of life. Chamula in particular has a very small permanent population, with many families driven out and forced to live in poverty for abandoning the traditional religion in favour of evangelical Protestantism. Should you opt to visit other villages in the vicinity, be aware that your presence may not be welcomed by everyone. Be extra courteous and find out as much as you can about practices, customs, and behavioural codes before visiting. It may also help to learn a few words of the native language. Villages to the west of San Cristóbal are generally **Tzotzil**-speaking, and those to the east speak **Tzetzal**, but each village has developed its own identity in terms of costume, crafts, and linguistics. Phonetic pronunciations of some simple words are given below.

Useful words in Tzotzil and Tzetzal

	Tzotzil	Tzetzal
To ask permission	Chíkhelav	Ya shka shan
Hello	Kúshee	Bish chee
Goodbye	Batkun	Bónish
Please	Avokoluk	Há wokolook
Thank you	Kalaval	Wókolawal
Sorry/Excuse me	Tsik bunjoomul	Pasbón
Yes	Chabal	Heech
No	Moo yuk	Ho'o

Transport and tours

Inexpensive *combis* leave frequently for Chamula and Zinacantán, less often but still several times a day for other villages, from the end of Utrilla, just north of the market in San Cristóbal. It's usually easier, more informative, and perhaps less culturally invasive to take an **organized tour** (US$15 per person), and countless tour companies, many located along Real de Guadalupe, will be queuing up for the privilege of taking you. Tours depart at 9.30am, taking in both villages and returning to San Cristóbal around 1.30pm (see "Listings", p.668, for recommendations). There is often little difference between companies and prices are standardized, though few have English-speaking guides. Marcos Ruíz (see "Listings", p.668) is the best of the local guides, a real character with an in-depth knowledge of the area and excellent English.

San Juan Chamula

SAN JUAN CHAMULA (usually referred to as just Chamula) is the closest of the villages to San Cristóbal and the most frequently visited. Traditional practices just about hang on here, especially in religion, and a visit to the **church** can be a humbling and moving experience. Before you enter, buy a ticket (US$1) from the "tourist office" in the Palacio Municipal to the right-hand side of the plaza as you face the church. The inside is glorious, with the floor covered with pine needles and the light of a thousand candles casting an eerie glow. Lining the walls are statues of the saints adorned with offerings of clothes, food, and mirrors, while above the altar, San Juan, patron saint of the village, takes pride of place. The rituals practised inside the church, incorporating aspects of Christian and Mayan practises, are unique – each villager prays by clearing an area of pine needles and arranging a "message" in candles, and rituals frequently involve tearful chanting and/or singing.

During the annual Kinta Jimultik, the **carnival** (Fri–Tues on the last weekend in February), representatives of all the villages in the county attend in traditional dress, marching in circles around the church and up to strategically placed crosses on the hillsides. On the final day, which coincides with the last of the five ill-fated days of the Mayan calendar, purification rites and fire-walking ceremonies take place.

Admission to the church also grants entry into the **Museo Etnográfico** (daily 8am–7pm) behind the palacio. Thatched rooms with mud and straw walls display artefacts of village life, musical instruments, and costumes from Chamula and other villages. Remember that taking **photographs** is expressly forbidden and no foreign visitors are admitted to the church after 7pm.

San Lorenzo Zinacantán

Just an easy 7km walk from Chamula and surrounded by steep, pine-forested hills, **ZINACANTÁN** is much more open than its neighbour. Far more Western in their outlook, the locals here have embraced flower farming as an export crop and the hillsides are dotted with greenhouses. Still, traditional practices have not completely disappeared. Some older men still wear the rose-pink ponchos with silver threads (called *pok 'ul*), decorated with tassels and embroidered flowers, and the same colours and designs feature in the women's costumes. Tours include a visit to a typical house, where you'll see the family altar, women weaving beautiful table mats decorated with large embroidered flowers, and the house fire where tortillas are prepared. Zinacantán also has a **museum**, the Museo Ik'al Ojov ("Our Great Lord"), which has displays of costumes from different hierarchical groups and a tableau of a house interior (daily 8am–6pm; donation).

San Cristóbal to Guatemala: Comitán and Montebello

Beyond San Cristóbal, the Panamerican Highway continues to the border through some of Chiapas' most scintillating scenery. On the way it passes through **Amatenango del Valle**, a Tzeltal-speaking village with a reputation for good unglazed pottery and a favourite stop for tour companies. Here, the pottery is prepared by the traditional pre-Hispanic method of building the fire around the piece, rather than placing it into an oven. **Comitán de Domínguez** (or just Comitán) is the only place of any size in this area – a jumping-off point not only for the **Guatemalan border** and for the **Lagos de Montebello National Park**, but for the Classic-period Maya site of **Tenam Puente**.

Comitán

One of the most beautiful towns in Chiapas, **COMITÁN** is spectacularly poised on a rocky hillside and surrounded by countryside in which wild orchids bloom. Once a major Maya population centre (the ruins of Bonampak and Yaxchilán, even Palenque, are not far away as the parrot flies across the jungle), Comitán was originally a Maya town known as Balún Canán (Nine Stars, or Guardians), renamed Comitán (Place of Potters in Nauhatl) when it came under Aztec control. The final place of any note before the border (Ciudad Cuauhtémoc is no more than a customs and immigration post with a collection of shacks), today Comitán is a market and supply centre for the surrounding agricultural area, a good place to rest if you've some hard travelling through the Lacandón forest or into Guatemala ahead of you.

The gateway to Comitán is marked by a statue of Dr Belisario Domínguez, the city's most important historical figure, and as you pass through, several more statues representing aspects of life of the various states of Mexico are placed at intervals along the central reservation.

Arrival and information

From Comitán's **airport**, a few kilometres south of town, a taxi into town runs about US$7. **Buses** stop along the Panamerican Highway, a long six or seven blocks from the centre. Only Cristóbal Colón has a terminal (with guardería); all the others just pull in at the roadside. To walk to the centre, turn left out of the terminal, cross the highway, then go right along Calle 1 Sur Pte after about three blocks. The zócalo is a further seven blocks east. **Taxis** are easy to find and any journey within the city boundaries costs US$1.50. To come to grips with the town's confusing layout, pick up a map from the **tourist office** (Mon–Fri 8am–7pm, Sat 8am–4pm; ⓣ963/632-4047), located on the east side of the plaza at no. 6, just along from the Palacio Municipal. If you are moving on to Guatemala and need a visa, the **Guatemalan consulate** is at the corner of Calle 1 Sur Pte and Avenida 2 Pte Sur, a couple of blocks southwest of the zócalo (Mon–Fri 8am–4.30pm; ⓣ/ⓕ963/632-2979).

Accommodation

Comitán has plenty of good-value **hotels** in all price ranges and those listed below are close to the centre. The cheapest places are just west of the zócalo, but of varying standards; we've noted the best below. Nights here are much cooler than days, so you'll need at least one blanket.

Hospedaje Montebello C 1 Nte Pte 10, a block northwest of the plaza ⓣ963/632-3572. The best of the budget options in this area. Large, clean rooms are set around a courtyard, some with private bath (US$1 extra per person), and the communal shower is really hot. Clothes-washing facilities available. ❸

Hospedaje San Francisco Av 1 Ote Nte 13 ⓣ963/632-0194, ⓔsamuel22f@prodigy.net.mx. A good-value budget option with en-suite bathrooms and some rooms with TV. Rooms on the front courtyard are bigger and brighter. ❸

Hotel Internacional Av Central Sur 16 ⓣ/ⓕ963/632-0110. Recently renovated, this is an attractive modern hotel with comfortable rooms, cable TV, and a good restaurant (*Girasoles*). ❺

Pensión Delfín Av Central Sur 21A, right on the plaza ⓣ963/632-0013. Pleasant, colourful, and spacious with large en-suite rooms and cable TV. There's safe parking and a quiet, flowery courtyard at the back. ❹

Posada El Castellano C 3 Nte Pte 12, a couple of blocks north of the plaza ⓣ963/632-3347, ⓕ632-0117. Friendly and rustic option, with a quiet courtyard containing a fountain and flower-filled horse cart. En-suite rooms come with telephone and cable TV, and there's a very good restaurant. ❺

Posada del Virrey Av Central Nte 13 ⓣ963/632-1811, ⓕ632-4483. This attractive colonial hotel has bright rooms with en-suite bathroom, laundry service, and cable TV. ❺

The Town

Comitán's spacious, highly manicured **zócalo** is arranged on several levels around a central bandstand. Surrounding it are a number of beautiful colonial buildings, notably the whitewashed **Palacio Municipal** which dominates the north side, and the Mudéjar **Templo Santo Domingo** to the east. The *portales* on the south side, painted in an attractive orange-and-brown style, are teeming with souvenir shops, while to the east several restaurants have tables under the arches. On the plaza's southeast corner, the stone **Casa de Cultura** (Mon–Fri 9am–7pm; free) has a pretty courtyard featuring a mural depicting the city's history. There are also exhibits in the building tracing local history, and several craft co-operatives operate from within here. On the same block, just off the plaza, the splendid little **Museo de Arqueología** (Tues–Sun 10am–5pm; free) offers a well-presented chronology of local Maya sites, through displays of jewellery and pottery, as well as some children's skulls deliberately deformed for ceremonial purposes. One block south of the zócalo, along Avenida Central Sur, is the best of the city's museums: the **Casa Museo**

Belisario Domínguez (Tues–Sat 10am–6.45pm, Sun 9am–1pm; US$0.50), housed in the former home of the local doctor and politician who was assassinated in 1913 for his outspoken opposition to Huerta's usurpation of the presidency. Most interesting is the pharmacy, its shelves lined with diverse lotions and potions, where he would administer free treatment to the poor. A block further south, the **Museo de Arte Hermíla Domínguez de Castellanos** (Mon–Sat 10am–6pm; US$0.20) is named after his wife, and houses a handsome collection of largely modern art by Mexican artists, many of them strikingly colourful and vibrant. Just around the corner, the domed **Templo de San José**, skirted with blue and gold, is the most unusual of the city's churches. Also worth seeking out is the Neoclassical **Templo de San Caralampio**, two blocks east of the plaza along Calle 1 Nte Pte, dedicated to a martyr who became an object of devotion after cholera and smallpox epidemics decimated the town in the nineteenth century. A fiesta in his name is celebrated in mid-February.

Eating and drinking

Apart from in the hotels, most of the best **places to eat** in Comitán are on the plaza. For really good-value Mexican food served in clean surroundings, try *Helen's Enrique*, which has tables under the arches, or *La Apujarra* for great pizzas and *licuados*, both on the west side. The *Café Quiptic*, on the east side next to the Casa de Cultura, serves hearty breakfasts, with very good coffee. Try the *desayuno Chiapanesco,* a spicy breakfast of tamales. The **market**, one block east of the zócalo, is filled with fruit stands and has some very good *comedores*. Finally, if you drink alcohol you should try **Comiteco**, a rich-tasting local spirit that's virtually unobtainable elsewhere. It's made from agave, like tequila, but is smoother and a good deal cheaper.

Nightlife

Comitán has a lively **nightlife** scene, with disco bars dotted around town, most of which play the standard mix of Latino pop, salsa, and Latino dance music. Among the more popular spots are the high-decibel *La Gum*, one block west of the main highway along Calle Central Pte, and the equally boisterous *Oxigeno*, a block south of the zócalo. *Jarra*, two blocks northwest of the plaza along Calle 1 Nte Pte, transforms from a quiet coffee bar during the day into a rock hangout at night.

Listings

Banks Bancomer, on the zócalo, is useful for currency exchange and dollar cash advances, and also has an ATM.

Buses Plenty of first- and second-class buses and *combis* leave from along the main highway to Ciudad Cuauhtémoc for the border, and San Cristóbal and Tuxtla to the west. For the Lagos de Montebello and the Frontier Highway, buses or *combis* run by Transportes Lagos de Montebello leave about every fifteen minutes from their terminal on Av 2 Pte Sur, between calles 2 and 3 Sur, about three blocks southwest of the plaza. Otherwise, you can just wait for one to come along on the highway heading south and flag it down.

Internet access Widely available throughout the city. Ciber@dicto (daily 9am–9pm; US$1 per hour), down the pedestrianized Pasaje Morales 13 on the north side of the plaza, has a fast connection, but there are plenty of other options on and around the plaza, including the clothes shop Mundo on the south side, where access is only US$0.50 per hour.

Post office One and a half blocks south of the zócalo on Central Sur (Mon–Fri 9am–3pm). If you're a little late look for the side door, which stays open until 3.30pm.

Travel agents Viajes Tenam, Pasaje Morales 8A (☎963/632-1654), can arrange domestic and international flights, as well as organize day-trips to local attractions.

The ruins of Junchavín and Tenam Puente

At the time of writing, visiting the Maya site of **Junchavín** (daily 8am–5pm; free), 45 minutes' walk northwest from Comitán's zócalo, was *not* recommended. Due to an ownership dispute, there is no security at the site and several tourists have been the victims of violent attacks. The site does remain open to visitors – check with staff at the Museo de Arqueológico for an honest appraisal of the current situation. Should you wish to visit, follow Avenida Central Nte for about 2km until you reach the church of Santa Teresita on the right, recognizable by its two tall bell towers. The road immediately past the church to the right, signposted **Quija** (and plied by *combis*), will lead you out of town into hilly farming country. The entrance to the site is on the left after 1500m. Hundreds of steps lead up to a small flat-topped pyramid about 5m high, flanked by two smaller structures. Views are superb from here, and it is said you can see Chinkultic, 45km to the southeast.

Tenam Puente (daily 9am–4pm; free) is a much larger site, 14km south of Comitán. A bus leaves for the *ejido* of Francisco Sarabia from 3 Ote Nte in Comitán at 8.30am, but any bus heading south passes the junction for the turn-off at Km 181, from where it is 3km to the village and a further 2km to the ruins. A path leads up beside the guard's hut, opening up into a meadow with a huge stone terrace. The site, discovered by Frans Blom in 1925, marks a settlement which was at its peak from 600 AD to 900 AD and finally abandoned around 1200 AD. The most important group of ruins, the acropolis, has three ball-courts and a twenty-metre-high pyramid that affords magnificent views of the Comitán valley. To get to it, keep climbing the stone terraces until you reach the highest point.

Comitán to Lagos de Montebello

The **Parque Nacional Lagos de Montebello** stretches along the border with Guatemala down to the southeast of Comitán, beautiful wooded country in which there are more than fifty lakes, sixteen of them very large. You could see quite a bit of the park in a long day-trip – buses cover the route all day from 5am, with the last bus leaving the park entrance around 7.30pm – but to really enjoy the scenic lakes and forest, and to visit the small but spectacular **ruins of Chinkultic**, you're better off staying in or near the park.

The road leading to the national park turns off the Panamerican Highway 16km from Comitán at the village of La Trinitaria, from where the park entrance is a further 36km. Once in the park this road becomes the **Carretera Fronteriza** – the Frontier Highway – roughly following the line of the Guatemalan border and paved all the way to Palenque. Transportes Lagos de Montebello **buses** from Comitán cover the whole route in about ten hours, and you can visit Bonampak and Yaxchilán (see p.688 and p.690) on the way. In the recent past, there were frequent **army checkpoints** along this road and you may still be asked for your passport at any time. The soldiers are invariably polite but make sure your tourist card is valid.

The road to the Parque Nacional Lagos de Montebello

The most comfortable of the several **places to stay** along the road to the park is the *Parador Museo Santa María*, 22km from the La Trinitaria junction, then 2km along a dirt track on the right (Ⓣ/Ⓕ967/678-0988; ❻). A former hacienda, it's a lovely place furnished with antiques and oil paintings and steeped in period atmosphere. There's hot water and electricity but rooms are also lit with oil lamps. A small chapel in the grounds is filled with religious paintings and other ecclesiastical works of art dating from the seventeenth century.

At Km 31 on the same road, a two-kilometre track leads off to the left to the Classic-period Maya ruins of **CHINKULTIC** (daily 9am–5pm; US$4). So far only a relatively small proportion of the site has been cleared and restored, but it's well worth a visit if only for the dramatic setting. Climb the first large mound, and you're rewarded with a view of a small lake, with fields of maize beyond and forested mountain ridges in the background. Birds, butterflies, and dragonflies abound, and small lizards dart at every step. A ball-court and several stelae have been uncovered, but the highlight is undoubtedly the view from the top of the tallest structure, **El Mirador**. Set on top of a steep hill, with rugged cliffs dropping straight down to a cenote, the temple occupies a commanding position; though peaceful now, this was clearly an important hub in ancient times.

You'll find a cluster of **budget accommodation** on the left-hand side at Km 32 – buses and *combis* will stop right outside – though note that none currently has phones. First, just a kilometre or so past the turning for Chinkultic (see p.675), there's the *Hospedaje and Restaurant La Orquídea* (❷), better known simply as *Doña María's*. Here, half a dozen simple cabins with electric light and very basic, shared cold showers are set among the pines. It's a very friendly place, run by Doña María Domínguez, who gave a lot of help to the Guatemalan refugees who fled the massacres across the border in the 1980s. Next door, and a step above in comfort, *Pino Feliz* (❸) has eight rooms in wooden cabins with shared, hot-water showers. Owner Roberta Alborres cooks good, simple meals and César Castellanos can guide you on foot or on horseback to lakes and caves you'd never find on your own.

The Parque Nacional Lagos de Montebello

The park entrance is at Km 36 (daily 9am–5pm; US$1 per person), but most *combis* terminate a few kilometres beyond the entrance at the **park headquarters**. The combination of pine forest and lakes is reminiscent of Scotland or Maine, with miles of hiking potential; for the less energetic, roadside viewpoints provide glimpses of many of the lakes, lent different tints by natural mineral deposits and the angle of the sun. The lakes themselves are actually a series of cenotes (sinkholes) formed by the erosion of limestone over millions of years. From the park entrance, the left-hand fork takes you past several smaller lakes to the end of the tarmac at **Laguna Bosque Azul**. From here two dirt tracks continue on, the left one leading down to a bridge signposted "Paso de Soldado" after a few hundred metres. To the right of this track just before the bridge, a path marked "Sendero de Grutas" heads into the jungle through an exquisitely forested gorge, under a massive limestone arch, and disappears into a cave in the cliff face. Back on the main track again, you can cross the bridge and climb the hill to the **restaurant** *Bosque Azul*. It is open only sporadically, but you can rent a very basic **cabaña** here (no phone; US$50 per person) or hire scrawny horses for US$10 per person.

Follow the right-hand fork from the park entrance to **Laguna Tziscao**, 8km on, where there is a tiny settlement. On the lake's edge the *Restaurant Tziscao* rents simple wooden **cabañas** (Ⓣ963/633-5244; US$75 per person), while *balsas* (**rafts**) are available to rent at most lakes from around US$40 per hour. The road continues on to **Laguna Internacional** where a white obelisk at either end of the lake marks the border with Guatemala. It is, however, not recommended that you try to cross the border here. In the opposite direction the Frontier Highway, served by buses from Comitán, winds through mountains with spectacular views and precipitous drops on its way around the border to Palenque.

The Frontier Highway east: Montes Azules Biosphere Reserve

The largest settlement along the road is **Las Maravillas de Tenejapa**, a pretty village with a restaurant but no accommodation, about two hours from Lake Tziscao. Beyond here the road climbs a steep limestone ridge and passes through an impressive tunnel before dropping down to the village of **Ixcán**, at the confluence of the Ixcán and Jataté rivers; downstream of here they form the Río Lacatún. A tourism project here, *Estación Ixcán* (Ⓦwww.ixcan.com.mx), enables you to visit the southern **Montes Azules Biosphere Reserve**, the largest remaining tract of rainforest in Chiapas. The brainchild of US-based Conservation International, it aims to promote conservation by developing economic alternatives to cutting down the forest. The *Estación* is beautifully located on the far bank of the Río Jataté, above some rapids in the turquoise river. **Accommodation** (❻) is in screened, shared-bath rooms (some with balcony) in a large thatched building and there's also limited space for **camping** (❷). Meals are taken in the unscreened dining room overlooking the river – and you'll be swatting insects as you eat. Local guides can take you along the impressive, jungle-lined rivers and show you the forest wildlife. Though you could just turn up in Ixcán and find a boat to take you downstream from the village (ask for Don Oscar, who heads the tourism committee), it's best to book ahead through the office in Tuxtla (Ⓣ/Ⓕ 961/613-9776, Ⓔreservaciones@ixcan.com.mx).

Beyond Ixcán the highway crosses the Río Ixcán on a new bridge high above the river and continues to **Benemérito** (3hr; see p.691), for Bonampak, Yaxchilán and **Palenque** (a further four hours). Be aware that this route traverses the "conflict zone" (see p.643) where the Zapatistas, paramilitaries and the Mexican army have been engaged in guerrilla warfare: you may well be stopped by any of them and questioned about your intentions.

Ciudad Cuauhtémoc and the Guatemalan border

A visit to the Lagos de Montebello is a good introduction to the landscapes of Guatemala, but if you want to see the real thing up close, it's only another 60km or so from the La Trinitaria junction (served by plenty of passing buses) to the **Mexican border post** at **CIUDAD CUAUHTÉMOC**. There's nothing here but a few houses, the immigration post, a restaurant, and the Cristóbal Colón bus station; the two hotels are not recommended.

The **Guatemalan border post** is at **La Mesilla**, a three-kilometre taxi ride away (about US$3). As always, the crossing is best attempted in daylight and you may not be able to get your passport stamped after 8pm. La Mesilla border post has been one of the worst in the country for exacting illegal charges from tourists. **Buses onwards** to Huehuetenango, Quezaltenango, and occasionally Guatemala City wait just over the border, leaving at least every hour until about 5pm. After this there are a couple more until midnight, when a comfortable Pullman run by Transportes Velásquez (the best company) leaves for Guatemala City. The **moneychangers** will give you reasonable rates for travellers' cheques or dollars, but not as good for pesos. **Getting into Mexico** is easy: the Mexican tourist card will be issued free, and vans or buses will be waiting to take you to **Comitán**.

San Cristóbal to Palenque

If you're heading from San Cristóbal to the Yucatán, the best route takes you to **Palenque** (5hr), via **Ocosingo**, along Hwy-199, a good paved road that's frequently used by buses and colectivos. It's an impressive and beautiful journey as the road winds around the spectacular mountain valleys, lush with greenery, and it's easier than ever to stop off here and visit **Toniná ruins** and the awesome waterfalls at **Agua Azul** along the way. Ocosingo is also the starting point for adventurous trips by light aircraft or by *combi* to the beautiful **Laguna Miramar**, at the heart of the **Montes Azules Biosphere Reserve**. At Ocosingo, a smaller road also heads south towards Comitán.

Ocosingo

OCOSINGO, its streets lined with single-storey, red-tiled houses and the air thick with the scent of wood smoke, makes a good place to escape the tourist crowds of San Cristóbal or Palenque. It's a town that has stayed close to its country roots, with plenty of farmers in from the ranches in their cowboy hats and local women selling *maiz* from great bubbling vats. It's also a base for visiting the amazing Maya site of Toniná. Central to town life is the **zócalo**, surrounded by *portales*, a big old country church on the east side, and the *ayuntamiento*, with its thoroughly incongruous tinted glass, opposite.

Buses stop on the main road or at a makeshift terminal nearby. To get to the zócalo turn left out of the terminal and walk down the hill for about four blocks until you reach Calle Central, then turn left for a further two blocks. You'll find pretty much everything you need within a block or two of here.

Accommodation options are plentiful. Hard to miss is *Hotel Central* (Ⓣ919/673-0024; ④), on the north side of the plaza, but though all rooms have fans, none has a/c. *Hotel San José*, just off the northeast corner of the plaza along Calle 1 Ote Nte (Ⓣ919/673-0039; ③–④), is a great budget option, with clean, comfortable rooms, some with cable TV and a/c. The best of the lot, however, is the colourful *Hospedaje Esmeralda* (Ⓣ919/673-0014, Ⓔinfo@ranchoesmeralda.net; ④), a block north of the plaza, which has a range of en-suite and shared-bath rooms. *Esmeralda* doubles as a **tourist information** office and the friendly staff can help you book flights over the ruins (US$420 for four people), horse-riding expeditions (US$20 per day), or visits to attractions farther afield. They also have a folder of newspaper reports documenting the seizure of the Rancho.

Several budget **places to eat** surround the square, most serving a standard Mexican menu of tacos and tortilla dishes. There is little to choose between them, but *El Campanario* on the north side is quite pleasant. The bright-yellow *El Desván*, on the opposite side of the zócalo, is a step up in class and also serves pizza. The **food market**, or *tianguis*, is where indigenous women sell fruit and vegetables and locally produced cheeses, including the round waxy *queso de bola* and the delicious creamy *queso botanero*. To get there turn right at the church for one block, then left along Calle 2 Sur Ote for another four.

There are a couple of **ATMs**, one at Banamex on the plaza, and another at Banco Santander opposite *Hospedaje Esmeralda* on Calle Central Nte. There are a few **Internet** cafés along this road as well, including Compuchat near the zócalo and Xanav (9am–2pm & 4–10pm; US$0.80 per hour; Ⓣ919/673-1334) at 40C, which doubles as a travel agent for domestic flights.

Leaving Ocosingo by road is easy enough until mid-evening, with frequent buses and *combis* to San Cristóbal (12 daily; 2hr) and buses to Palenque

(16 daily; 3hr 30 min). The last Autotransportes Tuxtla-Gutiérrez (ATG) buses in either direction officially leave at 7.30pm – though they're *de paso* and so are likely to be later. Cristóbal Colón services continue after midnight, with buses to Palenque at 3am and 4am, and San Cristóbal at 12.30am and 1.30am. There is a 24-hour left luggage service at the Cristóbal Colón terminal (US$0.50).

Toniná

The Classic-period Maya site of **TONINÁ** (daily 9am–4pm; US$3.20, includes museum entry), some 14km east of Ocosingo, is surprisingly big, and yet it sees few visitors. It centres on an enormous grassy plaza, once surrounded by buildings, and a series of seven artificial terraces climb the hillside above it. At the bottom are two restored ball-courts and an overgrown pyramid mound; as you climb the hill, passing corbel-arched entrances to two vaulted rooms on the right, you begin to get an impression of Toniná's vastness. The sixth and seventh terraces feature a total of thirteen temples and from the top there are fine views of the surrounding country.

There are also tombs on both the fifth and sixth levels, one of which contains an enormous mask of the Earth Monster, a powerful force in Maya cosmology. The most striking feature, however, is the enormous **Mural of the Four Suns**, on the sixth platform. This amazingly well-preserved stucco codex tells the story of Maya cosmology by following the four suns (or eras of the world) as they were created and destroyed. The worlds are depicted as decapitated heads surrounded by flowers. A grinning, skeletal Lord of Death presents a particularly graphic image as he grasps a defleshed human head.

In ancient times Toniná was known as "the place of (celestial) captives" and in the stunning **museum** (Tues–Sun 8am–5pm) several carved panels and sculptures portray bound (and sometimes headless) captives. Glyphs on the panels record the place where the prisoners were captured, while those on the loincloths of the captives may tell who they were.

The **road from Ocosingo** to Toniná is traversed by *combis* (US$1) leaving frequently from the market area, heading either for the site itself or the large army base by the turn-off to the site – look for "Predio" or "Ruinas". A taxi will cost US$7one-way. At the entrance to the site the *Restaurant Toniná* serves simple food, cold beer, and soft drinks, and also sells quality T-shirts and postcards.

For a spectacular **flight** over the ruins (around US$420 for four people) contact Servicios Aéreos de San Cristóbal through the *Hospedaje Esmeralda* (see p.677) or at their office on the street behind the *combi* terminal in Ocosingo (☎919/673-0188).

Laguna Miramar

A much more remote excursion is a visit to **Laguna Miramar**, over 100km southeast of Ocosingo, in the heart of the Lacandón forest. Miramar, at 40km long the largest lake in southeast Mexico, is now a pristine part of the **Montes Azules Biosphere Reserve**, and staying here enables you to experience the largest surviving area of rainforest in North America. There are no settlements on the lakeshore, and no motor boats are allowed. An island in the lake has traces of a fortress, which was a stronghold of the Maya until it was finally conquered in 1559. The high-canopy forest here is home to abundant wildlife, including howler and spider monkeys, tapirs, and jaguars, and there are rivers and caves to explore.

A trip to Laguna Miramar is a unique chance to visit one of the last truly remote corners of Mexico, and it's possible to visit on your own or as a member of an organized group. To **travel independently** you'll need to get a *combi* from the market in Ocosingo (leaving around 9am or 10am) to the *ejido* of **San Quintín**, about five hours down the mostly unpaved road, following the valley of the Río Jatatė. Here you'll be checked by the army and you'll need a guide from the community to lead you to **Emiliano Zapata**, another *ejido* a few kilometres away; some *combis* continue all the way. Alternatively you can **fly** to the *ejido* of San Quintín from Ocosingo, in a light aircraft from Servicios Aéreos de San Cristóbal (see p.677) for around US$30 one-way. It's still a nine-kilometre hike to the lake and you'll need to carry supplies and hire a guide from Emiliano Zapata – check with the *ejido* – for around US$15 per day. Fernando Ochoa at the *Casa de Pan* in San Cristóbal (☎967/678-0465), arranges superb, fully equipped three-day **expeditions** to Laguna Miramar which cost around US$300 including transport from San Cristóbal, flights from Ocosingo, guides, camping, and meals.

North to Palenque: Agua Azul and Misol-Há

A series of stunningly beautiful **waterfalls** is the chief attraction along the winding mountain road between Ocosingo and Palenque. And, although the awesome cascades on the Río Shumulhá at **Agua Azul** and the exquisite waterfall at **Misol-Há** are usually visited on a day-trip from Palenque, it's perfectly possible to visit them independently and stay nearby.

Agua Azul

AGUA AZUL, in the Parque Nacional Agua Azul, 4km down a track from the road and 64km before Palenque, is now a major tour-bus destination. If you come **by bus** (not on a tour), you'll be dropped at the crossroads, where there are usually taxis (US$1) waiting to take you to the base of the falls. Otherwise it's a 45-minute walk downhill to the waterfall (and at least an hour's sweaty hike back up). Local villagers have set up two tariff stations along the road, the first charging US$5 and the second at the entrance to the park charging US$10. Here, where the tour buses park, there are several basic **restaurants** and a **campsite** with hammock space. Simple **cabañas** (☎0155/5329-0995 ext 7002; ❹) are also available for rent – ask at the Modulo de Información near the car park. Make sure to keep a close eye on your belongings, though, and be warned that **violent attacks** on tourists have occurred away from the main area.

The whole area is exceptionally beautiful, with dozens of lesser falls above the developed area. If it's safe to walk upstream you'll come across a perilous-looking bridge over the river and eventually you'll reach an impressive gorge where the Río Shumulhá explodes out of the jungle-covered mountain. At the right time of year, the river is alive with butterflies. Higher up, the swimming is safer, too – though watch out for signs warning of dangerous currents as there are several tempting but extremely perilous spots, and people drown here every year.

Misol-Há

At **Misol-Há**, 18km from Palenque, a 25-metre waterfall provides a stunning backdrop to a pool that's safe for swimming (US$1). A fern-lined trail leads along a ledge behind the wide cascade – refreshing from the spray and mist even if you don't swim – and the air of the lush rainforest is filled with bird calls. It's an easy 1500-metre walk from the road, and there's inexpensive **accommodation** in some of the most beautiful wooden cabañas in Mexico (Ⓣ0155/5329-0995 ext 7006; ⑤). The cabins, and the **restaurant** catering to tour groups, are owned and run by the San Miguel *ejido*; each cabin has a private bathroom and electricity, and some also have kitchens.

Palenque

Set in thick jungle screeching with insects, **Palenque** is strongly linked to the lost cities of Guatemala while keeping its own distinctive style, and though it's not large – you can see everything in a morning – it is hauntingly beautiful. The **site**, in a national park 9km from the town of Palenque, was discovered by the priest Antonio Solís in 1790 and occupies the top of an escarpment marking the northern limit of the Chiapas highlands. The **town** of Palenque (officially Santo Domingo de Palenque), with its garish turquoise zócalo, is of little intrinsic interest to visitors and is best viewed simply as a base for exploring the ruins and the waterfalls in the nearby hills. Alternatively, since there are a number of camping sites and cabañas near the ruins, you may prefer not to stay in town at all.

Arrival and information

Arriving at any of the **bus terminals**, you'll be on Juárez, where the highway comes into town. If you plan to leave the same day, particularly on a first-class bus, get your onward or return ticket on arrival. The **airport** is 5km north, in

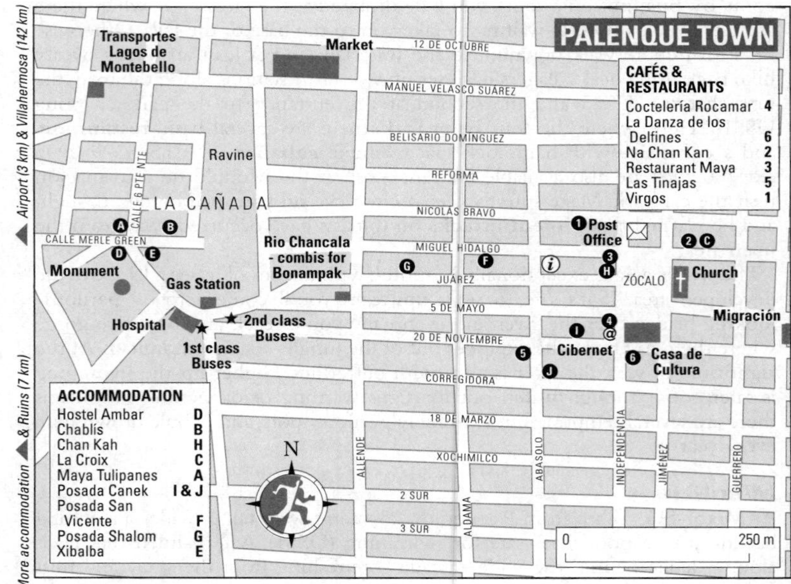

Tours and operators in Palenque

The surge in the numbers of tourists visiting Palenque has encouraged a dozen or so travel agencies to offer **tours** to the surrounding attractions. None can sell you an international air ticket, nor is there anywhere in town to rent a car. However, any of them can take you to the waterfalls at **Agua Azul** and **Misol-Há** (see p.679) and further afield to the ruins of **Bonampak** and **Yaxchilán** (p.688 & p690). Cheaper prices do not necessarily mean a better deal; be sure to check that your tour includes insurance, meals, English-speaking guides and even security guards. Most tours do not include entrance fees to the parks. Bear in mind that since the paving of the Frontier Highway, leading to Bonampak and Yaxchilán, and the opening of inexpensive accommodation and restaurants nearby, the sites can be **visited independently**. See the relevant accounts for details of how to get to Bonampak and Yaxchilán on your own.

Sample prices are US$14.50 per person for an all-day trip to Agua Azul and Misol-Há; US$65 for a one-day van-based trip to the Maya ruins at Bonampak and Yaxchilán; and US$105 for an overnight trip to both sites, including camping near Bonampak. To visit both sites by plane will cost around US$130. A **taxi to Bonampak** costs around US$100 and includes two hours of waiting time. Guided **horse riding** is also on offer, and some agencies can organize rafting and light aircraft flights as well.

The best **tour agent** in Palenque is Na Chan Kan (ⓣ916/345-0263, ⓔrosita_palenque@yahoo.com.mx), which has a small office on Juárez just up from the bus station and a main office behind the restaurant of the same name, on the corner of Hidalgo and Jiménez where they meet the zócalo; the manager Rosita speaks good English. Two rival companies, Colectivos Chambalu and Transportes Otolum, run *combis* and buses to the **Palenque ruins** (every 15min 6am–6pm; US$0.70) from their depots on Allende, between Hidalgo and the main road. Although they will try to sell you a round-trip ticket, it is advisable to buy just a one-way ticket so you don't have to wait for the same company on the return leg. They each also have three daily trips to **Agua Azul** (US$10).

a dusty settlement called Pakal Ná. Walk less than 100m to the highway to flag down a passing cab (US$3) to town – the airport taxis themselves will charge three times this.

Palenque's three main streets, avenidas Juárez, 5 de Mayo, and Hidalgo, all run parallel to each other and lead straight up to the **zócalo**, the Parque Central. There is a **tourist office** (Mon–Sat 9am–9pm, Sun 9am–1pm; ⓣ916/345-0356) in the Plaza de Artesanías on Juárez, a block below the zócalo, but all the staff can do is hand out a street map and some tour leaflets. You'll get better **information** from one of the recommended tour operators (see box above) or from Palenque's own interesting and very informative website, ⓦwww.palenquemx.com.

Accommodation

Palenque has seen a massive boom in **hotel** construction in recent years. There are plenty of places on the streets leading from the bus stations to the zócalo, especially Hidalgo (though the traffic noise makes these best avoided) and 20 de Noviembre. The most atmospheric area to stay in is La Cañada rainforest area, west of the town centre, set among the relative quiet of the remaining trees. It is generally more upmarket, though with some excellent budget hotels. You'll also find a host of excellent new hotels, in addition to the long-established *Mayabell* **campsite**, lining the road to the ruins. Note that some places will try to charge up to fifty percent more during peak times – July and August, Easter, and Christmas.

In town

Chan Kah corner of Juárez and Independencia ⓣ916/345-0489. The most upmarket hotel in town, this very comfortable hotel is under the same ownership as the *Chan Kah Resort Village* near the ruins (see below). Some rooms have the dubious advantage of balconies with views over the garish zócalo. ❻

La Croix Hidalgo, on the corner of the zócalo ⓣ916/345-0014. A long-established favourite and, though past its priime, still an atmospheric budget option. Rooms are arranged around a large jungly courtyard whose walls are decorated with murals of Palenque. ❹

Posada Canek 20 de Noviembre 43 ⓣ916/345-0150. One of several good options along this road, and great value if you're travelling alone. Dorms (US$5 per person) and huge double rooms, some with private bath. Luggage storage is available and there are views of the surrounding hills from the balconies. ❷

Posada San Vicente Hidalgo 100A ⓣ916/345-0856. A fantastic and remarkably cheap budget option halfway between the zócalo and La Cañada. Rooms are clean and comfortable and have en-suite bathrooms. ❷

Posada Shalom Juárez 158 ⓣ916/345-0944 and Corregidora ⓣ916/345-2641. Two hotels with the same name, both with clean rooms, cable TV, and tiled private bathrooms. Luggage storage and laundry service available. ❹

La Cañada rainforest area

Chablís Merle Green 7 ⓣ916/345-0870, ⓕ345-0365. Large, modern doubles in spacious white-washed rooms with a/c and cable TV. ❺

Hostel Ambar Hidalgo and C 6 Pte Nte ⓣ916/345-1008, ⓔambarhostel@hotmail.com. Dorms (US$6 per person and basic doubles. A popular backpacker hangout and the cheapest option in La Cañada. ❹

Maya Tulipanes Hidalgo ⓣ916/345-0201, ⓔmtulipan@tnet.net.mx. Opposite *Ambar* (above), a luxury hotel, with very comfortable, air-conditioned rooms, plus shady grounds, a small pool, and good restaurant. Has the only Internet access in La Cañada (available to non-residents), but rates are extortionate (US$2.50 per hour). ❽

Xibalba Merle Green 9 ⓣ916/345-0411, ⓔshivalva@tnet.net.mx. Opposite *Chablís* (above),offering lovely, tiled rooms with private bath-rooms in an A-frame building with a wooden deck upstairs; cable TV and a/c available. There's also a good restaurant and travel agency downstairs. ❺

On the road to the ruins

Cabañas Safari 1.5km from town, on the left ⓣ916/345-1145. Very comfortable, thatched, A-frame cabañas and suites with a deck and hammocks outside and beautifully decorated inside, run by the very friendly Uscanga family. The grounds are full of plants, including organic cocoa bushes and a small rubber plantation. Good value. ❺

Camping Chaac at the roadside 2km from the site entrance ⓔvtdeviaje@starmedia.com. Rustic, thatched, screened cabañas (❸, includes breakfast), plus camping (❶) and a small restaurant on the banks of two streams. The shared showers are clean, there's a river pool to bathe in, and also a *temazcal* – sweat bath – built by the friendly owner.

Chan Kah Resort Village 4.5km along on the left, just before the national park entrance ⓣ916/345-1100, ⓕ345-0489. Luxury brick and stone cabañas in a lovely forest and river setting, humming with birdlife. Amenities include three stone-lined swimming pools and a restaurant. ❼

Mayabell Camping and Trailer Park at the roadside 2km from the site entrance ⓣ916/345-0597, ⓔmayabell82@hotmail.com. A great favourite with backpackers and adventure-tour groups. In addition to palapa shelters for hammocks and tents *Mayabell* has vehicle pads with electricity and water, and some very comfortable private cabañas with hot water. The tiled, shared showers have hot water as well, and the site isn't crowded, so you'll usually get a space. Lockers are available. Hammock rental or tent camping per person ❶, RV for two ❷, cabaña ❹

El Panchan at the national park entrance, down a 200m track (3km from the ruins). A cluster of separate, great-value budget cabins and camping places (US$20 per person) set in the forest, with something of a New Age atmosphere. Definitely worth checking here to see what's available; follow the signs to the places below. *Chato's Cabañas* (ⓣ916/348-5820, ⓔelpanchan@yahoo.com; ❸), has neat, thatched cabañas and two-storey houses, some with private bath. There's also a pool and an observation deck for bird-watching, and a restaurant with Italian, Mexican, and vegetarian dishes at reasonable prices, and some live music. Nearby, *Rakshita's* (ⓔrakshitas@yahoo.com; ❸) has brightly painted, cosy cabañas, some with private bath and a deck with hammocks, in a lovely garden with a maze. It also has a great vegetarian restaurant and the owner offers massage and meditation. *Margarita and Ed's* (ⓔedcabanas@yahoo.com; ❸–❹) has comfortable, inexpensive thatched cabins and double rooms. *Beto's Cabins and camping* (❷) is the least expensive place here, with shelters for hammocks (with lockers) and simple, shared-bath cabins, a laundry, and a cheap café. Ask at the *Sol Luna* restaurant for information.

Eating and drinking

Food in Palenque town is fairly basic, and most restaurants serve up similar dishes, often just pasta and pizza, to customers who've really only come for the ruins; some of the best places are actually in *El Panchan* (see "Accommodation", opposite). The hotels in La Cañada invariably have a restaurant attached and, though standards are generally fine, prices are higher than in town. Bargains can be found among the set menus posted on boards outside most restaurants. **Juárez** also has several budget options between the bus stations and the zócalo, while **Hidalgo** has more Mexican-style food, with several taco places and even a couple of seafood restaurants. There's a good Mexican **bakery**, *Flor de Palenque*, on Allende next to the Chambalu colectivo terminal.

Coctelería Rocamar corner of Independencia and 5 de Mayo. Seafood is the specialty here. Hugely popular with locals for its generous portions and reasonable prices.

La Danza de los Delfínes corner of 20 de Noviembre and Independencia. Cheap and filling choice with shaded outdoor seating and a killer *salsa picante*.

Na Chan Kan corner of Jiménez and the zócalo. Good-value breakfasts and set meals. An enjoyable place for a coffee and watching the world go by.

Restaurant Maya corner of Hidalgo and the zócalo. Popular with tourists, but rather pricey. Set meals are better value at US$3.50.

Las Tinajas corner of 20 de Noviembre and Abasolo. Pleasant, family-run restaurant, rapidly gaining in popularity. Offers a wide menu of meats, fish, chicken, and pasta in addition to the usual Mexican fare.

Virgo's Hidalgo, opposite *Restaurant Maya*. Breezy outdoor seating and reasonable prices make this a good-value option for meats and Mexican food.

Listings

Banks Several along Juárez will change travellers' cheques and have ATMs.

Internet Cibernet (daily 9am–10pm; US$1 per hour) on Independencia, near 20 de Noviembre, is a good central bet with over twenty terminals. *Maya Tulipana* (daily 9am–9pm) has the only connection in the La Cañada area, and exploits it with a charge of US$2.50 per hour.

Laundry Several in town, including a good one on 5 de Mayo.

Post office On Independencia, a block from the plaza (Mon–Fri 9am–6pm, Sat & Sun 9am–1pm).

The ruins of Palenque

Palenque's architectural style is unique. Superficially, it bears a closer resemblance to the Maya sites of Guatemala than to those of the Yucatán, but its **towered palace** and **pyramid tomb** are like nothing else, and the setting, too, is remarkable. Surrounded by hills covered in jungle, Palenque is at the same time right at the edge of the great Yucatán plain – climb to the top of any of the structures and you look out, across the dark green of the hills, over an endless stretch of low, pale-green flatland. Founded around 100 BC as a farming village, it was four hundred years before it began to flourish, during the Classic period (300–900 AD). Towards the end of this time the city ruled over a large part of modern-day Chiapas and Tabasco, but its peak came during a relatively short period of the seventh century, under two rulers – **Hanab Pakal (Jaguar Shield)** and **Chan Bahlum (Jaguar Serpent)**. Almost everything you can see (and that's only a tiny, central part of the original city) dates from this era.

Getting to the site is no problem. Two *combi* services, Chambalu and Otolum, both on Allende between Hidalgo and the main street, run at least every fifteen minutes from 6am to 6pm (US$0.70 one-way), and will stop anywhere along the road, useful if you're staying at one of the hotels or campsites near the ruins. After 6pm, you'll have to either walk or take a taxi. For details of organized tours to Palenque, see box on p.681.

The ruins are in a **national park** (daily 8am–5pm; archeological zone daily 8am–4.30pm; US$3.70, includes museum) and guided tours are available from the entrance, costing around US$35 for groups of up to seven people and lasting about two hours. Arrive early, and climb the temples in the morning mist, if you want to avoid the worst of the heat and the crowds. There's a small **café** by the entrance (and some expensive lockers), and a toilet by the ticket office. At the entrance to the site, you'll find ranks of souvenir stalls and usually a group of Lacandón in white robes (or merely people in white robes imitating Lacandón) selling arrows and other artefacts. Signs inside the site are in English, Spanish, and Tzeltal, though Chol is the language spoken by most modern Maya in this part of Chiapas.

The site

A visit first to the **museum** (Tues–Sun 8am–4.45pm), on the road 1.5km before the site entrance, will give you a good idea of the scale of Palenque. The map of the site shows that only a quarter of the structures have been excavated, and an intricate model of the palace complex recreates how it would have appeared in the Classic period, with the tops of the buildings adorned with roof combs. Several carved panels removed from the archeological site are on display, as are numerous incense burners – large urns with elaborately stuccoed gods and mythological creatures – with explanations in Spanish and English. There's also a copy of Hanab Pakal's famous sarcophagus lid in the Templo de las Inscripciones, though it's no longer visitable.

As you enter the site itself, **El Palacio**, with its extraordinary watchtower, stands ahead of you. To the right, at the end of a row of smaller structures, stands the **Templo de las Inscripciones**, an eight-stepped pyramid, 26m high, built up against a thickly overgrown hillside. You are no longer permitted to climb the pyramid, which is a shame as the sanctuary on top contains a series of stone panels carved with hieroglyphic inscriptions relating to Palenque's dynastic history. Inside the pyramid is the **tomb of Hanab Pakal** (615–683 AD). Discovered in 1952, this was the first such pyramid burial found in the Americas, and is still the most important and impressive. Sadly, the huge numbers of visitors took their toll on the tomb and it has been closed to the general public. Some of the smaller objects found inside – the skeleton and the jade death mask – are on display at the Anthropology Museum in Mexico City, but the massive, intricately carved stone **sarcophagus** is still inside. One of the most renowned iconographic monuments in the Maya world, the sarcophagus lid depicts Pakal at the moment of his death, falling into the underworld, symbolized by a monster's jaws. Above the dead king rises the **Wakah Kan** – the World Tree and the centre of the universe – with **Itzam-Ye**, the Celestial Bird, perched on top representing the heavens. In order that the deified king buried here should not be cut off from the world of the living, a psychduct – a hollow tube in the form of a snake – runs up the side of the staircase, from the tomb to the temple. For now, though, you will have to be satisfied with the replica in the site museum.

In June 1994 another remarkable tomb was discovered, in **Templo XIII**, in a pyramid next to the Templo de las Inscripciones. This burial, currently the only one open to the public, is considered by archeologists to date from a similar period to that of Pakal, and its sarcophogus contains a number of jade and obsidian grave goods and food and drink vessels to sustain the deceased on her way to Xibalba, the Maya underworld. More recent excavations in the **South Acropolis** have revealed a painted tomb and a stone throne at **Edificio XX**, inscribed with over two hundred glyphs, among other rich grave goods, but there are no plans to open it for public viewing.

The centrepiece of the site, **El Palacio**, is in fact a complex of buildings constructed at different times to form a rambling administrative and residential block. Its square **tower** (whose top floor was reconstructed in 1930) is unique, and no one knows exactly what its purpose was – perhaps a lookout post or an astronomical observatory. Bizarrely, the narrow staircase that winds up inside it starts only at the second level, though you're no longer allowed to climb it. Throughout you'll find delicately executed relief carvings, the most remarkable of which are the giant human figures on stone panels in the grassy courtyard.

From here, the lesser buildings of the **Grupo del Norte**, and the **Juego de Pelota** (ball-court), are slightly downhill across a cleared grassy area. On higher

Moving on from Palenque

Leaving Palenque by **bus**, there are surprisingly few direct services **to Mérida** (4 daily; 9hr): departures via **Campeche** are at 8am, 9pm and 11.30pm. There's a first-class departure for **Oaxaca** (1 daily; 14hr) at 5.30pm; **Cancún** (5 daily; 12hr), with three first-class buses going via **Chetumal** and **Playa del Carmen**, at 5.30pm, 8.15pm, and 9.15pm, as well as overnight buses to **Mexico City** (2 daily; 17hr) at 9pm and 9.30pm. Buses for **Tuxtla** (10 daily; 7hr) all call at **Ocosingo** (3hr) and **San Cristóbal** (5hr). The main nearby transport hub is **Villahermosa** (15 daily; 2hr 30min), and you may find it easier to get there and change for your onward journey.

Transportes Comitán y Lagos de Montebello, on Velasco Suárez, just past the market, has services down the Usumacinta valley (see below) for **Bonampak** and **Frontera Corozal** (for Yaxchilán), and **Bethél** in Guatemala, with some services continuing all round the Frontier Highway to **Comitán**. Combis Río Chancala, on 5 de Mayo, also have services along the Usumacinta valley as far as **Benemérito**. Aerocaribe flies from the airport 5km north of the town to Mérida, Cancún, and Villahermosa, and to **Flores** (Guatemala). Check with one of the recommended travel agents on p.681.

ground in the other direction, across the Río Otulúm – lined with stone and used as an aqueduct in the city's heyday – lie the **Templo del Sol**, the **Templo de la Cruz**, and the **Templo de la Cruz Foliada,** half-obscured by the dense vegetation around them. All are tall, narrow pyramids surmounted by a temple with an elaborate stone roof-comb. Each, too, contains carved panels representing sacred rites – the cross found here is as important an image in Maya iconography as it is in Christian, representing the meeting of the heavens and the underworld with the land of the living. On the right-hand side of the Templo de la Cruz, God L is depicted smoking tobacco.

The **Templo del Bello Relieve** (**Templo del Jaguar**) is reached by a small path that follows the brook upstream – a delightful shaded walk. Beyond here, more temples are being wrested from the jungle. If you want to penetrate a bit further by following the path along the stream behind the **Templo de las Inscripciones**, you won't be permitted to pass without a guide. The path leads to the *ejido* of Naranjo, a little over an hour's walk away, and while you're on it it's easy to believe you're walking over unexcavated pyramids: the ground is very rocky and some of the stones certainly don't look naturally formed.

Downstream, the river cascades through the forest and flows over beautiful limestone curtains and terraces into a series of gorgeous pools – the aptly named **El Baño de la Reina** (**Bathing Pool of the Queen**) is the most exquisite. The path leading down beside the river, past more recently excavated buildings and across the river over a suspension bridge, eventually comes out on the main road opposite the museum and is an official **exit**; you can enter here if you already have a ticket (sold at the main entrance).

The Usumacinta valley and the Frontier Highway south

The obvious starting point for visits to the Usumacinta valley sites of **Bonampak** and **Yaxchilán** is Palenque, where several agencies offer overland or plane trips to the sites – you can also easily organize your own trip. If you do decide to head out on your own, you'll need to be prepared to walk, and possibly also to camp, although accommodation is increasingly available here, especially at the **Lacandón Maya** community of **Lacanhá Chansayab** (see box below), near the road to Bonampak.

The Usumacinta valley and the Lacandón forest form Mexico's last frontier. The **Carretera Fronteriza** (Frontier Highway) provides access to a number of new settlements whose inhabitants are rapidly changing the forest to farmland. The road is now paved all the way round to Comitán (see p.671), though there are several army checkpoints along its length, and there remains the risk of **armed robbery** in this wild region.

Exploring this route presents other options beyond Bonampak and Yaxchilán. From the riverbank settlement of Frontera Corozal, you can get a boat a short distance upstream to **Bethél** in Guatemala, and from the fast-expanding town of Benemérito you can occasionally take a longer trip on a trading boat upstream to **Sayaxché** (also in Guatemala), on the Río de la Pasión. The interior of this remote corner of Chiapas fortunately has some form of protection as the **Montes Azules Biosphere Reserve**.

Lacanhá and Bonampak

It's possible to visit **Lacanhá** and **Bonampak** independently on a day-trip from Palenque, and, as always, it's best to get an early start: Transportes Lagos de Montebello, on Velasco Suárez, and Combis Río Chancala, on 5 de Mayo in Palenque, have numerous departures to destinations along the Frontier Highway, beginning at 4.30am.

For both Lacanhá and Bonampak, you need to get off the bus at **San Javiér** (about 3hr), where there's an abandoned government control hut on the left

The Lacandón

You may already have encountered the impressively wild-looking **Lacandón Maya** selling exquisite (and apparently effective) bows and arrows at Palenque. Though the wearing of their simple, hanging white robes and uncut hair is today mainly for the benefit of tourists, the Lacandón were until recently the most isolated of all the Mexican tribes. The ancestors of today's Lacandón are believed to have migrated to Chiapas from the Petén region of Guatemala during the eighteenth century. Prior to that the Spanish had enslaved, killed, or relocated the original inhabitants of the forest. The Lacandón refer to themselves as "Hach Winik" (true people); "Lacandón" was a label used by the Spanish to describe any native group living in the Usumacinta valley and western Petén outside colonial control. Appearances notwithstanding, some Lacandón families are (or have been) quite wealthy, having sold timber rights in the jungle, though most of the timber money has now gone. This change has led to a division in their society, and now most Lacandón live in one of two main communities: Lacanhá Chansayab, near Bonampak, a village predominantly made up of evangelical Protestants, some of whom are keenly developing low-impact tourist facilities (see below); and Nahá, where a small group still attempt to live a traditional life.

The best source of information in Chiapas on the Lacandón is the *Casa Na-Bolom* in San Cristóbal de las Casas (see p.665), where you can find a manuscript of *Last Lords of Palenque* by Victor Perera and Robert Bruce (Little Brown & Co, 1982). *Hach Winik* by Didier Boermanse (University of Albany, 1998) is an excellent recent study of Lacandón life and history.

and a *comedor* on the right. The large, thatched visitors' centre here is not functioning; Lacandón taxi driver Chan Kin will probably be waiting here to drive you to Bonampak for US$10 round-trip. The Lacanhá community now has a *combi* and there's plenty of traffic heading for the village, so you won't have to walk. There are also several **places to stay**, though none currently has phones. For **Lacanhá Chansayab** take the paved side road bearing right. After 4km, at a right-hand bend in the road, you'll find *Camping Margarito* (❶; tents available), run by the friendly Chan Kayun family who also have a small **restaurant**. This is where most tours camp for the night; the road to Bonampak branches off left here. The side road continues a few more kilometres to Lacanhá village, passing *Camping Carmelo* (❶) on the way. The road enters the village at the airstrip and you'll see signs pointing to several purpose-built **campsites**, **cabins**, and **hammock shelters** (❶–❷). *Campamento Lacanhá* is to the left and others are a kilometre ahead, in the main part of the village. A few places also have simple dorm **rooms** (❷), with mosquito-netted beds and electric light. The best, in a grassy area on the bank of a clear, fast-flowing river, is run by Vicente Kin Paniagua. Don Vicente and his family produce some of the best artesanía in the village – clay and wood figurines and drums in addition to beautifully crafted bow and arrow sets. The villagers are eager to show you the gorgeous rivers and waterfalls in the forest, and you can reach the **Lacanhá ruins** in under two hours from here. Ask for Kin Bor or Carlos Chan Bor, at the house where the paved road enters the village; either of them will be able to fix you up with knowledgeable Lacandón guides to lead you. If you can, pick up an information sheet in the **Casa Na-Bolom** in San Cristóbal (see p.665) before you set off.

Back on the road to Bonampak itself, you pass through the entrance to the site a few hundred metres past *Margarito*'s, complete with mock corbelled arch across the road, a good **visitor centre**, and a café with clean toilets. There's also a **hiking trail** to the site (with some interpretive labels) and you'll have a less apprehensive trip through the forest if you do have a guide. The hike is wonderful in the dry season (Jan to late April) – be prepared for mud at other times.

After taking the **entrance fee** (daily 8am–4pm; US$3.20), the guards will not let you out of their sight – they're particularly vigilant near the Temple of the Frescoes. No flash photography is allowed and you will be charged an extra US$3 to use a video camera. Once you've seen the ruins, head back to the San Javiér junction, where you'll be able to catch a **bus** or *combi* to Palenque.

Bonampak: the site

The outside world first heard of the existence of **Bonampak** (Painted Walls) in 1946, when Charles Frey, an American conscientious objector taking refuge deep in the forest, was shown the site by the Lacandón, who apparently still worshipped at the ancient temples. The ruins themselves are not the most spectacular, but the famous **murals** make it worth the visit. American photographer Giles Healey was the first non-Maya ever to see these astonishing examples of Classic Maya art, shortly after Frey's visit.

After crossing the airstrip, you enter the site at the northwest corner of the main plaza, which is bounded by low walls – the remains of some palace-style buildings. In the centre of the plaza **Stele 1** shows a larger-than-life **Chan Muan**, the last king of Bonampak, dressed for battle – standing at 20m it is one of the tallest in the Maya world. You'll encounter other images of him throughout the site. Ahead, atop several steep flights of steps, lies the **Acrópolis**. On the lower steps more well-preserved stelae show Chan

Muan preparing himself for blood-letting and apparently about to sacrifice a prisoner.

Splendid though these scenes are, the highlight of the site is the famed **Temple of the Frescoes**. Inside, in three separate chambers, on the temple walls and roof, the renowned **Bonampak murals** depict vivid scenes of haughty Maya lords, splendidly attired in jaguar-skin robes and quetzal-plume headdresses, their equally well-dressed ladies, and bound prisoners, one with his fingernails ripped out, spurting blood. Musicians play drums, pipes and trumpets in what is clearly a celebration of victory. Dated to around 790 AD, these murals show the Bonampak elite at the height of their power: unknown to them, the collapse of the Classic Maya civilization was imminent. Some details were never finished and Bonampak was abandoned shortly after the scenes in the temple were painted.

In **Room 1**, an infant wrapped in white cloth (the heir apparent?) is presented to assembled nobility under the supervision of the lord of Yaxchilán, while musicians play trumpets in the background. **Room 2** contains a vivid, even gruesome, exhibition of power over Bonampak's enemies: tortured prisoners lie on temple steps, while above them lords in jaguar robes are indifferent to their agony. A severed head has rolled down the stairs and Chan Muan grasps a prisoner (who appears to be pleading for mercy) by the hair – clearly about to deal him the same fate. **Room 3** shows the price paid for victory: Chan Muan's wife, **Lady Rabbit**, prepares to prick her tongue to let blood fall onto the paper in a clay pot in front of her. The smoke from burning the blood-soaked paper will carry messages to ancestor-gods. Other gorgeously dressed figures, their senses probably heightened by hallucinogenic drugs, dance on the temple steps.

Though time and early cleaning attempts have taken their toll on the murals, work in the 1990s restored some of their glory. Sadly, you're no longer allowed to enter the rooms completely – you have to be content with peering in from just inside the doorway and no more than three people are permitted to enter at any one time, so be prepared to queue.

Frontera Corozal and Yaxchilán

Twenty kilometres beyond San Javiér, the turning for **FRONTERA COROZAL** is marked by a *comedor* and shop selling basic supplies. Corozal itself, another 19km down the paved side road and served by regular buses and *combis* from Palenque (last one back at 4pm), lies on the bank of the Usumacinta, where you need to catch a boat to get to Yaxchilán. There's a Mexican **immigration post** (see box, p.653, for border procedures): visitors to Yaxchilán will always be asked to show their passports, despite the fact that the site is in Mexico. On the right past the immigration post are the thatched and brightly painted **cabañas** of *Escudo Jaguar* (Ⓣ0155/5329-0995 ext 8057, in Mexico City; ❸ shared bathroom, ❺ en suite), named after Shield Jaguar, a king of Yaxchilán. The spacious rooms have comfortable beds with mosquito nets, hot water in the tiled bathrooms, and full-length windows opening onto the porch – a touch of luxury at a bargain price. There's also a good **restaurant** here, and you can **camp** nearby for US$35. More basic accommodation is available at Corozal's two **posadas** – the *Nueva Allianza* (Ⓣ0155/5329-0995 ext 8061; US$50 per person), near to the immigration post, is marginally the better and has a good *comedor*.

To reach the site, you need to get a ride in a *lancha* – a narrow riverboat with benches along the side and a tin roof for shade. Several companies now compete for business. Tickets are sold at *Escudo Jaguar* but are also available at the Tikal Chilan boat co-operative office next to the Museo Regional. You will also have to pay your entrance fee for the site here, as cash is no longer kept on site at the isolated ruins. Fares vary with group size, with one to four people paying US$50 between them, and no scope for bargaining. The journey downstream usually takes under an hour.

Yaxchilán: the site

A larger and more dramatic site than Bonampak, **Yaxchilán** (daily 8am–4pm; US$2.50, free on Sun) was an important Classic-period centre. From around 680 AD to 760 AD, the city's most famous kings (identified by their name-glyphs), Escudo Jaguar (Shield Jaguar) and his son Pájaro Jaguar IV (Bird Jaguar), began the campaign of conquest that extended Yaxchilán's sphere of influence over the other Usumacinta centres and made possible alliances with Tikal and Palenque.

From the entrance a path leads steeply off to the right, climbing 50m up the hillside to the **Pequeña Acrópolis**, the first set of buildings. A lintel on **Edificio 42** depicts Escudo Jaguar with one of his warriors. Beyond here a path leads down through the jungle, over several unrestored mounds, eventually forking towards the end. To the right it climbs steeply once again, until you reach **Edificios 39–41**, 90m above the river level – buildings that probably had some kind of astronomical significance and may have been observatories. The climb is worth the effort for the view alone.

The main path continues to the left to **Edificio 33**, overlooking the main plaza and the most significant building at the site. The lintels are superbly preserved and inside one of the portals is a headless statue of Pájaro Jaguar IV. In ancient times the building was a political court, but more recently served as a religious site for the Lacandón Maya.

Descending 40m down the terrace brings you to the **main plaza**. The temples here bear massive honeycombed roofs, and everywhere there are superb, well-preserved stucco carvings. These panels, on lintels above doorways and on stelae, depict rulers performing ritual events, often involving blood-letting to conjure up spirit visions of ancestors. Some of the very best lintels have been removed to the British Museum in London, but the number and quality of the remaining panels is unequalled at any other Maya site in Mexico. **Stele II**, originally sited at Edificio 41, has survived several attempts to translocate it to London and now lies at the west side of the plaza, where it shows the transfer of power from Escudo Jaguar to Pájaro Jaguar IV. When the water is low here, you can see (and climb) a pyramid built on a rock shelf on the river bed. Some archeologists suggest this was a bridge support, though this is unlikely as no corresponding structure has been found on the opposite bank, and the altar on top may indicate that it was used for religious rituals.

On from Frontera Corozal and Yaxchilán

Entering Guatemala is relatively easy, with plenty of *lanchas* between Corozal and **Bethél**, a thirty-minute boat ride upstream, plus any time spent waiting for the boat to fill up. Trips across to Bethél have a set fare of US$35 for one to four people. There's a Guatemalan **immigration post** (see box, p.653, for border procedure) in Bethél, from where buses leave at midday and 5pm for **Flores** (for Tikal), a five-hour ride, mostly along dirt roads. Alternatively, you can **stay** in the simple but comfortable *Posada Maya* cabañas (❸), on the riverbank amid the **ruins of Bethél**, camp here (tent or hammock provided; ❶), or get a bed at the very basic *hospedaje* (❶) in the village. The *lancheros* here in Bethél or in Corozal can arrange trips **downstream from Yaxchilán** to the impressive ruins of **Piedras Negras** on the Guatemalan bank, for which you'll need to get a group together as a two- to three-day trip will cost anything from US$75 to US$150 per person, depending on the number. There are rapids above the site, meaning you may well have to get out and walk along the bank at times. It's a beautiful journey, though, and well worth making if you have the time. Below the site the river speeds through two massive canyons: the **Cañon de San José**, where fearsome rapids shoot between cliffs 300m high, then the slightly less dramatic **Cañon de las Iguanas**.

The southern Usumacinta

Following the Frontier Highway south a further 35km from Frontera Corozal brings you to **BOCA LACANTÚN**, where a bridge carries the road over the enormous Río Lacantún. You can expect any bus along this road to be stopped by immigration officials or army checkpoints, so keep your passport handy. At the confluence of the Lacantún and Usumacinta rivers are some unusual Maya remains, the **Planchon de Figuras**, a great limestone slab of unknown origin, carved with Maya glyphs, birds, animals, and temples. If you're travelling by river, the beautiful **Chorro cascades** are just downstream.

Benemérito and onwards

The sprawling frontier town of **BENEMÉRITO**, 2km beyond Boca Lacantún, is the largest settlement in the Chiapas section of the Usumacinta valley, and an important centre for both river and road traffic. If you're **arriving by boat** from Guatemala you'll be met by Mexican soldiers who'll check your passport – the **immigration office** here is not always open, so you may be sent onwards to Frontera Corozal (see p.689) to complete the paperwork. There's a hospital, market, shops, *comedores*, and a few desperately basic **hotels**; you're better off heading on to Corozal (for Yaxchilán), Lacanhá (for Bonampak, see p.688), or even Palenque. The highway is the town's main street and in the centre, at the Farmacia Arco Iris, is the main road leading to the river, less than 2km away. **Heading north** is no problem: buses from Transportes Lagos de Montebello pull in opposite the *Hospedaje Montañero* and *combis* wait across from the *Hospedaje El Tapanco*. **Heading south** around the Frontier Highway, buses from Palenque pass through every couple of hours, eventually reaching the Lagos de Montebello and Comitán.

By river to Sayaxché

If you hope to get by boat **from Benemérito to Sayaxché** in Guatemala you'll need patience or a good deal of money. **Trading boats** (taking at least 12hr), are the cheapest method, but with no proper schedule you just have to ask for times. To reach Sayaxché in one day you'll need to leave early. Fast boats are now making the trip in less than three hours, stopping at the various sites en route, but you'll have to charter them at a cost of at least US$250. **Entering Guatemala**, you'll get your passport stamped at the army post at **Pipiles**, at the confluence with the Río de la Pasión. There's no Mexican immigration here (and probably none at Benemérito); make sure you get an exit stamp in Frontera Corozal (see p.653 for border procedure).

Tabasco

The state of **Tabasco**, crossed by numerous slow-moving tropical rivers on their way to the Gulf, is at last making determined efforts to attract tourists. These rivers were used as trade highways by the ancient **Olmec**, **Maya**, and **Zoque** cultures, and the state boasts dozens of **archeological sites**. Few of these pre-Columbian cities have been fully excavated, though **Comalcalco**, a Maya site north ofVillahermosa, and the Olmec site of **La Venta**, northwest of the capital, have been expertly restored and are certainly worth visiting. A visit to the restored Zoque site of **Malpasito**, in the remote Sierra Huimanguillo and easily the most attractive ancient city in the state, is perhaps more difficult but even more rewarding.

Villahermosa ("Beautiful Town"), the state capital, has undergone an amazing transformation in recent decades, with oil wealth financing the creation of spacious parks and several museums – the city is at last beginning to live up to its name. One excellent example is the **Parque Museo La Venta**, an outdoor archeological exhibition on the bank of a lagoon, which provides the most accessible glimpse of the Olmec civilization, while the ambitious **Yumká** is an expertly run safari park allowing you to take a step out into wild Africa.

Tabasco's **coast**, alternating between estuaries and sand bars, salt marshes, and lagoons, is off the beaten track to most visitors. A road runs very close to the shore, however, enabling you to reach the deserted beaches. As yet these have somewhat limited facilities – even the main coastal town, **Paraíso**, is a tiny place. Much of inland Tabasco is very flat, consisting of the flood plains of a dozen or so major rivers; indeed, most of the state's borders are waterways. Enterprising tour operators are running **boat trips** along the main rivers, the Grijalva and the Usumacinta, and these are the best way to see remote ruins and to glimpse the region's abundant birdlife. You can also travel by river into the Petén in **Guatemala**, leaving from La Palma, near **Tenosique**, in the far eastern corner of the state and near the Classic Maya site of **Pomoná**.

In the far south of the state, around **Teapa** and Villa Luz, the Chiapas highlands make their presence known in the foothills of the **Sierra Puana**. Overlooking the vast Gulf coast plain, these hills offer a retreat from the heat and humidity of the lowlands. Waterfalls spill down from the mountains, and a few small spas (*balnearios*) have developed. Village tracks provide some great **hiking trails** and, despite the proximity to Villahermosa, the state capital, you can enjoy a respite from the well-travelled tourist circuit.

Some history

Little is known about the **Olmec culture**, referred to by many archeologists as the mother culture of Mesoamerica. Its legacy, which included the Long Count calendar, glyphic writing, a rain deity – and probably also the concept of zero and the ball-game – influenced all subsequent civilizations in ancient Mexico, and the fact that it developed and flourished in the unpromising environment of the Gulf coast swamps 3200 years ago only adds to its mystery.

The Spanish Conquistador **Hernán Cortés** landed at the mouth of the Río Grijalva in 1519, and at first easily defeated the local Chontal Maya. However, the town he founded, Santa María de la Victoria, was beset first by indigenous attacks and then by pirates, eventually forcing a move to the present site and a change of name to "Villahermosa de San Juan Bautista" in 1596. For most of the colonial period, Tabasco remained a relative backwater, since the Spanish found the humid, insect-ridden swamps distinctly inhospitable. **Independence** did little to improve matters as local leaders fought among themselves, and it took the **French invasion** of 1862 and Napoleon III's imposition of the unfortunate Maximilian as Emperor of Mexico to bring some form of unity, though Tabasco offered fierce resistance to this foreign intrusion.

The industrialization of the country during the dictatorship of Porfirio Díaz passed agricultural Tabasco by, and even after the **Revolution** it was still a poor state, dependent on cacao and bananas. Though **Tomás Garrido Canabal**, Tabasco's governor in the 1920s and 1930s, is still respected as a reforming socialist whose implementation of laws regarding workers' rights and women's suffrage were decades ahead of the rest of the country, his period in office was also marked by intense **anticlericalism**. Priests were killed or driven out, all the churches were closed, and many of them, including the cathedral in Villahermosa, torn down. The region's **oil**, discovered in the 1930s but not fully exploited until the 1970s, provided the impetus to bring Tabasco into the modern world, enabling capital to be invested in the agricultural sector and Villahermosa to be transformed into the cultural centre it is today.

Villahermosa

VILLAHERMOSA, the state capital, is a major and virtually unavoidable road junction: sooner or later you're almost bound to pass through here on the way from central Mexico to the Yucatán or back, especially if you hope to see Palenque (see p.680). It's a large and prosperous city, and at first glance it can seem as bad a case of urban blight as any in Mexico. But the longer you stay, the more compensations you discover. Quite apart from the **Parque La Venta** and sudden vistas of the broad sweep of the **Río Grijalva**, there are attractive plazas and quiet ancient streets, impressive ultramodern buildings, and several new art galleries and museums. In the evening, as the traffic disperses and the city cools down, its appeal is heightened, and strolling the pedestrianized streets around the Zona Remodelada, where everything stays open late, becomes a genuine pleasure. This lively area, between the two main squares, the **Parque Juárez** to the north and the **Plaza de Armas** just beyond the southern end, is also known as Zona Luz – or simply La Zona.

Arrival and information

The Aeropuerto Carlos A. Rovirosa, Carretera Villahermosa–Palenque Km 13, east of the centre, is a very busy regional **airport**. No buses run to the centre from here; a taxi will cost around US$15. Arriving at one of the **bus stations**, you'll find things are pretty hectic as the highway thunders past through the concrete outskirts. The stations are pretty close to each other: the **first-class** (known simply as El ADO – pronounced El *AH-DAY-OH*), an efficient modern building just off the highway on Javiér Mina, and the two **second-class** terminals, busy, ramshackle affairs actually on the highway (for more on these, see below). Villahermosa's humidity might make you consider taking **taxis** more frequently – worthwhile as the set fare in the city is only US$1.40 (though there is a growing trend to try and charge tourists US$2) and plenty of *combis* ply the main streets.

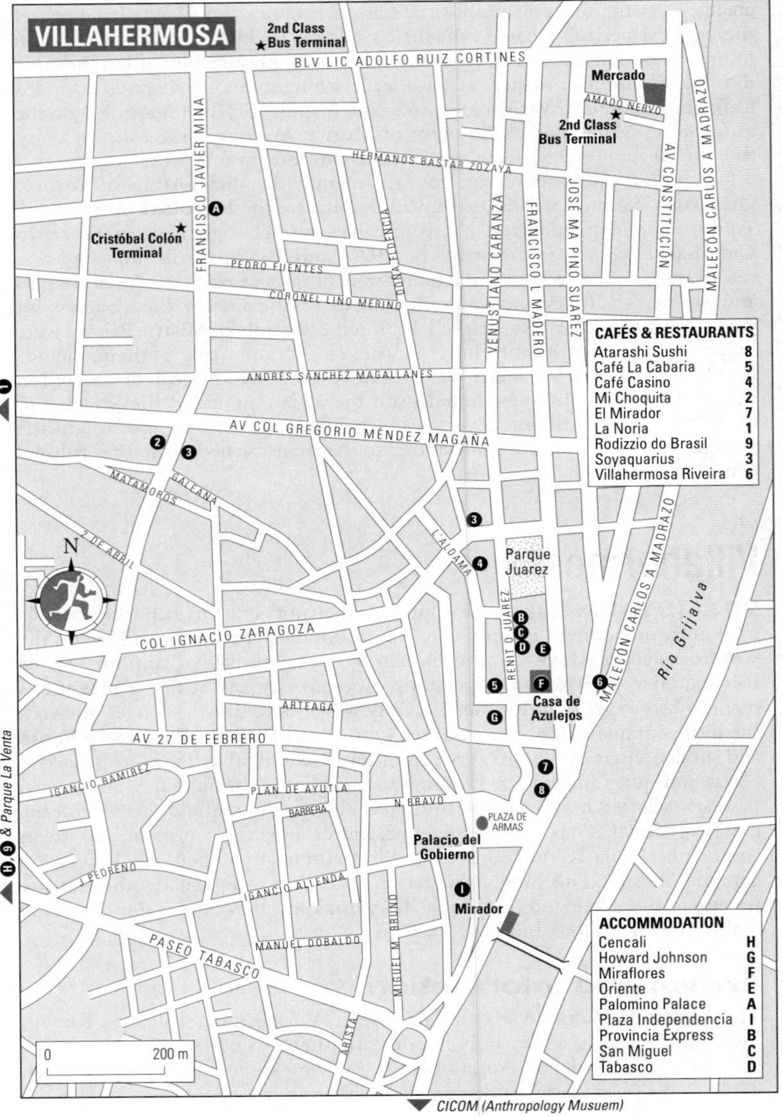

Despite the growth in visitor numbers, Villahermosa's tourist information remains inadequate. The small booths at the airport, history museum and at ADO can offer only a jumble of leaflets, and the main state and federal **tourist office** (Mon–Fri 8am–6pm, Sat 8am–1pm; ⓣ993/316-2889 ext 229), at the junction of Paseo Tabasco and Avenida de los Ríos, is too far away from the centre to be of much use. There's also a small tourist information office at the entrance to the Parque La Venta but they can do little more than give you a map.

The ADO bus terminal

There's a guardería at ADO (daily 7am–8pm; US$0.40 per item). To **get to the centre**, take a colectivo from outside the front of the terminal. There are also *combis* aplenty – look out for those labelled "Parque Juárez" or "Malecón". Otherwise, it's at least twenty minutes' walk to town: head up Merino or Fuentes, opposite the station, for six or seven long blocks, and then turn right at Madero, which will eventually get you to the zócalo (Plaza de Armas), past most of the cheap hotels. To get from ADO **to the second-class terminal**, turn left on Mina, walk three blocks down to the highway, Blv Adolfo Ruíz Cortines, turn right and cross it on the overpass – you can't miss the terminal.

The second-class bus terminals

Villahermosa's second-class terminals are much more crowded than ADO, with constant buses to main destinations. They are near each other on opposite sides of the main highway. To **get into the centre**, turn towards the river, then follow the highway to its junction with Madero. Colectivos are plentiful – you want one heading along Madero, for example, or to CICOM – but it's not easy to work out where they're going. Asking a local is the best way to find out. **Taxis** are around, too, but not always as easy to find as at ADO.

Accommodation

Accommodation in Villahermosa doesn't come cheap, though you will find some reasonable-value hotels in the centre if you look hard enough. Some of the best options are on Madero or Lerdo de Tejada, close to the heart of things. Along Constitución, a block or so from the river, it's possible to find rooms for very little, though the cheapest are distinctly dodgy. Several hotels now have an a/c option and it's always worth checking if free drinking water is available. The most **upmarket** hotels are around the Tabasco 2000 complex away from the centre.

Cencali Paseo Tabasco and Juárez ⓣ993/315-1999, ⓦwww.cencali.com.mx. The best-value hotel in this upmarket area, set in luxuriant gardens on the shore of a lagoon, the *Cencali* has a quiet location and an inviting pool. Comfortable, well-furnished a/c rooms and suites with beautiful tiled bathrooms; upstairs rooms have balconies. ❾

Howard Johnson Aldama 404 ⓣ/ⓕ 993/314-4645, ⓦwww.hojo.com.mx. Just what you'd expect from the chain: comfortable, modern a/c rooms and suites with great bathrooms; TV and phone. ❼–❾

Miraflores Reforma 304 ⓣ993/312-0034, ⓦwww.miraflores.com.mx. One of the better-value upmarket options in La Zona with all of the amenities that you would expect at this price, as well as a disco and video music bar on site. ❻

Oriente Madero 425 ⓣ993/312-0121, ⓕ312-1101. Clean, tiled rooms with modern, private bathrooms, some with a/c and TV; drinking water available. US$250–320.

Palomino Palace across from ADO terminal ⓣ993/312-8431. Conveniently located and usually has rooms available, but a bit overpriced. Rooms, some with a/c, all have private shower and TV. Bar and restaurant. ❺

Plaza Independencia Independencia 123 ⓣ993/312-1299, ⓔvillahermosa@hotelesplaza.com.mx. Comfortable, well-furnished rooms and suites in a quiet area just off the zócalo and handy for CICOM. Front rooms have balconies with views over the river and a safe-deposit box in every room. There's a lift, a pool, a good restaurant, a bar with live music, and secure parking. ❼

Provincia Express Lerdo de Tejada 303 ⓣ993/314-5376, ⓕ314-5442. New and tastefully furnished hotel right in the Zona Luz. All rooms have a/c, private bath, TV, and phone. ❺

San Miguel Lerdo de Tejada 315 ⓣ993/312-1500. Battered but serviceable rooms (some with a/c and TV) with clean sheets and private bath. This is the cheapest option in the area. ❸–❹

Tabasco Lerdo de Tejada 317 ⓣ/ⓕ993/312-0077. Spartan but functional rooms with TV and bathroom and good location in the Zona Luz. ❹

The Zona Remodelada and city centre museums

Though most visitors head straight out to the Parque La Venta, the centre of Villahermosa warrants some exploration. The pedestrianized **Zona Remodelada**, with some vestiges of the nineteenth-century city – the original colonial buildings were built mostly of wood and have perished – is as good a place as any to start your wandering. At its northern end the bustling Parque Juárez, at the junction of Madero and Zaragoza, is lively in the evenings as crowds swirl around watching the street entertainers. Opposite, on Madero, the futuristic glass **Centro Cultural de Villahermosa** (Tues–Sun 10am–8pm; free) has changing exhibitions of art, photography, and costume, as well as film screenings and concerts, and has a good café too. Pieces in the exhibitions are usually for sale.

In the centre of the Zona, on the corner of Sáenz and Lerdo, the distinctive pink and purple paintwork of **La Casa Siempreviva**, dating from the early 1900s, immediately catches the eye. Now a free gallery with a small café, it's one of the few fully restored houses from that era, with tiled floors, arched stained-glass windows, and some later Art Deco features. In the 1930s it was home to journalist and women's rights activist Isabel Rullan, and in the 1940s it became Villahermosa's first hotel with private bathrooms. The side streets here boast a number of other small **art galleries** – look around for signs of current exhibitions. The steps at the far end of Lerdo lead up to the small, tree-shaded **Parque Los Pájaros**, where budgerigars sing in a large, globe-shaped cage and water flows through a series of blue-tiled fountains and pools.

Villahermosa's small **history museum**, at the corner of 27 de Febrero and Juárez (Tues–Sat 10am–8pm; US$0.50), gives a quirky, detailed account of Tabasco's history, illustrated by such diverse objects as an early TV, the printing press for *El Disidente* (a newspaper from 1863), and archeological pieces from Comalcalco, and other information on the Maya sites. The main attraction, however, is the museum building itself (c.1900), which used to be a hotel. Popularly known as the "**Casa de Azulejos**", it is tiled from top to bottom with examples of patterns from all over Europe and the Middle East, forming an optical illusion on the lobby floor. Look up to see the statues of nymphs and classical figures perched on the railings around the roof.

The zócalo, the **Plaza de Armas**, with its river views, is a pleasant place to while away some time, especially in the cool of the evening when there may also be some music on offer. Here, the imposing white-painted **Palacio del Gobierno**, with its classical columns, turreted corners, and clock tower, faces the pretty little **Templo de la Concepción**. The first church was built here in 1799, but this and its successor were both demolished twice over – the present building dates from 1945. On the corner of the plaza the **Puente Solidaridad** footbridge over the Grijalva has a tower mirador that you can climb free for splendid views at sunset.

The CICOM complex

An easy walk along the riverbank from the Zona Remodelada brings you to Villahermosa's cultural centre, **CICOM** – Centro de Investigaciones de las Culturas Olmeca y Maya. The complex includes a concert hall, a beautiful theatre, a research library, and a fine restaurant, along with the **Centro de Estudios y Investigación de los Belles Artes** (daily 10am–2pm & 6–9pm; free), which hosts art and costume displays.

The highlight for most visitors, though, is undoubtedly the **Museo Regional de Antropología Carlos Pellicer Cámara** (Tues–Sun 9am–5pm; US$2) next door, where artefacts and models are displayed on four levels, proceeding chronologically from prehistoric times on the top floor to the Olmecs on the ground floor. In addition to the exhibits of Olmec and Maya ceramics and other artefacts (including a fascinating toy jaguar with wheels), you can also view a reproduction of the Bonampak murals. Carlos Pellicer, a poet and anthropologist born in Villahermosa, and the driving force behind the rescue of the stone carvings from the original La Venta, is commemorated by a bronze statue outside the museum. His house, at Calle Sáenz 203, in the Zona Remodelada, has also been turned into a museum – the **Carlos Pellicer Casa Museo** (Tues–Sat 10am–7pm, Sun 10am–4pm; free), with bits and bobs related to his life, including some of his old shirts and his bed.

Parque La Venta, the zoo, and the Museo de Historia Natural

Discovered by Pemex engineers while draining a marsh for oil, the Olmec site of La Venta – some 120km west of the city, at the border with Veracruz state – had most of its important finds transferred to the **Parque La Venta** (daily 8am–4pm; US$3, including museum and zoo, latter closed Mon), set inside the much larger **Parque Tomás Garrido Canabal**. The Parque La Venta is on the shores of a large lake, the **Laguna de Ilusiones**, where you can rent boats or climb the Mirador de los Águilas, a tower in the middle of the lake.

Although hardly the exact reproduction it claims to be, Parque La Venta does give you a chance to see a superb collection of artefacts from the earliest Mexican civilization in an appropriately jungly setting. The **museum**, housed under an enormous thatched roof just inside the entrance, allows you to familiarize yourself with the known facts of the Olmec culture and the history of the discovery of La Venta. The most significant and famous items in the park are, of course, the four gigantic **basalt heads**, which present such a curious puzzle with their African features. There's a whole series of other Olmec stone sculptures; follow the numbers as the path winds through the park. In their zeal to re-create an authentic jungle setting, the designers have introduced monkeys and coatis (members of the racoon family) which wander around freely, while crocodiles, jaguars, and other animals from Tabasco are displayed in the zoo's sizeable enclosures. The mosquitoes add an authentic but unplanned touch. Also in the park, opposite the La Venta entrance, the small **Museo de Historia Natural** (Tues–Sun 9am–5pm; US$1) has displays on the geography, geology, animals, and plants of Tabasco, focusing on the interaction between humans and the environment. **To get to the park** hop on one of the *combis* that run along Madero in the city centre ("Tabasco 2000", "Circuito 1", "Parque Linda Vista" among others); they also run along the highway from the second-class bus terminal. Beyond La Venta, many of the *combis* continue to Tabasco 2000.

Yumká

Villahermosa's latest ecological attraction, **Yumká** (daily 9am–4pm; US$4), is an ambitious combination of safari park and environmental studies centre. Its formal name, Centro de Interpretación y Convivencia con la Naturaleza, is a bit of a mouthful, so most people simply call it Yumká, after the Chontal Maya god, a dwarf who looks after forests. The park is large, covering more than six square kilometres, so after a guided walking tour of the Tabasco jungle, complete with monkeys, you board a train for a tour round enormous paddocks representing the savannas of Africa and Asia. Elephants, rhinos, giraffes, and antelopes are rarely displayed in Mexico and almost never in such spacious surroundings. After a stop at the restaurant (which serves the green-fleshed *pejelagarto* – alligator gar, a pike-like fish) and souvenir shop, you can take a boat tour of the lagoon (US$2), where, in addition to hippos, there are good bird-watching opportunities.

Yumká is 14km from the centre of Villahermosa, on the road to the airport. *Combis* (US$0.70) leave regularly from along Amado Nervo behind the market at the top end of Av Constitución. A taxi will set you back US$15.

Eating and drinking

Finding somewhere to eat in central Villahermosa can be a bit of a problem. Although there are plenty of food joints and juice bars around the bus station, for the most part the Zona Remodelada boasts only cheap *comedores* able to sell you little more than greasy tacos and fried chicken. For a wider choice, better quality and more cosmopolitan flavours you're best off travelling out towards Tabasco 2000, where the hotel restaurants are amongst the best in the city. As ever, the **market** is good for fruit, bread, and cheap tacos: you'll find it several blocks northeast of the Zona Remodelada, at the top end of Av Constitución. There are a couple of **cafés** at opposite ends of Juárez: *Café La Cabaña*, at the south end opposite the Casa de los Azulejos, is good but pricey, while at the northern end near the corner with Zaragoza, the *Café Casino* is almost as good but much cheaper.

Atarashi Sushi Vazquez Norte 203. Characterful sushi restaurant with the usual Japanese fare along with a selection of steaks. Rather pricey, but the *sushi combinación especial* allows you to sample ten different types of sushi without breaking the bank.

Mi Choquita Javiér Mina 304A. Good breakfasts from US$2.50 and regional dishes in a typical Tabascan style. A few blocks south of the bus station and opposite a branch of *Soyaquarius* (see below).

El Mirador Madero 105. Classy seafood restaurant with river views, and not unreasonable prices. Try the delicious *róbalo* (bass).

La Noria Av Gregorio Méndez 1008. Lebanese and Middle Eastern restaurant with very cheap prices and a menu containing items you are unlikely to find anywhere else in the state.

Rodizio do Brasil Paseo Tabasco 1102 in Tabasco 2000. Brazilian-style restaurant with plenty of grilled meats and an attentive staff.

Soyaquarius Fidencia 100 and another branch on Javiér Mina. Vegetarian food and health-food shop that, bizarrely, also sells hamburgers and fried chicken. Delicious, fresh sandwiches and daily specials.

Villahermosa Constitución 104. Classy and expensive – with main courses starting from US$11– but the food is fantastic. Puts on frequent live music and from the fourth floor the views along the river at sunset are magical.

Listings

Banks There are branches of all major banks at the airport and in the centre, on Madero or Juárez, and you can easily change cash and travellers' cheques. Most banks have ATMs.

Buses To get to the first-class terminal take a "Chedraui" *combi* – they go to a huge department store behind the terminal – and they generally also go past the second-class terminal. Between them, ADO and Cristóbal Colón operate dozens of services to all the main destinations: Campeche (15 daily; 6hr), Cancún (11 daily; 12hr), Chetumal (9 daily; 7hr), Mérida (18 daily; 9hr), Mexico City (27 daily; 12hr), Oaxaca (3 daily; 9hr), Tenosique (12 daily; 3hr), Tuxtla (10 daily; 7hr), Veracruz (15 daily; 7hr), and even the US border and Pacific coast, costing little more than to the capital. There

are several departures to Palenque (11 daily; 2hr 30min), and you can also easily get there from the second-class terminal, from where there are constant departures to all the same destinations, plus Comalcalco, Paraíso, and Frontera. For San Cristóbal (8–9hr), there are few direct services; its often easier to change at either Tuxtla or Palenque.
Internet access Internet cafés are widespread in the Zona Luz. Try *Naveghalia* (US$1 per hour), open until 3am and run by the friendly Marín family at Lerdo 608, up the steps past the Casa Siempreviva. Several others are along Aldama nearby.
Laundry Top Klean on Madero, near 20 de Noviembre, charges about US$2.50 per kilo.
Post office The main post office is in the Zona Remodelada at the corner of Sáenz and Lerdo (Mon–Fri 9am–3pm, Sat 9am–1pm).
Travel agents and tour operators There's no shortage of travel agencies in the Zona Luz, and all the big hotels have a tour desk to arrange domestic flights and trips to Palenque. Creatur, Paseo Tabasco 715 (Ⓣ993/315-3999, Ⓦwww.creaturviajes.com), is the best in the region, with multilingual staff.

South of Villahermosa

South of Villahermosa is an area of exceptionally beautiful highland. The foothills here are heavily farmed by banana plantations, but the surrounding hillsides retain the thick forest characterisitic of the area, and the roadside pools and wetlands – unsuitable for cultivation – are as wild as ever here. The highlights of this region are the numerous **caves and grottos**, while tectonic activity means there a number of **spas** that can be visited, especially in the region's main town, **Teapa**.

Teapa and the southern hills

Fifty-nine kilometres to the south ofVillahermosa, the small, friendly town of **TEAPA** is a lovely base for the spas and caves nearby. Cristóbal Colón **buses** leave Villahermosa for Tuxtla every couple of hours, calling at Teapa, but the best way to get there is to take the comfortable La Sultana service, which departs every half an hour from their terminal on the main highway, opposite the Delegación de Transporte building. La Sultana services also run regularly to Villahermosa, while there is an hourly service on the hour from the Cristóbal Colón terminal on Méndez right in the centre. Most second-class buses pull in at the **market** near the edge of town. To get to the centre, walk a couple of blocks down the hill and turn left at the green clock onto Méndez, which takes you past the hotels and on to the plaza. Teapa's **hotels** are good value: try the *Casa de Huéspedes Miye* (Ⓣ932/322-0420; ❸–❹), a clean, family-run place with private showers and (sometimes) hot water, and rooms round a tiny plant-filled courtyard, just across from the Cristóbal Colón terminal. Rooms with en-suite bathroom are very cheap, but you'll pay more than double if you want a/c as well.

There's swimming in the Río Teapa here, but it's better at the **Balneario Natural Río Puyacatengo**, a few kilometres east (walk or take the bus for Tacotalpa). Three kilometres west of Teapa, almost on the Chiapas border, the **Hacienda Los Azufrés spa** has a classy hotel (Ⓣ932/322-2031, Ⓦwww.haciendalosazufres.com.mx; ❻) and restaurant serving local specialities including *pejelagarto* (alligator gar). Besides taking the glorious and apparently beneficial spa waters, you can organize guided walks, rent bikes, and camp here, and fishing rods are also available for hire. Again, you can get here on foot, or catch a second-class bus towards Pichucalco. Colectivos run from behind the church near the plaza in Teapa to the spectacular **Grutas de Coconá** (daily 9am–5pm; US$15). Eight chambers are open to tourists, and others for potholing only. A stroll through the caves takes about 45 minutes, through surprisingly hot and humid terrain. Local children act as guides (US$4) and will point out interesting rock formations, including a supposedly miraculous representation of the face of Christ. You could also walk to the caves from Teapa (45min): from Méndez, head for the Pemex station and turn right, following the sign. When you get near the forested hills, the road divides; head left over the railway track.

The Sierra Puana: Tapijulapa and Oxolotán

Southeast from Teapa, you can get further away from the humidity of the lowlands by taking day-trips up the valley of the Río Oxolotán to Tabasco's "hill country". This is an extraordinarily picturesque area, with unspoilt colonial towns set in beautiful wooded valleys, and a turquoise river laden with sulphur cascading over a terraced cliff. You'll need to make a fairly early start to get the most out of the day. Buses to **Tacotalpa** from the second-class station on Méndez in Teapa (20min) connect with those to **TAPIJULAPA**, the main settlement (45min). The town is tiny, with narrow cobbled streets, red-tiled roofs, and unfortunately no accommodation. Turn right at the end of the main street, Avenida López Portillo, where steps lead down to the Río Oxolotán. Here you may find boats to take you upstream to visit the **Parque Natural Villa Luz**, with its spa pools, rivers, cascades, and caves. Even so, it's an easy **walk** of 3km to the park: cross the tributary river on the suspension bridge, head left on the concrete path, across the football field, then follow the track over the hill, keeping close to the main river – about 35 minutes in all.

In the park (open daily; free), signed trails lead to caves, but the outstanding feature – not least for its powerful aroma – is the river, which owes its colour to dissolved minerals, especially sulphur. The river exits from a cave and meanders for 1km or so until it reaches the cliff marking the valley of the Río Oxolotán. Here it breaks up into dozens of cascades and semicircular pools. Thousands of butterflies settle on the riverbanks, taking nourishment from dissolved minerals, and jungle trees and creepers grow wherever they find a foothold: a truly primeval sight. The **Cuevas de las Sardinas Ciegas** are not really open to the public, but you can peer into their precipitous entrances. In Maya cosmology the openings are believed to lead to the underworld (Xibalba) and abode of the Lords of Death. Beyond the caves are a couple of open-air **swimming pools** said to have therapeutic properties.

Trucks and *combis* frequently make the trip (25min) from Tapijulapa to **OXOLOTÁN**. Here the ruins of a seventeenth-century Franciscan monastery founded in 1633 contain a small museum (daily 10am–5pm; free) of colonial pieces and wooden sculptures. It occasionally also hosts performances by the Teatro Campesino y Indígena (The Peasant and Indian Theatre), a company that has taken part in cultural festivals throughout Mexico and abroad. **To get there** from Tapijulapa, climb the hill to the church, then descend to the road beyond, where there's a bus stop. The last bus back leaves at 6pm, but you're probably better off catching the 3pm bus if you're heading to Teapa.

West of Villahermosa

West ofVillahermosa the main attractions are a series of isolated ruins, the most famous being those at **La Venta,** although the best pieces now reside in Villahermosa. The mysterious Zoque culture also flourished in this area and the ruins at **Malpasito** are unique in the state and require several days to reach without your own transport.

La Venta

The small town of **LA VENTA**, on the border between Tabasco and Veracruz, would be of little interest were it not for the nearby **archeological ruins** (daily 10am–5pm; US$3.20). The town is served by a steady stream of **buses** from Villahermosa and Coatzalcoalcos, so there's no need or real reason to stay. The ancient site, the name of which remains unknown, was occupied by the Olmecs between 1200 BC and 400 BC. Most of the site's finest pieces, including the famous **basalt heads**, were transferred to Villahermosa's Parque La Venta in 1957 and 1958. The heads are all the more extraordinary because the material from which they were hewn does not occur locally in the region and must have been imported from what is now Veracruz, Oaxaca or Guatemala. The **museum** at the entrance has a model of the site, in a swamp surrounded by rivers, as well as glass cases with rather confusing displays of unlabelled pottery. The site retains a few weathered stelae and monuments, but the highlight is the huge grass-covered mound, about 30m high, clearly a pyramid, with fluted sides believed to represent the ravines on the flanks of a sacred volcano. The climb up is worth the effort for the views and the breeze. Paths below take you through the jungle – fascinating for its plants and butterflies, but haunted by ferocious mosquitoes.

Huimanguillo and the Zoque ruins of Malpasito

More than 100km southwest of Villahermosa, between the borders of Veracruz and Chiapas, a narrow triangle of Tabasco thrusts into the mountains. Known as the **Sierra Huimanguillo**, they're not that high, only up to 1000m, but they are rugged. To appreciate them at their best you have to hike: not only to caves, canyons, and waterfalls, but also to the **Zoque ruins of Malpasito**, with their astonishing **petroglyphs**. They're not that easy to reach independently and you may have to camp when you get there.

The best base for visiting the ruins is **HUIMANGUILLO**, a rather ugly town 68km southwest of Villahermosa. Buses leave Villahermosa for Huimanguillo frequently during the day, and arrive at the terminal on Gutiérrez, near the market. To get to the centre, turn left along Gutiérrez for seven blocks, then turn right onto Hidalgo, the main avenue, for a further six. Alternatively take a *combi* marked "Parque" or "Centro" from outside the terminal. Most of the **places to stay** are along Allende. By far the best is the superb-value *Hotel Guayacan* (Ⓣ917/375-0010; ❺) at no.124, with spacious ultra modern rooms with cable TV, a restaurant and a bar. Further along, the *Hotel Maya* (Ⓣ917/375-1813; ❸) is a budget option, with aging but clean en-suite rooms. Do not confuse it with the unfriendly *Maja* on the same street, which rents rooms by the hour! The owner of *Hotel Maya*, George Pagole del Valle, knows the ruins well and can provide worthwhile information (you'll usually catch him in the mornings).

Most of the **places to eat** in town are basic *taquerías* and *comedores*, but *BO-K2* on Escóbar, the continuation of Hidalgo, one block from the plaza, is clean and good value with nothing on the menu costing over US$3.20. A block further along on Escóbar is the first of several places with **Internet** access, S@rchs at no. 54 (US$1 per hour).

If you're not staying, get a bus heading to **Malpaso** and get off at the village of **Rómulo Calzada**, 70km south. Here you'll need to head west 5km to the *ejido* of **MALPASITO** – there may be a *combi* or a truck going to the village. By now you can see the peaks, with the great jungle-covered plateau of El Mono Pelón ("the bald monkey") dominating the skyline. This is the highest point in Tabasco, and the sheer sides look impossible to climb. In Malpasito ask for the Peréz Rincón family; they might have a room to rent and you can eat with them.

The site

A walk of just over 1km from Malpasito brings you to the post-Classic **Zoque** ruins of the same name (daily 10am–5pm; US$3.20), overlooked by jagged, jungle-covered mountains and reminiscent of Palenque (see p.680). Though the ruins bear resemblances, the Zoque were not a Maya group, and little is known about them. On the way in you pass terraces and grass-covered mounds, eventually arriving at the unique **ball-court**. At the top of the stone terraces forming the south side of the court, a flight of steps leads down to a narrow room, with stone benches lining either side. Beyond this, and separate from the chamber, is a square pit more than 2m deep and 1.5m square. This room may have been used by the ball-players, or at least one team, to effect a spectacular entrance as they emerged onto the top of the ball-court. Beyond the ball-court a grass-covered plaza leads to two flights of wide steps with another small plaza at the top, from where you'll have stunning views of mountains all around.

Perhaps the most amazing feature of this site are the **petroglyphs**. More than three hundred have been discovered so far: animals, birds, houses, and what are presumably religious symbols, etched into the rock. One large boulder has the most enigmatic of all: flat-topped triangles surmounted by a square or rectangle, and shown above what look like ladders or steps – stylized houses or launching platforms for the chariots of the gods, depending on your viewpoint. Beyond the ruins, a trail heads on to a clear pool beneath a twelve-metre waterfall, which is too good to miss if the hike around the ruins has left you hot and dirty. More trails lead up into the mountains; a relatively easy one heads to the base of **La Pava**, an almost perpendicular pillar of rock, the top of which is said to resemble the head of a turkey.

Higher up the valley the **La Pava waterfalls** are an hour's hike along the side of a gorge, during which you'll step between moss-covered boulders and cross the river on a suspension bridge. This is an utterly beautiful, tranquil place, perfect for enjoying the abundant wildlife.

Comalcalco and the north coast

The journey from Villahermosa along **the coast**, west to Veracruz or east to Campeche, is in many ways extraordinarily beautiful. The road hugs the shore so closely that in some places it's been washed away by storms (you may have to cross by boat) and it's never hard to find deserted beaches and lagoons. New bridges have replaced the ferries that used to cross the broad river mouths.

Attractive as the coastal route is, it's undeniably slow and almost no tourists travel it, preferring the inland route to the Yucatán in order to stop by Palenque on the way. Even if this is your intention, you'll be well rewarded by spending a day north of Villahermosa, at the ruins of **Comalcalco**.

Nacajuca and Cupilco

On the road north from Villahermosa to Comalcalco, you wind through the heart of the **cocoa-growing region**, with a few minior diversions along the way. Twenty kilometres on, just beyond the village of **NACAJUCA**, is the **Centro de Reproducción de Tortugas de Agua Dulce** (or simply Granja de Tortugas – Turtle Farm). A breeding centre for seven local species of freshwater turtle, it is the only one of its kind in Latin America (Tues–Sun 9am–6pm; free but donations welcome; ☎914/315-8020). Seven kilometres beyond here the main road passes through **CUPILCO**, notable for its roadside church, the **Templo de la Virgen de Asunción**. Decorated in gold and blue with floral patterns, it is perhaps the most beautiful church in Tabasco. In the area around Comalcalco several **cacao haciendas** have opened their doors to visitors. The first you will pass, 2km before Comalcalco, is Hacienda de la Luz (☎933/334-1126), while Hacienda Cholula (☎933/334-3815) is a further 3km beyond the ruins.

Comalcalco

The Classic-period site of **Comalcalco** (daily 10am–4pm; US$3.20, including museum) is an easy, very worthwhile trip from Villahermosa, 58km to the north. The westernmost Maya site, Comalcalco was occupied around the same time as Palenque (250–900 AD), with which it shares some features, and may even have been ruled by some of the same kings. The area's lack of building stone forced the Chontal Maya to adopt a distinctive, almost unique, form of construction – kiln-fired brick. As if the bricks themselves were not sufficient to mark this site as different, the builders added mystery to technology: each brick was stamped or moulded with a geometric or representational design before firing, with the design face deliberately placed facing inwards, so that it could not be seen in the finished building.

The **bus from Villahermosa** takes an hour and a quarter: ADO has two departures a day, and Transportes Somellera runs an hourly service from the second-class station. Faster and more frequent are the red, white and blue *combis* (US$0.70) that leave from the terminal one block behind the ADO. Once in Comalcalco you'll likely be dropped off at or near the ADO terminal. Green *combis* (US$0.45), found a block further, ply the route to the ruins, but any bus heading north will pass by. Ask the driver for *ruinas* or get off after about five minutes, when you see the sign. The ruins are on the right along a long straight paved road; some *combis* go all the way there, otherwise it's a fifteen-minute walk. There's a small **restaurant** and toilets at the site, and plenty of buses back to Villahermosa and on to Paraíso, running along the main road.

The museum and the site

You can see the astonishing designs on the bricks in Comalcalco's marvellous **museum**, though the labels are in Spanish only. Animals depicted include crocodiles, turtles, frogs, lizards, dogs, and mice, while those portraying the sculpted faces of rulers display an advanced level of artistic development. The most amazing figure, however, is of a skeleton which appears to be leaping out at you from the surface of the brick. The abundant clay that provided such a versatile medium for architects and artists here also formed the basis for many more mundane artefacts. Comalcalco means "place of the *comales*" – fired clay griddles for cooking tortillas – in Nahuatl, and these and other clay vessels have been found in great numbers. Some of the largest jars were used as **funerary urns** and several are on display here, including one with an intact skeleton.

There are no official guides, but Eugenio Martinez Torres (☎933/327-4629; US$20 per group) has collaborated on a book about Comalcalco's bricks, and he speaks some English. The accessible area is not large but you'll need to take water with you as the humidity can be extremely high, and insect repellent will come in handy. Though there are dozens of structures, only around ten or so of the larger buildings have been subjected to any restoration. Due to the fragile nature of the brickwork you're not allowed to climb many of the buildings, but you can follow a path up to Structure 3 and around the Palacio.

The first one you come to is the main structure of the **North Plaza Cluster**: Temple I, a tiered pyramid with a massive central stairway. Originally, the whole building (along with all of the structures here) would have been covered with stucco made from oyster shells, sculpted into masks and reliefs of rulers and deities, and brightly painted. Only a few of these features remain – the exposed ones protected from further erosion by shelters, while others have been deliberately left buried. Opposite Temple I is the **Great Acropolis**: it's 80m long, with more buildings being excavated, and there's a fine stucco mask of Kinich Ahau, the Maya sun god. At the far end of the site you'll come to **El Palacio**, where you can climb the mound and get a close view of the brickwork. There's a series of massive brick piers and arches here which once formed an enormous double corbelled vault, 80m long and over 8m wide – one of the largest enclosed spaces the Maya ever built. At the side of Temple V a small, corbelled room contains stucco reliefs of nine, richly dressed, half-life size figures apparently in conversation or even argument – they may represent the **Lords of Xibalba**, the Maya underworld.

The north coast

Skirting the coast and passing through areas of wetland teeming with wildlife, the little-travelled **north coast** road is a treat. Mangroves and lagoons are covered with flocks of feeding waterbirds, and if you look hard enough you may spot the odd crocodile. However, if its beaches that you've come for you are likely to be disappointed - the sand is grey-brown and, though generally clean, you've always got the oil refinery in sight to the east. There are few hotels along this stretch, but plenty of spaces for camping – and swarms of mosquitoes and sandflies.

Paraíso

If you want to travel the coastal route, catch one of the frequent buses passing the Comalcalco turn-off to **PARAÍSO**, 17km away on the banks of the Río Seco. It's a pleasant enough place, with some beaches nearby and a sleepy atmosphere if you need to wind down. Paraíso's ADO **bus station** is inconveniently located 1km south of the centre along Benito Juárez, the main road. Turn right out of the station and keep walking – eventually you'll see the town's most distinctive monument across the river up ahead – the twin-towered colonial church dominating the modern plaza. The main second-class station, with departures for points along the coast, is fifteen minutes' walk north of the centre and well served by *combis*. If you're walking from the second-class station to the centre, head south (left) and aim for the church tower, which is visible from just about everywhere. Most **hotels** here are not up to much: *Hotel Hidalgo* (☎933/333-0007; ❺), on the river at Degollado 206, at 2 de Abril, is the exception, with good, clean rooms with fan or a/c, private bathrooms with hot water, and drinking water. There are plenty of juice bars on and around the zócalo and a couple of decent, moderately priced **restaurants**: *Real de la Costa* on the east side is perhaps the best, with a wide selection of Mexican food, meats, pastas and seafood dishes. Internet access at Compucentro, on the west side of the plaza, is not cheap at US$1.20, but the connection is fast. The nearest beach, **Playa Limón**, is a twenty-minute *combi* ride north of Paraíso.

Puerto Ceiba and the coast road east

Ten kilometres east of Paraíso, the road passes through **PUERTO CEIBA** on the shores of the **Laguna de Mecoacán.** There's a *parador turístico* here offering ferry trips, outdoor activities, and a restaurant serving regional dishes and fish straight out of the lake. The road then crosses **Laguna Santa** to the east, and there are turn-offs for several good beaches before it meets Hwy-180, 50km or so north of Villahermosa. The first is **Playa Azúl**, a favourite for water-sports enthusiasts, while **Playa Pico de Oro,** 6km or so further on, is more tranquil. If you're travelling light you could easily camp at any of these and get back to the main road in the morning.

Frontera and the Reserva de la Biosfera Pantanos de Centla

About 50km beyond Paraíso the bus will drop you in **FRONTERA**, a pleasant if uninspiring working town and port. Visited by Graham Greene in 1938, it is little changed since then. **Arriving** by second-class bus, turn left out of the bus station and walk two blocks along Madero to get to the zócalo or, from the first-class bus station, left along Zaragoza, then right, and walk three blocks down Madero from the other direction. **Buses** for Villahermosa or Ciudad del Carmen leave every one or two hours during daylight hours, and four buses daily go to Veracruz. Everything you'll need is around the tastefully modernized zócalo, including a couple of nondescript **hotels**; *Marmor Plaza* (☎913/332-0001; ❺) is the best option, with reasonable, value rooms. For tasty shrimp or a good-value comida corrida, try *El Conquistador*, in an old colonial building, at Juárez 8. Perhaps the main reason for staying in Frontera is to visit the **Reserva de la Biosfera Pantanos de Centla**, an unspoilt wetland area positively teeming with wildlife. The Desarrollo Ecoturístico Punta Manglar (☎913/398-1688), 10km south of the town, offers guided walks, canoe and ferry trips, and other educational activities as well as a small restaurant for refreshment. North of Frontera, at the mouth of the Río Grijalva is the picturesque, palm-filled **Playa del Bosque**.

East to the Usumacinta and Guatemala

Heading east from Villahermosa, the toll road Hwy-186 (cars US$1.70) cuts across a salient of northern Chiapas before swinging north into Campeche to Francisco Escárcega, then east again as the only road across the base of the Yucatán peninsula to Chetumal. At Catazajá, in Chiapas, 110km from Villahermosa, is the junction for **Palenque**. If you've already been there and want to see Tikal in Guatemala's Petén, you can go via **Tenosique** and **La Palma** (see p.709), although it's quicker and cheaper to go from Frontera Corozal (see p.689); if you go this way, however, you could visit the nearby ruins of **Pomoná**.

Emiliano Zapata

Coming from either Palenque or Villahermosa, you'll pass through the town of **EMILIANO ZAPATA**, named after the Mexican revolutionary whose

Fiestas

The states of Chiapas and Tabasco are extremely rich in **festivities**. Local tourist offices should have more information on what's happening in your vicinity.

JANUARY

1 NEW YEAR'S DAY. **San Andrés Chamula** (Chiapas) and **San Juan Chamula** (Chi), both near San Cristóbal, have civil ceremonies to install a new government for the year.

19 At **Tenosique** (Chi) the El Pochó dancers perform, dressed as jaguars and men, to represent the struggle of good and evil. The celebration concludes on SHROVE TUESDAY with the burning of an effigy of El Pochó, god of evil.

20 DÍA DE SAN SEBASTIÁN sees a lot of activity. In **Chiapa de Corzo** (Chi) a large fiesta with traditional dances lasts several days, with a re-enactment on the 21st of a naval battle on the Río Grijalva. The event is big, too, in **Zinacantán** (Chi), near San Cristóbal.

FEBRUARY

2 DÍA DE LA CANDELARIA. Colourful celebrations at **Ocosingo** (Chi).

11–20 Fiesta de San Caralampio in **Comitán** (Chi).

27 In **Villahermosa** (Tabasco), a fiesta commemorates the anniversary of a battle against the French.

CARNAVAL (the week before Lent – variable dates Feb–March) is at its most frenzied in the big cities – especially **Villahermosa** (Tab) – but is also celebrated in hundreds of villages throughout the area. **San Juan Chamula** (Chi) has a big fiesta.

MARCH

1 Anniversary of the foundation of **Chiapa de Corzo** (Chi) celebrated.

HOLY WEEK is widely observed – particularly big ceremonies in **San Cristóbal de las Casas** (Chi). **Ciudad Hidalgo** (Chi), at the border near Tapachula, has a major week-long market.

APRIL

1–7 A feria in **San Cristóbal de las Casas** (Chi) celebrates the town's foundation. A Spring Fair is generally held here later in the month.

In the second half of the month **Villahermosa** (Tab) hosts its annual feria, with agricultural and industrial exhibits and the election of the queen of the flowers.

29 DÍA DE SAN PEDRO celebrated in several villages around San Cristóbal, including **Amatenango del Valle** and **Zinacantán** (Chi).

MAY

3 DÍA DE LA SANTA CRUZ celebrated in **San Juan Chamula** (Chi) and in **Teapa** (Tab), between Villahermosa and San Cristóbal.

8 DÍA DE SAN MIGUEL. Processions and traditional dances in **Mitontic** (Chi), near San Cristóbal.

15 DÍA DE SAN ISIDRO sees peasant celebrations everywhere – famous and picturesque fiestas in **Huistán** (Chi), near San Cristóbal.

Also, there's a four-day nautical marathon (variable dates) **from Tenosique to Villahermosa** (Tab), when crafts from all over the country race down 600km of the Usumacinta.

rallying cry "Tierra y Libertad" still rings out across Mexico on Revolution Day (Nov 20), and whose statue adorns the main plaza here. The town sits on the shores of **Laguna Nueva Esperanza**, with areas for swimming and excellent fishing opportunities. Great views of the lake can be had from the **bus stations**, in the same building on the edge of the town, and there are plenty of

JUNE

13 DÍA DE SAN ANTONIO celebrated in **Simojovel** (Chi), near San Cristóbal, and **Cárdenas** (Tab), west of Villahermosa.

24 DÍA DE SAN JUAN is the culmination of several days' celebration in **San Juan Chamula** (Chi).

JULY

7 Beautiful religious ceremony in **Comitán** (Chi), with candlelit processions to and around the church.

17 DÍA DE SAN CRISTÓBAL celebrated enthusiastically in **San Cristóbal de las Casas** (Chi) and in nearby villages such as **Tenejapa** and **Amatenango del Valle**, and this is just one highlight in over a week of festivities.

20 Strongly indigenous festivities, heavily influenced by the Zapatista movement, in **Las Margaritas** (Chi), near Comitán.

25 DÍA DE SANTIAGO provokes widespread celebration – especially in **San Cristóbal de las Casas** (Chi), where they begin a good week earlier.

AUGUST

6 Images from the churches of neighbouring villages are brought in procession to **Mitontic** (Chi), for religious ceremonies there.

10 FIESTA DE SAN LORENZO in **Zinacantán** (Chi), with much music and dancing.

22–29 Feria in **Tapachula** (Chi).

24 Fiestas in **Venustiano Carranza** (Chi), south of San Cristóbal.

30 DÍA DE SANTA ROSA celebrated in **San Juan Chamula** (Chi).

SEPTEMBER

14–16 Throughout Chiapas, celebration of the annexation of the state to Mexico, followed by Independence celebrations everywhere.

29 DÍA DE SAN MIGUEL is celebrated in **Huistán** (Chi).

OCTOBER

On the first Sunday, the DÍA DE LA VIRGEN DEL ROSARIO is celebrated in **San Juan Chamula** and **Zinacantán** (Chi).

3 DÍA DE SAN FRANCISCO in **Amatenango del Valle** (Chi).

NOVEMBER

29 DÍA DE SAN ANDRÉS celebrated in **San Andrés Chamula** (Chi).

DECEMBER

12 DÍA DE LA VIRGEN DE GUADALUPE is an important day throughout Mexico. There are particularly good fiestas in **Tuxtla Gutiérrez** and **San Cristóbal de las Casas** (Chi), and the following day another in nearby **Amatenango del Valle** (Chi).

17–22 **Pijijiapan** (Chi), on the coast highway to Tapachula, holds a feria and cheese expo.

first- and second-class services to Villahermosa (16 daily, last one 8.10pm) and Tenosique (11 daily, last one 8.35pm). If you do get stuck, try the *Hotel Ramos* (Ⓣ934/343-0600; ❺), opposite the bus station, which is at least comfortable and saves you going into town. Viajes Montecristo (Ⓣ934/343-1530), on the same street, is the only proper **travel agent** between here and Palenque.

Tenosique

The Río Usumacinta is crossed by the road and railway at Boca del Cerro, a few kilometres from **TENOSIQUE**, where the now placid river leaves some pretty impressive hills. **Buses** arrive at a small terminal close to the highway, just out of town. Inexpensive colectivos (US$0.45) run frequently to the centre; get off when you see a large white church with red trim on the right of the main street, Calle 26 (also known as "Pino Suárez"). Navigation around town can be difficult. Streets are numbered rather than named, and in no logical order. Calle 26 leads up to the zócalo, decorated with ridiculous giant fibreglass macaws, and Calle 28 runs parallel; pretty much everything you will need will be located along these two streets.

There's not a lot to do in Tenosique, whose main claim to fame is as the birthplace of Mexican national hero Pino Suárez (born here on September 8, 1869). His former house is on Calle 26, the blue and white building across the road from the church towards the zócalo. It now houses offices of Telcel, the Mexican telecom provider. If you have **to stay**, *Hacienda Tabasqueña*, C 26 no. 512 (Ⓣ934/342-2731; ❹–❺), is easily the best option, with comfortable, spacious en-suite rooms, some with a/c. *Roma*, a block closer to the plaza, on the parallel C 28 at no. 400 (Ⓣ934/342-0151; ❸), is rather battered, but cheaper and all rooms are en-suite. Calles 26 and 28 are also the main areas for shopping and **eating**. Most of the restaurants around here are unimpressive and cheap, and have similar menus. A row of inexpensive *comedores* lines the front of the market, just off the northwest corner of the plaza, while the slightly hyperbolic *El Paraíso*, next to the church on Calle 26, is better than most. *D'Manolo's*, opposite, also serves pizza. *La Palapa* restaurant overlooks the broad river. It's a good place for coffee and a snack whilst watching the boat traffic heading constantly back and forth. Several places with **Internet** access are found along Calle 28, including a place at no. 317, which charges US$1.20 per hour.

If you are going **to Guatemala** you'd be wise to stock up on provisions: there's a good **bakery** opposite the *Hotel Roma* and there are fruit stalls everywhere. The **banks** in Tenosique aren't interested in changing money, but Bancomer on the plaza has an ATM; for Guatemalan quetzales ask around in the shops on Calle 28, where you should find someone who will give better rates than the boatmen. For **moving on**, there are fifteen bus services to Villahermosa during the day, a first-class service to Mexico City at 5pm, and buses to Escárcega and points east at 6.15pm and 8pm, with no more services after 8pm.

The ruins of Pomoná and Reforma, and the Reserva Ecológica Cascadas de Reforma

On the road from Emiliano Zapata, about 30km west of Tenosique, the ruins of **Pomoná** (daily 8am–4pm; free) are reached 4km down a signed track. Although the site, located in rolling countryside with views of forested hills to the south, makes a pleasant diversion, a visit is really only for the dedicated. The restored structures date from the Late Classic period; the site's largest building is a stepped pyramid with six levels. Pomoná was a subject of the much larger city of Piedras Negras in Guatemala, further up the valley of the Usumacinta. The modern little **museum** houses some interesting carved panels and stelae, made even more mysterious by the omission of any explanations as to what you're seeing.

North of Tenosique a road heads about 70km through the **Reserva Ecológica Cascadas de Reforma**, where the Río San Pedro forms four pretty waterfalls. There's a *balneario* here with restaurants, toilets, and swimming opportunities in the naturally formed pools. A further 2km beyond here are the ruins of **Reforma** (daily 8am–5pm; free), which feature six Mayan stelae, seven large buildings, and a ball-court, as well as several other smaller and more minor constructions.

La Palma and the Río San Pedro to Guatemala

Buses (US$2) for **LA PALMA**, and the crossing to Guatemala, leave Tenosique approximately every two hours from 4.30am to 4.30pm from Calle 28 just behind the church. If you are in a group, or even if you're alone, a taxi is a much better bet, costing just US$2.50. They leave from the same place and are considerably more convenient than waiting for a bus to show up. Buses head due east through flat farming and ranching country and after an hour reach the Río San Pedro, stopping at the *Parador Turístico* restaurant by the dock for the **boat trip to El Naranjo** in Guatemala. The usual departure time is 8am, with boats returning at 1pm from El Naranjo (4hr; US$24), but you may have to wait until sufficient passengers turn up. The trip is, frankly, overpriced, and you'll have a much more interesting time crossing from Frontera Corozal to **Bethél**, visiting Bonampak and Yaxchilán en route (see box, p.653, for border procedure). There are some basic **rooms** at La Palma if you need to stay; ask at the restaurant.

Leaving for Guatemala, you hand in your Mexican tourist card at the immigration post at El Pedregal about halfway through the journey. Opposite the dock at **EL NARANJO** are some large, overgrown **ruins**, where the bigger pyramids are surmounted by posts bristling with machine guns. At least eight daily **buses** leave El Naranjo for **Flores** (4hr 30min; US$4); most will pass by the dock but if you get stuck here it's only a ten-minute walk to the main road and a number of rather desperate hotels and *comedores*.

Travel details

Buses

Departures given are for direct first-class services; there are likely to be at least as many second-class buses (and often *combis* as well) to the same destinations. See also the "Listings" sections of larger city accounts.

Palenque to: Campeche (3 daily; 6hr); Cancún (5 daily; 12hr); Mérida (4 daily; 9hr); Mexico City (2 daily; 17hr); San Cristóbal (10 daily; 5hr); Tuxtla Gutiérrez (10 daily; 7hr); Villahermosa (15 daily; 2hr 30min). Plenty of second-class buses run along the Frontier Highway for the junctions to Bonampak and Yaxchilán.

San Cristóbal to: Ciudad Cuauhtémoc, for Guatemala (at least 8 daily; 3hr 30min); Comitán, for Lagos de Montebello or the Guatemalan border (at least hourly; 2hr); Mexico City (5 daily; 18hr); Palenque (9 daily; 5hr); Tapachula (4 daily; 9hr); Tuxtla Gutiérrez (constantly; 2hr); Villahermosa, some direct, otherwise via Tuxtla or Palenque (6 daily; 8–9hr).

Tapachula to: Arriaga (at least 12 daily; 4hr); Guatemala City (2 daily; 5–6hr); Mexico City (12 daily; 18hr); Oaxaca (1 daily; 12hr); San Cristóbal (2 daily; 9hr); Tuxtla Gutiérrez (15 daily; 7hr); Veracruz (1 daily; 14hr); Villahermosa (2 daily; 13hr).

Tuxtla Gutiérrez to: Ciudad Cuauhtémoc, for Guatemala (6 daily; 6hr); Comitán, for Lagos de Montebello or the Guatemalan border (7 daily; 4hr); Mérida (1 daily; 14hr); Mexico City

(7 daily; 16hr); Palenque (hourly; 7hr); San Cristóbal (15 daily; 2hr); Tapachula (15 daily; 7hr); Tonalá (hourly; 3hr 30min); Villahermosa (9 daily; 7hr).
Villahermosa to: Campeche (15 daily; 6hr); Cancún (11 daily; 12hr); Chetumal (9 daily; 7hr); Mérida (18 daily; 9hr); Mexico City (27 daily; 11hr); Palenque (11 daily; 2hr 30min); San Cristóbal, some direct, otherwise via Tuxtla or Palenque (3 daily; 8–9hr); Tapachula (1 daily; 13hr); Tuxtla Gutiérrez (10 daily; 7hr); Veracruz (15 daily; 7hr).

International buses

Tapachula to: Guatemala (4 daily; 5–6hr).

International ferries

Frontera Corozal (Yaxchilán) to: Bethél, Guatemala (several daily, no schedule; 30min).
La Palma (near Tenosique) to: El Naranjo, Guatemala (1 daily; 4hr).

Flights

Villahermosa is the main regional airport, with international services to the US as well as services to some larger airports within Mexico. Most of the other airports run skeletal services of just a few flights, invariably to Mexico City, but occasionally to one or two minor destinations as well. If you are not flying from Villahermosa you will almost certainly have to change at Mexico City to get to other large Mexican cities by air. Servicios Aéreos San Cristóbal, based in **Ocosingo** (℗919/673-1088), operate light aircraft – from Palenque or San Cristóbal to Yaxchilán or Bonampak.
San Cristóbal to: Mexico city (1 daily).
Tapachula to: Mexico City (4 daily); Tuxtla Gutiérrez (1 daily).
Tuxtla Gutiérrez to: Mexico City (4 daily); Tapachula (1 daily).
Villahermosa to: Mexico City (9 daily); Mérida, Cancún, Tuxtla Gutiérrez and Oaxaca (1 daily); to Veracruz and Monterrey (1 daily).

10

The Yucatán

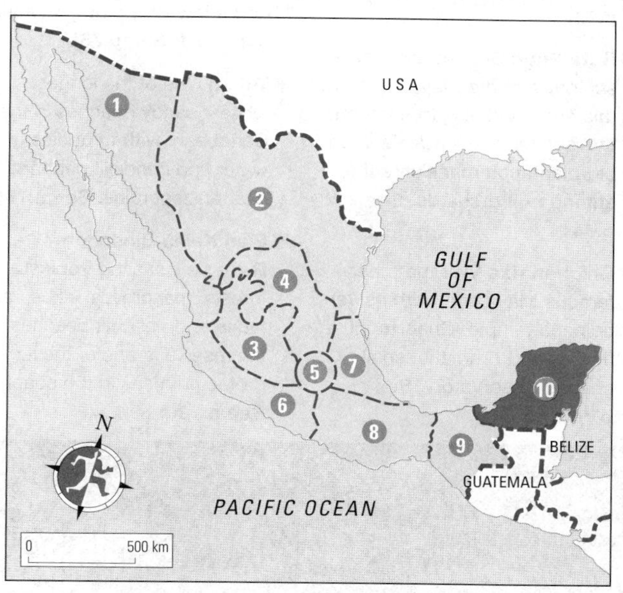

CHAPTER 10

Highlights

* **Campeche** This lovely walled city with narrow streets and pastel-coloured houses is immaculately kept by its proud citizens. See p.717

* **Mérida** Although the "White City" is the largest on the peninsula – alive with music and Sunday markets – it retains a tranquil charm. See p.727

* **Ruta Puuc** See the distinctive sculpture at the Maya sites in this area, and visit (or stay at) the isolated *Hacienda Tabi*, an old plantation mansion set among fruit orchards. See p.741

* **Chichén Itzá** Visit the most famous Maya site, with its vertiginous temple, Chac-mool figures and dramatic, snail-shaped observatory. See p.750

* **Cenotes** On a peninsula with no rivers and few lakes, these underground oases played an essential role in Maya survival and spirituality. Their clear waters make for a refreshing swim. See p.759

* **Cozumel** Some of the world's best snorkelling and scuba diving: crystal-clear visibility and a jaw-droppingly beautiful coral reef. See p.780

* **Tulum** One of the longest, whitest sandy beaches in the Caribbean, with turquoise water and candlelit cabañas near ancient ruins. See p.785

* **Sian Ka'an Biosphere Reserve** Boasting tropical forests, mangroves, lakes, rare fauna and unspoilt beaches, the reserve is one of the largest protected areas in the country. See p.790

△ Flamingoes, Celestún Natural Park

10

The Yucatán

The three states that comprise the Yucatán peninsula – Campeche, Yucatán and Quintana Roo – are among the hottest and most tropical parts of Mexico, though they lie further north than you might imagine: the sweeping curve of southern Mexico means that the Yucatán state capital, **Mérida**, is actually at a higher latitude than Mexico City. Until the 1960s, when proper road and train links were finally completed, the Yucatán lived out of step with the rest of the country and had almost as much contact with Europe and the US as with central Mexico. Tourism has since made major inroads, especially in the north around the great **Maya sites** and on the route from Mérida to the **Quintana Roo coast**, where development has centred on the "super-resort" of **Cancún**, the islands of **Isla Mujeres**, **Cozumel**, and, in more recent years, the once sleepy fishing village of **Playa del Carmen**. But away from the big centres, especially in the south, where townships are sparsely scattered in thick jungle, there's still a distinct pioneering feel.

Travelling around the peninsula, the changes in landscape are hard to miss. In Yucatán state, the shallow, rocky earth gives rise to stunted trees, and underground springs known as cenotes are the only source of water. At the opposite end of the scale, Campeche state boasts a huge area of **tropical forest**, the Calakmul Biosphere Reserve – though because a good portion of the reserve is still owned by *ejidos* (agricultural co-operatives), the forest is being thinned in spots for cattle ranching and timber. The entire peninsular coastline is great for spotting **wildlife** – notably turtles at the Sian Ka'an Biosphere Reserve in Quintana Roo, and the flocks of flamingoes at Celestún and Río Lagartos in Yucatán – but the most spectacular, white-sand **beaches** line the Caribbean coast, where magnificent offshore **coral reefs** form part of the second largest barrier reef system in the world.

Some history

The peninsula's modern boom is, in fact, a reawakening, for this has been the longest continuously civilized part of the country, with evidence of Maya inhabitants as early as 2500 BC, producing pottery and living in homes virtually identical to those you see in the villages today. **The Maya** are not a specifically Mexican culture – their greatest cities, indeed, were not in Mexico at all but in the lowlands of modern Guatemala, Belize and Honduras. But they did produce a unique style in the Yucatán and continued to flourish here long after the collapse of the "Classic" civilizations to the south. This they did in spite of natural handicaps – thin soil, heat, humidity and lack of water – and in the face of frequent invasion from

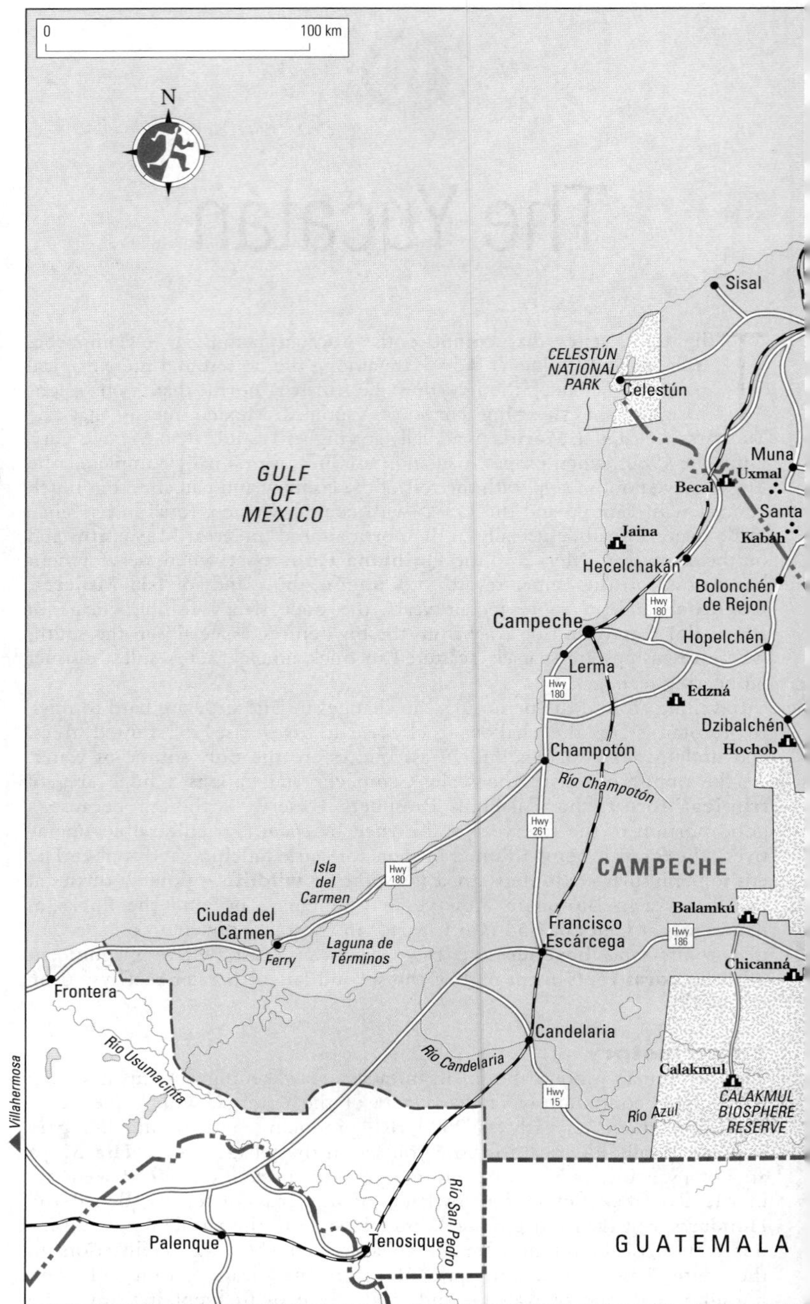

0
100 km
N
GULF OF MEXICO
Sisal
CELESTÚN NATIONAL PARK
Celestún
Muna
Uxmal
Becal
Santa
Jaina
Kabáh
Hecelchakán
Bolonchén de Rejon
Hwy 180
Campeche
Hopelchén
Lerma
Hwy 180
Edzná
Dzibalchén
Hochob
Champotón
Río Champotón
Hwy 261
CAMPECHE
Isla del Carmen
Hwy 180
Ciudad del Carmen
Balamkú
Francisco Escárcega
Hwy 186
Ferry
Laguna de Términos
Chicanná
Frontera
Candelaria
Río Usumacinta
Río Candelaria
Calakmul
Villahermosa
Hwy 15
CALAKMUL BIOSPHERE RESERVE
Río Azul
Río San Pedro
Palenque
Tenosique
GUATEMALA

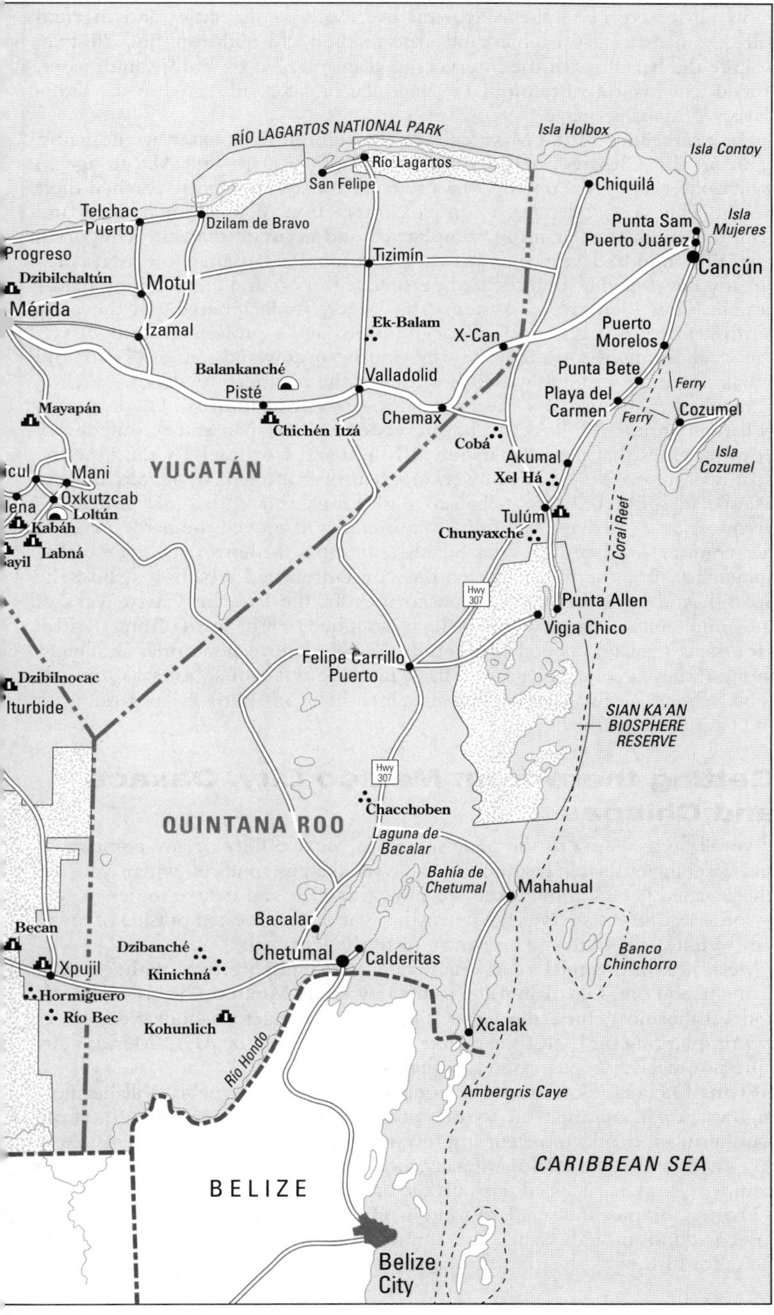

10 THE YUCATÁN

central Mexico. Here the Maya still live, both in the cities and in rural villages, in many cases remarkably true to their old traditions and lifestyle, despite the hardships of the intervening years: ravaged by European diseases, forced to work on vast colonial *encomiendas* or, later, subjected to the semi-slavery of debt peonage.

The florescence of the Maya culture, throughout their extensive domains, came in the **Classic period** from around 300 AD to 900 AD, an age in which the cities grew up and Maya science and art apparently reached their height. The Maya calendar, a complex interaction of solar, lunar, astral and religious dates, was far more complicated and accurate than the Gregorian one. Five hundred years before the European Renaissance, the Maya had already developed a sophisticated perspective in art and an elaborate mathematical and hieroglyphic system (still largely undeciphered). In the early ninth century AD, growing military tensions and a prolonged drought saw the abandonment of many of the southern lowland cities (Tikal and Calakmul among them), while the cities of the northern lowlands – such as Chichén Itzá, Uxmal and the Puuc sites – began to flourish. These in turn collapsed around 1200 AD, to be succeeded by Mayapán and a confederacy of other cities that probably included Tulum and Cozumel. By the time the Spanish arrived, Mayapán's power, too, had been broken by revolt, and the Maya had splintered into tribalism – although still with cities and long-distance sea trade that awed the Conquistadors. It proved the hardest area of the country to pacify. Despite Spanish attempts to destroy all trace of the ancient culture, the Maya carried out constant armed rebellion against the Spanish and later the Mexican authorities. In the last, the **Caste Wars** of the nineteenth century, the Maya, supplied with arms from British Honduras (Belize), gained brief control of the entire peninsula. Gradually, though, they were again pushed back into the wilds of southern Quintana Roo, where the final pockets of resistance held out until the beginning of the twentieth century.

Getting there from Mexico City, Oaxaca and Chiapas

If you'll be travelling to the peninsula from Mexico City or any point south and east, an invaluable resource is Ⓦwww.ticketbus.com.mx, where you can check schedules and buy tickets for most first-class and deluxe routes, as well as some second-class services. As many bus stations are located outside of town, this website will spare you an extra trip to the terminal.

Mérida, as the capital of Yucatán state, is a transport hub, with constant traffic in and out. The main route to the city **from Mexico City** is via Puebla and Villahermosa, then through Campeche – a nineteen-hour ride, so it's worth splurging on UNO, the deluxe bus line operated by ADO. Mérida's airport also receives frequent internal flights.

From Oaxaca, most buses head north and rejoin the Puebla–Villahermosa highway, then continue on to the lacklustre town of Escárcega. But from Villahermosa, thanks to recent improvements to the coast road, it's possible to take the more scenic (and marginally more direct) route hugging the water. If you drive, beware of speed traps on the bridges.

From Chiapas, the standard route is Hwy-199 to Escárcega, then back to the coast and through Campeche. On the way you'll pass Palenque, a touchstone for further exploration of Mayan ruins on the peninsula proper.

Central Yucatán: the great Maya sites

There's really only one main route around the Yucatán; the variation comes in where you choose to break the journey or make side trips off the trail. Whether you come from Palenque or along the beautiful coast from Villahermosa and **Ciudad del Carmen**, you'll find yourself on Hwy-180, which heads up to **Campeche**, from there to **Mérida**, and on via **Chichén Itzá** to the Caribbean coast. From Mérida the best of the **Maya sites** – Uxmal, Chichén Itzá and a trove of smaller, less visited ruins – are in easy reach.

The road that runs across **the south** of the peninsula, from **Francisco Escárcega** to **Chetumal**, is relatively new, passing through jungle territory rich in Maya remains, several of which have only been open to the public since the mid-1990s. The gem is the enormous site of **Calakmul**, located deep in a jungle reserve near the border with Guatemala; the view from its main pyramid, the tallest in the Maya world, takes in a sea of verdant tropical forest from horizon to horizon. You can get accommodation and arrange tours to all of the ruins at **Xpujil**, a village named after the nearby archeological site, on the border between Campeche and Quintana Roo states.

Campeche

CAMPECHE, capital of the state that bears its name, is another of the country's colonial gems. Elegant eighteenth- and nineteenth-century houses painted in pastel shades (hundreds of which have been recently restored to their former glory), interspersed with the occasional church, give it a distinctly European feel. At its heart, relatively intact, lies a colonial port town still surrounded by hefty defensive walls and fortresses; around are the trappings of a modern city that is once again becoming wealthy. The seafront is a bizarre mixture of centuries-old and twentieth-century modern: originally the city defences dropped straight into the sea, but now they face a reclaimed strip of land on which stand the spectacular concrete Palacio de Gobierno and State Legislature (spectacularly ugly in the eyes of most locals), a series of striking sculptures representing various aspects of the city – piracy, warfare at sea, fishing – and several big hotels. In the past, few tourists have stopped here, preferring to sweep by en route to Palenque or Villahermosa. Though more visitors are discovering the immaculately preserved and tranquil streets which compare favourably with Mérida's, for the moment at least Campeche remains unblighted by tourist overkill.

A Spanish crew of explorers under Francisco Hernández landed outside the Maya town of Ah Kin Pech in 1517, only to beat a hasty retreat on seeing the forces lined up to greet them. Not until 1540 did the second-generation Conquistador Francisco de Montejo the Younger found the modern town, and from here set out on his mission to subdue the Yucatán. From then until the nineteenth century, Campeche was the chief port in the peninsula, exporting mainly logwood (source of a red dye known as hematein) from local forests. It also became an irresistible target for the pirates who operated with relative impunity from bases on the untamed coast, hence the fortifications, built between 1668 and 1704 after a particularly brutal massacre of the local population. Although large sections of the walls have gone, seven of the eight original *baluartes* (bulwarks) survive.

Arrival and information

Campeche's **main bus station**, with separate halls for first- and second-class services, is 2km east of the colonial centre. To get to the centre, cross Avenida Gobernadores, the busy street in front of the station, and take a city bus marked "Centro" or "Gobernadores". Local buses leave from the market just south of the city walls. If you arrive at the **airport**, about 10km southeast of town, you'll have to take a taxi.

Within the city, even-numbered **streets** run parallel to the sea, starting with Calle 8 for some reason, just inside the ramparts; odd-numbered streets run inland. The zócalo, **Parque Principal**, is bordered by calles 8, 10, 55 and 57. Almost everything of interest to the visitor is within the old walls.

Campeche's **tourist office**, in the Plaza Moch Couoh on Avenida 16 de Septiembre opposite the imposing Palacio de Gobierno (daily 8am–4pm & 6–9pm; Ⓣ/Ⓕ981/981-9225, Ⓦwww.campechetravel.com), is helpful and there's usually someone there who speaks English. Although this is officially the tourism department for the whole state, specifics on activities outside the city are somewhat limited. It does have a list of independent **guides** (speaking various languages) who lead tours of the city and archeological zones, though you might be expected to provide the transport around town or to the sites; Betty Mena Pacheco is particuarly friendly and knowledgeable (Ⓣ981/811-0733). Other tourist **information booths** (at the bus station, in the Baluarte de San Pedro and in the Casa Seis cultural centre on the main plaza) have maps and details of activities and tours, and offer advice on accommodation.

Accommodation

Because Campeche is not yet fully on the tourist circuit, it still boasts plenty of reasonably priced **hotels**, though for the same reason the cheapest ones can be depressingly shabby. Avoid rooms overlooking the street, as Campeche's narrow lanes magnify traffic noise. Most of the budget hotels are within a couple of blocks of the zócalo; a couple more upscale choices are outside the old city walls facing the sea.

If you're travelling by car and want to **splurge**, the luxuriously restored eighteenth-century *Hacienda Uayamón* (Ⓣ981/829-7528, Ⓕ999/923-7963, Ⓦwww.starwood.com/luxury; ❾), 21km outside of town on the way to Edzná, is one of the only lodgings of its kind in Campeche state (there are plenty more in neighbouring Yucatán).

The unofficial **hostel**, the *Monkey Hostel* (Ⓣ981/811-6500, Ⓦwww.hostalcampeche.com; ❷), on the west side of the plaza, is especially clean and helpful, offering laundry, bike rental, transportation to nearby archeological sites and Spanish lessons. In addition to single-sex dorms, six private doubles are available for US$18 each.

América C 10 no. 252, between C 59 and C 61 Ⓣ981/816-4576, Ⓕ811-0556, Ⓦwww.hotelamericacampeche.com. Elegant colonial building with slightly threadbare rooms; the quietest ones overlook the small, pleasant courtyard. Continental breakfast included. ❹

Baluartes Av 16 de Septiembre 128, between C 59 and C 61 Ⓣ981/816-3911, Ⓕ816-2410, Ⓦwww.baluartes.com.mx. Recently renovated, with spacious modern rooms, a giant pool, TVs, a/c and an inexpensive breakfast café. ❼

Colonial C 14 no. 122, between C 55 and C 57 ⓣ981/816-2630. The best-value place in town, immaculately tidy and friendly, in a charming old building. Optional a/c. ❹–❺

Francis Drake C 12 no. 207, between C 63 and C 65 ⓣ981/811-5626. Opened in 2003, the only upscale choice in the colonial centre has plush rooms and a helpful staff; no pool, but more charm than the two oceanfront options. ❻

Hotel del Mar Av Ruíz Cortines 51, just north of *Baluartes* ⓣ981/811-9191, ⓕ811-1618, ⓔdelmar@camp1.telmex.net.mx. A decent upmarket hotel with a pool, restaurant and car rental facilities, catering to tour groups; not as nice as its neighbour, it's due for a remodelling. ❼

López C 12 no. 189, between C 61 and C 63 ⓣ/ⓕ981/816-3344, ⓔhotlpez@prodigy.net.mx. Attractive central hotel with nifty Art Deco details. Rooms are clean, with a/c and TV. Very basic continental breakfast included. ❺

Posada del Ángel C 10 no. 309, between C 53 and C 55 ⓣ981/816-7718. Rooms in this modern guesthouse near the cathedral are quite dark and kitschily decorated, but clean enough. Option of fan or a/c. ❺

Regis C 12 no. 148, between C 55 and C 57 ⓣ981/816-3175. Seven very large rooms, all with a/c, arranged around a small patio – a reasonable alternative to the *Colonial* or the *América*. ❺

The City

Though your time is well spent wandering Campeche's old streets or seafront, you could get the lie of the land by taking a **tour** on one of two open-sided buses (which were once used as city trams) that depart from the zócalo every two hours between 9am and 7pm. One route takes in most sites in the walled city, while the other runs along the seafront and up to Fuerte de San Miguel (see below). At US$7 for a 45-minute trip, the tour is no bargain, but it's a relaxing way to see the sights, with informed commentary in both Spanish and English.

Otherwise, the starting point for a stroll is often the **cathedral**, overlooking the zócalo. Founded in 1540, it is one of the oldest churches on the peninsula. The bulk of the construction, though, took place much later, and what you see now is not particularly striking Baroque. Across the plaza is **Centro Cultural Casa Seis** (daily 9am–9pm), which hosts art exhibits and performances, as well as an elegant permanent display of Baroque interiors. **La Mansión Carvajal**, on Calle 10 between calles 51 and 53, is also worth a brief visit – now government offices (Mon–Fri 8am–2pm), this Moorish-style colonial house once belonged to one of the city's richest families. Just beyond the zócalo, on Calle 8, between calles 55 and 57, the **Museo de las Estelas** (Tues–Sun 8am–7.30pm; US$2.40) is housed in the Baluarte de la Soledad and has a small but interesting collection of columns and faded stelae taken from Edzná and other local Maya sites, depicting religious and civil ceremonies amongst other things; explanations are in Spanish only. You could also spend some time at the **Baluarte de San Carlos**, which has cannons on the battlemented roof and, underneath, the beginnings of a network of ancient tunnels that runs under much of the town. Mostly sealed off now, the tunnels provided refuge for the populace from pirate raids, and before that were probably used by the Maya. The *baluarte* currently houses Campeche's **City Museum** (Tues–Sun 8am–7.30pm; donation), little more than a dusty collection of old photos and a scale model of the city, with Spanish commentary.

On a hill on the southwest side of town is **Fuerte de San Miguel**, which houses Campeche's particularly impressive **archeological museum** (Tues–Sun 8am–7.30pm; US$2.40). Again, plaques are in Spanish only, but the beautiful relics, from all over the peninsula, speak for themselves. Maya artefacts from Edzná and Jaina predominate, including delicate Jaina figurines, many of which are cross-eyed – a feature that the Maya considered a mark of beauty. There's also some fine sculpture and some pre-Hispanic gold, but the highlight is the treasure from the tombs at Calakmul. The jade death masks are mesmerizing and every bit as extraordinary as the death masks of Pacal from Palenque. Take a look at the views over the ramparts, too, which are wonderful at sunset. **Fuerte de San José**, on a hill on the opposite side of the city, is a museum that houses armaments and a collection of items from the colonial era.

Every Tuesday, Wednesday and Friday in front of the city's Puerta de Tierra, Campeche has its own **sound-and-light show** (8pm; free), which depicts various historical scenes and is heartfelt if not spectacular. If you're desperate for **beaches**, look for buses along the waterfront marked "Playa Bonita" or "Lerma", two seaside destinations just south of the city.

Eating and drinking

Restaurants abound in the centre of Campeche, especially along Calle 8 and Calle 10. **Seafood**, served almost everywhere, is a good bet; try the *pan de cazón* (a kind of lasagne made with layers of tortillas and shredded shark meat) or shrimps in spicy sauce. The café in the centre of the zócalo serves excellent coffee and homemade ice cream, and Campeche's **market**, just north of the walled city, is surrounded by *comedores* offering cheap and tasty comida corrida.

Casa Vieja C 10 on the plaza, above the zócalo's colonnade. Cuban-owned restaurant with well-appointed balcony overlooking the main square and varied international cuisine. Tasty, but prices match the classy setting.

La Iguana Azul C 55, opposite *La Parroquia.* Gorgeously decorated colonial house with a warren of rooms: up front is a large wooden bar; farther back, a lush courtyard. The reasonably priced menu includes local and Creole dishes.

Miramar C 8 and C 61. Flavourful seafood dishes, in an old-fashioned, wood-panelled setting. Not exactly the most affordable place in town.

La Palapa Av Resurgimento, 30min walk south along the malecón from the city centre. Large bar right on the water, where delicious *botanas* (bite-size snacks) are served with every drink.

La Parroquia C 55 no. 8, between C 10 and C 12. Traditional, family-run restaurant with high ceilings and a café atmosphere; excellent-value *pan de cazón* and other local dishes; very popular with locals. Open 24hr.

La Pigua Av Alemán 179-A. Follow C 8 north to find one of the city's most legendary restaurants, a pretty, somewhat elegant lunch spot with exceptionally delicious seafood. Daily 12.30–5.30pm.

Restaurante Campeche C 57, next door to the *Hotel Campeche.* Large, unfussy restaurant with extensive menu – Yucatecan specialities and Mexican food in general – and reasonable prices.

Listings

Airlines Aeroméxico (☎981/816-6656 or 5678) operates a variety of internal flights. A taxi out to the airport costs around US$8.

American Express Inside the VI-PS travel agency, C 59 between Av Ruíz Cortines and Av 16 de Septiembre (Mon–Fri 9am–8pm, Sat 9am–1pm; ☎981/811-1100, Ⓕ816-8333).

Banks Bital, at C 10 and C 55, is on the main square and has an ATM. Banamex is on C 10 at C 53.

Bicycle rental Rentamar, on C 59 opposite the American Express office, rents bicycles (US$6/2hr) and mopeds (US$15/2hr).

Buses First-class ADO and second-class Autobuses del Sur, ATP and TRP buses (all from the same terminal – see p.718) leave for Ciudad del Carmen (almost hourly; 3hr), Mérida (every 30min; 2hr), Chetumal via Escárcega and Xpujil (noon; 5–7hr), Villahermosa (10 daily; 6–7hr). There are also services to San Cristóbal de las Casas (via Palenque), Playa del Carmen, Veracruz, Mexico City and Coatzalcoalcos (for southern Veracruz) and second-class buses direct to Uxmal (4 daily; 1hr). Minibuses leave from the market just outside the southern end of the old city (C 53 and Circuito Baluartes Este), for local villages like the craft centres Becal and Calkiní, and for Edzná.

Car rental Maya Car Rental (☎981/811-1871) in the *Hotel del Mar.*

Internet and fax facilities There are Internet cafés on every street in the centre of Campeche, charging approx US$1 per hour. You can send a fax from Ah-Kim-Tel *caseta*, C 10 between C 57 and C 59.

Post office Av 16 de Septiembre at C 53, in the Oficinas del Gobierno Federal (Mon–Fri 9am–3pm).

Tours Servicio Turístico Xtampak (☎981/811-6473) runs day-trips to Edzná (US$20 transport only, or

US$75 with guide, lunch and time at the beach). The best way to see the Calakmul Biosphere Reserve and ruins is with Corazón Maya, located in the San Pedro Baluarte, C 18 and C 51 (Ⓣ981/816-8086, Ⓦwww.corazonmaya.cjb.net), which organizes excellent private tours (starting at US$50 per person) into the area and can also arrange customized bird-watching, camping or cycling trips.

The Campeche coast

South of Campeche, Hwy-180 splits into free (*libre*) and toll (*cuota*) roads. The old seafront route is winding and scenic, alternating between rolling hills fuzzy with sea grass and reeds, and striking vistas onto the green Gulf waters; the only flaw is the likelihood of tailing an underpowered delivery truck servicing the small towns along the way. The toll highway, however unremarkable, is straight and easy to **Champotón**, a growing fishing village and oil port renowned for its delicious and fabulously cheap shrimp cocktails and *ceviche*. Most visitors heading in this direction turn inland at Champotón, on their way southeast towards Escárcega for Chetumal or Palenque, but if you're heading to Villahermosa, opt for the improved highway south of Champotón en route to **Ciudad del Carmen**. Although the city itself isn't really a compelling destination, the drive down the coast is fast and pretty, passing along some lovely stretches of beach, particularly around Punta Xochen, where the water is a little farther from the highway. At **Isla Aguada**, the Puenta de la Unidad crosses the eastern entrance to the **Laguna de Terminos**, joining the **Isla del Carmen** to the mainland. If you're driving be careful not to exceed the speed limit; traffic cops posted at either end of the bridge are notorious for demanding heavy fines on the spot.

Ciudad del Carmen

CIUDAD DEL CARMEN, the only town of any size on the 35-kilometre-long Isla del Carmen, doesn't merit a special trip except perhaps during its lively **fiesta** in July, celebrating the town's namesake, Our Lady of Carmen. The city is pleasant enough, but hot and crowded and has much less historical atmosphere than Campeche. The Conquistadors landed here in 1518, but the first settlers were pirates in 1633. Nowadays it's home to a fishing fleet, catching, among other things, giant prawns for export (an enormous bronze shrimp presides over one central traffic circle). The oil industry (many rigs are offshore in the Gulf) has forced prices up, so you won't find any accommodation bargains here. The town's environs have suffered from oil pollution, though beaches are far cleaner than they were. Should you be interested, Carmen now has a small **museum** on Calle 22 (daily 8am–8pm; US$0.50) with an imaginative display charting the history of the city.

Practicalities

ADO (first-class) and Sur (second-class) **buses** use the same station on Avenida Periférica Oriente. To get to the centre, take a taxi or colectivo (5am–11pm; about 20min). The gleaming new **tourist office**, on the malecón in front of the central Parque General Ignacio Zaragoza (Mon–Sat 9am–9pm; Ⓦwww.carmen.gob.mx), is making a concerted effort to draw visitors and has plenty of information (English and Spanish) on Campeche state, but little about Ciudad del Carmen. The **post office** (Mon–Fri 9am–3pm) is on the corner of Calle 22 and Calle 27, while Banamex, on the corner of Calle 24 at the edge of the park, and Bancomer, Calle 24 at the corner with Calle 29-B, both have **ATMs**.

Most of the **accommodation** in town is on calles 20, 22 and 24 near the waterfront. At fiesta time places fill up, so book ahead. *Hotel Victoria* (☎938/382-9301; ⑤) and *Hotel Zacarias* (☎938/382-3506; ⑤), both on Calle 24, are comfortable enough and clean. More luxurious is the recently remodelled *Hotel del Parque*, on Calle 33 between the park and the waterfront (☎938/382-3046; ⑥), where all rooms have a/c, TV and phone. **Food** in Ciudad del Carmen is a mixture of specialities from the Yucatán peninsula and the state of Tabasco, with a stress on shellfish. Many low-priced restaurants are grouped together along Calle 33 by the park; also recommended is *La Fuente,* Calle 20 and Calle 29, on the waterfront, which serves cheap Mexican food round the clock. *Los Pelicanos,* Calle 24 between calles 29 and 29-A, has an attractive terrace and its Tex-Mex menu makes it popular with American oilmen.

Edzná and the Chenes sites

Some 60km from Campeche lie the impressive ruins of **EDZNÁ** (daily 8am–5pm; US$2.50), the only local site practically accessible by bus. Though this is an area where the **Chenes** style of architecture (closely related to the Puuc of Uxmal; see p.742) dominated – *chen* means "well" and is a fairly common suffix to place names hereabouts – Edzná is far from a pure example of it, also featuring elements of Río Bec, Puuc and Classic Maya design. For the real thing, you have to venture further south.

Edzná was a large city, on the main trade route between the Maya of the highlands and the coast. The most important structure is the great **Templo de los Cinco Pisos** (Temple of the Five Storeys), a stepped palace-pyramid more than 20m high built on a vast acropolis. Unusually, each of the five storeys contains chambered "palace" rooms: while solid temple pyramids and multi-storey "apartment" complexes are relatively common, it is rare to see the two combined in one building. At the front, a steep monumental staircase leads to a three-room temple, topped by a roof comb. The view from here is one of the most impressive in the Yucatán. As you look out over two plazas, the furthest of which must have been capable of holding tens of thousands of people, it is easy to imagine the power that the high priest or king commanded. Beyond lie the unexcavated remains of other large pyramids, and behind them, the vast flat expanse of the Yucatán shelf. A stele of the god of maize positioned here was illuminated by the sun twice a year, on the dates for the planting and harvesting of maize, and the whole temple is oriented to the rising sun.

Lesser buildings surround the ceremonial precinct. The **Casa Grande**, a palace on the northwest side, and some of the buildings alongside it, were cleared by archeologists in late 1986. Some 55m long, the Casa Grande includes a room used as a *temazcal* (sauna), with stone benches and hearths over which water could be boiled. There are two haunting masks of the gods of Day and Night in the **Templo de los Mascarones**. The rest of the site – including a large system of drainage (and possibly irrigation) canals – remains unexcavated.

Buses for Pich or Bon Fil leave from the huge market in Campeche (Calle 53 and Circuito Baluartes Este) every half-hour and will take you within 1km of the entrance to Edzná. Getting back is harder: buses pass, but they are erratic; ask the driver of your bus on the way out. Alternatively, you could join an **organized trip** from Campeche.

Other Chenes sites

The examples of true Chenes style are accessible only with a car or exceptional determination. The chief sites are reached on a poor road from the village of **HOPELCHÉN**, about 100km east of Campeche. It has has been host to a growing Mennonite community since the 1980s; the woodcarvings in the eighteenth-century Church of San Antonio de Padua are worth a visit. A bus follows this road as far as the Chenes sites of **Dzibalchén** and **Iturbide**, but it's not much use for visiting the ruins as it turns straight round on arrival. If you choose to **stay** in Hopelchén, the only option is *Los Arcos* (ⓣ982/822-0123; ❸), Calle 23 on the corner of the plaza, near where the buses stop.

The best of the ruins are some way from the paved road and substantially buried in the jungle. **Hochob**, just southwest of Dzibalchén (follow signs to Chencoh), has an amazing three-room temple (low and fairly small, as are most Chenes buildings), with a facade entirely covered in richly carved, stylized snakes and masks. The central chamber is surmounted by a crumbling roof-comb, and its decoration creates the effect of a huge mask, with the doorway as a gaping mouth. The remains of **Dzibilnocac**, 1km further east of Iturbide, demonstrate the ultradecorative facades typical of the Chenes style, and its restored western temple pyramid makes a trip out here very worthwhile.

Francisco Escárcega to Xpujil

Heading south from Champotón on the inland route, Hwy-261 meets the east–west Hwy-186 at **FRANCISCO ESCÁRCEGA** (always referred to as Escárcega), a hot, dusty town straggling along the road and old train tracks for a couple of kilometres. Generally known as the region's ugliest town, attempts have been made to spruce up the main street with a new median strip and streetlights, but it's still not an ideal stopover. However, Escárcega does provide a jumping-off point for a number of relatively unexplored **Maya sites** that are now beginning to be developed for tourism. Known as the **Río Bec sites**, many of them are in the **Calakmul Biosphere Reserve**, a vast area of tropical forest, once heavily populated by lowland Maya, which stretches all the way into the Petén region of Guatemala. Though the region's most famous ruins lie over the border at **Tikal**, others within Mexico are every bit as exciting as the sites of the northern Yucatán.

The ADO bus station is at the west end of town, at the highway junction; from there, it's 1500m east – a long walk or a short cab ride – to the centre and the Sur bus station (which will eventually be moved in with the ADO terminal). If you need to **stay**, the gaily painted *Hotel Escárcega* on the town's main drag as you leave towards Campeche (ⓣ982/824-0186; ❹–❺) has neat, modern rooms with a/c or fan. **Getting out of town** is relatively easy: at least seven buses run daily to Mérida (4hr 30min), and there are eight buses to Campeche (2hr), six to Palenque (though all but the 1.30pm service depart in the middle of the night; 4hr), and six to San Cristóbal de las Casas (7hr). Services to Xpujil (2hr) run at 8.30am, 12.30pm and 4.30pm, as well as very early in the morning; Chetumal (4hr) is more frequent, with seven daytime departures.

The ramshackle village of **XPUJIL**, 150km west on the border with Quintana Roo, is a slightly better base for exploring the region. Basically a one-street town straddling Hwy-186, it has a **tourist office** (with erratic opening hours) at the east end and a couple of perfunctory places to stay. The *Hotel Calakmul* (ⓣ983/871-6029; ❹–❺) offers slick a/c rooms or basic shared-bath cabañas.

The cabañas are a bit nicer at *Restaurant and Bungalows El Mirador Maya* (Ⓣ983/871-6005, Ⓔmirador_maya@hotmail.com; ❺), but the rooms are quite dark. The latter has a money-**exchange** counter. There are a couple of **restaurants**, an **Internet** café, several Ladatel **phones** and a small **post office**.

A far better option, if you have your own car, is to head 10km north to the tranquil village of Zoh-Laguna. *Cabañas and Restaurant Mercedes* (Ⓣ983/871-6054, Ⓕ871-6055; ❹) is the top choice here, with spotless cabañas, kindly owners and tasty meals on request. *Hotel del Bosque* (no phone; ❸) also rents basic rooms, and the money supports the village's Model Forest programme, which encourages sustainable use of woodlands. It is possible to reach Zoh-Laguna by public transport, but it's very hard to use the town as a sightseeing base this way: buses and colectivos run only twice a day, and passengers are usually dropped about 1km from the town proper.

Leaving Xpujil, there are, in theory, four ADO **buses** a day to Chetumal, and eight to Escárcega and onward. Colectivos also gather in front of the station. It is possible to catch a series of second-class buses through to Mérida via Dzibalchén, Hopelchén and the Ruta Puuc. This potholed road passes through the northern half of the Calakmul Biosphere Reserve, and is an interesting and little-travelled route north, if you have time to spare.

The Río Bec sites

The Río Bec style, characterized by long buildings with matching towers at each end and narrow roof-combs, can be seen at a number of sites in this region. The most accessible is **Xpujil**, just 1500m west along the highway from Xpujil village (8am–5pm; US$1.50). Dating from the Classic period, it is perhaps the least impressive of all the sites, though its three towers with almost vertical and purely decorative stairways are very striking.

The easiest way of taking a **trip** to the sites is with a taxi tour, arranged from the tourist office or either of the hotels in Xpujil. Expect to pay US$50 per head to go to Calakmul and Balamkú or to Kohunlich and Dzibanché, and US$30 for Chicanná, Becán and Xpujil, including waiting time. Alternatively you could take an organized tour from Campeche with Corazón Maya or Servicios Turísticos Xtampak for US$50–55 (see "Listings", p.720, for details). For small groups, renting a car in Campeche or Chetumal is an economical option, though the drive down the winding one-lane road to Calakmul is a slow and tedious one, requiring frequent braking for wild turkeys – it can be worth the extra money to leave the driving to someone else.

Becán

Becán (daily 8am–5pm; US$3.20), 6km west of Xpujil and then 500m north on a signed track, is unique among Maya sites in being entirely surrounded by a dry moat, 15m wide and 4m deep. This moat and the wall on its outer edge form one of the oldest known defensive systems in Mexico, and have led some to believe that this, rather than present-day Flores in Guatemala, was the site of Tayasal, capital of the Itzá. The site was first occupied in 600 BC, reaching its peak between 600 AD and 1000 AD. Unlike many of the sites in the northern Yucatán, many of the buildings here seem to have been residential – note the unusual use of internal staircases.

Chicanná and Balamkú

Chicanná (daily 8am–5pm; US$3.20), 3km west from Becán, is across the highway from the friendly *Chicanná Ecovillage Resort* (in Campeche Ⓣ981/811-

△ Palace of Masks, Kabáh

9191, Ⓕ811-1618, Ⓔinfo@delmarhotel.com.mx; ⑨), which offers rustic luxury at a reasonable price. The buildings at the site recall the Chenes style in their elaborate decoration and repetitive masks of Chac; the impressive Structure II gives the site its name ("House of the Serpent Mouth") with its gaping, square carved doorway. The main draw at **Balamkú** (daily 8am–5pm; US$3.20), 50km beyond Chicanná, just after the turn-off to Calakmul, is the elaborate, beautifully preserved seventeen-metre-long stucco frieze crawling with toads, crocodiles and jaguars. It's protected in a concrete shed; ask the caretaker to let you in. Additionally, two huge cross-eyed red stucco-coated stone masks adorn the central temple. These are larger than any you'll see in the north, though less impressive than the masks at Kohunlich in nearby Quintana Roo (see p.799).

Hormiguero and Río Bec

Hormiguero and **Río Bec**, which gives its name to the region's dominant architectural style, are accessible only by dirt road. Hormiguero (8am–5pm; US$3.20), 22km south from the main crossroads in Xpujil, fuses the Chenes style with the Río Bec. There are only two buildings that are completely excavated, the largest having a gaping mouth for its central doorway, surrounded by elaborate carving. In the village of Hormiguero, ask around for Margarita Cahuich and María Dzib, well-known residents who have rooms to rent and will help you find a local guide – although hiking through the ruins on your own is possible and can add to the sense of adventure. The scattered buildings of Río Bec, 10km east of Xpujil and south of the *ejido* of 20 de Noviembre, are closed for further excavation, but may reopen soon. Ask in the tourist office in Xpujil about arranging an expedition on horseback, an intrepid way to see all of the buildings scattered around the site. At the most accessible cluster of buildings, you'll see that, as with Xpujil, the "steps" on the twin towers were never meant to be climbed: the risers actually angle outwards.

Calakmul

Not only the most impressive of the Río Bec sites, **Calakmul** (daily 8am–5pm; US$3.20, plus US$2 for the protected biosphere reserve), which lies 60km south off Hwy-186 between Xpujil and Escárcega, is also one of the best of all of the Maya ruins for quiet contemplation of the culture's architectural legacy. Though the site is only partially restored, its location in the heart of the jungle and its sheer size make this Classic Maya city irresistible. The enormous ruined city is probably the biggest archeological area in Mesoamerica, extending for some 70km. It has nearly seven thousand buildings in the central area alone and more stelae and pyramids than any other Maya city; the great pyramid here is the largest Maya building in existence, with a base covering almost five acres. The view of the rainforest from the top of the principal pyramids is stunning, bettered only at Tikal, and on a clear day you can even see the tallest Maya pyramid of all, Danta, at El Mirador in Guatemala. Arrive early (the gate to the biosphere on Hwy-186 opens at 7am) to look for wildlife – there are wild turkeys, peccaries, toucans and even jaguars. If you don't spot anything, you'll likely hear booming howler monkeys and raucous frogs.

During the Classic period, the city had a population of about 200,000 and was the regional capital of southern Petén. A recently discovered *sacbe* (Maya road) running between Calakmul and El Mirador (another leads on to Tikal) has confirmed that these cities were in regular communication, as archeologists had long suspected. Calakmul reached its zenith between 500 AD and 850 AD but, along with most other cities in the area, it was abandoned by about 900 AD. The site was discovered in 1931, but excavations did not start until 1982 and only a fraction of the buildings have been uncovered so far, the rest being earthen mounds.

The treasures of Calakmul are on display in the archeological museum at Campeche (see p.719) and include two hauntingly beautiful jade masks. Another was found in a tomb in the main pyramid as recently as January 1998. You can also see the first mummified body to be found in Mesoamerica, from inside Structure no. 15, which was unearthed in 1995.

From Campeche to Mérida

From Campeche to Mérida there's a choice of two routes. First-class buses and all *directo* services take **Hwy-180** – once the colonial Camino Real. The highway now bypasses most of the towns, but signposts direct you to two worthwhile detours: **Hecelchakán**, about 80km from Campeche, which has a small **archeology museum** on the main square (Tues–Sat 10am–8pm, Sun 9am–noon; US$2), with figures from Jaina and objects from other nearby sites, and **Becal** (35km further), one of the biggest centres for the manufacture of baskets and the ubiquitous Yucatecan **jipis**, or "Panama" hats (the original Panama hats came from Ecuador). Shops throughout town sell them, and it's interesting to see a village so consumed with a single cottage industry – a fountain made of concrete hats even graces the town square. A little farther on, just over the border of Yucatán state near the town of **Granada**, is the small but luxurious *Hacienda Santa Rosa* (Ⓣ999/910-4875, Ⓕ923-7963, Ⓦwww.starwood.com/luxury; ⑨).

The longer route via Hopelchén and Muna, passing the great sites of **Sayil**, **Kabáh** and **Uxmal** (see p.741), is much better if you have the time. With a car you could easily visit all three, perhaps stopping also at **Bolonchén de Rejon**, a pretty village of stone houses, rolling hills and nine wells in the plaza, and the nearby **Grutas de Xtacumbilxunan**, 3km south, and still get to Mérida within the day. By bus it's slightly harder, but with a little planning – and if you set out early – you should be able to get to at least one site. Kabáh is the easiest because its ruins lie right on the main road.

Mérida

Even if practically every road didn't lead to **MÉRIDA**, it would still be an inevitable stop. Nicknamed the "White City" after its limestone buildings and sparkling-clean streets, the capital of the state of Yucatán is in every sense the leading town of the peninsula, and wonderfully calm and likeable for its population of nearly one million and all its thousands of visitors, both Mexican and foreign. Every street in the centre boasts a colonial church or mansion, while the plazas are alive with market stalls and free entertainment. You can live well here and find good beaches nearby, but above all it's the ideal base for excursions to the great Maya sites of Uxmal and Chichén Itzá (see p.742 and p.750).

Arrival, information and city transport

Mérida is laid out on a simple **grid** of numbered streets: even numbers run north–south, odd from east to west, with the zócalo, **Plaza Mayor**, bounded by calles 60, 61, 62 and 63. There's a dizzying amount of bus traffic and small second-class terminals, but tourists are most likely to use Mérida's main **bus**

stations, which lie around the corner from each other on the west side of town: the **first-class CAME**, at Calle 70 no. 555, between calles 69 and 71, or the **second-class** terminal, on Calle 69 between calles 68 and 70, which is inexplicably nicer than the first-class station, with air-conditioning and luggage storage. Some first-class buses arrive at the *Fiesta Americana* hotel, north of the centre and convenient if you're staying there or at the *Villa Mercedes*, but otherwise a slightly longer hike to the centre.

City buses don't go all the way from the bus stations to the Plaza Mayor; to walk takes about twenty minutes. With the main entrance to the second-class terminal at your back, the right-hand corner is Calle 68 and Calle 69; the Plaza Mayor is three blocks up (north) and four blocks right (east). Colectivos from the smaller places off the main highways terminate in Plaza de San Juan, on Calle 69 between calles 62 and 64. To get to the Plaza Mayor, leave Plaza de San Juan by the northeast corner and walk three blocks north up Calle 62.

Mérida's Manuel Crecencio Rejón **airport** is 7km southwest of the city. There's a tourist office (daily 8am–8pm), post office, long-distance phones and car rental desks. To get downtown, take a colectivo (buy a ticket at the desk) or bus #79 ("Aviación"), which drops off at the corner of Calle 67 and Calle 60.

Information

Mérida's main **tourist office** is in the Teatro Peón Contreras, on the corner of Calle 60 and Calle 57-A (daily 8am–8pm; Ⓦ www.cultur.com). Pick up a copy of the excellent *Yucatán Today* (Ⓦ www.yucatantoday.com), in English and Spanish, to find out what's going on around town and the state. There are also plenty of leaflets available and you'll usually find some English-speaking staff. Other **tourist information booths** are in the Palacio de Gobierno on the Plaza Mayor and on Paseo de Montejo just south of the *Fiesta Americana* hotel. Useful **websites** to check out in advance include Ⓦ www.cityview.com.mx and Ⓦ www.merida.gob.mx.

City transport

As most of the places of interest in Mérida are within walking distance, it really isn't worth the bother of using public transport to get around in the centre – though it can be fun to hop on one of the **horse-drawn carriages** (*calesas*) that cruise up and down the Paseo de Montejo; see p.733. To get out to some of the less central sites (the archeology museum, for example), you may want to catch a bus, but the bus system is remarkably convoluted and often on the brink of being completely revamped. Many buses and *combis* leave from Calle 54 and Calle 65, near the market; northbound buses often run up Calle 56. You can flag buses down at any corner; fares are posted on the doors – usually US$0.40. **Taxis** can be hailed all around town and from ranks at Parque Hidalgo, the post office, Plaza de San Juan and the airport. **Car rental** offices abound in Mérida, both at the airport and in the city (see "Listings" on p.737).

The Ruta Puuc bus

While at Mérida's second-class bus terminal you may want to buy a ticket for a transport-only **day-trip** by bus around the **Ruta Puuc** (see p.741), which can be difficult to visit without your own transport. Ask at the Autotransportes del Sur counter. The trip costs US$10.70 and leaves at 8am every day, visiting Uxmal, Labná, Sayil, Kabáh and Xlapak. You get just long enough at each site to form a general impression, but there's no guide or lunch included in the price.

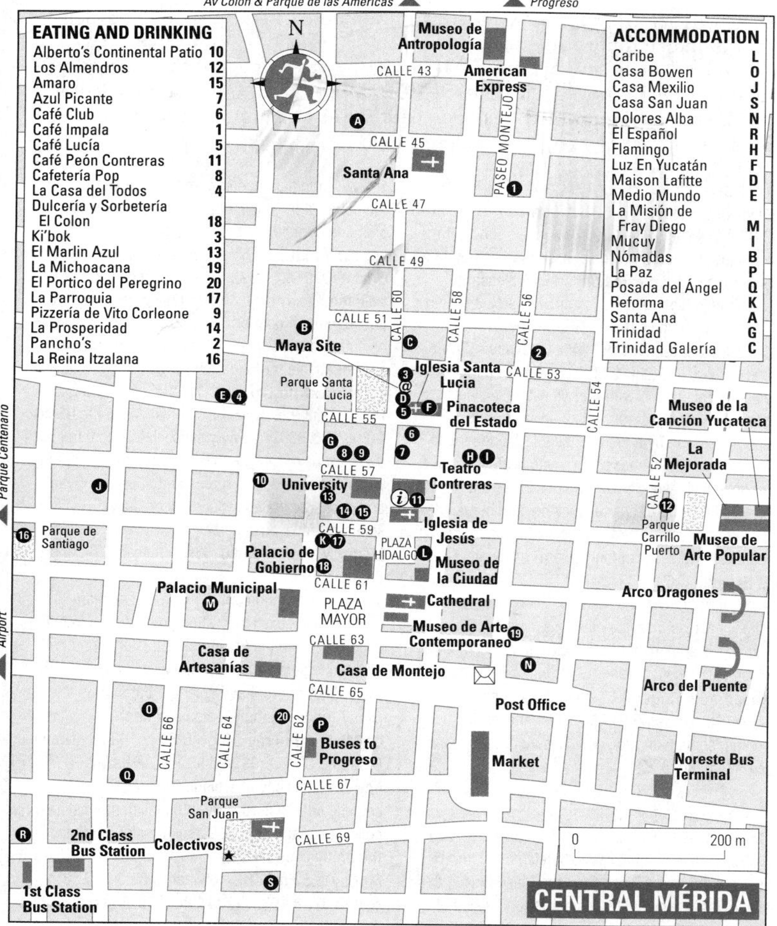

Accommodation

There are numerous **hotels** in Mérida, many housed in lovely colonial buildings and very reasonably priced. Although the city can get crowded at peak times, you should always be able to find a room. The cheapest hotels are concentrated **next to the bus station**, a noisy and grimy part of town, while a string of upmarket hotels lies along **Paseo de Montejo**, just north of the centre, most of them ultramodern and lacking in charm; the best-value hotels are in between, both geographically and in terms of price. A luxurious alternative is to stay outside town in a colonial **hacienda**, the closest of which is the eighteenth-century *Hacienda Xcanatun* (Ⓣ/Ⓕ999/941-0213, Ⓦwww.xcanatun.com; ⑨), 12km north on the road to Progreso, which has a particularly good restaurant. If you're happy to go further afield, check the state tourism website (Ⓦwww.mayayucatan.com) for a full list of converted haciendas all over Yucatán, ranging from ramshackle ruins to ultra-deluxe resorts and all quite atmospheric.

The best shoestring option in Mérida is the very attractive *Nómadas* **youth hostel**, Calle 62 no. 433 at Calle 51 (Ⓣ999/924-5223, Ⓦwww.nomadastravel.com; ❷), a clean and friendly spot with space to camp, six private rooms, a pool, live music and plenty of helpful advice.

Near the bus station

Casa Bowen C 66 no. 521-B, between C 65 and C 67 Ⓣ/Ⓕ999/928-6109. A travellers' favourite for years, this pretty colonial house is set around a bright courtyard. Spare but perfectly pleasant rooms with high ceilings (some with a/c), and two apartments with kitchens. ❹

Casa San Juan C 62 no. 545-A, between C 69 and C 71 Ⓣ999/986-2937. A variety of good-value rooms (some with a/c; all with excellent-quality bed linens) in a registered landmark colonial house, run by a knowledgeable Méridan who can arrange tailor-made tours with professional archeologists working in the field. There's a big shared kitchen, and prices include continental breakfast. Reserve ahead (two-night minimum), as it's often booked with longer-term residents. ❺

El Español C 69 no. 543-C, at C 70 Ⓣ999/923-2854, Ⓕ923-4319, Ⓦwww.hotelelespanol.com. Directly across from the main bus stations, *El Español* is an upmarket alternative to adjacent dives: clean, quiet rooms, powerful a/c and a small pool. ❻

Posada del Ángel C 67 no. 535, between C 66 and C 68 Ⓣ999/923-2754. Quiet and basic rooms (some with a/c), with a few pretty touches. On-site parking. ❹

In the centre

Caribe C 59 no. 500, Parque Hidalgo Ⓣ999/924-9022, Ⓕ924-8733, Ⓦwww.hotelcaribe.com.mx. In a small plaza a block from the Plaza Mayor, this place has a lovely patio restaurant and views of the cathedral and plaza from the rooftop pool. Travel agency; parking. ❻

Casa Mexilio C 68 no. 495, between C 59 and C 57 Ⓣ999/928-2505, or reservations in the US on 1-800/583-6802, Ⓦwww.mexicoholiday.com. This very attractive B&B in a restored colonial townhouse is a fascinating labyrinth of individually decorated rooms, tranquil gardens, sun terraces and a pool. The full breakfast (included) is delicious. ❻–❽

Dolores Alba C 63 no. 464, between C 62 and C 64 Ⓣ999/928-5650, Ⓕ928-3163, Ⓦwww.doloresalba.com. Popular mid-range hotel arranged round two courtyards and a large swimming pool. Rooms have TV, telephone and a/c. Parking and restaurant. Good value. ❺

Flamingo C 57 no. 485, between C 56 and C 58 Ⓣ999/924-7755, Ⓕ924-7070, Ⓦwww.hotelflamingo.com.mx. The modern rooms are a bit small, but a good price for a/c, pool and continental breakfast. ❺

Luz En Yucatán C 55 no. 499, between C 58 and C 60 Ⓣ999/924-0035, Ⓦwww.luzenyucatan.com. Delightful apartments in a rambling house with a pool; plenty of comfortable public space, as well as spa services, Spanish lessons and more. Rates are negotiable for longer stays. ❺

Maison Lafitte C 60 no. 472, between C 53 and C 55 Ⓣ999/928-1246, or reservations in the US on 1-800/538-6802, Ⓦwww.maisonlafitte.com.mx. An excellent new colonial-style hotel on the main drag, with comfortable, chic rooms and a lush courtyard and pool area. Rates include full breakfast. Spa services; travel agency. ❼

Medio Mundo C 55 no. 533, between C 64 and C 66 Ⓣ/Ⓕ999/924-5472, Ⓦwww.hotelmediomundo.com. A much-better-than-average book exchange shelf points to the interesting clientele (and owners) at this beautiful and hospitable small hotel. Ten colourful tile-floor rooms (fan or a/c) have splendid bathrooms and pillow-top beds; there's also a pool. ❻

La Misión de Fray Diego C 61 no. 524, between C 64 and C 66 Ⓣ999/924-1111, Ⓕ923-7397, Ⓦwww.lamisiondefraydiego.com. Very elegant colonial hotel with twenty minimalist, monastery-chic rooms and a good Spanish restaurant inside the pretty courtyard. ❽

Mucuy C 57 no. 481, between C 56 and C 58 Ⓣ999/928-5193, Ⓕ923-7801. Quiet and well run, with clean, good-value rooms and a truly hospitable owner. English-speaking staff and a laundry on premises. ❹

La Paz C 62 no. 522, between C 65 and C 67 Ⓣ999/923-9446. The best of the string of cheapies in this block, rooms are basic but bright and reasonably clean, with high ceilings. Parking. ❹

Reforma C 59 no. 508, at C 62 Ⓣ999/924-7922, Ⓕ928-3278, Ⓔhreforma@yuc1.telmex.net.mx. Long-established and well-kept hotel in a colonial building. Old-fashioned, high-ceiling rooms are arranged around a cool courtyard; a new wing, overlooking the pool, has brighter rooms with slightly less atmosphere. ❺

Santa Ana C 45 no. 503, between C 60 and C 62 Ⓣ999/923-3331, Ⓕ923-3332, Ⓦwww.hotelsantaana.com.mx. Good-value hotel with small colonial details on a quiet street that's still convenient to the main square. The 19 rooms have all the amenities – TV, extra-quiet a/c, phones – and there's a large pool. ❺

Trinidad C 62 no. 464, between C 55 and C 57 ⓣ999/924-9806, ⓕ924-1122, ⓦwww.hoteltrinidad.com. A wide range of rooms, including some dorm beds, decorated with modern paintings and antiques set round a plant-filled courtyard. Continental breakfast and use of the beautiful sunny pool at *Hotel Colón* (which also has steam baths) included; discounts for students or online bookings. ❷–❺

Trinidad Galería C 60 no. 456 at C 51 ⓣ999/923-2463, ⓕ924-2319, ⓦwww.hoteltrinidadgaleria.com. Wonderfully eccentric hotel crammed full of interesting artefacts, odd sculptures and paintings and much favoured by visiting artists. Rooms upstairs are lighter and more spacious, but all are individually decorated (some have a/c). Also has a pool, a small breakfast café and two art galleries. ❹–❻

Villa Mercedes Av Colón 500, between C 60 and C 62 ⓣ999/942-9000, ⓕ942-9001, ⓦwww.hotelvillamercedes.com.mx. Mérida's newest luxury hotel, in a converted Art Nouveau mansion; photos found during the renovation decorate the tasteful rooms. All the comforts, including full-size bathtubs, and more individual charm than others in this price range. ❾

The City

Founded in 1542 by Conquistador Francisco de Montejo (the Younger), Mérida is built over, and partly from, the ruins of a Maya city known as **Tihó** or Ichcansihó. Although, like the rest of the peninsula, it had little effective contact with central Mexico until the completion of road and rail links in the 1960s, trade with Europe brought wealth from the earliest days. In consequence the city looks more European than almost any other in Mexico – many of the older houses, indeed, are built with French bricks and tiles, brought over as tradeable ballast in the ships that exported henequen. Until the advent of artificial fibres, a substantial proportion of the world's rope was manufactured from Yucatecan henequen, a business that reached its peak during World War I.

In 1849, during the Caste Wars, the Maya armies had besieged Mérida and were within a hair's breadth of capturing the city and thus regaining control of the peninsula, when, legend has it, the Maya peasant fighters could no longer neglect their fields and left the siege lines to plant corn in hopes of an autumn harvest. It was this event, rather than the pleas of the inhabitants for reinforcements, that saved the elite from defeat; Yucatecan politicos quickly arranged a deal with the central Mexican government ceding the peninsula's independence in exchange for support against the Maya rebellions, which nonetheless ground on for some fifty years. By 1900, Mérida was an extraordinarily wealthy city – or at least a city that had vast numbers of extremely rich *haciendados* (estate owners). Much of this wealth was poured into the grandiose mansions of the outskirts of town (especially along the Paseo de Montejo) and into European educations for the children of the upper classes. Today, with the henequen trade all but dead, the city remains elegant and bustling, its streets filled with a vibrant mix of Maya, *mestizos*, Lebanese (who emigrated here in the early twentieth century) and more recent immigrants from Mexico City, drawn by Mérida's tranquil urbanity.

Plaza Mayor

Any exploration of Mérida begins naturally in the **Plaza Mayor**, the hub of the city's life, particularly in the evenings when couples meet on the park benches, and trios of *trovadores* in white *guayaberas* wait to be hired for serenades. The plaza is ringed by some of Mérida's oldest buildings, dominated by the **Cathedral of San Ildefonso** (daily 6am–noon & 5–8pm), built in the second half of the sixteenth century. Although most of the church's valuables were looted during the Revolution, the **Cristo de las Ampollas** (Christ of the Blisters), in a chapel to the left of the main altar, remains worth seeing. According to legend, this statue was carved from a tree in the village of Ichmul that burned for a whole night without showing the least sign of damage; later, the parish church at Ichmul burned down and the statue again survived, though blackened and blistered. The image is the focal point of a local fiesta at the beginning of October. Beside the cathedral, separated from it by the Pasaje San Alvarado, the old bishop's palace has been converted into shops and offices.

Next door to the cathedral is the **Museo MACAY** (Museo de Arte Contemporáneo Ateneo de Yucatán; daily except Tues 10am–6pm; US$2), the finest art museum in the state, with permanent displays of the work of internationally acclaimed Yucatecan painters Fernando Castro Pacheco, Gabriel Ramírez Aznar and Fernando García Ponce. Temporary exhibitions range from contemporary local photographers to European masters on loan from Mexico City museums. On the south side of the plaza stands the **Casa de Montejo**, a palace built in 1549 by Francisco de Montejo, the first Conquistador who attempted to bring the peninsula under the charge of Spain. His first effort, in 1527, failed, as did several later forays; however, his son, Francisco de Montejo the Younger, did what the father could not, securing the northern part of the peninsula in the 1540s and founding Mérida and Campeche. Until 1980 the building was inhabited by their descendants; it now belongs to Banamex, and most of the interior is used as office space. Visitors are welcome to see the restored dining room, off the back right corner of the Moorish-feeling courtyard. The facade is richly decorated in the Plateresque style, and above the doorway Conquistadors are depicted trampling savages underfoot. The **Palacio Municipal**, on the third side, is another impressive piece of sixteenth-century design with a fine clock tower, but the nineteenth-century **Palacio de Gobierno** (daily 8am–10pm), completing the square, is more interesting to visit. Inside, enormous murals by Fernando Castro Pacheco depict the violent history of the Yucatán, which is sometimes at odds with the explanatory texts in Spanish, English and Maya. One block east on Calle 61 is the small but informative **Museo de la Ciudad** (Tues–Fri 10am–2pm & 4–8pm, Sat & Sun 10am–2pm; free), which traces city history from ancient Mayan times to the henequen boom; texts are in Spanish and English.

North and east of the Plaza Mayor

Most of the remaining monuments in Mérida lie north of the zócalo, with Calle 60 and later the Paseo de Montejo as their focus. Calle 60 is one of the city's main commercial streets, lined with the fancier hotels and restaurants. It also boasts a series of colonial buildings, starting one block north of the plaza with the seventeenth-century Jesuit **Iglesia de Jesús**, on the corner with Calle 59, between the Parque Hidalgo and the Parque de la Madre. It was built using stones from the original Maya city of Tihó, and a few pieces of decorative carving are visible in the wall on Calle 59. In the same block of Calle 59, the **Pinacoteca del Estado Juan Gamboa Guzmán** (Tues–Sat 8am–8pm, Sun 8am–2pm; US$2.80) houses a collection of nineteenth-century portraits of prominent Yucatecans and Mexican leaders – would-be emperor Maximilian looks particularly hapless amongst the crowd of presidents. Back on Calle 60 and continuing north, you reach the **Teatro Peón Contreras**, a grandiose Neoclassical edifice built by Italian architects in the heady days of Porfirio Díaz and recently restored. Across the street is the **state university**, a highly respected institution that has existed, under various names, since 1624.

The **Museo de Arte Popular** (Tues–Sat 9am–8pm, Sun 8am–2pm; free), in the former monastery of La Mejorada, Calle 59 between calles 50 and 48, displays a fine collection of the different styles of indigenous dress found throughout Mexico. The rich wood and glass cases show *huipiles*, jewellery and household items, while old black-and-white photos provide glimpses of village life and ceremonies. At the rear of the museum you can stock up on souvenirs at the artesanía shop. Just around the corner is the **Museo de la Canción Yucateca** (daily 9am–5pm; US$1.50, free on Sun), detailing the diverse musical influences on the local *trovadores*, from pre-Columbian traditions to Afro-Cuban styles. The gift shop is an excellent place to pick up some romantic tunes.

Returning to Calle 60, one block north of the Teatro Peón Contreras, the sixteenth-century **Iglesia Santa Lucía** stands on the elegant plaza of the same name – a small colonnaded square that used to be the town's stagecoach terminus. Finally, three blocks further on, there's the **Plaza Santa Ana**, a modern open space where you turn right and then take the second left to reach the Paseo de Montejo.

Paseo de Montejo

The **Paseo de Montejo** is a broad boulevard lined with trees and modern sculptures by Yucatecan artists. It is bordered with the magnificent, pompous mansions of the grandees who strove to outdo each other's high-European style around the end of the nineteenth century. In one of the grandest, the Palacio Cantón, at the corner of Calle 43, is Mérida's **Museo de Antropología e Historia** (Tues–Sat 8am–8pm, Sun 8am–2pm; US$3.20). The house was built for General Cantón, state governor at the beginning of the twentieth century, in a restrained but very expensive elegance befitting his position, and has been beautifully restored and maintained. Given the archeological riches that surround the city, the collection is perhaps something of a disappointment, but it's a useful introduction to the sites nonetheless, with displays covering everything from prehistoric stone tools to modern Maya life. Obviously there are sculptures and other objects from the main sites, but more interesting are the attempts to fill in the background and give some idea of what it was like to live in a Maya city; unfortunately, most labels are only in Spanish. Topographic maps of the peninsula, for example, explain how cenotes are formed and their importance to the ancient population; a collection of skulls demonstrates techniques of facial and dental manipulation; and there are displays covering jewellery, ritual offerings and burial practices, as well as a large pictorial representation of the workings of the Maya calendar. Upstairs are temporary exhibits about Mérida's history and specific archeological sites. The **bookstore** has leaflets and guidebooks in English to dozens of ruins in Yucatán and the rest of Mexico.

The walk out **to the museum** from the plaza takes about half an hour – or you can get there on a "Paseo de Montejo" bus running up Calle 56, or in a horse-drawn **calesa** taxi (US$10 from the centre to the museum). The latter is not altogether a bad idea, especially if you fancy the romance of riding about in an open carriage (as many locals do), and if times are slack and you bargain well, it need cost little more than a regular taxi. Take some time to head a little further out on the Paseo de Montejo, to the **Monumento a la Patria**, about ten long blocks beyond the museum. It is a titan, covered in neo-Maya sculptures relating to Mexican history; you'll also pass it if you take the bus out to Progreso. You could also visit the **Parque de las Américas**, on Avenida Colón, which is planted with a tree from every country on the American continent, each carefully labelled.

Markets and handicrafts

Mérida's main **market**, a huge place between calles 65, 67, 56 and 54, is for most visitors a major attraction. A contentious reorganization plan may move the stalls into a more orderly area a couple of blocks south, but at the moment it's still an impressive maze of stuff. As far as quality goes, though, you're almost always better off buying in a shop – prices are no great shakes, either, unless you're an unusually skilful and determined haggler. Before buying anything, head for the **Casa de Artesanías** (Tues–Sat 9am–8pm, Sun 9am–1.30pm) in the Casa de la Cultura on Calle 63 west of the zócalo. Run by the government-sponsored Fonapas organization, it sells crafts from the peninsula that are consistently high quality, as well as a selection of delicate silver filigree jewellery; the clothing options are somewhat limited, though.

The most popular souvenir of Mexico is a **hammock** – and Mérida is probably the best place in the country to buy one. But if you want something you can realistically sleep in, exercise a degree of care and never buy from street vendors or even a market stall – they're invariably of very poor quality. Comfort is measured by the tightness of the weave and the breadth: because you're supposed to lie in a hammock diagonally, to be relatively flat, the distance it stretches sideways is far more crucial than the length (although obviously the woven portion of the hammock, excluding the strings at each end, should be at least as long as you are tall). A decent-size hammock (*doble* at least, preferably *matrimonial*) with cotton threads (*hilos de algodón*, more comfortable and less likely to go out of shape than artificial fibres) will set you back about US$20. ("Sisal" hammocks are generally fraudulent; this material is seldom used today.) For a **specialist dealer**, head to Tejidos y Cordeles Nacionales, one of the best and very near the market at Calle 56 no. 516-B, just north of Calle 65. More of a warehouse than a shop, it has hundreds of the things stacked against every wall, sold by weight rather than strictly by size; a high-quality, dense-weave *doble* weighs about a kilo. Buy several and you can enter into serious negotiations over the price. Similar stores nearby include El Campesino and El Aguacate, both on Calle 58, and La Poblana at Calle 65 no. 492, near Calle 60. The latter also sells *ahulado*, the bright, flower-patterned oilcloth popular all over Mexico.

Other good buys include *guayabera* shirts, Panama hats (known here as *jipis*) and *huipiles*, which vary wildly in quality, from factory-made, machine-stitched junk to hand-embroidered, homespun cloth. Even the best, though, rarely compare with the **antique dresses** that can occasionally be found: identical in style (as they have been for hundreds of years) but far better made and very expensive. Also look for fun smaller gift items, such as Spanish classroom vocabulary **posters** (Papelería El Estudiante, on Calle 63 between calles 62 and 64, has a good selection) or local foodstuffs, such as **coffee** and **honey** – visit the friendly women's co-op on Calle 60 near Calle 47 for these items and organic soaps and mosquito repellent.

Eating

Good **restaurants** are plentiful in the centre of Mérida, though the best (and some of the least expensive) are open only for lunch – plan accordingly if sampling local delicacies is a priority. Dinner restaurants are typically operated only by hotels, and frequented primarily by out-of-towners; prices are high and most menus verge on international-bland. Nonetheless, evening is the perfect time to visit the bustling sidewalk cafés on the **Plaza Hidalgo**, along Calle 60 between calles 61 and 59, and on **Paseo de Montejo**, which tends to be open later, with some glossier places popular with young locals.

Yucatecan cuisine

Typical **Yucatecan specialities** include *puchero*, a mutable stew that often includes chicken, beef, pork, squash, cabbage and sweet potato in a delicious stock broth seasoned with cinnamon and allspice, all garnished with radish, coriander and Seville orange; *poc-chuc*, a combination of pork with tomatoes, onions and spices; *sopa de lima*, which is not lime soup exactly, but chicken broth with lime and tortilla chips in it; *pollo* or *cochinita pibil*, chicken or suckling pig wrapped in banana leaves and cooked in a *pib*, basically a pit in the ground, though restaurants cheat on this; *papadzules*, tacos filled with hard-boiled eggs and covered in red and green pumpkin-seed sauce; and anything *en relleno negro*, a black, burnt-chile sauce. *Salbutes*, crisp corn tortillas topped with shredded turkey, pickled onions, avocado and radish, are ubiquitous at dinner time; *panuchos* are nearly identical but for an added dab of refried beans. For breakfast, *huevos motuleños* is an interesting sweet-savoury mix of fried eggs on a crisp tortilla with beans, topped with mild tomato salsa, ham, cheese, peas and fried banana slices. Little of this is hot, but watch out for the *salsa de chile habanero* that most restaurants have on the table – pure fire.

A number of less expensive spots surround the intersection of Calle 62 and Calle 61, at the northwest corner of the plaza, but cheapest of all are the *loncherías* in the **market**, where you can get good, filling comidas corridas. Around the Plaza Mayor several wonderful **juice bars** – notably *Jugos California*, on the southwest corner, and *La Michoacana* on Calle 61 and Calle 56 – serve all the regular juices and *licuados*, as well as more unusual local concoctions: try *guanabana*, *pitaya* or homemade root beer. Combine these with something from the **bakery** Pan Montejo, at the corner of Calle 62 and Calle 63, to make a great breakfast.

Alberto's Continental Patio C 64 no. 482 at C 57. A slice of old-world Mérida, with a beautiful interior courtyard and courtly service. The food is a little erratic, however: stick to the Lebanese specialties.

Los Almendros C 50 between C 57 and C 59, in the Plaza Mejorada. One of Mérida's most renowned restaurants, though it is marred by inconsistency. Delicious, moderately priced Yucatecan food, especially at Sunday lunchtime (when dressier *Gran Almendros*, around the corner, gets packed). The original *Los Almendros*, in Ticul, claims to have invented *poc-chuc* (see box above). Daily 10am–11pm.

Amaro C 59 no. 507, between C 60 and C 62. Set in a lovely tree-shaded courtyard with a fountain, and a romantic guitarist Wed–Sat. A little pricey, but interesting veggie options, such as *crepas de chaya*, offer a welcome change for vegetarians tired of endless quesadillas.

Café Club C 55 between C 58 and C 60. Small, very friendly restaurant specializing in natural and mostly vegetarian foods, with a bargain set lunch for US$4. Daily 7am–5pm.

Café Impala Paseo de Montejo at C 47. Sidewalk dining until late, with sandwiches, burgers, and Yucatecan standards. Daily 6pm–2am.

Café Lucía C 60 no. 474-A, across from Parque Santa Lucía, in the *Casa Lucía* hotel. Good Italian and international menu, reasonably priced frequented by city bigwigs. Worth a visit just for the excellent collection of modern Latin American art on the walls.

Café Peón Contreras C 60 adjacent to the Teatro Peón Contreras. One of the most pleasant outdoor spots in the city, with decent Mexican food and pizza. A great place to watch the world go by in relative peace.

Cafetería Pop C 57 between C 60 and C 62. A good breakfast joint with vintage 1960s decor that also serves hamburgers, spaghetti and Mexican snacks. It's a hangout for students and older intellectuals. 7am–midnight.

Dulcería y Sorbetería El Colón C 62 on the north side of the plaza. Popular spot for exotic fruit sorbets; try a *champola*, a big scoop of sorbet in a tall glass of milk. There's another branch on Paseo de Montejo between C 39 and C 41, a good refresher after you've been to the archeology museum.

Ki'bok C 60 no. 468, between C 53 and C 55. Modern, stylish coffee bar and restaurant serving large breakfasts and a varied dinner menu, which includes delicate treats like crepes with squash blossoms. Open until midnight; 2am on Fri and Sat.

El Marlin Azul C 62 between C 57 and C 59. Longtime local favourite for excellent but inexpensive seafood, including tasty fish tacos. Also serves breakfast. Closes at 4.30pm.

La Parroquia C 62 no. 507, between C 65 and C 67. *Lechería* serving blended milk drinks, yogurt and fruit plates. Great for a bargain breakfast or a late-night treat (try the cinnamon-laced chocolate milk).

Pizzería de Vito Corleone C 59 no. 508, at C 62. Inexpensive hole-in-the-wall pizza restaurant, complete with wood-burning oven, that also does takeaway.

El Portico del Peregrino C 57, next door to *Cafetería Pop*. Series of indoor and outdoor patios – a destination for romantic dinners, or at least drinks, as the food – primarily Yucatecan – is sometimes uninspired.

La Reina Itzalana Parque de Santiago, C 59 between C 70 and C 72. This and a couple of other cafés in the same market are some of the few places in town to get a casual, super-cheap dinner of *panuchos, salbutes* and *sopa de lima*. Packed with families until 10pm or 11pm; also open for lunch.

Entertainment and nightlife

Mérida is a lively city, and every evening you'll find the streets buzzing with revellers enjoying a variety of **free entertainment**. To find out what's happening on any particular night, pick up a free copy of the monthly *Mérida...en la cultura* schedule from the tourist office or bigger hotels. **Venues** include the plazas, the garden behind the Palacio Municipal, the Teatro Peón Contreras (next to the tourist office) and the Casa de la Cultura del Mayas, Calle 63 between calles 64 and 66. Things can change, but typical performances might include energetic and fascinating **vaquerías** (vibrant Mexican folk dances, featuring different regional styles, to the rhythm of a *jaranera* band); Glen Miller-style **big band** music; **marimba** in the Parque Hidalgo; **classical music** concerts; and the very popular **Serenata Yucateca**, an open-air performance of traditional songs and music.

Perhaps the best time to see the Plaza Mayor and the surrounding streets is Sunday, when vehicles are banned from the area and day-long music, dancing, markets and festivities take over – a delight after the usual traffic rumble. Street markets are set up along Calle 60 as far as the Plaza Santa Ana, and there's a **flea market** in the Parque Santa Lucía.

There's plenty to do of a more commercial nature too, from **mariachi nights** in hotel bars to **salsa dancing** in nightclubs. Those aimed at tourists will be advertised in hotels, or in brochures available at the tourist office. By far the best of these events is the **Ballet Folklórico de la Universidad de Yucatán**, a wonderful dance interpretation of traditional Mexican and Mayan ceremonies at the Centro Cultural Universitario, Calle 60 and Calle 57 (Fri 9pm; US$2). Less obviously, many big hotels have **video bars** and **discos**.

Apart from the hard-drinking *cantinas* (and there are plenty of these all over the city, including a couple on Calle 62, just south of the plaza) – many of Mérida's **bars** double as restaurants, with early closing times to match.

Bars, discos and live music

Azul Picante C 60 between C 55 and C 57. This small salsa club caters more to tourists than others listed, but offers free lessons early in the evenings, as well as Mexican- and Caribbean-theme nights.

La Casa del Todos C 64 at C 55. Very small student bar with a strong leftist bent – most nights there's a rousing folk singer or two on the tiny stage.

El Cumbanchero Paseo de Montejo at C 37. More convenient than *Mambo Café*, this small salsa bar is owned by the son of the late Rubén González, of Buena Vista Social Club. Dancing starts around dinner time, with an older crowd at first, then giving way to younger dancers around 10pm. Also open for brunch on Sundays.

El Establo C 60 between C 55 and C 57. In the same strip as *Azul Picante*, a popular and noisy bar with a pool table and rock music; light snacks served with the drinks.

Mambo Café in the Plaza Las Américas mall. Worth the cab ride if you're looking to mingle with salsa-mad locals in what's considered the city's best nightclub. Touring Dominican and Cuban bands often play here; cover is US$5.

Pancho's C 59, opposite the *Hotel Reforma*. A steak restaurant with a pricey Tex-Mex menu and a lively, if tiny, dance floor, *Pancho's* is a magnet for hip young Méridans and Americans homesick for "Mexican" food. The fun theme, with giant photos of Mexican revolutionaries and bandolier-draped waiters in sombreros, is ridiculously over the top. Try to hit the happy hour, 6–9pm.

La Prosperidad C 53 at C 56. Don't be deterred by the *restaurante turístico* label – this is a pleasant place for an afternoon beer, with a largely Mexican clientele. Drinks aren't cheap, but they come with substantial tasty snacks (*botanas*), and there's often live music starting around lunchtime. A small separate bar (entrance on C 56) has more of a men-only *cantina* feel. Both close at 8pm.

Listings

Airlines and flights Aerocaribe/Aerocozumel /Mexicana Internacional, Paseo de Montejo 500 ⓣ999/928-6790, at the airport 946-1678; Aeroméxico, Plaza Americana, *Hotel Fiesta Americana* ⓣ999/920-1260, at the airport 946-1400; Aviacsa, in the *Fiesta Americana* ⓣ999/925-6890, at the airport 946-1850; Aviateca, Paseo de Montejo 475-C ⓣ999/925-8059, at the airport 946-1296; Mexicana, Paseo de Montejo 493 ⓣ999/924-6633, at the airport 946-1332. Flights leave for most Mexican cities and some international destinations; to get out to the airport, catch bus #79 ("Aviación") going east on C 67. A taxi costs about US$10.

American Express Paseo de Montejo 492, between C 41 and C 43 (Mon–Fri 9am–5pm, Sat 9am–noon; ⓣ999/942-8200, ⓕ942-8210).

Banks Most banks are around C 65 between C 60 and C 64, have ATMs and are open 9am–4pm. The most centrally located is Banamex in the Casa de Montejo on the south side of the zócalo, which also has an ATM.

Books Librería Burrel, C 59 between C 60 and C 62, is good for maps; guidebooks are sold at Librería Dante across the street (another Dante branch is on the west side of the zócalo). Alternatively, check Arte Maya, on C 57 between C 60 and C 62, which has an extensive collection of used paperbacks in many languages, or borrow English-language books from the Mérida English Library, C 53 between C 66 and C 68, which also functions as a meeting point for the city's expat community.

Buses Because so many bus companies serve the city, routes and services are often duplicated at different terminals – therefore, the following is only a sampling of the schedules. From the first-class CAME, ADO runs to Campeche, Mexico City, Palenque and Villahermosa. Caribe Express provides a comfortable, a/c service with videos to Campeche and Villahermosa, as well as Cancún, Escárcega, Playa del Carmen and a number of other destinations. There are also services to Akumal, Villahermosa, Tulum and Playa del Carmen run by Autotransportes del Caribe. Caribe Express and Autotransportes del Caribe also have desks in the main second-class building, on C 69 between C 68 and C 70. Buses leave for: Campeche (Autotransportes de Sureste; 4hr); Cancún (Expreso de Oriente; 6hr); Escárcega (Autotransportes de Sureste; 6hr); Palenque (Autotransportes de Sureste; 10–11hr); Playa del Carmen (Expreso de Oriente; 7hr); Tuxtla Gutiérrez (Autotransportes de Sureste; 20hr); Valladolid (Expreso de Oriente; 3hr); and Villahermosa (Autotransportes de Sureste; 10hr). Of Mérida's smaller bus stations, the one at C 50 at C 67 is the most useful, with services (usually second-class) from Autobuses de Occidente en Yucatán, for destinations west of Mérida; Lineas Unidos del Sur de Yucatán; Autobuses del Noreste en Yucatán; and Autotransportes de Oriente. Buses leave for Celestún (5am–8.30pm; 2hr), Oxcutzcab (hourly; 2hr) and Sisal (2hr), as well as Río Lagartos (6hr), San Felipe (7hr) and Tizimín (4hr). There are also hourly buses to Cancún (6hr) and to Izamal, Pisté and Valladolid. Colectivos depart Plaza de San Juan, C 69 between C 62 and C 64, for Progreso, Dzibilchaltún and Dzitya, Oxcutzcab and Ticul, among other destinations.

Car rental Family-run Mexico Rent a Car, with offices at C 57-A between C 58 and C 60, and at C 62 no. 483-A, is friendly, with very good rates (ⓣ/ⓕ999/927-4916, ⓔmexicorentacar@hotmail .com). Otherwise, try Hertz, which has offices on C 60 between C 55 and C 57 (ⓣ999/924-2834), at the airport (ⓣ999/946-1355) and in the *Fiesta Americana* (ⓣ999/925-7595), where there are a number of other agencies to choose from as well.

Consulates Opening hours are likely to be fairly limited, so it's best to phone ahead and check. Belize, C 53 no. 498, at C 58 (ⓣ999/928-6152,

Ⓔdutton@sureste.com); Cuba, C 1-D no. 320, at C 42 (Ⓣ999/944-4216, Ⓔconsulcuba@yuc1.telmex.net.mx); France, C 33-D no. 528, at C 62-A (Ⓣ999/925-2886, Ⓔg_martin_mx@yahoo.com); Germany, C 7 Diagonal 217 (Ⓣ999/981-2976, Ⓔtautorant@sureste.com); Spain, C 13 no. 225 (Ⓣ999/944-8350); US, Paseo de Montejo 453, at Av Colón (Ⓣ999/925-5011).

Internet and telephone There are Internet cafés on every street in central Mérida – try Maya Site, C 60 between C 53 and C 55, which also has fax and long-distance services, or Chandler's, in the shopping complex on the north side of the zócalo. A small *caseta* in the *Fiesta Americana* mall has better-than-usual prices for calls to the US and Europe.

Laundry If your hotel doesn't do laundry, try Lavandería Agua Azul, C 70 no. 505 at C 61, which offers full-service washes, stain removal and ironing.

Post office C 65 between C 56 and C 56-A (Mon–Fri 8am–5pm, Sat 9am–1pm), but may be turned into a museum; use of the Lista de Correos (poste restante) is currently not recommended .

Travel agencies and tours Mérida's tourism bureau gives a free walking tour of the centre daily at 9.30am; make reservations at the office located inside the Palacio de Gobierno. A tour of the city by open-sided bus, operated by Carnaval, isn't incredibly gripping but can pass a pleasant few hours, as most of the riders are Mexican and it visits the out-of-the-way Parque de las Américas (from Parque Santa Lucía, Mon–Sat 10am, 1pm, 4pm and 7pm, Sun 10am and 1pm; US$8). For out-of-town trips, Deep Rock Adventures (Ⓣ999/987-8040) organizes caving expeditions to nearby cenotes; student travel agency Nómadas (Ⓣ999/948-1187, Ⓦwww.nomadastravel.com) has good-value trips to Uxmal and Chichén Itzá, as well as excellent plane fares to Mexico City. Otherwise try Yucatan Trails, C 62 no. 482, between C 57 and C 59 (Ⓣ999/928-2582, Ⓔyucatantrails@hotmail.com), where tour prices always include site admission fees; Cuba trips are also available. The knowledgeable Canadian owner offers luggage storage for US$1/day.

North of Mérida: the coast

From Mérida to the port of **Progreso**, the closest point on the coast, is just 36km – thirty minutes on the bus. About halfway between the two, a few kilometres east of the main road, lie the ancient ruins of **Dzibilchaltún**, with a **cenote** at the very middle of the city, fed with a constant supply of fresh water from a small spring, which you can swim in. The drive out of the city follows Paseo de Montejo through miles of wealthy suburbs and shopping malls before reaching the flat countryside where the henequen industry seems still to be flourishing. On the outskirts of Mérida is a giant Cordemex processing plant, and a nearby shop run by the same company sells goods made from the fibre.

It's easy enough to visit both Dzibilchaltún and Progreso in one trip from Mérida: **combis** for Chablecal stop at the ruins; they leave from Parque San Juan (Calle 62 and Calle 69) about every half-hour; from the ruins you can walk or hitch a ride back to the main highway, where you can flag down a Progreso bus. *Combis* return to Mérida from the corner of Calle 80 and Calle 31 near the post office, on the north side of Progreso's Parque Central (note that leaving on Sunday evenings in the summer, with the rest of the weekender crowds, you'll have a very long wait). To go straight to the coast from Mérida, **buses** leave from the terminal dedicated to Progreso services on Calle 62 between calles 65 and 67.

Dzibilchaltún

Unfortunately, the archeological importance of the ruins of the ancient city of **Dzibilchaltún** (daily 8am–5pm; US$5.50) is hardly reflected in what you actually see. Apparently the area was settled from 1000 BC right through to the Conquest, the longest continuous occupation of any known site. More than eight thousand structures have been mapped, and the city's major points were linked by great causeways – but little has survived, in particular because the ready-dressed stones were a handy building material, used in several local towns and in the Mérida–Progreso road.

In addition to providing the ancient city with water, the 44-metre-deep **Cenote Xlacah** was of ritual importance to the Maya: more than six thousand offerings – including human remains – have been discovered in its depths. A causeway leads from the cenote to a ramshackle group of buildings around the **Templo de las Siete Muñecas** (Temple of the Seven Dolls). The temple itself was originally a simple square pyramid, subsequently built over with a more complex structure. Later still, a passageway was cut through to the original building and seven deformed clay figurines (dolls) buried, with a tube through which their spirits could commune with the priests. In conjunction with the buildings that surround it, the temple is aligned with various astronomical points and must have served in some form as an observatory. It is also remarkable for being the only known Maya temple to have windows and for having a tower in place of the usual roof-comb. The dolls, and many of the finds from the cenote, can be seen in an excellent museum (8am–4pm; closed Mon) by the site entrance, which attempts an overview of Maya culture and the history of the region up to the present day. Around Dzibilchaltún, five and a half square kilometres have been declared an **eco-archeological park**, partly to protect a species of fish found only in the cenotes, including Xlacah. Nature trails take you through the surrounding forest, and it's a great place for bird-watching.

Progreso and around

First impressions of **PROGRESO** – a working port with a six-kilometre-long concrete pier – are unfavourable, especially at the end of a summer weekend when crowds of day-trippers have just pulled out, leaving beer bottles and food wrappers in their wake. But the beach is long and broad with fine white sand (though the water's not too clean), and it makes for a pleasant, non-touristy day out from Mérida. The shore front behind the beach is built up all the way to **Chicxulub Puerto**, an unremarkable fishing village some 5km east, and a walk between the two takes you past the mansions of the old henequen exporters, interspersed with modern holiday villas and condominiums.

Streets in Progreso are confusingly numbered using two overlapping systems: one has numbers in the 70s and 80s, the other in the 20s and 30s. However, it's a small place, and not difficult to find your way around. The main street is Calle 80, where you'll find the **tourist office** (Mon–Fri 8am–2pm, Sat 8am–1pm; Ⓣ969/935-0114), in the Casa de la Cultura; it's not terribly useful, however. Also on Calle 80 are a couple of **banks**, both with ATMs, and an Internet café. There are a few moderately priced **places to stay** on Avenida Malecón, which runs along the seafront between the beach and the hotels; because Progreso is a popular family destination, many have large rooms ideal for groups. The high season is July and August; outside of that, prices drop considerably. The less expensive hotels are a few roads back. Best bets include *Hotel Progreso,* Calle 29 no. 142, at Calle 78 (Ⓣ969/935-0039, Ⓕ935-2019; ❹–❺), with clean rooms and a choice of a/c or fan; and the new *Hotel Casa Quixote* (Ⓣ969/935-2909, Ⓕ935-5600, Ⓦwww.casaquixote.com; ❻), a little east of the centre, on Calle 23 between calles 48 and 50, which has a wide range of rooms and a pool. *Tropical Suites*, on the malecón at Calle 70 (Ⓣ969/935-1263; ❺), is a little seedy, but has some suites with kitchens.

For **eating**, try the lively *Eladio's*, on the malecón at Calle 80, where you can make a good meal of the tasty *botanas* that come free with beers. Also popular is *Sol y Mar*, across the street, for seafood snacks, and *Le Saint Bonnet*, a family restaurant on Calle 19 and Calle 78 that serves more elaborate local seafood specialities and has a pool for guests. For cheap comida corrida, the town's small, friendly market has several good *comedores*.

Beaches around Progreso

The **beach** stretches in either direction from Progreso, and though this coast is the focus of much new tourism development, it's never crowded. Indeed, in winter, when the holiday homes are empty, you'll have miles of sand to yourself. Check the numbers posted outside the villas and you may find bargain **long-term accommodation**.

The main highway east from Progreso runs behind **Chicxulub Puerto** and reaches, at Km 15, a smart **viewing platform** (free; follow signs for the *mirador turístico*) over the Río Huaymitún, which is a great place to see flocks of **flamingoes**. Go at sunrise or sunset (but before the 7pm closing time) for your best chance of spotting them – the caretakers will lend you binoculars. The coast road continues on to **Telchac Puerto**, one hour away, a laid-back seaside village popular in the summer with escapees from the city heat of Mérida. There's an excellent small hotel, *Posada Liz* (Ⓣ991/917-4125, Ⓔposadaliz_telchac@hotmail.com; ❹), as well as several very good seafood restaurants.

With more time and a detour inland at Chabiahu to avoid the washed-out coast road, it's possible to get even further east, first to **Santa Clara** – where *La Morena* restaurant serves excellent fresh fish, and the beach is tranquil – and on to **DZILAM DE BRAVO**, a remote fishing village at the end of the road, with no beach because of its sea-defence wall. *Hotel Capitán Jean Lafitte* (Ⓣ991/912-2548; ❹) is the only lodging option, but a good one, with a pool, restaurant and clean rooms. To visit **Bocas de Dzilam**, 40km away in the **San Felipe Natural Park**, you'll need to track down local guide Javier Nadar, better known as Chacate (ask around for him in the main square). He charges US$80 for a boat and a *ceviche* lunch (4–5hr; up to five people), US$35 for shorter trips (3–4hr). Set in 620 square kilometres of coastal forests, marshes and dunes, the *bocas* (Spanish for "mouths") are freshwater springs on the sea bed; the nutrients they provide encourage the wide biological diversity found here. Wildlife watching is superb: you may see turtles, tortoises, crocodiles, spider monkeys and dozens of bird species.

A more direct way to get to Dzilam de Bravo is to catch a second-class **bus** in Mérida from the Autobuses del Noreste terminal at the corner of Calle 50 and Calle 67. Three buses daily pass through on their way to and from Tizimín and Progreso, and four buses daily leave for Izamal.

West of Progreso, a number of hotels and holiday homes line the road to **Yucalpetén**, a busy commercial port and naval base 4km from Progreso. Further west, the small but growing resorts of **Chelem** and **Chuburná**, respectively fifteen and thirty minutes from Progreso and easy day-trips from Mérida, have clean, wide beaches and a few rooms and restaurants. *Hotel Sian Ka'an,* in Chelem, is one good option, offering big oceanfront rooms ideal for groups or families, with balconies and kitchenettes (Ⓣ/Ⓕ969/935-4017, Ⓦwww.hotelsiankaan.com; ❽).

Beyond Chuburná, the coast road, which was damaged by Hurricane Gilbert, is no longer negotiable and you'll have to turn inland. It's not worth making a detour back to the coast at **SISAL** – unbelievably Mérida's chief port in colonial times, but now quite shabby and practically deserted.

Celestún

CELESTÚN, at the end of a sand bar on the peninsula's northwest coast, would be little more than a one-boat fishing village were it not for its amazing bird-filled lagoon that boasts a large flock of flamingoes. To see them – as well as the blue-winged teals and shovellers that migrate here in the winter to take advantage of the plentiful fish in these warm, shallow waters – hire a boat at the official *parador turístico*, just past the the bridge on the main road into Celestún. Get the bus driver to drop you off, as otherwise it's a twenty-minute walk back from the main square. You'll need to purchase a group ticket (US$40) from the ticket booth and then individual tickets (US$4, maximum of six people per boat) for an eighty-minute tour. A longer trip (2hr 20min) – which heads farther up the lagoon and may give you time to swim in the rich red waters among the mangroves (bring your bathing suit) – is US$80 for the boat plus US$4 per person. If you're already in town and don't feel like trekking back out to the *parador*, you could arrange a trip from Celestún's beach with personable local guide Filiberto Couoh Cavich (also known as Ruso), which takes in seven different ecological sites of interest (2hr 30min–3hr; US$150 for eight people) – ask at the *Restaurant Celestún*.

Nominally protected by inclusion in the **Celestún Natural Park**, the flamingoes are nevertheless harassed by boats approaching too close in order to give visitors a spectacular flying display, disturbing the birds' feeding. Try to make it clear to your boatman that you don't wish to interrupt the birds' natural behaviour; you will still get good photos from a respectable distance.

There are first-class **buses** from Mérida for Celestún every two hours from the CAME. Second-class services leave from the terminal on Calle 67 at Calle 50. There are half a dozen **places to stay** in the village: the *Hotel Maria del Carmen*, Calle 12 no. 111, at Calle 15 (Ⓣ988/916-2170; ❺), has rooms with balconies, and some with a/c; *Hotel San Julio*, on Calle 12 at Calle 9 (Ⓣ988/916-2170; ❹), is more basic; and the *Ría Celestún* **hostel**, also on Calle 12 at Calle 13 (Ⓣ988/916-2219, Ⓔhostelriacelestun@hotmail.com; ❷), has decent dorm beds. Ten kilometres north of the town is a remote and lovely ecolodge, *Eco Paraíso Xixim* (Ⓣ988/916-2100, Ⓦwww.ecoparaiso.com; ❾), which operates primarily on wind and solar power and offers well-appointed cabañas, excellent showers and miles of deserted beach and wildlife-filled scrub to explore; rates include breakfast and dinner.

Several **seafood restaurants** can be found on the dusty main street and on the beach – the *ceviche* in Celestún is invariably good – and there's also a market, a bakery, a bank (but no ATM) and petrol station.

South of Mérida: Uxmal and the Ruta Puuc

About 80km south of Mérida in the **Puuc hills** lies a group of the peninsula's most important archeological sites. **Uxmal** (pronounced OOSH-mal) is chief of them, second only to Chichén Itzá in size and significance, but perhaps greater in its initial impact and certainly in the beauty and harmony of its extraordinary architectural style. Lesser sites include **Kabáh**, down the main road not far beyond; **Sayil**, nearby on a road running east; and **Labná**, further along this same road. Though related architecturally, each site is quite distinct from the others, and each is dominated by one major structure. From Labná you could continue to **Oxcutzcab**, on the road from Muna to Felipe Crrillo Puerto, and head back to Mérida via **Maní**, or take the new fast road past the Maya ruins of **Mayapán**.

Like Chichén Itzá, the Puuc sites are now regarded as being as authentically Maya as Tikal or Palenque, rather than the product of invading Toltecs, as was once believed. Though there are new stylistic themes both in the Puuc sites and at Chichén Itzá, the buildings also show marked continuities of architectural and artisitc technique, religious symbolism, hieroglyphic writing and settlement patterns. The newer themes are now believed to have been introduced by the **Chontal Maya** of the Gulf coast lowlands, who had become the Yucatán's most important trading partner by the Terminal Classic period (800–1000 AD). The Chontal Maya themselves traded extensively with Oaxaca and central Mexico and are thought to have passed on their architectural styles and themes to the Yucatán.

Getting to the sites

The sites are far enough apart that it's impractical to do more than a fraction of them by bus, unless you're prepared to spend several days and endure a lot of waiting around. The cheapest and most practical way to visit the sites is to take the "**Ruta Puuc**" **day-trip bus** (US$10.70), run by Autotransportes del Sur from the second-class bus station in Mérida (see p.728), and though you don't get much time at the ruins, Uxmal is the last-visited and it is possible to stay later and pay for a different bus back. Scores of Mérida travel agencies offer pricier Puuc route trips that include meals and a guide.

It's better still to **rent a car**: in two days you can explore all of the key sites, either returning to Mérida by evening or finding a room in Santa Elena or Ticul or around Uxmal. For details of car rental agencies, see p.737.

Uxmal

UXMAL – "thrice-built" – represents the finest achievement of the **Puuc architectural style**, in which buildings of amazingly classical proportions are decorated with broad stone mosaic friezes of geometric patterns, or designs so stylized and endlessly repeated as to become almost abstract. As in every Maya site in the Yucatán, the face of **Chac**, the rain god, is everywhere. Chac must have been more crucial here than almost anywhere, for Uxmal and the other Puuc sites, almost uniquely, have no cenote or other natural source of water, relying instead on artificially created underground cisterns, jug-shaped and coated with lime, to collect and store rainwater. In recent years these have all been filled in, to prevent mosquitoes breeding.

Little is known of the city's history, but what is clear is that the chief monuments, and the city's peaks of power and population, fall into the Terminal Classic period, and though there are indications of settlement long before this, most of the buildings that you see date from this period. Sometime after 900 AD the city began to decline, and by 1200 Uxmal and all the Puuc sites, together with Chichén Itzá, were all but abandoned. The reasons for this are unknown, although political infighting, ecological problems and loss of trade with Tula may have played a part. Later, the **Xiu dynasty** settled at Uxmal, which became one of the central pillars of the League of Mayapán (see p.749), and from here, in 1441, the rebellion originated that finally overthrew the power of Mayapán and put an end to any form of centralized Maya authority over the Yucatán. All the significant surviving structures, though, date from the Classic period.

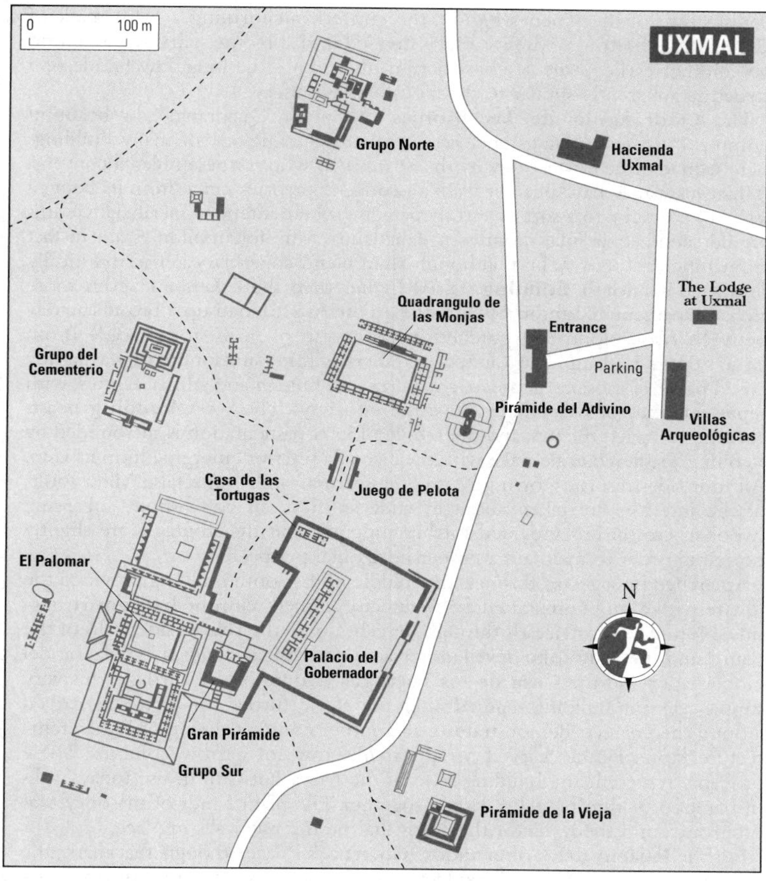

The site

Entering the site, the back of the great **Pirámide del Adivino** (Pyramid of the Magician) rises before you. The most remarkable-looking of all Mexican pyramids, it soars at a startling angle from its oval base to a temple some 30m above the ground, with a broad but steep stairway up either side. The structure takes its name from a legend that it was constructed in a single night by a magical dwarf, though in fact at least five stages of construction have been discovered – six if you count the modern restoration, which may not correspond exactly to any of its earlier incarnations.

Visitors are no longer permitted to climb the pyramid, but from the base of the rear (east) stairway you can see a tunnel, which reveals Templo III. At the top, surrounded by a platform, the summit temple has a facade decorated with interlocking geometric motifs. On the west face of the pyramid, the stairway runs down either side of a second, earlier sanctuary in a distinctly different style. Known as the **Edificio Chenes** (or Templo IV), it does indeed reflect the architecture of the Chenes region, the entire front forming a giant mask of Chac. At the bottom of the west face, divided in half by the stairway, you'll find yet another earlier stage of construction (the first) – the long, low facade of a structure apparently similar to the so-called "Nunnery".

The **Qudrángulo de las Monjas** (Nunnery Quadrangle), a beautiful complex of four buildings enclosing a square plaza, is one of many buildings here named quite erroneously by the Spanish, to whom it resembled a convent. Whatever it may have been, it wasn't a convent; theories range from its being a military academy to a sort of earthly paradise where intended sacrificial victims would spend their final months in debauchery. The four buildings are in fact from different periods and, although they blend superbly, each is stylistically distinct. The **north building**, raised higher than the others and even more richly ornamented, is probably also the oldest. Approached up a broad stairway between two colonnaded porches, it has a strip of plain stone facade (from which doors lead into the vaulted chambers within) surmounted by a slightly raised panel of mosaics: geometric patterns and human and animal figures, with representations of Maya huts above the doorways. The **west building** boasts even more varied themes, and the whole of its ornamentation is surrounded by a coiling, feathered rattlesnake with the face of a warrior emerging from its jaws. All four sides display growing Maya architectural skills – the false Maya vaults of the interiors are taken about as wide as they can go without collapsing (wooden crossbeams provided further support), and the frontages are slightly bowed in order to maintain a proper horizontal perspective.

An arched passageway through the middle of the south building provided the square with a monumental entrance directly aligned with the **ball-court** outside. Nowadays a path leads through here, between the ruined side walls of the court and up onto the levelled terrace on which stand the Palacio del Gobernador and the **Casa de las Tortugas** (House of the Turtles). This very simple, elegant building, named after the stone turtles (or tortoises) carved around the cornice, demonstrates well another constant theme of Puuc architecture: stone facades carved to appear like rows of narrow columns. These probably represent the building style of the Maya huts still in use today: walls of bamboo or thin branches lashed together. The plain bands of masonry that often surround them mirror the cords that tie the hut walls in place.

It is the **Palacio del Gobernador** (Governor's Palace), though, that marks the finest achievement of Uxmal's builders. John L. Stephens, arriving at the then virtually unknown site in June 1840, had no doubts as to its significance: "If it stood this day on its grand artificial terrace in Hyde Park or the Garden of the Tuileries," he later wrote, "it would form a new order ... not unworthy to stand side by side with the remains of the Egyptian, Grecian and Roman art." The palace faces east, away from the buildings around it, probably for astronomical reasons – its central doorway aligns with the column of the altar outside and the point where Venus rises. Long and low, it is lent a remarkable harmony by the architect's use of light and shade on the facade, and by the strong diagonals that run right through its broad band of mosaic decorations – particularly in the steeply vaulted archways that divide the two wings from the central mass, like giant arrowheads aimed at the sky. Close up, the mosaic is equally impressive, masks of Chac alternating with grid-and-key patterns and highly stylized snakes. Inside, the chambers are narrow, gloomy and unadorned; but at least the great central room, 20m long and entered by the three closer-set openings in the facade, is grander than most. At the back, the rooms have no natural light source at all.

Behind the palace stand the ruinous buildings of the **Grupo Sur** (South Group), with the partly restored Gran Pirámide (Great Pyramid), and El

Palomar (Dovecote or Quadrangle of the Doves). You can climb the rebuilt staircase of the **Gran Pirámide** to see the temple on top, decorated with parrots and more masks of Chac, and look across at the rest of the site. **El Palomar** was originally part of a quadrangle like that of the Nunnery, but the only building to retain any form is this, topped with the great wavy, latticed roof-comb from which it takes its name.

Of the outlying structures, the **Pirámide de la Vieja** (Pyramid of the Old Woman), probably the earliest surviving building at Uxmal, is now little more than a grassy mound with a clearly man-made outline. The **Grupo del Cementerio** (Cemetery Group), too, is in a state of ruin – low altars in the middle of this square show traces of carved hieroglyphs and human skulls.

Practicalities

Several **buses** a day run direct from Mérida to Uxmal, and any bus heading down the main road towards Hopelchén (or between Mérida and Campeche on the longer route) will drop you just a short walk from the entrance. At the modern **entrance to the site** (daily 8am–5pm; US$8, US$6 on Sun) the **tourist centre** includes a small museum, a snack bar and a shop with guides to the site, souvenirs, film and such. Uxmal's sound-and-light show (daily; US$3) starts at 7pm in winter and 8pm in summer and has a Spanish commentary – you can hire simultaneous translation equipment (US$2.50) – which is pretty crude, but the lighting effects are moderately impressive. Note that no buses run late enough to get you back to Mérida after the show (a taxi from Mérida costs around US$45 for a round-trip with waiting time).

There are several **hotels** nearby, none of them in the budget category. Two are right at the site's entrance: Club Med's *Villas Arqueológicas* (Ⓣ997/928-6020, Ⓕ976-2040, Ⓦwww.clubmed.com; ❼), which has a/c rooms, a pool and tennis courts, and *The Lodge at Uxmal* (Ⓣ997/923-2202, Ⓕ925-0087, Ⓦwww.mayaland.com; ❼), with similar facilities and a breezy restaurant and bar, *La Palapa*, a convenient spot for a cool drink. The most attractive option in the immediate vicinity is the colonial-style *Hotel Hacienda Uxmal* (Ⓣ997/976-2012, Ⓕ976-2011, Ⓦwww.mayaland.com; ❾), which is slightly further away on the main Mérida–Uxmal road. Further still, but much more lavish, is the ultra-luxurious *Hacienda Temozón* (Ⓣ999/923-8089, Ⓕ923-7963, Ⓦwww.starwood.com/luxury; ❾), on the sprawling grounds of which are two cenotes, a dramatic swimming pool and a gym in the old machine-works. It's located in Temozón Sur, about 45km south of Mérida and a half-hour drive from Uxmal.

For **lunch** after visiting the site, head about 1.5km back towards Mérida on the main road to *Restaurante Cana-nah*, in the otherwise dumpy *Rancho Uxmal* hotel. It's tasty and inexpensive, and restaurant guests are welcome to use the swimming pool. Another pleasant spot for a meal is the partially restored seventeenth-century *Hacienda Ochil*, just south of Temozón Sur on the main highway between Mérida and Uxmal. You can also tour the old henequen-processing machinery and take a dip in a cenote.

Santa Elena

A small town at a convenient point on the route from Uxmal to Kabáh, the village of **SANTA ELENA** is a handy base for exploring farther south. Two exceptionally nice **places to stay** make it more enticing: on Hwy-261 as it bypasses the village is the *Flycatcher Inn* (Ⓦwww.mexonline.com/flycatcherinn.htm; ❺–❻), a B&B with one suite and three rooms decorated with local craftwork. It's about fifteen minutes' walk south from the main square; if you're travelling by bus from Mérida, ask the driver to drop you off at the junction with Hwy-261 after you've gone through town. Just down the road towards Kabáh is *Sacbe Bungalows* (ⓣ985/858-1281, ⓔsacbebungalow@hotmail.com; ❶–❹), where a hospitable Mexican–French couple offer basic, spotless rooms, all with porches, dotted among the shady fruit trees. There is also some dorm accommodation, with a big shared kitchen, and limited space to camp. For a small additional charge the owners will cook you a delicious breakfast and supper. In between the two hotels is a small **restaurant**, *El Chac Mool*, which does decent local food (closes at 8pm). Note also that you may be able to hitch a ride to Santa Elena with Uxmal's workers after the sound-and-light show (though you should arrange your room ahead of time, as these two places fill up quickly).

Santa Elena itself is worth visiting for the magnificent view from its large **church** (daily until 3pm); ask for the sacristan, who will open the door to the spiral staircase that leads to the roof. Beside the church is a morbidly interesting small **museum** (daily 8am–6pm; free) that serves as a home for the 200-year-old mummified remains of four children that were discovered under the church floor in 1980.

Ticul

Located 80km south of Mérida on Hwy-184, **TICUL**, although not particularly scenic, is another good base for exploring the Puuc region. The town is an important centre of Maya shamanism as well as a pottery-producing centre and it's full of shops selling reproduction Maya antiquities, most too big to carry home. Visitors are welcome to watch the manufacturing process at the *fábricas*. The place is also renowned for its shoes, and the streets are lined with shoe shops. Despite all this, Ticul lives life at a slow pace, with more bicycles (and passenger-carrying *triciclos*) than cars.

On the main road between Mérida and Felipe Carrillo Puerto in Quintana Roo, Ticul is also an important transport centre, well served by **buses** to and from Mérida and with services to Cancún. If you're arriving by bus from Mérida, you'll be dropped on the corner of Calle 24 and Calle 25-A, behind the church. Buses **from Campeche** don't go through Ticul so you'll have to get off at Santa Elena to catch one of the colectivos that leave from the main square between 6am and 7pm; the trip takes about thirty minutes. **Trucks** for Oxcutzcab and surrounding villages set off when they're full from the side of the plaza next to the church; **combis** for Mérida leave from further down the same street.

Even-numbered roads run north to south, odd numbers east to west. Calle 23 is the main street, with the plaza at its eastern end at Calle 26. Half a block from the plaza, the *Sierra Sosa*, Calle 26 no. 199-A (ⓣ/ⓕ997/972-0008; ❹), has basic **rooms**, with shower and fan (upstairs is better), and a few new a/c rooms with TV. The English-speaking manager is a good source of information, and you can make international calls from reception. A smarter alternative is the *Hotel Plaza,* overlooking the main square at Calle 23 no. 202 (ⓣ997/972-0484, ⓕ972-0026, ⓦwww.hotelplazayucatan; ❺). It's the most comfortable and centrally located option, with TV, telephone and a/c in all rooms.

The best of the **restaurants** is *Los Almendros*, on Calle Principal heading out of town towards Oxcutzcab, which serves superb local dishes and even has a pool, which is packed with kids at weekends. The *Lonchería Carmelita*, two doors up from *Hotel Plaza* on the corner of Calle 23 and Calle 26, does an inexpensive comida. As usual, the least expensive places are the *loncherías* near the bus station. For night-time dining, don't miss the tortas at the front of the market on Calle 23 between calles 28 and 30.

Kabáh

Some 30km south of Uxmal and 25km from Ticul, the extensive site of **KABÁH** (daily 8am–5pm; US$2.90), meaning "Mighty Hand", stretches across the road. Much of it remains unexplored, but the one great building, the **Codz Poop**, or Palace of Masks, lies not far off the highway to the left. The facade of this amazing structure is covered all over, in ludicrous profusion, with goggle-eyed, trunk-nosed masks of Chac. Even in its present state – with most of the long, curved noses broken off – this is the strangest and most striking of all Maya buildings, decorated so obsessively, intricately and repetitively that it almost seems insane. Even the steps by which you reach the doorways and the interior are more Chac noses. A couple of lesser buildings are grouped around the Codz Poop, and on the other side of the road is an unusual circular pyramid – now simply a green conical mound. Known as the Great Temple, it is believed that the building, erected on a natural elevation, functioned as a "house of the gods", where priests offered sacrifices or interpreted divine messages. Just beyond the mound, a sort of triumphal arch marks the point where the ancient thirty-kilometre causeway, or *sacbe*, from Uxmal entered the city.

Leaving Kabáh, you may have to virtually lie down in the road to persuade a bus to stop for you – ask the guards at the site for the bus times. Hitching a ride with other visitors, though, is pretty easy, and with luck you may even meet someone touring all the local sites.

Sayil

A sober, restrained contrast to the excesses of Kabáh, the ruined site of **Sayil** (daily 8am–5pm; US$2.90) lies some 5km along a smaller road heading east off the highway, from a junction 5km beyond Kabáh. Once one of the most densely populated areas in the Puuc region, it is estimated that up to 17,000 people inhabited Sayil from 700 AD to 1000 AD. It is again dominated by one major structure, the extensively restored **Gran Palacio** (Great Palace), built on three storeys, each smaller than the one below, and some 80m long. Although several large masks of Chac adorn a frieze around the top of the middle level, the decoration mostly takes the form of bamboo-effect stone pillaring – seen here more extensively than at any other Puuc site. The interiors of the middle level, too, are lighter and airier than is usual, thanks to the use of broad openings, their lintels supported on fat columns. The upper and lower storeys are almost entirely unadorned, plain stone surfaces with narrow openings.

Few other structures have been cleared. From the Gran Palacio a path leads to the right to the large temple of **El Mirador**, and in the other direction to a stele, carved with a phallic figure and now protected under a thatched roof. On the opposite side of the road from all this, a small path leads uphill, in about ten minutes, to two more temples.

Xlapak and Labná

The minor road continues past the tiny Puuc site known as **XLAPAK** (daily 8am–5pm; US$2.90). Its proximity to the larger sites of Labná and Sayil means that Xlapak (Maya for "old walls") is seldom visited, but if you have the time, stop to see the recently restored buildings with their carvings of masks and yet more Chac noses. **LABNÁ** (daily 8am–5pm; US$2.90) is about 4km further.

Near the entrance to this ancient city is a palace, similar to but less impressive than that of Sayil, on which you'll see traces of sculptures including the inevitable Chac, and a crocodile-snake figure with a human face emerging from its mouth – thought to symbolize a god escaping from the jaws of the underworld. Remnants of a raised causeway lead from here to a second group of buildings, of which the most important is the **Arco de Labná**. Originally part of a complex linking two great squares, like the Nunnery at Uxmal, it now stands alone as a sort of triumphal arch. Both sides are richly decorated: on the east with geometric patterns; on the west (the back) with more of these and niches in the form of Maya huts or temples. Nearby is El Mirador, a temple with the well-preserved remains of a tall, elaborate roof-comb. An inner passageway at one time led to the site's principal temple.

If you're travelling by car, it's worth following signs just beyond Labná to the wonderfully romantic **Hacienda Tabi** (US$1.50), an abandoned sugar plantation which was declared a protected ecological reserve by the Mexican government in 1995 and is currently being restored. The seven-kilometre detour down a progressively more rutted road (nearly impassable if it has recently rained), through orange groves, leads to a sprawling ruined complex. The plantation's main house is still being restored, though you can make advance arrangements to **stay the night** in one of five enormous tiled bedrooms upstairs (❷–❹; the caretakers will provide three meals for an extra charge), and you should have the place, with its enormous park, swimming pool and ruined chapel, to yourself. There are also dorm beds and space to **camp**. For further information contact the Fundación Cultural Yucatán in Mérida, Calle 58 no. 249-D (Ⓣ999/923-9453, Ⓦwww.fcy.org.mx).

Oxkutzcab and around

From Labná, you can head back to Mérida on the fast new highway (look for signs just north of town) or you can stop off in the village of **OXKUTZCAB**, 25km from Labná. It's a decent rest stop after completing the Ruta Puuc, with a huge **fruit market**, bustling and lively in the mornings, selling most of its produce by the crate or sack. Calles 51 and 50 edge the main park and the *mercado*, with a large Franciscan church between them.

Buses to Mérida via Ticul (2hr) leave about every hour from the **bus station** at the corner of Calle 56 and Calle 51; colectivos come and go from beside the *mercado* on Calle 51. One basic **hotel**, *Hospedaje Trujeque* (Ⓣ997/975-0568; ❸), is centrally located on Calle 48 opposite the park, but the new *Hotel Puuc*, on Calle 55 and Calle 44 on the way out of town towards Labná (Ⓣ997/975-0103; ❹), is much preferable, with bright, clean rooms with a/c and TV. The Banamex **bank** on Calle 50, opposite the park, has an ATM. **Restaurants** and cafeterias skirt the market, but if you fancy a long, lazy lunch, try a few blocks back at the *Restaurante Su Cabaña Suiza*, Calle 54 no. 101, between calles 51 and 49, where comidas are served in the tranquillity of a spacious open-sided palapa.

Grutas de Loltún

Just outside Oxcutzcab on the road to Labná, the **Grutas de Loltún** (daily 9am–5pm; US$5), studded with stalactites and stalagmites (one in the shape of a giant corn cob), were revered by the Maya as a source of water from a time long before they built their cities. At the entrance, a huge bas-relief warrior guards the opening to the underworld, and throughout are traces of ancient paintings and carvings on the walls. Nowadays the caves are lit, with interesting guided tours available (officially at 9.30am, 11am, 12.30pm, 2pm, 3pm & 4pm; in practice it depends on who turns up, and when). The surrounding jungle is visible through the collapsed floor of the last gallery and ten-metre-long tree roots find an anchor on the cavern floor. There are two decent though pricey restaurants near the site, *El Guerrero* and *El Huimic de Loltún*.

Colectivos and trucks that pass the caves from Oxcutzcab leave from Calle 51 next to the market; if you get there by 8.30am you may be able to catch the truck taking the cave employees to work. Getting back is less easy, as the trucks are full of workers and produce, but if you wait something will turn up. The short taxi ride from the village will cost you approximately US$5.

Maní and Mayapán

Twelve kilometres north of Oxcutzcab lies the small town of **MANÍ**. Founded by the Xiu after they abandoned Uxmal, it was at the time of the Conquest the largest city the Spanish encountered in the Yucatán. Avoiding a major confrontation, Maní's ruler, Ah Kukum Xiu, converted to Christianity and became an ally of the Spanish. Here, in 1548, was founded one of the earliest and largest **Franciscan monasteries** in the Yucatán. This still stands, surrounded now by Maya huts, and just about the only evidence of Maní's past glories are the ancient stones used in its construction. In front of the church, in 1562, Bishop Diego de Landa held the notorious auto-da-fé in which he burned the city's ancient records (because they "contained nothing in which there was not to be seen the superstitions and lies of the devil"), destroying virtually all surviving original Maya literature. Méridans often come down here on day-trips to dine at *El Príncipe Tutul-Xiu,* a festive palapa-roof **restaurant** that has been serving Yucatecan standards for more than thirty years (daily 11am–7pm).

Forty-nine kilometres north of Ticul and 58km north of Maní are the ruins of **MAYAPÁN**, the most powerful city in the Yucatán from the eleventh to the fifteenth century. Its history is somewhat vague, but according to Maya chronicles, it was one of the three cities (the others being Chichén Itzá and Uxmal) that made up the **League of Mayapán**, which exercised control over the entire peninsula from around 987 to 1185. However, these dates, based on surviving Maya chronicles, are controversial, since archeological evidence suggests that Mayapán was not a significant settlement until the thirteenth century. The rival theory has Mayapán founded around 1263, after the fall of Chichén Itzá.

The league broke up when the **Cocom** dynasty of Mayapán attacked and overwhelmed the rulers of an already declining Chichén Itzá, establishing themselves as sole controllers of the peninsula. Mayapán became a huge city by the standards of the day, with a population of some fifteen thousand in a site covering five square kilometres, in which traces of more than four thousand buildings have been found – here, rulers of subject cities were forced to live where they could be kept under control, perhaps even as hostages. This hegemony was maintained until 1441 when Ah Xupan, a Xiu leader from Uxmal, finally led a rebellion that succeeded in overthrowing the Cocom and destroying their city – thus paving the way for the disunited tribalism that the Spanish found on their arrival, which made their conquest considerably easier.

What can be seen today is a disappointment – the buildings, anyway, were crude and small by Maya standards, at best poor copies of what had gone before. This has led to the society's widespread dismissal as "decadent" and failing, but a powerful case can be made for the fact that it was merely a changing one. Here the priests no longer dominated – hence the lack of great ceremonial centres – and what grew instead was a more genuinely urban society: highly militaristic, no doubt, but also far more centralized and more reliant on trade than anything seen previously.

Chichén Itzá

Chichén Itzá, the most famous, the most extensively restored, and by far the most visited of all Maya sites, lies conveniently along the main road from Mérida to Cancún and the Caribbean, about 120km from Mérida and a little more than 200km from the coast. A fast and very regular bus service runs all along this road, making it perfectly feasible to visit as a day's excursion from Mérida, or en route from Mérida to the coast (or even as a day out from Cancún, as many tour buses do). The site, though, deserves better, and both to do the ruins justice and to see them when they're not entirely overrun by tourists, an overnight stop is well worth considering – either at the site itself or, less extravagantly, in the nearby village of **Pisté** or in Valladolid (see p.757).

The route from Mérida: Aké and Izamal

If your pace to Chichén Itzá is fairly leisurely, scenic **IZAMAL**, the buildings of which are all painted a striking ochre yellow, is the one place that merits a detour. Now something of a backwater, this town 72km east of Mérida was formerly an important religious centre for the Maya, where they worshipped **Itzamná**, mythical founder of the ancient city and one of the gods of creation, at a series of huge pyramid-temples of the same name. Most are now no more than low mounds in the surrounding country, but several survive in the town itself, and are fascinating to see rising up right in the middle of the residential grid. The largest, **Kinich Kakmo** (daily 8am–8pm; free), dedicated to the sun god, has been partly restored. It's just a couple of blocks north of the two adjacent central plazas – ask for directions from any of the helpful brown-clad tourist police roaming the squares. Another pyramid had its top lopped off by the Spanish and was replaced with the vast **convent of St Anthony of Padua** (daily; free), which dominates the main squares. The porticoed atrium is particularly beautiful and photogenic in the late afternoon, and inside it is a statue of the Virgin of Izamal, patron saint of the Yucatán, whose presence brings pilgrims from all over the peninsula.

Neither of the very basic **hotels** on the zócalo can be recommended; better to head a few blocks east to *Macan Ché B&B* (Ⓣ/Ⓕ988/954-0287, Ⓦwww.macanche.com; ❺), an assortment of comfortable cottages on Calle 22 between calles 33 and 35. The same knowledgeable woman owns the rambling, artfully decorated *Hacienda Chalante* (❻), a few kilometres south, east of the town of Sudzal, and well worth the drive if you have your own transport. Back in town, you'll find a BanCrecen **bank** with ATM, as well as a **post office**, on the square on the north side of the convent. *Restaurante Portales*, facing the southwest corner of the convent, serves good basic local **food** and snacks, as well as hamburgers and the like; *Restaurante El Toro*, on Calle 30 just east of the convent, has a more purely Yucatecan menu, with a sit-down restaurant feel. Hecho a Mano, a particularly good craft and folk-art **shop**, is on Calle 31 facing the park. **Horse-drawn buggies** lined up around the zócalo will take you for a pleasant *recorrido* of the town (US$4) and Maya sites. **Buses to Izamal** leave Mérida every half-hour from the terminal at Calle 50 and Calle 67 (see p.737). They take a little over an hour and return to Mérida every thirty minutes, with the last one leaving at 7.30pm. It's therefore possible to visit Izamal in a comfortable afternoon trip from Mérida. Four buses a day go east to Valladolid and Cancún, and three run to Tizimín.

The Maya city of **Aké** (9am–5pm, closed Mon; US$3.20), which lies halfway between Izamal and Mérida on the highway, was probably in alliance with Izamal and is linked to it by one of the peninsula's largest *sacbes* (Maya roads).

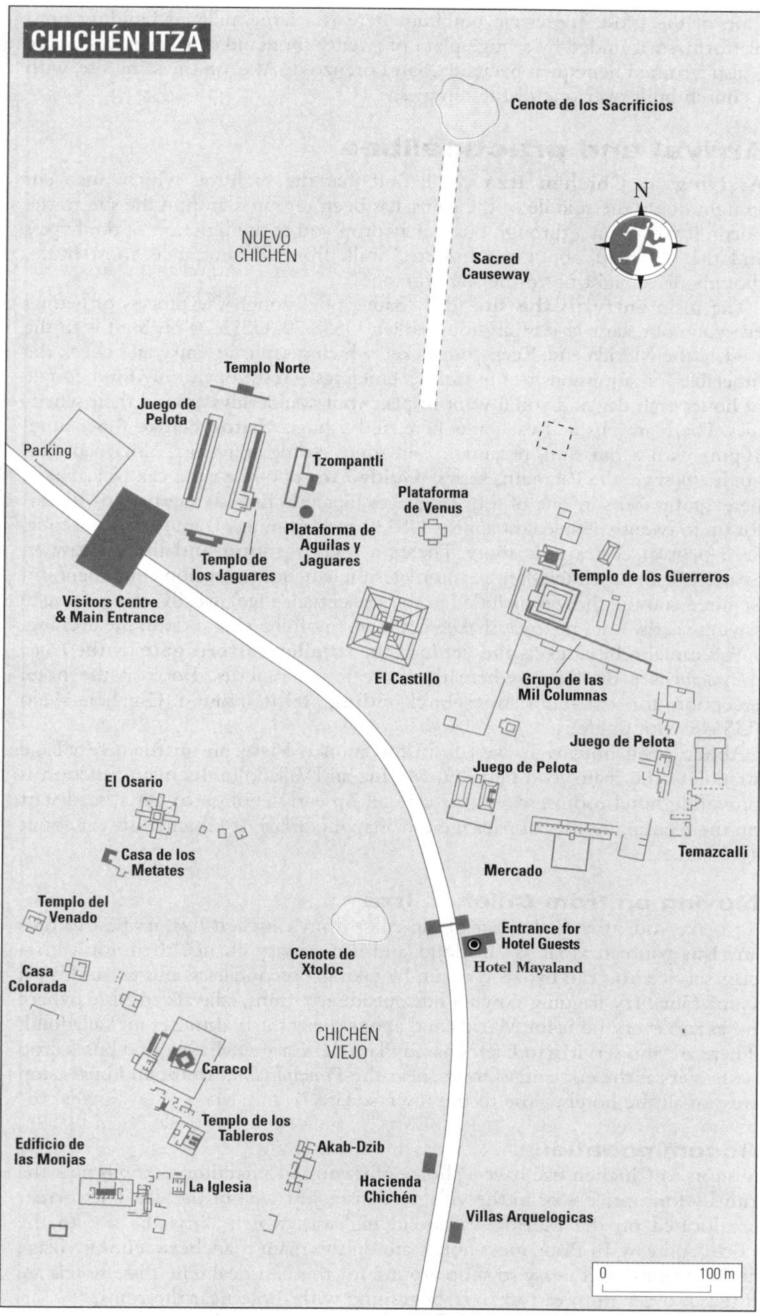
CHICHÉN ITZÁ
Cenote de los Sacrificios
N
NUEVO CHICHÉN
Sacred Causeway
Templo Norte
Juego de Pelota
Parking
Mérida
Tzompantli
Plataforma de Venus
Plataforma de Aguilas y Jaguares
Templo de los Jaguares
Visitors Centre & Main Entrance
Templo de los Guerreros
El Castillo
Grupo de las Mil Columnas
Juego de Pelota
Juego de Pelota
El Osario
Casa de los Metates
Temazcalli
Mercado
Templo del Venado
Entrance for Hotel Guests
Hotel Mayaland
Cenote de Xtoloc
Casa Colorada
CHICHÉN VIEJO
Caracol
Templo de los Tableros
Edificio de las Monjas
Akab-Dzib
La Iglesia
Hacienda Chichén
Villas Arquelogicas
0
100 m
Pisté, Valladolid & Highway to Cancún & Mérida

One of the most impressive buildings here is a large, pillared building on a platform, surrounded by a huge plaza of twenty thousand square metres. There is also a ruined henequen hacienda, San Lorenzo de Aké, on the same site, with a church built over one of the temples.

Arrival and practicalities

Arriving at Chichén Itzá you'll find that the highway, which once cut straight down the middle of the ruins, has been rerouted around the site to the north. If you're on a through bus it may drop you at the junction of the bypass and the old road, about ten minutes' walk from the entrance; most buses, though, drive right up to the site entrance.

The main **entry to the site** (daily 8am–5pm, though the process of getting everyone out starts at least an hour earlier; US$8.70, US$3.70 on Sun) is to the west, at the Mérida end. Keep your ticket, which permits re-entry, and check the timetable for admissions to the various buildings – most open only for a couple of hours each day, and you'll want to plan your wanderings around their schedules. There are bus and car parks here, and a huge **visitor centre** (open until 10pm) with a museum, restaurant, and shops selling souvenirs, film, maps and guides (best are the Panorama series). **Guided tours** of the ruins can be arranged here: group tours in one of four languages (Spanish, English, German or Italian) for up to twenty people cost approx US$30 and last ninety minutes; private tours (1–2 people) cost a little more. There's a nightly **sound-and-light show** in Spanish (7pm in winter; 8pm in summer; simultaneous translation equipment can be hired and the show is included in the site entrance fee), worth seeing if you're staying nearby – it's no great shakes, but there's nothing else to do in the evening.

You can also buy tickets and get in at the **smaller eastern gate** by the *Hotel Mayaland* (see opposite), where there are fewer facilities. Book at the hotel reception for two-hour **horseback-riding trips** around Chichén Viejo (US$48 with guide).

About a half-hour walk west from the ruins is **Pisté**, an unattractive village straddling the main road between Mérida and Valladolid. Its main function is providing hotel rooms, so visitors can get up early enough to get a head start on the teeming hordes of package tourists who arrive at Chichén Itzá at about 10.30am.

Moving on from Chichén Itzá

To make your way to the Caribbean coast from Chichén Itzá, it's best to take any **bus** you can as far as Valladolid, and if necessary change there for a first-class service. You can bypass Cancún by taking a second-class bus to Tulum via Cobá (3hr). Try flagging down a bus outside the ruins, or walk to Pisté, where buses run every hour for Mérida and about every thirty minutes for Valladolid. There are also services to Cancún and Playa del Carmen. Eastbound buses drop passengers at the east end of town, near the *Pirámide Inn*; westbound buses stop west of all the hotels, close to the town square.

Accommodation

Visitors to Chichén Itzá have a choice of staying in a handful of hotels near the ruins – for a price – or in the village of Pisté, just west of the site. The former are located on the Mérida–Valladolid highway, which skirts the site to the north and east. In Pisté, most hotels are on the main road, between the village and the ruins, so it's easy to shop around for the best deal. The Pisté hotels are listed in order from east to west, beginning with those near the ruins.

Near the ruins

Dolores Alba Hwy-180 *libre* Km 122 ⓣreservations in Mérida on 999/928-5650, ⓕ928-3163, ⓦwww.doloresalba.com. About 2km east of the ruins, and very good value, with clean, colourful rooms, a good restaurant and two swimming pools, one of which is made from a natural spring. The staff are very helpful and provide transport to the site (but not back). ❺

Parque Ikkil across from *Dolores Alba* ⓣ985/858-1525. Six swanky bungalows for rent on the grounds of this park with a cenote. Very private, but doesn't have all the amenities the larger resorts do. ❾

Villas Arqueológicas Hwy-180 *libre* Km 120 ⓣ985/851-0034, ⓕ851-0018, ⓦwww.clubmed.com. Not as aesthetically pleasing as its neighbours, but good value, with rooms set out round a patio enclosing a pool and cocktail bar; by night, its library of archeological tomes doubles as a disco (usually empty). ❼

Hacienda Chichén off Hwy-180, near the east entrance to the ruins ⓣ985/924-2150, ⓕ924-5011, ⓦwww.yucatanadventure.com.mx. Gracious old-colonial feel, with wrought-iron furniture and plenty of greenery, as well as a couple of small ruins within its grounds. Rooms, in individual cottages, are nice enough, but you're paying largely for location. ❾

Mayaland off Hwy-180, near the east entrance to the ruins ⓣ985/851-0100, ⓕ851-0129, ⓦwww.mayaland.com. High-end resort with a gorgeous hacienda-style dining room and luxurious thatched-hut suites dotted about the gardens. ❾

In Pisté

Pirámide Inn C 15-A no. 30, at C 20 ⓣ985/851-0115, ⓕ851-0114, ⓦwww.chichen.com. Conveniently situated near the eastbound bus stop and the western entrance to the ruins, with a pool, *temazcal*, extensive gardens and a somewhat New Age clientele. ❻

Stardust Inn 200m west of the *Pirámide Inn* ⓣ985/851-0275. A slightly faded air, but clean enough, with an enormous swimming pool. *Posada Novelo*, next door (❹), is under the same ownership, and guests there may also use the pool. ❻

Posada Chac-Mool 200m west of the *Stardust Inn* ⓣ985/851-0270. No frills, just nine small, sparkling-clean rooms, with choice of fan or a/c. ❹–❺

Chichén Itzá 100m west of *Chac-Mool*, across the street ⓣ985/851-0022, ⓕ851-0023, ⓦwww.mayaland.com. Recently renovated, with quite smart, comfortable rooms and a pretty pool, but not much atmosphere. ❻

Posada Olalde On C 6, south of the main road ⓣ985/851-0078. Basic, clean rooms with fans and hot water as well as a few rustic cabañas, all clustered around a garden; coming from the eastern bus stop, turn left by El Guayacan Artesanía. ❹

Posada Maya Oasis On C 6, north of the main road (no phone). Just three rooms with fans in this new guesthouse, but they're clean, quiet and off the main drag; turn right across from El Guayacan. ❹

Posada Carrousel Just east of the westbound bus stop ⓣ985/851-0078. A large courtyard for lounging and cheap beers draw budget travellers; the best rooms are in the back, away from the road; there's also space to hang your hammock. ❶–❹

Eating

For refreshment near the ruins, or if you're staying overnight, the **restaurant** at the *Hotel Dolores Alba* is good and affordable, and guests can use the pool. Across the road is the somewhat ritzy *Parque Ikkil* (8am–6pm; US$4), which has a buffet restaurant amid landscaped gardens. You can also take a dip in the large underground Sagrado Azul **cenote**; changing facilities are provided. In Pisté, the best dining options are *El Carrousel* and *Las Mestizas*, which does some good-value regional cuisine. The pricier hotels all have their own restaurants.

The site

Though in most minds **CHICHÉN ITZÁ** represents the very image of the Maya, in fact it is the site's very divergence from Maya tradition that makes it so fascinating, and so important to archeologists. Its history remains hotly disputed. Archeologists are fairly certain that the city rose to power in the Terminal Classic period (between 800 AD and 1000 AD), and was probably established about five hundred years before that, but what they are undecided about is exactly who built the city. Much of the evidence at the site – an emphasis on human sacrifice, the presence of a huge ball-court and the glorification of military activity – points to a strong influence from central Mexico;

considering the dates of Chichén's ascendancy, it seemed that this was the result of the city's defeat by the Toltecs, a theory reinforced by the resemblance of the Temple of the Warriors to the L-shaped colonnade at Tula, along with numerous depictions of the Toltec god-king, the feathered serpent **Quetzalcoatl** (Kukulcán to the Maya).

However, recent work at Chichén Itzá has revealed some continuity between Chichén Itzá and earlier Maya sites in the southern lowlands. It's now thought that Chichén Itzá was never invaded by the Toltecs, but occupied by Maya throughout its history, and only received Toltec and other central Mexican artefacts via its chief trading partner, the Chontal Maya or Putun of the Gulf coast lowlands. The Chontal were themselves influenced by central Mexico and Oaxaca through a thriving network of trade and political allegiances. This new theory is not without its own problems, though: while the **Itzá** kings who ruled Chichén Itzá were referred to by the contemporary Maya as "foreigners", the continuity of styles with the Maya sites of the southern lowlands suggests that the "foreigners" may actually have been Maya who moved north after droughts caused the abandonment of the forest cities.

Chichén Nuevo

The old highway that used to pass through the site is now a path dividing the ruins in two: **Chichén Nuevo** (New or "Toltec" Chichén) to the north and **Chichén Viejo** (Old Chichén) to the south. If it's still reasonably early, head first to the north and **El Castillo** (or the Pyramid of Kukulcán), the structure that dominates the site. This should allow you to climb it before the full heat of the day, and get a good overview of the entire area. It is a simple, relatively unadorned square building, with a monumental stairway ascending each face (though only two are restored), rising in nine receding terraces to a temple at the top. The simplicity is deceptive, however, as the building is in fact the **Maya calendar** rendered in stone: each staircase has 91 steps, which, added to the single step at the main entrance to the temple, amounts to 365; other numbers relevant to the Maya calendar recur throughout the construction. Most remarkably, at sunset on the spring and autumn equinoxes, the great serpents' heads at the foot of the main staircase are joined to their tails (at the top of the building) by an undulating body of shadow – an event that lasts just a few hours and draws spectators, and awed worshippers, by the thousands.

Inside the present structure, an earlier pyramid survives almost wholly intact. An entrance has been opened at the bottom of El Castillo, through which you reach a narrow, dank and claustrophobic stairway (formerly the outside of the inner pyramid) that leads steeply to a temple on the top. In the temple's outer room is a rather crude Chac-mool, but in the **inner sanctuary**, now railed off, stands one of the greatest finds at the site: an altar, or throne, in the form of a jaguar, painted bright red and inset with jade "spots" and eyes. This discovery was one of the first to undermine the Toltec theory: though the sculpture is apparently Toltec in style, it was found sealed in the inner temple, which predates the tribe's ostensible arrival.

The "Toltec" plaza

The Castillo stands on the edge of the great grassy plaza that formed the focus of Chichén Nuevo; all its most important buildings are here, and from the northern edge a *sacbe*, or sacred causeway, leads to the great **Cenote de los Sacrificios**. The **Templo de los Guerreros** (Temple of the Warriors), and the adjoining **Grupo de las Mil Columnas** (Group of the Thousand Columns), take up the eastern edge of the plaza. These are the structures that most recall the great Toltec site of Tula, near Mexico City, both in design and in detail – in particular the colonnaded courtyard (which would have been roofed with some form of thatch) and the use of Atlantean columns, representing warriors in armour, their arms raised above their heads. Throughout, the temple is richly decorated with carvings and sculptures (originally with paintings, too) of jaguars and eagles devouring human hearts, feathered serpents, warriors and, the one undeniably Maya feature, masks of Chac. On top are two superb **Chac-mools**: offerings were placed on the stomachs of these reclining figures, representing the messengers who would take the sacrifice to the gods, or perhaps the divinities themselves.

Once again, the Templo de los Guerreros was built over an earlier temple, in which some remnants of faded **murals** can be made out (the interior of the temple is very often closed to the public, however). The "thousand" columns alongside originally formed a square, on the far side of which is the building known as the **Mercado**, although there's no evidence that this actually was a marketplace. Near here, too, is a small, dilapidated ball-court.

Walking across the plaza towards the main ball-court, you pass three small platforms. The **Plataforma de Venus** is a simple, raised, square block, with a stairway up each side guarded by feathered serpents. Here, rites associated with Quetzalcoatl in his role of Venus, the morning star, would have been carried out. Slightly smaller, but otherwise virtually identical in design, is the **Águilas y Jaguares** platform, on which you'll see relief carvings of eagles and jaguars holding human hearts. Human sacrifices may even have been carried out here, judging by the proximity of the third platform, the **Tzompantli**, where victims' skulls were hung on display. This is carved on every side with grotesquely grinning stone skulls.

The ball-court

Chichén Itzá's **Juego de Pelota** (ball-court), on the western side of the plaza, is the largest known in existence – some 90m long. Its design is classically Maya: a capital "I" shape surrounded by temples, with the goals, or target rings, halfway along each side. Along the bottom of each side wall runs a sloping panel decorated in low relief with scenes of the game and its players. Although the rules and full significance of the game remain a mystery, it was clearly not a Saturday afternoon kick-about in the park. The players are shown processing towards a circular central symbol, the symbol of death, and one player, just right of the centre (whether it's the winning captain or the losing one is up for debate) has been decapitated, while another (to the left) holds his head and a ritual knife. Along the top runs the stone body of a snake, whose heads stick out at either end of this "bench".

At each end of the court stand small buildings with open **galleries** overlooking the field of play – the low one at the south may simply have been a grandstand, that at the north (the **Templo Norte**, also known as the Temple of the Bearded Man, after a sculpture inside) was almost certainly a temple and perhaps, too, the referee's stand. Inside are several worn relief carvings and a whispering gallery effect that enables you to be heard clearly at the far end of the court, and to hear what's going on there.

The **Templo de los Jaguares** also overlooks the playing area, but from the side; to get to it, you have to go back out to the plaza. At the bottom – effectively the outer wall of the ball-court – is a little portico supported by two pillars, between which a stone jaguar stands sentinel. Inside are some wonderful, rather worn relief carvings of Maya priests and warriors, and animals, birds and plants. Beside this, a very steep, narrow staircase ascends to a platform overlooking the court and to the **Upper Temple** (restricted opening hours), with its fragments of a mural depicting battle scenes.

The **Cenote de los Sacrificios** lies at the end of the causeway that leads off through the trees from the northern side of the plaza – about 300m away. It's a remarkable phenomenon, an almost perfectly round hole in the limestone surface of the earth, some 60m in diameter and more than 40m deep, the bottom half full of water. It was thanks to the presence of this natural well (and perhaps another in the southern half of the site) that the city could survive at all, and it gives Chichén Itzá its present name, "At the Edge of the Well of the Itzá". This well was regarded as a portal to the "other world", called Xibalba, and Maya would throw offerings into it – incense, statues, jade and especially metal disks (a few of them gold) engraved and embossed with figures and glyphs – as well as human sacrificial victims. People who were thrown in and survived emerged with the power of prophecy, having spoken with the gods. A cafeteria now overlooks the well and is a distraction for anyone contemplating the religious and mystical significance of the cenote.

Chichén Viejo

The southern half of the site is the most sacred part for contemporary Maya, though the buildings here are not, on the whole, in such good condition: less restoration work has been carried out so far, and the ground is not so extensively cleared. A path leads from the road opposite El Castillo to all of the major structures, passing first the pyramid known as **El Osario** (the Ossuary, also known as the High Priest's Grave). Externally it is very similar to El Castillo, but inside, most unusually, a series of **tombs** was discovered. A shaft, explored at the end of the nineteenth century, drops down from the top through five crypts, in each of which was found a skeleton and a trap door leading to the next. The fifth is at ground level, but here too was a trap door, and steps cut through the rock to a sixth chamber that opens onto a huge underground cavern: the burial place of the high priest. Sadly the shaft and cavern are not open to the public.

Near here, also very ramshackle, are the **Templo del Venado** (Temple of the Deer) and the **Casa Colorada** (Red House), with a cluster of ruins known as the Southwest Group beyond them. Follow the path round, however, and you arrive at **El Caracol** (the Snail, for its shape; also called the Observatory), a circular, domed tower standing on two rectangular platforms and looking remarkably like a modern-day observatory in outline. No telescope, however, was mounted in the roof, which instead has slits aligned with various points of astronomical observation. Four doors at the cardinal points lead into the tower and a circular chamber. A spiral staircase leads to the upper level, where sightings were made.

The so-called **Edificio de las Monjas** (the Nunnery) is a palace complex showing several stages of construction. Part of the facade was blasted away by a nineteenth-century explorer, but it is nonetheless a building of grand proportions. Its **annexe** has an elaborate facade in the Chenes style, covered in masks of Chac which combine to make one giant mask, with the door as a mouth. **La Iglesia** (the Church), a small building standing beside the convent, is by contrast a clear demonstration of Puuc design, with a low band of unadorned masonry around the bottom surmounted by an elaborate mosaic frieze and a roof-comb. Hook-nosed masks of Chac again predominate, but above the doorway are also the figures of the four **bacabs**, the mythological creatures that held up the sky – a snail and a turtle on one side, an armadillo and a crab on the other.

Beyond Las Monjas, a path leads in about fifteen minutes to a further group of ruins – among the oldest on the site, but unrestored. Nearer at hand is the **Akab-Dzib**, a relatively plain block of palace rooms which takes its name ("Obscure Writings") from some undeciphered hieroglyphs found inside. Red palm prints adorn the walls of some of the chambers – a sign frequently found in Maya buildings, the significance of which is not yet understood. From here you can head back to the road past El Caracol and the Cenote de Xtoloc.

Valladolid and around

The second town of Yucatán state, **VALLADOLID** is around 40km east of Chichén Itzá, still close enough to beat the crowds to the site on an early bus, and of interest in its own right. Although it took a severe bashing in the nineteenth-century Caste Wars, the town has retained a strong colonial feel and centres on a pretty, peaceful zócalo. The most famous of the surviving churches is sixteenth-century **San Bernardino**, 1km southwest of the zócalo (daily except Tues 9am–8pm; mass daily at 6pm); take scenic, pedestrianized Calle 41-A from two blocks west of the plaza. Built over the **Cenote Sis-Ha**, the buildings are very impressive, but there's little left inside as, like many of the Yucatán's churches, San Bernardino was sacked by the local Indians in the Caste Wars. Valladolid's other cenote, **Zací**, on Calle 36 between calles 39 and 37 (daily 8am–6pm; US$2), has become a tourist attraction, with a museum and an open-air restaurant at the entrance.

Arrival and information

First-class buses between Mérida and Cancún don't go into Valladolid, but stop at **La Isleta**, a small bus station on the highway, where you transfer to a local bus for the ten-minute drive into town. Valladolid's **bus station** is located on Calle 39 between calles 44 and 46, just a block and a half west of the zócalo. Buses run from here almost hourly to Mérida and four times daily to Cancún, and there are eight daily departures for Playa del Carmen, most of which are via Cancún, and four to Cobá and Tulum. All local second-class buses begin their journey here too, for the above destinations, Chichén Itzá and Tizimín. Most **colectivos** depart from Calle 44. You can catch one to Chichén Itzá for US$1.50, or a taxi for US$15.

The zócalo is bounded by calles 39, 40, 41 and 42. The **tourist office**, on the southeastern corner (Mon–Sat 9am–8.30pm, Sun 9am–1pm; Ⓦwww.chichen.com.mx/valladolid), in theory has plenty of information, including free maps of Valladolid and details of in-house **tour operator** Viajes Valladolid (Ⓣ985/856-1857, Ⓦwww.viajesvalladolid.com), though it's a pretty casual set-up and the office is often left unattended. However, most hotels and souvenir shops on the zócalo have maps. The **post office** is also on the zócalo, on Calle 40 near the corner of Calle 39 (Mon–Fri 9am–3pm), as is **Bancomer**, which changes travellers' cheques and has an ATM. In Supermaz, a shopping plaza at Calle 39 between calles 48 and 50, you'll find a supermarket and **laundry**. For national and international **telephone calls** Ladatel *casetas* are at the bus station and on the zócalo (daily 7am–10pm); the latter is also an **Internet** café. You can **rent bikes** from the Rey de Béisbol sports shop, Calle 44 no. 195, between calles 39 and 41, owned by Antonio "Negro" Aguilar, a one-time professional baseball star who is also a great source of local information.

Accommodation

Valladolid's budget hotels are serviceable, but for more atmosphere it's worth spending a bit more cash to stay in colonial style on the zócalo. There's an excellent **hostel** in Valladolid, *La Candelaria*, on the edge of Parque La Candelaria, on Calle 35 between calles 44 and 42 (Ⓣ985/856-2267, Ⓔcandelaria_hostel@hotmail.com; ❷), with a garden, Internet access, bike rental and a few private rooms. The owner of the Rey de Béisbol sports shop (see above) also rents out very inexpensive rooms.

Hotel Lily C 44 no. 192, between C 37 and C 39 Ⓣ985/856-2163. Small homely hotel with 21 basic rooms (upstairs has a little more light) at reasonable rates. ❹

María de la Luz C 42, on the zócalo Ⓣ985/856-2071, Ⓕ856-1181, Ⓦwww.mariadelaluzhotel.com. The best value on the plaza; clean, comfortable rooms with (somewhat noisy) a/c, arranged around a small pool. ❺

María Guadalupe C 44 no. 198, between C 39 and C 41 Ⓣ985/856-2068. The best of the cheapies, with clean, well-kept rooms with baths. Colectivos for the cenote at Dzitnup leave from outside. ❸

El Mesón del Marqués C 39 no. 203, on the zócalo Ⓣ985/856-2073, Ⓕ856-2280, Ⓦwww.mesondelmarques.com. Lovely hotel in a former colonial mansion, overlooking a courtyard with fountains and lush plants. There's a wonderful palm-fringed pool, and one of the best restaurants in town (full breakfast is included in the price). ❻

San Clemente C 42 no. 206, at C 41 Ⓣ/Ⓕ985/856-3161, Ⓦwww.hotelsanclemente.com.mx. Just off the zócalo. Prices and facilities are similar to the *María de la Luz* but the rooms are a bit dingy. ❹

Zací C 44 no. 193, between C 39 and C 37 Ⓣ985/856-2167. Pleasant hotel with a quiet, plant-filled courtyard and a small pool. Rooms have either a fan or, for a few dollars more, a/c and cable TV. ❺

Eating and drinking

Whatever your budget, to eat well in Valladolid you don't have to stray further than the zócalo, where you can get inexpensive snacks or treat yourself without going into debt.

El Bazar northeastern corner of the zócalo, C 39 at C 40. A dizzying selection of inexpensive *loncherías* and pizzerias, always busy and open late – about the only place to eat after 9pm.

Café de Carmelita C 42 no. 183, between C 35 and C 37. An inexpensive spot serving granola breakfasts and salads as well as more typical local fare; classic Mexican ballads on the stereo set a cosy, nostalgic tone. Closes at 9pm.

María de la Luz C 42, on the zócalo. Large, popular restaurant that opens onto the square and has a basic Mexican and Yucatecan menu, including Valladolid specialities like *longaniza*. Good-value (US$4.50) breakfast buffet daily.

El Mesón del Marqués C 39 no. 203, on the zócalo. Probably Valladolid's best restaurant, offering tranquillity and tables around the fountain of the hotel courtyard, though it's often packed with tour groups. Yucatecan specialities such as *sopa de lima* and *poc-chuc*.

Restaurante San Bernardino de Siena C 49 no. 227, two blocks behind Convento San Bernardino. Locally known as *Don Juanito's* and frequented mostly by Mexicans, this highly recommended, mid-price restaurant is a great place for a lazy lunch or dinner away from the hustle and bustle of the town centre.

Around Valladolid

From Valladolid the vast majority of traffic heads straight on to Cancún and the Caribbean beaches. A few places merit taking time out to explore, however. If you have the time, an alternative is to head north via Tizimín to see the flamingo colony at **Río Lagartos** or go to the beach at **San Felipe**. You'll need to make an early start if you want to co-ordinate your buses, go on a flamingo trip and get back to Valladolid in the same day – the last bus from Río

Lagartos for Tizimín leaves at 5pm, and the last bus for Valladolid leaves Tizimín at 6pm. You'll have to return to Valladolid to head on to the Caribbean coast.

Cenotes Dzitnup and Samula

Seven kilometres west of Valladolid, the remarkable **Cenote Dzitnup**, also called X'Keken (daily 7am–6pm; US$2), is reached by descending into a cave, where a nearly circular pool of crystal-clear turquoise water is illuminated by a shaft of light from an opening in the roof. A swim in the ice-cold water is a fantastic experience, but take a sweater as the temperature in the cave is noticeably cooler than outside. Equally if not more impressive is the **Cenote Samula** (daily 8am–5pm; US$2), almost directly across the road. While Dzitnup is frequently crowded and plagued by small boys asking for tips, you may well find yourself alone at Samula, which has the roots of a huge *alamo* tree stretching down into the pool.

Colectivos run direct to Dzitnup from outside the *Hotel María Guadalupe* in Valladolid (see previous page). Alternatively, any westbound second-class **bus** will drop you at the turn-off, 5km from Valladolid; then it's a walk of 2km down a signed track. You could also take a taxi or, best of all, **cycle** from Valladolid on the dedicated paved bike path.

Grutas de Balankanché

Thirty-four kilometres west of Valladolid, very close to Chichén Itzá and the *Dolores Alba* hotel (see p.753), you can visit the **Grutas de Balankanché**, where in 1959 a sealed passageway was discovered leading to a series of caverns in which the ancient population had left offerings to Chac. "Guided tours" (in English daily 11am, 1pm & 3pm; US$4.80) – in reality, a taped commentary – lead you past the stalactites and stalagmites, an underground pool and, most interestingly, many of the original Maya offerings. Be warned that in places the caves can be cold, damp and thoroughly claustrophobic. Charles Gallenkamp's book *Maya* has an excellent chapter devoted to the discovery of the caves, and to the ritual of exorcism that a local traditional priest insisted on carrying out to placate the ancient gods and disturbed spirits. Buses between Valladolid and Mérida will drop you at *las grutas*, or you can catch a **colectivo** from Calle 44 in Valladolid – or just take a taxi.

Ek-Balam

Little visited, but well excavated, **EK-BALAM** (daily 8am–5pm; US$3.20) is notable for the high quality and unique details of its sculpture. The compact site, enclosed by a series of defensive walls, is really only the ceremonial centre; the entire city, which evidence shows was occupied from the pre-Classic period to the Spanish Conquest, spreads out over a very wide area, punctuated by *sacbes* leading out in all directions. The entrance to the site is along one of these ancient roads, leading through a freestanding four-sided arch. Beyond are a long ball-court and two identical temples, called **Las Gemelas** (the Twins). The principal building is the massive structure called **La Torre**, the stones along its 200-metre-long base adorned with bas-relief carvings. Thatched awnings protect recently restored stucco: on the first level, two doorways, one to either side of the staircase, are marked by near-matching designs of twisted serpents and tongues. In the right-hand carving, the tongue is emblazoned with a glyph thought to represent the city of Ek-Balam. Just below the summit is the primary attraction, the fabulously intricate **Chenes-style doorway** that is believed to be the entrance to the tomb of Ukit-Kan-Lek-Tok, a powerful ruler of the Terminal Classic period around 800 AD. The giant gaping mouth is studded with protruding teeth – the lower jaw actually forms the floor of the doorway – and surrounded by stylized snakes and detailed human figures. Back on the ground, look for a remarkably clear stele in the plaza, believed to depict the same king.

No buses go directly to the site, but **colectivos** from Valladolid will stop here. Catch one on Calle 44 just west of the plaza.

Río Lagartos and Las Coloradas

Travelling by bus from Valladolid north to Río Lagartos, you have to change at the elegant colonial town of **TIZIMÍN**, 51km from Valladolid. The best of the modest **hotels** in the centre is *Hotel San Carlos*, on Calle 54 between calles 51 and 53 (Ⓣ986/863-2384; ❹). An easy walk from the two bus stations (around the corner from each other on Calle 47 and Calle 46), on the main square, is a great **restaurant**, *Los Tres Reyes*; it's a little pricier than you might expect, but free appetizers are served, and service is very good. Tizimín also has direct **bus** services to and from Mérida and Cancún.

The village of **RÍO LAGARTOS**, 100km north of Valladolid, juts into a lagoon in marshy coastal flatland, inhabited by vast colonies of **pink flamingoes**. Despite talk of turning the area into a new tourist centre, it still remains a backwater fishing village. It's manageable to visit on a day-trip from Valladolid, but if you want to **stay the night**, try the large rooms at *Posada Leyli* (Ⓣ986/862-0106; ❸), on Calle 14 at the north end of town. The smartest option is *Hotel Villa de Pescadores*, on the malecón (Ⓣ986/862-0020; ❺) on the northern tip; all rooms have balconies overlooking the water. A boat trip over to the seaward shore of the spit that encloses the lagoon will bring you to a couple of **beaches**, but they're not up to much, and in the end it's the flamingoes alone that make a visit worthwhile.

You're likely to be swamped by offers to take you out to see the flamingoes as soon as you get off the bus or out of your car. If not, the best place to start is the friendly *Restaurante Isla Contoy*, on the waterfront on the west side, where you can leaf through a book of photos and visitors' comments while waiting for your boat to turn up. A **boat** to visit the many feeding sites costs around US$35, with a maximum of seven people, but the price and length of the trip are infinitely negotiable. Make sure that your guide understands that you don't want to harass the flamingoes, as some will get too close if they think their passengers would prefer to see some action. Recommended is the amiable Marcel Flores (known as "Leches"), who will take you further out than other **guides**, perhaps as far as Las Coloradas (see below). Ask for him at *Los Negritos* restaurant, on the main street as you drive into town. As well as flamingoes, you're likely to see fishing eagles, spoonbills and, if you're lucky, one of the very few remaining crocodiles after which Río Lagartos was named.

The most spectacular flamingo colony is at **Las Coloradas**, on the narrow spit that separates the lagoon from the sea about 16km east of Río Lagartos. There's a small village and salt factory here, but you'll need your own transport, as the bus timetable does not give you a chance to stay long enough to see anything.

San Felipe

If it's beaches you're after, **SAN FELIPE**, 12km west of Río Lagartos, is a much better bet – many of the buses from Valladolid to Río Lagartos come out here as well. There's one good **hotel** in town, *Hotel San Felipe de Jesús,* Calle 9 between calles 14 and 16 (Ⓣ986/862-2027, Ⓕ862-2036, Ⓔsanfelip@prodigy.net.mx; ❺), which also has a decent restaurant and offers fishing trips and free boat service to the beaches on the offshore spit. Otherwise it's about US$5 for a boat, and you can set up **camp** on the beach. At Mexican holiday times – July, August, Easter week – the beaches are crowded; the rest of the year, quite deserted. If you do camp, be sure to bring protection against mosquitoes; if not, it's easy enough to arrange for the boat to collect you in the evening.

Isla Holbox

Although most traffic between Mérida and the coast heads directly east to Cancún, it is possible to turn north at Valladolid (on the bus) or just before the small town of Zaragoza (if you're driving) to reach **Chiquilá**, where you can board the ferry for **Isla Holbox**, a forty-kilometre-long island near the easternmost point of the Gulf coast. Sometimes touted as a new beach paradise to fill the place that Isla Mujeres once had in travellers' affections, it's still relatively unspoilt, with a genuinely warm feel, and will seem a relief to anyone who has come from the touristy resorts. Watch for the fearsome mosquitoes that arrive at the end of the summer and stay into October. From July to mid-September the huge and rare **whale sharks** arrive on the cape. Tours to see and swim with the gentle animals take the better part of a day (US$90 per person including lunch and snorkel gear); ask at your hotel or at *La Cueva del Pirata* (see overleaf). Any of them can probably also arrange tours for fishing or kayaking, and a dive shop at *Posada Mawimbi* does snorkelling excursions.

Arrival

The **bus for Chiquilá** leaves Mérida (6hr) and Valladolid (3hr) in the middle of the night and arrives in time for the 6am ferry. Transferring in Tizimín (3hr) is a little easier, with a choice of three daytime buses. Coming from the east, the easiest route to Chiquilá is the daily direct bus from Cancún (3hr), which leaves at 8am and returns to the city at 1.30pm (though it always waits for the 1pm Holbox ferry to dock before setting off). The **Chiquilá ferry** for Holbox leaves eight times a day, the first run at 6am and the last 7pm (30min; US$3), and returns as many times, from 5am until 6pm. Holbox is also served by a **car ferry**, leaving Chiquilá at 8am and 1.30pm daily and returning from Holbox at 11am and 3pm. It often doesn't run, for various reasons, and there's no sense in taking a car to the tiny island in any case. Secure parking is available near the ferry pier (though be certain you've set the price before you leave). Make sure you don't miss the boat: Chiquilá is not a place you want to get stranded. There's a restaurant, a store and a petrol station, but little else.

On Holbox, straight down Avenida Benito Juárez from the ferry dock is the central plaza, which has an **Internet** café and a **money-exchange**, but note that there is **no ATM** – plan ahead in order to have sufficient cash. There are very few cars in Holbox – the locals use tricycle taxis and electric **golf carts**, which are available to rent (US$12 per hour).

Accommodation

The hotels on the beachfront are all mid-range to luxury; the few decent cheaper options are in town. Out of season, room rates at some upscale hotels can fall by almost half.

Faro Viejo Av Benito Juárez at the beach ⓣ984/875-2217, ⓕ875-2186, ⓦwww.faroviejoholbox.com.mx. Pretty rooms directly on the beach (the only stretch in town that's free of fishing boats), plus a few suites ideal for groups, with kitchenettes and porches; full breakfast included. ❼

Hotel La Palapa Av Morelos 231 ⓣ984/875-2121. Attractive cabañas with bathrooms, some with kitchens. The helpful owners keep the rooms spotless and have a new separate rental house for longer stays. ❹–❺

Posada Los Arcos Av Benito Juárez on the plaza ⓣ984/875-2043. Clean, basic budget rooms around a little courtyard. Choice of a/c or fan, and some rooms have kitchenettes. ❹

Posada Mawimbi on the beach 15min east of town ⓣ/ⓕ984/875-2003, ⓦwww.mawimbi.com.mx. A great little collection of round, two-storey cabañas, beautifully decorated and tucked among dense greenery. ❻

Posada Playa Bonita Av Coldwell at Av Benito Juárez ⓣ984/875-2102. Another budget option, with a choice of rooms or cabañas, one block back from the beach. Has a casual, inexpensive restaurant and laid-back bar as well. ❺

Villas Chimay on the beach 1km west of town ⓣ/ⓕ984/875-2220, ⓦwww.chimay.info. Wonderfully isolated: the only lodging on the western beach, self-sufficient with wind and solar power. Thoughtfully decorated rooms, plus delicious bread with breakfast; guests have use of kitchen for other meals. Rents kayaks and runs jungle tours on the mainland. ❼

Villas Delfines on the beach east of town ⓣ984/874-4014, ⓦwww.holbox.com. Roomy cabañas with a casual atmosphere and an especially wide, white beach. There's a full-board option as well – the very good restaurant hosts a barbecue on Saturdays, with candlelit tables set throughout the orchid garden. ❼

Villas Los Mapaches on the beach two blocks west of Av Benito Juárez ⓣ/ⓕ984/875-2090, ⓦwww.losmapaches.com. One of a number of Italian-owned hotels, renting comfortable bungalows with kitchenettes, ideal for longer stays. ❻

Xaloc on the beach east of town, before *Delfines* ⓣ/ⓕ984/875-2154 or reservations in the US on ⓣ1-800/583-6802, ⓦwww.mexicoholiday.com. An architect owns this compact but well-designed property of eighteen steep-roofed cabañas with rough-hewn wood canopy beds and particularly nice bathrooms; there are two pools, free kayaks and snorkel gear. ❾

Eating and drinking

The island's village has several very good restaurants, and most hotels have their own offerings as well.

Antojitos Dafne Guadalupe in the centre of the plaza. Serves tasty *panuchos* and *salbutes* in the evenings.

Cariocas Beachfront bar that occasionally sees some dancing at weekends.

La Cueva del Pirata on the west side of the plaza. Truly wonderful Italian restaurant, complete with hand-made fresh pasta and a charming older proprietor.

La Isla de Colibri on the corner of the main square. Serves delicious fresh fruit juices and other healthy options; also a bit of a community centre, for meeting people and arranging tours.

Pizzas y Mariscos Edelyn on the east side of the plaza. Tasty, inexpensive pizzeria that hosts pretty much everyone on the island at some point or another.

Villamar on the beach at Av Juárez. Good laid-back, local-owned restaurant with inexpensive seafood and other Mexican dishes.

Zarabanda C Escobedo at Av Palomino, one block south of the plaza. The top choice for seafood.

Quintana Roo and the Caribbean coast

The coastal state of **Quintana Roo** was a forgotten frontier for most of modern Mexican history, its lush tropical forests exploited for their mahogany and *chicle* (from which chewing gum is made), but otherwise unsettled, a haven for outlaws and pirates and for Maya living beyond the reach of central government. In the 1970s, however, the stunning palm-fringed white-sand

beaches of the Caribbean coast and its magnificent offshore **coral reefs** began to attract **tourists**: the first highways were built, new townships settled, and the place finally became a full state (as opposed to an externally administered federal territory) in 1974.

The stretch of **coast** between Cancún and **Tulum** is the most heavily visited – and the focus of much recent, rapid hotel construction. Modern development is centred on the resorts of **Cancún** and **Playa del Carmen**, along with the islands of **Isla Mujeres** and **Cozumel**, which have become some of the world's most desirable package-tour destinations and increasingly overdeveloped as a result. You'll see images of the Maya everywhere here, but while their culture is shamelessly exploited as a tourist commodity, little of this money ever reaches the people themselves. Where locals haven't already been forced out by developers, they often live in poverty in small communal villages, growing maize and carving or weaving a few trinkets for tourists.

Further south things have remained quieter: the beaches within the **Sian Ka'an Biosphere Reserve** are nesting sites for sea turtles, and behind them are areas of mangrove swamp, home to numerous animals including jaguar and even manatee. The vast and beautiful **Laguna de Bacalar** was an important stop on the Maya's pre-Columbian trade routes and was later used as an outpost for arms shipments from Belize during the Caste Wars. **Chetumal**, the state capital and a duty-free border town, is of chief importance as a gateway to and from Belize. The coast south of the biosphere, while rewarding for naturalists and adventurers, is difficult to visit: only a couple of roads offer access, and public transport is minimal.

Inland, Quintana Roo is little visited. There are some spectacular **Maya sites**, though they are not as accessible or as fully restored as the pristine open-air museums of Yucatán state. **Cobá**, a lakeside Maya city just off the road to Valladolid, has some of the Maya world's tallest temples, but is only partially excavated, hidden in jungle swarming with mosquitoes. The early Classic site of **Kohunlich**, famous for its giant sculpted faces of the Maya sun god, lies in the heart of the Petén jungle that stretches into Guatemala and Belize; more remote are the ruins of **Kinichná** and **Dzibanché** and, north of Chetumal, **Chacchoben**.

Reef behaviour

Coral reefs are among the richest and most complex ecosystems on earth, but they are also very fragile. The colonies grow at a rate of only around 5cm per year, so they must be treated with care and respect if they are not to be damaged beyond repair. Remember to follow these **simple rules** while you are snorkelling, diving or in a boat.

Never touch or stand on corals, as the living polyps on their surface are easily damaged.

Avoid disturbing the sand around corals. Quite apart from spoiling visibility, the cloud of sand will settle over the corals and smother them.

Don't remove shells, sponges or other creatures from the reef, and avoid buying reef products from souvenir shops.

Don't use suntan lotion in reef areas, as the oils are pollutants and will stifle coral growth; look for special biodegradable sunscreen for use while snorkelling.

Don't anchor boats on the reef: use the permanently secured buoys instead.

Don't throw litter overboard.

Check ahead of time where you are allowed to go fishing.

If you are an out-of-practice diver, make sure you **review** your diving skills away from the reef first.

Cancún

CANCÚN is, if nothing else, proof of Mexico's remarkable ability to get things done in a hurry – so long as the political will exists. Between 1970 and 1974, a near-deserted stretch of beach was transformed into a viable resort destination, as the Mexican government built city infrastructure from scratch and funded three hotels. International hotel chains flocked to profit, workers and tourists arrived in droves, and now Cancún has a resident population of half a million and hosts almost two million visitors a year. The government chose the location well: the white-sand beaches are impeccable, and the city is marginally closer to Miami than it is to Mexico City. If you come on an all-inclusive package tour the place has a lot to offer – striking modern hotels, a hectic nightlife and high-energy entertainment including parachuting, jet skiing, scuba diving and golf – and from here much of the rest of the Yucatán is easily accessible. For the independent traveller, though, Cancún is expensive, and can be frustrating and unwelcoming. You may well be forced to spend the night here, but without pots of money the typical pleasures of the place will elude you.

The city has two quite separate parts: the *zona comercial* downtown – the shopping and residential centre which, as it gets older, is becoming genuinely earthy – and the *zona hotelera*, the strip of hotels and tourist amenities along "Cancún island", actually a narrow, 25-kilometre-long barrier island connected to the mainland at each end by causeways. It encloses a huge lagoon, so there's water on both sides.

Arrival, information and city transport

Charter flights from Europe and South America, and direct scheduled flights from dozens of cities in Mexico and North and Central America, land at the **airport**, 15km south of the centre. **Colectivos** take you to any part of the hotel zone or to the bus station for a fixed price (US$9 per person to downtown or the hotel zone) – buy your ticket from desks before or after customs. Taxis cost considerably more. There are **ATMs** and luggage lockers past customs in both the international and the domestic terminals. Arriving by bus, you'll pull in at the city's main **bus station**, in the heart of downtown, just by a roundabout at the major junction of avenidas Tulum and Uxmal.

Avenida Tulum, downtown Cancún's main street, is lined with the bulk of the city's shops, banks, restaurants and travel agencies, as well as many of the hotels – up side streets, but in view. The **city tourist office** is half a block south of the bus station, inside the city hall at Av Tulum 26 (daily 9am–8pm; ⓣ998/884-8073), and the friendly bilingual staff will help with even the smallest enquiries. They also dish out free maps and leaflets and copies of the ubiquitous promotional listings **magazines**, the glossiest of which is *Cancún Tips* – all information you can pick up at just about every travel agency and hotel reception. There are several other **tourist information kiosks** on Avenida Tulum and in the *zona hotelera*; some are genuine, but if you're asked if you want "tourist information" as you pass, it's almost certain you're being selected for a time-share sales pitch. Many hotels arrange **trips** to the chief Maya ruins – most commonly Chichén Itzá, Tulum and Cobá.

Most attractions in the downtown area are in walking distance, but you need some sort of transport to get to and around the *zona hotelera*. **Buses** marked "Tulum–Hoteles, Ruta 1" run along Avenida Tulum every few minutes; the flat fare is US$0.60. Alternatively, **taxis** are plentiful and can be hailed almost anywhere – the trip between downtown and the *zona hotelera* costs around

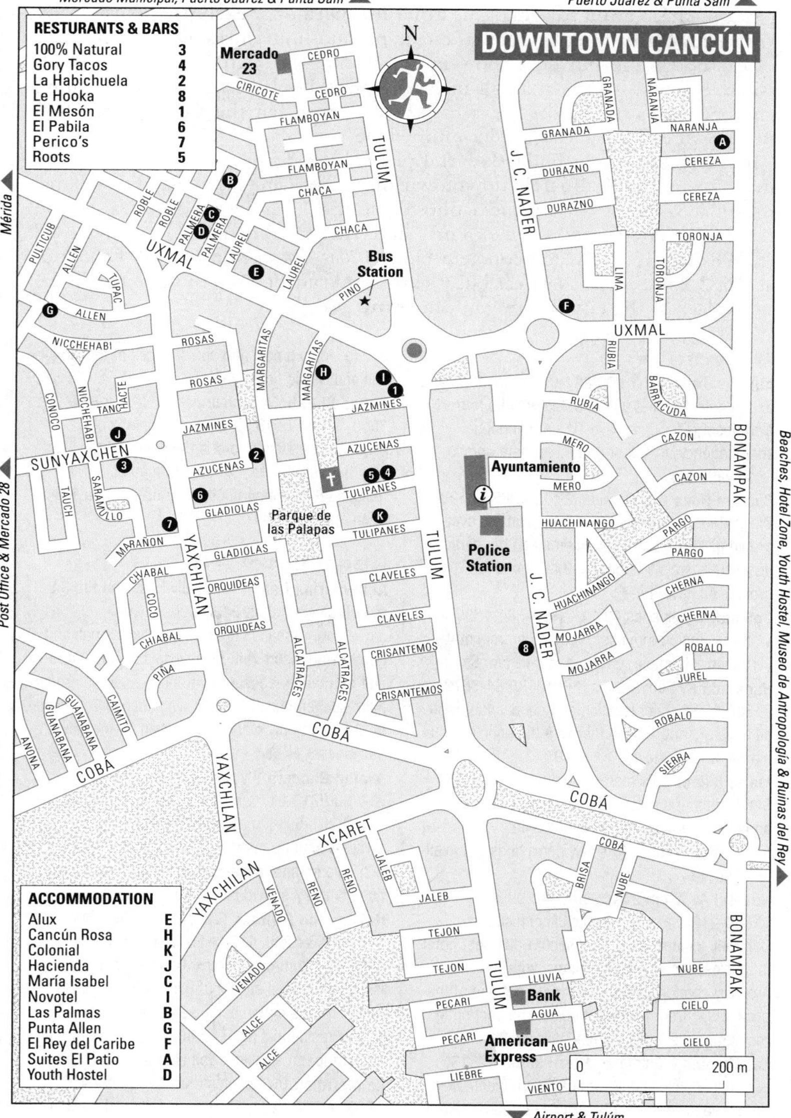

US$8. A car affords you more scope and makes day-trips as far as the ruins at Cobá perfectly feasible.

Accommodation

Cancún has plenty of choice, most of it very expensive for the casual visitor. **Downtown** holds the only hope of a decent budget room, while most of the glittering beachfront palaces of the **zona hotelera** offer exclusive luxury, many with extravagant interiors, glitzy restaurants and immaculate pools. A number of the hotels also put on a show in the evening or open a disco, or both. If you're bent on staying at an all-inclusive resort, book ahead and don't skimp: cheaper places may seem like a bargain on paper, but the facilities are often run-down and the meals border on inedible.

If you're on a tight budget, several places have dorm accommodation. The lively main **youth hostel**, downtown on Calle Palmeras at Avenida Uxmal (ⓣ998/887-0191, ⓦwww.mexicohostels.com; ❷), has several dorms, a rooftop terrace, Internet access, bike rental and laundry. There is another hostel (ⓣ998/883-1337; ❸), the concrete-block *Villas Juveniles* on Bulevar Kukulcán at Km 3.2 in the *zona hotelera*, but it's dirty and run-down – though it's still the only place in the city where you can **camp** (❶).

Downtown

Alux Av Uxmal 21 ⓣ998/884-6613. Comfortable and popular hotel, if a little dated with its mirror-clad decor; all rooms have TV and telephone. Travel agency next door and street café on site. Good value. ❺

Cancún Rosa C Margaritas 2 ⓣ998/884-0623. Old-fashioned, slightly faded hotel with an overgrown garden and a pool. Rooms can be a little dark, but there's a huge one that's good for groups. All have a/c. ❻

Colonial C Tulipanes 22 ⓣ/ⓕ998/884-1535. Well-lit, simple rooms set round a central courtyard with a fountain; choice of a/c or fan. ❺

Hacienda Av Sunyaxchen 39 ⓣ998/884-3672, ⓕ884-1208. Quiet location and good value; rooms all have a/c and TV and there's a big pool, a pretty garden and a café. ❻

María Isabel C Palmeras 59 ⓣ998/884-9015. Small hotel in a quiet side street with cheerful ambience (though rooms can be a little small) and a friendly, helpful staff; a few dorm beds are available too. ❺

Novotel Av Tulum 27 ⓣ998/884-2999, ⓕ884-3162, ⓦwww.novotelcancun.com. Centrally located, clean and secure; the best hotel in its class (book ahead). Rooms, with fan or a/c, are very comfortable, though try to get one at the back, away from the street noise. The cool patio restaurant overlooks a small garden. ❻

Las Palmas C Palmeras 43 ⓣ998/884-2513, ⓔhotelpalmascancun@hotmail.com. Clean, new dorm beds with a/c, or huge private rooms, with a communal kitchen downstairs. ❷–❺

Punta Allen C Punta Allen 8 ⓣ998/884-0225, ⓕ884-1001, ⓦwww.puntaallen.da.ru. Small but spotless rooms in a kitschy old house close to Av Yaxchilán. ❺

El Rey del Caribe Av Uxmal 24, at Av Nader ⓣ998/884-2028, ⓕ884-9857, ⓦwww.reycaribe.com. Sunny yellow rooms with kitchenettes, plus a pool and spa services at this small hacienda-style hotel. ❼

Suites El Patio Av Bonampak 51 ⓣ998/884-3500, ⓕ884-3540, ⓦwww.cancuninn.com. A quiet garden courtyard is the centre of this very hands-off hotel; situated in a quiet residential neighbourhood, it's more like staying in an apartment. ❻

Zona hotelera

Aquamarina Beach Hotel Blv Kukulcán Km 3.5 ⓣ998/849-4606, ⓕ849-4600, ⓦwww.aquamarina-beach.com.mx. Relatively small and good-value resort with pool, volleyball, miniature golf and thrice-weekly theme parties; some rooms have kitchenettes, for those who choose European or breakfast-only plans, rather than all-inclusive packages. ❽–❾

Avalon Baccara Blv Kukulcán Km 11 ⓣ1-800/713-8170 in Mexico, or in the US on 1-800/261-5014, ⓕ954/252-2088, ⓦwww.avalonvacations.com. Elegant, eclectic decor of rich colours and mosaics distinguish this smaller hotel with 27 individually styled rooms. ❾

Holiday Inn Express Paseo Pok-Ta-Pok 21 ⓣ998/883-2200, ⓕ883-2532, ⓦwww.hiexpress.com/cancunmex. Rooms are standard-issue chain hotel style, but this is an affordable *zona hotelera* option because it's located on a largely residential point on the lagoon side of the hotel strip; an excellent golf club is nearby. ❼

Le Meridien Blv Kukulcán Km 14 ⓣ998/881-2200, ⓕ812-2201, ⓦwww.meridiencancun.com.mx. Relatively understated luxury hotel with 213 rooms, three pools of different temperatures and rooftop tennis courts. The hotel's Spa del Mar is the best in Cancún, with hydrotherapy treatments, body wraps and massage from US$60 (open to non-guests). ❾

El Pueblito Blv Kukulcán Km 17.5 ⓣ998/881-8800, ⓕ885-2066, ⓦwww.pueblitohotels.com. A rare spot in Cancún that feels more Mexican than American, with colourful rooms and public spaces. Very friendly service; reasonable rates include all food and drink. ⑨

Suites Girasol Blv Kukulcán Km 9 ⓣ998/883-5045. The entry and public areas of this condo high-rise don't look promising, but the rooms are surprisingly large and clean, and all have kitchenettes. The pool is dismal, but the beach out front is gorgeous. ⑦

Villas Tacul Blv Kukulcán Km 5.5 ⓣ998/849-7060, ⓕ849-7070, ⓦwww.villastacul.com.mx. An older, smaller resort, refreshingly glitz-free: individual villas, each containing two or three private rooms, are scattered over a large area, with gardens, tennis courts and a pool. ⑨

The town and beaches

There's little in the way of sights in **downtown Cancún**. Most visitors head straight for the *zona hotelera* and the **beaches**. Though you're free to go anywhere, and signposted public walkways lead down to the sea at regular intervals, some of the hotels do their best to make you feel like a trespasser, and staff will certainly move you off the beach furniture if you're not a guest. To avoid being eyed suspiciously by hotel heavies, head for one of the dozen or so **public beaches** that are squeezed between the hotels. The beaches on the north coast of the *zona hotelera*, such as Playa Tortugas, are calm and shallow but often crowded, while those at the southeastern tip, such as Playa Ballenas and Playa Delfines, have more surf (and occasional dangerous currents) and are often near-deserted; a couple of beaches facing the bay – Playa Linda and Playa Langosta – are naturally quite calm and are very good for swimming. All are free but you may have to pay a small charge for a shower. Entertainment and expensive water sports are laid on all around the big hotels; if you venture further south, where more sites await construction, you can find surprisingly empty sand and occasional groups of nude sunbathers.

To catch a bit of culture while you're out here, the *Sheraton* boasts a small Maya ruin on its grounds, while the **Museo de Antropología**, behind the convention centre (Mon–Sat 9am–8pm, Sun 10am–7pm; US$2), has a small but absorbing outline of Mesoamerican and Maya culture and history, with information in English and Spanish. Cancún's largest Maya remains, **El Rey** (daily 8am–5pm; US$3.20), are at Km 18, overlooking the Nichupté Lagoon. They're not especially impressive – and if you decide not to take one of the guides at the entrance, there's no information available to explain them – but the area is peaceful and good for spotting birds and iguanas.

The best **snorkelling** in Cancún is at Punta Nizuc, next to Club Med. You aren't allowed to cross the grounds unless you're staying there, so you have to get off the bus at the *Westin Regina Resort*, cross the *Westin*'s grounds to the beach, then turn right and walk for about twenty minutes until you reach the rocky point. Walk over the rocks and snorkel to your heart's content. To join a **snorkelling tour** or go **diving**, contact Aquaworld (ⓣ998/848-8326, ⓦwww.aquaworld.com.mx). A one-tank dive costs about US$60 and a full PADI open-water certification course is around US$385. To view the colourful underwater life in a more leisurely fashion, take a trip on the *Subsee Explorer*, a glass-bottom **boat** that leaves from the Aquaworld centre at Bulevar Kukulcán Km 15.2 every hour from 9am to 3pm (US$35).

Both **jet skiing** (US$50 for 30min) and **parasailing** (US$40 for 10min) are very popular in Cancún and operators are dotted at frequent intervals in front of the big hotels on the beach.

Eating

Cancún's **restaurants** outnumber hotels many times over, and competition is fierce. Downtown, the bulk of the **tourist restaurants** line Avenida Tulum and its side streets: eat here and you can enjoy "fun" disco sounds with your meal. Though seafood and steak are the mainstay of many menus, you can also eat Middle Eastern, Yucatecan, Italian, Chinese, French, Cajun and Polynesian, not to mention international fast food and local chains. All the **hotels** in the *zona hotelera* have at least one formal restaurant, some of which are very elegant indeed, surrounded by tropical foliage with fountains and music. Many also feature a more relaxed beach or poolside dining room.

For **budget food**, follow the locals and make for the markets. The biggest in Cancún is **Mercado 28**, close to the city's main post office at the western end of Avenida Sunyaxchen, where there are plenty of food stalls and tiny cheap restaurants. Because Cancún draws workers from all over the country, the selection reflects a wide variety of regional specialties, and the atmosphere is lively, especially at weekends. The other market in Cancún, **Mercado 23**, is much smaller but makes a relatively peaceful venue for a decent Mexican lunch. From the bus station, walk a few blocks north along Avenida Tulum and then turn left on Calle Flamboyan or Calle Cerdo. For dinner, the **Parque de las Palapas** has a number of food stalls that are open late.

Almost all of the restaurants in the **zona hotelera** are geared towards one thing only: parting tourists from large amounts of cash. The few recommended here are good for a splurge, or are rare bargains. If you are staying on the beach, you're often better off taking a cab or the convenient "Hoteles" bus into downtown Cancún, where you'll find good food at reasonable prices, and more importantly, a congenial mix of people.

Downtown

100% Natural Av Sunyaxchen 26, at Av Yaxchilán. Not entirely vegetarian, but it serves fruit drinks, salads, yogurt and granola, as well as Mexican dishes, seafood and burgers. A nice enough place, if a little overpriced. Branches in Plazas Terramar and Kukulcán in the *zona hotelera*.

Gory Tacos C Tulipanes 26. Don't be put off by the name: this spotless and very friendly place serves good, inexpensive Mexican food, steaks, hamburgers and sandwiches, and a range of vegetarian meals. Closes at 8pm.

La Habichuela C Margaritas 25, in front of the Parque de las Palapas. Long-established and fairly expensive restaurant set in a walled garden. The menu is excellent, featuring such dishes as *cocobichuela*: half a coconut filled with lobster and shrimp in a curry sauce, accompanied by tropical fruits. Live jazz adds to the atmosphere.

El Mesón Av Tulum 75. Pavement café in front of the *Novotel Hotel,* with good breakfasts and special lunchtime offers. Great people-watching spot.

El Pabila Av Yaxchilán 31, in the *Hotel Xbalamque*. Mellow literary coffeeshop (a "*cafébrería*") with very good cappuccino, espresso and the like in a peaceful and sophisticated environment; at night there's low-key live music.

Perico's Av Yaxchilán 71. Strolling magicians, crooning mariachis, stilt-walkers and juggling barmen keep the crowds entertained at this *faux* hacienda serving tasty steaks and enchiladas. The atmosphere is so over-the-top (bordering on surreal) that even staunch tour-group-haters may be swayed.

Zona hotelera

La Casa de las Margaritas in La Isla mall. Upscale Mexican restaurant that has genuinely good food and isn't *quite* as wildly overdecorated as some. Live *mariachis* play at night.

Casa Rolandi in Plaza Caracol, Blv Kukulcán Km 8.5. Northern Italian specialities, many done in a wood-burning oven. Expensive, but good for a romantic dinner out.

Checándole in Plaza Flamingo, Blv Kukulcán Km 11. A satisfying and fresh-tasting inexpensive Mexican fast-food chain.

Dolcemente Pompeii Pez Volador. A rare casual restaurant catering to residents in the hotel zone: laid-back, with plastic chairs on the beach, serving high-quality (though not cheap) Italian food. A little hard to find because it's not affiliated with a mall or hotel: turn north in front of the giant Mexican flag.

Río Nizuc off Blv Kukulcán near Km 22. Hidden among the mangroves on the lagoon side is this cheap seafood specialist, where *ceviches* and *tikin-xic* (fish baked in banana leaves with achiote) are popular.

Entertainment and nightlife

As Cancún's goal is to encourage almost two million visitors each year to have fun, the entertainment scene in the **zona hotelera** is lavish – or remorseless, depending on how you look at it. There's everything from sports and gambling **bars** to romantic piano lounges to fun bars, even just plain drinking bars: enough choice to ensure that you can find a place to have a good time without being ripped off. Most of the **nightclubs**, on the other hand, are pricey, with a "no shorts or sandals" dress code, and the music usually painfully generic. **Downtown**, people often dance at weekends to traditional Mexican music at the Parque de las Palapas, and the stretch of Avenida Yaxchilán north of Avenida Sunyaxchen is quite lively – a few touts still push menus at tourists, but the clientele at the open-terrace restaurant-bars is mostly Mexican, and the entertainment limited to TVs, karaoke and roving *trovadores*. A couple of **cinemas** show new American releases subtitled in Spanish; the largest downtown is the multi-screen Cineapolis in Plaza Las Américas on Avenida Tulum south of Avenida Cobá; in the *zona hotelera*, there's a cinema in Plaza La Isla, Blv Kukulcán Km 8.5.

Bars and nightclubs

La Boom Blv Kukulcán Km 3.5, at the front of the *Aquamarina Beach Hotel*. Along with *Ma'ax'O*, the only place in the city that begins to approach Ibiza-style decadence, with international house hits on the sound system and an open-air chill-out room. No cover charge on Mon; US$25 open bar on Tues.

Coco Bongo in the Forum by the Sea shopping centre, Blv Kukulcán Km 9.5. Vast state-of-the-art rock and pop disco popular with US college kids, but with more diverse music than competitor *Dady O*. Cover charge at weekends only; open until 5am.

Dady O Blv Kukulcán Km 9.5, opposite the convention centre. Nightclub that favours American pop on its high-tech sound system – another spring-break staple. Casual dress but no shorts. The adjacent *Dady Rock* has all-you-can-drink deals for US$25.

Le Hooka downtown on Av Nader, opposite C Mojarra. Hipster Middle Eastern-theme café, open late with international DJ beats.

Ma'ax'O in La Isla mall, Blv Kukulcán Km 8.5. Newest member of the *Dady O* empire, with more European club music than most, and an excellent light show.

Pat O'Brien's in Plaza Flamingo, Blv Kukulcán Km 11. Live rock, blues and jazz in a larger-than-life version of the famous New Orleans establishment. Three rooms: a piano bar, a video lounge and an outdoor patio. Open until 2am.

Roots downtown on C Tulipanes 26, next to *Gory Tacos*. Funky little jazz and blues club which also serves dinner. Recommended.

Señor Frog's Blv Kukulcán Km 5.5. Practically synonymous with the name Cancún, the *Frog* is the first stop off the plane for the spring-break hordes. Go for live reggae or karaoke night, or just an anthropological experience.

Shows and dinner cruises

Ballet Folklórico Nacional de México at the convention centre, Blv Kukulcán Km 8.8 ⓣ998/881-0400. Buffet dinner nightly at 7pm followed by the colourful, verging-on-campy traditional dance of this world-renowned troupe. Tickets cost around US$40 including dinner.

Captain Hook El Embarcadero, Blv Kukulcán Km 4.5 ⓣ998/883-3736. Spanish galleon-style boat with pirate swordfighting and a lobster-and-steak dinner. Departs nightly at 7pm, returning at 10.30pm.

Corrida de Toros Plaza de Toros, Av Bonampak and Av Sayil. Weekly bullfights with a tacked-on folkloric show. Wed at 3.30pm (US$30).

Teatro de Cancún El Embarcadero, Blv Kukulcán Km 4 ⓣ998/849-4848. Hosts touring shows as well as regular local performances; call for schedule.

Listings

Airlines Aeroméxico ⓣ998/884-1097; American ⓣ1-800/904-6000; Aviacsa, Av Cobá 37 ⓣ998/887-4211, at the airport ⓣ998/886-0093; Delta ⓣ1-800/902-2100; Mexicana ⓣ998/881-9090; Northwest/KLM ⓣ1-800/447-4747.

American Express Av Tulum 208, at C Agua (Mon–Fri 9am–5pm; ⓣ998/884-4000).

Banks Most banks (usually Mon–Fri 9am–5pm, Sat 9am–1pm) are along Av Tulum between Av Uxmal and Av Cobá and in the biggest shopping malls – Kukulcán, Plaza Caracol – in the *zona hotelera*. The Bital bank, Av Tulum 192, stays open until 7pm on weekdays.

Car rental Available at most hotels and at the airport, or try Buster Rent a Car, Blv Kukulcán Km 3.5 (ⓣ998/849-7221, ⓕ849-4394, ⓦwww.busterrentacar.com) or Europcar, Av Nader 27 (ⓣ998/884-4714).

Consulates Canada, Plaza Caracol, Blv Kukulcán Km 8.5 (ⓣ998/883-3060); UK, *Hotel Royal Caribbean*, Blv Kukulcán Km 16.5 (ⓣ998/881-0100); US, Plaza Caracol, Blv Kukulcán Km 8.5 (ⓣ998/883-0272).

Internet Immediately across from the bus station and northwest on Av Uxmal are several Internet cafés; some are *casetas* as well.

Laundry Lavandería Las Palapas, on C Gladiolas, at the far side of the park (Mon–Sat 7am–8pm, Sun 8am–2pm), or Lavandería Martinez, across the street from *Las Palmas* hotel; in the *zona hotelera*, ABC Coin Laundry, west of *Aquamarina Beach Hotel* at Blv Kukulcán Km 3.5.

Post office Av Sunyaxchen at Av Xel-Ha (Mon–Fri 8am–6pm, Sat 9am–1pm); has a reliable Lista de Correos (postcode 77501).

Shopping The flea market on Av Tulum has an abundance of different goods – the usual blankets, ceramics and silver – but the sales pitch can be rather heavy. Mercado 23 (turn left off Av Tulum, three blocks north of the bus station) has a small range of arts and crafts from all over the country and is a more relaxed place to pick up reasonably priced souvenirs.

Travel agencies and tours Most hotels in the *zona hotelera* have in-house agencies. Otherwise, the student-friendly Mérida-based agency Nómadas has a branch at Avenida Cobá 5 (ⓣ998/892-2320, ⓦwww.nomadastravel.com) and leads affordable tours with guides to Chichén Itzá and other nearby attractions.

Moving on from Cancún

If you're heading west **by car** to Valladolid, Chichén Itzá and Mérida, you have a choice between the old free road (*libre*) or the new toll highway (*cuota*), running a few kilometres north of the old road for most of its length. From the bus station, drive north on Avenida Tulum about 1km, then turn left to join Avenida López Portillo; after a few kilometres you will have the choice of which road to join. For the toll road, you pay in advance, at the booths on the highway, for the sections you intend to travel along. The trip all the way to Mérida costs US$28.

First- and second-class **buses** go from the same well-organized terminal on the corner of Avenida Tulum and Avenida Uxmal. Destinations include Mérida, on the deluxe UNO service (2 daily; 3hr 30 min), first-class (12 daily; 4hr) and second-class (hourly round-the-clock; 6hr); Campeche, on the deluxe ADO GL service (daily 3pm; 9hr) and first-class (6 daily; 7hr); Chetumal, on deluxe ADO GL (daily at 4.30pm; 5hr) and second-class (hourly 5am–12.45pm; 6hr); Mexico City, on first-class (2 daily at 10am and 1pm; 18hr) and second-class (4 daily; 20hr); Playa del Carmen, on first-class (6 daily; 1hr) and second-class (every 30min; 1hr); Tizimín (6 daily; 4hr); Tulum, on first-class (9 daily; 2hr) and second-class (3 daily; 2hr); Valladolid (hourly; 3hr). International **flights** leave regularly from Cancún; from downtown and the *zona hotelera* a taxi to the airport costs about US$13.

The ferry to Isla Mujeres

The fast passenger **ferry** (15min; US$3.50) for Isla Mujeres officially leaves from Puerto Juárez every thirty minutes (6.30am–11.30pm) and the slow boat (45min; US$1.80) departs five times a day (5am–5pm). Schedules are supposedly set, but both services generally leave early if they're full. To get to the ferry terminal, catch a bus ("R-13" or "R-1 – Pto Juárez"; US$.60) heading north from the stop on Avenida Tulum opposite the bus station (15min), or take a taxi from Avenida Tulum (around US$4).

The car ferry (US$13 per car, plus US$2 for each passenger) leaves from Punta Sam, a few kilometres north of Puerto Juárez. There are five departures daily between 8am and 8.15pm, returning from Isla Mujeres between 6.30am and 7.15pm. However, it isn't really worth taking a car over to the island, which is quite small and has plenty of bicycles and mopeds for rent.

Isla Mujeres

ISLA MUJERES, just a couple of kilometres off the easternmost tip of Mexico in the startlingly clear Caribbean, is an infinitely more appealing prospect than Cancún. Its attractions are simple: first there's the beach, then there's the sea. And when you've tired of those, you can rent a bike, moped or even golf cart to carry you around the island to more sea, more beaches, a coral reef and the tiny Maya temple that the Conquistadors chanced upon, full of female figures, which gave the place its name. Unfortunately, however, Mujeres is no longer the desert island you may have heard about, and its natural attractions have been recognized and developed considerably. Several large hotels have sprung up, thousands of day-trippers visit from Cancún, and the once beautiful El Garrafón coral reef is now almost completely dead, and built into a small-scale amusement park. Inevitably, too, prices have risen and standards (in many cases) have fallen. All that said, the island can still seem a respite to those who've been slogging their way down through Mexico and around the Yucatán, or even to anyone who has tired of plastic Cancún – the wooden buildings and narrow streets have a genuine Caribbean feel, and the island is still very much on the backpacking circuit.

Arrival, information and island transport

The passenger **ferry** arrives downtown, at the main pier at the end of Avenida Morelos on Avenida Rueda Medina, which runs east to west; the car ferry comes in further east on Avenida Medina, at the end of Calle Bravo. Calle Madero, one block west from the passenger ferry dock, cuts north straight across the island; as you walk down it and away from the dock, the first street you cross is Calle Juárez, the second Calle Hidalgo and the third Calle Guerrero, the latter two of which lead west to Playa Norte and east to the zócalo. The boats leave from Puerto Juárez (10min in a taxi from central Cancún, or 15min on a bus) every half-hour, the last at 11.30pm. Aerocaribe and other airlines also occasionally fly out to Cancún or Cozumel from the small airstrip in the centre of the island.

From the pier, it's about a twenty-minute walk to the opposite side of the island and the farthest hotels. The zócalo is skirted by Calle Morelos, Calle Bravo, Calle Guerrero and Calle Hidalgo. The **tourist office** (Mon–Fri 8am–8pm, Sat & Sun 9am–2pm; Ⓦwww.isla-mujeres-mexico.com) is on Avenida Rueda Medina just west of the passenger-ferry pier. Here you can pick up leaflets, maps and copies of the free *Islander* magazine (in Spanish and English). The **post office** (Mon–Thurs 9am–4pm) is on Calle Guerrero at Calle Mateos, about ten minutes' walk from the centre; mail is held at the Lista de Correos for up to ten days (postcode 77400). There is a **caseta** on Calle Madero between Calle Hidalgo and Calle Juárez and an **Internet** café on Calle Hidalgo at Calle Abasolo. **Banks** are few: Bital is on Avenida Rueda Medina, with an ATM; there's also an ATM by the ferry dock. A couple of **lavanderías** are on Calle Abasolo.

The best way of getting around the island is by **moped** (US$8 per hour) or **bicycle** (US$8 per day): the island is a very manageable size with few hills. Alternatively hire a **golf cart** (US$14 per hour). At least a dozen places rent out all three forms of transport. There are several **dive shops** on the island – recommended is Coral at Calle Matamoros 13-A (Ⓣ998/877-0763, Ⓦwww.coralscubadivecenter.com), which offers a range of trips including some to the "Cave of the Sleeping Sharks", where tiger, bull, grey reef, lemon and nurse sharks are regularly encountered. You can also take **snorkelling** trips at the *lancheros* co-operative, south of the passenger-ferry landing (US$20; 2hr). The main day outing, to which scores of touts devote their efforts, is a boat trip to the island bird sanctuary of **Contoy** (with special permission, you may stay overnight). You can see colonies of pelicans and cormorants and occasionally more exotic sea birds, as well as a sunken Spanish galleon. The experienced captains at La Isleña Sea Tours, on Calle Morelos one block back from Avenida Rueda Medina, run a relaxed *faux*-castaway trip, with lunch caught straight from the sea, for US$40.

Accommodation

Isla Mujeres is short on good-value **budget places to stay**, and, though prices are lower than at Cozumel, so is the quality. Most of the reasonably priced options are on the northern edge of the island.

There is no official **campsite** on Isla Mujeres, but you can pitch your tent or sling up a hammock in the grounds of the *Poc Na* **youth hostel**, Calle Matamoros at Calle Carlos Lazo (Ⓣ998/877-0090, Ⓕ877-0059, Ⓔpocnahostel@yahoo.com.mx; ❷–❸), which has lots of other sleeping options, from dorms to rooms with a/c.

Belmar C Hidalgo 110, between C Madero and C Abasolo Ⓣ998/877-0430, Ⓕ877-0429, Ⓦwww.rolandi.com. Well-lit rooms with plenty of extras are a good deal – despite their potentially noisy location above the popular *Pizza Rolandi* on the main nightlife drag. ❻

Cabañas María del Mar C Carlos Lazo Ⓣ998/877-0179, Ⓕ877-0156, Ⓦwww.cabanasdelmar.com. Next to Playa Norte, with deluxe – if somewhat over-furnished – cabañas on the beach, or hotel rooms with a/c, refrigerator and private balcony or terrace. Lively restaurant, tours and car rental. ❼

Casa de los Sueños southern end of island, near Garrafón Ⓣ998/877-0651, Ⓕ877-0708, Ⓦwww.casadelossuenosresort.com. Far and away the most luxurious option on the island (rates, which include breakfast and dinner, start around US$400), with eight impossibly tranquil rooms with baths as large as the sleeping quarters. The Zen-inspired day spa is open to non-guests. ❾

Casa Maya Zazil-Há C Zazil-Há 129, at Playa Norte Ⓣ/Ⓕ998/877-0045, Ⓦwww.kasamaya.com.mx. An offbeat outpost of old-style Isla Mujeres (the owner's family pioneered tourism on the island), and the only reasonably priced option directly on the beach; prices significantly lower off season. ❻–❾

Francis Arlene C Guerrero 7, at C Abasolo Ⓣ/Ⓕ998/877-0310, Ⓦwww.hotelfrancisarlene.com. Pretty small hotel with gorgeous courtyards and clean (if rather brightly painted) rooms with plenty of comforts – good value, especially as there's a choice of a/c or fan. ❺–❻

Marcianito C Abasolo 10 Ⓣ998/877-0111. Spotless rooms, if not so well lit, with new bathroom fixtures. ❹

María Elena at southern end, near Garrafón Ⓣ998/877-0179, Ⓕ877-0156, Ⓦwww.cabanasdelmar.com. For those wanting to flee town, this new hotel near Garrafón offers a pool, a/c, a nice patch of beach and peace and quiet for a reasonable price. ❺

Na Balam C Zazil-Há 118, near Playa Norte Ⓣ998/877-0279, Ⓕ877-0446, Ⓦwww.nabalam.com. One of the island's most chic hotels, with a pool, a tropical garden on the beach, a very good restaurant and elegant, very large rooms. ❾

Las Palmas C Guerrero 20 Ⓣ998/877-0965. The cheapest option on the island; basic but acceptable rooms around a small courtyard. ❹

Playa La Media Luna on north coast Ⓣ998/877-0759, Ⓕ877-1124, Ⓦwww.playamedialuna.com. Pastel rooms, each with a balcony overlooking the beach (a bit rocky, but still swimmable). Nicely isolated, despite its proximity to town – walk straight up Av Mateos to the north shore. ❻

Posada Isla Mujeres C Juárez between C Abasolo and C Madero (no phone). Small new hotel with sparkling white rooms with fans. ❹

Roca Mar C Bravo at C Guerrero, behind the church next to the zócalo Ⓣ/Ⓕ998/877-0101. One of the island's oldest hotels, well maintained, with a restaurant overlooking the Caribbean; rocky beach, but there is a pool. ❻–❼

Suites Los Arcos C Hidalgo 58, between C Matamoros and C Abasolo Ⓣ998/877-1343, Ⓕ877-0236, Ⓔsuiteslosarcos@hotmail.com. Modern rooms with kitchenettes and a/c; quieter ones in the back have bigger balconies too; discounts for week-long stays. ❼

Vistalmar Av Rueda Medina at C Matamoros Ⓣ998/877-0209, Ⓕ877-0096. Very pink hotel opposite ferry pier and central downtown. Good value, with choice of a/c or fan. ❹

The island

Isla Mujeres is no more than 8km long, and even at its widest point is barely a kilometre across. A lone road runs its length, past the dead-calm waters of the landward coast – the other side, northeast-facing, is windswept and exposed. There's a small beach on this side in the town, but the currents even here can be dangerous. The most popular beach, just five minutes' walk from the town plaza, is **Playa Norte** – at the northern tip of the island, but protected from the open sea by a little promontory on which stands a giant all-inclusive resort.

If you've had enough of the beach, windsurfing and wandering round town (the grand tour takes little more than thirty minutes), rent a bike or moped to explore the south of the island. The tropical reef at the southern tip has seen significant damage from unsupervised day-trippers, and is now a family-fun nature park, **Garrafón** (daily 9am–6.30pm; US$15), with kayaking, restaurants and "snuba" set-ups. The entrance to the park is almost at the southern end of the island – beyond, the road continues to the old lighthouse, surrounded by *faux*-Caribbean houses containing shops and a restaurant. From there you can visit a somewhat gratuitous sculpture park and the **Maya temple** at the southernmost point (US$2.70; free with Garrafón ticket). It's not much of a ruin, but it is very dramatically situated on low rocky cliffs, and you can often spot large fish basking below.

On the way back, stop at **Playa Lancheros**, a small, palm-fringed beach that is virtually deserted except at lunchtime, when the day-trippers pile in. There's a restaurant here, specializing in seafood, and a clutch of souvenir stalls. Just north and inland lurk the decaying remains of the **Hacienda Mundaca** (9am–5pm; US$1), an old house and garden to which scores of romantic (and quite untrue) pirate legends are attached. The place has been restored with a few too many concrete paths, but the jungly shade makes for a prime picnic spot. Up the road fronting Laguna Macax is the government-run **turtle farm** and research centre, which breeds endangered sea turtles for release in the wild. An interactive exhibit teaches about the creatures, and you can even swim with a few of them. Entrance is pricey, but helps fund the preservation project (9am–5pm; US$20).

Eating and drinking

The area along and around Hidalgo between Morelos and Abasolo, lined with **restaurants** and crafts shops, is the best place to spend an evening on Isla Mujeres. Simply wander through the laid-back music-filled streets and see what takes your fancy. For inexpensive, basic Mexican food and great low-priced fruit salads, head for the **loncherías** opposite *Las Palmas* hotel. At night, food vendors set up shop on the main plaza.

Buho's Playa Norte. Very popular beach bar with loud rock music, swinging hammock chairs and a happy hour.

Café Cito C Juárez at C Matamoros. Healthy New Age breakfasts with good coffee and fruit-yogurt combos.

Cocktelería Picus Av Rueda Medina, just north of ferry landing. Small beachfront hut serving fresh and inexpensive *ceviches* and shrimp cocktails. Lunch only.

Le Bistro Français C Matamoros 29. Pseudo-French café with a varied, inventive and delicious menu (fish with fennel and capers, for instance) at reasonable prices. Good breakfasts too.

La Lomita C Juárez 25-B, two blocks south of the plaza. Locals line up for a helping of chef-owner Ophelia's daily lunch special, anything from bean soup and *chiles rellenos* to pan-fried fish with salsa verde. Fantastic home cooking, worth the hike up the hill.

Pizza Rolandi C Hidalgo between C Madero and C Abasolo. Part of a small family-run chain serving great wood-oven pizza, lobster, fresh fish and other northern Italian dishes with salads.

The east coast: Cancún to Playa del Carmen

Resort development along the spectacular white-sand beaches south from Cancún to the marvellous seaside ruins of Tulum has proceeded rapidly as landowners cash in on Cancún's popularity. The **Caribbean Barrier Reef** begins off **Puerto Morelos**, a quiet town with excellent beaches. Further south is **Punta Bete**, which is smaller and even quieter, while the phenomenal growth of **Playa del Carmen**, the departure point for boats to Cozumel, has transformed a village with a ferry dock into a major holiday destination renowned for its nightlife and gorgeous stretches of sand.

Finding a relatively deserted stretch of beach is increasingly difficult, though not impossible, and many visitors based in Cancún rent a car to explore the coast. Although a moped is feasible as far as the end of the divided highway at Playa del Carmen, it's a long trip for the underpowered bikes, and bus and truck drivers use little caution as they pass. Taking the bus is a better idea as the service along Hwy-307 is cheap and efficient.

Puerto Morelos and around

Leaving Cancún behind, the first town on the coast is **PUERTO MORELOS**, 20km south. Formerly of little interest except as the departure point for the car ferry to Cozumel, in recent years it has seen a surge in popularity, becoming a base for tours and **dive trips**. With a new direct bus service from the airport (9 daily, 8.30am–6.45pm), it's easier for visitors to bypass Cancún altogether, making Puerto Morelos their first stop along the Mayan Riviera. It is a good place to hang out for a while: despite a rash of new hotel and condo construction, it is a relaxing alternative to the bustle of Cancún, with some lovely beaches and pristine offshore reefs. Inland, on the dirt road to Central Vallarta, are some beautiful cenotes that are only just beginning to receive visitors. Puerto Morelos is also the only working fishing village between Cancún and Tulum that hasn't been entirely consumed by tourism.

Arrival and information

Buses going down the coast leave Cancún's bus station every 30–45 minutes (5am–10pm) and drop you at the highway junction, site of a **tourist information** kiosk with a helpful, enthusiastic staff. Taxis wait here to take you the 2km into town. The **car ferry** to Cozumel officially departs twice daily (except Sun), at 5am and 2pm, returning from Cozumel at 10am and 6pm. Given the price (US$75 per car, plus US$5 per passenger), the time required (at least 1hr wait, 2hr crossing) and the erratic nature of the service (Ⓣ998/871-0008 to check if it's running), it's hardly worth it.

There are several **long-distance telephones** by the police station on the corner of the plaza, an **Internet** café, a supermarket, a couple of **cambios** (7am–10pm) and an **ATM**, though no actual bank.

Accommodation

Almost all of the hotels in Puerto Morelos are right on the beach, but many of them are overpriced. If you want to **camp**, your only option is the pleasantly ramshackle *Acamaya Reef Trailer Park* (Ⓣ987/871-0132, Ⓦwww.acamayareef.com; ❷), on the beach a couple of kilometres north of town –

look for a signposted turn near the entrance to Crococun. Cabañas, with shared or private bath, are also available here (❻).

Amar Inn north of the main plaza, 500m along the seafront ⓣ998/871-0026. Very bohemian family-run hotel with large, well-furnished rooms and cabañas with kitchenettes around a shaded garden. Delicious breakfast included in rates. ❻

Casa Caribe four blocks north of the plaza, opposite the beach ⓣ998/871-0459, ⓦwww.us-webmasters.com/Casa-Caribe. Large peaceful house with six gorgeous rooms, kitchen facilities and sun decks. Highly recommended. ❼

Hacienda Morelos on the waterfront, south of the plaza ⓣ/ⓕ998/871-0015. Bright, airy rooms, all with kitchenettes, bathtubs and terraces right on the beach. ❼

Inglaterra Av Niños Héroes 29, 200m north of the plaza and two blocks back from the sea ⓣ/ⓕ987/871-0418, ⓔmichael@hotelinglaterra.freeserve.co.uk. Basic rooms, a little dark, but budget prices at this long-established hotel. ❺

Posada Amor Av Rojo Gómez, just south of the plaza ⓣ998/871-0033, ⓕ871-0178, ⓦwww.posadaamor.com. A few rooms are the least expensive option in town. Some others are worth the extra money; ask to see a few. Not on the beach, but friendly, with plenty of character. ❹–❻

Posada El Moro Av Rojo Gómez 17, just north of the plaza ⓣ/ⓕ987/871-0159, ⓔmorelos01@sbcglobal.net. Clean, new rooms, some with kitchens, in a pretty little house; amenities are excellent for the price. ❻

Rancho Libertad a 15min walk south of the plaza, beyond the car ferry dock ⓣ/ⓕ998/871-0181, ⓦwww.rancholibertad.com. Two-storey thatched cabañas in a tranquil beach and garden setting. Rates include large breakfasts with fruit and cereal. Guest kitchen facilities and massage available (US$45 per hour). No children. ❼

The Town

The turn-off from Hwy-307 ends at the small, modern **plaza** in the centre of Puerto Morelos. The only proper streets lead north and south for a few blocks, parallel to the beach. The plaza hosts a weekend market, known as a *tianguis*, and has a baseball court and a taxi rank. It's also home to the wonderful Alma Libre (Oct–April Tues–Sat 9am–noon & 6–9pm), probably Mexico's most extensive secondhand English-language bookshop. Ahead lies the **beach**, a wooden **dock** (the car ferry terminal is a few hundred metres south) and the **lighthouse**.

With the reef only 600m offshore and in very healthy condition, Puerto Morelos is a great place to learn to **dive**. Long-established Almost Heaven Adventures, on the square, offers certification courses and one- and two-tank dives (US$40–55), as well as sport-fishing charters (approx US$225 for up to four people; 5–6hr) and snorkelling trips (US$22 per person; 2hr).

If you want to learn more about the **natural and social history** of the area, contact **Maya Echo** (ⓣ987/871-0136, ⓦwww.mayaecho.com), a group dedicated to the conservation of the area's natural beauty and the preservation of Maya culture and spirituality. The group organizes tailor-made, one-day **tours** into the forest and to local villages, where the Maya will teach you about their way of life and their beliefs. Goyo Martín of Goyo's Info Center, on Calle Rojo Gómez (ⓣ998/871-0189, ⓦwww.mayajungle.com), one block north of the plaza, takes people into the forest and to a local cenote on half-day tours (US$40 including lunch). It's also possible to visit the nearby cenotes on your own – taxis cost about US$40 for a two-hour trip.

On the main highway just south of the turn-off to town, the **Jardín Botánico Dr Alfredo Barrera Marín** (daily 9am–5pm; US$7) features the native flora of Quintana Roo and is definitely worth a visit if you have the time. Exhibits are labelled in Spanish and English, and guides can explain the medicinal uses of the plants. Trails lead to a small Maya site and a reconstruction showing how *chicle* is tapped from the sap of the *zapote* (sapodilla) tree before being used in the production of chewing gum.

Eating and drinking

Most of Puerto Morelos' restaurants and nightlife centre around the town square, a cheerful spot for dinner, followed by a cold beer or an evening stroll. The *Hotel Ojo de Agua,* on Calle Rojo Gómez north of the plaza, occasionally hosts **live music** and parties.

Le Café D'Amancia south side of the square. Vegetarian café with salads, healthy breakfasts and fresh juices.

John Gray's Kitchen Av Niños Héroes, north of the plaza. Very good expat-owned restaurant with a diverse menu and a popular all-you-can-eat Sunday barbecue with chicken, ribs, guacamole, salads and the like.

La Pepita on the waterfront, north of the plaza. The local favourite for *ceviches* and fresh fish, with a great casual ambience.

El Pirata north side of the square. Open-air joint with Mexican staples – enchiladas, tacos, burritos and so on – at economical prices. A great hangout spot.

Posada Amor just south of the plaza. Friendly restaurant with tasty fresh fish, Mexican dishes and Sunday breakfast buffet. Good value.

Los Titos north side of the plaza. Inexpensive and delicious Yucatán-style fish tacos and shrimp cocktails.

Punta Bete

Tucked away between the more touristed resorts of Puerto Morelos and Playa del Carmen, the sedate **PUNTA BETE** is little more than a beach, several basic restaurants and a couple of small hotels; one expensive resort has been built up smack between the more rustic accommodation options. The beach is a bit rocky and nowhere near as beautiful as those in Cancún or Playa del Carmen, though it does have the advantage of being uncrowded. Punta Bete is some 4km east of the highway, with the turn-off signposted just south of the Cristal/Coca-Cola bottling plant around Km 62. Near the beach, the road forks: to the left you'll eventually find *Los Piños* (Ⓣ984/873-1506; ❺), a small, somewhat boring beach-front concrete block, and, a bit back from the sea, the more charming Swiss-owned *Coco's Cabañas* (Ⓣ998/887-0785, Ⓔmarsilhel@hotmail.com; ❻), with five individual cabañas, a small pool and a restaurant serving very good international cuisine. The right-hand road leads to Playa Xcalacoco and *Juanito's* (reservations in Cozumel on Ⓣ987/872-5009; ❶–❹), which has clean, simple rooms and no electricity. You can also **camp** here (❶). The **restaurant** dishes up reasonably priced basic Mexican food and fish from 7.30am until 8pm.

About 1km north of Punta Bete proper, adjacent to and reached through the entrance to *La Posada de Capitán Lafitte*, is the rare all-inclusive resort that appeals to independent travellers: casual, electricity-free *KaiLuum II* (reservations in the US on Ⓣ1-800/583-6802, Ⓦwww.mexicoholiday.com; ❾), a cluster of deluxe, palapa-sheltered tents, with good food and a wonderful staff.

Playa del Carmen

PLAYA DEL CARMEN (known simply as Playa), once a soporific fishing village, has mushroomed in recent years and now has the dubious distinction of being one of the world's fastest-growing towns. It's a bit pricey and can be overcrowded, not only with holiday-makers but also with thousands of day-trippers from Cancún and visiting passengers from cruise ships. As a result the town's main centre of activity, Avenida 5 (also called La Quinta), a long, pedestrianized strip one block back from the sea, is often packed to capacity with tourists rapidly emptying their wallets in pavement cafés, souvenir and silver-jewellery outlets and designer clothes shops. Nonetheless, Playa does retain a rather chic European atmosphere, due to the high number of Italian- and French-owned businesses, and compared to hyperactive, Americanized Cancún, it seems positively cosmopolitan and calm. The **beach** is one of the prettiest on the coast, with dazzling white sand and gloriously clear sea, and the central part of town – including the quieter, newer neighbourhood of North Beach (Avenida 5 north of Calle 20) – is compact and easily covered on foot. Playa also plays host to the best **nightlife** on the Mayan Riviera. The offshore reef is almost as spectacular here as in Cozumel, and of the scores of **scuba-diving** operations in Playa, recommended is Tank-Ha, Avenida 5 between calles 8 and 10 (ⓣ984/873-0302, ⓦwww.tankha.com), which offers PADI certification courses (US$275), one- and two-tank dives (US$40–60) and multi-day dive packages (from US$162) as well as twice-daily snorkelling tours (9am & 1.30pm; US$30; 3hr). **Cave diving** in the inland cenotes is also a major sport here – Sealife Divers (ⓣ984/877-8727, ⓦwww.sealifedivers.com), at Mamita's beach club in North Beach, is a specialist.

Arrival and information

Playa del Carmen has two **bus stations**: the central depot is at the corner of Avenida 5 and Avenida Juárez, the main street running east–west from the

highway to the beach, and deals mainly with shuttles from Cancún airport and services of the Riviera bus company; the other station, on Avenida 20 between calles 12 and 14, is primarily for ADO and affiliate companies handling some local services as well as destinations further afield. If you're heading into Playa from the international **airport** in Cancún, any number of private operators will take you on the hour-long trip in air-conditioned minibuses (approx US$15 per person; ask your hotel to organize pickup for your return). The **tourist information centre**, on Avenida Juárez at Avenida 15 (daily 9am–9pm; Ⓣ/Ⓕ984/873-2804, Ⓔturismo@solidaridad.gob.mx), is very helpful, with bilingual staff who'll do their best to answer any enquiries you may have. Pick up a copy of the useful *Playa del Carmen*, which has a quality map and hotel and restaurant listings. Look in upscale bars and restaurants for *La Quinta*, a free glossy magazine detailing the town's trendier side. The best way to visit local sites of interest is to hire a **taxi**, which will take you on a round-trip including waiting time for as little as half the price of any tour company.

Accommodation

You'll have no difficulty finding a room in Playa del Carmen – hotels are being built all the time – and as a result of competition, prices are coming down. The town has one hotel with camping facilities and several decent budget hotels (generally the further from the sea the cheaper the accommodation). *El Palomar* **hostel**, on Avenida 5 between Avenida Juárez and Calle 2 (Ⓣ984/803-2606, Ⓦwww.elpalomarhostel.com; ❷), is the best of the dorm-bed offerings, and has a few private rooms with a shared bath.

Baal Nah Kah C 12 between the beach and Av 5 Ⓣ984/873-0110, Ⓕ873-0050, Ⓦwww.playabedandbreakfast.com. Very popular and relaxed Italian-run house with charming, individually decorated rooms (breakfast not included, in spite of claims on website). ❻–❾

Cabañas La Ruina C 2 between Av 5 and the sea Ⓣ/Ⓕ984/873-0405, Ⓔlaruina@dicoz.com. Playa's most sociable and economical place to stay, on the beach with its own ruin in the grounds. Options include camping space, a few hook-ups for hammocks, and cabañas with or without private bath and a/c. ❷–❻

Casa de las Flores Av 20 no. 150, between C 4 and C 6 Ⓣ984/873-2898, Ⓦwww.hotelcasadelasflores.com. Worth the walk to the beach: beautiful grounds with colonial-style rooms and a swimming pool. ❻–❽

Deseo Av 5 at C 12 Ⓣ984/879-3620, Ⓕ879-3621, Ⓦwww.hoteldeseo.com. Ultra-trendy boutique hotel, with loads of clever details, like mellow electronica piped into the minimalist rooms. An equally chic clientele lounges at the bar. ❾

Kinbé C 10 between Av 5 and Av 1 Ⓣ984/873-0441, Ⓕ873-2215, Ⓦwww.kinbe.com. Small, friendly Italian-run hotel with beautifully designed rooms (all with a/c) overlooking a courtyard, and a nice ocean view from the small roof deck; guests get discounts at the hip *Mamita's* beach club in North Beach. ❻

Lunata Av 5 between C 6 and C 8 Ⓣ984/873-0884, Ⓕ873-1240, Ⓦwww.lunata.com. Attractive townhouse done up like a hacienda, with lovely rooms including a honeymoon suite. Continental breakfast served in walled garden. Overlooks the main street, so rooms at the front can be noisy. ❽

Playa Maya on the beach between C 6 and C 8 Ⓣ/Ⓕ984/803-2022, Ⓦwww.playa-maya.com. Newish beachfront hotel with a small pool, modern rooms and a gym. ❽

Posada Freud Av 5 between C 8 and C 10 Ⓣ/Ⓕ984/873-0601, Ⓦwww.posadafreud.com. Pretty rooms with colourful details smack in the middle of the action at reasonable (and negotiable) rates. ❻

Posada Mariposa Av 5 between C 24 and C 26 Ⓣ/Ⓕ984/873-3886, Ⓦwww.posada-mariposa.com. Quiet hotel filled with overgrown greenery in the new North Beach area. ❻

La Rana Cansada C 10 no. 132, between Av 5 and Av 10 Ⓣ984/873-0389, Ⓦwww.ranacansada.com. Friendly, laid-back hotel with communal living space, kitchen facilities and a range of room options. ❺–❼

Eating

Playa del Carmen is heaving with **restaurants** of every kind, and even the traditional Mexican places stay open late. The quality of food here is often very good (particularly **Italian**), but prices are high. The pedestrianized section of **Avenida 5** is lined end-to-end with dining tables where you can eat all sorts of cuisine – but if you're on a **budget** you'll need to search out where locals go, like the excellent taco carts on Avenida Juárez close to the beach or the inexpensive comida corrida and grilled-chicken places starting around Av 10 and going farther back from the sea.

Los Almendros Av 10 at C 6. No relation to the Ticul classic spot, but tasty food all the same: traditional Mexican restaurant with outdoor grill, delicious tacos and daily specials. Good value and unpretentious.

Babe's C 10 between Av 5 and Av 10. This Swedish-owned Thai noodle house typifies Playa's international hodgepodge – and the *mojitos* aren't bad either.

Buenos Aires Av 5 between C 4 and C 6. Argentinian steakhouse tucked away on a side street, the best place in town for grilled meat.

Café Sasta Av 5 between C 6 and C 8. Italian coffee house with pastries – the sidewalk tables are a good vantage point for people-watching.

La Cueva del Chango C 38 between Av 5 and the beach. Local favourite for long, late breakfasts, perfect after a morning stroll up the beach. Good granola and tasty empanadas. Mon–Sat 8am–2pm.

Don Pedro's Av 5 between C 22 and C 24. Very chummy, inexpensive little Italian place in the North Beach area.

Hot C 10 between Av 5 and Av 10. Bakery with small café serving fresh muffins, bagels and brownies as well as omelettes and sandwiches; there's another branch on C 14 north of Av 5.

Media Luna Av 5 between C 12 and C 14. Eclectic veggie and seafood restaurant with a well-priced lunch special and huge delicious breakfasts – fruit salad, French toast, pancakes.

Stone Island Av 5 between C 10 and C 12. Tiny *coctelería*, reasonably priced and good for a quick snack, particularly the inexpensive shrimp quesadillas.

Xtabentun C 2 between Av 10 and Av 15. Local family-run Mexican restaurant with tasty comida corrida, bean soup and burritos. Very good value. Lunch only.

Bars and nightlife

You can wander through Playa del Carmen well into the night, listening to all sorts of music, from salsa and reggae to 1970s classics. Drinks aren't cheap, but it's worth checking out the bar scene as it's easy to meet people. Plentiful happy-hour specials can ease you into the night without depleting funds too rapidly.

Bar Ranita C 10 between Av 5 and Av 10. Very mellow small space, with a crew of regulars hanging out at the horseshoe-shaped bar.

Blue Parrot on the beach at C 12. Friendly open-air bar with tables on the sand; live music in the afternoons and assorted dancers and fire-spinners at night. Open until 2am.

Calypso C 6 between Av 5 and Av 10. Cosy local atmosphere and a busy dance floor. Live Caribbean music on Fri and Sat evenings.

Capitán Tutix on the beach at C 2. *The* pick-up joint in town, jam-packed bar and disco with live music every night (10pm–midnight) and a predominantly young party crowd. For the after-party, *Kuba*, next door, takes over when *Tutix* closes.

Frida's Av 5 no. 217, at C 12. Kitschy and cool poolside bar with club music, all under the watchful gaze of wall-size portraits of Ché and Subcomandante Marcos.

Mil y Un Aluxes Av Juárez, three blocks west of the highway. Hip new club in an actual cave (the host will give you a tour); dinner begins at 7pm, dancing gets started around 10pm.

El Tigre C 2 between Av 10 and Av 15. Excellent local spot for beers and ridiculously generous *botanas*. Closes early.

Ula-Gula Av 5 at C 10. Small, trendy bar with DJ on ground floor; restaurant upstairs is uneven, but the simpler dishes are delicious.

Listings

Airlines The small airstrip just south of town handles short jaunts, chiefly to Cozumel, but also to Chichén Itzá and other key Maya sites; operators include Aeroferinco (☎984/873-0636) and Aeroméxico (☎984/873-0350, Ⓦwww.aeromexico.com).
Banks Bital, Av Juárez between Av 10 and Av 15 (Mon–Fri 8am–4pm); Bancomer, Av Juárez between Av 25 and Av 30 (Mon–Fri 9am–4pm). Both have ATMs.
Buses The distinction between Playa's two bus stations is somewhat fluid; typically, long-haul ADO-run trips go from Av 20 between C 12 and C 14, and short-haul services, including Riviera buses, leave from the central station, Av Juárez at Av 5. Either way, you can buy tickets for all routes at the central station – just ask which terminal the bus will leave from. Routes include Cancún (every half-hour; 1hr), Tulum (hourly; 1–2hr), Chetumal (hourly; 4hr), Mérida (hourly; 5hr), Valladolid (5 daily; 3hr), Villahermosa (10 daily; 12hr), and San Cristóbal de las Casas (5 daily; 17hr).
Car and bike rental All the large car rental companies have outlets in Playa – most are situated on the main coastal highway at the turn-off into town or in Plaza Marina near the Cozumel ferry pier. Try Localiza, Av Juárez between Av 5 and Av 10 (☎984/873-0580). Playa Bike, Av 1 Norte between C 10 and C 12 (☎984/806-0398), rents motorbikes (US$40 per day), bicycles (US$10 per day) and beach equipment like snorkels and boogie boards.
Internet and laundry There are a number of shops with Internet facilities on or around Av 5. Laundry & Internet del Carmen, C 6 between Av 5 and the beach, also has self-service washing machines and a drop-off laundry service.
Post office Av Juárez between Av 15 and Av 20 (Mon–Fri 8am–2pm); geared to dealing with tourists. There's a stamp machine outside. The Lista de Correos (postcode 77710) keeps mail for ten days.
Telephones Plenty of Ladatel phones on Av 5, and you can call long distance at Computel Caseta (daily 7am–10pm), next to the bus station.

Isla Cozumel

ISLA COZUMEL is far larger than Mujeres and has, unfortunately, been developed well beyond its potential. However, it offers the best **diving** in Mexico, with spectacular drop-offs, walls and swim-throughs, some beautiful **coral gardens** and a number of little-visited remote reefs where you can see larger pelagic fish and dolphins. The island is also good for **bird-watching** as it's a stopover on migration routes and has several species or variants endemic to Cozumel.

Before the Spanish arrived, the island appears to have been a major Maya centre, carrying on sea trade around the coasts of Mexico and as far south as Honduras and perhaps Panama; after the Conquest it was virtually deserted for four hundred years. This ancient community – one of several around the Yucatán coast that survived the collapse of Classic Maya civilization – is usually dismissed as being the decadent remnant of a moribund society, but that theory is not necessarily correct and was not the initial impression of the Conquistadors. Architecture might have declined in the years from 1200 AD to the Conquest, but large-scale trade, specialization between centres and even a degree of mass production are all in evidence. Cozumel's later rulers did not enjoy the same grand style as their forebears, but the rest of an increasingly commercialized population were probably better off. The island itself may even have been an early free-trade zone, where merchants from competing cities could trade peaceably.

Whatever the truth, you get little opportunity to judge for yourself. A US air base, built here during World War II, has erased all trace of the ancient city, and the lesser ruins scattered across the roadless interior are mostly unrestored and inaccessible. The airfield did, at least, bring a degree of prosperity: converted to civilian use, it remains the means by which most visitors arrive.

Arrival and information

Ferries depart from Playa del Carmen every two hours on even hours (8am–10pm, US$8 one-way, US$14.60 round-trip); they return on odd hours (7am–9pm). You can leave your car in the secure car park behind the bus station. **Arriving by boat**, you'll be right in the centre of town (officially **San Miguel**, but always known simply as Cozumel), with the zócalo just one block inland; from the **airport** you have to take the VW *combi* service (around US$4). The **tourist office** (Mon–Sat 8.30am–5pm; Ⓣ987/869-0212, Ⓔturismoczm@yahoo.com.mx) is in a kiosk just as you get off the ferry, and you can get a range of maps and brochures from the helpful staff; the ubiquitous *Free Blue Guide to Cozumel* is perhaps the most useful piece of literature. You'll probably need a map to get your bearings, as Cozumel's street-numbering system is slightly more complex than most Mexican towns. The main road along the water is Avenida Rafael Melgar. Avenida Benito Juárez runs perpendicular, straight from the plaza in front of the ferry pier, and divides the town: north of it, even-numbered streets run east–west; odd-numbered streets are to the south. Heading east from Avenida Melgar, you'll cross Avenida 5, Avenida 10 and so on.

The **post office** (Mon–Fri 9am–4pm, Sat 9am–1pm) is a fifteen-minute walk from the centre, on Avenida Melgar at the corner with Calle 7 Sur; for Lista de Correos use the postcode 77600. Cozumel has many **banks** (Mon–Fri 9am–4pm), most of them with ATMs. Bital, Avenida 5 at Calle 1 Sur, stays open until 7pm on weekdays; otherwise there are several **cambios** around the main square (daily 9am–10pm). The Crew Office, Av 5 no. 201-A between Avenida Salas and Calle 3 Sur, is a good **Internet, phone** and **fax** shop.

There are dozens of **dive shops** in town, the better ones using more experienced instructors and faster boats. Deep Blue, Avenida Salas at Av 10 (Ⓣ/Ⓕ987/872-5653, Ⓦwww.deepbluecozumel.com), is one of the best on the island, offering tailor-made small-group tours to some of the most interesting and remote reefs off the island (Las Palmas and Cedral Wall are popular advanced dive spots; Palancar Shallows is good for novices); a two-tank dive is US$65. They also run a full range of certification courses including PADI and IANTD (Nitrox) certifications and can help find accommodation, including longer-term house rental.

While Cozumel's principal activity is diving (as well as the ever-popular beach lounging), **snorkelling** and **sport-fishing** tours are both readily available. If you want to snorkel you'll need to organize a boat ride out to the reef – all of the dive shops in town should be able to take you (approximately US$25 for several hours in the water). The best spots are Palancar Shallows and Colombia Shallows – a little farther south, but a good way of judging your tour operator, if they're willing to make the extra effort. An exhilarating – if bumpy – way to see the wild, beautifully deserted side of the island is a **dune-buggy tour** of the uninhabited northeast coast. Jungle Buggy Tours, at Rentadora Isleña, Calle 7 between Avenida Melgar and Avenida 5 (Ⓣ987/872-0788, Ⓦwww.cozumelhomes.com), has built their own fleet of buggies (US$90; 8hr); trips include lunch and time to snorkel.

Town transport

Cozumel town has been modernized and is easy enough to get around on foot – there's even a pedestrian zone. Buses, however, are distinctly lacking, so to get further afield you'll have to go on a tour, take a taxi or rent a vehicle. **Cycling** is feasible on the surfaced roads, but it can be a bit of an endurance test if you aren't used to long-distance pedalling and positively unpleasant if you get caught in a sudden storm, which is likely from around July to October. **Mopeds** give you a bit more freedom and are easier to handle, while **jeeps** are available from numerous outlets (be sure to check the restrictions of your insurance if you want to go onto the dirt tracks). Prices vary little, but you may find occasional special offers. To rent per day, bikes cost around US$9, mopeds US$25–30 and jeeps around US$45. There is also no shortage of places on Cozumel to rent **cars**. Try Rentadora Isleña (info above) or Aguilar, in the lobby of the *Hotel Aguilar,* Calle 3 Sur 98 (ⓣ987/872-0307), which also rents out scooters and bicycles.

Accommodation

Hotels in Cozumel are divided into two distinct categories (with virtually all of them offering some kind of dive package). Most are expensive all-inclusive resorts strung out along the coast, particularly to the north of town. The others are the more affordable places in the centre, preferable if you're on a budget or don't want to be isolated from the social scene. But all of the latter are some way from the island's beaches, and nowhere has rooms for less than US$20 per night.

Aguilar C 3 Sur 98, between Av Melgar and Av 5 Sur ⓣ987/872-0307, ⓕ872-0769, ⓦwww.cozumel-hotels.net/aguilar. Quiet, slightly kitsch rooms, all with a/c, away from the road around a garden with small pool. Scooters and car rental available. ❺

Amigo's B&B C 7 Sur 571, between Av 25 and Av 30 ⓣ/ⓕ987/872-3868, ⓦwww.bacalar.net. Three separate cottages in a large garden with fruit trees. Continental breakfast is included in rates and served in the communal area, which also has TV, video and games. ❼

Las Anclas Av 5 Sur 325 ⓣ/ⓕ987/872-5476. Elegant, well-designed two-storey apartments with kitchenettes and a peaceful shared garden; rooms – all remodelled in 2003 – can sleep up to four people. ❼

Caribe Blu Costera Sur Km 2.2 ⓣ987/872-0188, ⓕ872-1631, ⓦwww.caribeblu.net. Hotel very close to town with an excellent dive shop, Blue Angel, and shallow dive training right off the hotel's beach. All rooms have sea views and private balconies; there's also a pool. ❼

Casa Mexicana Av Melgar 457, between C 5 and C 7 ⓣ987/872-9080, ⓕ872-9073, ⓦwww.casamexicanacozumel.com. Very stylish, state-of-the-art hotel overlooking the water, with pool, travel agency, business centre and gym; buffet breakfast is included. ❾

Flamingo C 6 Norte between Av Melgar and Av 5 Sur ⓣ987/872-1264, ⓦwww.hotelflamingo.com. Fun hotel popular with divers, with a roof terrace and bar and good dive packages; guests can use the beach at *Playa Azul.* ❼

Palapas Amaranto C 5 Sur between Av 15 and Av 20 ⓣ987/872-3219, ⓕ872-6190, ⓦwww.mexonline.com/amaranto.htm. Fanciful architecture and tasteful furnishings distinguish these three round stucco palapas and two apartments housed in a tower. Rooms – all with fridge and microwave, most with a/c – are clustered around a Mediterranean-influenced courtyard and small pool. ❻

Pepita Av 15 Sur 120, at C 1 Sur ⓣ987/872-0098. By far the best of the budget options, with clean attractive rooms, a pretty courtyard and complimentary coffee in the mornings. ❺

Playa Azul Zona Hotelera Norte Km 4 ⓣ987/872-0043, ⓕ872-0110, ⓦwww.playa-azul.com. Swanky resort on a picture-perfect stretch of beach north of town. Elegant rooms and all facilities, including a Jack Nicklaus-designed golf course. ❾

Saolima Av Salas 260, between Av 10 and Av 15 ⓣ987/872-0886. Basic but clean rooms away from the road – pretty unremarkable, but a decent option if *Pepita* is full. ❹

Vista del Mar Av Melgar 45, between C 5 and C 7 ⓣ987/872-0545, ⓦwww.hotelvistadelmar.com. Stylish new hotel done up in natural fibres; the plush rooms are very good value. Front rooms have ocean view; back rooms overlook a pretty pool and jacuzzi. Continental breakfast is included. ❼

The island

Downtown Cozumel is almost entirely devoted to tourism, packed with restaurants, souvenir shops, tour agencies and jewellery stores – exclusively set up to cater to the huge cruise-ship clientele. During the high season (Nov–April) up to twenty liners a week, each with several thousand passengers, dock at one of the island's five purpose-built piers. As a result the malecón is all too often an uncomfortably crowded throng of day-trippers and you may be hassled by aggressive sales people. The weekends, though, are blissfully free of cruise ships – none generally stops on Cozumel on Sunday, and only a couple arrive on Saturday and Monday.

If you decide to shop, don't buy **black coral**, an endangered and beautiful type of sea life which is unfortunately sold everywhere. Cozumel used to have one of the largest colonies of this rare, slow-growing species, but it has been severely depleted since the tourist trade started here in the 1960s. Don't, under any circumstances, go breaking it off the reefs.

The attractive **museum** (daily 9am–5pm; US$5) on the malecón, between avenidas 4 and 6, has small displays of the flora, fauna and marine life of the island, as well as a good collection of Maya artefacts and old photos. It occasionally hosts live music and theatre events – check with the tourist office.

Cozumel's eastern shoreline is often impressively wild; it remains undeveloped because, as on Isla Mujeres, it faces the open sea and is usually too rough for **swimming**. On the more placid west coast, which is additionally protected by a string of reefs, the easiest **beaches** to get to are north of the town in front of the older resort hotels. Far better, though, to rent a vehicle and head off down to the less exploited places to the south.

Heading **south**, you pass first a clutch of modern hotels by the car ferry dock; offshore here, at the end of the Paraíso Reef, you can see a rather alarming wrecked airliner on the bottom – it's a movie prop. There's accessible snorkelling off the pier at *Hotel Caribe Blu*, from where you can drift easily along a nice stretch of reef; equipment can be rented from the hotel's dive shop. A bit further south is the beach club **Dzul-Ha** (US$5), as yet unmobbed and with a stunning reef. Most visitors to the island are steered right to the **Parque Chankanaab**, or "Little Sea", recently designated a national park (daily 7am–5pm; US$10). The beautiful lagoon full of turtles and lurid fish feels somewhat exploited, but it's good for families, as there's a protected children's beach. Press on to **Playa Corona** if you want a cheaper day out: there's no charge for beach access, and the snorkelling here is on a par with Dzul-Ha (cruise-ship days bring crowds, however). Further south, **Playa San Francisco** is the best free beach for lounging and swimming, but if you're willing to pay, the quieter, elegant **Nachi-Cocom** club (US$10) has very fine facilities, including a swimming pool – but note that there's no snorkelling here.

You can complete a circuit of the southern half of the island by following the road up the windswept eastern shoreline. There are a couple of good, if basic (no running water or electricity), restaurants at **Chen Rio** and **Punta Morena** – the latter, a surfer hangout, also rents small bungalows (❶). The beaches here are often deserted, but swim only where you see others, as currents can be dangerous. The main road cuts back across the middle of the island to town; near the northern point, up a rough track, is the small Maya ruin of **Castillo Real**. Local legend has it that potential leaders went here to sit out 365 days and nights alone to test their fortitude and strength of character; we don't suggest you do the same.

More accessible – halfway across the island from town, 6km north of the main road – is the only excavated Maya site on the island, **San Gervasio** (daily 7am–5pm; US$5.50), built to honour Ixchel. Apparently modelled on Chichén Itzá, with several small temples connected by *sacbes* or long white roads, San Gervasio was, between 1200 AD and 1650 AD, one of the most important centres of pilgrimage in Mesoamerica – though it's not particularly impressive now. On the southern part of the island, the village of **Cedral** has a tiny Maya site near the old Spanish church and several **cenotes** reached only by horseback (US$25 per person for a 2hr tour); turn inland on the road shortly after passing San Francisco beach. In May, the village hosts a huge fiesta with bullfights, prize-winning livestock and dancing.

The southernmost point of the island is a protected reserve for diverse wildlife, the **Parque Punta Sur** (daily 9am–5pm; US$10). The site contains several lovely beaches, the Punta Celarain **lighthouse** and the **Templo El Caracol** – which may have been built by the Maya as an ancient lighthouse, and is worth visiting to hear the sounds produced when the wind whistles through the shells encrusted in its walls. You can climb to the top of the lighthouse for amazing views over the coast, or visit the adjacent **museum of navigation** (daily 10am–4pm; same ticket) in the former lightkeeper's house, which has a series of interesting displays on maritime history. A creaking wooden bus transports visitors between various sites (or you can rent bicycles), including viewing towers over a large network of lagoons and a beach restaurant serving good fried fish. This is also a prime spot for **bird-watching**, as the mangroves host a number of migratory species, as well as endemic ones. For additional fees, you can arrange a small-group night tour of the **crocodile** or **sea turtle reserve areas** and scientific monitoring stations in the park (US$30–35; reservations at ⓣ987/872-0914, or ask at the park entrance).

Eating and drinking

Eating tends to be expensive wherever you go in Cozumel, but there's plenty of choice if you've got money to spend. The zócalo downtown is a central focus for **nightlife** and, although it's an exuberant spot with food stalls, frequent **live music** and strolling **mariachis**, its restaurants are for the most part overpriced tourist traps. You're better off wandering several blocks back from the seafront for good food and local flavour. For a more laid-back atmosphere you can enjoy long, lazy lunches in the palapas dotted every few kilometres along the rugged eastern coast.

Arrecife at the *El Presidente Inter-Continental*, 6.5km south of town. The veranda bar at the island's ritziest hotel is an ideal spot for a sunset cocktail.

Chilangos Av Coldwell 30, between C 3 Sur and C Morelos. *Huaraches*, open-face quesadillas, are the house specialty; select your own combination of ingredients. 6pm–1am.

La Choza Av Salas at Av 10. Busy and popular mid-price restaurant serving Mexican home cooking. Good service and a buzzing atmosphere; off-the-menu lunch specials are a deal.

Coffeelia C 5 Sur between Av Melgar and Av 5. A proud local owner presides over breakfast and lunch from her homely kitchen in this sweet, small café. The menu mixes fresh Mexican dishes with fruit smoothies and whole-grain bread.

Conchita del Caribe Av 65 between C 21 and C 23. Well off the tourist track, in an unlikely-looking converted garage, this locally famous seafood spot is inexpensive and delicious – *ceviches* are particularly good. Closes at 6pm.

Diamond Café C 1 Sur at Av 15. Excellent bakery with an extensive breakfast menu, homemade ice cream and pastries.

Jeanie's Waffle House Av Melgar at C 11 Sur, in *El Acuario* restaurant on the beachfront. Residents love "La Casa del Wafle" for its giant fruit salads and its tables on the sand.

Las Palmas C 3 Sur at Av 25. Laid-back local favourite for an inexpensive lunch.

Paradise Café where the surfaced road meets the east coast on an anticlockwise circuit of the island. Palapa-roof restaurant and bar in the middle of nowhere, dishing up moderately priced Mexican food to the accompaniment of reggae. Good place to swing in a hammock, sipping a margarita. Daily 10.30am–5.30pm.

Prima Av Salas between Av 5 and Av 10. Very popular (and very loud) Italian restaurant with decent pizza and pasta and a rooftop terrace.

Tony Rome's Av 5 between Av Salas and C 3 Sur. Hilarious karaoke venue with the larger-than-life proprietor entertaining the crowds nightly Loads of fun, but better for drinks than dinner.

La Veranda C 4 Norte between Av 5 and Av 10 ⓣ987/872-4132. Beautiful garden behind an elegant Caribbean-style house. Worth a splurge. The food (entrees include jerk chicken and shrimp curry) is delicious and prepared with care, but service can suffer when it's crowded; reservations recommended.

Zermatt C 4 Norte at Av 5. Swiss-owned bakery serving huge sugar doughnuts, among other sweet treats.

From Playa del Carmen south to Tulum

Almost the entire stretch of coast **south of Playa del Carmen**, which includes a number of exquisite **beaches**, has been developed into a string of luxury all-inclusive resorts or condominium "villages" with private gated entrances and consequently little or no access for non-residents to the sea – principally **Puerto Aventuras**, 20km south of Playa, and **Akumal**, 15km further on, both of which are expensive, sterile and best avoided.

Six kilometres south of Playa is **Xcaret** (Mon–Sat 8.30am–9.45pm, Sun 8.30am–6pm; US$49; ⓦwww.xcaretcancun.com), tagged the "Incredible Eco-Archeological Park", but in fact a huge, somewhat bizarre theme park. There's a museum, tropical aquarium, aviary, "Maya village", botanical garden, some small authentic ruins, pools and beaches, and more than a kilometre of subterranean rivers down which you can swim, snorkel or simply float – along with scores of others – with the help of neon innertubes.

Twenty-five kilometres further south, **Xpu-ha** is the only piece of (relatively) unspoilt beach on this coast. An all-inclusive resort, *Hotel Copacabana*, breaks up the beautiful beach, but serves as a landmark for two smaller, less expensive **overnight** options. Just north is a sign and a narrow road marked "X-5" for *Villas del Caribe* (ⓣ984/873-2194; ❼), a small hotel adjacent to the excellent *Café de Mar* **restaurant** and bar, which is the only real focus of Xpu-ha's small community and serves healthy breakfasts and a tasty and diverse (gazpacho, Greek-style octopus) lunch and dinner menu. If you're on a budget you can stay in basic cabañas or camp on the beach at *Bonanza Xpu-ha* (no phone; ❶–❹) – look for a sign and the second narrow dirt road south of the *Copacabana*, marked "X-7".

Parque Xel-ha (daily 9am–6pm; US$27, or US$56 including all food and drink; ⓦwww.xelha.com.mx), 13km north of Tulum, is another theme park, this one proclaiming itself "the world's largest natural aquarium" and built around an extensive natural formation of lagoons, inlets and caves. It's a beautiful place, but like Xcaret it's usually crowded with day-trippers; get here early – after 10.30am you'll be fighting for space. You can rent snorkelling equipment on the spot and lockers are available. Across the other side of the highway, the small and only partly excavated **ruins of Xel Há** (8am–5pm; US$3.20), or "Place Where Water Is Born", are of little interest except for the Temple of the Birds, where faded paintings are still visible in places.

Tulum

Tulum, 130km south of Cancún, is one of the most picturesque of all Maya sites – small, but exquisitely poised on fifteen-metre-high cliffs above the impossibly turquoise Caribbean. When the Spanish first set eyes on the place in 1518, they considered it as large and beautiful a city as Seville. They were, perhaps, misled by their dreams of El Dorado, the glory of the setting and the brightly painted facades of the buildings, for architecturally Tulum is no match for the great Maya cities. Nevertheless, on account of its location, it sticks in the memory like no other. It is also an important Maya spiritual and cultural centre, and is one of the villages in the "Zona Maya", the central part of Quintana Roo that was once semi-independent.

If you want to take time out for a **swim**, you can plunge into the Caribbean straight in front of the site. Limitless further possibilities for a dip are strung out down a rough road to the south that runs along the beautiful and deserted-feeling coastline. The track continues, though passable only in a sturdy (and preferably 4WD) vehicle, all the way to Punta Allen at the tip of the peninsula. At the ruins, however, the beginning of the road has been blocked to protect the site from traffic damage, so you have to join it further south.

The site

The site (daily 8am–7pm, 6pm in summer; US$3.70) is about 1km from the main road – be sure to get off the bus at the turn-off to the ruins and not at the village 1.5km further south. **Entrance** is through a breach in the wall that protected the city on three sides; the fourth was defended by the sea. This wall, some 5m high with a walkway around the top, may have been defensive, but more likely its prime purpose was to delineate the ceremonial and administrative precinct (the site you see today) from the residential enclaves spread out along the coast in each direction. These houses – by far the bulk of the ancient city – were mostly constructed of perishable material, so little or no trace of them remains.

As you go through the walls, the chief structures lie directly ahead of you, with the Castillo rising on its rocky prominence above the sea. You pass first the tumbledown **Casa de Chultun**, a porticoed dwelling the roof of which collapsed only in the middle of the twentieth century, and immediately beyond it, the **Templo de los Frescos**. The partially restored murals inside the temple depict Maya gods and symbols of nature's fertility: rain, maize and fish. They originally adorned an earlier structure and have been preserved by the construction around them of a gallery and still later (in the fifteenth century) by the addition of a second temple on top, with walls which, characteristically, slope outwards at the top. On the corners of the gallery are carved masks of Chac, or perhaps of the creator god Itzamná.

The **Castillo**, on the highest part of the site, commands imposing views in every direction. It may have served not just as a temple, but also as a beacon or lighthouse – even without a light, it would have been an important landmark for mariners along an otherwise monotonously featureless coastline. You climb first to a small square, in the midst of which stood an altar, before tackling the broad stairway to the top of the castle itself. To the left of this plaza stands the **Templo del Dios Descendente**. The diving or descending god – depicted here above the narrow entrance of the temple – appears all over Tulum as a small, upside-down figure. His exact meaning is not known: he may represent the setting sun, or rain or lightning, or he may be the Bee God, since honey was one of the Maya's most important exports. Opposite is the **Templo de la Serie Inicial** (Temple of the Initial Series) – so called because in it was found a stele (now in the British Museum) bearing a date well before the foundation of the city, and presumably brought here from elsewhere. Right below the castle to the north is a tiny cove with a beautiful white beach, and on the promontory beyond it the **Templo del Viento** (Temple of the Wind), a small, single-room structure. This is reflected by a similar chamber – the **Templo del Mar** – overlooking the water at the southern edge of the site.

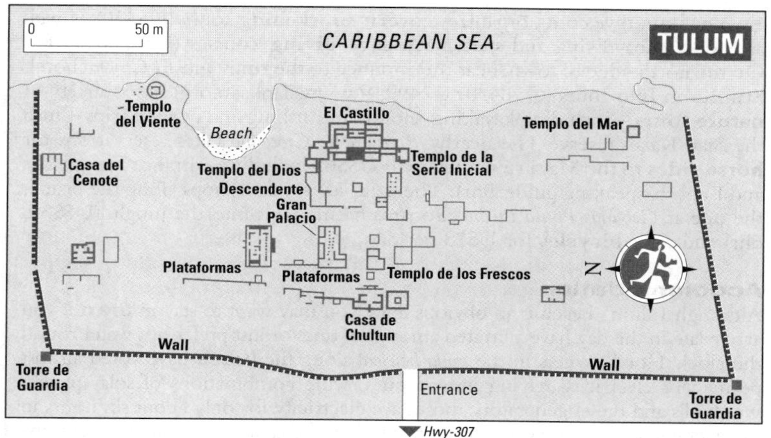

Tulum practicalities

Arriving in Tulum, by bus or private transport, can be confusing because there are two distinct parts to the community. The main coastal highway from Cancún turns slightly inland here, and the **village** proper, surprisingly nice for a sprawling waystation, straddles either side of this main road. The **ruins** and most of the local **accommodation** are situated right on the sea, with the hotels connected by an excruciatingly potholed road. Coming in on the highway from the north, pass the pedestrian entrance to the ruins, then the well-marked car and tour-bus entrance. At the next intersection (referred to as *el crucero* by everyone), dominated by a San Francisco de Asis supermarket, you reach the **sea** by turning left, following signs for "Boca Paila–Punta Allen"; it's 3km out to the beach road and the hotels.

The **bus** station in the village is at the southern end of town and open 24 hours. If you're heading to the ruins you'll want to get off before the terminal at the relevant turn-off. To the ruins themselves, it's an additional walk of nearly a kilometre. To get to the beach, you can find a taxi at the station – there's no public transport. Tulum's taxi drivers have a reputation for being particularly cutthroat, intimidating locals who pick up hitchhikers (consequently most don't) and denying the existence of hotels which don't pay them commission – if you've been given the name of a particular hotel, insist on being taken there.

Almost opposite the bus station is *The Weary Traveler* hostel (see overleaf). The helpful staff will do their best to answer your enquiries, and they help maintain a useful website about the area (Ⓦwww.intulum.com). A Bital **bank** with an ATM is in the middle of town, about 300m north of the bus station, and you can **change money** at one of several cambios on the main street. A good **laundry** service is Lavandería Burbujas, two blocks east of the main drag on Calle Jupiter, the street just south of the bus station. The **post office** is very small, on the right side just after the first *spead bump* coming from the north, and you can **rent a car** from Ana y José (Ⓣ984/871-2030, Ⓦwww.anayjose.com), on the west side of the street just south of the post office.

Most visitors to Tulum are happy to spend their days lying on the beach, but if you're looking for something more energetic, the Aktún Dive Center, at the intersection of the beach road and the road to Cobá (Ⓣ984/871-2311,

Ⓦ www.aktundive.com), organizes **cavern snorkelling** tours (US$30) as well as PADI scuba-diving and specialized **cave diving** courses (US$300–1100). On the north edge of town, near the entrance to the ruins and *El Crucero* hotel, Sian Ka'an Info Tours (Ⓣ984/871-2499, Ⓦ www.siankaan.org) has a variety of **nature tours** – including kayaking, snorkelling, fishing and cycling trips – into the Sian Ka'an reserve. The nearby *Restaurante Crocodilo* takes reservations for **horse rides** to the Maya ruins at Muyil (US$65 including entrance fees, snacks and English-speaking guide; 5hr). There are several dive shops along the beach; the one at *Cabañas Punta Piedra* also runs hiking trips into the jungle (US$30; 6hr) and rents **bicycles** for US$8 per day.

Accommodation

Although Tulum's beach is an obvious draw, you may want to stay in **town** if you arrive late in the day, have a limited amount of time or just prefer hot water round the clock. Hotel owners in the *zona hotelera* along the **beach** have voted against permanent electricity, relying instead on varying combinations of solar panels, windmills and diesel generators; most have electricity for only about six hours in the evening. Depending on your point of view, the candlelit ambience is charmingly rustic or expensive primitivism. Either way, the resulting calm – save for the crash of the surf – helps disguise the increasing development. The hotels closest to the ruins are some of the cheapest (and the ones that made this area famous with hippie backpackers), providing sand-floor cabañas with shared bathrooms and often little to no security – though this seems to be improving. Farther along, you'll see a few ritzier boutique resorts, with jet-set guests and prices to match.

For truly budget accommodation, the *Weary Traveler* (Ⓣ984/871-2389, Ⓦ www.theweary traveler.info; ❷), is your best choice and doubles as a backpacker **information** centre, which has **Internet** access, notice boards, and free maps of the area. On the beach, *Backpackers in Paradise*, just before *Papaya Playa*, offers dorm beds, but the price is higher (❸). You can **camp** at some of the cheaper cabaña spots very close to the ruins, or at *Camping Oasis Piedra del Sol* (❷), 5km south of the ruins on the road in from town, immediately past *Esmeralda K*.

In town

El Crucero just east of the highway, by the pedestrian entrance to the ruins Ⓣ984/871-2610, Ⓦ www.el-crucero.com. Fun, friendly hotel convenient to the ruins. Choose dorm beds, standard rooms or deluxe rooms with a/c and distinctive murals painted by a local artist. The bar-restaurant is extremely hospitable and even has a wireless Internet hub. ❷–❻

L'Hotelito on the main street, three blocks north of the bus station Ⓣ984/871-2061, Ⓔ hotelito@tulumabc.com. Small Italian-run, rustic-feeling hotel with a pretty garden and terrace restaurant. Upstairs rooms have high palapa ceilings with fans; downstairs rooms have a/c. ❺

On the beach

The hotels below are listed in order of their distance from the ruins, from closest to furthest.

Cabañas El Mirador left on the Punta Allen road, 1km from the ruins (no phone). Basic sandy-floor cabañas with beds or hammock hooks (bring your own or rent one of theirs). Shared bathroom with cold running water. The restaurant is perched on the cliff, with a wonderful view and cooling breezes. ❷–❹

Cabañas Don Armando's next door to *Cabañas El Mirador* Ⓔ cabanasarmandos@yahoo.com.mx. Sturdy, sandy-floored cabañas with security guards. Easily the most popular of the inexpensive places near the ruins (check in early) with a buzzing restaurant-bar, a constant party scene and a dive shop. ❹–❺

Diamante K 1.2km from the ruins Ⓣ984/871-2283, Ⓦ www.diamantek.com. Nicely decorated ecohotel run on solar energy with funky vegetarian restaurant, massage and sauna on site. A range of cabañas, from dorms to suites, are offered. ❹–❾

Papaya Playa right on the Punta Allen road, just south of the road that connects Tulum beach with the town Ⓣ984/804-6444, Ⓦ www.papayaplaya .com. Range of good accommodation, from spacious rooms with private bath and hot water to simple bamboo cabañas perched above the beach and tepees. Also has a small restaurant and bar playing chilled-out lounge beats. ❷–❻

Piedra Escondida 1.5km from the road junction ⓣ984/877-8288, ⓕ871-2217, ⓦwww.piedraescondida.com. Solid, comfortably furnished two-level cabañas with tile floors; each room has its own balcony and a view of the beach, a lovely sheltered cove. The Italian owners are very welcoming. Full breakfast is included. ❾

Cabañas Punta Piedra 2km from the junction ⓣ984/876-9167. Six rooms: one deluxe beachfront cabaña and five fairly basic cabins, but all with private bath. Bike rental and dive shop too. ❹–❻

Zamas 3km from the junction ⓕ984/871-2067, ⓦwww.zamas.com. Enormous rooms, some right on one of the prettiest stretches of beach in Tulum. Excellent Italian restaurant on site (see below) and trendy clientele. ❼–❾

Casa de Chio 500m from *Zamas* ⓣ984/806-1197, ⓔcasadechio@yahoo.com. Range of cabañas, from sand-floor basic to rustic suites with private bath, and an exceptionally friendly atmosphere. ❹–❻

Los Arrecifes 500m further south along the road ⓣ984/879-7307, ⓕ871-2092, ⓦwww.losarrecifestulum.com. Established some 25 years ago, this is one of the oldest places on this coast. Somewhat fancy cabañas with or without private bath in an idyllic setting with its own stretch of palm-fringed beach and a restaurant. ❺–❼

Esmeralda K 5km from the ruins ⓣ984/871-2283, ⓦwww.esmeraldak.com. Sister property of, and very similar to, *Diamante K*, with newer, handsome dark-wood cabañas on stilts. ❽

Nueva Vida de Ramiro 6.5km from the junction ⓣ984/877-8512, ⓕ871-2092, ⓦwww.tulumnv.com. Peaceful, rustic ecohotel with attractive and comfortable wooden cabins on stilts tucked among untamed greenery; the beach is splendid here, and the restaurant (guests only) serves tasty dishes. ❽

Las Ranitas 7.5km from the junction ⓣ/ⓕ984/877-8554, ⓦwww.lasranitas.com. This French-owned hotel is the fanciest on this coast, with all facilities – tennis courts, a pool and the like – as well as lovely rooms and an elegant restaurant and bar. ❾

Dos Ceibas next door to *Las Ranitas* ⓕ984/871-2335, ⓦwww.dosceibas.com. Small, attractive hotel with a variety of spacious, colourful cabañas in front of a turtle hatching beach. Yoga and meditation on site. ❻–❾

Eating

Because the accommodation in Tulum is spread over 10km and the village is 3km from the beach, almost every **hotel** in the place has its own restaurant – fittingly they range from cheap and grungy to very chic. Guests tend to stick to the restaurants in their hotels, but a couple **places to eat** along the coast road are worth making a trip to: *Gringo Dave's*, just north of the road into Tulum town, serves delicious fish and grilled meat in a clifftop setting; and *Que Fresco*, at the *Zamas* hotel is a very good Italian restaurant with a wood-fired pizza oven and fresh pasta. In the village, a number of cheap **cafés** serve comida comida and rotisserie chicken to the locals (and backpackers). *Charlie's*, opposite the bus stop, has good Mexican food, and *Il Giardino di Tony e Simone* rivals *Que Fresco* for the title of best Italian restaurant around (coming from the north, turn right before the first *tope* and the post office).

Cobá

Set in muggy rainforest 50km northwest of Tulum, the crumbling ancient city of **Cobá** (7am–6pm; US$3.70) is a fascinating and increasingly popular site. As it's scattered between two lakes and linked by a network of causeways, you'll need at least a couple of hours to see it all (although once inside you can rent bikes for US$3 per hour, or hire a *triciclo* cab) and it's well worth the effort, as much for the **wildlife** as for the ruins. The jungle around Cobá is home to toucans, egrets, herons and myriad tropical butterflies including the giant electric-blue morphius. There are plenty of vicious mosquitoes too, so bring lots of repellent.

The city's most surprising characteristic is a resemblance not to the great ruins of the Yucatán, but to those in lowland Guatemala and Honduras. Ceramic studies indicate that the city was occupied from about 100 AD up until the advent of the Spanish, and the site is even mentioned in the *Chilam Balam*, a book of Maya prophecy written in the eighteenth century and drawn from earlier oral tradition. Its zenith was in the Classic era (right up until about 800 AD) and most of the larger **pyramids** were built in this period, including the giant **Nocoh Mul**, tallest in the Yucatán and strikingly similar in its long, narrow and precipitous stairway to the famous Guatemalan ruins of Tikal. The city's influence and wealth during this period was derived from close links with the great cities of Petén, to the south, as the plethora of stelae, which are associated with Petén sites, and the style of almost all of the buildings and ceramics attest. Later, when the city maintained trade links with the Puuc cities to the west, the production of stelae ceased. In the early post-Classic era, from about 1000 AD, Cobá went into a brief decline, recovering in 1200 AD with a resurgence of new building which included the construction of the temple that crowns the Nocoh Mul pyramid.

If you turn right at the fork just before the ruins (following signs for Nuevo X-Can), you will reach after several kilometres the **monkey reserve** at Punta Laguna, which since 1994 has been a site for the scientific observation of one of the northernmost populations of spider monkeys. It's an informal affair, with a small entrance kiosk and often a neighbourhood child willing (for a small tip) to take you out to where the animals usually congregate.

Practicalities

Four **buses** a day run to Cobá from Tulum and continue on to Valladolid. The first one leaves Tulum at 7am and the next, which continues directly to Chichén Itzá after stopping in Valladolid, goes at 9am – therefore you could theoretically cover both sites via public transport from Tulum. Four buses run back to Tulum from Cobá, the last leaving at 5.30pm. Otherwise, a taxi from Tulum to Cobá costs US$21 each way.

The **village** of Cobá, where the bus stops, is little more than a cluster of houses and cabañas a few hundred metres from the site entrance. Two **hotels** represent the end points of the price spectrum: *Villas Arqueológicas* (Ⓣ/Ⓕ985/858-1527, Ⓦwww.clubmed.com; ❼), overlooking the lake, offers a wonderful bit of tropical luxury complete with swimming pool and archeological library. On the other end, *El Bocadito* (Ⓣ985/852-0052; ❸), right in the middle of the main street through the village, has very basic rooms. There's a good **restaurant** at the end of the village, *La Pirámide,* which sits beside the lake and serves Yucatecan specialities as well as other Mexican dishes. Other than this, there are several no-frills **cafés** by the entrance to the site. Don't swim in the lake here as it's full of crocodiles.

The Sian Ka'an Biosphere Reserve

Created by presidential decree in 1986, the 2400-square-kilometre **Sian Ka'an Biosphere Reserve** is one of the largest protected areas in Mexico. The name means "the place where the sky is born" in the Maya language, which seems utterly appropriate when you experience the sunrise on this stunningly beautiful coast. It's a huge, sparsely populated region, with only about a thousand permanent inhabitants, mainly fishermen, *chicleros* and *milpa* farmers.

Approximately one-third of the area is **tropical forest**, one-third **fresh- and salt-water marshes and mangroves**, and one-third marine environment, including a section of **the longest barrier reef in the western hemisphere**. The coastal forests and wetlands are particularly important feeding and wintering areas for North American migratory birds. Sian Ka'an contains examples of the principal ecosystems found in the Yucatán peninsula and the Caribbean, which include an astonishing variety of flora and fauna. All five species of Mexican wild **cat** – jaguar, puma, ocelot, margay and jaguarundi – are present, along with spider and howler **monkeys**, tapir, deer and the West Indian manatee. More than three hundred species of **birds** have been recorded, including flamingo, roseate spoonbill, white ibis, crested guan, wood stork, osprey and fifteen species of heron. The Caribbean beaches provide nesting grounds for four endangered species of **marine turtle**: the green, loggerhead, hawksbill and leatherback. Morelet's and mangrove **crocodiles** lurk in the swamps and lagoons.

The biosphere reserve concept, developed since 1974 by UNESCO, is an ambitious attempt to combine the protection of natural areas and the conservation of their genetic diversity with scientific research and sustainable development for local peoples. Reserves consist of a strictly protected **core area**, a designated **buffer zone** used for non-destructive activities, and an outer **transition zone**, merging with unprotected land, where traditional land use and experimental research take place. The success of the reserve depends to a great extent on the co-operation and involvement of local people, and the Sian Ka'an management plan incorporates several income-generating projects, such as improved fishing techniques, ornamental plant nurseries and low-impact tourism.

You can enter the reserve on your own (US$2), and there is accommodation at **Punta Allen**, the largest village in the reserve, or at the *Boca Paila Camps* (Ⓣ984/871-2499, Ⓦwww.siankaan.org; ❺), a new small-scale lodge run by the Centro Ecológico de Sian Ka'an, an organization started by an American ecologist who lives in the biosphere. The group funds its research and educational programmes with two **tours**, one starting around 8am and lasting until late afternoon, the other beginning shortly before sunset. Both begin with an instructive walk through mangroves and diverse ecosystems to a large cenote, followed by a boat ride across the lagoons and Maya-made canals, which criss-cross the reserve. It's a beautiful trip around the fringes of the reserve's vast open spaces, with excellent opportunities for bird-watching, especially on the sunset tour. You can reserve a place on either trip at Sian Ka'an Info Tours in Tulum (see p.788).

For further **information** on the biosphere, contact the Amigos de Sian Ka'an, a nonprofit organization formed to promote the aims for which the reserve was established. The Amigos support scientific research and produce a series of guide and reference books on the natural history of Sian Ka'an. Their main office is in Cancún (Ⓣ/Ⓕ998/880-6024, Ⓦwww.amigosdesiankaan.org).

Muyil (Chunyaxche)

The little-visited ruins of **Muyil** (daily 8am–5pm; US$2.40), also known as **Chunyaxche**, lie to the north of the reserve, about 20km south of Tulum. To get there catch any second-class **bus** heading between Tulum and Chetumal and ask to be dropped at the entrance. A sign on the west side of the highway points to the modest entrance, which has little more than a ticket booth and toilets. Despite the size of the site – probably the largest on the Quintana Roo coast – and its proximity to Hwy-307, you're likely to have the place to yourself.

Archeological evidence indicates that Muyil was continuously occupied from the pre-Classic period until after the arrival of the Spanish in the sixteenth century. There is no record of the inhabitants coming into direct contact with the Conquistadors, but they were probably victims of depopulation caused by European-introduced diseases. Most of the buildings you see today date from the post-Classic period, between 1200 AD and 1500 AD. The tops of the tallest structures, just visible from the road, rise 17m from the forest floor. There are more than one hundred mounds and temples, none of them completely clear of vegetation, and it's easy to wander around and find dozens of buildings buried in the jungle; climbing them is forbidden, however.

The centre of the site is connected by a *sacbe* to the small **Muyil lagoon** 500m away. This lagoon is joined to the large Chunyaxche lagoon and ultimately to the sea at **Boca Paila** by an amazing **canalized river**: the route used by Maya traders. If you travel along the river today you'll come across even less explored sites, some of which appear to be connected to the lagoon or river by **underwater caves**.

Leaving the site, particularly if you're making your way up to Tulum, should be easy enough, provided you don't leave it too late; continuing south could prove a little more difficult.

Punta Allen

Right at the tip of the peninsula, with a lighthouse guarding the northern entrance to the **Bahía de la Ascensión**, the remote Maya fishing village of **PUNTA ALLEN** is not the kind of place you stumble across by accident. The road south from Tulum is legendarily rutted in the rainy season, and is still slow going during the dry months. An alternative route is the somewhat better road through the reserve to El Playón (turn east off the highway 55km south of Tulum, or catch the 10am colectivo in Carrillo Puerto), where you can get a small launch to Punta Allen. Either way, the trip is so time-consuming that you will use half a day just getting there.

With a population of just four hundred, Punta Allen is the largest village within the reserve and a focus of initiatives by both government departments and nongovernmental organizations promoting sustainable development. During the summer, Earthwatch volunteers (see p.62) come here to assist scientists in gathering data.

Entering the village from the north, past the tiny naval station on the right and beached fishing boats on the left, the first of the **accommodation** options is *Cuzan Guest House* (Ⓣ983/834-0358, Ⓕ834-0292, Ⓦwww.flyfishmx.com; ❻), which specializes in bonefishing tours and rents tall conical cabañas and tepees, some with hot water. It has a bar and restaurant with information about the reserve, though you'll need to book meals if you're not staying there. At the far southern end of the village, the more bohemian *Posada Sirena* (Ⓣ984/877-8521, Ⓦwww.casasirena.com; ❺) has large cabañas with kitchens.

The village shop has a **long-distance phone** (Ⓣ984/871-2424), which serves the whole community – if you need to contact someone in Punta Allen this is the number to call. One small **restaurant**, the *Punta Allen,* serves basic seafood. A **mobile shop** in a truck travels the length of the peninsula on Thursdays and Saturdays, selling meat, bread, fruit and vegetables, reaching Punta Allen about 2pm. Although there's no dive shop, the hotels generally have some form of **water-sports equipment** for their guests, which they allow nonresidents to rent. Fishermen can be persuaded to take you into the reserve for a fee; they also go across the bay to El Playón. Victor Barrera is a recommended local guide who takes people fishing in the flat waters of Bahía de la Ascensión and organizes **eco-tours** (Ⓣ984/879-8040, Ⓦwww.macabimarch.com).

From Tulum to Chetumal

The road from Tulum to Chetumal skirts the Sian Ka'an Biosphere Reserve and heads inland, past Felipe Carrillo Puerto, a major crossroads on the routes to Valladolid and Mérida; through Limones, where there's a turn-off to the coastal towns of Mahahual and Xcalak; along the beautiful **Laguna Bacalar**; and on to **Chetumal**, the gateway to Belize and a good point from which to explore **Kohunlich** and other Maya sites.

Felipe Carrillo Puerto

FELIPE CARRILLO PUERTO, formerly known as **Chan Santa Cruz**, is a spiritual centre and the capital of the "Zona Maya" of Quintana Roo. During the Caste Wars, Maya from the north gathered forces here and took guidance and inspiration from a miraculous talking cross that told them to fight on against their oppressors. (Such talking crosses and statues are common in Maya mythology as conduits through which disincarnate spirits speak, or as manifestations of a soul, usually that of a shaman, when it has left the body during the state of trance; they are known as *way'ob* by the Yucatecan Maya.) Presumably as an attempt to disguise its rebellious past, the town was renamed after a former governor of the Yucatán who was assassinated in 1924. However, a monument to the martyrs of the Caste Wars still stands in the town. There are several reasonable **hotels** around the main plaza – try the cheery *Hotel Esquivel* (Ⓣ/Ⓕ983/834-0313; ❺) on the zócalo, only 100m from the small bus station, with a good, reasonably priced **restaurant** attached. If you're driving fill up with **petrol** in town, as it's the last filling station before Chetumal.

Laguna Bacalar

Further south, some 35km north of Chetumal, is the gorgeous **Laguna Bacalar**, the second largest lake in Mexico; 45km long and, on average, 1km wide, it links with a series of other lakes and eventually the Río Hondo and the sea. The village of Bacalar was a key point on the pre-Columbian trade route, and unexcavated **Maya remains** surround the lakeshore. The *Chilam Balam* of Chumayel, one of the Maya's sacred books, mentions it as the first settlement of the Itzá, the tribe that occupied Chichén Itzá. Near the village is a semi-ruinous **fort**: built by the Spanish for protection against British pirates from Belize (then British Honduras), it became a Maya stronghold in the Caste Wars, and was the last place to be subdued by the government, in 1901. The lake hosts a wide variety of **birdlife**, as well as huge fish that reach nearly 2m long. Nearby is the inky-blue "bottomless" **Cenote Azul**, which is busy with swimmers, picnickers and live musicians at weekends (8am–8pm; free).

There are several lakeshore **restaurants** in the village and a small range of options if you want to **stay overnight**. The wonderfully kitsch and comfortable *Hotel Laguna* (Ⓣ983/834-2206, Ⓕ834-2205; ❺–❻), south of town close to Cenote Azul, is done up with seashell-encrusted lacquer countertops and other obviously well-loved details. In town, *Hotelito El Paraíso* is a bargain lakefront choice, with big, clean suites and space for **camping** (Ⓣ983/839-2695; ❷–❺). Another good choice is *Amigos B&B* (Ⓣ983/834-2093, reservations in

Cozumel on 987/872-3868, Ⓕ872-4168, Ⓦwww.bacalar.net; ❻), which has a few lovely rooms overlooking the lake; breakfast is included in the rates. Several kilometres north of town, *Rancho Encantado* (Ⓣ983/753-3869, Ⓦwww.encantado.com; ❾ including breakfast and dinner) is a small New Age resort on the lakeshore, with a dozen very pretty cabaña suites and a resident massage therapist; it also organizes trips to Kohunlich and other Maya sites.

Chetumal and around

If you're heading south to Belize or Guatemala, you can't avoid **CHETUMAL**, capital of the state of Quintana Roo and about 15km from the Belize border. After being obliterated by Hurricane Janet in 1955, the place is finally beginning to reassert itself, but it still has no notable "sights" to speak of. Indeed, the city of Chetumal is largely oblivious to tourists – which can be refreshing after the rural hedonism of the Mayan Riviera. Moreover, everything is cheaper here, from gas to food to Internet cafés. Originally designated a duty-free zone and now levying only nominal customs charges, the city prospers in a brisk trade in an odd assortment of goods: Dutch cheese, Taiwanese hi-fis, American peanuts, reproduction Levi's from the Far East, Scotch whisky. Chetumal is clearly a border town, as everything from the language (many people speak English) to the clapboard houses demonstrates Belizean influence. Although it can't really be recommended as a destination, Chetumal does make a decent one- or two-day stop for resting, restocking at the numerous shops and strolling the revamped waterfront. You could also make day-trips to archeological sites west from here, though car rental is the one thing in Chetumal that's not a great deal.

The main attraction, on Avenida Niños Héroes at the northern edge of the centre, is the **Museo de la Cultura Maya** (Tues–Sun 9am–7pm; US$5). The numerous interactive displays and models provide a fascinating insight into ancient Maya society, mathematics and cosmology. The *Alegoría del Mestizaje* sculpture out front is one of the most striking depictions of the popular theme of the intermingling of Spanish and indigenous cultures, showing the Mexican born of a Conquistador and a Mayan woman. The **Centro Cultural de las Bellas Artes**, in a striking 1936 neo-Maya-style school, now houses the **city museum** (Tues–Sun 9am–7pm; US$2) as well as the state schools for the performing arts – plenty of live performances take place here. Avenida Héroes leads down to the bay and the shiny new malecón, popular for evening strolls and fishing. A few blocks east, behind the modern Palacio Legislativo on the malecón, is a small Caribbean house containing the fascinating **Maqueta Payo Obispo**: a hand-carved scale model of Chetumal as it looked in the 1920s.

Arrival and information

Chetumal's main **bus station** is on the north side of town, a short taxi ride from the centre, and the **airport** is only 2km west of town, at the end of Avenida Revolución. **Avenida Niños Héroes**, the town's main street, runs down from a big electricity-generating plant to the waterfront. The **tourist information** office, on Avenida 5 de Mayo at Avenida Carmen Ochoa (8.30am–4pm; Ⓣ983/835-0500), is helpful with information on buses, hotels and maps; they can also give information on Belize. The **bus ticket office** in town is on Avenida Belice between avenidas Gandhi and Colón.

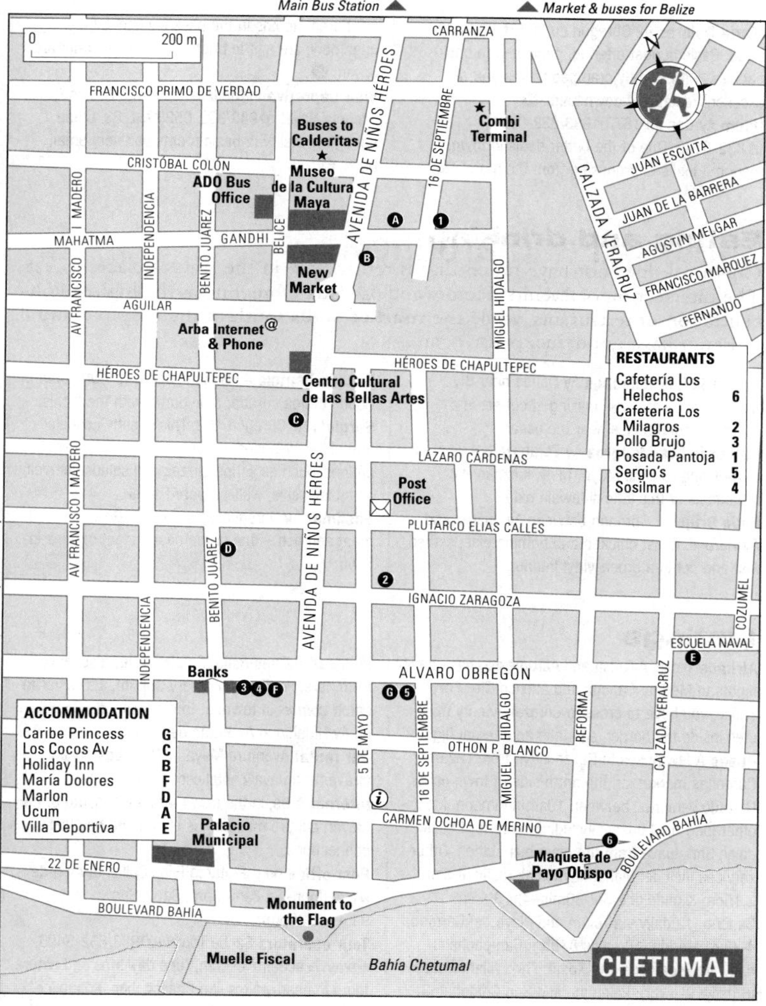

Accommodation

Most of Chetumal's **hotels** are on or near Avenida Héroes.

Caribe Princess Av Obregon 168 ⓣ983/832-0900. Best evidence of the city's time-warp ritz: shades of pink and smoky mirrors form the decorating scheme, but rooms are clean and all have a/c; free parking. ➎

Los Cocos Av Héroes 134 ⓣ983/832-0544, ⓕ832-0920, ⓔreservaciones@hotelloscocos.com. A better deal than the *Holiday Inn*, with large, comfortable rooms, a pool, a car rental agency and a sprawling terrace bar and restaurant. ➐–➒

Holiday Inn Av Héroes 171 ⓣ983/835-0400, ⓕ832-1676, ⓔhotel@holidayinnmaya.com.mx. The nicest luxury option in town, with all the comforts of a chain hotel, including a travel agency, though compared to the giant suites at *Los Cocos*, you're paying for the name. ➒

María Dolores Av Obrégon no 206 ⓣ983/832-0508. Basic budget offering, popular with backpackers, with slightly cramped rooms, but an excellent restaurant downstairs. ❹

Ucum Av Gandhi 167 ⓣ983/832-0711, ⓕ832-6185. One of the better deals in town, though it looks unpromising from the motel-like front area. Rooms in the back section, by the huge pool, are a little brighter and have either a/c or fan. ❹

Villa Deportiva in the local sporting club on C Escuela Naval ⓣ983/832-0525 ext. 23. Clean enough hostel with basic rooms and very small beds. ❶

Eating and drinking

Chetumal does not have much that is remarkable in the way of places to eat. The intersection of Avenida Héroes and Avenida Obregón has the highest concentration of restaurants, while the **market stalls** south of the Mayan cultural museum have good, inexpensive fare.

Cafetería Los Helechos Av Ochoa near Blv Bahía. Pretty café, specializing in coffee, in a scenic wooden house near the ocean.

Cafetería Los Milagros Av Zaragoza between Av Héroes and Av 5 de Mayo. Tasty, inexpensive breakfasts at this little sidewalk café.

Pollo Brujo Av Obregón between Av Juárez and Av Héroes. Roast chicken and nothing else, served fast and hot in a green-vinyl interior.

Posada Pantoja Av Gandhi, opposite *Hotel Ucum*. Good comida corrida, a favourite with the locals.

Sergio's Av Obregón 182. This slightly upscale (but still well-priced) restaurant has a few veggie options, such as soups, pizzas and salads, as well as inexpensive, well-prepared steak.

Sosilmar Av Obregón, in the *María Dolores*. Good meat and fish – one of the best budget options in town.

Listings

Airlines Tacsa, Aviacsa and Aeroméxico have daily flights to Mérida, Cancún and Mexico City. For Belize, you have to cross to Corozal, twenty minutes inside the border, and take an internal flight.

Buses A few buses to Belize leave from Lázaro Cárdenas market, on the north side of town on Av Calzado Veracruz, between 10am and noon. Most other long-haul buses, including more for Belize (5 daily; 3hr), leave from the main bus station. Other services include: Mahahual/Xcalak (daily at 6am, 3.15pm & midnight; 3hr 30min–4hr 30min); Cancún (12 daily via Tulum and Playa del Carmen; 4–6hr); Mérida (10 daily; 8–9hr); Campeche (1 daily via Escárcega and Xpujil; 7hr); Villahermosa (6 daily; 9–11hr); Palenque and San Cristóbal (3 daily; 7–10hr); Mexico City (2 daily; 24hr). Buses to Flores in Guatemala (2 daily; 12hr) also leave from here. For Bacalar (every 30min), it's easier to catch *combis* in town, at the Terminal de Combis on Av Hidalgo at Av Primo de Verdad.

Car rental Aventura Maya in *Hotel Los Cocos* ⓔaventuramaya@hotelloscocos.com.mx.

Internet Arba, in the new market just south of the Mayan culture museum, is cheap and has fast connections.

Post office on C Plutarco Elias Calles at Av 5 de Mayo (Mon–Fri 8am–6pm, Sat & Sun 9am–12.30pm).

Tour operators Sacbe Travel (ⓣ983/832-3496, ⓦwww.sacbetravel.com) runs day-trips and nature tours to nearby sites like Chacchoben, Kohunlich and Dzibanché, as well as some sites in Belize.

Around Chetumal

Near Chetumal are any number of refreshing escapes from the heat and dull modernity. At weekends, the town descends en masse on **CALDERITAS**, a small seaside resort just 6km north around the bay; there's only one **place to stay**, the *Sunrise on the Caribbean* trailer park, which has nice rooms (ⓣ983/834-4000, ⓕ834-4076; ❻) and a large picturesque garden with swimming pool right on the seafront. The **Laguna Milagros**, off the road towards Francisco Escárcega, is less spectacular than Bacalar, but is superb for bird-watching. Seven kilometres north of Calderitas, **OXTANKAH** (Mon–Sat 8am–5pm; US$2.20) is a small Maya site with the remains of a maritime city occupied principally in the Classic period (200–600 AD) and developed to exploit ocean resources – specifically salt. What remain are the ruins of several buildings around two squares, with an architectural style similar to that of the Petén region, and a chapel built by the Spanish conquerors. It's a peaceful wooded place with trees – *ceiba, yaxche* – and other flora neatly labelled, including one incredibly enormous *higo* tree just west of the chapel. You'll need your own transport to get there (follow the shoreline north through Calderitas) or a taxi, as there's no bus.

XCALAK is a tiny fishing community at the tip of the isthmus that stretches like a finger towards Belize on the other side of the huge Bahía de Chetumal. Unfortunately the village was flattened by the 1955 hurricane and still looks desolate and grim. It is without regular electricity or reliable phone lines, and there are no spectacular beaches or much else of note in the village. The reason to visit is the superb **fishing, snorkelling** and **diving** around the (as yet) pristine offshore reef as well as the vast atoll of **Banco Chinchorro** (though this area is more quickly accessible from Mahahual to the north). The best place in town to splash out is *Marina Mike's* (ⓣ983/831-0063, ⓦwww.hotelinxcalak.com; ❼–❽), at the northern end of the village, which has a handful of gorgeous rooms with fully fitted kitchens, huge balconies overlooking the sea and its own tiny beach. If you're on a budget, check out the palapas and **campsites** at the new *Mayan Village* (no phone, ask around town for Alan; ❶–❹), just over the bridge on the north side of town. Further north, on the very rough road to Mahahual, is a series of small hotels – the best of which is *Costa de Cocos* (ⓣ983/831-0110, ⓦwww.costadecocos.com; ❼), a laid-back spot with its own fishing boats and dive instructor and good snorkelling right off the dock; rates include a continental breakfast buffet, and their **restaurant**, which is the only place to eat in the area, is excellent and reasonably priced. Offering a bit more beachfront-luxury are *Tierra Maya*, 2km from Xcalak (ⓣ983/831-0404, ⓕ627-0089, ⓦwww.tierramaya.net; ❼); and the charming *Sin Duda Villas*, 8km further north (ⓣ983/831-0006, ⓦwww.sindudavillas.com; ❼–❾). In town, a PADI dive shop (ⓣ983/831-0461, ⓦwww.xcalak.com.mx) runs **snorkelling trips** (US$25; 2hr) and open-water certification courses (US$325). Otherwise the *San Jordi* bar in the village has information on **bird-watching and boat trips**.

MAHAHUAL, 55km north of Xcalak and now accessible by a fast road, has a small European expat community (Xcalak's foreign-born residents are almost exclusively North American), a tiny beach and, just outside of town, a new **petrol station**. It's slightly more cheerful than Xcalak, with a few basic *ceviche* restaurants in the centre of town. Though a cruise-ship pier has been built just to the north, it's had little effect on the slow pace here. You'll find a wider range of budget **accommodation** and it's slightly closer to the Chinchorro atoll if you want to go diving. About 15km north of town is *KaiLuumcito* (ⓣ1-800-538-6802 in the US, ⓦwww.mexicoholiday.com; ❾), an eight-tent version of *KaiLuum II,* the deluxe camping resort near Playa del Carmen. At the southern edge of Mahahual, you can **camp** or rent a basic room at *Las Cabañas del Doctor* (ⓣ983/832-2101; ❶–❹); a little farther on, *La Cabaña de Tío Phil* (ⓣ983/835-7166, ⓔtiophilhome@hotmail.com; ❺) also has comfortable rooms and can organize snorkelling and boat trips. Six kilometres south of town, along the bumpy old road to Xcalak, is new eco-sensitive *Balamku* (ⓣ983/838-0083, ⓦwww.balamku.com; ❻), which recycles wastewater, conserves trees and rents a few tasteful white thatch-roof cottages. A bit farther, *Garza Azul* (no phone; ❹) and *Kabah-Na*

Fiestas

JANUARY

The first week of January sees the festival of the Magi in **Tizimín** (Yucatán), an important religious and secular gathering.

6 FIESTA DE POLK KEKEN in **Lerma** (Campeche), near Campeche, with many traditional dances.

21 In **Dzitas** (Yuc), north of Chichén Itzá, an ancient festival with roots in Maya tradition.

Last Sunday In **Temax** (Yuc), between Mérida and Tizimín, this day is celebrated with a fiesta – the culmination of a week's religious celebration.

FEBRUARY

CARNAVAL (the week before Lent, variable Feb–March) is at its most riotous in **Mérida**, though it's celebrated, too, in **Campeche** and **Chetumal** and on **Isla Mujeres** and **Cozumel**.

MARCH

20 FERIA DE LAS HAMACAS in **Tecoh** (Yuc), a hammock-producing village near Mérida.

21 EQUINOX. Huge gathering to see the serpent shadow at **Chichén Itzá**.

APRIL

SEMANA SANTA (Holy Week beginning Palm Sunday, variable March/Apirl) is celebrated with particularly colourful Passion plays in **Mérida**, **Acanceh** and **Maní** (Yuc).

13-17 The traditional festival of honey and corn in **Hopelchén** (Cam).

MAY

3 DÍA DE LA SANTA CRUZ is the excuse for another fiesta in **Hopelchén** (Cam); also celebrated in **Celestún** (Yuc) and **Felipe Carrillo Puerto** (Quintana Roo).

12–18 Fiesta in **Chankán Veracruz** (QR), near Felipe Carrillo Puerto, celebrating the Holy Cross which spoke to the Maya here and gave inspiration for the Caste Wars.

20 FERIA DEL JIPI in **Becal** (Cam), celebration for the *jipi* hat which is the major industry in the town.

(Ⓣ983/838-2195, Ⓦwww.kabahna.com.mx; ❺) are attractive, good-value cabañas and can provide meals on request – though note that beaches down this way are not quite as nice. The coast's major dive outfit, well equipped with boats large enough to reach the Banco Chinchorro, is at the *Maya Ha* resort (Ⓣ983/831-0065, Ⓦwww.mayaharesort.com; ❾), about 15km from town. Foodwise, there's only the usual selection of *ceviche* restaurants.

Local **buses** to Mahahual and Xcalak leave Chetumal at 6am, 3.15pm and midnight daily from the main bus terminal. The bus runs only on the new inland highways – to reach lodging on the coast between the towns, you'll have to take a taxi or hitch a ride. Coming from Cancún you can connect with this service at Limones if you're there by 7.30am or 4.30pm. Buses to Calderitas leave from Avenida Cristóbal Colón, near the junction with Avenida Héroes. Travelling around this area, keep your passport and tourist card with you; as in all border zones, there are checkpoints on the roads.

JUNE

26–30 The Festival of San Pedro and San Pablo celebrated on **Cozumel** and in **Panaba** (Yuc), north of Tizimín.

JULY

15–30 Fiestas for the patron saint of **Ciudad del Carmen** (Cam).
At **Edzná** (Cam, date variable) a Maya ceremony to the god Chac is held to encourage, or celebrate, the arrival of the rains.

AUGUST

10–16 Feria in **Oxcutzcab** (Yuc).

SEPTEMBER

14 DÍA DE SAN ROMAN. In **Dzan** (Yuc), near Ticul, the end of a four-day festival with fireworks, bullfights, dances and processions. In **Campeche** (Cam) the Feria de San Roman lasts until the end of the month.
21 EQUINOX. Another serpent spectacle at **Chichén Itzá**.
29 DÍA DE SAN MIGUEL is celebrated with a major festival in **Maxcanu** (Yuc), on the road from Mérida to Campeche.

OCTOBER

The first two weeks of October in **Mérida** see processions and celebrations associated with the miraculous statue of Cristo de las Ampollas.
18 A pilgrimage centred on **Izamal** (Yuc) starts ten days of celebration, culminating in dances on the night of the 28th.

NOVEMBER

1–2 DAY OF THE DEAD celebrated almost everywhere in the country.
8–13 Feria in **Tekax** (Yuc), on the road from Mérida to Felipe Carrillo Puerto, with dances and bullfights.

DECEMBER

3–8 Popular fiesta with traditional dances in **Kantunilkin** (QR).
8 DÍA DE LA INMACULADA CONCEPCIÓN is widely celebrated, but especially in **Izamal** (Yuc) and **Champotón** (Cam), each of which has a fiesta starting several days earlier.

Kohunlich and other Maya sites in the south

The most direct route from Chetumal back towards central Mexico is across the bottom of the peninsula along Hwy-186 via Francisco Escárcega. Though the road enters the forests of the Calakmul Biosphere Reserve in Campeche state, in Quintana Roo most of the trees have been felled to ranch cattle for the fast-food and beef industries. The only worthwhile stop along the road is the Classic Maya city of **Kohunlich**, set some 60km from Chetumal, then another 9km off the road from the village of Francisco Villa (daily 8am–5pm; US$3.70).

The ruins, seldom visited by anyone other than butterflies and birds, are beautifully situated, peering out above the treetops. The buildings date from the late pre-Classic to the Classic periods (100–900 AD) and the majority are in the Río Bec architectural style. Foliage has reclaimed most of them, and those that are cleared are little more than pyramid-shaped piles of rubble, looted by grave-robbers before archeologists could preserve them. A notable exception is the Temple of the Masks, named after the four two-metre-high stucco masks that decorate its facade. Disturbing enough now, these wide-eyed, open-mouthed gods once stared out from a background of smooth, bright-red-painted stucco. Other structures, following recent reconstruction efforts, include a ball-court, the Pixa'an palace and an area called Ya'axna, which was a residential compound with a ceremonial centre and now offers wonderful views over the jungle canopy from its tall temples.

You can also visit other Maya sites in the south of Quintana Roo including the impressive Río Bec ruins at **Dzibanché** and **Kinichná**, as well as the recently opened excavations at **Chacchoben**. At present there is no public transport to any of these ruins (or to Kohunlich), but Chacchoben is the most accessible of the bunch, 9km west off Hwy-307, just south of the turn-off to Mahahual. The other two are north of Hwy-186, outside of Chetumal. If you're without a car the best way to see Dzibanché and Kinichná is to take a taxi tour from **Xpujil** (see p.723), though it's worth checking with the tourist office in Chetumal about alternative options.

Travel details

Buses

The most useful bus services are those between Mérida and Cancún and those provided by Mayab, which run at least every thirty minutes between Cancún and Playa del Carmen. Some places aren't served by first-class buses, but second-class buses and *combis* or colectivos will get you around locally and to the nearest major centre. The following frequencies and times are for both first- and second-class services, but you can also check ⓦwww.ticketbus com.mx for up-to-date schedules on major routes in the peninsula and to buy tickets from a number of different bus companies, including ADO, Autotransportes del Sur and Mayab.

Cancún to: Campeche (7 daily; 7hr); Chetumal (hourly 5am–midnight; 6hr); Mérida (hourly; 4–6hr); Playa del Carmen (every 30min; 1hr); Puerto Morelos (every 30min; 30min); Tizimín (6 daily; 4hr); Tulum (12 daily; 2hr); Valladolid (hourly; 3hr); Villahermosa (14 daily; 12hr).

Chetumal to: Bacalar (every 30min: 30min); Belize City via Orange Walk (5 daily; 3hr); Campeche (1 daily via Escárcega and Xpujil; 7hr); Cancún (12 daily via Tulum and Playa del Carmen; 6hr); Flores, Guatemala (2 daily; 12hr); Mahahual/Xcalak (3 daily; 3hr 30min–4hr 30min); Mérida (10 daily; 8–9hr); Mexico City (2 daily; 24hr); Palenque and San Cristóbal de las Casas (3 daily; 7–10hr); Villahermosa (5 daily; 9–11hr).

Playa del Carmen to: Cancún (every 30min; 1hr); Chetumal (hourly 6am–midnight; 4–5hr); Cobá (2 daily; 2hr); Mérida (13 daily; 5hr); Palenque and San Cristóbal de las Casas (5 daily; 11–17hr); Tulum (frequently; 1hr); Tuxtla Gutiérrez (4 daily; 18–19hr); Valladolid (5 daily; 3hr); Villahermosa (10 daily; 12hr).

Tulum to: Cancún (frequently; 2hr); Chetumal (8 daily via Bacalar; 3–4hr); Cobá (4 daily; 1hr); Mérida (6 daily; 4–7hr); Playa del Carmen (frequently; 1hr); San Cristóbal de las Casas (3 daily via Palenque; first-class: 10hr; second-class: 24hr); Valladolid (5 daily; 4hr).

Ferries

Ferry services run frequently to **Isla Mujeres, Cozumel** and **Isla Holbox**. Although there are car ferries to all three islands, it's hardly worth taking a vehicle to any – Holbox and Mujeres are small, and the Cozumel ferry is very expensive.

Passenger ferries

Chiquilá to: Isla Holbox (8 daily; 30min).

Playa del Carmen to: Cozumel (every 2hr 8am–10pm; 30min).

Puerto Juárez, Cancún to: Isla Mujeres (every 30min 6.30am–11.30pm; 15min).

Car ferries

Chiquilá to: Isla Holbox (2 daily; 1hr).

Puerto Morelos to: Cozumel – erratic, so call ahead (3 daily; 2hr 30min).

Punta Sam to: Isla Mujeres (5 daily).

Flights

Cancún and Cozumel both have busy **international airports** with several daily flights to Mexico City and regular connections to Miami and many other cities in the southern US. Mérida's airport also receives a few international flights, primarily from Miami and Houston, and Chetumal has daily direct services to Mexico City. Around the Caribbean coast various small companies fly light planes – frequently between Cancún and Cozumel, less often from these places to Isla Mujeres, Playa del Carmen and Tulum.

Contexts

Contexts

The historical framework

The nation of Mexico, with its current borders, has only existed around 150 years. The loose political entity known as Mexico dates back to the Spanish Conquest – but anything before the sixteenth century is largely a matter of oral histories recorded long after the events or of archeological conjecture, as the Spanish did their best to erase all traces of the cultures that preceded them.

The earlier cultures were not confined to present-day Mexico, but spread throughout the area known as **Mesoamerica**, which extends from the mid-north of Mexico well into Central America to the south. The north of this region was occupied by native peoples who never abandoned their nomadic, hunter-gatherer existence; the south was ruled by a succession of powerful empires including the Aztecs and the Maya (who at one time spread all the way from south-eastern Mexico into what is now Honduras). Within Mesoamerica some of the world's most extraordinary societies flourished, creating – without the use of metal tools, draught animals or the wheel – vast cities controlling millions of people, intricate statuary and sculpture and a mathematical and calendar system more advanced than those known in the "civilized" world.

The **prehistory** set out below is based on archeological theories which are generally, but by no means universally, accepted. There are still major questions – especially concerned with the extent and nature of the contact between the societies and their influence on each other – which, should they be solved, may overturn many existing notions.

Prehistory

The exact date when human beings first crossed the Bering Strait into the Americas is debatable, but the earliest widely accepted date is around 15,000 years ago. Successive waves of nomadic, Stone Age hunters continued to arrive until around 6000 BC, pushing their predecessors gradually further south.

The first signs of settled habitation – the cultivation of corn, followed by the emergence of crude pottery, stone tools and even of trade between the regions – seem to come from the **Archaic** period, around 5000–2000 BC. The first established civilization does not appear until the **pre-Classic** or **Formative** era (2500 BC to 250 AD) with the rise of the Olmecs.

Still the least-known of all the ancient societies, **Olmec** cities thrived in the low-lying coastal jungles of Tabasco and Veracruz. Many of the Olmec's political, cultural, artistic and architectural innovations can be observed in later Mesoamerican cultures. What you see of them in the museums today is a magnificent artistic style, exemplified in their sculpture and in the famous colossal heads. These, with their puzzling "baby-faced" features, were carved from monolithic blocks of basalt and somehow transported over ninety kilometres from the quarries to their final settings – proof in itself of a hierarchical society commanding a sizeable workforce.

Classic civilizations

By the end of the **pre-Classic** period, the Olmec civilization was already in decline – La Venta, the most important cultural centre, seems to have been abandoned around 400 BC, and the other towns followed over the next few hundred years. As the Olmec weakened, new civilizations grew in strength and numbers, establishing cities throughout central Mexico. However, these sites, such as Monte Albán, near Oaxaca, were obviously influenced by the earlier Olmec culture. To the north, in the great Valley of México (where Mexico City now stands, an area then known as Anahuac), many small cities grew. Tlatilco, one of the towns in Anahuac, hoarded Olmec objects, suggesting significant contact with the civilization to the south – at least through trade. Meanwhile there were hints of more important things to come: Cuicuilco (now in the capital's suburbs) was an important city until it was buried by a volcanic eruption around the beginning of the first century AD, and at the same time the first important buildings of Teotihuacán were being constructed.

The city of Teotihuacán rose in central Mexico and dominated during the **Classic Period** (250–900 AD) as the first truly urban society, with its architectural and religious influences reaching as far south as the Maya heartlands of Guatemala. Even today, the ruins of the city, with the great Pyramids of the Sun and Moon, are an impressive testimony to the strength of the civilization. Historically, little is known about Teotihuacán, including details about its people or rulers, or even its true name (Teotihuacán was coined later by the Aztecs – it means "the place where men became gods"). What is certain is that the city's period of greatness ended around 650 AD, and that within a century it had been abandoned altogether. Mysteriously, societies throughout Mesoamerica, and in particular the Maya, seem to have been disrupted at much the same time, and many other important sites were deserted.

The great **Maya** centres had also reached the peak of their artistic, scientific and architectural achievements in the Classic period, above all their cities in the lowlands of Guatemala and Honduras. These survived longer than Teotihuacán, but by around 800 AD had also been abandoned. In the Yucatán the Maya fared rather better, their cities revived from about 900 by an injection of ideas (and perhaps invaders) from central Mexico. The famous structures at Chichén Itzá mostly date from this later phase, around 900–1100 AD.

In general, the Classic era saw development everywhere – other important centres grew up on the Gulf coast at El Tajín and in the Zapotec areas around Monte Albán – followed by very rapid decline. There are numerous theories to account for this – and certainly the fall of Teotihuacán must have severely affected its trading partners throughout Mexico – but none is entirely convincing. In all probability, once started, the disasters had a knock-on effect, and probably they were provoked by some sort of agricultural failure or ecological disaster which led to a loss of faith in the rulers, perhaps even rebellion.

Toltecs and Aztecs

The start of the **post-Classic** era (900–1520 AD) saw the beginning of a series of invasions from the north which must have exacerbated any existing problems. Wandering tribes would arrive in the fertile Valley of México, like what they saw, build a city adopting many of the styles and religions of their predecessors in the area, enjoy a brief period of dominance and be subdued in turn by a new wave of invaders, or Chichimeca. All such marauding tribes were known as Chichimec, which implies barbarian (even if many of them were at least semi-civilized before they arrived), and all claimed to have set out on their journeys from the legendary seven caves of Chicomoztoc. Many cities were founded in the valley, and many achieved brief ascendancy (or at least independence), but two names stand out in this bellicose era – the Toltecs and the Aztecs.

The **Toltec** people, who dominated the central valleys around 950–1150 AD, were among the first to arrive – indeed some say that it was a direct attack by them that destroyed Teotihuacán. They assumed a mythical significance for the Aztecs, who regarded them as the founders of every art and science and claimed direct descent from Toltec blood. In fact, it appears that the Toltecs borrowed most of their ideas from Teotihuacán.

Nevertheless, there were developments under the Toltecs, and in particular the cult of **Quetzalcoatl** assumed new importance: the god is depicted everywhere at Tula, the Toltec capital (where he may have been embodied as a king or dynasty of kings), and it was from here that he was driven out by the evil god Texcatlipoca. The prediction of his return was later to have fatal consequences. The structure of Toltec society, too, was at least as militaristic as it was religious, and human sacrifice was practised on a far larger scale than had been seen before.

When the **Aztecs** (or Mexica) arrived in central Mexico around the end of the twelfth century they found numerous small city-states, more or less powerful, but none in a position of dominance. They spent some years scavenging and raiding until about 1345 – when legend has it that they found the prophesied sign (an eagle perched on a cactus devouring a snake) to build their own city.

The new city, **Tenochtitlán**, was to become the heart of the most formidable of all Mexican empires, but its birth was still not easy. The chosen setting, an island in a lake (now Mexico City), was hardly promising, and the city was at first a subject of its neighbours. The Mexica overcame the lack of arable land by growing crops on floating reed islands that they fashioned in the lake. This agricultural success led to self-sufficiency and a burgeoning population. They became the most powerful civilization in the valley, and around 1429 formed a triple alliance with neighbouring Texcoco and Tlacopán to establish the basis of the **Aztec empire**. Its achievements were remarkable – in less than a hundred years the Aztecs had come to control, and demand labour tribute and taxes from, the whole of central and southern Mexico. Tenochtitlán became huge – certainly the invading Spanish could not believe its size and grandeur – but however much it grew, the gods continued to demand more war: to suppress rebellious subjects, and to provide fresh victims for the constant rituals of human sacrifice.

Meanwhile, other societies had continued much as before. In present-day Oaxaca the Zapotecs were subjected to invasions by **Mixtecs** from the mountains in much the same way as was happening in central Mexico. By war and alliance the Mixtecs came eventually to dominate the region – developing the crafts of the potter and goldsmith as never before – and fell to the Aztecs only in the last years before the Spanish Conquest. In the Yucatán, the Maya were never conquered, but their civilization was in decline and any form of central authority had long since broken down. Nevertheless, they carried on trade all around the coasts, and Christopher Columbus himself (though he never got to Mexico) encountered a heavily laden boat of **Maya** traders, plying the sea between Honduras and the Yucatán. On the Gulf coast Aztec supremacy was total by the time the Spanish arrived, but they were still struggling to subdue the west.

The Spanish Conquest

Hernán Cortés landed on the coast near modern Veracruz on April 21, 1519 – Good Friday. With him there were just 550 men, a few horses, dogs and a cannon; yet in less than three years they had defeated the Aztecs and effectively established control over most of Mexico. Several factors enabled them to do so. First was Cortés himself, as ruthless a leader as any in history: he burned the expedition's boats within days of their arrival, so that there was literally no turning back. In addition, his men had little to lose and much to gain, and their metal weapons and armour were greatly superior to anything the Aztecs had (although many Spaniards adopted Aztec-style padded cotton, which was warmer, lighter and almost as protective). Their gunpowder and cannon could also wreak havoc on opposing armies – both physically and psychologically. The horses and trained attack dogs, too, terrified the Aztecs. None of these, though, in the end counted a fraction as much as Cortés' ability to form alliances with tribes who were fretting under Aztec subjugation and whose numbers eventually swelled his armies tenfold.

Moctezuma, the Aztec leader, could certainly have destroyed the Spanish before they left their first camp, since his spies had brought news of their arrival almost immediately. Instead he sent a delegation bearing gifts of gold and jewels which he hoped would persuade them to leave in peace. They served only to inflame the greed of the Spanish. By all accounts Moctezuma was a morose, moody and indecisive man, but his failure to act against Cortés had deeper roots: he was also heavily influenced by religious omens, and the arrival of Cortés coincided with the predicted date for the return of **Quetzalcoatl**. The invaders were fair-skinned and bearded, as was Quetzalcoatl, and they had come from the east, where the deity had vanished – moreover it seemed they bore a peaceful message like that of the god, for one of their first acts was always to ban human sacrifice. So although he put obstacles in their way, tried to dissuade them, and even persuaded his allies to fight them, when the Spanish finally reached Tenochtitlán in November 1519, Moctezuma welcomed them to the city as his guests. They promptly repaid this hospitality by taking him prisoner within his own palace.

This "phony war", during which Spanish troops skirmished with a number of other Indian tribes and made allies of many – most significantly the **Tlaxcalans** – lasted for about a year. In April 1520 news came of a second Spanish expedition, led by Pánfilo Narváez, which was under orders to capture Cortés and take him back to Cuba (the mission had always been unofficial, and many others hoped to seize the wealth of Mexico for themselves). Again, though, Cortés proved the more decisive commander – he marched back east, surprised Narváez by night, killed him, and persuaded most of his troops to switch allegiance.

Meanwhile the Spaniards left behind in Tenochtitlán had finally provoked their hosts beyond endurance by killing a group of priests during a religious ceremony, and were under siege in their quarters. Cortés, with his reinforcements, fought his way back into the city on June 24, only to find himself trapped as well. On June 27, Moctezuma (still a prisoner) was killed – according to the Spanish, stoned to death by his own people while attempting to appeal for peace. Finally Cortés decided to break out on the night of the 30th – still commemorated as the **Noche Triste** – when the Spanish lost over half their number on the causeways across the lake. Most of them were so weighed down with gold and booty that they were barely able to move, let alone swim in the places where the bridges had been destroyed.

Once more, though, the Aztecs failed to follow up their advantage, and the Spanish survivors managed to reach the haven of their allies in Tlaxcala where they could regroup. The final assault on the capital began in January 1521, with more fresh troops and supplies, and more and more Indians throwing in their lot with the Spanish. Tenochtitlán was not only besieged (the Spanish built ships which could be sailed on the lake) but ravaged by an epidemic of smallpox, among whose victims was Moctezuma's successor, Cuitlahuac. They held out for several more months under **Cuauhtémoc** – the only hero of this long episode in Mexican eyes – but on August 13, 1521, Tenochtitlán finally fell to the Spanish.

Although much of the country remained to be pacified, the defeat of the Aztec capital made it inevitable that it eventually would be.

Colonial rule

By dint of his success, Cortés was appointed Governor of **Nueva España** (New Spain) in 1522, although in practice he was watched over constantly by minders from Spain, and never therefore had much real freedom of action. There followed three hundred years of direct Spanish rule, under a succession of 61 viceroys personally responsible to the king in Spain. By the end of the sixteenth century the entire country had been effectively subjugated, and its boundaries stretched by exploration from Panama to the western states of the US (although the area from Guatemala down, including the Mexican state of Chiapas, was soon under separate rule).

When the Spanish arrived, the **native population** of central Mexico was at least 25 million; by the beginning of the nineteenth century the total population of Nueva España was just six million, and at most half of these were pure-blooded natives. Some had been killed in battle, a few as a result of ill-treatment or simply from being left without homes or land to live on, but the vast majority died as a result of successive epidemics of European diseases to which the New World had no natural immunity. The effects were catastrophic, and not only for the Indians themselves. The few survivors found the burden of labour placed on them ever-increasing as their numbers dwindled – for certainly no European man came to Mexico to do manual work – and became more and more like slaves.

The first tasks, in the Spanish mind, were of reconstruction, pacification and conversion. Tenochtitlán had already been destroyed in the war and subsequently pillaged, burned and its population dispersed. To complete matters – a conscious policy of destroying all reminders of Aztec power – the remaining stones were used to construct the new city, **México** (Mexico City). At first there was quite remarkable progress: hundreds of towns were laid out (on a plan, with a plaza surrounded by a grid of streets, as laid down in Spain); thousands of churches were built, often in areas which had been sacred to the Indians, or on top of their pyramids (there were over 12,000 in Mexico by 1800); and with the first Franciscan monks arriving in 1524, mass conversions were the order of the day. In a sense the indigenous peoples were used to all this – the Aztecs and their predecessors had behaved in a similar manner – but they had never experienced a slavery like that which was to follow.

At the same time **the Church**, which at first had championed indigenous rights and attempted to record native legends and histories and educate the children, grew less interested, and more concerned with money. Any attempt to treat the Indians as human was in any case violently opposed by Spanish landowners, to whom they were rather less than machines (cheaper than machinery, and therefore more expendable). By the end of the colonial era the Church owned more than half of all the land and wealth in the country, yet most native villages would be lucky to see a priest once a year.

In a sense Mexico remained a wealthy nation – certainly the richest of the Spanish colonies – but the riches were confined to the local elite and the imperialists in Spain. The governing philosophy was that "what's good for Spain is good for Mexico", and towards that end all **trade**, industry and profit was exclusively aimed. No local trade or agriculture that would compete with Spain was allowed, so the cultivation of vines or the production of silk was banned; heavy taxes on other products – coffee, sugar, tobacco, cochineal, silver and other metals – went directly to Spain or to still poorer colonies, and no trade except with Spain was allowed. Since the "Spanish Galleon" (actually more of a convoy) sailed from Veracruz just once a year and was even then subject to the vagaries of piracy, this was a considerable handicap.

It didn't prevent the growth of a small class of extraordinarily wealthy **hacendados** (owners of massive estates) and **mine-owners** – whose growing confidence is shown in the architectural development of the colonial towns, from fortress-like huddles at the beginning of the colonial era to the full flowering of Baroque extravagance by its end – but it did stop the development of any kind of realistic economic infrastructure, even of decent roads linking the towns. Just about the only proper road in 1800 was the one which connected Acapulco with Mexico City and Veracruz, by which goods from the far eastern colonies would be transported cross-country before shipment on to Spain.

Even among the wealthy there was growing **resentment**, fuelled by the status of Mexicans: only "**gachupines**", Spaniards born in Spain, could hold high office in the government or Church. There were about 40,000 of them in Mexico in 1800 out of the six million population, and some three million Indians – the rest were **criollos** (creoles, born in Mexico of Spanish blood) who were in general educated, wealthy and aristocratic, and **mestizos** (of mixed race) who dominated the lower ranks of the Church, army and civil service, or lived as anything from shopkeepers and small ranchers to bandits and beggars.

Independence

By the beginning of the nineteenth century Spain's status as a world power was in severe decline. In 1796 British sea power had forced the Spanish to open their colonial ports to free trade, and in 1808 Spain itself was invaded by

Napoleon, who placed his brother Joseph on the throne. At the same time new political ideas were transforming the world outside, with the French Revolution and the American War of Independence still fresh in the memory. Although the works of such political philosophers as Rousseau, Voltaire and Paine were banned in Mexico, the opening of the ports made it inevitable that their ideas would spread – especially as it was traders from the new United States who most took advantage of the opportunities. Literary societies set up to discuss these books quickly became centres of **political dissent**.

The spark, though, was provided by the French invasion of Spain, as colonies throughout Latin America refused to recognize the Bonaparte regime (and the campaigns of Bolívar and others in South America began). In Mexico, the "gachupine" rulers proclaimed their loyalty to Ferdinand VII (the deposed king) and hoped to carry on much as before, but creole discontent was not to be so easily assuaged. The literary societies continued to meet, and from one, in Querétaro, emerged the first leaders of the Independence movement: **Father Miguel Hidalgo y Costilla**, a creole priest, and **Ignacio Allende**, a disaffected junior army officer.

When their plans for a coup were discovered, the conspirators were forced into premature action, with Hidalgo issuing the famous Grito (cry) of Independence – ¡Méxicanos, viva México! – from the steps of his parish church in Dolores on September 16, 1810. The mob of Indians and *mestizos* who gathered behind the banner swiftly took the major towns of San Miguel, Guanajuato and others to the north of the capital, but their behaviour – seizing land and property, slaughtering the Spanish – horrified the wealthy creoles who had initially supported the movement. In spring 1811, Hidalgo's army, huge but undisciplined, moved on the capital, but at the crucial moment Hidalgo threw away a clear chance to overpower the royalist army. Instead he chose to retreat, and his forces broke up as quickly as they had been assembled. Within months, Hidalgo, Allende and the other ringleaders had been captured and executed.

By this time most creoles, frightened at what had been unleashed, had rejoined the ranks of the royalists. But many *mestizos* and much of the indigenous population remained in a state of revolt, with a new leader in the *mestizo* priest **José María Morelos**. Morelos was not only a far better tactician than Hidalgo – instituting a highly successful series of guerrilla campaigns – he was also a genuine radical. By 1813 he controlled virtually the entire country, with the exception of the capital and the route from there to Veracruz, and at the **Congress of Chilpancingo** he declared the abolition of slavery and the equality of the races. But the royalists fought back with a series of crushing victories, Morelos was executed in 1815, and his forces, under the leadership of **Vicente Guerrero**, were reduced to carrying out the occasional minor raid.

Ironically, it was the introduction of liberal reforms in Spain, of just the type feared by the Mexican ruling classes, which finally brought about **Mexican Independence**. Worried that such reforms might spread across the Atlantic, many creoles pre-empted a true revolution by assuming a "revolutionary" guise themselves. In 1820 **Agustin de Iturbide**, a royalist general but himself a *mestizo*, threw in his lot with Guerrero; in 1821 he proposed the **Iguala Plan** to the Spanish authorities, who were hardly in a position to fight, and Mexico was granted Independence. With Independence, though, came none of the changes which had been fought over for so long – the Church retained its power, and one set of rulers had simply been changed for another, local set.

Foreign intervention

In 1822 Iturbide had himself proclaimed emperor; a year later he was forced to abdicate, and a year after that he was executed. It was the first of many such events in a century which must rank among the most confused – and disastrous – in any nation's history. Not only had Independence brought no real social change, it had left the new nation with virtually no chance of successful government: the power of the Church and of the army was far greater than that of the supposed rulers; there was no basis on which to create a viable internal economy; and if the state hadn't already been bankrupted by the Independence struggle, it was to be cleaned out time and again by the demands of war and internal disruption. There were no fewer than 56 governments in the next forty years. In what approaches farce, the name of **General Santa Ana** stands out as the most bizarre figure of all, becoming president or dictator on eleven separate occasions and masterminding the loss of more than half of Mexico's territory.

Santa Ana's first spell in office immediately followed Iturbide – he declared Mexico a **republic** (although he himself always expected to be treated as a king, and addressed as His Most Serene Majesty) and called a constitutional convention. Under the auspices of the new constitution, the republic was confirmed, the country divided into thirteen states, and **Guadalupe Victoria**, a former guerrilla general, elected its first president. He lasted three years, something of a record. In 1829 the Spanish attempted a rather half-hearted **invasion**, easily defeated, after which they accepted the fact of Mexican Independence. In 1833 Santa Ana was elected president (officially) for the first time, the fifth to hold the post thus far.

In 1836 a rather more serious chain of events was set in motion when Texas, Mexican territory but largely inhabited by migrants from the US, declared its independence. Santa Ana commanded a punitive expedition that besieged **the Alamo** in the famous incident in which Jim Bowie and Davy Crockett, along with 150 other defenders, lost their lives. Santa Ana himself, though, was promptly defeated and captured at the battle of San Jacinto, and rather than face execution he signed a paper accepting **Texan Independence**. Although the authorities in Mexico refused to accept the legality of its claim, Texas was, de facto, independent. Meanwhile, in 1838, the French chose to invade **Veracruz**, demanding compensation for alleged damages to French property and citizens – a small war that lasted about four months, and during which Santa Ana lost a leg.

In 1845 the United States annexed Texas, and although the Mexicans at first hoped to negotiate a settlement, the redefinition of Texas to include most of Arizona, New Mexico and California made yet another war almost inevitable. In 1846 clashes between Mexican troops and US cavalry in these disputed western zones led to the declaration of the **Mexican–American War**. Following defeat for the Mexicans at Palo Alto and Resaca, three small US armies invaded from the north. At the same time General Winfield Scott took Veracruz after a long bombardment, and commenced his march on the capital. Santa Ana was roundly defeated on a number of occasions, and in September 1847, after legendary resistance by the Niños Héroes (cadets at the military academy) Mexico City itself was captured. In 1848, by the **Treaty of Guadalupe Hidalgo**, the US paid $15 million for most of Texas, New Mexico, Arizona and California, along with parts of Colorado and Utah; in

1854 the present borders were established when Santa Ana sold a further strip down to the Río Grande for $10 million under the **Gadsden Purchase**.

Reform

Mexico finally saw the back of Santa Ana when, in 1855, he left for exile in Venezuela, but the country's troubles were by no means at an end. A new generation had grown up who had known only an independent Mexico in permanent turmoil, who had lived through the American humiliation, and who espoused once more the liberal ideals of Morelos. Above all they saw their enemy as **the Church**: immense, self-serving, and far wealthier than any legitimate government, it had further sullied its reputation by refusing to provide funds for the American war. Its position enshrined in the constitution, it was an extraordinarily reactionary institution, bleeding the peasantry for the most basic of sacraments (few could afford official marriage, or burial) and failing to provide the few services it was charged with. All education was in church schools, which for 95 percent of the population meant no education at all.

Benito Juárez, a Zapotec Indian who had been adopted and educated by a priest, and later trained as a lawyer, became the leader of this liberal movement through several years of civil war in which each side became more bitterly entrenched in increasingly extreme positions. When the **liberals** first came to power following Santa Ana's exile they began a relatively mild attempt at **reform**: permitting secular education, liberating the press, attempting to distance the Church from government and instituting a new democratic constitution. The Church responded by obstruction and by threatening to excommunicate anyone co-operating with the government. In 1858 there was a conservative coup, and for the next three years **internal strife** on an unprecedented scale. With each new battle the liberals proclaimed more drastic reforms, churches were sacked and priests shot, while the conservatives responded by executing anyone suspected of liberal tendencies.

In 1861 Juárez emerged triumphant, at least temporarily. Church property was confiscated, monasteries closed, weddings and burials became civil affairs, and set fees were established for the services of a priest. It wasn't until 1867 that most of these **Reform Laws** were to be fully enacted – for the conservatives had one more card to play – but most are still in force today. Priests in Mexico, for example, are forbidden to wear their robes in public.

At the end of the civil war, with the government bankrupt, Juárez had suspended payment of all foreign debts, and in 1861 a joint British, Spanish and French expedition occupied Veracruz to demand compensation. It rapidly became clear, however, that the French were after more than mere financial recompense. Britain and Spain withdrew their forces, and Napoleon III ordered his troops to advance on Mexico City. The aim, with the support of Mexican conservatives, was to place **Maximilian**, a Habsburg archduke, on the throne as emperor.

Despite a major defeat at **Puebla** on May 5, 1862 (now a national holiday), the French sent for reinforcements and occupied Mexico City in 1863. The new emperor arrived the following year. In many ways, Maximilian cuts a pathetic figure. He arrived in Mexico with almost no knowledge of its internal feuds (having gleaned most of his information from a book on court etiquette), and expecting a victorious welcome. Proving to be a liberal at heart

– he refused to repeal any of Juárez's reforms – he promptly lost the support of even the small group which had initially welcomed him. While his good intentions seem undeniable, few believe that he would have been capable of putting them into practice even in the best of circumstances. And these were hardly ideal times. With Union victory in the **US Civil War**, the authorities there threw their weight behind Juárez, providing him with arms and threatening to invade unless the French withdrew (on the basis of the Monroe doctrine: America for the Americans). Napoleon, already worried by the growing power of Bismarck's Prussia back home, had little choice but to comply. After 1866, Maximilian's position was hopeless.

His wife, the Empress Carlota, sailed to Europe in a vain attempt to win fresh support, but Napoleon had taken his decision, the Vatican refused to contemplate helping a man who had continued to attack the Church, and the constant disappointments eventually drove Carlota mad. She died, insane, in Belgium in 1927. Maximilian, meanwhile, stayed at the head of his hopelessly outnumbered troops to the end – May 15, 1867 – when he was defeated and captured at **Querétaro**. A month later, he faced the firing squad.

Juárez reassumed power, managing this time to ride through the worst of the inevitable bankruptcy. The first steps towards **economic reconstruction** were taken, with the completion of a railway from Veracruz to the capital, encouragement of industry and the development of a public education programme. Juárez died in office in 1872, having been re-elected in 1871, and was succeeded by his vice-president **Lerdo de Tejada**, who continued on the same road, though with few new ideas.

Dictatorship

Tejada was neither particularly popular nor spectacularly successful, but he did see out his term of office. However, there had been several Indian **revolts** during his rule and a number of plots against him, the most serious of them led by a new radical liberal leader, **Porfirio Díaz**. Díaz had been a notably able military leader under Juárez, and in 1876, despite the re-election of Tejada, he proclaimed his own candidate president. The following year he assumed the presidency himself, and was to rule as dictator for the next 34 years. At first his platform was a radical one – including full implementation of the Reform Laws and a decree of no re-election to any political office – but it was soon dropped in favour of a brutal policy of **modernization**. Díaz did actually stand down at the end of his first term, in 1880, but he continued to rule through a puppet president, and in 1884 resumed the presidency for an unbroken stretch until 1911.

In many ways the **achievements** of his dictatorship were remarkable: some 16,000km of railway were built, industry boomed, telephones and telegraph were installed, and major towns, reached at last by reasonable roads, entered the modern era. In the countryside, Díaz established a police force – the notorious *rurales* – which stamped out much of the banditry. Almost every city in Mexico seems to have a grandiose theatre and elegant public buildings from this era. But the costs were high: rapid development was achieved basically by handing over the country and its people to **foreign investors**, who owned the vast majority of the oil, mining rights, railways and natural resources. At the same time there was a policy of massive land expropriation, in which formerly communal village holdings were handed over to foreign exploitation or simply grabbed by corrupt officials.

Agriculture, meanwhile, was ignored entirely. The owners of vast haciendas could make more than enough money by relying on the forced labour of a landless peasantry, and had no interest in efficiency or production for domestic consumption. By 1900 the whole of Mexico was owned by some three to four percent of its population. Without land of their own, peasants had no choice but to work on the haciendas or in the forests, where their serfdom was ensured by wages so low that they were permanently in debt to their employers. The rich became very rich indeed; the poor had lower incomes and fewer prospects than they had a century earlier.

Once the *rurales* had done their job of making the roads safe to travel, they became a further burden – charging for the right to travel along roads they controlled and acting as a private police force for employers should any of their workers try to escape. In short, slavery had been reintroduced in all but name, and up to a quarter of the nation's resources came to be spent on internal security. The press was censored, too, education strictly controlled, and **corruption** rife.

Revolution

With the onset of the **twentieth century**, Díaz was already old and beginning to lose his grip on reality. He had every intention of continuing in power until his death; but a real middle-class opposition was beginning to develop, concerned above all by the racist policies of their government (which favoured foreign investors above native ones) and by the lack of opportunity for themselves – the young educated classes. Their movement revived the old slogan of "no reelección", and in 1910 **Francisco Madero** stood against Díaz in the presidential election. The old dictator responded by imprisoning his opponent and declaring himself victor at the polls by a vast majority. Madero, however, escaped to Texas where he proclaimed himself president, and called on the nation to rise in his support.

This was an entirely opportunist move, for at the time there were no revolutionary forces, but several small bands immediately took up arms. Most important were those in the northern state of Chihuahua, where **Pancho Villa** and **Pascual Orozco** won several minor battles, and in the southwest, where **Emiliano Zapata** began to arm Indian guerrilla forces. In May 1911 Orozco captured the major border town of Ciudad Juárez, and his success was rapidly followed by a string of Revolutionary victories. By the end of the month, hoping to preserve the system if not his role in it, Porfirio Díaz had fled into exile. On October 2, 1911, Madero was elected president.

Like the originators of Independence before him, Madero had no conception of the forces he had unleashed. He freed the press, encouraged the formation of unions and introduced genuine **democracy**, but failed to do anything about the condition of the peasantry or the redistribution of land. Zapata prepared to rise again.

Emiliano Zapata was perhaps the one true revolutionary in the whole long conflict to follow, and his battle cry of **Tierra y Libertad** (Land and Liberty) and insistence that "it is better to die on your feet than live on your knees" make him still a revered figure among the peasants – and revolutionaries – of the present day. By contrast, the rest were mostly out for personal gain: Pancho Villa, a cattle rustler and bandit in the time of Díaz, was by far the most successful of the more orthodox generals, brilliantly inventive, and ruthless in victory. But his motivation seems to have been personal glory – he appeared to love fighting, and at one stage, when a Hollywood film crew was travelling with his armies, would allegedly arrange his battles so as to ensure the best lighting conditions and most impressive fight scenes.

In any case Madero was faced by a more immediately dangerous enemy than his own erstwhile supporters – US business interests. **Henry Lane Wilson**, US ambassador, began openly plotting with **Victoriano Huerta**, a government general, and **Felix Díaz**, a nephew of the dictator, who was held in prison. Fighting broke out between supporters of Díaz and those of Madero, while Huerta refused to commit his troops to either side. When he did, in 1913, it was to proclaim himself president. Madero was shot in suspicious circumstances (few doubt an assassination sanctioned by Huerta) and opponents on the right, including Díaz, either imprisoned or exiled. The new government was promptly recognized by the United States and most other foreign powers, but not by the important forces within the country.

Constitution versus Convention

Villa and Zapata immediately took up arms against Huerta, and in the north Villa was joined by **Alvaro Obregón**, governor of Sonora, and Venustiano Carranza, governor of Coahuila. Carranza was appointed head of the **Constitutionalist** forces, though he was always to be deeply suspicious of Villa, despite Villa's constant protestations of loyalty. At first the revolutionaries made little headway – Carranza couldn't even control his own state, although Obregón and Villa did enjoy some successes raiding south from Chihuahua and Sonora. But almost immediately the new US president, **Woodrow Wilson**, withdrew his support from Huerta and, infuriated by his refusal to resign, began actively supplying arms to the Revolution.

In 1914, the Constitutionalists began to move south, and in April of that year US troops occupied Veracruz in their support (though neither side was exactly happy about the foreign presence). Huerta, now cut off from almost every source of money or supplies, fled the country in July, and in August Obregón occupied the capital, proclaiming Carranza president.

Renewed fighting broke out straight away, this time between Carranza and Obregón, the Constitutionalists, on one side, and the rest of the revolutionary leaders on the other, so-called **Conventionalists** whose sole point of agreement was that Carranza should not lead them. The three years of fighting that followed were the most bitter and chaotic yet, with petty chiefs in every part of the country proclaiming provisional governments, joining each other in factions and then splitting again, and the entire country in a state of anarchy. Each army issued its own money, and each forced any able-bodied men it came across into joining. By 1920 it was reckoned that about one-eighth of the population had been killed.

Gradually, however, Obregón and Carranza gained ground – Obregón defeated Villa several times in 1915, and Villa withdrew to carry out border raids into the United States, hoping to provoke an invasion (which he nearly did: US troops pursued him across the border but were never able to catch up, and withdrew following defeat in a skirmish with Carranza's troops). Zapata, meanwhile, had some conspicuous successes – and occupied Mexico City for much of 1915 – but his irregular troops tended to disappear back to their villages after each victory. In 1919 he was tricked into a meeting with one of Carranza's generals and assasinated;Villa retired to a hacienda in his home state, and was murdered in 1923.

The end of the Revolution

Meanwhile Carranza continued to claim the presidency, and in 1917 set up a constitutional **congress** to ratify his position. The document they produced – the present constitution – included most of the revolutionary demands, among them workers' rights, a mandatory eight-hour day, national ownership of all mineral rights and the distribution of large landholdings and formerly communal properties to the peasantry. Carranza was formally elected in May 1917 and proceeded to make no attempt to carry out any of its stipulations, certainly not with regard to land rights. In 1920 Carranza was forced to step down by Obregón, and was shot while attempting to escape the country with most of the contents of the treasury.

Obregón, at least, was well intentioned – but his efforts at real land reform were again stymied by fear of US reaction: in return for American support, he agreed not to expropriate land. In 1924 **Plutarco Elias Calles** succeeded him, and real progress towards some of the ideals of the revolutionary constitution began to be made. Work on large public works schemes began – roads, irrigation systems, village schools – and about eight million acres of land were given back to the villages as communal holdings. At the same time Calles instituted a policy of virulent **anticlericalism**, closing churches and monasteries, and forcing priests to flee the country or go underground.

These moves provoked the last throes of a backlash, as the **Catholic Cristero** movement took up arms in defence of the Church. From 1927 until about 1935 isolated incidents of vicious banditry and occasional full-scale warfare continued, eventually burning themselves out as the stability of the new regime became obvious, and religious controls were relaxed. In 1928 Obregón was reelected, but assassinated three weeks later in protest at the breach of the "no reelección" clause of the constitution. He was followed by **Portes Gil**, **Ortiz Rubio** and then **Abelardo Rodriguez**, who were controlled behind the scenes by Calles and his political allies, who steered national politics to the right in the bleak years of the 1930s Depression.

Modern Mexico

By 1934 Mexico enjoyed a degree of peace, and a remarkable change had been wrought. A new culture had emerged – seen nowhere more clearly than in the great murals of **Rivera** and **Orozco** which began to adorn public buildings throughout the country – in which native heroes like **Hidalgo**, **Morelos**, **Juárez** and **Madero** replaced European ideals. Nowadays everyone in the republic would claim Indian blood – even if the Indians themselves remain the lowest stratum of society – and the invasion of Cortés is seen as the usurpation of the nation's march to its destiny, a march which resumed with Independence and the Revolution. At the same time there was a fear in these early days that Calles was attempting to promote a dynasty of his own.

With the election of **Lázaro Cárdenas** in 1934, such doubts were finally laid to rest. As the spokesman of a younger generation, Cárdenas expelled Calles and his supporters from the country, at the same time setting up the single broad-based party that was to rule for the next 71 years, the **PRI** (Party of the Institutionalized Revolution). Cárdenas set about an unprecedented programme of reform, redistributing land on a huge scale (170,000 square kilometres during his six-year term), creating peasant and worker organizations to represent their interests at national level, and incorporating them into the governing party. He also relaxed controls on the Church to appease internal and international opposition.

In 1938 he nationalized the **oil companies**, an act which has proved one of the most significant in shaping modern Mexico and bringing about its industrial miracle. For a time it seemed as if yet more foreign intervention might follow, but a boycott of Mexican oil by the major consumers crumbled with the onset of **World War II** (apart from Neville Chamberlain, who cut off diplomatic relations and lost Great Britain an important investment market as a result), and was followed by a massive influx of money and a huge boost for Mexican industry as a result of the war. By the time he stood down in 1940, Cárdenas could claim to be the first president in modern Mexican history to have served his full six-year term in peace, and handed over to his successor without trouble.

Through the war industrial growth continued apace under **Avila Camacho**, and Mexico officially joined the Allies in 1942. **Miguel Alemán** (1946–52) presided over still faster development, and a further massive dose of public works and land reform – major prestige projects, like the University City in the capital, were planned by his regime. Over the next thirty years or so, massive oil incomes continued to stimulate industry, and the PRI maintained a masterly control of all aspects of public life without apparently losing the support of a great majority of the Mexican public. Of course it is an accepted fact of life that governments will line their own pockets first – a practice which apparently reached its height under **Lopez Portillo** (1976–82) – but the unrelenting populism of the PRI, its massive powers of patronage, and above all its highly visible and undoubted achievement of progress, maintained it in power with amazingly little dissent.

All this is not to say that there were no problems. The year **1959** saw the repression of a national railway strike where ten thousand workers lost their jobs and their leaders were placed in jail, and in **1968** hundreds of students were massacred in Tlatelolco square in Mexico City to stem an active pro-democracy student movement that threatened Mexico's image abroad as the Olympic Games neared (Mexico's were the first Olympics to be held in the "Third World" and were seen as an opportunity to promote the regime abroad). The PRI was unable to buy off the students due to their rotating leadership, and unwilling to negotiate for fear of losing face. Although the massacre did put an end to student unrest, or at least any public manifestation of it, from Tlatelolco onwards the Mexican system lost a great deal of its legitimacy as the opposition saw fewer reasons for working within the system; guerrilla movements sprang up in Guerrero state, for example. The PRI was still, however, very much in control and had snuffed these movements out by the mid-Seventies. The government, who ran the union movement and the peasant organizations and delivered steady economic growth, appeared to have an unassailable hold on power, as well as being genuinely popular across a wide spectrum of the population.

Economic crisis

The government of **Miguel de la Madrid** (1982–88) found itself faced with economic crisis on a national and international scale. Mexico's enormous foreign debt (of almost $100 billion) had been run up in the heady days of the oil boom. Already a severe burden on the economy, the debt was greatly exacerbated by falling oil prices and revenues and rising international interest rates. At the same time the PRI seemed to be losing its populist touch: the twelve previous years, known as the "**Docena Trágica**" or tragic dozen, had seen flourishing corruption and economic mismanagement destroy the hopes brought about by the development of the oil industry. Also, De la Madrid was a US-educated financier who adopted the **austerity measures** imposed by the World Bank. Such policies won widespread acclaim from international bankers (Jesus Silva Herzog was voted "finance minister of the year" after his first year in office), but at home produced massive unemployment and drastically reduced standards of living – the average wage-earner lost fifty percent of his or her purchasing power – while struggling to keep inflation down to one hundred percent a year. An exploding population only added to the problems, and even the huge level of illegal **emigration** to the US had little impact on it. The business community suffered too. Outraged by the nationalization of the banks in 1982, they were further hit by a series of bankruptcies and by devaluation which made imported materials almost impossible to afford. With no sign of economic recovery, some of the wide panoply of interests covered by the PRI – from the all-powerful unions to the top businessmen – began to split off.

This movement against the PRI was exacerbated in 1985, when a huge **earthquake** hit the capital. The quake revealed widespread corruption, as the government attempted to prevent ordinary people from organizing their own rescue attempts to try and hide the inadequacy of official efforts. Furthermore, many of the buildings that collapsed were government-owned and although supposedly built to withstand earthquakes, turned out to have been constructed using inferior materials, with the profits siphoned off to construction companies and government officials. International relief aid was also diverted as the quake's victims were abandoned by the authorities.

Many grass-roots organizations were formed as the experience of the earthquake exposed the government's inability to provide anything other than rudimentary and poorly co-ordinated help. This marked the beginning of a modern civil society, as independent tenant groups, neighbourhood and women's groups, and small-scale trade unions began to press the government for specific rebuilding programmes and on wider social concerns such as lack of housing, basic services, police corruption and pollution.

Opposition also grew outside the capital. The right-wing opposition **PAN** won a string of minor election victories in the north (and were cheated out of the state governorship of Chihuahua by blatant fraud), while in the south a socialist/peasant alliance held power for a while in Juchitán (Oaxaca) before being ousted with traditional strong-arm tactics. These episodes highlighted a further danger – the increasing polarization of the country. In the north, life is heavily influenced by the US, and business and ranching interests hold sway. In the south, where peasants continue to press for more land redistribution, opposition is far more radical and left-wing: alternately inspired and intimidated by events in Central America.

De la Madrid's unpopularity was demonstrated at the **1986 World Cup** final, when the crowd – mainly middle-class Mexicans – booed and jeered at him as he took his seat. Considering the reverence traditionally accorded to the figure of the president, this was an unprecedented show of disrespect.

The **1988 election** was certainly dramatic, and may yet prove one of the most significant since the Revolution. Predictably, the PRI candidate, **Carlos Salinas de Gortari**, won. The extent of the opposition however, was significant, and into the traditional contest between PRI, PAN and a number of tiny splinter groups, a formidable new challenger emerged in the form of **Cuauhtémoc Cárdenas**, son of the legendary and much loved Lázaro. Cárdenas split from the PRI a year before the election and succeeded in uniting the Mexican left behind him (under the banner of the National Democratic Front, or **FDN**) for the first time since the Revolution.

The success of the FDN was spectacular, Cárdenas officially winning 32 percent of the vote, although the results took a week to appear after the "breakdown" of the electoral computer at a point when Cárdenas was clearly in the lead. Ballot rigging, voter intimidation and vote buying (typical of all Mexican elections) reached new heights. Cárdenas and his supporters claimed that he had won, and also claimed to have figures to support them. Salinas emerged from the tarnished contest with 50.36 percent of the vote and the PAN leader, **Manuel Clouthier** (previously the only serious challenger), came third with 17 percent. Opposition parties won seats in the Senate for almost the first time since the PRI came to power.

Salinas undertook to pave the way for a new multi-party democracy in Mexico. As a relatively young, untried, internally chosen candidate, he had little in the way of a following either within the PRI itself or the country as a whole, and began by announcing a clean-up **campaign against corruption**. On Salinas' orders, the head of the official PEMEX oil workers' union (a notoriously corrupt figure known as "La Quina") was arrested. He also created a human rights commission to investigate abuses, and ended direct government control over PIPSA, the official monopoly newsprint supplier. Salinas also upheld mid-term electoral triumphs by the opposition PAN in the states of Baja California and Guanajuato, despite opposition from local PRI activists.

Early signs were thus encouraging. Despite the death in mysterious circumstances of the PAN leader Manuel Clouthier in 1989 and controversial victories by the PRI in various state elections, Salinas managed to secure widespread support through the radical nature of his economic programme, as well as through traditional political patronage. Initially Salinas maintained the **economic policy** of his predecessor, strategically timing Mexico's privatization programme to maximize revenue, tightening up on tax avoidance and the black economy, and reducing the foreign debt by almost half in three years through restructuring and co-operation with the IMF and private banks.

The compliant **television media** also helped foster the image of the president. This was not a new phenomenon, but Salinas benefited media barons through deregulation of the media and the sale of the state-owned station (now Televisión Azteca), and their support helped the PRI to sweep the board during the 1991 mid-term elections. Economic growth, falling inflation and a large influx of foreign capital seemed to confirm the success of the government's agenda.

In the meantime the opposition had been trying to mount a coherent challenge to the PRI. Cuauhtémoc Cárdenas, building on his success in 1988, founded a party to harness his popular support. The **PRD** (Party of the Democratic Revolution) had a very radical platform, reflecting much of its support base, but has moved increasingly to the centre, no longer opposing privatization in principle, and accepting the need for reform of the *ejido* system (see overleaf). The PAN, with the PRI moving to the right, found its support base being eroded although it enjoyed unprecedented electoral gains.

The long-term consequences of the Salinas policy, however, were much less positive. **Social polarization** became even more extreme. By 1993, forty million Mexicans were living below the official poverty line (about half the population), while 24 Mexicans were listed in the Forbes list of the 500 richest men in the world. Most of these billionaires had acquired their wealth through buying privatized utilities. Salinas was committed to reducing the public debt and encouraging private investment, which he achieved by drastically cutting public spending and encouraging foreign companies by holding down wage levels. This involved expanding the "**maquiladora**" programme, which allowed foreign companies to set up assembly plants along the US–Mexican border (enjoying substantial tax concessions); a ban on union activity and relaxed health and safety and environmental requirements; and pushing through the North American Free Trade Agreement (**NAFTA**; **TLC** in Spanish), which creates a free market between Canada, the US and Mexico. This agreement has opponents in all the countries involved, with many in the US and Canada fearing job losses and lax environmental standards. Theoretically, a free market, with each country benefiting from its own comparative advantage, should increase trade levels to a degree in which all the participants would gain, spurring the Mexican economy to expand to the level of its partners and allowing Mexico to enter the "First World". Most Mexicans, with good reason, suspected that the agreement would provide little benefit, allowing US companies to offload polluting industries to Mexico and to take advantage of cheap labour – Mexico's "comparative advantage".

Salinas' response to the problems was to intensify his programme of reform, while at the same time introducing a social programme to ameliorate the effects of his economic programme. The national solidarity programme, or **PRONASOL**, directed a billion-dollar budget towards self-help programmes for the poor. Communities would typically supply free labour, while PRONASOL would provide materials and technical expertise for such projects as supplying basic amenities – electricity, piped water, street lighting – or making up for cuts in other government services such as school and hospital building. PRONASOL was supported by a huge advertising campaign, and its logo (like the PRI insignia, in Mexico's national colours) was painted upon every available surface to advertise the achievements of the programme – and by implication of the PRI – in the community. Most of the PRONASOL budget went to areas with strong PRD support such as Mexico City, the southern states and Cárdenas' home state of Michoacán, in an attempt to buy off opposition and co-opt self-help groups.

Another plan of the Salinas strategy was to modify much of Mexico's revolutionary legacy. Diplomatic relations with the Vatican, severed during the Revolution, were re-established, allowing the pope to visit Mexico for the first time. The national oil company, **PEMEX**, was split into smaller units to improve productivity, and foreign oil companies were allowed to prospect for new deposits, although the PEMEX monopoly is still more or less intact. The most important change in this direction was the amendment to article 27 of the constitution, which deals with land reform.

Land reform, as enshrined in the original article of the constitution, owed much to the legacy of Zapata. Land redistributed after the Revolution was parcelled out in communal holdings, known as "**ejidos**", which could not be sold as they belonged to the state. At a local level the land was held in common, divided up by the communities themselves, following the pre-Hispanic and colonial tradition. Salinas changed all that by allowing the sale of *ejido* lands. Many peasants and indigenous communities feared that their landholdings were now vulnerable to speculators, especially as many poor communities exist in a state of almost permanent debt, and believed that their land would be seized to cover outstanding loans, worsening their economic plight still further.

Despite, and maybe because of, these unpopular moves, Salinas began to be seen as a strong presidential figure, with a dynamic agenda for change. The successful negotiation of NAFTA, on which he had staked his reputation, went smoothly despite having to deal with two very different US presidents (George Bush and Bill Clinton), and this enhanced his reputation as a statesman. Even the opposition had to concede that economic progress had been made, and that Salinas had a clear agenda for Mexico and would leave the presidency in a much better state than he found it, giving the PRI a new lease of life.

There seemed little doubt that the PRI would go on to win the presidential election scheduled for 1994 with a minimum of fuss. In many areas, it wouldn't even have to resort to fraud. The crisis and upheavals of earlier days finally seemed to have been left behind.

Political crisis

All this changed on New Year's Day 1994, when an armed guerrilla movement known as the **Zapatista Army of National Liberation** (EZLN) took control of San Cristóbal de las Casas and four other municipalities in the southernmost state of Chiapas. The guerrillas were mainly indigenous villagers; they demanded an end to the feudal system of land tenure in Chiapas, free elections, the repeal of NAFTA and the restoration of article 27 of the constitution. The army reacted with a predictable use of force, committing human rights abuses along the way that included the bombing of civilians and the murder of prisoners. Long hidden from the world, the repressive side of the Mexican state – together with the plight of the indigenous peoples of Mexico – was suddenly front-page news throughout the world. To Salinas' credit, he rapidly prepared the ground for peace negotiations by ordering a cease-fire.

Negotiations progressed with remarkable speed to begin with. The government representative, Manuel Camacho Solís, ex-mayor of Mexico City and at one time potential PRI candidate for the presidency, made concessions to the guerrillas and upstaged the presidential candidate, Luis Donaldo Colosio, who remained silent about the conflict. Camacho was assisted by the Bishop of San Cristóbal, Samuel Ruíz, a champion of Indian rights in Chiapas and an advocate of liberation theology (many on the right have since accused the diocese of San Cristóbal of fostering the subversion, though with little apparent evidence; the Vatican even attempted to recall him in the middle of negotiations to explain himself, and calls from the right have insisted on his excommunication). The real star of the negotiations was **Subcomandante Marcos** of the EZLN, the main spokesperson for the Zapatistas. The Balaclava-clad, pipe-smoking guerrilla soon became a cult hero; his speeches and communiqués were full of literary allusions and passionate rhetoric and also revealed a strong sense of humour. Talks ended in March, when an accord was put together. The EZLN then sent the accord back to its community bases for them to vote upon it. Decisions regarding whether to fight or negotiate were not made any easier by the many different languages and dialects spoken and the inaccessibility of many villages, and the results were not ready until June. An uneasy truce between army and guerrillas was maintained, and Mexicans were given ample time to dwell upon events in Chiapas.

As the Mexican saying goes, "Nothing happens in Mexico . . . until it does." Something happened on March 23, when the presidential candidate for the PRI, Luis Donaldo Colosio, was shot dead on the campaign trail in the border city of Tijuana. This was the first **assassination** of such a prominent government figure since 1928. The assassin, a former policeman, was allowed by Colosio's bodyguards to shoot him from almost point-blank range, fuelling conspiracy theories about the murder on a scale similar to those surrounding the assassination of John F. Kennedy.

Despite the unexpected nature of the assassination, political violence in Mexico has a long history. This has been aggravated in recent years by a surge in drug-related crime among the Mexican **cocaine cartels**. In 1993, the archbishop of Guadalajara, Juan Jesús Ocampo, was shot dead at Guadalajara airport. He was reportedly caught in the crossfire between warring drug gangs, and some allege that drug cartels were also involved in the assassination of Colosio. Whatever the truth, and neither murder has been satisfactorily cleared up, it is clear that a huge amount of drugs are making their way across the Mexican border into the US, and that drug money has corrupted many in Mexican law enforcement and political circles. Although violence is nowhere near as widespread as in Colombia, say, the danger exists that the situation may deteriorate.

Another group suspected of carrying out drug murders consists of elements within the PRI itself. The so-called "**dinosaurs**" within the party, those committed to maintaining the status quo, felt threatened by moves to democratize the political system, which had been galvanized by the Chiapas negotiations. Colosio had pledged himself to democratic reforms, and his murder was calculated to remove this threat to the established system. The assassination of another prominent reformer in September 1994, José Francisco Ruíz Massieu (general secretary of the PRI), who was gunned down in Mexico City, seems also to have served as a warning against anyone trying to modify the system. Colosio's successor as presidential candidate, **Ernesto Zedillo Ponce de León**, was a minor PRI apparatchik, and in this climate of insecurity and violence the **elections of August 1994** did not augur well.

In June the EZLN rejected the accord with the government, and in July the PRD candidate for the governorship of Chiapas, Amado Avendaño Figueroa, met with a suspicious "accident" when a truck with no number plates collided with his car, killing three passengers. Avendaño lost an eye as a result of the crash. It was no surprise when the PRI again triumphed in the presidential elections: Zedillo gained 48 percent of the vote, Diego de Cevallos, the PAN candidate, 31 percent and Cárdenas for the PRD only 16 percent. The PRI also won all the senatorial races and the governorship of Chiapas. The scale of the vote (75 percent of voters participated, contrasting with traditionally high levels of absenteeism) and the presence of foreign observers at an election for the first time left little doubt that the PRI had managed yet again to defy all attempts to remove them; and despite high levels of fraud, it was clear that the governing party really had obtained popular backing. The Left were left in disarray as over 75 percent of votes cast were for the PRI and the PAN.

The results announced, the situation began almost immediately to deteriorate. In **Chiapas** the defeated Avendaño declared himself "rebel governor" after denouncing the elections as fraudulent. As many as half the municipalities in the state backed him, refusing to pay taxes to the official government, and both the PRD and the EZLN also supported his move. The EZLN warned that if the PRI candidate Eduardo Robledo was sworn in, the truce with the government would be at an end. Chiapas was anyway in a state of virtual **civil war**. Ranchers and landowners, who had long enjoyed the use of hired muscle to intimidate the peasantry, organized **death squads** to counter a massively mobilized peasantry. Land seizures and road blocks by one side were met with assassinations and intimidation by the other in a rapidly polarizing atmosphere. A build-up of Mexican troops in the state exacerbated the situation as Chiapas began to appear like an occupied Central American republic rather than a part of Mexico.

Post-electoral conflicts also developed after the governorship contests in **Veracruz** and **Tabasco**, both won in controversial circumstances by the PRI. Tabasco followed Chiapas' lead by declaring a "governor in rebellion". PRD supporters temporarily took over the centre of the state capital Villahermosa, and numerous PEMEX oil installations. In Veracruz, the PRD again claimed fraud in many of the municipalities in the south of the state. The PAN won in most of the urban centres, including the port of Veracruz itself.

On January 8, 1995, Zedillo attended the swearing-in of the PRI governor of Chiapas. Ten days later, the EZLN deployed their forces, breaking the army cordon surrounding their positions and moving into 38 municipalities (they had previously been confined to four). That they did it virtually undetected and later retreated, again without detection or a shot being fired, even under the watchful eyes of government troops, showed their familiarity with the terrain, the discipline of their troops and the folly of the "surgical strike" option contemplated by many in the military to wipe out the guerrillas.

The symbolic value of the EZLN action, combined with the apparent failure of the government to cope with the worsening political or economic situations, triggered a massive **devaluation of the peso**. Foreign capital started to flood out of the country, and at a stroke Mexican wages were cut by almost half in real terms. Meantime, higher interest rates hit Mexican business hard, unemployment rose drastically, and IMF austerity measures were again imposed on Mexicans to pay for a debt run up by their government. Not surprisingly, public anger turned to the government, and especially Carlos Salinas, who was now said to have kept the peso artificially high to hide economic problems from view. On this tide of discontent, the PAN prosecutor arrested **Raúl Salinas**, brother of the president, in February, and Ruíz Massieu's brother Mario later in the year. Both were accused of complicity in the murder of José Francisco Ruiz Massieu.

In March 1995, apparently under pressure from the US, Zedillo launched an offensive against the EZLN. A small-arms cache was uncovered in Veracruz, and supposed members of the EZLN were arrested. In Chiapas, the EZLN retreated and major confrontation was avoided. Thousands of peasants, terrified both by the army's incursions and by the violence of right-wing paramilitary groups, left their villages, becoming internal refugees. Although most of Chiapas' estimated 15,000 displaced people are Zapatista sympathizers, some are PRI supporters, and have fled from Zapatista-controlled areas. Exercising the military option was a high-risk strategy for Zedillo, and one that didn't really come off: the EZLN enjoyed considerable public sympathy, especially in view of their largely non-violent methods. Even unmasking Subcomandante Marcos as **Rafael Guillén**, a philosophy professor, failed to affect his popularity – indeed, cries of "Guillén for president" became common at opposition rallies. In a rapid U-turn, the government called off the army and set up **new negotiations**.

These proved to be even more protracted than the 1994 talks but eventually resulted in the **San Andrés Accords on Rights and Indigenous Cultures** (named after the village near San Cristóbal where the talks took place), signed in February 1996. Immediately prior to this agreement the Zapatistas proposed to establish a political front, the Zapatista Front of National Liberation (FZLN), at the same time stating that this political grouping would not contest elections. The San Andrés Accords guaranteed indigenous representation in national and state legislatures, but their implementation would require constitutional and legislative changes which Zedillo failed to push through Congress. Relations between the Zapatistas and the government negotiators, characterized by mutual distrust, were strained to breaking point, and in September the EZLN suspended further peace talks.

The spiral of armed political unrest was given a new twist in June 1996 with the appearance of the **Popular Revolutionary Army** (EPR) in Guerrero. During the rest of the year the EPR made its presence known, often by violent actions, in several states in the middle and south of the country. Despite the activities of two guerrilla groups (and each appears to disassociate itself from the other), however, there was never any real likelihood of a revolutionary end to the PRI's grip on power. The government's informal policy was one of containment and a gradual increase in military pressure rather than outright armed confrontation, in the hope that public support for the romantic notion of guerrillas fighting for "land and liberty" would gradually fade as the old political institutions continued to undergo reform.

Political neglect, accompanied by a remorseless increase of the military presence on the Zapatistas' perimeter appeared also to give the paramilitary groups even greater freedom to operate, further escalating the level of violence. This culminated in the December 1997 **massacre** at Acteal: 45 displaced Tzotil Indians, 36 of them women and children, were murdered by paramilitary forces linked to PRI officials in Chiapas. The killings brought worldwide condemnation, and Zedillo had to act to show that the federal government writ still ran in Chiapas. He announced an official investigation into the killings and ordered the arrest of those suspected of taking part in the massacre. Shortly after, in January 1998, Interior Minister Emiliano Chuayffet (and possible successor to Zedillo) and the Governor of Chiapas, César Ruíz Ferro, resigned.

The extra troops sent to Chiapas, ostensibly to stop more paramilitary killings, failed to prevent further violence and intimidation of Zapatista supporters, and the army even entered Zapatista strongholds on the pretext of searching for paramilitary arms. Emboldened by the militarily weak EZLN response to these incursions, the army began to move against the autonomous municipalities set up by the Zapatistas. This betrayal of the principles of a negotiated settlement finally provoked Bishop Ruíz to resign from his role as mediator in June 1998, causing the dissolution of the National Mediation Commission (CONAI). Negotiations broke down completely, leading some observers to conclude that the government had opted for a military strategy to overcome the Zapatistas by waging a "low-intensity" war in Chiapas.

One consequence of the increased international interest in Chiapas was the Mexican government's active campaign (supported by reports in some prominent sections of the media) against *simpático* **foreigners**, whom it accused of instigating political unrest in the state. Several dozen foreign journalists, church workers, human rights observers and even scientists were detained and deported, and immigration officials subjected anyone they suspected of being a Zapatista sympathizer to questioning and harassment.

Political reform

Despite the crisis in Chiapas, Mexico's **political reforms** continued. In July 1996 new election rules that imposed limits on campaign spending and established a fully independent federal electoral body (IFE) were agreed by the PRI and the main opposition parties. The new rules were brought into play for the first time in the July 1997 mid-term congressional elections, when the governorship of six states and Mexico City were also contested. The results were unprecedented: for the first time in its history PRI lost its majority in the Chamber of Deputies (the lower house of Congress) and lost control of Mexico City. Although the PRI had 239 of the 500 seats, the PRD, with 125 seats, became the second largest party, closely followed by the PAN with 122 seats. The opposition – which also included PT (Workers' Party) and PVEM (Green Party) representatives – could and sometimes did unite to defeat the PRI. The main opposition parties were separated by too wide an ideological gulf to form a permanent coalition, but the PRI government was unable to rely on Congress to rubber-stamp presidential decisions. The new Congress began cutting its new-found teeth in the spring of 1998 by insisting on greater control over monetary policy, and even the PRI-dominated upper chamber, the Senate, demanded – and received – more time to consider bills placed before it. With the PRI clearly losing their decades-long grip on the country the scene was set for change.

The new millennium

On July 2, 2000, **Vicente Fox Quesada**, the PAN candidate, was voted in as president and inaugurated in December that year. It was a landmark event. Not only was he the first opposition candidate ever to have been democratically placed in power, it was also the first peaceful transition between opposing governents since Independence. Furthermore, it was the end of seven decades of PRI rule – in fact, since the collapse of Communism in the Soviet Union, Mexico had been living under the world's longest-lasting one-party dynasty.

Once a Coca-Cola executive and a former governor of Guanajuato, the media-savvy Fox had wooed the business sector and wowed the general public with his campaign promise of *cambio* ("change"), encouraging hopes that he would shake up the system of political patronage and corruption. However, little of the much-vaunted *cambio* has been realized: Fox's ambitions for constitutional and structural reforms have been partly hampered by the fractured nature of PAN, with major differences existing between members, and partly by the PRI, which controls Congress, more than half the state governorships and most of the bureaucracy.

In spite of his political shortcomings, the president retains his popularity amongst most Mexicans, who still look to him with optimism. Domestically, the battle to crack down on police corruption, reform the judicial system, simplify the tax code and rein in the powerful drug cartels is ongoing. International politics have been difficult as relations between between the US and Mexico cooled after the events of September 11, 2001. Mexico did not support Bush's controversial war in Iraq, and the American focus on terrorism put immigration and regional trade issues on the back burner. In spite of this, Fox continues to work for a relaxation of immigration laws, a legitimization of cross-border Mexican labour in the US and a more balanced NAFTA. Overall, the Mexican government claims to be content with the effect of NAFTA, as Mexico has swelled into the world's ninth largest economy and now exports more than all other Latin American countries combined.

Chronology

20,000 BC ▸ First waves of Stone Age migrants from the north. Earliest evidence of man in the central valleys.

5000–2000 BC ▸ Archaic period. First evidence of settlement – cultivation, pottery and tools in the Valley of México.

2500 BC–250 AD ▸ Pre-Classic period. The first simple pyramids and magnificent statuary at the Gulf coast sites – San Lorenzo, La Venta and Tres Zapotes. Olmec influence on art and architecture everywhere, especially Monte Albán. Rise and dominance of the Olmecs. Early evidence of new cultures in the Valley of México – Cuicuilco (buried by volcano) and Teotihuacán.

250–900 AD ▸ Classic period. Teotihuacán dominates central Mexico, with evidence of its influence as far south as Kaminaljuyu in Guatemala. Massive pyramids at Teotihuacán, decorated with stucco reliefs and murals. Monte Albán continues to thrive, while El Tajín on the Gulf coast shows a new style in its Pyramid of the Niches. Maya cities flourish in the highlands of Guatemala and Honduras, as well as Mexican Yucatán. All the great sites – Uxmal, Palenque, Chichén Itzá, Edzná, Kabáh – at their peak. Puuc, Chenes and Río Bec styles are perhaps the finest pre-Hispanic architecture.

900–1520 AD ▸ Post-Classic. In central Mexico, a series of invasions by warlike tribes from the north. Toltecs make their capital at Tula (c.900–1150); new use of columns and roofed space – Chac-mools and Atlantean columns in decoration.

987 ▸ Toltec invasion of the Yucatán? New Toltec–Maya synthesis especially evident at Chichén Itzá.

C10 ▸ Mixtecs gain control of Oaxaca area. Mixtec tombs at Monte Albán, but seen above all at Mitla.

C11 ▸ League of Mayapán. Maya architecture in decline, as Mayapán itself clearly demonstrates.

C13 ▸ Arrival of the Mexica in central Mexico, last of the major "barbarian" invasions. Many rival cities in the Valley of México, including Tenayuca, Texcoco and Culhuacán.

1345 ▸ Foundation of Tenochtitlán – rapid expansion of the Aztec empire. Growth of all the great Aztec cities, especially Tenochtitlán itself. In the east, cities such as Cholula and Zempoala fall under Aztec influence, and in the south the Mixtecs are conquered. To the west, Purepecha (or Tarascan) culture developing, with their capital at Tzintzuntzan. Maya culture survives at cities such as Tulum.

1519 ▸ Cortés lands in present-day Veracruz.

1521 ▸ Tenochtitlán falls to Spanish. Spanish destroy many ancient cities. Early colonial architecture is defensive and fortress-like; churches and mansions in Mexico City and elsewhere, monasteries with huge atriums for mass conversions. Gradually replaced by more elaborate Renaissance and Plateresque styles – seen above all in churches in the colonial cities north of the capital.

1524 ▸ First Franciscan monks arrive.

1598 ▸ Conquest officially complete.

C17–C18 ▸ Colonial rulers grow in wealth and confidence. Baroque begins to take over religious building – great cathedrals at Mexico City and Puebla, lesser ones at, for example, Zacatecas. Towards the end the still more extravagant churrigueresque comes in: magnificent churches around Puebla and at Taxco and Tepotzotlán.

1810 ▶ Hidalgo proclaims Independence. The development of the Neoclassical style through the influence of the new San Carlos art academy, but little building in the next fifty chaotic years.

1821 ▶ Independence achieved.

1836 ▶ Texas declares independence – battles of the Alamo and San Jacinto.

1838 ▶ Brief French invasion.

1845 ▶ Texas allies itself with the US in the Mexican–American War.

1847 ▶ US troops occupy Mexico City.

1848 ▶ Half of Mexican territory ceded to US by treaty.

1858-61 ▶ Reform Wars between liberals under Benito Juárez and Church-backed conservatives. Many churches damaged or despoiled.

1861 ▶ Juárez triumphant; suspends payment of foreign debt. France, Spain and Britain send naval expeditions.

1862 ▶ Spain and Britain withdraw – invading French army defeated on May 5.

1863 ▶ French take Mexico City. Maximilian becomes emperor. Brief vogue for French styles. Paseo de la Reforma and Chapultepec Castle in the capital.

1866 ▶ French troops withdrawn.

1867 ▶ Juárez defeats Maximilian.

1876 ▶ Porfirio Díaz accedes to power. The Porfiriano period sees a new outbreak of Neoclassical and grandiose public building. Palacio de las Bellas Artes and Post Office in Mexico City. Theatres and public buildings throughout the country.

1910 ▶ Madero stands for election, sparking the Revolution. Another period of destruction rather than building.

1911 ▶ Díaz flees into exile.
1911–17 ▶ Vicious revolutionary infighting continues.

1920 on ▶ Modern Mexico. Modern architecture in Mexico is among the world's most original and adventurous, combining traditional themes with modern techniques. Vast decorative murals are one of its constant themes. The National Archeology Museum and University City in the capital are among its most notable achievements.

Ball-games and sacrifice: the pre-Columbian belief system

The Spanish Conquest and subjugation of Mesoamerica saw the destruction of more than just the physical remains of what at the time were some of the most advanced societies in the world. Still more pressing for the Spanish were the suppression of "alien" cultures and the propagation of Catholicism. All traces of traditional religion and culture were to be rooted out and systematically dismantled. In the process, hundreds of thousands of books were burnt, priests executed, temples overturned. Even now, when the state profits from the huge interest in the pre-Columbian world and pays lip service to multiculturalism, Mexican law forbids the teaching in schools of Yucatec Maya – the language of the people who built the pyramids. Such is the tenacity of traditional beliefs, though, that even five hundred years of effort have not been enough to eradicate them entirely, as anyone who has entered a rural Mexican church or witnessed the rituals of the Day of the Dead can attest.

Much of our knowledge of ancient Mesoamerican beliefs, then, is derived from the surviving traditions of contemporary indigenous groups, which have been handed down through the generations. Further fragments are gleaned from the various Spanish accounts, from hieroglyphs and images carved into the ruins of buildings, from sculpture and pottery, jewellery retrieved from tombs and the few surviving written records.

Shamanism: the root of Mesoamerican culture

The great **Mesoamerican civilizations** comprised some of the purest **theocracies** the world has ever known. Every aspect of life was sacred and formed part of a huge cosmic interplay between the everyday, material world and the dreamlike spirit world. This spirit world was home to a pantheon of gods, spirits and the souls of dead ancestors. The priests and kings who governed Mesoamerica so absolutely had privileged access to this realm, communicating with its denizens while in a state of trance, predicting the effect of the spiritual on the material from the motion of the stars, and maintaining the balance between the two worlds, thus avoiding misfortune or disaster. All was sacred – the days of the week, the cardinal points with their associated deities and spiritual properties – and every event from the planting of crops to the waging of war had to occur at the correct spiritual time.

This vast and elaborate belief system had its roots in **shamanism**, whose origins predate agriculture and settled village life. This is still the religion of the nomadic communities of Siberia, whose ancestors were the first to populate the Americas. In the shamanic universe everything is alive, not only in the material world but, more truly, in the spiritual. A rock has a soul every bit as much as a jaguar or a human being, and this soul can be separated from the physical form, a feat achieved by spiritually adept individuals known as shamans. The shaman's soul is able to travel through the spirit world, communing with gods, demons or ancestors or even appearing in the material world in another form, such as the shape of an animal. But the spirit world is an ambivalent place, containing both paradise and its opposite, inhabited by gods and demons and the souls of the evil as well as the good.

These malevolent and benevolent forces make the relationship between the **material and spiritual worlds** a delicate one. Disease, for instance, is not merely a physical condition, it is also a spiritual one which may result from the imprisoning of a soul by a malevolent spirit, or some other imbalance. The shaman, in a state of trance, can correct imbalances – journeying to free the soul from its prison, and thus making the material person well again. But in the shamanic universe, you rarely get something for nothing, and if a powerful spirit or a god is involved, sacrifice may be required to recompense that spirit.

The legacy of the shaman can be found in all Mexican religion. The Day of the Dead celebrations have their roots in a shamanic conception of the universe, as do the rituals of modern Mexican witchcraft. Nowadays, this legacy is most clearly seen in the belief systems of the tribes of northern Mexico, such as the **Yaqui** (whose shamanic traditions have been poetically immortalized by Carlos Castaneda) or the **Huichol**. It is worth taking a more detailed look at the practices and beliefs of the latter for the light it throws on ancient belief systems.

Huichol shamanism

In the province of Nayarit in the desert of northern Mexico, the **Huichol** have survived the dominance of the Aztecs, Nuño de Guzman's bloody conquest of western Mexico, the subsequent Spanish exploitation, the Revolution and the technological leaps of the twentieth century. More than any other people in Mexico, they have remained faithful to the spiritual beliefs of their ancestors, and their way of life has changed little in thousands of years, never really moving beyond the first stages of village life that their cousins to the south abandoned in about 1300 BC.

Like all shamanic communities, Huichols see the material and spirit worlds as two poles of one universe. The border between the two is blurred: the communities are in regular communication with their dead ancestors, most of whom live in the underworld, and who often sneak back into the world of the living to steal their maize beer. The spirit world is used as a constant reference for occurrences in the material, with shamans, known as **Maracames**, providing the readings that inform the community. Two facets of their cosmology – an orientation of their sacred buildings to the four cardinal points and a belief in a "first place" where their ancestors had been gods – stand out as distinctively Mesoamerican.

The most important Huichol buildings, **Xirikis**, are precisely oriented to the four cardinal points, each of which has a particular spiritual connotation. Each Xiriki is home to a disembodied ancestral shaman whose soul inhabits a quartz crystal attached to a ceremonial arrow lodged in its roof. Contemporary shamans use the spiritual strength of these crystals to travel to the Huichol spirit world, to confer with their ancestors, or with other spirits, and bring their wisdom into the community.

The centre of this spirit world is called **Wirikuta**. In the everyday, physical world, this is a dull stretch of desert in northwest Mexico, some 500km from Nayarit. In the spiritual world it is the Huichol womb of creation – the ground from which the sky and the stars emerged at the beginning of time, and the paradise where humans were created by the gods, and where for a while they lived with them as equals. The Huichol frequently visit Wirikuta in pilgrimages that involve taking peyote to induce trance-like states. A shaman guide orchestrates key rituals throughout the journey to protect the pilgrims from deceitful spirits, and interprets the landscape along the way: a waterhole becomes a spiritual gateway; shreds of cactus, the bones of ancestors. Plants, animals, rivers and mountains all have their associated spirits and their individual symbolic, sacred meaning.

Every aspect of Huichol life is filled with symbolism. Their bright weavings and intricate beaded masks reflect the spiritual reality behind the material, often depicting the three most sacred symbols of all – **corn**, the substance of creation, the **deer**, hunted for food but also revered, and **peyote**, the trance-inducing cactus. Gourds covered in brightly coloured beads, spelling out the wishes of their maker, are offered to the gods as sacrifices.

The Olmecs: the roots of Mesoamerican shamanism

Archeological research at **Olmec** sites tells us that many of the Huichol's beliefs were common to the first great Mesoamerican civilization, whose cities and preoccupations formed a template to be traced by subsequent cultures. The Olmecs were the first Mesoamerican civilization literally to set their cosmology in stone, making a permanent record of their rulers, and the gods and spirits with whom they communed. Like the Huichol, they had a Wirikuta, but the Olmec place of creation was in the shape of the mighty volcano of **San Martín** in the south of modern Veracruz state. They built a replica – a sacred artificial mountain, complete with fluted sides – in their city at **La Venta**. This was the original Mesoamerican **pyramid**, a feature that recurs in virtually every subsequent culture: the Classic Maya conceived of their cities as a living landscape of sacred artificial mountains and trees, while the Aztec Templo Mayor was a dual pyramid representing the two sacred mountains of Coatepec and Tonacateptl.

Into the base of their volcano pyramid the Olmecs embedded huge stone **stelae**, one portraying ruling dignitaries communicating with gods and spirits – shamans, who, because of their crucial importance in maintaining the balance between the material and spiritual, had come to govern Olmec society. Such stelae, the equivalent of the Huichol rooftop arrowheads, were regarded as embodiments of the gods or kings they represented – spiritual telephones to the dead and the divine, whose users operated them in a trance state. These were the first stelae in Mesoamerica, and later versions fill the plazas of ruined cities all over Mexico and Central America.

One stele at La Venta depicts a **World Tree**, a symbol of the "axis mundi" at the centre of the Mesoamerican universe: its roots in the earth, its branches in the heavens, linking the underworld of the dead with the earth and sky. Though this was perhaps the first such representation, World Trees have been found in cities all over Mesoamerica and are portrayed in Teotihuacán mythology and in the **Codex Borgia**, one of the most beautiful of the few surviving Aztec books. At Maya Palenque there are several, including one on the lid of a ruler's sarcophagus: here key symbols and events of Maya mythology are written in the patterns and motion of the stars, and the ruler is shown falling through a World Tree inscribed in the night sky – the Milky Way.

Opposite Mexico's first pyramid, the Olmecs built a **gateway** to the shamanic spirit world in the form of a sunken, court-shaped plaza with an enormous pavement of serpentine blocks. They added two large platforms on either side of the entrance into the court and deposited huge quantities of sacred serpentine inside. These two platforms were topped with mosaics and patterns depicting aquatic plants, symbols of a gateway to the spirit world. Such symbols appeared all over Mesoamerica in the ensuing centuries, often decorating ball-courts or ceramics.

Other surviving artefacts speak of stranger shamanic aspects to Olmec religion. **Statuettes** of half-jaguar, half-human babies probably depict the awakening of latent shamanic powers and associations with spirit animals – in the Mesoamerican pantheon each soul has its companion spirit animal. **Mirrors** found at Olmec cities were symbols of portals to the spirit world, an idea developed by the Aztecs, whose god, Tezcatlipoca ("Smoking Mirror") governs shamans and sorcerers in the Toltec and Aztec pantheon. In the Aztec creation myth, Tezcatlipoca assists Quetzalcoatl in the creation of the world.

The Olmec shaman-rulers also recompensed the gods and spirits through whom they kept the crucial balance between the material and the spiritual world. Human **sacrifice** and ritual blood-letting, those most Mesoamerican of practices, were probably developed by them for this purpose. And though there were different emphases, the basic structure of Olmec society – a theocracy ruled over by a priestly and regal elite who communicated with and propitiated the spirit world through sacrifice – would change little throughout Mesoamerica until the advent of Cortés. But there were some important developments. An increasing preoccupation with divining and balancing the material and the spirit world led to the invention of the calendar and writing, and the ball-game and sacrifice became ever more crucial, particularly in central Mexico, where the appetites of the malevolent and bloodthirsty Mesoamerican gods increased with each new civilization.

The calendar

The Mesoamericans believed that the relationship between the spirit world and the material was recorded in the stars, and that certain astronomical configurations were ominous. For the Maya and Aztecs, the stars themselves were embodiments of gods, and the constellations re-enactments of cosmic events. The Maya version of Wirikuta was in the night sky – they regarded the three stars below the belt of Orion as the place of creation itself. This preoccupation led to the invention of the **calendar**, probably by the Zapotecs of Monte Albán in about 600 BC. Subsequent depictions of calendars can be seen across the spectrum of Mesoamerican art, notably on the Aztec Piedra del Sol, now in the Museum of Anthropology in Mexico City, and in the paintings in Maya codices.

By the time of the Classic Maya (250–900 AD), the 260-day calendar had become the fundamental map of the relationship between the spirit and material worlds, and the highest tool of prediction and divination outside the trance state itself. Every number and day had its own significance; each of the twenty day names had a specific god and a particular direction, passing in a continuous anticlockwise path from one day to the next until a cycle of time was completed. This calendar was used alongside a 365-day calendar, roughly matching the solar year, but lacking the leap days necessary to give it real accuracy. This was divided into eighteen groups of twenty days plus an unlucky additional five days. Each twenty-day grouping and each solar year also had a supernatural patron. When the two calendars were set in motion and were running concurrently, it took exactly 52 years for the cycle to repeat. In addition to these two calendars, the pre-Classic Maya developed what is known as the **Long Count**, recording the total number of days elapsed since a mythological date when the first great cycle began. The mathematics required to administer this Long Count are advanced and complex – a stele at Copán in Honduras calculates the day of creation, recording it as a 29-figure number. For Mesoamerican civilizations, the ending of one cycle and the beginning of another heralded apocalypse and, afterwards, a new age and a reassertion of the ordered world from the disordered and demonic; one symbol of this new age was the construction of new temples over the old every 52 years. The Maya Long Count will end on December 23, 2012, and there are many who believe that this date will herald the end of the world that others predicted for the millennium.

Sacrifice

At the beginning of the 365-day cycle, the Aztecs extinguished all fires and smashed all ceramics throughout their empire. At midnight, if the stars passed overhead, priests ripped out the heart of a warrior and started a new fire in his chest – for the Aztecs, **sacrifice** was crucial in maintaining world harmony and the continuance of cosmic events. If the forces of the spirit world were not kept in balance with the proper appeasements, chaos and death would reign.

The ruling shaman-priests were vital to keep the world, and life itself, going, and sacrifice was one of their main tools: Mesoamericans believed that they were not so much living on borrowed time, but on time won by trickery from the gods of death. Maya vases, buried with the dead, often depict scenes from the Popul Vuh, the creation epic of the Quiché Maya, in which the Hero Twins defeat the **Lords of the Underworld** through a series of shamanic tricks and their skill at playing the ball-game. Central Mexican mythology went still further: life is not won from death by trickery, it is quite literally stolen. In one story, Quetzalcoatl and Xolotl descend to the underworld where they trick the god of death, Mictlantechutli, into giving them sacred bones left over from a previous creation. These bones are taken to the paradise of **Tamoanchán** – the central Mexican equivalent of the Huichol Wirikuta, or the Olmec San Martín – where they are ground into corn meal. The gods then let their blood into the ground meal, and humans are born. After the creation of people, the gods convene in darkness at Teotihuacán, where they decide to create a new sun. This, too, depends on sacrifice, and the two gods hurl themselves into a fiery furnace to become the sun and the moon.

The bloody creation mythology of central Mexico is filled with the presence of the Lords of the Underworld trying to regain the life that was stolen from them; none was more preoccupied with this than the Aztecs. The Aztec empire was enslaved to the Lords of the Underworld's seemingly insatiable appetite for **human hearts** – the price of continuing life and order. Bernal Díaz recounts the sacrifice of fattened children, women and captured warriors with horror, and concludes that the Aztec priests were slaves of the powers of darkness, an idea suggested even in their own mythology. The great Toltec prince **Quetzalcoatl Topiltzin**, renowned for his wisdom and holiness and founder of the great city of Tula, decided to make an end to human sacrifice and attempted to convince the inhabitants of Tula to give it up. He was unsuccessful, however, as the shamanic god, Tezcatlipoca, tricked the Toltecs and forced Quetzalcoatl Topiltzin into exile. Quetzalcoatl Topiltzin built a raft and left "for the east" from the Gulf coast, promising to return one day to banish false rulers and reinstate a higher order, where human sacrifice would play no part. It is a well-known irony that Cortés landed on the Gulf coast, where Quetzalcoatl Topiltzin was said to have left, at the time predicted for his return.

The ball-game

Like sacrifice and blood-letting, the Mesoamerican **ball-game**, once played all over pre-Hispanic Mexico and Central America, and still played in some villages in the Oaxaca valleys and the northwest, was imbued with shamanic symbolism and the Mesoamerican mythology of death. For though many Mesoamerican peoples saw the ball travelling through the alley of the court as the sun journeying in and out of the underworld, the game was primarily seen as a metaphor for life, death and regeneration.

Like so much of Mesoamerican religious tradition, the game was developed by the Olmecs, probably from an earlier prototype. A carving dating back to 900 BC, found at the Olmec city of **San Lorenzo**, depicts a ball-player kneeling to receive a ball; ball-players were depicted at Dainzú outside Oaxaca, sometime after 150 BC, and ball-courts appear in the pre-Classic Maya city of Izapa in the Chiapas mountains. The game was usually played in a ball-court shaped like a letter I. The players, in teams of two or three, would score points by hitting the ball with their upper arms or thighs, through hoops or at markers embedded in the walls of the court. Heavy bets were placed by supporters, and the penalty for losing the most important games was death (though there have been suggestions that the winners were sacrificed in some cities).

The Classic Veracruz civilization was obsessed with the ball-game, and there are more than seventeen courts in their most important city, **El Tajín**. Most are covered with superbly carved bas-reliefs showing all aspects of the game, including sacrifice: one depicts a ball-player having his chest cut open with an obsidian knife while a grinning skeleton rises from a pot. This figure appears in many of the carvings on the Tajín ball-courts, and is almost certainly an underworld lord – a personification of death. In Maya mythology, the ball-game is played against the Lords of the Underworld, most famously by the Hero Twins of the Popul Vuh. The largest court of all at **Chichén Itzá** is covered in bas-reliefs of aquatic plants, symbolizing an opening to the underworld. Still more depict the game and the death rituals that were associated with it. One shows a player holding the severed head of a captive. The stump of his neck spouts serpents – symbols of the spiritual life force contained in blood – which transform into water lilies, showing how the sacrifice opens the way to the spirit world.

Environment and wildlife

Mexico is one of the most biologically diverse countries in the world, with the second highest number of mammal species (450, after Indonesia), more than a thousand species of birds, at least 30,000 species of higher plants (including half of the world's pines), and more reptile species (700) than any other country. Many of these are endemic – found nowhere else – and this diversity, combined with its vast size (1,960,000 square kilometres) and tremendous range of natural environments, make Mexico an ideal location for the visiting naturalist, irrespective of expertise.

Specific wildlife highlights include: the grey whale calving grounds off the west coast of **Baja California** (at their best in Jan and Feb); the arid interior plains of **northern Mexico** and their diverse collection of cacti; the semi-tropical forests which line the **Gulf coast** near Veracruz; the lush tropical forests of **Chiapas** and **southern Yucatán**, containing the remaining populations of monkeys and large cats, and full of vividly coloured parakeets and toucans; the **Yucatán peninsula**, with its fabulous collection of migrating birds, including large flocks of greater flamingo, and the barrier reef and coastal islands in the Caribbean Sea, where the snorkelling reveals shoals of brilliantly coloured fish; the impressive colonies of sea birds along the **southern Pacific coastline**, including frigate birds and boobies. Dolphins are still commonly seen off all coastlines.

Unfortunately, as in many developing countries where economic hardship remains the prime concern, much of this natural beauty is under threat either from direct hunting or from the indirect effects of **deforestation** and **commercialization**. It is imperative that we, as paying visitors, show a responsible attitude to the natural environment where it remains, and endeavour to support the vital educational programmes which are seeking to preserve these remnants.

It should be stressed that not only is it extremely irresponsible, but it is also **illegal** to buy, even as souvenirs, most items that involve the use of wild animals or flowers in their production. This applies specifically to tortoiseshell, black coral, various species of butterfly, mussels and snails, stuffed baby crocodiles, cat skins and turtle shells. Trade in living animals, including tortoises, iguanas and parrots (often sold as nestlings) is also illegal, as is the uprooting of cacti.

Geography and climate

The distinct geographical pattern seen in Mexico, in conjunction with the climatic variation from north to south, creates a series of isolated **biomes**, each with its individual flora and fauna. The **Tropic of Cancer** divides the country laterally, technically placing half the country inside and half outside the tropics.

The predominant geographical features tend to be southward continuations of North American counterparts: the **Sierra Madre Oriental** range which lies to the east is an extension of the Rocky Mountain range, and the **Sierra Madre Occidental** range to the west is an extension of the **Sierra Nevada** range. The highlands that lie between and the intermontane basins form the lofty **Northern Plateau**, which extends from Mexico City to the western tablelands of the United States.

Further south (between latitudes 18 and 20 degrees north) lies the range of volcanoes known as the **Sierra Volcanica Transversal**, which rises in altitude towards its southern edge and runs from the Pacific coast, almost as far as the Gulf of Mexico. The lands south of this range are extensive coastal plains and plateaus (the low-lying Yucatán), with intermittent higher ranges, such as the **Oaxaca** and **Chiapas uplands**.

Most of the landmass is subject to the prevailing **trade winds** that blow from the northeast out across the Gulf of Mexico. Cool currents keep the Pacific coastal waters cooler and the air drier than the Atlantic coast, while the sharp escarpments of the Sierra Madre Oriental, creating a vast rain shadow, contribute to the aridity of the Northern Plateau.

Rainfall is variable across the landmass, scant in the arid deserts of the north Pacific and interior sierras and extremely heavy in the tropical cloud forests and rainforests of the southeastern slopes of the **Sierra Madre del Sur** and sections of the Gulf coast (the **rainy season** itself extends from late May to Oct or Nov).

Vegetation

The influence of long-term **deforestation** for charcoal cutting or slash-and-burn agriculture has substantially denuded the original forest which covered large areas of Mexico. Today the northern mountains contain tracts of conifer, cedar and oak, especially around Durango where the largest **pine forest** reserves are to be found. At lower altitudes, the grass-covered **savannas** are interrupted by the occasional palm or palmetto tree, and the riverbanks are graced with poplar and willow.

The **tropical rainforests** which border the Gulf of Mexico form a broad band that extends southwards from Tampico across the base of the Yucatán peninsula and the northern part of Oaxaca, containing mahogany, cedar, rosewood, ebony and logwood, but these reserves are being constantly depleted. **Seasonal tropical forest** and **dry scrub** cover the remaining areas of the Gulf coast and the lowlands of the Pacific coast. One particularly notable tree is a single **ahuehuetl** (or giant cypress), believed to have a bore of more than 50m in circumference and rumoured to be the oldest living thing in the Americas. Extensive **mangrove forests** once lined much of the Gulf coast and the Caribbean, and grew along sheltered reaches of the Pacific shore, but these are being destroyed throughout their range, as coastlines are developed for tourism.

The flatter lands of the north, the north Pacific and portions of central Mexico are characterized by dry scrub and grassland. The most conspicuous of the vegetation in these drier areas, however, are the **cacti**. Various species adorn these flat grasslands: the **saguaro** is a giant, tree-like growth which can exceed 15m in height, whereas the columns of the cereus cactus stand in lines, not dissimilar to fence posts, and can reach 8m in height. Another notable variety is the **prickly pear** (or nopal) which produces a fruit (tuna) that can be either eaten raw or used in the production of sweets. Other harvested varieties include the pulpy-leaved **maguey cactus** (one of the agave family), whose fermented juice forms the basis of tequila, *mescal* and pulque, and **henequen** (another agave), which is grown extensively on the Yucatán peninsula and used in the production of fibre.

The extensive temperate grasslands are composed primarily of clumped bunch grass and wiry, unpalatable **Hilaria grass**. Low-lying shrubs found amongst these grassy expanses include the spindly ocotillo, the **creosote** bush, the palm-like **yucca**, with low-lying **mesquite** and **acacia bushes** in the more sheltered, damper areas. Flowers are commonplace throughout Mexico and form an integral part of day-to-day life. Two flowers, **frangipani** and **magnolia**, were considered to be of such value that they were reserved for the Aztec nobility. Today the blue blossoms of **jacaranda** trees and purple and red **bougainvillea** still adorn the walls of cities and towns during their spring and summer blooms. Even the harsh arid deserts of the north are carpeted with wild flowers during the brief spring blooms which follow the occasional rains; the cacti blooms are particularly vivid. Many of these floral species are indigenous to Mexico, including **cosmos**, **snapdragons**, **marigolds**, **dahlias** and several species of **wild orchid** (over 800 species have been classified from the forests of Chiapas alone).

The tropical forests of Mexico provide supplies of both **chocolate** (from the cacao trees of the Chiapas) and **vanilla**, primarily for export. Also harvested are **chicle**, used in the preparation of chewing gum, from the latex of the **sapodilla** tree, and **wild rubber** and **sarsaparilla**. Herbs, used in the medicinal or pharmaceutical industries, include **digitalis** from wild **foxgloves** and various **barks** used in the preparation of purges and disinfectants. One plant, unique to Mexico, is **Discorea composita**, which is harvested in Veracruz, Oaxaca, Tabasco and Chiapas, and is used in the preparation of a vegetable hormone that forms an essential ingredient of the contraceptive pill.

Insects

Insect life is abundant throughout Mexico but numbers and diversity reach their peak in the tropical rainforests, particularly to the south of the country. Openings in the tree canopy attract a variety of colourful **butterflies**, **gnats** and **locusts** which swarm in abundance. For the most part, insect life makes itself known through the variety of bites and sores incurred whilst wandering through these areas: **mosquitoes** are a particular pest, with malaria still a risk in some areas. The **garrapata** is a particularly tenacious tick found everywhere livestock exists, and readily attaches itself to human hosts. A range of **scorpions**, whose sting can vary from extremely painful to definitively lethal, is found throughout the country.

Within the forests themselves, long columns of **leafcutter ants** crisscross the floor in their search for food, and surrounding tree trunks provide ideal shelter for the large, brown nests of termites. Further north in central Mexico, **army ants** have a direct bearing on the agricultural cycle: early cynicism by agronomists about the reluctance of peasant farmers to plant corn during certain phases of the moon has been forgotten with the realization that it is at these times that the ants are on the march. One species of ant, local to Tlaxcala, provides for seasonal labour not once but twice each year: firstly during the egg stage, when it is harvested to produce a highly prized form of caviar, and secondly during the grub stage, when it frequents the maguey cactus, which provides an equally prized food source. The most spectacular insect migration can be seen in winter in eastern Michoacán, where thousands of **Monarch butterflies** hatch from their larval forms en masse, providing a blaze of colour and movement (see p.249).

Fish, amphibians and reptiles

The diversity of Mexican inland and coastal habitats has enabled large numbers of both marine and freshwater species to remain mostly undisturbed. Among the freshwater species, **rainbow** and **brook trout**, **silversides** and **catfish** are particularly abundant (as are European **carp** in certain areas, where it has been introduced). The most highly regarded is a species of **whitefish** found in Lake Chapala and Lake Pátzcuaro, where it forms the basis of a thriving local fishing industry.

Offshore, Mexican waters contain over one hundred marine species of significance, including varieties of tropical and temperate climates, coastal and deep waters, surface and ground feeders and sedentary and migratory lifestyles. Among the more important species are **jewfish** (a type of giant sea bass), **swordfish**, **snapper**, **king mackerel**, **snook**, **tuna**, **mullet** and **anchovy**. **Shrimp**, **crayfish** and **spiny lobster** are also important commercial species. The marine fishing grounds on the Pacific coast are at their best off the coast of Baja California, where the warmer southern waters merge with subarctic currents from the north. Similarly, deep ocean beds and coastal irregularities provide correspondingly rewarding fishing in the waters of the Campeche bank on the Gulf of Mexico.

Reptiles are widely represented throughout Mexico. The lower river courses that flow through the southern forests are frequented by **iguana**, crocodile and its close relative, the **caiman**. Lizards range from the tiny **nocturnal lizards** along the Gulf coast to the **tropical iguanas**, which can reach up to 2m in length. **Marine turtles**, including the loggerhead, green, hawksbill and leatherback, are still found off many stretches of undeveloped waters and shores on both Atlantic and Pacific coasts. Hunting of both adults and eggs is now illegal, but numbers have been greatly reduced, as illegal hunting continues. Several kinds of **rattlesnake** are common in the deserts of northern Mexico, and farther south the rainforests hold a substantial variety of other snakes, including the **boa constrictor**, **fer-de-lance**, **bushmaster** and the small **coral snake**. Amphibian life is similarly abundant; varieties include salamanders, several types of **frog** (including several tree frogs in the southern forests) and one marine toad that measures up to 20cm in length.

Birds

More than five hundred species of tropical birds live in the rainforests and cloud forests of southern Mexico alone. Among these are resplendent **macaws**, **parrots** and **parakeets**, which make a colourful display as they fly amongst the dense tree canopy. The cereal-feeding habits of the parrot family have not endeared them to local farmers, and for this reason (and their continuing capture for sale as pets) their numbers have also been seriously depleted in recent times. Big-billed **toucans** perch on the lower branches and the occasional larger game birds, such as **curassow**, **crested guan**, **chachalaca** and **ocellated turkey** can be seen on the ground, amongst the dense vegetation.

Particularly rare are the brilliantly coloured **trogons**, including the resplendent **quetzal**, inhabiting the cloud forests of the Sierra Madre de Chiapas (in El Triunfo Reserve). The ancient Maya coveted its long, emerald-green tail feathers which were used in priestly headdresses; its current status is severely endangered. To the east, the drier tropical deciduous forests of northern Yucatán, the Pacific coastal lowlands and the interior lowlands provide an ideal habitat for several predatory birds including **owls** and **hawks**. The most familiar large birds of Mexico, however, are the carrion-eating **black** and **turkey vultures** – locally *zopilote* – often seen soaring in large groups. The Yucatán is also one of the last remaining strongholds of the small **Mexican eagle**, which features in the country's national symbol.

Large numbers of coastal lagoons provide both feeding and breeding grounds for a wide variety of aquatic birds – some of them winter visitors from the north – including **ducks**, **herons** and **grebes**. Foremost amongst these are the substantial flocks of graceful **flamingo** which can be seen at selected sites along the western and northern coasts of the Yucatán peninsula. In the north of Mexico, the harsher and drier environment is less attractive; outlying towns and villages form a welcome sanctuary from this harshness for a variety of **doves** and **pigeons**, and the areas with denser cover have small numbers of **quail** and **pheasant**. Any water feature in these drier zones, in addition to wetland areas further south, provides attractive migration stopover sites for large flocks of North American species, including **warblers**, **wildfowl** and **waders**.

Mammals

Zoologists divide the animals of the Americas into two categories: the **Nearctic** region of the mid-latitudes in which the native animals are of North American affinity, and the **Neotropical** region of the lower latitudes, in which the fauna is linked to that of South America. The Isthmus of Tehuantepec marks the border between these two regions, serving as a barrier to many larger mammalian species.

The northern Nearctic region is predominantly composed of open steppe and desert areas and higher-altitude oak and pine forests. Relatively few large mammals inhabit the highland forests, although one widespread species is the **white-tailed deer**, which is still overhunted as a source of food. The northern parts of the Sierra Madre Occidental mark the southernmost extent of several typically North American mammals, such as **mountain sheep**, and **black** and **brown bears**, though the latter are near extinction. Bears live in the Cumbres de Monterrey National Park and wild horned **sheep** can be seen at the San Pedro Mártir National Park in Baja California. Other mammals include **deer**, **puma**, **lynx**, **marten**, **grey fox**, **mule sheep**, **porcupine**, **skunk**, **badger**, **rabbit** and **squirrel**. A large array of smaller **rodents**, and their natural predators, the **coyote** and the **kit fox**, are also widespread throughout the forests. Nowadays the extensive grassland plains are frequented only by sporadic herds of white-tailed deer; the days of the pronghorn and even the bison have long passed under the burden of overhunting. Within the desert scrub, the **peccary** is still widely hunted, and rodents, as ever, are in abundance, forming an ample food supply for the resident **bobcats** and **ocelots**.

Baja California forms an outstanding wildlife sanctuary for marine mammals. Guadalupe Island is one of the few remaining breeding sites of the endangered **elephant seal**, and the only known mating and nursery sites of the **grey whale** are around Guerrero Negro. Although some southern species (notably the opossum and armadillo) have succeeded in breaching the Tehuantepec line, and now thrive in northern Mexico and the southern United States, on the whole the Neotropical region holds a very different collection of mammals. The relationship between these species and the lush vegetation of the tropical rainforest and the highland cloud forests is particularly apparent. Many species are arboreal, living amongst the expansive tree canopies: these include **spider** and **howler monkeys**, **opossums**, **tropical squirrels**, the racoon-like **coati** and the gentle **kinkajou**.

Because of the paucity of grass on the shaded forest floors, ground-dwelling mammals are relatively scarce. The largest is the **tapir**, a distant relative of the horse, with a prehensile snout, usually never found far from water. Two species of **peccary**, a type of wild pig, wander the forest floors in large groups seeking their preferred foods (roots, palm nuts and even snakes), and there's the smaller **brocket deer**. There are also large rodents, the **agouti** and the spotted **cavy**, which live in abundance along the numerous streams and riverbanks. These are hunted by the resident large cats, including **jaguar**, **puma** and **ocelot**.

The drier tropical and subtropical forests of northern Yucatán, the Pacific coastal lowlands and the interior basins produce a more varied ground cover of shrubs and grasses, which supply food for the **white-tailed deer** and abundant small rodents, including the spiny tree **rat** and the **paca**, which in turn provide food for a variety of predators such as the **coyote**, **margay** and **jaguarundi**. Other large mammals which can still be found in small numbers are large and small **anteaters**, **opossums** and **armadillos**. The reefs and lagoons which run along the Quintana Roo coast have small colonies of the large aquatic **manatee** or sea cow, a docile creature which feeds on sea grass.

Wildlife sites

It would be almost impossible to compile a comprehensive list of sites of wildlife interest in Mexico, particularly as so much can be seen all over the country. The following is a selection of some of the outstanding areas, particularly ones that are easily accessible or close to major tourist centres. The few zoos that exist in Mexico are generally depressing places, but there is one outstanding exception – the conservation-oriented **Zoológico Miguel Ál varez del Toro** in Tuxtla Gutiérrez.

Baja California

Easily accessible from the west coast of the United States, the peninsula of **Baja California** is a unique part of the Mexican landmass. Its exceptional coastline provides sanctuaries for a wide variety of marine mammals, including the major wildlife attraction of the area, the migratory grey whale (see overleaf). The lagoons where the whales gather can also offer superb views of other great whales, including blue, humpback, fin, minke, sperm and orca (killer whales). Dolphins and sea lions and a variety of sea birds, including pelicans, ospreys and numerous waders such as plovers and sanderlings also inhabit the lagoons. The sparse vegetation provides roosting sites for both jaegers and peregrines and even the occasional coyote may be seen wandering over the sandy shores.

Offshore, there are several small islands whose protected status has encouraged colonization by highly diverse animal communities. Furthest north is the island of **Todos Santos** where the sandy beaches, festooned with the remnants of shellfish, are used as occasional sunning spots by the resident harbour seals. The atmosphere is ripe with an uncommon blend of guano, kelp and Californian sagebrush. The Pacific swell frequently disturbs the resting cormorants, which bask in the hot sunshine, and the skies are filled with wheeling western gulls (similar to the European lesser blackback gull) from the thriving colony on the island.

Farther south lies the island of **San Benito**, which lies just to the northeast of the much larger island of Isla Cedros. The island provides ideal nesting grounds for migrating ospreys, which travel south from the United States. The hillsides are covered by the tall agave (century plants) whose brief, once-in-a-lifetime blooms add an attractive splash of colour to the surrounding slopes. These towering succulents produce a broad rosette of golden florets, which provide a welcome supply of nectar for resident hummingbirds, and ravens wheel above, searching for carrion. The island, along with Isla Cedros and the distant **Isla Guadalupe** (now a biological reserve), also provides a winter home to thousands of elephant seals, now happily recovering after years of overhunting. The large adult males arrive in December and the pebbly coves are soon crammed with the noisy and chaotic colony of mothers, calves and bachelor bulls, ruled by one dominant bull (or beach master) which can weigh

Grey whale migration and breeding

It is the **grey whales** and their well-documented migrations off the west coast of the peninsula that remain the outstanding spectacle of the region and continue to attract an estimated 250,000 visitors each year. Times have not always been so peaceful for these graceful leviathans; less than 150 years ago, the secret breeding grounds of the whales were discovered by **Charles Melville Scammon**. The Laguna Ojo de Liebre (renamed in recent times after the infamous whaler) was rapidly denuded of almost all of these magnificent beasts, and it wasn't until the establishment of **Scammon's Bay** as the world's first whale sanctuary in 1972 that their numbers began to recover. The population in the area is currently estimated at about 20,000 – a dramatic recovery within the time span.

The whale's **migratory route** runs the length of the American Pacific seaboard, from Baja to the Bering Sea and back; this is a round-trip of some 20,000km, which remains the longest recorded migration undertaken by any living mammal. They remain in the north for several months, feeding on the abundant krill in the high Arctic summer, and building up body reserves for the long journey south to the breeding lagoons. The migration begins as the days begin to shorten and the pack ice starts to thicken, sometime before the end of January.

Nowadays the human interest in the whales is purely voyeuristic, **whale-watching** being a million-dollar industry, and in 1988 the Mexican government extended the range of the protected area to include the nearby **San Ignacio Lagoon**, forming an all-embracing national park, the **Biosfera El Vizcaíno**. The San Ignacio Lagoon offers a daunting entrance of pounding surf and treacherous shoals, but once inside, its calmer waters flatten and spread inland for 15km towards the distant volcanic peaks of the Santa Clara mountains. Accessible points for land-based observation lie further north in the **Parque Natural de Ballena Gris** ("Grey Whale Natural Park"), 32km south of Guerrero Negro.

up to two tonnes. The males make a terrifying spectacle as, with necks raised and heads thrown back, they echo their noisy threats to any would-be rival who challenges the mating rights within their harem.

The interior of the peninsula has several areas of wildlife interest, many of which now have the protected status of nature reserve. Most significant of all are the national parks of the **Sierra San Pedro Mártir** and the **Desierto Central**. Here the chapparal-covered hills cede to forests of Jeffrey pine and meadow tables, interspersed with granite *picachos* (peaks) and volcanic mesas. The **Constitución de 1857** national park is another green oasis amongst the arid lowlands, where the coniferous woodlands form a picturesque border to the central **Laguna Hanson**. These sierras are renowned for the numerous palm-filled canyons which cut deep into the eastern escarpment; they make spectacular hiking areas with their miniature waterfalls, ancient petroglyphs, caves, hot springs and groves of fan palms.

Durango

Durango lies within a dry, hilly area where the intermittent oak and pine woodland is surrounded by large expanses of low-lying scrub. These areas are frequented by large numbers of birds, whose presence is an extension of their North American range. Typical species include red-tailed hawk, American kestrel and mockingbird. The denser, wooded areas provide the necessary cover for several more secretive varieties such as Mexican jay, acorn woodpecker, hepatic grosbeak and the diminutive Mexican chickadee. This is also an occasional haunt of the mountain lion (or puma) and the coyote. In the dry scrub, scorpions abound. Other nearby sites worthy of investigation include **El Salto** and **El Palmito**.

The Mazatlán estuary

The **Mazatlán estuary** is an extensive area of estuarine sands with marshy margins: ideal feeding grounds for a variety of waders and wildfowl, including marbled godwit, greater yellowlegs and willet. Large numbers of herons and egrets feed in the shallow waters (including little green and Louisiana heron and snowy and cattle egret), while further out to sea passage birds include laughing gull, gull-billed tern and olivaceous cormorant. Most spectacular of all are the aptly named magnificent frigate birds, which make a dramatic sight with their long wings, forked tails and hooked bills, as they skim over the water's surface in their search for fish.

The rocks offshore provide a suitable breeding site for both brown and blue-footed booby, and the pools at the northern end of the town, behind the large hotels, have some interesting water birds, including jacana, ruddy duck and canvasback.

San Blas

Immediately around **San Blas** are lagoons with wildlife very similar to that found in the Mazatlán estuary; boat tours from San Blas take you out to see herons, egrets and much more, with the possibility of a caiman the big attraction. Farther out the landscape forms areas of thicker scrub and dense forest at higher altitudes. Amongst the lower-lying scrub, it is possible to see the purplish-backed jay, gila woodpecker and tropical kingbird, whilst the skies above have the patrolling white-tailed kite. At higher altitudes, the birdlife includes the locally named San Blas jay, white-crowned parrot and cinnamon hummingbird. The town itself provides sufficient scraps for scavengers such as black and grey hawk and various rodents.

Veracruz and the Gulf coast

The eastern coastline of Mexico has particular attractions of its own, and none is more rewarding to the visiting naturalist than the final remaining tract of rainforest on the Mexican **Gulf coast**, southeast of **Veracruz**. The surrounding vegetation is lush, the tended citrus orchards yielding to rolling tropical forest, with its dense growth of ficus, mango and banana trees and the occasional coconut palm. These trees provide cover for a colourful underlying carpet including orchids, lemon trees, camellias, fragrant cuatismilla and gardenias. Even the roadsides are lined with banks of hibiscus, oleander and the pretty, white-flowered shrub known locally as "cruz de Malta". At the centre of the whole area, **Lake Catemaco** is outstandingly beautiful.

The surrounding forest has suffered much in recent times and many of the larger mammals are no longer found in the region. One sanctuary which remains amongst this destruction is the ecological research station of **Los Tuxtlas**. Although the institute's holding is fairly small, it adjoins a much larger state-owned reserve of some 25,000 acres on the flank of the **San Martín volcano**. Despite the problems of poaching and woodcutting, the area has the last remaining populations of brocket deer, black howler monkey, ocelot, jaguarundi, kinkajou and coati. It also boasts 92 species of reptile, fifty amphibians, thousands of insects and over three hundred species of birds.

With patience, it is possible to see such outstanding varieties as keel-billed toucan, black-shouldered kite, gold-crowned warbler, red-throated ant tanager, plain-breasted brush finch, red-lored parrot, ivory-billed woodpecker and the magnificent white hawk, to name but a few.

Palenque and the Chiapas uplands

In the **Chiapas uplands**, the absence of climatic moderation by lower altitudes and coastal breezes creates dense, lush vegetation that is truly worthy of the name of tropical rainforest. The **Sierra Madre de Chiapas** is of particular interest to visiting naturalists, particularly the Pacific slope at altitudes between 1500m and 2500m, as these are the last sanctuary of the endangered horned guan and azure-rumped tanager and even the quetzal. **El Triunfo Reserve**, at 1800m in the very southeastern corner of the country, less than 50km from the Guatemalan border, makes an excellent base camp for exploration of the area. The cloud forest is dense in this locality and the tall epiphyte-laden trees grow in profusion on the slopes and in the valleys, in the humid conditions which occur after the morning fogs have risen (generally by early afternoon).

Another area of interest in eastern Chiapas is the **Lagos de Montebello National Park** (see p.674), where the more determined bird-watcher may be rewarded with views of azure-hooded jay and the barred parakeet. Human encroachment has substantially reduced the number of large mammals in the area, but small numbers of howler monkey, tapir and jaguar (known locally as "el tigre") are a reminder of bygone days. Another speciality of the region is a vivid and diminutive tree frog, whose precise camouflage ensures that it is more often heard than seen.

At the archeological site of **Palenque** you're back among the tourists (and the howler monkeys), but the birding is unrivalled, and local specialities include the chestnut-headed oropendola, scaled ant pitta, white-whiskered puffbird, slaty-tailed trogon and masked tanager.

In the area of marshland around the **Río Usumacinta** about 25km east of the junction between the main Palenque road and Highway 186, pinnated bittern, everglade kite and the rare lesser yellow-headed vulture have all been recorded.

The Yucatán peninsula

The vegetation of the **Yucatán peninsula** is influenced by its low relief and the ameliorating effects of its extensive coastline which brings regular and fairly reliable rain along with year-round high temperatures. In the north it's predominantly dry scrub and bush, although large areas have been cleared for the cultivation of crops such as maize, citrus fruits and henequen. To the south is lusher tropical and subtropical forest, where the effects of agriculture are less obvious, and the dense forest of acacia, albizias, widespread gumbo limbo and ceiba is in parts almost impenetrable. These form an ideal shelter for scattered populations of both the white-tailed and brocket deer. The whole peninsula is a unique wildlife area, with the birdlife being particularly outstanding. Two specific sites worthy of thorough investigation are the archeological sites of Cobá and Chichén Itzá. The abundant and spectacular birds which fill the treetops include squirrel cuckoo, citreoline trogon and Aztec parakeet, whilst circling in the skies above are the resident birds of prey such as bat falcon, snail kite and the ever-present black and turkey vultures (these can be distinguished, even at great heights, as the wings of the latter are clearly divided into two bands – the darker primaries and the lighter secondaries being quite distinct). It is also possible to see all three species of Mexican toucan: collared aracari, emerald toucanet and the spectacular keel-billed. The denser areas of forest also hold small remnants of the original black howler and spider monkey populations.

The village of **Cobá** borders a lake with extensive reed margins along its eastern edge, which attracts a variety of water birds. Typical visitors, either migratory or resident, include the grebe, the elusive spotted rail, ruddy crake, northern jacana and the occasional anhinga – a cormorant-like bird which captures fish by spearing them with its dagger-like bill. The reed beds provide cover for several more-secretive species, including mangrove vireo, ringed kingfisher and blue-winged warbler, as well as several varieties of hirundine such as mangrove swallow and grey-breasted martin.

Chichén Itzá is a must on the list of any visitor, but save a little time at the end of the day for an exploration of the forested areas which lie to the south of the "Nunnery". The drier climate and lower altitude in this part of the peninsula encourages a sparser vegetation, where the oaks and pines are less obvious. Other colours amongst this greenness come from a variety of splendid flowers, such as the multicoloured bougainvillea, the aromatic frangipani and the eye-catching blue and mauve blooms of the jacaranda tree. Occasional splashes are added by the striking red flowers of the poinsettia (or Christmas flower) and the brilliant yellows of golden cups, during their spring and summer blooms. The resident birds appear oblivious to the busy tourist traffic, and amongst the quieter areas, to the south and southwest of the main site, the abundant birdlife includes plain chachalaca (surely a misnomer), ferruginous pygmy owl, cinnamon hummingbird, turquoise-browed motmot and numerous brilliant vireos, orioles and tanagers.

Cancún, Cozumel and the Caribbean coast

Even the mega-resort of **Cancún** has wildlife possibilities: the lagoons which line the outskirts have a variety of birds (such as great-tailed grackle and melodious blackbird). These wetland wastes form an ideal breeding ground for a number of brilliantly coloured dragonflies and damselflies, and the offshore scuba diving and snorkelling is quite stunning. More importantly the longest barrier reef in the Americas begins just south of the town. These extensive and spectacular reefs are formed by the limey skeletons of dozens of species of coral. The diversity of shape and form is spectacular, with varieties such as star, lettuce, gorgonian, elkhorn and staghorn being particularly widespread. The reefs provide food and shelter for over four hundred species of fish alone, including several species of parrotfish (which browse on the coral), butterfly fish, beau gregories, rock beauties and porkfish; the blaze of colour and feeling of abundance is unforgettable. The coral also provides protection for several other residents, such as spiny lobster, sea urchins, crabs and tentacled anemones, but this fragile environment requires cautious exploration if the effects of snorkellers and boat anchors are not to destroy the very thing that they seek to enjoy.

Puerto Juárez, where the ferries to Isla Mujeres leave from, and **Isla Mujeres** itself, offer a slightly less "touristy" environment in which to appreciate the natural beauty of the area. The birdlife is also quite spectacular, with frequent views of frigate bird, brown noddy, laughing gull, rufus-tailed hummingbird, tropical kingbird and the ubiquitous bananaquit.

A series of offshore islands and coastal sites in Yucatán are worthy of special mention. Natural parks and nature reserves include **Celestún**, on the west coast, and **Río Lagartos**, to the north. Both parks have spectacular flocks of migratory flamingoes, which winter here in the milder climate. **Isla Contoy** bird sanctuary off the northeastern tip of the peninsula is a worthwhile and popular day-trip from Cancún, and at **Puerto Morelos**, the largest botanic garden in Mexico provides a wonderful spot to observe numerous coastal and forest species.

Playa del Carmen is frequented by various wetland species including American wigeon, and the ferry trip to **Cozumel** island produces sightings of sea birds such as royal and Caspian terns, black skimmer, frigate birds and Mexican sheartails. On the island, the most rewarding sites are a couple of kilometres inland on the main road that runs across the island. The sparse woodland and hedgerows provide shelter for many typical endemics, such as Caribbean dove, lesser nighthawk, Yucatán and Cozumel vireo, the splendid bananaquit and a variety of tanagers. Elusive species which require more patient exploration (best through the mangroves which lie 3km north of **San Miguel** along the coast road) are the mangrove cuckoo, yellow-lored parrot, Caribbean ealania and Yucatán flycatcher.

The highlight of the peninsula's protected areas is the magnificent **Sian Ka'an Biosphere Reserve**, which includes coral reef, mangroves, fresh- and salt-water wetlands and littoral forest – possibly the widest range of flora and fauna in the whole of Mexico.

Chris Overington with Peter Eltringham

Mexican music

As in Cuba, the international boom in Mexican music took place in the 1940s and 1950s, when classic songs like "Besame Mucho" and "Cielito Lindo" crooned out from cinema screens and radios and were played by "Latin-style" orchestras all over the world. This so-called "golden age" had died out by the 1960s when the boom in Mexican cinema ended, and the music retreated to within its borders. Here live music continues to thrive, whether performed by romantic trios or twenty-piece dance orchestras, responding to a country that loves to dance and sing.

As Buñuel was making cinema history in the capital, **Celia Cruz** came from Cuba to seek her fortune along with **Beny Moré**, **Bienvenido Granda** and **Damasio Pérez Prado**, the last of whom developed the mambo rhythm between shifts as a session pianist at the Churrubusco film studios. These musicians were attracted by the bright lights of a city that didn't sleep: cosmopolitan and bohemian, Mexico City had long welcomed musicians from all over Latin America and taken their styles of music to heart. It's now the international capital of both **danzón**, originally from Cuba, and **cumbia**, from Colombia. Go to the Salón Los Angeles in the old centre of Mexico City on a Tuesday evening at 7pm, and you'll find seven hundred couples dancing, direct from the office. Sunday is the big night, however, when the enormous wooden floors carry the scent of shoe polish and perfume, and three different fourteen-piece orchestras play *danzones* old and new.

Despite its history as a centre of Latin music, Mexico was closed to **rock** music until the late 1980s, when a change in import regulations and in laws that specifically banned rock concerts resulted in a flood of music from north of the border and from Europe. A result of this influx in international rock, and arguably the most important musical phenomenon of the last few years, has been the emergence of Mexican rock bands. The boom began in the 1980s with middle-class rockers like **Los Caifanes** playing to middle-class audiences who knew about the outside scene because they, or their parents, travelled regularly to Europe and the States. Ironically, the Caifanes' massive hit was with a cover of a traditional Cuban *son*, "La Negra Tomasa", which appealed to a public that understands *son* and salsa better than rock.

In the 1990s, **Café Tacuba** and **Maldita Vecindad** began to reach a bigger audience, both bands with an interest, to some extent, in exploring Mexican roots and reinterpreting Mexican *son* in their own way, as Los Lobos did so successfully a decade earlier. Then came **Maná** from Mexico's second city, Guadalajara, and Mexican rock entered the superstar level, albeit with a style that hovers rather too closely above the pop ballads so keenly promoted by the media giant Televisa. Most recently, the emergence of the rap band **Molotov** has challenged the polite pulp of Televisa, and they have become controversial cult heroes, with a first CD that sold something like a million copies in Mexico alone. Rock, in its different guises, is booming, and new bands like **Plastelina Mosh**, **Control Machete** and **El Gran Silencio** are finding a home in the barrios of the world's biggest city.

Son

When Mexican rock bands like Café Tacuba look to their musical roots for the source of their inspiratation, they look to Mexican **son**. *Son* is a traditional music that grew out of the eighteenth-century encounter between Spanish, indigenous and African cultures – a style first popularized by the **mariachi** bands, those extravagantly passionate musicians who came originally from Jalisco state. Though the same encounter produced Cuban *son* and other Latin American styles like the Venezuelan *joropo*, Mexican *son* fast developed its own distinct sound.

In fact, Mexican *son* describes eight or nine different styles of music, all of which share certain aspects: all are country styles that rely on the participation of their public to add counter-rhythms through **zapateado** foot-stamping dancing, and all are incredibly creative – a *son* musician has to be able to make up lyrics on the spot in response to a comment from the dance floor, and the lead musician has to be able to create new flights on his violin or guitar that will satisfy a public that demands nothing less than inspiration. *Son* is almost always played by a string band, with lyrics, sung in four-line *coplas*, that are witty, more sexual than sensual, poetic and proud.

Most internationally famous are the **sones jaliscienses**, the original repertoire of the *mariachi* bands, although, sadly, few of the commercial bands now play this music, preferring the more simple ballads and *cumbias* that their public knows from the radio and TV. To hear the bands who still master the original *sones*, it's best to skip Mexico City's infamous Plaza Garibaldi and head off to southern Jalisco, where incredible twelve- or fourteen-piece *mariachis*, like **Los Reyes del Aserradero** and **Mariachi Tamazula**, offer spectacular violins, plenty of trumpet and vocal harmonies in a sophisticated version of the country *sones* that were orignally played on a harp and three guitars. *Mariachis* became nationally and internationally popular following the cinema boom, when regional music was being recorded by major labels, notably RCA – a few of these treasures can be found on cassettes in markets, and there's a healthy trade among collectors looking for the original vinyls, but little has been re-released on CD.

Apart from the *sones* from Jalisco, the **sones jarochos** from Veracruz also received a lot of attention. Many Jarocho musicians like **Andrés Huesca**, **Nicolás Sosa** and **Lino Chávez** tasted the big time in Mexico City before – as in the case of Nicolás Sosa – returning to the main square ofVeracruz to play to the public whose taste was less subject to fashion. Today, there is a new interest in *son jarocho*, and the first lady of this style is without doubt **Graciana Silva**, "La Negra Graciana", who was offering her *sones* for ten pesos a piece to the people drinking beers and eating fresh prawns in Veracruz's zócalo until one of such drinkers turned out to know more than she had expected about *son jarocho*. Eduardo Llerenas invited her to record for his staunchly independent label, Discos Corason, and the CD generated great interest in Europe. La Negra set off to play her *sones* at the Barbican Centre and Royal Festival Hall in London, at the Théâtre de la Ville in Paris and at the Harbourfront Centre in Toronto.

Around the port ofVeracruz, and in villages like Medellín de Bravo, where La Negra was born, the **African** influence has left its imprint on *son jarocho*, although further south the **indigenous** presence is much stronger and the harp virtually never played. Instead, the line-up consists exclusively of *requinto* and *jarana* guitars of different sizes and tunings. The *sones* are played more slowly and with a melancholy that is not so evident around the port. In the south of Veracruz, several young bands experimenting with fusions and creating new compositions gather annually on February 2 for the spectacular **Fiesta de la Candelaria in Tlacotalpan**. They set up a stage, and band after band is invited to play, several of whom invite the old *soneros* of the region to join their line-up. Leading this generation of Jarocho musicians is **Gilberto Gutiérrez** and his band, Mono Blanco, who have recorded with the Mexican label Urtext.

Perhaps most vibrant today is the **Huastecan** style of *son*, in which a virtuoso violin is accompanied by a *huapanguera* and a *jarana* guitar, the two guitarists singing falsetto vocals between flights of the violin. Each *son huasteco* is reinvented every time it's played: the singers compose new verses and the violinist creates new flourishes in response to the calls of a public who won't accept copies. There are literally hundreds of Huastecan *son* trios, the most outstanding being **Los Camperos de Valles**, **Trio Tamazunchale** and the youngsters **Dinastia Hidalguense**. Less known bands play in *cantinas* and at country fiestas throughout the Huastecan region and participate in a growing number of festivals in Huastecan towns like Pahuatlán, Huejutla, Amatlán and, most recently, Xilitla. In the cafés of Mexico City's Coyoacán barrio, trios sell their *sones* by the piece, offering impressive versions of "La Huasanga", "El Llorar" and "El Fandanguito", amongst other *sones*, which are technically very demanding.

Seldom heard in the city but enormously popular back home in the villages of the Sierra Gorda, the **arribeño** style is the most poetic form of *son*. Here, the *trovador* – who seems to be the natural successor of the medieval troubadour – is a country poet, often with no formal education, who composes verses about local heroes, the planets, the earth and the continuing struggles for land. Usually two *trovadores*, both playing the *huapanguera* guitar and each accompanied by two violins and the small *vihuela* guitar, confront each other on tall bamboo platforms that are erected on two sides of the village square. The poets enter into musical combat, improvising verses which are interspersed with the *zapateado* dancing. Each year on December 31, probably the greatest living *trovador*, **Guillermo Velázquez**, organizes a festival in his village which pays homage to the old musicians before starting the *topada* musical combat that lasts all night.

Based in the Mexican west, in the hotlands of the Río Balsas basin, the legendary violinist **Juan Reynoso** recently won the prestigious National Prize for Arts and Science, never before given to a country musician. Rebaptized by a local poet as "The Paganini of the Hotlands", Reynoso is an extraordinary violinist, even within the local tradition of *sones calentanos*, which are known for their complex melodies on the violin. Musicians find it hard to follow Don Juan, whose flights take unexpected turns, and whose genius, fortunately, has been recognized during his lifetime with a series of prestigious prizes, books, videos, concerts and tours.

Further west, in a region where the heat is so intense that it's known as "Hell's Waiting Room", **sones de arpa grande** (*sones* of the big harps) are one of Mexico's best-kept musical secrets. These bands – made up of a big harp, one or two violins and two guitars – don't thrive as they used to, but it's still possible to track down some great hair-raising harp by masters such as **Juan Pérez Morfín**, who plays with the legendary violionist **Beto Pineda**. In the brothels of Apatzingán and in the country fairs of the region, the sound boxes of the big harps are beaten in counter-rhythm by one of the musicians of the band or by a local fan who pays for the privilege. The harpist, meanwhile, must hold on to the melody – and his harp – with vocals that can sound something like a shout from the soul. Concerts are often organized by wealthy stable-owners who pride themselves on their dancing horses: although *norteño* music is very popular in this region, the horses will only dance to the big harp music, and they do so on wooden platforms, beating out the rhythm and counter-rhythm with their hooves.

Although *son* is basically *mestizo* music, several indigenous cultures play instrumental *sones* to accompany their ritual dances. **Sones abajeños** is the frenetic party music of the Purépecha of Michoacán, played on guitars, violins and a double bass. Between *abajeños*, the same musicians sing the hauntingly beautiful **Purépecha** love songs, *pirecua*, which are composed in honour of a girlfriend or of some local event. Outstanding Purépecha *son* bands include **Atardecer** (Sunset), from the lake village of Jarácuaro, and **Erandi** (Dawn). In the southern state of Oaxaca, the vibrant Zapotec culture has produced some of the country's great love songs and inspired mainstream Mexican romantic singers along the way. Sung in both Zapotec and Spanish, the **sones istmeños**, as they are known, are played to a slower 3/4 rhythm and are more melancholy than the *mestizo sones*. They boast some great solo passages on the *requinto* guitar and uniquely Zapotecan vocals, creating a very beautiful repertoire that has tempted some of Mexico's greatest urban vocalists to learn the Zapotecan lyrics and perform them in the big-city venues. **Lila Downs**, half-Mixtecan, half-American, is among the most successful and, typically, her repertoire also includes *rancheras*, *boleros* and jazz.

Ranchera

It's interesting that the great divas of Mexican music, of which there is a long tradition, are currently turning to Mexican traditional and country music to develop their own repertoire. Singers like **Tania Libertad** and **Betsy Pecanins**, enormously popular throughout the 1980s as **nueva canción** (new song) protest singers, are now singing their own versions of *norteños*, *mariachi*, *sones istmeños* and Mexican *boleros* to a more mature public. Outstanding among this illustrious company is **Eugenia León**, whose vocal range and passion encompasses a broad range of music styles. This diva tradition has a direct line back to the early days of *ranchera* music, an urban style that emerged alongside the new towns and cities in the early decades of the twentieth century and that became massively popular with the growth of film and radio.

"Ranchera" comes from the word *rancho*, farm, although the music was composed in the towns and cities for a public that wanted to remember how it used to be. The wit and freshness of the original *son* lyrics were replaced by bitter words about loss and betrayal, while musically the intensity shifted from the complex melody and rhythms of *son* to the melodramatic style of singing *ranchera*.

The first great diva of *ranchera* music was **Lucha Reyes**, whose emotionally charged voice hinted at her own inner turmoil. She died tragically in the style of Billie Holiday and others, but her work has been resuscitated by the great Mexican cabaret singer **Astrid Hadad**, who offered a postmodern take on Reyes for the early 1990s, carried off so successfully because of her particular blend of humour and a very fine voice. Although Astrid now includes a breadth of Latin cabaret music in her repertoire, her great moments were captured in her first CD of *ranchera* songs called, quite simply, *¡Ay!*.

Of the classic *ranchera* singers, the divas are now few and far between since the death of **Amalia Mendoza** and, more recently, of the great **Lola Beltrán** and of **María de Lourdes**. Today, fame and fortune has passed to a younger generation of male singers and, in particular, to **Alejandro Fernández**, a superstar who has left his father, the *ranchera* star Vicente Fernández, in the shade. Although musically there's little of the original *ranchera* left in Alejandro's repertoire, the melodrama and the association with ranch culture still exist – the *mariachi* trousers and sombrero hat are still in place; nonetheless Alejandro represents a different generation, more in the style of the new rock idols.

Norteño

Apart from *ranchera*, the style that has had most popularity throughout the country is probably **norteño**. Known north of the border as **Tex-Mex**, *norteño* has its roots in the *corrido* ballads that retold the battles between Anglos and Meskins in the early nineteenth century. The war turned out badly for Mexico, which lost half its territory, and Mexicans living in what is now California, Arizona, New Mexico and Texas found themselves with a new nationality.

The late 1920s were the golden age of the **corrido**, when songs of the recent Revolution were recorded in the hotels of San Antonio, Texas, and distributed on both sides of the border. The accordion, which had arrived with bohemian immigrants who came to work in the mines in the late nineteenth century, was introduced into the originally guitar-based groups by **Narciso Martínez** and **Santiago Jimenez** (father of the famous Flaco) in the 1930s, and the sound that they developed became the essence of *corrido* ensembles on both sides of the border.

When the **accordion** appeared, it brought the polka with it, and by the 1950s this had blended with the traditional duet-singing of northern Mexico and with salon dances like the waltz, mazurka and the *chotis* (the central European *schottische* that travelled to Spain and France before arriving in northern Mexico) to produce the definitive *norteño* style. The accordion had already pepped up the songs with lead runs and flourishes between the verses, but the *conjuntos norteños* needed to round out their sound to keep up with the big bands and so added bass and rolling drums – the basis of today's **conjuntos**.

Unlike most other regional styles, *norteño* is popular throughout the country. At a party in an isolated mountain community in central Mexico, the host takes out his accordion and plays *norteño corridos* until the dawn breaks. In an ice-cream parlour on the Pacific coast, the piped music is a *norteño* waltz. And waiting for darkness to cross the border at Tijuana, *norteños* are again the musical backdrop.

This countrywide popularity is most likely due to the **lyrics**. *Norteño* songs speak to people in words more real and interesting than the cozy pseudo-sophistication of Mexican pop music. The ballads tell of anti-heroes: small-time drug runners, illegal "wet-back" immigrants, a small-time thief with one blond eyebrow who defied the law. *Norteño* reflects the mood of a country that generally considers the government to be big-time thieves and hence has a certain respect for everyday people with the courage to stand up to a crooked system.

El Gato Felix (Felix the Cat)

I'm going to sing a *corrido*
About someone who I knew
A distinguished journalist
Feared for his pen
From Tijuana to Madrid

They called him Felix the Cat
Because the story goes that
He was like those felines
He had seven lives
And he had to see them through

He came from Choi, Sinaloa
That was the place he was born
He stayed in Tijuana
Because it took his fancy
And he wanted to help in some way
With what he wrote in the paper

He made the government tremble
He went right through the alphabet
A whole rosary of threats
He made his paper *Zeta* popular
With his valiant pen
He pointed to corruption
He always helped the people
And more than two presidents
Had their eyes on him
In a treacherous way
The Cat met his end
Death, mounted on a racehorse
A real beast
Rode him down

Now Felix the Cat is dead
They are carrying him to his grave
He will be another one on the list
Of brave journalists
That they've wanted to silence

Candles burn for Felix Miranda
To you I dedicate my song
But don't you worry
There will be other brave people
To take your place

Enrique Franco
(Los Tigres del Norte)

Groups like **Los Tigres del Norte** and **Los Cadetes del Norte** take stories from the local papers and convert them into ballads that usually begin "Voy a cantarles un corrido" ("I'm going to sing you a *corrido*") before launching into a gruesome tale sung in a deadpan style as if it were nothing to go to a local dance and get yourself killed. One of the most famous *corridos*, "Rosita

Alvírez", tells the story of a young girl who struck lucky: only one of the three bullets fired by her boyfriend hit and killed her.

Los Tigres are by far the most successful of all *norteño* groups – superstars, in fact – having won a Grammy and subsequently been adopted by Televisa. They now record in both the US and Mexico, having achieved superstardom on both sides of the border. Quite early in their career, the band modified the traditional line-up by adding a sax and mixed the familiar rhythms with *cumbias*; however, their nasal singing style and the combination of instruments identifies the music very clearly as *norteño*.

The banda boom

The enormous success of Los Tigres del Norte and their updated *norteño* sound resulted in a phenomenon that changed the face of Mexican music in the 1990s: **banda** music. This is a fusion of the *norteño* style with the brass bands that have played at village fiestas all over the country for the last century. There are now hundreds of *bandas* in Mexico – ranging in size from four to twenty musicians – all playing brass and percussion, with just an occasional guitar. Their repertoire includes *norteño* polkas, *ranchera* ballads, *cumbia*, merengue and salsa – all arranged for brass.

The most exciting of these groups is a fiery orchestra from Mazatlán, the **Banda del Recodo**. This is not a new band, indeed its former leader, Don Cruz Lizárraga, had been in the business for half a century, starting out in a traditional *tambora* marching band (the *tambora* is the huge, carried side drum) that played a straight repertoire of brass-band numbers. However, Don Cruz had always had an eye for musical fashions, adapting his material to merengue, *ranchera* or whatever anyone wanted to hear. His great *banda* hit was a version of Cuban bandleader Beny Moré's classic "La Culebra".

The *banda* boom currently dominates the TV music programmes and most places across the country except for the capital, where *cumbia* and salsa stay top of the bill. Elsewhere, it is the *bandas* that fill the stadiums and village halls, and it's their names you'll see painted in enormous multicoloured letters on any patch of white wall along the roads. The craze has brought with it a series of new dances, too, including the *quebradita* – a gymnastic combination of lambada, polka, rock'n'roll, rap and *cumbia*, which is danced with particular skill in all points north of Guadalajara.

In 1996, during a successful two-month tour of Europe, Cruz Lizárraga died, and the Banda del Recodo passed into the hands of two of his musician sons, Germán, now in his late fifties, and the young Alfonso. Changes were afoot. The band left the independent label where they had made about a hundred records and signed to the Televisa media empire. Several of the older musicians have been replaced with younger ones, and the original sound has suffered, although, ironically, record sales have never been better.

Cumbia

Although the *banda* line-up dates back to the village band tradition and the *tambora* music of northwest Mexico, todays *bandas* rely heavily on **cumbia** for

Discography

Mexican recordings are widely available in the US – less so in Europe. A label to look out for is **Corason**, who are recording and releasing consistently excellent CDs and cassettes of traditional sounds from all over the country. They are distributed in the US by Rounder and by Topic in Britain.

Compilations

Anthology of Mexican Sones (Corason, Mexico). This three-CD set is the definitive survey of Mexican traditional music, featuring wonderful recordings of rural bands. Excellent accompanying notes plus lyrics in Spanish and English.

Mexico – Fiestas of Chiapas & Oaxaca (Nonesuch Explorer, US). Atmospheric recordings from village festivities in southern Mexico. Marimba *conjuntos*, brass bands, some eccentric ensembles and great fireworks on the opening track. The next best thing to being there.

Mexique – Musiques Traditionnelles (Ocora, France). For those of a more folkloric inclination, music from the many little-known indigenous communities of Mexico.

The Rough Guide to Mexico (World Music Network, UK). This set examines a wide variety of both traditional and contemporary music, including *rancheras*, *corridos*, *boleros*, indie rock and various stylistic fusions.

Sones and mariachi

Conjunto Alma Jarochos, *Sones Jarochos* (Arhoolie, US). A fine disc, the first in a series of regional Mexican releases, featuring *sones* from Veracruz with harps and jarana guitars.

Juan Reynoso, *The Paganini of the Mexican Hotlands* (Corason, Mexico). The title is fair dues: Reynoso is Mexico's greatest country violinist, 80 years old now, but still in fine form on this recording, backed by vocal, guitars and drum.

La Negra Graciana, *Sones Jarochos* (Corason, Mexico). The first lady of Mexican harp plays solo and accompanied by her brother and sister-in-law.

Los Camperos de Valles, *Sones de la Huasteca* and *El Triunfo* (Corason, Mexico). The Huasteca *sones* are considered by many to be the most beautiful music in Mexico. Played on violin, guitar and the small *vihuela* guitar, an important element is the falsetto singing of love songs that are both rowdy and romantic.

Los Pregoneros del Puerto, *Music of Veracruz* (Rounder, US). Rippling *sones jaroches* from the Veracruz coast, where harp and *jarana* guitars still dominate. An enchanting album.

Mariachi Coculense de Cirilo Marmolejo, *Mexico's Pioneer Mariachis Vol 1* (Arhoolie, US). Wonderful archive recordings from the 1920s and 1930s of one of the seminal groups.

Mariachi Reyes del Aserradero, *Sones from Jalisco* (Corason, Mexico). An excellent *mariachi* band from Jalisco state play the original sones from this region where *mariachi* was born.

Mariachi Tapatió de José Marmolejo, *The Earliest Mariachi Recordings: 1906–36* (Arhoolie, US). Archive recordings of a pioneer *mariachi* band, featuring the great trumpet playing of Jesús Salazar.

Mariachi Vargas, *20 Exitos* (Orfeon, Mexico). Big-band style *mariachi* from Silvestre Vargas, who has managed to stay at the top of his field for over fifty years. Always flexible, his band released one disastrous album of *mariachi*-rock but has otherwise had hits all the way. They work much of the year in the US.

Various, *Pure Purépecha* (Corason, Mexico). A gem that brings together three duets of Purépecha peoples from Michoacán, singing sweet *pirecua* love songs, and some rowdy *abajeño sones* from Conjunto Atardecer.

Ranchera and norteño

Flaco Jimenez, *Ay te dejo en San Antonio* (Arhoolie, US). The best of Flaco's many recordings; he's a huge name in the Tex-Mex world north of the border.

José Alfredo Jimenez, *Homenaje a José Alfredo Jimenez* (Sony Discos, US). Jimenez was the king of *ranchera* and embodied the best and worst of Mexican machismo. As he predicted in one of his songs, everyone in Mexico missed him when he died.

Linda Ronstadt, *Canciones de mi Padre and Más Canciones* (Asylum, US). *Ranchera* classics sung very convincingly by the Mexican-American rocker, accompanied by Mariachi Vargas.

Los Lobos, *La Pistola y El Corazón* (Warner, US). The East LA band's brilliant 1991 tribute to their Mexican roots, with David Hidalgo pumping the accordion on their blend of *conjunto* and rock'n'roll.

Los Pingüinos del Norte, Conjuntos Norteños (Arhoolie, US). This album pairs up Tex and Mex *conjuntos*: Los Pingüinos, singing *corridos* live in a *cantina* in northern Mexico, and Fred Zimmerle's Trio from San Antonio, Texas, performing typical polkas and *rancheras*.

Los Tigres del Norte, *Corridos Prohibidos* (Fonovisa, US). A collection of *corridos* about Mexican low life and heroism from one of the best *norteño* groups in the business.

Narciso Martínez, *Father of the Tex-Mex Conjunto* (Arhoolie, US). The title says it all: a collection of 1940s and 1950s numbers, some instrumental, others featuring the leading vocalists of the day.

Santiago Jimenez Snr, *Santiago Jimenez Snr* (Arhoolie, US). One of the great accordion players, recorded in 1979 with his son Flaco on *bajo sexto*. Earthy, authentic sound.

Cumbia

Los Bukis, *Me Volvi a Acordar de Ti* (Melody, Mexico). The sound of soft *cumbia* – and the most popular Mexican record ever.

The Rough Guide to Cumbia (World Music Network, UK). The tunes on this compilation show why *cumbia* is such an infectious groove in Mexico and other regions of Latin America. The songs are licensed from the Sonolux label and date from the Sixties to the Nineties. Compulsively danceable, this is an essential party album and a solid overview of the genre.

Sonora Dinamita, *Mi Cucu* (Discos Fuentes, Colombia). Mexican *cumbia* performed by a breakaway group of artists who took the name of the Colombian originals. Their lyrics, full of double meanings, are performed with a zest that has brought huge success in Mexico.

Others

Agustín Lara, *Agustín Lara* (Orfeon, Mexico). The legendary crooner, the man who idolized prostitutes and married for love twelve times. One of Mexico's greatest composers of popular music, specializing in *bolero* ballads and music from Veracruz.

Various, *New Mexico*: *Hispanic Traditions* (Smithsonian Folkways, US). A good ethnographic recording from the Mexican diaspora in the US. Dances, songs, *corridos* and religious music in rustic style.

their repertoire, the simple dance music that came originally from Colombia but has taken deep root across Mexico.

Cumbia, now more popular in Mexico than in its native Colombia, has become simpler in its new home, more direct and danceable. For a long time, a national radio station used to call out "¡Tropi. . .Q!" – the last letter a "coooooh" that could unblock traffic jams – and then launch into the latest *cumbia* hit, which was played without reprieve for a month and then forgotten. A song about cellular telephones replaced "No te metes con mi cucu" (Don't Mess With My Toot Toot), which in turn had taken over from a song about fried chicken and chips – a thinly disguised treatise on how a macho likes his bird.

The flirtatious, addictive *cumbia* was the most popular music in Mexico in the 1980s, until *bandas* came along, and it remains a force throughout the country. Outside the capital, it tends to take on a more mellow, romantic tone, a sound closely associated with the band **Los Bukis**, who, before splitting up in the mid-1990s, made several albums, among them *Me Volvi a Acordar de Ti*, which sold 1.5 million legal copies and an estimated four million more in bootleg cassettes.

In the same line, an insipid mixture of *cumbia*, *norteño* and *ranchera*, which is sometimes known as **grupera** (or **onda grupera**), emerged in the late 1980s and continues to be enormously popular in small towns and villages – village populations have been known to swell four or five times over when a band like the **Yonics**, **Banda Machos** or the (now defunct) **Bronco** come to play. These musicians, like the *bandas* who share the same audience, arrive in a fleet of well-equipped coaches – one for them, one for the generator, one of lights and equipment and lavish leather suits and, quite often, one for their families. This music was despised by the media executives who, for many years, thought it common and continued to plug the familiar pretty faces of the pop idols that they manufactured. However, since the beginning of the 1990s, the phenomenal commercial success of the self-made *grupera*, *banda* and *norteño* musicians has forced the entertainment business to rethink. Groups like **Limite**, currently at the top of the lucrative country dance scene, are now regularly featured on TV shows and are invited to play in the hallowed halls of Mexico City's Auditorio Nacional, once the stronghold of protest singers and foreign ballet companies.

Mary Farquharson

Books

Mexico has attracted more than its fair share of famous foreign writers, and has inspired a vast literature and several classics. Until very recently, however, Mexican writers had received little attention; even now, when many new translations are being made available through small US presses, few are well known. Most big US bookstores will have an enormous array of books about, from, or set in Mexico, plus a few novels. In the rest of the English-speaking world there's far less choice, though the best-known of the archeological and travel titles below should be available almost anywhere. In the lists below, the UK publisher is followed by the US one; where only one publisher is listed it's the same in both places, or we've specified; o/p means a book is out of print, but may still be found in libraries or secondhand bookstores.

Books with a ★ symbol are highly recommended.

For the less mainstream, and especially for contemporary Mexico, there are a few useful **specialist sources**. In the UK the Latin America Bureau (LAB), 1 Amwell St, London EC1R 1UL (☎020/7278 2829, fax 7278 0165, Ⓦwww.lab.org.uk), publishes books covering all aspects of the region's society, current affairs and politics. Supporters receive a 25 percent discount off LAB books and a twice-yearly copy of *Lab News*. In the US, the Resource Center, PO Box 2178, Silver City, NM 88062-2178 (☎505/388-0208, fax 388-0619, Ⓦwww.irc-online.org), produces a wide range of publications, including a monthly magazine, *Borderlines*, which examines issues around the Mexican–American border (annual subscription US$12 in the States or US$17 internationally). In London you can freely visit Canning House Library, 2 Belgrave Square, SW1X 8PJ (☎020/7235 2303), which has the UK's largest publicly accessible collection of books and periodicals on Latin America, though you have to be a member to take books out and receive the twice-yearly *Bulletin*, a review of recently published books on Latin America.

If you're travelling to the **Maya** areas of Mexico or Guatemala, visit the library and resource centre at Maya – The Guatemalan Indian Centre, 94 Wandsworth Bridge Rd, London SW6 2TF (call ☎020/7371 5291 for opening times, Ⓦwww.maya.org.uk; closed Jan, Easter & Aug). Members (£5 annually) have use of the library (reference only) and video collection, and can access information of the monthly events and film shows held at the Centre. There is also a particularly fine textile collection. The Centre's director, Krystyna Deuss, is the acknowledged English authority on Guatemalan life, dress and contemporary Maya rituals.

Travel

Sybille Bedford *A Visit to Don Otavio* (Eland/Picador). An extremely enjoyable, often hilarious, occasionally lyrical and surprisingly relevant account of Ms Bedford's travels through Mexico in the early 1950s.

Frances Calderon de la Barca *Life in Mexico* (University of California). The diary of a Scotswoman who married the Spanish ambassador to Mexico and spent two years observing life there in the early nineteenth century.

Tom Owen Edmunds *Mexico: Feast and Ferment* (Hamish Hamilton/Viking Penguin, o/p). A coffee-table book of photographs, and a particularly good one, full of marvellous and unexpected images.

Charles Macomb Flandrau *Viva Mexico!* (Eland, o/p). First published in 1908, Flandrau's account of life on his brother's farm is something of a cult classic. Though attitudes are inevitably dated in places, it's extremely funny in others.

★ **Thomas Gage** *Thomas Gage's Travels in the New World* (University of Oklahoma Press, o/p). Unusual account by an English cleric who became a Dominican friar as he travelled through Mexico and Central America between 1635 and 1637, including fascinating insights into colonial life and some great attacks on the greed and pomposity of the Catholic Church abroad.

Graham Greene *The Lawless Roads* (Bodley Head/Viking). In the late 1930s Greene was sent to Mexico to investigate the effects of the persecution of the Catholic Church. The result (see also his novel on p.861) was this classic account of his travels in a very bizarre era of modern Mexican history.

Katie Hickman *A Trip to the Light Fantastic: Travels with a Mexican Circus* (Flamingo, UK). Enchanting, funny and uplifting account of a year spent travelling (and performing) with a fading Mexican circus troupe.

Aldous Huxley *Beyond the Mexique Bay* (Academy Chicago, o/p). Only a small part of the book is devoted to Mexico, but the descriptions of the archeological sites around Oaxaca, particularly, are still worth reading.

D.H. Lawrence *Mornings in Mexico* (Penguin/Peregrine Smith, o/p). A very slim volume, half of which is devoted to the Hopi Indians of New Mexico, this is an uncharacteristically cheerful account of Lawrence's stay in southern Mexico, and beautifully written.

John Lincoln *One Man's Mexico* (Century, o/p). Lincoln's travels in the late 1960s are an entertaining and offbeat read – travelling alone, often into the jungle, always away from tourists.

Patrick Marnham *So Far from God . . .* (Penguin, o/p). A rather jaundiced view, but nevertheless a humorous and insightful one, as Marnham travelled from the US to Panama in 1984. About half the book is occupied with his journey through Mexico.

James O'Reilly and Larry Habegger (eds) *Travelers' Tales Mexico* (Travelers' Tales, US). An anthology of Mexican travel writing. Disappointing considering the riches that are available: many pieces here are reprinted magazine articles. Nonetheless there's something for everyone somewhere.

Nigel Pride *A Butterfly Sings to Pacaya* (Constable, UK, o/p). The author, accompanied by his wife and 4-year-old son, travels south from the US border in a Jeep, heading through Mexico, Guatemala and Belize. Though the travels took place over 25 years ago the pleasures and privations they experience rarely appear dated.

John Lloyd Stephens *Incidents of Travel in Central America, Chiapas, and Yucatán* (Dover). Stephens was a classic nineteenth-century traveller. Acting as American ambassador to Central America, he indulged his own enthusiasm for archeology. His journals, full of superb Victorian pomposity punctuated with sudden waves of enthusiasm, make great reading. There have been many editions of the work. Many include fantastic illustrations by Catherwood of the ruins overgrown with tropical rainforest; the Smithsonian edition combines some of these with modern photographs.

Paul Theroux *The Old Patagonian Express* (Houghton Mifflin/Penguin). The epic journey from Boston to Patagonia by train spends just three rather bad-tempered chapters in Mexico, so don't expect to find out too much about the country. A good read nonetheless.

John Kenneth Turner *Barbarous Mexico* (University of Texas, o/p). Turner was a journalist, and this account of his travels through nineteenth-century Mexico exposing the conditions of workers in the plantations of the Yucatán, serialized in US newspapers, did much to discredit the regime of Porfirio Díaz.

Ronald Wright *Time Among the Maya* (Abacus/Grove). A vivid and sympathetic account of travels from Belize through Guatemala, Chiapas and Yucatán, meeting the Maya of today and exploring their obsession with time. The book's twin points of interest are the ancient Maya and the recent violence.

Mexican fiction

Mariano Azuela *The Underdogs* (University of Pittsburgh/Signet). The first novel of the Revolution (finished in 1915), *The Underdogs* is told through the eyes of a group of peasants who form a semi-regular revolutionary armed band. The story concerns their escapades, progress and eventual betrayal, ambush and massacre. Initially fighting for land and liberty, they end up caught up in a cycle of violence they cannot control and descend into brutal nihilism. The novel set many of the themes of post-revolutionary Mexican writing.

Carmen Boullosa *The Miracle Worker* (Jonathan Cape, o/p). One of Mexico's most promising contemporary writers, Boullosa's work focuses on traditional Mexican themes, often borrowing characters from history or myth. *The Miracle Worker* explores Mexican attitudes to Catholicism through the eyes of a messianic healer and her followers. The story can be seen as a parable about the Mexican political system, where ordinary Mexicans petition a distant and incomprehensible government machinery for favours, which are granted or refused in seemingly arbitrary decisions.

María Escandon *Esperanza's Box of Saints* (Simon & Schuster/Picador). A charming tale of female emancipation that starts when the eponymous heroine receives a message from the saints that her dead daughter is actually alive. Esperanza's quest to find her becomes a magical-realist odyssey that takes her from her small Mexican village to the dark and sleazy underworld of Tijuana and Los Angeles and forces her to question everything she thought she knew.

★ **Laura Esquivel** *Like Water for Chocolate* (Black Swan/Anchor). Adapted to film, Laura Esquivel's novel has proved a huge hit in Mexico and abroad. The book is even better: sentimental (schmaltzy, even), it deals with the star-crossed romance of Tita, whose lover Pedro marries her sister. Using the magic of the kitchen, she sets out to seduce him back. The book is written in monthly episodes, each of which is prefaced with a traditional Mexican recipe. Funny, sexy, great.

★ **Carlos Fuentes** *The Death of Artemio Cruz* (Penguin/Atlantic /Noonday), and *The Old Gringo* (Noonday). Fuentes is by far the best-known Mexican writer outside Mexico, influenced by Mariano Azuela and Juan Rulfo, and an early exponent of "magical realism". In *The Death of Artemio Cruz*, the hero, a rich and powerful man on his deathbed, looks back over his life and loves, from an idealist youth in the Revolution through disillusion to corruption and power; in many ways an indictment of modern Mexican society. Some of his other books are harder work: they include *Distant Relations* (Abacus), *Where the Air is Clear* (Noonday/Alfaguara), *A Change of Skin* (Deutsch/Farrar, Strauss & Giroux) and *Terra Nostra* (Penguin/Farrar, Straus & Giroux). *The Crystal Frontier* (Bloomsbury/Farrar, Strauss & Giroux) is a collection of stories examining the way personal contacts colour Mexicans' experiences of their unequal relationship with the US.

Sergio Galindo *Otilia's Body* (University of Texas). This prize-winning novel, published in Mexico as *Otilia Rauda*, traces the story of Otilia's passionate, tragic affair with an outlaw in post-revolutionary Mexico. Somewhat let down by an over-literal translation.

Jorge Ibargüengoitia *The Dead Girls*, *Two Crimes* and others (all Chatto & Windus/Avon, o/p). One of the first modern Mexican novelists translated into English, Ibargüengoitia was killed in a plane crash in 1983. These two are both blackly comic thrillers, superbly told, the first of them based on real events.

★ **Octavio Paz** (ed) *Mexican Poetry* (Grove). Edited by Paz (perhaps the leading man of letters of the post-revolutionary era) and translated by Samuel Beckett, this is as good a taste as you could hope for of modern Mexican poets. Some of Paz's own poetry is also available in translation.

Juan Rulfo *Pedro Páramo* (Serpent's Tail/Grove). Widely regarded as the greatest Mexican novel of the twentieth century and a precursor of magical realism. The living and spirit worlds mesh when, at the dying behest of his mother, the narrator visits the deserted village haunted by the memory of his brutal patriarch father, Pedro Páramo. Dark, depressing and initially confusing but ultimately very rewarding. Rulfo's short-story collection, *The Burning Plain and Other Stories* (University of Texas), is rated by Gabriel García Márquez as the best in Latin America.

Foreign fiction

There must be hundreds of novels by outsiders set in Mexico, all too many in the sex-and-shopping genre: apart from those below, others to look out for include a whole clutch of modern Americans, especially **Jack Kerouac**'s *Desolation Angels* (Flamingo/Riverhead) and several of Richard Brautigan's novels. And of course there's **Carlos Castañeda**'s *Don Juan* series (Arkana/Pocket Books) – a search for enlightenment through peyote.

Taisha Abelar *The Sorcerer's Crossing* (Penguin). The extraordinary true story of an American woman who joins an all-female group of sorcerers in Mexico and undergoes a rigorous physical and mental training process, designed to enable her to breach the limits of ordinary perception.

Tony Cartano *After the Conquest* (Secker & Warburg, o/p). An extraordinary fictional account of a fictional author who believes he is B. Traven's son and sets out to discover the truth about his father (see overleaf). A psychological thriller that is also full of Mexican history and politics.

Eduardo Galeano *Genesis*, *Faces and Masks* (both W.W. Norton). The opening parts of a trilogy by a Uruguayan writer, these anthologies of Indian legends, colonists' tales and odd snatches of history illuminate the birth of Latin America. Not specifically Mexican, but wonderful, relevant reading nonetheless.

Graham Greene *The Power and the Glory* (Penguin). Inspired by his investigative travels, this story of a doomed whisky priest on the run from the authorities makes a great yarn. It was a wonderful movie too.

Gary Jennings *Aztec* (Forge). Sex and sacrifice in ancient Mexico in this gripping bestseller. The narrator travels around the Aztec empire in search of his fortune, chancing upon almost every ancient culture along the way, and sleeping with most of them, until finally the Spanish arrive. Perfect beach or bus reading, and informative too.

D.H. Lawrence *The Plumed Serpent* (Wordsworth/Vintage). One of Lawrence's own favourites, the novel reflects his intense dislike of the country that followed on from the brief honeymoon period of *Mornings in Mexico* (see p.858). Fans of his heavy spiritualism will love it.

Haniel Long *The Marvelous Adventure of Cabeza de Vaca* (Picador). Two short stories in one volume – the first the account of a shipwrecked Conquistador's journey across the new continent, the second the thoughts and hopes of Malinche, Cortés' interpreter.

★ **Malcolm Lowry** *Under the Volcano* (Penguin/Plume). A classic since its publication, Lowry's account of the last day in the life of the British consul in Cuernavaca – passed in a *mescal*-induced haze – is totally brilliant. His *Dark as the Grave Wherein my Friend is Laid* is also based on his Mexican experiences.

James A. Michener *Mexico* (Crest). Another doorstop from Michener. Fans will love it.

★ **B. Traven** various works. Traven wrote a whole series of compelling novels set in Mexico. Among the best-known are *Treasure of the Sierra Madre* (Prion/Hill & Wang) and *The Death Ship* (L. Hill Books), but of more direct interest if you're travelling are such works as *The Bridge in the Jungle* and the other six books in the *Jungle* series: *Government*, *The Carreta*, *March to the Monteria*, *Trozas*, *The Rebellion of the Hanged* and *General from the Jungle* (all Allison & Busby/I. R. Dee, some o/p). These latter all deal with the state of the peasantry and the growth of revolutionary feeling in the last years of the Díaz dictatorship, and if at times they're overly polemical, as a whole they're enthralling. Will Wyatt's *The Secret of the Sierra Madre: The Man who was B. Traven* (Harcourt Brace) is the best of the books on the quest for the author's identity.

History

The sources below are all entertaining and/or important references; more standard **general histories** include Henry Bamford Parkes' *History of Mexico* (Houghton Mifflin); *Fire and Blood: A History of Mexico* by T.R. Fehrenbach (Replica); *A Concise History of Mexico from Hidalgo to Cárdenas* by Jan Bazant (CUP, o/p); and Judith Hellman's *Mexico in Crisis* (Holmes & Meier).

Inga Clendinnen *Ambivalent Conquests: Maya and Spaniard in Yucatán 1517 to 1570* (CUP). A product of meticulous research that documents the methods and consequences of the Spanish conquest of the Yucatán. The ambivalence in the title reflects doubts about the effectiveness of the conquest in subjugating the Maya, and the book provides insights into post-Conquest rebellions: over three hundred years after the Conquest the Maya rose in revolt during the Caste War, and almost succeeded in driving out their white overlords, while in January 1994, Maya peasants in Chiapas stunned the world and severely embarrassed the Mexican government by briefly capturing and controlling cities in the southeastern area of the state.

Hernán Cortés *Letters from Mexico* (Yale UP). The thoughts and impressions of the Conquistador, first hand. Less exciting than Díaz, though.

★ **Bernal Díaz** (trans. J.M. Cohen) *The Conquest of New Spain* (Viking). This abridged version is the best available of Díaz's classic *Historia Verdadera de la Conquista de la Nueva España*. Díaz, having been on two earlier expeditions to Mexico, accompanied Cortés throughout his campaign of conquest, and this magnificent eyewitness account still makes compulsive reading.

Adolfo Gilly *The Mexican Revolution* (Verso/Routledge, Chapman & Hall, o/p). Written in Mexico City's notorious Lecumberri jail (Gilly was later granted an absolute pardon), this is regarded as the classic work on the Revolution. Heavy going and highly theoretical though.

Brian Hamnett *A Concise History of Mexico* (CUP). The book kicks off with a brief examination of contemporary issues and then jumps back to the time of the Olmecs. A combined chronogical and thematic approach is used to analyse the social and political history of Mexico from then up until the present day. Some fairly large chunks of history are glossed over, but key events and issues are explored in greater detail, making for a good general introduction.

Michael Meyer, William Sherman and Susan Deeds, *The Course of Mexican History* (OUP). Comprehensive general history.

William Prescott *History of the Conquest of Mexico* (Cooper Square Press). Written in the mid-nineteenth century, and drawing heavily on Díaz, Prescott's history was the standard text for over a hundred years. It makes for pretty heavy reading and has now been overtaken by Thomas' account.

John Reed *Insurgent Mexico* (International Publications). This collection of his reportage of the Mexican Revolution was put together by Reed himself. He spent several months in 1913 and 1914 with various generals of the Revolution – especially Villa – and the book contains great descriptions of them, their men, and the mood of the times. It's far more anecdotal and easy to read than the celebrated *Ten Days that Shook the World*.

★ **Jasper Ridley** *Maximilian and Juárez* (Phoenix). This comprehensive, highly readable account of one of "the great tragicomedies of the nineteenth century" charts the attempt by Napoleon III to establish Archduke Maximilian as the Emperor of Mexico. The colourful narrative brings to life an unmitigated political disaster with huge consequences, including the execution of Maximilian, the insanity of his wife Carlota and the emergence of the United States as a world power.

Hugh Thomas *Conquest: Montezuma, Cortés, and the Fall of Old Mexico* (Touchstone); *The Conquest of Mexico* (Pimlico, UK). Same book, different title, but either way a brilliant narrative history of the Conquest by the British historian previously best known for his history of the Spanish Civil War. A massive work of real scholarship and importance – much of the archive material is newly discovered – but also humorous and readable, with appendices on everything from Aztec beliefs, history and genealogy to Cortés' wives and lovers.

James W. Wilkie and Albert L. Michaels (eds) *Revolution in Mexico* (University of Arizona Press, o/p). A fascinating anthology of contemporary and more recent writing on the Revolution and the years that followed.

Ancient Mexico

There are thousands of studies of **ancient Mexico**, many of them extremely academic and detailed, plus any number of big, highly illustrated coffee-table tomes on individual sites. Those below are of more general interest, and any of them will have substantial **bibliographies** to help you explore further.

Ignacio Bernal *Mexico Before Cortés* (Doubleday, US, o/p). The leading Mexican archeologist of the twentieth century, and one of the inspirations behind the Museo Nacional de Antropología (see p.401), Bernal did important work on the Olmecs and on the restoration of Teotihuacán, and has written many important source works. This book covers much the same ground as Davies', though in less detail, and is more dated, but it has the advantage of being widely available in Mexico. A more scholarly version is available in *A History of Mexican Archeology: The Vanished Civilizations of Middle America* (Thames & Hudson, o/p).

Warwick Bray *Everyday Life of the Aztecs* (P. Bedrick). A volume full of information about Aztec warfare, music, games, folklore, religious ritual, social organization, economic and political systems and agricultural practice. Although the book is now showing its age, and some of its conclusions are a bit dubious, its attractive comprehensiveness more than makes up for this. An excellent general introduction.

Inga Clendinnen *Aztecs: An Interpretation* (CUP). A social history of the Aztec empire that seeks to explain the importance – and acceptance – of human sacrifice and other rituals. Fascinating, though best to know something about the Aztecs before you start.

Michael D. Coe *The Maya* (Thames & Hudson). The best available general introduction to the Maya: concise, clear and comprehensive. Coe has also written several more weighty, academic volumes. His *Breaking the Maya Code* (Thames & Hudson), a history of the decipherment of the Maya glyphs, owes much to the fact that Coe was present at many of the most important meetings leading to the breakthrough, demonstrating that the glyphs actually did reproduce Maya speech. Aside from anything else, it is a beautifully written, ripping yarn, though the slagging-off of Eric Thompson gets a bit wearisome.

★ **Nigel Davies** *The Ancient Kingdoms of Mexico* (Viking). Although there's no single text that covers all the ancient cultures, this comes pretty close, covering the central areas from the Olmecs through Teotihuacán and the Toltecs to the Aztec empire. An excellent mix of historical, archeological, social and artistic information, but it doesn't cover the Maya. Davies is also the author of several more-detailed academic works on the Aztecs and Toltecs, including *The Aztecs, A History* (University of Oklahoma).

M.S. Edmonson (trans) *The Book of Chilam Balam of Chumayel* (Aegean, US, o/p). The *Chilam Balam* is a recollection of Maya history and myth, recorded by the Spanish after the Conquest. Although the style is not easy, it's one of the few keys into the Maya view of the world.

George Kubler *Art and Architecture of Ancient America* (Yale UP). Exactly what it says: a massive and amazingly comprehensive work, covering not only Mexico but Colombia, Ecuador and Peru as well. It's rather old-fashioned, however, and fails to take into account the ground-breaking epigraphic findings in Maya scholarship.

Diego de Landa *Yucatán Before and After the Conquest* (Dover). A translation edited by William Gates of the work written in 1566 as *Relación de las Cosas de Yucatán*. De Landa's destruction of almost all original Maya books as "works of the devil" leaves his own account as the chief source on Maya life and society in the immediate post-Conquest period. Written during his imprisonment in Spain on charges of cruelty to the Indians (remarkable itself, given the institutional brutality of the time), the book provides a fascinating wealth of detail for historians.

Maria Longhena *Splendours of Ancient Mexico* (Thames & Hudson, UK). Sumptuously illustrated coffee-table tome, with better than average text (translated from the Italian original) and excellent pictures and plans of all the major ancient sites.

Mary Ellen Miller *The Art of Mesoamerica: From Olmec to Aztec* (Thames & Hudson, UK). An excellent, wonderfully illustrated survey of the artisanship of the ancient cultures of Mexico, whose work reflects the sophistication of their civilizations.

★ **Mary Ellen Miller and Karl Taube** *The Gods and Symbols of Ancient Mexico and the Maya: An Illustrated Dictionary of Mesoamerican Religion* (Thames & Hudson). A superb modern reference on ancient Mesoamerica, written by two leading scholars. Taube's *Aztec and Maya Myths* (British Museum Press) is perfect as a short, accessible introduction to Mesoamerican mythology.

Chris Morton and Ceri Louise Thomas *The Mystery of the Crystal Skulls* (Thorsons, UK). Intriguing and accessible investigation into an ancient Amerindian legend that tells of a number of life-size crystal skulls said to contain vital information about the destiny of mankind. Following the discovery that such a skull actually exists, filmmakers

Morton and Thomas set off on a journey through Mexico and Central America, meeting experts in Maya culture, archeologists and modern-day shamans and finally coming to their own well-researched and thoughtful conclusions.

Jeremy A. Sabloff *Cities of Ancient Mexico* (Thames & Hudson). The best introduction to ancient Mexico currently available. Thoroughly up to date and easy to digest. Also worth checking is his *New Archeology and the Ancient Maya* (W.H. Freeman).

Linda Schele, David Freidel et al. The authors, in the forefront of the "new archeology", have been personally responsible for decoding many of the glyphs, revolutionizing and popularizing Maya studies. Although their writing style, which frequently includes re-creations of scenes inspired by their discoveries, is controversial to some fellow professionals, it has also inspired a devoted following. *A Forest of Kings: The Untold Story of the Ancient Maya* (Quill, US) in conjunction with *The Blood of Kings*, by Linda Schele and Mary Miller, shows that far from being governed by peaceful astronomer-priests, the ancient Maya were ruled by hereditary kings, lived in populous, aggressive city-states, and engaged in a continuous entanglement of alliances and war. *The Maya Cosmos* (Quill, US), by Schele, Freidel and Joy Parker is perhaps more difficult to read, dense with copious notes, but continues to examine Maya ritual and religion in a unique and far-reaching way. *The Code of Kings* (Touchstone, US), written in collaboration with Peter Matthews and illustrated with Justin Kerr's famous "rollout" photography of Maya ceramics, examines in detail the significance of the monuments at selected Maya sites. It's her last book – Linda Schele died in April 1998 – and sure to become a classic of epigraphic interpretation.

Robert Sharer *The Ancient Maya* (Stanford UP). The classic, comprehensive (and weighty) account of Maya civilization, now in a completely revised and much more readable fifth edition, yet as authoritative as ever. Required reading for archeologists, it provides a fascinating reference for the non-expert.

Dennis Tedlock (trans), *Popol Vuh* (Touchstone). Translation of the Maya Quiché bible, a fascinating creation myth from the only ancient civilization to emerge from rainforest terrain. The Maya obsession with time can be well appreciated here, where dates are recorded with painstaking precision.

J. Eric S. Thompson *The Rise and Fall of Maya Civilization* (Pimlico/University of Oklahoma, o/p). A major authority on the ancient Maya during his lifetime, Thompson produced many academic works; *The Rise and Fall . . .*, originally published in 1954, is one of the more approachable. Although more recent researchers have overturned many of Thompson's theories, his work provided the inspiration for the postwar surge of interest in the Maya, and he remains a respected figure.

Ptolemy Tompkins *This Tree Grows Out of Hell* (HarperCollins, o/p). An interesting attempt to piece together the mystery of Mesoamerican religion, which synthesizes and makes readable many of the recent findings in the area. The latter half of the book is a thoroughly unconvincing apology for the brutality of the Aztecs.

Richard F. Townsend *The Aztecs* (Thames & Hudson). Companion in the series to Coe's *Maya* book (see p.863), this is a good introduction to all aspects of Aztec history and culture.

Society, politics and culture

Tom Barry (ed) *Mexico: A Country Guide* (LAB/Resource Center). A comprehensive account of contemporary Mexico: Barry and ten other contributors impart their expertise to make this the best single-volume survey on the issues facing Mexico in the 1990s.

Rick Bayless *Mexican Kitchen* (Scribner/Absolute). Aimed at the ambitious chef, this weighty tome has over 150 recipes but no photos. The country's gastronomic heritage is explored in detail with a special focus on the myriad types of chile that form the heart of Mexican cuisine.

Harry Browne *For Richer, For Poorer* (LAB/Resource Center). A readable analysis of the background to NAFTA and the effects of and prospects for closer economic integration between the US and Mexico.

Miguel Covarrubias *Mexico South* (KPI). The people and popular culture of Veracruz and the Isthmus of Tehuantepec by the well-known Mexican artist and anthropologist. A good read, well illustrated.

Augusta Dwyer *On the Line* (LAB). A painstakingly detailed account of conditions on the US/Mexico border, where many of the most environmentally damaging factories on the continent poison lands and people on both sides of the frontier. The "line" is the only place in the world where the rich north directly borders the poorer south, and Dwyer documents the consequences of this economic discrepancy in case studies of *maquila* workers, legal and illegal immigrants and both victims and members of the US Border Patrol.

Clare Ferguson *Flavours of Mexico* (Ryland, Peters & Small). All the classics are here: tortillas, enchiladas, empanadas, *flautas* and tamales, along with party-food suggestions and a few vegetarian recipes. A colourful and straightforward cookbook that will inspire you to keep feasting on Mexican cuisine once back home.

Judith Adler Hellman *Mexican Lives* (The New Press, US). A compilation of interviews with fifteen Mexicans on the eve of the signing of NAFTA, offering a poignant insight into how ordinary people, rich and poor alike, cope with everyday life on the brink of enormous political and social change, with the voices of the interviewees themselves speaking so clearly that their personalities and emotions stand out from the pages. Underlying all the accounts is the reality of institutional corruption, which affects every sector of society but falls most heavily on the poor. Worth reading by anyone who wants to understand what modern Mexico is like behind the headlines.

Hayden Herrera *Frida* (Bloomsbury). This mesmerizing biography of Frida Kahlo brings to life a woman of extreme magnetism and originality. Starting with her childhood in Mexico City, the account goes on to describe the crippling accident she had as a teenager that left her unable to have children, her tempestuous marriage to Diego Rivera and the various men with whom she had affairs including, most notoriously, Leon Trotsky. The book contains numerous colour panels of her paintings.

Dan La Botz *Democracy in Mexico* (South End Press, US). Examines the political landscape of modern

Mexico and puts it into historical context by equating the rise of civil society and political consciousness with the major defining events of recent decades – the 1968 student massacre, the 1985 earthquake, and the 1994 Zapatista uprising amongst others.

★ **Oscar Lewis** *The Children of Sanchez* (Random House). These oral histories of a working-class family in the Mexico City of the 1940s are regarded as a seminal work in modern anthropology. The book is totally gripping, though, and doesn't read in the least like an anthropological text. Lewis' other works, including *Pedro Martinez* (Vintage, o/p/Penguin, o/p), *A Death in the Sanchez Family* (Vintage, US, o/p) and *Five Families* (Basic), use the same first-person narrative technique. All are highly recommended.

Patrick Marnham *Dreaming with his Eyes Open: A Life of Diego Rivera* (Bloomsbury). A gripping account of the extraordinary life of the great Mexican muralist in which truths are revealed and myths are unravelled.

Octavio Paz *The Labyrinth of Solitude* (Penguin/Grove). An acclaimed series of philosophical essays exploring the social and political state of modern Mexico. Paz, who died in 1998, won the Nobel prize for literature in 1990 and was universally regarded as the country's leading poet.

Elena Poniatowska various works. A pioneer in the field of testimonial literature and one of Mexico's best-known essayists and journalists. In *Here's to you Jesusa* (Farrar, Straus & Giroux) Poniatowska turns her attentions on her cleaning lady. Jesusa's story of her marriage, involvement in the Revolution and postwar period include her views on life, love and society. Narrated in the first person, the text is compelling, lively and at times ribald: Jesusa herself is now a celebrity on the literary circuit. Other works available in English include *Massacre in Mexico* (University of Missouri), a collage of testimonies of those present at the 1968 massacre of students in Tlatelolco; *Dear Diego* (Pantheon, US, o/p); and *Tinisima* (Farrar, Straus & Giroux/Penguin, US).

Gregory G. Reck *In the Shadow of Tlaloc* (Penguin/Waveland, o/p). Reck attempts a similar style to that of Oscar Lewis in his study of a Mexican village, and the effects on it of encroaching modernity. Often seems to stray over the border into sentimentality and even fiction, but interesting nonetheless.

Alan Riding *Mexico: Inside the Volcano* (IB Tauris, UK). In-depth analysis of modern Mexico by the British correspondent for the *New York Times*. Enlightening, though gloomy.

★ **John Ross** *Rebellion from the Roots* (Common Courage Press). A fascinating early account of the build-up to and first months of the 1994 Zapatista rebellion, and still the definitive book on the subject. Ross' reporting style provides a really detailed and informative background, showing the uprising was no surprise to the Mexican army. He's also the author of *Mexico in Focus* (LAB/Interlink), a short but authoritative guide to modern Mexican society, politics and culture – worth reading before a visit.

Guiomar Rovira *Women of Maize* (LAB). Rovira, a Mexican journalist, witnessed the Zapatista uprising in Chiapas on New Year's Day 1994. This book, which interweaves narrative, history and the personal recollections of numerous women involved in the rebellion, provides an extraordinary insight into the lives of indigenous people. The women interviewed reflect on how their previously traditional lifestyles were transformed when they joined up with the Zapatista National Liberation Army and gained access to education and other opportunities they'd never even dreamt of.

Chloë Sayer *The Arts and Crafts of Mexico* (Thames & Hudson/Chronicle). Sayer is the author of numerous books on Mexican arts, crafts and associated subjects, all of them worth reading. *The Skeleton at the Feast* (University of Texas), written with Elizabeth Carmichael, is a wonderful, superbly illustrated insight into attitudes to death and the dead in Mexico.

Joel Simon *Endangered Mexico* (Sierra Club Books). Eloquent and compelling study documenting the environmental crisis facing Mexico at the end of the twentieth century. Accurate and very moving, it's essential reading for those wanting to know how and why the crisis exists – and why no one can offer solutions.

David Rains Wallace *The Monkey's Bridge* (Sierra Club Books). When the Panama Bridge formed between North and South America three million years ago, plants and animals surged back and forth across it in an evolutionary intermingling that created one of the world's richest natural environments. This engaging account of Central Amercia's role as an evolutionary link between the two continents cleverly interweaves natural history, human history, travel writing and personal reflection.

Mariana Yampolsky *The Traditional Architecture of Mexico* (Thames & Hudson). The enormous range of Mexico's architectural styles, from thatched peasant huts and vast haciendas to exuberant Baroque churches and solid, yet graceful public buildings, is encompassed in this inspired book. While most of Mariana Yampolsky's superb photographs are in black and white, a chapter on the use of colour emphasizes its importance in every area of life; the text by Chloë Sayer raises it above the level of the average coffee-table book. (For guides to ecclesiastical architecture in Mexico see Richard Perry, below.)

Other guides

In Mexico itself, the best and most complete series of guides is that published by **Guías Panorama** – they have small books on all the main archeological sites, as well as more general titles ranging from *Wild Flowers of Mexico* to *Pancho Villa – Truth and Legend*.

Tim Burford *Backpacking in Mexico* (Bradt). Great on the practicalities of backpacking, with lots of information specifically relevant to Mexico, and a particularly good wildlife section. The hikes themselves cover all areas, including how to ascend Popocatépetl.

Carl Franz *The People's Guide to Mexico* (Avalon Travel). Not a guidebook as such, more a series of anecdotes and words of advice for staying out of trouble and heading off the beaten track. Perennially popular, and deservedly so.

Joyce Kelly *An Archaeological Guide to Mexico's Yucatán Peninsula* (University of Oklahoma). Detailed and practical guide to more than ninety Maya sites and eight museums throughout the peninsula, including many little-known or difficult-to-reach ruins; an essential companion for anyone travelling purposefully through the Maya world. Kelly's "star" rating – based on a site's archeological importance, degree of restoration and accessibility – may affront purists, but it does provide a valuable opinion on how worthwhile a particular visit might be.

★ **Richard Perry** *Mexico's Fortress Monasteries* (Espadaña Press, US). One in a series of expertly written guides to the sometimes overlooked treasures of Mexico's colonial religious architecture. This volume covers more than sixty cathedrals, churches and monuments in central Mexico, from Hidalgo to Oaxaca; *Maya Missions* deals with colonial Yucatán and *More Maya Missions* covers Chiapas. All are illustrated by the author's simple but beautiful drawings. These specialist offerings, ideal for travellers who want more information than most guidebooks can provide, are not widely available, though you can find them in tourist bookstores in the areas they cover.

D.G. Schueler *Adventuring Along the Gulf of Mexico* (Sierra Club Books, US). An entertaining read, with much general info on plants and animals along the Gulf coast.

R.J. Secor *Mexico's Volcanoes* (Mountaineers). Detailed routes up all the big volcanoes, and full of invaluable information for climbers.

Wildlife

Steve Howell *Where to Watch Birds in Mexico* (Christopher Helm). One for the enthusiast – over a hundred sites are listed, where more than 950 bird species can be seen. More general information on the recommended regions is also provided, along with tips on how to spot birds and identify them.

★ **Steve Howell and Sophie Webb** *The Birds of Mexico and Northern Central America* (Oxford UP). A tremendous work, the result of years of research, this is the definitive book on the region's birds. Essential for all serious birders.

C. Kaplan *Coral Reefs of the Caribbean and Florida* (Houghton Mifflin). Useful handbook on the abundant wildlife off the coasts of the Yucatán peninsula.

R.T. Peterson and E.L. Chalif *Mexican Birds* (Houghton Mifflin). The classic ornithological guide to Mexico. The text is excellent, but drawings are limited to indigenous examples only; migratory species are included in additional (North American) guides, which can be frustratingly impractical.

Language

Language

Mexican Spanish

Once you get into it, **Spanish** is actually a straightforward language – and in Mexico people are desperately eager to understand and to help the most faltering attempt. **English** is widely spoken, especially in the tourist areas, but you'll get a far better reception if you at least try to communicate with people in their own tongue. You'll be further helped by the fact that Mexicans speak relatively slowly (at least compared with Spaniards) and that there's none of the awkward lisping pronunciation.

Rules of pronunciation

Relative to English, the rules of **pronunciation** are clear-cut and, once you get to know them, strictly observed. Unless there's an accent, words ending in d, l, r and z are stressed on the last syllable, all others on the second last. All vowels are pure and short.

A	somewhere between the A sound of "back" and that of "father"
E	as in "get"
I	as in "police"
O	as in "hot"
U	as in "rule"
C	is soft before E and I, hard otherwise: *cerca* is pronounced "serka"
G	works the same way, a guttural H sound (like the ch in "loch") before E or I, a hard G elsewhere: *gigante* becomes "higante"
H	is always silent
J	the same sound as a guttural G: *jamon* is pronounced "hamon"
LL	sounds like an English Y: *tortilla* is pronounced "torteeya"
N	is as in English unless it has a tilde (accent) over it, when it becomes NY: *mañana* sounds like "manyana"
QU	is pronounced like an English K
R	is rolled, RR doubly so
V	sounds more like B, *vino* becoming "beano"
X	is slightly softer than in English – sometimes almost S – except between vowels in place names where it has an H sound, like México ("meh-hee-ko") or Oaxaca ("wa-ha-ka"). In Maya words, X sounds like sh – so Xel-Ha is pronounced "shel-ha"
Z	is the same as a soft C, so *cerveza* becomes "servesa"

Useful words and phrases

Although we've listed a few essential words and phrases here, if you're travelling for any length of time some kind of **dictionary** or **phrasebook** is obviously a worthwhile investment: the *Rough Guide to Mexican Spanish* is the best practical guide, correct and colloquial, and will have you speaking the language faster than any other phrasebook. One of the best small, Latin American Spanish dictionaries is the University of Chicago version (Pocket Books), widely available in Mexico. If you're using a dictionary, bear in mind that in Spanish CH, LL and Ñ are traditionally counted as separate letters and are listed after the Cs, Ls and Ns respectively. This has recently changed, but many dictionaries won't have caught up.

Basics

Yes, No	Sí, No	**Big, Small**	Gran(de), Pequeño/a
Open, Closed	Abierto/a, Cerrado/a	**Here, There**	Aquí, Allí
Please, Thank you	Por favor, Gracias	**More, Less**	Más, Menos
With, Without	Con, Sin	**This, That**	Este, Eso
Where?, When?	¿Dónde?, ¿Cuándo?	**Today, Tomorrow**	Hoy, Mañana
Good, Bad	Buen(o)/a, Mal(o)/a	**Now, Later**	Ahora, Más tarde
What?, How much?	¿Qué?, ¿Cuánto?	**Yesterday**	Ayer

Greetings and responses

Hello, Goodbye	¡Hola!, Adiós
Good morning	Buenos días
Good afternoon/night	Buenas tardes/noches
How do you do?	¿Qué tal?
See you later	Hasta luego
Sorry	Lo siento/disculpeme
Excuse me	Con permiso/perdón
How are you?	¿Cómo está (usted)?
Not at all/You're welcome	De nada
I (don't) understand	(No) Entiendo
Do you speak English?	¿Habla (usted) inglés?
I don't speak Spanish	(No) Hablo español
What (did you say)?	Mande?
My name is...	Me llamo...
What's your name?	¿Cómo se llama usted?
I am English	Soy inglés(a)
...American*	americano/a
...Australian	australiano/a
...Canadian	canadiense
...Irish	irlandés(a)
...Scottish	escosés(a)
...Welsh	galés(a)
...New Zealander	neozelandés(a)

*Mexicans are from the Americas too, so describing yourself as American can occasionally cause offence. Better to opt for "estadounidense" (from "Los Estados Unidos", Spanish for the United States) if you are a US American; and for Canadians, "canadiense".

Needs – hotels and transport

I want	Quiero
Do you know...?	¿Sabe...?
I'd like...	Quisiera... por favor
I don't know	No sé
There is (is there?)	Hay (?)
Give me...	Deme...
(one like that)	(uno así)
Do you have...?	¿Tiene...?
...the time	...la hora
...a room	...un cuarto
...with two beds/ double bed	...con dos camas/ cama matrimonial
It's for one person (two people)	Es para una persona (dos personas)
...for one night	...para una noche
...(one week)	(una semana)
It's fine, how much is it?	¿Está bien, cuánto es?

It's too expensive	Es demasiado caro
Don't you have anything cheaper?	¿No tiene algo más barato?
Can one...?	¿Se puede...?
...camp (near) here?	¿...acampar aquí (cerca)?
Is there a hotel nearby?	¿Hay un hotel aquí cerca?
How do I get to...?	¿Por dónde se va a...?
Left, right, straight on	izquierda, derecha, derecho
Where is...?	¿Dónde está...?
...the bus station	...el camionera central
...the railway station	...la estación de ferrocarriles
...the nearest bank	...el banco más cercano
...the ATM	...el cajero automático
...the post office	...el correo (la oficina de correos)
...the toilet	...el baño/sanitario
Where does the bus to . . . leave from?	¿De dónde sale el camión para . . .?
Is this the train for Chihuahua?	¿Es éste el tren para Chihuahua?
I'd like a (return) ticket to . . .	Quisiera un boleto (de ida y vuelta) para . . .
What time does it leave (arrive in...)?	¿A qué hora sale (llega en...)?
What is there to eat?	¿Qué hay para comer?
What's that?	¿Qué es eso?
What's this called in Spanish?	¿Cómo se llama este en español?

Numbers and days

1	un/uno/una
2	dos
3	tres
4	cuatro
5	cinco
6	seis
7	siete
8	ocho
9	nueve
10	diez
11	once
12	doce
13	trece
14	catorce
15	quince
16	dieciséis
20	veinte
21	veintiuno
30	treinta
40	cuarenta
50	cincuenta
60	sesenta
70	setenta
80	ochenta
90	noventa
100	cien(to)
101	ciento uno
200	doscientos
500	quinientos
700	setecientos
1000	mil
2000	dos mil

first	primero/a
second	segundo/a
third	tercero/a
fifth	quinto/a
tenth	decimo/a

Monday	Lunes
Tuesday	Martes
Wednesday	Miércoles
Thursday	Jueves
Friday	Viernes
Saturday	Sábado
Sunday	Domingo

Food and drink terms

Basics

Azúcar	Sugar	**Pescado**	Fish
Carne	Meat	**Pimienta**	Pepper
Ensalada	Salad	**Queso**	Cheese
Huevos	Eggs	**Sal**	Salt
Mantequilla	Butter	**Salsa**	Sauce
Pan	Bread		

Soups (Sopas) and starters

Caldo	Broth (with bits in)	**Sopa…**	Soup…
Ceviche	Raw fish pieces, marinated in lime juice	**…de arroz**	…with rice
		…de fideos	…with noodles
		…de lentejas	…with lentils
Entremeses	Hors d'oeuvres	**…de verduras**	…with vegetables

Eggs (Huevos)

A la Mexicana	Scrambled with tomato, onion and chile	**Rancheros**	Fried, served on a tortilla and smothered in a hot, red chile sauce
Con jamón	With ham		
Con tocino	With bacon	**Revueltos**	Scrambled
Motuleños	Fried, served on a tortilla with ham, cheese and salsa	**Tibios**	Lightly boiled

Antojitos

Burritos Wheatflour tortillas, rolled and filled

Chilaquiles Torn-up tortillas cooked with meat and sauce

Chiles rellenos Stuffed peppers

Enchiladas Rolled-up tacos, covered in chile sauce and baked

Enchiladas suizas As above, with sour cream

Flautas Small rolled tortillas filled with red meat or chicken and then fried

Gorditas Small, fat, stuffed corn tortillas

Machaca Shredded dried meat scrambled with eggs

Molletes Split torta covered in beans and melted cheese, often with ham and avocado too

Quesadillas Toasted or fried tortillas with cheese

Queso fundido Melted cheese, served with tortillas and salsa

Sincronzadas Flour tortillas with ham and cheese

Sopes Smaller bite-size versions of tostadas

Tacos Fried tortillas with filling

Tacos al Pastor Tacos filled with pork, sometimes served with a slice of pineapple

Tamales Corn-meal pudding, usually stuffed and steamed in banana leaves

Tlacoyo	Fat tortilla stuffed with beans	**Tostadas**	Flat crisp tortillas piled with meat and salad
Torta	Filled bread roll		

Fish and seafood (Pescado y mariscos)

Anchoas	Anchovies	**Langosta**	Lobster or crayfish (rock lobster)
Atún	Tuna	**Lenguado**	Sole
Cabrilla	Sea bass	**Merluza**	Hake
Calamares	Squid	**Ostión**	Oyster
Camarones	Prawns	**Pezespada**	Swordfish
Cangrejo	Crab	**Pulpo**	Octopus
Corvina	Sea bass	**Robalo**	Bass
Dorado	Mahi mahi	**Sardinas**	Sardines
Filete entero	Whole, filleted fish	**Trucha**	Trout
Huachinango	Red snapper		
Jurel	Yellowtail		

Meat (Carne) and Poultry (Aves)

Alambre	Kebab	**Costilla**	Rib
Albóndigas	Meatballs	**Filete**	Tenderloin/fillet
Barbacoa	Barbecued meat	**Guisado**	Stew
Bistec	Steak (not always beef)	**Higado**	Liver
Cabeza	Head	**Lengua**	Tongue
Cabrito	Kid	**Lomo**	Loin (of pork)
Carne (de res)	Beef	**Milanesa**	Breaded escalope
Carne adobado	Barbecued/spicily stewed meat	**Pata**	Feet
Carnitas	Spicy pork	**Pato**	Duck
Cerdo	Pork	**Pavo/Guajolote**	Turkey
Chivo	Goat	**Pechuga**	Breast
Chorizo	Spicy sausage	**Pierna**	Leg
Chuleta	Chop	**Pollo**	Chicken
Codorniz	Quail	**Salchicha**	Sausage
Conejo	Rabbit	**Ternera**	Veal
Cordero	Lamb	**Tripa/Callos**	Tripe
		Venado	Venison

Vegetables (Legumbres, verduras)

Aguacate	Avocado	**Chícharos**	Peas
Betabel	Beetroot (often as a *jugo*)	**Col**	Cabbage
		Coliflor	Cauliflower
Calabacita	Zucchini (courgette)	**Elote**	Corn on the cob
Calabaza	Squash	**Espárragos**	Asparagus
Cebolla	Onion	**Espinacas**	Spinach
Champiñones	Mushrooms	**Flor de calabaza**	Pumpkin flowers

Frijoles	Beans
Hongos	Mushrooms
Huitlacoche	A fungus that grows on corn cobs
Jitomate	Red tomato
Lechuga	Lettuce
Lentejas	Lentils
Nopales	Prickly pear fronds, something like squash
Papas	Potatoes
Pepino	Cucumber
Rajas	Strips of green pepper
Tomate	Green tomato
Zanahoria	Carrot

Fruits (Frutas) and juice (jugos)

Chabacano	Apricot
Cherimoya	Custard apple (sweetsop)
Ciruelas	Tiny yellow plums
Coco	Coconut
Durazno	Peach
Frambuesas	Raspberries
Fresas	Strawberries
Granada	Yellow passion fruit
Guanábana	Soursop, like a large custard apple
Guayaba	Guava
Higos	Figs
Limón	Lime
Mamey	Like a large zapote, with sweet pink flesh and a big pit
Mango	Mango
Melón	Melon
Naranja	Orange
Papaya	Papaya
Piña	Pineapple
Plátano	Banana/plantain
Sandía	Watermelon
Toronja	Grapefruit
Tuna	Prickly pear (cactus fruit)
Uvas	Grapes
Zapote	Sapodilla (chicu), fruit of the chicle tree

Sweets

Ate	Quince paste
Cajeta	Caramel confection often served with...
Crepas	...Pancakes
Ensalada de Frutas	Fruit salad
Flan	Crème caramel
Helado	Ice cream
Nieve	Sorbet

Common terms

Asado/a	Roast
Al horno	Baked
A la Tampiqueña	Meat in thin strips served with guacamole and enchiladas
A la Veracruzana	Usually fish, cooked with tomatoes and onions
Al mojo de ajo	Fried in garlic and butter
Barbacoa/pibil	Wrapped in leaves and herbs and steamed/cooked in a pit
Con mole	In mole sauce a thick concoction of chilies, chocolate and spices
A la parilla	Grilled
Empanado/a	Breaded

Glossaries

Terms and acronyms

Ahorita diminutive of *ahora* (now) meaning "right now" – usually an hour at least.

Alameda city park or promenade; large plaza.

Ayuntamiento town hall/government.

Aztec the empire that dominated the central valleys of Mexico from the thirteenth century until defeated by Cortés.

Barrio area within a town or city; suburb.

Camioneta small truck or van.

Cantina bar, usually men-only.

Cenote underground water source in the Yucatán.

Central camionera bus station.

Chac Maya god of rain.

Chac-mool recumbent statue, possibly a sacrificial figure or messenger to the gods.

Charreadas displays of horsemanship, rodeos.

Charro a Mexican cowboy.

Comal large, round flat plate made of clay or metal used for cooking tortillas.

Comedor cheap restaurant, literally dining room.

Convento either convent or monastery.

CTM central union organization.

Cuauhtémoc the last Aztec leader, commander of the final resistance to Cortés, and a national hero.

Descompuesto out of order.

Don/Doña courtesy titles (sir/madam), mostly used in letters or for professional people or the boss.

Ejido communal farmland.

Enramadas palapa-covered restaurants.

EPR Ejército Popular Revolucionario, the Popular Revolutionary Army. Guerrilla group, not allied to the Zapatistas; their first appearance was in Guerrero in 1996.

EZLN Ejército Zapatista de Liberación Nacional, the Zapatista Army of National Liberation. Guerrilla group in Chiapas.

Feria fair (market).

Finca ranch or plantation.

FONART government agency to promote crafts.

Fonda simple restaurant or boarding house.

Gringo not necessarily insulting, though it does imply North American – said to come from invading US troops, either because they wore green coats or because they sang "Green grow the rushes oh!..."

Guayabera embroidered shirt.

Güera/o blonde – very frequently used description of Westerners, especially shouted after women in the street; again, not intended as an insult.

Hacienda estate or big house on it.

Henquen hemp fibre, grown mainly in Yucatán, used to make rope.

Huipil Maya women's embroidered dress or blouse.

Huitzilopochtli Aztec god of war.

I.V.A. 15 percent value-added tax (VAT).

Kukulkán Maya name for Quetzalcoatl.

Ladino applied to people, means Spanish-influenced as opposed to Indian: determined entirely by clothing (and culture) rather than physical race.

Malecón seafront promenade.

Malinche Cortés' Indian interpreter and mistress, a symbol of treachery.

Mariachi quintessentially Mexican music, with lots of brass and sentimental lyrics.

Marimba xylophone-like musical instrument, also used of the bands based around it and the style of music.

Maya tribe who inhabited Honduras, Guatemala and southeastern Mexico from earliest times, and still does.

Mestizo mixed race.

Metate flat stone for grinding corn.

Mirador lookout point.

Mixtec tribe from the mountains of Oaxaca.

Moctezuma Montezuma, penultimate Aztec leader.

Muelle jetty or dock.

NAFTA the North American Free Trade Agreement including Mexico, the US and Canada; see also TLC below.

Nahuatl ancient Aztec language, still the most common after Spanish.

Norteño literally northern – style of food and music.

Palacio mansion, but not necessarily royal.

Palacio de Gobierno headquarters of state/federal authorities.

Palacio Municipal headquarters of local government.

Palapa palm thatch. Used to describe any thatched/palm-roofed hut.

Palenque cockpit (for cock fights).

PAN Partido de Acción Nacional (National Action Party), conservative opposition party; has gained several local election victories, mainly in the north.

Paseo a broad avenue, but also the ritual evening walk around the plaza.

PEMEX the Mexican national oil company, a vast and extraordinarily wealthy corporation, rumoured to be riddled with corruption, as is the powerful oil workers' union.

Planta Baja ground floor – abbreviated PB in lifts.

Porfiriano the time of Porfirio Díaz's dictatorship – used especially of its grandiose Neoclassical architecture.

PRD Partido Revolucionario Democrático (Party of the Democratic Revolution), the left-wing opposition formed and led by Cuauhtémoc Cárdenas; has the second largest number of seats in Congress.

PRI Partido Revolucionario Institucional (Party of the *Institutionalized* Revolution), the ruling party for the past eighty years.

PT Partido del Trabajo (Workers' Party), small party but with opposition seats in Congress.

PVEM Partido Verde Ecologista de México (Green Party), small opposition party.

Quetzalcoatl the plumed serpent, most powerful, enigmatic and widespread of all ancient Mexican gods.

Romería procession.

Sacbe Maya road.

Stele freestanding carved monument.

Tenochtitlán the Aztec capital, on the site of Mexico City.

Teotihuacán ancient city north of the capital – the first major urban power of central Mexico.

Tianguis Nahuatl word for market, still used of particularly varied marketplaces.

Tlaloc Toltec/Aztec rain god.

TLC Tratado de Libre Comercio, the Spanish name for NAFTA.

Toltec tribe which controlled central Mexico between Teotihuacán and the Aztecs.

Tula Toltec capital.

Tzompantli Aztec skull rack or "wall of skulls".

Virreinal from the period of the Spanish viceroys – ie colonial.

Wetback derogatory term for illegal Mexican (or any Hispanic) in the US.

Zapotec tribe which controlled the Oaxaca region to about 700 AD.

Zócalo the main plaza of any town.

Art and architectural terms

Alfiz decorative rectangular moulding over a doorway.

Arabesque elaborate geometric pattern of Islamic origin.

Artesonado intricate ceiling design, usually of jointed, inlaid wood.

Atlantean pre-Hispanic column in the form of a warrior – examples found at Tula.

Atrium enclosed forecourt of churchyard or monastery.

Azulejo decorative glazed tile, usually blue and white.

Churrigueresque highly elaborate, decorative form of Baroque architecture (usually in churches), named after the seventeenth-century Spanish architect.

Convento monastery residence which includes the cloister.

Dado ornamental border on the lower part of an interior wall.

Escudo shield-shaped decoration.

Espadaña belfry, usually on top of the front wall of a church.

Fluting vertical grooves in a column.

Fresco technique of painting on wet or dry plaster.

Garita ornamental pinnacle or battlement which looks like a sentry box.

Grotesque ornamental style depicting fantastic birds, beasts and foliage.

Herrerian imperial style named after sixteenth-century Spanish architect Juan de Herrera.

Lunette crescent-shaped space above a doorway or beneath a vault.

Merlón decorative pyramidal battlement.

Mudéjar Spanish architectural style strongly influenced by Moorish forms.

Ogee curved, pointed arch.

Pila font or water basin; also commonly found in domestic buildings.

Pilaster flattened column used as decorative element.

Pinjante glove-shaped decorative pendant, popular in eighteenth-century architecture.

Plateresque elaborately decorative Renaissance architectural style.

Portales arcades.

Portería entry portico to a monastery.

Predella base panel of an altarpiece.

Purista severe Renaissance architectural style, originating in sixteenth-century Spain.

Retablo carved, painted wooden altarpiece.

Tecali translucent onyx, also called Mexican alabaster.

Tequitqui early colonial style of sculpture using pre-Conquest techniques.

Zapata wooden roof beam, often decoratively carved.

Rough Guides

advertiser

...music & reference

Africa & Middle East
Cape Town
Egypt
The Gambia
Jerusalem
Jordan
Kenya
Morocco
South Africa, Lesotho & Swaziland
Syria
Tanzania
Tunisia
West Africa
Zanzibar
Zimbabwe

Travel Theme guides
First-Time Around the World
First-Time Asia
First-Time Europe
First-Time Latin America
Gay & Lesbian Australia
Skiing & Snowboarding in North America
Travel Online
Travel Health
Walks in London & SE England
Women Travel

Restaurant guides
French Hotels & Restaurants
London
New York
San Francisco

Maps
Algarve
Amsterdam
Andalucia & Costa del Sol
Argentina
Athens
Australia
Baja California
Barcelona
Boston
Brittany
Brussels
Chicago
Crete
Croatia
Cuba
Cyprus
Czech Republic
Dominican Republic
Dublin
Egypt
Florence & Siena
Frankfurt
Greece
Guatemala & Belize
Iceland
Ireland
Lisbon
London
Los Angeles
Mexico
Miami & Key West
Morocco
New York City
New Zealand
Northern Spain
Paris
Portugal
Prague
Rome
San Francisco
Sicily
South Africa
Sri Lanka
Tenerife
Thailand
Toronto
Trinidad & Tobago
Tuscany
Venice
Washington DC
Yucatán Peninsula

Dictionary Phrasebooks
Czech
Dutch
Egyptian Arabic
European
French
German
Greek
Hindi & Urdu
Hungarian
Indonesian
Italian
Japanese
Mandarin Chinese
Mexican Spanish
Polish
Portuguese
Russian
Spanish
Swahili
Thai
Turkish
Vietnamese

Music Guides
The Beatles
Cult Pop
Classical Music
Country Music
Cuban Music
Drum'n'bass
Elvis
House
Irish Music
Jazz
Music USA
Opera
Reggae
Rock
Techno
World Music (2 vols)

100 Essential CDs series
Country
Latin
Opera
Rock
Soul
World Music

History Guides
China
Egypt
England
France
Greece
India
Ireland
Islam
Italy
Spain
USA

Reference Guides
Books for Teenagers
Children's Books, 0–5
Children's Books, 5–11
Cult Football
Cult Movies
Cult TV
Digital Stuff
Formula 1
The Internet
Internet Radio
James Bond
Lord of the Rings
Man Utd
Personal Computers
Pregnancy & Birth
Shopping Online
Travel Health
Travel Online
Unexplained Phenomena
The Universe
Videogaming
Weather
Website Directory

Also! More than 120 Rough Guide music CDs are available from all good book and record stores. Listen in at www.worldmusic.net

North South Travel is a small travel agent offering excellent ersonal service. Like other air ticket retailers, we offer discount fares worldwide. But unlike others, all available profits contribute to grassroots projects in the South through the NST Development Trust Registered Charity No. 1040656.

NORTH SOUTH TRAVEL

For or queries, contact Brenda Skinner or her helpful staff. Recent made from the NST Development Trust include support to Djoliba Trust, providing micro-credit to onion growers in the Dogon country in Mali; assistance to displaced people and rural communities in eastern Congo; a grant to Wells For India, which works for clean water in ajasthan; support to the charity Children of the Andes, working for poverty relief in Colombia; and a grant to the Omari Project which works with drug-dependent young people in Watamu, Kenya.

Tel/Fax 01245 608 291.
Email brenda@northsouthtravel.co.uk
Website www.northsouthtravel.co.uk

North South Travel,
Moulsham Mill, Parkway,
Chelmsford,
Essex CM2 7PX,
UK

GREEN TORTOISE
ADVENTURE TRAVEL
Budget Camping Trips in
MEXICO
★Deserted Beaches★
★Jungle Waterfalls★
★Hidden Ruins★
1-415-956-7500 www.greentortoise.com

LATA
FTO
FEDERATION OF TOUR OPERATORS
Mexico &
Central America
tailor-made exclusively for you
TRIPS
worldwide
0117 311 4400
www.tripsworldwide.co.uk
info@tripsworldwide.co.uk
3150
ATOL
PROTECTED

ACADEMIA
FALCON
MEXICO

small print

and

Index

A Rough Guide to Rough Guides

In the summer of 1981, Mark Ellingham, a recent graduate from Bristol University, was travelling round Greece and couldn't find a guidebook that really met his needs. On the one hand there were the student guides, insistent on saving every last cent, and on the other the heavyweight cultural tomes whose authors seemed to have spent more time in a research library than lounging away the afternoon at a taverna or on the beach.

In a bid to avoid getting a job, Mark and a small group of writers set about creating their own guidebook. It was a guide to Greece that aimed to combine a journalistic approach to description with a thoroughly practical approach to travellers' needs – a guide that would incorporate culture, history and contemporary insights with a critical edge, together with up-to-date, value-for-money listings. Back in London, Mark and the team finished their Rough Guide, as they called it, and talked Routledge into publishing the book.

That first *Rough Guide to Greece*, published in 1982, was a student scheme that became a publishing phenomenon. The immediate success of the book – with numerous reprints and a Thomas Cook prize shortlisting – spawned a series that rapidly covered dozens of destinations. Rough Guides had a ready market among low-budget backpackers, but soon also acquired a much broader and older readership that relished Rough Guides' wit and inquisitiveness as much as their enthusiastic, critical approach. Everyone wants value for money, but not at any price.

Rough Guides soon began supplementing the "rougher" information about hostels and low-budget listings with the kind of detail on restaurants and quality hotels that independent-minded visitors on any budget might expect, whether on business in New York or trekking in Thailand.

These days the guides – distributed worldwide by the Penguin group – offer recommendations from shoestring to luxury and cover more than 200 destinations around the globe, including almost every country in the Americas and Europe, more than half of Africa and most of Asia and Australasia. Our ever-growing team of authors and photographers is spread all over the world, particularly in Europe, the USA and Australia.

In 1994, we published the *Rough Guide to World Music* and *Rough Guide to Classical Music*; and a year later the *Rough Guide to the Internet*. All three books have become benchmark titles in their fields – which encouraged us to expand into other areas of publishing, mainly around popular culture. Rough Guides now publish:

- Travel guides to more than 200 worldwide destinations
- Dictionary phrasebooks to 22 major languages
- History guides ranging from Ireland to Islam
- Maps printed on rip-proof and waterproof Polyart™ paper
- Music guides running the gamut from Opera to Elvis
- Restaurant guides to London, New York and San Francisco
- Reference books on topics as diverse as the Weather and Shakespeare
- Sports guides from Formula 1 to Man Utd
- Pop culture books from *Lord of the Rings* to Cult TV
- World Music CDs in association with World Music Network

Visit **www.roughguides.com** to see our latest publications.

Rough Guide Credits

Text editor: Thomas Kohnstamm
Layout: Ajay Verma, Jessica Subramanian
Cartography: Jasbir Kaur Sandhu, Karobi Gogoi, JP Mishra, Ashutosh Bharti
Picture research: Veneta Bullen
Proofreader: Derek Wilde
Editorial: **London** Martin Dunford, Kate Berens, Helena Smith, Claire Saunders, Geoff Howard, Ruth Blackmore, Gavin Thomas, Polly Thomas, Richard Lim, Lucy Ratcliffe, Clifton Wilkinson, Alison Murchie, Fran Sandham, Sally Schafer, Alexander Mark Rogers, Karoline Densley, Andy Turner, Ella O'Donnell, Keith Drew, Andrew Lockett, Joe Staines, Duncan Clark, Peter Buckley, Matthew Milton; **New York** Andrew Rosenberg, Richard Koss, Yuki Takagaki, Hunter Slaton, Chris Barsanti, Steven Horak
Design & Pictures: London Simon Bracken, Dan May, Diana Jarvis, Mark Thomas, Jj Luck, Harriet Mills; **Delhi** Madhulita Mohapatra, Umesh Aggarwal, Ajay Verma, Jessica Subramanian
Production: Julia Bovis, John McKay, Sophie Hewat
Cartography: **London** Maxine Repath, Ed Wright, Katie Lloyd-Jones, Miles Irving; **Delhi** Manish Chandra, Rajesh Chhibber, Jai Prakash Mishra, Ashutosh Bharti, Rajesh Mishra, Animesh Pathak, Jasbir Sandhu, Karobi Gogoi
Cover art direction: Louise Boulton
Online: **New York** Jennifer Gold, Cree Lawson, Suzanne Welles, Benjamin Ross; **Delhi** Manik Chauhan, Narender Kumar, Shekhar Jha, Rakesh Kumar
Marketing & Publicity: **London** Richard Trillo, Niki Smith, David Wearn, Chloë Roberts, Demelza Dallow, Kristina Pentland; **New York** Geoff Colquitt, Megan Kennedy
Finance: Gary Singh
Manager India: Punita Singh
Series editor: Mark Ellingham
PA to Managing Director: Julie Sanderson
Managing Director: Kevin Fitzgerald

Publishing Information

This sixth edition published July 2004 by
Rough Guides Ltd,
80 Strand, London WC2R 0RL.
345 Hudson St, 4th Floor,
New York, NY 10014, USA.
Distributed by the Penguin Group
Penguin Books Ltd,
80 Strand, London WC2R 0RL
Penguin Putnam, Inc.
375 Hudson Street, NY 10014, USA
Penguin Books Australia Ltd,
487 Maroondah Highway, PO Box 257,
Ringwood, Victoria 3134, Australia
Penguin Books Canada Ltd,
10 Alcorn Avenue, Toronto, Ontario,
Canada M4V 1E4
Penguin Books (NZ) Ltd,
182–190 Wairau Road, Auckland 10,
New Zealand
Typeset in Bembo and Helvetica to an original design by Henry Iles.

Printed in Italy by LegoPrint S.p.A

912pp includes index
A catalogue record for this book is available from the British Library

ISBN 1-84353-253-0

3 5 7 9 8 6 4 2

Help us update

We've gone to a lot of effort to ensure that the sixth edition of **The Rough Guide to Mexico** is accurate and up-to-date. However, things change – places get "discovered", opening hours are notoriously fickle, restaurants and rooms raise prices or lower standards. If you feel we've got it wrong or left something out, we'd like to know, and if you can remember the address, the price, the time, the phone number, so much the better.

We'll credit all contributions, and send a copy of the next edition (or any other Rough Guide if you prefer) for the best letters. Everyone who writes to us and isn't already a subscriber will receive a copy of our full-colour thrice-yearly newsletter. Please mark letters: "**Rough Guide to Mexico**" and send to: Rough Guides, 80 Strand, London WC2R 0RL, or Rough Guides, 4th Floor, 345 Hudson St, New York, NY 10014. Or send an email to **mail@roughguides.com**

Have your questions answered and tell others about your trip at **www.roughguides.atinfopop.com**

Acknowledgements

Adrien: thanks to my friend Cristina Gerez, the world's best travel companion, por su generosidad sin limites.
Dan: thanks to Stefan Hasselblad of CEDUAM and Armida Durán Aguilar.
Paul: thanks to Julia and Kai for the pool games, Marcos Ruiz for bringing Chamula to life, Navarra tours in San Cristóbal, Na Chan Kan tours in Palenque, and Carol (I love you). Hello to the thief who stole my bag – enjoy the binoculars – and thanks to Thomas Kohnstamm for his help and advice with the insurance claim!
Roger: thanks first to the wonderful Mexicans I met who made my time there so memorable and enlightening. Thanks as well to Thomas, Andrew and Chris for having faith in me and offering their guiding editorial pen. Also Stort Tack, Gaby, Hector, Mareike, Tara, Matt, Aaron, Brina, Delphine, Camille, Luke, Justin and Bryan. Extra special thanks to Jon, Jess, Aaron and Morgan for kick-starting my journey, and to my awesome parents for their support, encouragement and access to Western Union.
Ross: thanks to Thomas Kohnstamm for his careful editing, Chris Barsanti for his help in getting the project off the ground, and the following people for their time, advice, hospitality and logistical support in Mexico: Jean-Luc de France, Juan & Lisa Martinez, Nelly Allec, Frank & Ania Shattuck, Miriam Cordova, Arely Figueroa, Roberta Valdez, Yalila Radillo, Miguel Tejeda, Lupita Ayala, Christine Garsault, Rivelino Diaz, Alberto Martinez, Eloisa Rodriguez and Humberto Covarrubias López.
Sheelah: a huge thank you to Seth McAllister, Carlota McAllister and Jorge Uzon, Lilia Edith and Hugo Antonio in Oaxaca, Germán Ramos at Casa del Sotano, Susan McGlynn in Oaxaca, Gina Machorro Espinosa in Puerto Escondido, Victor and Michelle in Huatulco, Markus in Mazunte and all the bus and taxi drivers, hotel and restaurant managers and others encountered in Mexico who were incredibly kind and helpful.
Zora: thanks to Claudia Barrera and Lennard Struyk, Kristine and Santiago in Santa Elena, Eliane Tomasi, Andrés Limón, David and Ilana Randall, Gea Ubilla and Oscar Carreño, Pablo Da Costa, Stefania Cappelletti, Pedro and Eyal on Cozumel, José Lima, Ernesto Gutiérrez Alvarez, Verena Gerber, Dianne Dutton, Norma Pulido, Daniel Mellado, Janelle at Turquoise Reef, Lia Gonzalez, Andrea Arati, Alejandro Rueda, Rafael Micha, Anissa Lee, Will Warburton, Lupita Cupul, Verónica Carrillo.
The editor: For Mindy. And thank you to Chris Barsanti for getting the book started and helping throughout, Yuki Takagaki for picking up the slack, Hunter Slaton and Richard Koss for assisting time and again, and Andrew Rosenberg for steering the project and for his airtight editing. Thank you to Karoline Densley, Markie Rogers, Jules Sanderson and Katie Lloyd-Jones at RG London and Umesh Aggarwal at RG Delhi for their support, patience and toil. Also, Matt Harbison for backup info on the DF, Veneta Bullen for high-speed photo research and Nicky Agate for indexing work.

Readers' letters

Douglas Adamson, Amanda Ariss, Jillian Austin, Joan Ballentine, Janet Birnie, Oliver Bolt, Richard Boltz, Mason Bragg, Denis Carlin, Andrew Clough, Dan Delany, Kieran Dodd, Tamara Dukatz, Megan East, Nicole Eilers, Gregory Ferrell, Gabriel Frappier, Vanya Gerstemann, Ramiro Gomez, John L. Gresseth, Josef Gruber, Anna Jephcote, Kenneth Kay, Paul & Kathy Kester, Andrea Kunz, Bob Lowell, Gene Lui, Ricardo Luke, Sharon Maes, Mike Maloney, Jacob Maraya, Guy Moussali, Ken Nawrocki, Michael O'Brien, Roger Page, Vicki Paris, Richard Powell, Daniel Schwert, Mark Singer, Herb Streicher, Marion Wu, Ernesto Yunez, Jim Zosel. Apologies to anyone whose name was misspelled or omitted.

Photo Credits

Cover credits

Main front: Organ Pipe cactus, Baja California © Getty
Small front top picture: Chac-mool statue, Chichén Itzá © Pictures Colour Library
Small front bottom picture: Textiles © Powerstock
Back top picture: Cliff diving, Acapulco © Powerstock
Back bottom picture: Fiestas de Enero © Robert Harding

Introduction

Plaza de la Independencia at night, Mexico City © Randy Faris/Corbis
Watersports at Playa del Carmen © Borre Wickstrom/Travel Ink
Painted coconut shells, Oaxaca © Rose Hartman/Corbis
Cactus © Paul Whitfield
Mountain road through Copper Canyon © Robert Frerck/Robert Harding Library
Flag folding ceremony, Mexico City © Paul Whitfield
Copper Canyon train © Greg Evans International
Azulejos domes, Puerto Vallarta © Randy Faris/Corbis
El Tajín © Chris Sharp/South American Pictures
Oxkutzcab market © Paul Harris

Things not to miss

01 Diving © Greg Evans International
02 Great pyramid of Cholula © Iain Pearson/South American Pictures
03 Voladores de Papantla © Sue Carpenter/Axiom
04 Cenotes, Valladolid © Jerry Dennis
05 Sian Ka'an Biosphere Reserve © Robert Fried/Andes Press Agency
06 Silver jewellery from Taxco © S. Grant/Art Directors Trip
07 Football crowd © Empics
08 Tulum © Jerry Dennis
09 Whale-watching © Art Directors/Trip/Streano/Havens
10 Tortillas © Paul Harris
11 Museo Frida Kahlo © Dorling Kindersley Images
12 Field of blue agave, Tequila © Dorling Kindersley Images
13 Coffee beans © Carlos Reyes Manzo/ Andes Press Agency
14 Yaxchilán © South American Pictures
15 Monarch Butterfly Sanctuary © Alex Robinson
16 Guanajuato © Sue Carpenter/Axiom
17 Chiles © Alex Robinson
18 Rodeo, San Miguel de Allende © Powerstock/SuperStock
19 The Zócalo, Mexico City © E. Simanor/Axiom
20 Day of the Dead © Robert Francis/South American Pictures
21 Hammock at sunset © Powerstock/SuperStock
22 Chichén Itzá © Powerstock/Age fotostock
23 El Tajín © Chris Sharp/South American Pictures
24 Oaxaca market © Peter Wilson
25 Tula statue © Conor Caffrey/Axiom
26 Mariachis © World Pictures
27 Museo Nacional de Antropología © Dorling Kindersley Images
28 Xochimilco © Sue Carpenter/Axiom
29 Bonampak mural © Alex Robinson
30 Lago de Pátzcuaro © Dorling Kindersley Images
31 Templo de las Inscripciones, Palenque © Mirielle Vautier
32 Pacific Coast near Bahía Concepción © Art Directors/Trip
33 Calakmul © Alex Robinson
34 The zócalo in Veracruz © South American Pictures
35 Diego Rivera murals © M.Barlow/Art Directors/Trip
36 Oaxacan textiles © Alex Robinson
37 Train route over Copper Canyon © Guy Marks/Travel Ink
38 Santo Domingo church, Oaxaca © Tony Morrison/South American Pictures

Black and white photos

Baja California © Brian Garrett/Travel Ink (p.74)
Boats line Playa Norte beach, Mazatlán © Kelly-Mooney Photography/CORBIS (p.79)
Paquimé © Iain Pearson/South American Pictures (p.162)
Aerial view of Copper Canyon © South American Pictures (p.170)
Lago de Chapala fishermen © Tim Thompson/Corbis (p.218)
Morelia Cathedral © Conor Caffrey/Axiom (p.224)
General store in Guanajuato © Tony Morrison/South American Pictures (p.276)
Taxco silver jewellery © S. Grant/Art Directors/Trip (p.282)
Mariachis performing © Danny Lehman/Corbis (p.354)

Diego Rivera mural © South American Pictures (p.389)
Statues at Tula © Grazyna Bonati/Travel Ink (p.455)
Whale-watching © Art Directors/Trip/Streano/Havens (p.498)
Cliff diver, Acapulco © Greg Evans International (p.519)
Café life, Veracruz zócalo © South American Pictures (p.548)
Straw cowboy hats © Macduff Everton/Corbis (p.584)
Zapotec man, Tlacolula © Mirielle Vautier (p.610)
Church, San Juan Chamula © Sergio Pitamitz/Corbis (p.640)
Giant Olmec Head, Palenque © Danny Lehman/Corbis (p.647)
Flamingoes, Celestún National Wildlife Refuge © Robert Harding (p.712)
Palace of Masks, Kabáh © Robert Harding (p.725)

Index

Map entries are in **colour**.

D

E

INDEX

F

G

H

I

INDEX

INDEX

N

O

P

INDEX

U

V

W

X

Y

Z

Map symbols

Maps are listed in the full index using coloured text.

- International border
- State border
- Chapter division boundary
- Motorway
- Major Roads
- Minor Roads
- 4 Wheel drive
- Pedestrianised Street
- Steps
- Path
- Railway
- Ferry route
- Cable car and stations
- Metro Station
- River
- Spring/Spa
- Mountain peak
- Waterfall
- Viewpoint
- Lighthouse
- Ruin / Archeological Site
- Gardens
- Airport
- Inca Ruins
- Hospital/medical center
- Information center
- Post office
- Highway
- Church (regional maps)
- Bridge
- Point of interest
- Internet
- Bus stop
- Cave
- Parking
- Fuel Station
- Hill Shading
- Building
- Church (town maps)
- Cemetery
- Park
- Beach